MATERIALS ON
FAMILY WEALTH MANAGEMENT

Edited By

William J. Turnier
W.P. Mangum Professor of Law
University of North Carolina

Grayson M.P. McCouch
Professor of Law
University of San Diego

Contributing Authors

Patricia A. Cain
Aliber Family Professor of Law, University of Iowa

David G. Epstein
Professor of Law, Southern Methodist University

Robert H. Jerry II
Dean and Levin, Mabie and Levin Professor of Law, University of Florida

Richard L. Kaplan
Peer and Sarah Pedersen Professor of Law, University of Illinois

Michael J. Roberts
Senior Lecturer and Executive Director,
Arthur Rock Center for Entrepreneurship, Harvard Business School

Norman P. Stein
Douglas Arant Professor of Law, University of Alabama

AMERICAN CASEBOOK SERIES®

THOMSON
✳ ™
WEST

Mat #40180423

American Casebook Series and West Group are trademarks
registered in the U.S. Patent and Trademark Office.

© 2005 Thomson/West
    610 Opperman Drive
    P.O. Box 64526
    St. Paul, MN 55164–0526
    1–800–328–9352

ISBN 0–314–15005–6

TEXT IS PRINTED ON 10% POST
CONSUMER RECYCLED PAPER

Preface

The process of accumulating, managing and transmitting wealth raises issues of central importance for individuals and families. Faced with an ever-expanding array of financial instruments and investment choices, most people of modest or substantial means recognize the desirability, indeed the necessity, of achieving a basic level of financial literacy. Often, however, that need goes unmet throughout college and graduate school; far too many students emerge from years of higher education with little understanding of the financial facts of life. This volume aims to help students become familiar with fundamental principles and practices of personal finance and wealth management, so that they can make intelligent and responsible decisions for themselves and exercise sound judgment in advising or assisting others.

Technical aspects of wealth preservation, management and disposition have traditionally formed the subject matter of specialized courses in estate planning, federal taxation, and trusts and estates. In addition, a number of other courses focus on specialized areas such as disability and life insurance, employee benefits, elder law and asset protection. Few courses in the traditional curriculum provide students with a comprehensive exposure to issues and problems that they are likely to encounter in coping with the modern world of personal finance and wealth management. We believe that many students would benefit from a course in wealth management, and this volume is designed to fill the gap in published teaching materials for such a course. In addition, we hope that this book will stimulate interest on the part of other teachers to offer such a course regularly as an integral part of the curriculum.

In recent years there has been enormous political pressure to cut federal taxes, especially for taxpayers in the upper echelons of the income and wealth scale. The future of the federal estate tax remains especially controversial, as indicated by competing proposals to repeal the tax permanently or to raise the exemption substantially above the amounts provided under present law. As a result, estate planning courses may be forced to make significant changes in scope and emphasis if they are to retain their traditional importance and interest for students. By the same token, most individuals and families will confront a host of financial planning issues that are entirely independent of the existence of an estate tax or the size of an estate tax exemption. These issues relate to managing investments, protecting assets, meeting the costs of higher education, financing the purchase of a home, obtaining disability and life insurance coverage, providing for retirement security, and planning for incapacity and succession at the end of life. This book is intended to provide students with basic orientation and guidance in these and other related topics. The material presented in this book will be of value to lawyers and financial planners in providing advice to individuals and families; it should also be useful to students at a personal level as they enter their chosen professions and begin the process of accumulating and managing their own wealth.

To provide maximum flexibility, the book is designed so that each chapter stands on its own. The first four chapters provide an introduction to the fundamental topics of financial investing, succession, federal income taxation and federal estate and gift taxation, while subsequent chapters address specific topics: housing; higher education; life and disability insurance; retirement planning; elder law; and debt, credit and asset protection. As a result, a teacher can vary the order of assignments or even skip entire chapters. The sections within each chapter are also largely free-standing, so that the teacher can assign selected topics or portions of chapters for class discussion. The authors have intentionally structured the materials so that they may be used either in a conventional classroom setting or as an assigned text for a seminar. To facilitate use of the materials in a conventional classroom setting, the book includes numerous problems suitable for classroom discussion.

Although Professors Turnier and McCouch assumed primary editorial responsibility for the project as a whole, this volume is a truly collaborative endeavor. Each of the contributing authors brought significant expertise in a particular substantive area to the preparation of their respective chapters. Responsibility for the chapters was allocated as follows:

Chapter 1: Wealth and Personal Finance—Professor Roberts;

Chapter 2: Property and Succession—Professor McCouch;

Chapter 3: Federal Income Taxation—Professor Turnier;

Chapter 4: Federal Estate and Gift Taxation—Professor McCouch;

Chapter 5: Housing—Professor Cain;

Chapter 6: Higher Education—Professor Turnier;

Chapter 7: Life and Disability Insurance—Professor Jerry;

Chapter 8: Retirement Planning—Professor Stein;

Chapter 9: Elder Law—Professor Kaplan; and

Chapter 10: Credit, Debt and Asset Protection—Professor Epstein.

We wish to acknowledge the contributions of several individuals who provided significant help in preparing this book. Professor Turnier is grateful to Scott Little and Hanan Javid, who provided outstanding research assistance. Professor Roberts wishes to thank Matt Willis and Dan Heath for research assistance on investment strategies. Professor Cain thanks her colleague Pat Bauer, who reviewed an early draft of the housing chapter and provided useful comments. Professor Jerry is grateful to his colleague Dennis Calfee for sharing his expertise on the taxation of life and disability insurance. We also wish to thank Roxanne Birkel of West Group for her excellent work on production. Last, but not least, we wish to thank Pam Siege Chandler and her colleagues at West Group for their unfailing encouragement and support at every stage in the publication of this book, which we believe offers a novel, and we hope useful, approach to the teaching of wealth management.

WILLIAM J. TURNIER
GRAYSON M. P. McCOUCH

April 2005

*

Summary of Contents

*

Table of Contents

_____

*

Table of Cases

References are to paragraph number

Table of Statutes

---

*

MATERIALS ON
FAMILY WEALTH MANAGEMENT

*

Chapter 1

INTRODUCTION TO WEALTH AND PERSONAL FINANCE

A. WEALTH

[¶ 1,000]

This chapter will focus primarily on financial wealth. While health and happiness obviously constitute important aspects of wealth and well-being, the focus of analysis here is on the management of financial wealth.

[¶ 1,010]

1. What is Wealth?

Wealth is typically measured in dollar terms, and is often thought of as personal (or family) net worth. In that sense, it is analogous to the net worth of a business corporation, in that it includes various assets, from liquid (i.e., cash or near cash) to illiquid (i.e., assets that are difficult to turn into cash, such as a semi-restored wooden sailboat). For most individuals and families, wealth is derived from two main sources: savings—the excess of income over expenditures; and asset appreciation—the increase in value of owned assets. Finally, of course, inheritance and gifts can be an additional source of wealth for some individuals.

One of the key differences between personal and corporate wealth—and the financial theory that underpins them—is that, in the corporate context, the impact of most decisions can be, and is, measured in dollars. For instance, it may cost $1 million to construct and equip a new plant, and that plant may generate a cash flow of $150,000 a year for ten years. Those costs and benefits can be weighed, and an investment decision can be reached about whether to build the plant; a good decision will increase the wealth of the corporation. In the world of personal finance, an individual may decide to spend $10,000 to build a fireplace in the family room. The enjoyment such an investment creates—the pleasure of

1

sitting around with family and friends in front of a blazing fire on a chilly evening—cannot readily be measured in dollars, and yet surely it increases wealth in the broadest sense. As an even more pointed example, the decision to have a child clearly entails serious financial burdens, yet each year millions of couples willingly undertake those burdens because of the perceived non-financial benefits of having children.

A large portion of corporate financial theory focuses on investments in non-financial assets that provide a financial return, such as plant, equipment or new lines of business. In the realm of personal finance, almost all investment decisions relate to securities, such as stocks, bonds, mutual funds and, to a lesser extent, real estate. This book does not purport to elucidate the complex underpinnings of personal decisions concerning consumption or investments with non-financial returns. Economists and decision theorists do study such questions under the heading of "utility maximization," but they are beyond the scope of this book. We will assume that individuals are capable of making fairly sound decisions on this front. Rather, this book will address questions involving the accumulation, management, preservation, and transmission of personal wealth.

[¶ 1,020]

2. Personal Wealth

Typically, wealth increases during an individual's prime earning years, and then gradually decreases as wealth is depleted during the years of retirement. Individuals seek to increase their wealth not only by earning more money each year—increasing their income—but also by maximizing the rate at which the assets that comprise their wealth increase in value. For example, an individual may choose to invest in stocks (or equity mutual funds) rather than bonds, out of a belief that stocks are likely to produce a superior investment return over time. Similarly, individuals attempt to protect the wealth they have accumulated—as well as protect their earning power—through various forms of insurance.

This chapter will discuss several types of financial assets that typically represent major components of individual or family wealth, as well as the theory that underlies the choice of assets in an individual's portfolio.

[¶ 1,030]

3. Personal Financial Statements

Just as corporations have a standard set of financial statements—an income statement, balance sheet and cash flow statement—individuals have the need for similar summaries of their financial situation.

- The income statement gives a picture of the activity that occurred over a period of time—typically a year, but sometimes a month or a quarter. An income statement captures the "flows" that move through an individual's account—income that comes in during the year, expenses that go out.

- The balance sheet contrasts with the income statement in that it is a snapshot of the state of affairs that exists at a single point in time—it reflects the "stock" of an individual's wealth (not to be confused with shares of corporate "stock"). Thus, while an income statement will be dated (for example), January 1 through December 31, 2005, the balance sheet will be dated simply December 31, 2005. The balance sheet lists the individual's assets, liabilities, and net worth on that particular date.

- The cash flow or "sources and uses" statement uses information from both the balance sheet and income statement to derive a view of where cash actually came from and where it was used. So, for instance, withdrawing $50,000 from a bank account to make a down payment on a house would not show up on the income statement, but will show up on the cash flow statement both as a source of cash (from the bank account) and a use of cash (down payment on a home). Similarly, the purchase of a house will have no impact on net worth, but will show up on the balance sheet in the form of a new asset (and a new liability, if the purchase is financed with borrowed funds).

Thus, these three statements—the income statement, the balance sheet and the cash flow statement—can, in sum, present a reasonably accurate picture of an individual's finances at any point in time. An example of such a set of personal financial statements will be reviewed in more detail below.

[¶ 1,032]

a. *The Personal Balance Sheet*

The balance sheet lists an individual's assets, liabilities, and net worth. The balance sheet reflects the financial principle that:

$$\text{Assets} - \text{Liabilities} = \text{Net Worth.}$$

From a common sense perspective, assets represent "positive value," liabilities represent "negative value," and the difference is simply net worth. It also follows that the value of assets must always equal (or "balance") the sum of liabilities and net worth.

On a personal balance sheet like the one shown in Exhibit 1, below, assets are usually listed from most liquid to least liquid. *Liquidity* refers to the ability to convert an asset into cash. Thus, cash and cash-like instruments appear at the top of the asset column on the balance sheet, and less liquid assets, like cars, stamp collections, etc., appear near the bottom. Most securities are relatively liquid, and also appear near the top of the asset column. Certain investments—like shares in a private

[handwritten margin notes: —stock in privately owned corp's not as liquid; —debt ordered by what is due first; —cc payments top —mort, edu bottom]

corporation—may be less liquid, and would appear further down on the balance sheet.

On the liability side, in similar fashion, debts are listed in the order in which they will have to be met. Thus, credit card payments—usually due within 30 days—appear at the top of the liabilities column, and longer term debts—like a mortgage or educational loans—appear at the bottom. Note, however, that the "current portion," i.e., the portion of these debts due within one year, appears under the current liabilities heading. This convention helps the individual understand what debts will have to be paid within one year. By comparing current assets to current liabilities, one can determine whether there is sufficient cash to meet near-term obligations.

EXHIBIT 1: PERSONAL BALANCE SHEET AT DECEMBER 31, 2005

Assets

Current Assets

Checking Account (cash)	$ 5,000
Savings Account (cash)	10,000
Investment/Brokerage Account (cash)	60,000
IRA	300,000
Total Current Assets	$375,000
Automobile	$ 10,000
Real Estate: Primary Residence	290,000
Real Estate: Vacation Home	175,000
Total Assets	$850,000

Liabilities

Current Liabilities

Credit Card Debt	$ 7,000
Personal Loan (from brother)	2,500
Car Loan, current portion	1,000
Mortgage—Primary Residence, current portion	10,000
Mortgage—Vacation Residence, current portion	12,000
Total Current Liabilities	$ 32,500
Car Loan	4,000
Mortgage—Primary Residence	185,000
Mortgage—Vacation Home	135,000
Total Liabilities	$356,500
Net Worth	$493,500
Total Liabilities and Net Worth	$850,000

[¶ 1,034]

b. *The Personal Income Statement*

The personal income statement (see Exhibit 2, below) is simply a statement of an individual's annual revenue (earned and unearned income), minus expenses (food, clothing, housing, vacations, etc.), to yield a net surplus or deficit for the year. (Any net surplus is available for saving or investment; a net deficit reduces the individual's net worth accumulated in previous years.) The personal income statement is an important tool for understanding where money came from during the year, as well as where it went. Even more importantly, the personal income statement is an important planning tool for understanding what kind of resources will be required to support retirement, children's education and other planned expenditures, and whether that income is likely to be available from "earned" sources, or needs to be derived from some combination of borrowing and depletion of assets or savings.

EXHIBIT 2: PERSONAL INCOME STATEMENT FOR 2005

Revenue	
Salary	$100,000
Interest Income	2,500
Distributed Capital Gains	5,000
Gross Income	$107,500
Expenses	
Mortgage—Primary Residence (interest portion)	$ 5,000
Mortgage—Vacation Home (interest portion)	2,000
Food	12,000
Clothing	8,000
Insurance	4,000
Utilities	2,000
Entertainment	4,000
Interest	900
Miscellaneous	2,500
Taxes	30,000
Total Expenses	$ 70,400
Net Income	$ 37,100

Note that the interest portion of the mortgage payment is properly categorized as an expense. The remaining portion of the mortgage payment—the principal repayment—is not shown as an expense. Because the repayment of principal reduces both cash and debt by exactly the same amount, it is merely a set of balancing entries on the balance sheet, not an income or expense item. The repayment of principal would, however, show up on a cash flow statement.

[¶ 1,036]

c. *The Personal Cash Flow Statement*

A final financial statement is derived from these other two statements—it is called a cash flow or "sources and uses" statement. (See Exhibit 3, below.) In the corporate context, there are significant differences between income and cash flow for several reasons. First, assets are depreciated on the corporation's balance sheet, meaning that the corporation charges itself for a portion of the original purchase price each

reduces its
income

reduce its income

year, rather than ~~charging itself~~ the entire amount of the cost of the asset on the year it was purchased. This is done to more accurately match the expense with the income that will flow from it. So, for example, if a new plant is built at a cost of $20 million, with an expected useful life of 20 years, the corporation would charge itself only $1,000,000 (1/20 of $20 million) each year on its income statement. This charge would be referred to as "depreciation," and that amount would show up in the income statement as a cost each year. From a cash flow perspective, the entire $20 million was spent in the year in which the plant was built. As its name implies, a cash flow statement provides a more accurate picture of a corporation's actual cash gains and losses than does the income statement. Using the income statement as a starting point, the cash flow statement adds back depreciation (which is called a "non-cash charge") and subtracts the cash outflows associated with any investment. Similarly, cash that is generated from financing activity—raising money via debt (borrowing money) or equity (issuing new shares of stock in the corporation)—is also reflected on the cash flow statement as a source of cash. Paying off debt is a use of cash.

Note that the cash figure on the balance sheet—the sum of checking, savings and brokerage accounts—equals $75,000. Note that this figure "foots" to the $75,000 ending figure on the cash flow statement.

Because individuals are not businesses, different conventions are typically used, but some of these principles nonetheless continue to apply. For instance, if an individual purchases a house for $200,000, the asset labeled real estate on the personal balance sheet increases by $200,000. If the individual takes out a $160,000 mortgage loan to make that purchase, debt increases by the same amount. And, the remaining $40,000 (in this example) is presumably drawn from savings. So, on the asset side of the balance sheet, cash decreases by $40,000 and real estate increases by $200,000 for a net increase in assets of $160,000. Similarly, debt increases by $160,000 on the liabilities side of the balance sheet, so both sides have increased by $160,000. Any transaction that produces a change in assets will also produce an offsetting change in liabilities or net worth—this is why the balance sheet "balances."

In this example, the cash flow statement would show a "net cash outflow" of $40,000 in connection with the home purchase. Note that this $40,000 is different from an item of income or expense; it would not show up on the personal income statement as an expense, since it is not an expense—it is an *investment* in an asset. That is, the $40,000 in cash was exchanged for $40,000 of equity in the house (the $200,000 purchase price minus the $160,000 in debt). Each year, on the personal income statement, the interest cost associated with the mortgage payment is treated as interest expense; the principal portion of the mortgage payment (the amount which actually goes to reduce the outstanding balance of the mortgage) does not show up on the income statement. However, on the cash flow statement, it is a use of cash. Similarly, on the balance sheet, the liability labeled "home mortgage" decreases each year by the total amount of the principal payments made that year.

EXHIBIT 3: PERSONAL CASH FLOW STATEMENT FOR 2005

Gross Income	$107,500
Interest Expense, Credit Cards	(900)
Food	(12,000)
Clothing	(8,000)
Insurance	(4,000)
Utilities	(2,000)
Entertainment	(4,000)
Miscellaneous	(2,500)
Taxes	(30,000)
Mortgage—Primary Residence	(20,000)
Mortgage—Primary Residence (interest portion)	(5,000)
Mortgage—Vacation Home	(8,000)
Mortgage—Vacation Home (interest portion)	(2,000)
Increase (Decrease) in Cash	$ 9,100
Plus Cash at Beginning of Year	65,900
Equals Cash at End of Year	$ 75,000

[¶ 1,038]

Questions and Problems

1. Explain why the equation "Assets − Liabilities = Net Worth" makes sense. How else might you express the relationships in this equation?

2. Using the statements in Exhibits 1, 2 and 3 as a baseline, describe the effect on these statements of the following scenarios: (a) salary drops to $90,000; (b) an additional $10,000 payment is made towards the principal balance on the vacation home mortgage; (c) the personal loan from the brother is paid off in full; (d) a boat is purchased for $20,000, using $12,000 of borrowed funds and $8,000 withdrawn from the investment/brokerage account.

[¶ 1,039]

Exercise

Create your own personal financial statements, based on your assets, liabilities, net worth, income, expenses, and cash flow.

[¶ 1,040]

4. Financial Planning

Just as business firms employ skilled professionals to develop budgets and forecasts, and then make financial decisions about investing the surpluses (or financing the deficits) that may occur, individuals can avail themselves of the services of a personal financial planner. This chapter will not attempt to replicate the set of skills that such a person is likely to possess. Rather, the goal here is to introduce some basic principles of financial investing and to equip readers to understand and evaluate recommendations made by financial planners.

In general, financial planners make estimates of a family's future revenues—income—and prepare budgets for annual recurring expenses. They also try to project large expenditures or investments that may loom in the future—a second home, college tuition, care for a parent. Finally, they project future investment returns based on a specified investment strategy. Thus, they develop a picture of how much savings the family is likely to generate, as well as the adequacy of those savings and other available resources to maintain a desired standard of living through the working years and during retirement. Of course, these projections rely on all sorts of assumptions, but there is no other way to answer the fundamental question of whether the family can afford its projected level of consumption and whether it is saving enough to provide for the retirement years. In many cases, a financial planning exercise leads to the unhappy conclusion that the current rate of savings—when compared with foreseeable expenses such as a child's education—is insufficient to fund the desired standard of living up to and during retirement. Individuals often realize that they need to save more, earn a higher rate of return on those savings, and possibly, retire later (and with a lower standard of living) than originally planned. The sooner they realize the tradeoffs to be made, the better their position to bring their expectations into line with reality. Financial planners can make specific recommendations about how savings can be invested to maximize the pool of resources available during retirement.

Some financial planners provide this service for "free," and recommend products for which they receive a commission. The best way to obtain truly objective advice is to use a "fee only" financial planner. Such planners charge a fee for their services, but can render neutral, objective advice because their compensation does not depend on commissions received from products they recommend.

B. INTRODUCTION TO FINANCIAL ASSETS AND INVESTING

[¶ 1,050]

Subsequent chapters in this book will discuss the legal and tax issues confronting individuals and families in the course of financial planning. First, however, it is important to introduce the range of financial assets—stocks, bonds, and mutual funds—that make up a substantial portion of personal net worth for most individuals. In this connection, it is essential to develop a basic understanding of the financial principles that underpin such assets. Thus, the remainder of this chapter will discuss:

- The general characteristics of financial assets, as well as the features that distinguish them from one another;

- The principles of cash flow, risk, and return, and the application of those principles to stocks, bonds, and mutual funds; and

- The considerations that investors should have in mind when constructing a portfolio of investments.

[¶ 1,060]

1. Overview of Financial Assets—Some Definitions

Financial assets include a broad range of assets, the value of which can be denominated in dollars (or whatever local currency is relevant to the owner). As discussed above, this is a straightforward matter for assets like cash, near-cash equivalents, and publicly-traded securities. Certain types of assets, however, are less clearly members of this class of investment assets. A home, for instance, is bought and sold for a particular price, and often appreciates in value. It constitutes a significant component of the net worth of many families in the United States. However, it also provides another very important benefit—namely housing—to those who live in it. Thus, the house is a "mixed" asset in that it represents both investment and consumption. The same may be true for assets like a coin or stamp collection, or art, which can deliver a financial return in addition to important non-financial benefits. Because these assets are not easily analyzed through the standard financial lens, they will not be discussed in this chapter. Nonetheless, an asset that can generate financial returns on a par with a purely financial asset, while also delivering these kinds of consumption benefits to be enjoyed along the way, represents an attractive investment.

Many types of financial assets are broadly classified as "securities" (as in the "Securities and Exchange Commission"). A security is any financial instrument issued by an entity (a corporation, for example) in exchange for money invested by an individual. Securities represent a specified bundle of rights and interests. Stocks and bonds are the most common types of securities, and mutual funds are pools of these securities. Shares in mutual funds are themselves securities.

Bonds (also called "notes" or "debentures") are generally referred to as "fixed income" securities because they represent an obligation of the issuer to pay fixed amounts to the investor at fixed times. For instance, if an investor purchases a $1,000 bond that pays 5% interest annually, she will receive $50 in interest per year and a $1,000 principal payment when the bond matures. Most bonds have a life of 5 or 10 or even 30 years, and are then redeemed by the issuer for the original purchase price. The $1,000 figure is referred to as the *face* or *principal amount,* the 5% as the *yield or interest rate* (or *coupon rate,* referring to the days when people actually had to clip the coupon off the bond and send it in to receive a check for the interest payment), and the date of the final scheduled repayment of principal is called the *maturity.*

Stocks (or "equities") are securities that represent an ownership interest in a business. Publicly-traded corporations are those firms that sell their stock on a public market, available for anyone to buy. Obviously there are many corporations—including many large ones—that are

advantage of public = ascertainable value, liquidity

private. These "closely held" corporations are owned and controlled by a limited number of individuals or families, and the stock is not available for purchase on the open market. One advantage, of course, of a publicly-traded stock is that it has a readily ascertainable value, namely, the price at which the stock trades on the open market. Another advantage is liquidity—the ability to sell these shares for cash at any time. When an enterprise is organized not as a corporation but as a partnership or a limited liability company (LLC), the ownership stake is typically termed a "partnership interest" or an "LLC interest." Such private interests are often much more difficult to value and much harder to sell.

Mutual funds = pool of stocks and/or bonds

Mutual funds are simply collections of publicly-traded stocks, bonds or sometimes both, in a single investment pool, under the management of an investment professional who makes decisions about what to buy and what to sell.

liquidity = easily cash

illiquid = difficulty cash

An important principle relating to the ownership of financial assets involves the concept of liquidity. Assets that can readily be turned into cash are considered to be liquid, while those that can be turned into cash only with some difficulty are considered illiquid. So, for example, mutual funds and stocks traded on large exchanges (NYSE, NASDAQ) are considered very liquid. An investment in a brother-in law's pizza business would be considered very illiquid. A stamp collection or a piece of rental property falls somewhere in between.

liquid = easy to value

illiquid = hard to value

As a corollary, it follows that liquid assets are relatively easy to value because there is a market for them that prices them at least every day, if not every minute. An ownership interest in a private business or a piece of real estate, however, may be quite difficult to value, leading to widely differing appraisals in valuing such assets.

Techniques for valuing these securities and thinking about them as investment vehicles will be covered in more detail later in this chapter.

[¶ 1,070]

2. Basic Differences Among Securities—The Principle of Risk and Return

The differences between various types of securities and investments will be explained in more detail below, but first it is worth pointing out a fundamental relationship between the *risk* and the expected *return* of stocks, bonds, and other investments, which in turn affects the value of those investments.

Any security is backed by some form of promise that is spelled out in a series of documents—for example, a bond indenture or the by-laws of an equity issuer—all of which are essentially contracts. This promise is only as good as the issuer's ability to pay (the issuer's credit). So, for instance, General Motors or General Electric can make a "better" promise (i.e., a promise more likely to be upheld) than a start-up genetic engineering company that is betting all its hopes on a new drug under development. The value of any security depends in large part on the level of risk or uncertainty inherent in the issuing company and its business prospects.

Given a certain level of risk inherent in the company and its business, there are still very different kinds of promises that can be made. Some bonds, for instance, are backed up with specific guarantees. A company may guarantee a bond with a pledge of certain assets (all of its plant and equipment, for instance, or its accounts receivable), or it may give a certain class of bond holders a priority claim on the revenues from a particular project (e.g., the revenue that comes from licensing a particular technology, or the tolls collected on a particular stretch of roadway). So, a bond may be secured by very general or very specific assets or revenue streams.

These promises may also have a certain priority with respect to other promises the company has made. For example, a Series B bond may only pay interest after the Series A bonds have paid all of their interest. Again, the priority of claims will be laid out in detail in the bond indenture or description of securities in the prospectus.

Finally, promises can be of a fixed or variable nature. In contrast to debt, which represents a fixed obligation of the issuer, stocks represent a more variable commitment. The promise that a corporation makes to its shareholders is that these equity holders have a "right" to the money and assets that are left over each year after the corporation pays all of its fixed obligations, including debt service. Thus, the stock represents a residual claim on the corporation's earnings and profits, and this claim is subordinate to the claims of creditors (including bondholders). Shareholders typically receive payment on their claim in the form of dividends. However, shareholders have no enforceable right to receive a dividend until it is declared by the corporation's directors (or unless the corporation is taken over and liquidated by a "raider"). Absent such events, the only way for a shareholder to extract any cash from her investment is to sell her stock.

The risk of the security—the ability of the company to live up to its promise—is a function of the underlying cash flow of the business. In Exhibit 4 for instance, Line A depicts the cash flow of the company over 10 years. The cash flow varies over time as the company's operations are more or less successful. Year 4, for instance, is a tough one, and the company's cash flow dips. Now, imagine that the company borrows $1 million and promises to pay $100,000 per year in interest. This reduces the cash flow by $100,000 each year to the level shown as Line B. Still the company has positive cash flow in every year. Suppose, however, that the company borrowed $5 million, and promised to pay back $500,000 every year. In that case, the company would simply not have enough money in certain years to make the $500,000 payment. This is shown in Line C, which becomes negative in several years.

This chart also helps make another point. The equity holders in the business have the residual right to the money that is left over after the debt holders have been paid what they've been promised. (The area above the "zero" line in the graph.) You may be thinking, "Why would a company ever borrow money if, as a result, the real owners (i.e., the equity holders) get less money?" The answer is that the company should borrow the money only if it can put it to good use. That is, in the simple example above, the company is paying 10% interest per year for the use of $1 million in borrowed funds. If the company can use the borrowed funds to open a new factory and make more products and earn more than 10% on its investment, then it makes sense to borrow the funds; if it can't, then it does not.

EXHIBIT 4: A COMPANY'S CASH FLOW OVER TIME

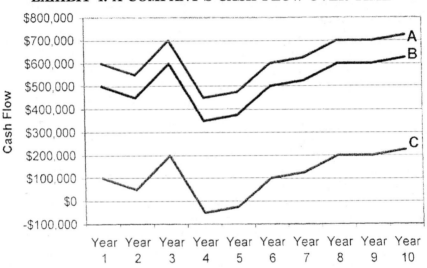

Later in this chapter we will look at some more complex questions of cash flow and investing, but for now it is simply worth noting that a financial investment involves you or your client—the investor—handing over cash today in exchange for a promise of payments or distributions to be received in the future. These promises can vary along many different dimensions, including—importantly—the underlying character of the firm (or individual) making the promise, as well as the exact nature of what they are promising to do and when.

In general, *risk is defined as the variation in expected returns*. That is, given what we know about the security markets overall, and the particular risks associated with a particular firm, we can make estimates—from past experience—about future returns and their variability, or volatility. The topic of risk is one we will return to later in this chapter (see ¶ 1,180). Many investors define a range of securities along a potential risk/reward spectrum as follows:

Cash	Short-Term Bond	Long-Term Bond	Large, Diversified Company Stocks	Small, Industry-Specific Stocks
Low	◄——————————————— Expected Risk ———————————————►			High
Low	◄——————————————— Expected Reward ———————————————►			High

[¶ 1,080]

3. Summary

Securities generally represent a promise to do something for the investor in the future, in return for the investor having turned over some cash in the present. Securities that pay a fixed amount in the future in the form of interest and principal payments are generally called bonds, notes or fixed-income securities, and securities that make a less certain promise to pay what's left after the fixed obligations have been paid are called stocks or equities. There are all sorts of hybrid securities that combine elements of these two general forms of promises: convertible bonds that can be converted into shares of stock at a given price; zero coupon bonds which don't pay any interest at all during the term of the bonds, but simply pay a lump sum at maturity; preferred stocks that pay dividends before any distributions on common stock; as well as other securities that are a blend of fixed and variable promises to pay. These will all be discussed later in this chapter.

There is such a large amount of cash available each year in the United States for investment, and this cash is so liquid—it can easily move to where an investor believes the highest returns are available—that many individuals and firms devote a lot of time and energy in the search for the "best" returns. Given that many of these securities vary along the dimensions mentioned above, a large part of that analysis consists of comparing different securities to determine which will yield the best returns. In an attempt to accomplish this, financial analysts have identified various principles that can be used to make these comparisons and evaluate securities. The next section will discuss the principles that underlie the valuation of securities and other investment opportunities.

[¶ 1,085]

Questions and Problems

1. What are the main differences between a stock and a bond?

2. What are the key features of a bond that an investor would want to know?

3. How would you define risk?

4. As an investor, would you expect to receive higher returns from a corporation's bonds or from shares of stock in the corporation?

[¶ 1,086]

Exercise

Look up the five most actively traded stocks on the NASDAQ for the most recent day for which this data is available. Evaluate the performance of these stocks over the past month, year and 5 years. How would you describe the stock's performance, and what factors have contributed to this performance?

C. KEY PRINCIPLES IN FINANCIAL INVESTING

[¶ 1,090]

Financial analysts use several key principles to analyze competing investment opportunities. They are explained below.

[¶ 1,100]

1. Cash is What Matters

The foundational principle is that cash is the only thing that matters. An investor contributes cash today in order to receive cash returns in the future. So, if you buy a share of stock, for instance, it is nice if the price of the stock goes up in the years after you own it, and your net worth could be computed each year using the then-current stock price. But, in reality, what matters is the cash you actually get when you sell the stock (and any cash you may receive in the form of dividends while you hold the stock).

[¶ 1,110]

2. Time Value of Money and Present Value

Another crucial principle is the time value of money—a dollar today is worth more than a dollar tomorrow.

Obviously, different investments have different return profiles— some require cash outflows (payments from the investor) in several years, then have no cash flows for several years, followed by several years of positive cash inflows (back to the investor). Other investments have one cash outflow and one positive cash inflow.

Analysts have developed the technique of *discounting* to compare cash flows over time. For instance, it is clear that an investor would prefer $100 today to $100 a year from now. If the investor receives $100 today she can invest it, and will have more than $100 in a year. A more complicated question is: would the investor rather have $100 today or $110 a year from now? Clearly, this is exactly the kind of question that one must be able to answer in order to compare potential investments. Imagine that an investor could take $100 today and invest it without risk for one year and then receive $110 in return, in exactly a year. Clearly, if someone offered $100 today or $107 or $108 or even $109 at the end of one year, the $100 today would be preferred; by investing it she could have $110 instead of the lesser sum being offered.

The general principle that emerges from the above example is that a dollar today is to be preferred to a dollar tomorrow. Put another way, the value of a dollar today is $1. The value today of a right to receive a dollar one year from now is less than $1.

The technique used to translate the value of future dollars back to the present is called *discounting*, and the value of those discounted dollars is called the *present value* or *present discounted value*.

Mathematically, the present value (PV) of a payment is the future value (FV) times a *discount factor* (D):

$$PV = FV \times D.$$

This of course leads to the question of what exactly the discount factor is. It may be helpful to think about the discount factor as the "opportunity cost" of capital. That is, the discount factor is the cost to the investor of *not* having the capital. It reflects the return (expressed as an annual rate of return or interest rate) that the investor could receive in the *best alternative use of the money*. So, for example, if an individual is trying to decide whether to buy a gas station or deposit the same amount of money in the bank, the discount factor used would reflect the interest rate the bank would pay—say, 5%. The topic of discount rates will be covered in more detail later in this chapter, but first, we'll see how discount rates are used.

Suppose that your client Charles has a right to receive $110 one year from now. To calculate the present value of $110 payable one year from now using a discount rate of 5%, the math is:

$$\frac{\$110}{(1 + .05)} = \$104.76.$$

Thus, using a discount rate of 5%, the present value to Charles of $110 a year from now is $104.76, which is higher than the present value of $100 today—which is of course $100.

In the general formula PV = FV × D,

$$D = \frac{1}{(1 + r)^n}$$

where r is the annual discount rate and n is the number of years from now until the time of payment. This formula is often used to compare alternative investment opportunities. For example, an investor has the option of: (1) investing $100 today and receiving $150 in five years; or (2) depositing $100 in a savings account at 4% interest. We can determine the present value of option 1 as follows:

$$PV = \$150 \times \frac{1}{(1 + .04)^5}$$

or, more simply,

$$\frac{\$150}{(1 + .04)^5} = \$123.29.$$

(Remember .04 is the same as 4%.) Because the present value of option 1 exceeds $100, we know that it has a positive present value and is superior to depositing the money at 4% interest.

Similarly, suppose your client Helen has the option of investing $2,500 in either: (1) a risk-free bond that pays 8% interest annually for 30 years and then repays the $2,500 principal amount; or (2) an investment that returns $20,000 in 30 years. We can calculate the present value of option 2 as follows:

$$\underline{PV} = \frac{\$20,000}{(1 + .08)^{30}} = \$1,987.55.$$

Because the present value of option 2 is less than the required investment of $2,500, you would advise Helen to choose option 1 in this scenario.

Present value calculations are an important part of many different kinds of financial analysis. Some of the earliest electronic calculators were developed in large measure to perform this kind of analysis, and indeed, various kinds of calculators are available for purchase today. Certainly, if you anticipate performing even basic financial analyses of the kind described in this chapter, you will find a calculator with financial functions—like present and future value—to be of significant assistance.

Before such calculators were developed, these calculations were done using "present value tables" like the one reproduced in Appendix A. In essence, a present value table shows the present value of $1 to be paid n years in the future at a discount rate r. It is worth doing a simple example of using present value tables just to understand how they work.

Suppose someone offers you the opportunity to invest $1,000 today in a real estate project and receive a stream of payments back as follows (assume the payments occur at the end of the years noted):

Year 1	$ 50
Year 2	$100
Year 3	$200
Year 4	Original sum of $1,000 returned

The question is, what is this opportunity worth to you?

As we've seen, answering this question requires that you determine your discount rate; let's say in this example that the best alternative—against which you are comparing the real estate investment—is 5%.

Looking at the present value table in Appendix A, we can see that the present value of $1 at a discount rate of 5% is as follows (over each of the four years of the investment):

Year 1	0.952
Year 2	0.907
Year 3	0.864
Year 4	0.823

Thus, at a 5% discount rate, $1 payable at the end of year 1 has a present value of $0.952, $1 payable at the end of year 2 has a present value of $0.907, and so on. Since we are analyzing the receipt of $50, $100, $200 and $1,000, in each of the 4 years, we must multiply the dollars we are getting by the discount factor for the relevant year.

Year 1	$ 50	× 0.952	$ 47.60
Year 2	$ 100	× 0.907	$ 90.70
Year 3	$ 200	× 0.864	$172.80
Year 4	$1,000	× 0.823	$823.00

In total, then, the investment has a present value of $1,134.10, making this real estate project preferable to an investment that yields 5%.

[¶ 1,115]

Questions and Problems

1. What is present value?

2. What is the present value of $100 payable in one year if the discount rate is 3%? $100 payable in one year if the discount rate is 7%? $100 payable in three years if the discount rate is 7%?

3. Assuming a discount rate of 5%, calculate the present value of the following streams of cash flows: $1,000 per year for 5 years; $100 in year 1, $200 in year 2; $300 in year 3.

[¶ 1,116]

Exercises

1.   If your discount rate is 5%, which is a more attractive stream of cash flows to you: $100 per year for 5 years, or $600 all in year 5?

2.   There is a bond that will pay you $100 each year for 25 years. If the discount rate is 15%, how much is the bond worth today?

3.   A client will receive a $7,500 payment each year for 30 years; she believes the present value of this stream of payments is $150,000. What discount rate is your client using?

[¶ 1,120]

3. Net Present Value

Net present value (NPV) is simply the present value of the return on the investment, minus the present value of the amounts invested to produce that return. Thus, another way of expressing the value of the investment in the first example in the previous section is to say that the NPV for Charles is $4.76 ($104.76 present value less $100 investment); for Helen, the NPV of option 2 is negative $512.55 ($1,987.45 present value less $2,500 investment).

For a more complicated example, still assuming a 5% discount rate, consider the following stream of cash flows associated with a real estate investment. The investor plans to buy an unimproved parcel of land for $100,000, to rent it out for five years as a parking lot at an annual rental of $5,000, and then to sell it for $100,000. Let's assume the projected cash flows are as follows:

	Year 0	Year 1	Year 2	Year 3	Year 4	Year 5
Purchase	($100,000)					
Rent		$5,000	$5,000	$5,000	$5,000	$5,000
Sale Proceeds						$100,000
Total	($100,000)	$5,000	$5,000	$5,000	$5,000	$105,000
Present Value	($100,000)	$4,762	$4,535	$4,319	$4,114	$82,270

If we sum the present value of all the cash flows and subtract the $100,000 initial investment we see that, assuming a discount rate of 5%, the NPV of the project is zero, meaning that as an investor we would be neutral between making this investment or not. Another way of saying the same thing is that the project has an implied return of 5%. That is, the project's cash flows, when discounted at their implicit rate of return, have an NPV of zero.

A more complicated example would be an investment in a trucking company where a $100,000 initial investment is required to purchase the company's trucks, annual maintenance on trucks is $1,000, cash flow (CF) from the operations of the company is $23,000 per year, and the trucks have a liquidation value of $10,000 at the end of year 5. Assuming a discount rate of 5%, the projected cash flows are as follows:

	Year 0	Year 1	Year 2	Year 3	Year 4	Year 5
Initial Investment	($100,000)					
Maintenance		($1,000)	($1,000)	($1,000)	($1,000)	($1,000)
Operations CF		$23,000	$23,000	$23,000	$23,000	$23,000
Sale of Assets						$10,000
Total	($100,000)	$22,000	$22,000	$22,000	$22,000	$32,000
Present Value	($100,000)	$20,952	$19,955	$19,004	$18,099	$25,073

If we sum the present value of each year's cash flows, we see that the investment has a NPV of $3,083 and is therefore an attractive investment opportunity, based on an assumed discount rate of 5%.

In analyzing a particular investment, the discount rate that is chosen can have a significant impact on net present value. In the above examples, the investments in the parking lot and the trucks, respectively, would each have a negative net present value if the discount rate were substantially higher (say, 8%).

[¶ 1,125]

Questions and Problems

1.   What is the difference between present value and net present value?

2.   If the cash flows of an investment have a present value of $7,500 but the investment required to attain those cash flows is $5,000, what is the NPV?

[¶ 1,126]

Exercises

1.   What is the net present value of an investment that costs $20,000 today and pays $45,000 in 5 years? Assume a discount rate of 10%.

2.   A salesman offers your client an investment in a real estate project. For an up-front investment of $250,000, your client can receive a $31,500 payment each year for 15 years. Assume the discount rate is 7.3%. Should your client make the investment?

3.   Your client has the opportunity to buy a snow-cone stand for $70,000. Assume that the stand will allow her to sell 10,000 snow cones each year, and that she will make $1 profit on each cone. Each year, she must spend $1,200 to sharpen the ice shaver. The discount rate is 4.5%. After 10 years, her snow-cone license expires and she can sell the stand itself for

$15,000. For simplicity, assume that all cash outflows and inflows happen on Dec. 31 of the relevant year (with the first profits coming in one year after your investment). Should your client buy the stand?

[¶ 1,130]

4. Special Types of Investments: Perpetuities

One useful shortcut involves what are known as *perpetuities*—that is, a stream of cash flows of a certain quantity that goes on forever. Imagine trying to determine the present value of a perpetual stream of $100 annual payments. (This is essentially the same as asking what capital amount is necessary to generate an annual cash flow of $100.) Assuming a 5% discount rate, we can express the present value of the stream of cash flows as follows:

$$\underline{PV} = \frac{\$100}{.05} = \$2,000.$$

(In other words, the capital amount of $2,000, invested at 5% interest, will produce annual cash flows of $100 in perpetuity.) The general formula is:

$$\underline{PV} = \frac{\text{Payment}}{r}$$

Another useful shortcut involves a *growing perpetuity*—say, $100 in year 1, growing at 2% per year forever. This has a present value of

$$\frac{\$100}{(.05 - .02)}$$

The general formula is

$$\underline{PV} = \frac{\text{Payment}}{r - g}$$

where g is the growth rate.

[¶ 1,135]

Exercises

1. For the cash flows in the real estate project described in the table above at ¶ 1,120, what is the NPV if the purchase price rises to $200.000? If the proper discount rate is actually 6%? 4%?

2. What is the present value of a perpetuity of $2,500, if the discount rate is 8%? What if the perpetuity grows at 3% annually (assuming the same discount rate of 8%)?

3. A company offers to sell your client a 10–year bond for $100,000 on Dec. 31, 2005. The bond pays $5,000 interest in each of the first five years, beginning Dec. 31, 2006. In years 6 through 10, the bond pays $20,000 interest each year. Also in year 10, the $100,000 is paid back. All payments are made on Dec. 31 of the relevant year. For your client to be indifferent about this investment (i.e., for the NPV to be 0), what must the discount rate be?

4. The present value of a perpetuity of $250 at a 4.5% discount rate is $7,812.50. What is the growth rate implied by this present value?

[¶ 1,140]

5. Future Value and Present Value

The concept of present value is designed to bring all cash flows back to the present. An analogous concept is *future value*, in which all present and intermediate cash flows are brought forward to the future. You can imagine applying this technique to figure how much money you will have to retire on if you save $1,000 per year for the 30 years between now and your retirement. The general formula to determine the future value (FV) of an ongoing investment (I) is $FV = I \times (1 + i)^n$, where i is the interest rate earned on the investment. Assuming an annual return of 5% on the cumulative investments, future value in this example can be expressed as follows: $FV = \$1,000 \times (1 + .05)^1 + \$1,000 \times (1 + .05)^2 \ldots \$1,000 \times (1 + .05)^{30} = \$69,761$. Future value tables appear in this volume as Appendix B.

Using basic algebra, we can manipulate the formula to calculate the amount that must be invested today to produce a defined future value. For example, if we know that a college education for a child who is born today will cost $250,000 in 18 years, we can manipulate the formula to determine the amount that must be invested today (I) to provide for the child's education:

$$I = \frac{FV}{(1 + i)^n}.$$

Assuming an interest rate of 10%, we would calculate:

$$I = \frac{\$250,000}{(1 + i)^{18}} = \$44,965.$$

[¶ 1,145]

Questions and Problems

1.   What is the future value of an investment of $1,000 that earns 5% for 4 years? For 7 years?

2.   How large an investment would be required to produce a future value of $1,000,000 in 10 years, assuming an interest rate of 5%?

[¶ 1,146]

Exercises

1.   Your client, Harold, is planning for his retirement. His goal is to have a nest egg of $1,500,000 in 30 years. He is going to invest $100,000 today in a CD with an interest rate of 3.1015%. Ten years from now, he will invest an additional lump sum, which will grow at 5% annually. What is the lump sum Harold must invest ten years from now, in order to reach his goal?

2.   At an annual interest rate of 10%, how many years will it take for a given amount of money to increase by thirty-four times (i.e., for $1 to grow to $34)?

[¶ 1,150]

6.   Simple Interest vs. Compounding

Another key concept is compounding, or compound interest. That is, the ability to earn interest on the interest accumulated in prior periods. This is a very important concept which has many applications in personal investing. *Simple interest* refers to the case where interest is paid simply upon the original principal amount of the loan or investment. So, for instance, if a bank offered to pay 5% simple interest on a $1,000 investment, it would pay $50 per year for the life of the investment.

Typically, most banks pay *compound interest*. That is, the bank computes the interest more frequently than once a year—say, monthly or daily—and then pays interest on the balance in the account, including interest accrued in prior periods. Thus, when the bank quotes interest rates, it will quote an interest rate in terms of an *annual percentage rate* (APR) and a compounding interval (e.g., "compounded daily" or compounded monthly").

The way to compare interest rates for different compounding intervals is to use the *effective interest rate*. The effective rate is the rate effectively paid if compounding were to occur just once per year. This allows the investor to compare rates on an "apples-to-apples" basis.

Where m is the number of compounding periods per year, the formula for computing the effective rate is as follows:

$$\text{Effective Rate} = \left(1 + \frac{\text{APR}}{m}\right)^m - 1$$

So, for instance, a 6% APR compounded monthly becomes

$$\left[1 + \frac{.06}{12}\right]^{12} - 1 = 6.1678\%.$$

The table below gives the effective annual rates for APRs of 5% and 10%, respectively, at various compounding intervals:

Compounding Interval (times per year)	Effective Rate (5%)	Effective Rate (10%)
1 (annual)	5.000	10.000
2 (semi-annual)	5.063	10.250
4 (quarterly)	5.095	10.381
12 (monthly)	5.116	10.471
365 (daily)	5.127	10.516

The principle of compounding is crucial for understanding how relatively small contributions can grow into large amounts over time. The more frequent the compounding interval, and the longer the term of the investment, the larger the compounded value at the end of the term. Individual saving for retirement frequently involves a compounding calculation. For instance, suppose you start saving for your retirement at the rate of $200 per month when you are 25, and you plan on retiring at 65. Let's assume that the contributions earn interest at an annual rate of 7%, compounded monthly. The annual rate is converted into a periodic rate by dividing the annual rate (7%) by the number of compounding periods in a year (12). The periodic rate is added to 1, and the result is raised to the power of the number of compounding periods from the time of the contribution to the end of the investment term. In this example, the math is as follows:

$$\text{FV} = \$200 \times \left(1 + \frac{.07}{12}\right)^{480} + \$200 \times \left(1 + \frac{.07}{12}\right)^{479} \ldots \$200 \times \left(1 + \frac{.07}{12}\right)^{0} = \$524{,}963.$$

Note that the $200 contributed in the first month of savings is worth $3,262 at the end of 40 years (480 months).

If you started saving when you were 35 instead of 25, not only would you lose 10 years of contributions, but you would also lose the benefit of compounding on those contributions over the succeeding years. So, $200 per month would become $243,994 over the 30–year period. On the other hand, $200 per month over a 50–year investment term would grow to $1,089,614 at the same 7% annual rate, compounded monthly.

For a table showing compounded future values, see Appendix B.

[¶ 1,155]

Questions and Problems

1. What is the difference between simple interest and compound interest? How can you properly compare two different interest rates with different compounding intervals?

2. What is the difference between effective rate and APR? If you were considering a new credit card offer, which would you care more about?

[¶ 1,156]

Exercises

1. What is the effective rate of 8% APR compounded monthly?

2. Which is a higher effective interest rate: 5% APR compounded annually, 4.9% APR compounded monthly, or 4.8% APR compounded daily?

3. What is the future value of $150,000 invested for 25 years at an annual interest rate of 10%, compounded daily? What is the value if the interest is compounded semi-annually?

[¶ 1,160]

7. **Rate of Return**

A *rate of return* is the figure that captures the effective interest earned, even when it is not paid out periodically as interest over time, but is simply paid back in a lump sum at the end of the investment term, or in some other sequence of payments during the term. For instance, an investment that requires an initial payment of $1,000 at time zero and produces a return of $100 per year in perpetuity has a rate of return of 10%. Similarly, if $1,000 is invested and $2,594 is returned in 10 years, with zero dollars returned in between, this investment also has a rate of return of 10%. The basic equation for the rate of return is the same as for NPV, except that the equation must be manipulated algebraically to solve for r, where the cash flow in the first year is CF, and so on through periods, and where I is the original investment:

$$\text{NPV} = \frac{CF_1}{(1+r)^1} + \frac{CF_2}{(1+r)^2} \cdots \frac{CF_\eta}{(1+r)^\eta} - I$$

The rate of return has a practical application in comparing bonds of different maturities and cash flows. Suppose an investor has a choice between two bonds: one bond costs $995.50, pays annual interest of $50.00, and repays principal of $1,000 in five years; the other bond costs $780.00, pays no annual interest, and repays the principal of $1,000 in five years. Solving for the rate of return in the two options above, an investor would find that both bonds have a rate of return of around 5.10%. (Note that a financial calculator makes these calculations much easier.)

Thus, rates of return are ways of making apples-to-apples comparisons between investments with different cash inflow and outflow patterns.

The technical term for the rate of return is *internal rate of return* (IRR). One way to think about IRR is that it is the rate of return that—when used as a discount rate—will result in a zero NPV. It is the "implicit" rate of return in the stream of cash flows generated by a project or investment. Thus, when the IRR is higher than the discount rate, an investment will have a positive NPV. In practice, calculating IRRs and NPVs can be complicated, especially when the cash flows are uneven and spread over a long period of time. Financial calculators have these functions programmed in to them, and can do these calculations easily.

[¶ 1,165]

Questions and Problems

1. What is the difference between IRR and NPV?

2. What is the IRR of a project with an NPV of $0?

[¶ 1,166]

Exercises

1. Using the "IRR" function in an Excel® Spreadsheet or a financial calculator, calculate the internal rate of return for a 10–year bond that is purchased on January 1 for $950, pays annual interest of $50 (at year-end), and returns the principal amount of $1,000 at the end of year 10.

2. A client is considering an investment that involves the following cash flows. What is the IRR?

Year 1	$(100)
Year 2	10
Year 3	20
Year 4	30
Year 5	40
Year 6	150

D. HISTORICAL PERSPECTIVE ON SECURITY RETURNS

[¶ 1,170]

Having introduced the general notion of financial return, we now consider the kinds of returns that investors actually seem to earn on different types of securities. Not surprisingly—given the vast amounts of money involved—economists have been studying rates of return on financial securities for many years. The most widely used data on this topic comes from the firm of Ibbotson Associates, who publish an annual yearbook of statistical data on the performance of the securities markets. Exhibit 5 presents data on rates of return for the period 1925 to 2002:

EXHIBIT 5: TOTAL VALUE OF $1 INVESTED IN 1925 AT END OF 2002

Type of Security	Value in 2002	Implied Annual Rate of Return
Small Company Stocks	$6,816.00	12.1%
Large Company Stocks	$1,775.00	10.2%
Long–Term Government Bonds	$ 59.70	5.5%
Treasury Bills	$ 17.48	3.8%
Inflation	$ 10.09	3.1%

[Source: Ibbotson Associates: Stocks, Bonds, Bills, and Inflation, 2003 Yearbook, pp. 33, 39, 87–89, 97–99 (2003).]

The above data illustrate the powerful effect of compounding. During the period from 1925 to 2002, the implied annual rate of return on small company stocks (12.1%) was slightly more than twice the rate on long-term government bonds (5.5%). If an individual started with $2 in 1925 and invested $1 in a pool of small company stocks and $1 in long-term government bonds, the first investment would have grown to $6,816 in 2002, while the second investment would have grown to $59.70—a difference of more than 100–fold in ending value, due to compounding over time. Moreover, an investor who started with $1 in 1925 would have had to receive $10.09 back in 2002 just to keep pace with inflation.

Clearly, something important is going on. What accounts for the dramatic difference in the rates of return on different types of investments? The answer revolves around *risk*—because stocks are riskier than bonds, they must pay a higher return to coax money out of investors. More generally, higher risk investments must offer higher returns to attract capital investment.

E. RISK AND RETURN

[¶ 1,180]

Economists recognize that there is no such thing as a free lunch. The only way to earn a higher return on a financial asset is to bear higher risk. So, for instance, the reason that stocks outperform bonds—on average, over time—is that they have higher risk. They *must* outperform bonds in order to induce investors to take that risk.

Risk may be thought of as variability or volatility in the range of expected returns from an investment in a security. Of course, the volatility in the expected returns is reflected in the price of the security. Analysts can study the price of a stock, and plot its volatility relative to the market overall (represented, for example, by a pool of the 5,000 most actively traded stocks). Volatility is simply measured by looking at the price movement of a stock on a given day and looking at the percentage increase or decrease relative to the market overall. So, if the stock in Acme Corp. tends to rise 2% when the market overall rises just 1%, and fall 2% when the market falls just 1%, then Acme is twice as risky as the market overall. It is said to have a *beta* of 2. (For the statistically minded, "beta" (β) is the coefficient in the regression equation that determines the slope of the line plotting the price movements of—in this example—one stock relative to the market overall.)

See Exhibit 6 for an example of the betas of some well-known large companies.

EXHIBIT 6: BETAS OF SOME PUBLIC STOCKS

Company	Symbol	Price/ Earnings	Market Cap($bn)	Beta
Caterpillar	CAT	24.41	26.70	1.06
Coca–Cola	KO	27.92	120.12	0.28
Dell	DELL	32.94	85.19	1.64
ExxonMobil	XOM	13.37	278.27	0.42
General Electric	GE	19.88	308.86	1.10
General Motors	GM	9.37	26.07	1.17
Microsoft	MSFT	30.67	270.18	1.62
Morgan Stanley	MWD	17.55	65.83	2.01
Pfizer	PFE	128.31	266.34	0.39
Time Warner	TWX	24.69	76.39	2.28
Wal–Mart	WMT	28.79	252.70	0.80
Yahoo!	YHOO	121.57	29.49	3.18

[Source: Yahoo! Finance on WSJ Online. Data for trailing twelve months as of 3/17/2004. Betas from Yahoo! Finance on 3/26/2004.]

Note that a stock with a beta of 1 is not risk free—it simply has the *average* level of risk relative to the market overall. Betas of more or less than 1 signify the level of risk *relative* to that average.

[¶ 1,190]

1. The Market Risk Premium

By looking at historical returns of stocks and bonds, analysts have tried to determine how much higher returns investors earn in exchange for bearing the extra risk inherent in stocks. In performing this analysis, they focus on the risk-free rate of return, which is the interest rate on Treasury bills. It is important to understand that this risk-free rate is the baseline one earns simply for giving up one's money, and putting it in what is essentially a risk-free instrument: a short-term bond backed by the full faith and credit of the U.S. government.

Over the long term, economists have determined that the entire stock market (again, represented by a pool of 5,000 stocks with an average beta of 1) earns a rate of return approximately *7% higher* than the risk-free rate of return earned by Treasury bills. This is called the *market risk premium*. Thus, the total expected return on stocks is equal to the risk-free rate plus a market risk premium.

We can plot a "security market line" (SML) on a graph (see Exhibit 7), using two reference points:

● Beta = 0, where the market risk premium is zero (i.e., investors earn only the risk-free rate); and

● Beta = 1, where investors earn a risk premium of 7%.

EXHIBIT 7: THE SECURITY MARKET LINE

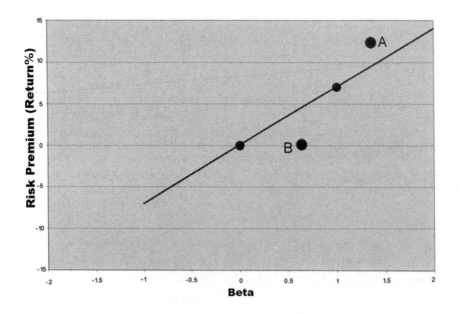

In this graph, the beta = zero point on the x-axis corresponds to the risk-free rate of return, with a market risk premium of zero. The risk level of beta = 1 corresponds to the risk of the entire stock market, with a 7% market risk premium. It makes sense that certain stocks—or investments—are less risky than the market overall, and should earn a lower return, and that certain riskier investments should pay a higher return. The SML is an "efficient frontier" which explains the valuation—and pricing—of all sorts of securities. Point A in the graph above is a stock that has the same beta—risk—as a stock on the security market line, but is earning a higher risk premium—a higher return. Thus, in an efficient market, money will flow away from all other stocks—depressing their price and thus, increasing their expected return slightly, and flow in to the security of company A, increasing its price and decreasing its expected return until the expected returns reach equilibrium, bringing company A's stock back to the SML. The same process would play out in reverse for the security of company B, whose stock was below the SML.

Note that as the risk-free interest rate moves, the total expected return on the stock market moves as well. That is, if the risk-free rate rises from 3% to 6%, the total expected return on stocks rises from 10% (3% + 7%) to 13% (6% + 7%).

[¶ 1,195]

Questions and Problems

1. What type of security has demonstrated the highest return over time, and why?

2. In an environment where the risk-free rate was 5%, what would be the total expected return on a broad portfolio of stocks?

3. A stock with a beta of 0.8 is trading at a price implying an expected return (risk premium) of 7.5%. Assuming an efficient market, would you expect the stock's price to rise, fall, or remain constant?

[¶ 1,196]

Exercises

1. Your client, Ted, invests $100 in an index fund (beta = 1.0). Another investor, Sally, invests $50 in a stock that is twice as risky as the overall market, and $50 in a stock that is half as risky as the overall market. A year later, the overall market has returned 10%. Does Ted or Sally have the higher return, or do they have the same return?

2. Can you think of an investment that might have a negative beta? Could you imagine any productive use for such an investment?

[¶ 1,200]

2. The Capital Asset Pricing Model

The *capital asset pricing model* (CAPM) is the formal term for the formula that is used to determine the expected rate of return on a specific stock. It depends on the logic expressed by the SML. Thus, the expected return (E) = risk-free rate + (beta × market risk premium). If we use a market risk premium of 7% (discussed above) and if the risk-free rate on Treasury bills is 3%, then a stock with a Beta of 1 should be expected to generate a return of 10% (over the long run).

Similarly, a stock with a lower beta (and therefore less risk) would be expected to generate lower returns. If a stock's beta was 0.1, we would expect a long-term annual return of 3% + (0.1 × 7%) = 3.7%. Many utility companies have low-beta stocks and have traditionally underperformed the broader markets. Stocks with higher betas (and therefore higher risk), represented by many "high-tech" companies, have a higher expected return. A stock with a beta of 3.18 (like Yahoo!) would be expected to return 3% + (3.18 × 7%) = 25.3% annually.

There is a very important corollary to CAPM. Since (in the first example) 10% is the expected rate of return demanded by investors, this 10% is also the *company's cost of equity capital*. That is, when a company analyzes its projects to determine the NPV of the project, it should use a cost of capital that is based on the returns that it will have to offer to investors to get that capital.

This is an outcome of the rule related to discounting that we began with. Namely, the proper rate at which to discount a stream of cash flows is the rate that reflects the *risk* of those cash flows. CAPM shows us how the risk determines the rate of return demanded by investors, and that this rate of return (from the investor's point of view) is the cost of capital (from the company's point of view). So, if a 10–year Treasury bond pays 3% interest, then this low 3% rate reflects the assumed safety—the lack of risk—of those payments. If a bond from a near-bankrupt asbestos manufacturer pays 25% interest, this reflects the riskiness of *those* cash payments. So, to extend this example, if an investor considers buying a $1,000, 10–year bond from each issuer described above, and then tries to discount the promised interest payments of $30 per year on the Treasury bond and $250 per year on the asbestos company bond, he would have to use two separate discount rates. Using a 3% discount rate for the Treasury bond, the investor would see that the present value of that investment would be:

$$\underline{PV} = \frac{\$30}{(1 + .03)^1} + \frac{\$30}{(1 + .03)^2} \cdots \frac{\$1,030}{(.1 + .03)^{10}}$$

and the present value of the asbestos company bond would be:

$$PV = \frac{\$250}{(1 + .25)^1} + \frac{\$250}{(1 + .25)^2} \quad \cdots \quad \frac{\$1,250}{(.1 + .25)^{10}}$$

Despite the higher cash flows of the asbestos company bonds, when the risk levels of the two bonds are taken into account, they have equal present value (equal to the original $1,000 face value).

Thus, every investment security needs to be looked at through the lens of the amount and timing of the promised cash flows as well as the riskiness of those cash flows. In an efficient market, securities will be "fairly" priced to reflect the consensus of beliefs on the part of buyers and sellers about the future. Of course, that consensus is rarely an accurate predictor of the future, although it may well be the best predictor available. Individual investors must make a decision about whether they want to make the same "bets" that the market is making, or if they wish to make investment decisions based on different assumptions.

[¶ 1,205]

Questions and Problems

1. Explain the capital asset pricing model.

2. Using the capital asset pricing model, determine the expected return of a stock that has a beta of 2.0, assuming the risk-free rate is 4% and the market premium is 7%. In an efficient market, is this stock a better investment than one with a beta of 1.5?

[¶ 1,206]

Exercise

A public company is considering launching a new business unit. The company expects that the unit will cost $20,000,000 to launch in year 1 and will yield a one-time $50,000,000 payout in year 7. Should the company launch the business unit? Assume that the company's stock has a beta of 2.1, the market premium is 7%, and the risk-free rate is 5.1%.

F.   THE INDIVIDUAL INVESTOR

[¶ 1,210]

Given an understanding of the key principles that guide investors in analyzing investments of all kinds, we now take a closer look at specific types of financial investments that dominate most investors' portfolios: stocks, bonds, and mutual funds.

Individuals can buy and sell securities in various ways. While there are rare instances where securities are purchased directly from the issuing corporation, far more frequently they are purchased through a stock brokerage account. Individuals can open a brokerage account with a major "full service" broker (full service equals full price) or with a "discount" broker (like Charles Schwab and others). An investor can buy shares of stock as well as bonds and other securities through a stockbroker. Individuals may have a real person whom they speak to and from whom they get advice (this is the "full service" type of broker). Or they may simply execute trades through an 800 number answered by a different customer service representative each time they call, or even over the internet.

In addition to the major brokerage firms, the major mutual fund companies—like Fidelity and Vanguard—also establish brokerage accounts for customers, through which they can purchase individual securities, as well as the mutual funds for which these companies are well known.

When an order is placed, the brokerage firm dispatches it to an employee on the floor of one of the stock exchanges, or—in the case of computerized exchanges like NASDAQ—simply enters it in a computer. When the order is executed on the floor of an exchange like the NYSE, there are individuals called specialists who actually make a market in the stock, setting a price at which they will buy and at which they will sell, (the "bid" and the "ask" price) in an attempt to "clear" the market (i.e., find a price at which the number of buyers equals the number of sellers).

There are all sorts of ways to buy stock. The most common approach is called a "market" order, when the broker is instructed to buy a certain number of shares at the market price, whatever that price may be. A "limit" order is an order for a certain number of shares, but only at a specified price. Thus, a limit sell order (for shares you already own) would be executed only at the limit price or higher; a limit buy order would be executed only at the limit price or lower.

The beneficial owner of the stock—the person who ultimately enjoys the financial returns (and bears the risk of loss) on the investment—is the individual who purchased the stock through a broker, or the shareholder in a mutual fund, or the participant of a pension fund that holds the stock in its portfolio. Relatively few individuals appear as shareholders "of record" on the books of issuing corporations, however, because most brokerage firms continue to hold the stock in their name; the issuing corporation knows only the name of the broker or institution that purchased the stock. (This is referred to as holding shares in "street name.")

In mid-March of 2004, for instance, the major holders of GE stock were a group of large institutions, most of them presumably holding stock in street name or in trust or pension trust funds for the benefit of individuals. The ten largest institutions collectively owned nearly 29% of GE's stock—nearly 2.9 billion shares out of slightly over 10 billion shares outstanding. See Exhibit 8 below.

EXHIBIT 8: MAJOR SHAREHOLDERS IN GE, MARCH 2004

Institutions	Shares	% Ownership	Market Value ($mil)
Barclays Bank	390,013,621	3.9%	$11,958
State Street Corp.	290,077,451	2.9%	$ 8,894
Fidelity Management & Research Corp.	249,708,633	2.5%	$ 7,656
Vanguard Group	194,204,316	1.9%	$ 5,954
Northern Trust Corp.	154,611,985	1.5%	$ 4,740
Capital Research & Management Co.	144,165,500	1.4%	$ 4,420
Wells Fargo & Co.	125,665,281	1.3%	$ 3,853
Axa	124,518,566	1.2%	$ 3,818
Mellon Bank	124,484,635	1.2%	$ 3,817
Citigroup	103,867,217	1.0%	$ 3,185
Mutual Funds	**Shares**	**% Ownership**	**Market Value ($mil)**
Vanguard 500 Index Fund	86,989,938	0.9%	$ .2,667
Fidelity Magellan Fund	72,238,400	0.7%	$ 2,215
CREF Stock Account	68,472,251	0.7%	$ 2,099
Washington Mutual Investors Fund	39,650,000	0.4%	$ 1,216
SPDR Trust Series 1	39,228,279	0.4%	$ 1,203
Vanguard Institutional Index Fund	37,298,703	0.4%	$ 1,144
Fidelity Growth & Income Portfolio	34,937,200	0.3%	$ 1,071
Putnam Voyager Fund	29,785,400	0.3%	$ 913
Vanguard Total Stock Market Index Fund	28,084,052	0.3%	$ 861
Fidelity Blue Chip Growth Fund	26,133,500	0.3%	$ 801

[Source: Yahoo! Finance, "GE: Major Holders for GENERAL ELEC CO," Yahoo! Finance Web site, accessed March 18, 2004.]

Of course, instead of buying individual stocks in specific corporations, an individual could purchase shares in a mutual fund in which a professional investment manager is assembling a portfolio of different stocks. The advantages of owning individual stocks as compared to shares in a mutual fund or index fund will be discussed later in this chapter. (See ¶ 1,390.)

As a practical matter, there are both institutional buyers and "retail" buyers of a stock. Retail investors include individuals who may decide they like shopping at Wal-Mart or Home Depot and therefore, that these are good stocks to buy, or who rely on reports in the business press to form opinions about particular stocks. In general, corporate management prefers to have retail investors as shareholders because they are viewed as more loyal and compliant than institutional investors. If the manager of a large mutual fund decides that she no longer likes a stock, she may dump hundreds of thousands of shares on the market, causing the price to drop. However, because the majority of stocks are held by institutions, it is important to have institutional demand for a stock as well.

It is also thought that institutions pay more attention to stock analysts. All of the major Wall Street brokers have "analysts" who follow various industries and stocks. Thus, a pharmaceutical analyst follows developments affecting the major drug manufacturers, visiting the company, talking to executives, and attempting to do sophisticated analysis on the forces affecting the company's sales and profits. Many of these people are quite knowledgeable about companies and the stock market.

In the late 1990's, however, a major scandal erupted in this arena as investors began to realize the full extent of the conflicting interests and pressures affecting these stock analysts. For instance, most of the major brokerage firms also have investment banking operations which generate fees for underwriting stock and taking a company public. The fees on these transactions can be very large, and most major firms covet this business. Thus, it was alleged that firms would put pressure on their analysts to make favorable assessments of actual or prospective investment banking clients as a way of currying favor with corporate management and attracting this investment banking business. In several investigations of these analysts and their firms, it was revealed that some analysts made highly negative assessments of these companies in private e-mails while still encouraging the public to buy the stock. Some reforms have been put in place, but it is wise to remember that there are inherent conflicts of interest at many of the Wall Street firms that serve two different sets of clients—corporate management seeking to maintain high stock prices, and investors seeking objective, independent advice.

G. APPLYING FINANCIAL PRINCIPLES TO BONDS

[¶ 1,220]

Earlier, a bond was described very generally as a promise to make a stream of payments and return the original capital invested, in exchange for the use of that capital. In essence, the buyer of a bond makes a loan to the issuer. To review, certain terms are key to understanding the economics of a bond:

- *Face value*, or *principal amount*, or *par value* of the bond: the amount that will be paid to the owner upon maturity.

- *Maturity*: the date when the principal amount is scheduled to be repaid to the investor.

- *Yield, interest rate or coupon*: the stated rate of interest on the bond.

To put all of these together, a bond may be described by reference to the issuer, maturity, face value and yield (e.g., a General Motors (GM) 10–year, $1,000, 5.25% bond). Once a bond is issued and begins trading, the fact that it is a 10–year bond doesn't really help the potential purchaser know how many years are left until maturity. For example, the original purchaser might have owned it for 4 years before reselling it on the market. So, bonds are typically described by the year in which they mature as well (e.g., a General Motors, $1,000, 5.25% bond, maturing March 2009).

While bonds may trade at exactly their face value, they most often do not. Suppose that General Motors issued the above described bonds in March of 1999, with an interest rate of 5.25%, and that the bonds were fully sold to investors at par value (i.e., the face amount). An investor buys a bond, holds it in his brokerage account, and decides to sell it one year later, by which time interest rates have risen to 6.0%. Another investor would be foolish to pay the full face amount of $1,000 for a 5.25% GM bond if for the same price she could go out and buy a "fresh," newly-issued bond with an interest rate of 6%. So, the price of the old bond must fall to the point where it has the same *effective yield* to a purchaser as the new bond. Thus, the March 2009 GM bond will sell at a "market discount" and will have a higher effective yield than the stated interest rate. The effective yield is known as the *yield to maturity* (YTM)—the actual yield on the bond, rather than its stated interest rate. In the above example, the 5.25% bond would trade at $948.99, with a YTM of 6%. Mathematically, this is calculated by the standard present value equation, except that in this instance, we know the PV and are trying to calculate r:

$$PV = \frac{CF_1}{(1+r)^1} + \frac{CF_2}{(1+r)^2} \cdots \frac{CF_\eta}{(1+r)^\eta}$$

Generally this calculation is so complex that the use of a financial calculator or spreadsheet is required.

Alternatively, interest rates may fall, and the market price of the bond may rise above par, reducing the yield to maturity below the stated interest rate. The *current yield* is the interest payment divided by the bond's actual price. So, if a 10–year bond's actual price was $980 and paid interest of $50 annually, the current yield would be

$$\frac{\$50}{\$980} = 5.1\%.$$

Note, however, that this is different than the YTM, which takes into account all of the bond's future cash flows, including the principal repayment. The YTM would be calculated as:

$$\$980 \ = \ \frac{\$50}{(1 + r)^1} + \frac{\$50}{(1 + r)^2} \cdots \frac{\$1,050}{(1 + r)^{10}}$$

Solving for r, we get 5.3%.

[¶ 1,225]

Exercises

1. How much should your client pay for a bond that pays annual interest of $50 for three years (at the end of each year) and then returns the original face amount of $1,000 (in addition to the final interest payment) at the end of the third year? Assume that the correct interest rate for such a bond is 4%.

2. Imagine a $1,000, 10–year, 5% bond issued at par one year ago today. Today, interest rates for similar bonds rise to 6%. What should a your client pay for this 2001 bond?

3. What is the current yield of a $1,000, 2–year bond selling for $900 that pays annual interest of $50? What is the bond's yield to maturity?

[¶ 1,230]

1. Bonds—Credit Risk

A key concern for the purchaser of a bond is the risk of default—the risk that the issuer will not make good on its promise to make timely and full payments of interest and principal. Several factors could cause a company to default on its debt: A large lawsuit or series of lawsuits that sap the company's assets (e.g., asbestos litigation), a sharp downturn in the company's business, or simple fraud (think of Enron, for example).

To help investors guard against such problems, several rating agencies make it their business to examine and report on the financial condition of debt issuers. These agencies—Standard & Poor's and Moody's—rate debt according to the risk of default. Exhibit 9 below outlines Standard & Poor's rating system.

EXHIBIT 9: S&P LONG–TERM ISSUER CREDIT RATINGS DEFINITIONS

AAA:	*Extremely strong* capacity to meet its financial commitments.
AA:	*Very strong* capacity to meet its financial commitments.
A:	*Strong* capacity to meet its financial commitments but is somewhat more susceptible to adverse effects of changes in circumstance.
BBB:	*Adequate* capacity to meet its financial commitments.
BB:	*Less vulnerable* in the near term than other lower-rated obligors. However, it faces ongoing uncertainties and exposure to adverse

	business, financial, or economic conditions which could lead to obligor's inadequate capacity to meet its financial commitments.
B:	*More vulnerable* to non-payment than obligations rated "BB," but the obligor currently has capacity to meet its financial commitment on the obligation.
CCC:	*Currently vulnerable*, and is dependent upon favorable business, financial and economic conditions to meet its financial obligations.
CC:	*Currently highly vulnerable* to non-payment.
C:	*Currently highly vulnerable* to non-payment.
R:	Under regulatory supervision
SD and **D:**	Has failed to pay one or more of its financial obligations.
N.R.:	An issuer designated N.R. is not rated.

[Source: Standard & Poor's, "S&P Long–Term Issuer Credit Ratings Definitions" (2004).]

Note that bonds rated BB or lower are not considered "investment grade." That is, the companies that issue these bonds face a good deal of business risk and have capital structure that places them at a significant risk of default on their bonds. These bonds are often referred to as "junk," or "high-yield" bonds, and are generally deemed unsuitable for risk averse investors.

Obviously, issuers with a lower rating must pay a higher interest rate to compensate investors for the higher risk of default on their bonds. Exhibit 10 below describes the spreads that existed in April 2004 between bonds with various credit ratings. As with stocks, a investor in bonds can minimize the risk of loss by diversifying (i.e., holding a portfolio of bonds from different issuers. One way to do this, of course, is with a bond mutual fund. This will be discussed further in ¶ 1,390.

EXHIBIT 10: YIELDS ON 10–YEAR BONDS OF VARIOUS RATINGS

Corporate Bond Yields, July 2004	**% Yield**
Corporate AAA	4.98
Corporate AA	5.11
Corporate A	5.23
Corporate BBB	5.73
High Yield: BB	6.90
High Yield: B	7.72
High Yield: CCC	9.32

[Source: Lehman US Aggregate Statistics, Bloomberg.]

[¶ 1,235]

Questions and Problems

1. What factors make a bond more or less risky?

2. What types of companies would you expect to have credit ratings of AAA or AA? What types would you expect to have ratings in the "high-yield" category?

3.   What additional return did holders of CCC bonds earn relative to AAA bonds in exchange for bearing that additional risk? (Use data in Exhibit 10.)

[¶ 1,236]

Exercise

Your client is trying to choose between two bonds. He will choose the bond with the highest NPV. One option is a $1,000 BB rated bond, which has 7 years to go until maturity and an interest rate of 7.0%. This bond is trading at $500 today. The second option is a $1,000 AA rated bond, with 5 years to go until maturity and an interest rate of 3.5%. This bond is selling for $400. (Use data in Exhibit 10.) Which bond should your client buy?

[¶ 1,240]

2.   Bonds—Interest Rate Risk

The Standard & Poor's ratings capture one dimension of risk inherent in a bond—the credit risk of the issuer. There is another significant risk that holders of bonds subject themselves to, and that is interest rate risk. Recall the earlier discussion (in ¶ 1,110) regarding the value of a bond, based on the present value of the payments (cash flows) discounted at the opportunity cost of capital. As we saw then, if the interest rate rises, the price of the bond must fall so that the rate of return is equivalent to new bonds being issued.

The longer the maturity of the bond, the longer it will take for all of its payments, including the return of principal, to be returned to the investor. This magnifies the effect of a change in interest rates, compared to the effect on a shorter-term bond. The following example illustrates the point.

An investor buys two newly-issued $1,000 bonds at par value. Both bonds pay annual interest of 5%, the prevailing market rate at the time of issuance. One bond has a 3–year term to maturity; the other has a 10–year term. At the end of the first year, the prevailing interest rate in the market rises to 7%, but the interest payments on the bonds remain at $50 per year. Using the YTM equation, we can calculate that the prices of the two bonds must have dropped to $963.84 and $869.70, respectively. Because so much more of the value of the longer-term (10–year) bond is tied up in interest and principal payments that will stretch out over the ensuing 9 years, the rise in interest rates has a much larger effect on its valuation.

[¶ 1,245]

Questions and Problems

1.   If interest rates fall dramatically, what would happen to the price of bonds? Would long-term bonds or short-term bonds be affected more by changes in interest rates? Why?

2. If a bond specifies a fixed payment schedule over a fixed timeline, why would its value change when the market interest rate changes? Explain your answer in common-sense terms.

[¶ 1,246]

Exercises

1. Imagine two different $1,000 bonds sold on January 1, 2003 at par value, each of which pays 5% annual interest. One bond is a 5–year bond and the other a 20–year bond. On January 1, 2005, interest rates rise to 7%. What price should a purchaser pay for each bond?

2. Consider two bonds with the same face value and term. The two bonds also have the same market price on January 1. The first bond initially has a corporate bond rating of B, but is subsequently downgraded to CCC on January 2. (Use the data in Exhibit 10.) The second bond has a rating of AA. On January 2, the market interest rate suddenly declines by 1.6%. Qualitatively, what will happen to the price of each bond?

[¶ 1,250]

3. The Yield Curve

At any point in time, investors have a set of expectations about future interest rates that can be captured in what is called the *yield curve*. Typically, the yield curve is drawn using data from U.S. Treasury bonds, where the default risk is assumed to be zero. Thus, the spreads in rates of return for bonds of different maturities are a function of the additional yield that must be paid to induce investors to buy bonds of longer maturities and to bear the interest rate risk associated with holding those bonds. In Exhibit 11 below, the difference between the 2–year and the 10–year bond is 2.23 percentage points—this is the price investors demand for bearing the additional risk.

If investors believe that interest rates are unusually low and are likely to rise significantly in the near future, then they will be less inclined to buy long-term bonds, and the spread will have to rise and the yield curve will have a steeper slope.

Occasionally, investors believe that interest rates are unusually high and are likely to fall. In this case, they will desire to hold the longest term bonds that they can, bidding up the price of these bonds, and actually creating a "negative spread" for longer maturities (that is, the longer maturities will actually pay a lower interest rate than the shorter maturities). This is known as an "inverted yield curve" and is relatively unusual.

EXHIBIT 11: THE YIELD CURVE

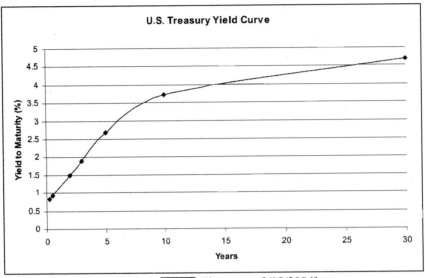

[Source: Treasury Yields from Yahoo! Finance on 3/18/2004]

[¶ 1,255]

Questions and Problems

1. Explain why the yield curve usually has the shape shown in Exhibit 11.

2. What set of expectations creates an inverted yield curve?

3. Suppose that financial analysts expect that the U.S. Federal Reserve Bank is likely to raise interest rates in the near future. What impact would you expect this to have on the yield curve? Why?

4. If the yield curve is relatively flat, what does that mean about the market's expectations with respect to interest rates?

[¶ 1,260]

4. Zero Coupon Bonds

Suppose that an investor is buying a bond and is content with the interest rate being offered but worried that this interest rate will not persist. As discussed above, this would lead to the decision to purchase a longer-term bond (a bond with a later maturity). But, the investor still faces what is called "reinvestment risk." That is, when she receives the interest payments, she may not be able to invest those funds in new bonds that pay the same rate of interest as is being received on the existing bond itself; interest rates may have fallen.

The investor can solve this problem by purchasing a *zero coupon bond*. Just as the name suggests, zero coupon bonds pay no periodic interest—they have a "zero" coupon rate. That is, the entire value of the bond is tied up in the principal repayment at maturity. Not surprisingly, these bonds trade for less than face value; they must be purchased at a discount to allow for a return in the form of capital appreciation. As the following example will show, a zero coupon bond can be "engineered" to offer a yield to maturity that is equivalent to a standard bond. The popularity of zero coupon bonds varies according to the same factors that drive the shape of the yield curve—investors' beliefs about the future direction of interest rates.

A zero coupon bond that pays $1,000 in 10 years and trades for $613.91 today would have a YTM of 5%, the same YTM as a 10–year bond that trades for face value of $1,000 and pays 5% interest each year.

When new zero coupon bonds are sold at a discount from face value, the discount is referred to as "original issue discount" (OID). Note that OID is really an estimate of the accumulated value of the forgone interest payments that will be paid to the investor at the bond's maturity. Although the investor receives this incremental value in the form of capital appreciation rather than as annual interest payments, the taxing authorities have figured out that OID is functionally equivalent to interest (i.e., compensation for the use of borrowed funds). Not surprisingly, the Internal Revenue Code recharacterizes OID as interest, with the result that taxpayers must report the return on zero coupon bonds as ordinary income rather than capital gain for federal income tax purposes. A further discussion of the taxation of OID can be found at ¶ 3,820.

Under § 163(f) of the Internal Revenue Code, issuers of corporate bonds are generally allowed to deduct the interest payments for federal income tax purposes only if the bonds are in registered form. As a result, almost all corporate bonds issued today are not sold as bearer bonds but rather are sold in registered form, and bearer bonds have virtually disappeared from the market.

[¶ 1,265]

Questions and Problems

1.   What is the difference between a zero coupon bond and a traditional bond?

2.   If you expect interest rates to rise in the near future, would you prefer to purchase a fairly priced zero coupon bond or a bond with annual interest payments? Why?

[¶ 1,266]

Exercises

1.   How much should an investor pay for a 10–year, $1,000 face amount zero coupon bond, if traditional bonds of similar risk are priced to yield 6%?

2.   What is the price for a 5–year, $10,000 face amount zero coupon bond, if traditional bonds of similar risk are priced to yield 6.3%?

[¶ 1,270]

5.   High–Yield Bonds

As discussed earlier, high-yield bonds, also referred to a "junk" bonds, are bonds rated BB or lower. These bonds are issued by companies that are viewed by the financial community as high-risk due to problems in the company's business, limited liquidity, or a capital structure that is overburdened with debt. These companies are at a significant risk of being unable to meet their debt obligations and potentially declaring bankruptcy.

A good example of high-yield bonds are the corporate bonds issued by Level 3 Communications. During the telecommunications bubble in the late 1990s, Level 3 accumulated more than $6 billion in debt. After the bubble collapsed it became clear that Level 3's limited profits and cash flow would make it difficult for the company to service its debt. By April of 2003, Level 3's debt was rated CCC. The company's March 15, 2010 maturity debt is a good example of high-yield debt. While the bonds bear interest at 11.250%, they have a YTM of 15.689%, reflecting the company's increased default risk.

[¶ 1,275]

Questions and Problems

1.   Why would a company's bonds be "high-yield" or "junk"?

2.   Why would an investor choose to invest in high-yield bonds over investment grade bonds?

3.   Imagine that you are an investor who bought a 10–year, $1,000 bond at face value when it was issued. Since then, the company has done very well, and its credit rating has improved. But the bond's YTM has decreased (i.e., the effective return to a new purchaser of the existing bond has fallen). Why does the company's success hurt the bond's YTM? Should you sell the bond?

[¶ 1,280]

6.   Tax–Exempt Bonds

While the taxing authorities are zealous in figuring out many of the loopholes that investors and their advisers have tried to find in the tax laws, there remains one widely used form of bond that is expressly tax free. These are generally referred to as *tax-exempt* or *municipal bonds*. In order to allow state and local governments avail themselves of lower financing costs, the Internal Revenue Code exempts the interest on state and local government bonds from federal income taxation. Moreover, the states typically provide similar exemptions for interest on their own bonds (but not for interest on bonds issued by other states).

State and local governments are able to issue tax-exempt bonds with stated interest rates below the rates on comparable taxable bonds, and investors—especially those in high income tax brackets—are willing to accept lower rates because they are concerned with the effective yield after taxes are taken into account. As it turns out, the effective yield on a tax-exempt bond is similar to the after-tax yield on a comparable taxable bond, though the yield comparison will vary according to the holder's marginal tax rate.

For example, a taxable bond with a $1,000 par value and a stated interest rate of 5% has an annual after-tax yield of 3.25% for a taxpayer in the 35% tax bracket ($1,000 × 5% = $50, and $50 × (1 − 35%) = $32.50). A tax-exempt bond with a par value of $1,000 and a stated interest rate of 3.25% has the same yield after taxes ($1000 × 3.25% = $32.50).

[¶ 1,285]

Questions and Problems

1. Why do tax-exempt bonds exist?

2. As an investor, would you prefer a par value tax-exempt bond with a current yield of 5.25% or a par value taxable bond with a current yield of 7%? Assume your tax rate is 28%.

[¶ 1,286]

Exercise

Assume a client's tax rate is 31%. The stated interest rate on a par value tax-exempt bond is 9.1%, and the after-tax yield on a taxable bond is also 9.1%. What is the stated interest rate on the taxable bond?

[¶ 1,290]

7. Callable Bonds

Just as investors have expectations about interest rates, so too do companies. A company may need to borrow money at a time when it believes interest rates are relatively high. It won't be able to pay the money back for some time, so it sells bonds with a relatively extended maturity date. However, if it wishes to preserve the option of refinancing—i.e., selling new bonds in a few years if interest rates fall and using the proceeds to pay off the old bonds before their stated maturity—the company can make the bonds *callable*. That is, the company can write the bond in such a way that after two or three years, it has the right to "call" the bonds back in and pay them off, usually at a slight premium over face value (e.g., 102% of face value). Your intuition tells you that if this is good for the company it must be bad for the investor, and you are right. Thus, companies usually must add some sweetener (such as a higher interest rate) to the callable bond to compensate for the risk of early redemption, and some investors will find this sufficiently enticing to accept the call feature.

[¶ 1,300]

8. Convertible Bonds

Convertible bonds are a type of hybrid security. Like a regular bond, a convertible bond has a specified maturity and interest payment. However, instead of simply paying back the face amount at maturity, the bond is convertible into a fixed number of shares of the issuer's common stock. For example, suppose that ABC Company issues convertible bonds with a par value of $1,000 and interest at 5%, at a time when its stock is trading at $10 per share. The convertibility feature may allow the holder to convert each bond into 50 shares of ABC stock at maturity. So, the convertibility feature is functionally equivalent to an option to buy ABC stock at $20. This clearly has some value, as—if the company does well—its stock could be worth more than $20 per share. Thus, ABC should be able to sell its convertible bonds with a lower interest rate than if the bonds did not have the convertibility feature, because the convertibility feature represents some additional value—some potential return—for investors.

H.   APPLYING FINANCIAL PRINCIPLES TO STOCKS

[¶ 1,310]

These basic financial principles involving cash flow and risk are also applicable in evaluating stocks.

A stock can be defined as a share of equity, which represents a residual claim on the profits and assets of the issuing corporation. Of course, while the equity owners have a "claim" on such funds, they don't often get them. The corporation's management may decide for legitimate business reasons to retain part or all of the corporation's profits and reinvest them in the business, buying more machinery and equipment, for example, or opening a new factory. In practice, the amount of money a corporation actually distributes to its shareholders is called a *dividend*. (When made by a partnership, such payments to equity owners are called *distributions*.) Dividends represent the primary means through which shareholders receive cash from the corporation in which they own an equity share.

[¶ 1,320]

1. Common Stock

A share of stock represents a fractional claim on the profits and cash flow of the issuing corporation. So, if a corporation has 1,000 shares of stock outstanding, then one share represents a 1/1,000 claim (0.1%).

Just as a bond has a yield—the interest paid divided by the price of the bond—a stock has a *dividend yield*. A bond that costs $1,000 and pays $80 per year in interest has an interest yield of 8%. A stock that costs $100 per share and has a dividend of $3 per share per year has a dividend yield of 3%. In practice, most stocks have a dividend yield that is significantly lower than the yield on a bond. Why is this? Because, while the price of the stock can go up, the price of the bond is less volatile. In general, stocks have more upside and more downside than bonds. To continue with the concept discussed above, if the performance of the corporation improves and it earns more profits and more cash, then the residual claim of the equity holders increases in value and the price of the stock also goes up. Of course, if an investor knew that the company was going to start performing much better and increase in value, she would want to buy the stock before this actually happened, in order to capture the appreciation in the share price. Thus, prices are determined as much by expectations about future performance as by actual performance. (Of course, expectations about future performance are influenced by past performance.).

The price of an actual share of stock at any given time is determined by the supply and demand for the stock. So, if a corporation announces good news ("We just discovered a cure for cancer"), the stock price will rise as more people attempt to buy than sell, and the price must rise to coax some holders to sell their shares. Of course, the number of shares bought on any given day must equal the number sold—every transaction requires both a buyer and a seller.

In evaluating a corporation's performance, the easiest aspect to understand—and relate to its value—is the corporation's earnings. Investors pay a great deal of attention to a corporation's earnings per share, which is simply the total amount of the corporation's earnings divided by the total number of shares of stock outstanding. The relationship between the price of a stock and a corporation's earnings performance is captured by what is called the *price/earnings ratio* (P/E ratio). This ratio is equal to the price of a share of stock divided by the corporation's earnings per share. So, for instance, a P/E ratio of 20 implies that a corporation with earnings per share of $1 (per year) would sell for $20 per share. In practice, a corporation's stock price rises or falls as a function of the market's expectations about its future earnings. So, a high growth corporation will have a higher P/E ratio than a low growth corporation because individuals (on average) believe that its earnings will grow at a more rapid rate.

Note that this relationship between P/E ratio and growth rate is a basic example of the principle of present value at work. Imagine two corporations, each of which has $1 of earnings per share today. Assume that the appropriate discount rate for these earnings is 10%. If Company A's earnings are forecast to grow at 3% a year forever, then its shares are worth

$$\frac{\$1}{.10 - .03} = \$14.29.$$

(Recall the formula for a growing perpetuity in ¶ 1,130).

If Company B's earnings per share are forecast to grow at 6% per year forever, then its shares are worth

$$\frac{\$1}{.10 - .06} = \$25.00.$$

More rapid growth indicates higher expected future earnings and thus increases the present value of the corporation's shares.

[¶ 1,325]

Questions and Problems

1. What does ownership of a share of stock represent?

2. What determines the price of a share of stock at any given time?

3. What does it mean if a stock has a P/E ratio of 12?

[¶ 1,326]

Exercises

1. What is the fair value of a stock with earnings per share of $15.00, a discount rate of 12%, and expected earnings growth of 2.5% per year?

2. The fair value of a share of Acme Widget is $7.50. The discount rate is 5%, and the market expects earnings growth of 4% per year. If the discount rate increases by two percentage points, and the company announces expected earnings growth of 6% per year, what is the new fair value of a share? Explain why this happened, in common-sense terms.

[¶ 1,330]

2. Valuing Stocks—Fundamental Analysis

Of course, it is easy to price a stock—one simply looks up its price in the newspaper or on the web. What is harder, of course, is valuing the stock—coming to a point of view on whether it is underpriced or overpriced. That is, does the stock represent a good investment based upon its prospects and its current stock price? Moreover, it is not enough to have a point of view on whether its price is likely to rise or fall. If the stock price simply rises along with the market overall, you could achieve the same return simply by investing in an index fund. What is crucial is coming to a point of view on whether the stock is likely to underperform or outperform "the market."

If you looked up a stock like Microsoft in the Wall Street Journal on Friday, March 26, 2004, you would see the following:

YTD % CHG	52-WEEK HI LO	STOCK (SYMB)	DIV	YLD %	PE	VOL 100s	CLOSE	NET CHG
-8.0	30.00 23.60	Microsoft (MSFT)	.16	.6	31	847049	25.19	.78

These figures are interpreted as follows:

- YTD % CHG: Year-to-date percentage change in the share price of the stock. Here we see that Microsoft's share price has declined 8.0%.

- 52–WEEK HI/LO: The highest and lowest prices of a share of the stock during the preceding 52 weeks.

- STOCK (SYMB): The name of the stock and the ticker symbol used to represent the stock on the exchange in which it trades.

- DIV: The annual cash amount of dividend payouts.

- YLD %: The dividend yield, the dividend payout as a percentage of the share price (dividend/share price = YLD %).

- PE: Price to earnings ratio.

- VOL 100s: The number of shares, or "volume," which traded the previous day, in hundreds of shares. In this example 84,704,900 shares of Microsoft traded the previous day.

- CLOSE: The share price at the end of the most recent trading day.

- NET CHG: The change in share price during the most recent trading day. Here we see that Microsoft's price appreciated $0.78.

Recall one of the principles of finance highlighted earlier—cash is what matters. Thus, when an investor purchases a share of stock, she pays with cash. What matters is how much cash comes back, and when.

There are basically two ways to get cash back:

- Dividends: Some corporations choose to distribute some of their profits to their shareholders, as quarterly or annual dividends. Dividends are declared on a per share basis as of a "date of record" (i.e., the date on which a shareholder must own the stock in order to be eligible to receive the dividend when it is subsequently paid out).

- Capital gain: If the price of the share goes up and the investor sells, her gain is a capital gain—the amount by which the stock has appreciated.

Of course, to say "if the price goes up and the stock is sold..." implies that the new owner has a set of expectations about the future cash flows that he will receive, that are largely based upon dividends. Thus, if you ignore the circumstance where the entire corporation is sold, taken over, or liquidated, the only money the corporation will ever distribute to its shareholders is in the form of dividends. The price at which any buyer will purchase an existing owner's shares is a function, in turn, of his expectations about future dividends.

Thus, it all comes down to dividends, which are driven by the corporation's earnings. The formula that captures this relationship is

$$R = \left[\frac{D}{P} \right] + g,$$

where R is the rate of return to the shareholder, D is the dividend, P is the price of the stock and g is the rate of dividend growth.

Corporations may choose not to pay dividends for many reasons, including poor financial performance. But many solid corporations choose not to pay a dividend because they believe they have excellent and productive uses for the cash—attractive investments they can make in their own business. Thus firms like online auction giant eBay pay no dividends. Often corporations that are considered "growth companies" do not pay dividends because they are plowing all of their earnings back into the growth of their business.

The school of thought that values companies based on the expectations of future earnings is called *fundamental analysis*. This is distinct from another school called "technical analysis," in which analysts chart the price of the company's stock on a daily or even hourly basis. Technical analysts (or "chartists") believe they can spot trends or patterns that signal an impending rise or fall in the price of the stock. This kind of analysis of stocks has waned in popularity, and is not considered further here.

Fundamental analysis, as its name implies, revolves around an analysis of the "fundamentals" of the company—its revenues, costs, earnings, and anticipated dividends. The vast majority of analysts who work at Wall Street brokerage houses and for mutual funds and investment firms employ fundamental analysis. Generally, they build models of the company's sales and earnings, based on knowledge of the company's products, markets, customers and competitors, as well as analysis of the costs and expenses associated with the company's business. Such knowledge comes from historical analysis of the company's financial statements and discussions with customers, as well as information the company may provide about its plans and prospects.

[¶ 1,335]

Questions and Problems

1. Under what circumstances would you expect a corporation to pay a high dividend? A low dividend?

2. If a corporation unexpectedly increases its dividend payout ratio (dividend per share divided by price per share) from 0.04 to 0.08, and the expected growth remains at 2%, how much has the expected rate of return changed?

3. What is fundamental analysis, and what kind of information is required to perform this type of analysis?

4. We note that many solid corporations choose not to pay a dividend because they can use the money to make attractive investments in their own businesses—usually investments yielding growth. Should we conclude, then, that the higher the dividends paid by a company, the worse its long-term prospects are? Why or why not?

[¶ 1,336]

Exercise

In an efficient market, two companies have exactly the same expected rate of return to the shareholder and the same share price. But Company A is expected to grow at 10% annually, while Company B is expected to have no growth at all. How is this possible?

[¶ 1,340]

3. Does Fundamental Analysis Work?

In the case of analysts who work for Wall Street brokerage firms, their analysis is generally published in the form of research reports on particular companies or sometimes an entire industry. Analysts who work at mutual fund companies or investment management firms don't publish their research, but use it to influence the investments made by the fund managers.

In his famous book, *A Random Walk Down Wall Street*, Princeton economist Burton Malkiel relates his assessment of the efficacy of fundamental analysis. He and his colleagues took the one-year and five-year earnings predictions from 19 different firms, and discovered that both the one-year and five-year predictions were "very little better than those that would be obtained by simple extrapolation of past trends, which ... are no help at all." (Malkiel, A Random Walk Down Wall Street, p. 167, 6th ed. 1996.) This general finding has been replicated in a variety of studies.

A similar analysis of mutual fund performance shows that these pools of professionally managed money rarely outperform passively managed "index funds" (see more on this topic in section ¶ 1,420). This general observation has led to a long-running feature in the Wall Street Journal in which the paper assembles a different portfolio of stocks each quarter—one selected by a series of well-known investment professionals, and the other chosen by someone who picks stocks by throwing darts at the stock pages. The "dart board portfolio" regularly beats the professionals.

All of this leads Malkiel to conclude: "No scientific evidence has yet been assembled to indicate that the investment performance of professionally managed portfolios as a group has been any better than that of randomly selected portfolios." Id. at 184.

[¶ 1,350]

4. Where and How to Research Stocks

Given the vast amounts of money that flow in and out of the stock market every day, it should come as no surprise that considerable time and resources are devoted to researching stocks. First, it's worth highlighting the fact that a very small percentage of business firms are actually public companies—that is to say, corporations whose stock trades freely on one or more of the markets established in the United States and elsewhere. Public companies are subject to SEC reporting requirements, as well as a host of other securities laws and rules imposed by the exchanges on which their shares are traded. Most companies are private, and many are organized not as corporations but rather in the form of a partnership, a limited liability company or a sole proprietorship. Even enterprises organized as corporations are likely to be privately owned, and financial information on such companies is rarely available. Some very large companies are private, including those listed in Exhibit 12 below.

EXHIBIT 12: LARGEST PRIVATE U.S. COMPANIES (BY REVENUE)

Rank	Company	State	Industry	Revenue ($mil)	Employees
1	Cargill	MN	Crops	59,894	98,000
2	Koch Industries	KS	Oil & Gas Operations	40,000	17,000
3	Mars	VA	Food Processing	16,800	31,000
4	Publix Supermarkets	FL	Retail (Grocery)	16,027	123,000

Rank	Company	State	Industry	Revenue ($mil)	Employees
5	Pricewaterhouse Coopers	NY	Business Services	15,900	125,000
6	Ernst & Young	NY	Business Services	13,100	106,000
7	Bechtel	CA	Construction Services	11,600	47,000
8	C & S Wholesale Grocers	VT	Retail (Grocery)	11,300	9,000
9	Meijer	MI	Retail (Grocery)	10,900	84,000
10	HE Butt Grocery	TX	Retail (Grocery)	10,700	56,000
11	TRW Automotive	MI	Auto & Truck Parts	10,630	63,000
12	Huntsman	UT	Chemical Manufacturing	9,000	15,000
13	Fidelity Investments	MA	Investment Services	8,937	29,142
14	Swift & Co.	CO	Food Processing	8,380	21,300
15	JM Family Enterprises	FL	Auto & Truck Manufacturers	7,600	3,500
16	Enterprise Rent-a-Car	MO	Business Services	6,900	53,500
17	Science Applications Intl.	CA	Aerospace & Defense	5,902	38,700
18	Unisource	GA	Forestry & Wood Products	5,900	8,000
19	Marmon Group	IL	Misc. Fabricated Products	5,756	30,000
20	Advance Publications	NY	Printing & Publishing	5,565	27,585
21	Menard	WI	Retail (Home Improvement)	5,500	33,300
22	SC Johnson & Son	WI	Personal & Household Products	5,372	12,000
23	MDFC Holding	CA	—	5,105	60,500
24	International Steel Group	OH	Iron & Steel	5,000	11,600
25	Alticor	MI	Personal & Household Products	4,900	11,500

[Source: "America's Largest Private Companies, 2003," accessed Apr. 11, 2004 at www.forbes.com/lists/results.jhtml.]

Shares in privately held companies do sometimes change hands. For example, a company may sell stock to a venture capitalist or a private investor in order to raise capital for expansion. Or a small firm may be acquired by another company in a stock-purchase transaction. These are negotiated transactions in which the price is determined in discussions between the company and the prospective investor, and the price may be affected by alternative sources of capital available to the company.

[¶ 1,355]

Questions and Problems

1. Why would you imagine a company would choose to stay private rather than "go public?"

2. Would you expect the price for shares of a private company's stock to be more or less "fairly" priced than a publicly traded security? Why?

3. Imagine that there are two very similar insurance companies, one public and one private. Your client has the chance to buy 10% of either company for $10,000,000. If the businesses are expected to generate roughly the same amount of cash flow for the foreseeable future, which company would you suggest she invest in? Explain your answer.

[¶ 1,360]

5. Dilution

We have already looked at the general relationship between a company's earnings and its value. This general relationship is captured in the ratio of the firm's market capitalization (price per share times number of shares outstanding) to the company's earnings. When both terms are divided by the number of shares, we get the P/E ratio: the price per share divided by the earnings per share (or EPS). In forecasting EPS then, the analyst must forecast not only the company's earnings but the number of shares outstanding. Generally, this is not especially difficult, because new shares are most commonly issued to employees pursuant to stock options.

Corporations give their employees stock options as a form of compensation, like a salary or a bonus. It is widely believed that stock options give employees (including senior management) an incentive that coincides with the interests of shareholders, namely, to increase the value of the corporation. Options are generally issued with an exercise price equal to the stock price at the time the option was issued. So, the option holder makes money only if the stock price rises. The issuance of options must be disclosed in the company's SEC filings, so it is possible to look up the number of options outstanding and determine the number of shares that may be issued.

When the number of potential new shares is added to the existing shares outstanding, and the resulting figure is used as the basis to compute EPS, the result is termed "fully-diluted earnings per share." That is, the EPS figure is "lowered" by the full number of shares that may be outstanding in the future, when existing options are taken into account. Of course, the higher the number of shares, the lower the EPS and the lower the likely stock price, to the extent stock price is a function of earnings per share. Most companies well understand this negative effect of option-induced dilution on their share price, but believe that the positive effects of being able to hire and retain good employees with options more than offset this cost.

[¶ 1,370]

6. Preferred Stock

Given that investors look at securities in terms of risk and return, it is not surprising that companies design securities to appeal to the different risk/return profiles of investors. Preferred stocks are one such instrument.

Preferred stocks are "preferred" in the sense that they guarantee that the holders of these securities will receive their dividends before any dividends are paid to the holders of common stock. When preferred stock is sold, it has a stated dividend amount per share, somewhat like the stated interest payment on a bond. However, unlike a bondholder, who typically has enforceable rights to fixed payments, a preferred stockholder is merely entitled to priority over the common stockholders in the payment of dividends, to the extent that any dividends are declared. Preferred stock is a form of equity, not debt, and it confers no fixed payment rights. Moreover, the preference is limited to the stated dividend amount. If the company does very well, the preferred stockholders do not share in that upside; that is, they have no claim on the residual value of the firm.

[¶ 1,380]

7. Relationship Between Interest Rates and Stock and Bond Prices

As we have discussed, the present value of a bond is the discounted value of a stream of promised future payments. The discount rate reflects the risk-free rate plus a "market risk premium" for the particular security. So, a 10–year corporate bond with a $1,000 face value may be priced at issuance to yield 5%, i.e., to pay $50 per year. But if, one year after issuance, interest rates have risen so that a comparable newly-issued bond would have to pay 10% interest, then in a reasonably efficient market, the price of the original 5% bond will simply fall until the effective interest rate is competitive. That is, no one will buy the 5% bond unless its effective interest rate is the same as other bonds of similar risk that are available in the market—10% in our example. Newly priced and issued bonds will simply have to pay the higher rate as their original interest rate.

In the above example, the newly issued bond would have a face value of $1,000 and an interest rate of 10%. Assuming the new bond has the same maturity as the original bond, the price of the original bond must drop to $712.04 in order to bring its YTM up to 10%—the same as the new bond.

The same principle holds true with respect to the price of a stock. If the price reflects the market's view of the value of the stream of future cash flows that will be generated by the stock (including dividends and any gain on sale), then a rise in interest rates will reduce the present value of any given set of expected cash flows. One major factor that should undoubtedly influence the choice of a discount rate for valuing the future cash flows from a stock is the interest rate—that is, the alternative return that could be achieved by investing in bonds instead of stocks. So, it makes sense that as interest rates rise, stock prices fall, because the discounted value of those future cash flows is less. Similarly, the price of outstanding bonds will fall as well. This makes sense, all else being equal—a high discount rate means that future cash flows are worth less than they are under conditions of a lower discount rate. So, all forms of investment—which involve investing cash today to get it back in the future—are worth less if the future cash flows remain the same in dollar terms and interest rates rise.

[¶ 1,385]

Questions and Problems

1. What is the relationship between interest rates and stock prices?

2. If the market interest rate falls, what should we expect will happen to the price of bonds, all other things being equal? What about stocks?

3. If the bond yield curve is steep, what is the market expectation about interest rates? Would you expect stock and bond prices to rise or fall if the market's expectation is correct?

I. MUTUAL FUNDS

[¶ 1,390]

A mutual fund is a pool of financial assets—stocks, bonds, options, or a mix of any of these—which is managed by an investment company on behalf of its shareholders (i.e., the investors in the mutual fund). The classic type of mutual fund is called an "open-end" fund. At the end of each and every trading day, the fund calculates a *net asset value*—the value of the entire portfolio, divided by the number of shares in the mutual fund. New or existing investors can buy additional shares in the fund at any time, and the fund stands ready to redeem (buy back) shares at the current net asset value. A "closed-end" fund is one in which the fund will not sell or redeem shares each day; the portfolio of securities being managed by the fund manager is more like a company, and an investor who buys a share in the fund must be prepared to "ride it out" for the life of the fund until the manager decides to liquidate. While shares in closed-end funds do trade on an exchange—like the stock of any company—they often trade at a discount from net asset value because of this uncertainty over when the investor can actually receive her money back.

[¶ 1,400]

1. Types of Equity Mutual Funds

Mutual funds are rated by Morningstar (www.mfb.morningstar.com). Each fund receives a rating between one star (the lowest) and five stars (the highest), based on the fund's overall performance relative to its peers. The ratings take into account the historical risk of the securities that make up the funds' investments, and the return that the fund earned. The overall rating is an attempt to assess the fund's risk-adjusted return.

Morningstar, and the mutual fund industry in general, attempt to classify most funds according to a three-by-three matrix based on the fund's investment style and the "capitalization" of the companies in the fund. See Exhibit 13 below.

EXHIBIT 13: MUTUAL FUND CLASSIFICATION CATEGORIES

Capitalization	Investment Style		
	Value	Blend	Growth
Large			
Medium			
Small			

Investment style refers to the type of companies in which the fund invests:

- "Value" investing consists of selecting stocks in companies with "below average" P/E ratios, based on the belief that these stocks are undervalued by the market and that their earnings will increase at a more rapid rate than that implicit in the P/E.

- "Growth" investing is the opposite style, consisting of investments in stocks with high P/E ratios and therefore, higher implicit growth rates of earnings. Managers of these funds believe they can identify stocks with high P/E ratios that are nonetheless undervalued because their growth rates will outperform the market's implicit estimates.

- A "blended" style is simply a mix of the two, i.e., the fund holds some stocks with high P/E ratios and others with low P/E ratios.

The other dimension of the matrix refers to the capitalization level of the companies in which the fund invests. Remember, a company's "market cap" is simply the price per share times the number of shares outstanding. There are three basic categories of capitalization:

- "Small cap" stocks are shares in companies whose total market cap is generally from $300 million to $2 billion. (Anything below $300 million is considered "microcap.")

- "Midcap" stocks are shares in companies with a market cap between $2 billion and $10 billion.

- Finally, "large cap" stocks are shares in companies with a market cap in excess of $10 billion.

One factor that generally affects a mutual fund manager's investment decisions relates to the size of the fund he or she is managing. A large fund—like Fidelity's Magellan Fund, for example—has $67 billion in assets under management. Selecting investments and monitoring their performance requires an investment of time and attention on the part of the fund manager, and that investment needs to be worthwhile. That is, having made a decision, the fund manager must be able to make enough money from that decision to "move the needle" on the overall return of the fund. If the fund manager wants to invest, say, 1% of the total fund assets in the stock of a particular company, he has to find a stock that can absorb $670 million in new investment.

Remember that the price of a stock is determined by the supply and demand in the market each day. Thus, it will be difficult for the manager of a large fund to deploy capital into small cap stocks. The fund manager has to buy enough shares so that—if his research is correct—the rising price of the stock will improve the performance of the fund. The manager can't afford to buy 10% or even 5% of a company's outstanding stock. Doing so would surely drive the price of the stock up as the fund manger is buying, and then drive the price down as he is attempting to sell.

See Exhibit 14, below for an example of companies that fall into the different market capitalization categories, as well as the number of shares outstanding and daily trading volume.

EXHIBIT 14: MARKET CAPITALIZATION—COMPANY EXAMPLES (FIGURES IN MILLIONS)

	Market Cap	Shares Outstanding	Daily Volume
Micro			
Boston Communications Group	193	18.52	0.414
OYO Geospace	93	5.58	0.009
Haggar Corp.	134	6.77	0.025
Small			
Corporate Executive Board	1,700	37.29	0.200
Frontier Oil	491	26.16	0.161
Hyperion Solutions	1,500	38.13	1.051
Mid			
A.G. Edwards, Inc.	2,930	80.10	0.525
Barnes & Noble	2,120	68.05	0.984
Washington Post Company	8,360	9.86	0.011
Large			
Ford Motor	23,940	1,830.00	11.331
General Electric	303,570	10,080.00	20.116
Hewlett–Packard	67,740	3,050.00	11.438

[Source: Yahoo! Finance, accessed March 26, 2004.]

[¶ 1,410]

2. Sector Funds

While many investors are willing to research individual stocks and develop a point of view on which ones they should own, this obviously requires a good deal of work. One technique that involves less analysis of individual stocks and fits with many investors' intuitive way of thinking about business, is to invest in industries or "sectors." That is, an investor may believe that industry sectors like energy or health care are poised to outperform the general market. Investors can buy sector funds which comprise stocks of companies selected by investment managers specializing in specific industries.

As an example of the wide variety of sector funds available, consider the 41 sector funds offered by Fidelity (in April, 2004), organized into seven different basic groups.

Sector	Sector Funds
Health Care	• Health Care
	• Biotechnology
	• Medical Delivery
	• Medical Equipment and Systems
	• Pharmaceuticals
Technology	• Technology
	• Business Services and Outsourcing
	• Computers
	• Developing Communications
	• Electronics
	• Software and Computer Services
	• Networking and Infrastructure
Utilities	• Utilities Growth
	• Telecommunications
	• Wireless
Consumer	• Consumer Industries
	• Food and Agriculture
	• Leisure
	• Multimedia
	• Retailing
Financial	• Financial Services
	• Banking
	• Brokerage and Investment Management
	• Home Finance
	• Insurance
Cyclicals	• Cyclical Industries
	• Air Transportation
	• Automotive
	• Chemicals
	• Construction and Housing
	• Defense and Aerospace
	• Environmental
	• Industrial Equipment
	• Transportation
	• Industrial Materials
Natural Resources	• Natural Gas
	• Natural Resources
	• Energy
	• Energy Service
	• Gold, Paper and Forest Products

[Source: Fidelity Website, <http://personal.fidelity.com/products/funds/> Accessed April 6, 2004.]

[¶ 1,415]

Questions and Problems

1. What are the main differences between the major categories of mutual funds?

2. Which type of mutual fund would you expect to have the lowest average P/E?

3. Why would a very large mutual fund be unlikely to hold many small cap stocks?

4. What are the relative advantages and disadvantages of a sector fund compared with a more traditional mutual fund?

5. Why is the P/E ratio of such importance to mutual fund managers, rather than another metric such as "total assets" or "price to sales"?

[¶ 1,420]

3. Index Funds

Index funds are an investment vehicle that became quite popular in the 1990's. The managers of index funds adopt a passive investment strategy—they simply buy every stock in the "index" in the same proportion in which it appears in the index. Thus, in the S & P 500, for instance there are 500 stocks. It is quite straightforward to have a computer program decide how many shares of particular stocks need to be bought or sold every day as new money flows into or out of the fund. This contrasts with "actively managed" funds in which the manager makes judgments about which securities to buy based on research and analysis. For the period 1993–2002, more than 75% of actively managed large cap stock funds underperformed the S & P 500 Index.

Exhibit 15 below shows the percentage of general "equity" mutual funds which outperformed the S & P 500 Index in recent years.

EXHIBIT 15: MUTUAL FUND PERFORMANCE

Year	% Funds Outperforming S & P 500 Index
1994	12%
1995	15%
1996	25%
1997	10%
1998	31%
1999	47%
2000	64%
2001	46%
2002	42%

[Source: Andre F. Perold, The Vanguard Group, Inc. (1998), HBS Case No. 9–299–005, p. 16., and Charles Schwab, "Equity Index Funds," 2003.]

There are two primary reasons for this performance: the general inability of "stock-pickers" to select stocks with superior returns, and the significant fees and expenses which active managers necessarily incur and pass along to fund shareholders.

A further performance problem is not captured in this data, but serves to erode the performance of active management to an even greater degree: the tax effect of higher turnover. Simply put, active management entails more frequent buying and selling—more turnover. When there is a net gain, this is passed through to the fund's owners, who must pay the resulting capital gains tax. Because an index fund holds a relatively stable pool of stocks (all the stocks in the index), there is much less turnover, less realized capital gain, and therefore less capital gains tax. Of course, a capital gains tax may be incurred when shares are ultimately sold at a profit, but the taxes are deferred until this point, allowing the advantages of compounding to work more effectively. Further discussion of the taxation of mutual funds can be found at ¶ 3,830. Exhibit 16 below describes various types of indexes on which index funds are commonly based.

EXHIBIT 16: TYPES OF INDEX FUNDS

S&P 500: Widely regarded as the standard for measuring large-cap U.S. stock market performance, this popular index includes a representative sample of leading companies in leading industries. The S & P 500 is used by 97% of U.S. money managers and pension plan sponsors. Some $626 billion is indexed to the S & P 500. Although the S & P 500 focuses on the large-cap segment of the market, with over 80% coverage of U.S. equities, it is also an excellent proxy for the total market.

NASDAQ Composite: The NASDAQ Composite Index measures all NASDAQ domestic and international common-type stocks listed on the NASDAQ stock market. The NASDAQ Composite includes over 4,000 companies, more than most other stock market indices. The NASDAQ Composite Index began on February 5, 1971, with a base of 100.00.

NYSE Composite: The NYSE Composite Index was established in 1966 to provide a comprehensive measure of market trends. The index consists of a composite index of all common stocks listed on the NYSE and four subgroup indexes—Industrial, Transportation, Utility, and Finance. The indexes are basically a measure of the changes in aggregate market value of NYSE common stocks, adjusted to eliminate the effects of capitalization changes, new listings, and delistings.

AMEX Composite: The Amex Composite Index reflects the aggregate market value of all its components relative to their aggregate value on December 29, 1995. The index was developed with a base of 550 as of Dec. 29, 1995. Components of the index include the common stocks or ADRs* of all Amex-listed companies, REITs, master limited partnerships, and closed-end investment vehicles. The market value of each component is determined by multiplying its price by the number of shares outstanding. The day-to-day price change in each issue is weighted by its market value (as of the start of the day) as a percent of the total market value for all components. Thus, the daily price change for each company influences that day's change in the index in proportion to the company's market value. The level of the composite index is not altered by stock splits, stock dividends, or trading halts, nor is it affected by new listings, additional issuances, delistings, or suspensions.

Wilshire 5000: The Wilshire 5000 Total Market Index represents the broadest index for the U.S. equity market, measuring the performance of all U.S. headquartered equity securities with readily available price data. The index was named after the nearly 5,000 stocks it contained when it was originally created, but it has grown to include over 5,000 issues, reflecting the growth in U.S. equity issues as a whole.

Wilshire 4500: The Wilshire 4500 Index was created in 1983 by removing the 500 stocks in the S & P 500 from the Wilshire 5000. Medium and small capitalization managers use the Wilshire 4500 as a performance benchmark.

Russell 2000: The Russell 2000 Index offers investors access to the small-cap segment of the U.S. equity universe. The Russell 2000 is constructed to provide a comprehensive and unbiased small-cap barometer and is completely reconstituted annually to ensure that larger stocks do not distort the performance and characteristics of the true small-cap opportunity set. The Russell 2000 includes the smallest 2000 securities in the Russell 3000.

Russell 3000: The Russell 3000 Index offers investors access to the broad U.S. equity universe representing approximately 98% of the U.S. market. The Russell 3000 is constructed to provide a comprehensive, unbiased, and stable barometer of the broad market and is completely reconstituted annually to ensure that new and growing equities are reflected.

Dow Jones Industrial Average: Prepared and published by Dow Jones & Co., the Dow Jones Industrial Average is an index of 30 corporate stocks designed to include the most important industrial corporations. In mid–2004 it included corporations such as Exxon, General Electric, IBM, Intel and Boeing.

Dow Jones Transportation: Prepared and published by Dow Jones & Co., the Dow Jones Transportation Index includes 20 stocks representing the airline, trucking, railroad, and shipping sectors.

* ADRs are "American Depository Receipts" and are used by foreign companies as a way for U.S. investors to buy their shares. The ADR is a proxy for the foreign share.

Dow Jones Utilities: Prepared and published by Dow Jones & Co., the Dow Jones Utility Index consists of 15 gas and electric utilities and is geographically representative.

NASDAQ Computer: The NASDAQ Computer Index includes computer software companies that furnish computer programming and data processing services, and firms that produce computers, office equipment, and electronic components and accessories. On November 1, 1993, the NASDAQ Computer Index began with a base of 200.00.

S&P Midcap 400: This index measures the performance of the mid-size company segment of the U.S. market. It is used by over 95% of U.S. managers and pension plan sponsors.

S&P 100 Index: This index measures large company U.S. stock market performance. It includes 100 major blue chip stocks across diverse industry groups, which are weighted by market capitalization.

[Sources: NASDAQ:http://dynamic.nasdaq.com/reference/IndexDescriptions. stm, Dow Jones, Standard & Poor's, Russell.]

[¶ 1,425]

Questions and Problems

1. What are index funds and what are the main indexes they track?

2. Why might an investor prefer to invest in an index fund rather than an actively managed mutual fund or individual stocks?

3. Why would a "value investor," such as Warren Buffett, be disinclined to invest a large part of his portfolio in an index fund?

[¶ 1,430]

4. REITs

A *real estate investment trust* (REIT) is a type of security that is similar to a mutual fund, but invests only in real estate companies. These real estate companies own properties like residential and office buildings, shopping centers and malls, as well as hotels, industrial properties, and even self-storage buildings. These companies are classified as "trusts" if they pay out over 90% of their taxable income each year in the form of distributions to their shareholders. The fact that REITs pay out their earnings gives their owners a dividend stream which—on average—has been between 6% and 8%, significantly higher than the average stock.

[¶ 1,440]

5. Mutual Fund Fees

Mutual funds can impose several different types of fees and charges on investors.

- Loads: First, there are a set of fees called front-end and back-end loads. These are in essence, a percentage commission that is charged upon buying shares in the fund (a front-end load or sales fee) or selling shares (a back-end load or redemption fee). Many funds, however, do not charge a load. On average, these "no-load" funds represent a more efficient use of the investor's money.

- 12b–1 fees: These fees are the costs associated with selling and distributing the fund. They are named after SEC Rule 12b–1, which authorizes such fees. Many (but not all) funds charge 12b–1 fees.

- Operating expenses: All mutual funds incur some level of operating expenses, including, for example, compensation paid to fund managers, office space rentals, and the cost of mailings sent to shareholders. Every mutual fund is required to list in its prospectus the fees and expenses associated with the fund.

As an example, the March 1, 2004 prospectus for the Third Avenue Small–Cap Value Fund offers the following information about its fees:

Shareholder Fees (fees to be paid directly from your investment):

Redemption Fee (as a percentage of amount redeemed)	1.00%*

Annual Operating Expenses (expenses that are deducted from Fund assets):

Management Fees	0.90%
Other Expenses	0.27%
Total Annual Fund Operating Expenses	1.17%

* These fees are charged only on redemptions of shares held less than one year.

Example

The following example is intended to help you compare the cost of investing in Third Avenue Small-Cap Value Fund with the cost of investing in other mutual funds. The example assumes that you invest $10,000 for the time periods indicated and then redeem all of your shares at the end of those periods. The example also assumes that your investment has a 5% return each year and that the Fund's operating expenses remain the same. Although your actual costs may be higher or lower, based on these assumptions your costs would be:

Year 1	Year 3	Year 5	Year 10
$119	$372	$644	$1,420

Thus, this fund charges a fee upon the sale of the shares in the fund—variously called a *redemption fee, deferred sales charge,* or *back-end load.* The example is offered to help potential investors understand the total dollar impact of this fee structure over time.

Compare these fees with those on a low-cost index fund like the Vanguard 500 Index. The prospectus for that fund lists fees and expenses, for two different categories of shares, as follows:

	Investor Shares	Admiral Shares
Shareholder Fees (fees to be paid directly from your investment)		
Sales Charge (Load) Imposed on Purchases:	None	None
Purchase Fee:	None	None
Sales Charge (Load) Imposed on Reinvested Dividends:	None	None
Redemption Fee:	None	None
Account Maintenance Fee (for accounts under $10,000)	$2.50/quarter	None
Annual Fund Operating Expenses (expenses deducted from the Fund's assets)		
Management Expenses:	0.16%	0.11%
12b-1 Distribution Fee:	None	None
Other Expenses:	0.02%	0.01%
Total Annual Fund Operating Expenses	**0.18%**	**0.12%**

Example

Expenses incurred over various periods if you invest $10,000 and fund earns 5% per year.

	1 Year	3 Years	5 Years	10 Years
Investor Shares	$18	$58	$101	$230

You can see the impact of the index fund's lower fee and expense structure by comparing the information from the two prospectuses above.

[¶ 1,445]

Questions and Problems

1. What are the main types of mutual fund fees?

2. Why are index fund fees lower than those of standard mutual funds?

[¶ 1,446]

Exercises

1. What is the difference in future value of a $100,000, 30–year investment in a mutual fund that charges fees of 1.18% compared to the same amount invested over 30 years in a mutual fund that charges fees of 0.18%? Assume that both funds return 10% annually (before fees).

2. Your client, Jake, buys one $125 share in Mutual Fund A, which has a 2.1% front-end load. Wendy buys one $510 share in Mutual Fund B, which as a 4% back-end load. Assume the share prices of both mutual funds grow at 12% annually, and that Jake and Wendy each keep their shares for exactly five years, then sell them. Calculate the IRR for Jake's and Wendy's investments, factoring in the fees paid. Who has the better IRR?

J. PUTTING IT ALL TOGETHER—PORTFOLIO THEORY

[¶ 1,450]

The fact that different securities have different levels of risk leads to the concept of what is called a "portfolio." That is, an investor who holds a diversified pool of securities reduces risk by not having all of her "eggs in one basket" (e.g., not investing all of her life's savings in Enron stock). Financial theorists who have studied the various components of risk conclude that the risks specific to a particular company can be "diversified" away, leaving only a general level of "market" risk (sometimes called systematic risk). This is the risk that is measured by beta, as discussed earlier.

To illustrate the advantages of diversification, imagine two companies in the mythical island resort of Bon Temps. One company sells umbrellas and the other sells suntan lotion. Every year, 10,000 tourists visit the island; in some years it rains throughout the tourist season, and in other years it never rains. Most years are partly sunny and partly rainy. In the rainy years, the umbrella company does well, but the suntan lotion company does poorly. And vice versa. Accordingly, there will be a high level of variance in the performance in these two companies and in the return on their respective stocks. Even if they don't go bankrupt, each company's earnings are very volatile and correspondingly risky. However, if you bought stock in both these companies, their combined earnings—and your returns—would be much less volatile. The counter-cyclical nature of each company's performance relative to the other would reduce the overall risk. Financial theorists have argued that investors should not be compensated for bearing this kind of risk—a risk that can easily be diversified away.

The kind of risk that remains is called systematic risk—risk related to the market and the economy overall. Certain kinds of stocks are more susceptible to these market risks, and thus have higher betas than other stocks. So, for instance, you can see the betas for a series of companies in Exhibit 17:

EXHIBIT 17: MARKET CAP AND BETA FOR VARIOUS PUBLIC COMPANIES

Company	Market Cap ($bn)	Beta
Caterpillar	26.70	1.06
Coca–Cola	120.12	0.28
Dell	85.19	1.64
ExxonMobil	278.27	0.42
General Electric	308.86	1.10
General Motors	26.07	1.17
Microsoft	270.18	1.62
Morgan Stanley	65.83	2.01

Pfizer	266.34	0.39
Time Warner	76.39	2.28
Wal–Mart	252.70	0.80
Yahoo!	29.49	3.18

[Source: From Yahoo! Finance on WSJ Online. Trailing Twelve Months as of 3/17/2004. Betas from Yahoo! Finance on 3/26/2004.]

A beta of 1 means that a company's stock will rise and fall in step with the stock market overall. A beta of more than 1 means that the company's stock will rise or fall more sharply. So, for instance, Dell's beta of 1.64 indicates that, if the stock market overall rises 10%, Dell's stock will rise 16.4%. Theorists estimate that a randomly chosen set of 100 or so stocks eliminates nearly all the firm-specific risks and leaves a portfolio with a beta of nearly 1. This fact helps explain the popularity and effectiveness of index funds. A broad index—like the S & P 500, has nothing *but* market risk in it. Of course, it is possible to put together diversified portfolios that have higher or lower levels of risk than the market overall. This then, leads to the question of how an investor can develop a point of view on how much risk she can bear in her investment portfolio.

All else being equal, a longer-term time horizon allows you to bear more risk. Given that we've defined risk as uncertainty, in any given year, the stock market—let's say the S & P 500—may go up or down. However, we know that over time, this increased risk—on average— yields a higher return than a risk-free investment in Treasury bonds. So, if you have $100,000 that you need for a down payment on a house in one year, it is highly risky to put the money into the stock market—you might make a quick profit, but you might just as easily lose a substantial part of your investment in one year. On the other hand, if you are saving for retirement in 25 years, then your time horizon allows you to take on more risk.

[¶ 1,460]

1. Inflation

Inflation refers to the general increase in prices for a particular basket of goods and services. It is generally expressed in terms of an inflation rate—the average annual rate of increase over the time period in question. The inflation rate can be calculated for a broad basket of goods purchased by the average consumer; this is the consumer price index, or CPI. Inflation rates can be calculated for specific items, such as wages, gasoline, or housing.

Inflation is important to the investor for two reasons.

First, inflation "eats away" at capital. If the ultimate purpose of saving and investment is to accumulate money to pay for future consumption (a house, a boat, a child's education), then a steady rise in the price of items to be purchased in the future can lead over time to an erosion of your purchasing power. Thus, you must earn a return on your investments equal to the rate of inflation just to "stay even." Putting your money under a mattress will surely erode its purchasing power.

Second, there is a relationship between interest rates and inflation. Investors want to earn a "real" rate of interest—interest above the inflation rate. So, if interest rates are below the perceived rate of inflation, money will flow away from interest-bearing securities to investments more correlated with "hard" assets such as company stocks and real estate. The resulting change in the supply of funds will push interest rates up until they are above the inflation rate.

[¶ 1,465]

Questions and Problems

1.   How does your investment strategy change if you are saving for the purchase of a car in one year or, alternatively, for your retirement in 30 years?

2.   If inflation decreases, what is the expected impact on the price of stocks and bonds?

3.   Explain why the market interest rate cannot stay below the inflation rate for long.

[¶ 1,470]

2.   The Life Cycle Theory of Investing

The relationship between time horizons and risk tolerance has given rise to the *life cycle theory of investing*. That is, individuals can bear more risk early in their lives because they have a longer time horizon over which to ride out the inherent year-to-year variations in returns on risky investments like stocks. According to the life cycle theory, as individuals age, they should gradually move more of their money to less risky forms of investments such as fixed-income securities.

As an example, one approach to life cycle investing is to allocate investment funds among the asset categories of equities, bonds, and cash as a function of the investor's age:

Asset Type	Early (Age 20 to 40)	Mid (Age 40 to 60)	Late (Over Age 60)
Equity	65 to 85%	40 to 65%	40%
Bonds	15 to 35%	30 to 55%	55%
Cash	0%	5%	5%

Similarly, it makes sense that individuals with lower incomes or wealth levels are generally more risk-averse. Having less to start with, they can ill afford to lose anything. Wealthier individuals, on the other hand, can more easily afford the risk of a loss, and that allows them to achieve the higher returns that compensate them (on average) for bearing this risk.

Diversification also allows you to achieve an optimal level of returns for a given level of risk.

For example, an investor with a long-term time horizon might construct the following portfolio for a large, diversified pool of dollar-denominated assets:

Component	*Allocation*
U.S. Equities	25%
Foreign Equities	20%
Venture Capital/Private Equity	10%
Bonds	25%
Commodities	10%
Real Estate	10%
	100%

There are several dimensions of diversification, beyond what is inherent in the large pool of stocks held in the equity investment account. International stocks are one source of diversification, as they are driven by the performance of other national and regional economies. The fact that these companies' values are denominated in their local currencies provides another form of diversification—if the dollar drops due to a weak economy in the United States, then other currencies will rise and the value of the international stock as measured in dollar terms will increase, even if the absolute price of the stock stays constant.

[¶ 1,475]

Questions and Problems

1. Why is diversification a good thing?

2. For an investor, what would be an efficient method to construct a diversified portfolio?

3. How could you minimize your costs of accomplishing this diversification?

[¶ 1,476]

Exercise

Assume that a 60-year-old client has $200,000 invested in stocks, representing 50% of his portfolio. As he nears retirement, he is ready to allocate more money to less risky assets. If he wants to match the allocation listed in the table above for investors over age 60, what percentage of his stock portfolio should he sell? Where should he invest the proceeds? Assume another 5% of his portfolio is already in cash.

K.   OTHER TYPES OF SECURITIES AND INVESTMENT STRATEGIES

[¶ 1,480]

There are a variety of other types of securities and investment strategies available to investors. The principal ones, discussed below, are arbitrage, short-selling, and financial derivatives.

[¶ 1,490]

1.   Arbitrage

Certain forms of investment opportunities are referred to as *arbitrage*. Technically, arbitrage refers to the opportunity to make a profit by buying and selling the same thing at the same time in two different markets. While this type of arbitrage is rare, the principle helps explain all sorts of transactions that do transpire and generally contribute to the efficiency of the market.

Imagine that a U.S. company's stock sells on the New York and Paris stock exchanges. On the NYSE it trades in dollars, and on the Paris Exchange it trades in francs. If demand for the shares in New York is high one day, and the price rises as a result, traders will look at the Paris market and at the dollar-to-franc exchange rate. As soon as it becomes advantageous to do so, they will sell dollars and buy francs, and use the francs to buy the company's stock on the Paris Exchange. The forces of supply and demand will cause the price in Paris to rise until the system is in equilibrium again. Of course, the fact that the market is, on average, efficient and in equilibrium does not mean that some investors cannot profit from these small imperfections that exist for brief periods of time.

[¶ 1,500]

2.   Short–Selling

It's tempting to think that an investor can only make money by buying a stock and holding it through a period when its price rises. In fact, an investor who expects the price of a stock to fall can "bet against" the stock by *short-selling* or "shorting" the stock.

This is accomplished by borrowing shares of stock and then selling the borrowed shares. As noted earlier, when an investor buys a stock, she typically does not take physical possession of the shares. They remain in the hands of the brokerage firm who executed the trade. The firm will "lend" that stock to a short-seller, who sells the stock but promises to return the stock to the firm in the future. In essence, the investor is betting that the price of the stock will drop, and that she can buy identical shares on the market at a lower price when the time comes to return the borrowed shares to the firm. Of course, if the price rises, this transaction will result in a loss for the short-seller.

[¶ 1,505]

Questions and Problems

1. What is the difference between an arbitrage profit and a normal profit?

2. Explain how an investor can bet against a stock.

[¶ 1,506]

Exercise

If two securities that had identical expected returns were trading in a market at different prices, how could an investor profit from buying and selling (shorting) those securities? If the price of one security was $25 and the price of the other security was $27 and both were expected to return $3 annually forever, how much arbitrage profit is available? What percent return does this represent for an investor?

[¶ 1,510]

3. Derivatives

A *derivative* is a security whose price is determined by the price of other securities. The most typical examples are securities called *options*, which may be "put" or "call" options.

A *put* is the right to sell a given stock at a given price during a specified period of time. A *call* is the right to buy a given stock at a given price during a specified period of time. For example, imagine a call option on 1,000 shares of General Electric stock. Let's say it's January 1, and the call is a 90–day right to buy GE stock for $60 per share. This $60 number is called the *strike price*. If on January 1, GE stock is selling at $50 per share, you clearly would not pay $50 for the right to buy it for $60. If you wanted to spend $50, you might as well buy the share of stock itself. On the other hand, you may think there is some chance GE will do some good things and that the stock will rise in the next 90 days. For example, if GE stock goes to $63 per share, the option will be worth $3. Once the price of the underlying security rises above the strike price, the option is said to be "in the money." Thus, the value of an option is a function of the length of the option period, the spread between the current price of the stock and the strike price, and the volatility of the stock. Clearly, a stock that is more volatile has more chance of rising a lot—just as it does of falling a lot. The formula that captures this relationship is called the Black–Scholes model, named after Fisher Black and Myron Scholes. The financial economist Robert Merton also did substantial work on developing this model, and Merton and Scholes were awarded the Nobel Prize in economics in 1997 for this work (Fisher Black had passed away prior to the award). The formula is complex and will not be reviewed here; suffice it to say that the Black–Scholes model represents a valuable tool for pricing options and other forms of derivatives.

Exhibit 18, for example, is a table of prices for a series of Microsoft options, all expiring on April 16, 2004. These are the prices as of March 26, 2004, approximately three weeks prior to expiration, when Microsoft stock itself is trading at $25.25. The table lists the price of a put (the right to sell) and a call (the right to buy) Microsoft stock at a series of specific strike prices. You can see that, with the expiration three weeks away and the stock at approximately $25, the right to buy the stock for any price over $30 is not worth much to potential option buyers. Conversely, the right to buy the stock for $5.00 is worth $19.20—a total purchase price of $24.20 ($19.20 to buy the option and $5.00 to exercise it), only slightly less than the current $25.25 price.

EXHIBIT 18: MICROSOFT (MSFT) OPTIONS, STOCK TRADING AT $25.25 ON 3/26/2004, FOR OPTIONS EXPIRING FRIDAY, APRIL 16, 2004

Strike Price	Call Price	Put Price
$ 5.00	$19.20	$ 0
7.50	16.70	0
10.00	14.20	0
12.50	11.70	0
15.00	9.20	0
17.50	6.70	0
20.00	5.20	0.05
22.50	2.65	0.05
25.00	0.65	0.40
27.50	0.05	2.35
30.00	0.05	4.90
32.50	0.05	8.15
35.00	0.05	10.80
37.50	0	13.30
40.00	0	15.80
42.50	0	18.30
45.00	0	20.60
47.50	0	23.10

[Source: Yahoo! Finance, accessed 3/26/2004.]

The options market has created liquid markets for all sorts of unusual investments. The ability to buy and sell such securities helps companies and investors manage their exposure to risk. As a simple example, imagine a company like Procter & Gamble, which owns the Folger coffee firm. It is not hard to imagine that a single penny increase in the per-pound price of coffee could cost P & G thousands of dollars.

Thus, they may want to hedge their exposure to coffee prices by purchasing a call option on the price of coffee at a specified future time. If coffee prices rise beyond the strike price on the option, P & G will lose money by having to pay more in the market for the coffee beans it is buying, but will have the opportunity to make some of that back in the option market, as its option gains value. Similarly, companies that do business in U.S. dollars, but sell their products overseas at prices denominated in local currency, can use options to hedge the risk of a fall in the value of those local currencies against the U.S. dollar.

[¶ 1,515]

Questions and Problems

1. Define the terms put, call, and strike price.

2. Looking at the table of option prices in Exhibit 18, explain why the price of the $47.50 call is 0, but the price of the $22.50 call is $2.65.

3. If an investor is concerned that the value of a stock she holds is likely to decrease in the near term, but believes that the stock is likely to appreciate in the long term, how can she use options to insure the near-term value of the stock? What type of option would the investor execute?

[¶ 1,516]

Exercise

The table below lists the strike prices and call prices for Acme Widget options. All the options expire in one week. A share of Acme Widget stock trades at $50. One of these call prices is mispriced and will quickly adjust. Which call price is wrong, how will it adjust, and why?

Option	Strike Price	Call Price
A	$47	$3.50
B	48	1.85
C	50	0.35

L. CONCLUSION

[¶ 1,520]

The three most important lessons to be drawn from the materials in this chapter are: (1) starting a program of regular saving and investing early in life is extremely important: (2) a rational investment strategy requires careful assessment and management of risks and rewards as they relate to the individual investor's profile, goals and stage in life; and (3) without taking on greater risks, an investor can significantly increase net return by minimizing investment costs.

Starting a program of saving and investing early in life is important for several reasons. First, the sooner one becomes committed to any worthwhile course of conduct, the more likely one is to internalize it as a regular part of one's behavior. Second, even if one ignores the range of possible investment returns, the longer one saves, the greater the accumulated funds that will be available when it becomes necessary to draw on savings (e.g., to purchase a home, pay for children's education, provide for retirement, etc.). Third, once one factors in the possibility of a decent return on investments, the "miracle of compounding" will accentuate the growth of investments over an extended period of saving and investing.

Managing risk is extremely important for investors and it is not possible to set down a simple rule of thumb that will be suitable for all investors. There are a number of reasons why this is so. First, some investors, because of their life situation, must necessarily be more risk averse than others. A young couple saving for a down payment on a home should take very little risk with their savings, whereas a well-established professional with substantial income and assets (and a life and disability insurance package to match) can afford to take greater risks. Moreover, an investor's time horizon can also have an important bearing on her choice of investments and her willingness to accept greater risk in exchange for a potentially higher rate of return. For example, although our young couple may decide to invest their savings for a down payment on a home in a money market account with their credit union, they would probably be wise to place most, if not all, of their retirement savings in a common stock fund. Similarly, as our established professional moves closer toward retirement, he may wish to consider shifting some of his growth-oriented assets into investment vehicles with lower risk and more stable returns.

Diversification is another important technique for managing risk. In recent years, the news has been filled with stories of individuals who invested most, or all, of their retirement savings in the stock of a single company (usually an employer), only to see those savings go up in smoke when the company filed for bankruptcy. A shrewd investor diversifies her portfolio not simply by picking a number of different stocks but by systematically allocating her assets across a range of investments with varying risk and return characteristics (including some interest-bearing securities). Moreover, an investor should periodically review her portfolio to make sure that the asset allocation is consistent with the investor's goals in light of advancing age and changing circumstances. Even in performing such routine chores, simple rules of thumb will no longer suffice. It once was common for investment advisors to recommend near total investment in bonds as retirement neared. Now, as more and more individuals survive into their 80's and 90's, even retirees may find it necessary to maintain significant equity holdings to guard against the ravages of inflation during a retirement that might last for two or three decades. Many investors achieve significant diversification at relatively low cost by investing in mutual funds or REITs. But even investors who choose to do so should consider investing in several different types of mutual funds to attain the desired type and level of diversification consistent with their investment goals and stage of life.

One of the most important things that an investor can do to maximize the net return on her investments is to keep administration and tax costs low. Many investors place their savings in mutual funds only to see a substantial portion of their returns eaten up by high brokerage commissions, management fees and taxes on realized capital gains. When such expenses are taken into account, few investors are able to beat the results obtained by low-cost index funds or "tax managed" mutual funds that seek to balance gains with losses and thus avoid taxes on capital gain distributions. In addition to tax managed funds, investors can avail themselves of several other techniques for minimizing taxes. Examples which will be discussed in the following chapters include various retirement savings plans, programs for meeting the costs of higher education, home ownership and life insurance. Some of these vehicles provide tax relief when funds are initially invested, others provide tax relief when money is eventually withdrawn, and most provide shelter from tax for the build-up in value while the funds remain invested.

Chapter 2

PROPERTY AND SUCCESSION

A. OVERVIEW

[¶ 2,000]

Over a lifetime, a person may accumulate many different types of property, including houses, furniture, jewelry, stocks, bonds, bank accounts, life insurance and miscellaneous personal effects. Property may be held by an individual in his or her own name as absolute owner, or co-owned with one or more other people as tenants in common or joint tenants with right of survivorship. Under the system of community property that governs marital property in several states, both spouses share equally in property earned by either spouse during the marriage. The forms and attributes of property ownership are governed primarily by state law, though in a few areas, notably private employee benefit plans, federal law plays a more prominent role.

This chapter introduces some basic methods of making gifts of property during life and at death. The main focus is on transfers occurring at death, which predominate over lifetime gifts in terms of size and planning significance. Over the course of a typical life cycle, most people earn enough to cover current living expenses, and many save enough to buy a house, pay for a child's education, and, with luck, maintain a decent standard of living during retirement. Few people, however, are in a position to give away substantial amounts of property during life, and even those who can afford to make large gifts tend to hold on to the bulk of their wealth until death. Thus, aside from routine lifetime gifts on birthdays, holidays and similar occasions, most major transfers of wealth are likely to occur at the owner's death. (Charitable contributions present a somewhat special case, due to the strong tax incentives favoring lifetime gifts.)

The traditional method of transferring property at death is by a duly executed *will*. A person who makes a will is called a *testator*; one who dies without a will is referred to as *intestate*. In order to effect a transfer of property, a will must be "proved" in a probate proceeding after the testator's death. (The word "probate" is derived from the Latin word for "proof.") If no will is admitted to probate, the decedent's property passes by default to his or her intestate successors. One obvious function of the probate system, therefore, is to determine whether the decedent left a valid will, in order to identify the persons who are entitled to receive his or her property.

The probate system also serves a related but distinct function. In order to settle a decedent's estate, it is necessary to have an orderly process for collecting the decedent's assets, paying creditors' claims, and distributing the remaining property to the appropriate recipients. Each state has its own statutory scheme governing the administration of decedents' estates. The main responsibility of administration falls on an executor or administrator, generally referred to as a *personal representative*, who is appointed by a probate court and often subject to close judicial supervision. The traditional process of estate administration, with its rigid technical requirements and arcane procedures, has earned a deplorable reputation for expense, delay and inefficiency. It should come as no surprise, therefore, that banks, insurance companies, brokerage firms and lawyers have sought to circumvent the probate system through alternative methods of transferring property. These so-called will substitutes include joint tenancies with right of survivorship, pay-on-death beneficiary designations, and revocable trusts.

The "nonprobate revolution" in turn has prompted a sustained effort to reform state probate laws. The Uniform Probate Code (UPC), promulgated by the National Conference of Commissioners on Uniform State Laws, is a comprehensive model statute dealing with intestacy, wills and administration of decedents' estates (as well as guardianships, conservatorships and durable powers of attorney). The UPC has been revised from time to time since it was first promulgated in 1969; in 1990, the drafters rewrote the provisions concerning intestacy, wills and donative transfers. Although the UPC is not self-executing, a number of state legislatures have adopted the UPC in whole or in part. Even in states that decline to adopt it, the UPC has influenced the debate over probate reform.

Trusts also occupy an important place in modern estate planning. They serve countless functions, ranging from simple probate avoidance to sophisticated tax reduction and asset protection. The basic concept is quite simple. A trust arises when one person (the *trustee*) agrees to hold property as a fiduciary for the benefit of one or more other people (the *beneficiaries*). The terms of the trust, specifying the nature and extent of the beneficiaries' interests and the trustee's powers and duties, are typically set forth in a written instrument signed by the person who created the trust (the *settlor*). A trust may last for a single lifetime or for several generations. Traditionally the law of trusts has been based largely on judicial decisions, supplemented by statutory enactments in specific areas. The Uniform Trust Code (UTC), promulgated in 2000, is a comprehensive model statute which has been adopted in several states.

This chapter provides an overview of the probate system and an introduction to the law of intestacy, wills and trusts. For a comprehensive discussion and analysis of these areas, see McGovern & Kurtz, Wills, Trusts and Estates (3d ed. 2004). For a concise overview, see Haskell, Preface to Wills, Trusts and Administration (2d ed. 1994); Lynn & McCouch, Introduction to Estate Planning (5th ed. 2004).

B. THE PROBATE SYSTEM

[¶ 2,010]

All of a decedent's property at death can be divided into two categories: probate assets and nonprobate assets. The decedent's *estate* (often referred to as the "probate estate," in contrast to the "gross estate" in the estate tax context) comprises assets passing by will or intestacy; implicitly excluded from the probate estate are assets given away during life or effectively transferred at death outside the probate system.

If the decedent left a valid will which is admitted to probate, the will governs the disposition of the net estate remaining after payment of creditors and other priority claimants. If there is no will, or if a will fails to dispose of the entire estate, the remaining property passes to the decedent's intestate successors as provided by statute. Thus, intestacy operates as a default disposition, which can be overridden only by a valid will. The probate system recognizes no other method of disposing of a decedent's estate.

The probate system performs two major functions. First, it provides a process to determine whether the decedent left a valid will and, if there are several wills, which one is controlling. Even a properly executed will has no effect unless it is admitted to probate. In the absence of a probate proceeding, a decedent is treated as having died intestate. Second, the probate system provides a process for collecting the decedent's probate assets, paying creditors, and distributing the remaining assets to the decedent's successors. These are the tasks of the personal representative charged with responsibility for administering the decedent's estate. Estate administration offers a measure of protection both to creditors and to successors, by providing a centralized mechanism for resolving claims and clearing title to probate assets.

By statute in most states, jurisdiction over the probate of wills and the administration of estates is lodged in a special probate court (sometimes called the surrogate's court or the orphan's court) or the probate division of a court of general jurisdiction. Proceedings in the probate court are required both to establish a will and to appoint a personal representative. Moreover, a personal representative, once appointed, remains subject to court supervision and may be required to seek court approval in order to sell land or to settle an accounting. While full-fledged judicial proceedings are clearly warranted in disputed matters (e.g., a will contest or a charge of misconduct against a personal representative), much of the probate court's routine business involves undisputed matters which can be handled with less formality. In some states a personal representative may be authorized at the time of initial appointment to administer the estate independently (i.e., with little or no further court supervision).

Given the elaborate rules and procedures for the probate of wills and the administration of estates, it may come as a surprise to learn that the vast majority of decedents' estates pass entirely outside the probate system. According to one study, only around 15% to 35% of decedents leave estates that undergo administration. See Stein & Fierstein, The Demography of Probate Administration, 15 U. Balt. L. Rev. 54, 62 (1985). A majority of the estates subject to administration are quite small in size. See id. at 87. In addition, individuals who leave a will tend to be older and wealthier than those who die intestate. See id. at 82–83; see also Sussman et al., The Family and Inheritance 62–82 (1970); Fellows et al., Public Attitudes About Property Distribution at Death and Intestate Succession in the United States, 1978 Am. B. Found. Res. J. 319, 324–25. These data do not tell us much about why the probate system is not more widely used. Perhaps most people die owning little or no property; perhaps they dispose of substantial assets through nonprobate transfers; or perhaps their affairs are wound up informally without the need to open an estate administration. In reading the following materials, consider why an individual might choose to make (or not to make) a will and why after death it may (or may not) be advisable to open a probate proceeding.

[¶ 2,020]

1. Proof and Contest of Wills

A will is a written instrument, executed in accordance with statutory formalities, which disposes of the testator's property at death. A will can also serve additional functions, including nominating a personal representative to administer the estate, regulating the powers and duties of the personal representative, appointing a guardian for minor children, apportioning estate tax liability, and directing burial or cremation of the testator's body. All of these functions are "testamentary" in the sense that they are to be carried out after the testator's death. A will has no operative effect during life, and becomes enforceable only if it is admitted to probate after the testator's death.

[¶ 2,025]

a. Proof of wills

A will cannot take effect unless its validity is established by an order of the probate court. See UPC § 3–102. If the decedent left a will, the original executed instrument is ordinarily filed with the probate court along with a petition for the appointment of a personal representative at the commencement of estate administration proceedings. The will is admissible to probate upon a showing that (1) the will was duly executed with the prescribed formalities (see ¶ 2,215), (2) at the time of execution, the testator was competent and was not acting under fraud, duress or undue influence, and (3) the will was not subsequently revoked before the testator's death.

The will may be probated either in "solemn form" after notice to interested parties and a hearing or in "common form" without prior notice or hearing. Probate in common form saves time and expense, but it also offers no protection against a will contest or a subsequent proceeding to establish another will. If there is any doubt about the validity of the will, probate in solemn form is advisable in order to achieve a prompt and final determination with binding effect on all interested parties.

In the case of an attested will, probate in solemn form traditionally required that the attesting witnesses, if available, appear in court and testify concerning the execution of the will. Today, most states permit a will to be "self-proved" by means of a sworn affidavit signed by the testator and the witnesses in the presence of a notary public and attached to or incorporated in the will. See UPC § 2–504. A self-proving affidavit raises a presumption of due execution so that the will can be admitted to probate without live witness testimony in uncontested cases. In the absence of fraud or forgery, the presumption is conclusive with respect to the signature requirements for execution, but the will can be contested on other grounds such as undue influence or lack of capacity. See UPC § 3–406.

The original executed will is ordinarily filed with the probate court and becomes a matter of public record. If the original will was last seen in the possession of the testator but cannot be found after the testator's death, it is presumed that the testator destroyed the will with the intent of revoking it. The presumption can be rebutted by evidence that the will was lost or destroyed by accident or was removed by another person. Even if the missing will is proved to have been duly executed and not revoked, it is still necessary to establish the contents of the will. This is usually accomplished by producing a "conformed copy" of the will (i.e., an unexecuted copy with the names of the testator and witnesses typed in place of the signatures) or, if none is available, by testimony of the drafter or the witnesses.

Some testators execute duplicate original wills in an attempt to guard against accidental loss or destruction. At first glance, it might seem that the existence of more than one original executed will would help to ensure probate after the testator's death, but this is not the case. An act of revocation performed by the testator on any one of the executed originals operates as a revocation of the entire will. Thus, the execution of duplicate original wills merely multiplies the chances of a contest on grounds of revocation if any one of the executed originals cannot be accounted for after the testator's death.

[¶ 2,030]

b. *Will Contests*

A will may be contested on grounds relating to the instrument itself, such as defective execution, forgery or revocation. Courts have traditionally required strict compliance with the statutory formalities for executing an attested will, especially with respect to signature by the testator and attestation by witnesses. A will that is not properly signed and attested may be challenged even if it is quite clear that the instrument accurately reflects the testator's intent. In some states, however, the doctrine of strict compliance has been relaxed by statute or judicial decision. (See the discussion of wills formalities at ¶¶ 2,215 and 2,225.)

By far the most common grounds of contest are that the testator lacked the requisite mental capacity or was subject to undue influence. The statutes typically provide simply that a testator must be at least 18 years of age and of "sound mind" to make a valid will. (Thus, a minor is categorically barred from making a will.) Courts have elaborated the test of testamentary capacity to require that a testator be able to form an orderly plan for the disposition of his or her property based on a general understanding of (1) the nature and extent of the property, (2) the persons who are the natural objects of the testator's bounty, and (3) the disposition being made of the property. The threshold for testamentary capacity is quite low—lower, indeed, than for capacity to enter into a contract or to make an inter vivos gift. Accordingly, a person who is incapable of managing his or her own affairs and who has been placed under a conservatorship may nevertheless be competent to make a will. Similarly, a person may show signs of senility, mental disorder or abuse of alcohol or drugs, yet still have the requisite mental capacity. The determinative question is whether at the time the will is executed the testator is able to understand the significance of the testamentary act. If testamentary capacity is lacking, the entire will fails.

A special type of incapacity arises if a testator is afflicted with an "insane delusion" which affects the disposition in the will. An insane delusion is a false belief resulting from a mental disorder and lacking any rational basis. Insane delusions usually involve imagined insults, threats or offenses which prompt the testator (who may be quite lucid and intelligent in other respects) to disinherit a close family member. Typical examples include a husband's false belief that his wife has been unfaithful to him, or a mother's false belief that her child is trying to harm her. It is not enough that the testator holds a mistaken belief; the contestant must show that the belief was groundless and irrational. If an insane delusion affects some portions of the will but not others, only the tainted portions will be struck down.

A will may also be set aside if it was procured by undue influence. Undue influence occurs when a testator is induced by another person through domination or coercion to make a will that does not reflect the testator's true wishes. In essence, the problem is one of substituted volition. A testator may be influenced in many ways by friends, family members and trusted advisers, and the line between legitimate advice or persuasion and improper pressure or manipulation is not always clear. Moreover, since the influencer is likely to act in secrecy, proof of undue influence usually rests on circumstantial evidence concerning the testator's physical and mental condition, the relationship between the testator and the influencer, the character of the influencer, and the apparent effect on the disposition in the testator's will. A rebuttable presumption of undue influence may arise if the testator and the influencer were in a confidential relationship and the influencer actively participated in procuring the will or otherwise acted in a suspicious or improper manner. The will is invalid to the extent it is found to have been procured by undue influence.

A lawyer who drafts a will naming the lawyer as a beneficiary not only invites a will contest on grounds of undue influence but also risks disciplinary sanctions for unprofessional conduct. The Model Rules of Professional Conduct (MRPC) prohibit a lawyer from preparing a will, trust or other instrument that makes a "substantial gift" from a client to the lawyer or a close relative of the lawyer, "unless the lawyer or other recipient of the gift is related to the client." MRPC 1.8(c). Even in the absence of undue influence, a lawyer who receives a benefit under a will or trust that the lawyer drafted for an unrelated client may be subject to sanctions under Rule 1.8(c). A separate rule prohibits a lawyer from representing a client if the representation may be "materially limited" by the lawyer's responsibilities to others or by the lawyer's own interests, unless the lawyer reasonably believes that he or she will be able to provide "competent and diligent representation" and the client gives "informed consent, confirmed in writing." MRPC 1.7. Any attempt by a lawyer to influence a client's testamentary scheme for the benefit of the lawyer or another person raises a serious conflict-of-interest problem under Rule 1.7. See McGovern, Undue Influence and Professional Responsibility, 28 Real Prop., Prob. & Tr. J. 643 (1994); Johnston, An Ethical Analysis of Common Estate Planning Practices: Is Good Business Bad Ethics?, 45 Ohio St. L.J. 57, 60–114 (1984).

Statistically, the number of will contests is not large—perhaps on the order of 1% of all wills offered for probate. See Schoenblum, Will Contests—An Empirical Study, 22 Real Prop., Prob. & Tr. J. 607, 614 (1987). Moreover, a substantial portion of will contests never go to trial, and a large majority of litigated contests fail. See id. at 625–27.

Nevertheless, will contests continue to provide a fertile source of acrimonious disputes, even in relatively small estates where the financial stakes are not high. A combination of substantive, procedural and evidentiary factors tend to encourage will contests, especially on grounds of incapacity and undue influence. The substantive rules in these areas are remarkably general, abstract and indeterminate; outcomes in particular cases are highly fact-dependent and difficult to predict. Memories and perceptions concerning the testator's condition and the circumstances surrounding the execution of the will may have become faded or distorted due to lapse of time, and in any event the most important witness—the testator—is unavailable to testify in support of the will. In most states one party or the other can request a trial by jury, and there is reason to believe that juries may be especially inclined to set aside a will in order to protect the rights of a deserving family member (typically a spouse or child) against an unworthy beneficiary. Indeed, in the absence of a forced share for children, a will contest may be the only avenue by which a disinherited child can hope to participate in a deceased parent's estate. These considerations, together with the prevailing rule that each party bears its own attorney fees and other costs of litigation, may encourage a disappointed heir to bring (or at least threaten to bring) a will contest not with any expectation of prevailing at trial but rather in the hope of extracting a pre-trial settlement from the beneficiaries named in the will. The beneficiaries, often close friends or relatives of the testator, may be willing to agree to a settlement out of all proportion to the strength of the contestant's case, simply to protect the testator's reputation or to spare themselves from embarrassing and vexatious litigation. It is difficult to gauge the impact of such strike suits because they do not show up in the reported cases. See Langbein, Living Probate: The Conservatorship Model, 77 Mich. L. Rev. 63, 64–66 (1978).

As a practical matter, the probability of a will contest is greatest in situations where there is a built-in rivalry between members of a blended family (e.g., children from a first marriage pitted against a second spouse), where one child fares substantially better or worse than another under the will, or where close family members are disinherited in favor of an outsider (e.g., a friend or caretaker). In such situations, a few elementary precautions at the time the will is executed may help to ward off a possible future contest. For example, it may be useful to create a contemporaneous record of the testator's physical and mental condition through affidavits of friends, family members and perhaps one or more attending physicians. It may also be appropriate for the testator to provide an explanation, in writing or on videotape, of the disposition made in the will. See Jaworski, Will Contests, 1 Baylor L. Rev. 87 (1958).

A testator might also consider including a "no-contest" clause in the will, providing that a beneficiary who brings a will contest shall take nothing under the will. Of course, this tactic is effective only if the potential contestant stands to receive a substantial benefit under the will by foregoing a contest; otherwise, the forfeiture condition is an empty threat. If the contestant goes forward and succeeds in setting aside the will, the no-contest clause has no effect. Moreover, in many states a no-contest clause is not enforceable if "probable cause" exists for bringing the will contest. See UPC § 3–905. The rationale is that a contestant with a reasonably strong (though ultimately unsuccessful) case should not be forced to risk forfeiting all benefits under the will in order to test the validity of the will in a judicial proceeding. There is no reason, however, not to enforce a no-contest clause against a litigant who brings a groundless will contest.

As a matter of professional responsibility, a lawyer may properly draft a will for a testator whose mental capacity appears to be borderline. In such cases, the lawyer should take steps to preserve available evidence concerning testamentary capacity. In contrast, if the lawyer reasonably believes that the testator lacks the requisite mental capacity, the lawyer should not prepare the will. See ACTEC, Commentaries on the Model Rules of Professional Conduct 218 (3d ed. 1999).

In an effort to improve the quality of the evidence and discourage groundless will contests, several commentators have proposed some form of a "living probate" proceeding in which questions concerning due execution, capacity and undue influence could be resolved by a court while the testator is alive and available to testify. In a "contest" model, the testator can request a judgment declaring the validity of the will; by giving notice to potential contestants, the testator can require them to come forward and contest the will in the testator's presence. See Fink, Ante–Mortem Probate Revisited: Can an Idea Have a Life After Death?, 37 Ohio St. L.J. 264 (1976). A "conservatorship" model contemplates a probate court proceeding along the lines of a voluntary conservatorship hearing, in which interested parties would have an opportunity to channel their concerns through a guardian ad litem instead of confronting the testator directly. See Langbein, Living Probate: The Conservatorship Model, 77 Mich. L. Rev. 63 (1978). An "administrative" model would dispense with notice and representation for potential contestants; the probate court would issue an order determining the validity of the will based on an investigation and report by a guardian ad litem. See Alexander & Pearson, Alternative Models of Ante–Mortem Probate and Procedural Due Process Limitations on Succession, 78 Mich. L. Rev. 89 (1979). Critics have pointed out problems relating to disruption of family relationships, fairness to potential contestants, and potential subsequent revocation or amendment of the will. See Fellows, The Case Against Living Probate, 78 Mich. L. Rev. 1066 (1980). A few states have enacted statutes to implement the "contest" model of living probate, but the procedure does not appear to be widely used.

[¶ 2,040]

2. Estate Administration

In addition to determining whether a decedent left a valid will, the probate court has exclusive jurisdiction over the administration of the decedent's estate. The basic tasks of estate administration—collecting the decedent's assets, paying creditors' claims, and distributing the remaining property to the appropriate recipients—are carried out by a personal representative. The personal representative is a fiduciary who must be appointed by the probate court and remains accountable to the court throughout the administration of the estate.

[¶ 2,045]

a. *Role of the personal representative*

Administration of a decedent's estate is opened by filing a petition in the probate court for the appointment of a personal representative. (Technically, the term "personal representative" includes both executors and administrators; the difference is that an executor, unlike an administrator, is named in a will.) The petition recites the essential facts concerning the decedent's identity and domicile, the date of death, the existence of any known wills, and the identities of known successors, and is usually filed by the person seeking appointment as personal representative or by some other interested person. The probate court appoints a personal representative by issuing "letters" (i.e., "letters testamentary" in the case of an executor, or "letters of administration" in the case of an administrator). See UPC § 3–103. The letters serve as documentary evidence of the appointment, and may contain special restrictions on the personal representative's powers. Upon the issuance of letters, the personal representative accepts authority and responsibility for administering the estate in accordance with the terms of the will, if any, and applicable laws. In general, no person has any authority to act on behalf of the estate prior to the issuance of letters, but the powers acquired by the personal representative upon appointment relate back to the decedent's death. See UPC § 3–701.

In many states, an individual must furnish a bond with sureties acceptable to the probate court in order to qualify as personal representative, unless the will provides otherwise. The amount of the bond is typically equal to the value of the personal property in the estate plus one year of estimated income, and the purpose is to ensure a reliable source of funds to make good any loss to the estate resulting from a breach of fiduciary duty by the personal representative. No bond is required of a corporate fiduciary, since a corporation must have substantial assets to act as a fiduciary. The cost of a bond can be substantial, often in the range of $5 to $10 per $1,000 of the covered amount for each year of coverage, and the will may include a provision waiving bond in order to avoid unnecessary expense. In several states, the bond requirement has been relaxed so that a personal representative can usually be appointed without bond, although the probate court has discretion to require a bond in appropriate cases. See UPC § 3–603.

Promptly after appointment by the probate court, one of the personal representative's first duties is to prepare and file an inventory listing the assets in the probate estate and their respective values, as well as any encumbrances. See UPC § 3–706. It may be necessary or desirable to obtain a professional appraisal of hard-to-value assets such as jewelry, art work, or interests in a closely held business. In some states, an appraisal is required for all of the inventoried assets; a court-appointed appraiser (or "probate referee") may be entitled to a statutory fee based on the value of the appraised assets (e.g., one-tenth of 1%).

The inventory serves as the foundation for the personal representative's duty to render an accounting of the estate administration. The personal representative is required to maintain clear and accurate records of all transactions involving the estate, including income received, payments of creditors' claims, taxes, commissions and other administration expenses, gain or loss on sales of estate assets, and distributions to beneficiaries. These records must then be compiled in an accounting which summarizes (1) the assets collected at the beginning of the estate administration, (2) receipts, disbursements, distributions and other transactions involving the estate during the period of administration, and (3) assets remaining on hand for distribution at the end of administration. A proper accounting provides the beneficiaries with the information they need in order to approve or object to the personal representative's management of the estate. In many states, an accounting must be filed with the probate court for its approval before the estate can be closed and the personal representative discharged. An accounting in court can be waived by the unanimous consent of the beneficiaries, if they are all adult and competent, and this is routinely done when there is no objection. A full-fledged court accounting can be a cumbersome and expensive proceeding, especially if a guardian ad litem must be appointed to represent the interests of minor or incompetent beneficiaries. In some states, the personal representative may be able to account directly to the beneficiaries without the need for a court accounting. See UPC § 3–1003.

Under traditional probate statutes, the personal representative took legal title only to the decedent's personal property; legal title to land passed directly to the decedent's testate or intestate successors at death, "subject to administration." As a practical matter, this meant that the personal representative could take possession of the land or sell it if necessary to carry out the administration of the estate. Many modern statutes provide for a unified treatment of real and personal property. For example, under the Uniform Probate Code, a decedent's property devolves at death to the testate or intestate successors, subject to statutory allowances, to creditors' rights, to the surviving spouse's elective share, and to administration. See UPC § 3–101. Furthermore, the personal representative is authorized to take possession and control of the decedent's property, "except that any real property or tangible personal property may be left with or surrendered to the person presumptively entitled thereto unless or until, in the judgment of the personal representative, possession of the property by him will be necessary for purposes of administration." UPC § 3–709.

Personal representatives traditionally had quite limited powers and were subject to close supervision by the probate court in administering decedents' estates. It has long been common practice in drafting wills to include a comprehensive grant of administrative powers so that the personal representative can sell land or other estate assets, pay creditors' claims and administration expenses, and make distributions to beneficiaries without prior court approval. Today many states have broadened the statutory powers of personal representatives (see UPC § 3–715), but it is still helpful to list administrative powers in the will, both to cover matters that may not be adequately addressed in a particular statute and to provide a convenient reference for the personal representative in managing the estate and dealing with third parties. In exercising powers conferred by statute or by will, the personal representative is subject to the same fundamental duties of loyalty, prudence and impartiality as trustees and other fiduciaries. (See ¶¶ 2,570–2,585.) In several states, the personal representative may be authorized by will to carry out an "independent" administration largely free of court supervision after the initial appointment. Even an independent personal representative, however, remains accountable to the probate court at the request of an interested party.

When a person dies, there may be any number of obligations—utility bills, credit card balances, mortgage or lease payments, even undiscovered tort liabilities—which are currently due or may become enforceable against the estate in the future. One of the most important functions of estate administration is to resolve these claims in a prompt and orderly manner. Under the "non-claim" statutes, most claims are barred unless they are presented to the personal representative within a fairly short time (e.g., four months) after notice of the commencement of administration. See UPC §§ 3–801, 3–803(a)(2). Thus, one of the first tasks of the personal representative after appointment by the probate court is to search through the decedent's personal and business financial records and mail a written notice to all of the known creditors, advising them of the deadline and the procedure for presenting claims against the estate. Constructive notice to unknown creditors is given by publication in a local newspaper of general circulation. As each claim is presented, the personal representative may either allow the claim and pay it or disallow the claim and require the creditor to sue. The Supreme Court has held, as a matter of constitutional due process, that creditors who are known or "reasonably ascertainable" are entitled to actual notice before their claims can be cut off by a non-claim statute. Tulsa Professional Collection Services, Inc. v. Pope, 485 U.S. 478 (1988). In response, many states have enacted self-executing statutes of limitation which automatically bar claims that are not presented within one year after the decedent's death, even if no notice is given. See UPC § 3–803(a)(1). These statutory bars do not affect the enforceability of a mortgage or other lien against estate assets, nor do they apply to administration expenses or claims arising at or after the decedent's death.

In making payments to creditors and other claimants, the personal representative should be careful to observe the order of priority prescribed by statute. If it is clear that there are sufficient assets in the estate to pay all liabilities, there is little risk in paying claims as they are presented or in making interim distributions to beneficiaries. If the estate turns out to be insolvent, however, the personal representative may be personally liable for any amounts improperly paid. A typical statute requires that assets of an insolvent estate be used to pay claims in the following order of priority: administration expenses; funeral expenses; debts and taxes with preference under federal law; expenses of the decedent's last illness; debts and taxes with preference under state law; and other claims. See UPC § 3–805.

The decedent's surviving spouse and minor or dependent children, if any, may be entitled to statutory allowances for homestead, exempt property and family support. The probate homestead typically consists of property, up to a specified dollar value or acreage, that was used as a residence by the decedent, while exempt property typically includes items of clothing, furnishings and personal effects up to a specified dollar value. The family support allowance is intended to meet basic support needs during the period of estate administration; the amount is often subject to the discretion of the probate court and may be payable in a lump sum or in installments. The provisions governing the availability, scope and procedure for claiming the statutory allowances vary widely from one state to another. The most important common feature of the statutory allowances is that they take priority over all claims and can therefore be paid promptly after the decedent's death without the need to determine whether the estate is solvent. In addition, the statutory allowances take precedence over the terms of the will. As a result, in a small estate with assets not exceeding the statutory allowances, claims against the estate need not be paid and the will does not control the disposition of the estate.

A personal representative is entitled to compensation for administering the estate. In many states, compensation is fixed by a statutory fee schedule based on the size of the estate being administered (e.g., 5% on the first $100,000, 4% on the next $200,000, 3% on the next $700,000, 2½% on the next $4,000,000, and 2% on amounts over $5,000,000). In other states, the personal representative is entitled to "reasonable compensation," which may take into account various factors including the size and nature of the estate as well as local custom. See UPC § 3–719. Lawyers are also entitled to compensation for services in connection with the estate administration, again either pursuant to a statutory fee schedule or under a reasonable compensation standard. As a practical matter, it appears that the method of computation makes relatively little difference in the amount paid as attorney fees. See Stein & Fierstein, The Role of the Attorney in Estate Administration, 68 Minn. L. Rev. 1107, 1193 (1984). In most states, a lawyer who serves as personal representative may also act (or engage his or her firm to act) as lawyer for the estate and claim dual compensation. See UPC § 3–715(21). Such arrangements may be justified on grounds of efficiency, but they inherently involve a conflict of interest and in some states dual compensation is prohibited or subject to special restrictions.

The final steps in settling a decedent's estate, after paying creditors' claims and administration expenses, consist of filing a final accounting and obtaining court approval for a final distribution of the remaining assets to the decedent's testate or intestate successors. If there are no objections to the final accounting and distribution, the personal representative can request an order from the probate court formally closing the estate and discharging the personal representative from liability.

Administration of a decedent's estate occurs primarily in the state where the decedent was domiciled at death. If the decedent owned land or other property located in another state, however, it may be necessary to open a separate, "ancillary" administration because a personal representative appointed in the state of domicile is not automatically authorized to take legal action in the courts of other states. The most common reason for ancillary administration is to clear title to out-of-state land owned by the decedent. Ancillary administration may also be necessary, for example, to collect assets in the possession of a person in another state, or to compel payment of a debt owed to the decedent by an out-of-state debtor. In addition, ancillary administration offers out-of-state creditors the convenience of reaching local assets in a local proceeding to satisfy their claims. In a number of states, an out-of-state domiciliary personal representative can collect debts and other personal property by affidavit without any court proceedings. See UPC § 4–201. Moreover, the out-of-state domiciliary personal representative can acquire the powers of a local personal representative simply by filing evidence of the original appointment with a local probate court. See UPC §§ 4–204, 4–205.

[¶ 2,050]

b. *The probate system in practical perspective*

In administering a decedent's estate, the personal representative acts as a fiduciary for the decedent's successors and for creditors of the estate. The personal representative is appointed by the probate court and is often subject to close judicial supervision. The personal representative is also confronted by a panoply of procedural safeguards (e.g., requirements of notice, hearing, bond, appraisal, accounting, etc.) which make it necessary, as a practical matter, to engage the services of a lawyer. As a result, the process of estate administration provides a high level of protection for all interested parties, but it does so at a price. Estate administration, and the probate process generally, have come to be widely perceived as slow-moving, expensive, and unnecessarily cumbersome. In some cases, the protective features of the probate system may be warranted to guard against incompetent or dishonest personal representatives. In the ordinary run of cases, however, there is little or no need for probate court involvement. Indeed, most decedents' estates are settled without ever opening a formal probate proceeding. This section examines some common methods of avoiding full-fledged probate proceedings, as well as some situations in which probate proceedings may be necessary or desirable.

Dissatisfaction with the traditional probate system has fueled the rise of will substitutes such as pay-on-death beneficiary designations and revocable trusts, which operate entirely outside the probate system. For an excellent discussion of will substitutes and their impact on the probate system, see Langbein, The Nonprobate Revolution and the

Future of the Law of Succession, 97 Harv. L. Rev. 1108 (1984). Today it is estimated that more wealth passes by will substitutes than through the probate system. Nevertheless, will substitutes have at least two inherent limitations which help to explain why they have not entirely displaced the probate system. First, will substitutes tend to be "asset-specific," meaning that they operate on particular assets (e.g., a bank account, mutual fund shares, or life insurance proceeds); they are not well suited to handle all the miscellaneous residual assets owned by a decedent, which accordingly fall into the probate estate to be disposed of by will or intestacy. Second, will substitutes are designed to carry out "easy" transfers, while leaving difficult or disputed cases to be resolved in the courts. Thus, "the nonprobate system rides 'piggyback' on the probate system." Id. at 1120. Will substitutes are discussed in more detail at ¶¶ 2,300–2,352.

Despite the rapid spread of will substitutes, the probate system continues to have an important role in the transfer of property at death. One obvious function involves the resolution of conflicts concerning the disposition of decedents' estates. The probate court provides a convenient and specialized forum for adjudicating disputes over whether or not a decedent left a valid will, owned a particular asset, or owed money to a creditor. Even if the parties do not proceed to litigation, the availability of a formal probate court proceeding is likely to affect how the parties assess the merits of their respective claims and the terms on which they can be induced to reach a settlement.

Even in the absence of a dispute, the decedent's successors may find it worthwhile to invoke the jurisdiction of the probate court in order to prove a will, to commence an estate administration, to establish their beneficial interests in the estate, or to obtain clear title to their respective shares of the estate assets. Consider the difficulties they must face if no probate proceedings are commenced. Initially, there is the question of whether the decedent died testate or intestate. Without a probate court proceeding, it is not clear whether the decedent left a will or, if so, whether it may eventually be admitted to probate. Thus, the rights of the intestate successors remain doubtful and unsettled. (In many states, a will may be offered for probate many years after the decedent's death, though the Uniform Probate Code imposes a general limitation period of three years. See UPC § 3–108.) This uncertainty may not be of immediate concern to the successors, especially if the decedent is known to have died intestate. In some cases, however, a potential purchaser is likely to insist on documentary evidence of title.

If the decedent held record title to property in his or her sole name, it may be difficult to clear title in the hands of the successors without opening a probate proceeding. This is because, in general, a testate or intestate successor can acquire record title only by a decree of the probate court or a deed from a duly appointed personal representative, after the presentation and payment of creditors' claims. Accordingly, administration is usually necessary if the estate includes land in the decedent's sole name; without proper documentation of title in the local land records, no purchaser will be willing to pay fair market value to a successor for the land. (In a few states, a probated will may be sufficient evidence of title, but this is not generally the case.) A similar situation may arise in the case of bank accounts, securities, motor vehicles, or other property held in registered form. A bank, brokerage firm or other entity that maintains ownership records will usually change record title only at the direction of a duly appointed personal representative.

Technically, all probate assets, including personal effects and household goods, are potentially subject to administration. As a practical matter, however, most items of tangible personal property (other than motor vehicles) are transferred simply by delivery of possession, without a formal record of title. For example, a purchaser of second-hand goods at a yard sale does not insist on documentary evidence of the seller's legal title. As a result, if the successors already have possession of items of unregistered tangible personal property and are able to agree on a division among themselves, there is ordinarily no need to open an estate administration on account of those items.

Regardless of the successors' preferences, creditors of the decedent may wish to open an estate administration to protect their own interests. One of the central functions of traditional estate administration is to make sure that creditors are given notice and an opportunity to have their claims paid in the prescribed order of priority before assets are distributed to the decedent's successors. If no other person opens a probate proceeding, a creditor has standing to do so, in order to present claims for payment. As a practical matter, however, it appears that creditors do not rely heavily on the probate system. In many cases, creditors are able to collect their claims promptly and informally; the successors voluntarily pay the decedent's routine debts (e.g., outstanding utility bills and credit card balances), either from instinctive rectitude or in order to protect their own credit ratings. (Of course, the very existence of the probate process gives creditors useful leverage in dealing with successors.) In other cases, the claims may be covered by credit life insurance or by a security interest. Accordingly, creditors tend to use the probate system primarily in disputed cases involving substantial amounts. See Langbein, The Nonprobate Revolution and the Future of the Law of Succession, 97 Harv. L. Rev. 1108, 1120–25 (1984).

In the absence of any disputes or unusual complications requiring judicial resolution, then, the main reason for opening a probate proceeding is simply to give the decedent's successors clear title to the assets remaining after payment of creditors' claims. Reacting to the phenomenal growth of will substitutes in the 1960's, the drafters of the original Uniform Probate Code sought to preserve a viable role for the probate system by making the process of administration more flexible and streamlined. To this end, the drafters introduced several informal procedures which make it possible to avoid a full-fledged, formal estate administration. The provisions for collection by affidavit and summary administration have influenced legislation even in states that have not adopted the Uniform Probate Code.

1. *Collection of personal property by affidavit (small estate).* If at least thirty days have elapsed since the decedent's death, the net estate does not exceed a specified amount (ranging from $5,000 up to $100,000 in some states), and no administration proceeding is pending, a successor entitled to personal property belonging to the decedent (including debts owed to the decedent) is authorized to collect the property by presenting an affidavit directly to the person in control of the property, without any probate court proceeding. A person who pays or transfers the property to the successor pursuant to the affidavit is protected to the same extent as in dealing with a personal representative. (If the person in control of the property refuses to turn it over to the successor, the successor can sue in court.) If a personal representative is subsequently appointed, the successor is accountable for the property received. See UPC §§ 3–1201, 3–1202. In some states, the collection-by-affidavit procedure can be used only by the decedent's surviving spouse or children. Also, many states have specialized collection-by-affidavit procedures for particular types of assets such as bank accounts or motor vehicles. Note that the procedure provides no protection to other interested parties against a purported successor who fraudulently collects property based on a false affidavit and then absconds.

2. *Summary administration.* After an estate administration has been opened, if it appears that the value of the estate, net of liens and encumbrances, does not exceed the sum of the statutory allowances (i.e., homestead, exempt property and family support) and preferred claims (i.e., administration expenses, funeral expenses and expenses of the decedent's last illness), the personal representative is authorized to disburse the estate to the appropriate recipients and file a closing statement. See UPC §§ 3–1203, 3–1204. Summary administration, as the name implies, is a short form of probate administration that allows the personal representative to wind up a small estate promptly, without requiring ordinary creditors to present claims that will not be paid in any event.

3. *Family settlement agreement.* The decedent's successors may agree among themselves to modify their respective interests in the probate estate. Such an agreement is binding, of course, only on the parties themselves; it has no effect on the rights of others such as creditors or taxing authorities. See UPC § 3–912. If the successors are all competent adults and are able to reach unanimous agreement, they can completely override the disposition set forth in the decedent's will or the intestacy statutes.

4. *Succession without administration.* In some states, no administration is required for community property passing to a decedent's surviving spouse. The spouse takes the community property subject to liability for the decedent's debts. (To limit potential liability to the decedent's creditors, the spouse may

choose to subject the property to administration.) The Uniform Probate Code also provides for succession without administration. The decedent's intestate successors or residuary beneficiaries under a will can join together in the probate court and qualify as "universal successors" with full powers of ownership over estate assets. To qualify, all of the intestate successors or residuary beneficiaries (except for minor, incompetent or unascertained persons) must assume personal liability for payment of claims and distribution of the remaining assets to the appropriate recipients. All of the universal successors are subject to the jurisdiction of the probate court and can be joined in a single proceeding by a creditor or other claimant, but the liability of each universal successor on a claim is proportional to his or her share of the estate. See UPC §§ 3–312 to 3–322.

Thus, in one way or another, most estates can be settled informally without a formal estate administration. Nevertheless, the probate system still performs a vital role in the transfer of wealth at death. The probate court provides a forum for judicial resolution of disputes, and even in routine, uncontested matters, estate administration provides a useful mechanism for clearing title to estate assets, paying statutory allowances and, if necessary, supervising the actions of the personal representative.

[¶ 2,052]

Problem

Yvonne died intestate, survived by her husband, one minor child and one brother. At her death, Yvonne owned an automobile (titled in her own name) worth $2,000, a bank account (in her own name) with a balance of $1,500, and miscellaneous personal effects and household items with an estimated value of $1,000. Yvonne also owned an insurance policy on her life, in the face amount of $200,000, which is payable to her surviving spouse as beneficiary. At her death, Yvonne owed various undisputed small debts totalling $500. Is it necessary or desirable to open an estate administration? If not, how will the surviving spouse obtain clear title to the automobile and the bank account? What difference would it make if Yvonne left a will in which she bequeathed the automobile by will to her brother?

C. INTESTATE SUCCESSION

[¶ 2,100]

The intestacy statutes provide an "estate plan by operation of law" for individuals who die without a valid will. Studies indicate that a majority of individuals die intestate, and accordingly the intestacy statutes have a broad field of application. Ideally, rules of intestate succession should be designed to carry out the probable intent of the average intestate decedent, but the actual rules on the books often fall short of this goal. Moreover, many individuals seem to have no very clear notion of how their own estates would be disposed of under the governing intestacy statutes. Any person who drafts or executes a will should have at least a basic understanding of intestate succession.

Intestacy statutes traditionally prescribed different rules for the *descent* of real property to a decedent's *heirs* and the *distribution* of personal property to the *next of kin*. Almost all modern statutes prescribe a unified system of "descent and distribution" for all types of property, and the term "heir" is widely used to refer to any intestate successor. The general outline of intestate succession is fairly well established, although the details vary widely from one state to another. In every state, the decedent's surviving spouse is entitled to an intestate share, and the rest of the estate (or the entire estate, if there is no surviving spouse) goes to the decedent's issue (i.e., lineal descendants), who take to the exclusion of all other relatives. If the decedent left no issue, the estate typically goes to the decedent's blood relatives based on proximity of relationship, i.e., first to the decedent's parents or their issue, then to the decedent's grandparents or their issue. See UPC § 2–103. If the decedent left no spouse or close blood relatives, some statutes cut off inheritance altogether and provide for escheat to the state. See UPC § 2–105. This approach avoids the burden of locating distant relatives ("laughing heirs") for whom grief at the decedent's death is likely to be outweighed by delight at receiving a windfall inheritance. Most statutes, however, allow remote blood relatives to inherit without limitation. If the decedent left no surviving spouse or close blood relatives, some statutes broaden the group of eligible takers to include a predeceased spouse's issue or other relatives.

Under general choice of law principles, intestate succession to personal property is governed by the law of the state where the decedent was domiciled at the time of death, while intestate succession to real property is governed by the law of the state in which the real property is located.

[¶ 2,110]

1. Spouse and Children

One striking feature of the intestacy statutes is that they allocate the estate to the decedent's surviving spouse and relatives in fixed proportions based on family status. A surviving spouse, for example, is entitled to an intestate share which typically ranges from one-third to one-half of the estate. Some statutes are considerably more generous. For example, the UPC never gives the surviving spouse less than the first $100,000 plus one-half of the balance of the estate; given the modest size of the average intestate estate, this means that the spouse is likely to be the sole heir, even if the decedent left surviving issue from a prior marriage. See UPC § 2–102.

The rigid statutory formulas for allocating a decedent's estate among the heirs may seem rather crude in operation. For example, in determining the intestate share of a surviving spouse, the statutes do not purport to take into account a host of factors that might be considered relevant: Was the spouse independently wealthy or destitute? Did the decedent make gifts to the spouse outside the probate system? Was the spouse married to the decedent for three months or 30 years? Nor do the statutes allow the probate court any measure of discretion to vary the rules of intestate succession to accommodate the financial needs or moral claims of individual family members. A more flexible approach involving a detailed case-by-case inquiry might produce better outcomes in particular cases, but such an approach would also impose heavy costs on the probate system. As long as the decedent had an opportunity to direct a different disposition of his or her property by will, considerations of certainty and efficiency may weigh in favor of a system of fixed default rules for intestate succession. The content of those default rules, however, remains controversial.

The intestacy statutes define the group of eligible heirs based exclusively on legally recognized family relationships, and thereby implicitly exclude individuals who may have had a close but informal family relationship with the decedent. For example, only a few states explicitly allow a domestic partner or an unadopted foster child to inherit from an intestate decedent. In the vast majority of states, these nontraditional family relationships are not recognized for purposes of intestate succession.

In general, children are eligible to inherit from their parents and vice versa. This is true regardless of whether the child is born out of wedlock; it is the parent-child relationship, not the marital status of the parents, that matters. Although an absolute bar on inheritance by an out-of-wedlock child would be unconstitutional, many statutes limit the type of evidence that can be introduced to prove paternity after the father's death. A parent-child relationship can be created or extinguished by legal adoption proceedings. In general, an adopted child is treated as the child of the adoptive parents and not of the natural parents. In the case of a step-parent adoption, however, most statutes permit the child to inherit from one or both of the natural parents as well as from the adoptive parent. See UPC § 2–114. For example, suppose a child's natural parents divorce, the mother remarries, and the child is adopted by the stepfather (with the natural father's consent). After the adoption, the child is eligible to inherit from the natural mother and the adoptive father, and in many states from the natural father as well. Inheritance rights are not necessarily reciprocal, however. Even if the child is eligible to inherit from the natural father, the natural father may be barred from inheriting from the child. See UPC § 2–114(b).

Advances in reproductive technology raise difficult questions concerning intestate succession. In the absence of statutory guidance, courts have struggled to sort out the parentage of children conceived through artificial insemination. The situation is even more complicated in situations involving surrogacy arrangements.

[¶ 2,120]

2. Representation

Frequently an estate must be divided among a decedent's surviving issue *by representation*. Basically, the takers are the oldest living descendants in each line of descent; if there is a deceased descendant with living issue, the issue collectively "represent" (i.e., take the place of) their deceased ancestor, but in no event do living issue compete with their own living ancestors.

Representation can take various forms. Several states follow a strict *per stirpes* system, which calls for the estate to be divided into equal shares, one for each surviving child and one for each deceased child with living issue; each deceased child's share is then redivided at each successive generation in the same manner until the entire estate has been allocated to living takers. Today the most common form of representation is the one set forth in the original UPC, which provides that the estate shall be

> divided into as many shares as there are surviving heirs in the nearest degree of kinship and deceased persons in the same degree who left issue who survive the decedent, each surviving heir in the nearest degree receiving one share and the share of each deceased person in the same degree being divided among his issue in the same manner. [UPC § 2–106 (1969).]

The two systems of representation often produce identical results. For example, suppose an unmarried decedent *D* dies survived by three children, *A*, *B* and *C*, and by *B*'s child *X* and *C*'s children *Y* and *Z*.

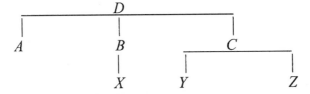

Under both systems of representation, *A*, *B* and *C* each take one-third of the estate; *B* and *C* take to the exclusion of their living issue. Now suppose that *B* and *C* are predeceased but their children are living. Under both systems, *A* takes one-third of the estate, *X* takes one-third, and *Y* and *Z* take one-sixth each.

To illustrate the difference between the two systems, suppose that all three children are predeceased. Under a per stirpes system, *X* takes one-half of the estate and *Y* and *Z* take one-quarter each. (*A* left no surviving issue and therefore drops out of the computation.) By contrast, under the original UPC, the initial division of the estate occurs at the grandchildren's generation; the children's generation is ignored because there are no living takers in that generation. Accordingly, *X*, *Y* and *Z* each take one-third of the estate. Note that the identities of the takers are always the same; the form of representation affects only the size of their respective shares.

A few states follow a third form of representation set forth in the revised Uniform Probate Code, which modifies the original UPC approach by requiring that in each generation the shares of any deceased members who left living issue must be recombined and then divided "in the same manner" among the living issue. See UPC § 2–106 (1990). The revised UPC approach ensures that in each generation the living takers who are related to the decedent in equal degree receive equal intestate shares. Thus, in the above example, if *D* was survived by *A* but *B* and *C* were predeceased, *A* would take one-third of the estate and the remaining two-thirds would be divided equally between *X*, *Y* and *Z*, who would take two-ninths each.

The same principles of representation apply in dividing an intestate share among collateral relatives (i.e., blood relatives other than the decedent's issue or ancestors). Moreover, courts often borrow the same rules in construing a class gift to "issue" in a will or a trust.

[¶ 2,130]

3. Ancestors and Collaterals

If the decedent left no spouse or close blood relatives, some statutes cut off inheritance altogether and provide for escheat to the state. See UPC § 2–105. Other statutes allow unlimited inheritance by the decedent's surviving blood relatives ("kindred" or "next of kin"). These statutes identify the intestate takers using either a "parentelic" system based on lines of descent or a "gradual" system based on degrees of consanguinity. (See the Table of Consanguinity, below.) A *parentelic* system gives categorical priority to nearer ancestors and their issue over more remote ancestors and their issue. For example, a great-grandparent would inherit to the exclusion of a great-great-grandparent. Similarly, a second cousin (the great-grandchild of the decedent's great-grandparents) would be preferred over a great-grand-aunt (the child of the decedent's great-great-grandparents). The living issue of a deceased ancestor take the ancestor's share by representation. See Tex. Prob. Code § 38.

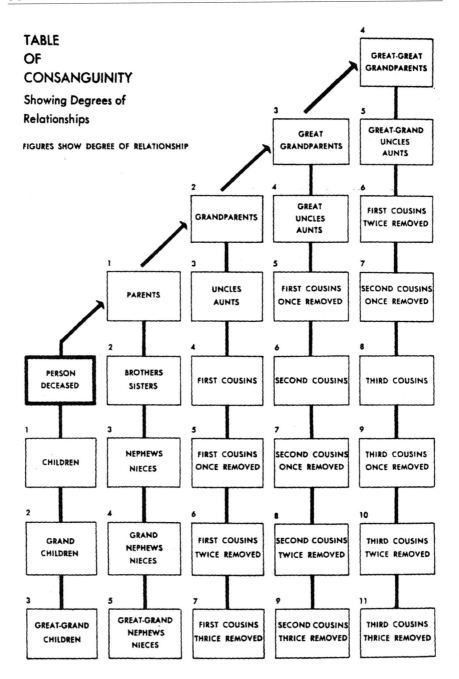

TABLE OF CONSANGUINITY
Showing Degrees of Relationships

FIGURES SHOW DEGREE OF RELATIONSHIP

This material is reproduced from *California Decedent Estate Practice, Vol. 1,* copyright 2004 by the Regents of the University of California. Reproduced with permission of Continuing Education of the Bar–California. (For information about CEB publications, telephone toll free 1–800–CEB–3444 or visit our Web site, CEB.com).

By contrast, in a *gradual* system, the estate goes to the surviving relatives who are closest to the decedent in degree of consanguinity. For this purpose, the degree of consanguinity is equal to the total number of generations, counting up from the decedent to the nearest common ancestor and then counting down from the common ancestor to the relative in question. For example, a great-grandparent is related to the decedent in the third degree, a great-aunt in the fourth degree, and a second cousin in the sixth degree. In a gradual system, a great-grand-aunt (related in the fifth degree) would inherit to the exclusion of a second cousin (related in the sixth degree). Two or more relatives in the closest degree of consanguinity share the estate equally, but some statutes include a tie-breaker provision that gives priority to relatives claiming through the nearest common ancestor. See Cal. Prob. Code § 6402(f).

[¶ 2,140]

4. Survival Requirement

To qualify as an heir, a person must be living at the decedent's death. Anyone who fails to survive the decedent is ineligible to share in the estate. In most cases it is clear whether or not the survival requirement is met, but occasionally two people die in circumstances that make the order of deaths difficult to determine. Under the traditional rule, if it can be proved that one person survived the other by even an instant, the survivor is entitled to inherit from the first decedent. If it is impossible to determine the order of deaths, a typical "simultaneous death" statute provides that "the property of each person shall be disposed of as if he had survived." Uniform Simultaneous Death Act § 1 (1940). Thus, if a husband and wife die together in an airplane crash and there is insufficient evidence that one spouse survived the other, the husband's estate would be disposed of as if he survived his wife, and the wife's estate would be disposed of as if she survived her husband. The rationale is to avoid multiple probate proceedings and to prevent one decedent's estate from being diverted to the other decedent's successors. The Uniform Probate Code goes further and provides that an individual is deemed to have predeceased the decedent unless it is established by clear and convincing evidence that the individual survived the decedent by 120 hours. See UPC § 2–104 (1990). The 120–hour survival requirement and the heightened burden of proof are intended to reduce the volume of litigation in cases where deaths occur in quick succession.

Similar principles apply in cases of simultaneous death involving property passing by will and property passing outside probate by right of survivorship or by beneficiary designation.

In general, an heir must be alive at the decedent's death in order to share in the estate. In the case of a child conceived while the father was alive but born after the father's death, the common law permits the child to inherit from the father by deeming the child's existence to "relate back" to the time of conception for purposes of inheritance. Courts have recently begun to address the more difficult question of whether a child conceived posthumously by artificial insemination using a decedent's frozen sperm is eligible to inherit from the decedent. See Woodward v. Commissioner of Social Security, 760 N.E.2d 257 (Mass. 2002).

[¶ 2,150]

5. Bars to Inheritance

Misconduct on the part of an heir, however morally objectionable, generally does not affect the heir's right to inherit. Courts have been reluctant to find implied exceptions to the rules of succession set forth in the intestacy statutes. Nevertheless, virtually every state by statute or judicial decision recognizes the principle that an heir who killed the decedent should not be allowed to profit from his or her wrongful conduct. A typical statute provides that a person who "feloniously and intentionally kills" a decedent automatically forfeits the right to inherit from the victim, and sets forth a similar rule for property passing by will, trust or right of survivorship. In general, the killer's interest passes as if the killer had predeceased the victim. UPC § 2–803.

In a few states, a surviving spouse may be barred by statute from participating in the estate of a deceased spouse on grounds of abandonment, non-support or adultery. With "no-fault" divorce widely available, however, a troubled marriage is likely to be formally terminated while both spouses are living. If the spouses were legally separated but not divorced at the decedent's death, the surviving spouse is usually entitled to a full intestate share. The Uniform Probate Code prevents a parent from inheriting from a deceased child unless the parent "openly treated the child as his [or hers], and has not refused to support the child." UPC § 2–114(c).

If an intestate decedent made gifts during life to a child or other heir in anticipation of the donee's inheritance, the gifts may be charged against the donee's intestate share. This is the doctrine of *advancements*, which serves to provide a rough equality of benefit between heirs who inherit their entire share at death and those who receive all or part of their share by gift during life. Mechanically, the doctrine requires that the total amount of gifts made by way of advancement be brought into "hotchpot," i.e., notionally added to the value of the actual estate for purposes of calculating the intestate shares, before reducing each heir's share by the amount of his or her advancements. For example, suppose Joelle gave $20,000 to her son Arnold, $10,000 to her daughter Barbara, and nothing to her son Charles during life by way of advancements, and then died intestate with an estate of $90,000. The grossed-up estate of $120,000 is divided into equal one-third shares, and each child's advancements are charged against his or her share. As a result, Arnold would receive $20,000, Barbara would receive $30,000, and Charles would receive $40,000. Note that advancements affect the computation of intestate shares but do not impair the validity of the lifetime gifts; the children do not actually return any of their advancements to the estate. Thus, if any child's advancements exceed his or her share of the grossed-up estate, the child simply drops out of the calculation and takes nothing by intestacy. The evidentiary problems of identifying a decedent's lifetime gifts and determining whether they were intended as advancements have prompted many states to enact statutes curtailing the scope of the doctrine. Under a typical statute, a lifetime gift is not treated as an advancement unless the decedent or the heir declared or acknowledged such an intent in writing. See UPC § 2–109. In these states, as a practical matter, the doctrine of advancements has been abolished.

Sometimes a person who becomes eligible to receive property by inheritance or other donative transfer finds it advantageous to disclaim the property and let it pass instead to another taker. This can happen, for example, if the person making the disclaimer wishes to keep the property out of the reach of creditors or to minimize gift or estate taxes that would otherwise be imposed on a subsequent transfer of the property. Many states have statutes setting forth the required formalities and the operative effects of a valid disclaimer. In the case of property passing from a decedent, the disclaimer typically must be made in writing and delivered or filed within a specified time after the decedent's death. The disclaimed property goes to the taker who would have received the property if the person making the disclaimer had died before the decedent. The disclaimer ''relates back'' to the decedent's death, with the result that the disclaimed property is treated as passing directly from the decedent to the ultimate recipient without ever going through the hands of the person making the disclaimer. For example, suppose that Diana dies intestate survived by her husband Robert and their child Clarence. If Robert makes a valid disclaimer of his intestate share, Clarence will receive the entire estate directly from Diana.

[¶ 2,160]

Problems

1. Greta dies intestate, survived by her husband and by: (a) one child; (b) one parent and two children; or (c) one parent. How should Greta's estate be distributed?

2. Mark is the child of Edmund and Grace. After Edmund's death, Grace remarried and her new husband adopted Mark. Edmund's parents die intestate. Is Mark entitled to an intestate share of their estates? If Mark dies intestate, do Edmund's relatives inherit from him?

3. *X* had issue as indicated in the following chart:

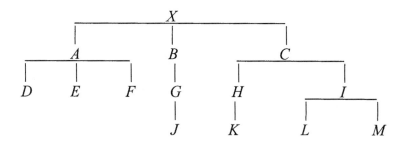

X dies intestate and unmarried, survived only by: (a) *A, G, H* and *I*; (b) *D, E, F, G, H* and *I*; or (c) *D, E, F, J, K, L* and *M*. How should *X*'s estate be distributed?

4. Karen dies intestate, unmarried, and without issue, survived by: (a) her mother and her paternal grandfather; (b) a maternal aunt and two paternal uncles; or (c) a maternal great-aunt and a paternal first cousin. How should Karen's estate be distributed?

5. Eustace and Marie, a married couple, died in an airplane crash. It is impossible to determine the order of deaths. Eustace left an estate of $100,000 and Marie left an estate of $200,000; in addition, they held Blackacre as joint tenants with right of survivorship, and Marie was the designated beneficiary of an insurance policy on Eustace's life. Eustace and Marie had no issue. They are survived by Eustace's brother and by Marie's parents. How should their estates be distributed? Who is entitled to Blackacre and to the life insurance proceeds?

D. WILLS

[¶ 2,200]

Many people put off making a will because they are reluctant to contemplate their own mortality or to go to the expense and inconvenience of consulting a lawyer; in addition, they often have only a limited understanding of the reasons for making a will. At first glance, a person may be content to rely on the intestacy statutes and may see little point in preparing a formal will. On closer examination, however, the intestacy statutes may produce undesirable results. For example, a married person may simply assume that his or her spouse will survive and take the entire estate by intestacy, without thinking of what would happen if the other spouse died first or if both spouses died in a common accident. A parent with minor children may fail to realize that the children could become entitled to an outright intestate share of the estate, resulting in expensive and cumbersome guardianship proceedings if the other parent failed to survive. (It may be appropriate to hold property in trust for the children during minority, but this will not happen under the intestacy statutes.) Family circumstances are likely to change over time: single individuals get married (or remarried); marriages end in divorce; domestic partnerships are formed and broken up; children are born or adopted.

Other circumstances also change: people of modest means may save substantial amounts over a lifetime (or receive windfalls overnight); married couples may migrate from a separate property state to a community property state or vice versa; a person may become infirm or disabled and need special care. In short, even if the intestacy statutes appear to provide a satisfactory default plan at the present time, making a will may be desirable as a precautionary measure, and the will should be drafted with a view to foreseeable changes involving the intended beneficiaries and the assets in the estate.

The primary function of a will is to direct the disposition of the testator's probate assets at death; any property not effectively disposed of by will passes under the intestacy statutes. The will also serves other purposes related to the settlement of the probate estate, such as nominating a personal representative, waiving bond, granting broad powers of administration to be exercised without prior court approval, nominating a guardian for minor children, apportioning liability for debts, taxes and administration expenses, and exercising any testamentary powers of appointment held by the testator. As a practical matter, instructions in a will concerning the disposition of the testator's body are usually carried out before the will is formally admitted to probate.

In general, a will deals with the disposition of probate assets and estate administration; it has no effect on the disposition or administration of property transferred outside the probate system. Will substitutes such as joint tenancies with right of survivorship, pay-on-death beneficiary designations and revocable trusts are effective to transfer specific assets outside the probate system, but they do not render a will superfluous. Even a person who has executed will substitutes for all major assets may still find it desirable to make a will to deal with residual assets as well as additional property acquired before death. Furthermore, in the event that a will substitute fails (e.g., because the intended beneficiary dies before the transferor) and the underlying property becomes part of the probate estate, a will serves to prevent the property from passing by intestacy.

[¶ 2,202]

Problem

Ellen is married and has a minor child. She presently owns a small bank account, an automobile, and miscellaneous personal and household effects. If Ellen is satisfied with the intestate scheme, should she nevertheless make a will? Why?

[¶ 2,210]

1. Execution

Most wills are formal instruments prepared by a lawyer which must be signed not only by the testator but also by two or more attesting witnesses in an elaborate execution ceremony. Many states also allow "holographic" (handwritten) wills, which can be executed by a testator without a lawyer or witnesses. In every state the formalities for executing a will are prescribed by statute. Courts have traditionally required strict compliance with the statutory requirements. A purported will may be denied probate due to a seemingly minor defect in execution, resulting in the failure of the decedent's entire testamentary plan.

[¶ 2,215]

a. Attested Wills

The statutory formalities for attested wills vary in detail from one state to another. Many modern American statutes, based on older English statutes (e.g., the Wills Act of 1837), specify that a will must be in writing and must be signed at the end by the testator (or by another person in the testator's presence and by the testator's direction); furthermore, the signature must be made or acknowledged by the testator in the presence of two or more witnesses present at the same time, and the witnesses must attest and subscribe the will in the testator's presence. The Uniform Probate Code adopts a somewhat simpler, more streamlined approach, and generally requires only that a will be:

(1) in writing;

(2) signed by the testator or in the testator's name by some other individual in the testator's conscious presence and by the testator's direction; and

(3) signed by at least two individuals, each of whom signed within a reasonable time after he [or she] witnessed either the signing of the will as described in paragraph (2) or the testator's acknowledgment of that signature or acknowledgment of the will. [UPC § 2–502(a).]

The requirement of a signed writing is relatively uncontroversial, though there is a body of case law involving the question whether a testator's written initials, nickname, or simple mark constitutes a valid signature. The most common problems involve the requirements of attestation and signing by the witnesses. The witnesses must observe either the testator's act of signing of the will or the testator's acknowledgment of a previously signed instrument as his or her will, and then they must sign the will. Expressly or by implication, the testator must sign or acknowledge the will in the presence of one or both witnesses. In addition, many statutes provide that the witnesses must sign the will "in the presence of the testator and each other." The presence requirement has generated much litigation. Some courts require that the testator actually be able to see the witnesses sign the will (the "line of sight" test), while others require only that the testator be near enough to be aware of what is going on (the "conscious presence" test).

Experienced will drafters always include an attestation clause at the end of the will. A typical attestation clause recites that the testator is of sound mind, that the testator has signed the will and has declared it as his or her will in the presence of the witnesses, and that at the testator's request the witnesses have signed the will in the presence of the testator and each other. Though not required by statute, the attestation clause serves two important functions. First, at the time of execution, it summarizes the steps to be followed by the testator and the witnesses and prompts them to observe the requisite formalities. In addition, when the will is offered for probate after the testator's death, the attestation clause provides persuasive evidence of due execution in the event of a will contest.

In most states a will can be made "self-proved" by a sworn affidavit signed by the testator and the witnesses in the presence of a notary public. The self-proving affidavit recites the facts necessary to show that the will has been duly executed and witnessed, in the form of a sworn declaration attached to or incorporated in the will. For a form of self-proving affidavit, see UPC § 2–504. The self-proving affidavit substitutes for live testimony from the witnesses when the will is offered for probate, and conclusively establishes compliance with the signature requirements for execution in the absence of fraud or forgery. (See ¶ 2,025.)

The attesting witnesses should be disinterested in the sense that they do not stand to receive a beneficial gift under the will. At one time beneficiaries under a will were disqualified from acting as attesting witnesses, with the result that the entire will failed unless it was attested by a sufficient number of disinterested witnesses. Modern wills statutes have abolished the harsh rule of disqualification, so that technically a will can be admitted to probate even if some or all of the attesting witnesses are named as beneficiaries. Nevertheless, under "purging" statutes found in many states, a testamentary gift to an attesting witness may be wholly or partially void. Some purging statutes simply invalidate a gift to an attesting witness. Other statutes allow the witness to take a gift not exceeding the share of the estate to which he or she would be entitled if the will were not established, and bar the witness only from taking any excess benefit under the will. Although the purging statutes are supposed to protect the testator from imposition by unscrupulous beneficiaries, they often operate as a trap for the unwary and deprive innocent beneficiaries of their intended gifts. "The requirement of disinterested witnesses has not succeeded in preventing fraud and undue influence; and in most cases of fraud and undue influence, the influencer is careful not to sign as a witness, but to procure disinterested witnesses." UPC § 2–505, cmt. The Uniform Probate Code abandons the approach of the purging statutes. A person who is "generally competent to be a witness" may act as an attesting witness to a will, and the signing of a will by an interested witness "does not invalidate the will or any provision of it." UPC § 2–505.

To minimize the choice of law problems, many states provide that a will is valid if it is executed in compliance with the law of "the place where the will is executed" or the law of "the place where at the time of execution or at the time of death the testator is domiciled, has a place of abode, or is a national." UPC § 2–506.

Given the variations in wills statutes and the possibility that a testator may move from one state to another or own property in more than one state, it is often recommended that wills be executed in compliance with the maximum statutory formalities. One recommended form of execution ceremony is as follows:

1. The testator reads through the entire will to ensure that he or she understands its terms.

2. The testator, three disinterested witnesses, the supervising lawyer and a notary public meet together in a room for the execution ceremony. No one else enters or leaves the room until the ceremony is completed.

3. Prompted by the lawyer, the testator declares in the presence of the witnesses that the instrument is the testator's will, that its terms have been explained to the testator, and that the will expresses the testator's intended disposition of his or her property at death.

4. Prompted by the lawyer, the testator requests the witnesses to witness the signing of the will.

5. The testator, observed by the witnesses, signs the will at the bottom of each numbered page and at the end of the will.

6. One of the witnesses reads aloud the attestation clause, and each witness declares that the statements in the clause are correct.

7. Each witness, observed by the testator and the other witnesses, signs the will and writes his or her address in the place provided following the attestation clause.

8. The testator and the witnesses, being sworn by the notary public, declare that the statements in a self-proving affidavit are correct. The testator and the witnesses sign the affidavit in the presence of the notary public, who also signs the affidavit and affixes his or her official seal.

See Restatement (Second) of Property (Donative Transfers) § 33.1, cmt. c. Some of the above steps are required by statute; others are recommended as precautionary measures. Consider the reasons for each step in the execution ceremony.

As a matter of professional responsibility, a lawyer who prepares a will or other estate planning instruments generally should supervise their execution or arrange for another lawyer to do so. If supervision by a lawyer is not practical, the lawyer may arrange to have the instruments delivered to the client with written instructions for execution, but only if the lawyer reasonably believes the client is sufficiently sophisticated and reliable to follow the instructions. See ACTEC, Commentaries on the Model Rules of Professional Conduct 22 (3d ed. 1999). In addition to disciplinary sanctions, a lawyer who fails to supervise the proper execution of a will may incur liability for malpractice. In most states, if probate is denied on grounds of defective execution due to the lawyer's negligence, the intended beneficiaries can sue the lawyer for damages equal to the gifts they would have received had the will been properly executed.

A separate issue of professional responsibility involves the safekeeping of a will. Some lawyers routinely offer to keep original, executed wills in the firm's vault as a convenience for their clients. On one hand, this practice serves the useful purpose of preserving the original will in a known location, safe from theft and accidental loss or destruction. On the other hand, the practice may inappropriately hinder the client from selecting a different lawyer to prepare a new will or codicil. At a minimum, therefore, a lawyer who retains a client's will for safekeeping should confirm in writing that the will is held subject to the client's order. See ACTEC, Commentaries on the Model Rules of Professional Conduct 190–91 (3d ed. 1999). See also Johnston, An Ethical Analysis of Common Estate Planning Practices: Is Good Business Bad Ethics?, 45 Ohio St. L.J. 57, 124–33 (1984).

[¶ 2,217]

Problems

1. Celine, in hospital, asks her friend Albert to witness her will. Celine has not yet signed the will, but Albert signs as an attesting witness. Later the same day, Celine signs the will. In the presence of witnesses Albert and Beatrice, Celine then acknowledges the instrument as her will and asks Beatrice to sign it. Beatrice does so. Celine dies. Is the will admissible to probate? See Burns v. Adamson, 854 S.W.2d 723 (Ark. 1993).

2. Kent, in hospital, signs his will in the presence of Lucy and Marvin and asks them to witness the will. Lucy signs the will, but in confusion of the moment Marvin leaves without signing. Kent dies. One week after Kent's death, Marvin signs the will as a witness. Is the will admissible to probate? See UPC § 2–502; In re Estate of Royal, 826 P.2d 1236 (Colo. 1992); In re Estate of Flicker, 339 N.W.2d 914 (Neb. 1983); Estate of Eugene, 128 Cal.Rptr.2d 622 (Cal. App. 2002); Estate of Peters, 526 A.2d 1005 (N.J. 1987).

3. Louis, a lawyer, prepares a will for his client Ted and supervises the execution of the will. Ted signs the will and acknowledges it before two witnesses, who sign a separate self-proving affidavit attached to the will but fail to sign the will itself. Ted dies. Is the will admissible to probate? See In re Will of Ranney, 589 A.2d 1339 (N.J. 1991); Boren v. Boren, 402 S.W.2d 728 (Tex. 1966). If not, is Louis liable to the intended beneficiaries for malpractice? See Auric v. Continental Casualty Co., 331 N.W.2d 325 (Wis. 1983); Guy v. Liederbach, 459 A.2d 744 (Pa. 1983). Has Louis violated the duty to provide competent representation under MRPC 1.1? See Attorney Grievance Comm'n v. Myers, 490 A.2d 231 (Md. 1985).

[¶ 2,220]

b. Holographic Wills

Many states recognize the holographic will as an informal alternative to the formal, attested will. Traditionally, a holographic will had to be written entirely in the testator's handwriting, dated and signed. Applied literally, these requirements often led to denial of probate in cases where the will was written on a paper containing extraneous printed matter (e.g., letterhead) or the date was ambiguous or incomplete. Accordingly, modern statutes take a more lenient approach, requiring only that the will be signed and that the "material portions" be in the testator's handwriting; the date requirement is often relaxed or omitted altogether. See UPC § 2–502(b).

The distinguishing feature of a holographic will is that no attesting witnesses are required. As a result, in states that recognize holographic wills, a testator can easily prepare his or her own will without the assistance of a lawyer. Indeed, almost all holographic wills are homemade. Problems can arise in determining whether a particular handwritten instrument was intended to operate as a will, or in interpreting garbled or ambiguous language used by an unsophisticated testator. Professional estate planners invariably caution against the use of holographic wills except in unusual circumstances where no attesting witnesses are available.

[¶ 2,222]

Problems

1. Vince purchases a "do-it-yourself" printed will form which contains standard testamentary language with blank spaces for the testator's name, dispositive provisions, date of execution and signature, as well as an attestation clause followed by signature lines for two witnesses. Vince fills in his name and dispositive provisions ("everything to Rosalie") by hand in the spaces provided on the form, and then writes the date and signs his name. The will is not witnessed, and the signature lines for the witnesses remain blank. After Vince's death, the instrument is offered for probate. Is it valid as a holographic will? Should it make a difference if a separate self-proving affidavit, executed by Vince and signed and sealed by a notary public, is found attached to the will? See In re Estate of Muder, 765 P.2d 997 (Ariz. 1988); In re Estate of Johnson, 630 P.2d 1039 (Ariz. App. 1981); UPC § 2–502(c).

2. Simone writes a chatty letter to her nephew Bert, discussing a recent vacation trip, home remodeling plans, weather conditions and local gossip. In describing the remodeling plans, she writes, "I'd like your opinion, since the house will be yours when I'm gone." The letter is dated, signed, and entirely handwritten by Simone. After Simone's death, Bert offers the letter for probate as a holographic will. Is there a valid devise of the house?

3. Patricia writes a letter to her lawyer Luke, stating, "I would like to make a new will leaving all my property to Marjorie. Please prepare the

necessary documents for me to sign before I leave town next week." The letter is dated and signed and entirely in Patricia's handwriting. Luke prepares a formal will the next day, but Patricia dies before the new will can be executed. Is the letter admissible to probate as a holographic will?

[¶ 2,225]

c. Curing Defects in Execution

Courts have traditionally demanded strict compliance with the wills formalities and have shown little tolerance for defects in execution. Professor Langbein has criticized this "harsh and relentless formalism" and has proposed a more flexible approach of "substantial compliance" which would allow courts to focus on the underlying purposes as well as the literal terms of the statutory requirements. See Langbein, Substantial Compliance with the Wills Act, 88 Harv. L. Rev. 489 (1975). In general, the wills formalities serve several purposes: to provide reliable evidence of testamentary intent and of the terms of the will after the testator's death; to channel the will into a standardized, easily recognizable form; to ensure that the testator executes the will with an appreciation of its significance and a deliberate and final intention that it take effect at death; and to protect the testator from imposition at the time of execution. Id. at 491–98. Under the doctrine of substantial compliance, a defect in execution would not lead automatically and inevitably to a denial of probate; instead, the proponent would have the opportunity to show that the instrument in question was intended as a will and that it satisfied the purposes of the wills formalities. Id. at 513–26. In essence, the doctrine would excuse harmless errors in the execution of wills.

Courts have hesitated to embrace the doctrine of substantial compliance fully and openly in the wills context. To encourage a more purposive approach to wills formalities, the drafters of the Uniform Probate Code have added a statutory "dispensing power" which allows a court to grant probate to a defectively executed will if the proponent establishes by clear and convincing evidence that the decedent intended the instrument to constitute his or her will. See UPC § 2–503. This provision "permits the proponents of the will to prove that the defective execution did not result from irresolution or from circumstances suggesting duress or trickery—in other words, that the defect was harmless to the purpose of the formality." UPC § 2–503, cmt. The dispensing power might be invoked, for example, to allow probate of a will that was not properly attested or to provide relief where two wills were prepared for simultaneous execution by a husband and wife and each spouse mistakenly signed the will prepared for the other. A few states have enacted a statutory dispensing power, but in most states courts continue to require strict compliance with the wills formalities.

[¶ 2,230]

d. Components of Wills

Under the wills statutes, a will must be in writing and executed in compliance with testamentary formalities. Moreover, a will must be executed with testamentary intent. Accordingly, a will consists of those writings which are physically present at the time of execution and which are intended by the testator to be part of the will. This is the doctrine of *integration*. Conversely, by implication, the will does not include material which is (1) not written, (2) written but not physically present at the time of execution, or (3) written and physically present but not intended to be part of the will. When a will consists of multiple pages or separate writings, they are usually connected both by physical means (e.g., a staple or other fastener) and by internal coherence (e.g., numbered pages and continuity of text). Problems can arise if pages from different versions of the will are jumbled together at the time of execution, or if revisions are marked on a single execution copy at the last minute, or if it appears that pages may have been added, removed or substituted after will was executed. To guard against uncertainty or tampering, it is common practice to prepare a single, clean execution copy and to have the testator sign or initial each page at the bottom next to the page number.

A *codicil* is a written instrument, executed with testamentary formalities, that amends an earlier will. (The Uniform Probate Code does not distinguish a codicil from a will, but defines a will to include a codicil. See UPC § 1–201(55).) A will and a codicil are read together, and the will remains in effect except to the extent the codicil revokes it expressly or by implication. (See ¶ 2,245.) Moreover, under the doctrine of *republication*, the will may be deemed to be reexecuted at the time the codicil is executed, unless this would be inconsistent with the testator's intent. Note that a codicil can republish a will only if the earlier will was duly executed. A purported will that is void due to a defect in execution cannot be republished, although in most states it can be given effect if it is incorporated by reference in a subsequent will or purported codicil (see infra). The doctrine of republication can apply in various situations. For example, if a gift in a will to an attesting witness would be invalid under a purging statute (see ¶ 2,215), the defect can be cured if the will is republished by a codicil that is attested by disinterested witnesses. Similarly, if a will purports to incorporate by reference a writing that is not in existence when the will is executed, the incorporation by reference can be given effect if the will is republished by a codicil after the writing comes into existence. If a child of the testator is born after the execution of a will and would be entitled to a share of the estate as a pretermitted heir (see ¶ 2,285), the child may lose his or her share if the will is republished by a codicil after the child's birth.

In most states, a will can *incorporate by reference* an extrinsic writing that is in existence when the will is executed, if the will sufficiently describes the extrinsic writing and manifests an intent to incorporate it. See UPC § 2–510. The incorporated writing is treated as having testamentary effect, although it is not part of the will in the physical sense. Incorporation by reference may be useful when a separate writing cannot conveniently be integrated into the will because it is not physically present at the time of execution. For example, a defectively executed will can be given effect if it is incorporated by reference in a later, duly executed will. (The doctrine of republication does not apply here because the first will was not properly executed.) Incorporation by reference is also sometimes used to give effect to a separate written list of specific gifts to be made at death to named beneficiaries. The utility of such an arrangement is limited, however, because the list must be in existence when the will is executed and must not be altered thereafter. To provide greater flexibility, some states have adopted a Uniform Probate Code provision that expressly authorizes a will to dispose of items of tangible personal property (other than money) by reference to a separate "written statement or list" signed by the testator, even if the writing is prepared or altered after the execution of the will. See UPC § 2–513. This provision should be used with caution. Even if the initial list seems simple and clear, nothing prevents a careless testator from making subsequent alterations or preparing additional lists with ambiguous or contradictory provisions.

Under the doctrine of *acts of independent significance*, a will may dispose of property by reference to "acts and events that have significance apart from their effect upon the dispositions made by the will." See UPC § 2–512. For example, provisions in a will leaving "$1,000 to each person in my employ at my death" or "all land owned by me at my death to my nephew Ned" are valid, even though the beneficiaries or property referred to in the will can be ascertained only by reference to extrinsic acts or events. The hiring, retention or dismissal of employees and the acquisition, retention or disposition of land are all matters within the testator's control which may change after the execution of the will up to the testator's death, but they clearly have significance independent of their effect on the gifts made in the will.

One of the staples of contemporary estate planning is a *pourover will* which typically leaves the residuary estate (i.e., the property remaining after payment of debts, expenses, taxes and gifts to other beneficiaries) to the trustee of a revocable inter vivos trust, to be administered and distributed as provided in a separate trust instrument executed by the testator. The pourover gift might be given effect under the doctrine of acts of independent significance, but only if the trust was funded with property before the testator's death. (For this reason, some estate planners insist on the formalistic step of funding the trust with $10 or some other nominal amount of property.) Alternatively, the terms of the trust instrument might be incorporated by reference in the will, but this would require that any trust amendments made after the execution of the will be ignored and would have the further undesirable effect of creating a testamentary trust instead of an inter vivos trust. To overcome these constraints and provide additional flexibility, every state has enacted legislation specifically authorizing pourover wills. The most widely followed approach is that of the Uniform Testamentary Additions to Trusts Act (UTATA), which also appears as part of the Uniform Probate Code. The UTATA validates a testamentary gift to the trustee of a trust, "regardless of the existence, size, or character of the corpus of the trust," if the trust is identified in the testator's will and its terms are set forth in a written instrument (other than a will) executed before, concurrently with, or after the execution of the will. The property added to the trust is to be administered and distributed in accordance with the terms of the trust, including any amendments. See UPC § 2–511. In effect, the UTATA authorizes the creation and funding of an inter vivos trust at death by means of a pourover will. Note that a pourover arrangement does *not* avoid probate. By definition, property passing under the will is included in the probate estate and is subject to administration before it reaches the hands of the trustee. Pourover wills are used not to circumvent probate administration but rather to consolidate probate assets with property flowing into the trust from other sources (e.g., life insurance proceeds), to allow the testator to modify the dispositive plan by amending the trust (rather than executing a new will or codicil), and to maintain privacy concerning the ultimate disposition of the residuary estate, since the trust instrument (unlike the will) does not become a matter of public record. See Lynn, Problems With Pour–Over Wills, 47 Ohio St. L.J. 47 (1986).

[¶ 2,232]

Problem

Rogelio prepares his own "will" which leaves his entire estate to Sandra; the instrument is typewritten and signed by Rogelio but not witnessed. Later Rogelio executes a typewritten "codicil" which leaves $10 to Neville and expressly states that the earlier will, as amended, is "confirmed and republished" by the codicil. The codicil is duly signed and witnessed. After Rogelio's death, the will and codicil are offered for probate. Of the following alternative statements, identify the one that most accurately describes the status of the will. The will is: (a) integrated with the codicil as part of a single testamentary instrument; (b) republished as amended by the codicil; (c) incorporated by reference in the codicil; (d) valid on other grounds (explain the grounds); (e) invalid. What difference does it make if the codicil is holographic?

[¶ 2,240]

2. Revocation

A will is said to be "ambulatory," meaning that the will is freely revocable and has no operative effect during the testator's life. If a will is validly executed and is not revoked, the will is eligible to be admitted to probate at the testator's death. In general, a will can be revoked either by a subsequent instrument or by a physical act, in accordance with prescribed statutory formalities. See UPC § 2–507. (For revocation by operation of law, see ¶ 2,260.)

[¶ 2,245]

a. *Revocation by Subsequent Instrument*

The most reliable method of revoking a will is by express language in a subsequent will. A professionally drafted will normally opens with a clause stating that the will "revokes all wills and codicils" previously made by the testator, leaving no doubt that the testator is beginning with a clean slate. As long as the new will is duly executed, the revocation is effective. (Indeed, if the testator wishes to revoke all previous wills and let the estate pass by intestacy, the new will need not make any affirmative new disposition.) In states that recognize holographic wills, a holographic will can revoke an attested will and vice versa.

A testator who wishes to modify the terms of an existing will without revoking it completely may do so by executing a codicil. A well-drafted codicil should clearly identify the will that is being modified, expressly state which portions of the will are revoked, set forth new provisions to be substituted for the old, and (usually) republish the remaining provisions of the old will. A codicil is appropriate if the modifications consist of a small number of discrete substitutions or deletions; if the modifications are numerous or complex, it is usually preferable to execute a new will that completely supersedes the old one.

In the absence of an express revocation, a will may be revoked in whole or in part by inconsistent provisions of a subsequent will or codicil. For example, suppose the original will leaves a valuable painting to Alice, $20,000 to Ben, and the residuary estate to Carmen. If the testator subsequently executes a codicil leaving the painting to Carmen, the original gift to Alice is revoked by implication. Problems arise when a codicil sets forth a new gift but fails to specify its effect on the earlier will. In the previous example, suppose the codicil leaves $10,000 to Ben, without any express language revoking the original gift of $20,000. Is Ben intended to receive a total share of $30,000 ($10,000 in addition to the original $20,000) or only $10,000 (i.e., $10,000 in place of the original $20,000)? The general presumption is that a codicil revokes the original will by implication only to the extent that its terms are necessarily inconsistent with those of the original will. Since both instruments are read together, and the $10,000 gift in the codicil is not necessarily inconsistent with the original $20,000 gift, Ben should receive $30,000. In contrast, a will or codicil that makes a complete disposition of the estate presumably revokes the earlier will by implication. See UPC § 2–507(b)-(d).

[¶ 2,250]

b. Revocation by Physical Act

A testator may also revoke a will by performing a physical act of "burning, tearing, canceling, obliterating or destroying" the will. See UPC § 2–507(a)(2). The act of revocation must typically be performed by the testator personally (or by another person in the testator's presence and by the testator's direction). If the testator tears up the will by mistake, or directs a lawyer in possession of the will to destroy it outside the testator's presence, the will is not revoked.

Revoking a will by physical act, though legally permitted, is generally not recommended. If a will is found in a mutilated condition after the testator's death, it may be unclear whether the act of burning, tearing or cancellation was performed by the testator or by another person. Moreover, even if the testator performed the physical act, it is usually necessary to resort to extrinsic evidence to determine whether the testator acted with the requisite intent to revoke, since the act of burning, tearing, etc. is inherently ambiguous. If the will was last known to be in the testator's possession but cannot be found at all after the testator's death, there is a presumption that the testator revoked the will by destroying it, but this presumption can be overcome by evidence that the will was destroyed by accident or was taken by another person. (See ¶ 2,025.) In short, it may be extremely difficult, especially after the testator's death, to determine whether the will was validly revoked by physical act. By comparison, an express revocation clause in a subsequent will or codicil provides much more reliable evidence of revocatory intent and for this reason is generally used in preference to physical acts of revocation.

In many states a testator can revoke specific portions of a will by physical act, while leaving the rest of the will intact. See UPC § 2–507(a). Partial revocation by physical act is usually done by cancellation, i.e., by drawing a line through the language to be deleted. Sometimes an unsophisticated testator attempts to go further and modify a formal, attested will by drawing a line through a word or phrase in the original executed instrument and writing substitute provisions by hand above the canceled words. The attempted modification generally fails because the new provisions can be given effect only if they are executed with the statutory wills formalities. Such interlineations are almost never signed and witnessed in the manner required for a formal will. Moreover, even if the new provisions are entirely handwritten and are accompanied by the testator's signature or initials in the margin of the will, they may fail to qualify as a holographic codicil—unless the handwritten portion constitutes a complete, coherent expression of testamentary intent, and this is seldom the case. (In contrast, a testator can modify a holographic will by making handwritten interlineations, even without signing the will a second time. The original signature is deemed adequate to validate the entire handwritten will, including the subsequent interlineations.)

[¶ 2,255]

c. *Dependent Relative Revocation and Revival*

If a testator purports to revoke all or part of a will based on a mistaken assumption of fact or law, the revocation is ineffective if the testator would have preferred to leave the will in effect had he or she known the truth. This is the doctrine of *dependent relative revocation.* (The purported revocation fails because the testator's revocatory intent "depends" on, and "relates" to, a mistaken assumption of fact or law. The doctrine also goes under the somewhat less confusing name of "conditional revocation," reflecting the fiction that the testator's intent to revoke is conditioned on an assumption of fact or law that turns out to be untrue.) In essence, the doctrine of dependent relative revocation is a limited equitable remedy for mistake. It commonly applies where a testator cancels or destroys an existing will in the mistaken belief that it is superseded by a new will. If the new will turns out to be void (e.g., due to a defect in execution), a court may invoke dependent relative revocation to keep the original will in force, if doing so appears closer to the testator's probable intent than allowing the estate to pass by intestacy. Note that the testator's actual intent cannot be carried out because the new will is void; dependent relative revocation permits a court to salvage a second-best outcome and avoid a result completely at odds with the testator's probable intent. Dependent relative revocation can also apply in cases of revocation by subsequent instrument. See Palmer, Dependent Relative Revocation and Its Relation to Relief for Mistake, 69 Mich. L. Rev. 989 (1971).

The question of *revival* arises when a testator executes a first will, subsequently executes a second will revoking the first will, and then revokes the second will. Assuming the first will remains physically intact, does the first will spring back to life upon the revocation of the second will, or does it remain permanently revoked? Put differently, does the revocation of the second will revive the first will? In most states the question of revival is governed by statute. A number of states have traditional "anti-revival" statutes which allow a revoked will to be revived only by reexecution or by a duly executed codicil, and then only to the extent the executed instrument shows an intent to revive. Other states take a more flexible approach and allow extrinsic evidence of the testator's intent if the second will is revoked by physical act; however, if the second will is revoked by a third will, the intent to revive must appear from the terms of the third will. See UPC § 2–509. To illustrate the application of the Uniform Probate Code approach, suppose a testator executes will #1 leaving the entire estate to Norma, and then executes will #2 which expressly revokes will #1 and leaves the entire estate to Otto. Still later, the testator revokes will #2 by destroying it, and then dies. If the circumstances of the revocation of will #2, including the testator's contemporary or subsequent declarations, indicate that the testator intended to revive will #1, the estate passes to Norma. In the absence of such evidence, the presumption is that will #1 remains revoked. See UPC § 2–509(a). If will #2 is revoked not by physical act but by the execution of will #3, will #1 is not revived unless the terms of will #3 indicate that this was the testator's intent. See UPC § 2–509(c).

[¶ 2,257]

Problems

1.   Danielle duly executes a typewritten will leaving her entire estate to her sister Marcia; the will expressly disinherits Danielle's only child Eldred. Later, Danielle crosses out the gift to Marcia and writes by hand in the margin, "everything to my brother Joseph." Danielle dies survived by Marcia, Eldred and Joseph. How should Danielle's estate be distributed? See Schneider v. Harrington, 71 N.E.2d 242 (Mass. 1947).

2.   David executes a will leaving $10,000 to Olga and the rest of the estate to Peter. David then executes a codicil revoking the bequest to Olga. Later, David revokes the codicil by tearing it up, and then dies. There is no extrinsic evidence to show whether David intended to revive the original gift to Olga. Is Olga entitled to $10,000? See Estate of Hering, 166 Cal.Rptr. 298 (Cal. App. 1980); UPC § 2–509(b).

[¶ 2,260]

d.   Revocation by Operation of Law

Today in most states revocation by operation of law is governed by statute. In almost all states, the termination of a testator's marriage by divorce or annulment automatically revokes all provisions for the former spouse in the testator's will, unless the will expressly provides otherwise. As a result, the will takes effect as if the former spouse disclaimed the revoked provisions or died immediately before the divorce or annulment. See UPC § 2–804. In many states, the revocation-by-divorce statute applies only to dispositions of property made by will to the former spouse, but several states have similar statutory rules for joint tenancies with right of survivorship, revocable trusts and other nonprobate transfers. A few states go even further and extend the revocation-by-divorce rule to relatives of the former spouse (e.g., the testator's stepchildren). The rule is based on the presumption that a testator who becomes divorced and then dies without revising his or her will probably would have wished to exclude a former spouse from receiving property under the will or being involved in the administration of the estate. If the testator remarries the former spouse, the revoked provisions are automatically revived.

In most states, divorce or annulment is the only change in family circumstances that gives rise to automatic revocation of provisions of a will. In several states, however, a testator's entire will is automatically revoked if the testator gets married (or gets married and has a child) after executing the will, unless the will indicates a different intent.

Again, the rule of revocation reflects a presumption that the testator failed to consider the possibility of a future spouse or child at the time the will was executed. The effect of the rule, however, is to obliterate the testator's entire testamentary plan and cause the estate to pass by intestacy. A less intrusive and more widely adopted method of protecting an omitted spouse or child against disinheritance is found in statutes that allow the omitted family member to take an intestate share of the estate under limited conditions. (See ¶ 2,285.)

[¶ 2,262]

Problem

Maria leaves her entire estate by pourover will to the trustee of her revocable trust. The sole beneficiary of the trust is Maria's husband Steven. The trust is unfunded. Several years later, Maria and Steven divorce. Maria dies, survived by her parents and by Steven. Is Steven entitled to the trust property? See Clymer v. Mayo, 473 N.E.2d 1084 (Mass. 1985); UPC § 2–804.

[¶ 2,270]

3. Interpretation of Wills

In drafting a will, it is important to ascertain the testator's intent and to express that intent clearly and accurately, keeping in mind that circumstances may change dramatically between the time of execution and the time of the testator's death. To that end, it is essential not only to determine the scope and nature of the testator's existing property and to identify the intended beneficiaries and their respective shares, but also to provide for events that may (or may not) occur before the testator's death: the testator may dispose of existing property or accumulate additional property; the testator may get married or divorced; beneficiaries who are currently living may die before the testator; additional beneficiaries may come into existence. Part of the planner's task is to assist the testator in thinking through these contingencies and making appropriate provision for them.

In general, the goal of interpretation is to discover and give effect to the intent of the testator as expressed in the will. If language in the will is garbled or ambiguous, courts routinely admit extrinsic evidence to clarify the intended meaning. However, if language which appears clear on its face is claimed to be the result of a drafting error, courts generally refuse to admit extrinsic evidence that would vary or contradict the "plain meaning" of the will and hold that the will cannot be reformed to cure the alleged mistake. In reality, the distinction between ambiguity and mistake is somewhat artificial and subject to manipulation. Arguably, the process of interpretation would be better served if courts abandoned the no-reformation rule for wills and granted relief for mistake in the same manner as for inter vivos transfers. See Langbein & Waggoner, Reformation of Wills on the Ground of Mistake: Change of Direction in American Law?, 130 U. Pa. L. Rev. 521 (1982).

If a will is ambiguous or completely silent, and the testator's intent cannot be ascertained from extrinsic evidence, it becomes necessary to resort to rules of construction. These rules generally deal with problems arising from changes in the testator's property holdings or in the status of beneficiaries identified in the will. Rules of construction are default rules which can be overridden by expression of a different intent in the will. Because rules of construction vary from one state to another and evolve over time, experienced will drafters do not rely on existing default rules but instead include express provisions in the will to make the testator's intent clear without the need for judicial construction proceedings. Mistakes in drafting a will or trust can deprive an intended beneficiary of his or her share and may also expose the drafter to liability for malpractice. (See ¶ 2,290.)

[¶ 2,275]

a. *Ademption, Satisfaction and Abatement*

In traditional terminology, a testamentary gift is referred to as a *devise* in the case of land, a *bequest* in the case of personal property, or a *legacy* in the case of an amount of money. (Some statutes refer to all testamentary gifts as devises. See UPC § 1–201(10).) A *specific* devise or bequest is a gift of specific, identifiable property (e.g., "my house at 279 Elm Street," "my diamond ring," or "my Liberty savings bonds"). A *general* devise or bequest is a gift of a certain amount or quantity of property, usually money, payable from general assets of the estate (e.g., "the sum of $10,000"). A *residuary* devise or bequest is a gift of the remaining property in the estate after all other gifts have been satisfied (e.g., "the rest, residue and remainder of my estate"). Finally, a *demonstrative* devise or bequest is a gift of a certain amount or quantity of property payable primarily from a particular source or, to the extent the designated source is insufficient, from general assets of the estate (e.g., "the sum of $10,000 payable from my account at the First National Bank"). Demonstrative gifts are a rarely used hybrid: they are treated as specific gifts to the extent they can be satisfied from the designated source and as general gifts as to the balance.

By definition, a specific devise or bequest can be satisfied only by delivery of the specific property identified in the will. In general, if the property is not part of the probate estate at the testator's death, the gift fails. This is the doctrine of *ademption*. For example, suppose a testator owns a house located at 279 Elm Street, which she devises to her son. Subsequently, the testator sells the house and invests the proceeds in savings bonds which she holds until her death. The devise is adeemed and the son takes nothing. The doctrine of ademption applies only to specific gifts, not to general or residuary gifts. Under the traditional "identity" theory of ademption, the doctrine applies automatically if the subject matter of a specific devise or bequest cannot be identified in the probate estate at the testator's death. To mitigate the harshness of the doctrine, courts have developed various exceptions in cases where the testator retains substantially the same property in a different form (e.g., new stock issued in a corporate reorganization), where the proceeds of a lifetime disposition remain unpaid at death, and where the property is disposed of by a conservator or agent acting on behalf of an incapacitated testator. See UPC §§ 2–605, 2–606. A few states have abandoned the identity theory of ademption in favor of the "intent" theory advanced in the Uniform Probate Code. In those states, the beneficiary of a specific gift of real property or tangible personal property is entitled to take property of a similar character that was acquired by the testator as a "replacement." See UPC § 2–606(a)(5). Moreover, a specific gift of property that was disposed of during life may be converted by statute into a pecuniary gift of the value of the property at the time of disposition, if it appears that the testator did not intend the gift to be adeemed. See UPC § 2–606(a)(6).

If a testator makes an inter vivos gift to a donee who is also a beneficiary under the testator's existing will, the inter vivos gift may offset or satisfy the testamentary gift, if the testator so intends. This is the doctrine of *satisfaction*, which is analogous to the doctrine of advancements in the context of intestacy (see ¶ 2,150). For example, if a testator executes a will leaving $25,000 to her nephew and subsequently gives $15,000 to the nephew, the nephew's bequest may be deemed to be partially satisfied by the inter vivos gift. By statute in many states, however, the doctrine of satisfaction does not apply in the absence of a will or other writing evidencing an intent that it do so. See UPC § 2–609. Such statutes make the doctrine inapplicable for most practical purposes.

The beneficiaries under a will are entitled to their respective gifts only after debts and other charges (including administration expenses and taxes) have been paid. Such payments implicitly limit the assets available for distribution, and may reduce or eliminate various classes of testamentary gifts. The allocation of this burden is governed by the doctrine of *abatement*. In the absence of a contrary provision in the will, testamentary gifts generally abate in the following order of priority: (1) assets not disposed of by the will (i.e., intestate assets); (2) residuary gifts; (3) general gifts (and demonstrative gifts, to the extent payable from general assets); and (4) specific gifts (and demonstrative gifts, to the extent payable from the designated source). If there are sufficient assets in the estate to pay some but not all of the gifts within a particular class, the gifts in the class usually abate ratably. See UPC § 3–902. For example, suppose a testator leaves her property as follows: "my house at 279 Elm Street to Abby; $10,000 to Basil; $20,000 to Carla; and the rest to Donald." If the total assets in the estate (including the house, valued at $100,000) are worth $200,000, and debts and other charges amount to $85,000, the residuary bequest to Donald is completely wiped out and Basil and Carla each receive only one-half of their general legacies ($5,000 and $10,000, respectively); the specific devise of the house to Abby is not affected. (In most states, Abby takes the house subject to any mortgage lien existing at the testator's death. The common law doctrine of *exoneration* has been widely repealed by statute. See UPC § 2–607.)

Related to, but separate from, the doctrine of abatement is the apportionment of estate taxes. Estate taxes are measured by the amount of property transferred at death, less certain deductions and credits, and represent a charge against the estate as a whole. Some states follow the traditional rule requiring that taxes be paid from the residuary estate without apportionment, unless the will provides otherwise. In contrast, many other states have adopted statutes providing for "equitable apportionment." See UPC §§ 3–9A–101 to 3–9A–115. In general, equitable apportionment means that the burden of estate taxes is spread among all beneficiaries receiving transfers subject to tax in proportion to the value of their respective shares. The statutory rule is a default rule which can be overridden by provision in the will for a different method of apportionment.

[¶ 2,280]

b. Survival and Lapse

A beneficiary must survive the testator in order to take his or her share under the will. In some states, the beneficiary must survive by a specified period (e.g., 120 hours) unless the will provides otherwise. See UPC § 2–702. If there is insufficient evidence that the beneficiary survived for the required period, the beneficiary may be deemed to have died before the testator, under the simultaneous death statute. (See ¶ 2,140.)

A gift in a will to a beneficiary who dies before the testator is said to *lapse* or fail. In general, a lapsed or failed gift, other than a residuary gift, becomes part of the residue. By statute in most states, a lapsed or failed residuary gift passes to the other residuary takers, if any, or by intestacy. See UPC § 2–604.

The rule is somewhat different for *class gifts*. A class gift is one which is to be divided among members of a class or group that may increase or decrease in number over time (e.g., a residuary gift to the testator's "children" or "issue"). If a class member dies before the testator, the deceased member's share lapses and is reapportioned among the other class members who survive the testator. A class gift as a whole fails only if there are no surviving class members.

In every state except Louisiana, the consequences of lapse are modified by "anti-lapse" statutes which preserve the lapsed gift for substitute takers, usually the deceased beneficiary's surviving issue. The anti-lapse statutes do not affect the basic survival requirement; in effect, they imply a substitute gift which preempts the general rule for the disposition of lapsed gifts. Most anti-lapse statutes apply only if the deceased beneficiary was a close blood relative of the testator, though some statutes reach more broadly. Furthermore, the statutes operate only if the testator is survived by at least one eligible substitute taker. The anti-lapse provision of the original Uniform Probate Code is typical:

> If a beneficiary who is a grandparent or a lineal descendant of a grandparent of the testator is dead at the time of execution of the will, fails to survive the testator, or is treated as if he predeceased the testator, the issue of the deceased devisee who survive the testator by 120 hours take in place of the deceased devisee and if they are all of the same degree of kinship to the devisee they take equally, but if of unequal degree then those of more remote degree take by representation. One who would have been a devisee under a class gift if he had survived the testator is treated as a devisee for purposes of this section whether his death occurred before or after the execution of the will. [UPC § 2–605 (1969).]

Like other rules of construction, the anti-lapse statutes are default rules which yield to an expression of contrary intent in the will. Courts have traditionally held that express words of survivorship in the will are sufficient to override the anti-lapse statute. For example, if the testator leaves $10,000 to her child Arthur "if he survives me" and Arthur dies leaving issue who survive the testator, most courts hold that the gift was intended to take effect only if Arthur survived and is not preserved for his surviving issue; as a result, the lapsed gift falls into the residuary estate. Similarly, if the will includes a gift to the testator's "surviving children," most courts hold that the gift is to be divided among the children who survive the testator; the share of a predeceased child is not preserved for the child's surviving issue.

The anti-lapse provision of the Uniform Probate Code was completely rewritten (and renumbered as § 2–603) in 1990. A few states have enacted the revised provision, which can fairly be described as "elaborate and intricate." Halbach & Waggoner, The UPC's New Survivorship and Anti–Lapse Provisions, 55 Alb. L. Rev. 1091 (1992). Among numerous other changes, the revised provision reverses the traditional rule concerning the effect of an express condition of survival in the will, stating that "words of survivorship ... are not, in the absence of additional evidence, a sufficient indication of an intent" to override the anti-lapse statute. UPC § 2–603(b)(3) (1990).

A careful will drafter should consider the possibility that one or more beneficiaries may die before the testator, and should include express provisions concerning the disposition of lapsed or failed gifts.

[¶ 2,282]

Problems

1. In her will, Pam leaves all of her property to her mother Linda "if she survives me by 30 days" and expressly disinherits her estranged husband Howard. Pam and Linda die together in an automobile accident, survived by Howard and by Pam's brother Frank. How should Pam's estate be distributed? See In re Estate of Stroble, 636 P.2d 236 (Kan.App. 1981); UPC § 2–605 (1969); UPC §§ 2–101, 2–603 (1990).

2.   In her will, Bella leaves $1,000 to each of her nieces and nephews and the residuary estate in equal shares to her brother George and her sister Inez, "and in the event either one of them predeceases me, then to the other surviving brother or sister." Both siblings were alive when Bella executed her will, but both of them predecease her. Bella is survived by George's only child and by four children of another sibling who was already dead when the will was executed. How should Bella's estate be distributed? See In re Estate of Ulrikson, 290 N.W.2d 757 (Minn. 1980).

[¶ 2,285]

c. *Omitted Heirs*

At one time, a testator's entire will was revoked by operation of law upon the testator's subsequent marriage or upon marriage and the birth of a child. This rule, which still survives in some states, served to protect the new spouse or afterborn child from inadvertent disinheritance, but it did so by causing the entire estate to pass by intestacy. (See ¶ 2,260.) A more narrowly tailored statutory approach, adopted in many states, leaves the will intact but allows the omitted spouse or child to take an intestate share of the estate before giving effect to the provisions of the will.

Under a typical statute, if a testator gets married after executing a will which fails to provide for the new spouse, the omitted spouse is entitled to receive an intestate share of the estate unless it appears from the will that the omission was intentional or the testator provided for the spouse outside the will in lieu of a testamentary provision. See UPC § 2–301 (1969). If the spouse's intestate share is equal to the entire estate, the testator's dispositive plan may be completely defeated. (Some states have adopted a revised version of this provision which prevents the surviving spouse from reaching property that the testator left to a child of a prior marriage. See UPC § 2–301 (1990).) Note that the statute protects the spouse only against unintentional disinheritance. The statute does not apply if the language of the will or the circumstances surrounding a nonprobate transfer to the spouse indicate that the omission was deliberate. This focus on inadvertent omission distinguishes the omitted spouse statutes from the protection against intentional disinheritance provided by an elective share or community property system. (See ¶¶ 2,400–2,430.)

Afterborn children enjoy similar statutory protection against unintentional disinheritance. Under a typical statute, a child of the testator who is born or adopted after the execution of the will and who is not provided for in the will is entitled to receive an intestate share of the estate unless it appears from the will that the omission was intentional, or the testator already had another child when the will was executed and left substantially all of the estate to the other parent of the omitted child, or the testator provided for the child outside the will in lieu of a testamentary provision. See UPC § 2–302 (1969). (Some states have adopted a revised version of this provision which seeks to give the omitted child an equal share of any property left to the testator's other children, and allows an intestate share only if the testator had no children living at the time the will was executed. See UPC § 2–302 (1990).) In several states statutory protection extends more broadly to any child or other descendant of the testator, whenever born, who is not mentioned or provided for in the will. Under these statutes, it becomes important to determine whether a child or other descendant who was in existence when the will was executed was deliberately omitted from the will. To avoid the application of such statutes, many drafters routinely include a statement in the will to the effect that the failure to mention or provide for any child or other heir, whether born before or after the execution of the will, is intentional and not due to inadvertence or mistake. Note that a testator who wishes to disinherit a child for any reason (or no reason) can do so by stating his or her intent unequivocally in the will and making a complete and effective disposition to other beneficiaries. Unlike a surviving spouse, a child is generally not entitled to a forced share of the estate.

[¶ 2,290]

d. *Professional Responsibility*

Most wills and trusts are drafted by lawyers. Indeed, a non-lawyer (e.g., a bank officer, life insurance agent or financial adviser) who prepares such documents for another person may be held to be engaged in the unauthorized practice of law. (Of course, a person may prepare his or her own will or trust, though as a practical matter homemade instruments often fail to operate as intended.) As a matter of professional responsibility, a lawyer owes a duty of "competent representation" to the client, including a reasonable level of "legal knowledge, skill, thoroughness and preparation." MRPC 1.1.

In addition to possible disciplinary sanctions, a lawyer who fails to exercise reasonable care in drafting a will or trust may incur malpractice liability to beneficiaries who lose their expected gifts as a result of the lawyer's negligence. In some states, the traditional requirement of privity shields the lawyer from liability to persons other than the testator (or the personal representative of the estate, after the testator's death). If the assets of the estate are not significantly diminished by errors in drafting, the damages in an action brought by the personal representative are likely to be limited to the lawyer's fee for preparing the will or the costs of a judicial construction proceeding. The damages sought by a beneficiary might be substantial, but the privity bar, where it persists, generally prevents the beneficiary from bringing an action against the lawyer.

The clear modern trend allows a beneficiary to bring an action against the lawyer for malpractice sounding either in tort or in contract. In most states, a beneficiary who loses an expected gift as a result of the lawyer's negligence in drafting or supervising the execution of a will can seek damages equal to the value of the lost gift. In addition, a lawyer may be liable for negligence in giving (or not giving) legal or estate planning advice that leads to unnecessary tax liability. The scope of liability is not unlimited, however. Ambiguous language in a will or trust does not necessarily indicate incompetence or negligence on the part of the drafter. To recover damages from the lawyer, a beneficiary must prove, often through extrinsic evidence, that the lawyer failed to exercise due care in advising the testator, drafting the will or supervising its execution, and that the beneficiary suffered a loss as a result of the lawyer's negligence.

In some states courts allow a beneficiary to bring a malpractice action only if the testator's intent *as expressed in the will or trust* is frustrated due to the lawyer's negligence. In effect, this approach limits the lawyer's liability to cases involving defective execution or void gifts, since it excludes extrinsic evidence which would be necessary to prove other drafting errors (e.g., the omission of an intended gift or the inclusion of a mistaken provision).

For commentary on professional responsibility and malpractice in the estate planning context, see ACTEC, Commentaries on the Model Rules of Professional Conduct (3d ed. 1999); Johnston, Legal Malpractice in Estate Planning—Perilous Times Ahead for the Practitioner, 67 Iowa L. Rev. 629 (1982); Begleiter, Attorney Malpractice in Estate Planning—You've Got to Know When to Hold Up, Know When to Fold Up, 38 Kan. L. Rev. 193 (1990).

[¶ 2,295]

4. Will Contracts

A testator may enter into a binding agreement to leave an existing will in place or to make a new will with specified provisions. Technically, under the law of wills, the will remains revocable and has no operative effect during the testator's life, but under the law of contracts the agreement may be enforceable if it complies with applicable formal requirements and is made for adequate consideration.

In a number of states, a will contract must be evidenced in writing. A typical statute provides that such a contract "may be established only by (i) provisions of a will stating material provisions of the contract, (ii) an express reference in a will to a contract and extrinsic evidence proving the terms of the contract, or (iii) a writing signed by the decedent evidencing the contract." UPC § 2–514. Such statutes serve the same purpose as the Statute of Frauds, namely, to guard against unsubstantiated claims of oral agreements.

A testator may promise to leave property by will to a beneficiary in exchange for personal services to be rendered by the beneficiary. For example, suppose a testator promises in writing to leave her estate to her niece to induce the niece to move in with the testator and take care of her for life. If the niece performs but the testator fails to make the will as promised, the niece should be able to enforce the promise by means of a constructive trust. Even if the promise was not in writing, the niece should be able to recover the value of her services.

Perhaps the most common type of will contract involves a husband and wife who execute mutual wills leaving all their property to the survivor and at the survivor's death to specified beneficiaries. In this situation there is evidently a common testamentary plan but it may be quite unclear whether the spouses intended or agreed not to modify or revoke their respective wills. In most states, the mere existence of mutual wills does not create a presumption of a will contract. See UPC § 2–514. Even if there is a written will contract, most courts hold that either spouse can repudiate the contract by giving notice to the other spouse while both spouses are living. Thus, the contract becomes irrevocable only at the death of the first spouse. For example, if the husband dies first and the wife receives all of his property under his will, she becomes contractually obligated to leave her will unchanged. If she dies with a new will making a different disposition, the original beneficiaries can enforce the will contract as third-party beneficiaries.

Will contracts are notoriously troublesome and are almost never used by experienced estate planners. Testators who bind themselves irrevocably not to modify or revoke an existing will often find themselves confined in a testamentary straitjacket, unable to make even minor adjustments in response to changing financial or family circumstances. Carelessly drafted will contracts breed litigation, with high costs and unpredictable results. Furthermore, in the case of spouses with mutual wills, any contractual limitations on the surviving spouse's rights may cause serious estate tax problems. As a practical matter, the goals of a will contract are almost always better served by a trust arrangement, which offers a reliable framework for interpretation and enforcement as well as flexibility to deal with changed circumstances.

E. WILL SUBSTITUTES

[¶ 2,300]

Will substitutes, as the name implies, are arrangements that achieve will-like results but do so outside the probate system. The range of available will substitutes and the amount of wealth passing under them have grown dramatically since the 1960's; today more wealth passes by will substitutes than through the probate system. The driving force behind the "nonprobate revolution" is a desire to avoid the costly and time-consuming procedures of the traditional probate system. Will substitutes flourish because they are able to carry out simple, routine deathtime transfers of property quickly, cheaply and reliably. Instead of a court-appointed personal representative, will substitutes make use of the administrative facilities of financial intermediaries such as banks, brokerage firms and life insurance companies. In effect, they have emerged as successful private-sector competitors of the probate system.

See Langbein,The Nonprobate Revolution and the Future of the Law of Succession, 97 Harv. L. Rev. 1108, 1115–20 (1984). Will substitutes are often conceptualized as inter vivos transfers of property, even though as a practical matter the owner may retain unfettered beneficial enjoyment and control during life. The legal fiction of a completed lifetime transfer furnishes a doctrinal basis for distinguishing will substitutes from "testamentary" transfers occurring at death, with two important consequences: will substitutes need not comply with the statutory wills formalities; and, perhaps more importantly, they operate outside the jurisdictional "monopoly" of the probate court over transfers occurring at death. See id. at 1125–34; see also McGovern, The Payable on Death Account and Other Will Substitutes, 67 Nw. L. Rev. 7 (1972).

[¶ 2,310]

1. Joint Tenancies with Right of Survivorship

The common law joint tenancy with right of survivorship has long been used by married couples and others to avoid probate of land or personal property. Conceptually, each joint tenant has an equal, undivided interest in the entire property from the inception of the joint tenancy; when one joint tenant dies, his or her interest simply expires, leaving the surviving joint tenant with absolute ownership of the entire property. Thus, each joint tenant acquires his or her interest at the creation of the joint tenancy, and no interest passes at death from the decedent to the survivor. The survivor receives full ownership of the property by operation of law, not through the probate system.

The main practical advantages of joint tenancy stem from the automatic right of survivorship. If the property is held in registered form, immediately after the death of the first joint tenant the survivor can have the property reregistered in his or her own name as sole owner simply by furnishing the registering authority with proof of survivorship (e.g., a death certificate). Moreover, because a joint tenant's interest in property expires at death, creditors generally cannot reach the decedent's interest after death. (Accordingly, mortgage lenders routinely require that both joint tenants subject their respective interests to the mortgage lien.)

[¶ 2,315]

a. Land and Other Property

Parties who wish to create a joint tenancy should express their intent clearly by taking title to property as "joint tenants with right of survivorship." If the property already belongs to one party, it is no longer necessary to go the formal step of a "straw man" conveyance; A can transfer her own property directly to A and B as joint tenants with right of survivorship. The form of title should include an express reference to the right of survivorship, since many states have a statutory presumption that property titled in the names of "*A* and *B*" or even "*A* and *B* as joint tenants" is owned by the parties as tenants in common with no right of survivorship. In some community property states, even more explicit language may be necessary to rebut a statutory presumption that property held jointly by a married couple is community property.

In creating a joint tenancy, parties should be aware of the immediate lifetime consequences of their arrangement. From inception, all joint tenants are equally entitled to possess and enjoy the entire property and any net income it produces. Decisions concerning the management or disposition of the property require the unanimous consent of the joint tenants; if they cannot agree, it may be necessary to go to court to partition the property or sell it and divide the proceeds. Each joint tenant is free to dispose of his or her interest at any time during life, and creditors of a living joint tenant can reach his or her interest. A transfer of a joint tenant's interest during life automatically severs the joint tenancy and converts it to a tenancy in common with no survivorship right. The interest of each tenant in common is transmissible by will or intestacy and includible in the owner's probate estate at death. Thus, as a practical matter, a party who contributes his or her own property to create a joint tenancy gives up ownership and control of an undivided one-half interest in the property.

Parties who think of joint tenancy simply as a will substitute should proceed with caution. The survivorship right is fragile, since it can be unilaterally destroyed by any joint tenant during life. The survivorship right is also inflexible, since it cannot be revoked or altered by will. If the joint tenancy remains intact at the death of the first joint tenant, the survivor becomes the absolute owner of the property by operation of law, regardless of any contrary provision in the decedent's will. As absolute owner, the survivor can freely dispose of the entire property during life or at death. If a parent puts property in joint tenancy with a child and the child unexpectedly dies first, the parent will end up owning the property outright and the purpose of the joint tenancy will be frustrated. If the order of deaths cannot be determined, a deemed severance occurs and an equal, undivided interest in the property is included in the probate estate of each party as if he or she had survived the other.

Before creating a joint tenancy, parties should also consider the potential gift and estate tax consequences. (See ¶ 4,230.)

The joint tenancy form is widely used by married couples as a means of pooling assets and avoiding probate at the death of the first spouse. Several states recognize the tenancy by the entirety as an alternative form of joint ownership for married couples. In general, a tenancy by the entirety resembles a joint tenancy with right of survivorship. The most important difference is that neither spouse can separately transfer his or her interest to another person, nor can creditors of one spouse reach that spouse's interest. A tenancy by the entirety can be terminated only by the consent of both spouses during the marriage or by the termination of the marriage on divorce or death.

[¶ 2,320]

b. *Bank Accounts*

An account in a bank or other financial institution (e.g., a savings and loan association or credit union) can also be held in joint form with right of survivorship. Applying traditional joint tenancy doctrine to a joint bank account raises special problems, however, since the balance in the account may fluctuate from day to day as amounts are deposited and withdrawn. Parties who open a joint bank account may intend that all amounts on deposit are to be owned equally by the parties during their joint lifetime, with the survivor to take the remaining balance at the death of the first party. This sort of pooling arrangement is probably most widespread among married couples.

The parties may have something quite different in mind, however. Suppose Elise opens a joint account in the names of herself and her son Gerald. If Elise exercises exclusive control over the account during her life, making all the contributions and withdrawals, her intent may be to give Gerald no beneficial interest in the account during Elise's life, but only the right to take the remaining balance at her death if Gerald survives her. If valid, this would be a pure will substitute. The problem with the intended arrangement is that an essential premise of a common law joint tenancy—shared beneficial ownership during the parties' joint lifetime—is missing. Accordingly, in the absence of statutory validation, the intended survivorship right is open to challenge. As a practical matter, however, if Gerald made no contributions to the account and did not attempt to withdraw any funds before Elise's death, it may be difficult to distinguish this arrangement from the joint pooling arrangement described above.

Alternatively, suppose that Elise contributes all of the funds on deposit, but Gerald occasionally withdraws funds to be used for Elise's benefit. Here the reason for creating the joint account may not be to give Gerald any beneficial interest or survivorship right at all, but merely to enable him to withdraw funds on behalf of Elise during her lifetime as a matter of convenience. Essentially, Gerald is acting as Elise's agent, and the account is intended to pass at Elise's death as part of her probate estate.

Some banks routinely recommend joint accounts to their customers as a sort of all-purpose vehicle, without inquiring whether a particular account is intended to serve as a true joint account, a pure will substitute or an agency account. In large part, this practice persists because a bank is generally protected by statute in paying amounts from a joint account to any living party, without regard to the beneficial interests of the parties between themselves. A party who withdraws amounts in excess of his or her beneficial interest in the account is liable to account to the other party, but this is a matter for the parties to settle between themselves; the bank is not involved.

A number of states have adopted the provisions of the original Uniform Probate Code for joint bank accounts. In general, a joint account is rebuttably presumed to belong to the parties during their joint lifetime in proportion to their respective net contributions (i.e., amounts deposited, plus a proportional share of interest received, less amounts withdrawn). See UPC § 6–103(a) (1969). At the death of a party, the amounts remaining on deposit are rebuttably presumed to belong to the surviving party; the presumption can be rebutted only by clear and convincing evidence of a different intent at the time the account is created. See UPC § 6–104(a) (1969). (In some states, the presumption of survivorship rights is conclusive, except in cases of fraud or undue influence.) In effect, these provisions treat each party's net contributions to a joint account as revocable transfers which become complete upon the contributing party's death (or upon earlier withdrawal by the other party with the consent of the contributing party). The joint account serves as a will substitute, but it is expressly declared to be "nontestamentary" and hence exempt from the wills formalities. See UPC § 6–106 (1969). Indeed, the survivorship right cannot be changed by will. See UPC § 6–104(e) (1969). Following the death of a party, the decedent's creditors can reach the decedent's share of a joint account to the extent the decedent's probate estate is insufficient to pay debts, taxes and administration expenses. See UPC § 6–107 (1969).

The provisions of the Uniform Probate Code concerning joint accounts were substantially revised in 1989. One innovation, adopted in a few states, invites banks to use account forms that explicitly indicate whether there is a right of survivorship and whether there is an agency designation. See UPC § 6–204 (1989).

[¶ 2,330]

2. Pay-on-Death Beneficiary Designations

Large amounts of property are transferred at death outside the probate system by various contractual arrangements with "pay-on-death" (POD) provisions. Familiar examples include life insurance policies, retirement plans, bank accounts, and other types of financial assets. Typically, funds or assets are held by a third party (e.g., an insurance company, bank, etc.) on behalf of the owner, subject to a written direction to make a payment or transfer at the owner's death to a designated beneficiary. Because the beneficiary designation is usually revocable and has no operative effect during the owner's life, it functions as a pure will substitute.

Courts have traditionally upheld beneficiary designations in life insurance policies but have struck down POD provisions in other contractual arrangements, labeling them as "testamentary," i.e., invalid for failure to comply with the wills formalities. In response, many states have enacted statutes that authorize POD provisions in particular types of arrangements and declare them to be "nontestamentary," i.e., valid despite the lack of compliance with the wills formalities. As the validity of POD provisions has become more firmly established, the volume and range of assets transferred through these arrangements have grown dramatically.

The terms of POD provisions are usually set forth in a standard printed contract form. In general, the designated beneficiary becomes entitled to receive a payment or transfer at the owner's death, if the beneficiary survives; if the beneficiary is not living, the underlying asset is payable to the contingent beneficiary, if any, or to the owner's probate estate. Thus, the POD provision functions much like a specific gift. Some of the subsidiary rules developed for wills have been extended by statute in many states to apply to nonprobate transfers as well; a common example is the effect of divorce on a designation of the owner's former spouse as beneficiary. See UPC § 2–804. Other provisions, such as the anti-lapse statute, are restricted to wills in most states, although the Uniform Probate Code includes a parallel provision for nonprobate transfers. See UPC § 2–706.

The formalities for revoking or amending a beneficiary designation are governed by the law of contracts, not by the law of wills. Although occasionally the terms of a POD provision may permit the owner to revoke or amend a beneficiary designation in his or her will, this is not typical. Ordinarily, the owner must comply with the formalities established by the insurance company, bank or other entity that maintains ownership records for the particular fund or asset.

[¶ 2,335]

a. *Life Insurance*

A life insurance policy is a contract in which an insurance company agrees to pay a specified amount of proceeds to a designated beneficiary at the death of a named person (usually the owner or a family member, employee or business associate), in consideration of premiums paid during the insured person's life (usually by the owner). There are many different types of policies, but two basic categories should be mentioned here. One is "term" life insurance, which covers the risk of the insured person's death during a fixed term (e.g., one year). Term life insurance is often renewable for successive terms until the insured person reaches a specified age limit (e.g., age 70). Premiums increase with the insured person's age, reflecting increasing mortality risk. A term policy represents "pure" life insurance; there is no cash surrender value. If the policy is not renewed at the end of the term, the insurance coverage lapses and the insurance company owes nothing.

A second category is commonly referred to as "ordinary," "straight" or "whole" life insurance. Here the premiums are calculated so that they remain constant throughout the life of the policy, which can remain in force indefinitely, i.e., until the insured person dies or the owner stops paying premiums. The premiums are higher than for a term policy, because each premium purchases a combination of pure life insurance (for the current period) and an incremental increase in cash surrender value. The cash surrender value of the policy builds up over time and represents a form of saving. The owner can borrow amounts from the insurance company up to the cash surrender value; if the owner decides to terminate the policy after several years, he or she is entitled to receive the cash surrender value. Various types of life insurance products are discussed further in Chapter 7.

Upon the death of the insured person while the policy remains in force, the proceeds generally become payable to the designated beneficiary, if living, or to the estate of the insured. Most life insurance policies offer various settlement options, including an immediate lump-sum payment, installment payments of principal and interest over a fixed term, fixed periodic payments over the beneficiary's life (i.e., an annuity), or interest only for the beneficiary's life with principal payable at death to another designated beneficiary.

A common estate planning technique involves the transfer of a life insurance policy to the trustee of an irrevocable trust, in order to divest the insured person of all incidents of ownership in the policy and remove the proceeds from his or her gross estate for estate tax purposes. (See ¶ 4,370.)

By statute in most states, life insurance proceeds are wholly or partially exempt from the claims of creditors of the insured person or the owner.

[¶ 2,337]

Problems

1. Paul takes out an insurance policy on his own life and names his wife Betsy as beneficiary. Several years later, Paul and Betsy divorce. In the divorce settlement, Paul receives ownership of the policy as his sole property. Paul subsequently remarries and executes a will which specifically leaves the proceeds of the life insurance policy to his new wife Clara. Paul dies survived by Betsy and Clara. Who is entitled to the proceeds? See Cook v. Equitable Life Assurance Society, 428 N.E.2d 110 (Ind. App. 1981).

2. Same facts as the preceding problem, except that shortly before his death, Paul writes a letter to the insurance company requesting that the beneficiary designation be changed from Betsy to Clara. The insurance company responds by sending Paul a standard "change of beneficiary" form to be signed and returned. Paul receives the form but dies before signing it. Who is entitled to the proceeds?

[¶ 2,340]

b. Validating Statutes

If *A* opens a bank account in the name of "*A*, pay on death to *B*," the arrangement is clearly intended as a pure will substitute. *B* is to receive the remaining balance in the account at *A*'s death if *B* is then living and if *A* has not previously revoked the beneficiary designation. Perhaps because the arrangement so clearly circumvents the probate system, courts have not hesitated to strike it down as "testamentary" in the absence of a validating statute. Following the original Uniform Probate Code, many states have enacted statutes that expressly authorize POD provisions in bank accounts. The statutes typically provide that the account belongs exclusively to the party who contributes funds during life, and that at that party's death the account belongs to the POD beneficiary. The arrangement is declared to be "nontestamentary" and hence not subject to the wills formalities. See UPC §§ 6–103, 6–104, 6–106 (1969). In substance, a POD account closely resembles a joint account that is funded and controlled exclusively by one party during life and then passes to another party by right of survivorship at the first party's death. The main difference is that the POD account leaves no doubt concerning the respective beneficial interests of the contributing party and the designated beneficiary.

A smaller number of states have also enacted statutes authorizing "transfer-on-death" (TOD) registration of securities, which allow nonprobate transfers of registered securities on similar (though not identical) terms. See UPC §§ 6–301 to 6–311 (1989).

The broadest type of validating statute, enacted in several states, provides:

> A provision for a nonprobate transfer on death in an insurance policy, contract of employment, bond, mortgage, promissory note, certificated or uncertificated security, account agreement, custodial agreement, deposit agreement, compensation plan, pension plan, individual retirement plan, employee benefit plan, trust, conveyance, deed of gift, marital property agreement, or other written instrument of a similar nature is nontestamentary. [UPC § 6–101 (1989).]

This statute authorizes various contractual arrangements that might otherwise be struck down as testamentary, including "self-canceling" provisions in a mortgage or promissory note. For example, if Emily sells land or lends money to her son Jim and takes back Jim's promissory note, the note may provide that if Emily dies before full payment is made the remaining balance will be canceled and the land or loan proceeds will belong to Jim. A companion statute imposes liability on recipients of a decedent's nonprobate transfers (other than a surviving joint tenant of real estate) for statutory allowances and claims to the extent the decedent's probate estate is insufficient to satisfy those items. The liability of each recipient is limited to the value of the nonprobate transfers that he or she received. See UPC § 6–102 (1989).

[¶ 2,342]

Problems

1. Monique executes a deed of land to her son Hank and leaves the deed in her safe deposit box where it is found at her death. Is the deed a valid nonprobate transfer under UPC § 6–101? See Estate of O'Brien v. Robinson, 749 P.2d 154 (Wash. 1988); First National Bank in Minot v. Bloom, 264 N.W.2d 208 (N.D. 1978); UPC § 6–101, cmt.

2. In a written contract between Blanche and her brother Carlos, Carlos promises to collect all of Blanche's assets at her death, pay her debts and distribute the remaining assets in accordance with any written instructions that Blanche may leave. Is this a valid nonprobate transfer under UPC § 6–101? Does it preclude Blanche's heirs or creditors from opening probate administration proceedings or challenging the terms of Blanche's written instructions?

[¶ 2,350]

3. Revocable Trusts

The revocable inter vivos trust (sometimes called a "living" trust) is undoubtedly the most versatile of all the will substitutes. It is simple to create; it can be used to coordinate the management and disposition of numerous different assets, including additions at death; to the extent funded during life, it avoids the costs and delays of the probate system; and its terms can be custom tailored to meet the needs and desires of the individual donor. Due to its unparalleled flexibility, the revocable trust has come into widespread use, especially among people with moderate or large estates. To achieve intended results and avoid potential pitfalls, two basic points should be kept in mind. First, a revocable trust must be funded with assets during life if it is to be effective as a will substitute; an unfunded trust may serve as a receptacle for assets that pour over by will at death, but such assets must necessarily go through probate on their way to the trust. Second, although a funded revocable trust avoids probate, it does not shelter assets from estate taxes or creditors' claims.

In creating a revocable trust, the settlor typically retains an express power to revoke or amend the trust at any time during life, as well as a right to receive the income from the trust property for life; at the settlor's death, the trust property is to be held in further trust or distributed outright to other beneficiaries. Conceptually, the validity of the arrangement as an inter vivos transfer rests on the notion that some equitable interest, no matter how fragmentary or contingent, passes from the settlor to the other beneficiaries before the settlor's death. Technically, even though the settlor retains beneficial enjoyment of the trust property for life, as well as the ability to recover absolute ownership at the stroke of a pen, nothing passes from the settlor to the beneficiaries at death. Instead, the settlor's retained interests and powers expire at death and the beneficiaries receive present enjoyment by virtue of the interest previously transferred by the settlor during life. Of course, the notion of a lifetime transfer is an elaborate legal fiction which serves to justify upholding the revocable trust as a valid will substitute. The settlor's dominion and control over the trust property during life are functionally indistinguishable from outright ownership. Nevertheless, the formal distinction between a revocable trust and a will has several practical consequences for planning, drafting and administration.

A settlor usually creates a revocable trust in one of two ways. The first method involves a transfer of legal title to property by the settlor to another person, who agrees to hold the property as trustee for the beneficiaries on terms set forth in a *deed of trust* or *trust agreement*. The second method involves a *declaration of trust* in which the settlor declares that he or she holds property as trustee on terms set forth in the declaration of trust. The main difference between the two methods is that a deed of trust requires a transfer of legal title to another person but a declaration of trust does not. In the former case, the required formalities are the same as for any inter vivos transfer of the property in question. In the latter case, there is no need for a formal change of legal title, since the settlor-trustee already owns the property and the settlor's declaration operates as a constructive transfer of an equitable interest to the other beneficiaries. Nevertheless, a formal retitling of property in the name of the settlor "as trustee" serves to identify the trust property and keep it separate from the settlor's other property.

The trust terms are ordinarily set forth in a written instrument signed by the settlor. The trust instrument should expressly provide that the settlor retains the power to revoke the trust. In the absence of a clear indication of the settlor's intent, the traditional presumption is that an inter vivos trust is irrevocable. In several states, however, the opposite rule has been adopted by statute. For example, the Uniform Trust Code provides that a trust may be revoked or amended by the settlor in the absence of a contrary provision in the terms of the trust. See UTC § 602. The trust instrument should also specify how the power to revoke or amend may be exercised. Typically the trust instrument permits revocation or amendment only by a written instrument, other than a will, which is signed by the settlor and delivered to the trustee during the settlor's lifetime. If the trust instrument is silent, it may be unclear whether the trust can be effectively revoked by oral declaration or by will. By statute in several states, termination of a settlor's marriage by divorce or annulment automatically revokes any provisions in a revocable trust for the settlor's former spouse, unless the trust instrument expressly provides to the contrary. See UPC § 2–804.

Not all of the rules of construction for wills apply to revocable trusts. Accordingly, a drafter should take care to coordinate the terms of a revocable trust with the settlor's will, especially if the two instruments are closely linked in operation as in the case of a pourover will. For example, if the beneficiary of a revocable trust was living at the creation of the trust but dies before the settlor, in the absence of an express or implied survival requirement, the beneficiary's share does not lapse but instead passes to the beneficiary's testate or intestate successors. Moreover, in most states, if the beneficiary's share fails due to a survival requirement, the anti-lapse statute does not preserve the deceased beneficiary's share for his or her surviving issue. These rules differ markedly from the rules concerning survival and lapse in the wills context (see ¶ 2,280). Although by statute in a few states the rules of construction for revocable trusts have been brought into line with those for wills (see UPC §§ 2–702, 2–707), a careful drafter should expressly include consistent provisions in the will and the revocable trust addressing questions of survival, alternative gifts and the like.

A "tentative" or "Totten" trust has long been recognized as a simple will substitute for savings bank accounts. In most states, A can create a tentative trust simply by opening a savings bank account in the name of "A in trust for B." By implication, the arrangement is treated as a valid gift to B of any balance remaining in the account at A's death if B is then living and A has not revoked the gift. See In re Totten, 71 N.E. 748 (N.Y. 1904); Restatement (Third) of Trusts § 26. In reality, no trust is funded during A's life, and the account passes to B at A's death without any action by a successor trustee. The purported trust is a legal fiction. The arrangement is essentially a common law version of a POD bank account, thinly disguised as a trust in order to avoid probate. See Friedman, The Law of the Living, the Law of the Dead: Property, Succession, and Society, 1966 Wis. L. Rev. 340, 368–69.

In addition to its primary function as a will substitute, a revocable trust may serve as a vehicle for lifetime asset management in the event the settlor becomes disabled or incapacitated during life. To this end, many drafters include provisions in the trust instrument authorizing the trustee to use income or principal for the settlor's benefit or even to make gifts from the trust to other beneficiaries to carry out the settlor's estate planning objectives. An alternative arrangement that serves much the same function is a *durable power of attorney*, by which an individual principal authorizes a designated agent to act on the principal's behalf in dealing with the principal's own property. The distinctive feature of a durable power, compared to an ordinary agency, is that it remains in force even if the principal becomes incapacitated; a durable power cannot serve as a will substitute, however, because it terminates automatically at the principal's death. An agent acts directly on behalf of the principal and is subject to control by the principal, but generally does not hold legal title to the principal's property. In this and other respects, the fiduciary relationship between principal and agent differs from a trust. In drafting a durable power or a revocable trust, special care should be taken to specify whether the agent or trustee is authorized to make gifts to himself or herself or to engage in other transactions involving a potential conflict of interest. See McGovern, Trusts, Custodianships, and

Durable Powers of Attorney, 27 Real Prop., Prob. & Tr. J. 1, 23–39 (1992). A revocable trust or a durable power is generally preferable to a *conservatorship*, on grounds of flexibility and efficiency.

Revocable trusts are often touted as a cure-all for the shortcomings of the probate system, but they should not be oversold. A revocable trust instrument may present drafting challenges equal to or even greater than those of a will, and the up-front charge for preparing a revocable trust usually exceeds the cost of a comparable will. Since a revocable trust almost never disposes of all the settlor's property, the settlor ordinarily bears the cost of preparing a revocable trust in addition to the cost of a will disposing of residual assets. If the settlor names a trust company or other professional trustee to administer the revocable trust, the trustee is entitled to compensation for its services, usually in the form of an annual fee as well as a separate termination fee based on the value of the trust property. Even if the settlor serves as the sole initial trustee under a declaration of trust, it is necessary to name a successor trustee to wind up the trust and distribute the trust property to the beneficiaries after the settlor's death, and the successor trustee is entitled to compensation.

The process of winding up a revocable trust is generally less cumbersome than the administration of a probate estate, but it can become protracted for any of several reasons. First, if there is any dispute about the validity or the terms of the trust, the trust may be challenged on much the same grounds as a will (e.g., fraud, undue influence, etc.) and mistakes or ambiguities in drafting may lead to litigation. Second, a revocable trust generally provides no protection against the settlor's creditors during life, and in a growing number of states, by statute or judicial decision, creditors can also reach the trust property after the settlor's death if the probate estate is insufficient. See UTC § 505; UPC § 6–102. Accordingly, it may be necessary to delay distribution to the beneficiaries until creditors' claims are paid or barred. Finally, since a revocable trust is included in the settlor's gross estate for estate tax purposes, distribution may be further delayed pending the resolution of any dispute concerning estate tax liability. More generally, as funded revocable trusts become more and more widely used as will substitutes, it can also be expected that some of the procedural safeguards of the probate system will be extended or adapted to apply to revocable trusts.

[¶ 2,352]

Problems

1. Ingrid executes a pourover will and a revocable declaration of trust. The will leaves Ingrid's entire probate estate to the trustee of the revocable trust, to be added to the trust and administered under its terms. The trust instrument directs the trustee to pay income to Ingrid for life and at her death to distribute the trust property to her child Olaf (expressly excluding her other child Kurt). Ingrid expressly reserves a power to revoke the trust

at any time during her life by a written instrument signed by her and delivered to the trustee. Ingrid funds the trust with $500,000. One year later, Ingrid dies survived by Olaf and Kurt, leaving a net probate estate of $1,000,000. The original will and the original trust declaration were last seen in Ingrid's possession, but at her death neither instrument can be found. (The terms of both instruments are proved by photocopies from the file of her lawyer.) How should Ingrid's probate estate and the trust property be distributed? See In re Estate and Trust of Pilafas, 836 P.2d 420 (Ariz. App. 1992).

2. Same facts as the Problem at ¶ 2,262, except that Maria funds the revocable trust with the bulk of her assets during life. Is Steven entitled to the trust property at Maria's death? See Clymer v. Mayo, 473 N.E.2d 1084 (Mass. 1985); UPC § 2–804.

3. Glenn executes a will and a revocable declaration of trust. The will leaves the entire probate estate in equal shares to Glenn's children Sara and Ted. The trust instrument directs the trustee to pay income to Glenn for life and at his death to distribute the trust property in equal shares to Sara and Ted. Glenn funds the trust with $500,000. One year later, Ted dies survived by his wife Olivia and his only child Ray; in his will, Ted leaves his entire estate to Olivia. Subsequently, Glenn dies survived by Sara, Olivia and Ray, leaving a net probate estate of $1,000,000. How should Glenn's probate estate and the trust property be distributed? See First National Bank of Bar Harbor v. Anthony, 557 A.2d 957 (Me. 1989); UPC §§ 2–603, 2–702, 2–707 (1990).

F. MARITAL PROPERTY

[¶ 2,400]

There are two basic marital property systems in the United States: a substantial majority of states have a system of *separate property* derived from the English common law, while a significant minority of states have a system of *community property* derived from the civil law of France and Spain. (The nine community property states are Arizona, California, Idaho, Louisiana, Nevada, New Mexico, Texas, Washington, and Wisconsin. In addition, Alaska has enacted an optional form of community property. Together, these states account for more than one-quarter of the total U.S. population.) Broadly speaking, in a separate property system, a husband and wife own property as separate individuals, in much the same way as unmarried persons, and each spouse is free to dispose of his or her property during life and at death. By contrast, in a community property system, any property earned by either spouse during the marriage automatically belongs to both spouses in equal, undivided shares. Thus, a separate property system emphasizes the individual autonomy of the spouses, while a community property system emphasizes the marital community as a sort of partnership in which both spouses share equally in their combined earnings.

During a harmonious marriage between spouses who pool their funds for current household consumption, the differences between a separate property system and a community property system are mainly symbolic. In the absence of a serious disagreement or misconduct by either spouse, the prospect of a dispute over marital property rights may seem remote. However, when the marriage eventually comes to an end, either by divorce or at the death of one spouse, problems may arise in determining the ownership and disposition of the spouses' accumulated property. Planners and drafters should foresee these problems and take steps to prevent them from materializing.

When a marriage ends in divorce, the divorce court will generally approve a property settlement agreed to by the parties. If the parties are unable to reach agreement, in most states the court may order an "equitable distribution" of all marital property. In a separate property state, this means that the court has broad discretion to award property acquired during the marriage to either spouse, regardless of title, based on the facts and circumstances of the particular case. The concept of equitable distribution has also been adopted in community property states, although in some states the court may be required to divide the community property equally between the spouses and may have little or no discretion to award one spouse's separate property to the other spouse.

If the marriage lasts until the death of one spouse, the contrast between a separate property system and a community property system emerges more starkly. In a separate property system, if the decedent failed to make adequate provision for the surviving spouse, the surviving spouse generally has a statutory right to claim an "elective share" of the decedent's property. The elective share (sometimes called a forced share) is the modern counterpart to the common law estate of dower. It provides a measure of protection for the surviving spouse against disinheritance at the death of the first spouse, and incidentally limits the decedent's freedom to dispose of his or her own property.

The situation is quite different in the community property states. Community property belongs equally to both spouses from the time of acquisition. Accordingly, when one spouse dies, only one-half of the community property passes under the decedent's will; the other half goes automatically to the surviving spouse. The surviving spouse's interest in community property is adequately protected without any need for a mechanism such as the elective share.

Federal law requires that most pension plans provide a survivor annuity for the surviving spouse of a deceased employee. The employee can select a different form of distribution (e.g., a single-life annuity payable to the employee or payment at the employee's death to a beneficiary other than the surviving spouse), but only if the spouse gives written consent. The survivor annuity protects only the surviving spouse of a deceased employee; a spouse who dies before the employee has no interest in the pension. In effect, the survivor annuity resembles a special type of forced share for pensions. (Retirement plans are discussed in Chapter 8.)

[¶ 2,410]

1. Elective Share

In each of the separate property states (except Georgia), a surviving spouse is entitled by statute to claim an elective share of the deceased spouse's property. The amount of the elective share and the manner of its payment vary considerably from one state to another, but in broad outline most statutes follow a recognizable pattern. Under a traditional statute, the surviving spouse may elect to renounce any benefits under the decedent's will and claim a specified portion (typically one-third or one-half) of the probate estate. After payment of the elective share, typically from the residuary estate, the rest of the probate estate passes under the will to beneficiaries other than the surviving spouse.

A number of states follow the original Uniform Probate Code, which modifies the traditional elective share in a few significant respects. The UPC defines the elective share as one-third of the "augmented estate," which embraces not only the decedent's net probate estate but also certain nonprobate transfers as well as the surviving spouse's own property (to the extent derived from the decedent). See UPC § 2–202 (1969). Moreover, the UPC allows the surviving spouse to claim an elective share without renouncing the decedent's will. It leaves undisturbed any transfers to the surviving spouse of property included in the augmented estate, and charges the value of those transfers against the elective share, dollar for dollar. See UPC § 2–207(a) (1969). As a result, the amount recaptured from other beneficiaries to satisfy the elective share is limited to the amount, if any, not satisfied by transfers to the surviving spouse. Any such shortfall is apportioned among the other beneficiaries of the augmented estate in proportion to the value of their respective interests. See UPC § 2–207(b) (1969). Thus, the UPC approach expands the elective share to cover most will substitutes, and also minimizes the disruptive effect of an election on the decedent's testamentary plan. In effect, the decedent can forestall an election by giving to the surviving spouse assets (selected by the decedent) with an aggregate value at least equal to the elective share.

A few states follow the revised Uniform Probate Code, which completely rewrote the original UPC's elective share provisions. The revised UPC defines the elective share as the greater of (1) a flat $50,000 amount, or (2) a percentage of the augmented estate, determined under a sliding scale according to the duration of the marriage. The maximum elective share is 50% of the augmented estate, in a marriage of 15 years or more. See UPC § 2–202 (1993). Under the revised UPC, the augmented estate includes all property of both spouses. Thus, the surviving spouse is entitled to one-half of the combined property of both spouses in a long-term marriage, or to a smaller portion in a short-term marriage. For a discussion of the rationale and operation of the revised UPC provisions, see Langbein & Waggoner, Redesigning the Spouse's Forced Share, 22 Real Prop., Prob. & Tr. J. 303 (1987).

Statistically, wives tend to be younger, to live longer, and to own less property than their husbands. Thus, the elective share, though formally gender-neutral, functions primarily to protect wives against disinheritance by their husbands. The UPC's concept of the augmented estate reinforces that protection by allowing the surviving spouse to recover property transferred by the decedent outside the probate system. Furthermore, by allowing the surviving spouse of a long-term marriage to reach up to one-half of the couple's combined property, the revised UPC's "accrual-type" elective share represents a step in the direction of equal sharing of marital property. Nevertheless, the elective share does not purport to implement a system of equal, shared ownership between the spouses. Under the UPC, the first spouse to die can select assets with an aggregate value equal to the elective share and leave them to the survivor, thereby preventing the survivor from reaching any assets that are left to other beneficiaries; the selection of assets rests with the decedent, not the survivor. Furthermore, only a *surviving* spouse can claim an elective share; if a wife with little or no separate property of her own dies before her husband, she has no right to enjoy or control any portion of her husband's property.

[¶ 2,420]

2. Community Property

In a community property system, property owned by a married person is classified either as community property or as separate property. In general, community property includes all property acquired by either spouse during marriage (other than by gift, bequest, devise or descent); conversely, separate property consists of all property acquired before marriage and any property acquired during marriage by gift, bequest, devise or descent. Separate property belongs to the spouse who acquired it, and can be disposed of during life and at death in much the same way as property owned by an unmarried person.

Each spouse has a present, equal, vested interest in the community property from the moment of acquisition. In most community property states, during the marriage, either spouse acting alone has full power to manage community property, except for certain transfers which require the consent of both spouses (e.g., conveyances of real property). (In Texas, community property is nominally subject to joint management by both spouses, but each spouse has sole management power over his or her own earnings, if they are kept separate.) In managing and disposing of community property, the spouses owe each other fiduciary duties of good faith and fair dealing. Some states follow the traditional rule which allows each spouse acting alone to make reasonable gifts of community property to third parties, as long as the gifts do not injure or defraud the other spouse; in other states, neither spouse may make any gift of community property without the other spouse's consent. If one spouse makes an unauthorized gift of community property, the nonconsenting spouse may act during the marriage to rescind the gift and recover the entire property for the community. However, if the gift is not challenged until after the donor spouse's death, the nonconsenting spouse can recover only his or her half of the transferred property.

If the marriage ends in divorce or at death, the community property must be divided between the spouses. On divorce, in the absence of a property settlement agreed to by both parties, the court in some states has discretion to order an equitable distribution of community property; in other states, the court's discretion is limited to allocating community property between the spouses to reach an equal division. The disposition of community property at the death of one spouse is discussed in ¶ 2,430.

In theory, a community property system reflects a notion of marriage as a partnership in which the husband and wife share equally in the fruits of their combined labor, effort and skill. This notion may seem fairer than a separate property system in which each spouse keeps whatever property he or she earns during the marriage (especially if one spouse does not work outside the home), but the equal sharing of marital property brings in its train problems of classification and tracing, discussed in ¶ 2,425. As more women enter the work force and two-earner couples become more prevalent, similar problems can be expected to arise in separate property states.

[¶ 2,425]

a. *Classification*

The rights of one or both spouses to enjoy, manage and dispose of property often depend on whether the property is classified as community property or separate property. In general, property acquired by either spouse before marriage, or during marriage by gift, bequest, devise or descent, is separate property; all other property is community property. Under the prevailing "ganancial" system derived from Spanish law, property acquired before marriage retains its original (i.e., separate) character after marriage. Moreover, property purchased during marriage generally takes the same character as the funds used to purchase it: property traceable to community funds is community property, and property traceable to separate funds is separate property. The general presumption is that property held by either spouse during the marriage is community property, even if it is titled in the name of one spouse, but the presumption may be rebutted if one spouse succeeds in tracing the property to a source of separate funds. If community funds and separate funds have been commingled (e.g., in a single bank account), making it impossible to trace the property to a single source, the community property presumption prevails.

In all community property states, income from community property is itself community property. The treatment of income (i.e., "rents, issues and profits") from separate property is not uniform. Some states follow the traditional rule that such income is community property, which can create a classification problem if the community income is commingled with the original separate fund (e.g., accumulated interest on a bank account). In other states, income from separate property is itself separate property.

A common law joint tenancy with right of survivorship is a form of separate property which is incompatible with traditional community property concepts. Nevertheless, all of the community property states (except Louisiana) recognize a special statutory form of "survivorship community property" which combines a right of survivorship (and automatic probate avoidance) with the traditional attributes of community property. Since married couples frequently take title as joint tenants without a clear understanding of the differences between community property and separate property, some states have enacted a statutory presumption treating any spousal joint tenancy as community property, at least for purposes of division on divorce, to reflect the probable intent of the parties.

Special problems arise when property is acquired with funds from different sources over time. For example, suppose one spouse initially takes title in his or her own name before marriage, and then subsequent payments are made from community funds during marriage. If it becomes necessary to determine the character of the property and disentangle the spouses' respective rights (e.g., on divorce or at death), courts generally follow one of two basic alternative approaches. Under the "inception of title" theory, property acquired before marriage is classified as separate property from the time of acquisition, and the community is entitled only to a right of reimbursement secured by an equitable lien on the property. The right of reimbursement may be limited to the amount of the community funds contributed to purchase the property, or may include interest or a portion of any subsequent appreciation in the value of the property. In contrast, the "apportionment" theory treats the marital community as a co-venturer with the spouse who furnished separate funds, and apportions the ownership of the property between them in proportion to their respective contributions.

Consider how the inception of title theory or the apportionment theory might apply in the following contexts:

1. *Ordinary life insurance.* Before marriage, Juliet took out an ordinary life insurance policy on her own life in the face amount of $500,000, with herself listed as the policy owner and her friend Kim as beneficiary. Juliet paid the premiums from her own separate funds until her marriage to Anton, and then paid subsequent premiums from community funds during marriage until her death. Of the total premiums paid before Juliet's death, $10,000 came from Juliet's separate funds and $40,000 came from community funds.

2. *Personal residence.* Before marriage, Judy purchased a house in her own name. She paid $20,000 in cash and took out a $180,000 mortgage loan to finance the balance of the $200,000 purchase price. At the time of her marriage to Edgar, Judy had paid down

$20,000 of the mortgage principal from her separate funds. During the marriage, she paid down another $40,000 from community funds. At Judy's death, the outstanding mortgage principal is $120,000 and the value of the house is $300,000.

3. *Closely held business.* Before marriage, Jonathan started a property management business with minimal capital. At the time of his marriage to Beth, the business was worth $100,000. During the marriage, Jonathan and Beth worked together in the business and both spouses drew a reasonable salary for their services. At Jonathan's death, the business is worth $500,000.

4. *Employee pension benefits.* For six years before his marriage to Janice and throughout their 24–year marriage, Ivan participated in a tax qualified pension plan sponsored by his employer. Upon retirement, Ivan became entitled to an annual pension benefit of $45,000 (1% × $150,000 final salary × 30 years of service). As required by federal law, the pension plan provides for distributions in the form of a "qualified joint and survivor annuity" payable to Ivan for life and then to Janice if she survives him. (Note that if Janice dies before Ivan, the Supreme Court has held that any right she might have under state law to dispose of a community property interest in undistributed pension plan benefits is preempted by federal law. See Boggs v. Boggs, 520 U.S. 833 (1997). Retirement plans are discussed in Chapter 8.)

Disentangling the interests of the spouses is complicated both by intricate characterization rules, which vary considerably from one state to another, and by factual uncertainties in tracing the contributions of each spouse. To avoid problems in this area, it is usually desirable to keep each spouse's separate property clearly labelled and segregated from the couple's community property.

In general, spouses may convert (or "transmute") community property to separate property or (except in Texas) vice versa. Transmutation may occur by agreement of the parties or by conveyance, partition or gift with the consent of both spouses. In some states, the intent to transmute must be expressly declared in writing. Prospective spouses may also agree in an antenuptial agreement to waive community property rights or to maintain all or part of each spouse's future earnings as separate property. Such an agreement should be in writing and voluntarily executed by each spouse; moreover, each spouse should receive a fair and reasonable disclosure of the other spouse's property and financial obligations. See Uniform Premarital Agreement Act § 6. As a practical matter, each spouse should be represented by separate counsel, to guard against duress or undue influence.

[¶ 2,430]

b. *Disposition at Death*

At the death of one spouse, the community property is automatically divided between the estate of the deceased spouse and the surviving spouse in equal shares. Under the "item theory" prevailing in most states, each item of community property belongs equally to the decedent's estate and to the surviving spouse. Accordingly, only one-half of each item of community property passes under the decedent's will; the other half already belongs to the surviving spouse. The decedent cannot leave specific community assets to another beneficiary and force the survivor to accept other community assets of equal aggregate value.

Nevertheless, the decedent may force the surviving spouse to choose whether to accept the terms of a will that purports to dispose of both halves of the community property or to renounce the will and take one-half of the community property outright. This technique, commonly known as a "widow's election," can be illustrated by a simple example. Suppose Henry dies survived by his wife Wendy. In his will, Henry creates a trust of both halves of the community property to pay income to Wendy for life with remainder at her death to their issue then living. Although Henry has no power to dispose of Wendy's half of the community property, he can put her to an election: if she accepts the will, she receives the income from both halves of the community property for life and allows the remainder in her half to pass to the issue at her death; alternatively, Wendy can assert her right to an outright one-half interest in the community property, but if she does so she forfeits any benefits under Henry's will. (This is a "forced" election, as compared to a "voluntary" election which would allow Wendy to receive benefits under Henry's will even if she asserts her rights in her half of the community property.) The widow's election is used for various purposes: to provide centralized management for a closely held business or other community property that is not suitable for divided ownership; to ensure professional management of community property on behalf of an inexperienced or disabled spouse; to avoid a second probate proceeding at the spouse's death; or simply to make a unified disposition of the community property and prevent the spouse from giving it to different beneficiaries.

If the spouses agree on a joint disposition of the community property while both are living, they can create a joint revocable trust. Such a trust typically pays income to the spouses jointly until the first spouse dies. At that time, the trust becomes irrevocable, and the income continues to be payable to the survivor for life, with remainder to other beneficiaries at the survivor's death. A joint revocable trust achieves many of the same objectives as a widow's election but avoids the appearance of one spouse unilaterally dictating the disposition of the community property.

[¶ 2,440]

3. Migratory Couples

Often a husband and wife accumulate property while domiciled in a separate property state and then move to a community property state, or vice versa. Because the character of marital property is generally fixed at the time of acquisition and is not affected by a subsequent change of the couple's domicile, planners and drafters in both community property states and separate property states should be familiar with the basic principles of both marital property systems.

When a married couple moves from a separate property state to a community property state, any property accumulated by either spouse retains its character as the separate property of the spouse who acquired it. At the death of the first spouse, however, the surviving spouse has no right to claim an elective share in the decedent's separate property. In general, the surviving spouse's rights are governed by the law of the decedent's domicile at death, and the community property states do not recognize an elective share. (Under general choice of law principles, succession to land is governed by the law of the situs rather than by the law of the decedent's domicile, but the situs law may refer back to the law of the domicile.) Thus, if the couple did not accumulate any community property while domiciled in the community property state (e.g., because they moved there to spend their retirement years), the surviving spouse may be left with no community property and no elective share.

To prevent this harsh result, a few states have adopted the concept of *quasi-community property*, which is generally defined as property which was acquired by either spouse while domiciled elsewhere and which would have been community property if the couple had been domiciled in a community property state. For most purposes, quasi-community property is treated during the marriage as separate property of the acquiring spouse. If the acquiring spouse is the first to die, half of his or her quasi-community property automatically belongs to the surviving spouse, in much the same way as if it were community property. (If the non-acquiring spouse dies first, he or she has no interest in the surviving spouse's quasi-community property.) In effect, the non-acquiring spouse has a deferred, inchoate one-half interest in the acquiring spouse's quasi-community property which ripens into possession if the non-acquiring spouse survives the acquiring spouse.

The situation is somewhat different when a married couple moves from a community property state to a separate property state. The couple's accumulated community property retains its character, despite the change of domicile, and each spouse retains his or her present, equal, vested interest in the property, unless the spouses agree to convert it to separate property. If community property is sold, the spouses should keep the proceeds clearly labelled as community property and segregated from their separate property (in a community property revocable trust, for example), in order to avoid confusion and uncertainty. Several states have statutes which recognize and preserve the rights of spouses in community property acquired in another state. For example, a typical statute provides that, at the death of one spouse, the decedent has testamentary power over one-half of the community property and the other half belongs to the surviving spouse. The decedent's one-half share of the community property is not subject to the surviving spouse's elective share. See Uniform Disposition of Community Property Rights at Death Act § 3.

G. TRUSTS

[¶ 2,500]

A trust is a device whereby a trustee holds legal title to property and manages the property for the benefit of one or more beneficiaries. In effect, the trust separates the burdens and the benefits of ownership, allocating the former to the trustee and the latter to the beneficiaries. A trust of the sort used in estate planning is typically created by a settlor who provides the original trust property and executes a written trust instrument setting forth the terms of the trust. The trustee usually has extensive management powers over the property, including powers of sale and investment. The trustee also has a fundamental fiduciary duty to administer the trust exclusively for the benefit of the beneficiaries, in accordance with the terms of the trust. The beneficiaries have no direct, legally recognized interests in the trust property itself. Instead, they have the right to compel the trustee to carry out the terms of the trust and the right to pursue equitable remedies against the trustee (or in some cases against a third party) for any breach of trust.

Because the trustee's duties and the beneficiaries' corresponding rights historically fell within the jurisdiction of courts of equity, the beneficiaries are said to have equitable interests in the trust, in contrast to the trustee's legal title to the trust property. A beneficiary's interest can be transferred or reached by the beneficiary's creditors, unless the interest is subject to a valid restraint imposed by the terms of the trust or by statute.

The drafter of a trust instrument has enormous flexibility in defining the interests of the respective beneficiaries. Beneficial enjoyment, in the form of distributions of trust income and principal, is generally spread out over time among various different beneficiaries, whose interests are commonly described in terms of estates in land and future interests (e.g., life estate, remainder, reversion, executory interest). The trustee may be given discretion to vary the time and amount of distributions to various beneficiaries, and the beneficiaries themselves may be given powers of appointment enabling them to designate the ultimate recipients of the trust property.

The versatility of the trust makes it an extremely useful vehicle for estate planning. Funded revocable trusts are widely used as a will substitute to avoid probate. (See ¶ 2,350.) A trust for a minor or incapacitated beneficiary can serve as a substitute for a guardianship or conservatorship while avoiding costly and cumbersome court proceedings. Long-term trusts provide a stable yet flexible means of preserving and managing property for successive generations of beneficiaries. Some trusts allow beneficiaries to enjoy the benefits of the trust property while sheltering their trust interests from the reach of their creditors. Moreover, a trust almost always has collateral income, gift and estate tax consequences which should be considered in planning the structure of the trust as a whole and in drafting particular provisions. Indeed, some trusts are designed primarily or exclusively to produce tax savings.

[¶ 2,510]

1. Trust Creation

In general, a trust is defined as "a fiduciary relationship with respect to property, arising as a result of a manifestation of an intention to create that relationship and subjecting the person who holds title to the property to duties to deal with it for the benefit of charity or for one or more persons, at least one of whom is not the sole trustee." Restatement (Third) of Trusts § 2. Unless otherwise indicated, the trusts considered here are those created by a settlor for the benefit of private beneficiaries.

A trust generally involves at least three parties. The *settlor* is the person who creates the trust, establishes its terms and furnishes the property with which the trust is initially funded. The *trustee* holds legal title to the trust property and administers it as a fiduciary for the benefit of one or more *beneficiaries*, who have standing to enforce the terms of the trust and to pursue remedies for any breach of trust. (The situation is somewhat different when a settlor creates a trust for charitable purposes. Since a charitable trust has no private beneficiaries, the state attorney general or a similar official has standing to enforce the terms of the trust on behalf of the general public.) Often one person fills more than one of these roles. For example, the settlor of a revocable declaration of trust acts as sole trustee and usually retains a life income interest in the trust as one of the beneficiaries. (See ¶ 2,350.) To be valid, however, the trust must have at least one beneficiary who is not also the sole trustee; it would be pointless to speak of fiduciary duties running from one person as sole trustee to the same person as sole beneficiary. A revocable declaration of trust does not run afoul of this rule as long as there is at least one other beneficiary, even if that beneficiary has only a contingent future interest (e.g., the right to receive beneficial enjoyment at the settlor's death if the beneficiary survives the settlor). In sum, *A* may create a trust with *A* as sole trustee for the benefit of *A* and *B*, or with *A* and *B* as co-trustees for *A* as sole beneficiary, but *A* cannot act as sole trustee of a trust for the benefit of *A* alone.

A trust does not come into existence until it is funded with property. Without property, the terms of the trust cannot be carried out because there is no subject matter for the trustee to administer on behalf of the beneficiaries. Moreover, the funding of the trust must coincide with the settlor's manifested intent to create a trust. A settlor can create an *inter vivos trust* during life either by transferring property to another person as trustee (a deed of trust) or by declaring that he or she holds property as trustee (a declaration of trust). (See ¶ 2,350.) A *testamentary trust* is created by will at the settlor's death. A trust funded by a pourover will is a sort of hybrid; it is treated by statute as an inter vivos trust, even though it is funded at death. (See ¶ 2,230.) Inter vivos trusts are generally administered without formal court proceedings, in contrast to testamentary trusts which in many states require probate court proceedings in connection with the appointment of trustees and the approval of accounts.

The terms of the trust are set forth in a written instrument executed by the settlor. If the trust property consists of land, a writing is generally required by the Statute of Frauds. For personal property, an oral agreement or declaration may be permissible, but a writing is almost always used, as a practical matter, in order to provide a reliable record of the existence and terms of the trust. Trust instruments range from preprinted fill-in-the-blank forms for specific assets (e.g., shares of a particular mutual fund) to professionally drafted forms with elaborate, custom-tailored dispositive and administrative provisions.

A trust is defined as a fiduciary relationship between the trustee and the beneficiaries. The settlor's role is generally limited to creating the trust, establishing its terms and contributing the trust property. Once the trust is created, the settlor has little or no continuing role in the operation of the trust, except to the extent that he or she serves as trustee, retains a beneficial interest, or reserves a power to revoke or amend the trust or to control the trustee in administering the trust.

A trust bears some resemblance to other fiduciary relationships, but it is distinguished by its broad scope and flexible structure. Unlike a personal representative, a conservator or a guardian, a trustee often has the responsibility of managing property for successive beneficiaries over an extended period of time, with little or no court supervision. In the case of a gift to a minor donee, a *custodianship* offers a simple and inexpensive alternative to a full-fledged trust. Under the Uniform Transfers to Minors Act (UTMA) (or its forerunner, the Uniform Gifts to Minors Act), which has been enacted in one version or another throughout the country, a donor can create a custodianship simply by transferring property in the prescribed form, "to A as custodian for B under the [State] Uniform Transfers to Minors Act." UTMA § 9. Technically, legal title to the custodial property is vested in the minor donee, but the custodian has broad fiduciary powers and duties resembling those of a trustee, including the power to "deliver or pay to the minor or expend for the minor's benefit so much of the custodial property as the custodian considers advisable for the use and benefit of the minor, without court order." UTMA § 14(a). The minor donee and certain other persons can request an accounting in court, but otherwise the custodian is not required to render an accounting. See UTMA § 19. In general, the custodian is required to turn over the custodial property to the minor donee when the minor reaches age 21. See UTMA § 20(1). In effect, the custodianship functions very much like a statutory trust for the minor donee.

[¶ 2,520]

2. Transfer of a Beneficiary's Interest

In the absence of a valid restraint on alienation, a beneficiary is free to transfer his or her interest in a trust, and the beneficiary's creditors can reach the interest to satisfy their claims. For example, suppose a settlor creates a trust to pay income to her son Alec for life with remainder at his death to his issue. Alec can give or sell his income interest to another person, with notice to the trustee, whereupon the transferee becomes entitled to receive the trust income for Alec's life. An involuntary transfer may occur if a judgment creditor of Alec brings an action to enforce the judgment. A court may direct the trustee to pay all or part of the income to the creditor until the judgment is satisfied, or may order that the interest be sold to a third party and the proceeds applied to satisfy the judgment. Alternatively, in the case of a future interest, the court may impose a lien on the interest, so that the creditor will be paid when and if the interest ripens into possession. In such proceedings, the court has discretion to determine the manner of payment or, if a fair price cannot be obtained for the interest, to deny relief altogether.

A creditor's ability to reach a beneficiary's interest may be limited by the terms of the trust. Spendthrift trusts, support trusts and discretionary trusts are commonly used to protect beneficial interests from creditors of the beneficiaries. Special rules apply in the case of interests retained by the settlor of a trust. (See ¶¶ 2,525–2,535.)

[¶ 2,525]

a. Spendthrift Trusts

A *spendthrift trust* is a trust which by its terms restrains the alienation of a beneficiary's interest. A typical spendthrift clause expressly prohibits the beneficiary from "anticipating, assigning, selling or otherwise disposing of" his or her interest in the trust. Courts in almost every state have held that such provisions are effective to prevent both voluntary and involuntary transfers of the beneficiary's interest. Thus, in general, the beneficiary of a spendthrift trust cannot transfer his or her interest, nor can the interest be reached by the beneficiary's creditors. The protection from creditors also extends to bankruptcy proceedings. See 11 U.S.C. § 541(c)(2).

Some states have statutes that make beneficial interests in trusts wholly or partially inalienable. Furthermore, as a matter of federal law, benefits under qualified pension plans cannot be assigned or alienated. See 29 U.S.C. § 1056(d)(1). In most states, however, a beneficiary's interest is freely transferable unless the terms of the trust include a spendthrift clause.

Spendthrift trusts have been controversial ever since they first appeared in the late nineteenth century. The main argument advanced in favor of spendthrift trusts rests on the freedom of the *settlor*, in creating a trust, to place whatever restrictions he or she chooses on the interest of the *beneficiary*. The paternalistic underpinnings of this argument emerge clearly from dictum in an early Supreme Court decision that paved the way for spendthrift trusts:

> Why a parent, or one who loves another, and wishes to use his own property in securing the object of his affection, as far as property can do it, from the ills of life, the vicissitudes of fortune, and even his own improvidence, or incapacity for self-protection, should not be permitted to do so, is not readily perceived. [Nichols v. Eaton, 91 U.S. 716, 727 (1875).]

The premise of the argument is questionable, since the dispositive freedom of any property owner is inherently bounded by considerations of public policy. Indeed, courts generally refuse to tolerate disabling restraints on alienation for other forms of property. Moreover, spendthrift trusts are by no means limited to beneficiaries who are spendthrifts or otherwise in need of special protection. Judge Learned Hand, starting from the premise of beneficiary autonomy, criticized spendthrift trusts in the following terms:

> We have no public concern for the preservation of family inheritances, and ought, I believe, have no tenderness towards expectants of rich reversions.... I find it hard to have patience with the waterish sentiment which seeks to make such a man the court's ward, and to protect him against the consequences of his own folly. If he is to have the enjoyment of great wealth, let him share its responsibility. If the prospect of a dollar so teased his appetite that the future ceased to be a reality, either let him be regarded as an incompetent and put in ward, or let us treat him as a person in a world of persons, and let him weave his fate as he will. [Provident Life & Trust Co. v. Fletcher, 237 F. 104, 110–11 (S.D.N.Y. 1916).]

For a contemporary assessment of spendthrift trusts, see Hirsch, Spendthrift Trusts and Public Policy: Economic and Cognitive Perspectives, 73 Wash. U. L.Q. 1 (1995). For a historical perspective, see Friedman, The Dynastic Trust, 73 Yale L.J. 574 (1964); see also Alexander, The Dead Hand and the Law of Trusts in the Nineteenth Century, 37 Stan. L. Rev. 1189 (1985).

Although spendthrift trusts have achieved widespread judicial acceptance, they do not provide absolute immunity to their beneficiaries from the claims of creditors. To begin with, the protection of a spendthrift clause extends only to a beneficiary's interest in *undistributed* trust income or principal. Upon receiving a distribution from the trust, the beneficiary becomes the absolute owner of the distributed amounts, and those amounts can be reached by creditors by the same process as any other assets owned by the beneficiary. In other words, spendthrift protection applies to property in the trustee's hands prior to distribution, but not to the same property in the beneficiary's hands after distribution. Thus, the main effect of a spendthrift clause is to force creditors to pursue assets in the hands of the beneficiary instead of collecting their judgments directly from the trustee. As a practical matter, of course, this puts creditors at a significant disadvantage in the ensuing game of hide-and-seek with the beneficiary.

By statute or judicial decision in many states, certain types of creditors are allowed to reach a beneficiary's interest in undistributed income or principal, even though the trust contains a valid spendthrift clause. For example, a child or spouse of the beneficiary is often allowed to reach the beneficiary's trust interest to satisfy a claim against the beneficiary for support or alimony. For reasons of public policy, these claims override any spendthrift protection that is effective against claims of ordinary creditors. Exceptions to spendthrift protection have also been found in cases involving claims for necessary services or supplies furnished to the beneficiary, claims for services which benefit the beneficiary's trust interest (e.g., the fee of a lawyer who successfully represented the beneficiary in trust litigation), and claims of federal or state governmental entities (e.g., for unpaid taxes).

[¶ 2,530]

b. *Support Trusts and Discretionary Trusts*

Even without an express spendthrift clause, the terms of a trust may define a beneficiary's interest in such a way that it has little or no practical value to any person other than the intended beneficiary. This is the effect of a *support trust*, which directs the trustee to distribute to a beneficiary whatever amounts are necessary for the beneficiary's support. A support trust implicitly prohibits a transfer of the beneficiary's interest because the interest is defined in terms personal to the beneficiary. Distributions to ordinary creditors or other transferees violate the terms of the trust unless they are made for the beneficiary's support. Thus, only certain types of creditors (e.g., those who furnished necessary services or supplies to the beneficiary) are entitled to reach the beneficiary's interest. The trustee of a support trust may have some flexibility in determining the precise level of required support (which may vary according to the beneficiary's "station in life"), but the trustee does not have discretion to withhold distributions altogether.

A *discretionary trust* by its terms gives the trustee broad discretion to make (or not to make) distributions of trust income or principal to the beneficiary. The trustee may be inclined to exercise such discretion quite liberally in favor of a financially secure beneficiary, but if a creditor forces a transfer of the beneficiary's interest or obtains a lien on it, the trustee can simply refuse to make any further distributions. Since the beneficiary had no enforceable right to compel the trustee to make distributions, the creditor (who stands in the beneficiary's shoes) stands in no better position. As a result, creditors may be discouraged from even attempting to reach a beneficiary's interest in a discretionary trust. A variation of this approach, commonly used in jurisdictions that do not recognize spendthrift clauses, is a *protective trust*, which provides for regular distributions of income to the beneficiary as long as no creditor attempts to reach the beneficiary's interest; however, upon an attempted voluntary or involuntary transfer, the trust automatically becomes a discretionary trust. If the creditor's claim is paid from other sources, the beneficiary may again become entitled to regular distributions under the original terms of the trust.

Both a discretionary trust (or a protective trust) and a spendthrift trust offer protection for a beneficiary's interest against creditors, but the two types of trusts operate quite differently. A discretionary trust shields trust assets from the beneficiary's creditors only as long as the trustee withholds distributions from the beneficiary. Just as the beneficiary's right to receive income or principal depends on the trustee's exercise of discretion, so the beneficiary's creditors (who stand in the beneficiary's shoes) cannot compel the trustee to make distributions from a discretionary trust. By the same token, however, a creditor may obtain a court order directing the trustee, if it decides to make any discretionary distributions, to pay the creditor before the beneficiary. Thus, the creditor may prevent the beneficiary from receiving any discretionary distributions until the creditor's claim is satisfied.

[¶ 2,532]

Problem

Under an irrevocable trust created by his mother, Laurence is entitled to receive all of the trust income for life as well as distributions of principal "at such times and in such amounts as the trustee in its absolute discretion deems appropriate." Any remaining trust property is payable at Laurence's death to his surviving issue. The trust includes an express spendthrift clause. Laurence was recently divorced and has fallen behind on support payments to his minor child Melissa. Also, while driving under the influence, Laurence caused an automobile accident in which Ralph, the driver of the other vehicle, sustained serious injuries. Melissa and Ralph have reduced their respective claims to judgment, only to discover that Laurence has no assets other than his trust interest. To what extent can either or both judgment creditors reach Laurence's trust interest to satisfy their claims?

[¶ 2,535]

c. *Self-Settled Trusts*

In most states, the protection against creditors provided by spendthrift trusts, support trusts and discretionary trusts does not apply to any beneficial interest retained by a trust settlor. To the extent the settlor of a trust retains a beneficial interest, the trust is said to be *self-settled*. By statute or judicial decision, the prevailing rule is that the settlor's creditors can reach any interest retained by the settlor (including any interest subject to the settlor's retained power to revoke), whether or not the trust includes a spendthrift clause. Moreover, in the case of a self-settled support trust or discretionary trust, the settlor's creditors can reach the maximum amount that the trustee could distribute to the settlor or apply for the settlor's benefit. See UTC § 505. In sum, a settlor cannot use a trust to shelter assets from his or her own creditors.

Even if a settlor creates an irrevocable trust and retains no beneficial interest, the settlor's creditors can reach the trust property if the creation of the trust constitutes a fraudulent transfer. For this purpose, the creation of a trust is treated the same as a gift of property. (See Chapter 10.)

The rules on self-settled trusts can have collateral consequences beyond the rights of the settlor's creditors. For example, property in a self-settled trust is counted as an available asset in determining the settlor's eligibility for public assistance benefits under means-tested programs such as Medicaid. (See ¶ 9,760.) In addition, to the extent the settlor's creditors can reach a beneficial interest in a self-settled trust, the creation of the trust may be treated as an incomplete transfer for gift and estate tax purposes. (See Chapter 4.)

A few states (notably Alaska and Delaware) have recently enacted statutes that override the traditional constraints on self-settled trusts. In these states, a settlor can shelter assets from most creditors by means of an irrevocable discretionary trust, even if the settlor is the sole current beneficiary. See Fox & Huff, Asset Protection and Dynasty Trusts, 37 Real Prop., Prob. & Tr. J. 287 (2002). These debtor-friendly statutes, which are apparently intended to attract new business for local trust companies, raise troublesome questions involving personal jurisdiction and choice of law. For example, if a New York settlor creates an Alaska asset protection trust with an Alaska trustee, creditors seeking to reach the settlor's interest will have no remedy under the substantive law of Alaska, and they are likely to have difficulty obtaining personal jurisdiction over the trustee in the courts of another state. Moreover, as a matter of constitutional law, an adverse judgment in an Alaska proceeding will be entitled to full faith and credit in the courts of other states. For creditors, the most practical remedy may lie in a federal bankruptcy proceeding. It remains to be seen whether interstate competition will induce states with large, established trust companies to enact more debtor-friendly statutes. See Sterk, Asset Protection Trusts: Trust Law's Race to the Bottom?, 85 Cornell L. Rev. 1035 (2000). Several off-shore jurisdictions with similar legislation have become well-known as havens for asset protection trusts. See Marty–Nelson, Offshore Asset Protection Trusts, 47 Rutgers L.Rev. 11 (1994); Sullivan, Gutting the Rule Against Self–Settled Trusts: How the New Delaware Trust Law Competes with Offshore Trusts, 23 Del. J. Corp. L. 423 (1998).

[¶ 2,537]

Problem

Andrew and Elena, a married couple, created separate discretionary trusts for the benefit of each other. The trust created by Andrew authorizes him, as sole trustee, to distribute income or principal to Elena "at such times and in such amounts as the trustee in his sole discretion deems appropriate." The trust created by Elena gives her, as sole trustee, similar authority to make discretionary distributions to Andrew. At the death of the primary beneficiary, the property of each trust is payable to the issue of Andrew and Elena. Both Andrew and Elena were solvent when the trusts were created, but Andrew, a surgeon, has just lost a medical malpractice suit brought by a former patient. Can the patient collect the malpractice judgment from either or both of the discretionary trusts created by Andrew and Elena?

[¶ 2,540]

3. Successive Beneficial Interests

In most long-term trusts, the enjoyment of trust property is divided among successive beneficiaries over time. The trustee is typically authorized or directed to distribute current income periodically to one or more beneficiaries and eventually to distribute principal to designated beneficiaries at specified times. Correspondingly, the interests of the respective beneficiaries are defined in terms of rights to receive trust income for a period of time (e.g., during the beneficiary's minority or for life) or to receive distributions of trust principal at specified times (e.g., when the beneficiary reaches age 30, or at the termination of a preceding income interest). The following sections provide a brief overview of some techniques commonly used by drafters to provide flexibility in response to changing circumstances during the term of the trust.

[¶ 2,545]

a. *Fiduciary Discretion*

The trustee is often given discretion to determine the timing and amount of distributions to various beneficiaries. For example, the trustee may have discretion to distribute current trust income to one or more beneficiaries or to accumulate the income and add it to trust principal. The trustee may also have discretion to invade trust principal for the benefit of one or more beneficiaries. The scope of the trustee's discretion may be very broad or limited by standards such as the "support," "comfort" or "need" of the beneficiary. In exercising (or failing to exercise) its discretion, the trustee is ultimately subject to judicial review. Even an express grant of "absolute" or "unlimited" discretion cannot insulate the trustee from accountability to the beneficiaries. Nevertheless, courts are generally reluctant to second-guess a trustee's judgment unless the trustee has abused its discretion by acting unreasonably or unfairly.

If the trustee has broad discretion to make or withhold distributions to a particular beneficiary, the rights of the beneficiary and his or her creditors are correspondingly limited. (See ¶ 2,530.) The beneficiary of a discretionary trust (other than a self-settled trust) may be eligible for public assistance benefits under a means-tested program (e.g., Medicaid). If the trust by its terms expressly prohibits the trustee from making distributions for the beneficiary's support but gives the trustee discretion to make distributions for "supplemental needs," the beneficiary's interest is not counted as an available asset or income in determining eligibility for public assistance. Thus, the beneficiary may be sufficiently needy to qualify for public assistance and yet also receive additional benefits from a discretionary trust. Medicaid and similar programs are discussed in Chapter 9.

[¶ 2,550]

b. Class Gifts

A trust may provide for gifts of income or principal to a class of beneficiaries (e.g., the settlor's children or issue). The distinctive feature of a class gift is that the number of beneficiaries in the class may increase or decrease over time as new members come into existence or existing members die. If the subject matter of the class gift is to be divided equally among the class members, the size of each member's share varies inversely in proportion to the size of the class.

The beneficiaries of a class gift are usually described in terms of their relationship to the settlor or another person (e.g., the settlor's children, or the issue of the settlor's siblings). The class description should be drafted with care to avoid ambiguities in identifying the members of the class. For example, it may be unclear whether a gift to the settlor's "children" includes an adopted child or a child born out of wedlock. Similarly, a question may arise as to whether a gift to "nieces and nephews" includes relatives by marriage as well as blood relatives. In some states, by statute or judicial decision, class gifts are presumed to accord with the corresponding provisions of the intestacy statutes. See UPC § 2–705. Ultimately, however, the scope of a class gift is a matter of interpretation which turns on the meaning of the words used in the governing instrument, and it is the responsibility of the drafter to make sure that the settlor's intent is clearly and accurately expressed.

In drafting a class gift, it is helpful to specify how long the class will remain open to admit new members and what conditions each member must meet in order to take possession of his or her share. The class "closes" when it can no longer expand to include new members; thus, any person born after the closing of the class is excluded from sharing in the class gift. As a general rule of construction, with respect to a class gift of principal, the class ordinarily closes when it is physically impossible for any additional members to come into existence or, if earlier, when any member of the class becomes entitled to possession of his or her share.

Often a beneficiary must reach a specified age or survive another person in order to receive his or her share. As a general rule of construction, courts traditionally have been reluctant to find an implied condition of survival except in certain multi-generation class gifts (e.g., "to A's issue" or "to A's heirs"). Ordinarily, in the absence of an express condition of survival, a beneficiary is not required to survive until the time for possession of his or her share. Thus, under a trust to pay "income to A for life, remainder to B," B's remainder interest is indefeasibly vested, and at A's death the trust property is payable to B if living, otherwise to B's estate. (The Uniform Probate Code reverses this rule and implies a survival requirement, coupled with a substitute gift to a deceased beneficiary's issue, for every future interest in trust. See UPC § 2–707. This provision has provoked considerable controversy. See Dukeminier, The Uniform Probate Code Upends the Law of Remainders, 94 Mich. L. Rev. 148 (1995); Waggoner, The Uniform Probate Code Extends Antilapse–Type Protection to Poorly Drafted Trusts, 94 Mich. L. Rev. 2309 (1996); Becker, Uniform Probate Code Section 2–707 and the Experienced Estate Planner: Unexpected Disasters and How to Avoid Them, 47 UCLA L. Rev. 339 (1999).) To avoid uncertainty, in creating future interests a drafter should state clearly whether a beneficiary is required to survive until the time for possession of his or her interest and, if so, who takes the interest if the beneficiary fails to survive.

The interest of a particular beneficiary is "vested" when the beneficiary is in existence and ascertained and all conditions precedent attached to the beneficiary's interest are satisfied. Note that the vesting of a beneficiary's interest does not necessarily mean that the beneficiary will actually receive a distribution from the trust; a vested interest may be subject to a condition subsequent which, if it occurs, will divest the interest and prevent the beneficiary from taking his or her share. A condition can be expressed either as a condition precedent or a condition subsequent; the difference is in the form of the words used. For example, a survival requirement may be expressed as a condition precedent (e.g., to A "if A reaches age 21" or "if A survives B"), or as a condition subsequent (e.g., to A "unless A dies before age 21" or "unless A dies before B"). In each case, the substance of the survival requirement is the same, but in the first formulation the interest is contingent, while in the latter formulation it is vested subject to divestment. The difference in classification, though highly formalistic, can be important in applying the Rule Against Perpetuities (see ¶ 2,560).

[¶ 2,552]

Problem

Teresa creates a testamentary trust to pay income to her son Brian for life with remainder at Brian's death to his children who reach age 21. Teresa dies survived by Brian and Brian's minor children Jake and Chris. Five years later, Brian dies, survived by three children—Jake (age 22), Chris (age 12), and Terry (age 2). Chris dies a year later at age 13, and Terry eventually reaches age 21. How should the trust principal be distributed? What difference would it make if Brian had a fourth child who survived Teresa but died before Brian at age 25?

[¶ 2,555]

c. *Powers of Appointment*

Many trusts provide flexibility by giving one or more beneficiaries a *power of appointment* over the trust property. A power of appointment is a power to designate ownership or beneficial enjoyment of the trust property. A *general* power is one which the holder can exercise for his or her own benefit (e.g., by appointing the property to the holder, the holder's estate, or creditors of the holder or the estate). For example, an income beneficiary who has a power to withdraw or consume trust principal has a general power of appointment. A power that cannot be exercised for the holder's own benefit is a *special* or *limited* power, even if it is very broad in scope. For example, if a trust provides income to Gilbert for life and gives Gilbert a power to appoint the remainder at death to any person other than himself, his estate, or creditors of himself or his estate, Gilbert has a special power of appointment.

In contrast to a trustee's discretionary power, which is subject to fiduciary constraints of fairness and good faith, a power of appointment is held in a nonfiduciary capacity and may be exercised in any way the holder wishes, subject only to any formal or substantive limitations in the terms of the trust. In creating a power of appointment, a drafter should consider not only the scope of the power (e.g., the persons in whose favor the power may be exercised) but also the manner of its exercise (e.g., by will or by deed) and the disposition of the underlying property in default of an effective exercise. In exercising a power of appointment, the holder may be required to refer specifically to the power or the trust instrument creating it. Such a requirement is intended to prevent an inadvertent or ill-considered exercise of the power.

[¶ 2,560]

d. *Rule Against Perpetuities*

The duration of trusts with private beneficiaries is limited in a roundabout way by the Rule Against Perpetuities. Under the common law version of the Rule, a future interest is valid only if it must vest, if it vests at all, within a period measured by some life in being at the creation of the interest plus 21 years. Conversely, if there is any possibility that a future interest might vest remotely (i.e., later than 21 years after some life in being at the creation of the interest), the interest is void from the outset. In the case of a class gift, the entire class gift fails unless it is certain that the class will close and each member's interest will become vested within the permitted period.

The Rule Against Perpetuities is not a rule of construction but rather a rule of law that may defeat the intent of a trust settlor. For example, suppose a testator leaves property to her *issue* who are living at the final distribution of her estate. Under a strict application of the Rule, this gift is void because at the testator's death it is possible (though highly unlikely) that the property could be distributed to afterborn issue more than 21 years after the death of all persons living at the testator's death; since the takers cannot be ascertained until the time of distribution, their interests might vest remotely. The gift is not saved even if the estate is distributed within one year after the testator's death; the Rule looks forward from the time the interest is created at what might happen, rather than at events as they actually occur. In contrast, a bequest to the testator's *children* who are living at the final distribution of the estate would be valid, because each child's share would necessarily vest or fail within the child's own lifetime and so each child can be used as a "life in being" to validate his or her share.

Suppose a testator leaves property in trust to pay income to her children for their lives, with remainder at the death of the last surviving child to the testator's grandchildren who reach age 30. The class gift of income is valid, since each child validates his or her own interest. The class gift of the remainder, however, is void because it is possible that a grandchild's interest might vest remotely (e.g., in the case of a grandchild born after the testator's death who reaches age 30 more than 21 years after the end of all lives in being at the testator's death). Note that this type of violation could be avoided by limiting the survival requirement to age 21 instead of age 30. The Rule bristles with technical traps for the unwary drafter, especially in connection with class gifts and powers of appointment. For comprehensive expositions of the common law Rule, see Leach, Perpetuities in a Nutshell, 51 Harv. L. Rev. 638 (1938); Dukeminier, A Modern Guide to Perpetuities, 74 Calif. Rev. 1867 (1986). For a discussion of the Rule's underlying policies, see Hirsch & Wang, A Qualitative Theory of the Dead Hand, 68 Ind. L.J. 1 (1992).

In many states the common law Rule has been modified by statute or judicial decision. Under the Uniform Statutory Rule Against Perpetuities (USRAP), a future interest is valid if it satisfies the common law Rule or if it actually vests or terminates within 90 years after its creation. See USRAP § 1. In effect, USRAP allows a 90-year "wait and see" period as an alternative to the common law Rule. Moreover, the statute authorizes a court to reform the terms of an interest that does not actually vest or terminate within the 90-year period. See USRAP § 3. In several states the Rule has been abolished altogether by statute.

A competent trust drafter should be familiar with the basic structure and operation of the common law Rule Against Perpetuities. To guard against inadvertent violations of the Rule (and avoid litigation over alleged violations), experienced drafters often include a "saving clause." A typical saving clause provides that, if a trust does not terminate earlier according to its terms, the trust shall terminate at the end of the common law perpetuities period (i.e., 21 years after the end of specified lives in being at the creation of the trust), and directs a terminating distribution to designated beneficiaries in the event the clause becomes operative. See McGovern, Perpetuities Pitfalls and How Best to Avoid Them, 6 Real Prop., Prob. & Tr. J. 155 (1971).

The Rule Against Perpetuities does not apply to purely charitable trusts. Because a charitable trust has no private beneficiaries, the problem of remote vesting of beneficial interests does not arise. As a result, charitable trusts can endure indefinitely.

[¶ 2,570]

4. Fiduciary Duties

In administering a trust, the trustee owes several fiduciary duties to the beneficiaries, including the duties of loyalty, impartiality and prudence. In addition, the trustee is generally required to exercise due care, to maintain reasonable records, and to keep the beneficiaries reasonably informed. If the trustee breaches a fiduciary duty, the beneficiaries may pursue several remedies: if the breach resulted in a loss to the trust or an improper profit to the trustee, they may sue the trustee for damages; in the case of an improper disposition of trust assets, they may recover the assets from the trustee or even from a third party (other than a bona fide purchaser for value); they may seek a court order to enjoin the trustee from a continuing or threatened breach of trust; and, in egregious cases, they may seek the removal of the trustee.

Sometimes a trust includes an exculpatory clause providing that the trustee shall be liable only for actions taken recklessly or in bad faith and not for ordinary negligence. Courts are inclined to interpret such a clause narrowly or to disregard it entirely if it appears to have been included as a result of overreaching on the part of the trustee.

Often a trust is administered by two or more co-trustees. Each co-trustee has a duty to participate in the trust administration and to take reasonable precautions against a breach of trust by another co-trustee. If there are multiple co-trustees, the trust instrument should specify whether they may act by majority vote and whether they may delegate certain functions to one of themselves or to third parties. Even if there is only one trustee, the trust instrument should also provide a mechanism for the resignation or removal of a trustee and the appointment of a successor.

[¶ 2,575]

a. Loyalty

The fundamental duty of *loyalty* requires that a trustee administer the trust solely in the interest of the beneficiaries. As a corollary, the trustee is not permitted to derive any personal gain (other than compensation for fiduciary services) from administering the trust. The trustee is also prohibited from engaging in self-dealing or in transactions affected by a substantial conflict of interest. A trustee who deals with trust assets on his or her own personal account (e.g., by purchasing trust assets or borrowing trust funds) commits a breach of trust, even if the trustee acted in good faith and the terms of the transaction were fair. By way of a remedy, the beneficiaries may sue the trustee for damages or set aside the transaction, whichever appears more advantageous. The trustee has no defense unless the transaction was authorized by the terms of the trust or by court order, or the transaction was entered into in good faith, on fair terms, and with the consent of the beneficiaries after full disclosure of the material facts.

The duty of loyalty is rigorous and burdensome. It is deliberately framed to discourage the trustee from participating in transactions in which his or her personal interests may conflict with those of the beneficiaries. In part this reflects the essence of the fiduciary relationship. The beneficiary should be entitled to rely unconditionally on the trustee's honesty and good faith. There are also strategic considerations at work, since fiduciary abuses are often hard to detect or prove, and a trustee is better situated than the beneficiaries to prevent abuses from occurring. Nevertheless, in some cases the duty of loyalty prevents the trustee from striking an advantageous deal on behalf of the beneficiaries. For example, if it becomes necessary to sell trust assets and the trustee is willing to offer better terms than any other purchaser (or if the trustee is the only potential purchaser), the trustee may be forced either to accept a less attractive offer or to seek advance court approval of the trustee's offer. In sum, protecting beneficiaries against unscrupulous trustees may involve real costs. The trust instrument may authorize the trustee to enter into transactions that would not otherwise be permitted, but the trustee cannot be relieved of the basic duty to act fairly and in good faith.

[¶ 2,580]

b. *Impartiality*

Most trusts have multiple beneficiaries with potentially divergent interests. The trustee has a duty to treat all beneficiaries fairly and *impartially*. This does not mean that all beneficiaries must receive precisely equal treatment, which is often neither possible nor desirable, but it does require the trustee to act evenhandedly in making discretionary distributions and in selecting trust investments. The trustee may not arbitrarily favor any particular beneficiary or class of beneficiaries over any other.

Special problems arise in connection with trust investments, since many types of investments tend to favor either income beneficiaries or principal beneficiaries. For example, a portfolio of municipal or corporate bonds may produce relatively high current income while allowing the real value of the principal to be eroded by inflation. Conversely, a portfolio of growth stocks may generate substantial capital appreciation with little or no current income. To permit the trustee to pursue an optimal investment strategy without violating the duty of impartiality, a trust drafter may give the trustee discretion to adjust the shares of the respective beneficiaries, either directly (i.e., by accumulating income or invading principal) or indirectly (e.g., by reallocating amounts between income and principal).

Another way of ensuring that the trustee's investment decisions do not unduly favor one beneficiary over another is to structure the beneficiaries' successive interests independently of the traditional trust accounting concepts of income and principal. For example, instead of requiring annual distributions of trust income, the trust instrument might provide for an interest in the form of an *annuity*, i.e., annual distributions of a fixed amount payable either from income or from corpus, with any remaining trust property payable to the remainder taker. Alternatively, the trust instrument might provide for an interest in the form of a *unitrust*, i.e., annual distributions of a fixed percentage of the total value of the trust property (determined annually), with any remaining trust property payable to the remainder taker. In an annuity trust, the current beneficiary is assured of receiving fixed payments, with the result that the remainder taker bears the risk of investment gain or loss. By contrast, in a unitrust, the beneficiaries participate ratably in the total investment return on the trust property. In both cases, the trustee is free to invest the trust property to achieve an optimal total return, regardless of whether the return takes the form of current income or capital appreciation.

[¶ 2,585]

c. *Prudence*

The trustee's duty of *prudence* generally requires the exercise of care, skill and caution in administering the trust property and specifically in investing trust funds. Courts have traditionally held that the trustee should "observe how men of prudence, discretion, and intelligence manage their own affairs, not in regard to speculation, but in regard to the permanent disposition of their funds, considering the probable income, as well as the probable safety of the capital to be invested." Harvard College v. Amory, 26 Mass. 446, 461 (1830). As a practical matter, this standard has encouraged trustees to pursue a markedly conservative investment strategy geared toward producing regular current income and avoiding principal loss rather than maximizing total return or managing risk.

The Uniform Prudent Investor Act (UPIA) embraces modern portfolio theory and encourages a flexible approach to investments, emphasizing the tradeoff between risk and return. Under the Act, the trustee is directed to invest as a "prudent investor" would, giving consideration to the "purposes, terms, distribution requirements, and other circumstances of the trust." UPIA § 2(a). Investment decisions concerning individual assets are to be evaluated "not in isolation but in the context of the trust portfolio as a whole and as part of an overall investment strategy having risk and return objectives reasonably suited to the trust." UPIA § 2(b). Categorical restrictions on permissible investments are removed; the trustee may invest in "any kind of property or type of investment" consistent with the standards of the Act. UPIA § 2(e). Moreover, the trustee generally has a duty to diversify trust investments and has authority to delegate investment functions to agents. See UPIA §§ 3, 9. See Langbein, The Uniform Prudent Investor Act and the Future of Trust Investing, 81 Iowa L. Rev. 641 (1996); Haskell, The Prudent Person Rule for Trustee Investment and Modern Portfolio Theory, 69 N.C. L. Rev. 87 (1990). For background on modern portfolio theory, see Macey, An Introduction to Modern Financial Theory (2d ed. 1998).

One likely consequence of liberalizing the guidelines for prudent investment will be to encourage trustees to invest in index funds in order to achieve a diversified portfolio that balances risk and return at relatively low cost. See Langbein & Posner, Market Funds and Trust–Investment Law, 1976 Am. B. Found. Res. J. 1; Langbein & Posner, Market Funds and Trust–Investment Law: II, 1977 Am. B. Found. Res. J. 1.

[¶ 2,590]

5. Modification and Termination

Trusts are often created to provide benefits for several generations of beneficiaries over an extended period of time. It is generally desirable to build some flexibility into the terms of the trust to respond to changing circumstances, either by giving the trustee discretionary powers over the management of the trust property and the timing and amount of distributions or by authorizing one or more beneficiaries to withdraw property or designate additional takers under a power of appointment. If the terms of the trust are drawn so narrowly and rigidly that they become unworkable or inconvenient, it may be necessary to resort to a formal modification or termination of the trust.

Under the doctrine of *deviation*, a trustee may seek court approval to deviate from the administrative provisions of a trust if, due to circumstances not anticipated by the settlor, compliance with the terms of the trust would defeat or substantially impair the accomplishment of the purposes of the trust. For example, if a trust instrument directs the trustee to retain a particular parcel of land or to invest only in government bonds, and if the investment restrictions no longer make sense due to unanticipated changes in markets and the economy, a court may authorize the trustee to sell the land or to invest in a more diversified portfolio. Courts have traditionally been willing to authorize deviation only in extreme cases; it is not sufficient that the terms of the trust are ill-considered or inconvenient. By statute in some states, however, deviation is available if a court finds that the existing terms of a trust are "impracticable or wasteful" or "impair the trust's administration." UTC § 412.

A trust may be *modified* or *terminated* by the unanimous consent of the owners of all beneficial interests, unless continuation on its original terms is necessary to carry out a material purpose of the trust. In theory, the beneficiaries, as equitable owners of the trust property, can compel a modification or termination on their own initiative, without the cooperation of the trustee and without court approval. In practice, however, this rarely happens. In order to consent to a proposed change, the owners of *all* beneficial interests must be competent adults. Even assuming that all of the existing beneficiaries reach an agreement among themselves, the possibility of future beneficiaries who are unborn or unascertained may present an insuperable obstacle. In a long-term trust, the ultimate remainder takers are frequently members of an open-ended class (e.g., children, issue or heirs) who cannot be identified with certainty before the scheduled termination date. A court can appoint a guardian ad litem to represent the interests of unborn or unascertained beneficiaries, but this will not make it easier to obtain unanimous consent, since the interests of those beneficiaries are likely to diverge from the interests of the existing beneficiaries.

Another, equally serious obstacle stems from the longstanding "material purpose" doctrine, which prevents the beneficiaries from modifying or terminating a trust if any material purpose of the trust remains unfulfilled. Courts have applied this rule quite expansively to prevent beneficiaries from interfering with the terms originally established by the settlor. For example, standard trust provisions such as a spendthrift clause, a trustee's discretionary power to accumulate income or invade principal, and a direction to distribute principal to a beneficiary at a specified age have all been held to constitute material purposes precluding modification or termination. Nevertheless, if the settlor is alive and consents to the proposed modification or termination, the material purpose doctrine does not apply. It would be pointless to insist on carrying out the settlor's original purposes if the settlor and all the beneficiaries agree that they are no longer material. However, the material purpose doctrine often prevents any modification or termination after the settlor's death.

In some states, the material purpose doctrine is modified by statute to permit modification or termination on somewhat more flexible terms with court approval. See UTC § 411.

Charitable trusts raise special concerns because they have no private beneficiaries and can endure indefinitely. Under the doctrine of *cy pres*, if it becomes impossible or impracticable to give effect to the specific terms of a charitable trust, a court may modify the terms of the trust to give effect as nearly as possible to a general charitable intent manifested by the settlor. See UTC § 413.

[¶ 2,592]

Problem

When Lily was 18 years old, her father died and left his entire estate to her. On the advice of a family friend, Lily created a trust and funded it with the property she inherited from her father. By its terms, the trust is irrevocable, and the trustee (a local bank) is authorized to distribute income or principal to Lily "as the trustee in its sole discretion deems appropriate." Lily is the sole beneficiary of the trust; any amounts remaining in the trust at her death are payable to her probate estate. Lily is now 25 years old and has joined a religious cult which requires that its members turn over all of their assets to the cult's leader. Lily asks the trustee to terminate the trust and distribute all of the trust property to her. The trustee refuses. Can Lily compel the trustee to cooperate? See Johnson v. First Nat'l Bank, 386 So.2d 1112 (Miss. 1980).

Chapter 3

INCOME TAXATION OF
THE FAMILY

A. INTRODUCTION

[¶ 3,000]

The federal income tax constitutes the primary financial obligation to government for most individuals and families. The body of federal law that sets forth an individual's obligations under the income tax is extensive and complex. Quite obviously, a thorough discussion of that law would take several volumes and even an introduction to the subject could take up a volume as large as this one which is devoted to a variety of subjects. The purpose of this chapter is not to substitute for even an introductory course in federal income taxation but rather to provide a modest introduction to some of the most important income tax concepts and issues that relate to personal and family wealth management. Fortunately, there are several helpful texts available for readers who wish to pursue specific topics in more depth, including, among others: Bittker et al., Federal Income Taxation of Individuals (3d ed. 2002); CCH, U.S. Master Tax Guide (published annually); and Chirelstein, Federal Income Taxation, A Law Student's Guide to the Leading Cases and Concepts (9th ed. 2002).

We begin this chapter by discussing what constitutes income and what are the principal statutory exclusions from income. We then examine the deductions and tax credits that are of primary interest to individuals and families, and consider the tax treatment of business expenses and major capital investments. Next, we discuss the concept of "basis" and its role in computing gain or loss for tax purposes. This is followed by a discussion of the preferential tax treatment accorded to capital gains. We also consider the various taxpaying entities and the topic of assignment of income. We address the tax treatment of investments, followed by a discussion of tax accounting methods. The chapter concludes with a brief overview of the alternative minimum tax.

B. WHAT IS INCOME

[¶ 3,004]

It will be useful to begin with a brief discussion of what economists generally agree is an acceptable working definition of income. This is important because the theoretical definition of income helps to explain why various items are taxed as income and why deductions are allowed for certain expenditures.

[¶ 3,008]

1. Income Defined

A group of early modern economists conceived of income as a flow of satisfactions consisting of intangible psychological experiences. In fact, most of us implicitly accept such a definition of income when we place value on intangibles such as climate, geography and cultural amenities in deciding where to live and what sort of job opportunities to pursue. The main difficulty with this approach is that it fails to provide a workable definition that can be used to allocate the tax burden among different individuals. For example, how should one assign value to highly subjective variables such as environment, demography and lifestyle? While one person may place great value on living in a large and diverse city with access to restaurants, theater, museums and sports events, another person may yearn to settle down in a small, homogeneous community surrounded by friends and family.

The need to develop a workable standard for measuring the flow of satisfactions that constitute income led theorists to equate income with the value of goods and services needed to produce the flow of satisfactions. For purposes of allocating tax liability among individuals, the generally accepted definition of income flows from the work of two prominent economists, Robert M. Haig and Henry C. Simons. The Haig–Simons definition of income posits that: "Personal income may be defined as the algebraic sum of (1) the market value of rights exercised in consumption and (2) the change in the value of the store of property rights between the beginning and end of the period in question." Simons, Personal Income Taxation 50 (1938). In brief, to ascertain a person's income for a particular year under the Haig–Simons definition, one would have to know the value of all goods and services that the person consumed during the year and add to that amount any increase in the person's net worth (or subtract any decrease in net worth) for the year.

The Haig–Simons definition expresses an abstract accounting identity (income equals consumption plus saving), but it does not provide a practical method for identifying or measuring specific items of income. To do this, we begin with a tally of an individual's measurable inflows of value in the form of money, goods and services, and then adjust that sum to reach as accurate a measure of income as is possible. Keeping this in mind will help to avoid the temptation to regard the Internal Revenue Code as a set of arbitrary rules. For example, suppose that Bob receives a salary of $100,000 and is ordered by a court to turn over $40,000 as alimony to his former wife Betty. Intuitively you may conclude that Bob's Haig–Simons income is only $60,000, and your instincts would be correct. The Internal Revenue Code produces this result not by measuring Bob's consumption of goods and services and his additions to (or subtractions from) savings, but by requiring Bob to include in income his full $100,000 salary and then allowing him a deduction for the alimony paid to Betty, with the result that he is taxed on only $60,000 of income. Because Betty is in a position to either consume or save the $40,000 received from Bob, she is treated as having $40,000 of income.

Keeping the Haig–Simons definition of income in mind will aid in understanding many of the results produced by the Internal Revenue Code as it attempts to tax income. For example, when an individual borrows money, regardless of whether she pledges property to secure the loan, we do not regard the loan proceeds as income because there is no increase in the borrower's net worth. If the borrower uses the loan proceeds to finance her living expenses, thereby decreasing her net worth, no deduction is allowed because the money has been spent on personal consumption. Under Haig–Simons, the decline in the taxpayer's net worth is offset by her consumption expenditures, resulting in no increase or decrease in her taxable income.

As we discuss what is taxed as income under the Internal Revenue Code, you will notice that statutory rules and judicial decisions often depart from the normative or ideal concept expressed in the Haig–Simons definition. These results may be inadvertent or may reflect a conscious policy decision. For example, we do not tax most annual changes in the value of investment assets, even though such changes directly affect net worth. Instead, we wait until the assets are sold or disposed of and then tax any resulting gains or allow a deduction for losses. This "realization" requirement rule flows from the Supreme Court decision in Eisner v. Macomber, 252 U.S. 189 (1920), which despite its questionable legal reasoning provides a pragmatic standard for determining the timing of taxable events. On other occasions, you will discover that Congress, for special policy reasons, has decided to exclude from income items such as scholarships or gifts which would otherwise be taxable as income. Understanding the breadth of the Haig–Simons definition of income helps to explain why Congress found it necessary to provide specific exclusions once it decided on the desired treatment of scholarships and gifts under the tax law.

[¶ 3,012]

2. Starting with the Internal Revenue Code

Section 61 of the Internal Revenue Code (the Code) is the starting point in determining what an individual must report as income. That provision requires that the taxpayer include in gross income various items from a non-exclusive list. The items mentioned include: compensation for services, income from a business, gains from sales of property, interest, rents, royalties, dividends, alimony, income from annuities, life insurance and endowment contracts, pensions, income from discharge of indebtedness, one's share of partnership profits, income in respect of a decedent and one's share of income from a trust or estate. Most of these items are likely familiar to most readers, but some items may require further explanation. Take, for example, income from discharge of indebtedness. Including such an amount in income makes sense in light of the Haig–Simons definition of income. Because forgiveness of indebtedness increases the net worth of the debtor as much as a salary or dividend of the same amount, it makes good sense to add it to the Code's list of items that constitute income. Income in respect of a decedent is a term that is probably unfamiliar to most people (other than tax lawyers and accountants). If an individual becomes entitled to receive income (for example, compensation for services rendered) but dies before receiving payment, in most cases she is not required to report it as her income. The item, however, retains its character as income and will eventually be taxed to the recipient when it is paid as "income in respect of a decedent."

In a typical federal income tax course, one would expect to spend considerable time and effort probing the outer limits of the concept of income. Here, however, such an exercise is unnecessary. In most cases families and individuals have little difficulty identifying various items as income. Indeed, the Internal Revenue Code employs § 61 as a broad brush which sweeps into the category of gross income virtually all positive inflows of value to an individual and then proceeds to exclude several items that would otherwise be included under § 61's broad brush. From this somewhat narrowed base, the Code allows deductions for specified items in computing taxable income.

[¶ 3,020]

3. Some Special Situations

Before turning to the principal exclusions and deductions which provide opportunities as well as headaches for taxpayers, tax lawyers and accountants, we look at a few special situations involving the definition of income.

In Kind Compensation. Most taxpayers who perform services receive compensation in cash, and the amount of cash received constitutes the measure of their income. Occasionally, however, taxpayers receive compensation in kind. For example, a developer who is short of cash may transfer one of the lots in a new subdivision to a contractor as compensation for construction services. Similarly, a lawyer who assists in setting up a start-up business may be compensated with stock in the new corporation. Where compensation consists of property other than cash, the taxpayer must report the fair market value of the property received as income in the year of receipt. If the taxpayer later sells the property, his gain or loss on that transaction will be measured by the difference between the sales proceeds and the amount previously included in income. For example, assume that the lot received by the contractor was worth $20,000 when received and that he reported that sum as income in the year of receipt. If he sells it two years later for $30,000, he will report the $10,000 gain as income in the year of sale.

Special rules apply to the taxation of restricted property such as stock options provided to executives under circumstances where the property may not be sold by the holder for a period of time. See I.R.C. § 83. Those interested in this topic are referred to the sources mentioned in ¶ 3,000.

Below Market Loans. Occasionally an employer or a family member makes a loan to an individual at no interest (or at an interest rate substantially below what a commercial lender would charge). By forgoing all or part of the interest that would have been charged in an arm's-length transaction, the lender is in effect conferring an economic benefit on the borrower. The Code recognizes this by treating the transaction as if the lender transferred the forgone interest to the borrower, who then paid interest back to the lender at the full market rate (determined by reference to the rate of interest on federal obligations). See I.R.C. § 7872. As a result, the lender must report interest at the full market rate; the borrower may or may not be allowed an offsetting interest deduction, depending on how she uses the loan proceeds. See ¶ 3,170.

Imputed Income. The Haig–Simons definition of income helps to explain a concept that economists refer to as "imputed income." When an individual performs services for herself or when she makes personal use of tangible property, she is consuming the value of the services or property in question. The Code does not require that she pay tax on the value of the services or property consumed. This implicit tax exemption for the imputed value of services and goods constitutes a significant tax break for individuals. For example, suppose that Mary is a lawyer who takes one day to prepare an estate plan for a client and bills $1,000 for her work. After paying her federal, state and local income taxes (as well as payroll taxes), she is left with $500 for her day's work. Mary has yet to do her own estate plan. She has two choices. First, she can hire her friend John, who also charges $1,000 for an estate plan. To pay John $1,000 Mary would have to work two days. Second, Mary can take one day off from work and prepare her own estate plan. She can then keep her after-tax earnings of $500 from the second day's work for her own use. The second choice is clearly preferable to the first choice because we do not tax Mary on the imputed income value of services that she performs for her own benefit. This approach rewards people who engage in do-it-yourself activities. It also explains the practical wisdom of people who say that they are better off staying home and caring for their children and performing domestic chores rather than earning a salary and paying someone else to perform the same services.

The value of imputed income with respect to consumer durables is equally important but slightly less obvious. To illustrate, suppose that in a subdivision with identical homes, you own a home outright and free of debt. To obtain a place to live you have two choices. First, you can rent out the home you own for $1,500 per month and then, after paying $500 tax on the rental income, you can live in an identical home that you rent from another owner for $1,500 per month. Second, you can simply live in the home that you own. Clearly you are better off living in your own home rather than renting out your home, paying tax on the income and then renting an identical home from someone else. The non-taxation of the imputed income from your use of your own home constitutes a significant tax advantage of home ownership and helps to explain the strong preference of most people for owning their own homes rather than renting. The tax advantage derived from the non-taxation of imputed income is not limited to home ownership but extends to all consumer durables such as household furnishings, automobiles and other personal possessions.

The Tax Benefit Rule. Assume that three years ago Betty gave $5,000 to a museum to build a new wing on the museum, and took a deduction for her charitable contribution. Having failed to meet its fundraising goals, the museum now decides that it must abandon the plans for a new wing and return all contributions previously received from donors during the fundraising campaign. How should Betty report this transaction on her tax return? The courts (and later Congress) have determined that Betty should simply include the $5,000 "refund" in income in the year of receipt. It would make no sense to force her to amend her tax return for the earlier year, because she originally made a completed gift with no strings attached and properly took a charitable deduction for $5,000. However, the return of the $5,000 three years later increases her net worth, putting her in the same position as if she had never made the original gift. Accordingly, the Code requires that she include in income an amount equal to the tax benefit or deduction previously allowed. See I.R.C. § 111(a). Now, let us assume that in the year that Betty made the gift of $5,000, her total itemized deductions exceeded the standard deduction for that year by only $4,000, so that her gift generated a tax benefit of only $4,000. (In other words, but for the gift to the museum she would have used the standard deduction.) In this case, the tax benefit rule of § 111(a) would only require that she include $4,000 in income when the museum returned her $5,000 gift.

The tax benefit rule raises several additional points. First, the amount the taxpayer is required to include is independent of the tax rates that prevailed in the year of deduction and in the year of correction. The relevant number is the amount of tax benefit (deduction) in the original year. See Alice Phelan Sullivan Corp. v. U.S., 381 F.2d 399 (Ct. Cl. 1967). Second, there is an income corollary of the tax benefit rule, but it seldom applies to individual taxpayers. Third, occasionally the item in question involves property other than cash (e.g., a gift of land to a charity). In such cases the amount that the taxpayer must include in income is limited to the lesser of the original tax benefit or the value of the property being returned. See Rosen v. Commissioner, 71 T.C. 226 (1978); Alice Phelan Sullivan Corp. v. Commissioner, supra. Fourth, taxpayers who itemize their deductions may encounter the tax benefit rule when they obtain an income tax refund from state or local tax authorities. They will commonly receive from state and local tax officials in the following year a notice informing them that if they itemize deductions they must include the amount of the refund in income to the extent it resulted in a tax benefit for them. This is the tax benefit rule in operation. This is such a common event that the basic federal income tax return (Form 1040) contains a separate line for reporting such income from the refund of state and local income taxes. In such circumstances it is important to recall the limitation imposed by § 111(a) on the tax benefit rule.

[¶ 3,025]

Problems

1.   Tom is an attorney who specializes in estate planning. Ricardo provides home improvement services. Tom recently discovered several safety hazards at his home that required prompt attention and asked Ricardo to give him a bid on the job. Ricardo told him that it would cost $1,500, plus materials to make the necessary repairs. Tom offered to provide Ricardo with estate planning services in exchange for Ricardo's performing the services after Tom purchases the necessary materials. Do Tom and Ricardo have any taxable income which would result from this arrangement and, if so, in what amount?

2.   Your sister Barbara has recently retired the mortgage on her home and bemoans the fact that she has thereby lost a major tax benefit of home ownership, the right to deduct mortgage interest on her residence. She said she is thinking of taking out a new home equity loan of $80,000 so as to "reacquire" this tax benefit. Advise Barbara.

3.   Last year Norma gave $8,000 to the city museum to enable it to purchase a painting. Because the museum is a charity, Norma took a charitable contribution deduction for the sum. Norma has considerable income and in the year of her gift she had itemized deductions in excess of $30,000. This year, just before the museum was about to go through with the purchase, it discovered that the seller's chain of title to the painting was clouded as a result of the painting having been seized by the Nazis during World War II. The museum backed out of the proposed purchase and recently refunded all donations. Norma asks you if she should amend her prior year's tax return to reflect the return of her gift.

[¶ 3,030]

4.   Social Security Benefits

The taxation of Social Security retirement benefits presents a special situation. Originally such benefits were completely exempt from income tax. Starting in 1984, Congress began to look to these benefits as a source of revenue as deficits grew under the weight of massive tax cuts put through in the first year of the Reagan administration. As deficits continued to grow over the years, so too did Congress's interest in these benefits as a source of tax revenue.

Under § 86 of the Code, Social Security benefits are initially not includible in gross income if the taxpayer's modified adjusted income (i.e., adjusted gross income plus tax-exempt interest and certain other items normally excluded from income) is less than $32,000 for a married couple or $25,000 for a single individual. Above these thresholds, taxpayers may find that anywhere from 50% to 85% of their Social Security benefits are subject to income tax. Most comfortably retired married couples normally find that by the time their modified adjusted gross income plus taxed Social Security benefits reaches about $60,000, they are subject to tax on 85% of their Social Security benefits.

C. EXCLUSIONS

[¶ 3,050]

For policy reasons Congress allows exclusions for a number of items which would otherwise be includible in gross income under the broad brush of § 61. We discuss here some of those exclusions, with particular attention to items that are likely to be relevant for individuals and families. The items discussed do not come near exhausting the full range of exclusions provided by the Code.

[¶ 3,060]

1. Gifts and Inheritances

Under § 102 of the Code, gifts and inheritances are generally excluded from the recipient's gross income. Sums paid out as settlements of claims of a will contest are also treated as if they had been paid out as an inheritance and are covered by the exclusion provided by § 102. See Lyeth v. Hoey, 305 U.S. 188 (1938).

The principal legal difficulties in this area arise in distinguishing tax-free gifts from taxable compensation. For example, people in a service industry often receive tips or gratuities equal to a percentage charge which is either included in the customer's bill or given by the customer out of appreciation for services well rendered. These and other similar items, such as honoraria paid to a clergyman or a lecturer, are not deemed to be gifts but rather are taxed as compensation for services rendered.

The exclusion of § 102 is subject to two important limitations. First, the exclusion does not apply to income on gifts and inheritances or to gifts or bequests consisting of income. I.R.C. § 102(b). This means, for example, that although a gift of stock is excluded from income, dividends subsequently declared and paid on the stock are taxed to the donee. Similarly, if a decedent devises land to A for life with remainder to B, A is taxable on the rental income collected during his life, even though he received his life estate by devise. The second limitation is found in § 102(c), which provides that—except in limited circumstances involving employee achievement awards (e.g. a safety award) of limited value or de minimis fringe benefits specifically excluded from income under § 132— the exclusion of § 102 does not apply to any amount transferred from an employer to an employee. This last provision was added to prevent abuses where an employer might seek to provide a tax-free bonus to an employee by labeling it as a gift rather than as compensation.

For our purposes, the principal significance of § 102 is to assure us that gifts and inheritances of property are free from income tax and to inform us that the exclusion does not extend to the income produced by gifted or inherited property.

[¶ 3,070]

2. Life Insurance

In most circumstances, life insurance proceeds paid out by reason of the insured person's death are excluded from the recipient's gross income under § 101 of the Code. Congress most likely chose to provide this exclusion from taxation to avoid imposing an additional burden on the decedent's survivors, who are often already suffering economic deprivation. Because insurance basically constitutes a device for shifting and spreading the risk of loss among a large pool of policy holders, a requirement that life insurance proceeds be included in gross income might have paved the way for allowing a deduction for premiums paid, in order to avoid taxing the same funds twice. Providing an exclusion for benefits can be viewed as a preemptive strike against such a rule.

There are several exceptions to the broad exclusionary rule of § 101. First, the exclusion does not apply to interest or other income earned on proceeds that are left with the insurance company after the insured's death. Second, when a life insurance policy is transferred for a "valuable consideration," the exclusion is available only for the purchase price paid by the new owner plus any subsequent premium payments. I.R.C. § 101(a)(2). This rule is intended primarily to reach situations where a person who owns a policy on his own life sells the policy to a new owner in order to raise money during his last days. There are two exceptions to the transfer-for-value rule: (1) where the basis of the transferred policy carries over in the hands of the new owner (typically a gift, bargain sale or other tax-free transfer); and (2) where the new owner of the policy is the insured, a partner of the insured, a partnership with the insured as a partner, or a corporation in which the insured owns stock. I.R.C. § 101(a)(2)(A), (B). The first exception typically covers a situation where the insured transfers a policy on her life to a family member in a bargain sale transaction. The second exception covers many transfers of policies among business associates for good business reasons—for example, to implement a buy-sell agreement among shareholders or partners, or to reward a retiring employee with a "key person" policy on her life when the policy is no longer needed by the employer. Clearly, neither of the two statutory exceptions involves the sort of speculation in life insurance policies that prompted the transfer-for-value rule of § 101(a)(2).

Since the AIDS crisis erupted in the 1980's, many individuals with policies on their lives have found it necessary to sell their policies either to the insurer or to a third party in order to obtain money for end-of-life medical care. As originally drafted, § 101 did not exclude any such amounts from income, and this resulted in a significant reduction in the amount of money available to cover medical expenses. In 1996 Congress responded by providing that, in the case of a terminally or chronically ill insured, amounts paid out under policies by insurers or as viatical settlements by persons in the viatical settlement business shall be deemed paid out by reason of death. Accordingly, such amounts, when paid to such individuals, are excluded from the recipient's gross income. I.R.C. § 101(g).

One final point concerning life insurance deserves mention. A premium statement may show a "dividend" that reduces the amount of premiums due under the policy; occasionally, the insurer may actually send out a check in the amount of the dividend. These "dividends" actually represent a refund of previously paid premiums that proved to be in excess of the amount needed to cover the mortality risk assumed by the insurer. As such, they do not represent income that is subject to taxation except in the rare case where the total "dividends" received exceed the total premiums paid over the life of the policy. For a more complete discussion of the income taxation of life insurance see ¶ 7,150.

[¶ 3,080]

3. Employment Related Exclusions

The Internal Revenue Code allows especially favorable treatment for a host of "fringe benefits" that employers routinely provide for their employees. The cost of such benefits is allowed as a deduction to the employer as an ordinary business expense, while the value of the benefits is excluded from the employee's gross income. This tax treatment reduces the effective cost to the employer of providing fringe benefits and also enhances the value to the employee, especially in the case of benefits such as health insurance, which the employee would otherwise purchase with after-tax dollars. Typically, employers acting on behalf of hundreds or thousands of employees can use their bargaining power to obtain dramatically lower per employee costs for benefits such as health insurance and group life insurance. In addition, as noted elsewhere, such employer provided insurance packages reduce the problem of adverse selection (see ¶ 7,020).

In comparing various job opportunities, an individual should pay close attention to the different fringe benefits offered by prospective employers, assuming that the benefits are of value to the individual. For example, suppose that Maria is offered a position with Acme Consulting at $100,000 per year and one with Baxter Industries at $93,000 per year. Baxter provides its employees with tax-free health insurance coverage, and Maria would have to pay $7,000 per year to purchase a comparable individual policy from a commercial insurer. Acme, on the other hand, provides no health insurance benefits. Assume that Maria's effective combined marginal federal and state tax rate is 30% and that she is not in a position to benefit from a medical expense deduction for any health insurance premiums. If Maria accepts the position with Acme, she will need $10,000 of pre-tax earnings to obtain a comparable health insurance policy ($10,000 salary less $3,000 tax leaves $7,000 after tax). After paying for an individual policy, the package offered by Acme will leave Maria with only $90,000 of (pre-tax) salary—$3,000 less than the package offered by Baxter. The lesson for employees is that a well-designed compensation package with substantial tax-free benefits is extremely valuable and can outweigh the initial appeal of a higher salary.

It is beyond the scope of this book to provide a detailed description of the requirements for the full range of tax-free fringe benefits. Instead, we will take a brief look at a few of the fringe benefits commonly offered by employers.

Health Insurance. Under §§ 105 and 106, health insurance benefits received by an employee under an employer-provided plan, as well as contributions made by the employer under such a plan, are excluded from the employee's gross income. Health insurance benefits are excluded regardless of whether they are paid by an insurance company under a contract with the employer or directly by the employer as a self-insurer.

Retirement Benefits. An employer is generally entitled to a deduction for contributions made to a qualified pension plan for the benefit of employees. Moreover, such contributions are not immediately taxable to the employees. The qualified plan itself is a tax-exempt entity, with the result that neither the employer's contributions nor the investment earnings thereon are subject to income taxation until distributions are made to the employees. Similar treatment is allowed for employee contributions to certain types of qualified plans sponsored by the employer. See §§ 401–404, 410–417. Retirement benefits are discussed in detail in Chapter 8.

Life Insurance. Many employers provide group term life insurance for their employees. Under § 79, the cost of the first $50,000 of coverage per employee is excluded from the employee's gross income if the group term life insurance is provided on a non-discriminatory basis. Moreover, although the employee is taxable on the cost of any coverage above the $50,000 limit, the method for valuing the excess coverage typically produces a lower cost than the employee would incur in purchasing comparable coverage in the open market.

Education Assistance Programs. Under § 127, an employee may exclude from gross income up to $5,250 of employer-provided education assistance. The employee may not be given a choice to accept such tax-free benefits in lieu of additional taxable compensation. Section 127 is discussed in more detail at ¶ 6,180.

Dependent Care. Under § 129, an employee may exclude from gross income up to $5,000 of dependent care expenses paid or incurred by the employer. (The limit is $2,500 in the case of a married individual filing a separate return.) The amount so excluded may not exceed the employee's earned income (or, in the case of a married employee, the earned income of the employee's spouse, if it is less). If such benefits are made available to the employee as part of a cafeteria plan under § 125, the employee may elect to receive tax-free dependent care in lieu of additional taxable compensation.

Adoption Assistance. Under § 137, an employee may exclude from gross income up to $10,000 paid by the employer to assist the employee in meeting qualified adoption expenses (adoption, attorney and court fees). The exclusion under § 137 phases out for employees with adjusted gross income between $150,000 and $190,000.

Moving Expenses. Employers often pay or reimburse moving expenses incurred by an employee in connection with taking a new job. Under § 132(a)(6), the employee may exclude such payment or reimbursement from gross income if the expenses would otherwise be deductible by the employee under § 217. Not all moving expenses meet the requirements of § 217, and employers often tailor their reimbursement programs to cover only expenses that would be deductible under § 217 if paid by the employee.

Miscellaneous Fringe Benefits. Under § 132, in addition to moving expenses, employees may receive free of tax certain job-related fringe benefits including: (1) no-additional-cost services such as standby airfare provided to employees by an airline; (2) qualified employee discounts such as the right to purchase a store's product line for a discount (as long as the discount does not result in goods being sold below cost); (3) "working condition" fringe benefits involving goods or services to the extent their cost would be deductible by the employee as a business expense (such as a Wall Street Journal subscription delivered to an investment banker at home); (4) de minimis benefits such as free incidental use of photocopy machines for personal purposes; (5) certain commuter transportation services such as van transportation, transit passes or qualified parking; and (6) certain retirement planning services.

Meals and Lodging. Under § 119, the value of meals and lodging provided to an employee (and the employee's spouse and dependents) for the convenience of the employer is excluded from the employee's gross income. In the case of meals, the meals must be provided on the employer's premises, and in the case of lodging, the employee must be required to accept the lodging on the employer's premises as a condition of employment. An example of qualifying lodging would be an apartment in a hotel that the hotel manager is required to occupy under her employment contract. Similarly, meals consumed by the manager in the hotel dining room would qualify for the exclusion under § 119.

Cafeteria Plans. Under § 125, an employer may offer employees a choice to receive certain qualified tax-free fringe benefits described above (such as health insurance, group term life insurance and dependent care services) in lieu of additional taxable compensation. The advantage of a cafeteria plan is that it enables employees to select the benefits that are most valuable to them in their particular circumstances. For example, a married employee with dependent children may elect to accept full family health insurance (as allowed by § 106) and up to $5,000 in child care (as allowed by § 129), while another employee whose spouse already has employer-provided health insurance may elect to receive $50,000 of group term life insurance (as allowed by § 79) and take all other compensation in cash, and a third employee who is single may simply prefer to take all compensation in cash.

Cafeteria plans often allow the employee to set aside a portion of her pre-tax salary in a so-called "flexible spending account" which can be drawn down to pay for medical expenses not covered by a health insurance plan (e.g., deductible amounts and co-payments) or for up to $5,000 of child care services. The employer may farm out the administration of such accounts to an outside agency, which receives documentation of qualifying expenses from employees and makes payment or reimbursement from funds provided by the employer. Because any unspent funds in the accounts are forfeited at year end, employees often fail to make optimal use of their accounts.

The Non–Discrimination Requirement. Many, but not all, of the above fringe benefits qualify for tax exclusion only if they meet specific economic non-discrimination requirements. For example, non-discrimination requirements apply to pension benefits, payments from self-insured health and accident plans (§ 105), the $50,000 employee group term life insurance benefit (§ 79), education benefits (§ 127), adoption assistance (§ 137), dependent care assistance (§ 129), and no-additional-cost services and employee discounts (§ 132). In certain other cases, an employer may provide fringe benefits on a discriminatory basis without jeopardizing the employee's tax exclusion. For example, an employer may provide health insurance and some work-related fringe benefits that favor highly-compensated individuals. Most employers are well aware of the importance to employees of the tax exclusion and design fringe benefit packages accordingly. Occasionally, however, in order to attract a particular employee, the employer may fashion a special individualized benefit package that does not qualify for tax exclusion.

[¶ 3,090]

4. Interest on State and Local Bonds

Under § 103 of the Code, interest on most state and local indebtedness is exempt from federal income taxation. Because the tax exemption is attractive to many investors, especially those in high tax brackets, these bonds bear interest at rates below the prevailing rates on comparable taxable bonds issued by private corporations. The interest rate on a tax-exempt bond is typically about 80% of the rate that one would expect to receive on a taxable bond of comparable quality. The lower interest rates on tax-exempt bonds, of course, offer an advantage to state and local governments that issue debt to finance public projects such as schools and highways. In some cases, investors may realize a higher after-tax yield on state and local bonds than they would on fully taxable corporate bonds of comparable quality. For example, assume that Norman, whose marginal federal tax rate is 35%, has the choice of purchasing, for $10,000, a taxable General Electric bond that pays 8% interest or a State of Indiana bond that pays 6.4% interest. If he purchases the GE bond he will owe tax of $280 (35% of $800) on the $800 of interest, leaving him with $520 after tax. On the other hand, if he purchases the Indiana bond he will receive $640 of interest completely free of federal income tax.

State and local bonds raise several additional issues. First, not all bonds issued by state and local governments are tax exempt. In response to abuses—for example, the use of municipal bonds to finance industrial and commercial development—Congress has sharply limited (but not entirely eliminated) tax-exempt status for "private activity" bonds, and investors should exercise caution when purchasing such bonds. Second, most states accord tax-exempt status to their own bonds and those of their local governments for state income tax purposes, thereby further enhancing the value of their bonds for their own residents. They do not, however, give the same favorable treatment to bonds of other states. This can lead to unpleasant consequences for an investor who holds a portfolio of tax-exempt bonds issued by his state of residence and then, upon moving out of state, discovers that the bond interest is no longer exempt from state income tax (although the federal tax exemption remains unimpaired). Finally, while many taxable corporate bonds are publicly traded, an investor may encounter difficulty in disposing of state and local bonds. Often the only practical way to dispose of such bonds is through a small regional investment banking house, which can involve unexpectedly high transaction costs.

[¶ 3,100]

5. Other Relevant Exclusions

The Code provides several other exclusions of interest here, relating to income from forgiveness of indebtedness, scholarships, and gain from the sale of a principal residence. The tax treatment of scholarships and home sales will be addressed in some detail in subsequent chapters, and accordingly will be mentioned only briefly here.

Forgiveness of Indebtedness. As mentioned above, because forgiveness of indebtedness increases the debtor's net worth, it makes sense to include the amount of the increase under the Haig–Simons definition of income. See I.R.C. § 108.

In some cases, however, debt forgiveness does not give rise to income. For example, if a debt is forgiven as a gift, the resulting increase in net worth is excluded from the debtor's gross income under § 102 (see ¶ 3,020). Suppose that, on Sally's graduation from law school, her parents, who had loaned her $5,000 toward the last semester's tuition, tell her that as a graduation gift they are forgiving repayment of the loan. The $5,000 is excluded from Sally's gross income under § 102. It is also common for a testator to cancel a family member's outstanding debt in her will. This too qualifies for the § 102 exclusion.

Another common situation in which debt forgiveness does not result in income to the debtor involves purchase price adjustments that are made after the time of sale when the buyer discovers that goods are defective or the seller retroactively reduces the amount due to match a competitor's lower price. See I.R.C. § 108(e)(5). For example, in Washington Package Store, Inc. v. Commissioner, 23 T.C.M. (CCH) 1805 (1964), a buyer of a business negotiated with the seller for a non-compete agreement and agreed to pay the purchase price in installments. The seller subsequently violated the non-compete agreement, and the buyer agreed not to seek an injunction against the seller in exchange for cancellation of the remaining installments. The court held that the debt forgiveness was merely a purchase price adjustment which did not constitute taxable income to the buyer.

A third exception to the basic debt forgiveness rule involves certain student loans that expressly provide for cancellation if the student borrower pursues a career in specified charitable or educational services. This sort of loan forgiveness program can, in essence, be viewed as a scholarship that is awarded after the completion of studies. See I.R.C. § 108(f)(2). For further discussion, see ¶ 6,190.

The last major type of tax-free debt forgiveness that we will consider involves economically distressed taxpayers whose debts are forgiven either due to insolvency (i.e., the creditor abandons collection efforts because the debtor's liabilities exceed her assets) or in a Title 11 bankruptcy proceeding. See I.R.C. § 108(a)(1)(A), (B). In the case of an insolvent taxpayer, the exclusion applies only to the extent that the taxpayer was insolvent prior to discharge. For example, assume that Carla had $50,000 of assets and owed $65,000 to a creditor who forgave the debt after unsuccessfully pursuing collection efforts. Because Carla's liabilities prior to discharge exceeded her assets by $15,000, the amount excluded from her gross income under § 108(a)(1)(B) is limited to $15,000; after discharge she has a positive net worth of $50,000, and she must include that amount in gross income. The insolvency and bankruptcy exclusions come at a cost to the taxpayer, who may have to give up several valuable tax attributes in order to take advantage of the exclusions. It is not necessary to explore those adjustments here, except to note that they are intended to compensate for the tax advantage of the exclusion from gross income under § 108. For example, an insolvent taxpayer who excludes $10,000 of debt forgiveness from gross income may be required to reduce by $10,000 the amount of certain unused tax losses carried forward from previous years. The practical significance of § 108 is that it shields insolvent or bankrupt taxpayers from immediate income tax liability when they obtain a discharge of debts that could not have been collected in any event. Unscrupulous creditors occasionally attempt to intimidate debtors or discourage them from filing for bankruptcy by telling them that debt forgiveness would have dire income tax consequences. Debtors familiar with the § 108 exclusion will not be misled.

Scholarships. Section 117 of the Code allows students at conventional educational institutions to exclude from gross income most scholarship aid in the form of assistance for tuition, books and related fees (but not for room and board). This exclusion is discussed in detail at ¶ 6,170.

Gain on Sale of a Residence. Section 121 allows a taxpayer to exclude up to $250,000 ($500,000 for a married couple filing jointly) of gain on the sale of a principal residence. Only gain from the sale of a principal residence qualifies for exclusion. Moreover, to obtain full benefit of the exclusion, the residence must have served as the taxpayer's principal residence for two out of the last five years, although the amount of the exclusion may be prorated in cases where it has served as a principal residence for less than two years and hardship such as a change of place of employment or health factors mandated a sale. A taxpayer who claims the § 121 exclusion for a sale of a residence may not claim the exclusion again for a subsequent sale within the next two years. For example, assume that Gail, a single taxpayer, purchased a home on May 1, 2002, leased the home to others until October 31, moved into the home on November 1, and made it her principal residence for one year; on November 1, 2003, in connection with a job transfer to a distant location, she sold the home for a profit of $150,000. Because Gail occupied the home as her principal residence for only 12 months, she can use only one-half of the $250,000 exclusion ($125,000) against the $150,000 gain, leaving her with $25,000 of taxable gain. She is not required to use the sale proceeds to purchase a new residence to obtain the benefit of the exclusion, but, if she does purchase a new residence she cannot take make use of the § 121 exclusion for any sale occurring before November 1, 2005. The § 121 exclusion is discussed in more detail in ¶ 5,710.

Compensation for Personal Injuries. Section 104(a)(2) of the Code excludes from gross income "any damages (other than punitive damages) received (whether by suit or agreement and whether as lump sums or as periodic payments) on account of personal injuries or physical sickness." The principal significance of this exclusion is that it represents a limited departure from the rules that normally govern the taxation of damages. In general, the taxation of damages is based on the nature of the item for which compensation is being made. For example, if a business is compensated for lost profits from a plant closure caused by a third party's tortious conduct, the full amount of the damages recovered from the third party to compensate for lost profits is subject to taxation. On the other hand, if an individual who was swindled out of $1,000 of after-tax earnings recovers the $1,000 in a court action, the individual should not be required to include the recovery in gross income (unless, of course, the recovery is subject to the tax benefit rule discussed in ¶ 3,020). Similarly, if an individual had just purchased a used car for $4,000 and the car was totally destroyed through the negligence of a third party whose insurer paid the car's owner $5,000 as compensation for loss of the car, the car's owner would have a gain of $1,000 on the recovery.

The principal significance of § 104(a)(2) for individuals who suffer physical injuries or sicknesses is that the exclusion for damages covers even those portions of recoveries based on lost earnings which would otherwise be taxable. Note that punitive damages (except where recovered as a substitute for wrongful death awards in Massachusetts and Alabama) are subject to taxation even if they are awarded in a case involving physical injury or sickness. Also outside the § 104(a) exclusion are damages for emotional distress (except to the extent that they cover medical care such as psychiatric services, medications to treat the condition and transportation to obtain such care). By making "physical injuries or physical sickness" an essential requirement for tax-exempt recovery, Congress has made subject to taxation recoveries for several whole classes of torts such as defamation, invasion of privacy, and discrimination on account of gender, age and race. It is important to note that emotional injuries that are the direct consequence of a physical injury are still exempt from taxation under § 104(a). For example, an individual who suffered severe facial scarring in an automobile accident would not be subject to tax on her damages for emotional distress.

When a lawsuit involves a combination of claims, some of which would qualify for exclusion, attorneys are often able to work out compromise arrangements with insurers that tilt in favor of nontaxable items. The resulting settlement, after taxes, may be more favorable for the client than a larger but more heavily taxed jury award.

[¶ 3,115]

Problems

1. The president of a nationally prominent university is retiring. As a member of the board of trustees of the university, you are asked if the university could make a tax-free gift of $200,000 to her in recognition of her leadership. One of your co-trustees thinks that any such gifts should be taxed as compensation. Another trustee suggests that perhaps the gift should be given to the husband of the president in gratitude for his sacrificing the pleasure of her company as she labored away on behalf of the university for so many years. Please comment on the tax consequences of the various proposals.

2. Peter retired as president of U.S. Industries last year and upon retiring was offered the opportunity of purchasing from the company a

$2,000,000 insurance policy that the company had on his life. Peter purchased the policy for its fair market value. This year he died and his widow Moira collected not only $2,000,000 on the policy that Peter had purchased from his former employer but also $50,000 on a policy that he had taken out years ago when they married. Are the proceeds collected under either policy subject to income taxation?

3.   When you graduate and enter the work force why should you care about any compensation related issues other than salary? What types of benefits should be of paramount interest?

4.   You have been asked to make a presentation to a local investment club about the value of investing in state and local tax-exempt bonds. Prepare yourself to discuss, in general, the benefits and drawbacks of such investments and the type of investors who should and who should not be interested in such bonds.

5.   As an inducement for you to accept employment with an employer in an area with high housing costs, the prospective employer offers you: (1) a $500,000 interest-free line of credit which may be drawn down to meet the cost of purchasing a principal residence; and (2) the promise that, if you remain in his employ for two years, for every additional year that you remain with the company, the employer will forgive $100,000 of the indebtedness. What are the tax consequences of this offer?

D.   PERSONAL DEDUCTIONS

[¶ 3,120]

There are two principal types of deductions available to a taxpayer in determining net taxable income. The first category involves expenditures that were necessary to generate income from a trade or business or from a transaction entered into for profit. In most (but not all) cases, these deductions can be viewed as implementing the Haig–Simons definition in arriving at net taxable income. These deductions, commonly referred to as business deductions, are discussed in more detail at ¶¶ 3,300 et seq. The second category consists of deductions for other expenses, which are commonly referred to as personal deductions. In some cases, such as the deduction for alimony, these deductions are consistent with the Haig–Simons concept of income. In other cases, such as the deduction for home mortgage interest, the deductions are not consistent with the Haig–Simons definition but rather reflect a policy decision by Congress to provide tax relief for certain types of expenditures or taxpayers.

The Internal Revenue Code measures income in three stages: (1) gross income, which is defined in § 61 and briefly discussed in ¶ 3,012; (2) adjusted gross income (AGI), which is equal to gross income less the deductions allowed by § 62 (discussed below); and (3) net taxable income, which is equal to AGI less the deductions allowed by other provisions of the Code. Many of the deductions allowed in computing net taxable income are subject to phaseouts or limitations based on AGI.

Gross income basically consists of gross receipts minus the cost of goods sold. For example, assume that a dealer in antique cars purchases a car from a supplier for $18,000 and sells it to a customer for $20,000 after incurring advertising expenses of $150. The dealer's gross income is $2,000, and his net income is $1,850 (gross income less costs incurred in connection with the sale).

Section 62 defines adjusted gross income as gross income minus numerous specified deductions. For most individuals, the most important items allowed as deductions in computing AGI are: (1) alimony; (2) interest on student loans; (3) losses on the sale of business or investment property; (4) contributions to qualified retirement savings plans; (5) moving expenses; (6) investment expenses; and (7) trade or business expenses.

After determining adjusted gross income, a taxpayer computes net taxable income by deducting either: (1) the standard deduction (a fixed amount based on filing status) and allowable personal exemptions; or (2) itemized personal deductions (e.g. state and local taxes, home mortgage interest and charitable contributions) and allowable personal exemptions.

Of principal concern here are the personal deductions for: (1) alimony; (2) charitable contributions; (4) state and local taxes; (3) home mortgage interest; (5) medical expenses; (6) casualty losses; and (7) education expenses.

[¶ 3,140]

1. The Standard Deduction

As noted above, after determining adjusted gross income, a taxpayer can elect either to take the standard deduction (which is inflation adjusted) or to itemize deductions. Normally, the taxpayer will choose whichever alternative produces the more favorable tax result.

Pursuant to § 63 of the Code, the standard deduction for 2004 was $4,850 for a single taxpayer, $7,150 for a head of household (typically an unmarried individual with at least one dependent child, step-child or grandchild), $9,700 for a married couple filing a joint return, or $4,850 for married individuals filing separately. If married couples file separate returns, both must either use the standard deduction or itemize deductions, and if one spouse itemizes deductions, the other spouse's standard deduction is reduced to zero. In addition, an individual who was claimed as a dependent on another taxpayer's return was allowed a standard deduction for 2004 of the greater of $800 or the sum of $250 and that individual's earned income (but not exceeding his or her basic standard deduction amount). For example, assume that Josh, who is 16 and was claimed as a dependent by his parents, earned $2,500 from a part time job and received $350 in interest income in 2004. Josh would be entitled to a standard deduction of $2,750. If Josh instead earned $5,000 and was still properly claimed as a dependent by his parents, he would be entitled to a standard deduction of $4,850. Historically the standard deduction for married couples filing jointly was less than double that of a single person. In 2003, Congress amended the statute to set the standard deduction for married couples equal to twice that of a single person. This change is effective through 2010.

A taxpayer who is blind or at least 65 years old was entitled in 2004 to an increase in her standard deduction ($950 for a married individual and $1,200 for an unmarried individual). These amounts and those noted in the preceding paragraph are all adjusted for inflation.

[¶ 3,150]

2. Alimony

Section 215 allows a taxpayer to deduct any alimony or separate maintenance payments made to a current or former spouse, to the extent such amounts are includible in the recipient spouse's income under § 71. As previously noted, the deduction for alimony is allowed in computing adjusted gross income. This means that a taxpayer who pays alimony gets the benefit of the deduction even if the taxpayer elects to take the standard deduction instead of itemizing his deductions. It is important to note that amounts paid as child support or as part of a marital property settlement are not deductible (nor are they includible in the recipient's income). These are important distinctions for taxpayers to keep in mind in negotiating the terms of a divorce or separation agreement. (In the following discussion, we use the term "alimony" to refer to alimony and separate maintenance payments, since both types of payments are subject to similar treatment for tax purposes.)

The deduction rule of § 215 is closely coordinated with the inclusion rule of § 71. To be deductible to the payor under § 215, an amount must qualify as alimony which is taxable to the recipient under § 71. For this purpose, payments qualify as alimony only if they are made in cash pursuant to a decree of divorce or separate maintenance. Moreover, payments do not qualify as alimony if they are designated in the decree as nondeductible, or if they are made between legally separated members of the same household, or if the payments are required to continue after the recipient's death. I.R.C. § 71(b)(1). These requirements were added to guard against what Congress deemed to be potential abuses. The cash payment rule stems from cases involving artists and craftspeople who paid alimony in paintings and handicrafts of dubious value; the separate household rule responds to cases involving legally separated spouses who shared living quarters; and the rule against post-death payments is intended to prevent taxpayers from converting nondeductible property settlements into deductible alimony.

Amounts paid as child support or as part of a marital property settlement do not qualify as alimony, and such amounts are neither deductible by the payor nor taxable to the payee. Nevertheless, divorced or separated parties sometimes find it mutually advantageous to substitute greater amounts of alimony for amounts that might otherwise be paid in the form of child support or a property settlement. For example, assume that Charles is in a 40% combined state and federal tax bracket and that his ex-wife Marion is in a 20% bracket. But for tax considerations, Charles and Marion would have agreed that he should pay Marion $20,000 in alimony and a property settlement of $80,000, resulting in an after-tax cost to Charles of $80,000 for the property settlement and $12,000 per year for the alimony ($20,000 minus the tax savings of $8,000 resulting from the deduction). Over five years, the total after-tax cost to Charles would be $140,000 ($80,000 property settlement plus $12,000 of alimony for 5 years). For Marion, the after-tax value of the five-year package would be $80,000 for the property settlement and $80,000 for the alimony ($20,000 minus $4,000 tax liability for 5 years), or $160,000. If Marion agrees to forgo the property settlement in exchange for higher alimony payments, despite the added tax burden for her, both parties might come out ahead after taxes. For example, suppose that the parties agree that Charles will pay nothing as a property settlement but instead will pay alimony of $48,500 per year for four years (a total of $194,000) and thereafter $20,000 per year. Over the five-year period, Charles would pay a total of $214,000 in alimony, but after deducting this entire amount at his 40% rate, Charles would have an after-tax cost of only $128,400, which is $11,600 less than the after-tax cost of the combined alimony/property settlement package. For Marion, the after-tax value of the five-year alimony-only package would be $171,200, which is $11,200 more than the after-tax value of the combined alimony/property settlement package. The only loser in this "win-win" scenario is the Internal Revenue Service. The same "win-win" strategy can also be applied to shift payments from child support (no deduction, no inclusion) to alimony (deduction to payor, inclusion to payee).

Section 71 imposes several rules to prevent taxpayers from disguising property settlement or child support payments as alimony. First, § 71(b)(1)(D) provides that there must be no continuing liability to make alimony payments after the payee's death. A payee who is concerned about the possibility of premature death might take out a policy of term insurance on her life with declining coverage over the payment period. In addition, § 71(c) provides that purported alimony may be recharacterized as child support payments to the extent that the divorce decree or separation agreement calls for a decrease or termination in payments on the occurrence of a contingency relating to a child (such as reaching age 18 or 21, leaving school, marrying or dying). Finally, § 71(f) provides an anti-front-loading rule to prevent deductible alimony from being substituted for nondeductible property settlement payments. There is no need to go into the details of § 71(f) here, except to note that, in general, if there is more than a modest decline in alimony payments during the first three years, a portion of the earlier payments must be added back into the payor's income and deducted from the payee's income. The anti-front-loading rule of § 71(f) does not apply where alimony payments terminate by reason of the payee's death or remarriage.

The "win-win" strategy has several potential dangers for the payor and the payee. For the payor, there is always the risk that his income and marginal tax bracket may decrease, thereby reducing the value of any tax savings. In an extreme case, the payor could actually end up paying more when after-tax savings are considered. The payor should also consider the possibility that child custody arrangements might change, leaving the payor with the combined burdens of raising children and unreduced alimony payments. Seeking relief from a court is likely to be time-consuming and expensive. Also, there is the emotional risk that young children may not grasp the tax considerations and may conclude from the terms of the agreement (perhaps with encouragement from an angry ex-spouse) that the payor is providing nothing for their support.

For the payee, the "win-win" strategy presents the risk that her income and marginal tax bracket may rise, reducing the after-tax value of the payments. Also, given the bad record of many payors in meeting their obligations, the payee may reasonably prefer to get a bird in the hand in the form of an immediate property settlement. Another risk for a payee is that in many states alimony automatically terminates if the payee remarries. A payee who buys into the "win-win" strategy may discover belatedly that remarriage will entail the loss of payments which were nominally designated as alimony but actually represented her share of a soon-to-be-forfeited property settlement.

[¶ 3,155]

Problems

1. Irene consults you about the dissolution of her marriage. Her husband, Carlos, is a highly compensated corporate executive and, during their marriage, Irene withdrew from employment to raise their children Maria (age 8) and Nicholas (age 6). Carlos has told Irene that in lieu of a property settlement and providing child support, he will pay her significantly more alimony than he would normally be expected to pay under the circumstances. Irene asks you to explain to her why he would make such an offer and what factors should be considered in evaluating the sums that finally emerge from discussions.

2. What factors should Carlos be considering as he enters negotiations with Irene and her attorney?

[¶ 3,160]

3. Charitable Contributions

Section 170 allows an itemized personal deduction for the value of charitable contributions made to a qualifying organization described in § 170(c). Many commentators view the charitable deduction as a feature of a normative income tax under the Haig–Simons definition because the donor diminishes her net worth without engaging in any personal consumption of the transferred property. The true consumers of the transferred property, it is said, are the beneficiaries of the charitable organization. Critics of this view argue that the psychic rewards of charitable giving constitute a form of consumption and that any justification for the deduction must rest on public policy considerations such as promotion of art, education, religion and other charitable purposes.

There is no need here to describe in detail the types of organizations which qualify as recipients of tax-deductible contributions under § 170. In general, gifts to domestic federal or state governments or their subdivisions and to most organizations that one would normally consider to be charities qualify as valid charitable contributions under § 170. For example, a gift of land to a city to be used as a park, and gifts of cash or securities to churches, museums, schools or other charitable organizations are deductible under § 170. If there is any doubt about the charitable status of a particular organization, a prospective donor can ask the organization to furnish a copy of its exemption letter from the I.R.S. The donor may also to check the status of the organization by consulting the "Cumulative List of Organizations" (Pub. 940), which is available on the I.R.S. website at <www.irs.gov>.

Subject to limitations discussed below, individual taxpayers are allowed to deduct the full amount of cash or the fair market value of most property given to a charity. Before examining the restrictions on the charitable deduction for in-kind gifts, we will consider the advantages and disadvantages of allowing a deduction for the full fair market value of such property.

If an individual taxpayer makes a charitable contribution of assets that, if sold, would generate long term capital gain, the taxpayer is generally entitled to deduct the full fair market value of the assets. In contrast, if the contributed assets would generate ordinary income, the deduction is normally limited to the taxpayer's adjusted basis. I.R.C. § 170(e)(1)(A). Assume that Rashad holds ABC stock worth $50,000, which he purchased several years ago for $5,000. Rashad's combined state and federal tax rate is 40% and that his combined effective rate on long term capital gain is 20%. Rashad wishes to make a charitable contribution of $50,000. If he sold the ABC stock to fund the gift, he would pay $9,000 of tax on the $45,000 long term capital gain (at the 20% rate), leaving him with only $41,000 after tax. To make the $50,000 gift that he had planned to make, he would have to top up the after-tax proceeds with an additional $9,000. The cash gift of $50,000 in cash would save Rashad $20,000 in taxes at his 40% marginal tax rate. If Rashad instead gives the ABC stock directly to charity, he will be entitled to a $50,000 deduction, which will save him $20,000 on his income taxes (at the 40% rate); moreover, he will have no taxable gain on the gift of the appreciated stock. Clearly Rashad is far better off using appreciated property rather than cash to satisfy his charitable impulses.

The tax advantage of charitable contributions of appreciated property stems from a combination of: (1) the non-taxation of accrued appreciation until gain is realized on a sale; and (2) the deductibility of the full fair market value (including unrealized appreciation) of assets contributed to charity. Remember, though, that this advantage is generally available only for assets that would generate long term capital gain if sold. Such assets typically consist of appreciated investment property such as securities or land. Moreover, in the case of tangible personal property (such as a painting), the full fair market value deduction is available only if the charity's use of the donated property is related to the charity's exempt purpose or function. I.R.C. § 170(e)(1)(B). Assume that Rita has an oil painting worth $50,000, which she purchased several years ago for $5,000. If Rita contributes the painting to a hospital (which will promptly sell it for cash), her charitable deduction is limited to $5,000, but if she contributes it to a museum (where it will be exhibited), she is entitled to deduct the full $50,000 value of the painting.

To guard against taxpayers assigning above market rules to property that is gifted to charities, Congress has added to § 170 a series of rules that require that appraisals be obtained when gifted property exceeds certain thresholds and that limit the amount allowed as a deduction in certain situations where it is likely a excessive value was assigned to gifted property.

It is unwise to make a charitable contribution of property that has declined in value (loss property). The reason is that, unless the taxpayer sells the property, he will never realize the built-in loss. For example, assume that Alicia owns XYZ stock which she purchased for $10,000 and which is now worth $2,000. If she sells the stock she will realize a loss of $8,000 which she can claim on her tax return. However, if she gives the stock to a charity, she will not realize the loss but will be allowed a charitable contribution deduction for the $2,000 value of the stock. Clearly Alicia will be better off from a tax standpoint if she sells the stock (thereby realizing the $8,000 loss) and then gives the charity the $2,000 sales proceeds (thereby also obtaining a $2,000 deduction for the charitable contribution). A taxpayer who holds loss property and contemplates making a charitable contribution is well advised to sell the property and make a charitable gift either of cash or of appreciated property, as discussed above.

The § 170 deduction is available only for gifts of cash or property and not for gifts of services to a charity. For example, a teacher who voluntarily tutors disadvantaged children after school hours, or a parent who volunteers as a Girl Scout troop leader, may not claim a deduction for the value of their services. However, they may claim a deduction for out-of-pocket expenses incurred in connection with such charitable activities (e.g., the cost of supplies).

If a taxpayer receives valuable consideration in connection with a charitable contribution, the charitable deduction is limited to the net value (i.e., the value of the property given to the charity minus the value of any property or services received by the taxpayer). This rule commonly applies to benefit performances and other charitable fundraising events. For example, assume that a local opera company holds a benefit performance; tickets that normally cost $75 are sold for $200 for that event only. An individual who purchases a ticket for $200 is entitled to a deduction of $125. If the consideration received by the taxpayer is honorific or nominal, there is normally no reduction in the charitable deduction. For example, Sarah gives $100,000 to her alma mater to fund a scholarship named in honor of her deceased mother. Sarah is entitled to a deduction for the full $100,000, with no reduction for the honorific value of naming the scholarship after her mother.

In most cases, the amount allowable as a charitable deduction in a given year is limited to 50% of the individual taxpayer's contribution base (i.e., adjusted gross income, without regard to net operating loss carrybacks). If the total amount of gifts exceeds the contribution base, the taxpayer may carry forward any excess amount for use in the following five tax years. In the case of gifts of appreciated property, the deductible amount is limited to 30% of the taxpayer's contribution base, with a five-year carryforward for any excess. For example, assume that James, who has a contribution base of $300,000, gives $200,000 of appreciated stock and $80,000 in cash to various charities. James is entitled to deduct $90,000 for the gift of stock (30% of $300,000) and $60,000 for the gift of cash, for a total deduction of $150,000 (50% of $300,000). He would be allowed to carry forward the excess amounts $110,000 for the stock and $30,000 for the cash, to be deducted in subsequent years. The 30% and 50% limits would still apply in those subsequent years. For example, if his contribution base in the first carryforward year is $350,000, he can deduct $105,000 of the carryforward amount for the gift of stock (30% of $350,000) and the full $30,000 carryforward amount for the gift of cash; the remaining $5,000 for the gift of stock would be carried forward to the next year. I.R.C. § 170(d). (Alternatively, the Code allows the taxpayer to elect to waive the deduction for the full value of appreciated property and deduct only its adjusted basis, in which case the 50% and not the 30% limitation applies. This election is normally used only in rare situations where there is negligible appreciation and the benefit of an immediate deduction outweighs the cost of a slightly larger total deduction spread over a longer period of time.)

Gifts to most charities are subject to the overall 50% limitation described above, but gifts to certain organizations (e.g., most veterans' posts and organizations and many private foundations) are subject to special restrictions which affect the amount, type and timing of deductible contributions to such organizations.

For many years it was common for wealthy individuals to make gifts to charities of partial interests while retaining other interests in the same property, in order to take advantage of the valuation rules applicable to split-interest gifts. For example, a taxpayer might create a trust to pay income to herself for life, with the remainder payable at her death to charity. Under the applicable valuation tables, the charitable remainder would be valued based on a uniform interest rate (such as 6%), even though the trust might actually be funded with junk bonds with a much higher yield (perhaps 12%). As a result, the charity might be lucky to receive even half the value of the original corpus at the end of the trust term.

Congress responded to such abuses in 1969 by enacting § 170(f), which allows a charitable deduction for split-interest gifts only in narrowly limited circumstances. To qualify for the deduction, a gift to charity of a remainder interest normally must take the form of: (1) a charitable remainder annuity trust, which pays a fixed amount to one or more noncharitable beneficiaries followed by the charitable remainder; (2) a charitable remainder unitrust, which pays a fixed percentage of the current value of the trust property, valued annually, to one or more noncharitable beneficiaries followed by the charitable remainder; or (3) a pooled income fund maintained by a public charity, which pays income to noncharitable beneficiaries for life followed by the charitable remainder. Similar rules apply to gifts of term interests to charities. These strict rules are subject to several significant exceptions, which allow, for example, a deduction in the case of a gift of a remainder interest in a personal residence or a farm or an undivided fractional interest in property (e.g., a 50% tenancy in common in land).

The rules concerning gifts of partial interests to charities are rigorous and complex, reflecting repeated attempts by Congress to prevent abuse of the charitable deduction. Although the brief discussion here provides only the most general introduction, it is worth noting that split-interest charitable gifts still offer a few planning opportunities. For example, a wealthy taxpayer who spends the winter in Miami and the rest of the year in Boston might arrange to give a museum a fractional interest in her art collection, thereby obtaining a deduction for the portion of the year she is out of town while also reducing her share of the cost of insurance. Also, consider the case of an individual who has substantially appreciated stock that pays no dividends. Instead of selling the stock, paying tax on the capital gain and living on the after-tax proceeds, the taxpayer might contribute the stock to a charitable remainder annuity trust. The trust, being a tax-exempt entity, can sell the stock without incurring any tax and then make annuity payments to the taxpayer for life. The taxpayer would not only avoid paying tax on the built-in gain, but also receive a charitable deduction to mitigate the burden of the tax on annual distributions from the trust—as well as basking in the warm glow of philanthropy.

[¶ 3,165]

Problems

1. Neighbors have been burned out of their house. As a good friend and neighbor, you wish to contribute to a collection being taken up in the

neighborhood to help them get back on their feet. Will your gift be tax deductible?

2. Your friend Joe is a high-income taxpayer who regularly itemizes his deductions. His church is seeking to expand its building and Joe wishes to make a gift in support of the endeavor. In general, Joe has been a very successful investor and his substantial portfolio is full of a number of highly appreciated securities. However, Joe made a very bad investment in a "dotcom" business several years ago (shares purchased for $12,000, presently worth $4,000) and wishes to rid himself of it. He has heard that there are tax advantages to giving property to a charity and asks if he should give the "dotcom" or some other stock from his portfolio to his church.

3. Liz, who is wealthy and advanced in years, is the owner of a collection of rare manuscripts. She has been courted by her alma mater to give the college her collection and is willing to do so either now or at her death. The development officer for the college has told her that it would be better for her to give the collection during her life because that way it will be out of her estate (thereby giving her the equivalent of an estate tax deduction) and she will also get an income tax deduction. Is this sound advice?

[¶ 3,170]

4. Interest

For many years the Internal Revenue Code allowed a deduction for most interest paid or incurred by the taxpayer. This lenient treatment was defended on the ground that the deduction was an appropriate means of arriving at net (rather than gross) income from business or investment activities. Because money is fungible, it was thought that it would be unduly burdensome to disallow the deduction for interest attributable to personal activities (such as the purchase of a personal residence or automobile). In 1986, however, under pressure for revenue-neutral tax reform, Congress imposed significant restrictions on the deductibility of interest.

In general, § 163(a) allows a deduction for interest paid or accrued during the tax year. But what is freely given by § 163(a) is severely restricted by other provisions such as § 163(d) and (h). Deductible interest falls into three categories, each with its own set of restrictions: (1) personal interest that is not connected with a taxpayer's trade, business or investment activities; (2) interest incurred in connection with investment activities; and (3) interest incurred in connection with a taxpayer's trade or business activities. Business deductions are discussed in ¶ 3,340. We are concerned here with the interest deduction as it relates to the taxpayer's personal and investment activities, as contrasted with trade or business activities.

Investment Interest. Section 163(d) limits the amount of the deduction for investment interest to the taxpayer's net investment income (i.e., investment income minus investment-related expenses other than investment interest). Any excess interest may be carried forward indefinitely and allowed as a deduction against net investment income in subsequent years. Net investment income typically consists of interest income on investments (and, optionally, qualified dividend income taxable at a rate of 15% or less), but does not include gains on sales of any investments unless the taxpayer waives capital gain treatment for such gains.

For example, assume that Jennifer received $2,000 in interest (taxable at her regular tax rate) and $1,000 in qualified dividends (taxable at a 15% rate) on her investments, and that she acquired these investments with $40,000 of borrowed funds on which she paid $4,500 of interest. She also realized a long term capital gain of $3,000 when she sold some of her stock. Jennifer can deduct $2,000 of the $4,500 interest expense and can carry forward the $2,500 disallowed interest deduction to offset investment income in subsequent years. If she wishes, she can elect to treat the $1,000 in qualified dividend income as investment income and waive capital gain treatment for $1,500 of her gain on the stock sale; this would allow her to deduct the remaining $2,500 of interest expense. In deciding whether elect such treatment, the taxpayer normally considers how rapidly she would be able to use the unused interest deduction against future investment income (which is usually taxed at higher rates than long term capital gains and qualified dividend income). For example, if Jennifer's marginal tax rate is 35% and her qualified dividend income and long term capital gains are taxed at 15%, she would probably prefer to carry forward the unused interest deduction and use it in the following year to offset investment income (taxable at a 35% rate) instead of using it in the current year to offset qualified dividend income and long term capital gains (taxable at a 15% rate). The cost of deferring the deduction for one year would probably not outweigh the benefit of offsetting higher-taxed income.

Personal Interest. Section 163(h) limits the deductibility of interest incurred in connection with the taxpayer's personal consumption activities. Section 163(h)(1) disallows the deduction for "personal interest," which is defined in § 163(h)(2) as interest other than: (1) interest connected with a trade or business; (2) investment interest (discussed above); (3) interest taken into account in connection with a "passive activity" under § 469 (see ¶ 3,840); (4) qualified residence interest; (5) interest on deferred estate tax liability; and (6) student loan interest deductible under § 221. For most taxpayers, the effect of this definition of personal interest is to restrict the deduction to interest on home mortgage loans and student loans. Interest on credit card balances, car loans and other consumer debt is not deductible under § 163.

Section 163(h)(3) allows a taxpayer to take an itemized deduction for "qualified residence interest"—interest on "acquisition" loans incurred to purchase or improve the taxpayer's principal residence and one other residence (typically a vacation home). The principal amount of all such loans may not exceed $1,000,000 ($500,000 for married individuals filing separately). In addition, a homeowner may take an itemized deduction for the interest on up to $100,000 of "home equity" loans. The home equity loans may not exceed the taxpayer's equity in the home (fair market value less outstanding mortgage debt). The deduction for acquisition loans and home equity loans is discussed in more detail at ¶¶ 5,610 et seq.

The deduction for interest on home mortgage loans provides homeowners with a significant tax benefit. Although one may reasonably ask why the Code privileges homeowners over renters in this regard, the home mortgage interest deduction undoubtedly provides material assistance to individuals and families in meeting their housing needs. The home equity feature of § 163(h) also allows homeowners to obtain a tax deduction for interest on loans incurred to finance consumer purchases such as cars and household appliances that would not otherwise qualify for tax deductibility.

As noted above, taxpayers are also allowed to deduct interest on loans incurred to finance higher education for the taxpayer (or the taxpayer's spouse or dependents). This deduction is especially valuable to eligible taxpayers because it is a so-called "above the line" deduction, meaning that it is allowed in determining adjusted gross income, and is therefore unaffected by whether the taxpayer uses the standard deduction or itemizes her personal deductions. This deduction is governed by § 221 and is subject to several limitations, the most important of which are: (1) the total amount of interest claimed as a deduction may not exceed $2,500 in any one year; and (2) the amount allowed as a deduction phases out as the taxpayer's adjusted gross income (modified by specified items) rises between $50,000 ($100,000 for a married couple filing a joint return) and $65,000 ($130,000 for a married couple filing jointly). The § 221 deduction is discussed in more detail at ¶ 6,140.

[¶ 3,175]

Problems

1. Jacob, who is in the highest income tax bracket, has an investment portfolio that consists entirely of common stocks. He occasionally borrows money from his broker to purchase stock. Last year he paid $4,000 in interest on such "margin" purchases. Last year he also received $3,000 in qualified dividend income and $15,000 of long term capital gains from his portfolio. Jacob has little use for interest-bearing investments and last year had only $500 in interest on bank accounts and money market funds. Consider what Jacob should do about claiming a deduction for the $4,000 in investment interest as he fills out his tax return for last year.

2. The Freunds have retired the mortgage on their Maryland principal residence, which is worth $550,000, and have purchased a Florida winter home, which has a $350,000 mortgage on it. They wish to purchase a summer cottage in Maine for $220,000. They need to borrow $80,000 to complete purchase of the Maine cottage. Would they be better advised to take a $80,000 mortgage out on the Maine property or to raise the $80,000 with a home equity loan on their principal residence?

[¶ 3,180]

5. State and Local Taxes

Section 164(a) allows an itemized deduction for certain state, local and foreign taxes not directly connected with the taxpayer's trade or business or with property held for production of income. The taxes covered by this deduction are: (1) state, local and foreign real property taxes; (2) state and local (but not foreign) personal property taxes; (3) state, local and foreign income, war profits and excess profits taxes; (4) the generation-skipping transfer tax imposed on income distributions (see ¶ 4,500); and (5) certain environmental taxes. In addition, for years 2004 and 2005, under § 164(b)(5) a taxpayer may elect to deduct general state and local sales taxes in lieu of deducting state and local income taxes. Taxes directly connected with an individual's trade or business or with property held for production of income are allowed as deductions under §§ 162 and 212 to the extent provided therein.

The primary significance of § 164(a) for most individuals and families (other than those using the standard deduction) is to allow a deduction for: (1) state and local income taxes; (2) state and local real property taxes on personal residences and vacation homes; (3) state and local personal property taxes (including intangibles taxes) on items such as automobiles, household furnishings, stocks and bonds; and (4) in states which do not have an income tax (e.g. Texas and Florida), or states with a low income tax where the state income tax burden may be less than the sales tax burden and an election to forgo deducting state income tax would make sense (e.g. Indiana and Tennessee), a deduction for general sales taxes. No deduction is allowed under § 164 for motor vehicle registration fees, estate or inheritance taxes, or excise taxes on cigarettes, alcohol, gasoline and the like.

The deduction for these taxes can be defended as a necessary adjustment to conform net taxable income to the Haig–Simons definition. Because there is no correlation between the amount of taxes that an individual pays and the public services that she consumes, if we seek to ensure that only her consumption and changes in net worth are subject to tax, we conclude that it is appropriate to allow a deduction for state and local taxes.

The deduction for real property taxes, when coupled with the deduction for home mortgage interest, provides an enormous incentive for individuals and families to own their own homes rather than to rent living quarters. This deduction is discussed in greater detail at ¶ 5,680. Moreover, the deduction for state and local taxes helps to lighten the burden of those levies, especially in high tax states. Interestingly, states which choose to finance their public services with nondeductible taxes actually saddle their residents with a somewhat heavier combined state and federal tax burden than if they relied on deductible taxes.

Several points are worth noting in connection with deductible taxes. First, although § 164 provides for the deduction of foreign income taxes, most individuals find it preferable to claim a credit for these taxes. (See ¶ 3,290. Of course, a taxpayer may not claim both a credit and a deduction for the same tax.) Second, when a taxpayer sells real property, it is necessary to apportion the deductible real property tax for the year. See I.R.C. § 164(d). Typically, the apportionment called for by statute is carried out at the closing. This issue is discussed in more detail at ¶ 5,680. Third, if an individual is self-employed, he is required to pay both the employee's share and the employer's share of Social Security and Medicare taxes on self-employment income. In 2004 the Social Security tax was computed at the rate of 12.4% on self-employment income up to $87,900 and the Medicare tax was computed at a rate of 2.9% on all self-employment income. For example, if an individual, acting as an independent contractor, performed translation services for fees aggregating $100,000, she would be obligated to pay $13,799.60 in self-employment taxes (12.4% on $87,900 and 2.9% on $100,000). Section 164(f) allows that individual to claim a deduction for one-half ($6,899.80) of those taxes. The deduction is not treated as an itemized deduction but rather as a trade or business deduction for the independent contractor. The reason for allowing this deduction is to put the self-employed individual on a par with an employee whose employer can claim the employer's share of the taxes as a deductible business expense. Fourth, in the case of cooperative housing, a tenant shareholder may deduct, as a property tax, amounts paid or accrued to the co-op to the extent they represent property taxes attributable to the taxpayer's own unit and his share of common property.

[¶ 3,190]

6. Medical Expenses

Under § 213, individuals may claim an itemized deduction for amounts paid for medical care for themselves (or their spouses or dependents), to the extent that the total of all such expenses, net of insurance reimbursements, exceeds 7.5% of adjusted gross income. For many families, routine annual medical expenses do not rise above the 7.5% floor and therefore do not qualify for the deduction. For example, assume that a married couple that files jointly has AGI of $150,000. The couple cannot claim a deduction under § 213 until unreimbursed medical expenses exceed $11,250, and then only the excess over $11,250 will qualify for the deduction. Unfortunately, such occasions arise all too frequently, especially for taxpayers who lack health insurance or who incur medical expenses that are not covered by health insurance. For example, a taxpayer who requires nursing home care may find, in the absence of long-term residential care insurance, that the medical expense deduction makes a significant difference in the after-tax cost of such care. Similarly, the cost of special education for a disabled child can easily drive a family's total medical expenses above the 7.5% threshold. Moreover, if a major health problem strikes an uninsured individual or family, the § 213 deduction may be very important.

Because individuals who obtain medical services clearly consume the value of medical services, it is somewhat difficult to justify the medical expense deduction under the Haig–Simons definition of income. Many commentators, however, view the deduction as a means whereby society refines its taxing mechanism to accommodate the varying ability to pay of different taxpayers with similar levels of income.

Issues occasionally arise over what types of items qualify as expenditures for "medical care." Amounts paid for prescription drugs and insulin, for the diagnosis, cure, mitigation, treatment or prevention of disease, for transportation to secure medical care, for long term care and for health insurance all qualify as medical care expenditures. I.R.C. § 213(b), (d)(1). Expenditures for physician mandated services that do not constitute medical care do not qualify for the deduction. For example, where the taxpayer's physician advised him to avoid mowing his lawn to alleviate an allergy problem, the taxpayer was not allowed to deduct the cost of lawn services as "medical care." See Taylor v. Commissioner, 54 T.C.M. (CCH) 129 (1987).

Section 213(d) imposes several additional limitations on the amounts that qualify for the medical expense deduction. Although expenditures for lodging while away from home to secure medical care from a physician in a licensed hospital are deductible, the amount allowed as a deduction is limited to $50 per night per person. I.R.C. § 213(d)(2). Expenditures for cosmetic surgery are not deductible unless made to correct for deformities arising personal injury, trauma, treatment of a disease or to correct a congenital abnormality. I.R.C. § 213(d)(9). For example, plastic surgery to correct a disfigurement arising from an auto accident, a breast implant to address the consequences of a mastectomy performed in the course of treating breast cancer, or nasal surgery to correct a deviated septum that impaired breathing functions would all constitute qualifying medical care. On the other hand, removal of "crow's feet," botox injections or "tummy tuck" surgery done to improve one's appearance would not be deemed qualifying medical care.

When an aged or disabled individual is institutionalized, all or a portion of the fees paid may qualify as deductible medical care expenditures. If an individual is placed in a nursing home because she suffers from a physical impairment such as partial paralysis caused by a stroke or from senile dementia so that she may not safely be left alone, then all of the monthly bill covering her stay in a nursing home (including lodging, meals and care) would be deductible. See Reg. § 1.213–1(e)(1)(v). On the other hand, if an individual moves into an assisted living facility in order to have access to custodial care should the need arise, or to be near a spouse who requires medical care at the facility, then only the portion of the monthly bill that is designated as covering medical services would be deductible. See Rev. Rul. 75–302, 1972–2 C.B. 86. Because the cost of skilled nursing home care normally runs from $4,000 to $6,000 per month, if a taxpayer (or her spouse or dependent) is placed in such a facility in circumstances where the full cost constitutes a qualifying medical care expenditure, the allowable deduction will quickly rise above the 7.5% floor for all but the very wealthy.

Families that have a learning disabled child may find that expenses for special education with tutors or at special institutions consume a large portion of their income. These expenses, when added to other expenses not covered by insurance, often result in such families having deductible medical expenses that exceed 7.5% of AGI. Only special education therapies that are designed to address the specific learning disabilities of the child will qualify for deduction. For example, tuition for attendance at a special school with programs for learning disabled children will qualify for deduction, whereas tuition for attendance at a school with conventional classes will not qualify, even if the classes are smaller than would be encountered at the local public school and would likely result in greater conventional individualized attention for the child. Compare Rev. Rul. 78–340, 1978–2 C.B. 124 (deduction allowed for portion of tuition at special school for learning disabled child), with Martin v. Commissioner, 548 F.2d 633 (6th Cir. 1977) (no deduction where deaf child attended private school with no special classes for deaf).

A common issue under § 213 involves capital improvements that are made to accommodate the needs of a sick or handicapped individual. With respect to improvements made to houses, such as adding a swimming pool for the exercise of an arthritic or crippled person, the general rule is that the taxpayer may deduct the full cost of such outlays minus the resulting increase in the value of the residence. For example, assume that an individual with severe arthritis is ordered by his physician to take daily swimming exercise, and that he installs a swimming pool at his home in order to obtain the needed exercise. The cost of the pool is $30,000 and it increases the value of the home by $12,000. In this case the taxpayer can treat $18,000 as a qualifying medical expense. See Rev. Rul. 83–33, 1983–1 C.B. 70. The I.R.S. has conceded, with some prodding from Congress, that residential barrier removals done for handicapped individuals, such as installation of ramps or door widenings, do not add to the value of a home and that the entire cost of such improvements should qualify as deductible medical expenses. See Rev. Rul. 87–106, 1987–2 C.B. 67. In keeping with the basic presumption that such outlays do not increase the value of a residence, the courts have applied the same rationale to the cost of making motor vehicles accessible to handicapped persons and have allowed a deduction for the full amount of any expenditures incurred to make a van or a car accessible to handicapped individuals. See Henderson v. Commissioner, 80 T.C.M. (CCH) 517 (2000).

Although the cost of health insurance is fully deductible, a special limitation applies in the case of long term care insurance. The cost of such insurance is deductible, but it is capped at rather modest levels that rises with the age of the taxpayer. I.R.C. § 213(d)(10).

Because of the 7.5% floor, even taxpayers who have health insurance find that they must pay deductible amounts and co-payments using after-tax dollars. To reduce the economic impact of such payments, many taxpayers use their employer's cafeteria plan to direct pre-tax compensation into flexible spending accounts that may be used to reimburse the employee for such expenses and for other medical expenses (such as eyeglasses) that are not covered by the employer's health insurance plan. Cafeteria plans are discussed in greater detail at ¶ 3,080.

As part of the Medicare prescription drug plan enacted in 2003, Congress authorized Health Savings Accounts (HSAs), which may be established by employers for employees and their family members under 65 years of age. Employees may make voluntary tax deductible contributions to the HSA to cover family medical expenses not covered by insurance. The deduction is taken in computing AGI, which means that it is available to taxpayers regardless of whether they use the standard deduction or elect to itemize deductions. Funds in an individual's HSA may either be used to cover current medical expenses or be carried over to cover retiree medical expenses, Medicare expenses and prescription drug expenses not covered by insurance. Any withdrawal of funds to pay for non-covered expenses (e.g. a plasma TV) is subject to income tax and if the individual is less than 65 an additional 10% penalty tax. The great advantage of an HSA over a traditional flexible spending plan is that, at year end, there is no forfeiture of unspent funds. The major drawback of the HSA is that it is available only if the health insurance plan that covers the employee has a rather high deductible (at least $1,000 for an individual and $2,000 for a family) which must be reached before any payment is made under the plan, as well as a high annual cap on out-of-pocket employee expenses ($5,000 per individual and $10,000 per family) above which an employee need not make further payments to cover co-pays or deductibles. As in the case of flexible spending accounts, funds paid out for appropriate medical expenses are excluded from income. The law also allows an employer to make tax deductible contributions to an HSA on behalf of an employee without the employee being required to ·include such sums in gross income. The total amount that can be contributed annually by employee and employer is limited to 100% of the underlying health plan deductible, up to a maximum of $2,600 for an individual and $5,150 for a family (with individuals between 55 and 65 being allowed to make catch up contributions of up to $500 per year). It remains to be seen how popular these HSAs will prove. Traditionally, high deductible policies have not been very popular with employees, although some in the health care industry predict that employers may adopt HSAs as a means of controlling rising medical costs.

[¶ 3,195]

Problems

1.   Grandma is a widow who has recently suffered a severe disabling stroke. She must enter a nursing home and has been told that normal monthly charges will run about $4,000. She has income from Social Security and a pension plan and at present, after paying income taxes, has about

$60,000 of disposable income left over. She also has a modest nest egg of about $200,000 which she had hoped to leave to her children. Grandma is worried that, although she will currently have $12,000 left over after covering nursing home costs, rising nursing home costs will soon exhaust all of her annual income and within a few years she will have to invade her nest egg possibly leaving her with little to pass on to her children. What advice can you offer Grandma?

2. The Hendersons, who have adjusted gross income of $80,000, recently learned that their son Ricky has a significant learning disability. Educational psychologists have advised that, if the couple can afford the $6,000 annual fee, they should enroll him in a special after-school program staffed by private specialists who are trained to help children such as Ricky develop coping skills. Typically the couple each year have about $3,000 in medical costs not reimbursed by insurance. If they enroll Ricky in the special program, how much, if any, of their medical expenses will be deductible, assuming that they normally itemize personal deductions? Grandpa Henderson, who is a successful real estate developer, on hearing of the situation, gave the Hendersons $10,000 to help them in this time of need and told them to do all they can for Ricky, who is the apple of his eye. He also said "Don't worry kids, there is plenty more where this came from." Does this change your analysis?

3. Your company has a fairly decent health insurance program, but the firm's director of Human Resources recently learned that there are other ways of helping employees with health care expenses at little or no extra cost to the company. She said that the company has also been getting pressure from employees about the need to provide some help with day care costs for employees with children. Are there any low cost options that you could recommend?

[¶ 3,200]

7. Casualty Losses

Section 165(a) allows a taxpayer to take a deduction for "any loss sustained during the taxable year and not compensated for by insurance or otherwise." This seemingly broad allowance is sharply narrowed by § 165(c), which limits the losses deductible by an individual taxpayer to: (1) losses incurred in a trade or business; (2) losses incurred in transactions entered into for profit but not connected with a trade or business; and (3) other losses arising from fire, storm, shipwreck, or other casualty, or from theft. Losses connected with a trade or business or transactions entered into for profit are discussed later in this chapter (see ¶¶ 3,580 et seq. and ¶¶ 3,660 et seq.). Our focus here is on the third category, commonly referred to as "casualty losses," which may be deducted even though they arise from a taxpayer's personal activities. For example, theft of personal jewelry, storm damage to a vacation home and the destruction by fire of a home or personal possessions all come within the category of casualty losses.

The theoretical justification for the casualty loss deduction is that such losses diminish the net worth of the taxpayer, do not constitute consumption by the taxpayer and are therefore appropriate adjustments to conform net taxable income to the Haig–Simons definition. Some commentators object to the deduction on the ground that the loss of consumer goods by any means represents a form of consumption.

Although it is fairly clear whether a loss arises from fire, storm, shipwreck or theft, it is not always clear what qualifies as a "casualty" loss. The courts have decided that, to qualify for the deduction, a loss must be of the same general nature as the enumerated types—it must be sudden and unexpected. Under this standard, losses arising from gradual erosion, such as damage to a roof caused by years of exposure to sun, rain and snow, do not constitute casualty losses; on the other hand, sudden damage to a roof in a storm would give rise to a deductible loss. Similarly, termite damage does not constitute a casualty loss because of the slow pace at which these pests consume wood. See Rev. Rul. 63–232, 1963–2 C.B. 97; cf. Rev. Rul. 79–174, 1979–1 C.B. 99 (allowing deduction for sudden and unexpected damage caused by southern pine beetles that, according to entomologists, eat quickly). A theft of jewelry qualifies as a casualty loss, but misplacing or mislaying jewelry does not.

The amount allowable as a casualty loss deduction is determined in three steps. First, the amount of the deduction is limited to the difference in the fair market value of the property immediately before and after the loss, and in no event may it exceed the taxpayer's adjusted basis in the property. See I.R.C. § 165(b); Reg. § 1.165–7(b). This rule can be illustrated by two examples. Suppose that Barbara's home, which she purchased for $200,000, is damaged by fire in a lightning storm. Before the storm the home was worth $240,000; after the storm it was worth only $210,000. The decline in value was derived from the cost of repairs. Barbara has a casualty loss of $30,000. Now, suppose that Carl owns a baseball card collection which he purchased many years ago for $5,000 and which is now worth $50,000. If the collection is stolen, Carl will be able to claim only $5,000 as a casualty loss. This limitation stems from the realization rule. Because Carl was never taxed on the unrealized appreciation, his deduction is likewise limited to his original cost. The amount of any casualty loss so determined must be reduced by the amount of any recovery from insurance or other sources. For example, if Barbara recovered $30,000 from her insurance company, she would have no deductible casualty loss.

The second step in the process requires that each casualty loss be reduced by $100. See I.R.C. § 165(h)(1). Thus, Carl would have to reduce the $5,000 casualty loss arising from theft of his baseball card collection to $4,900. If Carl also suffered a theft of $6,000 in cash, he would also have to reduce that loss by $100, leaving him with a casualty loss of $5,900 arising from the theft of cash.

Under the third step in the process, the taxpayer is allowed to deduct casualty losses only to the extent that their aggregate amount exceeds 10% of adjusted gross income for the year. See I.R.C. § 165(h)(2). If Carl had AGI of $80,000 for the year, his deductible casualty loss would be $2,800 ($4,900 + $5,900 − $8,000 = $2,800). The effect of the 10% floor and the automatic offset for insurance recoveries is that relatively few taxpayers actually claim a deductible casualty loss. Such taxpayers are often uninsured individuals who suffered damage to homes or automobiles. Due to the high cost and limited availability of flood insurance, flood damage also accounts for a significant number of deductible casualty losses.

[¶ 3,210]

8. Phaseout of Itemized Deductions

For high income taxpayers, much of the tax benefit of the itemized deductions mentioned above is negated by § 68. In general, this provision cuts back the amount allowable for itemized personal deductions as adjusted gross income rises above a specified threshold. The deductions for medical expenses, investment interest, casualty losses and wagering losses are exempt from the phaseout. Taxpayers are required to reduce the aggregate amount of their other itemized deductions by 3% of the amount by which their AGI exceeds $100,000 ($50,000 for married individuals filing separately). The threshold amount is adjusted annually for inflation, and in 2004 it stood at $142,700 ($71,350 for married individuals filing separately). The aggregate reduction in the itemized deductions subject to phaseout cannot exceed 80% of their original amount.

Assume that in 2004 Charles and Marie had AGI of $200,000 and had itemized deductions consisting of $4,000 in medical expenses, $15,000 in state income and local property taxes and $5,000 in charitable contributions. Although their itemized deductions total $24,000, the amount allowed as a deduction is limited to $22,281. The couple must reduce the amount of their combined $20,000 in state income and local property taxes and charitable contributions by 3% of $57,300 (the amount by which their AGI exceeds $142,700), or $1,719. This results in only $18,281 of their $20,000 outlays for property taxes and charitable contributions being allowed as a deduction. In addition, they can deduct the full $4,000 of medical expenses, which are not subject to phaseout, leaving them with total allowable itemized deductions of $22,281 after application of § 68. Note that if the couple's itemized deductions remain the same, regardless of how high their AGI rises, their allowable deductions cannot be reduced below $8,000. The reason for this is that due to the 80% cap, the charitable and property tax deductions cannot be reduced below $4,000, and the $4,000 of medical expenses are exempt from the phaseout under § 68.

Section 68 has been severely criticized by scholars and taxpayers alike, and it is scheduled to be phased out of existence beginning in 2006 and completely repealed in 2010.

E. PERSONAL AND DEPENDENT EXEMPTIONS

[¶ 3,250]

Regardless of whether taxpayers claim the standard deduction or elect to itemize their personal deductions, most will be allowed to deduct one personal exemption for themselves as well as additional exemptions for any eligible dependents. These exemptions are subject to a number of restrictions, as discussed below.

Under § 151 of the Code, an individual taxpayer is entitled to a personal exemption in the amount of $2,000, adjusted annually for inflation. In 2004, the amount of the exemption stood at $3,100. In addition, the taxpayer may claim a similar exemption for each dependent (as defined in § 152) whose gross income for the year is less than the exemption amount or who is a child of the taxpayer under age 19 (or under age 24, if a student). No additional exemption is allowed, however, for a dependent who is married and files a joint tax return. I.R.C. § 151(c). For example, in 2004, a family consisting of a husband and wife and their infant child (solely supported by the parents) would be entitled to three exemptions totalling $9,300.

In general, under § 152(a), an individual qualifies as a dependent of the taxpayer if the taxpayer provides more than half of the individual's support and the individual either comes within a prescribed group of relatives or is a member of the taxpayer's household with the taxpayer's home as his principal place of abode. The prescribed group of relatives includes, among others, the taxpayer's children, grandchildren, parents, siblings, stepchildren, step-parents, aunts and uncles, as well as a host of in-laws. It is also worth noting that no dependent exemption is allowed for an unrelated individual whose relationship with the taxpayer is "in violation of local law." I.R.C. § 152(b)(5).

In meeting the support test of § 152(a), the taxpayer may treat as support money and goods (such as groceries) provided to the dependent as well as the value of living quarters. In the case of students who are children or stepchildren of the taxpayer, amounts received as scholarships at conventional education institutions are ignored in determining the support provided by the taxpayer. I.R.C. § 152(d). The following examples, set in the year 2004 and based on an exemption amount of $3,100, illustrate the operation of § 152(a).

Klein Family. Bob and Gail Klein are a married couple who live at home with their only child Ben, Gail's mother Carla, and Bob's father Michael. Ben's income consists of $75 in interest from a savings bank account, Carla's income consists of $6,000 in Social Security benefits, and Michael's income consists of $7,000 in Social Security benefits and $5,000 in pension benefits. Bob and Gail provide more than half of the support for Ben, Carla and Michael in the form of food, clothing and lodging for all three. Bob and Gail are entitled to personal exemptions for themselves. They are also entitled to an exemption for Ben because he is their child and they supply more than half of his support. (Because Ben is their child and is under age 19, his own income is irrelevant.) In addition, they are entitled to an exemption for Carla because she satisfies the relational test, they provide more than half of her support, and her gross income (from which her Social Security benefits are excluded, as described in ¶ 3,030) is less than the exemption amount. However, they are not entitled to an exemption for Michael, even though he satisfies the relational test and they provide more than half of his support, because his gross income of $5,000 exceeds the exemption amount of $3,100.

Ramos Family. Enrique and Teresa Ramos have three children, Jose (age 16), Patricia (age 20), and Pablo (age 22). All three children live in their parents' house and their parents provide more than half of their support. Jose is a high school student who earned $3,500 from part-time work. Patricia, who graduated from high school two years ago, is a struggling artist who earned $4,000 selling paintings. Pablo is a student at State University who earned $5,000 working in the school bookstore and has used that money to purchase books and meet other incidental expenses. Pablo received a partial scholarship from State University in the amount of $4,000; his parents paid his remaining tuition of $2,000 and also provided additional support in the amount of $5,500. Enrique and Teresa are entitled to personal exemptions for themselves. They are also entitled to an exemption for Jose because he is their child and they provide more than half of his support. (Because Jose is their child and is under age 19, the amount of his income is irrelevant.) The situation with Patricia is different. She is a child of Enrique and Teresa (thereby satisfying the relational test) and they provided more than half of her support, but because she is over age 19 and no longer a student, her income of $4,000 ($900 more than the exemption amount) prevents her parents from claiming an exemption for her. However, Enrique and Teresa are entitled to an exemption for Pablo because he is their child, they provided more than half of his support, and, because he is a student under age 24, it does not matter that his income was greater than the exemption amount. Note that but for the rule of § 152(d) disregarding scholarship aid in determining the level of support provided to Pablo, Enrique and Teresa would not be entitled to an exemption for Pablo.

Boyd–Louis Family. Norma Boyd and Sally Louis have lived together in the same house for three years. They are registered as domestic partners but are prohibited from marrying under state law. Norma works outside the home and provides all of the couple's support; Sally keeps house. Norma should be allowed an exemption for Sally because she provides more than half of Sally's support, Sally does not have income in excess of the exemption amount, and the requirements of § 152(a)(9) for unrelated parties are satisfied. That provision requires that the unrelated individual have the taxpayer's home as her principal place of abode and that she be a member of the taxpayer's household. If Sally held a part-time job and earned income in excess of the exemption amount ($3,100), then Norma would not be entitled to an exemption for Sally. In discussing unmarried couples, of either the same or different sex, it should be recalled that § 152(b)(5) bars an exemption for an unrelated individual if her relationship with the taxpayer is in violation of local law. Unless the I.R.S. is prepared to hide under the bed or quiz people about their private lives (and rely on them to give candid answers), there is not much it can do to enforce this rule.

In the case of a fragmented family, § 152(e) provides special rules for determining which parent is entitled to claim the exemption for a dependent child. If the parents are divorced or legally separated (or live apart for the last six months of the year) and the child is in the custody of one or both parents for more than half of the year, the parent who has custody for a greater portion of the year is treated as providing more than half of the child's support. An exception applies where the custodial parent executes a written waiver of the right to claim the exemption and the other parent files the waiver with his tax return. The purpose of this provision is to keep the I.R.S. from becoming embroiled in disputes between divorced or separated parents as to which of them provided more support for their children.

Where several family members contribute to an individual's support and none of them provides more than half of the support, no one would be entitled to claim an exemption under the rules as outlined above, even if all the other requirements are met. Congress added § 152(c) to the Code to deal with such situations. In general, the support test is deemed to be satisfied with respect to an individual if: (1) no one person provides more than half of the individual's support; (2) a group of persons who would otherwise be entitled to claim the individual as a dependent provide more than half of the individual's support; and (3) each person providing at least one-tenth of the support agrees in writing to allow one of the group to claim the individual as a dependent. Assuming all other requirements are met, the designated person is entitled to claim the individual as a dependent on the condition that the written agreement is filed with the I.R.S. For example, assume that Sara and her brothers Mark and Rick each provide 25% of the support for their aged mother Martha who has no income other than modest Social Security benefits (which provide the rest of her support and under these circumstances are not taxable, as discussed in ¶ 3,030). The children may enter into a multiple support agreement allowing one of them to claim their mother as a dependent. They may decide to allow the child who is least well off or the child who will reap the greatest tax benefit to claim Martha as a dependent, or they may decide to rotate the tax benefit among them on an annual basis.

Section 151(d)(3) provides for phaseout of personal exemptions for high-income taxpayers. The aggregate exemption amount is reduced by 2% for every $2,500 ($1,250 for married individuals filing separately) or part thereof by which the taxpayer's adjusted gross income exceeds a threshold amount. The threshold amounts, which are adjusted annually for inflation, are $150,000 for married couples filing jointly, $125,000 for heads of household, $100,000 for single taxpayers, and $75,000 for married individuals filing separately. In 2004 those amounts (as adjusted for inflation) were, respectively, $214,050, $178,350, $142,700 and $107,025. For example, if a married couple with four dependent children had AGI of $250,000 in 2004, they could claim six exemptions (one for each parent and one for each child) totaling $18,600 before the phaseout. Because their AGI exceeded the $214,050 threshold by $35,950, they would be required to reduce that amount by 30%, leaving a deduction of $13,020. Note that the phaseout applies to the total amount of exemptions, so that a taxpayer with two dependents would lose the full benefit of her exemptions at the same AGI level as one with ten dependents. This sort of legislative irrationality and complexity is a product of a political environment in which there is a compelling need to raise revenue to meet budgetary shortfalls while at the same time sparing lawmakers the need to vote for an increase in tax rates. Fortunately, the § 151(d)(3) phaseout is itself scheduled to be phased out beginning in 2006 and completely repealed in 2010.

[¶ 3,255]

Problems

1.   Papa Vidal is a widower who is retired and receives only a Social Security check of $600 per month as well as about $200 in annual interest on a savings account. His children Emma and Raphael each contribute $7,000 per year to help him remain independent and living in his own apartment. They ask you, as a friend of the family, if it is possible for each of them to obtain one-half of a dependent deduction with respect to Papa or if you can recommend another approach.

2.   Would your reaction to the previous situation be any different if, in addition to his Social Security, Papa Vidal also received $400 per month of pension benefits from his former employer's pension plan?

F.   PERSONAL CREDITS

[¶ 3,260]

The Code allows tax credits for a number of outlays. A credit differs from a deduction because it reduces the taxpayer's tax liability on a dollar for dollar basis. In contrast, a deduction reduces the tax base (i.e., taxable income) on which tax liability is computed. Credits are equally valuable to all taxpayers whereas the value of a deduction varies according to the taxpayer's income level. For example, assume that Mary and Joy are single taxpayers; Mary's marginal tax rate (the rate at which her last dollar of income is taxed) is 15%, and Joy's marginal tax rate is 25%. Each woman has a child for which she is entitled to a $1,000 child tax credit (see ¶ 3,270), and each makes a deductible charitable contribution of $1,000. The $1,000 child tax credit saves each woman $1,000; the charitable contribution deduction of $1,000 saves Mary $150 but saves Joy $250.

A tax credit is refundable if it entitles the taxpayer to a net refund after the entire amount of the taxpayer's tax liability has been offset. For example, if a taxpayer has a refundable tax credit of $5,000 and a tax liability of $4,000 (before claiming the credit), the taxpayer is entitled to eliminate her entire $4,000 tax liability and then receive a payment of the remaining $1,000 from the Treasury. If the credit is not refundable, the benefit to the taxpayer is limited to offsetting her tax liability.

Our focus here is on two credits that are allowable to individual taxpayers without regard to business or investment activity. They are the child tax credit and the dependent care tax credit. Several other personal tax credits will also be discussed briefly.

[¶ 3,270]

1. Child Credit

Section 24 allows individual taxpayers a credit for each "qualifying child," which includes the taxpayer's children and stepchildren and their descendants, as well as foster children and certain other relatives whom the taxpayer cares for as her own children. In addition, a "qualifying child" must also be an individual under age 17 (and a U.S. citizen or resident alien) for whom the taxpayer is entitled to claim a dependent exemption. I.R.C. § 24(c). The amount of the credit stands at $1,000 per child through 2010 and is then scheduled to drop back to $500. I.R.C. § 24(a)(2). The credit may be used against the taxpayer's federal income tax liability and his alternative minimum tax liability. Moreover, if the credit exceeds the taxpayer's tax liability, a portion of the credit is refundable. I.R.C. § 24(d).

The child credit phases out as adjusted gross income increases above a specified threshold. The thresholds are $110,000 for married couples filing jointly, $55,000 for married individuals filing separately, and $75,000 for unmarried individuals. The amount of the credit is phased out at the rate of $50 for each $1,000 or part thereof by which the taxpayer's AGI (with certain modifications) exceeds the threshold amount. I.R.C. § 24(b). The child credit is of significant value to taxpayers and often provides an even greater tax benefit than the dependent exemption.

A major criticism of the child tax credit is that it is not fully refundable. If the credit is intended to help families meet the costs of raising children, clearly those in greatest need are the poorest families. Anything less than complete refundability shortchanges the purpose of enacting the credit in the first place and is a monument to either irrationality or Congressional mean-spiritedness toward the poor.

[¶ 3,280]

2. Dependent Care Credit

Section 21 provides a limited credit for some of the costs of obtaining custodial care for dependents where the care enables the taxpayer to be employed. Although the dependents covered by this provision are not limited to children of the taxpayer, most families that claim the credit do so because of dependent children, and the § 21 credit is commonly referred to as the child care credit. For the cost of the dependent's care to qualify for the credit, the dependent must be a member of the taxpayer's household and must be either: (1) a dependent under age 13 for whom the taxpayer can claim an exemption; (2) a physically or mentally incapacitated dependent who is incapable of caring for himself (e.g., an incapacitated parent) and for whom the taxpayer can claim an exemption (or would have been able to do so if the dependent did not have income in excess of the permissible threshold); (3) a mentally or physically incapacitated spouse of the taxpayer; or (4) a dependent child of a divorced taxpayer who has custody of the child but who has entered into a written agreement to allow the non-custodial parent to claim the exemption for the child.

Expenditures for dependent care qualify for the § 21 credit only if they are incurred to enable the taxpayer to be gainfully employed. Qualifying expenditures include outlays for care of a qualifying dependent as well as those made for household services. For example, Marge and Homer are gainfully employed and hire their neighbor Sue to watch their eight-year-old son Bart after school. As part of her employment arrangement, Sue is required to start dinner and perform light household duties such as picking up the family room and unloading the dishwasher. All compensation paid to Sue will qualify in determining the amount of the allowable credit under § 21. However, household services that are unrelated to dependent care (such as weeding and lawn mowing) will not qualify for the § 21 credit. Although the cost of custodial after-school care provided at the dependent's school or at a separate location such as a child care center or a summer day camp will qualify for the credit, expenses of attending an overnight camp will not qualify. I.R.C. § 21(b)(2)(A). This last restriction was added to prevent families from obtaining a tax credit for their children's attendance at summer boarding camps.

The allowable credit is limited to a percentage of the maximum qualifying amount spent on dependent care. Calculation of the allowable amount of the credit involves several steps. First, the maximum amount of qualifying expenses that may be taken into account in determining the credit is limited to $3,000 per year if there is only one qualifying dependent ($6,000 if there are two or more such dependents). This amount is then reduced by any amount excluded from income under § 129 under a dependent care program. Moreover, in no event may such amount exceed the taxpayer's earned income (and, in the case of a married couple, the earned income of the spouse earning the smallest amount of money). The amount of the allowable credit is a percentage of this base. For taxpayers with adjusted gross income of $15,000 or less, the percentage is 35% and it declines by one percent for each $2,000 or portion thereof by which AGI exceeds $15,000, but in no event can the percentage be reduced below 20% (which would occur at $43,001 of AGI). For example, assume that Connie has AGI of $17,500 and that she incurred child care expenses of $3,500 to enable her to be gainfully employed. Only $3,000 of her expenses would be able to be taken into account, and because her AGI exceeded $15,000 by $2,500, only 33% of the $3,000, or $990, would be allowable as a credit. The declining percentage feature is clearly intended to target the benefit of the credit at low-income taxpayers. It is also worth noting that the phaseout mechanism for married couples is identical to that for a single individual, resulting in a marriage penalty for married couples with small children or other dependents who require custodial care so that the couple may be gainfully employed.

The § 21 credit is coordinated with any child care expenditures made from flexible spending accounts for child care as part of a cafeteria plan (see ¶ 3,080). Amounts paid out under such plans are aggregated with the dependent care credit to ensure that neither provision's cap is exceeded and to prevent taxpayers from claiming an exclusion and a credit for the same expenditure.

Because of the phaseout feature, high-income taxpayers normally find it preferable to use child care spending accounts and to forgo use of the § 21 credit (or to use it only for amounts that exceed the $5,000 limit of § 129, where because two or more children are involved there is still room to use an additional $1,000 of such expenses under § 21). For example, assume that Joe and Trudy are a married couple with two small sons, a 35% marginal tax rate and $5,000 of child care expenses that would qualify for credit at the rate of 20%. Clearly, the couple would be better off using a child care spending account. (See ¶ 3,270.) However, if they had $12,000 of child care expenses for the two boys, the couple would find it advantageous to use the child care spending account to cover the maximum permissible amount under § 129 ($5,000) and then to claim a 20% credit for $1,000 of the remaining $7,000 of child care expenses that did not qualify under § 129. This is possible only because § 129 and § 21, although coordinated to avoid doubling of benefits, employ different caps.

The § 21 credit is not available where the caregiver is a child of the taxpayer who is under age 19 or an individual for whom the taxpayer is entitled to claim an exemption under § 151. The reason for this limitation is to bar taxpayers from claiming the credit for sums paid to relatives such as older siblings of the dependent who receives custodial care. Congress is understandably reluctant to step in and provide relief in situations where normal family relationships should suffice to encourage family members to do their part.

[¶ 3,285]

Problem

The head of your Human Resources Department asks you why the company should consider implementing a flexible spending account plan for child care services when the Internal Revenue Code already provides for tax relief for such costs in the form of a tax credit under § 21.

[¶ 3,290]

3. **Miscellaneous Personal Credits**

In addition to the child credit and the dependent care credit, the Code allows several other tax credits that may be of interest to families. The most important of these are summarized below.

Foreign Tax Credit. U.S. citizens are taxable on their worldwide income regardless of its source. To ameliorate the burden of double taxation where income from a foreign source is also subject to tax in the country of origin, the Code allows a credit against federal income tax liability for foreign taxes paid with respect to foreign source income. See I.R.C. §§ 901–908. Although the foreign tax credit provisions can become quite complicated, the credit can be important for U.S. taxpayers who invest abroad directly or indirectly through corporations or mutual funds with foreign holdings. Two points are worth noting here. First, a taxpayer may not take a deduction for foreign income taxes under § 164 and also claim a credit for the same taxes. In most cases, the credit provides a greater tax benefit. Second, the credit is available only for foreign income taxes (as contrasted with property or sales taxes) and is allowable only against U.S. income tax liability.

Education Tax Credits. Section 25A provides two important tax credits that are of considerable value in meeting the costs of higher education. The Hope Scholarship Credit and the Lifetime Learning Credit are discussed at ¶ 6,100.

Earned Income Tax Credit. The tax credit provided by § 32 has two distinct functions. Originally, it was intended to mitigate the burden of Social Security and Medicare taxes on low income wage earners. More recently, the credit has been restructured to provide a subsidy to working poor taxpayers with dependent children. In light of this second function, it should come as no surprise that, in the case of individuals with dependent children, the credit is refundable. Although the § 32 credit has an important public policy role and provides considerable relief for the working poor, its benefits phaseout rather quickly as income rises above modest levels, and the credit therefore has vanishing value for individuals and families at higher income levels.

Adoption Credit. Section 23 allows a refundable credit for qualifying adoption expenses of up to $10,000 for each eligible child. The benefit of the credit phases out as adjusted gross income rises above $150,000 and disappears completely when AGI exceeds $190,000. The phaseout range and the cap on qualifying expenses under § 23 are adjusted annually for inflation, so that in 2004 the maximum credit was $10,390 and the phaseout applied to taxpayers with AGIs between $155,860 and $195,860.

Other Credits. The Code allows several other credits, in addition to those mentioned above, which may be of interest to some taxpayers. These include: (1) the credit for elderly or permanently and totally disabled individuals (I.R.C. § 22); (2) the credit for contributions to individual retirement accounts and elective deferral plans (I.R.C. § 25B); and (3) the credit for interest on certain home mortgages (I.R.C. § 25). All of these credits are available only to low income individuals and therefore do not play a significant role in family wealth management. Other credits such as the credit for purchases of qualified electric vehicles (I.R.C. § 30) may be of occasional interest to a limited class of taxpayers at middle and high income levels.

G. BUSINESS EXPENSES

[¶ 3,300]

Section 162 of the Code allows a deduction for "ordinary and necessary expenses paid or incurred during the taxable year in carrying on any trade or business." Such deductions may be claimed either by individuals working as employees (including self-employed individuals) or by business entities such as partnerships or corporations. It is important to bear in mind that individual employees are viewed as engaged in business with respect to their employment. For example, an associate in a law firm is in the business of being a lawyer and a high school English teacher is in the business of being a teacher. We will see that the Code imposes a special limitation on the deduction of employee business expenses under § 162 (see ¶ 3,330). It is also important at outset to note that a taxpayer may only claim a deduction for his own business expenses and may not claim a deduction for the expenses of another. See Deputy v. Du Pont, 308 U.S. 488 (1940). For example, a parent may not take a deduction for office rent paid on behalf of a child who is opening a professional practice, but it may be possible to treat the payment as a gift from parent to child coupled with a constructive rent payment by the child.

The broad language of § 162 is qualified by several limitations in § 162 and elsewhere in the Code on the deductibility of expenditures in connection with trade or business activities. Our focus here is on some limitations that affect family wealth management.

[¶ 3,310]

1. Ordinary and Necessary Expenses

Section 162 allows a deduction for "ordinary and necessary expenses." The primary function of the term "ordinary" is not to limit deductions to conventional business outlays and thereby bar resort to new ways of conducting business operations. For example, advertising on the internet is a relatively recent phenomenon, but the "ordinary" requirement did not prevent the earliest internet advertisers from deducting their expenses. The primary practical function of the term is to disallow a deduction for "extraordinary" capital expenditures or investments. For example, the purchase of an office or factory is an extraordinary outlay which cannot be deducted as an ordinary business expense in the year of purchase. (We will see that the Code allows a depreciation deduction as a means of recovering the cost of such assets over a number of years.)

The courts have viewed expenses as "necessary" even if they are not absolutely essential to the continued operation of the business. The term "necessary" is construed, along with "ordinary," to mean that an expense must be "helpful or appropriate" to be deductible. See Welch v. Helvering, 290 U.S. 111 (1933).

The term "expense" should be understood as barring taxpayers from deducting outlays for "investments" as contrasted with ordinary and necessary "expenses." Thus, although a taxpayer may claim a § 162 deduction for items such as rent, utilities and wages that are all part and parcel of the day-to-day operations of a business, no deduction is allowed for the purchase of capital assets such as office furniture, automobiles or realty used in a business. The same rule also prevents taxpayers from claiming an immediate deduction for the cost of intangible assets. For example, the purchaser of a sole proprietorship who purchases both tangible assets (such as office furniture and a building) and intangible assets (such as goodwill and going concern value) may not deduct the cost of any of the purchased assets. He may, however, claim a depreciation deduction under § 168 for the cost of tangible assets such as the furniture and building that have a limited useful life. In addition, he may recover the cost of most of the purchased intangibles over a period of 15 years, under § 197. Due to the time value of money, taxpayers generally prefer to deduct the entire cost of assets immediately, if possible, instead of spreading out the deductions over a number of years.

[¶ 3,320]

2. Carrying on a Trade or Business

A taxpayer must be engaged in or "carrying on" a trade or business before she can deduct any expenses with respect to the business under § 162. For example, a dentist who hires a consultant to see whether it makes sense to acquire a new McDonald's franchise in an area adjacent to a national park cannot deduct the consultant's fees under § 162 because the dentist is not carrying on a fast food business. Moreover, the I.R.S. may successfully argue that, even if the investor operated several other fast food operations in other locations, the new franchise constitutes a different business and the consultant's fees were incurred to investigate entry into a new business rather than to expand an existing business. See Central Texas Savings & Loan v. United States, 731 F.2d 1181 (5th Cir. 1984); but cf. NCNB v. United States, 684 F.2d 285 (4th Cir. 1982). Recognizing that the "carrying on" requirement might deter taxpayers from entering into new business ventures, Congress added § 195 to the Code. That section now allows a deduction for the first $5,000 of any such expenses and provides that the balance shall be amortized over a period of fifteen years.

Because § 162 requires that expenses be paid or incurred in carrying on a "trade or business," the Supreme Court has held that an investor may not claim a § 162 deduction for expenses incurred in connection with investment activities (as contrasted with business activities). See Higgins v. Commissioner, 312 U.S. 212 (1941). Congress responded by enacting § 212, which allows a deduction for expenses paid or incurred for the production or collection of income, for the management, conservation or maintenance of income-producing property, or in connection with the determination, collection or refund of any tax. For example, a taxpayer who owns undeveloped real estate and a stock portfolio as investments may not claim a § 162 deduction for the cost of periodically clearing the land of brush that is a fire hazard or for investment or tax advice in connection with her portfolio. Nonetheless, these expenses are deductible under § 212. Section 212 adopts a rather generous position with respect to expenses for tax planning and return preparation services. As a result, it is common for divorce lawyers, estate planners, business lawyers, and others who provide tax advice to indicate what portion of their fees are attributable to such advice so that their clients can deduct at least a portion of their bills.

[¶ 3,330]

3. The Two Percent Haircut

In 1986, Congress sought to reduce tax rates without losing revenue. To accomplish this, it was necessary to raise revenue by curtailing various tax benefits. One of the revenue raisers was § 67, which basically requires taxpayers to aggregate their § 212 deductions and their employee business expenses and allows these items to be deducted only to the extent that they exceed two percent of adjusted gross income. This provision is commonly referred to as the "two percent haircut."

To illustrate the operation of § 67, assume that Sam, who is employed by a large corporation as an in-house attorney, had AGI of $90,000. He paid $750 to his accountant to prepare his tax return, $800 to his financial advisor, and $100 for a subscription to an investment newsletter. In addition, Sam paid $200 as bar association dues and $50 for a subscription to a corporate law journal. Under § 67, Sam must combine the $1,650 of § 212 expenses with $250 of employee business expenses for a total of $1,900, and then reduce this total by $1,800 (2% of $90,000 AGI). As a result, Sam can deduct only $100 of his $1,900 combined § 212 expenses and § 162 employee business expenses.

Because of § 67, many high-income taxpayers often derive little or no tax benefit from outlays for employee business expenses and § 212 expenses.

[¶ 3,335]

Problems

1. Graciana has just completed a residency in psychiatry at State University Medical School Hospital where she served as a member of the hospital staff. She has just signed a lease for a new office. She will be bringing several of her established patients over to her practice and State University has promised to provide her with a number of referrals from its student health services. Her parents have indicated that they are willing to spend $8,000 purchasing furniture to assist her in opening up her office. They have also told her that they are willing to help her out with the $1,000 per month office rent for the first few months until she can make it on her own. Do you have any reactions or suggestions to share with the family?

2. Graciana has also consulted an attorney to obtain advice about the best business form she should use from both a tax and asset preservation standpoint. She has paid him $4,000 for his advice. Will this sum, or a portion of it, be deductible by Graciana?

[¶ 3,340]

4. Personal versus Business Expenses

Expenditures for personal activities are clearly consumption by the taxpayer and any deduction for such outlays would be inconsistent with the Haig–Simons definition of income. Section 262 provides that, except as authorized by another provision of the Code, "no deduction shall be allowed for personal, living or family expenses." Some of the most contentious issues in this area involve travel and commuting expenses, entertainment expenses, meals and lodging expenses, business related clothing, and home office expenses.

Clothing. Any professional person who has purchased a dark pin-striped suit or other office apparel has a visceral feeling that the cost should be deductible as a business expense. Nevertheless, the I.R.S. and the courts have consistently held that the cost of clothing is not deductible under § 162 unless the clothing is: (1) required as a condition of employment; and (2) unsuitable for other non-business use. See Rev. Rul. 70–474, 1970–2 C.B. 34; Pevsner v. Commissioner, 628 F.2d 467 (5th Cir. 1980). Business suits fail this test because they can be worn to ceremonial events such as weddings, funerals, baptisms and bar mitzvahs. Examples of clothing that qualifies for deduction are uniforms worn by postal workers, law enforcement officers and flight attendants.

Travel and Commuting. The costs of commuting between the taxpayer's residence and her place of business are nondeductible personal expenses; they follow from the taxpayer's choice of residence. Once the taxpayer arrives at her office, the cost of travel to meet with customers and other necessary business trips are deductible as business expenses. Moreover, if the taxpayer, rather than going directly to work, first commutes from home to a client's place of business, the cost of that travel is fully deductible. Where the taxpayer works out of her home and travels to meet clients, the cost of all such travel is deductible as a business expense. See Rev. Rul. 99–7, 1999–1 C.B. 361. Similarly, the cost of travel away from the taxpayer's normal place of business for business purposes is deductible. In cases where the taxpayer must use extraordinarily expensive means of transportation to transport not only himself, but also cumbersome work equipment, from his home to a local work site, the additional transportation expenses above and beyond normal commuting expenses are deductible. See Rev. Rul. 75–380, 1975–2 C.B. 59.

Meals and Lodging. Section 162(a)(2) specifically allows a business expense deduction for meals and lodging, other than amounts that are "lavish or extravagant," while the taxpayer is "away from home in pursuit of a trade or business." The courts have applied an "overnight" test to all such expenses. For example, assume that two lawyers, Tom and Sally, fly to Washington, DC to review documents on file with the S.E.C. They eat lunch and dinner by themselves. Tom flies back to their home city so he can spend the evening with his family before returning to work the next morning. Sally, who is single, decides to stay overnight in Washington and flies back to their home city early the next morning. None of their expenses are reimbursed by their employer. Sally can deduct the costs of her travel and her meals and lodging, whereas Tom can deduct only his travel costs (taxi and air fare). We will later see that only half of the cost of Sally's meals is deductible due to special limitations on the deduction of business related meals and entertainment expenses.

The § 162 deduction is also available to individuals who are temporarily stationed at a distant location in pursuit of business, as long as the assignment does not last longer than one year. For example, a New York attorney who spends two months litigating a case in Cleveland may claim a deduction for his meals and lodging while in Cleveland. The deduction is also used by visiting professors who leave their home institutions for one or two semesters to teach at another institution. In such cases only the meals and lodging of the individual away from home for business purposes are deductible; the meals and lodging of accompanying family members are not. For example, if Jack travels to San Diego on a business trip, accompanied by his wife Melissa, and the couple stays in a hotel that charges a fixed price for a room regardless of the number of occupants, then the full cost of the room would be deductible. If the hotel charged an incremental amount for additional occupants, then only the base price of the room would be deductible. Similarly, although a married couple can claim a deduction for the full cost of a one-bedroom apartment where only one spouse is traveling for business purposes, a family of five that rents a four-bedroom house while one spouse is on a temporary assignment away from her place of employment can deduct only the portion of the cost attributable to the business traveler. Where business travelers do not go out to restaurants for meals, they frequently find it advantageous to use the standard allowance that the I.R.S. provides for meals away from home. See I.R.S. Pubs. 463 and 1542.

Entertainment. In some business settings it is customary (or even obligatory, as a practical matter) to spend substantial amounts to entertain clients. A dinner followed by a theater performance or a ball game may be good for business as well as enjoyable for both the taxpayer and the client. To guard against potential abuse, § 274 distinguishes entertainment activities that are directly related to the taxpayer's trade or business from those that are merely associated with a trade or business. Examples of directly related activities include a food manufacturer which offers free samples of its products to potential customers, or a hotel which offers complimentary meals, lodging and entertainment to solicit convention business from visiting members of a sponsor's selection committee. For entertainment directly related to a trade or business, the taxpayer must satisfy certain recordkeeping requirements.

Entertainment that is merely associated with business activities must meet a higher standard. To be deductible, such entertainment must be either preceded or followed by business discussions. I.R.C. § 274(a)(1)(A). For example, a manufacturer's representative who takes a retailer's purchasing agent out to dinner and a ball game could engage in business discussions with the agent during dinner or the next morning while visiting with the agent.

In response to widespread abuses involving entertainment on facilities such as yachts, beach homes and the like, § 274(a)(1)(B) prohibits all deductions for such facilities when used for entertainment. Before the enactment of this provision, some taxpayers sought to deduct all or most of the costs of owning such facilities, alleging that the facilities were used exclusively or primarily for client entertainment. Although the bar on deductions has effectively put an end to these abuses, the owner of such facilities may nevertheless deduct the indirect costs of using them for entertainment. For example, a taxpayer who invites weekend guests to his beach house to discuss business may deduct the cost of meals and other entertainment expenses, although he may not deduct any expenses associated with the house itself. The same treatment applies to membership in social, athletic and sporting clubs. Thus, although a taxpayer's initiation fee and membership dues at a country club are not deductible, greens fees, meals and beverages paid on behalf of a business client are allowable as deductions provided all other requirements are met.

Section 274 imposes recordkeeping requirements as a condition for deductibility of all travel expenses (including meals and lodging while away from home) and entertainment expenses. In general, taxpayers must maintain adequate records or other corroborating evidence to substantiate the amount of the expense, the location and time, the business purpose of the activities and the relationship of any entertained individuals to the business involved. In addition, in the case of associated entertainment, there must be a record that business discussions took place. I.R.C. § 274(d).

Section 274 imposes several additional limitations on the deduction of business expenses. First, the deduction for meals and entertainment is limited to 50% of the cost of such items. This limitation applies to all expenditures for food (including meals while away from home), and reflects the notion that these expenditures involve an element of personal consumption as well as business activities. As a result, individuals such as salesmen who buy their meals on the road can deduct only half of such expenses. Interstate truckers, commercial pilots and others whose hours are limited by the Department of Transportation have successfully lobbied for more favorable treatment with the result that, by 2008, such individuals will be allowed to deduct 80% of such expenses. I.R.C. § 274(n). Second, no deduction is allowed for travel as a form of education. I.R.C. § 274(h)(7). Thus, a French professor may not deduct the cost of an annual trip to France to soak up the culture (although a research trip is allowable), and an investor may not deduct under either § 162 or § 212 the cost of attending an weekend financial planning seminar aboard a cruise liner or at a mountain resort. Third, there are considerable limitations on the deduction for professional meetings abroad. These rules are aimed at abuses but are flexible enough to accommodate most situations where there are legitimate reasons for locating a meeting abroad. See I.R.C. § 274(h).

[¶ 3,345]

Problems

1. Daniel is employed as an associate at a law firm. His annual salary is $150,000. Daniel believes that his success in the courtroom is attributable to not only his legal skills but to his fine taste in clothing. He spent $5,000 last year on Brooks Brothers suits, fine silk ties and handmade white shirts. He only uses such attire in the courtroom and office and normally dresses in chinos and knit shirts. He also paid $300 out-of-pocket for membership dues in his state bar association, $400 for services related to management of his investments and $500 for tax preparation services. Because of investment income of $5,000 and his deduction of $30,000 for alimony to his ex-wife, Daniel's adjusted gross income is $125,000. He wishes to know if any of his expenses for clothing, bar membership, investment management and tax preparation services will be deductible as itemized expenses.

2. Sara, Hanan and Molly are forming their own consulting business which will be organized as a limited liability company. Molly has suggested

that rather than reimbursing employees for all expenses incurred on behalf of the firm, to simplify record keeping, the firm pay employees a good salary and tell them that they are expected to pay out of pocket for any single expense, including entertainment and travel, that is less than $250 for a single item or until all unreimbursed expenses, in aggregate, exceed $2,500 per employee. Hanan says that in addition to having adverse effects on employee morale, he believes that this may not make much sense from a tax standpoint. They seek your reaction.

3.   What concerns would you have about Molly's suggestion and the recordkeeping requirements of the Internal Revenue Code with respect to entertainment expenses?

[¶ 3,350]

5.   Reasonable Compensation

Under § 162(a)(1), the deduction for business expenses includes a "reasonable allowance for salaries or other compensation for personal services actually rendered." The primary function of this language is to disallow a deduction for excessive or unreasonable salaries paid by a business owner to family members. The problem of excessive compensation most commonly arises in a family-owned corporation, where executives sometimes attempt to avoid the burden of a corporate-level tax by labeling payments to themselves or family members as deductible salary rather than nondeductible dividends. In the case of a purported salary paid to a "no-show" employee, the entire payment is typically recharacterized as a nondeductible dividend. In the case of an excessive salary paid to an officer-shareholder who actually performs services for the corporation, the disallowance is limited to the portion of the payment that exceeds the reasonable value of the officer's services. (A preferable approach, if available, would be to organize the business at the outset as a partnership or an "S" corporation. The income earned by these entities generally passes through to investors, regardless of distributions, without a separate tax at the entity level. However, payment of unreasonable compensation to non-investors such as children still gives rise to disallowance of the deduction to the partnership or S corporation).

In closing it is worth noting that where an employer makes a legitimate bad business decision and overcompensates an individual (e.g., a major league baseball team that signs an aging shortstop to a multimillion dollar five-year contract and soon comes to regret its decision), the IRS does not add insult to injury by disallowing a deduction for a portion of the compensation.

[¶ 3,360]

6.   Education Expenses

In appropriate circumstances, individuals who are already employed may claim a deduction for education expenses that maintain or improve their skills or satisfy the requirements of an employer or a professional accrediting agency. The requirements for deductibility of such education expenses are discussed at ¶ 6,130.

[¶ 3,370]

7. The Public Policy Issue

Before 1969, it was not uncommon for the I.R.S. to challenge a claimed business expense deduction on the ground that the expense was contrary to public policy. The courts, however, had difficulty in agreeing on acceptable standards of business conduct. To provide more uniform and predictable results, Congress amended § 162 to specify limited circumstances in which deductions for certain business expenditures are disallowed. It is important to emphasize that, although the open-ended public policy doctrine has been preempted with respect to business expenses under § 162, it continues to flourish under other provisions of the Code. See Blackman v. Commissioner, 88 T.C. 677 (1987) (denying casualty loss deduction under § 165(c)(3), based on public policy considerations, where taxpayer's backyard revenge burning of spouse's clothing resulted in fire passing to uninsured residence).

The statutory disallowance rules of § 162 apply to: (1) fines or penalties paid to a government for violation of a law; (2) two-thirds of certain antitrust damages; (3) campaign contributions or other payments to influence elections or legislation, including many lobbying expenditures; (4) bribes or kickbacks to government officials; (5) commercial bribes or kickbacks in violation of generally enforced federal or state laws, if sanctioned by a criminal penalty or loss of professional license or right to engage in a business; and (6) kickbacks, rebates or bribes in connection with Medicare or Medicaid services. See § 162(c), (e), (f), (g).

H. DEPRECIATION AND DEPLETION

[¶ 3,400]

Allowing a deduction for the cost of capital assets in the year of purchase would violate the Haig–Simons definition of income. When a taxpayer purchases an asset, such as an office building or a piece of equipment, which will endure for many years, there is no immediate change in her net worth—the purchase affects only the composition of her assets. However, as business assets decline in value due to wear and tear and obsolescence over time, there will be a corresponding decline in the taxpayer's net worth. The depreciation deduction is intended to allow the taxpayer to recover the cost of certain assets over time. The deduction is available for assets that are either used in a trade or business or held for the production of income, and the applicable rules are found primarily in §§ 167, 168, 179 and 195 of the Code.

The discussion here focuses on four principal issues concerning the depreciation deduction: (1) whether the asset in question is one that will decline with the passage of time due to obsolescence, wear and tear or the passage of time; (2) when the taxpayer is entitled to begin taking the depreciation deduction; (3) what is the period of time over which the taxpayer can recover the cost of the asset; and (4) how fast the cost of the assets can be recovered over the recovery period.

[¶ 3,410]

1. Wasting Assets

To qualify for the depreciation deduction, an asset must be one that declines in value over time. The decline in value may be attributable to wear and tear, obsolescence or the asset's having a limited useful life. An example of a capital business asset that does not qualify for the depreciation deduction is land. Nevertheless, a building located on land and used in a trade or business has a limited useful life and qualifies for the depreciation deduction. For example, a taxpayer who pays $800,000 for land and an office building must apportion the purchase price between the land and the building; only the cost of the building qualifies for the depreciation deduction. A patent is an example of an asset that declines in value due to the passage of time. Scientific equipment, which may not be subject to significant wear and tear but will eventually lose value due to technological innovation, is an example of equipment that declines in value due to obsolescence.

[¶ 3,420]

2. Placed in Service

A taxpayer may not claim a depreciation deduction for a qualifying asset under § 167 until the asset is "used in a trade or business" or "held for the production of income." The mere acquisition of assets for future use in a trade or business or for the production of future income does not entitle the taxpayer to an immediate depreciation deduction. The assets must be placed in service. For example, a taxpayer who is constructing a building for industrial or rental use cannot deduct any depreciation until the building is available for use in the business or for rental to tenants, and this generally occurs when the taxpayer receives a certificate of occupancy from local authorities.

[¶ 3,430]

3. Useful Life

The shorter the useful life assigned to a depreciable asset, the faster the taxpayer's recovery of his cost and the greater the benefit of the depreciation deduction. Initially, taxpayers claimed depreciation for an asset based on their estimate of the asset's useful life, and the I.R.S. often concluded that a longer useful life was appropriate. To stem the ensuing flood of litigation, the I.R.S. published a bulletin the size of a small telephone directory listing useful lives for many thousands of assets, and later published a series of guideline class lives for all assets used in certain industries and business applications. For example, instead of assigning separate lives for different types of office equipment (e.g., desks, files and office safes), the I.R.S. initially assigned a single life of 10 years for all office equipment. The guideline class lives, and the corresponding cost recovery periods have been modified from time to time by the I.R.S. through the issuance of Revenue Procedures or by Congress through legislation. For example, property such as office equipment, which initially had a guideline life of 10 years, is now classified as 7–year property for purposes of tax depreciation. See I.R.C. § 168(e); Rev. Proc. 87–56, 1987–2 C.B. 674.

[¶ 3,440]

4. Depreciation Methods

Section 168 prescribes a "modified accelerated cost recovery system" (MACRS) for computing the recovery period and annual computation method for depreciation of tangible assets. Depreciation of intangible assets, such as patents and copyrights, is governed by § 167, which allows straight line depreciation over the asset's actual remaining useful life. Intangible assets acquired in the purchase of a business are assigned a useful life of 15 years for depreciation purposes under § 195.

MACRS allows two principal methods for computing annual depreciation deductions: (1) the straight line method; and (2) the declining balance method. Under the straight line method, the annual depreciation deduction is equal to a fixed fraction of the taxpayer's original basis (typically cost) for the asset in question. For example, a taxpayer who paid $8,000 for an asset which is depreciable over 10 years using the straight line method can deduct depreciation of $800 per year.

Under the declining balance method, the taxpayer applies a constant percentage (either 200% or 150%) against her original basis reduced by the sum of all previously claimed depreciation. For example, if the taxpayer in the previous example uses the 200% declining balance method on the asset with a 10–year life and an original cost of $8,000, the depreciation deductions would be $1,600 in the first year (1/10 × 2.00 × $8,000), $1,280 in the second year (1/10 × 2.00 × $6,400), $1,024 in the third year (1/10 × 2.00 × $5,120), and so on. Under the 150% declining balance method, a factor of 1.50 would be substituted for 2.00 in the above computations.

MACRS not only allows shorter recovery periods and front-loaded depreciation deductions but also attempts to simplify the computation of depreciation deductions in several ways. First, although the declining balance method accelerates cost recovery in the early years, a taxpayer who persists in using it for the entire cost recovery period will find that he has not recovered his original basis in full. To remedy this, MACRS automatically switches the taxpayer who uses the declining balance method over to the straight line method as soon as it is more advantageous to do so. Second, MACRS provides a series of charts with depreciation schedules for various cost recovery periods, including the automatic switch from the declining balance method over to the straight line method. The charts are structured based on the assumption that a taxpayer on average will acquire assets mid-way through the tax year. This results in taxpayers having to depreciate assets over one more year than their assigned recovery period. To guard against a taxpayer's attempt to back-load purchases of assets in a tax year (for example purchasing a fleet of trucks in December), § 168 provides mechanisms for reducing the amount of depreciation allowed in the first year.

[¶ 3,450]

5. Automobiles and SUVs

Taxpayers are allowed to depreciate automobiles used in their trade or business over a 5–year recovery period. Automobiles are often used for mixed business and personal purposes, and the tax law attempts to guard against potential abuses in several ways. First, records of business and personal use must be kept for all vehicles, and the allowable depreciation is reduced in proportion to any personal use. Taxpayers whose use of a vehicle is divided between business and personal use may elect to forgo depreciation and instead claim a deduction based on the number of business miles of use (37.5¢ per mile in 2004). Second, if personal use of a vehicle exceeds 50% of total use, accelerated depreciation is not available. Third, if a vehicle is converted from predominantly business to predominantly personal use, any previously claimed accelerated depreciation in excess of straight line depreciation must be recaptured (in essence, retroactively disallowed). Fourth, to discourage the purchase of luxury automobiles by businesses, the allowable depreciation for any automobile used in a trade or business is limited to specified dollar amounts, which are adjusted for inflation. The allowable amounts are so modest that only low-cost cars, such as Chevy Cavaliers and Toyota Corollas, are likely to be fully depreciated in the normal 5–year period. Any amount not recovered by the end of the 5–year recovery period can still generate depreciation deductions, but all subsequent depreciation is limited to the amount allowed in the last year for which a full depreciation deduction was permitted. I.R.C. § 280F. Thus, a taxpayer who purchases a Porsche as a company car may well reach retirement age before the car is fully depreciated. These limitations on depreciation for "luxury" vehicles do not apply, however, to vehicles above a certain weight limit (3 tons). This 6,000 pound exception, originally created to allow heavy expensive vehicles (such as limos purchased by a limo service) to be fully depreciated over a 5–year recovery period, has in recent years allowed taxpayers who purchase expensive sport utility vehicles for business use to depreciate their vehicles fully over the 5–year recovery period. Moreover, a taxpayer who is fortunate enough to qualify under § 179 (discussed below) may buy a 4–ton Hummer for business use and under § 179 claim a deduction for $25,000 of the cost and then deduct the balance of the cost over the 5–year recovery period that applies to automobiles. Keep in mind that the proud owner of this gas-guzzler will also be able to deduct the cost of fuel as a business expense.

[¶ 3,460]

6. Section 179

It clearly would be burdensome for a small business owner such as a carpenter or a landlord with one or two residential rental units to calculate depreciation and maintain the required records for wasting assets of modest value. To simplify the tax affairs of small businesses, Congress added § 179 to the Code. This section, which applies only to otherwise depreciable tangible assets used in the United States, allows a taxpayer to elect to deduct up to $100,000 in the year of purchase through 2007, however in the case of vehicles in excess of 6,000 pounds the maximum amount deductible is $25,000. For tax years beginning after 2007, the $100,000 maximum deductible amount is scheduled to fall back to $25,000, but it appears unlikely that the $25,000 limitation will actually be allowed to take effect. To limit the benefit of the § 179 deduction, the maximum allowable deduction is cut back as the cost of qualified property placed in service in a given year rises above certain thresholds ($400,000 for years 2003 through 2007 and $200,000 thereafter). Both the $100,000 cap and the $400,000 phaseout threshold that apply for tax years 2003 through 2007 under § 179 are adjusted for inflation.

[¶ 3,465]

Problems

1. Karen is interested in purchasing a townhouse under construction to hold as an investment asset. The developer is asking $200,000 for units such as the one Karen is considering purchasing. She believes that, with the attractive financing package the developer is offering (95% financing on a 30–year mortgage with a favorable interest rate), she will be able to rent out the unit for $300 per month in excess of the cost of servicing her mortgage (including the escrow for real property taxes and insurance). Because of the prime location of the project, Karen anticipates that the value of the unit will increase at a rate of about 5% per year. Her friend Nicko has told her that because of the depreciation she will really have a better cash flow from the unit than $3,600 per year. Karen knows nothing about "depreciation" and seeks your advice. She asks whether depreciation is such a good deal that she should buy now and start claiming the deduction right away. She also asks if the amount of her depreciation deduction will be based on the full $200,000 cost of the property.

2. Todd is a successful real estate agent. He operates his own business and until recently had used a rented car as his business car. Todd is considering purchasing, as a business car, either a Mercedes–Benz or a

Humvee to impress clients. He tells you that he will use the car all day for business purposes, but it is a sure bet that if he purchases the Humvee his children will make great use of it on evenings and weekends. He says that the advantage to him of a Mercedes is that the children would find it as stuffy as he found his father's Oldsmobile and would avoid using it. Advise him of the tax consequences of his choices and the consequences of personal use of the vehicle.

3.   Your brother-in-law Bob is starting a construction business and is concerned about all the bookkeeping that will be involved in calculating depreciation each year on equipment that he purchases. His friends tell him it is a real headache. What can you tell him that will ease his anxieties?

[¶ 3,470]

7. Depletion

Mineral, oil and gas deposits can be viewed as wasting assets because individual deposits are limited and will be exhausted through extraction. To measure income accurately, the taxpayer must be allowed to reduce the gross receipts from extractive operations by a portion of his basis (typically cost) in the deposits in question. This is done in two ways: (1) the cost depletion allowance; and (2) the percentage depletion allowance. See I.R.C. §§ 611–613A.

Cost depletion allows the taxpayer to claim a portion of his cost against gross receipts realized from extractive operations. For example, assume that a taxpayer paid $2,200,000 for a tract of land that is known to contain 1,000,000 tons of coal and that the residual value of the land after the coal has been extracted will be $200,000. The taxpayer would be allowed to claim a depletion deduction of $2.00 against each ton of coal sold from the mine.

Percentage depletion allows the taxpayer to claim a statutory percentage of the gross receipts realized from extractive operations, regardless of his cost for the particular deposit. See I.R.C. § 613. For example, assume that a taxpayer purchased land for $100,000 and later began to mine silver ore, which is eligible for a 15% depletion allowance under § 613(b)(2). In his first year of operations, he realized $2,000,000 in gross receipts from sale of the ore. The taxpayer would have been allowed to claim a depletion deduction of $300,000 (15% of $2,000,000) in calculating net taxable income. Moreover, despite the fact that his allowable percentage depletion exceeded his entire investment in the property, he will still be allowed to claim percentage depletion in subsequent years on his mining operations for those years.

I. BASIS

[¶ 3,480]

"Basis" is a term of art that refers to the base amount used in measuring two important income tax characteristics of an asset: (1) the amount allowable as depreciation or cost depletion, in the case of a depreciable or depletable asset (see ¶¶ 3,440 and 3,470); and (2) the amount of gain or loss on the sale of the asset. When a taxpayer sells an asset, gain or loss is simply the difference between the sales proceeds and the taxpayer's basis in the asset. We will consider five basic rules for determining basis: (1) the cost basis rule (§ 1012); (2) the basis rule for property transferred by inter vivos gift (§ 1015); (3) the basis rule for inherited property (§ 1014); (4) the basis adjustment rules (§ 1016); and (5) the basis rules for property transferred between spouses or incident to a divorce (§ 1041).

[¶ 3,490]

1. Cost Basis

Under § 1012 of the Code, a taxpayer who purchases property generally has a basis in the property equal to its cost. The taxpayer's cost may consist of: (1) cash paid for property; (2) the value of other property provided as consideration for the purchase; (3) the value of services provided by the taxpayer to acquire property; and (4) the amount of any indebtedness assumed on the purchase of property or secured by the property, even if the taxpayer is not personally liable on the debt. For example, assume that Alice, as part of her compensation, receives stock of her employer worth $25,000 for a bargain purchase price of $10,000. Alice is deemed to receive compensation income of $15,000 in the transaction, and she has a cost basis of $25,000 in the stock. Assume that Frank purchases Blackacre by paying $25,000 in cash and assuming an existing mortgage debt of $75,000 on the property. Frank has a cost basis in Blackacre of $100,000. The result would be the same if he took title to Blackacre subject to the mortgage rather than assuming personal liability on the mortgage.

[¶ 3,500]

2. Property Acquired by Gift

Under § 1015, an individual who acquires property by inter vivos gift takes the property with what is commonly called a carryover basis. In the simplest case, this means that the donor's basis carries over to the donee, but § 1015(a) actually provides that the donee's basis "shall be the same as it would be in the hands of the donor or the last preceding owner by whom it was not acquired by gift, except that if such basis . . . is greater than the fair market value of the property at the time of gift, then for purposes of determining loss the basis shall be such fair market value."

If at the time of the gift the property is appreciated—its fair market value is equal to or greater than its basis in the donor's hands—the donee merely takes the donor's basis in the property. Where the fair market value is less than the donor's basis, the donee is entitled to use the donor's basis for the purpose of depreciation deductions, but the donee must wait until she sells the property to ascertain her basis for the purpose of determining gain or loss. If the property is sold for less than its fair market value at the time of the gift, the donee must use that fair market value as her basis and report a loss on the sale. For example, assume that Gene gave his daughter Moira property in which he had a basis of $10,000 but which, at the date of gift, was worth only $8,000. If Moira later sells the property for $5,000, she must use $8,000 as her basis in computing her loss of $3,000. On the other hand, assume that all of the facts are the same but that after Moira receives the property it appreciates in value and she sells it for $13,000. In this case, because there is no loss on the sale, Moira can use the donor's basis in the property and report a gain of only $3,000. If instead she sells the property for $9,000, she reports neither gain nor loss. See Reg. § 1.1015–1(a)(2).

Donors are often advised against making gifts of property that would be subject to the loss limitation rule of § 1015(a). It is generally preferable for the donor to sell such property, make a gift of the sale proceeds, and claim the resulting loss on his tax return. If the property is given to the donee, then, unless the property dramatically increases in value, the opportunity to use the donor's full basis in the property may be lost.

If gift tax was paid on a gift of appreciated property, § 1015(d) allows the donee to increase her basis in the property by a portion of the gift tax paid. The adjustment is limited to the amount of gift tax which is attributable to the net appreciation in the property (i.e., the difference between the property's fair market value and the donor's basis at the time of the gift). For example, if the donor makes a gift of property with a fair market value of $50,000 and a basis of $20,000, and he pays $10,000 of gift tax on the transfer, then the donee takes a basis of $26,000 in the property (the donor's $20,000 basis plus 60% of the gift tax).

Where property is sold to an individual at a bargain price, the transaction is part gift and part sale, and the regulations indicate that the donee takes either a carryover basis or a cost basis, whichever is greater. See Reg. § 1.1015–4. For example, if Marie owns a parcel of land with a fair market value of $50,000 and a basis of $25,000, and sells it to her daughter Paola for $10,000, Paola takes a carryover basis of $25,000 in the land. If Marie instead sold the land to Paola for $35,000, Paola would have a basis of $35,000.

[¶ 3,510]

3. Property Acquired from a Decedent

Under § 1014(a), an individual who acquires property from a decedent generally takes the property with a basis equal to its fair market value at the date of death. This is usually the same as the value reported on the estate tax return, if one is required to be filed. (Special rules apply where property was valued for estate tax purposes using the alternate valuation date of § 2032, the special valuation rules of § 2032A for certain farm or business assets, or the exclusion for qualified conservation easements under § 2031(c).) The rule of § 1014(a) is commonly referred to as a basis "step-up" rule. However, where assets have declined in value, the basis of assets acquired from a decedent must be "stepped-down" to their date of death value.

Section 1014(e) provides an exception to the general basis "step-up" rule of § 1014(a) where the decedent received a gift of appreciated property from a donor within one year before death and the property then passes at death back to the donor (or the donor's spouse). The exception also applies if such property is sold by the decedent's estate and the proceeds are distributed back to the donor (or the donor's spouse). The purpose of this provision can be illustrated by the following example. Assume Dad has $500,000 worth of XYZ stock which he purchased years ago for $50,000 and that Mom, who is on death's doorstep, has an estate of about $5,000,000. Her will provides that her child Sue will receive property in an amount equal to the estate tax exemption and that Dad will receive the rest of her estate. The ABC bank, as Mom's executor, is given discretion to determine what property should be allocated to each of the beneficiaries. Absent § 1014(e), Dad could make a gift of the XYZ stock to Mom shortly before her death (which will escape gift tax due to the marital deduction, as described in ¶ 4,340) and then stand by to receive it back with a stepped-up basis at her death, assuming that ABC would honor his suggestion that the stock be allocated to him. In this particular case, the executor could easily sidestep § 1014(e) by simply allocating the XYZ stock to Sue and other property to Dad. If Dad were the sole beneficiary of Mom's estate, or if the executor were required to allocate the XYZ stock to Dad, then § 1014(e) would perform its intended function.

Because of the different basis rules for property acquired by purchase, by gift and by inheritance, estate planners have developed some simple rules of thumb to maximize tax benefits for older individuals. Assets that have appreciated considerably should be retained to obtain the benefit of a stepped-up basis. Assets that have declined in value should generally be sold. Cash or assets that have only declined or appreciated modestly in value are good candidates for inter vivos gifts.

Beginning in 2010, the basis step-up rule of § 1014(a) for property acquired from a decedent is scheduled to be replaced by a new, modified carryover basis rule. In general, the recipient will take such property with a carryover basis equal to the decedent's basis or fair market value at death, whichever is less. Appreciated assets, however, will generally be eligible for a basis step-up of up to $1,300,000 (but not in excess of fair market value), and appreciated assets passing to the decedent's surviving spouse will generally be eligible for an additional basis step-up of up to $3,000,000 (but not in excess of fair market value). As a practical matter, appreciated assets in all but the largest estates will be completely sheltered from the carryover basis rule and will receive a full basis step-up. It appears likely that this carryover basis rule for property acquired from a decedent will be modified or even repealed before it takes effect in 2010.

[¶ 3,520]

4. Basis Adjustments

Section 1016 requires several adjustments to the basis of assets in a taxpayer's hands. The most important of these are: (1) an upward adjustment for improvements made to an asset and for other capital items; and (2) a downward adjustment for any depreciation claimed or allowable with respect to the asset. The downward adjustment for allowable depreciation applies even if the taxpayer, through ignorance or bad planning, fails to claim the full amount of depreciation to which she is entitled. For example, assume that a taxpayer purchased a rental unit for $120,000, properly claimed straight line depreciation of $20,000, made $8,000 of improvements, and then sold the unit for $150,000. The taxpayer would have an adjusted basis of $108,000 in the rental unit and would realize a gain of $42,000 from the sale. If the taxpayer failed to claim any depreciation on the rental unit, her basis would still be subject to a $20,000 downward adjustment and she would still be taxed on $42,000 of gain from the sale. If an asset could have been depreciated using an accelerated method, such as 200% declining balance, and the taxpayer failed to claim any depreciation, she would only be required to reduce basis using the straight line method. I.R.C. § 1016(a)(2).

[¶ 3,530]

5. Property Transferred Between Spouses

For many years, when a marriage ended in divorce and the spouses divided their property, there was a good chance that one spouse or the other would recognize taxable gain. If, for example, in a property settlement incident to divorce, a husband who owned stock with a basis of $40,000 and a fair market value of $100,000 transferred it to his wife in exchange for her release of other marital property rights, the husband would have had to report gain of $60,000. Depending on the type of property that the husband received from the wife, she too might have had to report a taxable gain. The transaction was analyzed as if one spouse had sold his or her interest in the property to the other in exchange for any property received in the property settlement. The resulting tax burden often came as an unwelcome surprise not only to the divorcing parties but also to their attorneys, who could find themselves at the wrong end of a malpractice suit due to their failure to pay attention to the tax consequences of the property settlement.

The divorce bar lobbied for a change in the tax law, and Congress responded in 1984 by adding § 1041 to the Code. Section 1041 basically provides that no gain or loss shall be recognized by spouses on a transfer of property between them during the marriage or on a transfer incident to divorce. A transfer is incident to a divorce if it occurs within one year of the date a marriage ceases or is related to the cessation of the marriage. If a transfer satisfies these conditions, the transferee takes the property with a basis equal to the transferor's basis. I.R.C. § 1041(b). Special rules apply, however, if one of the spouses is a non-resident alien. I.R.C. § 1041(d).

Section 1041 ensures that there is no immediate recognition of gain on any property division incident to a divorce. That provision does not provide permanent relief, however, but merely puts off the day of reckoning until the property is sold. Divorce attorneys must now focus their attention upon the basis rules. An attorney who is ignorant of § 1041 may feel he has done well for his client if he negotiates a satisfactory division of property based on fair market values. However, the attorney may be accepting a less favorable settlement than is appropriate, if the client ends up with property having a low basis (or other unfavorable tax characteristics). For example, assume that a married couple owns a parcel of land and shares of stock which are to be divided in a divorce settlement. Both assets have a fair market value of $800,000, but the land has a basis of $800,000 while the stock has a basis of only $50,000. If husband's attorney proposes that the husband should receive the land and the wife should receive the stock, the wife's attorney should object vigorously to the proposal. If the husband sold the land for its fair market value he would receive $800,000 after taxes, but if the wife sold the stock she would have a taxable gain of $750,000 which might easily generate a combined federal and state tax liability of more than $100,000. The tax characteristics of property—in this case, the basis under § 1041—can have a significant impact on the valuation of property in such situations, and the wife's attorney should either reject the proposal or ask for additional property in the exchange.

[¶ 3,535]

Problems

1.   Adam purchased a residential rental unit for $200,000 by paying the seller $40,000 in cash and taking out a $160,000 purchase money mortgage. He then spent $20,000 enclosing a carport to turn it into an additional room. Adam rented the unit for several years and claimed $15,000 of straight-line depreciation on the property. He recently gave the property, which was appraised at a value of $250,000, to his daughter Christine. What is the Christine's adjusted basis in the property? Would your answer change if you discovered that, during his ownership, Adam had also spent $3,000 making necessary repairs on the unit?

2.   Paola purchased stock in Micro Industries Inc. for $10,000. When the fair market value of the stock had declined to $6,000 she gave it to her son Mark. What would be Mark's gain or loss on the stock if he later sold it for: (1) $5,000; (2) $8,000; or (3) $13,000?

3.   Elsie is 82 years old and her grandson Harold is s senior in law school. He told her that in his estate planning class he recently learned that, generally speaking, she should leave in her estate assets that are vastly appreciated, make gifts from cash and property that has not changed much in value since she purchased it, and sell property that has declined in value. Elsie did not wish to let Harold show off too much in front of her and told him that she has known that for years. She asks you, as her friend and financial adviser, to tell her if Harold knows what he is talking about and why that would be so.

4.   You have been invited by a local support group for individuals who are going through divorce to explain to the group the tax issues that are involved for couples in dividing assets incident to a divorce. Other individuals on a panel will be addressing the issues of alimony and child support. Prepare yourself to address the group.

J.   SALES AND DISPOSITIONS OF PROPERTY

[¶ 3,540]

We will discuss three major issues involving sales and dispositions of property. First, when does an event occur that makes an individual subject to tax with respect to property that has increased or decreased in value? Second, how is gain or loss to be calculated? Third, what are the principal non-recognition rules that apply to such transactions?

[¶ 3,550]

1.   Taxable Event

Under the realization rule, property held by a taxpayer is not subject to tax merely because it fluctuates in value, even though the fluctuations are reflected in the holder's net worth. However, when the holder transfers the benefits and burdens of ownership in property in exchange for something of value, in the absence of a non-recognition rule, gain or loss must be recognized. In most circumstances it is easy to identify such taxable events. They typically occur when a taxpayer sells property to another for a valuable consideration such as cash. Exchanges of property (unless covered by a non-recognition rule) can also constitute a taxable event. For example, assume that Bob owns $10,000 of Vanguard S & P 500 Index Fund shares which he purchased several years ago for $4,000. If he swaps those shares for shares in another Vanguard mutual fund, the transaction will be treated as if he had sold his shares for cash and then used the proceeds to purchase shares in a new fund. Similarly, if a taxpayer transfers appreciated property to another in exchange for services or in satisfaction of a debt, the transferor must recognize gain on the exchange. For example, if Larry accepts an improved lot from Builder in exchange for services rendered, Larry will be treated as receiving compensation from Builder equal to the fair market value of the lot, and Builder will have to recognize gain on the difference between his basis in the lot and its fair market value. This rule also applies where an executor satisfies a pecuniary bequest (a bequest of a specified amount of cash) with property of equal value held by the estate. The estate must recognize gain on the post-death appreciation in the property because it has distributed the property in satisfaction of an obligation to make a cash payment.

[¶ 3,560]

2. Amount Realized

The amount realized on a sale or other disposition of property is the sum of cash plus the fair market value of any other property received. The amount of gain or loss is then determined by subtracting the basis of the transferred property from the amount realized. For example, if Martha receives land worth $400,000 in exchange for a painting that she had purchased for $150,000, she has realized a gain of $250,000 on the sale of the painting.

Occasionally a taxpayer who owns encumbered property transfers it to a purchaser who either assumes personal liability on the debt or takes the property subject to the debt. In such a case, the face amount of the debt is treated as part of the amount realized in the sale. For example, assume that Rick owns a tract of land with a basis of $20,000 and a fair market value of $50,000, subject to a $15,000 mortgage loan. He sells the land to Martina, who pays him $35,000 in cash and takes the property subject to the mortgage. Rick has a taxable gain of $30,000 ($35,000 cash + $15,000 debt − $20,000 basis). The result would be the same if, instead of taking the property subject to the mortgage, Martina assumed the debt and thereby relieved Rick of any further personal liability in the event of default.

It is worth noting a few special situations involving dispositions of property. First, a gift of encumbered property can give rise to taxable income if the debt exceeds the donor's basis in the property. For example, if George gives his grandson Peter a vacation home which has a basis of $30,000 and a fair market value of $250,000 and is subject to a mortgage loan of $65,000, George will realize $35,000 of taxable gain ($65,000 debt − $30,000 basis). See Rev. Rul. 70–626, 1970–2 C.B. 158. Second, if a taxpayer makes a bargain sale of appreciated property to a charity, her basis is apportioned between the gift and sale components in proportion to their respective values, resulting in gain to the transferor. For example, if Roy makes a gift to charity of land with a basis of $10,000 and a fair market value of $60,000, subject to a $30,000 mortgage loan, he is treated as selling half of the property for the amount of the mortgage debt for a taxable gain of $25,000 ($30,000 amount realized minus a prorated basis of $5,000) and as making a deductible charitable contribution of the other half worth $30,000. See I.R.C. § 1011(b). Finally, the rule concerning encumbered property applies even if the liability exceeds the property's fair market value. For example, assume that Donna owns a building with a basis of $100,000 and a fair market value of $200,000, subject to a mortgage loan of $220,000. If Donna walks away from the property and turns it over to the lender, she will have taxable gain of $120,000 ($220,000 mortgage − $100,000 basis), regardless of whether she was personally liable on the mortgage loan. See Commissioner v. Tufts, 461 U.S. 300 (1983).

[¶ 3,565]

Problems

1. You have been appointed the executor of your late uncle's estate. His will directs that $20,000 be given to his alma mater State University. Your uncle's estate is short on cash but has a substantial amount of other liquid assets. What would be the income tax consequences if you, as executor, satisfied his bequest to State University with $20,000 of stock in Cree Industries which your uncle purchased for $4,000 and which was worth $18,000 on the date of his death (and was the value listed for the stock on his estate tax return)?

2. Pursuant to your uncle's will, his daughter Sally was entitled to receive half of his residuary estate. What would be the income tax consequences if instead of transferring the Cree stock to State University, you transferred it to Sally in partial satisfaction of this bequest to her?

3. Paul purchased a house as a rental unit for $200,000 by paying the seller $20,000 and financing the rest of the purchase price with a purchase money mortgage. During the last few years Paul has claimed $40,000 in allowable straight line depreciation deductions on the property. Because the mortgage is a 15–year balloon mortgage, Paul has not retired any of the debt on which he is still liable. The home is now worth $250,000 and Paul intends to transfer it, subject to the mortgage, to his daughter Ming as a wedding gift. No gift tax will be owed on the transfer. Although Paul assumes that Ming will live in the home with her new husband, he does not care if she sells it or continues to rent out the property. What are the income tax consequences for Paul? What will be Ming's adjusted basis in the home?

[¶ 3,570]

3. Non–Recognition Provisions

Of the various non-recognition provisions in the Code, we are here concerned primarily with those involving: (1) like kind exchanges; (2) involuntary exchanges; and (3) exchanges of stock on certain corporate acquisitions, divisions and stock dividends.

Like Kind Exchanges. Under § 1031, neither gain nor loss is recognized if a taxpayer who holds business or investment property exchanges it for other property of "like kind" and equal value to be used in his trade or business or held as an investment. For example, if Tom holds land as an investment and exchanges it for an office building of equal value to be used by him in his business, Tom will recognize no gain or loss on the exchange. Moreover, the taxpayer's basis in the old property is transferred to the new property received in the exchange. Thus, if Tom had a basis of $100,000 in the land held for investment, he would take the office building received in the exchange with the same basis, thereby preserving his built-in gain in the office building. This provision is important for real estate investors because it allows them to move from one investment to another without incurring any immediate income tax liability.

The term "like kind" is construed fairly liberally and refers to the nature and character of property rather than its quality. Without going into detail on what qualifies as a like kind exchange, two points are worth making here. First, an exchange of personal property for real property does not qualify as a like kind exchange. Second, most intangible and several tangible assets are ineligible for like kind exchange treatment. The prohibited assets include: (1) stock in trade, such as inventory, and other property held primarily for sale; (2) stocks, bonds, notes and other securities or evidences of indebtedness; (3) partnership interests; (4) certificates of trust or beneficial interests; and (5) choses in action. I.R.C. § 1031(a)(2).

When, as commonly occurs, the exchanged properties are unequal in value, one party must contribute some additional cash or other property to equalize the exchange, and the party who receives such nonqualifying consideration ("boot") must recognize gain to the extent of the lesser of the built-in gain in the transferred property or the boot received. For example, if Ellen transfers a tract of investment realty with a basis of $400,000 and a value of $750,000 to Scott in exchange for $50,000 cash and a residential rental unit with a basis of $300,000 and a value of $700,000, Ellen must recognize $50,000 in gain and she will take the residential unit with a basis of $400,000. Moreover, Ellen must either use the residential unit in a trade or business or hold it as an investment asset; if she uses the property as her personal residence, the transaction will not qualify as a like kind exchange.

Until recently, the most common barrier to the vigorous use of § 1031 arose from the difficulty of finding two parties who were willing to exchange properties. In some cases creative lawyers and developers managed to work out three-party swaps in which a would-be buyer who had agreed to "purchase" property from a seller would acquire other property desired by the seller and swap it with the seller for the seller's property. To make life simpler for sellers who wished to acquire "like kind" replacement property without recognizing gain, Congress added § 1031(a)(3), which allows a seller of investment or trade or business property to enter into a contract of sale that obligates the purchaser to arrange for the transfer to the seller of property of a specified value to be identified by the seller within a limited time frame. Under § 1031(a)(3), the seller has 45 days after the transfer of his property to identify replacement property, and the buyer must effect the transfer to the seller by the earlier of: (1) 180 days after the transfer of the seller's property to him; or (2) the time for filing the seller's tax return (including any extensions). The property so acquired in the "swap" must, of course, be used by the seller in his trade or business or held as an investment. Because of the vast profits which are often involved in sales of commercial real estate investments, this provision is of great importance to real estate investors.

Involuntary Exchanges. Section 1033 allows an individual to use the proceeds of an involuntary conversion of property to acquire replacement property that is of equal or greater value and "similar or related in use or service" (or to acquire control of a corporation which owns such property) without recognizing gain. Were it not for this provision, taxpayers who received insurance or condemnation proceeds for property that was lost in a fire or other casualty or taken in a condemnation proceeding might be hit with such a large tax bill that they might be unable to rebuild or replace their property.

Section 1033 requires that any reinvestment be made within a specific time frame. Specifically, the replacement property must be acquired within a period commencing at the earlier of loss of the property or the threat of condemnation and ending two years after the close of the tax year in which gain was realized. I.R.C. § 1033(a)(2)(B).

The replacement property must have virtually the same use as the converted property to be considered "similar or related in use or service." For example, a taxpayer may not replace a billiard parlor that was destroyed in a fire with a bowling alley; apparently the taxpayer would have to invest the insurance proceeds in another billiard parlor. See Rev. Rul. 76–319, 1976–2 C.B. 242. Nevertheless, § 1033(g) provides that where business or investment property is taken in a condemnation proceeding, property which is "of a like kind" shall be deemed to meet the "similar or related in use or service test." This more liberal rule for condemnations is necessary because frequently the location of a business that was seized is crucial to the success of a business of that character, and it would be impossible to run another business of the same type successfully at another location. It is important to bear in mind that the taxpayer need not use the proceeds of an insurance or condemnation settlement to acquire qualifying replacement property; § 1033 requires only that he acquire such qualifying property within the required time frame. For example, if a taxpayer owned an office building that was destroyed in a fire, he can satisfy the test and avoid recognizing gain if he keeps the insurance proceeds on deposit in the bank and borrows funds to build a replacement building of equal or greater value within the required time frame.

Under § 1033(b), if the taxpayer acquires qualifying replacement property of equal or greater value within the required time frame, her basis in the lost property is transferred to the replacement property, thereby preserving the taxpayer's built-in gain. For example, if a taxpayer had a basis of $300,000 in a rental property which was destroyed by fire, and she used the insurance proceeds and $150,000 of additional cash to acquire another rental property, her basis in the replacement property would be $450,000.

It is worth noting that taxpayers often welcome the news of condemnation proceedings because they see a tax-favored opportunity to change not only the location but also the character of a business or investment by investing in property that is "of like kind" in a new location with more potential for success.

Corporate Acquisitions, Divisions and Stock Dividends. It is impossible to discuss all the situations in which investors may escape gain recognition upon receipt of stock as a stock dividend, in a corporate division, or as a replacement for stock in another corporation. What is important here is to note that such events are commonplace for investors in publicly traded corporations. For example, an individual who purchased 200 shares of stock in Citibank in the early 1990's would find that because of a subsequent merger with another financial institution and a series of stock dividends, he would now own 1,000 shares of stock in a new corporation, Citigroup. Moreover, because of a corporate division by Citigroup, he would have held stock in Travelers Insurance Company which subsequently merged into St. Paul Insurance Company. All of this would have occurred without any income tax liability for the investor.

[¶ 3,575]

Problem

Your aged grandfather has held a warehouse for years in a decaying part of the city's old industrial quarter. To retain the local major league baseball team, the city has agreed to acquire a large tract of land that includes your grandfather's warehouse. Initial discussions indicate that your grandfather will be paid about $2,200,000 for the land and building, in which he has an adjusted basis of about $100,000. Your grandfather is in poor health and had hoped to hold the property until his death to be able to pass it to his children with a stepped-up basis. He considers the $2,200,000 to be a very good price, far more than he would have received had it not been part of a site for a new stadium. He also believes firmly in holding real estate as an investment and would reinvest the sales proceeds in replacement realty in a trendier area. What suggestions do you have for your grandfather to consider? If he sells the property what steps would you recommend he take? Is there any reason why you might advise him to wait for the city to threaten condemnation and then take their offer?

K. LOSSES

[¶ 3,580]

Pursuant to § 165(c) of the Code, individual taxpayers may deduct losses only on: (1) transactions entered into for profit; (2) trade or business activities; and (3) casualty losses. We will now look at several types of transactions to gain a better understanding of deductible losses.

[¶ 3,590]

1. Personal Losses

Section 165(c) makes it quite clear that, except for casualty losses, no deduction is allowed with respect to personal losses. For example, if an individual purchases a painting to hang in her living room and later sells the painting at a loss, she cannot claim any deduction for the loss. The theoretical justification for this result is that the loss flows from the taxpayer's decision to spend her money on personal consumption. Because the loss is a fair measure of personal consumption, at least with respect to that particular asset, allowing a deduction for the loss would be inconsistent with the Haig–Simons definition of income. Of course, it may seem unfair that had the taxpayer turned a profit on the sale she would have been required to include that in income. However, it must be recalled that the Code taxes all income from whatever source derived (see ¶ 3,012), and life is not always fair.

[¶ 3,600]

2. Gambling Losses

Under § 165(d), gambling losses are allowed as a deduction only to the extent that they offset the taxpayer's gambling winnings for the year. For example, if Dan had gambling winnings of $3,000 for the year and also had gambling losses of $4,500, he would be allowed to claim $3,000 of the losses to offset the gains, but the balance of his losses would not be deductible. Moreover, he would not be allowed to carry forward any of the unused losses to a subsequent year. The theory for allowing only a limited use of the losses is that gambling represents a combination of personal consumption and a series of transactions entered into for profit, and allowing losses only to the extent that they offset gains represents a fair compromise. Another way of looking at it is to say that the losses in excess of gains are a fair measure of the taxpayer's personal consumption. In closing, it should be noted that the courts have carved out an exception for professional gamblers, who are allowed to deduct their losses even when they exceed winnings on the basis that the losses are "trade or business" losses which are fully allowable under § 165(c).

[¶ 3,610]

3. Bad Debts

The treatment of bad debts is governed by § 166(a), which indicates that business and other bad debts that become worthless are allowed as a deduction in the year in which they become worthless. Section 166(a) also states that the I.R.S. may allow a taxpayer to deduct a partially worthless bad debt if it is satisfied that the debt is only partially collectible, in which case the deduction is limited to the amount that is written off as uncollectible.

In the case of non-business bad debts, § 166(d) indicates that such debts are not deductible as an ordinary loss but are allowed only as a short term capital loss. The tax treatment of short term capital losses is discussed later at ¶ 3,660. For now it is sufficient to note that this is considerably less advantageous to the taxpayer than if he could claim the loss as an ordinary loss. The most troublesome issue in this area involves situations where the taxpayer lends money with a dual motive. For example, assume that a taxpayer who is both a significant shareholder and an officer of a corporation lends money to the corporation during hard times and the corporation defaults on the loan. The courts have indicated that in such cases the outcome depends on the taxpayer's dominant motive. See United States v. Generes, 405 U.S. 93 (1972). To resolve the issue, one must determine whether in making the loan the taxpayer was motivated predominantly by fear of losing his employment (resulting in a business loss) or by concern about protecting his investment (resulting in a short term capital loss on a non-business bad debt).

[¶ 3,620]

4. Hobby Losses

When dealing with activities that some pursue for profit and others pursue for pleasure, it may be difficult to determine whether losses should be treated as trade or business losses—in which case they should be fully deductible (even to the extent of offsetting income from other sources)—or as nondeductible personal losses. Examples of such activities include farming, horse and dog breeding, and various racing and collecting activities.

Section 183 addresses this problem by disallowing a deduction for "hobby losses" with respect to activities not engaged in for profit. If the taxpayer's gross income from an activity exceeds the deductions attributable to the activity for at least three of the last five years (at least two of the last seven years, in the case of horse breeding, training, showing or racing), then the activity is rebuttably presumed to be engaged in for profit. The factors to be considered in determining whether an activity is engaged in for profit are discussed in Reg. § 1.183–2.

Even if an activity is determined to be a hobby (i.e., not engaged in for profit), the taxpayer may still claim all deductions to which he would be entitled as personal deductions (e.g. real property taxes) and may also claim other deductions to offset any remaining receipts from the activity. For example, assume that Bob, a Wall Street lawyer, spends his weekends as a gentleman farmer in activities not engaged in for profit. He received $8,000 from sales of organic produce and paid expenses of $1,500 for seeds and $4,000 for labor as well as $6,000 in real property taxes on the "farm." From the $8,000 in receipts, Bob can deduct the full $6,000 of property taxes as well as $2,000 of the remaining $5,500 in expenses, leaving no net gain or loss from the farm. On the other hand, if Bob had only $5,000 in receipts he would still be allowed to claim a deduction for the full amount of the real property taxes but would be allowed no further deductions.

Because the taxpayer is allowed to offset income from a hobby activity with deductions from the same activity, it is possible to obtain a limited benefit from hobby losses. For example, assume that Louise, who collects vases, sells a vase for a gain of $4,000. If she sells another vase in the same year for a loss of $3,000, she can use the loss to reduce her taxable gain to $1,000. Of course, if she instead sold another vase for a loss of $5,000, she would be allowed to use only $4,000 of that loss to offset the gain on the earlier sale; the remaining $1,000 of loss would be disallowed. This aspect of § 183 encourages collectors to match gains against losses on a yearly basis.

[¶ 3,630]

5. Vacation Homes

At one time taxpayers who used a vacation home for a portion of the year would hold it available for rent during the rest of the year and claim a deduction for most of their repair, insurance and maintenance costs (and even for depreciation). Congress added § 280A to the Code to curtail such deductions. Pursuant to § 280A(g) no deduction shall be allowed with respect to any personal use residence that is actually rented for less than 15 days during the year, nor is the income from any such rental required to be included in gross income. If the taxpayer's use of the residence exceeds the greater of 14 days or 10% of the number of days the home is actually rented, § 280A essentially treats the rental as a hobby activity with deductions being allowed first to the extent that they would be allowed as personal deductions and then to the extent of any remaining income not offset by such personal deductions. If the taxpayer's use falls below the statutory threshold, expenses are apportioned between the personal use and the business or rental use and a corresponding portion of the expenses are allowed as a business deduction or a § 212 deduction. For more detailed discussion, see ¶ 5,830.

[¶ 3,640]

6. Wash Sales

A taxpayer who owns a stock or other security that has declined in value may wish to sell the asset and then purchase an identical asset shortly before or after the sale, with the thought of realizing a deductible loss for tax purposes while maintaining an essentially unchanged investment position. For example, assume that Marge holds 100 shares of XYZ stock which she purchased for $8,000 and which is worth $5,000. Although Marge would like to sell her XYZ stock and deduct the loss, she wishes to maintain her position in the stock because she considers XYZ to be a likely takeover candidate. She sells her XYZ stock and almost immediately purchases another 100 shares of XYZ stock. If she does so, she will run afoul of the "wash sale" rule of § 1091, which disallows any such losses where the taxpayer also acquired an economically identical position in the same investment within 30 days before or after the sale.

[¶ 3,650]

7. Losses on Transactions with Related Parties

Suppose that, instead of engaging in a wash sale, the taxpayer seeks to achieve a similar result by selling the asset either to a family member or to an entity in which the taxpayer has a significant ownership stake (such as a corporation controlled by the taxpayer or members of his family). Section 267 is designed to prevent just such attempts at circumventing the realization rule with the aid of family members or controlled entities. Section 267 disallows losses between a taxpayer and an elaborate network of related individuals and entities. For our purposes, it is sufficient to note that the related parties covered by § 267 include: members of the taxpayer's family (siblings, ancestors, lineal descendants, and spouse), corporations controlled by the taxpayer and certain family members, partnerships in which he has a requisite ownership interest, and certain trusts. If the taxpayer engages in such a sale, the loss is disallowed, but the purchaser is, in essence, entitled to use the disallowed loss to offset any gain on a subsequent sale of the property. I.R.C. § 267(d). (This resembles the treatment of gifts of property where the donor's basis was greater than the property's value at the time of the gift, as discussed at ¶ 3,500.) For example, if Dad purchased stock for $9,000 and sold it to Son for $4,000, and Son then sells the stock to a third party for $3,000, Son has a loss of $1,000. If instead Son sells the stock to a third party for $5,000, he has no gain or loss, and if he sells it to a third party for $10,000, he has taxable gain of $1,000. The loss disallowance rules of § 267 make it unadvisable for most taxpayers to sell assets with built-in losses to related parties.

[¶ 3,655]

Problems

1. Three years ago you loaned a friend $20,000 to help him get through a difficult period with his business. Not only has your friend not paid you any interest on the debt, but he also recently filed for bankruptcy, showing no assets whatsoever and debts in excess of $400,000, most of which were secured by assets which he sold as his own to naive and trusting friends (fortunately you are not among these "friends"). To obtain the funds to loan to your friend, you had borrowed $20,000 as a home equity loan. The whole experience has made you more cautious about carrying debt and you have decided to sell your relatively new bass boat and retire the home equity loan. You had purchased the boat two months ago for $25,000 and "fortunately" you were recently able to sell it for $20,000. Can you claim any deduction for the loss on the loan to your friend and, if so, how should it be treated? What are the tax consequences of the loss on the sale of your bass boat? Would your answer depend on whether you sold it to a stranger or to your brother?

2. You have a vast collection of Wedgewood items and recently sold, at a loss of $2,000, an item that was determined to be a fake. You sometimes sell off lesser items in your collection, almost always at a profit, to raise money to enhance your collection. What should you now consider doing, besides being more careful about the authenticity of your next purchase?

3. Your spouse has just returned from visiting friends at their beach house. There your spouse met a high-powered salesperson who said that such homes, while expensive, could be purchased with assistance from the U.S. Treasury. According to the salesperson, not only are the real property taxes and interest deductible, but as long as you advertise the home "for rent," even if you do not get any takers, you will be able to depreciate the home and its contents and deduct all repairs and insurance, even though you and family members use the home for the summer months. What is your reaction to the sales pitch that your spouse received?

L. CAPITAL GAINS AND LOSSES

[¶ 3,660]

The Code provides special treatment for sales and dispositions of capital assets, including taxation at preferential rates. The discussion here focuses on the following topics: (1) the rules for determining the amount of capital gains and losses; (2) the preferential rates applicable to various types of capital gains; (3) the types of assets that qualify as capital assets for such purposes; (4) the sale or exchange requirement; (5) the special class of assets eligible for even more favorable treatment under § 1231; and (6) the "recapture" rules which treat some or all of the gain on depreciable assets as ordinary income.

[¶ 3,670]

1. Netting Rules

In determining the tax treatment of gains and losses from the sale of capital assets, it is necessary to know whether the assets sold were held for one year or less (short term) or for more than one year (long term). The taxpayer's holding period normally runs from her purchase of an asset. However, in the case of gift property, the donee is permitted to tack on the donor's holding period. I.R.C. § 1223(2). For example, if Max purchased stock for $4,000 and held it for eight months, then gave it to Cora when it was worth $4,500, and Cora sold the stock six months later, Cora's sale gives rise to long term gain or loss. In the case of most inherited property, the one-year holding period is deemed satisfied even if the combined holding period of the decedent and the heir is less than one year. I.R.C. § 1223(11). Moreover, a taxpayer who acquired stock in a tax-free transaction (such as a tax-free acquisition, division or stock dividend) can typically tack on the holding period for her original stock that was the source of the stock acquired in the tax-free transaction. See ¶ 3,570.

Because long term capital gains are taxed at lower rates than short term capital gains, it is important to understand the "netting rules" for determining the amount and character of gain subject to tax. First, the taxpayer must classify all capital gains and losses as long term or short term, and then compute the net amount of long term gain or loss as well as the net amount of short term gain or loss. If the netting process results in both long term capital gains and short term capital gains, the long term gains are taxed at the appropriate preferential rate and the short term gains are taxed as ordinary income. If the netting process resulted in both long term capital losses and short term capital losses, the taxpayer can deduct up to $3,000 of such losses against ordinary income (using short term losses before long term losses). Any remaining losses retain their short term or long term character and can be carried forward indefinitely for use in a subsequent year.

If the netting process results in a net short term capital loss and a net long term capital gain, or a net short term capital gain and a net long term capital loss, the gain and the loss are offset against each other. If the result is a long term gain, it is taxed at the preferential rate for long term capital gains, and if the result is a short term gain, it is taxed as ordinary income. If the result is a long term or a short term capital loss, the taxpayer is permitted to deduct up to $3,000 of such losses as a deduction against ordinary income and to carry forward the unused balance to be used in subsequent years.

[¶ 3,680]

2. Preferential Rates

In most cases, long term capital gains are taxed at a maximum rate of either 15% or 5% until 2008. The 5% rate applies only to taxpayers whose top marginal rate on ordinary income is either 10% or 15%, and the 15% rate apples to taxpayers whose ordinary income is taxable at rates above 15%. In 2008 the 5% rate will be reduced to 0% and the 15% rate will remain unchanged. Then in 2009 and 2010, the long term capital gains rates will rise to 10% for taxpayers whose top marginal rate on ordinary income is either 10% or 15% and to 20% for taxpayers whose ordinary income is taxable at rates above 15%.

These preferential rates do not apply to collectibles such as antique cars or comic books (or similar items that are the mainstay of the "Antiques Road Show"). Long term gains from such items are taxed at 28% for taxpayers whose ordinary income is taxed at 28% or higher, and at the same rate as ordinary income for other taxpayers.

The preferential rates for net long term capital gains should be contrasted with the generally higher rates applicable to ordinary income and net short term capital gains.

[¶ 3,690]

3. Capital Gains Defined

The starting point for any definition of capital assets is § 1221, which defines capital assets as all assets other than certain specified items such as: (1) inventory and property held for sale to customers; (2) notes or receivables derived from the performance of services or sale of inventory or property held for sale to customers; (3) depreciable real property used in a trade or business (see ¶ 3,710); and (4) self-created literary or artistic works (or such works acquired by gift). In addition, capital asset status is denied to other more esoteric investments such as certain hedging transactions and commodity and derivative transactions by dealers.

In Arkansas Best Corp. v. Commissioner, 485 U.S. 212 (1988), the Supreme Court indicated that the statutory exclusions from capital asset status are to be broadly construed. For example, if a business purchases commodity future contracts for grain in lieu of purchasing inventories of the same grain, the future contracts will be classified as inventory in the hands of the company and will therefore be denied capital asset status. On the other hand, a similar future contract purchased by a dentist would be treated as a capital asset in the dentist's hands.

For our purposes, it is sufficient to note that the vast bulk of capital assets consist of investment assets or personal use assets (such as a personal residence or automobile). Of course, one should remember that, although gains on personal use assets are taxable, losses on such assets are generally disallowed by § 165(c), except to the extent allowable under the hobby loss rules (see ¶ 3,620).

[¶ 3,700]

4. Sale or Exchange

To qualify for capital gain (or loss) treatment, § 1222 requires that the gain or loss arise from the "sale or exchange" of a capital asset. This requirement is met if the taxpayer surrenders "all substantial rights" in the capital asset in the transaction. For example, if the holder of a patent transfers all his rights under the patent to a manufacturer in exchange for the right to receive royalty payments, the transaction is treated as a sale even if the holder reserved the right to revoke the transfer in the event of a default by the manufacturer. However, if the holder merely licensed the patent to a manufacturer and reserved the right to "make, use or sell" under the patent, the sale or exchange requirement would not be met due to the holder's retained rights. Similarly, if the patent had ten years left to run and the holder transferred all his rights for only two years, retaining rights for the balance of the ten-year term, the sale or exchange test would not be met.

[¶ 3,710]

5. Section 1231

Section 1231 provides special tax treatment for depreciable personal property used in a trade or business, as well as real property used in a trade or business, that does not qualify as a capital asset under § 1221. Gains and losses from the sale of such assets are netted (along with certain involuntary conversions of business assets), and any resulting net gain is taxed as a capital gain while any net loss is treated as an ordinary loss. For example, assume that Bob held a tract of land and a piece of equipment, both of which were used in his business for several years. Bob sold the equipment for a loss of $200,000 and the land for a gain of $300,000. The net $100,000 gain is taxable as long term capital gain. If, on the other hand, the land had been sold for a gain of only $150,000, the resulting net loss would be treated as an ordinary loss.

[¶ 3,720]

6. Recapture

The amount allowable as depreciation with respect to an asset for tax purposes often exceeds the economic decline in the value of the asset. To correct for this phenomenon, Congress added §§ 1245 and 1250 to the Code, which basically amount to an extension of the tax benefit rule discussed at ¶ 3,020. Under § 1245, gain on the sale of tangible personal property (or certain tangible real property) that was used in a trade or business or held for the production of income is taxed as ordinary income to the extent the gain is attributable to allowable depreciation deductions; only the remaining gain, if any, qualifies for preferential capital gain treatment. For example, assume that Martin purchased a piece of business equipment for $40,000 and deducted $15,000 of depreciation, leaving him with an adjusted basis of $25,000. If he sells the equipment for $50,000, the resulting gain of $25,000 must be bifurcated into an ordinary income component of $15,000 (under § 1245) and a capital gain component of $10,000 (under § 1231).

Section 1250, which applies to depreciable real property not covered by § 1245, is similar to § 1245 in operation except that it recaptures only the excess of accelerated depreciation over straight line depreciation. This provision has very limited application, however, because only straight line depreciation has been allowed for real property placed in service since 1986. Instead, the Code provides a special capital gains rate of 25% for gain attributable to straight line depreciation on property placed in service since 1986, which serves as an imperfect proxy for a recapture rule. To illustrate, assume that Rosa held a building which she purchased six years ago for $400,000 for use in her medical practice. She has claimed $55,000 of depreciation deductions, reducing her adjusted basis to $345,000. If Rosa sells the building for $600,000, assuming she has no other § 1231 gains or losses, she will realize $255,000 of gain,

with $55,000 of the gain taxed at 25% and the remaining $200,000 of
§ 1231 gain taxed at her capital gains rate of 15%.

[¶ 3,725]

Problems

1.   You sold 2,000 shares of XYZ stock that you had held for three years
as an investment. You sold the stock for a loss of $5,000 and had no other
capital gains or losses during the year to date. On a cable TV investment
program you heard commentators talking about matching up gains and
losses at year end. It is late December and except for tax reasons you would
not sell anything else in your portfolio which is full of stocks that show nice
gains. What should you do and what are those talking heads really talking
about?

2.   You have long favored investing in both improved and unimproved
real estate. When you invest in improved realty you normally look for
property such as an office building that requires little management, produces
a positive cash flow and has good potential for appreciation. In the case of
unimproved realty virtually your sole consideration is the property's potential for short-term (3–5 years) appreciation. Your brother-in-law recently told
you over drinks, "You don't know what you are doing, recent changes in the
tax laws have made investing in realty a sucker's deal. I personally am
heavily into antiques, gold and stock in gold mining companies—the only
real protection against the doomsday that is coming." What, besides too
many Coronas, is prompting your brother-in-law to speak as he does and
does he know what he is talking about?

3.   You and your two siblings are equal investors in the Apex LLC,
which is taxed as a partnership. Apex owns and operates "Quik Lube"
stations in several states. Apex has received an attractive offer from a group
of investors to purchase all of the assets at one location and you wish to
accept the offer. They have offered the following: (1) $50,000 for inventory
(basis of $35,000); (2) $60,000 for equipment (cost of $50,000, basis of
$30,000); (3) $200,000 for an advantageous assignable leasehold with 8 years
to run (no basis); (4) $100,000 for goodwill (no basis); (5) $200,000 for a
regional franchise; and (6) $250,000 for a 5–year non-compete agreement.
Your siblings say that they want to take the money and run but turn to you
to advise them how it will be taxed to Apex.

M.   TAXPAYING ENTITIES

[¶ 3,730]

The fundamental taxpaying unit in our federal income tax system is
the individual, but in the case of a married couple, the spouses can elect
to file a joint return (in effect, as a single taxpaying unit) or to file
separate individual returns. Because of the economic cohesiveness of
families, there are special rules for taxing the income of children who are
members of a family unit. We will examine the tax rules that apply to

single individuals, married couples and children, and then look briefly at the income taxation of trusts.

[¶ 3,740]

1. Single and Married Taxpayers

Our income tax rate structure is progressive, meaning that as income rises, so does the marginal rate of tax. Historically, married couples in community property states enjoyed an income tax advantage over their counterparts in separate property states. This arose because, in a community property state, each spouse is generally treated as earning one-half of the couple's combined income and is taxed accordingly. In contrast, in a separate property state, each spouse was historically taxed on his or her own individual earnings. As a result, where one spouse earned all or significantly more than half of the couple's combined income, a couple in a community property state paid substantially less tax than a similarly situated couple in a separate property state. For example, if a married couple in California had combined income of $200,000, earned entirely by the husband, the couple was taxed as if the husband earned $100,000 and the wife earned $100,000. A similarly situated couple in New York, however, was taxed on the husband's individual income of $200,000. The California couple was able to use two sets of low rate brackets and avoid being taxed at the marginal rates for income over $100,000, but the New York couple incurred tax at the higher marginal rates for an individual with $200,000 of income.

In 1948, Congress responded by introducing the joint return, which makes the tax benefits of income-splitting available to married couples in all states, thereby ensuring that married couples with equal combined incomes would bear the same tax burden regardless of whether they lived in community property states or separate property states. The introduction of the joint return, however, introduced a new disparity. In the previous example, assume that the New York husband had a sister who also earned $200,000. Before 1948, she and her brother each paid the same amount in income tax. After 1948, however, the brother paid substantially less than his sister due to his married status.

In 1969, Congress adjusted the tax rate schedule to ensure that the taxes paid by a single individual would be no more than 120% of those for a married couple with the same income filing jointly. This rate adjustment reduced the tax burden for many single individuals, but also produced an unfortunate result for some couples contemplating marriage. If each prospective spouse had a substantial income of his or her own, the couple would find that they had a higher aggregate tax bill after marriage than before marriage. This is an example of what is commonly called a "marriage penalty." It is worth noting that, even after 1969, there were many married couples who still benefitted from filing a joint return—typically, those where one spouse earned all or a disproportionate share of the couple's combined income.

In 2003, Congress adjusted the tax rate schedule to eliminate the marriage penalty for married couples in the 10% and 15% brackets. This was done by setting the tax for a married couple in the 10% or 15% bracket equal to twice the tax for a single taxpayer with half the couple's taxable income. See I.R.C. § 1(f)(8). The standard deduction for a married couple was also set equal to twice that of a single taxpayer. (For couples in higher tax brackets, however, the marriage penalty remains in place.) To limit the resulting revenue loss, Congress originally made these changes effective only for 2003 and 2004, but in 2004 they were extended to apply through 2010.

Married taxpayers can elect to file separate individual returns, but the special rate structure for separate filers ensures that they derive no tax advantage from doing so. See I.R.C. § 1(d). The principal factor that prompts married individuals to file separately is marital discord, especially if one spouse suspects that the other may be fraudulently concealing income and wishes to avoid joint and several liability for filing a false joint tax return.

In addition to providing separate rate structures for single individuals, married couples filing jointly and married individuals filing separately, the Code also provides a special rate structure for single individuals who are heads of household, typically single parents with a dependent child. This rate structure, although not as beneficial as that provided for married couples filing jointly, is somewhat more favorable than that provided for single individuals. See I.R.C. §§ 1(a), (b), (c).

To prevent high-bracket parents from assigning income-producing assets to their young children to make use of the children's lower marginal rates, Congress enacted the so-called "kiddie tax." See § 1(g). This provision imposes tax on the unearned income of a child under age 14 at the parents' rate, if higher, after first allowing the child a modest exclusion and taxing a de minimis amount at the child's rate. In 2004, the exclusion and the de minimis amount each stood at $800. For example, assume that in 2004 Alexander is 4 years old, has $3,600 of interest income and his parents' marginal tax rate is 35%. The first $800 of his interest would be free of tax, the next $800 would be taxed at 10%, and his remaining $2,000 in interest income would be taxed at 35%. The total tax due would be $780 (10% of $800 plus 35% of $2,000). If his one-year-old brother Ethan had only $450 of interest, Ethan would not owe any tax.

[¶ 3,750]

2. Taxation of Trusts

For tax purposes, there are two principal types of private trusts: grantor trusts and non-grantor trusts. The rules for taxing trust income are found in Subchapter J of the Code (I.R.C. §§ 641 et seq.). Charitable trusts are subject to special rules that are beyond the scope of this discussion.

Grantor trusts. Under the grantor trust rules (I.R.C. §§ 671–679), income is taxed to the grantor rather than to the trust itself or to any beneficiary to whom trust income is distributed. In essence, grantor trusts are ignored for income tax purposes.

Although the grantor trust rules are detailed and complicated, it is possible to indicate in general terms when a trust will be deemed a grantor trust.

- If the grantor retains a reversion (for either herself or her spouse) that is worth more than 5% of the trust corpus at inception, the trust is generally treated as a grantor trust. (I.R.C. § 673.)

- If the grantor (or her spouse) retains a beneficial interest in trust income, the trust is generally treated as a grantor trust. (I.R.C. § 677.) This rule applies where a trustee (with no beneficial interest in the trust) has discretion to distribute income to the grantor or the grantor's spouse, even if the income is actually distributed to other beneficiaries. The grantor is also taxable on any trust income that is actually used for the support of a minor child whom the grantor is legally obligated to support.

- A power to control beneficial enjoyment of the trust income or corpus, even if only for the benefit of others, can also cause the trust to be treated as a grantor trust, depending on the scope of the power and the identity of the power holder. (I.R.C. § 674.)

- A power to revoke the trust and thereby revest the trust property in the grantor (or her spouse) can cause the trust to be treated as a grantor trust. (I.R.C. § 676.)

- A foreign trust established by a U.S. grantor, with U.S. beneficiaries, is typically taxed as a grantor trust. (I.R.C. § 679.)

Non-Grantor Trusts. Aside from charitable trusts, which are taxed under special rules, there are two types of non-grantor trusts: simple trusts and complex trusts. In general, a simple trust is a non-grantor trust that by its terms is required to distribute all income annually to one or more noncharitable beneficiaries and which does not distribute any corpus in a given year. A complex trust is a non-grantor trust that is neither a simple trust nor a charitable trust. Most noncharitable trusts permit the accumulation of trust income for distribution in subsequent years or make distributions of corpus in a given year and are therefore classified as complex trusts.

The tax rates for non-grantor trusts escalate rapidly under § 1(e). In 2004, non-grantor trusts with taxable income exceeding $9,550 were subject to the top marginal rate of 35%. The tax brackets for trusts and estates are adjusted for inflation, as are the brackets for individuals. The steep rate progression under § 1(e) is intended to discourage the use of trusts as tax sheltering devices. Moreover, to deter taxpayers who seek to avoid tax by creating multiple trusts with identical beneficiaries, the Code requires that such trusts be aggregated and treated as a single trust, thereby negating the possibility of obtaining multiple exemptions or repeated trips up the rate ladder. I.R.C. § 643(f).

Non-grantor trusts are treated as separate taxable entities for income tax purposes, and are entitled to an exemption of $300 (in the case of simple trusts) or $100 (in the case of complex trusts). Decedents' estates are entitled to an exemption of $600, but in most other respects are taxed in the same manner as complex trusts. See I.R.C. § 642(b).

Many provisions of the Code discussed above in connection with individual taxpayers are equally applicable to trusts. For example, a trust may deduct trade or business and § 212 expenses that would normally be allowed to an individual taxpayer. The § 212 deduction is subject to the 2% haircut (see ¶ 3,330), except that administration expenses that are incurred solely because assets are held in trust are not subject to the limitation. The major difference between trusts and individuals is that a trust is a "pass-through" entity which is allowed a deduction for current income that is distributed to beneficiaries. See I.R.C. §§ 651, 661. Accordingly, in most cases, a trust's taxable income typically consists only of any accumulated income and undistributed capital gains.

What constitutes income for trust accounting purposes is determined under "the terms of the governing instrument and applicable local law." See I.R.C. § 643(b). This has practical importance because the tendency of corporations to retain a large part of their earnings and declare only modest dividends has led many planners and legislatures to embrace the concept of "total return" investment (see ¶ 2,580). Under this approach an income beneficiary, for example, might be entitled not only to ordinary trust accounting income such as interest and dividends, but also to a portion of trust corpus.

Income distributed to a beneficiary retains its character and is taxed to the beneficiary accordingly. For example, if trust income of $30,000, consisting of $20,000 of interest and $10,000 of dividends, is distributed to a beneficiary, the beneficiary is taxed on $20,000 of interest and $10,000 of dividends. Where beneficiaries have "separate and independent shares" in a trust, a special rule treats the shares as if they were separate trusts for purposes of determining the amount and character of income that passes through to the beneficiaries. See I.R.C. § 663(c).

Where a trust retains income for distribution in a subsequent year (making it a complex trust), the trust income is taxable to the trust as a taxpaying entity. In general, distributions of accumulated income to beneficiaries in later years will not be subject to a second level of tax in the beneficiaries' hands. Similarly, distributions of corpus are generally received tax-free by the beneficiaries by virtue of the exclusion for gifts and inheritances in § 102 (see ¶ 3,060).

The income tax treatment of trusts and beneficiaries assures that trust income is taxed only once. In addition, however, the fiercely progressive tax rates that apply to trust income assure that trusts no longer offer significant opportunities for income tax avoidance by wealthy families.

N. ASSIGNMENT OF INCOME

[¶ 3,760]

Because of the progressive rate structure and various provisions that limit tax benefits based on income, high-bracket taxpayers may seek to assign income to family members in lower tax brackets. To prevent this type of income-shifting, the courts have developed several doctrines that apply to income from the performance of services as well as income from the ownership of property.

[¶ 3,770]

1. Income From Services

In essence, the assignment-of-income doctrine, as it applies to income derived from the performance of services, requires that income be taxed to the individual who earned it. The leading case in this area involved a husband and wife who agreed to split their earnings equally. Although the contract was enforceable under state law, the Supreme Court held that the income earned by each spouse should be taxed to that spouse. See Lucas v. Earl, 281 U.S. 111 (1930).

Despite the holding of Lucas v. Earl, if a taxpayer in a business context agrees to forgo income to which he is entitled in exchange for valuable consideration, the agreement will be given effect. For example, where a teacher in a law school clinic agreed, in exchange for a guaranteed salary, to assign to the school all legal fees to which the teacher would become entitled, the agreement was given effect and the fees generated by the teacher were not taxed to the teacher. See Rev. Rul. 74–581, 1974–2 C.B. 25.

One difficult situation involves related parties who are partners in a business venture. In general, the income of a partnership (or S corporation) passes through to the partners (or S corporation shareholders), who are taxed based on their respective ownership interests in the entity. In the absence of a special rule, taxpayers who wished to get around the doctrine of Lucas v. Earl could merely perform services through a partnership (or S corporation) and give some of their ownership interest in the entity to a family member. For example, assume that Mary, the sole owner of an S corporation that provides consulting services, gives 50% of her stock to her 15–year–old son Tom. If Mary performs personal services for the partnership for inadequate compensation, half of the forgone compensation would increase Tom's share of the corporation's taxable income. The so called "family partnership rules" and comparable rules that govern the taxation of S corporations discourage the most serious abuses in this area by requiring that the share of income to be taxed to other family members be determined after attributing a reasonable salary to the service provider. See I.R.C. §§ 704(e), 1366(e). Moreover, in the case of a partnership where capital is not a significant income producing factor and the donee contributes neither capital nor services, case law requires that the income be taxed to the donor unless there is a good faith business reason for the transaction. See Commissioner v. Culbertson, 337 U.S. 733 (1949). For example, if parents, who are partners in a thriving consulting business, admit their 32–year–old son, who has an M.B.A. and relevant business experience, as a 25% partner to share their substantial workload, such an arrangement has a good chance of passing muster.

[¶ 3,780]

2. Income Derived from Property

With respect to income derived from property, the assignment-of-income doctrine essentially requires that the income be taxed to the owner of the property. This means that an owner who wishes to shift investment income to another person must transfer the income-producing property to the donee. The owner may transfer a portion of her ownership interest to the donee and thereby successfully assign a corresponding portion of the income for tax purposes. For example, if a parent owns an apartment building and wishes to shift some of the rental income from the building to a child in a lower tax bracket, the parent may do so by transferring an undivided interest in the building (or specific rental units) to the child. However, if the parent sought to assign income by merely giving the child a portion of the rents in perpetuity or for a limited number of years (while retaining ownership of the building), then all of the income would be taxed to the parent. See Blair v. Commissioner, 300 U.S. 5 (1937); Helvering v. Horst, 311 U.S. 112 (1940). It is often said that a taxpayer may effectively assign a "vertical slice"—but not a "horizontal slice"—of income for tax purposes. Another common way of putting the point is to say that the fruit is taxable to the owner of the tree that produced it.

A parent who owns appreciated property can successfully assign the unrealized appreciation by making a gift of the property to a child. Under the basis rule for inter vivos gifts (see ¶ 3,500), the parent's basis in the property carries over in the child's hands, and any gain on a subsequent sale will be taxed to the child at the child's marginal rate. In using this technique, it is important to make sure that the child is old enough to avoid the reach of the "kiddie tax" (see ¶ 3,740).

[¶ 3,785]

Problems

1. Your consulting business has been highly successful. That is more than you can say for your son Eric, who is a well-read individual with an

M.A. in comparative literature and an aversion to any kind of work. You have been paying the rent on Eric's apartment and have provided him with an allowance. Your spouse has suggested that you stop indulging Eric and instead employ him at a no-show job with your consulting business. That way it is hoped that you will in essence get a deduction for the funds you are providing for his upkeep and help qualify him for Social Security when the time for his "retirement" arrives. In addition to being concerned about further enabling your son, what is your reaction to your spouse's proposal?

2. As an alternative to the proposal in the previous question, your spouse proposes that you give Eric an apartment in a 22–unit apartment structure that you own and either assign to him the rent from 10 units until he "straightens out" or give him the 10 units outright and allow him to collect the rents to "get by." Again, putting aside concerns about enabling your son, what is your reaction to these proposals? Would contribution of several of the units to a trust for Eric's benefit make more sense if you decide to "help" him more permanently?

3. Phil and Nancy Young are equal owners of all the stock of Marvel, Inc., an S corporation. Several years ago Phil and Nancy obtained a patent for a device that they had been developing for several years. They formed Marvel for the purpose of exploiting the patented device, and contributed the patent to Marvel in exchange for all of its stock. Phil is a professor at a major university and Nancy left her position as a researcher at the same institution to develop Marvel into a successful company. To save on Social Security and Medicare taxes, Nancy, who puts in about 50 hours per week managing Marvel, draws no salary. Last year Marvel earned $300,000. As 50% owners, they each reported $150,000 as income form their ownership of Marvel. The Youngs have twin sons, Ronnie and Donnie, who are about to enter college. Nancy asks your opinion about the possibility of making a gift to each son of 25% of the stock in Marvel and thereby shifting half of Marvel's future income to the twins so that they could afford to pay for their own higher education (and a good deal more).

O. TAXATION OF INVESTMENTS

[¶ 3,790]

Many types of investments are subject to special tax treatment. We will discuss some specific rules relating to the following investments: (1) annuities and life insurance; (2) stocks; (3) bonds; (4) mutual funds; (5) real estate; and (6) collectibles.

[¶ 3,800]

1. Annuities and Life Insurance

The taxation of annuities is governed by § 72 of the Code. A portion of the periodic payments received by the annuitant over time represents a recovery of her original capital investment, which is excludable from income, while the balance of the payments represents a taxable return on the investment. Under § 72, the annuitant's investment in the contract (basis) is recovered ratably over her projected life span, and the portion of each payment that is excluded from income is referred to as the "exclusion ratio." For example, assume that Apex Insurance Co. agrees to pay Bella an annuity of $12,000 per year for the rest of her life, in exchange for a purchase price of $100,000. If Bella's projected life span is 10 years, the exclusion ratio is ($100,000 ÷ 10) ÷ $12,000, or 83.33%. Bella is entitled to exclude $10,000 of the annual payments (83.33% of $12,000) from income for each of the first 10 years of the contract. Very few people actually die at the precise end of their projected life span; some die earlier and some live longer. For annuity contracts entered into after 1986, if the annuitant outlives her projected life span, she cannot continue to exclude any of the subsequent annuity payments from income. For example, if Bella is still alive at the end of 10 years, each subsequent payment of $12,000 that she receives will be fully taxable. In the case of annuitants who die prematurely, a loss is allowed for the amount of the unrecovered investment, and this loss can be carried back to prior tax years of the decedent by the executor, resulting in a potential tax refund.

In a sense, a life insurance contract is the mirror image of an annuity. From a strictly financial standpoint, the return on a life insurance policy is highest if the insured dies shortly after taking out the policy and lowest if he outlives his projected life span by many years. The exact opposite is true for an annuity. The income taxation of life insurance benefits is discussed briefly at ¶ 3,070 and in greater detail at ¶¶ 7,150 et seq.

[¶ 3,810]

2. Stocks as Investments

The financial return on an investment in corporate stock comes in two forms: (1) dividends received while the investor holds the stock; or (2) capital appreciation realized when the investor sells the stock.

Dividends. Amounts received as dividends are almost always fully taxable. (It is possible, but extremely rare, for all or a portion of a dividend to be nontaxable.) Since 2003, dividends on both common and preferred stock have generally been taxed at preferential rates (below the taxpayer's normal marginal tax rates). Until 2009, taxpayers in brackets higher than 15% will be taxed on dividends at a 15% rate. Taxpayers in the 10% or 15% brackets will be taxed on dividends taxed at a 5% rate through 2007 and at 0% in 2008. Beginning in 2009, all dividend income will be taxed at the taxpayer's normal marginal rates ranging from 10% to 35%. See I.R.C. § 1(h).

Capital Gains. Net long term capital gains on the sale of stock are taxed at preferential rates (see ¶¶ 3,670–3,680). From 2003 through 2008, the maximum rate applicable to all such gains for taxpayers in brackets higher than 15% is 15%; beginning in 2009, they will be taxed at a 20% rate. From 2003 through 2007, taxpayers in the 10% or 15%

brackets are taxed on their net long term capital gains at a maximum rate of 5%, which will drop to 0% in 2008 and then rise to 10% beginning in 2009. See I.R.C. § 1(h).

Investors who hold substantially appreciated stock must decide whether to sell their stock, pay tax on the gain and then invest the remaining after-tax proceeds in an investment that promises a higher yield. For example, assume that Charles holds $50,000 worth of Alpha stock which he purchased several years ago for $10,000, and that he is receiving a 4% dividend on the stock ($2,000 annually). He believes that Beta stock would be likely to appreciate at a rate of 7.5%, whereas he expects his Alpha stock to appreciate at 7% per year. The Beta stock has a dividend payout of 4.5%. Should Charles opt for the higher expected return on the Beta stock or hold on to a larger investment in the Alpha stock? Assuming a combined state and federal tax rate of 20% on both dividends and long term capital gains, he has the following choices. If he continues to hold the Alpha stock, he expects to receive a dividend of $2,000 in the first year (which would be taxed at 20%) and to see the stock appreciate by $3,500 (7% of $50,000). On the other hand, if he sells the Alpha stock, he will owe tax of $8,000 (20% of the $40,000 capital gain), leaving him with $42,000 to reinvest. On a $42,000 investment in Beta stock, he would receive a dividend of only $1,890 (4.5% of $42,000), and the 7.5% capital appreciation would amount to only $3,150. Clearly, Charles is better off holding onto his original investment. A dramatically higher projected yield on the Beta stock, in the form of either dividends or capital appreciation, could produce a different result. This phenomenon is sometimes referred to as "lock-in." The calculus for taxpayers becomes even more difficult when they must also factor into their decision the age of the investor and the availability of a stepped-up basis at death. See ¶ 3,510.

[¶ 3,820]

3. Bonds

A bond investor has two basic promises from the issuer—a promise to pay interest for the use of the investor's funds, and a promise to repay a specified principal amount at a future date. The value of the bond depends not only on the likelihood that both of these items will be paid as promised but also on fluctuations in the general market rate of interest.

Except in the case of interest paid by state and local governments that is exempt from tax under § 103 (see ¶ 3,090), interest typically is taxed as ordinary income to the investor. Repayment of principal by the issuer at the maturity of the bond is normally tax-free.

Difficulties in analysis arise where: (1) the holder sells the bond and realizes a gain or a loss due to fluctuations in the general market rate of interest or changes in the issuer's creditworthiness; (2) the bond was issued with a stated rate of interest below the appropriate market rate and was issued at a discount from face value; or (3) the bond was issued with a stated rate of interest above the appropriate market rate and was issued at a premium over face value.

Value Fluctuation. The value of a bond fluctuates due to changes in the general market interest rates and the issuer's creditworthiness. For example, assume an investor paid an issuer $1,000 for a 20–year non-callable bond bearing interest at a rate of 6% (equal to the market rate) and that, because the bond was properly priced, it traded for $1,000 immediately after issuance. Several years later, due to a rise in market interest rates, the bond might trade for $850. Alternatively, if interest rates had instead fallen, the bond might trade for $1,100. If the investor sold the bond, any resulting gain or loss would be taxed as a capital gain or loss.

Original Issue Discount. If an issuer offers bonds at a stated interest rate below the rate determined in the open market, the bonds will sell at a discount. For example, assume that an issuer offers a new issue of 20–year, non-callable, AAA-rated bonds bearing stated interest of 5% when the market rate for such bonds is 6%. Clearly, no investor will be willing to buy such bonds for the full face amount (the amount to be repaid at maturity). If the newly-issued 5% bonds, with a face amount of $1,000, bond sell for only $850, the $150 difference is called "original issue discount."

At one time investors who purchased bonds with original issue discount claimed that any amount realized in excess of the purchase price, whether on redemption at maturity or on an earlier sale, should be taxed as a capital gain. This created a powerful incentive for issuers to offer "zero coupon" bonds that bore no stated interest whatsoever. Although such bonds would trade at deep discounts, the opportunity to convert the yield on the bonds from ordinary interest income to capital gain would make such bonds significantly more attractive, to issuers as well as investors, than conventional bonds bearing stated interest at a market rate. Congress reacted by adding several provisions to the Code to deal with original issue discount. See I.R.C. §§ 1271 et seq. Without going into detail here, it is enough to say that most original issue discount is now taxed as ordinary income. Moreover, the investor is taxed on original issue discount as it accrues during his holding period (even if he is a cash basis taxpayer); the income cannot be deferred until the bonds are sold or paid at maturity. The issuer is required to inform holders of the amount accrued each year as original issue discount. The original issue discount rules are subject to a de minimis exception where the difference between price of a bond and its face amount does not exceed ¼% for each year of the bond's term. For example, a $1,000, 20–year bond that is originally issued for $950 or more does not result in original issue discount.

Bond Premium. Occasionally an issuer offers bonds that bear interest at a rate above the market rate. Such bonds trade at a premium over the face amount. For example, if the market dictates a 6% interest rate on $1,000 bonds issued by Apex Inc. but the issuer pays stated interest of 7% or $70.00 per year, investors may be willing to pay $1,100 for a bond that will repay only $1,000 to the holder at maturity. The $70.00 per year in interest is taxable as ordinary income to the investor. However, § 171 allows the investor to elect either to take a loss deduction for the $100 at maturity or to amortize the premium (apportion the deduction) over the term of the bond and reduce his basis in the bond each year by the amount claimed as a deduction under § 171. Most investors prefer to amortize the premium over the life of the bond. The election to amortize must be made on the first tax return filed after purchasing the bond.

Convertible Bonds. An individual who purchases convertible bonds is taxed on the bond interest as ordinary income and, in the event she exercises the conversion privilege, she is not taxed on the difference in value between what she paid for the bond and the value of the stock received. See Rev. Rul. 72–265, 1972–2 C.B. 222. Any gain or loss on the stock received will occur when the stock is eventually sold or redeemed. When an investor acquires stock by exercise of a conversion privilege, her basis in the stock is determined by reference to her total cost for the investment package, and her holding period for the stock dates back to her purchase of the convertible bond. For example, assume that Rachel paid $1,000 for a Magna Inc. convertible bond that bore 4% interest and was convertible into 40 shares of Magna stock. She collected $40 in interest for each of the first three years, and then exercised her conversion privilege to acquire 40 shares of Magna common stock worth $45 per share (a total value of $1,800). Rachel has a basis of $1,000 in the Magna stock and her holding period dates back to her purchase of the bond three years ago, so if she sells the stock she will realize a long term capital gain of $800.

[¶ 3,830]

4. Mutual Funds

An investor in a mutual fund receives an annual report from the fund that indicates, among other things: (1) the total amount of any distribution; (2) the amount of the distribution that is taxable as long term capital gain; (3) the amount that is taxable as a dividend; (4) the amount that is taxable as ordinary income; (5) the amount of allocated (undistributed) capital gains; (6) the amount that is treated as tax-exempt interest on state or local indebtedness; (7) the amount that is treated as interest on federal indebtedness; (8) the amount of any gain that is treated as a tax free distribution; and (9) any tax credits that are available on account of foreign income taxes paid or amounts allocable to capital gains.

To understand the significance of the reported items it is helpful to gain a general understanding of how mutual funds are treated under §§ 851–855 of the Code. In general, mutual funds are treated as conduits which pass their investment income through to investors. This is a bit of an oversimplification, of course, but it is a good starting point. In fact, most income received by a mutual fund is distributed to investors and is taxed to them based on the character of the income in the hands of the fund. For example, a distribution of interest on corporate bonds passes through to investors as ordinary income, dividends are taxed at the lower rate for dividends, and interest on state and local bonds retains its exempt character in the hands of investors. Similarly, if a fund invests in securities of foreign corporations, any resulting foreign tax credit passes through to investors. There are two significant exceptions to this general rule. Short term capital gains are simply taxed as ordinary income, without any netting at the level of the fund. Also, a fund may elect either to distribute capital gains as a capital gains distribution or to allocate capital gains without actually distributing them. In the latter case, the fund pays a 35% tax on the allocated capital gains, and investors are required to treat their allocable shares of those capital gains as a capital gains distribution subject to a credit for the 35% tax paid by the fund.

Mutual fund investors can elect to receive their distributions in cash or to reinvest them automatically in the fund. Reinvested amounts increase the investor's basis in her shares. For example, assume that Amy invested $10,000 in Wallace Mutual Fund (WMF). Instead of receiving distributions in cash, Amy elected to have her distributions automatically reinvested in WMF. Shortly after year end WMF sent her a report summarizing her distributions for the year as follows: $600 of capital gains, $200 of dividends, and $100 of interest on corporate bonds. Amy, who is in a 35% bracket, will pay tax on $600 of long term capital gain at a rate of 15%, on $200 of dividend income at a rate of 15%, and on the remaining $100 of interest at a rate of 35%. The $900 reinvested distribution increases Amy's basis in her WMF shares to $10,900. However, assume that her WMF shares are now worth $12,000, due to appreciation in fund investments during her holding period as well as her reinvested distributions. If Amy sells her shares (having held them for more than 1 year), she would have $1,100 of long term capital gain on the sale.

Most mutual funds distribute capital gains to shareholders rather than allocating them to distributions. Where funds do decide to allocate capital gains to distributions, the shareholders are allowed to increase their basis in their stock by 65% of any such gain.

A shareholder who reinvests capital gain distributions and increases her basis in her shares must pay tax on the reinvested amount. Many investors overlook this cost and in fact would be better off if their funds traded securities less aggressively or if the funds engaged in a bit of tax management with respect to their investments. Funds that are "tax managed" attempt to offset capital gains by selling loss securities, thereby minimizing the net amount of capital gain that passes through to investors. Index funds have also become popular as an alternative to actively managed funds. The principal advantage of index funds is that, because they are passively managed, they avoid a large portion of the administrative costs incurred by actively managed funds. In addition, index funds have relatively low portfolio turnover (usually stocks are sold only when the issuing corporation is dropped from the relevant index) and therefore seldom pass through large capital gains to investors. The resulting cost savings enhance the net investment returns to investors, with the result that few actively managed funds can consistently outperform index funds over the long term.

Mutual fund investors have a choice as to how their basis in their shares is determined. They may elect either to use their average cost basis for each fund in which they hold shares or to keep basis records with respect to specific holdings in each fund. For example, an investor who wishes to liquidate some (but not all) of his shares in a particular fund might elect to redeem specific shares with the highest cost basis, to minimize his taxable gain (or maximize his loss). Having done so, he would then be barred from using the average cost method with respect to any remaining shares in such fund.

In point of fact, investors who use the average cost basis method have their choice of two averaging conventions: the single category method and the dual category method. Under the single category method (which is by far the more commonly used of the two), an investor creates an average basis for all his shares in a fund and any sales are deemed to come from the first acquired shares. This ordering rule generally results in either long term capital gains or losses for the investor. Under the dual category method, the taxpayer creates an average basis for shares held for less than one year and another average basis rule for shares held for more than one year. The investor is then free to choose from which block of shares any sales should come. This method is favored by very sophisticated investors who can tolerate the record keeping burdens and wish to have more control over both the amount and the character (long term or short term) of any gains or losses. Once a taxpayer uses one of the two averaging conventions for a fund, she is required to continue using that method for that fund.

Financial advisers often warn investors against purchasing shares in a mutual fund late in the year because the new purchaser will receive a year-end distribution that carries tax liability for a share of the fund's capital gains for the full year (even though he has held the shares for only a brief period of time). This can be a serious concern if the investment is substantial. However, any capital gain that is taxed to the investor will increase his basis and eventually reduce his taxable capital gain when he finally redeems his shares. In most cases, the real cost to the investor is the float on the taxes paid with respect to the initial year-end distribution. Moreover, if one is investing in a tax managed fund or an index fund, there often may be no, or only modest, gains reported as distributions, in which case there will be modest or no tax costs incurred in investing at year end.

[¶ 3,840]

5. Real Estate

Several rules concerning the taxation of real estate have been discussed already. The most basic are the taxation of rents as ordinary income and the deductions for various expenses associated with holding the property (real property taxes, depreciation, repairs, maintenance, etc.). One provision that deserves mention here is § 469, which limits a taxpayer's ability to claim losses from a "passive activity" (such as rental of real property) against any other income (such as portfolio income or income from a trade or business, including employment income). Under § 469, a taxpayer may claim losses from passive activities only against income from such activities. Although there is an exception that permits up to $25,000 of such losses to be claimed against income from other sources, that exception phases out as adjusted gross income exceeds $100,000 and disappears when AGI exceeds $150,000. Any loss deduction that is disallowed under § 469 may be carried forward indefinitely for use in subsequent years against passive income that is not portfolio income.

Individuals who wish to invest in real estate without the headaches of being a landlord might consider investing in a real estate investment trust (REIT). The rules governing the taxation of REITs appear in §§ 856–859 of the Code. There are essentially two different types of REITs—those that basically serve as financing vehicles for real estate projects, and those that take major ownership positions in real estate projects. Of course, one will occasionally encounter a hybrid REIT that participates in both types of real estate investments. REITs function as conduits for income tax purposes, but as investment vehicles they are generally less popular than mutual funds.

[¶ 3,845]

6. Collectibles

Occasionally individuals will purchase coins, stamps or other items of tangible personal property, such a oriental rugs or antiques, and view the purchases as investments. This is a bad idea for several reasons. First, the rise in future values of such items is quite unpredictable and is more often a matter of fad and fashion. Predicting what will be the fad or fashion twenty years from now is difficult to say the least. Second, actually realizing on the alleged value of such items can be rather difficult. For example, stamp dealers often will pay little above face value even for rather old stamps. The advent of the internet and trading sites such as eBay has somewhat improved the limited opportunities that individuals have to turn such collections into cash at a reasonable price. Third, recall that although most capital gains qualify for markedly reduced rates, long term gains on collectibles are taxed at a rate of 28% (or lower if the taxpayer's normal marginal rate is below that rate). See

¶ 3,680. Fourth, it is most likely, although not certain, that such collections will be taxed as hobby activities with the result that losses on sales of such items will only be allowed to the taxpayer to the extent that they do not exceed gains on such activities in the current tax year. See ¶ 3,620. Putting these four factors together makes it quite apparent that one should only acquire collectibles (generally works of art, rugs, antiques, gems, stamps, coins, alcoholic beverages and most other personal property the use of which is personal in nature) if one genuinely finds the venture personally rewarding and enjoyable and should look on any profits as a windfall that under appropriate circumstances may qualify for a modest tax break.

[¶ 3,848]

Problems

1. Your aunt Martha has recently been widowed and asks your help in deciding how she should invest about $1,000,000 of life insurance proceeds that she received at her husband's death. Between her Social Security survivor benefits and the benefits from her husband's qualified pension plan, she will receive about $180,000 per year, and most of that amount will be taxable. Martha seeks your advice on the following:

- An insurance agent for the company that issued the policy on the husband's life recommended that Martha invest the proceeds in an annuity. Martha was impressed with his pitch that this would result in her receiving most of the payments from the company free of tax.

- An agent for a retail brokerage house has recommended that, because Martha is already in a fairly high marginal tax bracket, she should favor tax-exempt state and local bonds and common and preferred corporate stock, while avoiding corporate and federal bonds (except for high-quality convertible corporate bonds that are likely to be converted). He also mentioned something called "original issue bonds" and said that some of these bonds that are being issued at a deep discount would also make good sense for her to consider.

2. When you start accumulating investment funds, what types of mutual funds will you consider most strongly as good candidates for your investments? You will probably want to combine what you learned in this chapter with what you learned in Chapter 1 in formulating your answers to this question. When you finally do decide to make some investments in mutual funds, why may you wish to wait until the beginning of the next calendar year to make your investment? Would your answer to the previous question be any different if you were investing in a tax managed mutual fund?

P. ACCOUNTING

[¶ 3,850]

Having looked at what constitutes income, what deductions are permitted, who is taxed on the resulting net taxable income, and the tax rates applicable to certain classes of income, we now turn to a basic question of timing: In what year will income be taxed and deductions allowed? In general, taxpayers are required to account for income and deductions using one of two methods: the cash method or the accrual method. It is possible, however, for a taxpayer who is involved in two distinct businesses to use the cash method for one business and the accrual method for the other business. For example, an attorney who sells office supplies on the side could use the cash method for his legal practice and the accrual method for the sale of supplies.

[¶ 3,860]

1. The Concept of Annual Accounting

Section 441 of the Code requires that taxpayers account for income on an annual basis. While this may seem obvious, it is worth noting that there is no compelling reason to use an annual accounting period. For example, many states require either quarterly or monthly reporting for sales tax purposes. Almost all individual taxpayers use the calendar year as their taxable year, but business reasons may dictate the use of a fiscal year. For example, a sole proprietor who owns a clothing shop in a ski area might well find it more justifiable to use a fiscal year commencing in the spring or summer.

[¶ 3,870]

2. The Cash Method

Most individual taxpayers use the cash method, which requires the taxpayer to take an item into income when he receives cash or its equivalent. Similarly, the taxpayer is entitled to claim a deduction for an expense only when he actually pays it. In most cases, application of the cash method is quite simple. For example, if a taxpayer worked for an employer for the month of December 2004 but is not paid until the tenth day of the following month, the taxpayer takes her December 2004 salary into income for the 2005 tax year. Similarly, if the employer uses the cash method, he must wait until 2005, when he actually pays his employees, to deduct the salary they earned in December 2004. See I.R.C. § 446.

Special problems arise in connection with checks and other notes, credit card payments, charitable gifts, sales of securities, the acquisition of capital assets with a useful life of more than one year, and situations where the taxpayer has constructive receipt of income.

Constructive Receipt. Where income is basically the taxpayer's for the asking, he is deemed to be in constructive receipt of the income and is taxed accordingly. See Reg. § 1.451–2. For example, if an employer regularly distributes paychecks to employees at the end of the month, an employee may not avoid taking his salary into income by refusing to pick up the paycheck. Nevertheless, an employee may negotiate a compensation agreement with the employer that defers payment of all or part of the employee's compensation until later years. This is commonly done by cash basis professional athletes who thereby avoid reporting compensation until the year of receipt. A taxpayer may even amend an existing deferred compensation agreement to stretch out further the schedule for future payments. See Oates v. Commissioner, 18 T.C. 570 (1952).

Checks, Notes and Credit Cards. Technically speaking, a check is a note. Generally, a taxpayer should include a check in income in the year of receipt, even if she receives the check on the last day of the year after the drawee bank has closed. The reason for this is that the taxpayer is in receipt of cash or its equivalent (a negotiable note that can readily be reduced to cash). See Kahler v. Commissioner, 18 T.C. 31 (1952). Where a taxpayer is in receipt of a note other than a check, the courts generally look at whether the note was intended as payment or merely as an acknowledgment of an existing debt. For example, if an client was unable to pay a professional for services rendered and provided the professional with an IOU for the purpose of acknowledging the debt, the professional would not be required to treat the note as income.

A taxpayer who uses a check to pay bills or make charitable contributions is entitled to a deduct such sums when he puts the check in the mail, provided that his bank subsequently honors the checks (even though the check may not clear until the next year). See Rev. Rul. 80–335, 1980–2 C.B. 170. Similarly, payments or charitable contributions made by credit card are deemed made in the year in which the item is charged, despite the fact that the card holder may wait until the next year to pay the credit card charge. See Rev. Rul. 78–38, 1978–1 C.B. 67.

Sales of Securities. The Code provides special rules for income and losses derived from the sale of securities. Section 453(k) requires that all gains and losses from the sale of publicly traded stock or securities (and certain other intangible investment assets) must be accounted for in the year of disposition, regardless of when the proceeds are received. For example, if Marisa sells stock on December 30, 2004 and does not receive payment through her broker until January 2, 2005, she must account in 2004 for the resulting gain or loss. This is a modest departure from the general cash basis rule which would have required that gain be reported in 2005 (but would have allowed loss to be reported in 2004). The general rule still applies to sales of other items such as livestock or realty. The change in the law with respect to securities was made primarily to enable the I.R.S. to use electronic information filed by brokers in conducting "electronic audits" of tax returns.

Capital Items. Neither cash nor accrual accounting rules affect the prohibition discussed above on deducting outlays for capital expenditures. See ¶ 3,400. For example, a cash basis taxpayer who prepays two years of insurance coverage is not allowed to deduct the full cost of the insurance in the year of payment. See Commissioner v. Boylston Market Ass'n, 131 F.2d 966 (1st Cir. 1942).

[¶ 3,880]

3. The Accrual Method and Inventory Accounting

Because our focus here is on individuals, and individuals rarely use the accrual method of accounting, we will mention this topic only in passing. Under the accrual method, a taxpayer takes an item of income or deduction into account when all events have occurred that establish her right to an item of income or her liability for an expense and the amount thereof can be determined with reasonable accuracy. For example, an accrual-method taxpayer who receives a bill for utilities in her business would be allowed to deduct the expense before she actually pays the bill. Similarly, a business that receives an order for goods would accrue income either when it shipped goods to satisfy the order or at some other point such as the mailing of a sales invoice, and would not wait until actual payment. Regardless of the event chosen by the taxpayer to accrue income in a business (e.g., shipment of goods, delivery to customer, passage of title, etc.), the taxpayer must be consistent and must use the same event to account for all items of income in the business. See Reg. § 1.446–1(c)(1)(C).

Businesses that keep an inventory are required by law to use accrual accounting rather than cash method accounting. Businesses often have inventories of goods that were purchased at different times and for different prices, and in accounting for gain or loss from sales some convention is needed to identify which goods have been sold. The two basic conventions for this purpose are "last in, first out" (LIFO) and "first in, first out" (FIFO). See I.R.C. § 471. LIFO assumes that the goods sold were those most recently acquired, whereas FIFO assumes that goods sold were those first acquired. Because we live in an economy that is generally inflationary, businesses typically report lower taxable income under the LIFO method. However, if LIFO is used for tax purposes, the business must also use it for financial accounting purposes. See I.R.C. § 472(c). While this is of no consequence for closely held businesses, it often deters publicly traded businesses from using LIFO.

[¶ 3,890]

4. Installment Method

Section 453 of the Code allows a taxpayer who sells property with payment due in one or more future years to spread out gain over the payment period. Section 453 applies both to dealers in property and to taxpayers who make casual sales of property. The discussion here is limited to the rules as they apply to casual sales of property.

A taxpayer who elects to report gain using the installment method basically spreads out the gain ratably over the projected payments. For example, assume that Ramon sells a tract of land in which he had a basis of $32,000 in exchange for three payments: $25,000 payable in the year of sale, $25,000 payable in the following year, and $50,000 in the final year. The notes all bear interest at a fair market rate. Ramon will recognize $17,000 of gain in the year of sale, $17,000 of gain in the following year, and $34,000 of gain in the final year.

The installment method applies only if the taxpayer elects to use it. Making the election is simple. All the taxpayer must do is, instead of reporting all of the gain in the year of sale, to report only the amount of gain that is required to be reported under the installment method in the year of sale. For example, if no payment is due in the year of sale, mere failure to mention the sale in that year's tax return would constitute an election to use the installment method. Taxpayers should keep in mind that the deferred payments should always bear interest at a fair rate; failure to do so may cause a portion of the sales proceeds to be recharacterized as interest.

The installment method offers several advantages. First, payment of tax is delayed, allowing the taxpayer to keep the float on the deferred tax payments. Second, the taxpayer may be able to defer reporting income until a year when he expects to be in a lower tax bracket (e.g., during retirement). Third, deferring gain may enable the taxpayer to avoid a phaseout based on adjusted gross income (or some other income-sensitive threshold such as a needs-based formula for higher education assistance). Fourth, because the installment method defers only gains, not losses, it allows a taxpayer who is selling business assets with a mix of § 1231 losses and § 1231 gains (e.g., at liquidation of a business) to separate the losses from the gains and to deduct the losses immediately while deferring the gains. Without the installment method, the losses would first be netted against the gains and lose their ability to offset ordinary income.

Several points are worth noting concerning the installment method. First, if property is sold to a related party who resells the property within two years, the initial seller must recognize gain on the subsequent sale to the extent that the amount realized on that sale exceeds the payments made under the initial sale. Second, most dispositions by the holder of an installment note will result in gain recognition. For example, factoring the installment notes at a local bank or giving them to a child triggers gain recognition. Third, in rare circumstances where the proceeds of an installment sale exceed $150,000 and the face amount of all installment obligations held by the vendor which arose during the year (and are outstanding at year end) exceeds $5,000,000, the holder of the notes must pay interest on the deferred tax. See § 453A. The purpose of this provision is to strip away one of the advantages of tax deferral from sellers who are engaged in large scale operations involving installment sales. Finally, a seller who takes a purchaser's installment note instead of an immediate cash payment assumes a real risk of loss. Sellers should normally enter into installment sales only with reliable purchasers and should always insist on having a security interest in the property sold (and other assets, if possible). Although it might make good sense to accept installment notes of General Electric for a factory site, it is highly risky to accept the notes of a contractor-subdivider on the sale of land for a future housing development even if the seller retains a security interest in the property sold. Pursuing a debtor in bankruptcy can be costly and tiresome even for a secured creditor.

[¶ 3,895]

Problems

1. Tom is a consultant who is a cash basis taxpayer. Because of an extraordinary one-time contract with a major foreign company, last year was shaping up to be a banner year for him and he expected to be in the top marginal tax bracket for the first time in his life. Toward year end he did several things that he hoped would either generate extra deductions for last year or shift income into the present year. Give your reaction to each.

- Tom prepaid the remaining three years of rent on his business office. The normal monthly rental is $2,000 so Tom signed a check for $72,000 to his landlord and delivered it to him in early December. The landlord was delighted and promptly cashed the check.

- In late November of last year, Tom decided to delay billing clients for work done in the rest of the year and to send out the bills in January.

- During the last two weeks of last year, Tom did not deposit in his business's bank account any checks that he received from clients as payment on their accounts. He placed the checks in his office safe and deposited them in the bank on the January 2 of the new year.

2. Sally, who is a medical doctor and a cash basis taxpayer, was in need of cash and late last year decided to sell several stock holdings and some of her collection of primitive American paintings. She asks your advice as to whether the gains or losses should be reported in this year or last year.

- On December 30 of last year she sold through her broker: (1) 1,000 shares of Ridge Industries (basis $10,000) for $25,000; and (2) 500 shares of Big Box Stores (basis $15,000) for $10,000. Although both sales went through on December 30, Sally did not receive a check from her broker for the sales proceeds (less commissions) until January 3 of the following year.

- Sally sold to a Hilda, a wealthy art collector, two paintings that she had held for several years in her private collection: (1) "Catfish Fry" (basis $2,000) for $15,000; and (2) "High Cotton" (basis $6,000) for $3,000. Hilda signed a contract to purchase the paintings and took possession of both on December 28 of last year but was not obligated to make payment for 30 days. She gave Sally a check for $18,000 on January 15 of the year following sale.

3. Bob is an aging farmer who just received an offer from Sam Adams Brewery to purchase his farm for the site of a new brewery. He has asked you to help him in the negotiations. The assets that Bob holds consist primarily of farm equipment and buildings on which he would show a modest loss and land on which he would show a large gain. After the sale goes through, Bob intends to retire from farming and live on the sales proceeds (which should be substantial) and Social Security retirement benefits. Although he wants you to get as good a price as you can for him, he is also interested in structuring the deal so as to minimize taxes. His sister told him that she heard somewhere about using installment sales in such situations and he wants you to explain how an installment sale could be helpful.

Q. THE ALTERNATIVE MINIMUM TAX

[¶ 3,900]

In Congressional hearings in 1969 it was revealed that large numbers of wealthy individuals regularly paid little or no federal income tax. Congress reacted by enacting a minimum tax (MT), which took the form of a 10% "add-on" tax on certain tax preference items to the extent that such items exceeded $30,000, plus the taxpayer's income tax liability.

In 1982, Congress replaced the original MT with an alternative minimum tax (AMT). Taxpayers are liable for the AMT to the extent it exceeds their normal income tax liability. Under the AMT, taxpayers must add back to their net taxable income certain tax deductions and set aside certain other tax benefits. After deducting certain favored items, the taxpayer is then allowed a substantial fixed exemption which varies based on marital status. Over the years, the AMT has been adjusted but little attention has been paid to the exemption, and due to inflation this tax is rapidly becoming the bane of many middle-income taxpayers.

To determine a taxpayer's AMT base, one starts with the taxpayer's taxable income and then adds back a number of items, including: (1) a portion of the accelerated depreciation claimed on most assets; (2) any claimed percentage depletion to the extent that it exceeds the taxpayer's basis in the mineral assets; (3) state and local taxes claimed as personal deductions; (4) medical expenses to the extent they do not exceed 10% of adjusted gross income; (5) any deductions allowed for employee business expenses and § 212 expenses; (6) tax-exempt interest on certain state and local bonds; (7) personal exemptions; and (8) the standard deduction if claimed by the taxpayer. These are only some of the more common adjustments that must be made to taxable income to compute the taxpayer's tentative AMT base.

The taxpayer is then allowed to claim a fixed exemption. In 2005, the exemption was $40,250 for single taxpayers and $58,000 for married taxpayers ($29,000 for married individuals filing separately). The AMT is then imposed at a rate of 26% on the first $175,000 ($87,500 for married taxpayers filing separately) and 28% on the excess, with the exception that net long term capital gains and dividends are not to be subject to these higher rates but are to remain taxable at their low preferential rates. Several credits such as the child tax credit are allowable against the AMT. See I.R.C. §§ 55–59.

The only thing more painful than paying the AMT is calculating it with any degree of accuracy. If the tax is to perform its original task, insuring that the highest-income taxpayers do not avoid paying their fair share of tax, and if it is not to become a nightmare for ordinary citizens, Congress must at least raise the basic exemptions by amounts which would come close to preserving the real inflation-adjusted value of the original exemption.

Chapter 4

FEDERAL WEALTH TRANSFER TAXATION

A. OVERVIEW

[¶ 4,000]

Gratuitous transfers of wealth, whether made during life or at death, are generally not subject to the federal income tax. Instead, such transfers are subject to one or more of the federal estate, gift and generation-skipping transfer taxes. Together these three taxes constitute a separate, free-standing system of wealth transfer taxation. The wealth transfer taxes have their own distinctive history and structure, and for the most part they operate independently of the income tax. At the same time, transfers that are subject to wealth transfer taxation frequently have significant collateral income tax consequences. More broadly, it is important to remember that the wealth transfer taxes coexist with the income tax (as well as payroll and excise taxes) as integral parts of a larger federal fiscal system. The federal tax system has undergone dramatic changes in recent years, most notably under the Economic Growth and Tax Relief Reconciliation Act of 2001 (the 2001 Act), and some of those changes have not yet taken full effect. Changes in one part of the tax system often have significant and unforeseen effects on the behavior of taxpayers and on the operation of the tax system as a whole.

This chapter provides an overview of the federal wealth transfer taxes and introduces some basic estate planning techniques. For a succinct discussion of these areas, see McNulty & McCouch, Federal Estate and Gift Taxation (6th ed. 2003). For more comprehensive treatments, see Bittker & Lokken, Federal Taxation of Income, Estates and Gifts, vol. 5 (2d ed. 1992); Stephens, Maxfield, Lind & Calfee, Federal Estate and Gift Taxation (8th ed. 2003); and Price, Contemporary Estate Planning (2d ed. 2000).

[¶ 4,005]

1. General Background

The central component of the wealth transfer tax system is the federal *estate tax*, which was originally enacted in 1916. As its name implies, the estate tax is imposed on the privilege of transferring property at death and is graduated according to the size of the decedent's entire estate. (At the state level, many states have also adopted an estate tax, often with provisions conforming closely to the federal statute. In contrast, some states have an *inheritance tax*, which is imposed on the privilege of receiving property from a decedent and is graduated for each beneficiary according to the beneficiary's relationship to the decedent and the size of his or her share.) During its formative years, prior to the enactment of the gift tax, the estate tax became established as the workhorse of the federal wealth transfer tax system. To fulfill its mission effectively, the estate tax reaches not only transfers which are "testamentary" in the usual sense (i.e., property passing from a decedent by will or intestacy), but also various nonprobate transfers occurring at death and certain lifetime transfers that are treated for tax purposes as testamentary substitutes.

To prevent easy avoidance of the estate tax by means of lifetime gifts, Congress enacted the federal *gift tax* in 1932. The gift tax reaches gratuitous transfers of property made in each year during the donor's life, and functions primarily as a backstop to the estate tax. For many years the estate and gift taxes operated as components of a dual system, with each tax having its own separate exemption and rate schedule. Since the gift tax rates were substantially lower than the estate tax rates, the dual system offered substantial tax advantages to wealthy taxpayers who could afford to make large lifetime gifts. In 1976, Congress finally enacted a "unified" system which applies a single schedule of graduated rates to all cumulative taxable transfers, whether made during life or at death, above a specified exempt amount. Under the unified gift and estate tax system, a donor's taxable gifts in each year are cumulated with his or her taxable gifts for preceding years and are taxed at progressively higher marginal rates under the graduated rate schedule; at death, the taxable estate is similarly cumulated with the decedent's lifetime taxable gifts and is taxed under the same rate schedule.

Transfers made by one spouse to the other are generally sheltered from gift and estate taxes by the *marital deduction*. Congress first enacted the marital deduction in 1948 (along with the gift-splitting election and the joint income tax return), to allow married couples in separate property states to enjoy the benefits of gift and estate "splitting" on more or less the same terms as their counterparts in community property states. In its original form, the marital deduction was limited to one-half of the value of separate property transferred from one spouse to the other. However, this limitation was removed in 1981, and today spouses can make unlimited transfers of property to each other during life or at death without incurring gift or estate tax liability. Effective use of the marital deduction lies at the heart of contemporary estate planning for married couples.

There is also an unlimited *charitable deduction* for transfers made during life or at death to qualifying charitable organizations. As a result, such transfers to escape gift and estate tax entirely.

The final component of the wealth transfer tax system is the *generation-skipping transfer tax* (GST tax), which was enacted in 1986. (The current GST tax replaces an earlier version enacted in 1976 in connection with the unification of the estate and gift taxes.) As its name implies, the GST tax is intended to ensure that wealth does not escape tax as it passes from one generation to the next. The GST tax reaches transfers that shift property to beneficiaries two or more generations below the transferor without attracting a gift or estate tax at the level of the intervening (or "skipped") generation. The GST tax functions as a supplement to the estate and gift taxes, but it has its own special exemption and rate structure. The GST tax can have a significant impact on the planning and drafting of long-term trusts for successive generations of beneficiaries.

[¶ 4,010]

2. The Unified Estate and Gift Tax System

Since 1976 the estate and gift taxes have been "unified" in the sense that they share a cumulative base, a single graduated rate schedule, and a single exemption. At the same time, the two taxes remain formally separate. The estate tax appears in Chapter 11 of the Internal Revenue Code (I.R.C. §§ 2001 et seq.); the gift tax appears in Chapter 12 (I.R.C. §§ 2501 et seq.). Largely due to their separate historical evolution, the two taxes are not perfectly correlated with each other, and they occasionally overlap in their application to a single transfer. Nevertheless, the mechanics of computing gift and estate tax liability under the unified system are relatively straightforward.

[¶ 4,015]

a. Gift tax

The gift tax is imposed annually on the "transfer of property by gift" by an individual donor during each calendar year. I.R.C. § 2501. The concept of a "gift" is defined broadly for gift tax purposes (see ¶ 4,100), but not all gifts are taxable. The total amount of gifts made by the donor during the year must be reduced by allowable *exclusions* and *deductions* to arrive at the donor's *taxable gifts*. I.R.C. § 2503.

The *annual exclusion* allows a donor to make tax-free gifts up to a specified dollar amount per donee per year. The exclusion amount—$11,000 in 2005—is indexed for inflation. Thus, in that year a donor could make tax-free gifts of up to $11,000 to each donee, with no limit on the number of donees. (This amount can be doubled in the case of a married donor, if the donor's spouse makes a "gift-splitting" election and thereby consents to be treated as making one-half of the donor's gifts.) In addition, the gift tax allows an unlimited exclusion for payments of qualified educational and medical expenses on behalf of any donee. Note that amounts covered by these exclusions are completely removed from the gift tax base and do not count against the gift tax exemption described below. The gift tax exclusions are discussed in ¶¶ 4,150 and 4,160.

The gift tax allows deductions for gifts made to the donor's spouse or to a qualified charitable organization, thereby removing such gifts from the taxable base. The marital deduction and the charitable deduction are discussed in ¶¶ 4,340 and 4,350.

The donor's taxable gifts for the current year must be cumulated with his or her taxable gifts for all preceding years, to ensure that successive gifts are taxed at progressively higher rates under the unified rate schedule. This is accomplished by computing a "tentative tax" under the rate schedule on the total amount of the donor's taxable gifts for the current year and all preceding years, and then subtracting a "tentative tax" computed under the same rate schedule on the total amount of the donor's taxable gifts for all preceding years. I.R.C. § 2502. In effect, each year's taxable gifts are stacked on top of those made in preceding taxable years and then subjected to tax under the unified rate schedule.

Each individual transferor is allowed a gift tax exemption in the form of a *unified credit*. I.R.C. § 2505. The unified credit applies to offset the gift tax computed under the graduated rate schedule on taxable gifts up to a specified amount. The unified credit is cumulative; it is allowed only to the extent not used in preceding years. Furthermore, the credit is not elective; it applies automatically against the gift tax imposed on the donor's taxable gifts in each year until it is exhausted. Beginning in 2002, the unified credit was set at $345,800, which is equal to the amount of gift tax that would be imposed on a taxable gift of $1,000,000 under the graduated rate schedule. In effect, the credit is equivalent to an exemption for cumulative taxable gifts up to $1,000,000, and the amount sheltered from tax by the credit is often referred to as the "exemption equivalent" (or the "applicable exclusion amount"). By casting the exemption in the form of a credit rather than a deduction, Congress ensured that the exemption would apply at the lowest brackets of the graduated rate schedule and would provide a uniform tax benefit to all donors regardless of their marginal rate brackets.

The unified credit eliminates gift tax liability on cumulative taxable gifts up to $1,000,000 and thereby effectively establishes a zero rate bracket for the first $1,000,000 of taxable transfers. As a practical matter, beginning in 2002, only the following portion of the unified rate schedule set forth in I.R.C. § 2001(c) is relevant:

Cumulative taxable transfers	Tax
Not over $1,000,000	None
Over $1,000,000 but not over $1,250,000	$345,800 plus 41% of the excess over $1,000,000
Over $1,250,000 but not over $1,500,000	$448,300 plus 43% of the excess over $1,250,000
Over $1,500,000 but not over $2,000,000	$555,800 plus 45% of the excess over $1,500,000
Over $2,000,000 but not over $2,500,000	$780,800 plus 49% of the excess over $2,000,000
Over $2,500,000	$1,025,800 plus 50% of the excess over $2,500,000

Thus, taxable gifts in excess of $1,000,000 are subject to gift tax at marginal rates beginning at 41%. Under the 2001 Act, the top marginal rate fell to 49% in 2003, to 48% in 2004 and to 47 percent in 2005, and is scheduled to drop by another percentage point each year until it reaches 45% in 2007.

In general, a donor who makes any taxable gifts during a calendar year is required to file a gift tax return and to pay any resulting gift tax by April 15 of the following year. A gift tax return must be filed even if the tax is entirely offset by the unified credit, so as to document the cumulative amounts of taxable gifts made and credit used by the donor. However, no return is required for gifts that are entirely covered by an available exclusion (e.g., the annual exclusion).

[¶ 4,020]

b. Estate tax

The estate tax is imposed on the "transfer" of a decedent's "taxable estate." I.R.C. § 2001. The starting point in computing the estate tax is the *gross estate*, which includes property actually owned by the decedent at death as well as other enumerated transfers that are deemed for this purpose to occur at death (e.g., revocable trusts, joint tenancies, and life insurance proceeds). I.R.C. § 2031. From the gross estate certain *deductions* are allowed, including administration expenses, creditors' claims, and amounts passing to a surviving spouse or to a qualified charitable organization, to arrive at the *taxable estate*. I.R.C. § 2051.

The estate tax computation resembles the cumulative gift tax computation described above. The decedent's taxable estate is cumulated with all "adjusted taxable gifts" (i.e., post–1976 taxable gifts that are not otherwise included in the gross estate), and a "tentative tax" is computed under the unified rate schedule. This tentative tax is then reduced by the amount of gift tax that would have been "payable" on the total amount of the decedent's post–1976 taxable gifts, computed under the same rate schedule in effect at death. I.R.C. § 2001(b). In effect, the taxable estate is treated as a single, final deathtime transfer which is stacked on top of the decedent's (post–1976) taxable lifetime gifts and then subjected to tax under the unified rate schedule.

The final step in computing the amount of estate tax due is to apply any available estate tax credits against the tax determined under the unified rate schedule. The most important credit is the unified credit, which is available to the extent not already used during life. I.R.C. § 2010. Since the unification of the gift and estate taxes in 1976, the unified credit had been the same for purposes of both taxes, although the amount of cumulative taxable transfers sheltered from tax by the credit—the exemption equivalent—has increased from time to time. The 2001 Act, however, introduced a new complication by "decoupling" the gift and estate tax exemptions. Beginning in 2004, the exemption rises to $1,500,000 for estate tax purposes but remains frozen at $1,000,000 for gift tax purposes. As a result of this decoupling, wealthy taxpayers will have a powerful incentive to limit their lifetime taxable gifts to $1,000,000 and retain any additional assets until death, so as to take advantage of the increased estate tax exemption. (This incentive will become even more pronounced under the 2001 Act, as the estate tax exemption rises to $2,000,000 in 2006 and then to $3,500,000 in 2009.) Since the unified credit is nonrefundable, it is not possible to apply the increased deathtime credit against gift tax liability incurred during life.

In addition to the unified credit, the estate tax allows credits for estate taxes paid on certain prior transfers to the decedent (I.R.C. § 2013) and for foreign death taxes imposed on property included in the gross estate (I.R.C. § 2014). Beginning in 2005, the credit formerly allowed under I.R.C. § 2011 for state death taxes is replaced by a deduction for such taxes under I.R.C. § 2058.

An estate tax return must be filed if the decedent's gross estate (combined with any adjusted taxable gifts) exceeds the estate tax exemption equivalent. Accordingly, a return may be required even if no estate tax is due—for example, where allowable deductions reduce the taxable estate below the exemption equivalent. The decedent's personal representative is primarily responsible for filing the estate tax return and paying any tax. The deadline for filing the estate tax return and paying the estate tax, if any, is nine months after the decedent's death, though extensions for filing and payment are available in some circumstances.

[¶ 4,025]

c. *Illustrative computation*

At this point it may be helpful to illustrate the operation of the gift and estate taxes with a simple example. Suppose that Laura (who has no previous gift tax history) makes taxable gifts of $1,000,000 in 2002, makes additional taxable gifts of $500,000 in 2003, and then dies in 2006 leaving a taxable estate of $1,500,000. Note that the gift tax exemption is $1,000,000 in 2002 and 2003 when Laura makes her gifts; in 2006, the year of Laura's death, the estate tax exemption is $2,000,000 and the top marginal rate under the unified rate schedule is 46%.

Laura's gifts in 2002 are fully covered by her available gift tax exemption. Accordingly, she owes no gift tax for that year, but still she must file a gift tax return. Laura's gift tax computation for 2002 is as follows:

tentative tax on cumulative taxable gifts ($1,000,000)	$345,800
less tentative tax on prior taxable gifts (none)	(0)
less available unified credit	(345,800)
2002 gift tax payable	0

Having exhausted her gift tax exemption in 2002, Laura must pay a gift tax on the gifts made in 2003. Her gift tax computation for 2003 is as follows:

tentative tax on cumulative taxable gifts ($1,500,000)	$555,800
less tentative tax on prior taxable gifts ($1,000,000)	(345,800)
less available unified credit	(0)
2003 gift tax payable	$210,000

When Laura dies in 2006, she incurs an estate tax liability. Her estate tax computation is as follows:

tentative tax on sum of taxable estate and adjusted taxable gifts ($3,000,000)	$1,240,800
less gift tax payable on post–1976 taxable gifts	(210,000)
less available unified credit	(780,800)
2006 estate tax payable	$ 250,000

These computations suggest several observations concerning the unified estate and gift tax system. First is a technical point involving the unified credit. Initially it may appear that the unified credit has been counted twice: the 2002 gift tax computation shows an allowable credit of $345,800 (equivalent to a $1,000,000 exemption), and the 2006 estate tax computation shows an allowable credit of $780,800 (equivalent to a $2,000,000 exemption). Nevertheless, there is no double counting. To see why this is so, recall that the tentative estate tax is reduced by the sum of (1) the gift tax "payable" on post–1976 taxable gifts (taking the gift tax unified credit into account) and (2) the full amount of the estate tax unified credit. An alternative way of expressing the same computation is to reduce the tentative estate tax by the sum of (1) the gift tax on post–1976 taxable gifts (ignoring the gift tax unified credit) and (2) the estate tax unified credit less the gift tax unified credit used during life. The statutory language calls for the former approach in the estate tax computation, but the latter approach produces the same result. In each case the unified credit allowed at death is adjusted, directly or indirectly, for the amount of credit used during life.

A second observation involves the method of computing the gift and estate taxes. The gift tax is imposed on the net value of the transferred property exclusive of the gift tax, while the estate tax applies to a base that includes the amount of the estate tax. In tax parlance, the gift tax is "tax-exclusive" and the estate tax is "tax-inclusive." Although both taxes use the same rate schedule, the gift tax imposes a lighter burden than the estate tax. To illustrate the difference, suppose that gift and estate taxes are imposed at a flat 50% rate. If a donor makes a taxable gift of $100, the resulting gift tax is $50 ($100 × 50%); the donor's total out-of-pocket cost is $150, and the donee receives $100 after tax. In contrast, if the same donor dies with a taxable estate of $150, the resulting estate tax is $75 ($150 × 50%); the decedent's total out-of-pocket cost is again $150, but the beneficiary receives only $75 after tax. In effect, the gift tax is paid with pre-tax dollars, while the estate tax is paid with after-tax dollars.

Recall the computation of Laura's gift and estate tax liability. At first glance, it may appear that it makes no difference whether Laura transfers her property during life or at death. She makes cumulative taxable transfers of $3,000,000, and incurs a total tax liability of $460,000; in effect, the $1,000,000 of taxable transfers in excess of the $2,000,000 exemption allowed at death are taxed at a 46% rate under the unified rate schedule. On closer examination, however, it is clear that Laura reduced her overall tax burden by making taxable lifetime gifts and paying the resulting gift tax. Had she made no lifetime gifts and instead retained all of her property—including the $210,000 gift tax—until death, her taxable estate would have been $3,210,000, and she would have owed an estate tax of $556,600 (tentative tax of $1,337,400 less unified credit of $780,800). By paying a gift tax of $210,000 and removing that amount from her taxable estate (which would have been taxed at a rate of 46%), Laura reduced her overall tax burden by $96,600 ($210,000 × 46%).

A third observation involves the imperfect coordination of the gift and estate tax rules concerning the timing of completed transfers. Although most transfers can be clearly classified either as lifetime transfers subject to gift tax or deathtime transfers subject to estate tax, in some situations a single transfer may be subject to both taxes. In the above example, if Laura's 2002 and 2003 transfers took the form of contributions to an irrevocable trust under which Laura retained a life income interest, the transfer would be treated as a completed gift for gift tax purposes (hence subject to gift tax), but the same property would be drawn back into her gross estate and subjected to estate tax at her death. (See I.R.C. § 2036, discussed in ¶ 4,280.) Although this might reflect poor tax planning on Laura's part, the result would not be "double taxation" of the same property. Instead, the property would be included in Laura's gross estate (at its deathtime value) but would be excluded from Laura's "adjusted taxable gifts" (defined in I.R.C. § 2001(b) as taxable gifts made after 1976 *that are not otherwise included in the gross estate*, see ¶ 4,020). If the property, originally worth $1,500,000 at the time of the lifetime gifts, appreciated to $1,800,000 by the time of Laura's death, the estate tax computation would be as follows:

tentative tax on sum of taxable estate and adjusted taxable gifts ($3,300,000)	$1,378,800
less gift tax payable on post–1976 taxable gifts	(210,000)
less available unified credit	(780,800)
2006 estate tax payable	$ 388,000

The net result is that the full value of the property at Laura's death is included in the estate tax base, but the gift tax paid during life is allowed as an offset against the resulting estate tax under I.R.C. § 2001(b). The net increase of $138,000 in the estate tax is entirely attributable to the $300,000 of appreciation between the time of the lifetime gifts and the time of Laura's death ($300,000 × 46% = $138,000). In effect, the gift tax on the 2003 gift is treated as a downpayment on the estate tax liability. To avoid the problem of overlapping gift and estate taxation, experienced estate planners usually are careful to structure a transfer so that it is subject to one tax or the other but not to both.

More generally, it should be observed that despite the unification of the estate and gift taxes, lifetime gifts are often taxed differently from deathtime transfers. Lifetime gifts enjoy some obvious tax advantages, such as the annual exclusion and the exclusion for qualified educational and medical transfers, which are found only in the gift tax (see ¶¶ 4,150 and 4,160). Another, less obvious advantage is implicit in the structure of the tax base—despite the unified rate schedule, lifetime gifts subject to the tax-exclusive gift tax are in effect taxed at lower rates than deathtime transfers subject to the tax-inclusive estate tax. These and other features of the tax system undoubtedly induce many taxpayers to make larger or more frequent gifts than they would otherwise do, but studies suggest that most people prefer to retain ownership and control of the bulk of their wealth until death, even at the cost of incurring a somewhat heavier estate tax burden. This instinctive reluctance to give away property during life is reinforced to some extent by tax provisions that tend to favor deathtime transfers. For example, the provisions allowing a fresh-start income tax basis, special use valuation for farm or business real property, and deferred payment for closely held business interests, are available only for property passing from a decedent.

[¶ 4,030]

3. Relationship to the Income Tax

A gratuitous transfer of property is generally not a taxable event for income tax purposes. The transferor generally realizes no gain or loss, and the transferred property is expressly excluded from the recipient's gross income under I.R.C. § 102. Nevertheless, the transfer has collateral income tax consequences, particularly in determining the recipient's basis in the transferred property.

The Code specifies substantially different basis rules depending on whether property is transferred by gift during life or passes from a decedent at death. In the case of property transferred by gift, the property generally has a "carryover" basis in the donee's hands equal to the donor's basis, except that for purposes of determining loss on a subsequent disposition the donee's basis cannot exceed the fair market value of the property at the time of the gift. I.R.C. § 1015(a). Thus, for example, if Frances makes a gift to James of property with a fair market value of $10,000 and a basis of $8,000, and James subsequently sells the property for $12,000, James realizes $4,000 of gain. If instead the property had a value of $8,000 and a basis of $10,000 at the time of the gift, and James subsequently sold it for $6,000, his loss would be limited to $2,000. (And if James sold the property for $9,000, there would be no realized gain or loss.) In the case of a gift of appreciated property (i.e., property with a value greater than its basis at the time of the gift), the donee is entitled to increase his or her basis by the amount of gift tax, if any, paid with respect to the gift and attributable to the unrealized appreciation. I.R.C. § 1015(d). In the case of gifts between spouses, the donor's basis carries over in the hands of the donee without limitations or adjustments. I.R.C. §§ 1015(e), 1041.

In the case of property passing from a decedent, the property in the beneficiary's hands generally takes a "fresh start" basis equal to the fair market value of the property at the time of the decedent's death. I.R.C. § 1014(a). (This is often referred to as a "stepped-up" basis, even though the basis may actually be stepped down if the value of the property at the decedent's death was less than its basis in the decedent's hands.) In effect, the fresh start basis launders out any pre-death appreciation for income tax purposes; on a subsequent sale or disposition of the property, the beneficiary's taxable gain is limited to post-death appreciation. The fresh start basis rule applies not only to property acquired by bequest, devise or inheritance, but also to other property that is includible in the decedent's gross estate. I.R.C. § 1014(b). The value of the property in the decedent's estate as appraised for estate tax purposes generally governs the fresh start basis in the beneficiary's hands.

The fresh start basis rule gives rise to some interesting planning opportunities. In deciding whether to sell or retain particular assets, a taxpayer has an incentive to sell investment assets with built-in losses in order to enjoy an immediate tax benefit and avoid a stepped-down basis at death. Conversely, a taxpayer has an incentive to retain appreciating assets until death in order to pass them on with a stepped-up basis and eliminate income tax on the appreciation accrued before death. Studies suggest that this "lock-in" effect may substantially distort the investment decisions of elderly taxpayers, inducing them to hold on to assets that they would otherwise be inclined to sell and thereby creating liquidity problems. Furthermore, estate planners often advise clients to retain appreciating assets until death and make gifts during life of assets with little or no appreciation. Suppose that Louise owns appreciated property and gives the property to her elderly father Bill. In due course Bill dies and devises the property back to Louise. Does Louise receive a stepped-up basis in the property at Bill's death? The statute attempts to block this sort of deathbed basis laundering by requiring that Louise take a carryover basis in the property if Bill dies within one year after Louise's initial gift. I.R.C. § 1014(e). However, if Bill survives for more than one year, Louise would be entitled to a stepped-up basis.

By making a fresh start basis available for property included in the decedent's gross estate, the Code provides a loose linkage between the income and estate taxes. However, that linkage is quite attenuated, since there is no direct relationship between the income tax benefit of a fresh start basis and the potential burden of an estate tax liability. For example, any appreciated property owned by a decedent will receive a stepped-up basis equal to fair market value, even though in an estate of moderate size the estate tax liability may be fully offset by the unified credit. Even in a very large estate, appreciated property passing from a decedent to his or her surviving spouse receives a full basis step-up even though the property may be sheltered from estate tax by the unlimited marital deduction. In this connection, it should be noted that community property receives a special tax benefit. In general, community property is treated as owned equally by both spouses, and accordingly when one spouse dies only one half of such property is included in his or her gross estate. Nevertheless, for purposes of the fresh start basis rule, both halves of the community property are treated as passing from the decedent, with the result that the surviving spouse automatically receives a fresh start basis in the entire community property at the decedent's death. I.R.C. § 1014(b)(6).

The fresh start basis rule is subject to one significant limitation. It does not apply to tax-deferred retirement accounts, accrued but unpaid earnings or other items of "income in respect of a decedent" to which the decedent became entitled during life but which were not realized before death for income tax purposes. Such items are subject to income tax in the hands of the recipient, who steps into the decedent's shoes and takes a carryover basis rather than a fresh start basis. I.R.C. §§ 691, 1014(c).

[¶ 4,035]

4. The Role of Wealth Transfer Taxation

The estate tax was originally enacted in 1916, primarily to raise revenue for the national war effort as the United States prepared to enter World War I, and for several years the estate tax (and eventually the gift tax) provided a modest but significant source of federal revenues. Since World War II, however, the contribution of the wealth transfer taxes has rarely exceeded two percent of annual federal revenues. In 2000, these taxes yielded around $29 billion, out of total federal revenues of over $2 trillion. While $29 billion is not a trivial amount, it pales in comparison to the yield of the income and payroll taxes (or even the excise taxes on alcohol and tobacco). Compared to the broad impact of the income and payroll taxes, the wealth transfer taxes are concentrated among a small but relatively wealthy group of taxpayers. In 2000 the number of taxable estate tax returns was only 52,000, representing around two percent of adult deaths. In view of their narrow impact and their limited revenue yield, the wealth transfer taxes play only a minimal role as an instrument of fiscal policy.

As an instrument of social policy, the wealth transfer taxes may be viewed as a means of limiting concentrations of inherited wealth and enhancing equality of opportunity. In fact, however, there is little evidence to suggest that these taxes have had a significant impact on the concentration of wealth in the United States; if anything, the trend since the 1980's appears to be toward increasing inequality of wealth and income. Nevertheless, these inequalities would presumably be even more pronounced in the absence of the wealth transfer taxes. Perhaps the strongest argument for maintaining and strengthening these taxes is that they contribute to the progressivity of the overall tax system and compensate for imperfections in the income tax system.

In recent years the wealth transfer taxes have come under sustained attack by opponents who seek to repeal them altogether. One charge often leveled against these taxes is that they constitute unfair "double taxation" of earnings that have already been subjected to income taxation, though this argument is undermined by the fact that a large portion of the value of large estates subject to estate tax consists of unrealized appreciation that would otherwise go completely untaxed as a result of the basis step-up under § 1014. Another charge is that the wealth transfer taxes threaten the existence of family-owned farms and businesses because these enterprises must be sold to pay the tax imposed at the owner's death. Seldom mentioned, however, are the relief provisions of existing law that allow special use valuation and deferred payment for family-owned farms and businesses, or the small proportion of taxable estates that actually face liquidity problems, or the overwhelming non-tax factors that undermine the economic viability of such enterprises. Moreover, only a small percentage of taxable estates consist predominantly of closely held businesses or family farms. Yet another charge is that the wealth transfer taxes are unduly complex and costly to administer, but there is no reason to think that these taxes fare any worse in this regard than, say, the income tax.

Arguably the most serious charge against wealth transfer taxation is that it discourages work, saving and investment and thereby impedes capital formation and economic growth. This argument undoubtedly has some force, but in reality the situation is not nearly so clear-cut. A parent facing a heavy estate tax burden may seek to avoid the tax by retiring early and consuming his or her accumulated wealth (the "substitution effect"), but the opposite result is equally plausible; the parent may be spurred to overcome the tax burden by working harder and saving more (the "wealth effect"). In addition, it is possible that the estate tax encourages work, saving and investment on the part of a child whose inheritance is reduced by the tax. In other words, in the absence of the tax, a child who received a larger inheritance might opt for more leisure and higher consumption. Furthermore, the government's use of tax revenue should be compared with alternative uses of the same funds by taxpayers. If the government would use those funds to build infrastructure or pay down the national debt, the net result may be to stimulate capital formation and economic growth. Finally, wealth transfer taxes cannot be evaluated in isolation; they must be viewed in the larger context of federal budget decisions. If the existing taxes were repealed, the lost revenue would presumably have to be made up from other taxes, imposed either currently or in the future, which might well prove to be no more conducive to capital formation and economic growth. Given the current state of theoretical and empirical research concerning the incidence of the wealth transfer taxes, the behavior of wealthy individuals, and alternative uses of tax revenue, it is hardly surprising that the economic impact of these taxes remains uncertain and hotly contested.

For an excellent discussion of the role of wealth transfer taxation, see Graetz, To Praise the Estate Tax, Not to Bury It, 93 Yale L.J. 259 (1983). The economic effects of the taxes are discussed in Aaron & Munnell, Reassessing the Role for Wealth Transfer Taxes, 45 Nat'l Tax J. 119 (1992); Gale & Slemrod, Overview, in Rethinking Estate and Gift Taxation (Gale et al. eds., 2001); and the essays by Boskin and Jantscher in Death, Taxes and Family Property (Halbach ed. 1977).

[¶ 4,040]

5. The 2001 Act and the Future of Wealth Transfer Taxation

In recent years wealth transfer taxes appear to have become increasingly unpopular, not only among farmers and small business owners but also among the population at large. Polls indicate that two out of three respondents say they favor complete repeal of the taxes. This level of opposition is somewhat puzzling, since the taxes directly affect a small group of wealthy taxpayers—only around two percent of decedents each year leave taxable estates large enough to incur an estate tax liability. Public opinion about the estate tax is shaped by several factors: unrealistically high estimates by most people of their own relative wealth and upward mobility; widespread ignorance about the operation and impact of the tax; and the pervasive mythology of the "American dream." For an illuminating account of "the fight over taxing inherited wealth," see Graetz & Shapiro, Death by a Thousand Cuts (2005).

The 2001 Act made significant changes in the wealth transfer taxes. The top marginal rate in the unified rate schedule dropped to 50% in 2002 and then falls by one percentage point each year until it reaches 45% in 2007. Meanwhile, the exemption equivalent for estate and GST tax purposes jumped to $1,000,000 in 2002 and rises further in subsequent years, reaching $1,500,000 in 2004, $2,000,000 in 2006 and $3,500,000 in 2009. The gift tax exemption equivalent, however, remains frozen at $1,000,000.

If the 2001 Act takes effect as originally written, the estate and GST taxes will be completely repealed in 2010. (The gift tax, however, will remain in effect with a top marginal rate of 35%, equal to the top marginal income tax rate then in force. In effect, beginning in 2010, the gift tax will be imposed at a flat rate of 35% on cumulative taxable gifts over $1,000,000.) At the same time, the existing rule of I.R.C. § 1014, providing a fresh start income tax basis for property acquired from a decedent, will be replaced by a modified carryover basis rule set forth in new I.R.C. § 1022. Under the new rule, property passing from a decedent will generally have a basis in the recipient's hands equal to the lesser of the decedent's basis or the fair market value of the property at death. Nevertheless, in the case of appreciated property "owned" by the decedent at death, the statute allows a tax-free basis increase of up to $1,300,000, regardless of the relationship (if any) between the decedent and the recipient, as well as a separate basis increase of up to $3,000,000 for property passing from the decedent to his or her surviving spouse. Due to these generous exemptions, only a small fraction of all property passing from decedents will actually take a carryover basis; the vast bulk of such property will continue to receive a fresh start basis, as under current law. For a critical assessment of the new carryover basis provisions, see Burke & McCouch, Estate Tax Repeal: Through the Looking Glass, 22 Va. Tax Rev. 187 (2002).

It remains to be seen whether the repeal of the estate and GST taxes will actually take effect in 2010. Under a special "sunset" provision, the substantive changes made by the 2001 Act will automatically expire at the end of 2010, thereby reinstating prior law for 2011 and subsequent years. (The sunset provision was inserted in the 2001 Act to limit projected revenue losses and to avoid a procedural challenge under the Senate budget rules.) In effect, the 2001 Act calls for a temporary one-year repeal of the estate and GST taxes and leaves open the controversial question of whether to make the repeal permanent. Even if Congress acts to extend repeal beyond 2010, a subsequent Congress may revisit the matter and decide that it is preferable to retain the existing taxes with lower rates and higher exemptions. Given the deteriorating federal budget outlook and the pressing revenue demands for military engagements, national security, Social Security and Medicare, any prediction concerning the future of the wealth transfer taxes would be little more than a guess. For the balance of this chapter, the focus will be on those taxes as they exist under current law.

B. THE GIFT TAX

[¶ 4,100]

I.R.C. § 2501(a) imposes the gift tax on the "transfer of property by gift." The statute does not offer a specific definition of a transfer by gift for this purpose, but provides that the tax applies "whether the transfer is in trust or otherwise, whether the gift is direct or indirect, and whether the property is real or personal, tangible or intangible." I.R.C. § 2511(a). The legislative history confirms the expansive reach of the gift tax, noting that the term "property" is used in the "broadest and most comprehensive sense" to embrace "every species of right or interest protected by law and having an exchangeable value." S. Rep. No. 665, 72d Cong., 1st Sess. (1932), reprinted in 1939–1 (pt. 2) C.B. 496, 524.

The regulations provide that "any transaction in which an interest in property is gratuitously passed or conferred upon another, regardless of the means or device employed, constitutes a gift subject to tax." Reg. § 25.2511–1(c)(1). Thus, a gift subject to tax may arise from "the creation of a trust, the forgiving of a debt, the assignment of a judgment, the assignment of the benefits of an insurance policy, or the transfer of cash, certificates of deposit, or Federal, State or municipal bonds." Reg. § 25.2511–1(a). The tax applies only to a "transfer of a beneficial interest in property"; it does not apply to a "transfer of bare legal title to a trustee." Reg. § 25.2511–1(g)(1).

To determine the federal tax consequences of a particular transaction, it is usually necessary to ascertain the interests and rights of the parties under applicable state law. "State law creates legal interests and rights. The federal revenue acts designate what interests or rights, so created, shall be taxed." Morgan v. Commissioner, 309 U.S. 78, 80 (1940). Note that a transaction need not be classified as a gift under state law to constitute a "transfer by gift" for federal gift tax purposes. The regulations give several examples:

1. Elsa pays Henry to render services to Donald. Elsa has made an indirect gift to Donald (and possibly to Henry as well, if the payment exceeds the value of Henry's services).

2. Peggy opens a joint bank account for herself and Thomas. Later, Thomas withdraws funds for his own benefit, without any obligation to account to Peggy. The amount withdrawn is a gift from Peggy to Thomas.

3. Diane purchases land with her own funds and has title conveyed to herself and Gustav as joint tenants with right of survivorship. Diane has made a gift to Gustav of half the value of the land.

4. Elaine takes out a life insurance policy on her own life and irrevocably assigns all ownership rights in the policy to Brian. After the assignment, Elaine continues to pay the premiums as they come due. Elaine has made a gift to Brian of the value of the policy at the time of the assignment, and each subsequent premium payment constitutes a separate gift from Elaine to Brian.

Reg. § 25.2511–1(h).

Indirect gifts often occur in connection with the creation or operation of a family business entity. For example, suppose that Edgar is the sole shareholder of a corporation that provides lawn care services. If Edgar causes additional shares of stock to be issued to his 15–year-old son Paul at a bargain price, he has made a gift to Paul equal to the difference between the fair market value of the stock and the consideration paid by Paul. If Edgar hires Paul as an assistant at a monthly salary of $1,000, even though Paul has no skills and rarely shows up for work, Edgar has made a gift in the amount of the monthly payments. And if Edgar allows Paul to use the company car after business hours, without charge, he has made a gift of the fair rental value of the car. Note that the gift tax is imposed on individual taxpayers, and gratuitous transfers made to or by an entity (e.g., a corporation or partnership) are attributed to the individual owners (shareholders or partners) in proportion to their respective interests in the entity. Thus, in the example just given, the donor for gift tax purposes is Edgar, even if the transfers to Paul are made by Edgar's corporation.

A transaction that is formally structured as a loan can also have gift tax consequences. If a parent lends money to a child and later forgives interest or principal payments as they come due, the parent clearly has made a gift to the child of the amounts forgiven. Suppose instead that the parent lends funds interest-free to the child and retains an enforceable right to require repayment of the outstanding principal balance from the child on demand. In Dickman v. Commissioner, 465 U.S. 330 (1984), the taxpayer argued that the parent made no "transfer" for gift tax purposes, either by initially making the loan (which could be recalled at any time) or by allowing the loan to remain outstanding over time without demanding repayment. The Supreme Court rejected this argument and held that by allowing the interest-free loan to remain outstanding, the parent periodically made completed gifts of the forgone interest. The *Dickman* holding is now codified in I.R.C. § 7872, which generally applies to loans with a below-market rate of interest. Under § 7872, the transaction in *Dickman* would be recast as if the parent transferred the forgone interest to the child as a gift and the child transferred the same amount back to the parent as interest at the end of each year while the loan remains outstanding. I.R.C. § 7872(a). For the parent, the transaction gives rise not only to gift tax on the deemed annual gifts to the child, but also to income tax on the annual interest payments constructively received from the child. The amount of forgone interest is measured by the difference between the prevailing rate on certain U.S. Treasury obligations and the rate at which interest actually accrues on the loan. I.R.C. § 7872(e). If the loan is made for a fixed term (instead of being payable on demand), the gift tax is imposed at the outset on the discounted present value of the forgone interest over the term of the loan. I.R.C. § 7872(b)(1), (d)(2).

Although the Code now provides detailed rules concerning the tax treatment of below-market loans, the Supreme Court's decision in *Dickman* remains important for its underlying premise that gift tax liability may arise when a donor's failure to exercise a right or power enhances the value of property previously transferred to another person. Thus, for example, the Service has found taxable gifts where a parent permitted a statute of limitations to run on enforcement of a child's debt, Rev. Rul.

81–264, 1981–2 C.B. 185; where a parent accepted a smaller amount than she was entitled to receive under her deceased husband's will, thereby augmenting the residuary share passing to her child, Rev. Rul. 84–105, 1984–2 C.B. 197; and where the controlling shareholder of a corporation acquiesced in a recapitalization that shifted value from her own shares to shares held by a trust for her issue, Rev. Rul. 89–3, 1989–1 C.B. 278.

One significant limitation on the gift tax is that the donor must make a transfer of "property." For gift tax purposes, the term "property" does not include uncompensated services. Accordingly, a person can perform all kinds of valuable services that directly benefit another—free investment advice, business contacts, assistance with home repairs or child care—without incurring any gift tax liability. The exclusion of uncompensated services presumably rests not only on the definitional question of what constitutes property, but also on a pragmatic recognition that it would be administratively unworkable (and undesirable as a matter of policy) to impose a gift tax on routine acts of kindness. Moreover, there are natural limits on the level of services that any one person can perform.

For gift tax purposes, a gift of property is valued "at the date of the gift." I.R.C. § 2512(a). It is therefore important to identify the particular property or interest that is the subject of the gift and to determine when the gift becomes complete, in order to report the gift accurately for gift tax purposes. If a gift is not adequately disclosed on a gift tax return, the statute of limitations for assessing the gift tax will not run. I.R.C. § 6501(c)(9).

[¶ 4,105]

Problem

Robert died leaving a marital bequest to his surviving spouse Amanda and the rest of his estate to their child Sam. The will names Amanda as executor, and under applicable state law she is entitled to reasonable compensation for her services. Amanda, however, decides to serve without compensation and promptly waives her right to commissions. As a result of Amanda's waiver, Sam's residuary share of the estate is increased by the forgone commissions. Does Amanda's waiver give rise to a deemed gift of the forgone commissions for gift tax purposes? See Rev. Rul. 66–167, 1966–1 C.B. 20. Suppose instead that Amanda enters on her duties as executor intending to claim compensation, but changes her mind and waives the commissions two years later when she submits her final account at the end of the estate administration. Same result?

[¶ 4,110]

1. Completed Gifts

The gift tax applies only to completed transfers. For gift tax purposes, a transfer generally becomes complete when the donor relinquishes dominion and control, retaining no power to revoke the transfer or change the interests of the beneficiaries in the underlying property. Reg. § 25.2511–2(b). Conversely, a transfer remains incomplete to the extent that the donor retains control over beneficial enjoyment of the transferred property. Reg. § 25.2511–2(c). If a donor retains enough control to prevent the transfer from becoming complete during life, the retained control will generally cause the property to be included in the donor's gross estate at death. (See I.R.C. § 2038, discussed in ¶ 4,270.) Accordingly, the donor may avoid an immediate gift tax by retaining dominion and control of transferred property, but the transfer will eventually be subject to gift or estate tax upon the termination or relinquishment of the power. Rev. § 25.2511–2(f).

An important distinction should be drawn between "dispositive" powers which directly affect the beneficial enjoyment of transferred property and "administrative" powers which involve the management of transferred property. Ordinarily, only dispositive powers are relevant in determining whether a transfer is complete for gift (or estate) tax purposes. Typical examples of dispositive powers include a power to accumulate trust income, to invade trust principal, to reallocate the shares of existing beneficiaries or to designate new beneficiaries. In contrast, normal administrative powers, such as a power to select trust investments, to sell or exchange trust property or to allocate receipts and disbursements between income and principal, have no bearing on whether a transfer is complete.

The most obvious example of an incomplete transfer is one where the donor reserves an unrestricted power of revocation that allows the donor to recover the transferred property at the stroke of a pen. Thus, the creation of an ordinary revocable trust is not a completed transfer for gift tax purposes, regardless of whether the trustee is the donor or another person. Burnet v. Guggenheim, 288 U.S. 280 (1933). Less obviously, a retained power that allows the donor to name new beneficiaries or to change the interests of the original beneficiaries (but not to recover beneficial ownership) is also sufficient to prevent a completed gift. Estate of Sanford v. Commissioner, 308 U.S. 39 (1939). In either case, any amounts of income or principal subsequently distributed to other beneficiaries while the trust remains subject to the donor's retained power would constitute completed gifts at the time of distribution, and a relinquishment by the donor of the retained power during his or her life would constitute a completed gift of the remaining trust property.

Not every dispositive power retained by a donor prevents a transfer from being complete for gift tax purposes. The gift tax regulations recognize a few situations where a retained power is so circumscribed that it does not rise to the level of dominion and control. The most important example is "a fiduciary power limited by a fixed or ascertainable standard." Reg. § 25.2511–2(c). To illustrate, suppose that Kate declares herself trustee of property for her adult children Igor and Dmitri. In her capacity as trustee, Kate retains a power to distribute income or principal as needed for the "support," "education" or "health" of the respective children. If Kate retains no other dispositive powers, the creation of the trust constitutes a completed gift. (The result would be different if Kate also retained a discretionary power to make distributions for the "welfare" or "happiness" of the beneficiaries.) The "ascertainable standard" rule can be useful to a donor who wishes to retain a restricted dispositive power without being treated as having retained dominion and control for gift (or estate) tax purposes.

Another power that does not prevent gift completion is "a power to change the manner or time of enjoyment." Reg. § 25.2511–2(d). This type of power refers to the manner or time of enjoyment by a single beneficiary; a discretionary power to shift enjoyment from one beneficiary to another falls outside the "time or manner" rule. Thus, if Conrad creates a trust with Lester as the sole beneficiary, and Conrad retains a power to determine the timing and amount of distributions to Lester (and no other dispositive powers), Conrad has made a completed gift of the entire trust property.

Sometimes a donor retains a power that can be exercised only with the consent of another person, as, for example, where the donor creates a trust with himself and another person named as co-trustees. Such a joint power is treated as if it were held by the donor alone, unless the other person has a "substantial adverse interest" in the underlying property. Reg. § 25.2511–2(e). The rationale for this rule is that any person selected by the donor to exercise a joint power can generally be expected to be responsive to the donor's wishes, unless the other person stands to lose a substantial beneficial interest in the underlying property. Suppose that Julia names herself and Karl as trustees of a trust for the benefit of Ludwig. Julia retains the power, exercisable with Karl's consent, to revoke the trust. Karl has no incentive to resist a revocation of the trust because he has no beneficial interest that would be adversely affected. Accordingly, Julia is treated as having retained an unrestricted power of revocation and there is no completed gift. However, if Karl were the trust beneficiary, his beneficial interest would give him an incentive to block any revocation of the trust; the joint power would be disregarded, and Julia's gift would be complete.

Powers lodged solely in a person other than the donor generally do not prevent gift completion. For example, if Yvette creates an irrevocable inter vivos trust for the benefit of Michael and Lucia, and names Daniel as trustee with discretionary power to make or withhold distributions to either or both of the beneficiaries, there is a completed gift of the entire trust property. For gift tax purposes, it makes no difference whether Daniel is an independent trustee or a close family member (e.g., Yvette's spouse); as long as Yvette has no retained beneficial interests or dispositive powers, the gift is complete. However, in some cases a donor may be treated as having indirectly retained an interest or power that prevents gift completion. Thus, in the above example, if Yvette retained an unlimited power to remove Daniel and substitute herself as trustee, the trustee's powers would be attributed to Yvette and the gift would be incomplete.

Suppose that Mary creates an irrevocable inter vivos trust and names another person as trustee with discretionary power to distribute the trust property among a class of beneficiaries including Mary. Although Mary has no right to compel the trustee to make any distributions, under state law Mary's creditors may be able to reach the maximum amount that the trustee could distribute to Mary. (See the discussion of self-settled trusts at ¶ 2,535.) If so, Mary has retained the ability to reach the trust property by running up debts and relegating her creditors to the trust property as a source of repayment. In effect, she has indirectly retained a power of revocation which prevents the gift from being complete to the extent the trust property remains subject to claims of her creditors. Paolozzi v. Commissioner, 23 T.C. 182 (1954). However, if state law does not allow Mary's creditors to reach the trust property (because, for example, Mary is not included in the class of permissible distributees), the gift would be complete.

A gift may be partially complete and partially incomplete. That is, a donor may make a completed gift of certain interests in property while retaining other interests in the same property. Reg. § 25.2511–1(e). The most flexible and commonly-used device for splitting up beneficial ownership of property in this manner is a trust, though similar results can be accomplished with other arrangements (e.g., a joint tenancy, corporation or partnership). For gift tax purposes, the various interests must be identified and analyzed separately to determine the extent of the completed gift. To illustrate, suppose that Claire creates an irrevocable inter vivos trust to pay income to herself for life with remainder at her death to Mark. As to the remainder interest, the gift is complete, since Claire has relinquished dominion and control; but as to the life income interest, there is no completed gift. (Claire cannot make a gift to herself.) Suppose instead that the trust is to pay income to Mark for life with remainder at Mark's death to his surviving issue, and Claire retains a power to accumulate income during Mark's life for the remainder beneficiaries. Here Claire is not a beneficiary of the trust, but she has retained a power to change the beneficial enjoyment of the trust income during Mark's life. Accordingly, the gift is complete as to the remainder but not as to the life income interest.

Note that the test of completion focuses on the *donor's* dominion and control; there is no requirement that the *donees* be identified or their respective shares ascertained. Indeed, in the case of a contingent future interest, there may be no assurance that a beneficiary will ever receive possession of his or her share. Suppose that Roger creates an irrevocable inter vivos trust to pay income to Monica for life, and then to distribute principal at Monica's death to Roger if living or if Roger is not living to Monica's appointees or heirs. The gift is clearly complete as to Monica's life income interest and incomplete as to Roger's reversionary interest. As to the contingent remainder in Monica's appointees or heirs, the beneficiaries cannot be identified until Monica's death, and even then they will receive nothing if Roger is still living. Nevertheless, the gift of the contingent remainder is complete because Roger retains no power to change beneficial enjoyment of that interest. Smith v. Shaughnessy, 318 U.S. 176 (1943). In this case, the values of the transferred and retained interests, respectively, can be determined by actuarial methods. However, if the gift is structured in a way that makes the donor's retained interest "not susceptible of measurement on the basis of generally accepted valuation principles," the retained interest may be deemed worthless and a gift tax may be imposed on the entire value of the underlying property. Reg. § 25.2511–1(e). For example, if Roger creates an irrevocable inter vivos trust, retaining a reversion which will become possessory only if his 30–year–old child should die leaving no issue who reach age 21, the reversion has no ascertainable value. Therefore, the entire value of the trust property is attributed to the transferred interests and is subject to gift tax. Robinette v. Helvering, 318 U.S. 184 (1943).

Overall, the rules concerning gift completion allow donors considerable flexibility. If a donor wishes to transfer property to other beneficiaries without incurring an immediate gift tax liability, the donor can retain a power of revocation (or some other power affecting beneficial enjoyment) that prevents the gift from being complete. Of course, the underlying property will eventually be subject to gift or estate tax when the retained power expires. Alternatively, the donor may prefer to pay gift tax at the outset and avoid a subsequent gift or estate tax liability. The donor can accomplish this by giving up all beneficial interests and by lodging exclusive control over beneficial enjoyment in another person such as a spouse or a trusted family member. If the donor retains (directly or indirectly) any interests or powers, it is important to structure the transfer in a way that will not attract an estate tax at death. It is possible for the same transfer to give rise to both gift and estate taxes, but such an overlap is almost never desirable and can usually be avoided through competent planning.

[¶ 4,115]

Problems

1. Alice sends a check for $10,000 to her son Bruno as a holiday gift. Bruno receives the check on December 23, 2005 and deposits it in his own account on December 31, 2005. The check clears on January 4, 2006. Has Alice made a completed gift in 2005 or in 2006? Does it make a difference if Bruno waits until January 2 to deposit the check? What if Alice dies before Bruno deposits the check? See Estate of Metzger v. Commissioner, 38 F.3d 118 (4th Cir. 1994); Estate of Dillingham v. Commissioner, 903 F.2d 760 (10th Cir. 1990); Estate of Newman v. Commissioner, 111 T.C. 81 (1998), aff'd mem., 203 F.3d 53 (D.C. Cir. 1999); Rev. Rul. 96–56, 1996–2 C.B. 161.

2. In 2005 Larry created an irrevocable inter vivos trust with himself and Judith as trustees. The trust is to pay income to Judith for life with

remainder at Judith's death to Richard. Larry initially retained two separate powers: one, exercisable with the consent of either Judith or Richard, to change the beneficial interests in favor of any person other than himself; and the second, exercisable with Judith's consent, to invade the trust principal for Judith or to accumulate income for Richard. In 2006 Larry relinquishes the first power, and in 2007 he relinquishes the second power. To what extent has Larry made completed gifts in 2005, 2006 and 2007? See Camp v. Commissioner, 195 F.2d 999 (1st Cir. 1952).

[¶ 4,120]

2. Valuation

When a donor makes a gift of property, the amount of the gift is the "value" of the transferred property at the time of the gift. I.R.C. § 2512(a). In general, the regulations define value as "the price at which such property would change hands between a willing buyer and a willing seller, neither being under any compulsion to buy or to sell, and both having reasonable knowledge of relevant facts." Reg. § 25.2512–1. This "fair market value" standard is relatively easy to apply if there is an active market for the property in question. For example, shares of stock in a publicly traded company are valued at the mean between the highest and lowest quoted selling prices on the date of the gift. Reg. § 25.2512–2. A newly-issued life insurance policy is valued at its cost (or the cost of a comparable policy); if the policy has been in force for some time and further premium payments are to be made, the value is ordinarily the amount the insurance company is required to set aside under the policy to cover the risk of death (the "interpolated terminal reserve") plus an adjustment for the unearned portion of the most recent premium at the date of the gift. Reg. § 25.2512–6. The value of real estate is usually determined by appraisals, which may be based on comparable sales, capitalized income or a combination of both methods. Historical cost may be relevant if the property was recently purchased in an arm's-length transaction, but the assessed value for local property tax purposes is not controlling. In general, fair market value is based on the gross price, without adjustments for broker's commissions or other selling expenses.

[¶ 4,123]

Problem

Beatrix takes out a $100,000 life insurance policy on the life of her husband Eric, and designates her son Jaime as the beneficiary of the policy. Beatrix, as the owner of the policy, has the right to change the beneficiary designation at any time during Eric's life, but she does not do so. Eric dies, survived by Beatrix and by Jaime, and the insurance company promptly pays the $100,000 proceeds to Jaime. Has Beatrix made a gift to Jaime? If so, when does the gift occur and how is the amount of the gift determined? See Goodman v. Commissioner, 156 F.2d 218 (2d Cir. 1946). What result if

Beatrix irrevocably assigns all incidents of ownership in the policy to Jaime while Eric is still alive?

[¶ 4,125]

a. Income interests, remainders and annuities

When beneficial ownership of property is carved up into successive interests (e.g., a life income interest and a remainder), the values of the respective interests are generally determined using actuarial principles. The regulations provide valuation tables that make it possible to calculate the discounted present value of an income interest for life or a fixed term, a private annuity, a remainder or a reversion. I.R.C. § 7520; Reg. §§ 25.2512–5(d), 20.2031–7(d). Excerpts from the tables are reproduced in Appendices A and C. The tables reflect some crucial simplifying assumptions concerning the life expectancy of individuals, the value of property and its current income yield, and the time value of money (i.e., the rate of interest). Although these assumptions may depart dramatically from actual expectations in particular cases, both the government and the taxpayer are ordinarily required to use the tables where they apply. The mortality assumptions of the tables do not apply, however, in valuing an interest that depends on the life expectancy of an individual who is "terminally ill" at the time of valuation (i.e., suffering from an incurable illness or other condition that is likely to cause death within one year). Reg. §§ 20.7520–3(b)(3), 25.7520–3(b)(3).

To illustrate the operation of the tables, consider a trust of $100,000 which is to pay income to Shana for 10 years, with remainder at the end of the term to Brad. Since the income interest and the remainder taken together comprise full beneficial ownership of the underlying property, the present value of the income interest can be calculated by subtracting the present value of the remainder from the value of the entire property. If the current interest rate is 5%, the tables indicate that the remainder has a present value of $61,391. (The tables assume that the remainder is equivalent to a right to receive $100,000 in 10 years, and $61,391 is the amount which, if invested at an annual interest rate of 5%, will grow to $100,000 at the end of 10 years.) According to the tables, then, the income interest has a present value of $38,609 ($100,000 − $61,391).

Suppose that Shana creates the trust described above, retaining an income interest for a 10–year term and making a gift of the remainder to Brad. Shana will report a taxable gift of $61,391, the value of the remainder according to the tables. If the assumptions built into the tables hold true, Shana will receive annual income distributions of $5,000 and Brad will receive property worth $100,000 at the end of the 10–year term. However, if the trust is funded with property that generates an investment yield consisting of capital appreciation rather than current income (e.g., "unproductive" real property, or shares of a corporation that pays no dividends), the tables will overstate the value of Shana's retained income interest and correspondingly understate the value of the remainder given to Brad. In an extreme case, Shana might receive nothing and the full value of the appreciated property might pass to Brad at an artificially low gift tax value. During the 1980's, this type of "grantor retained income trust" (GRIT) became widely known as a gift tax avoidance technique.

The special valuation rules of I.R.C. § 2702, enacted in 1990, significantly alter the traditional gift tax treatment of a donor's retained interests and powers in trust property. The special rules apply where the donor carves up beneficial ownership of property into successive interests and gives some interests to family members while retaining other interests in the underlying property. Under the special rules, subject to a few exceptions, the donor's retained interest is deemed to have a value of zero, with the result that the full value of the underlying property is attributed to the transferred interest. Thus, in the above example, Shana's retained income interest would be ignored and she would be treated as making a taxable gift to Brad of a remainder with a value of $100,000. Note that § 2702 supersedes the general rules for valuing gifts of partial interests, but does not affect the timing or extent of the completed gift. In addition, the special rules apply only for gift tax purposes; they do not change the estate tax treatment of the trust. Thus, if Shana died during the 10–year term, the trust property might still be subject to estate tax (with an adjustment for the earlier gift tax).

There are three escape hatches from the harsh zero-value rule of § 2702. One is a specific exception for "qualified" retained interests, such as an annuity interest (i.e., a right to receive fixed annual payments for life or a specified term of years) or a unitrust interest (i.e., a right to receive annual payments equal to a fixed percentage of the value of the underlying property, determined annually, for life or a specified term of years). These qualified interests pose relatively little risk of abuse and therefore are allowed to be valued under the tables. The statute also provides a second exception which allows the retained income interest in a GRIT to be valued under the tables if the trust property consists of a personal residence to be used by the donor. (The requirements for a "qualified personal residence trust" are set forth in Reg. § 25.2702–5.) As a result, a GRIT remains viable as an estate planning technique for transferring a personal residence at an artificially low gift tax cost (see ¶ 4,370). Finally, § 2702 applies only if an interest is transferred to a member of the donor's "family." For this purpose, the donor's family includes his or her spouse, ancestors, descendants, siblings, and certain in-laws. Thus, a gift to an unrelated person or a non-family member (e.g., a niece or nephew) falls outside the reach of the zero-value rule.

Section 2702 has a major impact on the planning and drafting of trusts. Aside from transfers covered by one of the exceptions mentioned above, the zero-value rule makes it undesirable in most cases for a donor to retain interests or powers in a trust involving completed gifts of partial interests to other family members. Instead, a donor will usually do better to make a completed gift of all interests in the trust and incur an immediate gift tax on the entire value of the underlying property (taking care to avoid inclusion of the property in the gross estate at death), or, alternatively, to retain a sufficient degree of dominion and control to prevent any completed gift from occurring at the creation of the trust (recognizing that the property will eventually be subject to gift or estate tax).

[¶ 4,130]

b. Closely held business interests

Interests in a closely held corporation or partnership raise special valuation problems. The interests are rarely if ever sold in an arm's-length transaction, and there may be distinctive features of the business or its capital structure that make it difficult to find comparable transactions. Appraising such interests is a highly fact-sensitive exercise, and valuation experts may arrive at dramatically different results depending on their assumptions and methodology. Courts routinely allow substantial valuation discounts to reflect lack of marketability, and, in the case of a "minority" interest, lack of voting control. Estate planners often structure transactions to take advantage of these valuation discounts, which often add up to 30% or 40% of the value of the entity's underlying assets. Similar discounts are available, though on a slightly smaller scale, for undivided ownership interests in a joint tenancy or a tenancy in common.

Each gift made by a donor is valued separately from other gifts made at different times or to different donees. As a result, the value of an entire property may be greater than the sum of its parts for gift tax purposes, and a donor may be able to achieve substantial tax savings by making a series of small gifts rather than a single large gift. For example, suppose that Lily, the sole shareholder of a corporation with assets worth $1,000,000, wishes to give her shares to Omar. If she makes a single gift of all of her shares, the gift will be valued at around $1,000,000; there is no reason to allow much of a discount, since the transferred shares carry unrestricted voting control and the ability to liquidate the corporation. However, if Lily makes four separate gifts to Omar of 25% minority blocks of stock, each gift will probably be eligible for a substantial discount. At one time the Service attempted to take aggregate family voting control into account in valuing a gift of a minority interest, but it now concedes that "a minority discount will not be disallowed solely because a transferred interest, when aggregated with interests held by family members, would be a part of a controlling interest." Rev. Rul. 93–12, 1993–1 C.B. 202.

[¶ 4,135]

c. Restrictions and conditions

The value of property for gift or estate tax purposes may be affected by restrictions on the use or disposition of the property. For example, the owners of a closely held business may enter into a "buy-sell" agreement that requires that any interest in the business be offered to insiders at a specified price before it can be sold to outsiders. Although such an agreement may be motivated by business exigencies (such as a desire to maintain cohesive control and continuity of management), there is a risk of abuse if it sets an unrealistically low price for a permitted sale to insiders. I.R.C. § 2703, enacted in 1990, responds by disregarding restrictions on the "right to sell or use" property (or any right to acquire or use property at a below-market price) for gift and estate tax purposes unless three conditions are met: (1) the restriction must be a "bona fide business arrangement"; (2) it must not be a "device" to transfer property to family members for less than full and adequate consideration; and (3) its terms must be "comparable to similar arrangements entered into by persons in an arm's length transaction." Suppose that Fred and his son Greg, each owning half of the stock of a family corporation, agree that during their joint lifetime neither of them will sell any stock to an outsider without first offering it to the other at a price determined by formula, and that at the death of either of them the survivor will be entitled to purchase the decedent's stock for a price determined under the same formula. Upon Fred's subsequent death, Greg exercises his right to purchase Fred's stock at the specified price. If the arrangement has a bona fide business purpose, is not a testamentary device, and is fair and reasonable in its terms, the formula price will probably be effective to establish the value of Fred's stock for estate tax purposes, even if an unrestricted sale of the stock on the open market might have brought a higher price. In contrast, if the arrangement was designed to produce an artificially low value for tax purposes, the stock will be valued under § 2703 without regard to the restrictions.

Occasionally a donor attempts to impose a self-executing limitation on the amount of a taxable gift. For example, suppose that Sybil, the sole shareholder of a corporation, wishes to make a gift of stock worth $15,000 to her son Peter, and obtains an appraisal indicating a value of $100 per share. Sybil makes a gift of 150 shares to Peter, subject to a saving clause which provides that if the Service determines a value of more than $15,000 for the shares, the gift shall be reduced so that the value of the transferred shares does not exceed $15,000. The saving clause is intended to place a ceiling on Sybil's potential gift tax liability, even if the stock turns out to be worth substantially more than $100 per share. Not surprisingly, the Service takes a different view. It argues that such "conditions subsequent" are contrary to public policy, noting that they "tend to discourage the enforcement of federal gift tax provisions, because operation of the provisions would either defeat the gift or otherwise render examination of the return ineffective." Rev. Rul. 86–41, 1986–1 C.B. 300.

[¶ 4,138]

Problems

1. Nina conveys Blackacre to Carlos on condition that Carlos pay the resulting gift tax. Carlos accepts the transfer and pays the gift tax. Blackacre

has a fair market value of $600,000. If the gift tax is imposed at a flat rate of 50%, what is the amount of Nina's taxable gift and what is the amount of the gift tax? What difference does it make if Blackacre is subject to a nonrecourse mortgage liability of $150,000? See Rev. Rul. 75–72, 1975–1 C.B. 310.

2.   Nathan, who owns all 1,000 outstanding shares of a corporation, gives 150 shares to his daughter Silvia and reports a gift of $15,000, relying on an appraised valuation of $100 per share (reflecting discounts for lack of marketability and control). The instrument of gift includes the following saving clause: "If the value of the transferred shares for federal gift tax purposes is finally determined by a federal court to be greater than $15,000, the transfer shall be limited to the number of shares equal in value to $15,000, and any excess shares shall be excluded from the transfer and shall remain the property of Nathan." The Service revalues the 150 shares at $150 per share and assesses a gift tax based on a total gift of $22,500. Nathan argues that his total gift is limited to $15,000 because he transferred either (a) 150 shares worth $100 per share, or (b) 100 shares worth $150 per share (pursuant to the saving clause). What result? See Commissioner v. Procter, 142 F.2d 824 (4th Cir. 1944); Ward v. Commissioner, 87 T.C. 78 (1986). Does it make any difference if there is no saving clause, but Silvia agrees to pay Nathan an amount equal to any value in excess of $15,000 as finally determined for federal gift tax purposes? See King v. U.S., 545 F.2d 700 (10th Cir. 1976); Rev. Rul. 86–41, 1986–1 C.B. 300.

[¶ 4,140]

3.   Donative Intent and Consideration

In general, a transfer of property by gift is valued at the time the gift becomes complete. The amount of the gift is equal to the value of the transferred property, reduced by any consideration "in money or money's worth" received by the donor. I.R.C. § 2512. If the donor receives "full and adequate consideration in money or money's worth," the gift tax does not apply. Reg. § 25.2511–1(g)(1).

The gift tax concept of "consideration" differs in important ways from the common law concept of the same name. Consideration, as used in the gift tax, has nothing to do with determining the enforceability of a promise. Instead, its primary function is to measure the net decrease in a donor's net worth when he or she receives something of monetary value in return for a transfer of property (or, in the case of a sale for full and adequate consideration, to negate the existence of a gift). Since consideration functions as an offset in measuring the amount of the gift, it must enhance the donor's net worth in some measurable way. It is not enough that the donee relinquishes a benefit or incurs a detriment in reliance on the donor's transfer, nor that the donee reciprocates with gratitude or affection. If Ruth transfers $100,000 to Albert in exchange for Albert's promise to marry Ruth or to refrain from using alcohol and tobacco, Ruth has made a gift of $100,000. Commissioner v. Wemyss, 324 U.S. 303 (1945). Similarly, if Ruth transfers $100,000 to Albert in exchange for Albert's promise to transfer property of equal value to another person, there is no consideration for Ruth's gift because the benefit from Albert's promise flows to a third person, not to Ruth. (In effect, Albert serves as a conduit for Ruth's gift. From Albert's perspective, the transfer made to the third person is offset by the payment received from Ruth.) In this connection, it makes no difference that the transaction is enforceable as a contract under state law or that Ruth lacks donative intent.

A payment made to discharge an enforceable obligation founded on a promise or agreement is ordinarily not a gift, if the obligation was "contracted bona fide and for an adequate and full consideration in money or money's worth." I.R.C. § 2053(c)(1)(A). Thus, a borrower who repays a debt does not make a gift; the repayment merely discharges an existing liability and leaves the borrower's net worth unchanged. Similarly, there is no gift when a person pays money or property to satisfy a legal obligation to support a spouse or a minor child; the discharge of a legal support obligation is treated as the receipt of money's-worth consideration. Rev. Rul. 68–379, 1968–2 C.B. 414.

Transfers of property in exchange for a release of marital property rights raise special problems. In general, a relinquishment by one spouse of the right to claim an elective share or similar "marital rights" in the other spouse's property or estate is not treated as money's-worth consideration for gift tax purposes. Reg. § 25.2512–8. For example, if pursuant to an antenuptial agreement Kevin transfers $100,000 to Anne in exchange for Anne's release of her right to claim an elective share of Kevin's estate, Kevin has made a gift of $100,000 to Anne. Merrill v. Fahs, 324 U.S. 308 (1945). (Of course, the gift may be sheltered from gift tax by the marital deduction.) The rule disqualifying inchoate marital property rights as consideration does not apply to interests in community property. If Giles transfers property to Rose in exchange for Rose's release of her share of the couple's community property, Giles has made a gift only to the extent that the value of the transferred property exceeds the value of the rights relinquished by Rose.

The gift tax statute provides a special exemption for marital property settlements incident to divorce, subject to certain formal requirements. To qualify for the exemption, the spouses must enter into a written agreement relative to their marital and property rights, and divorce must occur within two years after (or one year before) the date of the agreement. If these requirements are met, any transfer made pursuant to the agreement "to either spouse in settlement of his or her marital property rights" or "to provide a reasonable allowance for the support of issue of the marriage during minority" is deemed to be made for full money's-worth consideration. I.R.C. § 2516. Divorce settlements are commonly structured to come within the statutory exemption, thereby avoiding the need to determine the values of transfers actually made or received by the respective spouses. Note that the exemption is available only if the spouses actually divorce within the specified time period; a separation agreement, without more, does not provide automatic protection from gift tax, though transfers between spouses during marriage may qualify for the marital deduction. A property settlement that calls for transfers to adult children ordinarily gives rise to gift tax liability. If one spouse dies before making a promised exempt transfer to the other spouse, the estate tax allows a parallel deduction for the resulting claim against the decedent's estate. I.R.C. §§ 2043(b)(2), 2053(a), (c)(1)(A).

The gift tax regulations declare that "a sale, exchange, or other transfer of property made in the ordinary course of business (a transaction which is bona fide, at arm's length, and free from any donative intent), will be considered as made for an adequate and full consideration in money or money's worth." Reg. § 25.2512–8. The exemption for ordinary business transactions makes good sense. Without it, every purchase or exchange would have to be examined; there would be potential gift tax consequences whenever a person made a bad investment or found a good bargain, and the gift tax would become unworkable. The exemption allows ordinary business transactions to proceed unimpeded, and avoids the need to value property given or received in such transactions. At the same time, the exemption raises a potential problem concerning the treatment of business transactions between family members—for example, a sale of a closely held business interest to a family member. If the sale is really bona fide, at arm's length and free from any donative intent, the seller should be deemed to have received full money's-worth consideration. But if the relationship of the parties, the terms of the sale or other circumstances suggest the possibility of a disguised gift, then it becomes necessary to determine the respective values of the transferred property and the consideration received. Similarly, if a person transfers property to another family member to settle a dispute, it may be difficult to determine whether the transfer is an ordinary business transaction or a gratuitous transfer.

[¶ 4,145]

4. Deductions and Exclusions

Not all gifts are taxable. Gifts that qualify for a deduction or an exclusion are removed from the donor's taxable gifts and therefore do not absorb any of the donor's unified credit. The gift tax marital deduction and charitable deduction allow a donor to make unlimited tax-free gifts to a spouse or to a qualified charitable organization. These deductions mirror their estate tax counterparts, which are discussed at ¶¶ 4,340 and 4,350. The annual exclusion allows a donor to make tax-free gifts in a specified dollar amount to an unlimited number of donees each year. Finally, a separate exclusion allows a donor to make unlimited tax-free payments for qualified educational and medical expenses.

[¶ 4,150]

a. *Annual exclusion*

The annual exclusion applies to "gifts (other than gifts of future interests in property) made to any person by the donor during the calendar year," up to a specified dollar amount per donee. I.R.C. § 2503(b). The basic exclusion amount was set at $10,000 in 1981, and has been indexed for inflation since 1999; in 2005, the exclusion amount was $11,000. This is the maximum amount of excludable gifts that a donor can make to a particular donee in a single year. However, there is no limit on the permissible number of donees, nor on the number of successive years in which excludable gifts can be made to the same donees. Gifts that are fully covered by the annual exclusion are completely free of gift tax. Such gifts do not enter into the donor's taxable gifts, do not count against the gift tax exemption equivalent, and need not be reported on a gift tax return.

To illustrate, a donor with six donees (e.g., two children and four grandchildren) can make tax-free gifts totalling $66,000 each year without even filing a gift tax return. For married couples, the utility of the exclusion is enhanced by the "gift-splitting" provision of I.R.C. § 2513, which treats any gift made by a married donor to a donee (other than his or her spouse) for gift tax purposes as made one-half by the donor and one-half by the spouse, if both spouses consent. Thus, a married individual with two children and four grandchildren can make gifts of $132,000 per year with no gift or estate tax consequences (other than filing a gift tax return containing the spouse's consent to gift-splitting).

The annual exclusion was originally justified on grounds of administrative convenience. According to the legislative history, the exclusion was intended "on the one hand, ... to obviate the necessity of keeping an account of and reporting numerous small gifts, and, on the other, to fix the amount sufficiently large to cover in most cases wedding and Christmas gifts and occasional gifts of relatively small amounts." S. Rep. No. 665, 72d Cong., 1st Sess. (1932), reprinted in 1939–1 (pt. 2) C.B. 496, 525–26. Over the years, however, the exclusion has come to play a prominent role in estate planning. Indeed, some planners recommend a program of annual gifts in the full amount of the exclusion, apparently on the heroic assumption that the donor makes no other gifts (e.g., for birthdays, holidays or similar occasions) that use up any portion of the available exclusion.

One obvious way to stretch the annual exclusion is to spread a large gift of property over several years. For example, suppose that Bianca has an available exclusion amount of $10,000 and wishes to make a tax-free gift to David of property worth $100,000. She can give David a one-tenth undivided fractional interest in the property in the current year, and then make similar gifts in each succeeding year until the entire property has been transferred to David. This approach may require periodic appraisals to ensure that the annual gifts are covered by the available exclusion. To avoid the burden of periodic appraisals and put the entire property in David's hands at once, Bianca might structure the transfer as an arm's-length sale to David. Bianca can then return the purchase price to David through a series of annual exclusion gifts.

Occasionally a donor goes too far in attempting to exploit multiple annual exclusions. For example, if Carmen transfers separate blocks of stock, each worth $10,000, to 30 different friends and family members, and each transferee promptly turns around and retransfers the stock to Gerald, the transaction can easily be recast as a single gift to Gerald of stock worth $300,000; the intermediate transfers will be disregarded and Carmen will be allowed only one annual exclusion. Heyen v. U.S., 945 F.2d 359 (10th Cir. 1991).

To be eligible for the annual exclusion, a gift must give the donee an immediate, unrestricted right to the use, possession or beneficial enjoyment of property. Reg. § 25.2503–3(b). An outright gift of property ordinarily meets the "present interest" requirement without difficulty, even if the property consists of a contractual right to future payments (e.g., a bond or a life insurance policy). Gifts in trust, however, require careful planning. The donees of a gift in trust are the beneficiaries, and the exclusion is available only to the extent that one or more beneficiaries receive immediate, ascertainable, unrestricted beneficial rights in the trust property or its income. If a donor creates an irrevocable trust of income-producing property and the trustee is required to distribute all of the income to a single beneficiary for life with remainder payable at death to other beneficiaries, the income beneficiary has received a present interest and the donor is entitled to one annual exclusion. Similarly, if the trustee is required to distribute the income to two or more beneficiaries in ascertainable shares, the donor is entitled to an annual exclusion for the gift of income to each beneficiary. The exclusion is allowed for the present value of each beneficiary's income interest, up to the dollar amount specified in the statute.

No exclusion is allowed for a gift of a "future interest" that is "limited to commence in use, possession, or enjoyment at some future date or time." Reg. § 25.2503–3(a). This disallowance extends not only to interests conventionally classified as future interests under state law (e.g., remainders and reversions), but also to any gift that imposes restrictions on the donee's immediate right to the use, possession or beneficial enjoyment of property. For example, if a donor creates an irrevocable trust and authorizes the trustee to make or withhold distributions of trust income or principal in the trustee's unfettered discretion, the donor is generally not allowed to claim any annual exclusions because none of the beneficiaries can compel a distribution of any ascertainable amount; they have only future interests within the meaning of the statute.

This obstacle can be overcome, however, if one or more beneficiaries have an immediate, unrestricted power, under the terms of the trust, to withdraw property from the trust. Whether or not exercised, such "demand powers" create present interests which can qualify for the annual exclusion. This form of trust is often called a *"Crummey* trust," after the leading case of Crummey v. Commissioner, 397 F.2d 82 (9th Cir. 1968), which allowed annual exclusions based on unexercised demand powers held by minor beneficiaries. Technically, a demand power is a general power of appointment which would ordinarily cause the holder to be treated as the owner of the underlying property for gift and estate tax purposes under I.R.C. §§ 2514 and 2041 (discussed in ¶ 4,310). The statute, however, provides a special exception for certain powers that lapse during the holder's life. I.R.C. § 2514(e). For this reason, demand powers are usually designed to remain exercisable for only a brief period—commonly 30 to 60 days—before they lapse automatically. As a practical matter, demand powers are almost never exercised. They are intended only to generate one or more annual exclusions for the donor, not to facilitate withdrawals of trust property by beneficiaries. As long as the demand powers are legally enforceable and there is no prearranged agreement or understanding prohibiting their exercise, the courts have upheld the resulting annual exclusions.

Gifts to minors raise special problems. Most donors are reluctant to make substantial outright gifts directly to minors, although there is no legal impediment to doing so. One alternative is a custodianship under the Uniform Transfers to Minors Act (or its forerunner, the Uniform Gifts to Minors Act), which has been enacted in one version or another throughout the country (see ¶ 2,510). Such gifts are eligible for the annual exclusion, notwithstanding the custodian's broad discretionary powers over beneficial enjoyment of the property. Rev. Rul. 59–357, 1959–2 C.B. 212. (Note that if the donor dies while acting as custodian during the term of the custodianship, the property will be includible in the donor's gross estate for estate tax purposes. For this reason, it is generally recommended that the donor consider naming someone else as custodian.)

A gift of property that would otherwise not meet the present interest requirement of I.R.C. § 2503(b) may still be eligible for the annual exclusion if it comes within the safe harbor of I.R.C. § 2503(c), which treats the donee as having a present interest if the transferred property and its income "may be expended by, or for the benefit of, the donee before his attaining the age of 21 years" and must, to the extent not so expended, "pass to the donee on his attaining the age of 21 years" (or, if the donee dies before reaching age 21, "be payable to the estate of the donee or as he may appoint under a general power of appointment"). This provision permits the donor of a trust for a minor beneficiary to lodge control of the trust property in the hands of a trustee with broad discretion, without losing the tax benefit of the annual exclusion. In effect, the minor beneficiary is treated for gift tax purposes as the constructive owner of the trust property because he or she is entitled to claim absolute ownership upon reaching age 21 and no distributions can be made from the trust to any other person during the interim. The trust need not actually terminate when the minor beneficiary reaches age 21. As long as the beneficiary has the right to compel a distribution of the trust property at that time, the beneficiary may elect to terminate the trust or to permit it to continue by its own terms. Donors who are reluctant to give a beneficiary unfettered access to large amounts of property at age 21 may prefer to use a *Crummey* trust, which provides considerably more flexibility. Unlike a § 2503(c) trust, a *Crummey* trust can have multiple current beneficiaries and can give the trustee broad discretion to make or withhold distributions throughout the beneficiaries' lives following the expiration of their demand powers.

[¶ 4,155]

Problems

1. Basil, the owner of an insurance policy on his own life, irrevocably assigns the policy to his son Rodney, retaining no incidents of ownership. After the assignment Basil continues to pay the annual premiums on the policy. Is Basil entitled to annual exclusions for (1) the gift of the policy and (2) the subsequent premium payments? See Reg. § 25.2503–3(a), (c); Rev. Rul. 55–408, 1955–1 C.B. 113.

2. Celeste gives $10,000 to her own child and $10,000 to her brother Arthur's child. On the same day, Arthur makes gifts of equal amounts to the same donees. Are Celeste and Arthur each entitled to two annual exclusions? Have they each made any taxable gifts as a result of these transfers? See Schultz v. U.S., 493 F.2d 1225 (4th Cir. 1974); Rev. Rul. 85–24, 1985–1 C.B. 329.

3. Paula transfers Blackacre, with a fair market value of $100,000, to Jack in exchange for Jack's promissory note in the principal amount of $100,000 with no cash downpayment. The note is secured by a mortgage on Blackacre, bears interest at a market rate, and provides for level payments of principal and interest totalling $10,000 per year. In the year of the transfer and each succeeding year, Paula forgives the payments of principal and interest as they come due. Has Paula made any taxable gifts? If so, in what year(s) and in what amount(s)? See Haygood v. Commissioner, 42 T.C. 936 (1964); Estate of Kelley v. Commissioner, 63 T.C. 321 (1974); Deal v. Commissioner, 29 T.C. 730 (1958); Rev. Rul., 77–299, 1977–2 C.B. 343. Does it make any difference if in each year after the initial transfer, Paula gives $10,000 in cash to Jack and Jack uses the cash to make the annual payments on the note?

4. Carol creates an irrevocable inter vivos trust and funds it with property worth $100,000. The trust income is payable in equal shares to Carol's three children during her life, with remainder at her death in equal shares to her children then living; if any child fails to survive, the child's share is to be distributed to the child's surviving issue. At the creation of the trust, in addition to her three children, Carol has seven living grandchildren. The trust instrument gives each child and each grandchild has an unrestricted power to demand a distribution of $10,000 from the trust at any time during a 30–day period from the creation of the trust; any power that is not exercised at the end of the 30–day period will lapse. Has Carol made a taxable gift? If so, in what amount? See Estate of Cristofani v. Commissioner, 97 T.C. 74 (1991). Does it matter whether the beneficiaries are aware of the creation of the trust or of their demand powers? What if the demand powers are exercisable for only two days following the creation of the trust? See Rev. Rul. 81–7, 1981–1 C.B. 474; Rev. Rul. 83–108, 1983–2 C.B. 167.

[¶ 4,160]

b. *Educational and medical expenses*

In addition to the annual exclusion, the gift tax allows a separate exclusion for certain educational and medical expenses paid on behalf of an individual beneficiary. I.R.C. § 2503(e). The exclusion is unlimited in amount. It covers amounts paid directly to an educational organization as tuition for the beneficiary's education or training, but not for books, room and board, or other incidental expenses. The exclusion also covers amounts paid directly to a medical care provider as payment for the beneficiary's medical care (including expenses incurred for the diagnosis, treatment and prevention of disease, and medical insurance premiums). Reg. § 25.2503–6. In each case, the exclusion applies only to amounts paid by the donor directly to the educational organization or the medical care provider for current expenses; it does not cover funds set aside (e.g., in an irrevocable trust) for future payment of such expenses, nor does it cover amounts paid to reimburse the beneficiary for his or her own payment of current expenses.

[¶ 4,165]

5. Disclaimers

In general, a person who becomes entitled to receive property by gift, devise, inheritance or other gratuitous transfer may disclaim the property and let it pass instead to another taker under applicable state law. (See the discussion at ¶ 2,150). For federal tax purposes, a "qualified disclaimer" may offer significant tax benefits. Under the federal disclaimer statute, if a person makes a qualified disclaimer with respect to any interest in property, the federal wealth transfer taxes apply as if the disclaimed interest "had never been transferred to such person." I.R.C. § 2518(a). As a result, the disclaimed interest is treated as passing directly from the original transferor to the ultimate recipient in a single transfer. Note that I.R.C. § 2518 controls only the federal tax treatment of the qualified disclaimer; the dispositive effect of a disclaimer (whether qualified or non-qualified) is governed by state law.

To illustrate, suppose that Gail dies intestate, leaving her brother Dustin as her sole heir. Dustin disclaims his intestate share, which passes under applicable state law to his issue. If Dustin's disclaimer is a "qualified disclaimer" under I.R.C. § 2518, Gail's estate will be treated for gift, estate, and GST tax purposes as passing directly to Dustin's issue without passing through Dustin's hands. In contrast, if Dustin's disclaimer is not qualified, the transfer will be taxed as if Dustin had accepted his intestate share and then retransferred it to his issue by gift. In either case Gail's estate will attract an estate tax, but if Dustin's disclaimer is qualified the property will escape a separate gift tax in Dustin's hands.

A qualified disclaimer must be irrevocable, unconditional, and made in writing. The disclaimer must be made by the disclaimant within nine months after the date of the transfer creating the interest (or, if later, within nine months after reaching age 21). The disclaimant must not have accepted the disclaimed interest or any of its benefits. Finally, the interest must pass as a result of the disclaimer, without any direction on the part of the disclaimant, to the original transferor's spouse or to some person other than the disclaimant. I.R.C. § 2518(b). The federal tax requirements for a qualified disclaimer are independent of, and in some respects more restrictive than, the general requirements for a valid disclaimer under state law. For example, the nine-month disclaimer period under federal tax law may expire long before the time allowed under state law. Indeed, the federal disclaimer period may expire before the disclaimant learns of the existence of the interest. Reg. § 25.2518–2(c). In addition, unlike most state laws, federal tax law generally requires that a disclaimer be effective to put the disclaimed interest beyond the disclaimant's ownership and control. Reg. § 25.2518–2(e). Finally, federal tax law imposes stricter limits than most state laws on the use of partial disclaimers. Reg. § 25.2518–3. Thus, in planning and executing a disclaimer it is important to make sure that the disclaimer not only is valid under state law but also complies with the requirements of federal tax law.

A qualified disclaimer may be especially useful in fine-tuning a decedent's estate plan after death so as to make the best use of the marital deduction. For example, if a decedent's surviving spouse disclaims a bequest, which passes instead to other beneficiaries, the disclaimed bequest will not be eligible for a marital deduction. The reverse is also true: if the decedent's child disclaims a bequest, which passes instead to the decedent's surviving spouse, the bequest may become eligible for a marital deduction. If the disclaimed interest passes to the original transferor's grandchildren or more remote descendants, the transfer may become subject to a GST tax.

[¶ 4,170]

Problems

1.   Donna used her own funds to purchase Blackacre and took title in the names of herself and her adult son Nick as joint tenants with right of survivorship. Several years later Donna died survived by Nick, who became entitled to full ownership of Blackacre as surviving joint tenant. Nick proposes to disclaim his survivorship interest in Blackacre. Under applicable state law, the disclaimer would leave Nick with a one-half undivided interest in Blackacre; the other half would belong to Nick's issue. Will the proposed disclaimer be a qualified disclaimer? If Nick died first and Donna proposed to make a similar disclaimer, would her disclaimer be a qualified disclaimer? See Reg. § 25.2518–2(c)(4).

2.   Trina's father died in 1977. In his will, he left property in trust to pay income to Trina for life, with remainder at her death to her issue then living. Trina is still alive, and her 25–year–old son Rudy has recently learned of the existence of the trust. Rudy proposes to disclaim his interest. Under

applicable state law, the disclaimer would be effective to pass the disclaimed interest to Rudy's own issue. Will the proposed disclaimer be a qualified disclaimer under § 2518? Does it make any difference if Rudy is only 20 years old? See I.R.C. § 2518(b); Jewett v. Commissioner, 455 U.S. 305 (1982).

C. THE ESTATE TAX

[¶ 4,200]

Broadly speaking, the gift and estate taxes function as complementary components of a single system for taxing gratuitous transfers made during life or at death. To be sure, the estate tax includes several special provisions that have no counterpart in the gift tax (and vice versa), and the two taxes occasionally overlap in their application to a single transfer, but for the most part the structure and method of computation are closely similar. Both taxes allow deductions for property passing to the transferor's spouse or to a qualified charitable organization, and both taxes make use of the unified rate schedule and the unified credit.

The first step in computing the estate tax is to identify and value the property included in the gross estate, which embraces various categories of property that were actually or constructively transferred at death by the decedent. I.R.C. §§ 2031–2044. Allowable deductions (e.g., administration expenses, creditors' claims, and transfers to a surviving spouse or to a qualified charitable organization) are then subtracted from the gross estate to arrive at the taxable estate. I.R.C. §§ 2051–2058. A tentative tax is computed under the unified rate schedule on the decedent's cumulative taxable transfers (i.e., the taxable estate plus adjusted taxable gifts), and a similar tax is computed on the decedent's post–1976 taxable gifts. I.R.C. § 2001. The difference, less allowable credits (e.g., the unified credit), is the estate tax actually payable. I.R.C. §§ 2010–2014. For an illustrative computation, see ¶ 4,025.

[¶ 4,210]

1. The Gross Estate

The gross estate includes not only property actually passing from the decedent by will or intestacy but also several enumerated types of property that are treated for estate tax purposes as testamentary substitutes, such as joint tenancies, survivor annuities, life insurance proceeds, certain lifetime transfers subject to retained interests or powers, and property over which the decedent held a general power of appointment. Property included in the gross estate is ordinarily valued at its fair market value as of the date of death. I.R.C. § 2031. (In some cases where the gross estate drops in value after death, however, property may be valued as of an "alternate valuation date" up to six months after death. I.R.C. § 2032. And certain real property used in a farm or a closely held business may be eligible for "special use" valuation to alleviate liquidity problems at death. I.R.C. § 2032A.)

In a general sense, the estate tax inclusionary rules defining the gross estate complement the gift tax rules concerning the timing of lifetime gifts. To the extent that a donor retains sufficient dominion or control to prevent a transfer from constituting a completed gift during life, the transfer generally must be included in the gross estate at death. Because the two taxes are not perfectly correlated, however, it is possible for the same transfer to be subject to overlapping gift and estate taxes. In such cases, the estate tax computation under I.R.C. § 2001(b) automatically allows an offset for any gift tax imposed during life (see ¶ 4,025), with the result that only the appreciation in value between the time of the completed gift and the date of death is exposed to the estate tax.

[¶ 4,220]

a. *Property owned at death*

The central component of the gross estate consists of property owned at death. The operative provision is I.R.C. § 2033, which includes "all property to the extent of the interest therein of the decedent" at death. This provision applies to property of all kinds—real property, personal effects, cash, stocks and bonds—in which the decedent had a beneficial interest (as opposed to bare legal title) at death. It also includes various items earned but not yet collected by the decedent at death (e.g., wages due, accrued interest, and dividends payable to the decedent as stockholder of record). Section 2033 applies only to transmissible interests, i.e., those which survive the death of the decedent. For example, a life estate that terminates at the decedent's death is not included under this provision, nor is a contingent remainder which is defeated by the decedent's death.

From an early date, the courts have viewed § 2033 as reaching more or less the same assets as those which are included in the decedent's probate estate. Had the courts taken a more expansive view of this provision (along the lines of "dominion and control" or "substantial ownership" under the income tax), it might have been possible to dispense with several of the inclusionary provisions discussed below.

[¶ 4,225]

Problems

1. Several years ago Susan and Oliver, the parents of Dorothy, created a trust to pay income to Dorothy for life, with remainder at her death to Susan if living, or if Susan does not survive Dorothy then to Oliver or his estate. Oliver dies, then Susan dies, then Dorothy dies. What interest, if any, is includible in the gross estate of each trust beneficiary under I.R.C. § 2033? What difference would it make if Dorothy also held a general power

of appointment exercisable by will? See Helvering v. Safe Deposit & Trust Co., 316 U.S. 56 (1942).

2. Zoe purchased a lottery ticket for $1 and told a friend that she was holding it for her son Ralph. At the lottery drawing one week later, the ticket purchased by Zoe was selected as the winner of a $10 million jackpot. On hearing the good news, Zoe suffered a heart attack and died later the same day. The lottery proceeds are payable in twenty annual installments of $500,000, and are protected from creditors by a statutory prohibition on sale or assignment. What property is includible in Zoe's gross estate under I.R.C. § 2033, and how should it be valued? See I.R.C. § 7520; Estate of Cook v. Commissioner, 349 F.3d 850 (5th Cir. 2003); Estate of Gribauskas v. Commissioner, 342 F.3d 85 (2d Cir. 2003); Shackleford v. U.S., 262 F.3d 1028 (9th Cir. 2001); Estate of Winkler v. Commissioner, 73 T.C.M. (CCH) 1657 (1997); Aghdami, The Morning After: Tax Planning for Lottery Winners, 90 J. Tax'n 228 (1999).

3. At the time of his death, Geoff, a former U.S. serviceman, had in his possession several works of art (with an estimated value of $50 to $100 million) which he had stolen while stationed abroad. When his heirs attempted to sell the works, the true owner came forward to reclaim them and paid a $2.75 million "finder's fee" to the heirs. What interest, if any, did Geoff own at death, and what amount is includible in his gross estate under I.R.C. § 2033? See Tech. Adv. Memo. 9152005 (Aug. 30, 1991); Turnier, The Pink Panther Meets the Grim Reaper: Estate Taxation of the Fruits of Crime, 72 N.C. L. Rev. 163 (1993).

4. Deirdre, a best-selling popular author, died while she was working on the latest in a series of novels. After Deirdre's death, her executor entered into an agreement with her publisher, in which the publisher was authorized to hire a ghost writer to complete the unfinished novel and write additional novels to be published under Deirdre's name, based on characters and situations taken from her earlier works. The estate was to receive an advance of $200,000 and a royalties equal to 10% of net revenues from sales of the new works. What property is includible in Deirdre's gross estate under I.R.C. § 2033, and how should it be valued? See Estate of Andrews v. U.S., 850 F.Supp. 1279 (E.D. Va. 1994).

[¶ 4,230]

b. *Joint Tenancies*

Many people think of a joint tenancy with right of survivorship primarily as a convenient will substitute, without considering how the arrangement is treated for gift and estate tax purposes. While both tenants are alive, either of them can unilaterally sever the joint tenancy at any time and convert it to a tenancy in common. For gift tax purposes, each joint tenant is treated as owning an equal share of the underlying property. Accordingly, the creation of a joint tenancy may give rise to a completed gift if one tenant contributes a disproportionate share of the consideration for the jointly owned property. Similarly, a deemed gift may occur upon the termination of a joint tenancy if one tenant keeps a disproportionate share of the property or its proceeds. If the joint tenants are husband and wife, a gift on creation or termination has little significance, since such gifts are sheltered from tax by the unlimited marital deduction.

The estate tax treatment of joint tenancy property is governed by I.R.C. § 2040, which distinguishes between spousal and nonspousal joint tenancies. If the joint tenants are husband and wife, each spouse is treated as owning an equal share of the underlying property for estate tax purposes. Accordingly, at the death of the first spouse, one-half of the property is includible in the decedent's gross estate. I.R.C. § 2040(b). Since an equivalent amount automatically qualifies for the unlimited marital deduction, the net effect is to remove the decedent's share of the joint tenancy property from his or her taxable estate. Thus, under current law, spousal joint tenancies do not give rise to any gift or estate tax liability. (The estate tax treatment is important for income tax purposes. Since only one-half of the property is includible in the decedent's gross estate, the surviving spouse receives a fresh start basis only in the half of the property acquired from the decedent, under I.R.C. § 1014.)

In the case of a nonspousal joint tenancy, the estate tax consequences are a bit more complicated. At the death of the first tenant, the statute generally requires that the full value of the joint tenancy property be included in the decedent's gross estate, "except such part thereof as may be shown to have originally belonged to [the surviving joint tenant] and never to have been received or acquired by the latter from the decedent for less than an adequate and full consideration in money or money's worth." I.R.C. § 2040(a). The includible amount may be expressed as $V \times [1 - (p_s \div p_t)]$, where V is the value of the joint tenancy property at the decedent's death, p_s is the surviving joint tenant's contribution toward the purchase price, and p_t is the total purchase price of the property. (If the decedent and the survivor originally acquired the joint tenancy property by "gift, bequest, devise, or inheritance," a ratable share of the property is includible in the decedent's gross estate, just as if the joint tenants had made equal contributions toward the purchase price.) In theory, once the respective contributions of the decedent and the survivor toward the total purchase price are known, it is a simple matter to compute the includible portion of the property's deathtime value. However, the estate has the burden of proving the surviving joint tenant's contributions, and in the absence of meticulous recordkeeping this burden may be difficult to sustain.

To illustrate the operation of I.R.C. § 2040(a), suppose that Janet, using $100,000 of her own funds, purchases Blackacre for herself and her son Frank as joint tenants with right of survivorship. The creation of the joint tenancy results in a completed gift of $50,000 (which constitutes a present interest for purposes of the annual exclusion). Janet dies a few years later, when Blackacre is worth $150,000. The full deathtime value of Blackacre is includible in Janet's gross estate, but the resulting estate tax is partially offset by the gift tax that Janet paid when she created the joint tenancy (see I.R.C. § 2001(b)). In effect, the full value of Blackacre is taxed in two stages, with a portion payable during life and the balance at death. If Frank subsequently dies owning Blackacre, it will be includible in his gross estate under I.R.C. § 2033.

In effect, in the case of a nonspousal joint tenancy, each tenant is treated for estate tax purposes as owning a share of the property in proportion to his or her contributions toward the total purchase price. This tracing rule made sense, before the enactment of the gift tax, as a means of guarding against the use of joint tenancies to circumvent the estate tax on deathtime transfers. With the enactment of the gift tax, it would seem sensible to treat each joint tenant as owning an equal share of the property for both gift and estate tax purposes, but this has been done only in the case of spouses. For others (e.g., parent and child, brother and sister, or unmarried cohabitants), the potential overlapping gift and estate taxes on joint tenancy property may come as an unwelcome surprise.

[¶ 4,235]

Problems

1.   Christine, using $100,000 of her own funds, purchases Blackacre for herself and her son Alex as joint tenants with right of survivorship. Alex unexpectedly dies survived by Christine, when Blackacre is worth $150,000. What amount is includible in Alex's gross estate under I.R.C. § 2040(a)? When Christine subsequently dies owning Blackacre, how much is includible in her gross estate under I.R.C. § 2033?

2.   Mabel and her daughter Betty purchase Blackacre (worth $100,000) as joint tenants with right of survivorship. Each joint tenant contributes $20,000 in cash, and they take the property subject to a $60,000 recourse mortgage on which they are jointly and severally liable. Mabel pays off $30,000 of the principal balance of the debt. Later, when Blackacre is worth $200,000 and the outstanding principal balance of the debt is $30,000, Mabel dies survived by Betty. What amount is includible in Mabel's gross estate under I.R.C. § 2040(a)? See Rev. Rul. 79–302, 1979–2 C.B. 328.

3.   Fabio gives stock worth $30,000 to Gillian. A few years later, when the stock is worth $50,000, Gillian sells the stock to a third party in exchange for bonds of equal value, taking title to the bonds in the names of herself and Fabio as joint tenants with right of survivorship. Subsequently, when the bonds are worth $150,000, Fabio dies survived by Gillian. What amount is includible in Fabio's gross estate under I.R.C. § 2040(a)? See Reg. § 20.2040–1(c)(4).

[¶ 4,240]

c.   *Survivor annuities*

Under I.R.C. § 2039, a decedent's gross estate includes survivor benefits payable to beneficiaries under a "contract or agreement," if the decedent was entitled under same contract or agreement to receive an "annuity or other payment" for life. The survivor benefits are includible to the extent attributable to contributions made by the decedent (or on the decedent's behalf by his or her employer) toward the purchase price. This provision is aimed primarily at survivor benefits under employee benefit plans and individual retirement accounts. (A special exemption for qualified plans and individual retirement accounts was repealed in 1984.) Section 2039 also applies to amounts payable under commercial survivorship annuities and other contractual arrangements. It does not reach life insurance proceeds, survivor benefits under statutory programs (e.g., social security), or "pure" death benefits under an arrangement that made no provision for payments to the decedent during life. Also, if the decedent purchased a single life annuity payable to himself or herself for life, with no survivor benefits payable to another beneficiary, nothing is includible in the gross estate.

[¶ 4,250]

d. *Life insurance*

I.R.C. § 2042 governs the estate tax treatment of proceeds of insurance on the decedent's life. If the proceeds are payable to the decedent's estate, they are fully includible in the gross estate. I.R.C. § 2042(1). However, if the proceeds are payable to any other beneficiary (as is typically the case), they are includible only if the decedent possessed at death any of the "incidents of ownership" in the policy. I.R.C. § 2042(2). The term "incidents of ownership" is not limited to ownership in the technical legal sense; it refers generally to "the right of the insured or his estate to the economic benefits of the policy," and includes, for example, "the right to change the beneficiary, to surrender or cancel the policy, to assign the policy, to revoke an assignment, to pledge the policy for a loan, or to obtain from the insurer a loan against the surrender value of the policy, etc." Reg. § 20.2042–1(c)(2). The term also includes a reversionary interest in the policy or its proceeds if immediately before death the value of the interest exceeded 5% of the value of the policy.

A person may hold incidents of ownership without having full legal ownership of the insurance policy. For example, if Bernice is named as the owner of a policy on Justin's life, but under the terms of a trust or other agreement Justin has the right to change the beneficiary or to surrender the policy (or if Justin's consent is required for any such action), then Justin is treated as holding an incident of ownership even if he has no beneficial interest in the proceeds. If Justin continues to hold that right at death, even if he holds no other incidents of ownership, the entire proceeds will be includible in his gross estate. Similarly, if Justin is the controlling shareholder of a corporation that owns a policy on his life, and an object of Justin's bounty is named as the beneficiary of the proceeds at his death, the corporation's incidents of ownership may be attributed to Justin for estate tax purposes. Reg. § 20.2042–1(c)(6).

If a husband and wife hold a policy on one spouse's life as community property, and the insured spouse dies first, only half of the proceeds are includible in the insured spouse's gross estate. Reg. § 20.2042–1(c)(2), (c)(5). The noninsured spouse is treated as the owner of the other half of the policy (or proceeds) for gift and estate tax purposes. To illustrate, suppose that Harold and Wendy own a community property policy on Harold's life, with their child Candice named as beneficiary. Harold dies survived by Wendy and by Candice, and the proceeds become payable to Candice. Half of the proceeds are includible in Harold's gross estate under I.R.C. § 2042, and Wendy is treated as making a completed gift of the other half of the proceeds at Harold's death. (If Wendy died first, one half of the value of the policy would be includible in her gross estate under I.R.C. § 2033. Section 2042 has no application to policies owned by a decedent on the life of another person.)

Under current law, a person who holds an insurance policy on his or her own life can put the proceeds beyond the reach of § 2042 simply by transferring the policy and relinquishing all incidents of ownership. The incentive to make such a transfer is especially strong if the present value of the policy is substantially less than the proceeds payable at death and the insured policy holder expects death to occur relatively soon. To foreclose this gambit, the statute provides a three-year look-back rule for life insurance: if a decedent transfers or relinquishes an incident of ownership in a policy on his or her own life and then dies within three years, the life insurance proceeds are includible in the gross estate just as if the decedent had retained the incident of ownership until death. I.R.C. § 2035(a). As a result, the policy holder must survive for at least three years after the transfer to remove the proceeds definitively from the gross estate. Note that it is irrelevant for estate tax purposes whether the premiums on a life insurance policy are paid by the insured person or by someone else. If an insured decedent held no incidents of ownership in a policy at death or during the preceding three-year period, the proceeds are not includible in the gross estate under §§ 2042 or 2035 even if the decedent paid all of the premiums up to the date of death.

The estate tax treatment of life insurance gives rise to the widespread use of irrevocable life insurance trusts which allow an insured settlor to pay all of the premiums during life while keeping the proceeds out of the gross estate at death. See the discussion at ¶ 4,370.

Note that § 2042 applies only to policies of insurance on the decedent's own life. Policies on the life of a third party are governed by other provisions. For example, if Edith dies owning a policy on the life of her surviving child Gilbert, the value of the policy at Edith's death (i.e., the "interpolated terminal reserve" plus the unearned portion of the most recent premium, see ¶ 4,120) is includible in her gross estate under § 2033. If Gilbert died first and the proceeds became payable to Franz as the designated beneficiary under the policy, Edith would be treated as making a gift of the proceeds to Franz.

[¶ 4,255]

Problem

Raquel arranges for her husband Martin to take out an insurance policy on Raquel's life. Raquel selects the policy, dictates the terms, signs the application as the insured person, and pays all of the premiums. Martin is named as the sole owner and beneficiary of the policy. Raquel dies one year later. Are the proceeds includible in her gross estate under I.R.C. §§ 2042 or 2035? See Estate of Leder v. Commissioner, 893 F.2d 237 (10th Cir. 1989); Estate of Headrick v. Commissioner, 918 F.2d 1263 (6th Cir. 1990); Estate of Perry v. Commissioner, 927 F.2d 209 (5th Cir. 1991).

[¶ 4,260]

e. *Lifetime transfers*

From the earliest days of the estate tax it has been clear that if wholesale avoidance is to be prevented, some provision must be made for taxing transfers which, although technically operative during life, function as testamentary substitutes. Prior to the enactment of the gift tax, such transfers would go completely untaxed unless they were included in the gross estate. Accordingly, the original estate tax statute drew two types of transfers made by the decedent during life back into the gross estate at death: transfers "intended to take effect in possession or enjoyment at or after death" (the predecessor of I.R.C. §§ 2036–2038), and transfers made "in contemplation of death" (the predecessor of I.R.C. § 2035).

The original postponed-possession-or-enjoyment provision was aimed at lifetime transfers which remained "incomplete" in some respect until death due to interests or powers held by the decedent. Through a complicated dialectic of judicial interpretation and legislative revision, the postponed-possession-or-enjoyment provision gradually evolved into the considerably more detailed provisions of I.R.C. §§ 2036–2038, which cover more or less the same territory under current law. (The focus here is primarily on current law. However, many trusts established long ago are still in existence today and remain subject to the provisions of prior law. Given the checkered history of these provisions, the tax consequences of a particular transfer may vary substantially depending on when the transfer was made.) Section 2036 deals with transfers under which the decedent retained rights and interests in the property or its income for life. Section 2037 deals with transfers in which the decedent retained a reversionary interest and the interests of other beneficiaries are conditioned on surviving the decedent. Section 2038 deals with transfers in which the decedent reserved a power affecting beneficial enjoyment. Each of these provisions, like their common predecessor, is predicated on a "transfer" of property made by the decedent during life (though not necessarily a completed gift for gift tax purposes) which left the decedent holding some specified taxable "string" (e.g., a life estate or power to revoke). The three provisions are not mutually exclusive; indeed, they often overlap, e.g., where a decedent retained both a life estate and a power to revoke. The amount includible in the gross estate may vary depending on the type of interest or power involved.

The contemplation-of-death provision was replaced in 1976 by a bright-line rule that drew back into the gross estate any transfers made by the decedent within three years of death. In addition, to discourage tax-motivated deathbed gifts, a new "gross-up" provision required that any gift tax paid by the decedent on such transfers also be included in the gross estate. With the unification of the estate and gift taxes, it soon became clear that there was little reason to draw most deathbed gifts back into the gross estate as long as the gross-up provision captured the gift tax on such gifts. The 1981 Act therefore repealed the three-year inclusionary rule for most transfers but left the gross-up provision intact. The current version of the three-year rule appears in I.R.C. § 2035 (discussed in ¶ 4,300).

Each of the inclusionary provisions of §§ 2035–2038 contains an exception for a "bona fide sale for an adequate and full consideration in money or money's worth." The bona fide sale exemption, like its counterpart in the gift tax, avoids double counting where the transferred property is replaced by property of equivalent value in the transferor's hands. If the decedent received less than full consideration for the transfer, the amount of consideration received is allowed as a dollar-for-dollar offset against the amount includible in the gross estate under §§ 2035–2038. I.R.C. § 2043(a). Because the consideration offset under § 2043 is measured at the time of the lifetime transfer while the property included under §§ 2035–2038 is valued at the time of death, the offset for partial consideration fails to take account of any appreciation accrued in the meantime. Therefore, if a transaction is structured as a sale, it is important to establish an accurate valuation for the transferred property and to ensure that the transferor receives money's-worth consideration of equal value.

[¶ 4,270]

(1) Revocable transfers

Under I.R.C. § 2038, the gross estate includes any property transferred by the decedent during life, to the extent that the decedent at death held a power to "alter, amend, revoke, or terminate" the beneficial enjoyment of the property. The courts have given this provision an expansive interpretation. It has been applied to reach property transferred in trust by the decedent during life not only where the decedent retained a power to revoke the trust and recover the property, but also where the decedent retained a "nonbeneficial" power to alter or amend the trust in any way other than for his own benefit. Porter v. Commissioner, 288 U.S. 436 (1933). Moreover, the decedent's power need not be presently exercisable during life; § 2038 has been held applicable where the settlor of an irrevocable inter vivos trust retained only a special testamentary power to appoint the trust property among her descendants. Commissioner v. Chase Nat'l Bank, 82 F.2d 157 (2d Cir.), cert. denied, 299 U.S. 552 (1936).

Section 2038 applies to "any power affecting the time or manner of enjoyment of property or its income, even though the identity of the beneficiary is not affected." Reg. § 20.2038–1(a). Thus, if a person creates a custodianship for a minor child under the Uniform Transfers to Minors Act (or the Uniform Gifts to Minors Act) and then dies while serving as custodian before the child reaches the age of majority, the custodianship property is includible in the custodian's gross estate under § 2038. Similarly, if a settlor creates an irrevocable inter vivos trust for the sole benefit of a minor child, and retains a fiduciary power to accumulate income or distribute corpus, the trust property is includible in the settlor's gross estate. Lober v. United States, 346 U.S. 335 (1953). (Note that such a retained "time or manner" power would not prevent the transfer from being complete for gift tax purposes.) However, if the decedent's power was "subject to a contingency beyond the decedent's control which did not occur before his death," then § 2038 does not apply. Reg. § 20.2038–1(b). For example, suppose that Emily creates an inter vivos trust for the benefit of her son John and John's issue, retaining a power to revoke the trust only in the event that John dies before Emily. If Emily dies survived by John, the trust property is not includible in Emily's gross estate under § 2038 because her retained power was not exercisable at the time of death.

By its terms, § 2038 applies to a power held by the decedent alone or "in conjunction with any other person." It is immaterial whether the other person has a substantial beneficial interest which would be adversely affected by the exercise of the power. For example, if a settlor creates an inter vivos trust, reserving a power of revocation exercisable only with the consent of one of the beneficiaries, and then dies holding the reserved power, the trust property is includible in the settlor's gross estate. Helvering v. City Bank Farmers Trust Co., 296 U.S. 85 (1935). Nevertheless, § 2038 does not apply to a decedent's power that is exercisable "only with the consent of all parties having an interest (vested or contingent) in the transferred property" and "adds nothing to the rights of the parties under local law." Reg. § 20.2038–1(a). (But for this exception, even an irrevocable trust with no retained powers might fall within the reach of § 2038, because under state law a trust can always be terminated with the consent of the settlor and all of the beneficiaries. See ¶ 2,590.)

For purposes of § 2038, it generally makes no difference whether a decedent held a power as an individual or as a fiduciary; by its terms, the provision applies to a power exercisable by the decedent "in whatever capacity." Nevertheless, courts have held § 2038 inapplicable where the decedent held a fiduciary power, exercisable for the benefit of other beneficiaries, that was limited by an "ascertainable standard" enforceable in a court of equity. For example, if George declares himself trustee of an irrevocable inter vivos trust for the benefit of his adult children, and retains a fiduciary power to distribute income or principal as needed for the "support," "education" or "health" of the respective children, the retained power will not draw the trust property into George's gross estate. As in the gift tax context, the ascertainable standard doctrine rests on the premise that a retained power does not amount to dominion or control if it is limited by an objective, external standard and constrained by fiduciary duties (with the implicit sanction of enforcement by a court of equity). Although the premise may be questionable, the doctrine has become firmly established in case law and in the Service's own rulings.

Section 2038 reaches only powers affecting beneficial enjoyment; it has no application to purely administrative powers. Thus, property transferred by a decedent in trust is not drawn back into the gross estate merely because the decedent retained standard fiduciary powers to select trust investments, to sell or exchange trust property, or to allocate receipts and disbursements between income and principal.

Section 2038 does not apply to "a power held solely by a person other than the decedent." Reg. § 20.2038–1(a). Thus, a transferor can ordinarily avoid the reach of § 2038 by giving another person (such as a spouse or a trusted family member) complete control over beneficial enjoyment of the transferred property. In some cases, however, powers held by another person may be attributed to the decedent. For example, if the decedent held "an unrestricted power to remove or discharge a trustee at any time and appoint himself as trustee," the decedent would be treated as holding the powers vested in the trustee. Id.

[¶ 4,275]

Problem

Daria creates an irrevocable inter vivos trust for the benefit of Ugo and Flora. XYZ trust company is named as trustee, with absolute discretion to distribute income and principal to one or both of the beneficiaries. In her capacity as settlor, Daria retains a power to remove the trustee and appoint another independent trust company as trustee. Is the trust property includible in Daria's gross estate under I.R.C. § 2038? What if Daria could remove the original trustee and appoint anyone other than herself as successor trustee? What if Daria could not remove the original trustee, but could appoint anyone, including herself, as successor trustee if the original trustee resigned? See Reg. § 20.2038–1; Estate of Wall v. Commissioner, 101 T.C. 300 (1993); Rev. Rul. 95–58, 1995–2 C.B. 191.

[¶ 4,280]

(2) Transfers with retained life interest

If a decedent made a lifetime transfer and retained possession or enjoyment of the transferred property or its income for life, I.R.C.

§ 2036 requires that the property be included in the gross estate, even if the decedent retained no power of revocation or amendment. In effect, the statute treats a retained life estate as equivalent to retained ownership of the underlying property and the transfer as a testamentary substitute. Section 2036(a) provides:

> The value of the gross estate shall include the value of all property to the extent of any interest therein of which the decedent has at any time made a transfer (except in case of a bona fide sale for an adequate and full consideration in money or money's worth), by trust or otherwise, under which he has retained for his life or for any period not ascertainable without reference to his death or for any period which does not in fact end before his death—
>
>> (1) the possession or enjoyment of, or the right to the income from, the property, or
>>
>> (2) the right, either alone or in conjunction with any person, to designate the persons who shall possess or enjoy the property or the income therefrom.

If § 2036 applies, the amount included in the gross estate is not the value of the decedent's retained interest or right (which ordinarily expires at death) but rather the value of the underlying property in which the decedent retained the interest or right. The regulations offer the following explanation:

> If the decedent retained or reserved an interest or right with respect to all of the property transferred by him, the amount to be included in his gross estate under section 2036 is the value of the entire property, less only the value of any outstanding income interest which is not subject to the decedent's interest or right and which is actually being enjoyed by another person at the time of the decedent's death. [Reg. § 20.2036–1(a)].

For example, if Barbara transferred Blackacre to Neil subject to a reserved life estate in Barbara, the full value of Blackacre at Barbara's death would be includible in her gross estate. Instead, suppose that Barbara gave Neil a life estate followed by a reserved life estate in Barbara and a remainder in Connie or her estate. If Barbara died while Neil was still living and in possession of the property, the value of the property includible in Barbara's gross estate would be reduced by the present value of Neil's outstanding life estate. Reg. § 20.2036–1(b)(1). Thus, the constructive deathtime transfer under § 2036 is limited to the interests that follow or depend on the decedent's retained life estate; these are the only interests that take effect in possession or enjoyment at or after the decedent's death.

To determine whether § 2036 applies to a lifetime transfer, it is necessary to identify the interests and rights, if any, retained by the decedent "under" the transfer. The most obvious examples of a § 2036 transfer are an outright transfer subject to a reserved life estate or a transfer in trust with a retained income interest for life. (For this purpose, a right to receive the income from trust property is equivalent to possession or enjoyment or the property itself.) There is no requirement that the decedent's interest be expressly retained in the terms of the transfer, however. It is sufficient that the decedent retained actual possession or enjoyment under an informal understanding or agreement at the time of the transfer. To illustrate, suppose that Bella conveys her house to her son Stephen with the understanding that Bella may continue to live there as long as she wishes to do so. If Bella dies while still in possession, the house is includible in her gross estate even though the lifetime conveyance to Stephen was absolute on its face, because Bella retained possession for a "period which [did] not in fact end before [her] death." (Note also that the lifetime conveyance is a completed gift, and any resulting gift tax will be allowed as an offset against the estate tax imposed at Bella's death under I.R.C. § 2001(b).)

For purposes of § 2036, a decedent is treated as having retained possession and enjoyment of property "to the extent that the use, possession, right to the income, or other enjoyment is to be applied toward the discharge of a legal obligation of the decedent, or otherwise for his pecuniary benefit." Reg. § 20.2036–1(b)(2). For example, if Ernest created an inter vivos trust with himself as a discretionary income beneficiary, and under applicable state law the trust property could be reached if necessary to satisfy claims of his creditors, the trust property would be includible in Ernest's gross estate under § 2036. The result would be the same if the trust terms directed the trustee to apply the trust income for the support of Ernest's minor child and Ernest died before the child reached the age of majority.

Even if the decedent retained no beneficial interest in the property or its income, the statute applies where the decedent retained a power "to designate the persons who shall possess or enjoy the property or the income therefrom." I.R.C. § 2036(a)(2). This provision overlaps to a large extent with I.R.C. § 2038, and the courts have reached identical results under both provisions in cases involving joint powers, powers subject to ascertainable standards and administrative powers (see ¶ 4,270). Nevertheless, the two provisions are not entirely congruent. Section 2036(a)(2) is aimed at powers affecting the beneficial enjoyment of property or income during the decedent's life, while § 2038 reaches powers over the property itself which do not affect the enjoyment of income earned or received during the decedent's life. Reg. § 20.2036–1(b)(3). Moreover, the amounts includible under the two provisions are not necessarily identical. In analyzing the estate tax treatment of retained powers, therefore, it is important to consider the applicability and effect of each provision separately.

Section 2036 may also apply where a decedent transferred shares of closely held stock while retaining voting rights in the transferred stock. The statute provides that, for purposes of § 2036(a)(1), "the retention of the right to vote (directly or indirectly) shares of stock of a controlled corporation shall be considered to be a retention of the enjoyment of transferred property." I.R.C. § 2036(b). For this purpose, a corporation is "controlled" if the decedent or certain related parties held at least

20% of the combined voting power of all classes of stock. This provision was enacted in 1976 to overrule the holding of United States v. Byrum, 408 U.S. 125 (1972), in which the Supreme Court concluded that a controlling shareholder's lifetime transfers of stock subject to retained voting rights fell outside the scope of § 2036(a). Note, however, that § 2036(b) operates only where the decedent retained voting rights in stock that was transferred during life; if the transferred shares carried no voting rights that could be exercised by the decedent, the provision does not apply.

[¶ 4,285]

Problems

1. Lydia conveys her house, worth $250,000, to her son Bruce for an interest-bearing promissory note in the same amount, secured by a mortgage on the property. On the same day, Bruce leases the property back to Lydia for a fair market rent. As it happens, Bruce's interest payments under the note and Lydia's rental payments under the lease are almost identical in amount, with the result that the cash flows offset each other. Moreover, at the time of the sale and in each subsequent year, Lydia forgives $10,000 of the principal on the note. Lydia dies four years later when the outstanding principal balance on the note is $200,000 and the fair market value of the property is $500,000. In her will, Lydia forgives the remaining principal on the note. What amount is includible in Lydia's gross estate? See I.R.C. §§ 2033, 2036, 2043; Estate of Maxwell v. Commissioner, 3 F.3d 591 (2d Cir. 1993).

2. Therese creates an irrevocable inter vivos trust of $100,000 to pay income to her brother Patrick for life with remainder at Patrick's death to other named beneficiaries. On the same day Patrick creates a similar trust of $100,000 to pay income to Therese for life with remainder at Therese's death to the same beneficiaries. Therese dies survived by Patrick, when each trust is worth $500,000. What amount, if any, is includible in Therese's gross estate? What result if Therese's trust named Patrick as trustee with a discretionary power to make distributions to named beneficiaries and Patrick's trust named Therese as trustee with a similar power? See United States v. Estate of Grace, 395 U.S. 316 (1969); Estate of Bischoff v. Commissioner, 69 T.C. 32 (1977); Estate of Green v. Commissioner, 68 F.3d 151 (6th Cir. 1995).

3. Adam, the sole shareholder of Dotcorp, transferred nonvoting Dotcorp shares irrevocably in trust for his grandchildren. By the terms of the trust, the trustee was prohibited from selling any Dotcorp shares without Adam's consent, and Adam never consented to a sale while he was alive. Adam retained all of the voting shares of Dotcorp in his own name outside the trust until his death, and at no time while he was alive were any dividends declared or paid by Dotcorp to its shareholders. Is any portion of the trust property includible in Adam's gross estate? See I.R.C. § 2036; Rev. Rul. 81–15, 1981–1 C.B. 457; United States v. Byrum, 408 U.S. 125 (1972).

[¶ 4,290]

(3) Transfers taking effect at death

If the decedent made a lifetime transfer of an interest that takes effect in possession or enjoyment at or after the decedent's death, subject to a retained future interest in the same property, the transferred interest may be drawn back into the gross estate under I.R.C. § 2037. This provision applies only if two requirements are met: the holder of the transferred interest must be able to obtain possession or enjoyment of the property "only by surviving the decedent"; and the decedent's reversionary interest must be worth more than 5% of the value of the underlying property immediately before death. I.R.C. § 2037(a). For this purpose, the value of the reversionary interest immediately before death is determined, without regard to the fact of death, by "usual methods of valuation, including the use of tables of mortality and actuarial principles," as prescribed in the regulations. I.R.C. § 2037(b).

To illustrate the type of transfer at which § 2037 is aimed, suppose that Pablo creates an irrevocable inter vivos trust to pay income to his wife Miranda for life and then to distribute the trust property at Miranda's death to Pablo if living, or if Pablo is not living to Celia or her estate. If Pablo dies while Miranda is still alive, his reversion fails and Celia's remainder becomes indefeasibly vested. The "necessary survivorship" requirement of § 2037 is met because Celia must survive Pablo to obtain possession or enjoyment of the trust property; in no event could Celia's interest become possessory during Pablo's lifetime. If the value of Pablo's reversion immediately before death was more than 5% of the value of the trust property—in other words, if the actuarial probability of Pablo surviving Miranda was greater than 5%—then the transfer is subject to § 2037. Under § 2037, if applicable, the includible amount is not the value of the decedent's reversionary interest (which may have been extinguished at death) but rather the value of the other beneficiaries' interests which can be possessed or enjoyed "only by surviving the decedent." Thus, the amount includible in Pablo's gross estate is limited to the value of Celia's remainder (i.e., the value of the trust property reduced by the value of Miranda's outstanding life estate at Pablo's death). Reg. § 20.2037–1(e).

In the above example, Pablo failed to survive Miranda. Because Pablo's reversion failed at his death, nothing was includible in his gross estate under § 2033. If Pablo survived Miranda, his reversion would become possessory and the property would eventually be includible under § 2033.

With the above example, compare an irrevocable inter vivos trust created by Dennis to pay income to Naomi for life and then to distribute the trust property at Naomi's death to Carla if living, or if Carla is not living to Dennis or his estate. Here the "necessary survivorship" requirement is not met because Carla need not survive Dennis to possess or enjoy the property; if Carla survives Miranda, she will receive the property at Miranda's death, regardless of whether or not Dennis is then living. Reg. § 20.2037–1(e).

As a practical matter, § 2037 is far less important than §§ 2036 and 2038. Transferors often wish to retain possession or enjoyment, or a power affecting beneficial enjoyment, of transferred property until death, but seldom have a similar desire to retain a reversionary interest except as a last resort upon the failure of all other interests. As a result, the type of transfer reached by § 2037 has little if any planning significance other than as a trap for the unwary.

[¶ 4,300]

(4) Transfers within three years of death

In its current form, I.R.C. § 2035(a) operates in conjunction with four enumerated provisions (§§ 2036, 2037, 2038 and 2042) to reach certain transfers which would otherwise escape inclusion in the gross estate. Section 2035(a) applies only if, within three years of death, the decedent transferred an interest in (or relinquished a power with respect to) property which would have been includible in the gross estate under §§ 2036, 2037, 2038 or 2042 if the decedent had retained the interest (or the power) until death. If § 2035(a) applies, the property is includible in the gross estate just as if the decedent had actually retained the interest (or power) until death; in effect, for estate tax purposes, the deathbed transfer is disregarded. The three-year rule most commonly operates to draw proceeds of life insurance on the decedent's life back into the gross estate where the decedent once held incidents of ownership in the policy but relinquished them within three years before death. (See ¶ 4,250.)

Section 2035(a) also applies where the decedent initially transferred property subject to a retained "string" of the type described in §§ 2036–2038 and then cut the string within three years of death. For example, if Jorge transferred property at age 50 subject to a retained life estate, then at age 70 released his remaining life estate and died within three years thereafter, the full value of the underlying property is includible in Jorge's gross estate.

In its current form, § 2035(a) has no application to ordinary outright gifts made within three years of death. If the decedent had held the property until death instead of giving it away, the property would have been includible under § 2033, not under §§ 2036–2038 or 2042. As a result, the three-year rule does not apply. Similarly, a termination of a joint tenancy within three years of death falls outside the scope of the three-year rule. Any distribution of property from a revocable trust within three years of the settlor's death is treated as "a transfer made directly by the decedent." I.R.C. § 2035(e). This provision was added in 1997 to ensure that a gift made through a revocable trust is not treated as a relinquishment of the settlor's power of revocation for purposes of the three-year rule.

The gross-up rule of I.R.C. § 2035(b) requires inclusion in the gross estate of the amount of any gift tax paid by the decedent (or by the estate) on gifts made by the decedent or the decedent's spouse within three years of death. Note that this provision applies regardless of whether the gift property itself is drawn back into the gross estate. Thus, for example, if Gervase makes an outright gift of $50,000, pays the resulting gift tax of $20,000, and dies within three years after the date of the gift, his gross estate must be increased by the $20,000 gift tax payment. The gross-up rule puts deathbed gifts more or less on a par with testamentary transfers by neutralizing the benefit of the tax-exclusive gift tax base.

[¶ 4,305]

Problems

1. Terry directs the trustee of her revocable trust to pay $10,000 to each of her children from the trust property. The trustee makes the payments, which qualify for the gift tax annual exclusion under I.R.C. § 2503(b). If Terry dies within three years after making the gifts, are the payments from the revocable trust drawn back into her gross estate under I.R.C. § 2035(a)? See I.R.C. § 2035(e); Estate of Jalkut v. Commissioner, 96 T.C. 675 (1991).

2. Victor made a gift of $100,000 to his wife Cynthia, and Cynthia immediately used the funds to create an irrevocable life insurance trust for the couple's children. Cynthia reported the creation of the trust as a taxable gift and filed a return showing a gift tax liability of $40,000. Victor transferred an additional $40,000 to Cynthia, who immediately used the funds to pay the gift tax. Victor died less than three years after the date of the gift. What amount, if any, is includible in Victor's gross estate? See Brown v. United States, 329 F.3d 664 (9th Cir.), cert. denied, 540 U.S. 878 (2003).

[¶ 4,310]

f. Powers of Appointment

Unlike I.R.C. §§ 2035–2038, which are concerned with interests or powers retained by a decedent with respect to lifetime transfers of his or her own property, I.R.C. § 2041 deals with "powers of appointment" exercisable by the decedent to designate the beneficiaries of property that the decedent never actually owned or transferred. Most powers of appointment arise in connection with the creation of a trust. For example, if Pat's parent created a trust to pay income to Pat for life with remainder at Pat's death to her surviving issue, and Pat is entitled to withdraw or consume the trust property during life or to designate one or more different beneficiaries to take the trust property at her death, Pat holds a power of appointment. A power of appointment may be held in an individual or a fiduciary capacity. Thus, a trustee's discretionary power to sprinkle income among a class of beneficiaries or to invade principal for one or more beneficiaries is also a power of appointment, but a purely administrative power held in a fiduciary capacity is not a power of appointment. Reg. § 20.2041–1(b)(1).

Powers of appointment are classified as general or as non-general (i.e., special or limited). A general power is broadly defined as one which is exercisable in favor of the holder, the holder's estate, the holder's creditors, or creditors of the estate. I.R.C. §§ 2041(b)(1), 2514(c). By implication, a power exercisable solely in favor of one or more other beneficiaries is a non-general power. For example, if Lynn, the life income beneficiary of a trust created by her parent, has a power to appoint the remainder "to any person other than Lynn, her estate, her creditors or the creditors of her estate," the trust property will not be includible in Lynn's gross estate under § 2041. Moreover, the statute expressly provides that "[a] power to consume, invade, or appropriate property for the benefit of the holder which is limited by an ascertainable standard relating to the health, education, support, or maintenance of the [holder] shall not be deemed a general power of appointment." I.R.C. §§ 2041(b)(1)(A), 2514(c)(1). Thus, in the above example, Lynn may also be given a power to withdraw trust property for her own health, education, support or maintenance without incurring any estate or gift tax liability. The statute also provides a separate exception for joint powers exercisable in conjunction with the creator of the power or an adverse party. I.R.C. §§ 2041(b)(1)(C), 2514(c)(3).

Broadly speaking, a person who holds a general power of appointment over property is treated as the constructive owner of the property for estate and gift tax purposes. Thus, if a decedent dies holding a general power of appointment, the property subject to the power is includible in the gross estate, whether or not the power is exercised. I.R.C. § 2041(a)(2). A parallel provision applies for gift tax purposes, with the result that the holder of a general power who exercises or releases the power in favor of another person during life is treated as making a transfer of the underlying property. I.R.C. § 2514(b). With one exception discussed below, these provisions have no application to non-general powers.

If a decedent exercised or released a general power during life, the underlying property may be drawn back into the gross estate—even though the decedent no longer held a general power at death—if the disposition is "of such a nature that if it were a transfer of property owned by the decedent, such property would be includible in the decedent's gross estate under sections 2035–2038." I.R.C. § 2041(a)(2). To illustrate, suppose that Lee, the life income beneficiary of a trust created by her parent, had a power to appoint the trust property to any person including herself or her estate, and that during her lifetime she released the power but continued to receive trust income until death. In addition to gift tax on the release of the power, the trust property would be drawn back into the gross estate at death (just as if Lee had made a transfer of her own property subject to a retained life estate under § 2036). Of course, if Lee retained the power until death, the underlying property would be includible in her gross estate whether or not she exercised the power.

In general, when a power lapses by its terms during the holder's life (e.g., when the holder reaches a specified age, or at the end of a specified period of time), the lapse is treated as a release of the power, which may result in gift or estate tax liability. However, the statute expressly allows a tax-free lapse in any calendar year to the extent that the property subject to the lapsed power does not exceed the greater of $5,000 or 5% of the value of the property subject to the power. I.R.C. §§ 2041(b)(2), 2514(e). This special "5–or–5" exemption makes it possible to set up a trust in which the income beneficiary holds a non-cumulative power to withdraw the greater of $5,000 or 5% of the trust corpus in any year without any adverse gift or estate tax consequences (except in the year of death) to the holder of the power.

The only occasion for subjecting a non-general power to gift or estate tax arises when such a power is exercised to create a second power of appointment "which under the applicable local law can be validly exercised so as to postpone the vesting of any estate or interest in such property, or suspend the absolute ownership or power of alienation of such property, for a period ascertainable without regard to the date of the creation of the first power." I.R.C. §§ 2041(a)(3), 2514(d). This rather arcane provision, sometimes referred to as the "Delaware tax trap," is aimed at a situation in which a chain of successive powers might be used to postpone the vesting of interests (or suspend ownership or alienability) for an indefinite period. For example, suppose that under the will of her deceased parent, Michelle holds a non-general power of appointment, which she exercises to create a new non-general power in her child Sean (born after the death of Michelle's parent). Although the creation of Sean's new power would be void under the common law Rule against Perpetuities (see ¶ 2,560), it would be valid in a jurisdiction (e.g., Delaware) where the perpetuities period runs from the date of a non-general power's exercise rather than its creation. See, e.g., Del. Code tit. 25, § 501. To make sure that such powers do not escape gift and estate tax indefinitely, the statute treats Michelle's exercise of her power as a transfer for estate and gift tax purposes.

As a practical matter, most estate planners intentionally create general powers of appointment only in a few situations where they serve a specific tax objective (e.g., to generate a present interest for purposes of the annual exclusion, to qualify a transfer for the marital deduction, or to avoid a GST tax). In most cases, a broadly-drafted non-general power (e.g., a power exercisable in favor of any person other than the holder, the holder's estate, the holder's creditors or creditors of the estate) offers nearly as much flexibility as a general power without subjecting the power holder to estate or gift tax liability. This flexibility can be enhanced, with no adverse tax consequences, by naming the holder of such a non-general power as a permissible beneficiary of a separate non-general power held by a third person.

[¶ 4,320]

2. Deductions and Credits

In computing the taxable estate, the statute allows deductions from the gross estate for various items, including funeral and administration expenses and creditors' claims (I.R.C. § 2053), casualty losses (I.R.C. § 2054), charitable transfers (I.R.C. § 2055), transfers to the decedent's surviving spouse (I.R.C. § 2056), and state death taxes (I.R.C. § 2058). The deductions for expenses, claims, losses and state death taxes reflect the principle that the estate tax is imposed on the net amount passing from the decedent to beneficiaries. In contrast, the marital and charitable deductions allow a decedent to leave unlimited amounts of property free of tax to a surviving spouse or to eligible charitable organizations, as long as such transfers are made in qualifying form.

The estate tax is imposed on the taxable estate under the cumulative computation provided in I.R.C. § 2001(b) (see ¶ 4,020). The resulting estate tax is then reduced by the unified credit (I.R.C. § 2010) and by any other available credits.

[¶ 4,330]

a. Administration expenses, creditors' claims and state death taxes

I.R.C. § 2053(a)(2) allows a deduction for executor commissions, attorney fees and miscellaneous expenses (e.g., probate court costs), to the extent such items are allowable under applicable state law and are "actually and necessarily incurred in the administration of the decedent's estate." Reg. § 20.2053–3(a). For example, fees charged by appraisers or accountants in connection with valuation of assets or preparation of tax returns are generally deductible, but carrying costs of the decedent's residence incurred for the convenience of beneficiaries are not. Interest incurred on estate borrowing and expenses of selling assets may be deductible if the borrowing or sale is necessary for the settlement of the estate. If an administration expense also qualifies for an income tax deduction, the executor must elect to claim the deduction either on the estate tax return or on the estate's income tax return; a "double deduction" is not allowed. I.R.C. § 642(g).

I.R.C. § 2053(a)(3) allows a deduction for creditors' claims which represent personal obligations of the decedent existing at the time of death. Reg. § 20.2053–4. In the case of any claim "founded on a promise or agreement," the deduction is allowable only to the extent the claim was contracted "bona fide and for an adequate and full consideration in money or money's worth." I.R.C. § 2053(c)(1)(A). The purpose of this requirement is to prevent a taxpayer from converting a taxable bequest into a deductible claim. For example, suppose that Joseph borrows funds from a bank and then dies before repaying the loan. Because Joseph received full money's-worth consideration when he took out the loan, the bank's claim against his estate is fully deductible. However, if Joseph promised to leave property to his child by will, without receiving adequate money's-worth consideration, the estate is not entitled to a deduction for payment of the child's claim under § 2053, even if the claim is enforceable under state law. The estate tax result mirrors the gift tax treatment that would apply if Joseph paid the child's claim during life rather than at death.

No deduction is allowed for the amount of any federal estate tax liability. (Thus, the estate tax computation is "tax-inclusive.") However, beginning in 2005, a deduction is allowed under I.R.C. § 2058 for state death taxes. This deduction replaces the limited state death tax credit formerly allowed under I.R.C. § 2011. While the credit was in effect, almost all states had "pick-up" death taxes geared to the allowable amount of the credit. The pick-up taxes did not impose any additional net tax burden, since they generated a dollar-for-dollar credit against the federal estate tax; in effect, they merely shifted a portion of the estate tax revenue from the federal government to the states. With the repeal of the credit, the pick-up taxes have automatically disappeared as well, and many states have moved to enact independent death taxes.

[¶ 4,335]

Problem

Over a period of several years, Tracey made annual cash gifts to her son Ben in amounts equal to the allowable annual exclusion. Promptly after receiving each gift, Ben lent back the same amount of cash to Tracey in exchange for Tracey's unsecured promissory note. Each note bears interest at a market rate and is payable when Tracey reaches age 100 or on her earlier death. Tracey dies at age 80, when the outstanding balance of the notes is $100,000. Ben files a claim against Tracey's estate, which is allowed and paid by the executor. Is Tracey's estate entitled to a $100,000 deduction under I.R.C. § 2053? See Estate of Flandreau v. Commissioner, 994 F.2d 91 (2d Cir. 1993).

[¶ 4,340]

b. *Marital deduction*

The estate tax allows a marital deduction for property passing from a decedent to his or her surviving spouse. I.R.C. § 2056. A parallel provision in the gift tax allows a marital deduction for lifetime gifts made by one spouse to the other. I.R.C. § 2523. The marital deduction is unlimited in amount, with the result that spouses can make unlimited tax-free transfers between themselves during life or at death. Moreover, the marital deduction makes it possible for a married couple to avoid paying any estate tax at the death of the first spouse, although any property left to the surviving spouse will eventually be subject to gift or estate tax along with the spouse's other property.

For purposes of the marital deduction, marital status is generally determined by reference to applicable state law concerning intestate succession and probate administration. Thus, a person who is entitled to receive a surviving spouse's intestate share of a decedent's probate estate is generally recognized as the surviving spouse for federal estate tax purposes as well. Note, however, that the federal "defense of marriage" act denies recognition to same-sex couples for federal tax purposes even if the couple has entered into a valid marriage, domestic partnership or civil union under state law. See 1 U.S.C. § 7. Special rules apply in the case of a spouse who is not a U.S. citizen, to ensure that the marital deduction cannot be used to remove property from the reach of the federal transfer tax system. See I.R.C. §§ 2056(d), 2056A, 2523(i).

Although it is sometimes said that the unlimited marital deduction treats a married couple as a single taxable unit, this is a bit of an overstatement. Even if the couple elects gift-splitting treatment for gift tax purposes under I.R.C. § 2513, each spouse's rates and exemptions are determined based on his or her individual record of cumulative lifetime gifts. A spouse who dies without using all of his or her unified credit or low rate brackets cannot directly assign those attributes to a surviving spouse. Nevertheless, in general terms it is fair to say that the marital deduction relieves spouses from gift and estate tax liability on transfers between themselves and defers tax liability until property passes to a third person.

To qualify for the marital deduction, a transfer to a spouse must be made in qualifying form. There is usually no difficulty when one spouse transfers his or her entire interest in property to the other spouse. However, if the transferor carves up beneficial ownership of property into successive interests and gives, for example, a life estate to the spouse with remainder to a third person, the transfer may be disqualified under the so-called "terminable interest rule." Technically, that rule denies the marital deduction if three conditions are met: (1) the transferee spouse's interest might terminate or fail upon the occurrence (or nonoccurrence) of some event or condition; (2) an interest in the same property passes from the transferor spouse to another beneficiary; and (3) the other beneficiary's interest might become possessory after the termination of the transferee spouse's interest. I.R.C. §§ 2056(b)(1), 2523(b). Consider the common case of a decedent who leaves property in trust to pay income to a surviving spouse for life, with remainder to the couple's issue. The spouse's life estate satisfies the first condition because it will terminate when the spouse dies, and the remainder interest satisfies the second and third conditions because it gives the couple's issue the right to receive the underlying property at the spouse's death. Under the terminable interest rule, such a bequest, without more, does not qualify for the marital deduction. As a result, the full value of the property, including the spouse's income interest, is taxable at the decedent's death. The same result would hold in the case of a bequest to the spouse "for ten years," or "until remarriage." In contrast, if a decedent leaves property in an "estate trust" to make discretionary distributions to a surviving spouse during life, with any corpus and accumulated income remaining at death to be paid to the spouse's estate, the terminable interest rule does not apply and the entire transfer qualifies for the marital deduction.

The terminable interest rule is premised on the notion that the marital deduction should be available only if the surviving spouse will ultimately become the beneficial owner of the property passing from the decedent. In theory, at least, the rule ensures that any property that escapes tax in the decedent's estate by virtue of the marital deduction will eventually become subject to tax in the hands of the surviving spouse. (Of course, the surviving spouse may make substantial tax-free lifetime gifts, or remarry and pass on property to a new spouse.) In some cases the terminable interest rule produces harsh results. For example, amounts paid to a decedent's surviving spouse as a statutory support allowance pursuant to a probate court order may be nondeductible if, at the time of the decedent's death, the allowance would have terminated on the spouse's subsequent death or remarriage, even if these contingencies did not in fact occur. Jackson v. United States, 376 U.S. 503 (1964). In addition, if a married couple enters into a binding will contract, the marital deduction may be unavailable at the first spouse's death for property that passes to the surviving spouse subject to restrictions on disposition or to rights of other beneficiaries.

To mitigate the rigors of the terminable interest rule, the statute provides several exceptions which have significance for estate planners. Suppose that Corinne leaves property by will "to my husband Pierre, but if he fails to survive me by 30 days, to my issue then living." This bequest would ordinarily violate the terminable interest rule because it is not certain, as of the moment of Corinne's death, whether Pierre will survive for 30 days. However, a special statutory exception allows a decedent to impose a survival requirement of up to six months on a bequest to a surviving spouse without jeopardizing the marital deduction—provided, of course, that the spouse actually survives for the required period. I.R.C. § 2056(b)(3). Thus, assuming Pierre survives Corinne by at least 30 days and becomes entitled to the property, the transfer is deductible.

If a decedent gives a surviving spouse a life estate in property coupled with a general power of appointment exercisable by the spouse "alone and in all events" in favor of the spouse or the spouse's estate, the transfer qualifies for the marital deduction under an exception to the terminable interest rule. I.R.C. § 2056(b)(5). Such a disposition is commonly made in trust, but a legal life estate coupled with the requisite power of appointment also suffices. To satisfy the requirement that the spouse be "entitled for life to all the income," care must be taken to avoid giving the trustee any discretion to accumulate income; indeed, the income must be "payable annually or at more frequent intervals," and any limitation on the spouse's right to receive current income may jeopardize the deduction. Moreover, the requirement of a general power exercisable by the spouse "alone and in all events" means that the spouse must have exclusive and unfettered control over the ultimate disposition of the property. The combination of a life estate and a general power of appointment gives the spouse rights approximately equivalent to those of a full owner, and ensures that the marital deduction allowed to the decedent will eventually be matched by a corresponding inclusion in the surviving spouse's gift or estate tax base. A parallel provision is found in the gift tax. I.R.C. § 2523(e).

A separate exception to the terminable interest rule allows a decedent to obtain a marital deduction for the value of "qualified terminable interest property" (QTIP) in which the surviving spouse has only a life estate but no power to dispose of the underlying property. I.R.C. § 2056(b)(7). To obtain the marital deduction, the decedent's executor must elect QTIP treatment. If the election is made, the spouse who actually receives only a life estate—a quintessential terminable interest—is treated as the constructive owner of the entire property for gift and estate tax purposes. As a result, the full value of the underlying property qualifies for the marital deduction in the decedent's estate, and—in accordance with the general premise of the marital deduction—the value of the same property is eventually subject to estate tax at the spouse's death or to gift tax if the spouse disposes of the income interest before death. I.R.C. §§ 2044, 2519. A parallel provision appears in the gift tax. I.R.C. § 2523(f).

According to the legislative history, the QTIP provisions were intended to spare the decedent from being "forced to choose between surrendering control of the entire estate to avoid imposition of estate tax at his death or reducing his tax benefits at his death to insure inheritance by the children." Allowing the decedent to obtain a marital deduction without giving up control over the ultimate disposition of property was justified on the grounds "that the tax laws should be neutral and that tax consequences should not control an individual's disposition of property." H.R. Rep. No. 201, 97th Cong., 1st Sess. 160 (1981), reprinted in 1981–2 C.B. 352, 378. From the surviving spouse's perspective, the QTIP provisions may seem less benign. Indeed, it has been suggested that in equating a mere life estate with full ownership for tax purposes, the QTIP provisions "encourage husbands to transfer less than a full property interest to their wives." Gerzog, The Marital Deduction QTIP Provisions: Illogical and Degrading to Women, 5 UCLA Women's L.J. 301, 327 (1995).

[¶ 4,345]

Problems

1. Jeanne died survived by her husband Bernard. In her will, Jeanne left property in trust to pay income to Bernard for life with remainder at his death to their surviving issue. Jeanne's executor filed an estate tax return and elected to treat the trust as qualified terminable interest property under I.R.C. § 2056(b)(7). The return was accepted as filed and the marital

deduction was allowed for the value of the trust property. Subsequently it was discovered that Jeanne's will gave the trustee a power to accumulate income during Bernard's life. This power was never exercised, but its existence violated the statutory requirement that the income from qualified terminable interest property be "payable annually" to Bernard. At Bernard's death, his executor excludes the trust property from Bernard's gross estate, claiming that it never met the definition of qualified terminable interest property and thus is not includible in the gross estate under I.R.C. § 2044. What result? See Estate of Letts v. Commissioner, 109 T.C. 290 (1997).

2. Edward died survived by his wife Nora. In his will, Edward left property in a discretionary trust for the benefit of Nora and their issue. Nora renounced her rights under the will and claimed an outright elective share equal to one-third of Edward's net probate estate. Is Edward's estate entitled to a marital deduction? If so, in what amount? See Reg. § 20.2056(c)–2(c); First Nat'l Exchange Bank of Roanoke v. United States, 335 F.2d 91 (4th Cir. 1964).

3. Amelia died survived by her husband Boris. In her will, Amelia left all her separate property, worth $2,000,000, to Boris and all the couple's community property, worth $2,000,000, to their surviving issue. Thus Boris was put to a forced election: he could either accept the transfer of $2,000,000 and allow the community property to pass to the issue, or renounce his rights under the will and keep his half of the community property. Boris accepted the terms of the will. Is Amelia's estate entitled to a marital deduction? If so, in what amount? See I.R.C. § 2056(b)(4); United States v. Stapf, 375 U.S. 118 (1963).

[¶ 4,350]

c. Charitable deduction

From an early date the estate and gift taxes have allowed a deduction for transfers made to qualifying charitable organizations or for charitable purposes. In general, a transfer is treated as charitable if it is made to the United States or a political subdivision thereof for public purposes, or to a corporation, trust or foundation organized and operated exclusively for religious, charitable, scientific, literary or educational purposes. I.R.C. §§ 2055(a), 2522(a). If the organization or purpose for which a charitable contribution is made satisfies the statutory criteria, there is no limit on the amount which may be given.

Outright gifts to a charitable organization seldom give rise to serious problems. The deduction may be jeopardized, however, if property is transferred for mixed charitable and noncharitable purposes. Long-standing regulations generally require that the charitable interest be "presently ascertainable" and that any contingency that might defeat it be "so remote as to be negligible." Reg. § 20.2055–2(a), (b). Moreover, under a set of statutory rules added in 1969, if a transfer creates both charitable and noncharitable interests in the same property, no charitable deduction is allowed at all unless the transfer is in qualifying form. I.R.C. §§ 2055(e)(2), 2522(c)(2).

In the case of a charitable remainder interest following a noncharitable interest, a qualifying transfer commonly takes one of two forms: (1) a charitable remainder annuity trust that provides for annual payments of a fixed amount to noncharitable beneficiaries, followed by an irrevocable charitable remainder; or (2) a charitable remainder unitrust that provides for annual payments of a fixed percentage of the current value of the trust property (calculated annually) to noncharitable beneficiaries, followed by an irrevocable charitable remainder. I.R.C. § 664(d). A qualifying interest may also take the form of a "charitable lead" trust in which the charitable interest consists of an annuity or unitrust interest, followed by a remainder in noncharitable beneficiaries. In addition, the statute allows a deduction for a charitable remainder interest following a life estate in a personal residence or farm, and for an undivided portion of the transferor's entire interest in the underlying property. I.R.C. § 170(f)(3)(B).

The statutory rules concerning split-interest transfers are intended to guard against valuation abuses and to ensure that charitable beneficiaries will receive the full value of an interest for which a deduction is allowed. To assist in planning and drafting such transfers, the Service publishes standard forms of trust instruments that comply with the detailed requirements of the statute and regulations.

[¶ 4,360]

3. Planning and Practice

Estate planners have developed various techniques to reduce the gift and estate tax burden on wealth transfers. In their most sophisticated versions, these techniques can become exceedingly complex, but the underlying concepts are not difficult to grasp. The following materials introduce some basic principles of estate planning and examples of common planning techniques involving trusts, private annuities and family limited partnerships. In each case, the opportunity for tax reduction rests on the transferor's ability to make value disappear from the tax base without impairing the ultimate value of the transferred property in the hands of the recipients. Of course, while income and transfer tax savings play a prominent role in estate planning, they are by no means the only consideration. A competent planner should seek to ascertain and carry out the transferor's intent reliably and efficiently, taking care to avoid unnecessary taxes, fees, litigation and other transaction costs.

[¶ 4,370]

a. *Transfers in trust*

Trusts are extremely flexible vehicles for holding, managing and distributing property. In creating a trust, the choice of trustee, the decision to retain or relinquish particular interests or powers, and even the selection of assets to fund the trust may all have significant gift and estate tax consequences. In general, if the trust property is to escape inclusion in the settlor's gross estate at death, the settlor should avoid retaining a power to revoke the trust or alter the interests of the beneficiaries, even in a fiduciary capacity, unless the power is limited by an ascertainable standard and cannot be exercised for the settlor's own benefit. Similarly, the settlor should avoid retaining an income interest for life or a substantial reversionary interest preceding a remainder interest in other beneficiaries. Any transfer that removes property from the gross estate is likely to incur a gift tax, though the gift tax burden may be reduced by use of one or more annual exclusions.

Estate planners frequently recommend the use of trusts to hold life insurance on the settlor's life. To keep the life insurance proceeds out of the gross estate, the insured settlor should avoid holding any incidents of ownership in the policy for at least three years before death. This can be done by creating an irrevocable inter vivos trust and having the trustee take out the policy for the benefit of the trust beneficiaries. The settlor should have no beneficial interest in the trust and no power to alter the interests of the beneficiaries. The trust instrument should expressly prohibit the settlor from acting as trustee or having any power to control the trustee. The settlor may make regular contributions to the trust to cover premiums on the life insurance policy. Such contributions will be completed gifts, which may be eligible for one or more annual exclusions if the trust beneficiaries are given unrestricted powers to withdraw a ratable share of each contribution as it is made to the trust. (If each beneficiary's power of withdrawal is limited to the greater of $5,000 or 5% of the value of the trust property, the lapse of the power will have no gift or estate tax consequences to the holder.) Thus, if properly structured, the trust allows the insured settlor to make substantial tax-free gifts to cover premiums on the policy during life while avoiding inclusion of the proceeds in his or her gross estate at death.

Another type of trust that has become prominent in recent years is the "qualified personal residence trust" (QPRT). The QPRT is a purely tax-driven phenomenon; its only function is to reduce the gift and estate tax cost of transferring a personal residence. The key statutory provision is I.R.C. § 2702(a)(3)(A)(ii), which makes the special valuation rules of § 2702 inapplicable to a transfer in trust if the underlying property is "to be used as a personal residence by persons holding term interests in such trust." This provision allows the settlor to create a grantor retained income trust funded with a personal residence and to value the retained income interest under the Treasury tables. The regulations set forth detailed requirements concerning the type, use and disposition of property held in a QPRT. Reg. § 25.2702–5. (For a sample form of trust declaration that meets the requirements of the regulations, see Rev. Proc. 2003–42, 2003–1 C.B. 993.) To illustrate the operation of a QPRT, suppose that Fern, age 40, transfers her personal residence (including appurtenant structures and a "reasonably appropriate" amount of adjacent land) in trust, retaining possession and enjoyment of the property for a fixed term of 20 years; at the end of the term, the trust will terminate and the property will be distributed to Fern's daughter Amy or Amy's estate. The property is worth $1,000,000 and is expected to appreciate rapidly. If the trust qualifies as a QPRT, Fern can value the gift of the remainder interest under the Treasury tables. Assuming an applicable interest rate of 5%, Fern's taxable gift is just under $380,000. Reg. § 20.2031–7(d)(6) (tbl. B). At the end of the 20–year term, if Fern is still living, Amy receives the property (now worth, say, $4,000,000) with no further gift or estate tax consequences. The only potential problem is that if Fern dies during the 20–year term, the property will be drawn back into her gross estate at its appreciated value under I.R.C. § 2036(a). However, assuming that Fern is in good health and likely to survive, the potential tax savings are impressive. If she wins the mortality gamble, she will have successfully frozen the value of the property for gift tax purposes at $1,000,000 and obtained a discount of more than 60% for the future interest under the Treasury tables, while retaining the right to occupy the property as it appreciates. Indeed, if she wishes to remain in possession of the property after the end of the 20–year term, she can enter into a lease with Amy and pay a fair market rent, thereby removing the rental payments from the reach of the estate tax.

[¶ 4,380]

b. *Private annuities*

Annuities are widely used to provide a stream of fixed payments for one or more lives. In planning for retirement, a person may purchase an annuity from an insurance company or other commercial issuer to provide a stream of payments that is guaranteed to last until death. Unlike ordinary life insurance which replaces lost savings in the event of premature death, a single-life annuity offers protection for a person concerned about outliving his or her savings. In a typical "private annuity" transaction, Joan transfers cash or other property to Jeff in exchange for Jeff's promise to make fixed annuity payments to Joan for her lifetime. If properly structured as a bona fide sale for full money's-worth consideration, the private annuity escapes both gift and estate taxation. As long as the value of the property transferred by Joan does not exceed the value of the promised stream of annuity payments to be made by Jeff, there is no gift on Joan's part. For gift tax purposes, the annuity payments are generally valued under the Treasury tables; the special valuation rules of I.R.C. § 2702 do not apply because Joan has not retained any interest or power with respect to the transferred property. At Joan's death, the annuity payments automatically terminate, leaving no asset (other than annuity payments received during life and not consumed before death) includible in her gross estate under I.R.C. § 2033. Moreover, since no amounts are payable to a surviving beneficiary, the survivor annuity provisions of I.R.C. § 2039 have no application. There is a risk that the transferred property might be drawn back into the gross estate under I.R.C. § 2036, however, if the promised payments are secured by an interest in the transferred property (e.g., a mortgage or other lien) or are geared to the income actually produced by the transferred property, since the transaction might then be recast as a transfer with a retained right to income from the transferred property. To avoid this result, the transaction is usually structured to ensure that Joan retains no rights or interests in the transferred property and that the promised annuity payments represent full money's-worth consideration for the transfer. Within these constraints, the private annuity offers substantial estate tax savings if Joan dies before she has recovered full consideration for the transferred property in the form of annuity payments. In other words, if Joan loses the mortality gamble through premature death, she will nevertheless have made an advantageous bargain for estate tax purposes. By the same token, if she outlives her life expectancy, the transaction may prove to be a bad deal for the family.

[¶ 4,385]

Problem

Jerry sells Blackacre (recently purchased for $100,000) to his daughter Karen for $20,000 cash and Karen's unsecured promissory note for $80,000. The note provides for payment of the full principal amount in 10 years if Jerry is still living; if Jerry dies during the 10–year period, the note will automatically be cancelled. The note bears interest, payable annually, at a rate reflecting a premium for the risk that Jerry may die within the 10–year period; the fair market value of the note is equal to its face value. In fact, Jerry dies five years after the sale. What amount is includible in Jerry's gross estate? See Estate of Moss v. Commissioner, 74 T.C. 1239 (1980).

[¶ 4,390]

c. *Family limited partnerships*

The "family limited partnership" has achieved notoriety as a technique for transferring assets at steeply discounted values for gift and estate tax purposes. The family limited partnership transaction typically occurs in two stages: family members form the partnership and contribute assets in exchange for pro rata partnership interests; and subsequently, the donor partner transfers his or her partnership interests during life or at death. The transaction is generally structured to make sure that capital accounts are properly maintained and that allocations are proportionate to each partner's percentage interest. To illustrate, suppose that Olivia contributes $990,000 to a newly-formed partnership in exchange for a 99% limited partnership interest, and her two children, Trevor and Winston, each contribute $5,000 in exchange for a 0.5% general partnership interest. (Alternatively, the general partner might be a corporation owned by Olivia, Trevor and Winston.) If the transaction is properly structured, the courts have held that the formation of the partnership does not give rise to any taxable gift because there is no capital shift from any partner to any other partner. Furthermore, when Olivia subsequently transfers her limited partnership interest to Trevor and Winston during life or at death, the interest is valued with substantial discounts for lack of marketability and lack of control. For example, assuming a 40% combined discount from her capital account of $990,000, Olivia's limited partnership interest would be valued at $596,000. Eventually, Trevor and Winston can liquidate the partnership and recover outright ownership of the underlying assets. In reality, the partnership is nothing more than a temporary vehicle for transferring assets at discounted values; it often has no independent business purpose and no lasting effect on the value of the assets in the donee's hands. Courts have occasionally disregarded the existence of the partnership and have required that a deceased partner's share of the underlying assets be drawn back into his or her gross estate under I.R.C. § 2036 where the decedent retained unfettered possession, enjoyment or control of the assets until death. If § 2036 applies, the effect is to disallow any valuation discount and defeat the entire purpose of the partnership. To avoid this unwelcome result, taxpayers should take care to observe scrupulously the formalities of the partnership arrangement.

[¶ 4,400]

d. *Marital transfers*

Using the unlimited marital deduction, a married couple can easily arrange to avoid incurring any estate tax at the death of the first spouse, but it is not always advisable to do so. Whether it makes sense to take advantage of the marital deduction at all, and if so, to what extent, depends on the circumstances of the particular case. For example, suppose that Horace dies survived by his wife Winifred, neither spouse having previously made any taxable gifts. To avoid wasting Horace's unified credit, it is necessary to ensure that his taxable estate (after the marital deduction) is at least equal to the exemption equivalent (see ¶ 4,020); this implies a ceiling on the amount of property that Horace should leave to Winifred in deductible form. If Horace leaves property worth $5,000,000 and Winifred has no property of her own, it may make sense for Horace to leave all of his property in excess of the exemption equivalent to Winifred, either outright or in the form of qualified terminable interest property (see ¶ 4,340). In contrast, if Winifred already has property of her own worth $5,000,000, there may be little point in reducing the estate tax at Horace's death to zero if the result will be to subject his property to tax at the highest marginal rate in Winifred's gross estate.

Under a progressive rate schedule, it appears that the overall tax burden can be minimized—if that is the primary goal—by equalizing the spouses' respective estates (e.g., through deductible gifts from the richer spouse to the poorer spouse), so that neither spouse ends up in a higher marginal tax bracket than the other. However, the compressed tax rates under the 2001 Act reduce the benefits of estate equalization. Moreover, a strategy of estate equalization—which must be implemented no later than the death of the first spouse—requires a good deal of guesswork about future events which cannot be predicted with confidence. How long will the surviving spouse live? Will the value of the survivor's property go up or down over time? Will the survivor acquire substantial additional property through personal effort, astute investment, inheritance, or blind luck? Will the survivor run up large expenses for support or medical care? Will the survivor make substantial tax-free gifts during life? Will the estate tax rates go up or down in the future? Will the tax be repealed? Perhaps, in view of these imponderables, it is not surprising that many couples forgo the potential tax benefits of estate equalization and settle instead for a strategy of tax deferral, i.e., leaving just enough property to the surviving spouse to produce a zero estate tax in the first spouse's estate.

In drafting a will or trust, it is common practice to define the size of the marital bequest by means of a formula clause. This allows the drafter to specify the size of the marital bequest in terms of the desired tax result, despite the inevitable uncertainties concerning the size and composition of the estate at the time of the testator's death. The drafting of formula clauses involves a host of federal income, estate, gift, and GST tax issues as well as considerations of estate and trust administration under state law. Moreover, as scheduled increases in the exemption equivalent under the 2001 Act take effect, formula clauses drafted under prior law may produce unexpected results. For example, suppose that Hubert, whose will was drafted in 1996 when the exemption equivalent was $600,000, leaves an amount equal to the exemption equivalent in a nondeductible family trust and the rest of his estate to his wife Wanda. If Hubert dies in 2006 with an estate worth $2,000,000, the formula clause will allocate the entire estate to the family trust and nothing to Wanda. Perhaps this is what Hubert intended, though it seems equally plausible, based on the law as it existed when the will was executed, that he intended to leave a major portion of his estate to Wanda as residuary beneficiary.

[¶ 4,405]

Problem

Barry died survived by his wife Eloise. The couple held the bulk of their property as joint tenants with right of survivorship, with the result that Eloise became entitled to all of the joint property at Barry's death. Barry's will left his entire probate estate in trust to pay income to Eloise for life with remainder to their surviving issue. As it turns out, the joint property is worth $4,900,000 and Barry's probate estate is worth only $100,000. Eloise is named as executor and trustee in Barry's will. What actions might Eloise take to avoid wasting Barry's unified credit?

D. THE GENERATION–SKIPPING TRANSFER TAX

[¶ 4,500]

The third and final component of the federal transfer tax system is the generation-skipping transfer (GST) tax, which functions as a supplement to the gift and estate taxes. Although closely linked with the other two transfer taxes, the GST tax stands apart from them. It has its own separate exemption and rate structure, and makes use of its own special terminology to identify the timing and amount of taxable transfers. In general, the GST tax is aimed at transfers which shift beneficial enjoyment of property to beneficiaries who are at least two generations younger than the transferor without attracting a gift or estate tax at the intervening generation. The basic premise is that persons with substantial means should not be able to avoid transfer taxes by creating long-term trusts which spread beneficial enjoyment over several generations or by transferring property directly to remote generations: transfer taxes should be imposed as property passes from one generation to the next.

[¶ 4,510]

1. Taxable Events

The GST tax is imposed on every "generation-skipping transfer." I.R.C. § 2601. There are three types of generation-skipping transfers: a "direct skip," a "taxable termination," and a "taxable distribution." I.R.C. § 2611(a). Each of these taxable events involves a transfer of property from an individual in whose hands the property was subject to gift or estate tax (the "transferor") to a beneficiary two or more generations younger than the transferor (a "skip person").

In general, beneficiaries related to the transferor by blood or marriage are assigned to generations based on the family relationship. For example, the transferor's spouse is always treated as a member of the transferor's own generation; children are assigned to the generation below their parents; grandchildren to the second generation below their grandparents; and so on. Unrelated beneficiaries are assigned to generations based on their age: a person born within 12½ years of the transferor belongs to the transferor's generation; a person born more than 12½ years but not more than 37½ years after the transferor belongs in the next lower generation; and so on, with new generations at 25-year intervals. I.R.C. § 2651.

In general, a *direct skip* is "a transfer subject to [gift or estate tax] of an interest in property to a skip person." I.R.C. § 2612(c)(1). For example, if Fiona dies survived by her son Bertram and leaves a bequest directly to Bertram's child Abigail, the bequest is a direct skip which attracts a GST tax (in addition to the estate tax) at Fiona's death; the result would be similar in the case of a lifetime gift. A transfer in trust may also constitute a direct skip, if all of the beneficiaries who are currently entitled or permitted to receive distributions of income or corpus from the trust are skip persons. Thus, if Fiona creates a testamentary or inter vivos trust which bypasses Bertram and provides benefits exclusively for Abigail and her issue, the creation of the trust constitutes a direct skip subject to GST tax. In each case, the GST tax stands in for the additional gift or estate tax that would have been imposed if the property had passed through Bertram's hands on its way from Fiona to the ultimate beneficiaries. (The result is different, however, if Bertram is already dead at the time of the transfer. In that case, a special rule provides that Abigail moves up one generation and is no longer treated as a skip person for GST purposes. I.R.C. § 2651(e).)

By definition, taxable terminations and taxable distributions involve property held in trust. In general, a *taxable termination* is "the termination (by death, lapse of time, release of power, or otherwise) of an interest in property held in a trust," unless "immediately after such termination, a non-skip person has an interest in such property" or "at no time after such termination may a distribution (including distributions on termination) be made from such trust to a skip person." I.R.C. § 2612(a)(1). Note that, for GST tax purposes, a person has an "interest" in a trust if he or she is currently entitled or permitted to receive distributions of income or corpus from the trust. I.R.C. § 2652(c)(1). A *taxable distribution* is "any distribution from a trust to a skip person (other than a taxable termination or a direct skip)." I.R.C. § 2612(b). To illustrate these provisions, consider a discretionary trust created by Alma to distribute income and corpus to her son Pedro and his issue, with remainder at Pedro's death to his issue then living. No GST tax is imposed on the creation of the trust because at that time Pedro (who is not a skip person) is a permissible current beneficiary; hence, the creation of the trust does not constitute a direct skip, and distributions to Pedro do not constitute taxable distributions. At Pedro's death, however, the termination of his interest constitutes a taxable termination which attracts a GST tax. (If Pedro had a sibling who was permitted to receive distributions of income or corpus after Pedro's death, the taxable termination would be deferred until the sibling's death, when all of the remaining beneficiaries would be skip persons.) Furthermore, if the trustee distributes income or corpus to any of Pedro's issue while Pedro is still living, each such distribution constitutes a taxable distribution subject to GST tax.

Over the course of a long-term trust, the GST tax may apply several times as beneficial interests shift from one generation to the next. For example, suppose that Gordon creates a trust to pay income to his daughter Dora for life, then to Dora's child Oscar for life, with remainder at Oscar's death to his issue then living. For purposes of the GST tax, the first taxable event involving the trust is the taxable termination occurring at Dora's death, which triggers a GST tax on the value of the underlying trust property. To prevent the imposition of another GST tax within the same generation, a special rule reassigns Gordon, the original transferor, to the generation immediately above that of Oscar, the current income beneficiary. I.R.C. § 2653(a). As a result, after Dora's death Oscar is no longer treated as a skip person and distributions to Oscar do not constitute taxable distributions. However, another taxable termination will occur at Oscar's death, when Oscar's income interest terminates and the remainder becomes payable to his issue.

[¶ 4,520]

2. Computation and Liability

The amount of GST tax due with respect to a particular generation-skipping transfer is computed by multiplying the "taxable amount" by the "applicable rate" of tax. I.R.C. § 2602. In the absence of an allocation of the transferor's GST exemption (discussed below), the GST tax is imposed at a flat rate equal to the maximum estate tax rate. (For the sake of simplicity, the examples below assume a maximum estate tax rate of 50%.)

The taxable amount is generally equal to the value of the property involved in the particular generation-skipping transfer, subject to certain adjustments. The primary liability for paying the GST tax, however, depends on whether the taxable event is a direct skip, a taxable distribution, or a taxable termination. In the case of a direct skip, the taxable amount is equal to the value of the property received by the beneficiary and the tax is ordinarily payable by the transferor (or his or her estate). I.R.C. §§ 2603(a)(3), 2623. Thus, if Tim leaves a $100,000 bequest to his grandchild Raoul (a direct skip), Tim's estate is liable for the resulting $50,000 GST tax. Note that in the case of a direct skip, the taxable amount does not include the resulting GST tax; the base is tax-exclusive.

In the case of a taxable distribution, the taxable amount is generally equal to the value of the property received by the beneficiary, and the tax is payable by the beneficiary. I.R.C. §§ 2603(a)(1), 2621. In the case of a taxable termination, the taxable amount is generally equal to the value of the underlying trust property, and the tax is payable by the trustee. I.R.C. §§ 2603(a)(2), 2622. Thus, if Inez creates a discretionary trust for her son Raymond and his issue, and the trustee distributes $100,000 to Raymond's daughter Delores (a taxable distribution), Delores is liable for the resulting $50,000 GST tax. Furthermore, if the trust property is worth $100,000 at Raymond's death (a taxable termination), the resulting $50,000 GST tax is payable by the trustee from the trust property. Note that in the case of a taxable distribution or a taxable termination, the base is tax-inclusive; the amount distributed or held in trust is subject to a built-in GST tax liability in the hands of the beneficiary or the trustee.

The applicable rate at which the GST tax is actually imposed on a particular generation-skipping transfer depends on how the transferor's GST exemption is allocated. Each individual transferor is entitled to a GST exemption. Beginning in 2004, the amount of the GST exemption is scheduled to rise in lockstep with the estate tax exemption equivalent, reaching $1,500,000 in 2004, $2,000,000 in 2006, and $3,500,000 in 2009. I.R.C. § 2631. This exemption applies solely for purposes of the GST tax and operates independently of the estate tax unified credit. The transferor can freely allocate his or her GST exemption, in whole or in part, to any property transferred outright or in trust; in the absence of an affirmative allocation, the GST exemption is allocated under statutory default rules. I.R.C. § 2632.

The link between the GST exemption and the applicable rate of GST tax can be illustrated by a simple example. Suppose that in 2005 Rhoda leaves a $1,500,000 bequest to her grandchild Damien (a direct skip), and allocates her entire available GST exemption of $1,500,000 to that bequest. The allocation is sufficient to cover the entire bequest, and the GST tax is imposed at an applicable rate of zero. Technically, the applicable rate is equal to the maximum estate tax rate multiplied by an "inclusion ratio" which represents the portion of the transferred property that is not covered by the transferor's GST exemption. I.R.C. §§ 2641, 2642. Thus, in the preceding example, if Rhoda allocated only $300,000 of GST exemption to her bequest to Damien, the bequest would have an inclusion ratio of 80% (($1,500,000 − $300,000) ÷ $1,500,000) and the applicable rate of GST tax would be 40% (50% × 80%). Thus, depending on how much of the transferor's GST exemption is allocated to particular property, the applicable rate of GST tax may range from zero to 50%.

Ordinarily an allocation of GST exemption to particular property occurs at the time the transferor makes a completed transfer of the property for gift or estate tax purposes. In the case of a trust, an allocation of GST exemption may occur many years before a taxable termination or taxable distribution actually gives rise to GST tax. Such an allocation establishes an applicable rate of GST tax for all generation-skipping transfers which occur with respect to the trust, until the trust property next becomes subject to gift or estate taxation in the hands of a new transferor. Thus, if Brigitte creates a discretionary trust of $1,500,000 to pay income to her son Claude and his issue, and immediately allocates $1,500,000 of GST exemption to the trust property, the allocation will establish an applicable rate of zero for all subsequent taxable events involving the trust. In effect, no matter how many taxable terminations or taxable distributions may occur, or how far the value of the trust property may rise in the future, the trust will remain completely exempt from GST tax for the entire duration of the trust.

[¶ 4,530]

3. Planning Considerations

Any transfer of property involving beneficiaries more than one generation younger than the transferor has potential GST tax implications. Because the tax may be imposed at a relatively high rate (i.e., the maximum estate tax rate), estate planners go to considerable lengths to make optimal use of available exemptions and exclusions. In this connection, the allocation of the transferor's GST exemption is of central importance. An allocation of GST exemption to property transferred in a direct skip directly and immediately reduces the applicable rate of tax on that particular transfer, but the tax savings tend to be greater if the allocation is made instead to property held in trust for multiple generations of beneficiaries. This is because an allocation of GST exemption generally has the effect of sheltering all or a fractional portion of the trust property from GST tax for the duration of the trust; as the trust property appreciates over time, the value of the exempt portion increases correspondingly. Moreover, the initial allocation remains effective until the property ends up in the hands of a new transferor, no matter how many taxable distributions or taxable terminations occur as beneficial enjoyment shifts from one generation to the next. Indeed, a major incentive for creating a perpetual "dynasty" trust (in jurisdictions where such trusts are permitted) is the possibility of complete and permanent avoidance of GST tax on the trust property.

Making effective use of the GST exemption raises a special problem in connection with a marital deduction trust. Suppose that Hector dies survived by his wife Wilma and leaves property in trust to pay income to Wilma for life with remainder to the couple's grandchildren, and Hector's executor makes a QTIP election with respect to the trust. Although Hector is the original transferor of the trust for GST tax purposes, it ordinarily makes no sense to allocate his GST exemption to the trust property. The reason is that Wilma will become a new transferor when the trust property is included in her gross estate at her death, making it necessary to use her own GST exemption to shelter the trust from GST tax. Nevertheless, to provide greater flexibility, I.R.C. § 2652(a)(3) allows Hector's executor to elect to ignore the QTIP election in applying the GST tax to the trust. The effect of such a "reverse QTIP" election is that, for GST tax purposes, Hector (not Wilma) will be treated as the transferor of the trust property when a taxable termination occurs at Wilma's death. This allows Hector to make effective use of his own GST exemption and leaves Wilma free to allocate her GST exemption to other property.

Some transfers automatically escape the GST tax without using any of the transferor's GST exemption. An outright gift made directly to an individual skip person is ordinarily exempt from GST tax to the extent covered by the gift tax annual exclusion. (This exemption is unavailable, however, for a gift in trust unless the trust is effectively limited to a single beneficiary.) I.R.C. § 2642(c). Payments of qualified tuition or medical expenses on behalf of a skip person, to the extent excludable from taxable gifts under I.R.C. § 2503(e), are expressly exempt from GST tax. I.R.C. § 2611(b)(1). As a result, a transferor can make substantial lifetime gifts to skip persons without incurring any gift tax or GST tax liability.

For a transferor who has exhausted any available exemptions and exclusions, there is still another way to sidestep the GST tax, namely, by arranging for the transferred property to be subject to gift or estate tax in the hands of a beneficiary who is only one generation younger than the transferor. Recall that the GST tax serves essentially as a backstop to the gift and estate taxes; it applies only where a transfer puts property in the hands of a beneficiary at least two generations younger than the transferor without incurring a gift or estate tax at the intervening generation. Thus, to the extent that property is subject to gift or estate tax in the hands of a beneficiary who is only one generation younger than the transferor, there will be no generation-skipping transfer. In the case of a trust, for example, this can be accomplished by providing for distributions to such a beneficiary or by giving the beneficiary a general power of appointment. A more flexible and sophisticated approach calls for the creation of a special power of appointment which the beneficiary may exercise by creating a new, presently-exercisable general power in another person. Because the exercise of a presently-exercisable general power would start a new perpetuities period running, the creation of such a power is technically subject to gift or estate tax pursuant to the Delaware tax trap (see ¶ 4,310). This technique allows the beneficiary who holds the special power of appointment to wait and see whether it is more advantageous to leave the underlying property exposed to a GST tax or to incur a gift or estate tax. If a gift or estate tax would be imposed at a lower marginal rate, for example, the beneficiary can deliberately spring the Delaware tax trap by creating a new power; if not, the beneficiary can leave the power unexercised and allow the underlying property to remain subject to the GST tax.

A large number of trusts in existence today were established before the current version of the GST tax was enacted in 1986. By the terms of the enacting legislation, trusts that were already "irrevocable" on the relevant effective date are permanently exempt from GST tax, even if they give rise to generation-skipping transfers occurring after the effective date. Reg. § 26.2601–1. A significant amount of planning is devoted to maximizing the duration and value of grandfathered trusts while protecting their exempt status.

[¶ 4,540]

Problem

Magda dies and leaves her entire estate to her surviving child Brandon. Brandon disclaims the bequest, which passes to his daughter Jessie under the applicable state disclaimer statute. Assuming Brandon's disclaimer is a qualified disclaimer, does a generation-skipping transfer occur at Magda's death? See I.R.C. §§ 2518, 2654(c).

E. INCOME TAXATION OF TRUSTS

[¶ 4,600]

In general, a trust is recognized as a separate taxable entity for federal income tax purposes, and the rules governing the computation of taxable income are, with some important exceptions, the same for trusts as for individual taxpayers. (The same is true for decedents' estates, which resemble trusts in important respects.) The most significant income tax problems involve the question of who should be taxed on the income from property held in trust. Usually there are three obvious candidates: the grantor, the beneficiaries, or the trust itself. Although the applicable provisions of the statute and regulations can be quite complex, any person involved in planning or drafting wills and trusts should be familiar with a few basic concepts.

Ordinarily, where the trust is irrevocable and the grantor has severed virtually all strings over the trust property, the trust is treated as a separate taxpayer and its income, deductions, and other taxable items either stay with the trust or "pass through" to the beneficiaries under I.R.C. §§ 641–663. However, if the grantor retains significant interests or powers with respect to the trust, the grantor may be treated as the substantial owner of all or a portion of the trust and taxed on the trust's income pursuant to the "grantor trust" provisions of I.R.C. §§ 671–677. Moreover, if a person (other than the grantor) has a power to withdraw income or corpus from the trust, that person may be treated as a substantial owner under I.R.C. § 678.

In the case of an ordinary trust (i.e., one which is not treated as substantially owned by the grantor or another person), the trust's income is generally allocated between the trust and the beneficiaries based on the amounts distributed to beneficiaries in the current taxable year. This is accomplished by allowing a deduction to the trust for such distributions and then including an equivalent amount in the gross income of the recipients. I.R.C. §§ 651, 652, 661, 662. In this sense, the trust may be viewed for income tax purposes as a "conduit" to the extent of its current distributions; the trust itself incurs tax only on amounts retained in the trust. An important limitation on the conduit principle is the tax concept of "distributable net income" (DNI), which establishes a ceiling on the amount of distributions to be deducted by the trust (and included by the beneficiaries). Roughly speaking, DNI corresponds to current income (as defined for trust accounting purposes) and normally excludes capital gains (which therefore remain taxable to the trust). Distributions are classified as mandatory or discretionary; items entering into DNI are prorated first among beneficiaries receiving mandatory distributions, and then among beneficiaries receiving discretionary distributions.

To the extent that a trust does not distribute all of its income currently, the conduit principle does not apply and the trust is taxable on its accumulated income. As a practical matter, there is no other way to ensure payment of the tax on income accumulated in the current year, since the beneficiaries who will ultimately receive it may well be unborn or unascertainable. Under current law, when the trust eventually distributes the accumulated income in a subsequent year, the beneficiaries ordinarily are not liable for any additional tax.

At one time trusts offered significant income shifting advantages. Taxpayers sought to spread income among several different taxable entities so as to take advantage of each trust's low rate brackets and separate exemption. In recent years, however, as income tax rates have generally fallen and brackets have become more compressed, the tax incentives for creating multiple trusts have all but disappeared. Moreover, under a special anti-abuse rule, multiple trusts that have "substantially the same" grantors and primary beneficiaries and have tax avoidance as "a principal purpose" may be aggregated and treated as a single trust for income tax purposes. I.R.C. § 643(f).

For a concise overview of the income taxation of trusts and decedents' estates, see Sherman, All You Really Need to Know About Subchapter J You Learned from this Article, 63 Mo. L. Rev. 1 (1998).

Chapter 5

HOUSING

A. INTRODUCTION

[¶ 5,000]

Home ownership has been part of the American dream for decades. Today, more than two-thirds of the people in the United States own their own homes. Home ownership provides a way for families of modest means to build economic security. As the value of the home rises, the net worth of the homeowner increases. Homeowners have access to borrowed funds at lower interest rates because they can use their homes as security for the loans. Parents who own their own homes can provide stability for their children as they grow up and, once the children have moved out of the home, the parents can sell the home to provide funds for retirement and decide either to rent or to purchase a less expensive home. Neighborhoods with high levels of owner-occupied housing experience lower crime rates and higher property appreciation because owners have a greater stake in the future of the neighborhood than do renters or transients.

In 1862, Abraham Lincoln signed the Homestead Act, evidencing a strong national policy of promoting home ownership. Under the Act anyone who was at least 21 years of age could apply for ownership of land that was currently in the public domain. To gain ownership of a 160–acre tract, the claimant had to build a home and farm the land successfully for at least five years. Under this Act, which remained a part of American law until the 1970's, 270 million acres were converted from public lands to privately owned homesteads.

This strong national policy in favor of home ownership did not benefit every segment of the population equally. Racial discrimination by homeowners, private lenders and even the federal government contributed to lower rates of home ownership by African–Americans and other racial and ethnic minorities. See, e.g., Shelley v. Kraemer, 334 U.S. 1 (1948) (striking down the enforcement of private racial covenants that prohibited white homeowners from selling to persons of other races); see also William Ming, Racial Restrictions and the Fourteenth Amendment:

The Restrictive Covenant Cases, 16 U. Chi. L. Rev. 203, 203–04, 226–27 n.61 (1949) (describing the FHA practice of refusing to finance new housing unless the property was subject to racially restrictive covenants).

Despite many years of racial discrimination by those in the housing industry, people of color now own homes at record rates (approximately 50%) and that number is increasing. The American Dream Downpayment Act of 2003 authorizes up to $200 million per year for four years (2004–2007) to be made available to first time low-income or minority home buyers. Awards of up to $10,000 (or 6% of the purchase price, whichever is greater) will be made to help purchasers with downpayments, closing costs, and rehabilitation assistance. The ability to access these funds is predicted to produce at least 40,000 new homeowners.

For most families, the home is the primary form of family wealth. It is an asset that provides current support in the form of housing. It may be the only asset available late in life to help provide nursing home options. And it is often the single most valuable asset that parents devise to their children. Managing home ownership starts with the purchase and ends with a final disposition by sale, inter vivos gift, or devise by will. In between the purchase and final disposition, the asset is a form of wealth that should be managed for the benefit of the family. This chapter will focus on the financial and tax aspects of homeownership, emphasizing ways to maximize the benefits of homeownership over the life of the owner.

B.   COSTS AND BENEFITS OF HOME OWNERSHIP

[¶ 5,010]

The best way to understand the costs and benefits of home ownership is to compare two options, renting and buying. Assume that Adam is debating whether or not to rent a three bedroom home for $750 per month or to buy a comparable home for $175,000. He has $35,000 he can use as a down payment (20% of the purchase price) and he has located a mortgage broker who says he can borrow enough to cover the balance ($140,000) over a 30–year period at 5% fixed interest. His mortgage payments will be $751.55 per month. He understands that each $750 rental amount is money down the drain that he can never recover. It pays only for his right to occupy the home. (Of course, as an economic matter, so long as the rental *value* of the home is equal to the rental *cost* of $750, there is no economic loss to Adam on the payment of monthly rent.) But now he realizes that for a mere $1.55 more per month, plus the $35,000 down payment, he not only gets the right to occupy the home, but certain other advantages as well. Are those other advantages sufficient to warrant the difference? Should he buy or rent?

The most obvious advantage of purchasing rather than renting is that by purchasing, Adam will not only be paying for the right to occupy the home (which is all that rent pays for), but he will also be making an investment. If the value of the home increases, he will realize an investment gain when he sells it. On the other hand, as the owner, he also runs the risk that the value of the home will decrease. If it does, he stands to lose not only the $751.55 per month (which is a cash loss only to the extent it exceeds the $750 he otherwise would have paid for rent), but also the $35,000 down payment.

Another advantage of home ownership is stability and certainty. Adam knows that he can live in his purchased home as long as he wishes. As a renter, he would be subject to the wishes of his landlord. While a long term lease or a renewable lease with a guarantee of limited rent increases can also provide stability and certainty, renting will never provide the same degree of stability and certainty as home ownership. The importance of stability is a subjective factor that Adam will have to take into account, based primarily on how long he plans to stay in one place.

Other considerations in making the decision to buy or rent include property taxes, insurance against property damage, and estimates about future repair and maintenance. As a general rule, residential renters do not have to pay additional sums to the landlord for property taxes and insurance. But homeowners must be concerned about these expenses and the risk that they may increase. Thus, in addition to mortgage payments that cover principal and interest, the home buyer needs to plan for annual payments of property taxes and insurance. Lenders often require home buyers to make monthly escrow payments to ensure that there are sufficient funds to make these annual payments. In Adam's case, that means that monthly mortgage payments are likely to be higher than $751.55 a month.

Homeowners also bear the risk that repairs may be required to maintain the property. Renters don't bear this risk since most residential leases require the landlord to make repairs. Thus, when a furnace stops working or the roof starts leaking, the renter can merely call the landlord, while the homeowner must arrange for the repair and pay for it.

To analyze the benefit of home ownership, one must first fully understand all the costs in buying a home. Costs include the purchase price, the cost of financing the purchase price, insuring against property damage caused by casualties such as fires and storms, property taxes, and repair and maintenance costs. Utilities may be a factor as well. If a renter pays a monthly rent that includes utilities, then a comparison of the difference between renting and homeownership will need to include the cost of utilities.

Finally, when analyzing the costs attributable to the purchase and maintenance of a home, one must also understand certain tax rules that affect these costs. For example, interest payments are deductible whereas rental payments are not. If Adam were to compare the $750 rent to the $751.55 mortgage payment, he should do so on an after-tax basis.

After payment of taxes, the $750 rental cost remains $750. But for the early years of payment most of the monthly mortgage payment (initially approximately $580) represents mortgage interest, which is specifically allowed as an income tax deduction by § 163 of the Internal Revenue Code. If Adam's marginal tax rate was 28%, then his out-of-pocket, after-tax cost for the monthly mortgage payment would be 72% of the $580 interest payment and 100% of the $170 principal payment (figures are rounded). That means the after-tax cost is only $418 plus $170 or $588 (again, figures are rounded). The fact that Adam's monthly payments are actually less for the mortgage than for the rental agreement should make home ownership the more attractive option. Even after taking account of property taxes, insurance and other costs of home ownership, Adam is likely to find that buying a home is a better deal than renting.

[¶ 5,020]

Problem

To do a complete analysis of the advantages of buying versus renting, one would want to compare the total out-of-pocket expenses over time with the total return. Adam has $35,000 in cash which he could either invest in a home or somewhere else. In addition, he has sufficient monthly income that he could either pay in rent or pay towards a mortgage liability. What additional facts would you want to know in order to make a realistic comparison of the two options?

C. UNDERSTANDING THE HOUSING MARKET

[¶ 5,030]

Housing markets vary greatly by geographical location. The mix between renters and homeowners is one factor that varies. At the national level, and in most states, there are twice as many homeowners as renters. According to the 2000 census, however, in the state of New York, the number of renters is almost the same as the number of homeowners. Other states with high renter populations include California, Hawaii, Massachusetts, Nevada, and the state of Washington. The lowest rates of homeownership occur, not surprisingly, in large cities. For example, according to the census, the homeownership rate is only 23.8% in Newark, New Jersey, 30.2% in New York City, and 32.2% in Boston, Massachusetts. Not all large cities contain a majority of renters. Philadelphia's homeownership rate is 59.3% and San Antonio's is 58.1%. No one set of factors can explain the difference, but it is worth noting that both Newark and New York City have rent control laws that give their renters more rights than other cities do. Boston had rent control until 1994.

The National Association of Realtors (website at www.realtor.org) reports that in 2003 the median sales price for existing homes throughout the United States was $170,000. But the median price varied widely among geographical regions. In the northeast, the median was $190,500, in the midwest, it was $141,300, in the south, $157,100, and in the west, $234,200. Coldwell Banker Real Estate Corporation does an annual survey of home prices and provides an online calculator that demonstrates relative market prices. For example, a $150,000 home in Cedar Rapids, Iowa can be expected to cost $281,000 in Seattle, $690,000 in Nassau, New York, $832,000 in San Francisco, and $1,009,000 in Palo Alto, California. See www.Coldwellbanker.com.

Rental prices also vary according to geography. In 2003, the U.S. Census Bureau reported a national median rent of $900–$1,000 per month for apartments containing two or more bedrooms. In Iowa City, Iowa, the median rent was $572; in San Francisco, it was over $2,000.

Prices depend on such variables as supply and demand. Housing starts have increased in recent years, contributing to the overall supply, but demand has also increased. The Office of Federal Housing Enterprise Oversight issues a quarterly House Price Index (HPI) which tracks the increase in average house prices of single-family properties.

Based on that data, average housing prices increased approximately 8% per year for a total of 41.73% over the five-year period from March 31, 1999 to March 31, 2004. That makes the appreciation benefit of home ownership very attractive. But appreciation in home values also varies considerably by geography. For example, during this same period, house price appreciation in Massachusetts climbed 75.5%, whereas in Utah appreciation for the entire five-year period was only 9.98%.

In viewing the purchase of a home solely as an investment, one must estimate the value of the future appreciation and the value of the current consumption or use of the home. If those two benefits outweigh the costs, then purchasing a home is a good decision. The costs of home ownership are explored further in the following sections.

D. PURCHASING A HOME

[¶ 5,040]

The purchase of a home typically begins with a contract for sale. Performance under the contract occurs at a real estate closing, when the purchaser pays the purchase price and the seller delivers a deed to the purchaser. If the purchase price is financed with borrowed funds, the lender will be represented at closing and will take a security interest in the purchased property. The deed and mortgage are then recorded to protect the purchaser's title and the lender's security interest. The purchaser may also purchase title insurance at closing to ensure that the title conveyed is marketable.

The primary direct cost of home ownership is the purchase price of the home. But there are additional indirect costs. These include the costs of closing the real estate purchase and costs related to acquiring good title (e.g., the attorney's fee for the title examination). If the purchase is financed through a bank or a mortgage broker, there are additional indirect costs attributable to the financing portion of the transaction.

[¶ 5,050]

1. The Real Estate Contract

Any two persons can negotiate the terms of a contract for sale of real property. Usually, however, sales of homes occur through real estate agents and brokers, who typically have access to a multiple listing service, listing all homes for sale that are being handled by local brokers. In recent years, however, prospective purchasers have gained direct access to listings through the web. See, for example, www.realtor.com, which provides full listing information on over 2 million properties throughout the United States. While purchasers may still negotiate the real estate contract through a broker, they are less dependent on brokers for initial information about homes that are for sale. Brokers nonetheless continue to play an important role in interpreting the information available on the web for properties in their own communities. For a discussion of how a multiple listing service (MLS) works and the antitrust issues it raises, see Marianne M. Jennings, Multiple Listing Services—Antitrust and Policy, 32 Real Est. L.J. 140 (2002).

Some sellers may elect to sell the property on their own, a process that is typically referred to as a "for sale by owner" (FSBO) transaction. Most sellers, however, sell their property through real estate professionals. Recent surveys show that over 80% of homeowners use real estate professionals to help them sell their homes. See generally National Association of Realtors Profile of Home Buyers and Sellers, published annually.

[¶ 5,060]

a. The role of brokers and agents

In the early nineteenth century, sales of real property were handled primarily by lawyers. Since that time, however, the role of real estate brokers and agents has become more central. The terms "broker," "agent," and "realtor" are often used interchangeably. According to one definition, a real estate agent is "[a]n agent who represents a buyer or seller (or both, with proper disclosures) in the sale or lease of real property. A real estate agent can be either a broker (whose principal is a buyer or seller) or a salesperson (whose principal is a broker)." Black's Law Dictionary (7th ed. 1999). A real estate professional cannot use the title "realtor" unless the individual is a member of the National Association of Realtors or one of its affiliates. See Pope v. Mississippi Real Estate Comm'n, 872 F.2d 127 (5th Cir. 1989).

State law regulates the real estate profession. In every state, a person who wants to sell real estate will need to acquire a license. To become a broker, however, the licensed professional will typically have to take a course of study and hold the license for a number of years. Terminology varies from state to state, but as a general rule, licensed salespersons are at the bottom of the hierarchy, followed by agents, and brokers are at the top. Sometimes salespersons are called agents. All brokers are necessarily also agents and have sales licenses. The terms "broker" and "agent" are thus often used interchangeably. State law generally requires the person who is merely licensed to sell real estate to work under the authority of a broker.

Typically the seller will sign a "listing agreement" with the broker which gives the broker the right to list the property for sale, to show it to prospective purchasers, and, in the event of a successful sale, to collect a commission for the services performed. Brokers often employ other real estate agents to help perform the duties required under the listing contract and agree to split the commission with such agents. Often there is an agreement among brokers in a community that the commission will be split evenly with any broker (or agent) who produces a willing buyer. Thus, for example, if Adam were to use a broker (or agent) to help him locate a home to purchase, his broker (or agent) would be entitled to half of the commission that the seller had agreed to pay to the listing broker, whether or not his agent worked for the listing broker. In many areas, the typical listing commission is 6%. At closing, the listing broker would take 3% and the broker for the purchaser would take the other 3%.

[¶ 5,070]

b. Whom do brokers and agents represent?

At common law, the listing broker represents the seller and owes no duties to the buyer. Under this rule, the buyer cannot sue the listing broker for failure to inspect for defects or to verify the seller's statements. Nor can the buyer sue her own agent because there is usually no contract between them. The agent promises nothing to the buyer and the buyer promises nothing to the agent, although there is often an understanding that the buyer will not work with other agents. The buyer does not pay the agent for services. Rather the agent's services are paid for by the seller, out of the commission bargained for by the listing broker and the seller. The effect of this arrangement is that the buyer's agent is viewed as working for the seller by helping the seller to find a willing buyer.

Several problems arise from the fact that brokers traditionally represent sellers and not buyers. An agent owes a duty of disclosure to the principal, which in our case is the seller. If the agent that Adam thinks is working for him is actually working for the seller, then Adam must be careful what he tells his agent. Suppose Adam is thinking of making an initial offer to purchase at $150,000, but is willing to go as high as $175,000 if necessary to get the property. Can he share this information with an agent who is really working for the seller? In addition, since the commission to be paid to Adam's agent is a percentage of the selling price, there is an immediate conflict of interest. Adam wants to pay as little as possible for the home while his agent has a personal stake in having Adam pay a larger sales price (and thus produce a larger commission).

To deal with this problem, a number of states have recently enacted statutes that authorize agents to work as the "buyer's agent." In such cases, it is imperative that the broker (or salesperson) clarify the arrangement to the client. For example, under Texas law, all brokers and salespersons must notify the client in writing to explain what sort of broker/buyer arrangement they are operating under. Specifically, each buyer must be given the following notice:

> Before working with a real estate broker, you should know that the duties of a broker depend on whom the broker represents. If you are a prospective seller or landlord (owner) or a prospective buyer or tenant (buyer), you should know that the broker who lists the property for sale or lease is the owner's agent. A broker who acts as a subagent represents the owner in cooperation with the listing broker. A broker who acts as a buyer's agent represents the buyer. A broker may act as an intermediary between the parties if the parties consent in writing. A broker can assist you in locating a property, preparing a contract or lease, or obtaining financing without representing you. A broker is obligated by law to treat you honestly.

> IF THE BROKER REPRESENTS THE OWNER: The broker becomes the owner's agent by entering into an agreement with the owner, usually through a written listing agreement, or by agreeing to act as a subagent by accepting an offer of subagency from the listing broker. A subagent may work in a different real estate office. A listing broker or subagent can assist the buyer but does not represent the buyer and must place the interests of the owner first. The buyer should not tell the owner's agent anything the buyer would not want the owner to know because an owner's agent must disclose to the owner any material information known to the agent.

> IF THE BROKER REPRESENTS THE BUYER: The broker becomes the buyer's agent by entering into an agreement to represent the buyer, usually through a written buyer representation agreement. A buyer's agent can assist the owner but does not represent the owner and must place the interests of the buyer first. The owner should not tell a buyer's agent anything the owner would not want the buyer to know because a buyer's agent must disclose to the buyer any material information known to the agent.

> IF THE BROKER ACTS AS AN INTERMEDIARY: A broker may act as an intermediary between the parties if the broker complies with The Texas Real Estate License Act. The broker must obtain the written consent of each party to the transaction to act as an intermediary. The written consent must state who will pay the broker and, in conspicuous bold or underlined print, set forth the broker's obligations as an intermediary. The broker is required to treat each party honestly and fairly and to comply with The Texas Real Estate License Act. A broker who acts as an intermediary in a transaction: (1) shall treat all parties

honestly; (2) may not disclose that the owner will accept a price less than the asking price unless authorized in writing to do so by the owner; (3) may not disclose that the buyer will pay a price greater than the price submitted in a written offer unless authorized in writing to do so by the buyer; and (4) may not disclose any confidential information or any information that a party specifically instructs the broker in writing not to disclose unless authorized in writing to disclose the information or required to do so by The Texas Real Estate License Act or a court order or if the information materially relates to the condition of the property. With the parties' consent, a broker acting as an intermediary between the parties may appoint a person who is licensed under The Texas Real Estate License Act and associated with the broker to communicate with and carry out instructions of one party and another person who is licensed under that Act and associated with the broker to communicate with and carry out instructions of the other party.

If you choose to have a broker represent you, you should enter into a written agreement with the broker that clearly establishes the broker's obligations and your obligations. The agreement should state how and by whom the broker will be paid. You have the right to choose the type of representation, if any, you wish to receive. Your payment of a fee to a broker does not necessarily establish that the broker represents you. If you have any questions regarding the duties and responsibilities of the broker, you should resolve those questions before proceeding.

Tex. Occupations Code § 1101.558(d).

For an excellent history of the traditional role of brokers and the ways in which those roles are changing, see Ronald Benton Brown & Joseph M. Grohman, Real Estate Brokers: Shouldering New Burdens, 11 Prob. & Prop. 14 (May/June 1997).

[¶ 5,080]

c. *Brokers' and owners' duty to disclose defects*

Under the common law doctrine of *caveat emptor*, a seller generally had no duty to warn a prospective purchaser about defects in the property. Courts in this country have chipped away at that doctrine, creating exceptions for latent defects and particularly hazardous defects. In some states, courts have abolished the doctrine altogether. See, e.g., Strawn v. Canuso, 657 A.2d 420 (N.J. 1995). In other states, the move away from *caveat emptor* has been accomplished by statute. Over half the states have adopted a version of the "Residential Property Disclosure Act," requiring the seller to disclose facts about the condition of the property. In some states, however, disclosure is voluntary. For example, the owner can elect not to disclose by checking an appropriate box on the form. Presumably this action would serve as a warning of some sort to the purchaser.

Usually the requirement is placed on the seller, which means that the broker is protected from liability. But see 60 Okla. Stat. § 836, which provides: "A real estate licensee has the duty to disclose to the purchaser any defects in the property actually known to the licensee which are not included in the disclosure statement or any amendment." See also Haw. Rev. Stat. § 508D–7.

Brokers can be held liable for active misrepresentations about the condition or quality of the realty, but are not generally liable for merely inflating a sales pitch. See, e.g., Williamson v. Realty Champion, 551 So.2d 1000 (Ala. 1989) (buyer's agent not liable for saying that home was "well built" even though home turned out to have many defects); Patch v. Arsenault, 653 A.2d 1079 (N.H. 1995) (listing agent not liable for saying condo was in "excellent condition" when in fact it had electrical and water drainage problems). The modern trend under both decisional law and statutory law is to hold sellers and their brokers to a higher standard of disclosure than required by the common law. This duty extends to off-site conditions, such as nearby hazardous waste dumps, that might affect the value of the property. See Annot., Liability of Vendor or Real–Estate Broker for Failure to Disclose Information Concerning Off–Site Conditions Affecting Value of Property, 41 A.L.R.5th 157 (1996).

Despite these trends, it is still very difficult for a buyer to assert liability against either the listing broker or the buyer's agent. For this reason, it is imperative that the buyer either hire someone to inspect the property thoroughly before purchasing it or obtain a warranty from the seller that the property is in fit condition (or both). Termite inspections are probably the most common, since termite activity is often difficult to detect. Other "invisible" threats to property that should be checked out before closing a purchase include radon (a radioactive byproduct of natural soil decay that can produce harmful gas inside a home), asbestos (which can cause lung-related diseases), and mold (high mold counts inside a home, even if not hazardous to health, may indicate moisture penetration that can lead to additional problems). Some states have specific requirements about disclosure of these threats. See, e.g., 33 Me. Rev. Stat. § 133.4 (requiring the seller of residential real estate to disclose presence or prior removal of both asbestos and radon). For additional information about owner and broker responsibilities, see generally Ann Morales Olazábal & René Sacasas, Real Estate Agent as "Superbroker": Defining and Bridging the Gap Between Residential Realtors' Abilities and Liabilities in the New Millennium, 30 Real Est. L.J. 173 (2002); Craig W. Dallon, Theories of Real Estate Broker Liability and the Effect of the "As Is" Clause, 54 Fla. L. Rev. 395 (2002).

[¶ 5,090]

d. Commissions under the contract

The terms of the commission payable to the broker are determined by the listing agreement. Typically, the contract provides for payment upon production of a ready, willing and able buyer. A ready, willing and able buyer is one who is willing to buy at the price and terms set in the listing offer and who has the financial and legal ability to do so. If the seller agrees to an offer from a buyer at a price below the listing price, then the seller is agreeing that the buyer is ready and willing and the broker's right to the commission is fixed at that time.

Once a contract for sale is negotiated, the terms for payment of the commission can be altered by mutual agreement between the seller and the broker. For example, if the seller is willing to accept an offer in which the buyer will give the seller a promissory note rather than cash, as contemplated by the original listing agreement, the seller might condition her acceptance of buyer's offer on the broker's agreement to change the terms of the listing agreement and accept a deferred payment of the commission. If the broker agrees, the new terms will apply to the payment of the commission.

If the broker's commission is conditioned solely on the production of a ready, willing and able buyer, then the broker is entitled to the commission even if the sale is never completed. See Dworak v. Michals, 320 N.W.2d 485 (Neb. 1982) (seller refused to complete sale); see also Kuga v. Chang, 399 S.E.2d 816 (Va. 1991) (buyer defaulted). In some cases, however, the listing contract may require consummation of the sale before the broker can recover. For a general discussion of this topic, see Kurtis A. Kemper, Cause of Action by Real Estate Broker to Recover Commission, 7 Causes of Action 485 (2004).

While the commission is technically paid by the seller, the economic impact of the commission passes through to the purchaser. Sellers set a selling price understanding that the commission, typically 6% of the purchase price, will be paid off the top to the agents who bring the deal to closure. Property that is listed for sale by the owner does not have to carry that built-in 6% cost off the top, although there is no assurance that the owner has in fact listed the property at a lower price than he would choose if using a listing agent. The owner may instead feel that since he is willing to do the work of advertising the home and showing it, he should be paid the full asking price, including any amount that would otherwise be payable to an agent. According to the National Association of Realtors, the number of sellers who list their homes for sale by owner is declining. At least one-third of those who try to sell without the aid of a broker report that the hardest task is "understanding and completing the necessary paperwork."

Sometimes sellers who prefer to list their property for sale by owner are willing to offer a 3% commission to any agent who brings them a ready, willing and able buyer. In such cases, agents who work with prospective buyers should have an equal incentive to show their clients properties for sale by owner along with listed properties because their ability to earn a commission is the same.

[¶ 5,100]

Problems

1. Otis Owner owns a home that he purchased many years ago for $160,000. The home is subject to a mortgage with an outstanding principal balance of $100,000. Otis believes the home is now worth $200,000 and intends to list it for that amount. If he lists the property through a broker who charges a 6% commission, how much cash will he receive if he actually sells it for $200,000? How much cash will he receive if he sells it for $200,000 without using any real estate brokers or agents?

2. Assume that Otis decides to sell the property himself without hiring a listing broker or agent. He receives two offers from two different prospective purchasers at the same time. Purchaser #1, who is not represented by an agent, offers him $190,000. Purchaser #2, who is represented by an agent, offers him $195,000 with a provision in the offer that requires Otis to pay the purchaser's agent 3% out of the sales proceeds. What should Otis do?

[¶ 5,110]

e. *Terms of the contract*

A contract for the sale of real estate must be in writing to satisfy the Statute of Frauds. In most states, a contract for the sale of real estate is not enforceable unless it contains: (1) the names of both buyer and seller; (2) a description of the realty to be sold; (3) the essential terms of the sale, such as the selling price; and (4) the signatures of both buyer and seller.

Most real estate contracts for the purchase of residential realty are set forth on form contracts available to brokers and agents through their professional organizations. In addition to the purchase price, the contract also provides the terms of the sale, e.g., whether the seller expects cash at closing or is willing to finance part of the purchase price, the expected time within which closing must occur, and any conditions added by the seller or the purchaser.

The buyer is the first to fill in the terms of the proposed contract in the initial offer. To indicate that the buyer is serious, the buyer usually offers to make a good faith deposit, to be held by the seller's broker/agent until the contract is completed. Typically the buyer will include a condition that closing is contingent on the buyer's ability to obtain mortgage financing. The seller, not wanting to take the property off the market for too long a period of time, will generally be interested in seeing that that condition is met within a reasonable time. Other conditions that buyers typically include are proof of marketable title and physical inspection of the premises by experts (e.g., for termites, soundness of the foundation, etc.). If the buyer has doubts about the value of the property, the buyer may include a condition that closing is contingent on a professional appraisal at the selling price or higher.

If the seller agrees to the terms and conditions offered by the buyer, the seller will accept the offer. If the seller disagrees, the seller is free either to reject the offer completely or to propose a counter offer. Sometimes the seller will ask for a higher good faith deposit. Ultimately, if the contingencies listed by the buyer are not met, the deposit will be returned.

For more information about performance under the contract, see ¶ 5,370 (appraisals), ¶ 5,380 (requirement of good faith attempt to meet contingencies), and ¶ 5,410 (breach before closing).

[¶ 5,120]

2. Determining the Purchase Price

The most important term in the real estate contract is the purchase price. Sellers often list properties at prices that are higher than what they expect to receive at closing. Real estate professionals (e.g., brokers and agents) can be useful advisors in determining what price to offer since they have ready access to information about recent sales of comparable property in the local area. While their estimates may be highly reliable, depending on the competence of the particular realtor, their opinions are not formal appraisals. A purchaser may wish to hire an independent appraiser in order to obtain a more reliable estimate of value before making an offer, but formal appraisals take time. If a purchaser is working without an agent, it would be advisable to consult a professional to do an analysis of recent comparable sales in the neighborhood before making an offer.

Property tax records, although publicly available, are not a particularly good index of current fair market values because assessed values for property tax purposes are typically much lower than fair market value. Knowing the assessed property tax value, however, can be useful. The assessed value should, in any event, set a floor for determining current market value.

If the purchase of the property is contingent on the buyer's ability to obtain satisfactory mortgage financing, the buyer could wait to see what the lender's appraiser says the property is worth. In that event, the offer by the buyer should state an explicit condition that the property be appraised at the offering price or higher. Mortgage lenders usually require a recent appraisal because they apply a loan-to-value ratio that will determine the terms of the loan. Higher ratios result in lower equity investments and correspondingly higher risks to the lender. Thus, a lower loan-to-value ratio will result in a loan with a lower interest rate and may also avoid the need for private mortgage insurance.

Example: Mort is purchasing a $200,000 home. If he can make a down payment of only $20,000 (10% of the purchase price), his equity will be only 10% and the loan-to-value ratio will be 90%. A higher down payment of $40,000 (20%) produces a lower loan-to-value ratio of 80%.

E. MORTGAGE FINANCING

[¶ 5,130]

Mortgage financing has become a complex business. Thirty or forty years ago, a first-time home buyer seeking a mortgage would likely make an appointment with a loan officer at a local bank, credit union or savings and loan association to discuss what sort of mortgage financing was available. The understanding would be that the financial institution would provide the mortgage funds to the borrower on terms that were mutually agreeable and the borrower would make payments to the financial institution. A first-time purchaser with little cash on hand might prefer a loan with a higher interest rate in exchange for a lower down payment and closing costs. Other borrowers with sufficient cash might be willing to pay higher costs at closing, including "discount points," in exchange for a lower interest rate throughout the term of the loan, resulting in a lower overall cost. (Note: The benefit of a lower overall cost will be realized only if the loan remains outstanding long enough for the borrower to recoup the points paid up front and then to enjoy the lower interest payments. A sale of the home or a refinancing of the loan will prevent realization of the full benefit. For this reason, purchasers of "starter homes" and those who are likely to change job locations often avoid, if possible, loans with discount points.)

In shopping for the right mortgage, borrowers often focus on what the monthly payments will be as the most important factor. A 30–year mortgage will produce smaller monthly payments than a 20–year mortgage, but the trade-off is typically a higher interest rate for the longer mortgage term. A borrower who needs low monthly payments will opt for the longer term even though the overall costs are higher. These sorts of considerations affect what sort of loan package a particular borrower will want.

The array of loan packages has expanded significantly in the past few decades. Today, however, rather than sitting down to discuss the options with a local banker, borrowers are much more likely to deal with mortgage brokers. According to the U.S. Department of Housing and Urban Development, over 60% of all mortgages originate through mortgage brokers. See 67 Fed. Reg. 49,134 at 49,140. And, today, even if the loan process begins with an application to a loan officer at the local bank, the loan is likely to be sold to another institution and serviced by someone other than the bank. (For further details, see ¶¶ 5,150 and 5,180.)

The following are some key terms in mortgage financing:

- *Amortization:* A mortgage loan is paid off over a set period, typically 30 or 15 years. Over this amortization period, monthly payments are applied first to accrued interest with the balance of each payment credited to reduce the outstanding principal amount. Amortization tables show the amount of each payment that is credited to interest and principal during the term of the loan.

- *Contract for deed:* See Installment Land Contract.

- *Default:* Failure to meet the terms of the loan agreement, e.g., when the buyer/mortgagor fails to make mortgage payments in a timely fashion.

- *Equity:* The amount by which the fair market value of the home exceeds the outstanding principal owed on the mortgage debt.

- *Equity of redemption:* Once the borrower/mortgagor has defaulted and foreclosure proceedings are underway, the borrower has the right to pay off the debt and gain clear title to the realty. Some states give the borrower the right to redeem for a limited period of time after foreclosure.

- *Foreclosure:* The primary remedy for a mortgagee upon a default by the mortgagor. Usually there are statutory requirements of notice to the owner and other interested parties, after which the mortgagee can offer the property for sale in a public auction in order to recover the amount of the lien.

- *Home equity loan:* A homeowner borrows money and gives the lender a second mortgage to secure the loan. The loan may be taken out for a purpose related to the home (e.g., for home improvements or to provide additional purchase money funds that the lender is unwilling to include in the first mortgage), but usually it is taken out for an unrelated purpose (e.g., to purchase an automobile).

- *Installment land contract:* Under this arrangement, the buyer agrees to pay the purchase price in installments and the seller agrees to give immediate possession to the buyer and to convey legal title once the payments are completed. The seller can reclaim possession of the realty from the purchaser if the purchaser defaults. Retention of legal title by the seller serves the same function as a mortgage, but this form of protection for the seller/lender is better than a mortgage because no foreclosure proceedings are necessary to establish legal title. This arrangement is sometimes referred to a "contract for deed."

- *Lien:* A security interest in the property arising from a loan of money. The lien entitles the lienholder to institute foreclosure proceedings against the property if the debt is not repaid.

- *Mortgagee:* The lender, whether a bank or a mortgage company.

- *Mortgagor:* The borrower, i.e., the purchaser.

- *Origination fee:* A fee charged up front by some lenders and expressed as a percentage of the loan amount. Unlike points, however, this fee is for services performed by the lender in arranging the loan and is not tied to the interest rate. It is a cost of acquiring the loan.

- *Points:* Mortgagees often charge "discount points" at closing, which typically are an extra cost for buying down the interest rate. One point is equal to one percent of the loan amount. Conceptually, points can be viewed as prepaid interest since they are paid at closing for the benefit of acquiring the loan.

- *Prime:* This refers to the interest rate that banks charge their best (i.e., most creditworthy) customers. Most banks use the same prime rate and adjust their rates at the same time. In recent years, "prime" has varied from as low as 4% in 2004 to as high as 9.5% in 2000 and early 2001.

- *Private mortgage insurance:* When the purchaser provides less than 20% as a down payment, then there is more risk that the purchaser will default on the mortgage note (i.e., lower down payment means less incentive to invest more in the form of mortgage payments). In such cases, the mortgagee will usually require the borrower to purchase private mortgage insurance (PMI) to protect against default. Premiums for PMI are added to the borrower's monthly mortgage payments. Under the Homeowners Protection Act of 1998, borrowers can cease PMI payments once they have made principal payments sufficient to reduce the loan balance to 78% of the original value of the property. See 12 U.S.C. §§ 4901, 4902.

- *Purchase money mortgage:* When the loan funds are used to purchase the property, the mortgage securing the loan is called a purchase money mortgage.

- *Subordination:* When there is more than one lien securing a loan against the property, the priority of the lenders must be determined in the event of a foreclosure. Typically, the first in time has priority over subsequent lenders. However, one lien may by agreement be subordinated to others.

[¶ 5,140]

1. The Mortgage Transaction

Most mortgage arrangements involve a simple transaction between borrower and lender in which the borrower signs a note promising to pay to the lender the amount that is borrowed. The note will specify the amount of the loan, the interest rate to be paid on any outstanding balance, the term of the loan, and the amount of the monthly payments. In addition, the note will usually provide other details such as where the monthly payments are to be made, the legal consequences of failing to make payments on time, and what constitutes a default. Most notes create personal liability on the part of the borrower. These loans are called "recourse loans." When a borrower signs a note creating personal liability, the lender has the right to seek recourse against the borrower as well as against the property. This right will make a huge difference to the lender whenever foreclosure against the property fails to produce sufficient funds to pay off the mortgage balance. Any deficiency can be collected personally against the borrower. Note, however, that states protect borrowers against deficiency judgments in a variety of ways, especially when the foreclosure is of a single family residence. See, e.g., Ariz. Rev. Stat. § 33–729 (deficiency judgments allowed only if borrower was responsible for a diminution in value of the mortgaged property). For further discussion of antideficiency relief, see ¶ 5,490; see also John Mixon & Ira B. Shepard, Antideficiency Relief for Foreclosed Homeowners: ULSIA Section 511(b), 27 Wake Forest L. Rev. 455 (1992).

A separate legal document is signed by the borrower conveying a security interest to the lender in the property that is being purchased with the loan proceeds. The type of document varies from state to state. In some states, the security interest is transferred by using a mortgage deed. In others it is transferred in a security deed or a deed of trust. The effect of these documents is basically the same, however. The security interest in the home is transferred to the lender to protect the lender against default on the note. If default occurs, and is not cured within the time limits set forth in the documents, then the lender has the right to foreclose the security interest. Foreclosure can occur only after the lender has given notice as required by state law. Then typically there is a foreclosure sale, usually on the front steps of the local courthouse, in which the mortgagee bank offers the property for sale and usually bids on its own behalf in the amount of the outstanding balance on the mortgage note. Many lenders, however, prefer remedies other than foreclosure. The most common is a deed in lieu of foreclosure (see ¶ 5,510).

During the term of the loan, the borrower makes monthly payments to the lender as promised in the note. Each monthly payment is part interest and part principal. In some cases, monthly payments will include a payment for mortgage insurance and for amounts to be escrowed to pay for insurance and property taxes, which are typically billed annually. Interest is calculated based on the outstanding principal balance of the loan. As a result, in the early years, before much principal has been repaid, most of the monthly payments are interest. In the later years, once the principal has been reduced, the portion of the monthly payment attributable to interest is lower and the portion attributable to the repayment of principal increases. For example, a $200,000 loan at 6% amortized over five years would create monthly payments of $3,866.56, allocated between interest and principal as follows:

Monthly Payment	Interest	Principal	Principal Balance
1	$1,000.00	$2,866.56	$197,133.44
2	985.67	2,880.89	194,252.55
3	971.26	2,895.30	191,357.25
4	956.79	2,909.77	188,447.48
5	942.24	2,924.32	185,523.15
6	927.62	2,938.94	182,584.21

Monthly Payment	Interest	Principal	Principal Balance
7	912.92	2,953.64	179,630.57
8	898.15	2,968.41	176,662.16
9	883.31	2,983.25	173,678.91
10	868.39	2,998.17	170,680.75
11	853.40	3,013.16	167,667.59
12	838.34	3,028.22	164,639.37
13	823.20	3,043.36	161,596.01
14	807.98	3,058.58	158,537.43
15	792.69	3,073.87	155,463.55
16	777.32	3,089.24	152,374.31
17	761.87	3,104.69	149,269.62
18	746.35	3,120.21	146,149.41
19	730.75	3,135.81	143,013.60
20	715.07	3,151.49	139,862.11
21	699.31	3,167.25	136,694.86
22	683.47	3,183.09	133,511.77
23	667.56	3,199.00	130,312.77
24	651.56	3,215.00	127,097.77
25	635.49	3,231.07	123,866.70
26	619.33	3,247.23	120,619.48
27	603.10	3,263.46	117,356.01
28	586.78	3,279.78	114,076.23
29	570.38	3,296.18	110,780.06
30	553.90	3,312.66	107,467.40
31	537.34	3,329.22	104,138.17
32	520.69	3,345.87	100,792.30
33	503.96	3,362.60	97,429.71
34	487.15	3,379.41	94,050.29
35	470.25	3,396.31	90,653.99
36	453.27	3,413.29	87,240.69
37	436.20	3,430.36	83,810.34
38	419.05	3,447.51	80,362.83
39	401.81	3,464.75	76,898.08
40	384.49	3,482.07	73,416.01
41	367.08	3,499.48	69,916.53
42	349.58	3,516.98	66,399.56
43	332.00	3,534.56	62,865.00
44	314.32	3,552.24	59,312.76
45	296.56	3,570.00	55,742.76
46	278.71	3,587.85	52,154.92
47	260.77	3,605.79	48,549.13
48	242.75	3,623.81	44,925.32
49	224.63	3,641.93	41,283.38
50	206.42	3,660.14	37,623.24
51	188.12	3,678.44	33,944.80
52	169.72	3,696.84	30,247.96
53	151.24	3,715.32	26,532.64
54	132.66	3,733.90	22,798.74
55	113.99	3,752.57	19,046.18
56	95.23	3,771.33	15,274.85
57	76.37	3,790.19	11,484.66
58	57.42	3,809.14	7,675.53

Monthly Payment	Interest	Principal	Principal Balance
59	8.38	3,828.18	3,847.34
60	19.24	3,847.32	0.02

[¶ 5,150]

2. Loan Origination and the Primary Mortgage Market

Mortgage loans originate with two primary types of institutions: (1) those that have deposits (e.g., commercial banks and thrifts), and (2) those that do not have deposits (e.g., mortgage banks). The number of mortgages any institution can offer is dependent on the total amount of funds available to make loans. Deposits provide one source of loan funds. Borrowed funds provide another source. The originator of the loan can also sell the loan, after it has been funded, to an investor in the secondary market. The proceeds from this sale will either replenish deposits that were used to fund the loan or will pay off the line of credit that was used to fund the loan.

Mortgage loan originators participate in the primary mortgage market by taking applications, verifying the applicant's creditworthiness and the adequacy of the property as security, and closing the loan by preparing legal documents and recording them. After the loan is closed, the original lender should receive the monthly mortgage payments, see that property taxes and hazard insurance premiums are paid, and give notice to the borrower whenever payments fall behind. If the borrower defaults, the lender is responsible for foreclosing on the security interest in the property.

Primary lenders hold some mortgage loans in their own portfolios and sell others in the secondary mortgage market. Indeed, in most cases, the lender uses automated underwriting services to determine that the loan can be sold in the secondary market. In some cases, it is difficult to tell whether the primary lender has funded the loan on its own and then sold it or has merely acted as the agent of the purchaser in the secondary market. The distinction can make a difference in terms of the borrower's legal rights. It is a fine-line distinction when mortgage brokers and bankers are involved.

[¶ 5,160]

a. Acquiring a loan through a mortgage broker

Mortgage brokers arrived on the scene in large numbers as the securitization of mortgage loans increased. Securitization is a process in which mortgage notes are sold to entities that pool similar notes from many different borrowers and convert them into investments that can be sold on the securities market. These investments are known as mortgage-backed securities (MBS) or sometimes merely as mortgage securities. The sale of mortgage notes to investors creates additional funds for new mortgage loans. It is this additional source of funding which has helped to make mortgages more accessible to a broader segment of the American population.

Mortgage brokers do not lend funds directly to borrowers. Rather, a mortgage broker offers services to customers who are looking for lenders to provide mortgage funds. Brokers counsel borrowers about available types of mortgages and help them obtain the best lender for their specific circumstances. The borrower makes an application directly to the broker and the broker matches the borrower with a suitable lender, who actually provides the mortgage funds. Or, in some cases, the broker initially provides the funds and then immediately after closing transfers the mortgage note and supporting documents to another lender who essentially purchases the note from the broker. In either event, the mortgage funds come from a source other than the broker, and the borrower will make payments on the mortgage to the ultimate lender or to a third-party servicer rather than to the broker.

Brokers can be very helpful for first-time buyers and for buyers with credit problems. As a general rule, borrowers should be able to find better mortgage packages through brokers since brokers have access to a wide array of lenders and have more information about the market than a single borrower has.

The challenge for borrowers is to pick the right mortgage broker. Many borrowers don't understand the role that the broker plays. The broker appears to be acting as the borrower's agent in looking for the best loan package. But at the same time, the broker will be paid out of amounts charged by the lender who funds the mortgage loan. This situation creates a conflict of interest similar to that of the real estate broker who is helping a purchaser to find the right home but will be paid out of the proceeds of the sale. The higher the sales price, the higher the payment to the real estate broker. Similarly, with mortgage brokers, higher origination fees or higher interest rates usually create an opportunity for the broker to be paid more.

Often the broker's fee is difficult to ascertain because it is hidden in the cost of the loan. Brokers are not required to explain their fees to borrowers, although they are required to provide certain information to the borrowers prior to closing on the loan. See ¶ 5,240. Some mortgage brokers charge a flat fee up front and some experts think this is the fairest way to deal with borrowers. Others are paid out of the interest charged on the loan. For example, the lender might be willing to make a loan at 5.5%, but the broker quotes a rate of 5.75% with the understanding with the lender that the 0.25% premium will compensate the broker for services rendered. This form of compensation is known as the yield spread premium and need not be disclosed to the borrower.

Example: Betsy is looking for a lender who will lend her $100,000. Broker X offers to work with her for a fee equal to two points of the loan, which would be $2,000. Broker Y offers to work for her for no upfront fee and to find her the best loan available. If Broker X finds her a loan at 5.25% over 30 years and no points and Broker Y finds her a loan at 5.25% over 30 years plus two points at closing, then the cost to Betsy will be the same. The problem is that Betsy has no way of knowing in advance which broker will obtain the best loan for her out of all possible loans available.

b. Acquiring a loan directly from the lender

Homebuyers who have established relationships with a local bank or credit union may want to use a loan officer at the bank or credit union as a broker. Dealing with someone local and known to the borrower can be safer than working through an unknown broker. Some banks fund mortgages directly but then sell them in a secondary market, which means that all future payments and questions about the mortgage will be handled through a stranger rather than the local bank. In any event, the loan officer, like the mortgage broker, will be compensated for putting the loan together. That compensation will be paid by the borrower in the form of loan costs, in much the same way that mortgage brokers are paid. As with mortgage brokers, the loan officer is not required to identify the officer's compensation to the borrower. However, unlike the situation with mortgage brokers, the loan officer may have an ongoing relationship with the borrower in connection with other banking transactions. Desirous of sustaining trust with their banking customers, loan officers have an added incentive to be open with their borrowers about loan costs.

Dealing with a local bank no longer means what it used to mean when borrowers made monthly payments to the bank for the full term of the loan. Today most mortgage loans are sold in the secondary market to large institutional investors. The end result to the borrower in such cases is not really different from using a mortgage broker who is handling the loan for a national company.

3. The Secondary Mortgage Market

Most loans originate with mortgage companies and commercial banks. After initial funding, however, most loans are sold to investors. The original lender often works with the purchaser from the time the borrower submits a loan application to be sure that the loan will meet the purchaser's requirements. Fannie Mae (see below) is the largest purchaser. The purchaser may keep the loan in its portfolio or it may pool the loan with others to create mortgage securities.

In 2003, approximately 55% of the residential mortgage debt outstanding in this country was held in the form of mortgage securities. To pool mortgage notes and convert them into securities, the notes must meet certain requirements. Securitization has resulted in a certain amount of standardization of mortgage loans. Loans that don't fall within the guidelines required by the purchaser are usually the loans that are retained by the original lender, typically a bank.

There are a number of key actors in the secondary mortgage market. Fannie Mae, Freddie Mac, and Ginnie Mae, all connected to the federal government in some way, serve as important conduits. They either guarantee the payment of the mortgage notes, buy them in the secondary market, or bundle purchased notes together and convert them into mortgage securities. Mortgage securities are then purchased by investors. Different investors purchase different types of mortgages. The role of key participants is outlined below.

[¶ 5,190]

a. FHA mortgages

During the depression in the 1930's, the number of mortgage defaults rose sharply and banks were reluctant to make loans to new home purchasers. In response, the federal government created the Federal Housing Administration (FHA) to provide insurance against default. The FHA guaranteed payment of loans that conformed to its "30–year fixed rate mortgage" requirements, and the FHA continues to provide that guarantee today for any mortgage that meets its underwriting requirements. In return, the borrower pays slightly more for the loan in the form of an up-front fee and in monthly mortgage insurance premiums. The premium is paid by the borrower for the benefit of the lender. As a result, the lender is willing to make a loan that is somewhat riskier than the conventional mortgage loan. Thus, for home purchasers who cannot meet the 10% to 20% down payment required by conventional private mortgagees, the FHA mortgage is an attractive option. The FHA mortgage is aimed at low to middle income home purchasers, and its loan limits are accordingly low compared with other mortgage options.

[¶ 5,200]

b. VA home loans

At the end of World War II, the Veterans Administration (VA) began a loan guarantee program similar to that of FHA but for the sole benefit of veterans. The program has changed over the years, but it still offers the possibility of a zero down payment with interest rates that are competitive with FHA and conventional loans. The maximum amount guaranteed is $60,000, but guidelines allow lenders to lend up to $240,000 (four times the guaranteed amount).

[¶ 5,210]

c. Conventional mortgages

Conventional lenders include savings and loan associations, savings banks, credit unions, commercial banks, and mortgage companies. Conventional or private mortgage loans are not guaranteed by the government. In the case of a risky loan (e.g., one with a small down payment), the lender may require the borrower to purchase private mortgage insurance. The cost of the private mortgage insurance is then added to the monthly payment of interest and principal until such time as the equity in the mortgaged property has been built up sufficiently. Conventional mortgages are typically for a fixed term (e.g., 20 or 30 years) and carry a fixed interest rate throughout the term of the loan.

[¶ 5,220]

d. Fannie Mae, Ginnie Mae, and Freddie Mac

The Federal National Mortgage Association (FNMA or Fannie Mae) was created in 1938 to purchase FHA-insured loans. Fannie Mae began purchasing VA loans in 1948 and conventional mortgage loans in 1970, and it remains the primary purchaser in the secondary market. Some of the loans it purchases are retained in its own portfolio, but most are securitized.

In 1968, federal legislation converted the entity into a stockholder-owned, privately-managed corporation. The same legislation created the Government National Mortgage Association (GNMA or Ginnie Mae). Ginnie Mae does not buy and sell loans in the way that Fannie Mae does. Its primary role is to guarantee mortgage securities that are created from pools of FHA and VA loans. Ginnie Mae mortgage securities are backed by the full faith and credit of the federal government.

Freddie Mac (Federal Home Loan Mortgage Corporation) was created by Congress in 1970 to share responsibility with Fannie Mae for stabilizing the mortgage industry by providing liquidity. Like Fannie Mae, it acts in the secondary market as a purchaser of mortgage loans that conform to its requirements and it also converts pools of loans into mortgage securities.

Fannie Mae and Freddie Mac (but not Ginnie Mae) are participants in the secondary market for conventional loans. Because private lenders look to Fannie Mae and Freddie Mac as a source of mortgage funding, they prefer to make loans to borrowers that conform to the requirements set forth by these two organizations. The most important requirement is the amount of the loan. Fannie Mae and Freddie Mac were formed to help low to middle income home buyers by providing sufficient liquidity and thus keeping mortgage rates on such loans lower than they would otherwise be. Thus they purchase loans only at or below certain loan maximums. For 2004, the loan limit for a single family mortgage was $333,700. Higher limits apply to Alaska, Hawaii, Guam, and the Virgin Islands. Loans above these limits are typically called "jumbo loans" (or "non-conforming loans") and carry a slightly higher interest rate because they are not available for purchase by Fannie Mae or Freddie Mac.

[¶ 5,230]

4. Home Equity Loans

People use the term "home equity loan" to refer to a number of different mortgage arrangements. In concept, a home equity loan is something other than a loan that is taken out to purchase a residence. In tax law, "home equity indebtedness" is a statutory term that means any indebtedness up to $100,000 secured by the residence that is not acquisition indebtedness and that does not exceed the equity in the home (i.e., the difference between the value of the home and the acquisition indebtedness). Some people refer to all second mortgages as home equity loans, even though some people use the proceeds from the second mortgage to help finance the purchase of the property.

In any event, home equity loans are almost always second liens on the home and are structured as a line of credit rather than as a fixed term mortgage. The line of credit makes it easy for the homeowner to use the value in the equity of the home as a liquid asset, drawing down cash as needed and paying it back on a monthly basis. The interest rate is adjustable and usually tied to a specified rate (e.g., prime rate or the yield on one-year Treasury bills).

Home equity loans can be used for any purpose, for example, to pay for a new automobile, a vacation, medical expenses, or a child's college education. Interest rates are low compared with other sources of instant credit such as credit cards. And interest is deductible so long as the loan falls within the parameters of I.R.C. § 163(h). See ¶¶ 5,610 and 5,620.

[¶ 5,240]

5. Statutory Protections for Borrowers

Borrowers, whether they are acquiring a purchase-money mortgage or a home equity loan, have surprisingly little knowledge about the cost of credit. The unsophisticated borrower is protected by a patchwork of state and federal legislation. Usury laws were imported from England in colonial times. These statutes placed a limit on the rate of interest that can be charged on loans. But with the deregulation of the credit industry in the 1980's, these state statutes were preempted as federal legislation lifted the limits for loans that were made to purchase a home. In 1982, Congress enacted the Alternative Mortgage Transaction Parity Act, 12 U.S.C. §§ 3801 et seq., similarly lifting limits that had applied to home equity loans.

By removing restrictions on how lending institutions structured loans, Congress encouraged creative lending techniques, which were thought to be essential to the survival of the consumer home credit industry. Despite deregulation, borrowers still enjoy some statutory protections.

[¶ 5,250]

a. Truth in Lending Act

The Truth in Lending Act (TILA), 15 U.S.C. §§ 1601 et seq., was originally enacted in 1968 and has been amended numerous times since then. To make the cost of credit more accessible to consumers, the statute requires that lenders disclose certain credit terms to borrowers before the loan is finalized. This is a pure disclosure statute. It does not set limits or restrictions. It presumes that consumers will be able to bargain better with lenders (or decide to forgo borrowing altogether) if they know the true cost of the credit. The disclosure rules apply to the extension of loans that are primarily for personal, family or household purposes. Specific requirements are contained in Regulation Z. See 12 C.F.R. §§ 226.1 et seq.

Regulation Z requires disclosure of a number of terms, but the most important ones are the finance charge and the annual percentage rate. A finance charge is defined as "the cost of consumer credit as a dollar amount. It includes any charge payable directly or indirectly by the consumer and imposed directly or indirectly by the creditor as an incident to or a condition of the extension of credit. It does not include any charge of a type payable in a comparable cash transaction." 12 C.F.R. § 226.4. The term includes interest, points, and mortgage broker fees, among other things. In addition, the lender must state the finance charge as an annual percentage rate (APR). To compute the APR, one must add up all finance charges, including points paid at closing, and adjust the stated interest rate on the loan to account for these additional payments. For example, a loan in the face amount of $100,000 at a stated interest rate of 7%, but with a total of $2,000 in additional finance charges, actually costs more than 7% per year. If the borrower pays the finance charges out of the loan proceeds, then the net amount loaned is only $98,000. Assuming a 30–year loan, the monthly payments, calculated on the basis of a $100,000 loan at 7%, will be $665.30. However, monthly payments of $665.30 on a net loan of $98,000, means that the APR is 7.2%. Under TILA, the lender must show that the finance charges add 0.2% to the APR.

There is no requirement that the costs included in the finance charge be separately stated. The disclosure can't tell you whether you are paying the right "price" by any objective standard. Rather the point of the disclosure is to allow you to compare options.

There is also no requirement that the borrower be informed of any "yield spread premium" that might be paid in connection with the loan. A "yield spread premium" occurs whenever the broker or loan officer handling the loan application acquires a loan from a secondary lender at an interest rate lower than that which the broker or loan officer charges the borrower. If X is willing to loan money at 5% to the prospective borrower and the broker is able to close a loan with that borrower at

5.25%, then the broker will pocket the extra 0.25% of interest. There is nothing wrong with this arrangement provided the broker either covered up front costs of the loan or provided services worth the 0.25% premium. But the borrower may never know that the ultimate lender was willing to make the loan at 5% because disclosure only requires that the actual interest rate of 5.25% be reported to the borrower.

The idea that disclosure will inform borrowers who can comparison-shop is valid in the abstract. In reality, borrowers do not understand the nature of the disclosures, they usually do not have time to comparison-shop, and they often experience the disclosures as "information over-load." For example, there would be little reason for concern about the "yield spread premium" if borrowers did enough comparison shopping to discover that their credit record was sufficient to buy them a loan at 5% rather than 5.25%. See generally William N. Eskridge, Jr., One Hundred Years of Ineptitude: The Need for Mortgage Rules Consonant with the Economic and Psychological Dynamics of the Home Sale and Loan Transaction, 70 Va. L. Rev. 1083, 1133–34 (1984).

[¶ 5,260]

b. *Real Estate Settlement Procedures Act*

Another disclosure statute that applies to home loans is the Real Estate Settlement Procedures Act (RESPA), 12 U.S.C. §§ 2601 et seq., which was originally enacted in 1974. It is also an anti-kickback statute. RESPA requires lenders and mortgage brokers to provide prospective borrowers certain information at the time they apply for a loan. They must provide a "Good Faith Estimate" (GFE) of settlement costs and a "Mortgage Servicing Disclosure Statement" which indicates whether the lender intends to service the loan or transfer it to a third party lender.

At closing a "settlement statement" is required which should show the actual settlement costs. A copy of the HUD form can be found in Appendix E. The form provides for settlement costs that are charged to the borrower to be separately stated, including fees for loan origination, loan discount, appraisal, credit report, lender's inspection, mortgage insurance application, and assumption of the mortgage (if applicable). Although the current rules require full disclosure of total settlement costs, they do not require a specific explanation of what those costs cover. A borrower may agree to pay a one point loan origination fee without considering whether that is a fair fee for the services provided by the loan officer or broker.

The anti-kickback provisions of RESPA prohibit anyone from receiving a premium payment for the purpose of steering settlement business toward the payor. For example, if a bank as lender agreed to split its loan origination fee with real estate agents who steered mortgage customers to the bank, the arrangement would violate RESPA.

Payments to loan officers and brokers who actually provide services are generally permissible so long as they payments are for actual services rendered. One of the shortcomings of RESPA is that it doesn't adequately monitor the value of services rendered. As a result, borrowers often pay settlement costs in excess of the value received.

An additional problem arises when loan officers or brokers are paid out of the interest charged to the borrower. This occurs when the interest actually charged is higher than the interest the ultimate lender would have been willing to charge. This "yield spread premium" need not be disclosed under either TILA or RESPA. Nonetheless, if the "yield spread premium" is in fact a payment of a kickback then it ought to be covered by the anti-kickback provisions of RESPA. Often, however, brokers are able to escape these provisions because of the exception for mortgages that are sold on the secondary market. Assume that Broker makes a loan to a client at 6%, knowing that he will ultimately sell the loan to Mortgage Company and that Mortgage Company will pay a premium for the loan because Mortgage Company would have been willing to make a loan to this client at 5%. Unless Broker provided services equal in value to the premium, the premium looks like a kickback. But if Broker funded the loan from his own funds or from any source other than Mortgage Company, the sale to Mortgage Company after the loan is closed is exempt from RESPA because it is a "bona fide secondary market transaction." See Chandler v. Norwest Bank Minnesota, 137 F.3d 1053 (8th Cir. 1998).

[¶ 5,270]

Question

A frequent complaint about the mortgage lending industry is that unsophisticated borrowers pay too much for mortgage loans. The current disclosure rules are not sufficient protection for such borrowers. Can you suggest some ways to improve the protections?

In answering the question, consider the following critique by Professors Engel and McCoy:

> Both RESPA and TILA have loopholes that hinder effective disclosure. Under TILA, significant costs are excluded from the finance charge and APR, meaning that the reported total cost of credit is too low. These exclusions include fees for credit reports, appraisals, inspections by lenders, flood certifications, document preparation, title searches, and title insurance, as well as notary fees, recording fees, and government taxes. RESPA's disclosure system has flaws in timing and enforcement. GFEs [good faith estimates] do not have to be provided until three days after application, after an application fee has already been paid. Furthermore, since lenders face no liability for errors on the GFE, estimates sometimes bear little relationship to actual costs. Both flaws mean that GFEs are not useful tools for comparison shopping. Similarly, while borrowers may request their HUD–1 settlement statements a day before closing, they do not need to be informed of that right. Furthermore, just as with the GFE, there is no requirement that HUD–1 statements be accurate. [Kathleen C. Engel & Patricia A. McCoy, A Tale of Three

Markets: The Law and Economics of Predatory Lending, 80 Tex. L. Rev. 1255, 1269 (2002).]

[¶ 5,280]

c. *Home Ownership and Equity Protection Act*

The most vulnerable borrowers are low to middle income families. They cannot borrow from the same sources that borrowers with solid credit ratings can. Lenders who make loans in this "sub-prime" market often structure loans that the borrower has no real chance of paying off. Making a loan to someone who has assets but no cash flow to make loan payments (asset-lending) is one common tactic. Another tactic is to keep refinancing the loan when payments aren't made on time, adding closing costs to the principal of the loan. Eventually the borrower will default and lose his or her home in the process. To combat some of these predatory lending techniques, in 1994 Congress amended the Truth in Lending Act to reinstate some protections for borrowers who were vulnerable to such practices. For a description of which loans are covered, see 15 U.S.C. § 1602(aa). Among other things, this statute prohibits the lender's use of prepayment penalties, balloon payments, and similar devices that were causing many homeowners to default on their loans and lose their homes. See 15 U.S.C. § 1639.

[¶ 5,290]

6. Types of Interest Arrangements

Lenders offer different arrangements for the payment of interest and principal. For example, a borrower might pay only interest for a period of time, followed by a balloon payment of the principal. Additionally, the lender and borrower may negotiate different interest rates, depending on whether the rate is fixed for the term of the loan or adjustable.

[¶ 5,300]

a. *Paying discount points*

The rate of interest can be adjusted if discount points are paid in advance at closing. A "point" is a shorthand way of referring to a fee paid at closing in the amount of 1% of the loan amount. "Discount points" are in effect prepaid interest. If you pay 1% on a $100,000 loan to acquire an interest rate of 5% rather than 5.25%, then you are paying $1,000 up front for the more attractive interest rate. One simple way to determine whether the payment of points is advisable is to ask how much money you will save each month by buying down the interest rate. On a $100,000 loan, for example, paying 5% rather than 5.25% will save you $15.38 per month in mortgage payments. You won't recoup your $1,000 up-front payment unless you hold on to the mortgage for a little over five years (65 months). So if you think you might refinance or sell within five years, paying the point for the lower rate would not make sense.

[¶ 5,310]

b. Adjustable rate mortgages

An adjustable rate mortgage (ARM) is a mortgage loan on which the interest rate can fluctuate. The terms of the fluctuation are set when the loan is made. These terms state the starting interest rate and how long it will remain fixed before any change occurs. This initial fixed rate period may be as short as 30 days or may last several years. The ARM borrower is agreeing to take the risk of rising interest rates in exchange for a lower starting interest rate. Because the ARM puts the risk on the borrower rather than the lender, ARM rates will always start out lower than fixed rates. The shorter the initial fixed rate period, the lower the starting interest rate will be.

While there is also some risk to the lender that the rates will fluctuate downward, lenders often protect against that risk by including a minimum rate or "floor" below which the rate will not fluctuate. And, if market rates do fall below those floors, then borrowers always have the option of refinancing at those lower rates, assuming that there is no prepayment penalty and that the transaction costs of refinancing are covered by the saving from the lower interest rate on the new loan.

In addition to specifying how long the initial rate will remain fixed, the ARM specifies how the new rate will be determined. In other words, changes in the rate are not left to the discretion of the lender, but rather are determined by an external standard, referred to as the index (e.g., prime rate or the yield on one-year Treasury bills) plus a margin adjustment (e.g., one point). When the initial fixed rate period ends, the new rate will kick in at the designated index plus margin adjustment. Future rate changes will occur in the same way periodically (e.g., annually) throughout the life of the loan.

Most ARMs also provide for a cap on rate increases, both at the time the rate changes and over the life of the loan. For example, an ARM might provide that the interest rate will be set each year at prime plus one point, but in no event will it increase more than two points in a year nor will it ever exceed 14%. The ARM may also provide for a minimum rate.

[¶ 5,320]

Problem

Barry is trying to decide how best to finance the $200,000 he needs to borrow to purchase a new home. He has sufficient savings to provide the estimated $35,000 needed at closing for down payment and closing costs. He is focusing on the costs and benefits of a fixed rate mortgage compared with an ARM. His banker tells him he can get a 30–year, fixed-rate mortgage at 5.75% plus payment of an additional point at closing. Monthly payments would be $1,167.15. Alternatively, he can get a one-year ARM at 4.25% for zero points at closing. Key terms of the ARM are: (1) the interest rate adjustment period is one year (i.e., rate changes occur once a year on the anniversary date of the loan); (2) the rate fluctuates at prime plus one; (3) the maximum increase each year is capped at 1%; (4) the rate will not fall below 4%; (5) the rate will not rise above 12%; (6) the loan will be amortized over 20 years. For the ARM, the monthly payments will start out at $1,238.47. The current prime rate is 3.25%. What are the pros and cons of each alternative and what do you think Barry should do?

Assume that Barry's lender offers him the following option on the fixed-rate mortgage: instead of paying one point at closing, Barry agrees to pay 1% of the outstanding balance on the loan in the event the loan is prepaid any time within the next 5 years. What are the pros and cons of this alternative and how does it affect the comparison of the fixed-rate loan with the ARM?

[¶ 5,330]

c. *Balloon mortgage*

A balloon mortgage requires the borrower to pay the loan in full prior to the full amortization period. It is really a short term loan, with a longer amortization period in order to create smaller monthly payments. For example, a borrower might borrow $200,000 at 5.75%, amortized over 30 years, but payable in full at the end of seven years. Monthly payments for the seven-year period would be the same as any 30–year mortgage, which in this example would be $1,167.15. At the end of seven years, however, the remaining principal (the balloon amount) would have to be paid in full. The amount of principal remaining after seven years of monthly payments (84 payments in all) would be $178,466.59. This sort of mortgage makes sense if the borrower thinks he will either want to refinance or sell within the seven-year period. Interest rates on balloons are slightly lower than a full 30–year term mortgage.

Balloon mortgages more closely resemble ARMs. For example, a five-year balloon that will have to be refinanced at the end of five years is similar to a five-year ARM with interest that remains at a low fixed rate for five years and then fluctuates according to the market. If the five-year interest rate were the same on the balloon and on the ARM, which type of loan would be preferable? The answer is: it depends. If one believes that interest rates will increase enough to trigger an increase in the rate of the ARM, then one should focus on the caps that apply to the ARM. Interest rates have not exploded in recent years, but in the late 1970's they rose by almost 9% over a five-year period. If interest rates increase by 9% over five years and the ARM has a cap that limited the increase to 6% over five years, then the ARM will turn out to be better than the balloon, which will have to be refinanced at whatever the market rate is. In other words, the caps available in the ARM give the borrower an element of protection that is not available in a balloon. In addition, the balloon requires a refinancing at the end of the term, which means that additional closing costs will be incurred. In contrast, the ARM merely adjusts the interest rates at the end of the term without charging additional costs. If the borrower believes that interest rates will go down in the future, perhaps even below the floor in a competitive ARM, then the balloon, followed by a refinancing, will make sense even if it does create some additional closing costs at the time of refinancing. In general, balloon loans do not offer protections such as caps and they can cause extra costs if they need to be refinanced. But they often offer lower interest rates than ARMs. Thus, if the borrower plans to sell within the balloon period, the balloon mortgage would be the preferred alternative simply because of the lower interest rate. In other cases, the benefit of the lower interest rate should be weighed against the potential extra costs of refinancing.

[¶ 5,340]

d. *Down payments, equity, and loan-to-value ratios*

In a conventional mortgage, the lender typically requires 20% of the price of the home to be paid at closing. If a buyer wants to make a lower down payment, then the lender will require the borrower to pay for private mortgage insurance (PMI). FHA guaranteed loans can be acquired with smaller down payments and VA loans sometimes provide a zero down payment option. Fannie Mae and Freddie Mac also influence what lenders will require as down payments. These two entities offer to purchase loans in the secondary market if they conform to certain requirements. Mortgages with low down payments will not bring as high a price on the secondary market. Knowing how much cash the mortgage will bring on the secondary market in advance of closing allows the direct lender to adjust closing costs accordingly.

Down payment requirements are usually expressed in terms of the loan-to-value ratio (sometimes called the loan-to-price ratio). Twenty percent down means that the lender is providing 80% of the selling price so the loan-to-value ratio is 80%. Zero down payment loans have a loan-to-value ratio of 100%.

The risk of default is extremely high with 100% loans because the purchaser has so little at risk. In addition, a borrower who has not managed to accumulate any funds to contribute to the down payment is likely to be a poor credit risk. From the lender's perspective, a 100% loan may make sense in a market in which home values are appreciating rapidly. But if values fall, the lender may not be able to recoup the amount of the loan at foreclosure. While the buyer/borrower is personally liable, as a legal matter, for any amount of the loan that is not realized through a foreclosure sale, the likelihood of recovering against such an individual is low. First of all, if the purchaser had any assets, he or she would not need a 100% loan. Secondly, the lender must first prove that the loan obligation was not satisfied in full as a result of the foreclosure sale and then institute legal proceedings against the borrower to recoup the balance. These activities take time and cost money. Finally, in some jurisdictions deficiency judgments are either strictly limited or completely barred.

For example, § 580b of the California Code of Civil Procedure provides:

> No deficiency judgment shall lie in any event after a sale of real property or an estate for years therein for failure of the purchaser to complete his or her contract of sale, or under a deed of trust or mortgage given to the vendor to secure payment of the balance of the purchase price of that real property or estate for years therein, or under a deed of trust or mortgage on a dwelling for not more than four families given to a lender to secure repayment of a loan which was in fact used to pay all or part of the purchase price of that dwelling occupied, entirely or in part, by the purchaser.

Arizona has a similar rule for certain residential property:

> If trust property of two and one-half acres or less which is limited to and utilized for either a single one-family or a single two-family dwelling is sold pursuant to the trustee's power of sale, no action may be maintained to recover any difference between the amount obtained by sale and the amount of the indebtedness and any interest, costs and expenses.

Ariz. Rev. Stat. § 33–814; see also Ariz. Rev, Stat. § 33–729 (deficiency judgment allowed only if borrower was responsible for a diminution in value of the mortgaged property).

As a result, home purchasers in California and Arizona are at risk of losing only their down payments, any other up-front costs paid at closing, and any equity in the property arising from subsequent payments.

As a general rule, borrowers will have to maintain sufficient funds in bank accounts to show that they have the resources to make the down payment. If the borrower is required to pay $20,000 down and expects to borrow half of that amount from a friend or family member, difficulties arise. The source of the down payment must not create additional obligations on behalf of the borrower and cannot create any possible liens against the property that will compete with the mortgagee's lien. If funds are being contributed by a friend or family member, the mortgagee typically requires that contributor to sign a statement verifying that the amount is a gift and not a loan.

Borrowers can borrow funds for the down payment if the borrowed funds are secured by something other than the new home. If the borrower already owns a home and is looking for a new home, then a "bridge loan" or "swing loan" may be the best way to borrow the money for the down payment on the new home. These loans are similar to home equity loans. The current home is used as security for the short-term loan and then when the current home is sold the "bridge loan" can be repaid. Using a "bridge loan" is preferable to making an offer to the seller of the new home that is contingent on selling the old home. Sellers typically view such contingencies unfavorably because they are not willing to take their property off the market for the period of time it might take to find a suitable buyer for the purchaser's old home.

[¶ 5,350]

e. Qualifying for a mortgage loan

To qualify for a loan the borrower must prove that he or she has the funds for the down payment and sufficient income to make the required monthly payments. Lenders typically determine how much a borrower can afford to pay for housing by applying a formula that tests estimated mortgage expenses against disposable monthly income. If the initial lender intends to sell the mortgage to an entity in the secondary market, then the requirements of the secondary mortgage purchaser will effectively determine whether the borrower can qualify for the mortgage. These formulas are available to lenders, to mortgage brokers, and to real estate agents. A home buyer can consult with his or her real estate agent to determine how much he or she is likely to be able to borrow. This process is called "pre-qualification," often shortened to "pre-qual."

Pre-qualification is not the same thing as pre-approval. A "pre-qual" is based on information that the borrower provides. To be approved, the information must be verified. The lender will want to verify the borrower's employment, income, debts, assets, and credit history. Once the necessary facts have been verified, the lender should issue the borrower a letter stating that the mortgage is approved on certain specific terms and that the approval is good for a specified time period.

To demonstrate the ability to make monthly payments, formulas usually look at the availability of monthly income after other debt service has been satisfied. Fannie Mae guidelines call this the "debt-to-income ratio." There is no set formula or ratio. Nonetheless guidelines typically specify a 25% to 30% mortgage-debt-to-income ratio and a 35% to 40% total-debt-to-income ratio. Thus, a person with monthly gross income of $4,000 should be able to qualify for a loan with monthly payments of $1,000 (25% of gross income) so long as his other debt payments are no higher than $600 per month. In this scenario, total debt would be $1,600, which is 40% of $4,000.

[¶ 5,360]

Problem

Reconsider Barry's situation in the problem at ¶ 5,320. He is looking at a proposed mortgage loan payment of approximately $1,200 per month for a $200,000 loan. Assume further that the mortgage will require monthly escrow payments for taxes and insurance of an additional $200 per month. Furthermore, Barry is already making payments of $700 per month on other debts (e.g., student loans, car payments). He has gross income of $5,000 per month. Will he qualify under the Fannie Mae guidelines?

[¶ 5,370]

f. Appraisals

The lender will want to be sure that the home being purchased is valued high enough to justify the amount being borrowed to finance the purchase. For example, in a conventional mortgage the lender will typically lend up to 80% of the value of the home without charging an additional fee for private mortgage insurance. Since the mortgage is likely to be sold on the secondary market, the appraisal must be done by an appraiser who will be approved by the ultimate purchaser of the loan. For example, HUD maintains a list of certified appraisers for FHA mortgages. The appraisal is for the direct benefit of the lender, although it obviously benefits the borrower as well.

Appraisers are professionals licensed by the state. They will usually prepare a detailed appraisal report using one of two methods, the sales comparison approach and the cost approach, to determine a value for the subject property. The sales comparison approach identifies a number of comparable properties ("comps"), usually at least three, that have sold recently and then makes adjustments for the differences between the "comps" and the subject property. Remodeled kitchens, extra fireplaces, number of bedrooms, and location can all affect the price of properties and should be taken into account. The cost approach estimates the cost of constructing a replacement property and then adjusts for the age of the subject property by applying a depreciation factor. The borrower pays for the appraisal and should receive a copy of the final report.

[¶ 5,380]

7. Preparing for Closing

The real estate contract is not binding as long as it is subject to contingencies. Contingencies, in addition to the buyer's ability to qualify for mortgage financing, may include such things as a satisfactory home inspection, sale of the buyer's current principal residence, or completion of specified repairs by the seller. When the ability to meet these contingencies is within the control of either the seller or the buyer, there is an obligation to make a good faith effort to meet the contingency. See Bushmiller v. Schiller, 368 A.2d 1044 (Md. Ct. Spec. App. 1977) (buyer must engage in reasonable efforts to obtain financing even if efforts are likely to be fruitless).

[¶ 5,390]

a. Title opinions and title insurance

Unless the contract calls for something less (or more) than marketable title, the seller must be able to convey "marketable title" by the time of closing. Marketable title is a title that is free and clear of encumbrances or other title defects. If encumbrances show up in a title search, then it is the seller's responsibility to remove them before closing. If the property is subject to a current mortgage that will be paid off from the sales proceeds at closing, then the documents at closing should include a release of that encumbrance.

Most buyers protect themselves by purchasing title insurance at closing. Most lenders require title insurance before they will fund the loan. Much of this is driven by the secondary mortgage market, including Fannie Mae and Freddie Mac. Purchasers of mortgage loans in the secondary market uniformly require title insurance as a pre-requisite for purchase. By contrast, local banks may be willing to rely on a lawyer's opinion letter certifying marketable title. Even in areas where title insurance is not customarily used, lenders will often require borrowers to obtain title insurance to make the mortgage loan marketable in the secondary market.

[¶ 5,400]

b. Title insurance and recording

Title insurance, even though now commonly required by mortgagees, is subject to much criticism. Insurance is thought to be a product that protects against risks. Thus, title insurance should protect purchasers against the possibility of defects in title that could make the property unmarketable. Critics of the title insurance industry point to the fact that most policies contain exceptions for any risks that are discovered in the title examination process.

If an unencumbered chain of title is established from a close examination of the deed records, then the purchaser is entitled to rely on the record of clear title. A good title examination should uncover any potential clouds on the title, including misfiled deeds so long as they are in the grantor/grantee index. If a review of the deed records does turn up an impediment to the title (e.g., an outstanding lien or other encumbrance), then the seller should be required to remove the impediment. Title insurance does not insure against these types of impediments.

Title insurance does insure against negligent title examinations. So if the examiner fails to discover a defect that later is discovered and creates a cloud on the title, the title insurance company would be liable. A lawyer who does a title examination negligently would also be liable, but title insurance companies tend to have deeper pockets than individual lawyers and thus are more likely to be able to satisfy such liabilities. In addition, title insurance does protect against such things as forged and misfiled deeds that the most diligent title examiners are unlikely to discover.

[¶ 5,410]

c. Breach before closing

Failure to meet any of the contingencies listed in the sales contract does not create a breach unless the party relying on the contingency failed to make a good faith effort. A seller may breach by refusing to convey or failing to provide marketable title. A buyer may breach by failing to purchase. Remedies include specific performance (e.g., the buyer may require the seller to convey), damages (e.g., the seller recovers from a recalcitrant buyer an amount equal to the benefit of the bargain), or rescission (e.g., the seller may keep the good faith deposit if the buyer breaches, or the buyer may demand return of the deposit if the seller breaches).

[¶ 5,420]

8. The Closing

At closing, the buyer pays the purchase price and the seller conveys the property by deed. While financial arrangements are made before closing, the documents (e.g., note and mortgage) are executed at closing. All documents from the closing that affect title are then promptly recorded.

The agent in charge of the closing may be a representative of the title insurance company, the buyer's attorney, or the attorney or loan officer for the lending institution. The agent prepares a closing statement in advance of the closing which should be reviewed by both buyer and seller. This statement allocates certain crucial closing costs to one party or the other. Closing statements vary greatly according to local practice. Often standard forms used by lenders are difficult to understand and don't reflect anything other than the borrower's view of the transaction. Attorneys should draft closing statements that state the details of the transaction in a format that their clients can understand. Some sample statements follow. Note the interdependence of the two statements regarding pro-ration of property taxes. The statements assume that the purchaser will pay the property tax bill when it is received (probably in the fall) because it is the purchaser as owner who will be at risk of losing the property in the future if taxes are not paid. Property taxes are assessed once a year, typically on January 1, but when a transfer in ownership occurs during the year, the liability for the taxes is prorated between the owners based on their respective periods of ownership. These sample statements assume a June 1 closing date. As a result, the seller is liable for the first five months of the current year's property tax. Since the tax will in fact be paid by the purchaser, the purchaser is in effect assuming this tax liability of the seller. As a result the amount to be paid to the seller by the purchaser at closing should be reduced by the five months of tax liability.

Note that the sample borrower's mortgage closing statement reproduced below does not reflect the five months' tax payment that the purchasers (borrowers) will be making on behalf of the seller. That amount, $1,470.00, is charged to the seller on the seller's statement and reduces the amount of cash due to the seller. The purchasers, James and Ellen Smith, will pay the total tax bill of $3,528.00 when it falls due. When they file their federal income tax return, however, they will only be entitled to deduct their share of the total tax bill, which is $2,058.00. If all they have from the closing is their own closing statement, it may be difficult for them to calculate how much of the $3,528.00 should be deducted under I.R.C. § 164. See ¶ 5,680.

Some buyers' statements will also reflect the mortgagee's requirement that property taxes and hazard insurance be paid by the mortgagee as the buyer's agent. This arrangement will require the establishment of an escrow reserve from which the payments will be made by the mortgagee. To protect the mortgagee against rising property taxes and insurance costs, the escrow must truly function as a reserve. That means there must be a sufficient balance available to make these payments, even when the amounts increase. A prepayment equal to three months worth of estimated costs is typically required. This amount is charged to the borrower at closing.

The monthly contribution to the reserve is calculated based on current costs and is added to the monthly mortgage payment of principal and interest (PI). Once the charges for taxes and insurance (TI) are added, the total monthly charge is referred to by shorthand as PITI.

Paying these funds to the mortgagee in advance of the time the payments are due to the taxing authority and insurance company allows the mortgagee to collect the interest earned on these funds while held in escrow. For sufficiently affluent borrowers, mortgagee banks will agree to forgo the escrow. Whenever possible, the borrower should request this treatment in order to keep the interest earned on the funds. Low interest rates have made this benefit less attractive in recent years, however. And some borrowers prefer the forced savings caused by the escrow requirements and the security of knowing that the bank is taking care of the payment of taxes and insurance.

Compare the following sample closing statements with the HUD–1 form in Appendix E. For most sellers and purchasers, a HUD–1 form must be made available, unless they waive their right to it. The form can be modified in accordance with local practice. And, information that is only relevant to one of the parties need not be disclosed to the other party.

Which form do you find easier to understand? Can you make suggestions that would improve the sample statements? Can you make suggestions that would improve the HUD form?

SAMPLE MORTGAGE CLOSING STATEMENT

Date: June 1, 2005

Address of Property: 2214 Branch Lane, Marshalltown
Borrowers: Smith, James and Ellen
Lender: First Bank of Marshalltown

Type of Mortgage FHA ( ) GI ( ) Convent (X)	Amount of Loan	$200,000
Payments to Lender:		
Application Fee	$	50.00
Appraisal Fee		250.00
Credit Report		50.00
Service Fee		0.00
Processing Fee		0.00
Origination Fee		500.00
Points		0.00
Other		0.00
Total	$	850.00
Payments to Lender to establish escrow reserve		
Taxes 3 months @ 294.00	$	882.00
Insurance 3 months @ 86.00		258.00
Mtg. Ins.		0.00
Total	$	1,140.00
TOTAL Payments to Lender	$	1,990.00
Payments to Third Parties:		
Property Taxes and Assessments	$	0.00
Title Examination		0.00
Survey		0.00
Title Insurance		985.00
Attorney Fees		250.00
Recording Fees		14.00
Broker/agent commission		0.00
Real estate transfer tax		0.00
Paid to Seller		198,000.00
Total	$	199,249.00
TOTAL Payments on behalf of borrower	$	201,239.00
Less Loan Amount		(200,000.00)
Closing costs due from borrower at closing	$	1,239.00
Payment to seller due from borrower at closing*		44,530.00
TOTAL CASH NEEDED AT CLOSING	$	**45,769.00**

* See Seller's Closing Statement.

SAMPLE SELLER'S CLOSING STATEMENT

Date: June 1, 2005

Address of Property: 2214 Branch Lane, Marshalltown
Sellers: Brown, Virginia
Buyers: Smith, James and Ellen

Total Sales Price		$ 245,000.00
Less Earnest Money Deposit	$ (1,000.00)	
Balance Due at closing	$ 244,000.00	
Add for adjusted items		
Unearned insurance	0.00	
Escrow adjustment	0.00	
Credit for interest	0.00	
Subtract for Items Charged to Seller		
Proration of 2005 taxes (5 months)	$ (1,470.00)	
Adjusted Sales Price (due Seller)		$ 243,530.00
Due Seller from First Bank	$ 198,000.00	
Due Seller from Buyer	44,530.00	
Due Seller from Escrow	1,000.00	
Total due Seller	$ 243,530.00	
Disbursement of Total due Seller:		
Pay off mortgage to Second Bank	$ 154,000.00	
Abstract Costs	120.00	
Transfer Stamps	275.00	
Attorney fee	50.00	
Real estate commission—6%	14,700.00	
Total Disbursements	$ 169,145.00	
Cash Balance Due Seller after Disbursements		$ 74,385.00

F.   TAKING TITLE TO REAL PROPERTY

[¶ 5,430]

Title should be conveyed at closing by a warranty deed. A general warranty deed is most common, although sometimes a special warranty deed is used. A quitclaim deed offers no warranty of title and is usually used only to convey contingent interests rather than fee title.

How should the grantee be listed on the deed? If there is only one grantee, the answer is usually simple. However, since some states provide rights to a grantee's spouse in property acquired during marriage, it is often wise to indicate whether the grantee is married or single.

If the grantees are a married couple, the deed should indicate that they are married and should also state whether they take as joint tenants with right of survivorship, as tenants in common, or, in states where the estate is recognized, as tenants by the entirety. In community property states, the deed should indicate whether the property is to be held as community property or separate property. In some community property states (e.g., California and Texas) it is possible to hold community property with right of survivorship, so if survivorship rights are intended, that should be stated explicitly.

Unmarried couples often purchase homes together. In such cases, it is especially important to be clear about the purchasers' intent. State laws presume that property taken jointly is held as tenants in common. So if the couple wants to hold as joint tenants, the deed should say "as joint tenants with right of survivorship and not as tenants in common."

Married couples who own property jointly and then decide to split up generally have the benefit of state divorce laws to help them determine how the property is to be divided upon divorce. Unmarried couples have no such system to resolve their disputes. However, at least two states (Vermont and California) allow certain couples who cannot marry (e.g., same-sex couples) to form an alternative relationship that confers similar property rights, including the right to a judicial division of property upon dissolution of the relationship.

Absent such procedures, a person who jointly owns a home with another needs to plan in advance for the contingency that the relationship may end and the partners may not want to continue living together. Signing a buy-sell agreement to cover such a contingency is a good plan. Alternatively, at the time the relationship ends, either partner can seek to have a court partition the property and order a sale, in order to divide the sales proceeds. A court-ordered sale of one's home is not a particularly attractive solution. Court oversight imposes additional transaction costs when compared with a voluntary sale. To protect unmarried couples who purchase homes together, lawyers should draft contracts that explain in advance exactly what will happen if one of the partners decides to end the relationship and sell the property. A typical buy-sell agreement would provide that if one of the partners elects to sell, the other partner has an option to purchase the property. The contract should either specify the terms of the purchase or set forth a clear process for determining the terms when the option arises. If purchasing on credit is contemplated, the contract should specify the terms of the loan as well.

[¶ 5,440]

1. Joint Tenancy versus Tenancy in Common

The primary advantage of joint tenancy is that upon the death of the first joint tenant, full ownership of the property vests in the survivor without having to go through probate. Probate proceedings vary from state to state, but often they can be time-consuming and costly. Joint tenancy is not always preferred, however. Sometimes couples do not want the jointly owned residence to be owned outright by the survivor. This would be true in the case of a second marriage where the joint tenants want to benefit their separate families rather than the surviving spouse at the death of the first spouse. At the same time, a tenancy in common may not be the preferred solution because at the death of one spouse, the surviving spouse would become a co-owner with the deceased spouse's heirs or devisees.

Joint tenancy can also create estate tax problems. Assume, for example, that husband and wife hold all of their property, with a combined value of $10 million, as joint tenants with right of survivorship. At husband's death, the wife will become the sole owner of all of the property, which will pass to her free of estate tax by virtue of the unlimited marital deduction. But at the wife's subsequent death, all of the property will be included in her gross estate. And since everything passed to the wife by right of survivorship, the husband's estate tax exemption ($1.5 million in 2005 and increasing to $3.5 million in 2009) will be wasted. See ¶¶ 4,020, 4,230 and 4,400.

The right of survivorship incident to the joint tenancy can be defeated by severance. At common law, the joint tenancy was thought to be dependent upon the four unities of interest, title, time, and possession, and if any one of the unities was destroyed, then the joint tenancy was destroyed. A conveyance by one of the joint tenants to another party destroys the unity and automatically severs the joint tenancy whether or not the parties so intend. A severance causes the joint tenancy to be converted into a tenancy in common. Unintentional severances can occur when one joint tenant executes a contract to sell the property or to mortgage it. While the results vary based on state law, any act that conveys an interest in the jointly owned property runs the risk of destroying the unity of title, as well as the unity of possession. Thus, it is important to consider this possibility before agreeing to sell or mortgage the property. And it is always advisable to execute a will that leaves any potentially devisable interest in the joint property to the intended beneficiary, i.e., the other joint tenant.

[¶ 5,450]

Problems

1. Harry and Wanda were married five years ago. It is a second marriage for both of them. They have discussed their estate plans with each other and they agree that that Harry's children, Clem and Claude, should inherit his wealth and that Wanda's daughter, Debby, should inherit hers. They currently own their home, purchased jointly, as joint tenants with right of survivorship. They both agree that the survivor should have the right to live in the home until the survivor's death if he or she desires. What do you advise them to do about title?

2. Father and son own investment property as joint tenants with right of survivorship. They agree to sell the property and execute a contract of sale to Polly Purchaser for a sales price of $500,000. If father dies before closing, will son be entitled to the entire $500,000 or will half of that amount belong to father's estate? If father's estate is entitled to half of the proceeds, but father intended son to receive the full amount, what should they do to effectuate that intent?

[¶ 5,460]

2. Tenancy by the Entirety

At common law, under the doctrine of coverture, a married woman's right to own property was practically nonexistent. If property was conveyed to both husband and wife, the presumption was that they took as tenants by the entirety. The tenancy by the entirety estate carried a right of survivorship that could not be severed unilaterally. As with any other property owned by the wife, the husband had full management power of the estate. When married women's property acts were enacted in the late 1800's and early 1900's, many states refused to recognize the tenancy by the entirety estate, reasoning that its existence stemmed from the doctrine of coverture, which the married women's property acts were intended to abolish. Today about half the states recognize the tenancy by the entirety. The rights of management have been altered by the married women's property acts, but in all cases the estate is characterized by an indestructible right of survivorship.

[¶ 5,470]

3. Community Property versus Separate Property

There are eight community property states (Arizona, California, Idaho, Louisiana, Nevada, New Mexico, Texas and Washington). Wisconsin has adopted the Uniform Marital Property Act, which applies community property rules to marital property in much the same way that the community property states do. More recently Alaska has adopted the Uniform Marital Property Act, but unlike Wisconsin and the eight traditional community property states, Alaska makes the regime optional rather than automatic. It is not yet clear whether Alaska community property will be recognized as community property for federal tax purposes. In all of these states there is a strong presumption that property acquired during marriage is community property even if title is taken in some other form (e.g., by the husband alone or by husband and wife as joint tenants).

There are tax advantages to community property, the primary one being that when the marital community terminates at the death of one spouse, both halves of the community property get a "fresh start" basis under I.R.C. § 1014(b)(6) (providing a basis in the entire community property equal to its fair market value, so long as half of it is included in the deceased spouse's gross estate). Joint tenancy property, by contrast, only enjoys a step-up in the 50% of the property that is included in the decedent's estate under I.R.C. § 2040(b).

Example: Husband and wife own Sea-acre, a coastline retreat that they use as a second home. They purchased it for $200,000 and it is now worth $1,200,000. Husband dies leaving Sea-acre by will to wife, and wife wants to sell the property at its current fair market value. If the property is held as community property, wife's basis in the property will be $1,200,000. When she sells it for $1,200,000, she will have no gain. But if they held the property as joint tenants or as tenants in common, wife would have received a step-up in basis only as to the half that was included in husband's gross estate ($600,000); combined with her original basis in her half ($100,000), this would leave her with a total basis of $700,000. The sale for $1,200,000 would produce a gain of $500,000.

If Sea-acre was the wife's principal residence at the time of sale, I.R.C. § 121 would allow her to exclude a portion of the gain. But § 121 limits the exclusion to $250,000 of gain. See ¶ 5,710.

This benefit of stepping up the basis to fair market value at death is sufficiently valuable that couples who buy property in non-community property states with community funds should be careful to preserve the community character of the new property. Many states will recognize that claim either under conflict of laws principles or under statutory authority. See the Uniform Disposition of Community Property Rights at Death Act, adopted by almost a third of the states. See, e.g., Ore. Rev. Stat. §§ 112.705 et seq.

[¶ 5,480]

4. Rights of Unsecured Creditors

Secured creditors can enforce their rights against the property that secures the payment of the loan. Unsecured creditors are a different story. As a general rule, an unsecured creditor who pursues his claim to judgment can reach any interest in property that the debtor can reach. Many states, however, provide special protection for homesteads. In some states (e.g., Texas and Iowa), unsecured creditors cannot reach the homestead. In other states, the homestead protection is limited to a set dollar figure (e.g., in California the limit is $50,000 to $150,000 depending on the family status of the debtor; in Georgia the limit is $10,000 to $20,000 depending on marital status). In a handful of states, homesteads are not protected from creditors' claims (e.g, Pennsylvania and Delaware). See ¶ 10,255.

For non-homestead property, the unsecured creditor's rights will vary depending on how the debtor holds title to the property. In the case of a joint tenancy, a creditor who attaches one joint tenant's interest cannot succeed to the debtor's contingent right of survivorship. Under the doctrine of unities, a conveyance of the debtor's interest to a creditor severs the joint tenancy and thereby creates a tenancy in common between the non-debtor tenant and the creditor.

Tenancies by the entirety are somewhat different. Under the common law doctrine of coverture, the husband's creditors could reach the entireties property but the wife's creditors could not. Once states began to recognize the principle of gender equality in marriage, they were faced with the question of whether to equalize the spouses' respective rights by allowing each spouse's creditors to reach the property or, alternatively, by denying each spouse's creditors the right to reach the property. Most states have adopted the latter rule. As a result, the tenancy by the entirety provides special protection for married couples with debts. Vermont extends this benefit to same-sex couples who enter into a civil union. Hawaii extends this benefit to any couple that registers as reciprocal beneficiaries. See Haw. Rev. Stat. § 509–2.

The rights of unsecured creditors in community property states vary depending on whether the debt is a separate debt of one spouse or is a debt of the community. Community property is liable for community debts in all community property states. Whether community property can be seized to satisfy the separate debts of one spouse varies from state to state. In some states the debtor spouse's interest in community assets can be reached to satisfy any debt that arose during the marriage and in other states, the community assets can be reached only for debts that were incurred for the benefit of the community. As a general rule, one spouse's separate property cannot be reached by a creditor of the other spouse to satisfy that spouse's separate debts.

G. FAILURE TO PAY THE MORTGAGE

[¶ 5,490]

Failure to make timely payments on the mortgage debt constitutes an event of default and causes the remaining balance of the debt to become due. Once this acceleration of the mortgage debt occurs, the borrower will have to pay the full amount of the outstanding debt to "redeem" the property from the lender.

Defaults can sometimes be cured if the lender is willing to work with the borrower. But if the lender is not willing to restructure the loan or to accept past due payments after default has occurred, and if the borrower cannot pay off the mortgage, the lender will seek an alternative way to satisfy the loan. The most common remedy in these situations is foreclosure. The mortgage documents give the lender the right to foreclose loans in default, usually by auctioning off the property at a public sale to the highest bidder. In practice, the highest bidder is often the mortgagee bank. As a result, the lender will end up with title to the property. Most mortgagees do not want to become property managers, so their aim is to resell the property as soon as possible. In fact, most mortgagees would prefer to avoid a foreclosure sale.

There are two primary alternatives to foreclosure available to the mortgagee: (1) restructure the original loan arrangement so that the borrower can keep the realty and pay off the debt under terms that are possible for the borrower, or (2) accept a deed in lieu of foreclosure.

[¶ 5,500]

1. Restructuring the Debt

Borrowers who have trouble paying their bills often deal first with small debts (e.g., credit card balances). But the most important debt to worry about is the mortgage, which can cause the borrower to lose his or her home. Because lenders may not be interested in becoming property owners and landlords, borrowers are often in a better position than they may realize in seeking to renegotiate a mortgage. This is particularly true if the mortgagee is a local bank or thrift institution.

There are two ways to restructure the debt. One is to refinance the outstanding debt on new and different terms. A lower interest rate or a longer amortization schedule will decrease the monthly payments. In this event the borrower is really paying off the existing loan with a new loan.

There are several key income tax questions that arise in such refinancing cases. You may not be able to answer these questions until you have studied the income tax rules that apply to mortgaged property (see ¶ 5,520.) But it is important to refer here to one rule regarding the deductibility of interest. To qualify for the home mortgage deduction, the interest must be incurred either on indebtedness to purchase the property or on a home equity loan. The question that arises when original purchase money debt is refinanced is whether the interest on the new debt qualifies as interest paid on acquisition indebtedness. The answer is that the interest does qualify so long as the outstanding loan amount is not increased. If additional closing costs are added to the outstanding balance, the additional amount is not acquisition indebtedness, but it should nonetheless qualify as home equity indebtedness. That would make it deductible under the provision allowing for interest deductions on home equity loans of up to $100,000 (see ¶ 5,610).

The other way to restructure the debt is for the mortgagee to reduce the principal amount of the outstanding loan. A reduction in principal amount generally gives rise to cancellation of indebtedness income because the cancellation "frees up" assets in the debtor's hands. See United States v. Kirby Lumber Co., 284 U.S. 1 (1931); I.R.C. § 61(a)(12). The Internal Revenue Service has ruled that cancellation of indebtedness income occurs in such cases whether the mortgage loan is recourse or nonrecourse. See Rev. Rul. 82–202, 1982–2 C.B. 35; Rev. Rul. 91–31, 1991–1 C.B. 19. Unless some exception to recognition is available under I.R.C. § 108, the income must be recognized for tax purposes. To the extent the cancelled debt is of accrued interest that, if paid, would have been deductible, the cancellation does not trigger taxable income. See I.R.C. § 108(e)(2). For further discussion of debt cancellation, see ¶ 3,100.

[¶ 5,510]

2. Deed in Lieu of Foreclosure

Once the borrower is in default, the mortgagee has the right to institute foreclosure proceedings. In a foreclosure the mortgagee sells the property for a sum that in most cases will satisfy the outstanding indebtedness. But if the property is worth less than the outstanding mortgage balance, the mortgagee also has the right to collect the deficiency from the mortgagor, provided the mortgage note was a recourse one.

Often, however, to avoid the costs of those proceedings, the mortgagee will be willing to accept a deed in lieu of foreclosure. In addition, mortgagees are often willing to forego their right to collect deficiencies because defaulting mortgagors generally do not have ready funds or liquid assets available to satisfy the deficiency. The specific details of such arrangements can vary widely, but they often include the mortgagee's agreement to accept the realty in full satisfaction of the outstanding debt, even if the property is worth less than the outstanding loan amount. If the property is worth more than the outstanding loan balance, then the borrower should either refinance the loan to protect his equity or sell the property to pay off the loan and cash out the equity.

[¶ 5,520]

3. Income tax consequences

A deed in lieu of foreclosure is a transfer of the property to the lender in exchange for the lender's agreement that the outstanding debt has been satisfied. In such an exchange, the transferor's gain or loss is determined under I.R.C. § 1001 by subtracting the basis in the transferred property from the "amount realized." In Commissioner v. Tufts, 461 U.S. 300 (1983), the Supreme Court held that, in the case of a nonrecourse mortgage loan, the "amount realized" under § 1001 is the face amount of the outstanding loan, even if that amount is greater than the value of the property. By contrast, in Rev. Rul. 90–16, 1990–1 C.B. 13, the Internal Revenue Service has taken the position that, in the case of a recourse mortgage loan, a deed in lieu of foreclosure should be bifurcated into two transactions: (1) a disposition of property under § 1001 with an "amount realized" equal to the value of the transferred property, and (2) forgiveness of indebtedness income to the extent the face amount of the outstanding loan exceeds the value of the property.

Example: Dora Debtor purchased a vacation home for $100,000, subject to a nonrecourse mortgage of $90,000. Five years later, when the balance on the mortgage was still $90,000 and the fair market value of the property had declined to $80,000, she voluntarily conveyed the property to the mortgagee bank by deed in lieu of foreclosure. The transaction is viewed as a sale to the mortgagee bank in the amount of $90,000. Since her basis in the property was $100,000, she realizes a loss of $10,000 on the transaction. But the loss is not deductible because the home is held for personal use rather than for business or profit. On the other hand, if the $90,000 mortgage loan had been fully recourse, the transfer to the mortgagee bank should be bifurcated into two transactions: (1) a sale for $80,000, producing a nondeductible loss of $20,000, and (2) cancellation of indebtedness income in the amount of $10,000.

Note: If the taxpayer is insolvent or otherwise qualifies under I.R.C. § 108, the cancellation of indebtedness income may be excluded from gross income. See ¶ 3,100.

[¶ 5,530]

Questions

1.   Does this difference in tax result between recourse and nonrecourse mortgages make sense?

2.   Although most home mortgages are recourse, some states prohibit deficiency judgments when a foreclosure sale fails to produce a sufficiently high sales price to satisfy the mortgage in full. Should these mortgages be treated as nonrecourse?

3.   Should we have one single tax rule for all foreclosures and deeds in lieu of foreclosure whenever the fair market value of the property is less than the outstanding balance? If so, what should that rule be?

H. TRANSFERS OF MORTGAGED PROPERTY

[¶ 5,540]

When a homeowner sells his or her home to a new owner, the buyer typically obtains his or her own financing and, at closing, the existing mortgage on the property is paid in full. However, it is sometimes desirable to sell the property "subject to" the existing mortgage. This alternative would be particularly attractive to a buyer who might have trouble securing his own financing or who might be facing a higher interest rate on a new mortgage than the one on the existing mortgage. If buyer and seller can agree, seller might transfer the property to the buyer in exchange for a cash down payment and the buyer's agreement to continue making mortgage payments. There are some risks in this transaction. From the seller's point of view, for example, if the buyer fails to make the mortgage payments, the seller's credit rating will be negatively affected.

[¶ 5,550]

1. Due on Sale Clauses

Mortgages typically include a provision that causes the outstanding balance of the mortgage debt automatically to fall due whenever the mortgagor transfers the property. This provision is called a "due on sale" clause, although it usually applies to any type of transfer, including gifts and long-term leases. There are at least two reasons for a lender to include a "due on sale" clause in a mortgage. First, the loan was made on the basis of the original borrower's credit record. If the property is to be sold to a new owner with the understanding that the new owner will make the mortgage payments, the lender will want an opportunity to approve the new owner. The typical "due on sale" clause requires that the lender be notified of any intended transfer and approve the new owner. A second reason for including a "due on sale" clause is that, in times of rising interest rates, the lender will not want to continue holding the mortgage at the lower interest rate. Accelerating the mortgage will allow the lender to refinance at the higher interest rate.

In the 1970's, during a time of rapidly increasing interest rates, several states struck down the application of "due on sale" clauses when they were enforced by lenders primarily to gain a higher interest rate. The theory was that the clauses created an unreasonable restraint on alienation or, alternatively, that they were unconscionable. The federal government responded by defending such clauses in federal mortgages. Ultimately Congress enacted the Garn–St. Germain Depository Institutions Act in 1982, validating the "due on sale clause" and preempting state law with respect to all mortgages. 12 U.S.C. § 1701j–3. Today, "due on sale" clauses are generally enforceable.

The standard "due on sale" clause in a Fannie Mae mortgage instrument provides as follows:

> *Transfer of the Property or a Beneficial Interest in Borrower.* If all or any part of the Property or any interest in it is sold or transferred (or if a beneficial interest in Borrower is sold or transferred and Borrower is not a natural person) without Lender's prior written consent, Lender may, at its option, require immediate payment in full of all sums secured by this Security Instrument. However, this option shall not be exercised by Lender if exercise is prohibited by federal law as of the date of this Security Instrument.

> If Lender exercises this option, Lender shall give Borrower notice of acceleration. The notice shall provide a period of not less than 30 days from the date the notice is delivered or mailed within which Borrower

must pay all sums secured by this Security Instrument. If Borrower fails to pay these sums prior to the expiration of this period, Lender may invoke any remedies permitted by this Security Instrument without further notice or demand on Borrower.

Note that the clause applies to any transfer of the property *or any interest* in the property. The regulations provide that "a sale or transfer means the conveyance of real property or any right, title or interest therein, whether legal or equitable, whether voluntary or involuntary, by outright sale, deed, installment sale contract, land contract, contract for deed, leasehold interest with a term greater than three years, lease-option contract or any other method of conveyance of real property interests." See 12 C.F.R. § 591.2(b).

Certain transfers are excluded:

(1) the creation of a lien or other encumbrance subordinate to the lender's security instrument which does not relate to a transfer of rights of occupancy in the property;

(2) the creation of a purchase money security interest for household appliances;

(3) a transfer by devise, descent, or operation of law on the death of a joint tenant or tenant by the entirety;

(4) the granting of a leasehold interest of three years or less not containing an option to purchase;

(5) a transfer to a relative resulting from the death of a borrower;

(6) a transfer where the spouse or children of the borrower become an owner of the property;

(7) a transfer resulting from a decree of a dissolution of marriage, legal separation agreement, or from an incidental property settlement agreement, by which the spouse of the borrower becomes an owner of the property;

(8) a transfer into an inter vivos trust in which the borrower is and remains a beneficiary and which does not relate to a transfer of rights of occupancy in the property; or

(9) any other transfer or disposition described in regulations prescribed by the Federal Home Loan Bank Board.

See 12 U.S.C. § 1701j–3(d).

Thus, a homeowner may give or sell an interest in his home to his spouse or child without triggering the due on sale clause, but a transfer to a homeowner's domestic partner or sibling should be cleared with the lender. Transfers at death are excluded, although when exclusions three and five are considered together, they suggest that unless the transfer is by means of a joint tenancy (which most scholars would argue is not really a "transfer"), the transfer at death must be to a relative. It is yet to be determined whether a same-sex spouse, a partner in a civil union who is given spousal status under Vermont law, or a domestic partner in California who is given similar status, can qualify as a "relative." Recall that the defense of Marriage Act, 1 U.S.C. § 7, denies recognition to same-sex marriages for purposes of federal law.

Exception number 8 is important for homeowners who wish to put their property in a revocable inter vivos trust in order to avoid probate. See ¶ 2,350. The transfer will not trigger the due on sale clause. Nonetheless, some practitioners routinely inform mortgagees whenever such transactions occur, just to make sure that there is no misunderstanding.

The risk in making any transfer is that the lender will discover the transfer and exercise the right to accelerate the mortgage and demand payment of the full balance. Of course the lender will first have to find out about the transfer. And if the owner does not notify the lender, how will the lender learn of the transfer? While discovery of the transfer by the lender may be only a remote possibility, it can happen. During the 1970's, some lenders were known to spend time checking recently recorded deeds to determine whether one of their borrowers might have violated the provisions of a due on sale clause.

The safest course of action is to notify the lender of the transfer and ask for verification that the transfer will not trigger the due on sale clause. In cases in which there is a new purchaser, clearly triggering the due on sale clause, and the purchaser wishes to assume the existing mortgage, the lender will have to be a party to the transaction. If the lender agrees to substitute the purchaser on the mortgage at an interest rate that is satisfactory to the lender, then the due on sale clause cannot be enforced. "Upon such agreement ..., a lender shall release the existing borrower from all obligations under the loan instruments, and the lender is deemed to have made a new loan to the existing borrower's successor in interest." See 12 C.F.R. 591.5(b)(4).

[¶ 5,560]

Problem

Which of the following do you think literally triggers the Fannie Mae "due on sale" clause?

(a) Ann's sister Betty comes to live with her for an indeterminate amount of time after the death of Betty's husband.

(b) Ann and Betty execute a written lease agreement giving Betty the right to share the home with Ann for as long as Ann lives in the home.

(c) Ann and Betty enter into a written agreement under which Betty will pay half the mortgage payments and household expenses for upkeep, and will be entitled to a pro rata share of the proceeds from any sale of the home.

(d) Ann signs a deed transferring title in the home to herself and Betty as joint tenants with right of survivorship. She does not record the deed.

(e) At Ann's death, Betty's survivorship rights kick in.

Would you recommend, in any of the above cases, that Ann notify the mortgagee bank about her sister's presence and rights in the home?

[¶ 5,570]

2. Wraparound Mortgages

A wraparound mortgage may be an attractive arrangement for some sellers and buyers who want to take advantage of a low interest rate on an existing mortgage. Assume for example, that Seller's home is on the market for $200,000. It is currently subject to a $100,000 mortgage held by a local bank at 4%. Buyer is interested in the home, but determines that she will need to borrow $180,000 to make the purchase and that the likely interest rate on her loan will be 8%. At that rate, a 30–year mortgage will require monthly payments of $1,320.78. Buyer had counted on spending closer to $1,000.00 per month. If she could borrow the $180,000 at 6% rather than 8%, the monthly payments would be $1,079.19, an amount she feels she could handle.

Seller offers Buyer the following deal: He will transfer possession of the property, but not title, to her in exchange for a $20,000 down payment and a promissory note for $180,000 with interest at 6%. Seller promises to continue making payments to the bank on the existing $100,000 mortgage. Upon payment of the full selling price, Seller will convey legal title to Buyer. This arrangement is a contract for deed with a wraparound mortgage.

The transaction gives Buyer what she wants, lower monthly payments. It gives Seller the right to capitalize on the benefit of the low rate mortgage. He gets the full 6% interest on $80,000 of the mortgage debt and pockets the 2% interest spread on the $100,000 that is owed to the mortgagee bank.

To determine whether this option is worthwhile for Seller, one would need to compare Seller's return on this investment with other available options. It should be kept in mind, however, that mortgages are not liquid investments, especially if there is no ready secondary market in which the mortgage can be sold. If Seller could find a purchaser for this wraparound mortgage, it would likely sell at a steep discount. Additionally, if the original mortgage contains a due on sale clause of the sort contained in Fannie Mae mortgages, it would clearly be violated by this arrangement. As a result, both Seller and Buyer run the risk that the bank will demand full payment.

From Buyer's perspective, the arrangement is quite risky. She is making payments to Seller and trusting him to make payments to the bank. If payments are not made to the bank, foreclosure may occur and she would stand to lose her interest in the property. To ensure that payments are made on "wraps," borrowers often insist on making the payments themselves or paying through an escrow agent. However, direct payments to the bank from someone other than the original borrower would surely alert the bank to the fact that something has changed. The bank might then pursue enforcement of the due on sale clause. On the other hand, if the mortgage is assumable, and Buyer does make payments directly to the bank, Seller will want to make sure that the payments are made to protect Seller's own security interest in the property.

I. INCOME TAX RULES AND HOME OWNERSHIP

[¶ 5,580]

There are a number of income tax rules that affect the costs and benefits of home ownership. Perhaps the most valuable tax aspect of home ownership is the fact that the imputed value of living in a home is not considered taxable income. This point can be demonstrated by the following example: Dee and Dum each have $100,000 to invest. Each is looking for a return of at least 5%. Dee purchases a home for $100,000, with a fair rental value of $5,000 a year. She could either rent the home to someone else for $5,000 or she could live in the home herself. If she rents the home, the $5,000 will be taxable income to her. She will be able to offset that income by certain deductions connected with the rental, but she will ultimately have taxable income and have to pay a tax, thereby reducing her after-tax return on her investment. She decides it is better to live in the home and to personally consume the $5,000 rental value tax-free. In the end, her full $100,000 is invested, she has no positive cash flow from her investment, and she has a place to live rent-free. Dum, on the other hand, is averse to owning real estate. He invests his $100,000 in a secure trust fund, which produces a return of $5,000. He spends the $5,000 to rent a personal residence similar to the one that Dee purchased for herself. In the end Dum, like Dee, has invested the full $100,000 and has no positive cash flow because he must spend the full amount as rent. But Dum will be out of pocket additional funds at tax time because the $5,000 investment income is taxable and he must pay the income taxes on it.

Another way to describe their relative positions is to say that Dee has invested in something that produces an after-tax benefit of $5,000 (the rent-free use of the home). Dum, on the other hand, has invested in something that produces an after tax benefit of less than $5,000. If Dum had to pay federal and state taxes combined of at a rate of 30%, then he would retain after taxes only 70% of the $5,000 income or $3,500. Of course, if Dum could find an alternative investment at $100,000 that would produce after-tax income of $5,000, Dum would be in the same position as Dee.

Other tax benefits of home ownership include the deductibility of mortgage interest, the deductibility of property taxes, and the exclusion of gain upon the sale of a principal residence.

[¶ 5,590]

1. The Interest Deduction

Because most mortgage interest is deductible (see I.R.C. § 163(h)(3)), the cost of borrowing for the purpose of purchasing a home is lower than it otherwise would be. The benefit of this lower cost of borrowing is not necessarily captured by the purchaser/borrower, however. More likely, most of this benefit is captured by the homebuilding industry, including real estate brokers and lenders. Since the cost of home ownership is lowered by the interest deduction, purchasers can pay more for the product and for the costs of acquiring it. The same analysis can be applied to all tax benefits that support homeownership, including the property tax deduction (see I.R.C. § 164) and the exclusion of gain upon sale of the home (see I.R.C. § 121).

[¶ 5,600]

a. Some history

The first Revenue Act, passed in 1913, provided that all interest was deductible, without regard to how the borrowed funds were used. Thus, until the law was changed in 1986, personal interest was fully deductible on an individual's tax return. This deduction included interest on mortgages, on car loans, and on credit card debt.

There is no persuasive reason to allow a deduction for personal interest since it represents nothing more than an additional cost of personal consumption. As a general rule, personal consumption expenditures are not deductible for income tax purposes. Thus, interest incurred on loans used for personal consumption should not be deductible.

When the interest deduction was included in the tax law in 1913, consumer credit of the kind we have today was virtually unknown. Most interest expenses were incurred in business or investment loans. The only major category of consumer interest was interest paid on home mortgages. Most non-mortgage consumer debt did not charge a specific amount of interest because the debt was extended in the form of installment plans that charged purchasers a higher price for buying on credit than for cash purchases. Remarkably, that difference in price was not recognized as interest and thus was not deductible for income tax purposes. See, e.g., Hogg v. Ruffner, 66 U.S. 115 (1861) (holding that the difference between a cash price and a deferred payment price was not interest under usury statutes). Courts followed this precedent in tax cases involving purchasers who claimed that the difference in price should be treated as deductible interest. See, e.g., Daniel Brothers v. Commissioner, 28 F.2d 761 (5th Cir. 1928). In 1937, the Board of Tax Appeals created an exception to this "no interest deduction" rule. So long as interest was separately stated by the parties to the contract as part of the deferred sales price, the interest could be deducted. See

Hudson–Duncan & Co. v. Commissioner, 36 B.T.A. 554 (1937); Kingsford Co. v. Commissioner, 41 T.C. 646 (1964). This line of cases, holding that deferred sales prices did not include unstated interest, remained valid until 1964, when § 483 was added to the Internal Revenue Code.

By 1986, taxpayers were deducting interest on all forms of personal loans, mortgages, car loans, short term consumer loans, and credit card debt. If interest was not stated on the loan, it would be imputed at a reasonable rate, and the purchase price would be reduced accordingly to reflect that it included an interest factor. But the law changed abruptly in 1986 when § 163(h) was added to the Internal Revenue Code.

[¶ 5,610]

b. Current law: I.R.C. § 163(h)

Today, § 163(h) states the controlling law regarding the deductibility of interest on personal debt. As a general rule, personal interest cannot be deducted. There is one exception to this rule. Within certain limits, taxpayers can deduct interest paid on mortgage loans secured by their personal residences. The interest must satisfy the statutory definition of "qualified residence interest." Qualified residence interest is interest on a mortgage debt of up to $1,000,000 that was incurred to acquire a residence. The $1,000,000 cap is intended to reduce the benefit for wealthy taxpayers, although, given the geographical differences in cost of housing, the limitation is likely to hurt taxpayers in California, Hawaii, and Alaska more than those in Iowa, South Dakota or Wyoming.

Qualified residence interest also includes interest on up to $100,000 of home equity indebtedness. Home equity indebtedness is any debt secured by the equity in the home. For this purpose, the equity is the fair market value of the home minus any outstanding acquisition indebtedness. Home equity loans can be taken out for any purpose.

The primary justification for allowing a deduction for interest paid to acquire a home is that the deduction provides an indirect governmental subsidy to encourage home ownership. The underlying assumption is that increased rates of homeownership are good for the country as a whole.

[¶ 5,620]

Questions and Notes

1. What is the justification for allowing a deduction for interest on a home equity loan which may be used for purposes unrelated to the purchase or improvement of the home?

2. Does allowing a deduction for interest on home equity indebtedness discriminate unfairly against renters who must borrow cash from other sources to purchase such things as automobiles?

In considering the scope and operation of I.R.C. § 163(h), you may find it helpful to refer to the statutory language allowing a deduction for qualified residence interest.

INTERNAL REVENUE CODE § 163(h)

(3) Qualified residence interest.— For purposes of this subsection—

(A) In general.— The term "qualified residence interest" means any interest which is paid or accrued during the taxable year on—

   (i) acquisition indebtedness with respect to any qualified residence of the taxpayer, or

   (ii) home equity indebtedness with respect to any qualified residence of the taxpayer.

For purposes of the preceding sentence, the determination of whether any property is a qualified residence of the taxpayer shall be made as of the time the interest is accrued.

(B) Acquisition indebtedness.—

   (i) In general.— The term "acquisition indebtedness" means any indebtedness which—

      (I) is incurred in acquiring, constructing, or substantially improving any qualified residence of the taxpayer, and

      (II) is secured by such residence.

   Such term also includes any indebtedness secured by such residence resulting from the refinancing of indebtedness meeting the requirements of the preceding sentence (or this sentence); but only to the extent the amount of the indebtedness resulting from such refinancing does not exceed the amount of the refinanced indebtedness.

   (ii) $1,000,000 Limitation.— The aggregate amount treated as acquisition indebtedness for any period shall not exceed $1,000,000 ($500,000 in the case of a married individual filing a separate return).

(C) Home equity indebtedness.—

   (i) In general.—The term "home equity indebtedness" means any indebtedness (other than acquisition indebtedness) secured by a qualified residence to the extent the aggregate amount of such indebtedness does not exceed—

      (I) the fair market value of such qualified residence, reduced by

      (II) the amount of acquisition indebtedness with respect to such residence.

   (ii) Limitation.— The aggregate amount treated as home equity indebtedness for any period shall not exceed $100,000 ($50,000 in the case of a separate return by a married individual).

(D) Treatment of indebtedness incurred on or before October 13, 1987.— * * *

(4) Other definitions and special rules.— For purposes of this subsection—

(A) Qualified residence.—

   (i) In general.— The term "qualified residence" means—

(I) the principal residence (within the meaning of section 121) of the taxpayer, and

(II) 1 other residence of the taxpayer which is selected by the taxpayer for purposes of this subsection for the taxable year and which is used by the taxpayer as a residence (within the meaning of section 280A(d)(1)).

(ii) Married individuals filing separate returns.— If a married couple does not file a joint return for the taxable year—

(I) such couple shall be treated as 1 taxpayer for purposes of clause (i), and

(II) each individual shall be entitled to take into account 1 residence unless both individuals consent in writing to 1 individual taking into account the principal residence and 1 other residence.

(iii) Residence not rented.— For purposes of clause (i)(II), notwithstanding section 280A(d)(1), if the taxpayer does not rent a dwelling unit at any time during a taxable year, such unit may be treated as a residence for such taxable year.

(B) Special rule for cooperative housing corporations.— * * *

(C) Unenforceable security interests.— Indebtedness shall not fail to be treated as secured by any property solely because, under any applicable State or local homestead or other debtor protection law in effect on August 16, 1986, the security interest is ineffective or the enforceability of the security interest is restricted. * * *

Note that there is nothing in § 163(h) that requires that the home equity loan be enforceable in order to deduct the interest. See I.R.C. § 163(h)(4)(C). When this provision was enacted in 1986, Texas law strongly protected homeowners from foreclosure under state homestead laws. The Texas constitution prohibited second mortgages in the form of home equity loans unless they were incurred to provide part of the purchase price of the home, to pay for home improvements, or to pay for property taxes. As a result, Texas banks would not make home equity loans since they were not enforceable. But with the creation of the tax benefit allowing interest deductions for home equity loans, Texas banks were pushed to make such loans. The prohibition of such loans under Texas law, however, prevented banks from moving forward. Ultimately the issue was settled in 1995 when the voters approved an amendment to the Texas constitution making home equity loans legal in the state. As a result the tax benefit available under § 163 is now available in Texas and homestead protections have been greatly weakened.

Also note that the taxpayer can deduct the interest on mortgage indebtedness with respect to two homes, a principal residence and one other residence. For this purpose, a dwelling unit is treated as a residence if it is used by the taxpayer for personal purposes for the greater of 14 days or 10% of the number of days during the tax year for which the unit is rented at a fair rental. See I.R.C. §§ 163(h)(4)(A)(i)(II), 280A(d)(1). Personal use includes use by certain family members such as children, parents, and siblings. See I.R.C. § 280A(d)(2)(A).

The $1,000,000 limitation for acquisition indebtedness and the $100,000 limitation for home equity indebtedness apply to each taxpayer. A married couple, however, must share the $1,000,000 and $100,000 limitations. The two-home limit also applies to each married couple. As a result, unmarried cohabitants could arrange their home purchases in a way that would allow them to have $2,000,000 in total acquisition indebtedness and $200,000 in total home equity indebtedness (provided these amounts were split evenly between the two taxpayers). It would also be possible for an unmarried couple to deduct interest on mortgage indebtedness on a total of four homes.

One final question is: who can claim the interest deduction? According to Treas. Reg. § 1.163–1(b), interest is deductible if it is "paid by the taxpayer on a mortgage upon real estate of which he is the legal or equitable owner, even though the taxpayer is not directly liable upon the bond or note secured by such mortgage." For example, if Paul purchases an interest in Tina's home but Tina never transfers legal title to Paul and Paul never assumes Tina's mortgage indebtedness, he will nonetheless be entitled to an interest deduction under § 163 provided he actually pays the interest. On the other hand, if Paul is merely living with Tina and Paul makes the mortgage payments on her behalf, he is not likely to be considered an equitable owner of the property and he will not be entitled to take a mortgage interest deduction.

If Paul does not have an ownership interest, but he is the one making the mortgage payment, what happens to the interest deduction? Can anyone claim the deduction? What arguments support your conclusion?

[¶ 5,630]

Problems

1. Carl wishes to purchase a home for $2 million. He will pay $500,000 down and borrow the remaining $1.5 million, payable over 20 years at an interest rate of 5%. His monthly payments are $9,899.34. (See the amortization schedule below to see how much of each payment for the first 12 months is attributable to interest and how much is attributable to repayment of the $1.5 million principal.) Assume he makes his first payment on Sept. 1, 2005, so that he makes only 4 monthly payments in tax year 2005. How much interest does he pay in 2005 and how much of it can he deduct?

Amortization Table — First Year — 1.5 million at 5% over 20 years

Monthly Payment	Interest	Principal	Principal Balance
1	$6,250.00	$3,649.34	$1,496,350.66
2	6,234.79	3,664.55	1,492,686.11
3	6,219.53	3,679.81	1,489,006.30
4	6,204.19	3,695.15	1,485,311.15
5	6,188.80	3,710.54	1,481,600.61
6	6,173.34	3,726.00	1,477,874.61
7	6,157.81	3,741.53	1,474,133.08
8	6,142.22	3,757.12	1,470,375.96
9	6,126.57	3,772.77	1,466,603.18
10	6,110.85	3,788.49	1,462,814.69

Monthly Payment	Interest	Principal	Principal Balance
11	6,095.06	3,804.28	1,459,010.41
12	6,079.21	3,820.13	1,455,190.28

2.   Donna purchased her own home four years ago for $150,000, paying $45,000 down and borrowing the $105,000 balance. It is now 2005 and the home is worth $190,000. The outstanding mortgage balance is approximately $100,000. Because interest rates have decreased from 7% to 5%, she can refinance the mortgage for a new 30–year term, increase the face amount of the loan to $120,000, and her monthly payments will be about $50 lower. She wants the extra $20,000 to spend on travel to exotic places. Should she refinance? If she does, can she deduct all her interest payments? Would she do better to refinance only the $100,000 balance of her existing mortgage and take out a $20,000 home equity loan to satisfy her wanderlust?

3.   Ellen has decided to buy a new car for $35,000. She has only $5,000 in cash. One option for financing the balance of the purchase price is to borrow from the car dealer for 60 months at a fixed rate of 3.5%. Another option is to take out a home equity loan against her home. The current rate on the home equity loan is 4%. Which should she do? What additional facts do you need to advise Ellen?

4.   Fred and Flora (husband and wife) own a home in Wisconsin that is currently valued at $800,000. The balance on their mortgage is $400,000, down from the original loan amount of $480,000. They own a vacation home on the Cape that is worth $600,000 and subject to a mortgage of $200,000. Flora's mother still lives in the old family home in Texas, but her health requires that she move closer to town and preferably live in a one-story residence. It will take some time to sell the family home, so Flora and Fred have agreed to buy a new home for Flora's mother. They have located an ideal residence at the reasonable price of $225,000. They have $25,000 for the down payment. To finance the remaining $200,000, they can choose either (1) to take out a purchase money mortgage from a Texas bank to buy the home, or (2) to use the open line of credit that they have on the Wisconsin home. If their primary goal is to maximize their interest deduction, which alternative should they choose?

5.   Would your analysis for Fred and Flora be any different if they were not husband and wife, but instead were long-time committed cohabitants?

[¶ 5,640]

c.   *What is interest?*

A borrower who takes out a purchase money mortgage loan to acquire a home pays many different costs at closing. Purchasing a home is a personal choice. It is not a business activity and it is not a profit seeking activity, although the potential for future appreciation in a home is one reason for purchasing rather than renting. Because the purchase is personal, none of the costs associated with the purchase, other than interest, are deductible.

Typically, a borrower is charged for a credit report, an appraisal, various other banking services, and origination points or just plain "points." Interest is defined as the amount a borrower promises to pay for the use of borrowed money, or more generally as the amount paid for "the use or forebearance of money." See Deputy v. Du Pont, 308 U.S. 488, 498 (1940). Charges that are for services, such as doing a credit check, are not considered interest. Discount points, however, are paid for the use of the borrowed funds. That is, they directly compensate the lender for the money loaned and not for anything else.

Points paid at closing represent prepaid interest. A borrower can obtain a lower fixed interest rate by paying points at closing. The trade-off is a matter of timing, namely, whether the interest is paid up front in a lump sum or in monthly installments over the term of the loan.

As a tax accounting matter, prepaid expenses, including prepaid interest, are usually capitalized and deducted over the period to which they relate. In the case of prepaid interest, that period should be the term of the loan. However, I.R.C. § 461(g)(2) provides an exception for points paid by a cash basis taxpayer "in connection with the purchase or improvement of, and secured by, the principal residence of the taxpayer." Note this exception does not apply to any points paid to refinance a principal residence.

Suppose Paul Purchaser can't find desirable financing at the time he needs to buy a new home. Interest rates are unusually high and he expects them to come down soon. He decides in the short run that it is better to borrow the purchase price on a balloon note that will fall due in three years. He pays a slightly lower interest rate for the loan than for a conventional 30–year loan. Two years later, interest rates have dipped sufficiently and he decides to enter into a permanent 30–year loan and pay off the balloon. He pays three points at closing to obtain a lower interest rate for the term of the loan. Can he deduct the three points under § 461(g)(2)?

The I.R.S. would definitely say that he cannot. The points were not paid "in connection with the purchase or improvement" of his principal residence but rather were paid in connection with a refinancing. The Court of Appeals for the Eighth Circuit disagrees. See Huntsman v. Commissioner, 905 F.2d 1182 (8th Cir. 1990). The court determined that so long as the permanent loan was acquired for the purpose of paying off the short-term purchase-money mortgage it was sufficiently connected with the purchase of the residence. No other circuit court of appeals has had the opportunity to consider the issue.

[¶ 5,650]

Problem

Paul Purchaser, a cash-basis taxpayer, borrows $200,000 from First Bank to help with the purchase of a new principal residence. In order to obtain a lower interest rate on the loan, Paul is willing to pay two points ($4,000) up front at closing as prepaid interest. First Bank offers to add the $4,000 to the loan amount so that he can pay it off over time. How would you advise him? See Schubel v. Commissioner, 77 T.C. 701 (1981).

[¶ 5,660]

d.   Imputed interest

Any sale of property for a deferred payment includes an interest element, even if the interest is not explicitly stated. The Internal Revenue Code requires that the unstated interest be imputed at specified rates. For example, § 483 applies to deferred sales of property for less than $250,000, deferred sales of residences, and deferred sales of farms for under $1,000,000; § 1274 applies to all other sales of property for deferred payments.

In structuring a deferred payment sale that is covered by one of these imputed interest rules, the parties should be sure to state interest at least equal to the current "applicable federal rate" that is used by the I.R.S. to impute interest. These rates are determined each month by reference to the average yield on certain U.S. Treasury obligations and are published in the Internal Revenue Bulletin. When the sale occurs between family members and the sales price is $500,000 or less, the maximum imputed interest rate is 6%. See I.R.C. § 483(e).

Imputed interest is treated the same as stated interest. It can be deducted when it is paid so long as it qualifies under § 163(h)(3).

[¶ 5,670]

Problems

1.   Carl purchases a widget for a stated sales price of $110, to be paid one year from the date of purchase. If the going rate of interest is 10% on consumer loans of this sort, how much of the $110 is interest and how much of it is the purchase price of the widget?

2.   Donna purchases a farm from Farmer for a stated sales price of $500,000, to be paid over a two-year period at $250,000 a year, with the first payment due one year after the sale. If the applicable federal rate is 10% per year, how much of each payment will be interest and how much will be purchase price?

Note: To determine the present value (PV) of a dollar that is to be paid in the future, you can use the formula $PV = 1/(1 + i)^n$, where i is the annual interest rate and n is the number of years.

[¶ 5,680]

2.   The Property Tax Deduction

I.R.C. § 164 allows an income tax deduction for all "state, local, and foreign real property taxes." Like the interest deduction, this deduction represents an indirect federal subsidy for the homebuilding industry.

To claim the deduction, the taxpayer must own the property subject to the tax and must pay the tax. In the words of the regulations, "taxes are deductible only by the person upon whom they are imposed." Treas.

Reg. § 1.164–1(a). When the tax is a property tax, the tax is imposed on the person who owns the property. Property taxes, however, do not generally create personal liability. They are nonrecourse liabilities and therefore are more accurately conceived as being imposed upon the property itself which is always the ultimate recourse for payment of the tax. The tax is deductible by any person who risks losing the property for nonpayment of the tax. The person need not hold legal title to the property. For example, the holder of an equitable life estate is entitled to deduct property taxes that she pays on the property even if legal title to the property is held by a trustee. See Horsford v. Commissioner, 2 T.C. 826 (1943). In addition, if one co-tenant pays 100% of the tax bill, she will be entitled to a deduction for the full amount. Under common law, co-tenants have the right to use the entire property and so one co-tenant has an interest in the whole tract of property and not just a fractional share. Furthermore, if the taxes are not paid in full, the taxing authorities can foreclose the tax lien that arises for unpaid taxes and sell off the entire tract, not just the interest of the one co-tenant. As a result, the co-tenant is sufficiently liable for the full tax bill to warrant a deduction if she pays it in full. See Powell v. Commissioner, 26 T.C.M. (CCH) 161 (1967). However, she cannot deduct any amounts for which she receives reimbursement from her co-tenants. See Daya v. Commissioner, 80 T.C.M. (CCH) 743 (2000).

I.R.C. § 164(d) provides a special rule for apportioning the property tax deduction when real property changes ownership during the tax year. Under this provision, the tax allocable to the period of time that the property is owned by the seller is treated as a tax imposed on the seller, and the tax allocable to the period of time that the property is owned by the purchaser is treated as a tax imposed on the purchaser. This apportionment rule satisfies the requirement that the taxes be imposed upon the person who claims the deduction. In addition, to claim a deduction, the taxpayer must also *pay* the tax. Typically, the purchaser pays the tax if the sale occurs before the tax bills are sent out and the seller will have paid the tax if the sale occurs later in the year, after the tax has been paid. Section 164(d) allows the seller to deduct his or her apportioned share of the tax even if the tax was actually paid by the purchaser, and vice versa.

[¶ 5,690]

Problems

1. George owns a personal residence and usually pays the property tax each year. To avoid probate at death, George transfers the residence to his daughter, Debra, with the understanding that he will continue to live in the residence as long as he wishes. If he pays the property taxes, can he claim a deduction?

2. Hal and Hank (a gay couple) own a home together as joint tenants with right of survivorship. Hal is out of work and is being supported by

Hank. Hank pays the full amount of property tax due on the home. Can Hank deduct the full amount? What would happen to Hank's interest in the property if he fails to pay the full property tax?

3. Irene sold her home to Jack on December 1, 2005. In October she paid her 2005 property tax bill (assessed on owners of property as of January 1, 2005) in the amount of $1,200. The closing statement failed to apportion the property taxes. Jack wants to know if he can claim a property tax deduction for his one month's share of the taxes for 2005. What do you think? See I.R.C. § 164(d); Treas. Reg. § 1.164–6(d)(2).

[¶ 5,700]

3. Cashing Out Home Equity

One strong reason to invest in a home is for its future appreciation. Of course, if one stays in the same home indefinitely, it may be hard to realize the value of this appreciation other than by continuing to consume the rental value of an increasingly expensive home. Nonetheless, the principal residence is usually one of the most valuable assets in an estate plan. There are several ways for the owner to cash out on the appreciation other than by selling the home. In many cases, however, selling may be the most attractive option. For example, the homeowner may want to retire from the family farm and move into a smaller apartment or condominium in the city. Or the family home may be too large for one surviving parent who would prefer to sell the home and buy something smaller. In these cases, the homeowner will have excess cash from the larger, older home, which can be used to supplement Social Security and retirement benefits.

[¶ 5,710]

a. Sale of the principal residence

A home is a capital asset under the tax code. It is property, but it is not inventory or property used in a trade or business or any of the other items that are listed as "non-capital assets" in I.R.C. § 1221. When Alice purchases property for $100,000 and sells it for $200,000, she realizes gain in the amount of $100,000. Most gains are recognized for tax purposes when they are converted into cash. Because the $100,000 gain results from a sale of a capital asset, it appears to be a capital gain. See I.R.C. § 1222. In most cases, however, the gain will not be taxable. See I.R.C. § 121, which provides as follows:

(a) **Exclusion.**— Gross income shall not include gain from the sale or exchange of property if, during the 5–year period ending on the date of the sale or exchange, such property has been owned and used by the taxpayer as the taxpayer's principal residence for periods aggregating 2 years or more.

The exclusion is limited to the first $250,000 of gain, or, in the case of qualifying spouses, to the first $500,000. For spouses to be entitled to the

$500,000 limit, only one spouse has to meet the ownership requirement, but both spouses must meet the use requirement.

If a taxpayer fails to meet the two-year ownership and use requirements because of a change in employment or health or due to unforeseen circumstances, the taxpayer may nonetheless qualify for exclusion of the gain. The maximum amount of gain that can be excluded, however, will be reduced proportionately. For example, assume Taxpayer owns and uses the home for only one year rather than two, and then sells it at a gain. So long as the sale was due to a change in employment, health, or unforeseen circumstances, the maximum allowable exclusion will be cut in half ($125,000 for a single taxpayer and $250,000 for certain married couples). Whether a sale is due to a change in employment (e.g., being transferred to a new location) or health or unforeseen circumstances is a question of fact. For descriptions of safe harbors and examples of unforeseen circumstances, see Treas. Reg. § 1.121–3.

The full exclusion can be claimed only once every two years. For example, assume Sam Seller owns a home and has met the two-year ownership and use requirements. Before selling the home, Sam purchases a condominium and moves into it. The next year he sells the home. Sam is entitled to an exclusion of the gain on the home. But if he then sells the condo for a gain within two years after selling the home, he cannot claim another exclusion of gain, unless he can show that the second sale occurred because of a change in employment or health or due to unforeseen circumstances. Assume Sam sold the condo because his employer transferred him to a branch office hundreds of miles away in another state. In this event he could exclude gain, but the maximum allowable exclusion will be reduced. The allowable exclusion is determined by multiplying the full amount of the exclusion by a fraction in which the numerator is the period of time between the first and second sales and the denominator is two years. Thus, if Sam had sold the home on January 1, 2005, and then sold the condo on July 1, 2006, he could exclude gain to the extent it did not exceed $187,500 ($250,000 × 18 months/24 months).

[¶ 5,720]

Problem

Neal purchased a home for himself 10 years ago. The purchase price was $250,000. In addition to the purchase price, Neal incurred the following closing costs (which were not deductible as interest): $250 for a title opinion from a local lawyer, and $300 for a credit check. Two years later, he added an outdoor swimming pool at a cost of $30,000. If Neal sells the home this year for $545,000, how much gain must he report? Assume he pays a 6% commission to the listing agent and incurs closing costs in the amount of $1,000.

To answer the above question, you will need to know the rules for computing the tax basis of property. In general, basis is the original cost

(I.R.C. § 1012) plus any amounts that are properly attributable to the acquisition of the property (I.R.C. § 263). The $250 payment for the title opinion should qualify as an acquisition cost of the property. See Treas. Reg. 1.263(a)–2 providing that "the cost of defending or perfecting title to property" is a capital expenditure. But the $300 for the credit check was spent primarily to acquire the mortgage, which makes it too indirect to add to the basis of the home. The swimming pool is clearly an additional cost that should be added to basis.

Since gain is computed by subtracting basis from the "amount realized" on the sale (I.R.C. § 1001), you will need to know how to compute the "amount realized." The question is how to treat selling expenses such as the broker's commission. As a general rule, selling expenses are deducted from the amount realized, thereby decreasing the gain on the sale. Presumably any amounts that a seller pays to enable the sale to go through would be selling expenses and should reduce the "amount realized."

[¶ 5,730]

(1) Sale of a partial interest

I.R.C. § 121(d)(8)(A) provides as follows: "At the election of the taxpayer, this section shall not fail to apply to the sale or exchange of an interest in a principal residence by reason of such interest being a remainder interest in such residence, but this section shall not apply to any other interest in such residence which is sold or exchanged separately."

Shortly after the enactment of this provision, there was much debate over whether this apparent ban on the sale of partial interests (other than a remainder) would apply to an owner who wanted to sell an undivided fractional interest in the property rather than his entire interest. It seemed perfectly clear that joint owners should be able to sell off their interests, either at the same time or at different times, and claim the exclusion so long as they were selling their entire interest in the property. For example, if A and B owned a home as tenants in common and together they sold their interests to a new purchaser, each seller should be entitled to the exclusion so long as the other statutory requirements were met. Similarly, if A sold his interest in the home to a new purchaser who became a co-tenant with B, A should be entitled to the exclusion. Confusion arose, however, when one person who owned 100% of the home sold a carved-out interest to another person. Did the sale run afoul of § 121(d)(8)(A)? If not, what was the maximum exclusion? If the seller sold a one-half interest was the exclusion reduced by half? If she sold a 10% interest, was she limited to 10% of the exclusion amount? If she was otherwise entitled to the $250,000 exclusion and owned a home with a built-in gain of $500,000, could she sell half of it now and claim the $250,000 exclusion and then sell the other half later and claim an additional $250,000 exclusion? In other words, did the exemption limit apply "per sales transaction" or "per property?"

Finally, the Treasury issued regulations to clarify the application of § 121 to sales of partial interests in property. Under the regulations, a sale of a partial interest qualifies up to the maximum amount of the exclusion ($250,000 or $500,000). The limit on the exclusion amount applies "per property." Thus the total amount that can be excluded as a result of sales of partial interests in the same property by the same person is $250,000, or $500,000 in the case of qualifying spouses. Additionally, the "once every two years" restriction does not apply in cases where the taxpayer sells a partial interest in one year and sells another partial interest within two years thereafter.

Example: In 1991 Albert buys a house that he uses as his principal residence. In 2004 Albert's friend Ben moves into Albert's house and Albert sells a 50% interest in the house to Ben, realizing a gain of $136,000. Albert may exclude the $136,000 of gain. In 2005 Albert sells his remaining 50% interest in the home to Ben, realizing a gain of $138,000. Albert may exclude $114,000 ($250,000 − $136,000 exclusion previously claimed) of the $138,000 gain from the sale of the remaining interest. See Treas. Reg. § 1.121–4(e)(3).

[¶ 5,740]

Problems

1. Sandy owns a home worth $600,000, which she purchased years ago for $100,000. She and Kit have just become domestic partners and want to continue living in Sandy's home. Kit wants to have an ownership interest in the home. What is the tax result to Sandy if she sells Kit a one-half interest in the home?

2. What result if 10 years later Sandy and Kit sell the home to Paula for $1,000,000, net of selling costs?

3. Morton purchased a home 10 years ago for a total cost (including additions to basis) of $200,000. It has recently been appraised at $800,000. Morton and Jane are planning to marry. Jane thinks it is only fair for her to buy into ownership of the home. She sells her home and pays Morton $400,000 for a half interest in his home six months before their wedding. Does Morton have to recognize income on the sale to Jane? What result if Jane waits to purchase an interest in Morton's home after they marry? See I.R.C. § 1041. What do you advise them to do?

[¶ 5,750]

(2) Subdividing acreage surrounding the residence

The ability to exclude up to $500,000 per couple of capital gain on property that has been used as a residence is a huge benefit. In cases involving acreage surrounding the residence, opportunities arise to maximize both gain and the § 121 exclusion. For example, assume a husband and wife have owned a farm for many years and are now thinking of retiring. The farm consists of a residence, 20 acres of land surrounding the residence primarily used for personal gardening and recreation, 180 acres of crop land, and numerous farm buildings. A sale of the entire property comprises the principal residence as well as the farming business. The sale of the business will be taxable, whereas the sale of the residence will qualify for the $500,000 gain exemption. How much of the sales proceeds should be allocated to the sale of the residence and how much to the farming business? Is the 20 acres used for personal gardening and recreation properly accounted for as part of the residence?

To determine what qualifies as a principal residence, one must consider all the facts and circumstances. The building that is used as a home will qualify as a principal residence, but what about the surrounding acreage? If the 20 acres surrounding the home are used for personal gardening rather than for crops, that acreage should qualify as part of the residence. To determine the amount of gain attributable to the sale of the principal residence, the owners would need to allocate both basis and the amount realized on the sale between residential acreage and farm acreage. It may well be that the value of the 20 acres surrounding the home is worth more than the 180 acres used for farming. In other words, a sale of the entire acreage for an agreed upon sales price does not necessarily result in an allocation of 10% of the sales price to the residential acreage and the other 90% to the farmland just because the use of the total acreage is split that way. In addition, if the sale of the 20 acres could be divided into two separate transactions, one sale of the residence with accompanying acreage and the other sale of undeveloped land that could serve as a building site for another residence, the seller may be able to realize more gain. As a general rule, subdividing a large lot into two smaller lots will produce higher sales revenue than selling a single lot.

In situations involving extra acreage, the regulations provide special rules that help the taxpayer to maximize the amount of nontaxable gain. Treas. Reg. § 1.121–1 allows a taxpayer to sell unimproved land adjacent to the residence in a separate transaction and count it as part of the sale of the residence, provided the two sales occur within two years of each other. For example, Farmer Jones and wife can carve out from their 20–acre homestead a 10–acre vacant lot and sell it to a developer. Normally, this sale would produce taxable capital gain. But if the 10–acre lot is part of the residence, and if they sell their residence within the next two years, the gain on both sales is exempt to the extent that the combined gain does not exceed $500,000.

[¶ 5,760]

(3) Combining § 1031 deferral with the § 121 exclusion

As originally enacted, § 121 created a "loophole" for individuals who acquired property in a § 1031 like-kind exchange and then converted that property into a principal residence. Under § 1031, an exchange of any real estate for other real estate is tax-free at the time of exchange so long as both the property exchanged and the property acquired is held either for productive use in a trade or business or for investment purposes. For example, exchanging one rental home for another would produce no immediately taxable gain even though a sale of the rental property would have produced gain. Section 1031, however, is not a true exclusion provision. It is a deferral of gain provision. Ultimately, when the newly acquired property is sold, or otherwise disposed of, the deferred gain on the first transaction should be recognized. See ¶ 3,570. Converting investment or business property to personal use, however, is not considered a disposition of the property. And, if the new personal use of the property were to qualify under § 121 (e.g., use as a principal residence for at least two years), the taxpayer could then dispose of the property for cash and use § 121 to exclude up to $250,000 of the gain ($500,000 for a married couple).

Example: Tom, a single taxpayer, exchanges Blackacre, basis $100,000, for Goldacre, worth $300,000. The exchange qualifies for nonrecognition under § 1031, because both properties were used for investment purposes. Tom takes Goldacre with a basis of $100,000, which should ensure that the $200,000 gain will ultimately be taxed when he cashes out of his investment. After renting Goldacre for a year, Tom converts Goldacre into his principal residence. Two years later he sells Goldacre for $350,000, producing a gain of $250,000, which he claims is excluded under § 121, despite the fact that $200,000 of the gain is attributable to his earlier investment in Blackacre, which was never used as a principal residence.

Before 2004, Tom could use § 1031 and § 121 to accomplish the desired result of excluding the original $200,000 gain as well as the $50,000 of gain that accrued during the time that he used the property as his principal residence. Congress closed this loophole in 2004 by amending § 121 to provide that on the sale of a principal residence originally acquired in a § 1031 exchange, no exclusion would be available unless the taxpayer had used the home as a principal residence for at least 5 years.

[¶ 5,770]

Questions

Does the Congressional action completely close the loophole or is it still possible to use § 121 to exclude gain that accrued on property while it was used for investment or business purposes? Do you think the Congressional response was a sound way to deal with the problem? Why or why not?

[¶ 5,780]

b. Cashing out equity without vacating the home

In many cases, a retired homeowner will want to use the cash buildup in the home's equity, but will not want to move out of the home he or she has lived in for most of his or her life.

[¶ 5,790]

(1) Reverse mortgages

Reverse mortgages are designed for older homeowners who either own their homes outright or have substantial equity in the home. For an elderly homeowner in need of cash, the reverse mortgage is a way to access that cash without having to sell the home, thereby allowing the homeowner to remain in the home. Basically, the lending institution forwards cash to the homeowner and agrees to let the homeowner retain possession. The loan will not be repaid until the home is sold, which may be after the death of the homeowner. The amount of cash available to the homeowner depends on several factors, the most important being the amount of equity in the home and the homeowner's age. The cash may be paid out in installments or in a lump sum. Or, the lender may open a line of credit for the homeowner so that cash can be withdrawn as needed.

The key difference between reverse mortgages and other home equity loans is that the outstanding balance and accrued interest need not be paid until the home is sold. The cash received is not taxable because it is a loan. If the home is sold during the owner's lifetime, § 121 is available to exempt the gain if it is within the maximum limits. If the home is sold after the death of the homeowner, the sale should produce no gain because the basis in the home is increased at death to fair market value. When the mortgage is paid off, the accrued interest can be deducted to the extent it qualifies under § 163(h)(3) as home equity interest.

The Home Equity Conversion Mortgage is the most popular reverse mortgage and it is the only one insured by the federal government. The Federal Housing Administration (FHA) sets the guidelines for these loans. The homeowner must be at least 62 years old and the value of the home must be sufficient to cover the obligation. The credit history of the homeowner is not determinative since the loan is essentially nonrecourse. It will eventually be paid out of the sales proceeds of the home and the borrower will not have to make up any difference if the home sells for less than the outstanding loan balance.

Another reverse mortgage product is the "Home Keeper" loan. This is a nonrecourse adjustable rate mortgage sponsored by Fannie Mae. This means the homeowner can take out the loan from a local lender and the lender can then sell the mortgage to Fannie Mae. Fannie Mae will make payments to the original lender and the original lender will make payments to the homeowner. See Jacqueline Queener, Note: Finding the Gold to Finance the "Golden Years": Options for Financing Long–Term Care in Arizona, 45 Ariz. L. Rev. 857 (2003).

[¶ 5,800]

(2) Sale and leaseback

Another way to realize the cash value of home equity is to structure a sale and leaseback transaction. Typically, the aging parent or parents will sell the home to the children either for a lump sum or for a promissory note payable over time. If there is a mortgage balance outstanding, the children can take title to the property "subject to" the mortgage, as transfers to children are exempted from "due on sale" clauses.

If the children make a lump sum payment, the parent can purchase an annuity or make a similar investment to create needed cash flow. Alternatively, the children can make installment payments of the purchase price and interest, providing the parent with monthly payments as needed. Or, the children might buy the home by agreeing to pay a life annuity to the parent. In this event, payments will cease at the death of the parent, whereas payments under an installment note continue after the parent's death and thus become an asset in the parent's estate. Some parents forgive these installment obligations at death and some structure the installment notes so that they will automatically cancel at death, making them functionally similar to a life annuity.

The most important thing in any of these arrangements is to be sure that the amount paid, whether in a lump sum or in installments, is equal to the fair market value of the residence. A sale at fair market value coupled with a leaseback of the premises will not create unintended or harmful tax results. But, if the parent sells the residence for less than it is worth, the sale will be partly a gift and subject to the estate inclusion rules of I.R.C. § 2036(a)(1) (transfer with retained life estate). See ¶ 4,280. If the home is the only remaining major asset, however, estate taxes may not be an issue because the estate is likely to be under the taxable threshold. If estate taxes are an issue, and the transaction runs the risk of being classified as part sale/part gift, then the parent may want to plan the transaction so as to meet the requirements of a "qualified personal residence trust." See ¶ 4,370.

In a sale-leaseback, the installment payments by the children provide needed cash flow to the parents, provided the installments exceed the rent that is charged to the parents under the "leaseback" part of the transaction. Installment notes (as well as annuities) include an interest factor, so the parent will have taxable interest income upon receipt of the payments, while the payments of principal will be tax-free to the extent they represent recovery of basis or excludable gain under § 121. The children, as lessors, will be entitled to tax deductions for interest, as well as other expenses related to the rental of the home (e.g., depreciation, repair, and maintenance) so long as it is rented at a fair rental value. See I.R.C. § 280A(d)(3).

If the parent is in need of additional support, the children may agree to offer the home at a reduced rent, or rent-free. In that case § 280A will treat the home as a personal residence of the children (see ¶¶ 5,820 and 5,830). Section 280A limits deductions for rental property that is used personally to the amount of rental income produced by the property. If the home is provided to the parent rent-free, the children would be able to deduct the interest on the purchase money installment obligation as qualified residence interest (subject to the overall limitations of § 163(h)(3)). They would also be entitled to deduct fully the property taxes as another itemized personal deduction. If rented at a reduced rate, they could deduct other allocable expenses against the rental income, but could not deduct expenses in excess of the rental income. For allocation formulas for rental property, see ¶ 5,830.

If there are no children who are capable of purchasing the property and leasing it back, the homeowner may look for an unrelated investor. The homeowner will want to be certain, however, that the investor is willing to sign a lease that will allow the owner to remain in the home as long as he or she wants.

[¶ 5,810]

(3) Sale of a remainder interest

Section 121 excludes the gain on a sale of a remainder interest. Thus, if there are children who are willing to purchase the home and let the parents remain in the home rent-free, the most direct way to accomplish that is for the parent to sell the remainder interest, retaining a life estate. As with the sale-leaseback, the parent should be careful to sell the remainder for full value to avoid the pitfalls of § 2036(a)(1).

[¶ 5,820]

4. Business Use of the Home

Some homeowners are able to get double service out of a home, using it for business purposes as well as for a personal residence. To the extent the home is used for business purposes, a portion of the cost of maintaining the home can be deducted against business income in the same way that the cost of maintaining a separate office can be deducted against business income. To qualify for these deductions, however, the taxpayer must meet the requirements of I.R.C. § 280A.

Section 280A was enacted in 1976 to reduce a taxpayer's ability to claim business deductions for certain expenses relating to the mixed personal and business use of the home. For example, under prior law, a school teacher who graded papers at the dining room table might claim deductions for part of the cost of the dining room (e.g., a portion of the rent if the teacher was a renter, or depreciation if the home was owned).

Under § 280A, deductions for such things as repairs and maintenance, utilities, hazard insurance, and depreciation are allowable only if the portion of the dwelling that is used for business purposes is used regularly and exclusively for business purposes. In addition, the dwelling space must be either the taxpayer's principal place of business, a place where the taxpayer meets with patients or clients, or a separate structure. Thus, there are three separate requirements that must be met before the taxpayer is entitled to any home office deductions: (1) exclusive use, (2) regular use, and (3) principal place of business.

Employees generally cannot claim that a portion of their dwelling is their principal place of business because most employers provide their employees with work space. Thus, classrooms are provided for teachers and offices for university professors. If the employer fails to provide adequate work space and expects the employee to do some of the work at home, then the dwelling might qualify. For example, a university professor who is expected to write scholarly works, but is not given a private office in which to conduct research, may claim that the office at home is the principal place of business rather than the shared classrooms and offices at the university. See Weissman v. Commissioner, 751 F.2d 512 (2d Cir. 1984) (allowing deduction for such home office expenses).

A person can have more than one trade or business, however. Thus, a taxpayer can have more than one principal place of business. For example, a lawyer might also be a novelist. The law office would be the principal place of his law practice, but his home office could be the principal place of his business as a novelist. Provided that writing novels is a real trade or business (and not just a hobby or hopeless quest for fame and fortune), the lawyer/novelist should be able to deduct home office expenses on his or her Schedule C, where income from that trade or business is likely to be reported.

When the lawyer/novelist sells the mixed-use property, questions arise about the applicability of the gain exclusion under § 121. Under earlier versions of § 121, the I.R.S. viewed the sale of a principal residence that had also been used as a home office as a sale of two separate properties: a principal residence and a business office. Prior to 1997, sales proceeds in such cases had to be allocated between the two properties and taxable and nontaxable gain computed accordingly. One way around this rule was for the homeowner to cease using the dwelling as a home office for a period of time and then claim that it qualified exclusively as a principal residence at the time of sale.

Under current law, whenever the sale of a dwelling includes a home office that is part of the dwelling, the full transaction qualifies for the gain exclusion, but § 121(d)(6) provides for recapture of any depreciation claimed for the home office. The recapture provision applies even if the property is not being used as a home office at the time of sale.

Example: Steve purchases a home in 2001 for $200,000 and uses part of the dwelling as a home office that qualifies for deductions under § 280A. He claims $10,000 in depreciation over the following years and ultimately sells the home in 2005 for $250,000. He can exclude $40,000 of the gain and must report $10,000 of depreciation recapture as ordinary income.

Assume, instead, that Steve retired in 2005 and ceased using part of his home as a home office. He also ceases taking home office deductions. When he sells the home in 2009, he will nonetheless have to report $10,000 of his gain as depreciation recapture.

[¶ 5,830]

5. Vacation Homes

It is not uncommon for persons of moderate wealth to acquire a second home, which may be used for personal recreational purposes (e.g., a vacation home) and also rented out for gain. Renting the property produces valuable rental income which can offset the cost of owning the property. Before § 280A was enacted in 1976, taxpayers could claim that their primary purpose in owning the second home was for investment or for income-producing purposes, even though the home was also used for personal purposes. If they could satisfy the primary purpose requirement, typically by showing that rental use of the property exceeded personal use, then they could claim an allocable portion of expenses as deductible expenses for the production of income. See I.R.C. § 212(1)–(2), allowing a deduction for expenses incurred for the production of income or the management of income-producing property whether or not the investment activity constitutes a trade or business. Taxpayers regularly deducted expenses under these provisions, usually in excess of the rental income produced by the property, thereby creating a loss that could be offset against other income. In effect, vacation homes were used as a tax shelter.

To combat this abuse, § 280A now limits the deductibility of expenses related to rental property that is also used by the taxpayer as a personal residence. These limitations generally apply to any dwelling that is used more than 14 days during the year for personal purposes. However, if the dwelling is rented out for more than 140 days, then the limitations apply only if the personal use days exceed 10% of the number of rental days. "Personal purposes" includes use by the taxpayer, family members, or others to whom the dwelling unit is rented at less than fair rental value. See I.R.C. § 280A(d).

Once the personal use of the dwelling unit triggers the application of § 280A, then deductions are limited as follows:

1. Otherwise allowable deductions (e.g., mortgage interest, property taxes, casualty losses) must first be allocated between rental use and personal use.

2. Provided that these expenses do not exceed rental income for the year, then other deductions allocable to the rental use of the dwelling can be deducted. Section 280A(e)(1) provides the allocation formula. It is a fraction in which the numerator is the number of days rented and the denominator is the number of days the unit is used. These expenses include such things as

hazard insurance, utilities, repairs, maintenance, and depreciation.

3. Deductions that do not reduce the basis of the property (i.e., anything other than depreciation) are to be taken first. If these expenses, together with the expenses in paragraph (1) above do not offset income, then depreciation may be claimed.

4. In any event, deductions cannot exceed rental income for the year.

An issue has arisen about how to compute the amount of "otherwise allowable deductions" (e.g., mortgage interest and property taxes) that are attributable to the rental activity. The regulations state a rule that is consistent with the statutory provision for the deduction of expenses that are not otherwise allowable (e.g., insurance, utilities, repairs, and depreciation). That rule is described in paragraph (2) above. It requires an allocation using a fraction in which the numerator is the number of days rented and the denominator is the total number of days used. But the statute does not provide for such an allocation. The statute is silent on how to allocate mortgage interest and taxes. It would be just as reasonable to allocate on the basis of a ratio of number of days rented to number of days in the year. After all, both mortgage interest and property taxes are paid over the full 365 days of the year and can be viewed as benefiting the property each day. Indeed, when a taxpayer claimed the right to use this allocation formula, the Court of Appeals for the Ninth Circuit agreed. See Bolton v. Commissioner, 694 F.2d 556 (9th Cir. 1982). There are times when the *Bolton* approach would be beneficial for the taxpayer and times when it would not be.

Example 1 (beneficial to the taxpayer): Assume the owner of the vacation home uses the dwelling for 20 days during the year and it is rented for 180 days. The restrictions of § 280A will apply. Now assume the gross rental for the 180 days is $18,000 ($100 per day). All of this $18,000 will be reported on Schedule E of the 1040 and will be included "above the line" except to the extent it can be offset by deductions. Otherwise allowable deductions (interest and property taxes) total $15,000. Under the *Bolton* rule, the taxpayer will deduct half of these expenses (180 days rented/360 days in the year) or $7,500. The advantage to the taxpayer is that the other $7,500 can be deducted as an itemized deduction on Schedule A. The taxpayer will win under the *Bolton* rule so long as she has additional deductions attributable to the rental of the vacation home that will wipe out all taxable income from the rental use. For example, assume expenses for maintenance, insurance, utilities, etc. total $5,000 for the year. She can deduct 180/200ths of that amount, or 90%, for a total deduction of $4,500. Now assume that depreciation for the year would be $10,000. She can deduct 90% of that, or $9,000. Thus, her $18,000 rental income will be reduced first by $7,500, bringing it down to 10,500. Then it will be further reduced by $4,500, bringing it down to $6,000. The depreciation deduction will offset this amount completely, eliminating the taxable income from the rental.

In addition, the taxpayer will be entitled to claim the remaining $7,500 of the interest and property taxes as an itemized deduction. Under the I.R.S. approach, she would be forced to deduct 90% of the $15,000 against the rental income and so would only have an additional $1,500 to claim as an itemized deduction. Total deductions under *Bolton* are $25,500 ($18,000 + $7,500). Total deductions under the I.R.S. approach are only $19,500 ($18,000 + $1,500).

Example 2 (not beneficial to the taxpayer): When the taxpayer does not have enough in total deductions beyond the mortgage interest and property taxes to offset all of the rental income, it may not be to the taxpayer's advantage to allocate the smaller portion of those deductions (50%) rather than the larger portion (90%) to the rental income. Assume rental income of $18,000 and allocable deductions other than interest and property taxes of only $4,000. That would leave $14,000 of rental income to be taxed and a 50% deduction for mortgage interest and taxes ($7,500) would leave taxable rental income of $6,500, whereas a 90% deduction ($13,500) would leave taxable income of only $500. Claiming the deduction "above the line" on Schedule E rather than "below the line" on Schedule A is usually more valuable because "above the line" deductions reduce adjusted gross income and "below the line" deductions are subject to additional limitations (and may trigger an alternative minimum tax).

J. SUMMARY OF COSTS AND BENEFITS OF HOME OWNERSHIP

[¶ 5,840]

Now let's return to our initial question: should Adam purchase a home or rent? While we can't know with certainty all the costs and benefits in advance, we can estimate them. And to do a close comparison, we should ask something like the following question: Let's assume that Adam wants to know which investment is better for the next three years. At the end of those three years, will the total payments for purchasing a home put him in a better situation than the total payments he would have had to make to rent a similar home for the same time period? And to make an accurate comparison, we would have to compute both costs and benefits in terms of present value—or in terms of future value. But in any event we would need to adjust dollar amounts to account for the time value of money.

Key questions that we would need to answer to make this determination for Adam during the first three years of owning the home are:

1. What is the total after-tax cost of acquiring the home in terms of present value? That is, what is the cost, expressed in year one values, of the down payment, the three years of mortgage payments (adjusted for the benefits of the income tax deduction for interest), and other incidental costs of acquisition paid during the first three years?

2.   What would have been the total cost of rent during the first three years to acquire the use of a similar home?

3.   What will be the value of the ownership interest (or the leasehold interest, if it has any value, which it might if the lease was renewable at a low rental rate) at the end of the three years?

Based on our initial assumptions, Adam was planning to spend $35,000 as a down payment in year one. Over three years, he would spend a total of $27,055.80 (36 × $751.55). Approximately $20,000 of those payments constitute interest. So the rough, after-tax cost of these mortgage payments is really $7,000 plus 70% of $20,000 (assuming a 30% marginal tax rate) or $21,000. Assume that property taxes are $1,000 a year. After taxes that would be $700 per year for a three-year total of $2,100. Assume other costs that Adam would have to bear as an owner rather than a renter amount to $4,000 over the three-year period. Then his total outlay is:

Down payment in year one	$35,000
After-tax cost of monthly mortgage payments	21,000
After-tax cost of property taxes	2,100
Additional home-owner costs (e.g., insurance, repairs)	4,000
Total costs invested by the end of year three	$61,100

If monthly rental payments for a similar home were $800 per month, then he would have paid out $28,800 (36 × $800) for rent during the same three-year period. And if he had invested the $35,000 rather than spending it for a down payment, he would have presumably been able to earn a return on it. The same would be true for amounts he might have saved by paying less in rent than in mortgage and other homeowner costs. As it turns out, in Adam's case projected rental costs are $28,800 over the three-year period, while home purchasing costs (other than the down payment) total $27,100. The costs are almost equal.

So the question in Adam's case boils down to this: how much is the $35,000 investment in the home worth at the end of three years compared to the $35,000 invested at an 8% after-tax return. Recall that on average home prices have increased in recent years by 8% per year. And remember that in the case of the home purchase, the 8% is not a return on just the $35,000 equity investment. Rather it is a return on the overall value of the home. A home that Adam buys for $175,000 in year one will have appreciation of $14,000 (8% of $175,000) in the first year, $15,120 (8% of 189,000) in the second year, and $16,330 (8% of 204,120) in the third year.

Adam's return as homeowner:

Fair market value of investment at end of year three	$220,450
Minus amount owed to bank at end of year three	(133,481)
Minus estimated selling expenses (at least 6% of listing price)	(13,227)
Total cash available	$ 73,742

Adam's return on the $35,000 if he rents:

Return of 8% in year one	$ 2,800
Return of 8% in year two	3,024
Return of 8% in year three	3,266
Total gain	$ 9,090
Total cash available (gain plus original investment)	$ 44,090

Question: Which looks like the better investment?

K.   AUTOMOBILES: TO PURCHASE OR TO LEASE?

[¶ 5,850]

While home purchases are almost always preferable to renting because of the ability to build up equity in the home, different considerations arise in the financial analysis of whether to purchase or lease a new automobile. Most automobiles, other than the rare classics, do not present opportunities for equity investments that will appreciate. A new car depreciates in value dramatically the moment it is driven off the lot. It suddenly becomes a "used car" and worth much less. Because automobiles are thought to depreciate rapidly in the early years of use and less rapidly in later years, the question of whether to purchase or lease depends heavily on how long the driver expects to keep the automobile before trading in for a newer model.

To make a comparison, however, one would need to go through the same steps as with Adam's proposed purchase of the home. First, compare the overall out of pocket expenses during the proposed term of use (say three years for someone who likes to change cars whenever the warranty runs out). Then ask what the residual value is at the end of the three years. In a lease, there is likely to be no residual value at the end of three years. In fact, some leases may actually require an additional cash payment by the lessee if the car is returned at the end of three years. In that case, there would be a negative value.

If the same car is purchased by making monthly payments over a three-year period, then at the end of the three years there will be some residual value. In almost all cases, a person who intends to use a car for a long period of time will be better off in the long run purchasing than leasing. In general, the advantages of leasing include lower monthly payments and the ability to acquire a new car every three or four years. Even though in the long run, leasing costs a bit more, it may be worth it to people who want to drive new cars rather than continuing to maintain their own cars over a long period of time.

When deciding how to finance a car, it is worth looking at the options available from car dealers that provide low interest rates. While a home equity loan is often a smart way to finance the purchase of a car because the interest is deductible, even a 4% home equity loan costs more after taxes than a 1.5% car loan. However, before deciding which financing opportunity to select, the car purchaser should verify whether there are additional costs for the 1.5% car loan and also whether the dealer is willing to take a lower price for a cash offer. Drawing on a home equity loan enables the purchaser to make a cash offer to the dealer and sometimes that offer will lead to a reduction in the price that is ultimately negotiated.

Chapter 6

MEETING THE COST OF HIGHER EDUCATION

A. INTRODUCTION

[¶ 6,000]

For most families, the cost of providing for the higher education of offspring is the family's second most onerous economic burden, eclipsed only by the cost of housing. Despite the effort required, most families willingly struggle to meet the burden for a variety of reasons, not the least of which is economic. Recent studies indicate that college graduates will earn up to one million dollars more, over a lifetime, than will individuals who only graduate from high school. For those who go on to attend professional and graduate schools, the difference can be even greater. There are also a variety of non-economic reasons for pursuing higher education. A college degree brings enhanced social standing and prestige. Moreover, a college education enriches the graduate's personal life by fostering a greater appreciation and understanding of the culture in which the graduate lives.

[¶ 6,005]

1. The Cost

According to the College Board, in the 2004–2005 academic year, the average in-state tuition and fees charged by public four-year colleges and universities was $5,132, up 10.5% from the year before, and the average for four-year private institutions was $20,082, up 6% from the previous year. Several things are worth noting about these data. First, the increases exceeded the increase in the Consumer Price Index for the year 2004 by 7.2% and 2.7% respectively. See College Board, Trends in College Pricing 2004 (2004). Second, because the data reflect average increases, they may understate the costs that families will actually confront when students are placed in the institutions to which they aspire. For example, as discussed below, tuition at elite private and flagship public institutions typically exceeds the average.

Although there was little real growth in tuition and fees over normal inflation during the 1970's, tuition and fees increases rapidly began to outstrip inflation in the 1980's. During most of the 1980's and 1990's public institutions provided families with relatively affordable options for educating their children. In recent years, however, due to mounting financial pressures, many states have raised tuition and fees at public institutions of higher learning at rates that vastly outstrip inflation. If this trend continues, it creates real concerns for families with young children that, when the college years arrive, even the cost of attending an average four-year public institution may be beyond their means.

It may be useful to put some flesh on the bones of the above mentioned averages by considering recent tuition and fees for some representative institutions. The tables below provide 2004–2005 data provided by typical schools in various categories.

Elite Private Institutions

Institution	Tuition and Fees	Room and Board
Cal Tech	$25,551	$9,939
Harvard	30,620	9,260
Smith	29,156	9,730
Stanford	29,847	9,503

Non–Elite Selective Private Institutions

Institution	Tuition and Fees	Room and Board
Creighton	$21,118	$7,200
Guilford	20,670	6,330
Ithaca	23,690	9,704
Wabash	22,274	7,050

Flagship Public Institutions

Institution	Tuition and Fees		Room and Board
	Resident	Non-resident	
University of Iowa	$5,396	$16,048	$6,350
University of North Carolina	4,444	15,920	6,756
University of Texas	6,786	14,490	7,088

As the above data indicate, tuition and fees plus room and board at elite institutions typically aggregate about $39,000, and those expenses at non-elite selective private institutions average about $8,000 to $12,000 less. Interestingly enough, families with a child at a private school may discover that the cost of a junior year abroad may amount to as much as $10,000 less than the cost of a junior year spent at the student's school. This is typically only the case if the student is able to enroll in a program (often run by another institution such as the state university of the student's home state) in which tuition and fees are charged at the rate that prevails at the foreign institution, most of which charge tuition, even to non-citizens, that is dramatically less than that charged by many U.S. private universities. If the student enrolls in a program abroad run by the U.S. private university that he or she attends, the family may discover that the same tuition and fees are charged with the home school pocketing the difference. Occasionally home schools will not permit students to attend programs abroad and still receive school-provided aid unless the student enrolls in the more expensive program sponsored by the home institution.

Tuition, fees and room and board at flagship public institutions for state residents typically aggregate about $11,000 to $13,000, and for non-residents they aggregate about $20,000 to $41,000. Moreover, enrollment in a study abroad program for students attending a state institution seldom results in any financial savings for the family. Often its effect is to increase aggregate costs by several thousand dollars.

To the above cost estimates for both private and public institutions, one must add average costs of about $1,000 to $2,500 for books, supplies, plane tickets home and other incidental expenses. One must bear in mind that the figures reported above are current costs. Most experts estimate that for a child born in 2004, the cost to a state resident of attending a typical public institution for four years will be about $150,000 and for an elite private institution such costs will approximate $400,000. Clearly, few families will be able to meet such costs from current income. Savings, use of tax-favored devices, borrowing and grants must all be used to bridge the gap between money available from current family income and the costs of higher education.

[¶ 6,010]

2. Elements Contributing to Escalating Costs

There are several reasons why we should anticipate that the cost of college tuition will increase at a rate in excess of the rate of inflation. Mark Kantrowitz, an expert on the topic, offers the following explanations. First, so-called tuition discounting accounts for about 30% of college tuition increases. Tuition discounting occurs when colleges decide to fund aid to less well-off students with tuition dollars paid by well-to-do families. Although the practice may seem strange at first blush, without it, many low-income families could not afford college. Second, declines in non-tuition income (such as endowments or licensing opportunities) relative to college operating expenses mean that tuition must rise to make up the difference. Third, declining state support for public institutions of higher education results in significant tuition increases at public institutions. Fourth, a general decline in the heady level of giving to colleges and universities that prevailed in the boom days of the 1990's leads to tuition increases as colleges struggle to fill the void left by the decline. Fifth, increases in the cost of instruction account for a significant portion of tuition increases. Sixth, relatively modest increases in the level of federal aid to colleges through grants and contracts have contributed to an escalation in the rate of tuition increases. See Mark Kantrowitz, Causes of Faster-than-Inflation Increases in College Tuition, 78 College & University 3–10 (Fall 2002). To the above one could also add, among other things, the rising cost of medical and psychological services that constitute a component of student fees.

[¶ 6,015]

3. The Roadmap to Meeting Expenses

The average middle or upper middle class family will find it very difficult, if not impossible, to meet college expenses for several children, even at a state institution, unless the family has planned and saved for a prolonged period of time. Injecting private institutions into the picture only compounds the family's problem, yet few families would willingly tell a child who is offered a place at an elite school to forgo all thought of attending such a school solely on economic grounds. Fortunately, federal and state governments are aware of these difficulties and have responded by providing a number of tax-favored savings plans as well as tax breaks for amounts spent on higher education. In addition, students may be eligible for financial assistance under federal and state grant-in-aid programs as well as government-sponsored loan programs. This chapter will first explore various tax-favored savings programs and then examine tax-favored spending programs, governmental grant-in-aid programs and government-sponsored loan programs. Many higher education institutions also have their own programs of assistance, such as scholarships and loan programs, but because such programs are unique to each institution they will not be discussed here.

B. TAX SHELTERED SAVINGS

[¶ 6,020]

The federal government provides several tax-favored means whereby families may save to meet the cost of higher education. Generally tax-favored savings programs make a good deal more sense for families than do conventional saving activities of children and parents. Nonetheless, some families prefer to steer clear of tax-favored programs so that they can seek higher yields, preserve flexibility and, in some cases, avoid penalties if money is withdrawn for non-qualifying use. The discussion below will first deal briefly with non-sheltered savings activities and then concentrate on several tax-sheltered programs provided by the Internal Revenue Code.

[¶ 6,025]

1. Traditional Non–Tax Sheltered Savings

Many families engage in traditional savings programs that are intended to meet future goals and needs, including higher education for their children. These savings programs may be conducted at the level of the child or the parents with either designated as the saver in whose name the assets are kept. Saving by the parents in this manner has both advantages and disadvantages. Among the principal advantages are the following. The parents retain complete control of the assets and may ultimately do with them as they wish, with no penalty or adverse tax consequences if the parents eventually use the funds for purposes other than the child's education. Moreover, in assessing financial need, the federal government and many institutions of higher learning expect that a lower percentage of assets held in the name of the parents must be dedicated to meeting educational expenses, whereas a higher percentage of assets held by the student must be dedicated to meeting such expenses. (See ¶ 6,230). Parents who hold assets in their own names should be aware, however, that most additional aid provided by institutions comes in the form of loans rather than grants-in-aid, so that the net result of such a strategy may simply be to send children off into life with even more debt than is necessary. The principal disadvantage of holding assets in the parents' names is that income derived from those assets will most likely be subject to tax at a significantly higher rate than if the assets were held by the child. Indeed, the principal advantage of placing investment assets in the hands of children who are likely at some point to attend college or university is that the income from the assets will be taxed to the children (who are invariably in lower tax brackets than their parents). There are several caveats worth noting. First, the child as owner of the property is free to use the funds for non-educational items, and the family may awake one day to find a shiny new Harley parked in the driveway (or worse, up a tree). Second, depending on the age of the child, "kiddie tax" consequences may follow (see ¶ 3,740), although, even if the kiddie tax applies because of the age of the child and the amount of unearned income in a given year, some tax savings are nevertheless available. Third, as noted above, the federal guidelines and those used by most colleges for allocating additional aid require that a higher percentage of student-held assets be dedicated to satisfying educational expenses before aid is made available.

Parents and others who do not wish to avail themselves of any of the tax-sheltered college savings devices described below and who do not feel comfortable putting assets directly in the hands of minors may wish to consider the following strategy often used by individuals who have such concerns. Under § 1015 of the Internal Revenue Code, appreciated assets acquired by gift have a carryover basis in the hands of the donee. When college bills arrive, parents or others who are in high tax brackets and who hold appreciated assets that are ripe for sale may simply transfer those assets to the student, who may then sell them and pay the resulting tax at what are likely to be significantly lower rates. In doing so, donors should be mindful of their gift and estate tax situation. For example, a married donor who intends to make a gift in excess of the annual per donee exclusion allowed under the gift tax should take care to obtain the consent of his or her spouse so that the couple may make use of the spouse's exclusion and preserve the donor's lifetime exemption. See ¶¶ 3,500 and 4,150.

[¶ 6,030]

2. Series EE U.S. Savings Bonds

Series EE U.S. savings bonds are zero-coupon bonds that pay no interest currently but accumulate accrued interest for payment at maturity. The taxation of Series EE savings bonds is unique in several respects. First, under § 454 of the Code, at the election of the taxpayer, interest income on such bonds, rather than being taxed to the holder on redemption of the bond, may be taxed to the holder annually as the interest accrues. If the bond is held by a minor who would be taxed at a low tax rate or escape tax altogether, it often makes good sense to make this election with the result that, on redemption, none of the proceeds will be subject to taxation. If this is not done, the holder runs the risk that on redemption all or a large portion of the increase in value of the bond reflecting interest will be subject to tax, perhaps at higher rates than would otherwise have been the case had the election been made. This feature of Series EE bonds allows them to be intelligently used as a vehicle for accumulating income at relatively low tax rates or completely free of tax. Families occasionally use Series EE bonds to accumulate savings for meeting future education expenses of a child. To obtain such an advantage, the bond must be placed in the name of the minor (often with the parent as custodian), who presumably will be taxed at a lower rate than her parents.

A second unique feature of Series EE bonds is that under § 135 of the Code, redemption proceeds of such bonds that are used to satisfy higher education expenses may partially or completely escape federal income taxation. Obviously § 135 will be of little interest to individuals who elect to be taxed annually on the income accruing on Series EE bonds.

There are a number of conditions attached to the income exclusion feature of § 135. Only so-called "qualified U.S. savings bonds" (hereafter QSB) are eligible for the special treatment accorded by § 135. To be deemed qualified, a bond must be a Series EE savings bond and must have been issued after 1989 to an individual who had attained age 24 before issuance of the bond. Although a QSB may be held by a married couple which holds the bond as joint tenants with rights of survivorship, interest on such a bond does not qualify if the bond is held by married taxpayers filing separately. Because of the age requirement for holders, the typical QSB will likely be held by parents or grandparents who will use bond proceeds to meet the educational costs of offspring. However, an individual who has attained 24 years of age could purchase a Series EE bond for the purpose of later using it to pay for the further education of the individual or the individual's spouse. If a parent intends to take advantage of § 135 and purchases a bond in the name of a minor child, intending to use the proceeds to meet college expenses for that child, the bond will not qualify as a QSB because it was acquired by an individual less than 24 years of age.

To qualify for exclusion, proceeds of the redemption of a qualifying Series EE bond must be used exclusively to pay for "qualified higher education expenses" (135QE). Section 135(c)(2) defines 135QE as tuition and fees, at an institution of higher learning or certain vocational schools, of the taxpayer, the taxpayer's spouse or any dependent of the taxpayer that the taxpayer is entitled to treat as a dependent under § 151 of the Code. It is worth noting that room and board do not qualify as 135QE and that "qualified higher education expenses" for § 135 purposes are slightly different from "qualified higher education expenses" as defined elsewhere in the Code. Because of the § 151 dependent requirement and the narrow definition of qualifying expenses under § 135, the § 135 exclusion is typically used by a parent or grandparent who held a QSB and redeemed it to meet the tuition and fees of a child or grandchild whom the parent or grandparent is entitled to claim as a dependent under § 151.

If the redemption proceeds (original invested capital plus accrued interest) do not exceed the student's tuition and fees and the taxpayer pays the educational institution in question an amount at least equal to the redemption proceeds to cover all or part of the tuition and fees of the holder, her spouse, dependent child or grandchild, the full amount of the accrued interest on the QSB will escape taxation as long as the holder does not run afoul of certain income limits which will be discussed later. If the redemption proceeds of the QSB exceeds the 135QE paid in a given year, then only a portion of the interest on the QSB will be excluded. Under § 135(b)(1) the portion of interest that may be excluded is determined by using the following formula:

$$\frac{\text{135 QE Paid by Taxpayer in Year}}{\substack{\text{Aggregate QSB Redemption Proceeds} \\ \text{Received by Taxpayer in Year}}} \times \substack{\text{Aggregate Accrued Interest} \\ \text{Received in Year}}$$

For example, if the total tuition and fees or 135QE paid by a married couple (Mary and Bob) for their son Paul in the year are $4,000 and Mary or Bob redeemed in the same year a QSB receiving $6,000 in redemption proceeds of which $1,500 was accrued interest, only $1,000 of the interest would qualify for exclusion under § 135.

Further complicating the calculations is the limitation imposed by § 135(d)(1) in situations where the student has qualified for scholarship aid as described in § 117 or for any of several other assistance programs (veteran benefits, employer payments excluded under § 127 and payments made under § 529 plans). In such cases, the amount paid as a scholarship or other benefit is subtracted from the tuition and fees for the purpose of determining 135QE and making the required calculations. If in the prior example Bob and Mary still receive the same $6,000 of redemption proceeds but Paul received a scholarship of $1,000, 135QE would be reduced to $3,000 and only $750 of the total $1,500 in accrued interest received by Mary and Bob would qualify for § 135 exclusion.

Extremely significant limitations on the use of Series EE bonds as tax-favored savings vehicles are the income-based exclusion phase-out rules of § 135(b)(2). These phase-out rules operate with respect to "modified adjusted gross income" (adjusted gross income modified by several additional adjustments). For the year 2004, the inflation-adjusted phase-out ranges for the exclusion were from $89,750 to $119,750 for a married couple and from $59,850 to $74,850 for all other taxpayers. The amount of accrued interest that is otherwise excludable is reduced proportionately as one's modified adjusted gross income (MAGI) rises within the phase-out range. For example, if in 2004 our married couple Mary and Bob had MAGI of $104,750, then only one-half of any accrued interest on the QSB that would otherwise be excluded would qualify for exclusion. This would then operate to further reduce the amount of accrued interest qualifying for exclusion from $750 to $375.

The income-based phase-out feature severely limits the usefulness of § 135 as a savings device with predictable value for parents. Because investors must purchase Series EE bonds a good many years in advance of their projected redemption date if the bonds are to accumulate a significant amount of accrued interest, at the time of purchase it will be virtually impossible to estimate with any accuracy the taxpayer's MAGI at the time of redemption. Section 135 provides the taxpayer with a hit-or-miss tax savings device about which the taxpayer can make few plans as to its future real value. Quite possibly, many individuals who purchase Series EE bonds expecting to reap the exclusion benefit of § 135 will find that because of improvements in their employment or financial situation, the expected tax saving benefit will have completely evaporated when college bills come due. Indeed, § 135 may be most useful to taxpayers who purchased Series EE bonds years earlier for investment purposes and discover that, when tuition bills fall due, they fit comfortably within the profile of those for whom § 135 is of maximum value.

Because Series EE bonds provide only modest rates of return, many families are more interested in savings options that promise the hope of higher rates of return. Such families will typically be interested in exploring the options made available by § 529 and Coverdell Education Savings Accounts. Those topics are explored in the materials that follow.

[¶ 6,033]

Problems

1. Every year for the last ten years, Paul's grandparents have given him a $1,000 face amount Series EE savings bond as a birthday present, and they have always told him that the bonds were to be used for his college education. Paul is now 19 years old and will begin attending college in the fall. He has heard that Series EE savings bonds can be advantageously used to meet higher education expenses and asks you to explain how he may do so with the bonds he holds.

2. Sally recently gave birth to a baby girl Molly. She and her husband Dan ask you whether you think they should buy Series EE savings bonds to save for Molly's college education. Dan is an accountant with a major accounting firm with audit responsibilities and Sally is a buyer for a department store, and consequently neither of them has extensive knowledge of tax laws.

3. Mary is a single parent school teacher with MAGI of $50,000. This fall her daughter Rita will be attending State University, where annual tuition is $6,000 ($3,000 due in August and $3,000 due in December). Mary holds two $5,000 face amount Series EE savings bonds that she purchased 10 years ago for $2,500 each and each are now worth $4,500. Mary asks you if the tax consequences would be the same if she redeemed both bonds this year or redeemed one this year and the second the next year.

[¶ 6,040]

3. Section 529 Qualified Tuition Plans

There are essentially two distinct types of qualified tuition plans that are encompassed by § 529, which was added to the Code in 1996. The two types of tuition plans are: (1) the prepaid tuition credit plan (PTC plan); and (2) the education savings plan (ESP). A PTC plan enables families to purchase, in advance, tuition credits on behalf of a designated beneficiary which may be used by the beneficiary to pay for future qualified higher education expenses. The basic goal of the PTC plan, as originally conceived, is to enable a family to purchase tomorrow's college costs at today's prices. Under an ESP, the individual makes contributions with after-tax dollars to an account which invests those contributions free of tax and later pays out accumulated funds without any further income taxes to satisfy qualified higher education expenses.

[¶ 6,045]

a. *Prepaid tuition credit plans*

By 2003, eighteen states had adopted prepaid tuition credit plans as authorized under § 529(b)(1)(A)(i). The plans vary considerably but, in general, they enable families to prepay tuition costs to a state agency. Most such plans require that participants be residents of the sponsoring state. The appeal of the plans is that they allow families to cover the cost of future years of higher education with their present payment. Under a PTC plan as originally intended and in its simplest form, the family pays tuition for college credit hours at today's rates and then uses the prepaid credits years later when the child is admitted to college. For example, assume that a family had used a PTC plan to prepay 24 credit hours of college at a state university several years ago, having paid the then required $100 per credit hour for a total of $2,400. Assume that the child commenced university last fall when tuition was $150 per credit hour and that the child enrolled for 15 credit hours of courses during the fall for which the family was billed $2,250. The family would simply use 15 of the prepaid credits to satisfy the bill and would owe no additional money to the university. In the spring when the child enrolled for 15 additional credit hours of courses, the family would again receive a bill for $2,250 and would use the remaining 9 prepaid credits to satisfy a portion of the bill but would be obligated to pay the university $150 per credit hour for the remaining 6 credit hours that were not satisfied by use of prepaid credits. The principal tax advantage of PTC plans under § 529 is that neither the individuals purchasing credits for designated would-be college students nor the designated individuals themselves are taxed on the increase in value of the credits as they accrue or as they are used. The tax advantages of PTC plans are discussed in more detail at ¶ 6,070.

States typically established PTC plans to assure parents of young children that they would be able to afford to pay for higher education at a state institution when their child reached college age. By purchasing tuition credits over the years, parents would approach the college years with all, or a large part of, the college tuition costs already satisfied. The plans originally came into favor when tuition at state institutions was not rising at a significant rate. Moreover, during the late 1990's the states were able to invest funds collected from parents at a rate of return that generally outstripped, or at least kept up with, the rate of tuition increases at state institutions. The post–2000 economic decline placed extraordinary economic burdens on the states, most of which saw budget surpluses turn into massive budget shortfalls. In a political environment in which tax increases were anathema, many states were forced to raise additional revenue by imposing double-digit annual increases in tuition at state colleges and universities. The result is that some states have recently imposed significant surcharges on prepaid tuition plans to enable them to meet future estimated tuition. For example, some states now charge a premium of about 20% per prepaid credit hour over the current cost of credit hours. Other states have frozen their plans to new entrants or new contributions by already enrolled members.

Although these PTC plans can, in the right circumstances, provide families with a valuable opportunity to meet future college expenses, the plans do present a number of difficulties. First, in only a small minority of the participating states are the plans backed with the full faith and credit of the state. In several other states the legislature is required by law to appropriate funds annually to cover any shortfalls, but such legislation is subject to change. Second, if a child decides to attend a private institution or an out-of-state public university, then the family will receive credit for the private or out-of-state institution based on the plan's pre-existing formula. Typically these formulas give the family credit for funds paid plus a modest rate of interest, making them a bad vehicle for saving for college in such circumstances. Occasionally state PTC plans are more generous. Illinois, for example, provides credit toward tuition at non-qualifying institutions at a level equal to the average tuition and mandatory fees at Illinois public institutions. Third, should a family discover that it will not be using accumulated credits for college expenses, most state plans, in addition to providing a refund with only modest interest, also impose a penalty fee.

In 2001, Congress authorized private higher educational institutions, either singly or acting in groups, to establish PTC plans. In 2003, TIAA–CREF launched an independent PTC plan ("Tuition Plan Consortium" or TPC) covering about 240 elite and selective institutions of higher learning. The Internal Revenue Service ruled that the plan qualified as a § 529 prepaid tuition plan in Priv. Ltr. Rul. 200311034. Under the plan, families may purchase credits toward tuition costs at any of the participating schools based on the tuition rates prevailing at the time of purchase. For example, assume that a family paid $10,000 into the plan in a year in which annual tuition at colleges A and B were $20,000 and $30,000 respectively and that, when their child reached college age, annual tuition at A was $28,000 and annual tuition at B was $48,000. Because, at the time of prepayment, the family had paid an amount equal to one-half of the tuition at A, it would owe college A an additional $14,000 (½ of the $28,000 tuition). Whereas, if the child enrolled in college B, because the family at the time of prepayment had prepaid an amount equal to one-third of the annual tuition at B, $16,000 or ⅓ of the $48,000 tuition bill at B would be deemed prepaid and the student's family would be responsible for the remaining two-thirds or $32,000.

An added advantage of the TPC is that participating schools have pledged to provide a discount of at least one-half percent on tuition to plan participants, with some schools promising to provide discounts in the range of 2–3%. Also, in contrast with a state sponsored PTC plan, the range of schools at which the TPC credits may be used is considerably larger and not geographically limited. For example, consortium members include: Princeton, Notre Dame, MIT, Smith, Chaminade, Furman, Middlebury, Emory, Guilford and Stanford. The two most widely cited disadvantages of the plans are: (1) families may be able to make private investments that outpace the rate of private school tuition increases; and (2) under Department of Education guidelines, prepaid tuition credits (either PTC or TPC), to the extent used, basically reduce a child's overall financial need on a dollar-for-dollar basis. (See ¶ 6,230.) These criticisms of the TPC (which are also leveled at state-sponsored PTC plans) themselves suffer from several weaknesses. First, unless a family invests in one of the tax-sheltered plans described at ¶¶ 6,050–

6,085, the savings will be subject to taxation. Beating a tax-sheltered investment with a taxed investment (after payment of taxes) is a feat that few investors will be lucky enough to accomplish. Second, as discussed at ¶ 6,260, the present subsidized government loan program makes available such a relatively small amount of money each year that many students from middle class families will find that they fully qualify for the maximum available loan amount regardless of how Department of Education guidelines treat prepaid tuition credits and the gap must be filled by non-subsidized loans. Also, as previously stated, there seems to be little reason for a cohesive family to launch a child into life burdened with vast amounts of debt while the parents bask in the glow of a large pool of investment assets held in their names. See "Beware of Hidden Pitfalls in 529 Plans," Employee Benefit News 1 (Jan. 1, 2003).

[¶ 6,050]

b. *Education savings plans*

In addition to prepaid tuition credit plans, § 529 also provides for state-sponsored tax-sheltered education savings plans. See I.R.C. § 529(b)(1)(A)(ii). In general, under an ESP individuals make contributions to state-sponsored savings plans on behalf of designated would-be college students. The amounts so contributed are invested by the states or other organizations operating on behalf of the states and, when the designated individual attends an institution of higher learning, the funds accumulated in each individual's account are made available to satisfy qualified undergraduate, graduate or professional school expenses. The principal tax advantage of such plans is that neither the individual making contributions to the plan nor the designated beneficiary is taxed on the increase in value of the account as it accrues or as it is drawn down to meet qualifying expenses. The tax advantages of ESPs are discussed in more detail at ¶ 6,070.

An ESP is managed either by a state agency or by various private financial service management companies designated by a state. Only a small number of states (such as Virginia) actually manage their funds themselves through state agencies, and most of those states also offer one or more ESPs that are managed by private financial service companies which we will refer to as the plan manager (PM). Choosing the correct ESP for a consumer is probably more difficult than choosing the best mutual fund for normal non-sheltered investment. See Chapter 1. Just as investors in mutual funds often confront a variety of commissions, management fees and exit fees that may greatly diminish their actual net return, so too does the individual seeking to make a contribution to an ESP. Among the fees that may be levied on an ESP are: (1) a front-end load commission or charge; (2) a fixed minimum management fee that is often waived when the accumulated investment in a fund exceeds a given threshold; (3) annual management fees charged by the PM; (4) a management fee charged by the fund in which the PM chooses to invest the funds; and (5) an exit fee charged by the PM based on a percentage of the funds paid out of the fund in a given year. Not all ESPs impose all the fees listed above.

Individuals looking to place funds with an ESP confront a difficult task in assessing and balancing all the competing factors and weighing the costs and benefits. It is important to keep in mind that individuals are not limited to using only an ESP sponsored by the individual's state of residence. Most, but not all, states welcome investments in their ESPs by non-residents. Moreover, some states (e.g., New York, Michigan, Missouri, Utah and Wisconsin) offer limited tax deductions for funds invested in an ESP (the federal government does not do so), and the resulting enhancement in the after-tax investment yield can act as a powerful inducement for individuals who reside in such states to invest in their ESPs.

Individuals are well advised to avoid placing an ESP with a PM that has high management fees and either commissions or exit fees. The importance of this advice is illustrated by the following two examples.

Example 1. Michigan's College Savings Program is managed by TIAA–CREF, which charges neither a commission nor an exit fee. The fund is subject only to a 0.65% annual fee on accumulated capital. Nora, who is not a state resident and therefore has no benefit from a state tax deduction, places $1,000 in the fund for the benefit of her daughter Gloria. If the fund realizes a 6% annual rate of return over a ten-year period, after allowing for the 0.65% management fee, the fund will have grown to $1,684.

Example 2. At the same time that Nora made the above investment for Gloria's benefit, Nora's husband Tom placed $1,000 in an ESP sponsored by Arizona which charged a $10 enrollment fee and a 5.75% commission resulting in a net investment of $932.50. The PM of the Arizona plan charged a 0.91% annual management fee and placed the investment in a fund that was subject to annual management expenses of 0.85%. The fund, like the fund in *Example 1*, realized a gross annual return of 6% before management fees and expenses. The combined annual management fee of the PM (0.91%) and the annual management expenses of the investment fund (0.85%) will reduce the net investment return to 4.24%. Over a period of ten years Tom's initial investment of $1,000 will grow to $1,412.51, or $271.49 less than the investment made by Nora in *Example 1.*

As the above examples indicate, it is not enough to simply save for a child's education with the aid of an ESP. It is important that the investor thoroughly research the various investment opportunities available. Both *Examples 1* and *2* are based on actual state-approved ESPs. See Richard Feigenbaum & David Morton, The 529 College Savings Plan and "How to Pick the Right College Plan," Business Week 88 (March 11, 2002). The results in *Example 2* are so bad that most investors could probably achieve better after-tax results using a conventional investment vehicle such as a tax managed index fund. For example, assume that

Tom instead invested $1,000 in a tax managed index fund that charges no commissions and realizes annual dividend income of 1% as well as annual capital appreciation of 5% (none of which is subject to capital gains tax due to the tax management skills of the fund manager). Assume that dividends are subject to combined state and federal taxes of 20% and that the investor withdraws from the fund only an amount equal to the tax on the dividends so that he can hold the fund at no out-of-pocket annual cost to himself. Moreover, assume that at year end the fund charges a management fee of 0.2% (as is typical of a well managed index fund), and that at the end of ten years Tom liquidates his investment in the mutual fund and pays combined state and federal tax of 20% on the capital gains that he realized in the fund. Under these circumstances, he would have $1,598.75 available after tax to be used toward Gloria's tuition expenses, leaving him $186.24 ahead of where he would have been under the ESP illustrated in *Example 2*. For a good discussion of this issue, see Lynn Asinof, "Hefty Fees Can Crimp Your College Savings," Wall Street Journal D2 (April 17, 2002) (recommending the New York, Missouri, Minnesota and Michigan plans, all then using TIAA–CREF with 0.65% annual fee). Recently some states have become more aware of the significance of keeping plan costs low and net yields high and have made changes in plan structures to help investors maximize yields. For example, in 2003, New York switched to Upromise Investments Inc. as its provider (with the Vanguard Group as investment manager), thereby lowering the annual fee for its plan to 0.58%. A good internet site for keeping current on various state plans is <www.savingforcollege.com>.

Most noteworthy in the above examples is that, because of the high fees associated with the ESP in *Example 2,* a family is actually likely to be better off forgoing investing in such a fund. Also, it is interesting that even the low-cost fund in *Example 1* outperforms the fully taxed savings vehicle by only $85.25 or 14.2%. As we will see later, when we explore other tax-favored educational spending devices which provide for deductions and credits, most of these do not allow a deduction or a credit, if the funds in question come from a tax-sheltered § 529 plan, with the result that, in some circumstances, a fully taxed savings vehicle may actually be superior to a tax-sheltered § 529 ESP for meeting at least a portion of educational expenses.

As the above discussion indicates, it pays for families to shop around when choosing an ESP. Families must not only examine a great number of competing products but also take into account the advantages of any potential tax deduction (or credit) provided at the state level. For example, if Nora and Tom resided in Michigan, which provides a state income tax deduction for contributions to the state's ESP and also provides a limited $1 for $3 matching credit for first-year participants with family incomes below $80,000, the benefit to the couple from investing in the Michigan plan would be all the greater.

The investment strategies of ESPs vary considerably. Some states offer only one investment plan while others offer a great variety. For example, the only available option under one state's plan consists of certificates of deposit, whereas other states offer a choice of investment opportunities. It is not uncommon to find that a state's plan adjusts investments based on the age of the designated beneficiary. For example, although a plan may allow contributions to be initially allocated to a growth stock fund, it may require that, when the beneficiary reaches age 14, the funds shall be reallocated to a federal funds investment pool so as to minimize market risk as the beneficiary approaches college age. It is also worth noting that some state plans are restricted to residents whereas other plans accept contributions from any resident of the United States (and several impose higher fees on out-of-state participants).

Proponents cite as an additional advantage of ESPs the fact that they receive favorable treatment for the purpose of federal aid and loan determinations. Assets held in an ESP established by a parent are not deemed assets of the child but rather are deemed assets of the parent. As a result, under federal guidelines (see ¶ 6,230), a lower percentage of such assets must be used to fund a child's education than would be the case if the child were treated as the owner. The same caveats noted above (see ¶¶ 6,025 and 6,045) about not placing too much weight on such considerations are equally applicable here in making long term decisions about saving for higher education.

Finally, in formulating a saving strategy, families should keep in mind the very liberal federal income tax rates accorded to dividends and capital gains by the Jobs and Growth Tax Relief Reconciliation Act of 2003. In general, under the 2003 Act, long term capital gains on equity investments and dividends are taxed at a maximum rate of 15%; for taxpayers in the 10% and 15% brackets, such gains and dividends are subject to tax at 5% (and at 0% only in the year 2008). Under sunset provisions of the 2003 Act, these favorable rates will expire in 2009 and long term capital gains on such investments will revert to being taxed at 20%, except for taxpayers in the 10% and 15% brackets who will be taxed at 10% on such gains. In 2009 all dividend income will be taxed at the taxpayer's normal rates. (See ¶ 3,810.) A taxpayer who wishes to take advantage of these low rates can place assets in the name of a child or hold the assets herself. If a tax managed index fund is used, the major concern is the taxation of dividends which normally would be expected to run around 1½% of the principal amount in the fund. On a $100,000 investment this might only produce annual dividend income of about $1,500. The federal income tax to a parent who kept the investment in his own name would be $225. Even if the assets were placed in the name of a child subject to the kiddie tax, only nominal tax would be due. For example, in 2004, only $35.00 in tax would have been due (nothing on the first $800 and 5% on the next $800). See ¶ 3,740. This should be contrasted with the results under even a good state ESP such as the Michigan plan in *Example 1* where the fund is subject to a management fee that is typically 0.45% above that of a well managed index fund. The resulting additional fee of $450 would exceed any federal tax due in either scenario. The situation changes a bit if one allows for some significant appreciation in the investment assets and injects capital gains into the picture. For example, assume that after about four years the investment appreciates to $150,000 and is sold. This would result in a capital gains tax of $7,500 if the assets are held by the parent (or by a child subject to the "kiddie tax" who had used up the $800 standard deduction and $800 low rate bracket available under the "kiddie tax"). No tax would be due if the gain were realized by an ESP, and even five years of management fees at the rate of 0.45% above typical index fund management fees would not come close to equaling the tax burdens of either parent or child. Slightly more favorable tax results would be obtained if the child was not subject to the "kiddie tax," but the ESP would still produce superior results overall. If one injects a state income tax into the picture for a state whose tax law is in conformity with federal law, the relative after-tax advantages of using a low cost ESP would be even greater.

[¶ 6,060]

c.   *Qualifying requirements for § 529 tuition plans*

Section 529 imposes a number of requirements on both PTC plans and ESPs that qualify for the tax benefits accorded these plans. The most important of these requirements are discussed below, and the tax benefits are discussed in more detail at ¶ 6,070.

Under § 529(b)(2) a qualified ESP or PTC plan may accept only contributions in cash. This requirement is apparently imposed to foreclose any attempt by taxpayers to avoid recognizing gain on contributions of appreciated assets and to simplify administration of § 529 plans by their PMs. For example, this requirement makes it unnecessary for PMs to concern themselves with valuing contributions of land or closely held stock. Moreover, existing participants in § 529 plans need not be concerned about potential dilution of their interests resulting from overvaluation of assets contributed in kind. Lastly, if assets such as restricted stock could be contributed to a plan, the PM not only would have difficulty in valuing the stock but would also be constrained in dealing with the stock as long as it remained subject to restrictions on sale.

Section 529 plans are required to maintain separate accounts for each designated beneficiary. See I.R.C. § 529(b)(3). Nonetheless, the contributor (not the beneficiary) is deemed to be the owner of a § 529 plan. A contributor to a § 529 plan, however, may not have any direct or indirect control over the investment of contributions to the plan or the income therefrom. See I.R.C. § 529(b)(4). Although this latter requirement is of little consequence in the case of a PTC plan, it has significance for a contributor to an ESP. Such accounts are not like self-directed IRAs where the owner exercises direct control over investments, or conventional IRAs where the owner may change the fund in which his IRA is invested. Nonetheless, depending on the state plan to which contributions are being made, it may be possible for a contributor to make contributions to various types of accounts with differing investment strategies. It is not uncommon to encounter state plans which provide a broad range of investment options such as a growth fund, an index fund, several sector funds and a money market fund. Moreover, funds in a § 529 plan may be switched to another investment fund within the plan or to another § 529 plan as long as this is done more than 12 months after the date of inception of the account and any transfer of funds to the account. See I.R.C. § 529(c)(3)(C). The ability to make such changes gives the owner of the account some limited control over strategy for investing the funds in the account. For example, if a contributor-owner of a § 529 account that is invested in an index fund is concerned that the market may be close to topping out and if she has not switched into the existing fund in the last 12 months or made new contributions to the account within 12 months, she could move the § 529 account from the index fund into a bond fund or money market fund. After having made such a switch, however, she would have to leave the account in the new fund for the next 12 months. In addition, a contributor who makes relatively frequent periodic contributions (e.g. monthly rather than annually) thereby retains a different type of flexibility. For example, if three months after commencing contributions to an ESP growth fund there was a severe market downturn, the contributor could shift new monthly contributions into a money market or similar funds.

Section 529 imposes two additional requirements. Under § 529(b)(5) neither an ESP nor a PTC plan may allow any interest in the program or a portion thereof to be used as a security for any loan. Moreover, a program will lose its status as a qualified tuition program, thereby jeopardizing the status of its ESPs and PTC plans, unless it provides adequate safeguards to ensure that contributions on behalf of a designated beneficiary will not exceed an amount necessary to meet the qualified education expenses (generally tuition, fees, books, supplies and equipment required for enrollment, as well as room and board for students enrolled at least half time and special needs services for special needs students) of individual designated beneficiaries. See I.R.C. § 529(b)(6), (e)(3). States normally meet this obligation by determining the maximum amount required to meet such expenses at the most expensive institution of higher learning in their given state and prohibiting any new contributions that would bring the account accumulations per beneficiary above that amount. For example, in Wisconsin in 2004 no additional contributions may be made to a § 529 plan account with one beneficiary if total accumulations equal or exceed $246,000; if the account had two designated beneficiaries then the account cap would be $492,000. These caps on contributions are of little consequence for most families who are likely to be more concerned with making adequate contributions to a § 529 plan than with exceeding allowable limits.

[¶ 6,070]

d. Income, gift and estate tax benefits of § 529 plans

Neither the contributor to a qualified § 529 plan nor the designated beneficiary of such a plan derives any federal income tax advantage (such as a deduction or a credit) on the occasion of a contribution to a qualified § 529 plan. However, a handful of states do provide a deduction (or credit) for state income tax purposes for contributions to their state-sponsored plans. Of prime importance to families saving for higher education is the fact that § 529 plans are exempt from income taxation with the result that all internal build-ups in account value from ordinary income or capital gains are exempt from income tax. See I.R.C. § 529(a). Equally important is the fact that funds and credits withdrawn from a qualified § 529 plan are free of income tax to the extent they are used to satisfy "qualified higher education expenses" of a designated beneficiary. See I.R.C. § 529(c). The contributor to the § 529 plan, as the owner of the § 529 account, has control over when and how much of the accumulated funds and credits are to be applied toward qualifying expenses in any given year. Although most states also allow tax-free withdrawal from § 529 accounts to meet such expenses, several do not. In recent years, as states have searched for new sources of revenue, some states have passed legislation that limits the privilege of tax-free withdrawal at the state level to situations where the beneficiary attends an institution of higher education located within the sponsoring state.

Under § 529(c)(3)(A) and (c)(6), distributions which are not made to meet qualified higher education expenses (QHEE) subject the distributee to income tax on the portion of the distribution that reflects internal build-up in the value of the account and in most cases to a 10% penalty tax. To avoid such adverse tax consequences, it is therefore essential that all distributions be made only for QHEE. Section 529(e)(3)(A) defines QHEE as tuition, books, supplies and equipment (e.g. a computer) required for enrollment and attendance of the designated beneficiary at an eligible educational institution. If the designated beneficiary is a special needs student, special needs expenses are also deemed to qualify as QHEE. In addition, limited amounts paid for room and board of a designated beneficiary who attends school at least half-time may also be deemed QHEE. See I.R.C. § 529(e)(3)(B). To guard against funds in a § 529 plan being used to finance lavish room and board, § 529(e)(3)(B)(ii) provides a mechanism for limiting room and board to reasonable amounts for the college attended by the beneficiary. Primarily to accommodate PTC plans, § 529(c)(3)(B)(i) also allows for in-kind distributions of QHEE by a § 529 plan.

Normally, one would anticipate that most designated beneficiaries would be individuals related to the contributor. However, there is no requirement that this be the case. A contributor could, if she wished, designate a complete stranger or other unrelated individual, such as a domestic partner, as the beneficiary of a § 529 plan. Moreover, the contributor, as owner of the § 529 plan, may designate a new beneficiary without adverse tax consequences as long as the new beneficiary is a member of the old beneficiary's family. See I.R.C. § 529(c)(3)(C)(ii). The primary justification for allowing a change of beneficiary is to enable families to respond to changing circumstances. For example, assume that Mary initially designated her son Paul as the beneficiary of a § 529 plan and Paul either decided not to attend college or won a scholarship so that the family did not need to use the § 529 plan to finance Paul's education. Mary can designate Paul's sister Sara as the new beneficiary of the § 529 plan without suffering any adverse tax consequences. Section 529(e) describes "member of the family" as: (1) the spouse of the beneficiary; (2) any individual bearing a relationship to the beneficiary described in § 152(a)(1)-(8); (3) a spouse of any individual described in § 152(a)(1)-(8); and (4) any first cousin of the beneficiary.

It is important to bear in mind that an owner of a § 529 account (normally the contributor) is not obligated to use the funds in the account to meet QHEE of the beneficiary. However, if the funds are withdrawn for another purpose, then the owner of the account will be taxed on the portion of the withdrawn amount that reflects any increase in value of the account and in most cases will be obligated to pay a 10% penalty tax on such sum. See I.R.C. § 529(c)(3)(A), (c)(6).

Contributions to both ESPs and PTC plans also qualify for very favorable gift tax treatment. Under § 529(c)(2), a contribution to a qualified § 529 plan on behalf of a designated beneficiary is treated as a completed gift of a present interest to the beneficiary, thereby qualifying the contribution for the annual per-donee exclusion which in 2004 was $11,000. Moreover, if the contributor makes a contribution to the § 529 plan in excess of the annual per-donee exclusion in any calendar year, the contribution will be deemed to be spread out over a five-year period beginning with the year of contribution if the contributor so elects. The advantage of this is that it enables a contributor to give an amount in one year that exceeds the annual per-donee exclusion by up to five times the exclusion without using up any of the donor's unified credit. (See ¶ 4,150). For example, assume that grandmother transferred $55,000 to a qualified tuition plan in 2004 when the annual per donee exclusion was $11,000. If the donor elects to have her contribution deemed spread out over five years, none of the contribution would be subject to gift tax nor would any of the donor's unified credit be used unless she made additional gifts in 2004 or in any of the four subsequent years. (Of course, any inflation adjustment to the annual per-donee exclusion in a subsequent year would free up an additional amount that could qualify for the annual per-donee exclusion in the years to which it applies). Section 529(c)(2)(A)(ii) indicates that contributions to a qualified § 529 plan for a designated beneficiary shall not impair the ability of the contributor to make use of the education and medical exemption provided by § 2503(e). For example, in 2004, grandmother could pay directly to the University of Illinois all grandson's tuition and could also in that year contribute, with grandson as the designated beneficiary, $55,000 to the Illinois § 529 PTC plan, *College Illinois*, without incurring any gift tax liability or using any of her unified credit. It also should be borne in mind that the § 2513 split-gift election may be available, thereby enabling grandmother to double the amount of any gift tax exclusion if her spouse is still alive and consents to have any contribution to a § 529 plan treated as if one-half of the gift was made by him and the other half was made by grandmother. See ¶ 4,150. If this is the case, then $110,000 could be contributed to the § 529 plan in a single year free of any gift tax and without using any of the donor's unified credit.

Gift and generation-skipping transfer tax liability is triggered if the owner of the plan decides to change beneficiaries and selects, as the new beneficiary, an individual who belongs to a generation below that of the original beneficiary. See I.R.C. § 529(c)(5). For example, assume that Grandma Miller had designated her daughter Dora as the beneficiary of a § 529 account and that Dora did not attend college. Grandma Miller subsequently decided to designate Dora's son Manuel as the beneficiary of the § 529 account. Because Manuel is of a younger generation than Dora, the change in beneficiaries will be subject to the gift tax and the generation-skipping transfer tax. To minimize transfer tax liability, Grandma Miller could transfer an amount equal to the per-donee annual gift tax exclusion to another § 529 plan with Dora as beneficiary and then designate Manuel as the new beneficiary of that plan. She would need to follow this procedure annually until she had transferred all funds from the original § 529 plan. The generation-skipping transfer tax may not be avoided so easily, but because of its large lifetime exclusion (see ¶ 4,520) this may not prove too much of a problem.

If the contributor to a § 529 plan dies while there are unexpended funds in the account, pursuant to § 529(c)(4)(A), such funds generally are not included in the contributor's gross estate for estate tax purposes. However, if the contributor made excess contributions to the § 529 plan, elected to treat such contributions as being spread out over a five-year period, and then died within the five-year period, the portion of those contributions allocable to post-death years must be included in the contributor's gross estate. I.R.C. § 529(c)(4)(C). Of interest to wealthy individuals whose estates are likely to be subject to the estate tax is the fact that § 529 permits contributors to retain at death control over assets that would normally make those assets subject to estate tax. For example, if a grandparent established a trust and then died holding a retained power to decide when distributions from the trust would be made and which of her grandchildren would have access to trust assets to meet undergraduate or professional school expenses, the corpus of the trust would be included in the grandparent's estate for estate tax purposes under §§ 2036 and 2038. See ¶¶ 4,270 and 4,280. However, rather than establishing such a trust, a grandparent could retain a similar degree of control with the aid of a § 529 plan and avoid estate tax exposure under § 529(c)(4). In the event of a designated beneficiary's death, all amounts that are paid to the beneficiary's estate by the terms of the § 529 plan are included in the beneficiary's gross estate for estate tax purposes. See I.R.C. § 529(c)(4)(B). For all but dynastically wealthy families this last point is likely to be of no consequence. Except for such families, it is difficult to imagine many situations where an individual would be motivated to make contributions to a § 529 plan for a beneficiary with a net worth that would make him or her subject to the estate tax given the magnitude of the exemption that applies to that tax. See ¶ 4,020. For further discussion of the gift and estate tax treatment of § 529 plans, see Gazur, Abandoning Principles: Qualified Tuition Programs and Wealth Transfer Taxation Doctrine, 2 Pittsburgh Tax Rev. 1 (2004).

Given the array of saving and spending incentives provided for educational expenses in the Code, there is a significant risk that taxpayers might attempt to double up on benefits and claim, for example, tax relief under § 529 in addition to a credit under § 25A (Hope Scholarship and Lifetime Learning Credits) or a deduction under § 222 for the same expenditures. Congress, in general and sometimes rather imperfectly, has attempted to block any doubling of benefits for the same expenditures while at the same time still allowing the taxpayer to coordinate the various forms of relief so that expenditures only partially covered by one provision are, in most circumstances, accommodated under other provisions of the Code. Consistent with this general goal, § 529(c)(3)(B)(v) provides that the amount that qualifies as QHEE shall be reduced by any amounts that were used in calculating the Hope Scholarship or Lifetime Learning Credits under § 25A. For example, assume that a designated beneficiary is enrolled as a full-time student in her first year of college and that she incurs tuition expenses of $8,000. Because $2,000 of the student's tuition was used to qualify for $1,500 of Hope Scholarship Credit, only $6,000 of her tuition would qualify as QHEE. Section 529(c)(3)(B)(vi) provides for similar coordination with the Coverdell Education Savings Account to guard against doubling up. Section 222 (which provides a limited deduction for higher education expenses) requires that any amount that qualifies for deduction under that provision shall be reduced by the amount of any distribution from a § 529 plan that is not merely a return of capital as determined under § 529. Similarly, § 135(d)(2) provides for coordination with both the Hope Scholarship and Lifetime Learning Credits and § 529 to prevent the taxpayer from using the same expenditure to qualify for benefits under those sections.

In closing discussion of the tax and economic features of § 529, it is worth calling attention to two matters. First, the feature of § 529 that allows for tax-free distributions from ESPs for the purpose of paying QHEE was added to the Code in 2001 under legislation that makes it subject to sunset for tax years beginning after December 31, 2010. It is therefore theoretically possible that a family could make contributions to a § 529 plan and discover that, when distributions are made from the ESP after December 31, 2010, income tax is due on any portion of the distribution representing ordinary income or capital gain. Most observers, however, believe that Congress is unlikely to allow the tax-free distribution feature of § 529 to expire in 2010. Second, some commentators warn that the extremely favorable tax rates enacted in 2003 for dividends and capital gains (see ¶ 3,810) have made § 529 plans less attractive as a method of saving for college. These commentators generally recommend that families adopt either of two different saving strategies. First, they recommend that funds be saved in a parent's name in an index fund or some other account with low annual management costs. The account could be in the form of a tax-managed mutual fund, in which case the parent would typically be taxed only on dividend income and at only a maximum rate of 15%. When the child enrolled in college the parent could either liquidate the fund and pay tax on any capital gains at 15% or transfer the fund to the child who could liquidate it at the child's (potentially lower) tax rate (see ¶ 3,780). Second, it is recommended that the mutual fund be placed in the name of the child rather than the parent, thereby reaping the benefit of lower tax rates from the start. Proponents of this strategy note that the present $800 exclusion under the "kiddie tax" and the taxation of the next $800 at lower rates (see ¶ 3,740) offer substantial tax savings. Once the child attains age 14 and is no longer subject to the kiddie tax, assuming that he has no other significant income, the highly favorable tax rates applicable to low-income individuals on dividends and capital gains should provide even more tax shelter for income from the investment. Advocates of these strategies believe that the modest amount of additional income taxes on a taxable investment will be more than offset by the lower management fees that are generally available in a well-managed index fund. Such fees typically run around 0.20% of fund assets per year, as compared with annual management fees of 2% or more in many § 529 plans. See Jonathan Clements, "The Case Against 529s: New Tax Law Boosts Other College–Savings Plans," Wall Street Journal D1 (Eastern Edition, June 18, 2003). Although such a strategy is preferable to placing funds in a § 529 plan with high management fees, a well managed § 529 plan with a low management fee such as those sponsored by New York, Michigan, Missouri, Minnesota, and Utah is likely to achieve comparable or better results over time, especially if a family wishes, as college enrollment draws near, to attain a degree of security by shifting assets to a bond fund (which, if it were taxable, would not qualify the income interest for the low rates applicable to dividends and capital gains). Placing assets in a child's name also provides the child with access to the assets when the child reaches majority. The decision as to what use should be made of the assets then rests entirely with the child. See ¶ 6,025. It might be helpful at this point to reread the discussion at the end of ¶ 6,050 on the impact of the 2003 Act on investment decisions.

[¶ 6,080]

e. A property law caveat

The contributor is deemed to be the owner of a § 529 account for purposes of state property law. It is important that contributors keep this in mind as they plan their estates. Because the contributor is the owner of any such account, a general durable power of attorney that is intended to become operative on incapacity will enable the holder of the power to make any appropriate changes in the identity of the designated beneficiary in light of changed circumstances. Many § 529 plans, like most mutual funds, set forth their own rules as to who will become the successor owner of an account upon the death of the original owner. Typically forms used to open accounts will ask the contributor to designate who is to become the successor owner in the event of the owner's death. If there is no valid designation of a successor owner, then the ownership of the account will be determined under state property law. Depending on the terms of the contributor-owner's will or, in the absence of a will, state intestacy law, an account may pass to several individuals as successor owners. This could prove problematic. It is therefore important that the contributor or her estate planner guard against such an occurrence.

[¶ 6,083]

Problems

1. Grandpa Turner, who is a widower, retired with a large bonus and wishes to use some of the money to set up ESPs under § 529 for each of his two grandchildren Alex and Ethan, who are the children of his daughter Polly. He is thinking of contributing $25,000 to two separate § 529 plans with one grandchild named as the beneficiary of each plan. He has several concerns about this course of action and seeks your advice. First, he wishes to know what are the real income tax benefits of such plans. Second, he wishes to know about the estate and gift tax consequences of his plans. Third, he is concerned that, if his younger, newly-married daughter Norma eventually has children, he may lack sufficient funds to provide similar treatment for them. He asks if it is possible to solve this problem by also naming any additional grandchildren as beneficiaries of the § 529 plans that he intends to set up for Alex and Ethan.

2. Norman and Martha are about to set up a § 529 plan to use as a savings vehicle to help them meet the cost of higher education for their children, Peter (age 5) and Betty (age 3). They ask you to advise them on how they should go about selecting a § 529 plan for their use.

3. Norman and Martha also have been told by Norman's cousin, Ben, that he hears that parents may actually be better off saving funds in taxable custodian accounts for the benefit of each child. They ask you to explain what might prompt Ben to offer such advice.

[¶ 6,085]

4. Coverdell Education Savings Accounts

Under § 530 individuals may fund what the Code calls "Coverdell Education Savings Accounts." As is the case with § 529 plans, income on a Coverdell account is not subject to taxation when earned and distributions made for QHEE (as defined in § 529(e)(3)) are exempt from taxation. In contrast to § 529 plans, funds may also be withdrawn from a Coverdell account to pay for qualified elementary and secondary education. See I.R.C. § 530(b)(2), (4). Because the focus of this chapter is on meeting higher education costs, this feature of the Coverdell account will not be discussed further.

As is the case with § 529 plans, contributions may be made to Coverdell accounts only in the form of cash. The Coverdell account has several significant limitations. First, contributions to a Coverdell account are limited in aggregate to $2,000 per year per beneficiary. In the event that several individuals each contribute $2,000 to Coverdell accounts with the same individual as beneficiary, under § 4973, the same penalty mechanism that applies to overfunding of IRAs would apply and the excess funding would be subject to a 6% penalty tax for each year that it remained in a Coverdell account. (Nevertheless, § 530 permits the penalty tax to be avoided if all overfunded amounts and any earnings thereon are returned to the contributor within a specified grace period.) Second, the Coverdell account must have as its trustee a bank or other person who demonstrates its capacity to administer such an account (or a conventional IRA) to the satisfaction of the Treasury. Third, funds may not be invested in life insurance contracts. Fourth, as the adjusted gross income of the contributor exceeds statutory limits, the maximum amount that may be contributed to a Coverdell account is phased down. The $2,000 limit is phased down if the contributor's adjusted gross income falls in a range from $95,000 to $110,000 ($190,000 to $220,000 for joint returns). Fifth, no additional contributions may be accepted in a Coverdell account after the designated beneficiary reaches age 18 and the entire account balance must be distributed by the time the designated beneficiary reaches age 30. If the beneficiary dies before reaching age 30 and funds still remain in the account, the funds must then be distributed within 30 days of the beneficiary's death.

As in the case of a § 529 plan, the contributor to a Coverdell account is regarded as the owner of the account for property law purposes. It is therefore important to make sure that the contributor's will designates a successor owner of the account in the event of the contributor's death. Unless this is done, several individuals may be deemed owners of the account under state intestacy law or the residuary clause of the contributor's will. Section 530 also allows the owner of the account to change the designated beneficiary of the account, free of tax. Under § 530(d)(6), the beneficiary designation may be changed without any tax consequences if the new beneficiary is a member of the family of the original beneficiary (as defined in § 529(e)(2)) as long as the new beneficiary has not yet reached age 30. Moreover, distributions from § 529 plans and Coverdell accounts are subject both to income tax and to a 10% penalty tax unless made solely for QHEE. Under § 530(d)(3), Coverdell accounts are subject to the same estate and gift tax treatment as § 529 plans. This means that, as in the case of a § 529 plan, designation of an individual as the beneficiary of a Coverdell account is deemed to be a completed gift.

However, because of the $2,000 per year cap on contributions to Coverdell accounts, this is unlikely to present a problem unless the contributor makes additional gifts to the beneficiary in excess of the available annual per donee exclusion for the year in question. As in the case of § 529 plans, for estate tax purposes, Coverdell accounts are not included in the taxable estate of the owner-contributor at his or her death and designation of a new beneficiary who is of a generation below that of the existing beneficiary gives rise to potential generation-skipping transfer tax liability.

The Coverdell account has several advantages over a § 529 plan. First, the contributor to a Coverdell account may have the same control over the choice of account investments as does the owner of a conventional self-directed IRA. Second, the Coverdell account assets may be used to pay for elementary and secondary education of the beneficiary as well as QHEE, whereas § 529 plans may only be used for QHEE. Third, the ability to make distributions from the account to meet QHEE free of income tax is not subject to the same sunset provisions as in the case of a § 529 plan, although the Coverdell account is subject to several other sunset provisions. Offsetting these advantages of the Coverdell account are the following advantages of the § 529 plan. First, § 529 plans are not subject to any contributor income limitations. Second, in contrast to the Coverdell account, there is no annual per beneficiary limitation on the amount that may be contributed to a § 529 plan. Third, contributions may be made to a § 529 plan regardless of the age of the designated beneficiary.

As is the case with § 529 plans, families considering whether to establish a Coverdell account should carefully examine all fees imposed by the institutions that manage the funds as well as those imposed by any mutual funds or other accounts in which the funds may be placed. Low-cost providers such as Vanguard and Fidelity may offer Coverdell accounts whose tax sheltered results will outdistance the results produced by low-cost non-tax sheltered investments, but high-cost providers of Coverdell accounts are unlikely to match the after-tax returns on a tax managed taxable index fund. This is especially likely to be true if the taxable account is eligible for the low rates accorded dividends and capital gains under the 2003 Act. If the investor intends to make use of interest-bearing investments, a Coverdell account is more likely to outperform the after-tax results obtained even with a low-cost provider of such investments. Again, as was mentioned in the case of § 529 accounts (see ¶ 6,070), careful consideration should be given to placing a taxable mutual fund with a low-cost provider in the name of a child to reap the advantage of lower tax rates and exclusions that may be available to the family.

All of the coordination features of the Code that are described above at ¶ 6,070 to prevent doubling of tax benefits also apply in the case of Coverdell accounts. In rereading those materials, note that in theory it is possible to use § 135, funds in a § 529 plan, funds in a Coverdell account and either the Hope Scholarship or Lifetime Learning Credits, all at the same time, as long as there is no overlap. In essence, they may be stacked one on top of the other. The deduction provided by § 222 is a far less accommodating device, since amounts that escape taxation under any of the other devices (such as a Coverdell account) count against the dollar ceiling of § 222.

[¶ 6,088]

Problems

1.   Grandma Murray has a net worth of $4,000,000 and annual income of $200,000. She has already established § 529 ESPs for each of her grandchildren and asks you if it would be advisable for her in addition to set up Coverdell Education Savings Accounts for each of her grandchildren.

2.   Paul's grandparents established a Coverdell Education Savings Account for his benefit. The account is now worth $20,000. Paul's parents had also created a § 529 ESP for his benefit and it is now worth $40,000. He recently received a $12,000 tuition bill for his first year of college and intends to use the first $2,000 of tuition to claim a Hope Scholarship Credit which will save him $1,500 in income taxes. He asks you how much of the $12,000 tuition bill may sensibly be paid out of either the Coverdell account or the § 529 ESP.

[¶ 6,095]

5.   Roth IRAs

Occasionally financial planners suggest that parents consider using what is called a "Roth IRA" as a vehicle to save for both education and retirement. When Senator Roth headed the Finance Committee, he saw to it that a special type of IRA was added to the Code (§ 408A) and that it bore his name. A perceptive reader will note that although senators and members of Congress in positions of power eagerly name various Code provisions that bestow tax breaks after themselves (e.g. Archer MSA in § 220) or their deceased colleagues (Coverdell), to date none has chosen to have a Code section that imposes a tax named after himself or herself, although some have probably contemplated naming one after a political opponent.

In general, under § 408A, Roth IRAs must be established with after-tax dollars and no deduction is allowed for contributions to a Roth IRA. As is the case with a conventional IRA, no tax is imposed on income realized by the Roth IRA. Unlike a conventional IRA, however, no income tax is imposed on funds that are withdrawn from a Roth IRA as a "qualified distribution." See I.R.C. § 408A(d). Any withdrawal after age 59½ is a qualified distribution, as are certain other distributions (e.g. those attributable to disability or to provide for certain first home purchases). A penalty tax of 10% is imposed on withdrawals that are made prior to age 59½ unless they qualify for a special statutory dispensation. See I.R.C. § 72(t). One of the special circumstances under which a withdrawal may be made from a Roth IRA without a penalty tax is where the funds are needed to pay for QHEE of the taxpayer, his spouse, child or grandchild. See I.R.C. § 72(t)(2)(E), (t)(7). There is, however, no dispensation from income taxation for an early withdrawal from a Roth IRA.

Some financial advisors occasionally suggest that taxpayers set up Roth IRAs and use them as flexible savings accounts that may be tapped to meet college costs of a child or held until retirement. See Kristin Davis, "Saving for College: Tuition Submission," Kiplinger's Personal Finance 72, 74 (May 2003). However, unless a distribution from a Roth IRA will be deemed a "qualified distribution" that avoids income tax under § 408A(d) (e.g., if the account owner has reached age 59½), it is generally desirable to avoid making any distributions. Because a distribution from a Roth IRA for a QHEE that is not also a "qualified distribution" avoids only the 10% penalty tax and not the regular income tax, the owner of a Roth IRA should hesitate to use it as a flexible savings account that may be tapped to meet educational expenses.

C. THE HOPE SCHOLARSHIP CREDIT AND THE LIFETIME LEARNING CREDIT

[¶ 6,100]

In 1997 Congress added § 25A to the Code. That section provides two separate tax credits to help defray the cost of higher education—the Hope Scholarship Credit and the Lifetime Learning Credit. In general, the Hope Scholarship Credit (HSC) allows an income tax credit for up to $2,000 (adjusted for inflation) of the cost of tuition and related expenses for the first two years of higher education. The amount of the credit allowed is 100% of the first $1,000 per year of such expenses and 50% of the balance of such expenses with the aggregate allowable credit effectively capped at $1,500 per year (adjusted for inflation). In general, the Lifetime Learning Credit (LLC) is allowed at the rate of 20% of the cost of tuition and related fees for higher education expenses for the first $10,000 per year of such costs. Both the HSC and the LLC are non-refundable tax credits (i.e., they are available to the taxpayer only to the extent of his federal income tax liability). Section 25A imposes a number of conditions on taxpayers who seek to take advantage of each of these credits. These conditions are discussed below.

In examining the HSC and the LLC, we are concerned primarily with four elements: (1) the nature of the expenses that qualify for the credits; (2) qualification as an eligible student with respect to whom the expenses are incurred; (3) the relationship of the eligible student to the party claiming the credit; and (4) the phaseout features of the HSC and the LLC.

Only expenses for "qualified tuition and related expenses" at an "eligible educational institution" qualify for credit. See I.R.C. § 25A(f).

Qualified tuition and related expenses means tuition and fees required for the enrollment or attendance, at an eligible educational institution, of the taxpayer, the taxpayer's spouse or any dependent of the taxpayer for whom the taxpayer is allowed a deduction under § 151. Fees for instruction involving sports, games or hobbies do not qualify unless incurred for a course that is part of the student's degree program. Moreover, fees for non-academic items such as room and board or health insurance do not qualify. An eligible educational institution generally includes traditional institutions of higher education, vocational schools and other post-secondary educational institutions that are accredited and are eligible to participate in federal financial aid programs under Title IV of the Higher Education Act of 1965. This requirement would appear to exclude foreign educational institutions, with the result that expenses incurred directly for enrolling in a foreign educational institution will not qualify. That does not mean that tuition and related expenses for study abroad may not qualify for tax credit relief under § 25A. If a student enrolls in a U.S. educational institution's study abroad program and pays tuition and related fees to the U.S. institution, thereby gaining access to courses at a foreign college or university, such expenditures will constitute "qualified tuition and related expenses." An important restriction on qualifying for tuition payments for tax credit under § 25A is the requirement of § 25A(g)(2) that any tuition paid be reduced by the amount of any scholarship aid or other tuition assistance that is excluded from income. For example, if tuition at State University is $4,000 and the student is awarded a tuition scholarship of $2,500 that is excluded from income under § 117, only the $1,500 that the student or her family pays out of pocket will qualify for tax credit under § 25A. Other assistance awards, such as Pell grants, will also reduce the amount of otherwise qualifying tuition. Tuition paid with proceeds of a loan (e.g., a loan obtained under the Stafford Guaranteed Student Loan Program or a PLUS loan) or with an inheritance or gift is deemed paid by the taxpayer.

The HSC and the LLC have different classes of students who are eligible for credit relief under each program.

A student will qualify under the HSC if five basic criteria are satisfied. First, the student must be enrolled at an eligible educational institution in a program leading to a post-secondary degree or certificate. Second, the student must carry at least half the normal full-time load for the degree sought for at least one of the academic periods beginning during the tax year. See I.R.C. § 25A(b)(3). Third, at the beginning of the tax year, the student cannot have completed the first two years of post-secondary education; for the purpose of making such determinations, credit awarded for proficiency on performance tests such as advanced placement tests is ignored. Fourth, the HSC is available for only two years per student, regardless of whether the student has actually completed the first two years of post-secondary education. For example, if a student's family claimed the HSC for tax years 2002 and 2003, even if the student had only successfully completed a little more that one full year of college studies in those years, the HSC would no longer be available. Fifth, the student must not have been convicted of a state or federal felony offense for possession or distribution of controlled substances. This last requirement may seem out of place in a society that claims to wish to rehabilitate its criminals, but it is typical of the sort of thing that gets added to legislation to gain leverage at election time. Students who do not qualify as eligible students under the HSC program nonetheless may qualify under the LLC program if they meet that program's less demanding standards.

To qualify as an eligible student under the LLC program a student need only be enrolled in any course at an eligible educational institution for the purpose of acquiring or improving job skills. See I.R.C. § 25A(c)(2)(B). For example, all of the following qualify as eligible under the LLC: (1) an individual who has completed her bachelor's degree in accounting and enrolls in a single advanced accounting course to improve her skills; (2) a college freshman who has a prior felony conviction for selling LSD; (3) an individual who enrolls in a three-credit-hour computer studies course at a local community college to enable her to qualify for additional responsibilities at her place of employment. Unlike the HSC which is available for only two years, the LLC is available for an unlimited number of years. See Reg. § 1.25A–4(b).

The tax credits available under the HSC and the LLC may be claimed by the individual who pays the qualified tuition and related expenses as long as the payor is the student, the spouse of the student or an individual who is entitled to a dependent deduction under § 151 with respect to the student. See I.R.C. § 25A(b)(1), (c)(1), (f). If the taxpayer forgoes claiming a dependent deduction under § 151 with respect to an eligible student, the student may be deemed to be the payor of the tuition and related fees paid by the taxpayer and the student may then be entitled to claim the benefit of either the HSC or the LLC. See Reg. § 1.25A–1(f)(2). This would typically be done in circumstances where, under the phaseout rules discussed below, the taxpayer-parents would not be entitled to claim a credit or the credit would be reduced to an insignificant amount. Moreover, if any individual claims the eligible student as a dependent, any payments made by the student will be treated as made by the individual who is entitled to claim the student as a dependent for the purpose of enabling such individual to claim the benefit of either the HSC or the LLC. See Reg. § 1.25A–5(a). For example, this would enable a parent whose dependent child paid for tuition with earnings from a job to claim the benefit of any allowable credit. Also if an individual who is not entitled to claim a dependent deduction for the student makes payment of tuition and related expenses directly to an eligible educational institution, then solely for the purposes of § 25A such payment is deemed to be made first to the student who is then treated as making payment to the institution. See Reg. § 1.25A–5(b). This means, for example, that if a grandparent pays tuition to a college on behalf of a grandchild-student, the parents of the grandchild would be entitled to claim the benefit of the HSC or the LLC, assuming that the parents are entitled to claim the student as a dependent and in fact do so.

Eligibility for the HSC and the LLC is limited to taxpayers whose "modified adjusted gross income" (MAGI) falls within certain bands. Neither credit is available to a single taxpayer whose MAGI exceeds $50,000 or to a married couple whose MAGI exceeds $100,000. Moreover, both credits are phased out as MAGI exceeds $40,000 for a single taxpayer or $80,000 for a married couple. See I.R.C. § 25A(d). The phaseout ranges are adjusted for inflation commencing with tax years after 2001. See I.R.C. § 25A(h). MAGI is defined as adjusted gross income (as defined by § 62), increased by any amounts excluded from income under § 911 (certain income earned abroad), § 931 (income derived from certain U.S. possessions) and § 933 (income from sources within Puerto Rico). For most taxpayers, MAGI is the same as adjusted gross income. The phaseout features of § 25A are significant because they often limit the benefits of § 25A. As noted above, families who find that they will lose some or all of the benefit of § 25A because parental income is either too high or too low may wish to consider whether it would be worthwhile for the parents to forgo claiming the student as a dependent and allow the student to claim the benefit of the HSC or the LLC. Since neither credit is refundable, only a small minority of such families are likely to find such a strategy advantageous because few students are likely to have sufficient tax liabilities against which the credits may be used to justify the parents in forgoing the dependent deduction for the child.

In closing discussion of the conditions that must be met for either the HSC or the LLC to be available to a taxpayer, several other items should be noted. First, the HSC is allowed on a per student basis whereas the LLC is allowed on an aggregate basis. For example, a taxpayer parent who has three children enrolled in college as a freshman, a sophomore and a senior may be entitled to claim the HSC with respect to the freshman and the sophomore and the LLC with respect to the senior. On the other hand, if a family had one child in graduate school and a second enrolled as a senior in college, only a total of $10,000 from both students in tuition and related expenses would qualify for the LLC. See Reg. § 1.25A–3(b). Second, a taxpayer may not claim both the HSC and the LLC in the same tax year with respect to the same student. For example, if a parent spends $5,000 on tuition for the first semester of school, she may not claim the HSC on the first $2,000 of tuition and then claim benefit of the LLC on the $3,000 balance. See I.R.C. § 25A(c)(2). Third, any prepayment of tuition made during the year for an academic period that begins during the first three months of the following year shall be treated as made during the year in which payment is made. See I.R.C. § 25A(g)(3). The significance of this provision is that a student who defers an eligible course of study until the spring semester but who pays a tuition bill in the fall of the previous year may qualify the payment for either the HSC or the LLC in the year in which tuition was paid. Similarly, if a student commences study in the fall and pays the fall tuition bill in August and continues studies through the academic year, paying the spring semester tuition bill in December of her first year of study, both the August and December payments are aggregated for purpose of determining the amount of the credit allowed for that tax year. Fourth, no credit will be allowed if the taxpayer is married and does not file a joint return. See I.R.C. § 25A(g)(6). Fifth, the credit is unavailable for taxpayers who are treated as nonresident aliens under the Code. See I.R.C. § 25A(g)(7).

Because of the array of federal tax provisions aimed at assisting taxpayers in meeting education expenses, Congress has taken steps to prevent doubling up of benefits. Some of these features of the Code are discussed above as they apply to § 529 plans, Coverdell accounts and Series EE savings bonds. See ¶¶ 6,070 and 6,085. As previously noted, a taxpayer may not use both the HSC and the LLC with respect to the same student in a given tax year. A taxpayer may use one of the § 25A credits along with funds withdrawn from a § 529 ESP or tuition credits drawn from a § 529 PTC plan. However, doubling up is forbidden. For example, assume that a family receives a tuition bill of $10,000 covering the first year of college at State University. The parents may claim the HSC for the first $2,000 of expenses and may withdraw $8,000 free of tax from an ESP. On the other hand, if the family claimed the HSC for $2,000 of expenses and then withdrew $10,000 from an ESP, assuming no additional qualified educational expenses existed, the family would find that $2,000 of the withdrawal from the ESP would be considered a nonqualified withdrawal under § 529(c)(3)(B)(v). Similar rules now apply for withdrawals from Coverdell accounts and § 25A credits; however, this coordination provision is scheduled to sunset for tax years beginning after 2010. See I.R.C. § 530(d)(2)(C). Section 135(d)(2) of the Code contains similar coordination provisions that are also scheduled to sunset. Section 222 of the Code, which provides a modest deduction for qualifying educational expenses (see ¶ 6,120), does not provide for coordination with § 25A and taxpayers must elect to have the benefit of either § 222 or § 25A.

Due to the phaseout features of § 25A, the provision is not very helpful for families who wish to plan in advance how they will meet future college expenses for young children. By the time that tuition bills come due, families may discover that they are completely phased out of the benefits provided by § 25A. The provision is basically a public assistance program aimed at middle and lower income families and individuals. That having been said, it is rather difficult to justify the non-refundable nature of the credits provided by § 25A. It seems rather curious that Congress decided to aid middle income families with their college costs while at the same time turning its back on students from poor families who wish to better their lot through education but who do not earn enough taxable income to be able to avail themselves fully of the tax credits provided by § 25A.

[¶ 6,105]

Problems

1. Margaret is a single mother with AGI (and MAGI) of $38,000. She claims her son Josh as a dependent, and paid the tuition for his freshman year at a local community college. The tuition amounted to $1,800. Her federal taxes for the year were $3,800. May Margaret claim the HSC? If she does so, what is the amount that she will be allowed?

2. Greg is married to Penny. He is a high school teacher and she works as a retail clerk. Their combined AGI (and MAGI) for the year amounted to $75,000. Greg, who has completed his bachelor's degree, wishes to study for a masters degree at State University and this year he incurred $3,000 in tuition expenses. Do these expenses qualify for the HSC or the LLC? If so, what is the amount of the credit that the couple will be allowed against their federal tax liability of $5,200 for the year? Does it matter whether the couple itemizes their personal deductions?

3. Sandy and Jim Fischer have a large family of six children. Sandy is a pediatrician and Jim is a real estate agent. Their AGI (and MAGI) exceeds $250,000. Their children range from 2 to 12 years of age. They have heard that the Code provides several devices to help couples provide their children with higher education, ranging from tax credits to tax sheltered savings plans and special prepaid tuition programs. They consult you generally to point them in the right direction as to the various options that may be available to them in the future. Please advise them based on what you have learned so far.

D. DEDUCTIONS FOR EDUCATION EXPENSES

[¶ 6,110]

Taxpayers may qualify expenditures for education as deductions under either § 162 which provides a deduction for business expenses or § 222 which provides a limited deduction for qualified tuition and related expenses (as defined under § 25A). In addition, interest on student loans may qualify for deduction under § 221. Each provision has its own set of rules which are discussed below.

[¶ 6,120]

1. Section 222

In 2001 Congress added § 222 to the Code to provide a limited deduction for education expenses. The legislative history indicates that Congress believed that for some taxpayers a deduction would provide greater relief than would the system of credits under § 25A. Accordingly, Congress added § 222 to the Code to maximize tax benefits for education while providing taxpayers with a new choice for obtaining tax relief. Because Congress sought to provide taxpayers with a choice and not with supplemental tax relief, it should come as no surprise that § 222(c)(2) requires that a taxpayer must choose between claiming a tax credit under § 25A or a deduction under § 222.

Section 222 allows a deduction for "qualified tuition and related expenses," which it states "has the same meaning given such term by section 25A(f) [HSC and LLC]. Such expenses shall be reduced in the same manner as under section 25A(g)(2)." This incorporation of §§ 25A(f) and 25A(g)(2) into the definition of what qualifies as a deductible expense under § 222 has several significant consequences. First, the expenditures must be for tuition and fees required for the attendance or enrollment of: (1) the taxpayer; (2) the taxpayer's spouse; or (3) a dependent of the taxpayer for whom the taxpayer is entitled to claim a dependent deduction under § 151, at an eligible educational institution (as defined in § 25A(f)) for courses of instruction of such individual at such institution. Second, the same exclusion of fees for non-academic courses and activities that applies under § 25A also prevails under § 222. That means, for example, that room and board and health insurance fees are not eligible for deduction under § 222. Third, the incorporation into § 222 of the § 25A(g)(2) reduction feature with respect to qualified tuition and fees means that the deductible amount of tuition charged by the institution must be reduced by various forms of assistance such as scholarships and Pell grants that are used to pay for tuition. Similarly, taxpayers may claim as their contributions any loan proceeds, inheritances and gifts that are used to pay qualified expenses. Section 222 is actually somewhat more restrictive than § 25A concerning the type of educational institution attended by the student. Under § 222(d)(3)(A), the institution must not only meet the "eligible educational institution" definition of § 25A but also must be an "institution of higher education," thereby excluding some post-secondary institutions such as vocational training programs from its coverage. No deduction is allowed under § 222 to any individual with respect to whom a dependent deduction is allowable to another taxpayer under § 151. Section 222 also incorporates other features of § 25A. As is the case under § 25A, the taxpayer claiming the benefit of § 222 may not be a nonresident alien and if married must file a joint return. Similarly, as long as classes commence within three months after the start of a tax year, any prepayments of tuition and fees made in the preceding tax year qualify for deduction in the year of payment. See I.R.C. § 222(d)(3)(B).

The amount deductible under § 222, as in a number of other pieces of recent tax legislation, is the result of overly ambitious tax cutting. To meet the overriding goal of cutting taxes while remaining within agreed upon limits on projected revenue losses, Congress has resorted to a various gimmicks such as phasing in deductions, rate cuts and credits over a number of years so as to minimize their immediate impact, enacting temporary relief measures that operate for only a few years before they expire, and imposing automatic repeal ("sunset") on entire pieces of legislation. One senator has described the endeavor as an attempt to fit 20 pounds of sugar into a 10 pound sack. The deduction rules of § 222(b) provide a prime example of this featuring phase-ins, phase-outs and a short-fuse sunset provision.

During 2002 and 2003, the maximum amount deductible under § 222 was $3,000 with no amount being deductible for taxpayers with adjusted gross income (as specially defined in § 222) above certain limits. For purposes of § 222, adjusted gross income is defined to include the items of foreign source income added to AGI under § 25A and after taking into account the exclusions, deductions and limitations provided by § 86 (social security and certain railroad retirement benefits), § 135 (see ¶ 6,030), § 137 (adoption assistance program benefits), § 219 (deductible IRA contributions), § 221 (deductible student loan interest) and § 469 (limitation on passive activity losses and credits). In addition, to avoid the benefit of a double deduction, any tuition expenses deductible under another provision (such as § 162) must be added back to adjusted gross income. No deduction is allowed under § 222 for any qualifying education expenses in 2002 and 2003 if § 222 AGI exceeds $65,000 for single individuals or $130,000 for married couples filing jointly. In 2004 and 2005, for taxpayers whose § 222 AGI does not exceed $65,000 ($130,000 for married couples filing jointly), the maximum deductible amount is capped at $4,000 per year. For taxpayers whose § 222 AGI falls between $65,000 and $80,000 (between $130,000 and $160,000 for married couples filing jointly), the maximum amount deductible is limited to $2,000. If the taxpayer's § 222 AGI exceeds $80,000 ($160,000 for married couples filing jointly), no deduction is allowable under § 222. See I.R.C. § 222(c). Section 222(e) provides that § 222 will expire at the end of 2005. It was the hope of many who placed such sunset provisions in the Code that when time came for sunset, a way would be found to extend the provisions even if only on a year-by-year basis. Therefore, readers who are interested in determining the status of § 222 after 2005 should be careful to check a current version of the Code to see if § 222 has been given a legislative reprieve.

Section 222 is not as flexible as § 25A in terms of who in the family may claim benefit of the tax break. If a parent claims a child-student as a dependent then the parent may claim the § 222 deduction only if he or she actually paid the qualified expenses in question. Moreover, in contrast to § 25A, a taxpayer who is entitled to claim a child-student as a dependent may not choose to forgo doing so and thereby enable the student to get the benefit of the § 222 deduction. In addition, even if the child-student actually pays the qualified expenses, if the student's parents (or another person) were able to claim the student as a dependent and did not do so, the student is not entitled to claim the qualified expenses as a deduction. A student may claim a deduction for the qualified expenses only if no one is eligible to claim the student as a dependent and the student pays the qualified expenses or another person pays the expenses and the payment is regarded as a gift to the student. For example, if a student is over age 24 and is not claimed as a dependent by another, the student may claim the benefit of the § 222 deduction if the student pays the qualified expenses or if they are paid by another person such as a parent or grandparent. In the latter case the student is regarded as the payor and the payments by the parent or grandparent are regarded as gift from that party to the student. See I.R.S. Pub. 970, Tax Benefits for Education 26 (2002).

An important feature of § 222 is that the deduction is claimed in determining adjusted gross income and therefore is available even if the taxpayer does not itemize deductions. This could theoretically be of significance for many low income individuals and families who find themselves below the threshold for itemizing and therefore use the standard deduction. However, in most such cases, these taxpayers will find that they will be better off claiming either the HSC or the LLC because their marginal income tax rates will be sufficiently low that the value of a § 25A credit will exceed the value of any tax deduction allowed under § 222.

Section 222 contains its own prohibitions on the taxpayer obtaining double benefits. Several of these "double dip" prohibitions have already been discussed above briefly at ¶¶ 6,070, 6,085 and 6,100. A more detailed discussion of how they apply in particular to § 222 is included below.

Because Congress added § 222 to enhance the choices of a taxpayer who was otherwise generally eligible to claim the benefit of either the HSC or the LLC under § 25A, it makes perfect sense that a taxpayer must choose between claiming a credit provided by § 25A or the deduction provided by § 222. See I.R.C. § 222(c)(2)(A). It is important to realize that this prohibition against double benefits does more than merely prohibit the taxpayer from obtaining a credit for the balance of tuition not deductible under § 222. The taxpayer must affirmatively elect to use either the § 25A credit or the § 222 deduction for each individual student. However, because the prohibition operates on a per student basis, the taxpayer could, for example, claim a § 25A credit for one student and a § 222 deduction for another student. Assume that Charles is a junior at Private College and that his family pays out-of-pocket tuition expenses of $14,000. Charles' sister Deborah attends State University Law School for which the family pays $8,000 in tuition. Under these circumstances, assuming that all other requirements of both sections are satisfied, it would be possible for their parents to claim the LLC for Charles' tuition and the § 222 deduction for Deborah's tuition.

Taxpayers are sometimes able to obtain a deduction for education expenditures as trade or business expenses under § 162. See ¶ 6,130. It should therefore come as no surprise that § 222(c)(1) bars a taxpayer from claiming a deduction under § 222 for an education expenditure if the same expenditure is also claimed as a deduction under another provision of the Code.

Section 222(c)(2)(B) provides a means whereby a taxpayer may take advantage of several other provisions of the Code that are in aid of education (the § 135 Series EE saving bond exclusion, § 529 plans and

Coverdell accounts) while also claiming a deduction under § 222. However, the price of enjoying such multiple benefits is that the benefits accorded under these other provisions of the Code are considered in determining the amount of any deduction allowable under § 222. For example, assume that a family would otherwise be entitled to a deduction of $4,000 for $9,000 of tuition paid for a child but that $3,000 of the tuition bill was paid with funds withdrawn from an ESP. Also assume that only $600 of the $3,000 represented untaxed gain in the ESP and that the balance represented a return of capital originally contributed to the ESP. Under these circumstances, the amount allowable as a deduction under § 222 would be reduced by $600 with the result that $3,400 of qualified expenses would be deductible under § 222.

The double benefit denial rules of § 222 may present the taxpayer with difficult decisions as to how best to maximize her tax benefits. It is virtually impossible to provide a simple set of guidelines to determine whether the taxpayer will be better off opting for one form of relief over another, but a few observations may prove helpful in focusing attention on some of the more important considerations that may be involved. Because § 25A has a relatively low phaseout range ($40,000–$50,000 for single taxpayers and $80,000–$100,000 for married couples filing jointly) and because the cut-off for deduction under § 222 operates at a higher level of income ($65,000 or $80,000 for singles and $130,000 or $160,000 for married couples filing jointly), some taxpayers may find that they in effect have no choice and that only the § 222 deduction provides any benefit for them. The decision will be more difficult for those who find themselves operating within the phaseout ranges of § 25A. Their only alternative will be to work out the results for the § 25A credit and the § 222 deduction and to then choose the alternative that is most advantageous for them. Normally, a taxpayer who is eligible to claim the HSC will find it preferable to opt for that alternative because of the extremely generous nature of that credit. However, the different phaseout ranges noted above may cause a taxpayer to opt for the deduction if she finds herself at an income level where that would be more advantageous. Of course, a taxpayer who finds that she is fully phased out under § 25A may find that the § 222 deduction is her best option. However, she should remember that § 25A offers her the option to forgo claiming the student as a dependent and allow the student to garner the tax savings of the HSC if that proves more advantageous for the family. Taxpayers who find themselves choosing between the LLC and the § 222 deduction will find that they must weigh the different phaseout ranges of each provision, the value of a credit at 20% versus a deduction at the taxpayer's marginal rate, the possibility of forgoing the dependent deduction and thereby shifting the § 25A credit to the child-student, and the relatively low limit on the amount of qualifying expenses allowable as a deduction under § 222 ($2,000 or $4,000) compared to the amount eligible for credit under the LLC ($10,000). The permutations are seemingly endless and, as already noted, in most cases taxpayers will have to be careful to evaluate all possibilities before reaching a decision.

In closing, it may be worth noting that, although phaseouts of tax credits or deductions may make sense from a standpoint of distributive justice, such phaseouts make it difficult, if not impossible, for taxpayers to incorporate the available tax benefits in sensible and effective long term planning for meeting the educational needs of their children.

[¶ 6,125]

Questions

1. Under what circumstances would you normally expect to find families resorting to use of the § 222 deduction rather than making use of the HSC or the LLC?

2. Section 222 requires that the total amount of qualified tuition and related expenses under that provision must be reduced by the amount of any tax benefit realized under §§ 135, 529 and 530. What is the likely impact of this requirement on the opportunities of taxpayers to make use of § 222?

3. Sections 135 (Series EE savings bonds), 222 (deduction) and 530 (Coverdell Education Savings Accounts) all have phase-out provisions based on income, whereas § 529 (ESPs and PTC plans) does not. What is the justification for making such distinctions and why should the various provisions that employ phaseout features use different amounts to trigger their phaseout mechanisms?

[¶ 6,130]

2. Education Costs as Deductible Business Expenses

In general, § 162 of the Code provides a deduction for ordinary and necessary business expenses. In some situations, education expenses may qualify as deductible business expenses under this provision. As a practical matter, the requirements of § 162 limit its usefulness for taxpayers seeking to deduct expenses of post-secondary education. However, when the § 162 deduction is available, it often provides greater tax benefits than some of the other Code provisions. Moreover, § 162 sometimes presents taxpayers with the only available avenue of relief.

Taxpayers encounter three principal barriers in seeking to claim a deduction for education expenses under § 162, which allows a deduction for "all ordinary and necessary expenses paid or incurred . . . in carrying on any trade or business. . . . " First, the "ordinary and necessary expenses" language has been construed to preclude a deduction under § 162 for capital investments. In general, expenditures which result in a capacity to produce income for more than one year are not allowed as deductions under § 162. Such expenditures are regarded as "investments" (as contrasted with "expenses") and are typically deemed to be "extraordinary" (as contrasted with "ordinary") expenditures. It is easy to see that many outlays incurred to obtain an education (such as a higher education degree or professional training) would fail to satisfy such a test. Second, under the quoted language a deduction is allowed only for expenses incurred "in carrying on" certain prescribed activities. Many outlays for education are made before a student has entered the career for which the education is being sought. For example, an individual who graduates from college and enters law school can hardly be deemed to be carrying on the legal profession. On the other hand, after the student graduates, is admitted to the bar and commences the practice of law, expenses incurred for periodically pursuing continuing legal education are likely to qualify for deduction under § 162. Third, because § 162 allows a deduction only for expenses incurred in carrying on a "trade or business," and because § 262 states that "[e]xcept as otherwise expressly provided, no deduction shall be allowed for personal, living, or family expenses," large amounts of education which advance the intellect and enrich the personal life of a student are not deductible under § 162.

Fortunately, the Treasury has promulgated comprehensive regulations under § 162 to help taxpayers sort out which education expenses are deductible and which are not. Basically, the regulations provide a deduction for economic outlays by the taxpayer that: (1) enable the taxpayer to maintain or improve skills required by the taxpayer's trade or business (with the taxpayer's line of employment or profession considered as the taxpayer's trade or business); or (2) meet the requirements of the taxpayer's employer, profession or applicable law as a condition of retaining the taxpayer's position, professional status or rate of compensation. See Reg. § 1.162–5(a). Moreover, education expenses are not deductible if they: (1) are made to satisfy the minimum education requirements for qualification in the taxpayer's employment or trade or business; or (2) qualify the taxpayer for a new trade or business. See Reg. § 1.162–5(b).

There are several important points worth making about the requirements of § 162 for deducting education expenditures. First, any expenses which qualify must be paid by the student to enable the student to obtain an education. Tuition payments made by parents on behalf of a child do not entitle the parent to a deduction even if all of the other requirements are satisfied. It may be possible for the family to argue that the payment by the parent was in fact a gift to the child who, assuming all conditions are met, is entitled to a deduction. In arguing this, they would find considerable support in the position taken by the Service regarding similar payments under § 222. See ¶ 6,120 (discussing I.R.S. Pub. 970). Second, most undergraduate and professional education expenses are unlikely to be deductible under § 162 for several reasons. Typically such education (especially undergraduate education) is undertaken for the personal enjoyment and enrichment of the student and merely satisfies the basic minimum requirements for entry into a profession or line of employment. Moreover, because most students are not in the trade or business for which they are obtaining an education, they fail the "carrying on" test of § 162. Third, educational expenses that qualify for deduction under § 162 are incurred after the student has entered into the line of employment for which the taxpayer's education had prepared the taxpayer; deductible outlays either maintain or enhance the taxpayer's job or business skills and do not prepare the taxpayer for a new trade or business.

The following are all examples of the types of education expenses that are likely to qualify for deduction under § 162: (1) a high school social science teacher attends summer classes at State University to earn a masters degree in history; (2) a middle school Spanish teacher goes back to university after her first year of teaching and pursues a masters program in Spanish to improve her skills and to qualify for a higher level of pay as a school teacher; and (3) a resident in psychiatry, at the suggestion of her department, undergoes a year of psychoanalysis not for purposes of obtaining treatment but to gain an understanding of the process so as to be a better psychiatrist. On the other hand, the following are examples of education expenses that are not likely to qualify for deduction under § 162: (1) a student, on graduating from high school, enrolls in an undergraduate curriculum in accounting; (2) a student who has obtained her undergraduate degree in business enrolls in law school; and (3) an accountant who prepares tax returns decides to attend law school at nights to better enable him to function as an accountant, thereby also qualifying him for entry into a new trade or business.

There are several things that should be kept in mind with respect to deduction of education expenses as business expenses under § 162. First, if the expenses are claimed by an individual as an employee, the so-called 2% haircut under § 67 will apply. This means that affected individuals are allowed to deduct § 162 employee business expenses and § 212 expenses only to the extent that they exceed 2% of adjusted gross income. For example, assume that Sam earns $40,000 as a high school French teacher and that he spends $1,400 taking summer courses to improve his skills as a teacher and also spends $100 to purchase a subscription to a financial newsletter to assist him in planning his investment and retirement strategies. Under these circumstances, Sam can claim a deduction for only $700 of the aggregate $1,500 in expenses. Sam would likely find it preferable to claim a deduction under § 222, assuming that he was eligible to do so, because the full $1,400 in education expenses would be deductible.

Second, because § 222 has a cap on deductions whereas § 162 does not, a taxpayer with substantial expenses may find that § 162 provides greater relief. For example, assume that Clara is a middle school science teacher in Miami and that after three years of teaching she decides to take a year off and obtain a masters degree in biology to improve her skills as a teacher. When Clara takes her leave of absence in 2005 to commence her studies, she has earned a total of $30,000 and has no other income for the year. Clara pays $8,000 in tuition in 2005 and in addition incurs $6,000 in room and board expenses while studying at Florida State University in Tallahassee. Only $4,000 of her $8,000 tuition would be deductible under § 222 because deductions under that provision for education expenses are capped at $4,000. Clara would clearly be better off claiming her education expenses as an employee business expense under § 162, despite being subject to the 2% haircut of § 67. Moreover, when Clara considers that a small portion of her room and board expense (which will qualify for a deduction under § 162 as meals and lodging expenses incurred while away from home in pursuit of a trade or business) will absorb the 2% haircut, she will clearly be better off claiming a deduction for her tuition under § 162.

Third, § 222 has phaseout features which may make its benefits entirely unavailable to certain taxpayers. Although § 162 employee deductions are subject to the 2% haircut rules of § 67, even after their application a taxpayer who was totally denied the benefits of § 222 may find that § 162 still provided him some (albeit modest) relief. For example, a single taxpayer who has AGI of $80,000 per year and incurs $3,000 of tuition expenses in 2005 at a local college in keeping up his job skills will find that although after the 2% haircut he will only be allowed a deduction for $1,400 of his education expenses. This, however, surely beats the zero deduction allowance provided under § 222 because his income exceeds the cap on earnings imposed by § 222(b)(2)(B).

In closing, we note that § 162 seldom provides relief to families as they seek to put their children through their undergraduate years. In most such cases, the student will fail to satisfy the tests of maintaining or improving skills in an established line of employment. Nor is such education likely to be incurred to maintain a position as required by an employer or profession. Typically, undergraduate education provides the student with no more than the bare essentials (if even those) needed to enter a trade or business or qualifies the student to enter a new trade or profession. The same can also be said of most graduate education such as that obtained by attending law or medical school. Section 162 will most likely to be of assistance to individuals such as school teachers, doctors or lawyers who have already embarked on a professional career and who seek additional education to maintain or improve skills. From a planning standpoint, individuals who have obtained the minimum education required to enter a profession may wish to enter that profession and then obtain any additional education that will enable them to function at the highest level in their profession. For example, an individual who plans a career in secondary school teaching, rather than obtaining all available advanced education in her specialty (M.Ed. or D.Ed.) before commencing her career in teaching, might first start teaching and, after a year or two, take time off to pursue an advanced degree. In doing so, care must be taken to assure that the additional education does not qualify the student for a new trade or business.

[¶ 6,133]

Problems

1. On graduating from college Josh took up carpentry as a trade. He progressed well in the field and within a few years was made a site superintendent by his firm which specialized in residential home construc-

tion. After a few years he concluded that the entire field of residential home construction could be revolutionized by the application of modern business practices. He then decided to attend business school to obtain an M.B.A. to enable him to seize the opportunities which he saw within his grasp. He took a prep course to prepare him for the GMAT. Josh was admitted to a top level business school and obtained his M.B.A. within 18 months. May Josh take a deduction under § 162 for one or more of: (1) the cost of his undergraduate education; (2) the cost of his prep course; and (3) the cost of his M.B.A. including tuition, food and lodging?

2. Your state requires that all lawyers take 20 hours per year of continuing legal education to retain their license to practice law. To date your firm has required all associates to pick up the cost of such CLE (normally $800 per year). Why might you, as a partner who is a member of the firm's managing committee, wish to suggest that the firm absorb the cost of all such CLE as a business expense?

[¶ 6,140]

3. Interest on Education Loans

Section 221 provides a limited deduction for interest on education loans. The maximum amount deductible as interest on a student loan under this provision for 2001 and subsequent years is $2,500. See I.R.C. § 221 (b)(1). Any deduction allowed under § 221 is a so-called "above-the-line deduction," which means that it is taken into account in determining adjusted gross income and is allowed regardless of whether the taxpayer itemizes deductions or claims the standard deduction. See I.R.C. § 62(a)(17). Moreover, no deduction is allowed under § 221(e)(1) for interest that may have been allowed as a deduction under another provision of the Code (e.g., interest on a home equity loan used to finance education and for which a deduction was claimed).

This deduction, like several other allowances for education expenses, is subject to phaseout. The phaseout for § 221 is based on the taxpayer's § 221 modified adjusted gross income (§ 221 MAGI), which is the same as § 222 adjusted gross income except that instead of adding back any interest allowed as a deduction under § 221 the taxpayer is required to add back any tuition and related fees allowed as a deduction under § 222. For years beginning after 2001, phaseout commences as § 221 MAGI rises above $50,000 ($100,000 for married couples filing jointly) and is complete when § 221 MAGI exceeds $65,000 ($130,000 for married couples filing jointly). See I.R.C. § 221(b)(2). The phaseout amounts for § 221 are adjusted for inflation. See I.R.C. § 221(f). Married couples who do not file joint returns are barred from claiming any deduction under § 221.

Only interest on a "qualified education loan" is allowed as a deduction under § 221. Generally, qualified education loan interest is interest paid by the taxpayer on a loan incurred by the taxpayer to pay for "higher education expenses" for the taxpayer, the taxpayer's spouse or a person who was a dependent of the taxpayer when the loan was incurred. No deduction is allowed with respect to any individual if any person other than the taxpayer claimed a dependent deduction with respect to such individual under § 151. See I.R.C. § 221(c). It is worth noting that both a parent and a child-student can qualify as parties who may claim deductions for interest on qualified education loans. Consequently, it would be possible for each to deduct up to $2,500 (but not the same $2,500) of interest, assuming each satisfies all other statutory requirements. The student must have been enrolled at least as a half-time student in a program leading to a degree, certificate or other recognized educational credential. The lender may not be a party related to the taxpayer nor may the loan be one from certain employer loan plans. See I.R.C. § 221(d). Qualified education loans include not only conventional student loans but also refinanced student loans such as a consolidated loan (a loan used to refinance more than one student loan of the same borrower) and a collapsed loan (two or more loans of the same borrower that lender and borrower treat as one loan).

To qualify for a deduction, the party paying the interest and the student must have the requisite relationship described in the preceding paragraph. In addition, the deduction is allowed only for "interest paid by the taxpayer." The "paid by the taxpayer" requirement means, for example, that a parent is not allowed a deduction for interest paid by the child-student on a student loan incurred by the child-student even if the student qualifies as a dependent of the parent. However, if the parent pays interest on a loan that is a loan of the child-student, it may be possible for the child to claim that the payment by the parent was intended as a gift to the child and that the child is entitled to a deduction, assuming that all other requirements are met. This would be consistent with the Service's concession that payment of tuition by a parent may be treated as a gift by the parent to the child and may entitle the child to a deduction for tuition under § 222. See ¶ 6,120.

Only interest on loans incurred to pay for "qualified higher education expenses" at an "eligible educational institution" may be deducted under § 221. In general, qualified higher education expenses include the costs of: (1) tuition and related fees; (2) room and board actually charged by an eligible educational institution or the amount allowed as reasonable by such an institution; (3) books, supplies and equipment; and (4) other expenses (such as transportation). I.R.S. Pub. 970, Tax Benefits For Education 20 (2002). The sum of the foregoing items at a qualifying institution must be reduced by any amounts excluded from income under § 127 (employer education assistance programs, see ¶ 6,180), § 135 (Series EE savings bonds), § 529 (PTC plans and ESPs), § 530 (Coverdell accounts) and certain scholarships described in § 25A(g)(2). For example, assume that Sean's only qualified higher education expenses are $12,000 of tuition and $6,000 of room and board, and that he receives a full tuition scholarship from the college that he is attending and borrows $7,000 to pay for room and board and incidental expenses such as cable TV service and fraternity dues. Only 6/7ths of the interest on the student loan would qualify for deduction under § 221.

According to the I.R.S.: "An eligible educational institution is any college, university, vocational school, or other post-secondary educational institution eligible to participate in a student aid program administered by the Department of Education. It also includes virtually all accredited public, non-profit, and proprietary (privately owned profit-making) post-secondary institutions." Id. The term also includes any institution conducting an internship or residency program leading to a degree or certificate from a higher education institution or a health care facility (e.g. a hospital) that offers postgraduate training. Id. Interestingly, § 221 is broader than most other relief provisions both in terms of the types of qualifying education expenses and the range of eligible educational institutions. In that regard, § 221 is perhaps one of the broadest relief devices provided by the Code.

In closing discussion of § 221, it is worth noting that, unlike many other provisions of the Code, § 221 provides relief only after an individual or family has arranged to pay for education expenses. Moreover, the cap on deductible interest ($2,500) makes the value of the relief in terms of the dollar value of loans covered highly sensitive to the prevailing interest rates at the time the loans are either incurred or refinanced by conventional means or by consolidation. Lastly, the phaseout provisions of § 221 may preclude many families and individuals from obtaining relief under § 221 when the time comes for repayment of eligible loans. Accordingly, instead of being regarded as a basic component in a family's financial plan for meeting higher education expenses, § 221 should be regarded as a means-tested, after-the-fact form of relief for those lucky enough to have figured out how they would meet education expenses and unlucky enough to have to borrow to do so.

E.   EXCLUSIONS OF EDUCATIONAL BENEFITS FROM INCOME

[¶ 6,160]

The Code also provides assistance for education by excluding from taxation three items which, under normative definitions of income, would be included in gross income. Under § 117 of the Code, most scholarships for higher education are excluded from taxation. Section 127 of the Code provides a limited exclusion for up to $5,250 per year per employee of certain employer-provided education benefits. Section 108(f) of the Code excludes from income cancelled student loans where cancellation is pursuant to the terms of the loan and additional conditions have been satisfied. Although tax benefits derived under any of these provisions will be of considerable economic benefit to qualifying individuals, in most circumstances they provide little help for families in formulating a plan for meeting future education expenses. Because most families have virtually no way to know in advance whether their child-student will garner a scholarship or will work for an employer who offers an education assistance plan, neither § 117 nor § 127 provides much by way of up-front assistance in planning for the future. Moreover, because the loan forgiveness programs that qualify under § 108(f) are typically geared to students who enter a specific field of employment that the government wishes to encourage because of public need (e.g., teaching severely handicapped people) and because few students are certain that they will pursue such a career, this provision also provides little help for families in planning how best to meet future education expenses. In some cases a family may have a well-founded expectation that a child will qualify for a scholarship (typically where there is a narrowly defined program for which the child will qualify) or that because of definite career plans of the child-student a loan will be forgiven. It is only in such circumstances that §§ 117 and 108(f) provide assistance in planning to meet higher education expenses. Nonetheless, even where this is not the case, §§ 117, 127 and 108(f) can all provide significant relief for families struggling to meet the costs of higher education and a grasp of these provisions can therefore be of real value for students who are fortunate enough to qualify for the benefits they provide.

[¶ 6,170]

1. Scholarships

There are two principal sources of scholarship aid for students attaining higher education: (1) the higher education institutions themselves and their alumni organizations or other affiliated tax exempt organizations; and (2) philanthropic institutions that have no connection with the higher education institution that a student attends.

Many colleges and universities use scholarships to engage in what is sometimes called differential pricing. Just as airlines use various pricing mechanisms (e.g., advance purchase, duration of stay, Saturday night stayover) to maximize revenue yield from passengers based on the varying ability of different passengers to pay for an airline ticket, so do universities attempt to maximize the yield among admitted students to produce an optimal enrolled class. The chief means of achieving the desired mix is by granting scholarships and other forms of aid to certain groups of students. Although airlines are interested in maximizing gross revenue yield, colleges and universities have a different goal when they engage in differential pricing. Indeed, higher education organizations often pursue several different goals when they admit and offer aid to potential enrollees. These goals include, but are not limited to, the following: successfully competing with other schools for a highly qualified student body; enabling needy qualified students to attend the school of their choice; attracting students with special talents (e.g., athletes); obtaining a diverse and interesting student body; and setting different prices for education based on family income and wealth so as to optimize revenue yield, quality and mix of the student body. This last mentioned factor could almost serve as a catch-all to describe any scholarship program run by institutions of higher education and their affiliates were it not for the fact that some such organizations are actually concerned with only one factor when they award a scholarship. For example, a university-affiliated foundation that was established to support an athletic program is concerned with only one factor (athletic ability) when it awards a scholarship; and a college concerned only with enrolling the most gifted student body it can will award all of its scholarships based on a single factor or series of factors (e.g., SAT score and GPA).

Some organizations that are not affiliated with any college or university award scholarships to further the goals of the organization. Such scholarships may enable a student to attend any one of several colleges designated by the granting organization. For example, an organization formed to assist women pursuing careers in science may award scholarships to eligible women to study science at an institution of their choice, and an organization founded to assist needy residents of a particular area or ethnic group may provide assistance to qualifying students to attend any one of a limited number of colleges or universities. Students who first obtain a commitment of need-based financial aid from the college of their choice and subsequently obtain a scholarship from an independent source should not be surprised when the level of support provided by their school is reduced. Typically, to encourage students on financial aid to seek independent sources of support, schools do not reduce their own scholarship awards on a dollar-for-dollar basis. For example, if a college offered an enrolled student a need-based scholarship of $10,000 covering 50% of the tuition and the student then obtained a partial scholarship of $6,000 from a fraternal organization, the student might expect to see the amount of the college scholarship reduced by 75% of the independently provided $6,000 scholarship ($4,500), leaving him with a school-provided scholarship of $5,500. If the scholarship from an independent source is nominal in value when compared to the cost of education being borne by the student's family, schools rarely reduce the amount of the aid that they provide. Assume that the student in the previous example obtained a scholarship of only $300 from a fraternal organization. In such a case most schools would not reduce the amount of aid that they provided. Where a student's financial aid package consists of several items (e.g., loans, work, scholarship), schools often feel at liberty to determine which, if any, of the items of support should be reduced. For example, where a student's aid package consists of loans and scholarship, it is entirely plausible that a school might react to a student's obtaining a scholarship from an independent source by reducing the amount of the loan that a student is expected to incur or perhaps reducing both the scholarship and amount of the loan by an amount that in aggregate is less than the value of the independently provided scholarship. This is another means whereby schools create incentives for students to seek scholarships from independent sources.

In general, a student who seeks and obtains an offer of a scholarship from an independent organization not affiliated with an institution of higher education will have no success in reapproaching the institution to ask if it can possibly increase the size of its scholarship award. This is not always the case with colleges and universities that make an offer of scholarship aid to a student who they hope will enroll at their institution. If a student obtains an offer of a scholarship and related aid package from another college or university that makes attending that institution more affordable than attending the student's preferred institution, this could provide an opportunity to ask the preferred institution if it could possibly increase its level of support. This is typically done by informing the preferred institution of the disparity in costs and politely asking if the preferred institution could reexamine the student's situation. Depending on the preferred institution's policy, the availability of additional aid and the degree of interest that a school has in the particular applicant, schools in such situations may be willing to increase either the amount of their scholarship offer or the level of other components of their aid package.

In recent years, many schools have become obsessed with their annual ranking in the U.S. News & World Report. This has had an unfortunate impact on the financial aid policies of some institutions. In the past, schools typically used scholarship aid to provide resource sensitive differential pricing for higher education. This was done by providing aid which varied inversely with family wealth, i.e., the higher a family's income and wealth, the less likely it was that an admitted student would receive aid. Because the SAT and GPA of enrolled students are important components in most systems for ranking undergraduate schools, schools concerned about raising their ranking in such studies have begun to shift toward granting aid based primarily on SAT scores and GPA rather than on need. The same pattern of shifting financial aid criteria has recently commenced in law and medical schools.

There are several sources of information on scholarship aid that are not tied to or provided by the school that a student is attending. Two good web-based free sources are: <http://www.fedmoney.org/0–scholarships.htm> and <http://www.college-scholarships.com/free scholarship searches.htm>. A good reference book on the subject is Joseph Russo, "The College Board Scholarship Handbook 2004" (2003, normally updated annually). Students and their families should be very careful about paying for assistance in locating scholarship aid. Generally, the most that the paid provider of information will do is to run searches of the above data bases and pass the results back to the family in exchange for a hefty fee. In many cases the student and her family will receive only a duplicated list of the data bases covered by the second mentioned free data base. In some cases, all the student and her family will get back from the so-called information provider will be a cancelled check. Needless to say, most college and university aid offices recommend against paying to obtain assistance in locating scholarships and other forms of financial aid.

In 1954 Congress added § 117 to the Code to provide an exclusion from gross income for qualifying scholarships. Prior to 1954, an individual who received a scholarship had to include the benefit in gross income unless it qualified as an excludable gift under § 102. Section 117 now provides the sole avenue for excluding scholarships from gross income.

Under § 117, a taxpayer may exclude from gross income an amount received as a "qualified scholarship by an individual who is a candidate for a degree at an educational organization described in section 170(b)(1)(A)(ii)." For an educational organization to be so described, it must maintain a regular faculty, curriculum and student body that is in attendance at the location where the organization's educational activities are regularly carried on. Moreover, because of the requirement that the student be a candidate for a degree, the organization must also be a degree-granting institution. However, the student may pursue credits at an institution other than the one granting the degree, as long as they count toward receiving a degree at the degree-granting institution. See Prop. Reg. § 1.117–6(c)(4).

The term "qualified scholarship" covers only amounts received as scholarship or fellowship grants for tuition and fees required for enrollment as well as fees, books, supplies and equipment required for courses of instruction. See I.R.C. § 117(b). Conspicuously absent from the list of qualifying education expenses are awards that cover room and board. To protect the exclusion of their awards, most organizations that offer scholarships provide in their grant awards that the grant is being made to cover tuition, fees, books and any other items that qualify for exclusion. In the event that a student receives a flat dollar amount as an award, the student should take steps to establish, as well as he can, that the award was used to meet expenses that qualify for exclusion. See Prop. Reg. § 1.117–6(c)(1). However, to the extent that an award is specifically made to cover non-qualifying expenses such as room and board or to the extent that the award prohibits its being used to meet qualifying expenses, such amounts do not qualify as an excluded scholarship award. See Prop. Reg. § 1.117–6(c)(1).

One of the most significant limitations imposed on the exclusion of scholarships under § 117 is the prohibition against the recipient being required to perform services as a condition of the scholarship grant, except in two limited circumstances. See I.R.C. § 117(c). The two limited circumstances involve awards received under certain Armed Forces and National Health Services scholarship programs. At first blush, it would appear that the prohibition on the performance of services would adversely affect athletic scholarships. The Service has ruled that Ivy League type scholarships (solely need based) granted to athletes that do not require that students play a sport are eligible for the exclusion. See Rev. Rul. 77–263, 1977–2 C.B. 47. Because traditional NCAA athletic scholarship grants require that the grantee play a specified sport to retain the award, the ruling on Ivy League type scholarships provides no guidance as to how such scholarships should be treated. However, the Service, perhaps recognizing that any move to tax such athletic scholarships would be met with severe Congressional reaction, has refrained from attempting to tax traditional NCAA athletic scholarships.

Section 117(d) provides an exclusion from gross income for certain tuition reductions provided by educational organizations described in § 170(b)(1)(A)(ii) to an employee, the spouse of an employee or an employee's child who is less than 25 years of age for the pursuit of education below the graduate level. The tuition reduction may be provided at the employing institution or at another § 170(b)(1)(A)(ii) educational organization. Section 117(d)(3) provides that for such tuition programs to qualify for exclusion, they may not discriminate in favor of highly compensated individuals. Occasionally, individuals will seek employment at a college or university with such a program for the purpose of being able to obtain free or much reduced tuition for themselves, a spouse or child. Even if the college's or university's plan does discriminate in favor of highly compensated individuals and does not qualify for exclusion, as long as the employee qualifies for participation, she will still find it advantageous to receive the tuition reduction even if it is subject to income taxation. Section 117(d)(5) provides a special rule for individuals whose employment status at a university is based on their status as teaching or research assistants. In such cases, the tuition reduction may be provided for the pursuit of graduate studies. This source of tax-free tuition relief can be very useful for individuals pursuing graduate studies.

In closing discussion of scholarship relief, it should be emphasized that § 117 provides little help to families in planning how best to meet future education expenses. More important and more difficult than obtaining tax relief for scholarship aid will be positioning the student to be on the receiving end of a scholarship grant. Few families can count on having a child who is bright enough to win a merit scholarship or talented enough to win an athletic scholarship. More than likely, if a student qualifies for a scholarship it will be based on need, and few families willingly seek to ensure that their financial situation makes such a scholarship a strong likelihood. Nonetheless, for those families who find that a member is eligible for a scholarship qualifying for exclusion under § 117, the tax relief provided can prove to be of considerable value.

[¶ 6,180]

2. Employer Provided Education Benefits

Under § 127, an employee may exclude from gross income up to $5,250 of employer-provided education assistance furnished pursuant to a program that meets certain statutory conditions. The $5,250 cap is personal to each individual employee. This means, for example, that if an individual works for two employers and one employer provides the employee with $2,000 of qualifying education benefits, only $3,250 of education benefits received from the second employer during the same year will qualify for the exclusion. Typically, an employee will be informed by her employer if any education benefits provided by the employer are excludable from gross income.

The educational assistance that qualifies for exclusion under § 127 includes (but is not limited to) tuition, fees, books, supplies and required equipment for study at vocational training programs and higher education at both undergraduate and graduate institutions (including professional schools such as law and medical schools). Education and training (including books, supplies and equipment) provided by an employer also qualify for the education assistance exclusion. See I.R.C. § 127(c). Expenditures for education that do not qualify include tools or supplies that may be retained by an employee after training, meals, lodging and transportation. Moreover, expenditures for education and training involving sports, games or hobbies do not qualify for exclusion.

In general, for an educational assistance program to qualify under § 127, there must be a written plan. In providing benefits the plan must not discriminate in favor of highly compensated employees, and no more than 5% of the benefits under the plan may be provided for shareholders or owners (or their spouses or dependents) who hold more than 5% of the ownership interest in the employer. See I.R.C. § 127(b)(1)–(3). The purpose of imposing such conditions is to prevent business owners from setting up educational assistance programs primarily for the benefit of themselves or family members.

Section 127, like most other tax incentives for education, bars an employee from obtaining a deduction or tax credit for any amounts excluded from income under § 127. See I.R.C. § 127(c)(7).

In closing discussion of § 127, we note that Congress has traditionally imposed short-term sunset limits on § 127 and periodically renewed the provision. In 2001, Congress extended the operation of § 127 through the year 2010.

[¶ 6,190]

3. Loan Cancellation

Normally, cancellation of indebtedness results in income to the debtor. See I.R.C. § 61(a)(12). An exception relevant to financing the cost of higher education is provided by § 108(f). Under this provision, forgiveness of qualifying student loans does not give rise to cancellation of indebtedness income if certain conditions are met. For a loan to qualify under § 108(f), the lender must be one of the following: (1) the federal government, a state, a local government or an instrumentality or agency thereof; (2) a public benefit corporation that has assumed control over a state, county or municipal hospital, provided that the employees of such corporation are deemed public employees under state law; or (3) an educational institution described in § 170(b)(1)(A)(ii) (see ¶ 6,170), if the loan is made as part of an agreement with organizations described in (1) or (2) to use funds provided by such organizations for educational purposes or under a program designed to encourage students to enter certain occupations or serve in areas where skilled persons are in short supply as long as such students serve as employees of governmental or charitable entities. To qualify for benefits under § 108(f), the loan must include a provision that all or part of a student's loan will be cancelled if the student works for a certain period of time in certain professions for a broad class of employers. It is important to note that only loans of the student (as contrasted with parental loans to fund a child's education) qualify for exclusion under § 108(f).

Typically the occupations that a student must enter to secure the benefits of this provision are those for which there is a critical shortage of willing participants such as teachers of severely retarded children and medical doctors in rural areas or in the military. Because few students, on entering college, know that they are likely to enter such careers, this provision provides little help for families in planning to meet future higher education expenses. Obviously, there are situations where students and their families can plan to take advantage of § 108(f). For example, § 108(f) can prove useful for families with a child who wishes to enter medical school and must borrow considerable amounts of money to obtain a medical education. By borrowing those funds from a governmental agency that provides loans with cancellation features conditioned on the student serving as a doctor in the military or in a rural area, the student can position himself or herself to take advantage of the loan forgiveness feature of § 108(f).

F. GIFTS

[¶ 6,200]

Occasionally a wealthy individual, such as an aunt, uncle or grandparent, outside of the student's immediate family may be willing to provide financial assistance to the student and her family. If this is the case, an advisor will seek to minimize any income or gift tax liability of the donor.

The primary opportunity for minimizing income taxes arises where the donor holds significantly appreciated assets that are ripe for sale. Rather than having the donor sell the assets, pay tax on the gain and transfer the proceeds to the student for use in paying tuition or other bills, it is often recommended that the donor transfer the appreciated assets to the student who can then sell the assets with gain being taxed at the student's (presumably lower) bracket. See ¶¶ 3,500 and 3,780 (discussing § 1015 gift basis rules and assignment of income). If property that has declined in value in the hands of the donor is involved, in virtually all cases it makes sense for the donor to sell the property, claim the resulting tax loss and transfer the sale proceeds to the donee or an eligible transferee under § 2503(e) which is discussed below.

When contemplating a gift for educational purposes it is important to keep in mind two gift tax exclusions: (1) the annual per-donee exclusion provided by § 2503(b) which in 2004 stood at $11,000 per donee per year; and (2) the exemption for education and medical expenses provided by § 2503(e). See ¶¶ 4,150 and 4,160. Normally there is little difficulty in taking advantage of the $11,000 annual exclusion, and married donors should bear in mind that, by taking advantage of the gift-splitting election under § 2513, if the donor obtains the consent of his or her spouse, the gift can be treated as if one-half came from each spouse. The primary advantage of this is that the amount excludable under the annual per-donee exclusion may be doubled. See ¶ 4,150. The exclusion provided by § 2503(e) for transfers for education and medical expenses is available in addition to the $11,000 annual per-donee exclusion. This exclusion is available only for tuition that is paid by the donor directly to the educational institution that the student is attending (or, in the case of medical expenses, for amounts paid directly to the person providing medical care). With respect to the so called "ed and med" exclusion, it is important to bear two things in mind: (1) payment must be made directly to the provider and cannot be made to the student or her parents; and (2) payment may be made only for tuition or for medical care (as defined in § 213(d)). For example, this provision enables a donor to pay for both tuition and student health insurance (which qualifies as medical care under § 213(d)). A donor of considerable means would be well advised to use the "ed and med" exclusion first, thereby keeping intact his annual exclusion under § 2503(b) so as to enable him to make a gift to the student of up to $11,000 to pay for room, board, books or other expenses.

After exhausting the § 2503(e) "ed and med" exclusion and the $11,000 annual exclusion of § 2503(b), and where possible, doubling that sum with the aid of § 2513, a donor will then have to fall back on the $1,000,000 lifetime exemption provided by § 2505 to shelter additional gifts from gift tax. See ¶ 4,015.

[¶ 6,210]

Problem

Grandmother Stuart has a net worth in excess of $8,000,000. She was thrilled when her grandson Floyd was accepted as a student at Stanford University and his twin sister Hyacinth was accepted at Smith College. Although her son John and his wife Kelly, who both have high-paying professional positions, could manage to sent the twins through both Stanford and Smith by making payment out of earnings, invading savings, borrowing and having the children work at the colleges, Grandmother Stuart does not want the family to stretch its resources when she can so easily afford to supply the needed funds. She seeks your advice as to how she may do so with minimal gift tax consequences. Before advising Mrs. Stuart you may wish to consult ¶ 6,005 to refresh your recollection of what sums of money Mrs. Stuart may be dealing with annually.

G.   FEDERAL LOANS AND GRANTS

[¶ 6,220]

Approximately two-thirds of all students or their families incur debt to finance higher education. About 80% of all student loans are made available under federal educational loan programs with most of the balance consisting of loans provided by the college or university that a student attends. To obtain a loan under a federal program and under most college and university run loan programs, a student and her family must complete a Free Application for Federal Student Aid (FAFSA). Moreover, to qualify for a Pell Grant, a need-based grant provided by the federal government, a FAFSA must also be completed. The FAFSA gathers required information about student and family finances which is used to assess the expected family contribution (EFC). The general intent is that loans, scholarships, work study aid and other forms of assistance will be made available to bridge the gap between the EFC and the cost of obtaining an education at a given college or university. Nonetheless, it must be borne in mind that neither the government nor institutions of higher education are obligated to bridge the gap and unfortunately many students will not be financially able to attend the college of their choice; for some, the pursuit of higher education will be barred solely for financial reasons.

Because of the centrality of EFC in the aid process, it will be helpful first to explore, in general, how that sum is determined before examining the degree to which Pell Grants and loans may be available to assist families in meeting college costs.

[¶ 6,230]

1.   Expected Family Contribution

In January of a student's senior year in high school (or, for students who have already graduated, in January of the year in which they anticipate commencing classes in the fall), a family will be asked to complete a FAFSA based on income and financial information for the previous calendar year. Because most of the information reported on the FAFSA is based on information that a family will receive in January to enable it to file its federal and state income tax returns, most families will first have to accumulate a variety of information returns that filter in during January before being able to complete the FAFSA. The information so provided is used by the federal government to determine EFC. Moreover, some colleges will ask that a supplementary form (either the PROFILE form or a special form peculiar to the school or a group of schools) be completed by student applicants. Because colleges are not bound to use the EFC figure produced by the federal government when they provide aid, they often use the information provided by the supplementary form to make their own aid assessment solely for determining the level of aid that they will provide in addition to the loan and other aid made available though federal programs which use the federal EFC to determine the appropriate level of Pell Grants and federally supported loans. For example, although the FAFSA is unconcerned with the amount of money parents may have accumulated in a 401(k) or other pension plan, the annual level of tax-sheltered contributions to a pension plan, or the make and value of cars owned by a family, individual schools may be interested in obtaining such information to determine the appropriate level of aid that the school should offer to provide from its own resources in the form of loans, grants or work opportunities. Also, although the federal EFC formulae make no allowance for private primary and secondary school tuition commitments for younger siblings, many private colleges are understandably willing to make an accommodation for such expenses. Families should be aware that providing such information is not a one-shot affair and that a FAFSA and perhaps supplementary forms will have to be filed for each year that a student attends school and wishes to obtain federally supported loans, a Pell Grant or aid from a college that the student is attending.

The FAFSA will ask for information about, among other things, the financial and business assets that both parents and the child own, the income of parents and the child from their tax returns, the state and federal taxes paid by each, child support received, payments made to retirement plans, tax exempt interest received, and housing as well as other allowances paid to the child and family. There are two formulae used for determining EFC. The simplified formula is used if neither the parents nor child was required to file form 1040 with the I.R.S. for the purpose of determining federal income tax liability and the parent's AGI (for tax filers) or income earned from work (for nonfilers) was less than $50,000. If the student is independent of her parents, then she will qualify for the simplified formula if she and her spouse meet the forgoing tests as applied to their tax returns and income. The conventional formula is applied in the case of students and families who do not qualify for the simplified formula. The principal difference between the simplified and the conventional formulae is that in many cases in which the simplified formula is used, assets will not be considered in calculating EFC.

The precise formulae used to determine EFC are unimportant for our purposes, although those interested in exploring them in detail are referred to the U.S. Department of Education Information for Financial Aid for Professionals Library (available on the internet at <http://ifap.ed.gov/sfahandbooks/attachments/0203Volch6.pdf>). What is important for our purposes is that in determining EFC, family and student income and assets are all evaluated. The higher the level of income, the greater the amount that a family is expected to contribute after making allowances for payment of living expenses, taxes and employment-related expenses. Similarly, after making an allowance for a base level of protected assets (based on the age of the oldest parent) deemed necessary to provide a family with minimal security in retirement and an allowance for business assets based on a sliding scale, families are expected to contribute up to 5.64% percent of unprotected assets each year to meet college costs. In the case of students, it is expected that 35% of any financial assets will be used each year to meet college expenses. The asset calculation is performed annually. For example, if a student had $10,000 in savings, in his first year of college he would be expected to use $3,500 of his savings to meet college costs. If his grandmother then made him a gift of $500, raising his remaining savings to $7,000, the student would be expected to contribute 35% of $7,000 or $2,450 of his savings toward the cost of his second year in college. The sum of anticipated student contributions from assets and income as well as the sum of parental contributions from their assets and income constitute the EFC in most cases. This sum is then subtracted from the anticipated cost of attending the various colleges to which a student has been admitted to determine the student's level of need. It bears repeating here that there is no guarantee from government or from higher education institutions that a student's need will be met. The primary function of the EFC at most schools is to set a cap on the value of a loan, grant and work package to be offered to a student and not to determine the level of support that will actually be provided. In a few cases involving extremely well-endowed schools, the school may wish to undertake the commitment to provide worthy students with whatever financial aid is necessary to enable the student to attend the school. These situations are so rare that they should not loom large in a family's plans for meeting the cost of higher education for young children. The schools which are able to make this sort of commitment are often among the most competitive colleges and universities, and few families can count on admission to them as a means of solving the problem of how to meet the cost of higher education for their middle and high school children. Moreover, these schools also typically employ a supplementary form for calculating EFC which may consider items such as voluntary parental contributions to tax-sheltered retirement plans as available income that can be tapped to meet EFC, something which the federal EFC formula ignores.

Journalists who write financial aid columns and authors of books on financing higher education often cannot resist including in their materials tips on how families can game the EFC formulae and thereby obtain financial aid above the level to which a family would normally be entitled. There are at least two reasons to be skeptical of attempts to game the system. First, in some cases the steps undertaken are misleading at best and unethical at worst. Second, the authors who suggest gaming the system imply that winners in the process will emerge with baskets of scholarship and grant support indirectly resulting in money in the pockets of the families who follow their advice. In fact, however, any additional aid obtained in this manner typically comes in the form of loans rather than scholarship or grant aid. The result of such schemes, more often than not, is to ensure that the student starts out professional life burdened with an unnecessarily large load of debt.

Despite the previously stated misgivings about providing advice on gaming the EFC, we offer the following advice for those interested in exploring the issue. Because the starting place for income under the federal EFC formulae is adjusted gross income (AGI) as shown on the prior year's federal tax return, families may wish to undertake steps to suppress AGI. For example, AGI may be diminished by increasing the amount of money contributed to a tax-sheltered retirement plan (such as a 401(k) or a 403(b) plan), a deferred compensation arrangement or a flexible spending account to meet medical or child care expenses (see ¶ 3,080). Also, any income of a child less than 14 that is subject to the kiddie tax (see ¶ 3,740) and is reported on the parent's return will boost the AGI shown on the return. By simply reporting the income on a separate return for the child, a parent will reduce the AGI shown on the parent's return. Careful timing of sales of parent-owned assets may also reduce AGI. For example, by selling appreciated assets in December of the year before the base year used for determining the first EFC, rather than in January of the base year, a family may be able to present a more favorable financial picture on the initial FAFSA. Although investing in a tax-managed mutual fund is always a prudent choice, it can have a double payoff by keeping down AGI reported on a FAFSA. Families that own their own businesses have additional opportunities to decrease AGI by scheduling of billing of receivables and purchases of deductible items, especially depreciable assets that may be written off under § 179 (see ¶ 3,460). In addition, owners of businesses may consider hiring younger siblings of the student both as a means of assigning income to them to be taxed at a lower rate (see ¶ 3,770) and reducing parental AGI reported from the business, although care must be taken that the added FICA taxes do not cancel out any resulting benefits. Moreover, because refunds of state income taxes are, for most middle class families, added back into income for purposes of computing AGI (see ¶ 3,020), care should be taken to minimize excessive withholding of state taxes in order to reduce the amount of the refund that must subsequently be included in AGI.

Because assets owned by the student and her family are also used in determining EFC, those interested in gaming the calculation of their EFC will have to consider asset shifting that will result in lowering their EFC. The federal aid formulae exclude home equity and that of a family farm as well as tax-sheltered retirement accounts and the cash surrender value of life insurance policies from the owner's asset base. Although there may be a temptation to force money into these assets, for example by paying down a mortgage on a home, to exclude it from EFC calculations, the payoff to a family hardly seems to be worth the loss of flexibility that results. For example, a transfer of $10,000 will only reduce the EFC by $564. Moreover, bear in mind that a family that does so will likely discover that all they have done is to increase the amount of educational loans that they or their child will be allowed to incur. To the extent that the additional $564 in debt is subsidized student loan debt on which no interest will accrue until after studies have terminated, the family may reap some small financial advantage. However, because the amount of subsidized student loans that one may incur is quite small (see ¶¶ 6,260 and 6,270), families that play the game may find that all they are doing is incurring additional interest-bearing debt which, because of the phaseout provisions of the rules allowing for deduction of interest on student loans and the $2,500 cap on such interest, may not result in deductible interest for the student. See ¶ 6,140.

Occasionally families attempt to reduce family assets by going on a buying spree. This is a foolish strategy for a family that is about to face a heavy multi-year commitment for college education of their offspring. As the example in the previous paragraph indicates, a family must spend a considerable sum to produce even a modest reduction in the EFC. Moreover, if the family must eventually resort to the purchased assets to meet expenses in subsequent years, it is likely to find itself in a real financial bind as it attempts to liquidate a cache of Persian rugs or a bass boat bought in a moment of ill-conceived do-it-yourself financial planning.

In fact the most sensible gaming of the asset component in the EFC formula that a family can undertake is to ensure that most assets being saved for higher education are placed in the name of the parents rather than in the name of the would-be student. The advantage in doing so is that parent-owned assets are assessed at a rate of 5.64% whereas student-owned assets are assessed at the rate of 35%. Unfortunately, doing so is likely to deprive the family of the advantage over the years of having assets in a student's name taxed at the student's (presumably lower) income tax rate. Another step that can be taken in this regard is to make sure that student-owned assets (rather than parent-owned assets) are used to pay for some high-cost items associated with college attendance. For example, student savings should first be tapped to purchase a required computer or a car needed by the student for commuting. However, one should still bear in mind that in most cases all a family will be doing is increasing the burden of education loans on the student to be paid off after graduation.

[¶ 6,240]

2. Pell Grants and Federal Supplemental Educational Opportunity Grants

The federal government has two principal grant programs aimed at the most needy students to enable them to meet a portion of their costs of attending college. These programs are the Pell Grant Program and the Federal Supplemental Educational Opportunity Grant Program. Because these programs provide only modest assistance and are limited to the most needy, they should not figure prominently in the plans of families that are making a long-term assessment as to how best to provide for the cost of a child's higher education. They are best viewed as a default benefit for families of modest income levels who lack any meaningful savings that can be tapped to meet college expenses.

Pell Grants (named after the late Senator Claiborne Pell, a strong advocate of assistance to poor students to enable them to attend college) are typically awarded to needy undergraduate students based on data reported on the FAFSA. Because this is a grant and not a loan program, there is no requirement that Pell Grant awards be repaid. The amount awarded to a student depends on the cost of attending the school of his choice and the EFC determined by the federal government for the student. The maximum amount of Pell Grant awards is determined each year by Congress. For the academic year 2004–2005 the maximum award was $4,050 and the minimum award was $400. To be eligible a student must be pursuing his first undergraduate degree, or be pursuing a post-baccalaureate teacher certificate, must not be incarcerated and if a male must have registered with the Selective Service. Grants are awarded for both full and part time study and are typically paid directly to the college or in some cases to the student. Only one Pell Grant may be received by a student in an award year and Pell Grants may not be received for attending more than one school in an award year.

Students who are eligible for Pell Grants may also be eligible for a Federal Supplemental Education Opportunity Grant (FSEOG). The primary difference between the Pell and the FSEOG programs is that Pell Grants are awarded as of right to qualifying students whereas FSEOG money is awarded to colleges and universities based on past patterns of need for their student bodies. The schools then award FSEOG money based on a student's EFC after taking into account the Pell Grant awarded to the student. The awards have recently ranged from $100 to $4,000 with the amount of an award being dependent on, among other things, the student's unmet need, the funds available to the college in question and the policies of the college's financial aid office.

[¶ 6,250]

3. Borrowing to Fill the Gap

After spending what it can out of family income, savings and taking advantage of any available scholarships, the family of the average student finds itself left with unmet higher education costs that may only be met through borrowing. The principal sources of loan money available to close the gap between costs and assets are: (1) Stafford Student Loans; (2) Perkins Loans; (3) Parent Loans for Undergraduate Students (PLUS); (4) private loans, including but not limited to EXCEL loans, Sallie Mae Signature Loans, Alternative Loans from The Education Resources Institute (TERI) and loans against other family held assets such as insurance policies, retirement assets and home equity. Helpful information on a variety of borrowing options is provided by Kristen Davis, Kiplinger's Financing College (2002).

[¶ 6,260]

a. *Stafford student loans*

Under the Stafford loan program, students (and not their parents) may borrow a limited amount each year up to an aggregate cap to fund undergraduate and graduate higher education. The annual as well as the aggregate limit on loan principal amount is a function of whether the student is dependent on her parents or is deemed to be independent of her parents. As of academic year 2004–2005, dependent undergraduate students may borrow $2,625 for their freshman year, $3,500 for their sophomore year and $5,500 annually for their junior, senior and any subsequent years, with a cap of $23,000 imposed on total borrowing for undergraduate education. Independent students may borrow $6,625 for their freshman year, $7,500 for the sophomore year and $10,500 annually for their junior, senior and any subsequent years, with a cap of $46,000 imposed on total borrowing for undergraduate education. Graduate students may borrow up to $18,500 per year up to an aggregate of $138,500 for undergraduate and graduate education combined. The funds are borrowed either under the Federal Direct Student Loan Program (FDSL) or under the Federal Family Education Loan Program (FFEL). Whether a student borrows under the FDSL or the FFEL depends on the loan program available at the school he attends. Under FDSL the student borrows directly from the federal government, whereas under FFEL the student obtains a government guaranteed loan from a private lending institution. FDSL and FFEL may be either subsidized or unsubsidized. Subsidized loans are made available based solely on need. If the loan is subsidized, the federal government pays the interest on the loan while the student is enrolled in school and for the first six months following graduation. If the student enrolls in graduate or professional school, the obligation to pay interest also abates. If a student does not qualify for a subsidized loan or has a level of need below the maximum amount of Stafford loan available based on his year in college, he will be eligible for an unsubsidized Stafford loan up to the balance of the maximum loan amount available for his year in college. For example, assume that Jane and Joe are both dependent students in their sophomore years. Jane does not qualify for a subsidized Stafford loan and Joe qualifies for a $2,000 subsidized Stafford loan. Jane will be able to borrow $3,500 in the form of an unsubsidized loan and Joe will be eligible to qualify for an unsubsidized $1,500 Stafford loan in addition to his $2,000 subsidized loan.

The interest rate on Stafford loans is adjusted every year starting in July. The rate is equal to the July 91–day T-bill rate plus 1.7% while the student is attending school and 2.3% on graduation or withdrawal from school. For example, in July 2004 the 91–day T-bill rate was 1.07%, the in-school rate for the 2004–2005 fiscal year was 2.77%, and the post-graduation rate was 3.37%. By law the cap on Stafford loans is 8.25%. The in-school interest on unsubsidized loans may either be paid as it comes due or be added to the principal amount of the loan. A 4% loan origination fee is charged on all Stafford loans with 3% going to the lender and 1% going to a loan guarantee fund. Because of the origination fee, students will only receive 96% of the principal amount of any loan. For example, a sophomore who borrows $3,500 will actually receive only $3,360 which may be used to meet the cost of higher education. Obviously, subsidized Stafford loans are very valuable and in most cases it makes little sense to pass them up. Unsubsidized Stafford loans are also valuable because in most circumstances families will be unable to borrow money at a lower rate than that which applies to Stafford loans.

[¶ 6,270]

b. *Perkins loans*

Students with a high level of need may qualify for a loan under the federal Perkins Loan Program. Perkins loans are offered by the school that the student attends from a pool of federally provided funds and are available in addition to Stafford loans. The maximum amount of money that students may borrow under the Perkins Loan Program is $4,000 per year for undergraduate study with an aggregate cap of $20,000, and $6,000 per year for graduate or professional study with an aggregate cap of $40,000 for undergraduate and graduate study combined. The interest rate on Perkins loans is 5%. Loan repayment obligations do not commence until nine months after graduation or the student drops below half-time status. Perkins loans may be forgiven if the student is employed in certain jobs or professions such as nurse, medical technician, teacher in a low-income area or as a special-ed, science or math teacher, a law enforcement officer, a Peace Corps volunteer or in certain social service positions in low-income areas.

[¶ 6,280]

c. *PLUS loans*

Another important federal loan program is the Parent Loans for Undergraduate Students (PLUS) program. PLUS loans are made to parents to finance the undergraduate education of their children. After accounting for all student aid and loans, creditworthy parents are allowed to borrow the balance of the unmet cost of their child's undergraduate education (tuition, books, supplies, room and board). Like Stafford loans, the interest rate on PLUS loans is based on the rate on 91–day T-bills. It is set at 3.1% over the rate on 91–day T-bills and is capped at 9%. For loans disbursed during the 2004–2005 school year, the rate was 4.17%. Since PLUS loans do not require collateral, they are available, for example, to creditworthy parents who do not own their own home and lack other assets to secure the loan. Borrowers must be either U.S. citizens or permanent residents of the U.S. and the student with respect to whom the loan is incurred must be at least a half-time student. The obligation to repay a PLUS loan commences 60 days after funds have been disbursed under the loan and normally runs for 10 years, although it is possible (but perhaps not generally advisable) to extend the repayment period for up to 30 years. As in the case of Stafford loans, if the school attended by the student participates in the Federal Direct Student Loan Program, the PLUS loan will be made by the federal government which will send the loan proceeds directly to the school. Any excess not needed to meet direct school expenses, such as tuition, room and board, will be paid over to the parents to cover other indirect expenses such as books. If the student's school does not participate in the Federal Direct Student Loan Program, then, as is the case under the Stafford Loan Program, the borrower must make arrangements with a private bank to obtain a PLUS loan. PLUS loans carry a loan origination fee of 4%, of which 3% is remitted to the lender to cover expenses and 1% is paid into a loan guarantee fund.

[¶ 6,290]

d. *Other loan options*

In most cases it is advisable to exhaust the sources of borrowed funds mentioned above before students and their families explore other loan sources to finance higher education. Normally, the above sources will provide students and their families with all funds that are necessary and prudent to borrow. Moreover, in most cases federal education loans will provide families with the lowest available interest rates. However, in some circumstances it may be necessary for families to borrow even more money and in other circumstances it may make good economic sense to borrow elsewhere. For example, because § 221 of the Code caps deductible interest on student loans at $2,500 per borrower, a family that has incurred PLUS loans with annual interest payments of at least $2,500 may wish to consider a home equity loan to cover additional needs. Moreover, depending on the interest (and loan origination fees, if any) charged on such loans, it may actually make more sense to incur a home equity loan than a PLUS loan. For example, one inquiry at a local credit union revealed that during the 2003–2004 academic year, when the rate on PLUS loans was 4.22% with a 4% loan origination fee, the credit union would have made a variable rate home equity loan at 3.75% with no loan origination fee (although there was no cap on future interest rates on the loan as there would be with a PLUS loan). During the fall of 2004 that credit union raised its home equity loan rate to 4.75% which may still be preferable for a family that is itemizing personal deductions. Of course, any positive advantage of a lower effective rate on a home equity loan because of tax deductibility must be weighed against the consideration that the rate on a home equity loan may be raised during the period it is outstanding.

Home equity loans are, perhaps, the first non-federal loan source to which a family should turn because in most circumstances the interest on such loans will be deductible in determining federal and state income tax liability. See ¶ 3,170. As is the case with any loan, it makes good sense to shop for the best rate and terms that are available. The borrower may obtain funds either as a second mortgage for a fixed interest rate or as a variable rate loan. The latter will normally carry a lower interest rate but will carry with it the risk of future rate increases.

Other sources of private loans worth noting are Nellie Mae <www.nelliemae.com>, Sallie Mae <www.salliemae.com> and The Educational Resources Institute (TERI) <www.teri.org>. Nellie Mae offers creditworthy families EXCEL loans which are variable rate loans with interest rates adjusted either monthly or annually. Annually adjusted rate loans are available at a rate 2.25% above prime and monthly adjusted rate loans are available at a rate 1% above prime. EXCEL loans are available regardless of financial need for an amount up to college costs minus financial aid as long as payments on all parental debt (including a home mortgage) do not exceed 45% of gross family income. A loan guarantee fee of 2–7% is charged on EXCEL loans, making them considerably more expensive than they would appear at first blush. Sallie Mae offers Signature Loans which are variable rate loans at an interest rate of up to 9.85% in excess of the prime rate with a loan origination fee that can be as high as 6%. Signature Loans are made available up to the following amounts when combined with all other education loans: (1) $100,000 for undergraduate study; (2) $150,000 for graduate study; and (3) $200,000 for medical school. TERI provides students with educational loans called Alternative Loans through various lending institutions at a rate of prime minus 0.5% with a loan origination fee of up to 6.5%. Alternative Loans typically require a co-signer and are made available for up to $15,000 per year up to an aggregate amount of $45,000.

In addition, students and their families may wish to consider borrowing against various assets such as retirement accounts and life insurance policies. This is generally not advisable for several reasons. First, one may only borrow against certain types of retirement accounts and in many cases it will simply not be possible to do so. Moreover, even when it is possible to do so, there are often significant and possibly onerous conditions imposed. For example, if the borrower terminates employment or is dismissed, the loan becomes due and failure to repay it can result in a 10% penalty as well as imposition of income tax on the borrowed sum if the employee is under 55 years of age. Also, money may be borrowed from such accounts only once each year. Second, the interest paid on such loans will not be deductible in calculating federal income taxes except to the limited extent allowed under § 221 of the Code. Third, the actual cost of such loans vastly exceeds the stated rate on the loan. For example, assume that a parent borrows $10,000 against a 401(k) or 403(b) retirement account, that the account was normally earning 10% per year and that the parent borrows from the plan at a rate of 6% per year. The actual cost is the 6% interest paid plus the 4% additional yield that the borrowed funds would have earned in the plan. Similarly, with whole or universal life insurance policies (loans are not available against term policies), when one borrows against the policy value the real interest cost should reflect not only the interest paid but also the forgone yield on the investment component of the policy.

In summary, with the exception of home equity loans, it is generally best to resort to these other lines of credit only as a last resort after exhausting all of the federal loan options mentioned in ¶¶ 6,260–6,280.

[¶ 6,295]

Problems

1. Your sister's daughter, Nicki, is considering applying for a subsidized Stafford student loan for which she will readily qualify. As a matter of principle, your sister opposes borrowing for any purpose other than to acquire a home. She feels that Nicki should work part-time in lieu of borrowing. Advise them both on the benefits of a subsidized Stafford student loan.

2. Bob and Christine's son Mark has borrowed the maximum amount for which he is eligible under the Stafford student loan program. The couple is now considering applying for a PLUS loan or a home equity loan to cover the balance of Mark's educational costs not met from income, savings and the Stafford student loan. The couple is taxed at the highest marginal tax rate. They seek your advice as to the relative merits of PLUS loans and home equity loans.

H.   STATE ASSISTANCE

[¶ 6,300]

Because of the great variety of different forms and levels of state provided relief, it is not possible to explore this topic in depth here. Perhaps the best place to start in finding out what assistance may be available is <www.finaid.org/otheraid/state>. A few state programs will be mentioned to give an idea of the range of possibilities. One of the most ambitious aid programs is the Georgia Hope Scholarship Program. Under this program, graduates of Georgia high schools who have attained a 3.00 GPA or its equivalent and have taken the required courses may attend a Georgia state institution of higher learning tuition free. To remain eligible from year to year during college, the student must maintain a 3.00 GPA. Eligible students attending a Georgia private college or university are given cash grants of $3,000 plus an additional $1,050 toward tuition expenses. North Carolina provides state residents who attend a North Carolina private institution of higher learning with a North Carolina Legislative Tuition Grant to be applied against tuition at the college or university attended. For the 2004–2005 academic year the amount of the grant was $1,800 and was available to all state residents regardless of need.

I. FURTHER THOUGHTS

[¶ 6,310]

Having surveyed in some detail the myriad sources of assistance available to enable students to pursue higher education, it may now be appropriate to consider whether we as a society are in effect spending our student aid dollars in the most socially responsible fashion. For example, although it may be appropriate to provide aid in the form of tax relief, why do we not provide refundable tax credits? If it is appropriate to provide assistance in the form of a Hope Scholarship Credit or a Lifetime Learning Credit to a family with $75,000 of income, why is it appropriate to deny the same benefit to a family that earns $18,000 and has no federal income tax against which the credit may be claimed? Moreover, although many, but not all, tax relief provisions phaseout as income rises, none of the phaseout formulae take into account the number of dependents in a family or the number of them that may be pursuing higher education. Could something better not be designed? The amount of money provided to the poorest families under the Pell Grant Program is likely not proportional to the burden the family experiences in meeting college costs, as compared with the income and gift tax benefits that a wealthy family may reap from the use of a § 529 plan and, if necessary, the proceeds of a PLUS or home equity loan to meet its higher education expenses. Is this justifiable?

The following essay provides further food for thought.

EDUCATING FOR PRIVILEGE
Gene Nichol
The Nation (Oct. 13, 2003)

As a law school dean, I was much taken with a statement from Justice Sandra Day O'Connor's landmark opinion in the University of Michigan case: "Law schools represent the training ground for a large number of our nation's leaders . . . ; it is necessary that the path to leadership be visibly open" to every segment of society. In a powerful way, that sentiment breaks new ground. It recognizes that more is at stake in our affirmative-action battles than the quality of the classroom experience. The graduates of the country's strong law schools enjoy a hugely disproportionate access to opportunity and authority in the private and public sectors of our economy. Selective professional schools constitute distinctive pipelines to our principal corridors of power. The processes designed to distribute these remarkable resources, Justice O'Connor reminded, must be open to all.

The Michigan case, of course, explored the accessibility of selective higher education when it comes to race. The Justices concluded, thankfully, that universities need not be agnostic about the effective integration of their halls. But what if we cast O'Connor's inquiry more broadly? What if we asked about the diversity of selective student bodies on the basis of class? I think we'd find that the great institutions of American higher education, and their law schools, are constructed on a foundation of economic advantage that is bad—and getting worse. We aren't doing much about it. And we're behaving in ways to widen the breach.

Here's what I mean.

The Educational Testing Service recently published a study of the nation's 146 most selective colleges and universities. This is the pool into which law schools cast their nets. ETS concluded that only 3 percent of those students come from the bottom economic quartile. Only about 10 percent of the cohort comes from the bottom 50 percent. A stunning 74 percent hails from the top quarter. The pool of undergraduates from which we choose is badly skewed toward the economically privileged.

And the bias is increasing. A 2003 Education Department study found that the lion's share of the past decade's financial aid increases has gone to students in the top economic quarter. In 1995, 41 percent of private university aid went to high-income students. By 1999 it was 51 percent. The Lumina Foundation's recent study of tuition discounting draws similar conclusions. Eight years ago, students from families making $20,000 or less received, on average, 2 percent more than students from families making $60,000 or more. Today, wealthier children get 29 percent more than poorer ones. The high tuition, high aid model is backfiring.

And then there are the law schools. Tuition increases have dramatically outpaced inflation over the past decade. Public school tuition rose a staggering 141 percent. Inflation was 31 percent. The average private law school tuition bill is now about $25,000 a year. Public ones charge about $19,000 for nonresidents, $10,000 for residents; 86 percent of law students borrow to pay for their studies. Last year, the median private law graduate debt burden was $84,000. And that doesn't include undergraduate loans, which can also be daunting. The typical starting salary for public-sector jobs nationally is about $35,000—requiring an impossible 40 percent of monthly income for debt repayment.

As private law school tuition has skyrocketed, some of the best public law schools have, in effect, privatized—Michigan and Virginia being ready examples. Average per-student expenditures at American Bar Association-approved schools quadrupled over the past two decades—rising from about $5,000 to $20,000 per student. The money fueled what one dean calls "a positional arms race." We compete on U.S. News & World Report's terms—offering more high-end and fewer need-based scholarships; paying extraordinary salaries to star faculty and deans; spending huge sums on facilities, technology and brochures bragging about our accomplishments—raising the price of education for everyone. No one even thinks of expanding our student bodies or reducing the costs of instruction. That would be heresy. This elevator only goes up.

This crescendo of rising costs and expenditures cannot be thought acceptable. It fences out a huge segment of our community on the basis of wealth. It allows students' dreams to be swamped by their debts— forcing them into career paths they wouldn't otherwise choose. It increases the ultimate cost of representation in a legal regime that already prices too many out. It results in a system of legal education that radically penalizes the bottom half, in the service of a system of justice that has long done exactly the same thing.

No single formula will push back the mounting exclusion. But altered admissions and financial aid practices could work to assure that poor students matter. And meaningful loan forgiveness programs, at both state and federal levels, could help return public-sector jobs to viability. State legislators must recall that even given budget difficulties we face, an economically polarized democracy can't afford to abandon public higher education. And the academy itself has to remember that professional education is a public good, not merely a private one. After all, educating for privilege is powerfully at odds with who we say we are.

Chapter 7

LIFE AND DISABILITY INSURANCE

[¶ 7,000]

A. INTRODUCTION: THE IMPORTANCE OF INSURANCE

Is insurance important? Justice Hugo Black answered the question succinctly: "Perhaps no modern commercial enterprise directly affects so many persons in all walks of life as does the insurance business. Insurance touches the home, the family, and the occupation or the business of almost every person in the United States." United States v. South–Eastern Underwriters Association, 322 U.S. 533, 540 (1944). Indeed, insurance is a global enterprise that is inextricably intertwined with the well-being of individuals and businesses almost everywhere on the planet. This is because insurance protects against the consequences of the destruction of wealth, and, in doing so, facilitates the expansion and enhancement of wealth.

Although primitive insurance mechanisms can be found in most ancient societies throughout the world, the modern insurance business finds its roots in maritime commercial activities in the Mediterranean beginning in the late medieval period. As business enterprises expanded in Europe, the insurance business grew along with them. Economic growth brought not only increased affluence but also new risks of loss, which prompted individuals and business entities to enter into arrangements to limit their exposure to potential losses. When economic prosperity generates discretionary income, individuals and businesses can set aside funds in pooling mechanisms to provide compensation for those who suffer disproportionate losses. This, in brief, is what insurance does: a group of similarly situated individuals contribute to a pool of resources out of which those who contribute and suffer loss are compensated.

The loss compensation function of insurance has a direct, positive impact on economic activity and productivity. Imagine an aspiring entrepreneur who is considering starting a business that requires significant physical space. She can afford to purchase the building she needs, but

480

she is concerned about the risk of fire and other perils that could destroy it. If this were to occur, she would lose her investment of time, energy, and financial resources. In a world without insurance, she might choose not to start this business and instead choose a less risky investment, thereby avoiding the possibility of a catastrophic loss in the event the worst-case scenario unfolds. In a world with insurance, she can pay a modest periodic premium in exchange for an insurer's promise to restore her building in the event of its destruction and to make up her financial losses if her business is interrupted. In other words, insurance makes it possible to substitute a predictable, periodic business expense (i.e., the insurance premium) for the risk of an unlikely but potentially catastrophic loss. Because the insurance premium is predictable, the entrepreneur can budget for it by building it into the cost of doing business, and this ultimately encourages her to proceed with her more ambitious plan of starting the new business. This story, of course, plays out millions of times in a complex economy and illustrates the basic point that insurance plays an important role not only in protecting against loss but also in promoting economic activity.

The role of insurance in compensating for damage to and loss of physical assets has been important for centuries. This role was particularly important two to three generations ago in the United States when "hard capital," such as a farm or a small business, was the staple of many families' wealth. But physical assets have never been the exclusive mainstay of most American families. Human capital was necessary to work the fields, tend the herd, or run the business. In the late nineteenth century, the breadwinner in many households was one who held a blue-collar job in the steel mill or the coal mine. In these families, human capital was the principal family asset. The absence of insurance protection for family wealth when the worker was killed or disabled on the job explains the advent early in the twentieth century of workers' compensation and various social welfare programs to help families cope with these economic calamities.

The protection of physical assets was important in the past and remains important today, but in recent years human capital has become increasingly significant in the generation of wealth. For example, for many firms, the most important assets take the form of intellectual property and the skilled employees who create it. In the service sector as well, human capital is the primary factor of production. This trend is evident in many families where wealth is generated by someone with advanced education or professional training (e.g., a doctor, lawyer, architect, businessperson, etc.). In the twenty-first century, insurance is necessary to protect against the loss of that human capital, just as it has been necessary for many years to protect homes, automobiles, and physical structures.

Even if one were to ignore the connection between insurance and the protection and generation of wealth, the insurance business would command attention simply because of its enormous size. At the end of 2003, total life insurance coverage in force in the United States reached

$16.8 trillion, and approximately 370 million policies and group insurance certificates were in force. ACLI Life Insurance Fact Book 2004, at 92. In 2001, 69% of all families in the United States owned some kind of life insurance. Id. at 81. In 2003, life insurers paid over $102 billion to beneficiaries in proceeds, surrender values and other payments (excluding annuities); when annuities are included, the figure exceeded $301 billion. Id. at 62. In 2000, the average amount of life insurance coverage per insured household was $196,200, a figure equal to approximately 35 months of disposable personal income for the average household. ACLI Life Insurance Fact Book 2001, at 104. Disability insurance is less prevalent, but it adds billions of dollars more to the calculus.

Thus, for individuals and households across the nation, life and disability insurance is a major expenditure. Millions of Americans depend on insurance policy payments for their financial well being, and countless more rely on the promise of payments to provide security against the risk of financial loss associated with premature death or a disabling illness or accident. This chapter will discuss both life insurance and disability insurance. Portions of this chapter are based on Robert H. Jerry, II, Understanding Insurance Law (3d ed. 2002).

[¶ 7,002]

Problem

Joshua is an 18–year–old high school senior who is blessed with height, speed, agility, and intellect. He is extraordinarily talented with a basketball, and he makes the most of this talent. He has practiced for countless hours during his teenage years, and is actively recruited by coaches from NCAA Division I colleges and universities. In fact, he has caught the attention of some National Basketball Association scouts, as NBA teams in recent years have been drafting players directly from high school rather than waiting for them to mature in college. Joshua does not appear to be a first-round NBA pick out of high school, but there is reason to think that he will soon be one of the top ten basketball players in the college ranks.

Should Joshua be thinking about insurance? What risks should he be worried about? As an 18–year–old high school student with great promise, what assets is he at risk of losing? What kind of insurance products would you recommend that he consider? Karen is one of Joshua's classmates. She is Joshua's equal in intellect; although she plays a solid game of volleyball, a career beyond the high school team is out of the question. Should Karen be thinking about insurance? For what risks? To protect what assets? What kind of products would you recommend to her?

[¶ 7,005]

1. The Nature of Risk

Life is inherently uncertain. It is impossible to know precisely what the future holds, but it is also true that future events are not completely random. We can predict with varying degrees of accuracy a range of probabilities for particular events, even if their precise timing, location, and impact are unknown. Thus, we know from history that hurricanes, earthquakes, fires, and accidents will occur in the future, and we know from past experience approximately how many will occur in any particular interval of time. We can even make reasoned predictions of the magnitude of these events based on our knowledge of the past. But much is unknown. Although, for example, it is certain that a major earthquake will hit the west coast of the United States sometime in the future, we do not know exactly where or when it will strike or how severe it will be. This event may not happen in our lifetimes or even in the next 100 years, but it is certain to happen some day.

Similar observations can be made about two of the most significant personal risks faced by individuals—death and disability. Every person is certain to die at some future time, but neither the time nor the manner of death can be predicted with certainty. For every person a risk of death exists, and the risk increases as the person ages. We know from past experience that most people die due to illness; only a small percentage— less than 6%—die from accidents, suicide, murder, or other causes unrelated to illness. We know that each person has a risk of becoming disabled due to illness or accident, although we cannot know with certainty who will become disabled in any particular interval of time. In a sufficiently large group of individuals, it is possible to make a fairly reliable prediction of how many persons in the group will die or become disabled each year, although it is impossible to know exactly who will suffer that fate.

The inherent uncertainty of events is typically described in terms of probability or chance. In insurance, this uncertainty is usually described in terms of *risk*. Not all risk events in life are adverse; for example, if a person purchases a lottery ticket, it can be said that the person has a risk of winning a prize. But the risk of a positive or beneficial gain is not an event for which an individual will purchase insurance (although there are examples of mechanisms that spread the risk of beneficial events—a simple example would be a group of persons combining their resources to purchase a lottery ticket). Insurance exists to spread the risk of negative or adverse events such as death, disability, liability, or damage to property.

[¶ 7,006]

Problem

The following problem is based on an example given by Professor A. Mitchell Polinsky in his excellent book, An Introduction to Law and Economics (3d ed. 2003). You have just graduated from law school, and you receive one job offer, which you decide to accept despite its unusual compensation arrangement. You agree to work on one case for your first year, which is a case that the firm has accepted under a contingency fee arrangement. Assume that your first year salary will be $120,000 if you win the case, but nothing if you lose the case. You and the firm are confident that you have a 50% chance of winning the case—and a 50% chance of losing it. Does this arrangement make you nervous? The expected value of your compensation is $60,000. (Why?) How much less than $60,000 would you be willing to accept as a certain payment in order to avoid the 50% chance of earning no salary next year? What does your answer to the Polinsky hypothetical tell you about the value of security in a world of risks?

[¶ 7,010]

2. Responding to Risk

Insurance is one of several ways of responding to risk, and in some respects it is a "last resort." For example, before purchasing an insurance policy, a rational consumer will evaluate whether there are low-cost ways to limit the probability of loss. When a person confronts two or more alternatives and opts for the safest alternative (as when a skier of modest ability chooses the beginner's slope to descend the mountain instead of the expert slope), a choice has been made to reduce the risk of injury, disability, or death by reducing the probability that a loss will occur. Another risk management technique involves limiting the effects of loss. Wearing a seat belt will not prevent an auto accident from occurring (the probability of loss), but it does reduce the likely effects of loss (death, disability, or injury) should an accident happen.

Setting up a reserve is another way to respond to risk. For example, a person might set up and contribute to a savings account that is maintained for the purpose of compensating for the effect of a loss (e.g., disability) should one occur, but which is available for other purposes (e.g., funding a bequest at death) in the event the loss never materializes. This method of responding to risk is commonly called "self insurance." Diversification is another means of responding to risk. This is a common practice with regard to investments and property ownership, but when the parents of young children decline to fly or travel together to reduce the risk that both will be killed in an accident, they are also engaged in a form of diversification.

A rational consumer will invest in loss prevention or mitigation strategies whenever the marginal cost of such strategies is less than the cost of purchasing insurance. At a certain point, however, the cost of such strategies becomes prohibitive or the effort required to implement them is excessive. (For example, staying at home on one's sofa and eschewing all travel would reduce risk, but life would be quite boring). And some risks can be reduced but not eliminated (i.e., the risk of death). When it is no longer desirable to invest marginal resources in managing risk, it may be preferable (or, as economists would say, "efficient") to pay for the transfer of the risk and its assumption by someone else. Insurance companies are in the business of assuming the risks of others for a price (i.e., the premium charged for the insurance contract).

[¶ 7,011]

Problem

If you own an automobile, have you purchased a policy of insurance on it? If so, for what kinds of potential losses? Unless you live in a no-fault jurisdiction, your automobile insurance has four major components: (1) medical payments coverage, which provide compensation to you or your passengers for medical and hospital expenses you suffer as a result of an accident; (2) liability coverage for bodily injury or property damage you cause third parties as a result of your negligent operation of the vehicle; (3) uninsured motorist protection that provides compensation to you in the event you suffer bodily injury in an accident caused by the negligence of a third party and that party is uninsured (or perhaps "underinsured," meaning that the negligent party has less liability insurance than you carry); and (4) collision damage for property damage your automobile suffers in an accident and "comprehensive damage" for property damage your automobile suffers in a non-accident situation, such as if a tree were to fall on the vehicle. If you live in a no-fault jurisdiction, your medical payments coverage may be broader in terms of amount and types of loss covered, and your right to sue third parties whose negligence results in your bodily injury will be curtailed to some extent (meaning you must look to your own medical payments coverage for compensation in these instances when you cannot sue a third party). How much coverage do you have in each of these categories? Why did you choose these amounts? Do you have deductibles? If so, why? What do these choices you have made tell you about your attitude toward the risk of loss you might suffer in each of these categories?

[¶ 7,015]

3. Insurance as a Means to Transfer Risk

Consumers transfer risk to insurers because they are risk averse with respect to many risks, especially large ones. For example, for an average 40–year–old male, the risk of death during the current year is low—approximately 1 in 600. But if that individual has dependent children at home, the financial consequences of premature death could be devastating. If the financial loss to the children from the loss of the parent's future income has an estimated present value of $1 million, the 1 in 600 risk of death translates into an expected loss of $1,666. Of course, the odds are overwhelming that this loss will not occur, but the parent might be willing to pay considerably more than $1,666 as an annual insurance premium in order to eliminate the 1 in 600 risk of a devastating financial loss resulting from the parent's death. In this example, it is reasonable to assume that the parent might be willing to pay as much as $2,000 in annual premiums for the knowledge that if he died during the year the insurer would pay $1 million for the children's benefit.

The business of the insurer is to assume the parent's risk in exchange for the parent's payment of a premium (in this example,

$2,000 for a $1 million insurance policy). By entering into similar transactions with thousands of other similarly situated individuals, the insurer is able to distribute the risks of death across a large pool of insureds and achieve certainty. In other words, the law of large numbers gives the insurer a very high degree of confidence about expected losses. For example, in our hypothetical, if the insurer assembles a pool of 60,000 males all aged 40, it is probable that 100 members of the pool (give or take a few) will die during the year. In this example, the insurer will pay $1 million to each of those insured's beneficiaries, or a total of $100 million (give or take a few million dollars). But the insurer will also collect $2,000 in premium from each of the insureds, or $120 million, leaving around $20 million for the costs of administering the insurance arrangement, overhead, and profit (or in the case of a mutual company, a dividend that can be returned to the policyholders in lieu of profits).

This discussion has used the example of life insurance to illustrate the point, but the same analysis applies to disability insurance. In that situation, the risk is not death, but becoming unable due to illness or accident to work in gainful employment and earn income. A risk averse person would prefer to transfer the risk of lost income to a disability insurer, which would assume the risk in exchange for the payment of a premium.

Insureds transfer their risk to insurers because insureds are risk averse, but this does not mean that insurers are risk preferring. On the contrary, insurers are among the most risk averse of all economic actors. The essential point is that insurers are able to achieve a high degree of confidence about the number of losses that will occur in the future among a large group of insureds. When the pool of insureds is sufficiently large, the insurer can predict with considerable accuracy how many losses will occur in a given period within that group. This enables the insurer to set a price for its assumption of risk that is large enough to pay all claims that the group is likely to submit, pay the costs associated with administering the insurance plan, and earn a reasonable return (in the case of a for-profit company).

Many contracts transfer risk (for example, a sale of goods accompanied by a warranty involves the seller "insuring" the performance of the good for a particular period of time), but insurance contracts have two distinctive features: (1) risk itself is the subject of the exchange; and (2) the risk is distributed across a large pool of insureds. Thus, an insurance contract is "an agreement in which one party (the insurer), in exchange for a consideration provided by the other party (the insured), assumes the other party's risk and distributes it across a group of similarly situated persons, each of whose risks has been assumed in a similar transaction." Robert H. Jerry, II, Understanding Insurance Law 20 (3d ed. 2002).

[¶ 7,016]

Problem

Professor Polinsky suggests the following variation on the problem in ¶ 7,006. Suppose that you are willing to accept a guaranteed salary of as little as $45,000 (regardless of the outcome of the case) in place of a 50% chance of $120,000 and 50% chance of nothing. Dealmaker approaches you with this proposition: Leave the firm's compensation arrangement as it is, but assign to Dealmaker your right to the receipt of compensation from the firm; in exchange, Dealmaker will pay you $50,000. In the course of your conversation with Dealmaker, you learn that he has started similar negotiations with 999 other persons who are working for other firms under exactly the same arrangement and who are also willing to accept a certain payment of $45,000. Who is Dealmaker in this hypothetical? Why is he interested in making these proposals? Is Dealmaker an "insurance company"?

[¶ 7,020]

4. Economic Consequences of the Transfer and Distribution of Risk

As noted above, a contract of insurance is an economically beneficial transaction. The insured is better off because he or she achieves security by transferring risk to the insurer. The insurer is better off because it distributes risk in a large pool of similarly situated insureds, achieves certainty by virtue of the operation of the law of large numbers, and earns a profit when premiums exceed losses. But such transactions can also have undesirable effects.

History demonstrates that the insurance mechanism can be used inappropriately or unlawfully. For example, there are many examples of insureds being murdered by beneficiaries who stand to receive proceeds of insurance on the victim's life. Also, even when foul play is not involved, the presence of insurance increases the probability of loss. This is most obvious in property insurance, where the presence of insurance discourages the insured from taking precautions to prevent loss. It is unlikely that the presence of life insurance will decrease the insured's precautions against life-ending injury or illness, but history shows that disability claims increase when the economy is in a recession. The inherent tendency of insurance to increase the probability of loss, due either to intentional conduct, the increased frequency of claims, or to the insured's reduced incentive to take precautions, is called "moral hazard." Many things insurers do in the underwriting process, such as asking the applicant questions about her past experiences before deciding to assume the risk, represent efforts to address the problem of moral hazard. Some common insurance policy provisions, such as the suicide exclusion in life insurance (which eliminates coverage in the event the insured commits suicide within two years of a policy's issuance), also represent responses to the phenomenon of moral hazard.

Another concept that influences insurer behavior is "adverse selection." This term refers to the fact that every pool of insureds has a disproportionate number of higher-risk insureds. People tend to seek insurance if and when they think they need it; people who believe they are unlikely to suffer loss are less likely to purchase insurance. Thus, a person who knows she is at high risk for cancer may be more likely to apply for life insurance; one who has a history of missing work due to illness is more likely to seek to obtain disability insurance; one who lives in a flood plain is likely to be interested in buying flood insurance; and so on. This means that risk pools tend to attract a disproportionate number of higher risk people. Insurers try to respond to this phenomenon by subdividing risk pools into lower-risk and higher-risk pools and adjusting premiums based on the relative risk. There is, of course, expense involved in making the subdivision. Information must be gathered and analyzed, and the sorting of insureds into lower-and higher-risk pools involves transaction costs. Insurers will subdivide risk pools as long as the premium differential that can be made between the lower-risk and the higher-risk pools is greater than the cost of subdividing the pool. If the cost of making the distinction is larger than the resulting benefits, the subdivision will not be made. Even if the pool is subdivided, however, there will be a disproportionate number of higher-risk insureds within each of the smaller, subdivided pools.

The concept of adverse selection helps to explain the insurer's difficulty when the insured has more information than the insurer about her risk. The insured may appreciate the greater risk of loss, but the insurer, lacking access to this information, faces the possibility that a risk pool may be overpopulated with higher-risk insureds. Many practices in insurance underwriting represent insurers' efforts to combat adverse selection. For example, the information gathering process in connection with applications for coverage is part of the insurer's effort to deal with adverse selection. Coverage provisions also sometimes reflect that effort, as is the case, for example, when the insurer excludes from coverage some high-risk activities and thereby makes the pool less attractive to individuals who engage in those activities.

[¶ 7,025]

5. The Fortuity Requirement

A fundamental principle of insurance is that one cannot purchase insurance for events that are certain to occur. This is why, for example, a person cannot purchase automobile insurance for the consequences of an accident after the accident has occurred, and this is why a person cannot purchase fire insurance on her home while the home is burning. This principle also explains why, if the insured knows that a loss is about to occur (as is the case where the insured actually plans to cause the loss after securing the insurance), the insurer is not obligated to pay for the loss. This is commonly referred to as the "fortuity" principle, and it operates to prevent coverage even in the absence of specific policy provisions excluding coverage in those circumstances. For example, it is common for policies to explicitly exclude coverage for losses intentionally caused by the insured (although this issue becomes more complicated in life insurance, as discussed below), but even if policies did not include such provisions, the fortuity principle would operate to avoid coverage for the loss in question.

The very first life insurance policies encountered some resistance from courts under the logic that death is certain to occur at some future time and therefore cannot be an insurable event. The limitation in this analysis is that the *timing* of death is uncertain, i.e., one cannot be certain when death will occur, and in some cases the timing will be especially inopportune, at least in economic terms. Thus, when one recognizes that life insurance is designed to insure against the risk of *premature* death—an inherently uncertain event—it becomes clear that the fortuity principle presents no problem for the validity of a life insurance contract.

The same can be said of disability. It is certain that every employee or worker, regardless of age, will eventually become disabled in the sense of being unable, due to health, old age, or accident, to carry on his or her occupation. As a theoretical matter, the timing of the onset of disability is uncertain, and this is enough to meet the fortuity requirement. As a practical matter, no insurer would be willing to renew a disability policy indefinitely and without regard to the fitness and health of the insured.

[¶ 7,026]

Problem

Shortly after midnight on Monday, April 15, 1912, the first wireless message was sent and received that the *Titanic* had struck a giant iceberg but all passengers were safe. At 4:15 a.m., the Canadian Government Marine Agency received a wireless message that the *Titanic* was sinking but was being towed to shoal waters where it would be beached. Through noon on Monday, wireless messages reported that the *Titanic*'s passengers were being transferred to the nearby steamer *Carpathia*; these reports indicated that between 800 and 1,200 persons were already transferred, that a second ship, the *Parisian*, was assisting in the rescue, and that three other ships were near the scene. Later reports indicated that the *Titanic* was badly damaged but still afloat, and that there was uncertainty as to whether it could make shore. An official of White Star, the company that operated the *Titanic*, said that he expected the passengers would reach Halifax by Wednesday and that no loss of life had occurred. On Tuesday, the true fate of the *Titanic* and its passengers became known.

Jane, a resident of Liverpool, hears the first wireless messages. Her husband David is a passenger on the ship. Even though the reports are that all passengers are safe, she is apprehensive. She purchases a £50,000 life insurance policy on David's life for the benefit of herself and their three young daughters after the first wireless report but before Tuesday's news, which is followed on Wednesday by a report that David is among the missing and is presumed drowned. Jane's fears are later realized when David is not found among the survivors. Is the insurance policy valid?

[¶ 7,030]

6. Insurance in the Group Setting

Modern group insurance dates back to the early twentieth century, when several forward-thinking employers negotiated life insurance contracts for the benefit of their employees through master contracts with an insurer. Under these arrangements, the employer (the group representative) contracts with an insurer, and the employees (the "certificate holders") are third party beneficiaries of the contract. In the usual arrangement, the employees are the insureds, and each of them is authorized to designate a beneficiary who will receive the proceeds at the employee's death. Approximately 44% of all life insurance in force in the United States—$7.2 trillion in 2003—is provided under group contracts. ACLI Life Insurance Fact Book 2004, at 82. A large amount of disability insurance is provided under group contracts. According to the Bureau of Labor Statistics, 30% of all workers had long-term disability insurance through their employers in 2003. Id. at 101. Group insurance contrasts with individual insurance, where an individual contracts directly with the insurer without the employer or another group representative acting as an intermediary.

Group insurance is attractive to insurers because the employment setting itself assists the insurer in the underwriting. By making eligibility for the coverage dependent on the employee being "actively at work" or some equivalent standard, the insurer limits coverage to persons who are healthy enough to maintain a full-time occupation. Group insurance is attractive to employers because they can deduct the employer-paid premiums as a business expense for income tax purposes. Employees also receive favorable tax treatment because they can exclude from gross income the cost of the first $50,000 of employer-paid group term life insurance as long as it is provided on a non-discriminatory basis. See ¶ 3,080.

B. LIFE INSURANCE

[¶ 7,035]

1. Reasons for Purchasing Life Insurance

Generally, an individual should consider purchasing life insurance in one of the following situations:

(a) The individual has persons who depend on his or her income. The most common example is an adult whose spouse, child, or other dependent (perhaps an aged parent) would suffer financial loss if the adult died prematurely. This is the most common role of life insurance— providing replacement income for those who depend on the income

earned by the insured while he or she is living. If, for example, a couple owns a home encumbered by a mortgage, the death of the income-earning spouse may leave the surviving spouse without sufficient funds to pay the outstanding debt. Life insurance proceeds can be used to pay the debt, essentially replacing the income that would have been used to pay the debt if the income-earning spouse had survived. By the same logic, an adult may have children who expect to rely on the adult's income to pay for the children's college tuition; life insurance can be used to meet the children's tuition expenses in the event of the income-earning parent's death.

To determine how much insurance is needed, one begins by calculating the current and future requirements of the purchaser's dependents. This calculation will depend on various assumptions. The starting place is determining what standard of living the purchaser wishes to provide for the dependents. For example, does the purchaser wish to fund a moderately-priced college education, or does the purchaser wish to give the children the means to attend any college at any price? If there is a mortgage to be paid, how large is it? Once the needs are established, the sources of funds to meet these needs must be evaluated. These sources may include Social Security benefits, retirement plan benefits, and income from other investments. To the extent these needs exceed available resources, life insurance can be used to make up the difference. Whether the entire difference can be made up will depend, of course, on the purchaser's ability to pay the premiums. The mix of term and permanent insurance will come into play, both in terms of ability to pay and the time frame for meeting particular needs. These considerations are discussed in more detail in ¶¶ 7,070 and 7,245.

(b) The individual provides services to others, and those who depend on these services would need to employ another person to provide the services in the event of the individual's death. The most common example is the parent-spouse who maintains the household while the other parent-spouse works outside the home for the family's income. In the event of the at-home parent-spouse's premature death, it would be necessary to hire providers to maintain the household, take care of the children, etc. Insurance on the life of the at-home parent-spouse can provide funds to pay for these services in the event of his or her premature death.

(c) Life insurance can be used to provide a predictable amount of wealth at death. In contrast to, for example, property insurance, where a fundamental premise of the coverage is that the benefit should not exceed the loss (e.g., if a car is worth $40,000, it is generally inappropriate to pay the insured a sum larger than $40,000 in the event the car is completely destroyed), it is possible to use life insurance to create a fund that benefits a survivor in an amount exceeding the economic loss caused by the insured's premature death. In other words, whereas the principle of indemnity is strong in property insurance (i.e., the benefit of the coverage should not exceed the amount of the loss), the principle of indemnity is weak in life insurance, in the sense that the proceeds paid

at the insured's death are not necessarily limited to the resulting economic loss.

To illustrate, for most low- or middle-income families with young children, it is probable that an income-earning parent who dies prematurely will not leave sufficient assets in his or her estate to create a trust to pay for the college education of surviving children. By purchasing life insurance, however, the parent can provide for such a fund. Likewise, an individual may desire to make end-of-life gifts to charities, educational institutions, or other organizations. This can be accomplished by designating the charity as a life insurance beneficiary. For example, with life insurance, a person who has made annual gifts to a charity can endow the gift in perpetuity with an insurance-created fund that comes into existence upon the insured's death.

(d) Life insurance can provide needed liquidity at the time of the insured's death. If the assets in a decedent's estate cannot easily be sold in a short period of time, which is often the case with real estate and closely held business interests, other assets may be needed to pay estate taxes and other expenses of administering the estate. In many situations, purchasing life insurance for the payment of estate taxes may be preferable to borrowing funds or using other assets to pay the tax. Life insurance can also be used to cover a variety of other end-of-life expenses, such as medical or hospital bills and the costs of a funeral and burial.

(e) Life insurance can preserve or enhance the value of a business. Life insurance also has significant business uses. In a partnership, for example, the continued survival of all the partners may be essential to the continued viability of the business. Rather than terminate an on-going business enterprise when one partner dies, an insurance policy that pays proceeds to the partnership upon the death of a partner can be used to create a fund that substitutes for the financial contribution the deceased partner would have made to the business had he or she lived. Where a business has co-owners, in the absence of insurance the interest of a deceased owner may pass to his or her heirs, which may have the practical effect of bringing the business to an end. But if the business insures the life of each co-owner, the proceeds payable at the death of any one of them can be used by the survivors to purchase the decedent's interest, which means the business can continue with the surviving owners as a going concern.

In these circumstances, the business's purchase of a life insurance policy on the life of each owner of the business protects the business from the consequences of the death of any owner. It may be costly, however, to purchase policies on the lives of all owners. Thus, businesses often buy renewable "first to die" policies, which pay proceeds whenever the first owner dies. Sometimes these policies have escalating policy limits as the circle of surviving owners grow smaller, so that the proceeds payable at the death of each remaining owner are sufficient to meet the cost of buying out each decedent's enhanced share of the business.

Sometimes each partner in a business purchases insurance on the lives of the other partners. These "cross purchase" arrangements make it possible for the surviving partners to buy out the deceased partner's interest. Sometimes life insurance is purchased on the life of a key employee whose continued existence is vital to the success of the business. If the business depends on the credit status of an individual owner, a life insurance policy could be useful to protect the business's ability to borrow in the event of that owner's death.

Also, a business may want to obtain life insurance as a fringe benefit for employees. By providing insurance for employees and their beneficiaries, the business secures the good will of its employees. Also, the tax advantages of paying some compensation in the form of benefits rather than salary allow a business in effect to increase the value of the total compensation package, which is beneficial to employees as long as they prefer increased in-kind benefits to increased salary. See ¶ 3,080.

[¶ 7,040]

2. Types of Life Insurance

There are hundreds of different kinds of life insurance policies that are marketed today, but in general structure they fall into two basic categories: term insurance or permanent insurance.

[¶ 7,045]

a. Term insurance

Term insurance is a kind of life insurance contract whereby the insured purchases coverage for a specified time period and the designated beneficiary collects the proceeds only if the insured dies during the term. The term is typically less than a lifetime. It is common, for example, for term insurance to expire when the insured reaches age 65 or 70, although some policies run into later years. Alternatively, term insurance may be sold for a specified time period ranging from one to 25 or 30 years. Term insurance, unlike permanent insurance, does not have a savings component that allows the insured to get some money back if the insured decides to surrender the policy before death (commonly referred to as "cashing in" the policy). With term insurance, as the insured ages, either the amount of the premium increases or the amount of coverage declines. This is because as the insured ages, the risk of death increases. If the premiums are level over a particular period of years, the premium will be the average of the premiums that would have been paid during that period if the premiums had been adjusted annually.

Most term insurance is renewable, typically for one-year or five-year terms. This is a particularly valuable feature because it protects the insured from being left without coverage if he or she becomes uninsurable due to poor health. Sometimes premiums rise annually, but in many policies premiums rise in five-year cohorts. Many term policies terminate somewhere between age 65 and 75. This is because the cost of protection rises very steeply, and the policy typically becomes unaffordable at older ages. This is usually not a problem, however, because the need for term insurance (e.g., to care for dependents, cover a mortgage, etc.) typically disappears at higher ages, and with luck any remaining needs can be covered by Social Security benefits or other assets.

[¶ 7,046]

Problems

1. Steve and Sara, husband and wife, have twins aged 7. They wish to protect their children against the consequences of either parent's premature death, and wish to do so through the twins' college years. They are interested in term insurance. How long a term should they purchase?

2. Bob has a term life policy that he purchased from Teachers Insurance Company. The policy has a face value of $500,000 and is renewable through age 70. The second year he has the policy, he is offered a "Supplemental Inflation Coverage" that provides him with an additional $15,000 of coverage based on the prior year's 3% increase in the Consumer Price Index (i.e., 3% of $500,000 is $15,000). Bob is advised that if he turns down the supplement, he will not be offered the supplement again. Further, if he accepts the supplement, he will be entitled to purchase increasing sums of coverage in future years based on increases in the CPI without any medical examination or other underwriting, but if he fails to renew the supplemental coverage in any future year, the supplemental benefit will be canceled and he will not be offered a supplemental benefit again. The cost per $1,000 of coverage under the supplemental policy is higher than the cost per $1,000 of coverage under the $500,000 base policy, but is competitive with other term policies available in the market. Why does the supplemental policy cost more than the base policy per $1,000 of coverage, and why is the supplemental policy offered on the terms presented? Under what circumstances should Bob consider purchasing the supplemental coverage?

[¶ 7,050]

b. Permanent insurance

Permanent insurance (often referred to as "whole life," "straight life" or "ordinary life" insurance) is essentially a policy of term insurance combined with a savings plan, except that the policy lasts for the insured's entire life. Part of each premium covers the cost of the insurance, and the remainder goes into the savings component of the product. Under most policies, a relatively small portion of the premium goes into savings in the early years. (Unless a policy is purchased directly from a company, most of the excess over what is needed to cover the risk of death in the early years is used to pay the agent's commission.) In later years an increasingly large portion of each premium becomes a part of the savings component. The amount of the savings is called the policy's "cash value" or "surrender value." The insurer will pay interest on this amount, usually in the range of 3% to 4% per year. After the policy has been in force for two or three years, the insured typically has the right to borrow against the cash value at a designated interest rate, which is usually very favorable to the insured, or cash in the policy and receive the surrender value. If the insured dies after borrowing part of the cash value, the outstanding amount of the loan is deducted from the face amount of the policy in determining the proceeds payable to the beneficiary.

Some whole life policies pay dividends, and these are called "participating policies" (to be distinguished from "nonparticipating policies," which do not pay dividends). Unlike a dividend that an investor receives on a stock or mutual fund, the dividend on a life insurance policy is a return of premiums previously paid, which is made possible because the insurer's investments have done well enough to allow this refund to occur. Typically, participating policies require a higher premium, and the dividends are not guaranteed. Under a participating policy, the insured customarily has four choices concerning how dividends are paid: (a) the dividends may be paid in cash to the insured; (b) the dividends may be used to reduce the premium; (c) the dividends may be kept on deposit with the insurer and earn interest; or (d) the dividends may be used to purchase additional coverage, meaning that the premiums would not increase, but the amount paid to the beneficiary at the insured's death would increase by the amount of the additional coverage.

Figure 7–1 illustrates how cash value grows over time in a permanent policy with a face value of $100,000 that is issued to an insured at age 40. The policy has an annual premium of $1,800, and will pay dividends that are projected but not guaranteed.

Figure 7–1: Whole Life Policy Illustration

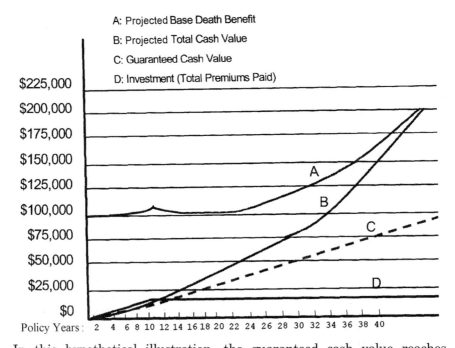

In this hypothetical illustration, the guaranteed cash value reaches $100,000 when the insured reaches age 80. If dividend projections are reached, the policyholder will be required to make premium payments for only the first 10 years; thereafter, the annual premium will be covered by dividends. If dividend projections are not met, however, the policyholder may have put as much as $72,000 into the policy by way of premium payments by the time the insured reaches age 80. The insurance guarantees a modest return on the insured's investment. This may seem meager, but if the insured survives to age 80, it is important to realize that throughout the period up to age 80 the insured was protected by a $100,000 death benefit and a portion of the premium paid for this protection. Thus, if the insured died in policy year 5, the insured would have invested only $9,000 in the policy, but the insurer would have paid proceeds of $100,000 to the designated beneficiary. Thus, a portion of each $1,800 premium is used to provide life insurance, and it is the remainder that goes into the cash value and on which the insurer pays interest. The insured hopes, of course, that the cash value will grow according to the "total cash value" projection. Indeed, if the cash value grows fast enough, this projection calls for the insured to stop paying premiums after policy year 10. (The death benefit in the illustration dips slightly after policy year 10, when a portion of the projected cash value begins to be used to pay the policy's mortality expense, i.e., to pay the premium.) Note that the death benefit includes a return of the accumulated cash value, so if the cash value grows to a sum that is greater than face value, the policy will pay a death benefit in excess of face value.

Note also that the cash value grows relatively slowly in the early years of the policy (a disproportionate part of early premiums goes to pay the selling agent's commission), so that if the insured cancels the policy soon after purchasing it, the insured will receive very little cash back.

The foregoing relationships can also be illustrated numerically. In Table 7–1, assume a 35–year–old healthy male nonsmoker purchases a policy with a $250,000 death benefit and a $2,795 annual premium:

Table 7–1: Terms of $250,000 Whole Life Policy (35–Year–Old Healthy Male Non–Smoker)

Policy Year	Premium	Guaranteed Cash Value	Projected Dividends (Paid-Up Accumulation)	Total Cash Value
1	$ 2,795	$ 0	$ 1	$ 0
5	2,795	5,108	473	5,580
10	2,795	17,800	3,926	21,726
15	2,795	33,215	13,625	46,840
20	2,795	51,598	31,756	83,354
25	2,795	72,678	61,730	134,407
30	2,795	96,048	108,528	204,575
35	2,795	120,595	178,826	299,421
40	2,795	145,058	280,344	425,402
50	2,795	187,100	612,460	799,560
60	2,795	220,228	1,178,808	1,399,036

Source: LifeQuoteCenter.com, http://www.lifequotecenter.com/instype_wholelife.htm (Oct. 23, 2004).

Note that under the policy's dividend projections, the total premiums paid are more than the total cash value at policy years 5 and 10; but by policy year 15, the total cash value exceeds the total premiums paid. The policy's guarantees, however, are considerably less; it is not until sometime between policy years 20 and 25 that the cash value exceeds the total premiums paid. If the policy were to be surrendered in one of the early years, the cash value would be less than total premiums paid, which means that if return on investment were the only objective, the insured would have been better off putting the money into an alternative investment vehicle. Of course, throughout those early years, the insured had insurance protection of $250,000, the amount that would have been paid to the designated beneficiary in the event of the insured's death.

The insured hopes, of course, to receive dividends at an increasing rate over the life of the policy. It may be that dividends will be used initially to pay the premium of the policy. If dividends are added to cash value, the cash value will grow at an increasing rate, as the table shows. Some of this increasing cash value takes the place of the insurer's obligation to pay the death benefit—which is why the premium can remain level over the life of the policy even though the insured's risk of death increases with each passing year. If the cash value grows fast enough, it may be that the death benefit will actually increase over the life of the policy. Eventually, the total cash value will equal the death benefit, at which point it can be said that the policy is fully paid up. If the policy continues in force past this time, the cash value may grow to a number much larger than the death benefit, which is what happens with the policy in Table 7–1.

One of the features of a policy with a cash value is that the cash value is not subject to forfeiture. Thus, if the insured decides to cancel the policy, the insured can receive the cash value as a lump-sum cash payment or perhaps some other settlement option that involves payments to the insured or a designated beneficiary. Likewise, the insured can decide to apply the cash value to purchase prepaid insurance, either permanent (with a reduced face amount and no subsequent premium payments) or term.

Permanent insurance is more expensive per unit of coverage because part of the premium goes into the savings component of the product. However, the premium does not increase over time, and the amount of the policy's coverage does not decline, which is sometimes viewed as an advantage. As a result, permanent insurance in its traditional form (i.e., "whole life," as opposed to "universal life" or "variable life," which are discussed below) is sometimes described as insurance written for a fixed amount on a person's entire life for a fixed premium. In reality, however, the cost of the term insurance portion of the whole life product does increase over time. This is because the policy's cash value increases as the insured ages, resulting in a corresponding decline in the difference between the policy's face amount (i.e., the proceeds payable if the insured dies while the policy is in force, without having borrowed any of the cash value) and its cash value. This difference, which declines over the policy's life, is actually the term insurance component of the product. Thus, as the insured ages, the premium remains the same but less term insurance is provided each year, which means the effective cost of the insurance component of the product increases. There are many different variations on permanent policies, but each involves the same combination of two basic elements: term insurance and a savings plan.

If permanent insurance is the functional equivalent of term insurance plus a savings plan, why should a consumer not purchase a term insurance policy and then make his or her own investments with the premiums saved by not purchasing a more expensive whole life policy? This is, in fact, what many people do. Many people use term insurance to provide protection against the economic loss of death in their early years, and then use the funds they saved by not purchasing whole life insurance to make contributions to a tax-sheltered retirement plan (e.g., a 401(k) plan or an IRA). Under this approach, if the insured dies at a young age, the risk of early death is covered by the term insurance. If the insured lives past retirement age, the tax-sheltered plan is available to provide income during retirement. This underscores the fact that individuals face dual risks: the risk of early death and the risk of living too long. To cover the risk of early death, one typically purchases term life insurance. To protect against the risk of living too long, one might have a whole life policy with an accumulated cash value or an annuity or tax-sheltered retirement plan to provide a source of income during retirement.

[¶ 7,055]

c. Pricing elements of an insurance policy

There are two key components reflected in the price of a life insurance policy. The *mortality cost* is essentially the sum needed to provide a reserve for payment of the death benefit. The *policy expense cost* is the share of the company's expenses (overhead, administrative costs, agent commissions, etc.) that is allocated to the policy. The mortality cost will increase as the insured ages, but the policy expense cost will remain relatively constant.

With term insurance, the increased mortality cost means that the overall premium must rise (or the amount of the coverage must decline if the premium remains level). With permanent insurance, in essence, the insured pays more than the mortality cost in the early years of the policy, and the overpayment is kept in the policy's cash value. The insurer earns a return on the cash value over time, and can therefore charge a premium that is less than the mortality cost in the later years of the policy without sacrificing the adequacy of reserves or the insurer's profit. From the insured's perspective, the premium appears level, but the actual insurance coverage purchased declines as the cash value grows.

Premiums are lower for term life insurance than for permanent life insurance, especially in the early years of the policy. Not surprisingly, agent commissions for selling permanent life insurance are much higher than for selling term, and this leads many agents to recommend that their customers purchase permanent instead of term, often in circumstances where the customer would be better off purchasing term insurance.

[¶ 7,060]

d. Variations on term insurance

There are several significant variations on the basic concept of term insurance. *Credit insurance* is a form of coverage for debtors: if the insured debtor dies or becomes disabled before a debt (such as a home mortgage) is paid, the insurer either pays the debt in full or makes periodic payments on the debt until the debt is paid in full. Thus, the coverage is functionally equivalent to term life insurance (or term insurance accompanied by a disability endorsement). As the debt is paid down (which will happen while the insured is simultaneously aging and becoming a higher risk), the amount of coverage declines and the premium remains constant. There is no accumulation of cash value. Most states have statutes requiring that the unearned premiums be refunded to the debtor if the debt is paid off early. If the insured dies while the amount of insurance in force exceeds the amount of the debt, the usual result is for the amount of proceeds exceeding the amount of the debt to be paid to the insured's estate. This kind of insurance is often marketed on a group basis, typically by a lending institution that may have a master policy with an insurer, and the coverage is made available to the lender's debtors as a way to ensure that the debt is paid. The Uniform Consumer Credit Code ("UCCC") regulates to some extent the use of term insurance to secure debt; for example, the UCCC provides that the amount of credit life insurance sold cannot exceed the amount of the debt and requires certain disclosures to the insured. See UCCC § 4.201 (regulating duration of consumer credit insurance), § 4.202 (regulating amount of insurance).

The policy in credit life insurance is typically tied to the existence of the debt; once the debt is paid, the insurance coverage terminates. Also, the premium charged per $1,000 of coverage in credit life insurance is generally much more than a term insurance policy with equivalent coverage. Adverse selection is one likely reason for this. If most people qualify for term insurance to cover most of their needs, including their need to discharge unpaid debts upon death, the persons who would most likely be interested in credit life coverage are those who cannot qualify for other products. Consequently, to cover the increased risks associated with those who are inclined to purchase credit life insurance, the policies must carry higher premiums. It is also likely that consumers entering into credit transactions do not anticipate that life insurance coverage will be offered to them and are not well prepared to assess the merits of the coverage when they take out a loan or to make rational decisions about whether to purchase the coverage. Also, such individuals may be vulnerable to predatory practices at the time a loan is closed (e.g., pressure from the lender with comments such as "who will pay this debt if you die?" or "are your prepared for your children to lose your home if you die and your spouse can't pay the mortgage?"). For most people, it is generally preferable to determine how much coverage they need to pay a debt in the event of premature death and then purchase the amount of term insurance required to cover the debt.

Another variation on term life insurance is "deposit term insurance." This type of policy blends whole-life and term insurance. The coverage looks like renewable term coverage with a large first-year premium; the premium drops in the second year, and then slowly increases over time, all while the amount of coverage remains the same. The first premium includes a deposit that sets up a small cash value. This deposit is forfeited if the policy lapses (typically due to nonpayment of premium) before the term expires. If the policy is kept in force for the length of the term, the deposit plus interest is returned to the insured. If the insured dies before the end of the term, the face amount of the policy plus the deposit is paid to the beneficiary. Also, it is customary for the policy to have various conversion options at the end of each term.

Term insurance, because it is pure insurance, is less expensive per $1,000 of coverage than permanent insurance. There are variations on permanent insurance (discussed below) that try to make permanent insurance more affordable in the policy's early years, but for consumers who cannot afford permanent insurance even when initial premiums are reduced, some insurers offer "convertible term" insurance. In essence, convertible term gives the insured an option at a specified future time to convert the term policy to whole life by agreeing to pay thereafter the regular whole life premium charged to individuals of the attained age. An alternative approach allows the term policy to be converted into whole life if the insured pays the difference between what the premiums on the term insurance were and what premiums on a whole life policy would have cost, plus interest. Conversion is expensive, but what the insured purchases with convertible term is protection against the risk that the insured might later become uninsurable (due, for example, to worsened health) and unable to purchase whole life insurance when he or she is financially ready to do so.

[¶ 7,061]

Problem

Joe, a 25–year–old recent law school graduate, has several credit cards, including the National Express platinum card issued by a local bank. Joe receives an offer in the mail from National Express stating that for $0.29 per month per $100 of his unpaid balance on the card, Reliable Insurer will pay the outstanding credit card balance in full in the event of Joe's accidental death. In addition, 5% of the outstanding balance up to $5,000 will be paid each month for one year if, due to an accident, Joe is disabled for 60 days or more. Should Joe accept the offer? Would your answer change if the insurer's promise extended to death or disability due to illness or accident?

[¶ 7,065]

e. Variations on permanent life insurance

Most permanent life insurance products are similar, with the key differences being how the premiums or benefits are calculated. In the simplest form of permanent life policy, the insured pays premiums for life or until the insured reaches a specified age, such as 65, or maybe even 100 (which for most people equates to paying premiums for life). If the insured lives to the specified age, the cash value will have grown to equal the face value. At this point, the policy might be terminated with the insured receiving the accumulated cash value in a lump sum, or the policy might continue into the future with an increasing cash value.

If the insured wants to pay for the policy on an accelerated basis, the insured might purchase a "limited-payment life" policy. Under this arrangement, the insured pays premiums for a fixed number of years, a number which is sometimes coordinated to match a pre-planned event such as retirement. The most extreme version of limited-payment life is "single premium life," where the entire cost of the policy is paid in one lump sum. The advantage of limited payment life is that the premium payments are ordinarily completed prior to retirement, but the premiums are correspondingly larger.

Because permanent insurance is more expensive than term, many consumers are unable to afford permanent insurance early in their careers. Thus, some insurers offer variations on whole life policies that reduce the size of the premium in the policy's first years. In a "graded premium" whole life policy, the premium increases in the first five years and remains level thereafter. This arrangement is essentially a redistribution of the premiums across the life of the policy; the level premium paid after the fifth year will be slightly higher than whole life policies without the graded premium feature. To the extent the initial premium (which might even be flat for the first three or five years) is lower, the premium jump for the later years of the policy will be correspondingly higher.

"Endowment life insurance" is essentially limited-payment life insurance. Under this type of policy, the insured pays premiums until a specified age at which time an "endowment" exists, i.e., the policy's cash value equals the face value. When the policy matures, the insured typically has the option to take the cash value in a lump sum or in the form of an annuity. This kind of policy is usually marketed as one that will create a fund to support the insured during his or her retirement years. Functionally, this product is very similar to an annuity or retirement plan, except that some insurance protection greater than the cash value is provided during the policy's early years.

One of the reasons mentioned above for the purchase of insurance is to provide liquidity upon the death of the insured. In the case of a married couple, this need for liquidity may not arise until the death of the surviving spouse, especially if the couple makes use of standard estate planning techniques involving the unlimited marital deduction. (See ¶¶ 4,340 and 4,400.) To meet this need, insurers began in the 1980's to offer what is called "last-to-die" or "survivorship" insurance. In this type of policy, the death benefit is payable at the death of the survivor of two or more persons (typically, husband and wife). In some situations, this type of policy may not be what a couple needs; if the first death creates financial hardship for the surviving spouse, survivorship insurance is the wrong product. Some insurers, however, sell a policy which provides a death benefit payable at the death of the first spouse to die, with the remainder of the proceeds payable at the death of the surviving spouse.

In the late 1970's and early 1980's, as interest rates skyrocketed, consumers searched throughout their portfolios for assets that they could invest in high-earning money market and other interest-paying accounts. Interest paid by insurers on the cash value of life insurance was relatively low (while insurers were earning high returns on the funds on deposit with them), and knowledgeable consumers borrowed against cash values to earn higher returns elsewhere or avoided purchasing permanent insurance altogether. To become more competitive with other financial institutions, insurers began to market a variant of whole life insurance called "universal life." Many kinds of universal life insurance policies have been created through the years, but this type of insurance is best understood as a more flexible variety of whole life insurance. A universal life policy allows the insured to adjust, within limits, the premium payments and the death benefit over the life of the policy, which means the cash value component of the policy will also reflect increases or decreases in premium payments.

The typical universal life policy works as follows. The insurer credits the insured's premium to a "cash value account." Each month, the insurer deducts from this account the cost of insurance protection, which increases as the insured ages. The remainder of the account accumulates with interest. The insurer guarantees a minimum interest rate, but typically pays a rate competitive with other financial instruments (such as U.S. Treasury bills). The rate of return on a universal life policy is often higher than on a whole life policy, but the universal life policy has greater risk because it is more sensitive to declining interest rates. If interest rates go down, the insured may have to pay more in premiums in order to maintain the policy's stated death benefit. Over the long term, however, the cash value of a universal life policy will probably grow faster and larger than the cash value of a whole life policy. Normally the insured can modify the amount of the death benefit and change the timing and amount of the premium payments to respond to changing economic conditions.

A universal life policy gives the insured the ability to invest assets and have the cash buildup accrue on a tax-deferred basis, much like other kinds of investment accounts. Because a portion of the policy's cash value will come from investment returns that grow on a tax-deferred basis, it is possible to pay for the term insurance portion of the policy with pre-tax dollars. Doing so, of course, will reduce the amount of cash value in the policy; if the investment returns fall below the mortality costs and expense costs, the insured will either have to pay an increased premium to keep the death benefit in force or simply allow the policy to lapse. Whenever a consumer is interested in purchasing a universal life policy, the insurer will prepare an illustration of the projected cost, coverage, and cash values for a person of the insured's age and general health status. These illustrations, which are typically about ten pages long, come with two sets of numbers. One set represents the policy's future performance based on "current values"; this is a projection of the policy's performance if interest rates remain at the illustrated levels and if the company's cost of insurance (based upon the company's experience in paying death claims) remains unchanged. The second set of numbers represents the policy's "guaranteed values," i.e., the minimum guarantees made by the insurance company (typically an interest rate between 3% and 4.5%) based on an assumed cost of insurance derived from actuarial tables, as opposed to the insurer's mortality experience. The actual terms of the policy, when issued, will contain the guaranteed values, not the current values, which underscores the fact that the insurer does not promise that the projected current values will be attained.

In practice, universal life is a more sophisticated and more complex type of whole life policy. As with whole life, the insured can withdraw the cash value entirely (upon surrender of the insurance coverage); unlike whole life, the insured can withdraw portions of the account, which is a major advantage of universal life (but note that in a whole life policy the insured can tap a portion of the cash value by borrowing against the policy). In addition, the insured can alter the premium levels from time to time and the timing of payments. Although universal life is an intensively marketed alternative to whole life insurance, it does not vary the permanent life insurance policy's basic formula: part of the premium pays for a policy of term insurance, and the remainder is deposited in some sort of savings account, from which the insured can make withdrawals prior to death. The distinguishing feature of universal life is that the savings account is more like an investment account managed by the insurance company. The price of this added flexibility is increased risk. With whole life, the insured has no risk: the insurer guarantees the premium for life and bears all of the risk of changes in mortality costs and expense costs. A guaranteed rate of return on the cash value is promised, but the rate will be low—usually in the range of 3.5% to 4.5% for life. (If the insured purchases a participating policy, the insured shares to some extent in the good years through the payment of dividends.) With universal life, the risk of changes in mortality costs, expense costs, and interest rates is borne for the most part by the insured. If interest rates rise or costs decrease, the insured gets the benefit, but the insured bears the loss if interest rates decline or costs increase, subject to some limits (i.e., the insured has a guaranteed minimum interest rate—usually fairly low—and is protected by a limit on how high costs can go).

"Variable life" is a more recent evolution of the universal life policy. It is basically identical to universal life insurance, except that the cash value account is invested in instruments of the insured's choice, such as stocks, bonds, money market funds, or a combination thereof. This allows the insured to increase the level of investment risk and (it is hoped) achieve higher returns. If the investments do poorly and the cash value declines below the amount needed to pay the insurance premium, the insured is required to contribute additional sums to the account in order to maintain the insurance protection. The assumption underlying variable life policies is that, over the long term, alternative investments (e.g., corporate stocks) will consistently outperform other kinds of investments. There are still further variations on the universal/variable theme; some insurers market "flexible premium variable" or "variable-universal life" insurance, which typically refers to a policy that combines most of the elements of universal and variable life.

In a permanent insurance policy, the rate at which the cash value increases can vary, depending on the face value of the policy and the size of the premium. There are some combinations of face value and premium that essentially generate enough return that the policy can eventually pay for the premium itself. Where the policy's projections predict that the dividends paid over time or the increases in cash value will be sufficient to pay the premium in its entirety, the policy is frequently referred to as a "vanishing premium" policy. In the 1980's and 1990's, these policies were the subject of much litigation, primarily due to agents marketing the policies with scenarios based on projections for the future that were not always realized. Before purchasing any policy, a consumer should carefully analyze the assumptions on which its projected earnings and returns are based.

To summarize the various permanent life options, one might say that permanent insurance in its most basic iteration carries no risk. In the traditional whole life policy, the insurer guarantees that the premium will not change over the life of the policy. If mortality costs rise, the insurer bears these expenses; by the same token, if mortality costs decrease, the insurer keeps the extra profits. Expense costs also remain a constant; so if the insurer reduces expenses, it profits, but, by the same token, additional expenses cannot be passed along to the insured during the life of the policy. The rate of return on the cash value in a traditional or pure whole life policy will be low. If the insured is willing to bear more risk, it may be possible to achieve higher returns through universal or variable life insurance, but the type and level of risk that are appropriate for a particular investor will depend on the investor's financial position, asset allocation, time horizon, risk preference, and other variables.

[¶ 7,066]

Problem

Kara and Steve have one child, Stacy, who is two years old. Both Kara and Steve are employed in the public school system, Kara as a secretary and Steve as a custodian. Each has life insurance coverage provided by the school district equal to 1.5 times the amount of his or her salary. Able Agent visits Kara and Steve and proposes that they purchase a $10,000 whole life policy on Stacy's life. The annual premium is $240, and Able produces tables showing that by the time Stacy is 22 years old, the policy will have a cash value of $3,200. Stacy will also have the option to raise the coverage in $10,000 increments (with an accompanying increase in premium) at designated times—when she reaches age 16, when she reaches age 21, when she marries, and when she has her first child. Is purchasing a policy on Stacy a wise investment for Kara and Steve?

[¶ 7,070]

f. Choosing between term and permanent insurance

As its name suggests, permanent life insurance provides coverage over the insured's entire life and is therefore better suited to covering long-term financial needs. For example, term insurance becomes extremely expensive if one lives past the average life expectancy. Thus, whole life can better accomplish end-of-life goals, such as paying for end-of-life expenses (e.g., funeral costs, legal costs at the end of life, etc.), covering estate taxes at death, or providing a supplemental retirement fund for a surviving spouse. Term insurance, which by its nature is not permanent, is a more cost-effective way to provide protection for specific, short-term needs, such as mortgage payments, children's college costs, or other expenses associated with raising children.

In deciding whether to invest in permanent insurance, a consumer should understand that what he or she is purchasing is term insurance coverage (which may or may not be needed, either now or in the future) plus a savings account. As a result, the coverage will be more expensive. Table 7–2 below compares the approximate costs of various insurance products according to on-line quotes. The hypothetical male applicant for a life insurance policy with a $100,000 face value was of average height and weight, with normal blood pressure and cholesterol readings and no negative health history either personally or in his family. Comparing whole life products is particularly difficult, because the specific terms of the coverage can affect the value of the product and hence its cost. But these data provide some sense of what one would expect to pay for a 10–year term life insurance policy, a 20–year term policy, and a whole life level-premium policy:

Table 7–2. Annual Premium for $100,000 Face Value Policy (Male, No Negative Health History)

Age at issuance	10–Year Term	20–Year Term	Permanent
25	$ 84	$109	$ 310
40	101	144	649
60	400	730	1,582

Source: Approximate average of quoted policies on www.insure.com (Oct. 2004).

A consumer who purchases permanent insurance is choosing the insurance company as the manager of the assets placed in the savings account. There are many other kinds of investments that a consumer can make with the portion of a premium that goes into the savings account (i.e., the cash value). If the consumer believes that he or she can get a better after-tax return on other kinds of investments than in the insurer-managed savings account, the consumer should purchase a pure term insurance policy in whatever amount is needed to protect against premature death and use the savings resulting from lower insurance premiums to acquire alternative investments.

If the choice is to purchase permanent insurance, the question becomes whether the policy should be a traditional whole life policy or a universal life product. Universal life allows flexibility in setting premiums and the death benefit, so it may be a good choice for someone who anticipates needing varying amounts of coverage in the future but who does not wish to switch policies over time or purchase multiple small policies. For example, a young person who has no home mortgage or dependents but who expects to take on such obligations in the future may wish to consider this option. Universal life is more expensive than term, but it is typically less expensive than whole life, and the consumer may find universal life to be a more attractive, lower cost way to start a permanent insurance program. If the insured chooses to increase the death benefit, he or she may be subject to additional physical examinations to demonstrate continued insurability. As discussed above, an insurer issuing a universal life policy only commits to the "guaranteed values," which will be much less than the "current values" shown in the illustration prepared for the applicant. How well the policy performs in the future will depend on many variables, including general economic conditions. One should not expect that the current values will be achieved, but, by the same token, it is unlikely that the worst case scenario—that the policy generates only the guaranteed values—will materialize. The chances are that the policy's performance will be somewhere between the two predictions, much as one would predict with any investment.

Most states now require that insurers provide consumers with cost indexes to assist in making comparisons among different whole life insurance policies. One index is the "Life Insurance Surrender Cost Index." This index is more useful if the consumer is primarily interested in the level of cash values that will be accumulated. This index provides a standardized way to compare costs of a policy if at some future time (e.g., 10 or 20 years later) the insured surrenders the policy and takes its cash value. A second index is the "Life Insurance Net Payment Cost Index." This index is more useful if the consumer is primarily interested in death benefits rather than cash value. The cost index comparisons can be helpful if similar life insurance plans with essentially identical terms are compared. It is important to realize that small differences in cost may be offset by other policy features not reflected in the indexes.

[¶ 7,071]

Problem

Evan and Chris have an estate that is conservatively valued at $3 million and they are concerned about a potential estate tax obligation. Under federal tax law, the unlimited marital deduction allows property to pass tax-free at the first spouse's death to the surviving spouse, but those assets then become part of the surviving spouse's estate and may be subject to tax at the second spouse's death. Evan and Chris have reciprocal wills in which each spouse leaves one-half of his or her assets to the other at death. How can life insurance assist Evan and Chris in this situation?

[¶ 7,075]

3. Common Terms and Provisions of a Life Insurance Contract

Several provisions are common in virtually all life insurance contracts. This section describes some of the more important clauses, plus a couple of endorsements that frequently appear in life insurance contracts.

[¶ 7,080]

a. Incontestability clause

The policy commonly provides that the insurer will lose the right to contest the coverage—i.e., the policy becomes "incontestable"—after it has been in force for a specified period during the lifetime of the insured. In virtually every jurisdiction, a state statute mandates this provision and specifies a contestability period of no more than two years (although there are a few lines of insurance in some states where the statute specifies that defenses become incontestable after one year). Assuming a two-year contestability period, this means that after two years the insurer no longer has the right to deny coverage based on the insured's concealment, misrepresentation, or misstatement in the application. In some jurisdictions, the incontestability clause also reaches fraudulent statements.

Life insurance contracts in many instances are long-term contracts, and they often remain in force for decades. The incontestability provision prevents an insurer from asserting at the time of the insured's death, which could be a half-century or longer after the policy was issued, that the policy is invalid because of a misstatement made on the application. The risk of unfairness to beneficiaries who must argue over something that happened decades earlier is essentially deemed to outweigh the unfairness to insurers from being forced to pay proceeds despite learning after the end of the incontestability period that there was, in fact, an irregularity in the insured's statements that induced the making of the contract.

[¶ 7,085]

b. Misstatement of age

If the insured misstates his or her age, this misrepresentation does not invalidate the policy, but instead results in the policy's proceeds being adjusted to the amounts that the premiums paid would have purchased if the insured had provided the insurer with his or her correct age at the time the policy was sought. In some jurisdictions, this regulation also extends to misstatements of sex.

The modern significance of this provision, which is routinely required by state statutes dating back to the early 1900's, is quite limited. The origin of the age regulation can be found in the fact that in the late nineteenth century birth records were often incomplete and many people were genuinely uncertain about their birth date and age. These statutes prevented insurers from taking advantage of beneficiaries in these situations by pointing to a misstatement of the insured's age on the application. Where the same regulation exists with respect to misstatements of sex, the rationale is probably that inadvertent mistakes of this sort should not be a bar to coverage, particularly when the sex of the applicant should be apparent to the insurer at the time of contracting or to the medical examiner at the time of any examination.

[¶ 7,090]

c. *Suicide exclusion*

It is common for a life insurance policy to exclude coverage if the insured commits suicide within two years after the policy is issued. This means that if death is caused by suicide more than two years after the policy is issued, the beneficiaries can collect the proceeds. The purpose of this clause is to discourage an individual who might be contemplating self-destruction from purchasing insurance as a means of generating a financial windfall for his or her beneficiaries.

[¶ 7,095]

d. *Grace period*

Most policies state that if a premium is not paid within 31 days after the due date, the policy will lapse. This 31–day period is called the "grace period"; a payment during this period is late, but the policy will not lapse during this period. If death occurs during the grace period, the premium will be deducted from the proceeds paid.

With respect to permanent insurance, the lapse of a policy does not terminate the insured's right to the cash value. An insured who intends to let a policy lapse may cancel it and give directions on how the cash value should be disbursed (e.g., returned to the insured, used to purchase term coverage for some period in the future, etc.). But often when a policy lapses for nonpayment, the insured may simply not be paying attention to the policy or its cash value and may not be familiar with the policy's terms. The typical default in these circumstances is for the accumulated cash value to be used to purchase a paid-up term policy for whatever term the cash value is sufficient to acquire.

[¶ 7,100]

e. *Accidental death rider*

One common endorsement or rider on life insurance is the so-called "accidental death" or "double indemnity" endorsement. Typically, this provision requires the insurer to pay twice the face value of the policy if the insured perishes in an accident. In most instances, it is apparent whether the insured's death is accidental, but there are occasionally situations where the circumstances are not so clear. Policy language has changed over time to promote greater clarity, with mixed success. In any event, double indemnity insurance is rarely a wise investment for the insured, given that only a very small portion of decedents (approximately 3%) die in accidents. Moreover, the cause of death has nothing to do with family need.

Accidental death insurance has its roots as a travel insurance product in England in the mid-nineteenth century. Early railroad travel was prone to accident, sometimes with devastating consequences, which led to the emergence of a type of policy which covered death due to accident while traveling. The product came to America in roughly the same form, and it survived as a substitute for the lack of a tort remedy in situations where death resulted from accident. Also, during periods when workers were at risk in hazardous occupations and workers' compensation programs had not yet been developed, the coverage provided some protection for the worker's family when death occurred in the workplace. The coverage became bundled with dismemberment coverage, which also served a purpose, before the era of workers' compensation, of providing some financial relief for the families of workers who were severely injured on the job. Understandably, when policies were written to cover dismemberment, it was natural for the policies to cover arguably the most serious of all accidental injuries—death. Finally, these policies had some attraction early in the twentieth century when health insurance was relatively undeveloped, as these policies could help pay for medical expenses, whether end-of-life or associated with injury, incurred as a result of an accident. With the development of modern workers' compensation programs, a more elaborate tort liability system, and the growth of health insurance, most of the historical reasons for the existence of accidental death insurance are no longer present.

[¶ 7,105]

f. *Waiver of premium endorsement*

Another common rider is the "waiver of premium" endorsement, which eliminates the insured's need to pay the premiums on the policy in the event the insured becomes disabled. When waived, such premiums are not taxable as income to the insured; they are expressly excluded from gross income as "amounts received through accident or health insurance ... for personal injuries or sickness." I.R.C. § 104(a)(3). Under the same logic, benefits received under a disability insurance rider on a life insurance policy should be tax exempt.

[¶ 7,106]

Problems

1. Your client calls you to report that a $100,000 whole life insurance policy was found in records of his recently deceased father. The client indicates that he and his mother, who predeceased his father, are named as beneficiaries. According to the decedent's bank records, no insurance premiums had been paid in the last seven years, and no earlier records were in the deceased's possession. This is why your client was surprised when the insurance policy, which was issued in 1977, was found. Your client asks what he should do about this old policy. What would you say to your client?

2. Reliable Insurance Company issued a policy of group life insurance to Hot Air Heating and Cooling Company, a small heating and air conditioning firm with about 20 employees. The master policy issued to the employer provided coverage for all "full-time employees of the company," and "full-time employee" was defined as "any employee whose regular work schedule is at least 30 hours per week." Mrs. Hurd, the president and owner of the company, employed her son Adam as a half-time secretary at the company. In no week did he work more than 20 hours. Adam had been a half-time employee for four years when he died in an auto accident. In the enrollment form which Adam filled out to receive the group coverage, Adam checked the box that he was a "full-time employee" and named his mother as the beneficiary of his coverage. The Reliable group policy had been in force for three years at the time of his death. Is Mrs. Hurd entitled to proceeds on account of her son's death?

3. Arthur, the deceased husband of Amy, died on September 1, 2004 of a self-inflicted gunshot wound. On July 1, 2003, he had purchased a $250,000 term life insurance policy on his own life, naming Amy as beneficiary. At the time of his death, Arthur was taking a prescription medication that is known to exacerbate depression in those who are predisposed to the condition. Arthur's physician testified that he had no knowledge of Arthur's previous episodes of depression and that it was very probable that Arthur was subject to an "irresistible impulse" brought on by the medication to take his own life. Amy argues that the suicide exclusion does not apply in these circumstances, but the insurer disagrees and has denied coverage. What result?

4. Kathy, the wife of Donald, died on September 1, 2004 of carbon monoxide poisoning. On July 1, 2003, she had purchased a $250,000 term life insurance policy on her own life, naming Donald as beneficiary. The coroner's report indicates that Kathy died in her car, which was left running in her garage with a hose attached to the tailpipe which channeled the poisonous gas into the vehicle's passenger compartment. The report also indicates that the position of Kathy's body showed that at the time of her death she had made an unsuccessful effort to unhook the hose, presumably in an effort to stop the deadly chain of events she had set in motion. Based on this report, Donald wishes to show that Kathy changed her mind in the middle of her suicide attempt and unsuccessfully tried to abort the attempt.

Assuming Donald can establish this fact by a preponderance of the evidence, is the insured's death outside coverage by virtue of the suicide exclusion?

5. Jack was a skilled high diver. On many occasions he had made spectacular dives from great heights into small pools of water. One of his most notorious dives was from the top of the Coolidge Dam to a pool of water a great distance below. Unfortunately, when he attempted to repeat this feat a second time, Jack lost his life. Was Jack's death a suicide? If not, is Jack's beneficiary entitled to recover under the accidental death benefit rider on his life insurance policy?

[¶ 7,110]

4. Interests Protected in a Life Insurance Policy

Life insurance is essentially a special type of contract between the owner of the policy and the issuer of the policy, which provides for the payment of proceeds to one or more beneficiaries at the death of the person whose life is insured. The following discussion explores the relationship between the parties and the rights created by the contract of insurance.

[¶ 7,115]

a. *Owners and insureds*

The person whose life is insured is sometimes called the "cestui que vie" (or CQV), which roughly translated from the old French means "the one whose life" is the subject of the contract, i.e., the insured. This person may or may not be the same person who *owns* the policy. In other words, the rights that attach to the policy belong to the policy's *owner*, who may be but need not be the same person as the insured. If a person purchases insurance on his or her own life, that person is *both* the owner and the insured. But if, for example, a wife purchases insurance on her husband's life, the wife is the owner and the husband is the insured. The insurer becomes obligated to pay proceeds at the death of the *insured*, not the death of the owner. Typically, it is the owner who purchases the policy and pays the premiums, but a person may succeed to the owner-ship rights by virtue of an assignment, which occurs when the original owner of the policy *assigns* his or her rights to someone else.

[¶ 7,120]

b. *The insurable interest requirement*

It is a fundamental principle of insurance that the owner of a policy must have an "insurable interest" in the subject matter of the insurance in order for the policy to be valid. In life insurance, this test is met in one of two ways: either (1) there is a sufficiently close family relationship to establish the insurable interest, or (2) the owner of the policy has a pecuniary interest in the life of the insured such that the owner will derive an economic benefit from the insured's continued life (or will suffer a loss in the event of the insured's death). Although it is sometimes said that the purpose of the rule is to prevent wagering on someone's continued existence, the underlying policy of the rule is grounded in the concept of moral hazard. If someone could purchase insurance on a life in which he or she has no interest, the policy owner would lack incentives to preserve the life and might even be tempted to help end it prematurely. Interestingly, in life insurance, it is commonly said that the insurable interest must exist at the time that the contract is made, and the lack of the interest at the time of the insured's death is irrelevant. The rule's focus is on ensuring that policies are not *issued* in the absence of an insurable interest, although it is at least arguable that whether a person has an incentive to hasten the insured's death depends on the relationship at the time of the death. (The analogous rule in property insurance requires an interest at the time of the loss, and not at the time of contracting.) As a practical matter, there are few situations where an insurable interest will exist at the time of contracting and thereafter terminate, so this quirk in the rule ultimately has little significance.

The insurable interest doctrine has its roots in eighteenth-century England, where insurance became a cover for wagering practices. For example, a person might bet on whether a particular ship would successfully finish its voyage by insuring the ship or its cargo, even though the insured did not own the ship or the cargo or have any other relationship with the ship. In fact, some insureds were thought to have passed intelligence to enemy nations about ship locations and dates of travel during wartime to facilitate the enemy's destruction of the ship—and thereby make it possible for the insured to recover. When Parliament enacted a statute in 1746 that rendered void any policy of insurance on property in which the insured had no interest, the wagering practice switched to life insurance. People would purchase insurance on the lives of persons accused of capital crimes—essentially betting whether the accused would be convicted and executed. Other policies were taken out on the lives of well-known individuals who were known to be ill, essentially making a bet on whether the individual would survive his current malady. Naturally, the concern arose that owners of the policies might engage a physician or attendant to hasten the individual's death to facilitate a recovery on the policy, and in its most sordid manifestation, policies were issued to applicants whose sole purpose in procuring the policy was to murder the insured and collect the proceeds. In 1774, Parliament enacted a statute that rendered invalid any life insurance policy where the policy owner had no interest in the life of the insured. The insurable interest doctrine was recognized early on in the United States by courts, although eventually many states would enact statutes on the subject as well.

As the rule has developed, every person has an unlimited insurable interest in his or her own life. Of course, no one expects to suffer pecuniary loss as a result of his or her own death, given that death ends finally and completely all of one's earthly pursuits. It could be said that the family relationship one has with himself or herself is uniquely close, but the crucial point is that when someone takes out insurance on his or her own life, society has only a minimal concern that the insured is wagering on his or her continued existence or is inclined to self-destruct for the purpose of bestowing a financial benefit on others. A person who takes out insurance on her own life has the power to designate any beneficiary; it is presumed that she will not designate a beneficiary who is likely to murder her. It is not necessary that the named beneficiary have an insurable interest in the life of the insured. (This rule is not without exception, however. If a third person named as beneficiary encouraged the insured to take out the policy on the insured's own life and pay the premiums, there is case law voiding the policy as a wager.)

Where an individual takes out insurance on the life of another, there is a greater risk that the evils against which the insurable interest doctrine was created—destruction of the insured and wagering—will occur. However, if a strong familial or economic relationship exists, a court is likely to conclude that the person taking out the insurance possesses the requisite insurable interest. The closer the familial relationship, the more likely it is that an insurable interest exists. It is not denied anywhere that one has an insurable interest in the life of his or her spouse. This relationship is so close and the affection normally so great that it is presumed that the evils at which the doctrine is directed will not occur. The insurable interest of each spouse in the other's life ordinarily ends at divorce, although a divorce decree may give rise to an economic relationship that replaces the insurable interest previously grounded in the love and affection presumed to exist between spouses. This would occur, for example, if the divorce decree required one spouse to pay alimony to the other. For the same reasons that spouses have an insurable interest in each other's life, courts also agree that a parent and minor child have an insurable interest in each other's life. However, beyond the spousal and parent-minor child relationships, courts are not in agreement on the degree of family relationship that will support the existence of an insurable interest. If an economic interest combines with a weak family relationship, it is more likely that a court will find the insurable interest requirement satisfied. Where there is no family relationship to support the existence of an insurable interest, courts sometimes find the insurable interest requirement satisfied by a pecuniary interest alone. Thus, if one person is likely to suffer an economic loss because of the death of a business associate or someone with whom that person is in a contractual relationship, courts generally hold that the person has an insurable interest in the life of the other person. Under this reasoning, a partner has an insurable interest in the life of his or her partner, and an employer and employee can have an insurable interest in each other's life, although as an organization becomes larger and the relationships between employers and employees more distant, the likelihood of finding an insurable interest diminishes. A creditor— even an unsecured creditor (who lacks an insurable interest in the property of the debtor)—has an insurable interest in the life of the debtor.

Where the insurable interest is based on a family relationship, no limit exists on the amount of insurance that may be purchased. However, where the insurable interest is based only on an economic interest, most courts hold that the value of the pecuniary involvement fixes a limit upon the amount of insurance that can be purchased. If the amount received by the creditor is equal to the debt, there is no objection on the ground of a "gambling contract." If the amount received is greater than the debt, the debtor's estate may be entitled to any amount exceeding the debt (plus interest), thereby preventing the creditor from being unjustly enriched.

Last but not least, it is important to recognize that statutes in some states have codified aspects of the insurable interest rules for life insurance. Many of these statutes state broad principles, leaving it to courts to sort out the details. Other statutes are more restrictive, and some have specific provisions requiring an economic interest or dealing with particular situations, such as whether a charitable organization that takes a policy by assignment must have an insurable interest in the assignor's life. Some statutes deal specifically with the matter of the insured's consent to issuance of the policy, indicating the circumstances under which consent is required or under which consent will suffice to satisfy the insurable interest requirement.

Consider these examples from two of the nation's largest states. New York defines "insurable interest" in the case of persons closely related by blood or law as "a substantial interest engendered by love and affection," and in the case of other persons as "a lawful and substantial economic interest in the continued life, health or bodily safety of the person insured, as distinguished from an interest which would arise only by, or would be enhanced in value by, the death, disablement or injury of the insured." N.Y. Ins. L. § 3205(a). New York also has a consent requirement:

> No contract of insurance upon the person, except a policy of group life insurance . . . [or some others], shall be made or effectuated unless at or before the making of such contract the person insured, being of lawful age or competent to contract therefor, applies for or consents in writing to the making of the contract, except in the following cases:
>
> > (1) A wife or husband may effectuate insurance upon the person of the other.
> >
> > (2) Any person having an insurable interest in the life of a minor under the age of fourteen years and six months or any person upon whom such minor is dependent for support and maintenance, may effectuate a contract of insurance upon the life of such minor, in an amount which shall not exceed the limits specified in [§ 3207].
>
> [N.Y. Ins. L. § 3205(c).]

California's statute is more succinct:

> Every person has an insurable interest in the life and health of:

(a) Himself.

(b) Any person on whom he depends wholly or in part for education or support.

(c) Any person under a legal obligation to him for the payment of money or respecting property or services, of which death or illness might delay or prevent the performance.

(d) Any person upon whose life any estate or interest vested in him depends. [Cal. Ins. Code § 10110.]

[¶ 7,121]

Problem

Albert was a unemployed person who lived in the streets. Albert was befriended by Steve, who suggested that Albert and Steve form a business partnership under which Steve would produce an advertising magazine that would be distributed for free, and Albert would be responsible for leaving stacks of the magazine in various key locations and personally handing them out in some of the locations. Albert had no assets, so Steve agreed to put up all of the money to start this business. Steve also persuaded Albert to take out a $50,000 insurance policy on his own life, with the premiums to be paid by Steve, and with Steve to be named as the beneficiary. Albert agreed, and Ace Insurance Company issued the policy to Albert. After the policy had been in effect for two months, Steve invited Albert to go on a hunting trip with him. The two hunted alone, but only Steve returned alive. He claimed that while they were handling guns in the woods, one of the guns accidentally discharged, killing Albert instantly. Albert's mother would testify that Albert hated hunting and since his childhood had been disgusted by the notion of shooting animals, but the prosecutor concluded that the evidence was insufficient to charge Steve with any kind of criminal conduct in connection with Albert's death. Steve now submits a claim for proceeds under the policy. Ace Insurance Company is your client, and they ask you whether they should pay the proceeds to Steve. How would you advise the company?

[¶ 7,125]

c. *Designating and changing the beneficiary*

A life insurance policy confers valuable rights on its owner, and one of the most valuable of these rights is the right to designate a *beneficiary*. The term "beneficiary" is usually used in insurance law to describe the person who, although not a party to the contract (in the sense that the owner of the policy contracts with the insurer, and the owner and the insurer are therefore the contracting parties), is entitled to receive the proceeds of the insurance. An individual who takes out insurance on his or her own life is allowed to name anyone as the beneficiary. The rights of a person who takes out insurance on the life of another to name a beneficiary are more limited, as discussed in more detail below. A beneficiary may be an individual, a business, a charity, a trust, or an estate.

It is common to designate different "levels" of beneficiaries; these are typically referred to as "primary beneficiaries" and "contingent beneficiaries." A primary beneficiary is the beneficiary with the highest priority; in other words, if the primary beneficiary is alive and otherwise qualified to receive the proceeds, the proceeds will be paid to that beneficiary. It is common, however, to also designate contingent beneficiaries, i.e., beneficiaries who will receive the proceeds only if the primary beneficiary is deceased or otherwise disqualified. A common formulation is for a married individual with children to designate his or her spouse as the primary beneficiary, with the children as contingent beneficiaries. If the designated spouse is alive at the time of the insured's death, the surviving spouse receives the proceeds; but if the designated spouse is deceased (or disqualified, as would be the case if the beneficiary-spouse murdered the insured), the proceeds would go to the children.

It is possible to designate more than one person at each level. For example, one could name two persons as the primary beneficiaries and "all my children" as the contingent beneficiaries. Under those formulations, the proceeds are first divided equally among any surviving beneficiaries at the level in question. Most modern policies provide that in the event there are no surviving, qualified beneficiaries, the proceeds are paid to the estate of the insured. Thus, the failure of the owner to designate a beneficiary (a rare occurrence, as the insurer is likely to insist that a designation be made) simply means that the proceeds will be paid to the insured's estate.

Other rights that belong to the owner of the policy are the right to receive the policy's cash value, to take out loans against the cash value, to surrender or terminate the policy in exchange for the cash value, and to assign the policy. In modern policies, all of these rights, including the right to change the beneficiary, can be exercised by the owner without the designated beneficiary's consent. In other words, beneficiaries under modern policies do not have vested rights, and have only an expectancy of receiving the proceeds under the insurance. Thus, it is possible that the owner-insured of a life insurance policy might assign the policy to a third party (for example, a charity), and the assignee would then be free to designate itself as the new beneficiary of the policy. This would quash the rights of the original beneficiary, and would not require the consent of the original beneficiary.

Language in policies dealing with assignments varies, but most modern forms contain a provision that states that the owner has the right to assign the policy, that the insurer will not be deemed to have knowledge of the assignment unless the owner complies with certain procedures (including filing the assignment with the insurer), and that the rights of the owner and any beneficiaries will be subject to the assignment. This language is understood, and is treated by most courts, as making the assignee's rights superior to those of the beneficiary. When an assignment occurs to secure a debt, most courts hold that the assignee's rights supersede the beneficiary's rights only up to the amount of the debt, but there are some cases to the contrary. It is incumbent on the owner-assignor to be clear in the assignment; a limited assignment of a portion of life insurance proceeds and an explicit reference to the amount of the debt can easily accomplish this purpose.

Generally, a person who takes out insurance on her own life can designate any beneficiary she chooses. Spouses and children are the most frequent designees, but sometimes employers, partnerships, corporations, trustees, and charitable organizations are designated. In recent years, some charitable organizations (particularly educational and religious institutions) and some associations (such as fraternities and sororities), at the urging of insurance agents and brokers, have encouraged their members to purchase life insurance policies and name the organization as the beneficiary. This does not guarantee that the organization will actually receive the proceeds, because the beneficiary designation is subject to change at the owner's discretion. But if the beneficiary designation is accompanied by an assignment of the policy to the organization, the organization acquires both the ownership rights and the entitlement to proceeds, and thus can rest assured that the beneficiary designation will not be changed.

The owner's right to designate freely any beneficiary is subject to limitations in some situations. First, the rules change when an individual purchases a policy on someone else's life. As discussed above, the person purchasing insurance on someone else's life must have an insurable interest in the other person's life; otherwise, the policy is void. If the owner has an insurable interest in the life of the insured, the owner can designate himself or herself as the beneficiary; but if the owner chooses to designate a third party as the beneficiary, that party must also have an insurable interest in the life of the insured. Second, in a community property state, the owner's power to designate a beneficiary is not absolute when the policy is purchased with community funds. Third, with respect to group insurance, many state statutes prohibit the person whose life is insured from designating the owner of the policy as the beneficiary. The logic of this prohibition is presumably that most group insurance is offered by employers as a benefit to employees; it would defeat the purposes for which such insurance is encouraged if the employer, through either direct or implicit coercion, could convert the employee benefit to an employer benefit. Fourth, if the beneficiary designation or change is made under undue influence or as a result of fraud or other misconduct, the designation may be invalid. A designation or change may also be invalid if the policyholder was incompetent or insane at the time of the designation or change.

Potential gift tax consequences can also be relevant to how a beneficiary is designated. For estate planning reasons, it may be useful for an individual to take out and hold a policy on the life of another, such as his or her spouse. If the policy is not assigned to a life insurance trust or if the beneficiary designation is revocable (which is generally the case under modern life insurance forms), the owner may be deemed to have made a completed, taxable gift of the policy proceeds at the death of the insured. This was the situation in Goodman v. Commissioner, 156 F.2d 218 (2d Cir. 1946), where the wife, who owned a policy on her husband's life, was deemed to have made a gift of the proceeds to the beneficiaries upon her husband's death. If she had placed the insurance in an irrevocable trust (with no retained interests or powers) or had irrevocably designated the beneficiaries when she acquired the policy, she would have incurred a gift tax on the value of the policy at that time, which would have been considerably less than the proceeds which were subject to tax at the husband's death. (Note that this problem does not arise if the owner designates herself as the beneficiary.)

Because modern life insurance forms contemplate that beneficiary designations are revocable, how does one make an irrevocable beneficiary designation? Under the law of third-party beneficiaries, it is possible for an owner and insurer to agree that a beneficiary designation cannot be changed or can be changed only with the consent of the beneficiary, but this kind of agreement is extremely rare. Insurers are typically not interested in assuming additional burdens under policies, and in this case the obligation to make sure that a beneficiary change was not inadvertently accomplished in the future could create liability for the insurer. If the owner assigns his or her interest in the policy to the beneficiary, the beneficiary, as owner, can control future changes of beneficiary, thereby protecting his or her interest. This approach, however, does not work if the owner wants to continue to hold the policy for some reason, such as making sure the premiums are paid in circumstances where the beneficiary is a minor. The owner and the beneficiary can enter into a binding contract pursuant to which the owner agrees not to revoke the designation, but the insurer will not be bound by this arrangement. Presumably, the gift tax benefits will be enough incentive to ensure that the owner performs the agreement, but should this not be the case and if the insurer pays the proceeds to a different beneficiary, the original beneficiary's remedy will be against the estate of the deceased, not the insurer. In most cases, a transfer of the policy in trust will be the preferred method of making a beneficiary designation irrevocable.

Usually, the insurer can pay the designated beneficiary of record without liability, assuming the insurer has no knowledge of a possible adverse claim or a reason to believe that the designated beneficiary is disqualified. Therefore, it is important to the owner that the beneficiary designation be clear and current. Some common techniques for designating beneficiaries work well in some situations and cause confusion in others. For example, it is common for beneficiary designations to contain descriptions of the individual, e.g., "John Jay, husband of the insured." If the owner-insured and John Jay subsequently divorce, there may be a question concerning the meaning of the designation. Does it mean "John Jay, and if there is doubt as to which John Jay is intended, it is the one who is the husband of the insured"? Or does it mean "John Jay, but only so long as he is the husband of the insured"? Courts usually hold that the phrase "husband of the insured" is descriptive only, and that the name itself is controlling. Sometimes a class of people, such as "my nieces and nephews," is designated as the beneficiary. This enables nieces and nephews who are born after the policy is issued to be members of the class of designated beneficiaries and eliminates the need to change the beneficiary each time a new niece or nephew is born. On the other hand, if the class is large, the payment of proceeds may be held up until each member of the class can be accounted for. Moreover, where there are relations by marriage (e.g., the children of the insured's wife's sister), disputes may arise as to who is a "nephew" or a "niece." A designation of "all my children" may work well in many situations, but disputes can arise if children of an insured are born or adopted into or out of a particular family. In large families, identifying all the members of a class can be extremely difficult. (Imagine the difficulty with a designation of "all my cousins.") Thus, it is generally wise to be specific about the designation. A beneficiary designation that is vague (such as "to my family") and incapable of interpretation may end up being disregarded altogether; contingent beneficiaries or the insured's estate would then receive the proceeds.

Most modern policies allow the owner to change the beneficiary, but there are some limitations on this right. Community property rules sometimes limit the ability of one spouse acting alone to designate a new beneficiary; divorce decrees often limit the policy owner's ability to make future changes; and individuals who are incompetent entirely lack the power to make valid changes. Furthermore, with respect to life insurance issued under the Federal Employee Group Life Insurance program and the Servicemen's Group Life Insurance program, Congress has specified that beneficiaries can be changed only in accordance with special statutory and regulatory requirements, and courts have been unwilling to depart from these mandates even though the rationale for them is unclear.

Insurance policies usually indicate the procedure for changing a beneficiary. Most policies require that the insured execute and deliver to the insurer a written request for a change and that the insurer endorse this change on the policy. (Some policies also require that the policy itself be submitted along with the written request, but this requirement appears less frequently today.) If the policyholder complies with these procedures, the change of beneficiary is effective, even though the change is made without the knowledge or consent of either the original beneficiary or the new one.

In most jurisdictions, the change will be deemed effective if the owner "substantially complies" with the procedures specified by the insurer. This test involves essentially two elements: first, the owner must have intended to change the beneficiary; and second, the owner must have taken all practically feasible steps to manifest that intention. Thus, if the owner took all possible steps to comply with the specified procedures but nevertheless failed to comply due to circumstances beyond the owner's control, the change can be given effect despite the failure to comply strictly with the policy's change-of-beneficiary provisions. The rule is grounded in equity; it is designed to work fairness by carrying out the intent of the insured. Thus, if the owner seeks to change the beneficiary from his ex-wife to his mother, but his ex-wife intercepts the owner's mail, including the forms necessary to process the change, and the owner dies before discovering the ex-wife's interference, the change will be deemed effective under the logic that the owner substantially complied with the change-of-beneficiary procedures. See Standard Life & Accident Ins. Co. v. Pylant, 424 So.2d 377 (La.App. 1982). The tension in the change of beneficiary cases is the classic one between form and substance: should the intent of the insured be paramount, or should the formal requirements of the policy control? The substantial compliance doctrine attempts to strike a balance between these two interests.

An attempt to change a life insurance beneficiary by will is generally held void where the policy (as is typically the case) sets out specific procedures for making beneficiary changes. In most of these cases, the attempt to name a new beneficiary in the will does not satisfy the requirements of the substantial compliance test because at the time the insured executed the will the insured was fully capable of changing the beneficiary under the specified procedures. Also, a will does not become operative until the death of the testator-owner. At the moment of death, the designated beneficiary under the life insurance contract becomes entitled to the proceeds; there is no obvious reason why a will should take precedence over a beneficiary designation, since both arrangements become operative at death.

Except where the rule is changed by statute (discussed below), divorce, in and of itself, does not change a beneficiary designation. Moreover, the general rule is that a divorce decree or property settlement does not, in and of itself, automatically terminate a spouse's right as a designated beneficiary. But if a divorce decree expressly directs who is to receive the insurance proceeds, the decree ordinarily controls, even if the beneficiary designation is not changed to conform with it (or is subsequently altered). The decree is binding with respect to the owner's rights in a life insurance policy, just as it is with respect to the owner's other assets. Under the same logic, the owner's right to change a beneficiary may be limited by divorce decree, property settlement, or other contractual arrangement. If the beneficiary change mandated by the decree is not actually made, or if the beneficiary designation is subsequently altered in violation of the decree, the persons entitled to the proceeds under the decree will have an equitable right to the proceeds. The language of the divorce decree must, however, be very clear; if the decree is framed in general terms and does not specifically require a change of beneficiary, the beneficiary designation will be enforced according to its terms. Any person who is mandated to receive insurance proceeds under a divorce decree or property settlement would be wise to forward a copy of the decree or settlement to the insurer to put the insurer on notice of its terms.

Several states, following the lead of the Uniform Probate Code, have enacted statutes addressing the effect of divorce on a life insurance policy where one spouse is the owner-insured and the other spouse is the designated beneficiary. In general, these statutes treat the divorce as automatically revoking the original beneficiary designation unless the insurance policy, a court order, or a property settlement agreement expressly provides otherwise. As a result, the beneficiary-spouse is generally treated as having disclaimed his or her right to the insurance proceeds. See UPC § 2–804(b), (d). This means that a contingent beneficiary (or if there is none, the estate of the insured spouse) becomes entitled to the proceeds. This provision extends the revocation-by-divorce rule, which traditionally applied only to wills, to reach life insurance and other will substitutes (including beneficiary designations in revocable trusts, bank accounts, and retirement plans). The life insurance industry has vigorously opposed this provision due to concerns about administrative burdens and the risk of liability for paying proceeds to the wrong beneficiary. The Uniform Probate Code, however, provides protection for insurers and other payors who make payments in good faith reliance on the terms of a life insurance policy or other written instrument without notice of the divorce. See UPC § 2–804(g).

Private employee benefit plans must take some additional rules into account. Because ERISA preempts all state laws insofar as they "relate to any employee benefit plan" except for those laws that regulate insurance, several federal circuit courts have held that state laws dealing with beneficiary designations in private employee benefit plans are preempted, including state law dealing with the effect of divorce on beneficiary designations. This analysis was approved by the U.S. Supreme Court in Egelhoff v. Egelhoff, 532 U.S. 141 (2001). The Court reasoned that the state statute—in this case, the Washington version of UPC § 2–804—would have interfered with ERISA's goal of national uniformity in the administration of plans and benefits, and was therefore preempted with respect to plans covered by ERISA.

The federal circuit courts have split on the question of whether ERISA itself supplies the relevant rule of law or whether judges must look to federal common law for the controlling principles. (See Manning v. Hayes, 212 F.3d 866 (5th Cir. 2000), describing the split of authority.) This question was not resolved in *Egelhoff*. If a state court enters a judgment, decree, or order (including approval of a property settlement agreement) in a domestic relations proceeding that overrides the beneficiary designation or otherwise alters the right to receive benefits under an ERISA plan, the court action may nevertheless survive ERISA preemption. ERISA provides a specific exemption from the preemption clause for a "qualified domestic relations order" (QDRO). See 29 U.S.C. §§ 1056(d)(3), 1144(b)(7). Thus, if the court order meets the requirements of a QDRO, it will not be subject to preemption. See, e.g., Metropolitan Life Ins. Co. v. Wheaton, 42 F.3d 1080 (7th Cir. 1994). To avoid uncertainty as to who is entitled to the proceeds of insurance on the life of a former spouse, it is important to pay attention at the time of divorce to the terms of a divorce decree or marital property settlement that may affect beneficiary designations on existing life insurance policies.

[¶ 7,126]

Problems

1. Alex created a revocable trust that provided for income to be paid after his death to his wife Doris for life, with remainder to their children. Doris purchased an insurance policy on Alex's life and named the trustee of Alex's trust as beneficiary. Doris, as the owner of the policy, retained all rights, including the right to change the beneficiary. Doris also paid all the premiums. Alex dies, survived by Doris. How would you describe the tax consequences at Alex's death?

2. Juan and Catrina were engaged to be married, but their plans for an early wedding were disrupted when Juan's National Guard unit was deployed in Bosnia for one year. Before leaving for Bosnia, Juan purchased a $10,000 policy of whole life insurance on his own life, naming "Catrina, my fiancée" as beneficiary. Three months after he arrived in Bosnia, Juan received a letter from Catrina in which she expressed "serious doubts" about her readiness for marriage and wrote that "although I still have affection for you, I can't marry you." Juan was distraught; he informed his sergeant about the letter, and asked the sergeant what he should do about the life insurance policy. The sergeant said he "didn't know," but that Juan should probably "check into it." Two weeks later, Juan was killed in an freak accident. Catrina now claims the proceeds of the policy as the designated beneficiary, but Juan's father insists that he is entitled to the proceeds because Catrina had broken off her engagement with Juan and was no longer his fiancée. The insurer asks you what it should do in these circumstances. How would you advise the insurer?

[¶ 7,130]

d. Disputes between beneficiaries and creditors

Disputes sometimes arise between the beneficiary and someone else claiming the proceeds of a policy. One common situation involves the beneficiary and creditors of the owner who make competing claims to the proceeds. For example, during the life of the insured, a creditor of the owner might attempt to attach the policy's cash value, or after the insured's death, creditors might claim an interest in the proceeds. If a creditor has no interest in the insurance contract, either as owner of the policy, assignee, or beneficiary, the creditor cannot make a claim on the contract itself. Of course, nothing prevents a creditor from owning a policy or being designated as the beneficiary or assignee, but in the absence of such ownership or designation, the creditor's claim on the policy is no different than the claim the creditor would make on any other property of the owner, whether it be the owner's car, boat, or bank account.

Statutes in most states exempt insurance policies from the claims of creditors in varying degrees. The purpose of these statutes is to protect the debtor's family, who often depend on the debtor's purchase of insurance for their financial needs in the event of the debtor's death. The state statutes providing the insurance exemption vary widely in their content, and it is difficult to generalize about them. (See ¶ 10,250; 7 Collier on Bankruptcy (15th rev. ed. 1996).) In many states, if an individual takes out a policy of insurance on her own life and names immediate family members as beneficiaries, the proceeds are exempt from the claims of the owner-insured's creditors. In these jurisdictions, cash values ordinarily cannot be seized during the life of the insured either, but contrary results have been reached in states where the statutes exempt only proceeds. If the owner-insured names herself or her own estate as beneficiary, the cash value or proceeds are less likely to be immune to creditor's claims. Such an insurance policy looks like the owner-insured's asset, much like a bank account; accordingly, the public policy shifts in favor of allowing creditors to attach such policies. For a discussion of the exemption for life insurance proceeds in bankruptcy, see 2 Epstein et al., Bankruptcy 515–19 (1993).

In most cases, no problem is created by designating a creditor as the beneficiary, assuming the proceeds do not exceed the amount of the debt. However, if the proceeds exceed the amount of the debt, another person (such as a family member) may assert a claim to the excess proceeds. Most courts handle the situation by drawing the inference, which may be accomplished by interpreting the underlying contract documents that created the debt and established some kind of security arrangement, that the owner intended to designate the creditor as a beneficiary only to the extent of the debt. If this inference is drawn, the excess proceeds are held in trust by the creditor for the benefit of the insured's estate. A minority of courts, however, allow the creditor to retain the proceeds, particularly in circumstances where the creditor procured the insurance and designated itself as beneficiary. Some courts that follow the minority rule recognize an exception where there is evidence other than the owner's designation of the beneficiary showing that the owner intended that the creditor would be entitled to proceeds only up to the amount of the debt. Also, if the amount of the proceeds greatly exceeds the debt, the contract resembles a wagering contract, and it might be held wholly or partially invalid for lack of an insurable interest.

[¶ 7,135]

e. Assignments

In life insurance, assignment of the policy does not involve designating a new insured or a new beneficiary. Rather, an assignment of a life insurance policy is ordinarily viewed as a transfer of the ownership rights to the policy, such as the right to borrow against the cash value, the right to surrender the policy for cash, the right to designate a different beneficiary, and the right to select the settlement option. Most modern policies contain a provision setting forth both the procedures for effecting an assignment and its legal effect. One form in common use provides: "You may assign this policy. We assume no responsibility for the validity of any assignment, and we will not be considered to have knowledge of it unless it is filed in writing at our Home Office. When it is filed, your rights and those of any Beneficiary will be subject to it." Whole Life Policy, in Alliance of American Insurers, Policy Kit: A Collection of Sample Policy Forms (1999) (hereinafter "Policy Kit"), at 158 (Form AM–26.08 E 9–81). This language indicates that if the assignment is filed with the insurer, the assignee's rights supersede those of the beneficiary, and the assignee (rather than the beneficiary) will receive the proceeds. If the assignment is not filed with the insurer and the insurer pays the proceeds to the beneficiary of record, the insurer will not be liable to the assignee. Usually, a certificate holder's interest in a group insurance policy is not assignable.

Although the language in policies dealing with assignment varies and some policies have provisions considerably more elaborate than the passage quoted above, most courts in interpreting such clauses have held that when the policy owner complies with the procedures specified in the policy for assigning it, the assignee's rights supersede those of the beneficiaries. This approach gives preference to the rights of the owner of the policy. Indeed, the beneficiary's expectancy interest is subject to being extinguished at any time during the life of the insured if the owner simply changes the beneficiary, so the fact that a beneficiary's interest can be superseded by assignment of the policy is not particularly remarkable. Often an assignment is made to secure a debt. In such cases, some courts have held that the assignee's rights are superior only up to the amount of the debt, with any excess proceeds belonging to the designated beneficiary. Other courts have held that the creditor is entitled to all the proceeds, under the reasoning that the assignment itself functions as a change of beneficiary.

Most courts allow a person who has taken out insurance on his or her own life to assign the policy to anyone, even a party lacking an insurable interest. This result is defended on the ground that if the insured can designate any beneficiary desired, no reason exists to preclude the insured from assigning the policy to any particular assignee. Under the same logic, if someone has a policy on someone else's life, that person should be allowed to assign the policy only to another person possessing an insurable interest. Because one cannot validly purchase insurance on someone else's life without possessing an insurable interest in that life, allowing assignment of the policy to one lacking such an interest would frustrate the purposes of the insurable interest doctrine.

One area where assignments have become very important in life insurance involves a practice called "viatical settlement." Beginning in the 1980's, the AIDS epidemic led many insurers to include in their policies a mechanism through which an owner-insured who is terminally ill can receive life insurance proceeds prior to death. The somewhat more controversial practice of "viatical settlement," which is a particular kind of assignment, arose during the same period. The essence of the transaction is that a terminally ill owner-insured will assign his or her policy to a third party, a viatical settlement firm, in exchange for a lump sum payment, which will be the face amount discounted to present value. Some firms purchase the policies for their own account, while other firms function as brokers that, for a commission, match the insured with one or more persons willing to purchase the policy. Normally, the acquiring purchaser is designated as assignee and beneficiary, and the viatical company may obtain releases from previously named beneficiaries. Depending on the insured's life expectancy, the cash payment might range anywhere from 50% to 80% of the expected death benefit. Because the viatical firm will lack an insurable interest in the life of the insured, the viatical arrangement is permissible only if the insured is permitted by law to assign a policy on his or her own life to someone lacking an insurable interest in his or her life.

On the plus side, viatical settlement arrangements, like accelerated benefits, provide a means for insureds with terminal conditions to liquidate policies in order to meet immediate needs. The interests of designated beneficiaries are eliminated, but beneficiaries have no vested right to proceeds in any event. Moreover, the person who owns the policy should be the one to decide how her assets can best be deployed for the benefit of those who depend on the insured. In effect, from the beneficiary's perspective, a viatical settlement is little different in form from what would occur if the insured opted to change the beneficiary to her own estate. In addition, the viatical settlement arrangements give owner-insureds additional options; if a viatical settlement firm will provide a more generous benefit than the insurer would provide through accelerated benefits, the insured is better off with the viatical settlement option.

On the negative side, many have expressed concern that viatical settlement firms exploit the terminally ill by paying low benefits at a time when the owner-insured is in great need. For this reason, some advocate banning the viatical settlement industry altogether. In 1993, the National Association of Insurance Commissioners (NAIC)—an association of state insurance commissioners—proposed the "Viatical Settlements Model Act." The model act calls for the licensing of viatical settlement providers, regulatory approval of viatical settlement contracts to be used in the respective states, examination of the financial resources of the provider, disclosure by the provider to the owner-insured of alternatives to viatical settlement and other information, and other regulation. As of 2004, legislation based on the model act was enacted in 36 states. The premise of the model act is that appropriate regulation of viatical settlement arrangements is preferable to prohibiting the option altogether. See IV Nat'l Ass'n of Insurance Comm'rs, Model Laws, Regulations, and Guidelines 697–1 (2004).

[¶ 7,140]

f. Beneficiary disqualification

A principle that applies to all kinds of insurance is that no insured can recover proceeds for a loss that the insured has intentionally caused. It follows from this principle that a beneficiary who intentionally and unlawfully causes the death of the insured (or is an accomplice in the slaying) cannot receive the proceeds of the insurance. In some jurisdictions, the general rule also disqualifies all of the slayer's relatives, under the reasoning that otherwise the beneficiary might have an incentive to slay the insured for the benefit of the slayer's relatives. Typically exempted from this broad disqualification rule are the slayer's children if they are also the children of the victim. In contrast, there is authority for the slayer's relatives being disqualified upon a finding that allowing the relatives to receive proceeds would confer a significant benefit on the slayer.

Some jurisdictions have statutes that disqualify slayers, and a substantial number have adopted Uniform Probate Code § 2–803, which provides that the "felonious and intentional killing of the decedent" has the effect of revoking any "revocable ... disposition ... made by the decedent to the killer in a governing instrument," which includes a life insurance policy and its beneficiary designation. Even in the absence of a slayer statute, courts have long held that a beneficiary who kills the insured is not entitled to keep the resulting life insurance proceeds, based on the equitable doctrine that prohibits a wrongdoer from profiting by his or her own wrongful action. New York Mutual Life Ins. Co. v. Armstrong, 117 U.S. 591 (1886). The slayer statutes were enacted in response to some early judicial decisions that reached a different result in the case of slaying heirs who claimed their victims' estates under the intestacy statutes. Today, most states have slayer statutes that apply to property passing by intestacy or by will, but some states still rely on case law to establish the rules of beneficiary disqualification.

If the beneficiary kills the insured and is thereby disqualified, this does not mean that the insurer need not pay proceeds to anyone. In the ordinary case where the slaying beneficiary is not the owner of the policy, the disqualified beneficiary is treated as having predeceased the insured, which means that the proceeds go to any remaining primary beneficiaries or, if there are none, to the contingent beneficiaries. If there are no surviving qualified beneficiaries, most policies provide that the proceeds are paid to the estate of the insured. An alternative approach, followed by a very few courts, is to have the slaying beneficiary hold the proceeds as constructive trustee for the insured's estate. This approach is less desirable because it is less likely to fulfill the insured's intent, as expressed in the beneficiary designations, with regard to how the proceeds should be distributed. If the slaying beneficiary is the only named beneficiary, it is correct to pay the proceeds to the insured's estate, and this may explain why the rule continues to be articulated from time to time.

A different result might be reached if the murdering beneficiary purchased the insurance on the life of the insured and paid the premiums. It is often said that a policy of insurance purchased on the life of another with intent to murder the insured is void ab initio. The underlying rationale is that the purchaser of the insurance has committed a kind of fraud, which prevents a valid contract from coming into existence.

[¶ 7,141]

Problem

Kevin, a soldier in the U.S. Army, was the insured under two policies: a term life insurance contract issued by Reliable Insurance Company in the amount of $100,000, and a policy of term life insurance issued by Florida Mutual in the amount of $50,000. The Reliable policy named Kevin's wife Gina as the primary beneficiary, and Kevin's stepson Steven (Gina's son from a previous marriage) as the contingent beneficiary. At the time of Kevin's death, Steven was 13 years old and had lived with Kevin and Gina throughout the 11 years of their marriage. The Florida Mutual Policy also named Gina as the primary beneficiary, but it named Gina's sister Betty as the contingent beneficiary. Neither policy mentioned Crystal, Kevin's 14–year–old daughter, who was born out of wedlock before Kevin's marriage to Gina. Kevin had never lived with her nor acknowledged the relationship, which was established by DNA after Kevin's death. In his will, Kevin devised his estate to Steven, describing him as "my son." Kevin was murdered by Gina's 18–year–old lover at the direction of Gina. Gina was convicted of murder and was sentenced to life in prison without parole. The evidence also shows that Betty was estranged from Gina and had not had a conversation with her for at least seven years. Who is entitled to the proceeds of the life insurance?

[¶ 7,145]

g. *Impact of community property laws*

Ten jurisdictions—Arizona, California, Idaho, Louisiana, Nevada, New Mexico, Texas, Washington, Wisconsin, and (on an opt-in basis) Alaska—have community property laws. These laws vary, but their essence is that a husband and wife each own present, equal, vested interests in community property. Community property comprises all property acquired by the spouses during marriage except property acquired separately by one of them through gift or inheritance. When one spouse dies, the other has a right to one-half of the community property, with the other half belonging to the decedent's estate. The principal significance of community property laws for life insurance is that any insurance acquired with community funds affects the rights to the proceeds of the policies.

Whether life insurance is community property will depend on the time when the policy was acquired and the source of the funds that were used to purchase it. Generally, life insurance acquired after marriage with community funds is presumed to be community property, even if only one of the spouses is designated as the owner of the policy. Simply designating the noninsured spouse as a policy owner will not in and of itself rebut the presumption; there must be clear and convincing evidence that the policy was intended by the spouses to be the separate property of the policy owner under his or her sole control and discretion. Likewise, if one spouse applies for and is issued a policy of life insurance on his or her own life during marriage, pays the premiums out of community funds, and designates someone other than the other spouse as the beneficiary, the policy constitutes community property. If the estate of the spouse who applied for the insurance is the designated beneficiary or the beneficiary by default, the proceeds are also community property. But if one spouse purchases a policy of insurance on his or her own life during the marriage with community funds and designates the other spouse as the beneficiary, the proceeds are usually considered the other spouse's separate property on the theory that the insured-spouse has made a gift of his or her half of the community proceeds to the other spouse. By the same logic, if life insurance proceeds are community property, when the insured spouse dies first only one-half of the proceeds are includible in the deceased spouse's gross estate for estate tax purposes, regardless of whether the proceeds are payable to the estate, the surviving spouse, or some other beneficiary. Reg. § 20.2042–1(b)(2).

In a community property jurisdiction, the owner-insured's right to designate and change the beneficiary is not absolute. The owner-insured in a community property state who names someone other than his or her spouse as beneficiary on a policy that is purchased with community funds has, in effect, made a gift to the third party. If the owner-insured's spouse does not consent to the making of the gift, the spouse may challenge the beneficiary designation and recover either all of the proceeds for the community (during the insured's life) or one-half of the proceeds for the spouse (after the insured's death). Similarly, if the owner-insured elects a settlement option contrary to the wishes of the owner-insured's spouse, the spouse may be able to defeat the chosen option.

In community property states, because the spouse of a named policy owner may claim that the owner designated a beneficiary without the spouse's consent and therefore the spouse is entitled to a share of the proceeds, legislatures have provided insurers with a "safety net" for circumstances where the insurer, acting in good faith and without knowledge of adverse claims, pays the proceeds to the designated beneficiary. So-called "exoneration statutes" excuse the insurer from liability if a spouse makes a claim for proceeds paid to a third party where the insurer had no notice of the adverse claim and otherwise acted reasonably.

[¶ 7,150]

5. Income Tax Consequences of Life Insurance

If a policy qualifies as a "life insurance contract" for federal tax purposes, the policy receives unusually favorable treatment under the Internal Revenue Code. In general, both the cash value build-up inside the policy during the insured's life and the proceeds payable at the insured's death are exempt from federal income tax. This tax-favored treatment makes life insurance a more desirable investment than it would be if it were taxed in the same manner as other financial products.

[¶ 7,155]

a. *Exclusion from income of proceeds payable at death*

One of the most significant advantages of life insurance is that life insurance proceeds payable "by reason of the death of the insured" are excluded from the recipient's gross income in calculating federal income tax (and most state income taxes as well). I.R.C. § 101(a)(1). This is true regardless of who paid the premiums or who owned the policy, and regardless of whether the policy was an individual or group policy. Under some circumstances, benefits paid prior to the death of a chronically or terminally ill insured qualify for this exclusion as well. I.R.C. § 101(g)(1). In contrast, death benefits under an annuity contract are not proceeds of life insurance and do not qualify for the exclusion.

In general, when life insurance proceeds are paid under an optional settlement method, the amount that the insurer would have paid in a lump sum at the insured's death is prorated over the applicable payment period. This portion is viewed as principal which the beneficiary may exclude from gross income, but any interest on this amount (i.e., any payment in excess of the prorated amount) is taxable to the recipient as ordinary income. I.R.C. § 101(d)(1). For income tax purposes, it is irrelevant whether the life insurance policy is a single premium policy or is a more usual multiple premium policy arrangement. As long as the policy qualifies as a "life insurance contract" for tax purposes (see ¶ 7,170), proceeds payable at the insured's death are generally free of income tax. For a more detailed discussion of the income tax treatment of life insurance proceeds, see Miner et al., 2004 Tax Facts on Insurance & Employee Benefits (2004).

[¶ 7,160]

b. *Exclusion for cash value build-up*

If the life insurance policy meets the definition of a "life insurance contract" for tax purposes, the annual increase in the policy's cash value will not be included in the recipient's gross income for federal income tax purposes. I.R.C. § 7702(g). The logic of this rule is that the policy's cash value cannot be reached unless the owner surrenders or transfers the policy, which means that the inside build-up of cash value is not constructively received until the policy is surrendered or transferred. If the policy fails to meet the definition of "life insurance contract," the following will be taxable to the insured each year as ordinary income: the excess of (1) the sum of (a) the increase in "net surrender value" (i.e., cash surrender value less any surrender charges) during the year and (b) the cost of life insurance protection for the year, over (2) premiums paid under the contract during the year. I.R.C. § 7702(g)(1).

If the owner withdraws the cash value, this withdrawal will not be treated as gross income unless and until the amount of withdrawals and the dividends paid to the owner exceed the premiums and consideration paid for the policy. I.R.C. § 72(e)(5)(A). Likewise, a loan from the insurer out of the cash value and secured by the policy will not result in taxable income. I.R.C. § 72(e)(5)(C).

In the 1980's, as Congress began to close down various tax shelter arrangements for high-income taxpayers, life insurance companies began to market single-premium policies aggressively as an investment device that could generate tax-deferred earnings and tax-free access to accumulated cash values. Congress responded by imposing special guidelines that restrict the tax-sheltering advantages of single-premium policies. These guidelines appear in I.R.C. § 7702 and are discussed in ¶ 7,170.

[¶ 7,161]

Problem

Sarah is a 38–year–old female who owns a $200,000 whole life insurance policy on her own life. The policy does not pay dividends. Sarah purchased the policy ten years ago, and has been paying premiums of $1,800 per year. The cash value of the policy is now $16,500. Sarah has decided to let the policy lapse. Her options are: (1) to receive $16,500 as a lump sum cash payment; (2) to convert to a fully paid-up whole life policy with a face value of $40,000; or (3) to convert to a fully paid-up term insurance policy equal to $250,000 for 30 years. What option should Sarah choose? What factors might influence her choice of options?

[¶ 7,165]

c. *Transfers for value*

The most significant exception to the income tax exclusion for life insurance proceeds payable at the insured's death is the *transfer-for-value rule*. Under this rule, if the owner of a life insurance policy transfers it to another person, by assignment or otherwise, for "valuable consideration," the transferee must include in gross income the proceeds paid at the insured's death to the extent they exceed the consideration the transferee paid for the policy plus premiums the transferee paid to keep the policy in force after the transfer. I.R.C. § 101(a)(2). The consideration paid for the policy includes any cash or property transferred in the exchange plus the amount of any debt secured by the policy at the time of the transfer.

There are two important exceptions to the transfer-for-value rule. First, the rule does not apply if the transferee's basis in the policy is determined in whole or in part by reference to the transferor's basis in the policy. I.R.C. § 101(a)(2)(A). This exception would apply, for example, if the transferee acquired the policy from the transferor by gift, in which case the transferee's basis would be determined by reference to the transferor's basis. Second, the transfer-for-value rule does not apply if the transferee is a "permissible transferee." A permissible transferee is the insured, a partner of the insured, a partnership in which the insured is a partner, or a corporation in which the insured is an officer or shareholder. I.R.C. § 101(a)(2)(B).

[¶ 7,170]

d. The "life insurance contract" requirement

Prior to 1985, the definition of life insurance for tax purposes was a matter of common law. In determining whether a particular arrangement qualified as life insurance, courts generally insisted that it involve bona fide risk-shifting in the sense that the insurer must bear the financial risk of the insured's premature death, as happens when the proceeds payable at death exceed the cumulative value of the premiums plus interest. See Helvering v. Le Gierse, 312 U.S. 531 (1941). The underlying purpose of the rule was to distinguish life insurance contracts from contracts of deposit which are designed to pay a return to the owner, but never to pay more on account of the owner's death than the cumulative premiums plus interest.

In the 1970's and early 1980's, many high-income taxpayers took their taxable investments and converted them to life insurance contracts in order to take advantage of the tax deferral available for life insurance contracts. For example, a taxpayer might take $80,000 from a certificate of deposit or other taxable investment and purchase a life insurance policy with a $100,000 death benefit. The taxpayer might have no desire for more life insurance but merely be interested in exploiting the life insurance policy to convert a taxable investment into a tax-deferred investment.

To eliminate this abuse, Congress in 1984 revised the Code to provide that if proceeds of a life insurance policy payable at the insured's death are to qualify for the income tax exclusion of I.R.C. § 101, the policy must meet the statutory definition of a "life insurance contract." This means that the policy must be a life insurance contract under applicable state law *and* meet one of two alternative tests: *either* the "cash value accumulation" test *or* the "guideline premium and cash value corridor" test. I.R.C. § 7702(a). The "life insurance contract" test must also be met if the cash value build-up is to be exempt from income tax. These tests are complicated and are subject to some exceptions, but if a policy fails to meet the statutory requirements, the tax exemption for inside build-up of cash value and for proceeds from the beneficiary's gross income will be lost. In effect, Congress's purpose was to take private investment vehicles masquerading as life insurance and deny these vehicles the favorable tax treatment otherwise available for life insurance. Section 7702 applies to contracts issued after 1984. There is no need to describe the statutory requirements of § 7702 in detail here, since virtually all policies issued since 1985 are carefully structured to comply with those requirements.

[¶ 7,175]

e. Dividends

Dividends received by the policy owner are not included in gross income until the amount of dividends paid is more than the amount of premiums and any other consideration paid for the policy. Reg. § 1.72–11(b)(1). If the dividend is kept in an account maintained by the insurer, any interest paid on the account will be taxable income to the owner if the owner is entitled to withdraw the interest. The same rule applies to any interest payment made on proceeds held by an insurer. I.R.C. § 72(j).

[¶ 7,177]

Problem

Jim recently received a notice from Apex Insurance that because of good experience with his age cohort in his group term policy, he will be eligible for a $400 dividend on his policy and this will be used to reduce the normal expected premium of $650 to $250. Jim wishes to know if he will have to report this dividend as income for income tax purposes and, if so, whether it will qualify for the lower tax rate that now applies to dividends.

[¶ 7,180]

f. Exchanges

Certain life insurance exchanges are subject to special rules. Sometimes, for example, a policyholder may desire to exchange an existing life insurance policy for a new life insurance policy. Absent an exemption, such an exchange would be a taxable event, and the policy owner would have ordinary income to the extent the policy's value exceeds the premium and consideration paid for the policy (i.e., the basis). But the Code permits tax-free exchanges of life insurance policies, endowment contracts, and annuities in circumstances where the replaced policy and the new policy apply to the same person. I.R.C. § 1035(a).

[¶ 7,185]

g. Nondeductibility of premiums

In general, premium payments by the owner of a life insurance policy are personal expenses and are therefore not deductible. I.R.C. § 262(a). It makes no difference whether the premiums are paid by the owner of the policy or by another person on behalf of the owner; for example, the premiums paid by the owner's spouse for a policy on the owner's life are not deductible. (Nevertheless, the cost of group term life insurance provided by an employer for its employees is deductible by the employer as a business expense.) Moreover, interest paid on debt incurred to purchase or carry a life insurance contract is generally not deductible, although this rule is subject to some limited exceptions. See I.R.C. § 264(a), (d). The nondeductibility of premiums does not change in circumstances where the policy is procured for the benefit of a creditor, regardless of whether the debt is a business or non-business debt.

There are two situations where premiums may be deductible. First, a policy owner who transfers all ownership rights in the policy to a charity and continues to pay premiums may be able to deduct the premium payments as a charitable contribution, subject to the requirements of § 170. Second, premium payments required by a divorce decree or separation agreement may be deductible as alimony, subject to the requirements of § 215.

[¶ 7,190]

h. Life insurance provided in the employment setting

If an employer pays for life insurance owned by the employee, the employee receives compensation equal to the amount of the premiums paid. Reg. § 1.61–2(d)(2)(ii)(a). If the policy is a group-term life insurance plan, the value of the first $50,000 of life insurance coverage is generally exempt from taxation. I.R.C. § 79(a). Accordingly, many employers routinely offer group coverage as a fringe benefit, even though some individual employees might prefer to receive a different type of benefit or an equivalent value in the form of taxable wages.

[¶ 7,195]

i. Taxation of amounts received before death

I.R.C. § 72 governs the income tax treatment of amounts received during the life of the insured as proceeds from life insurance policies and endowment contracts. This provision applies to three different classes of payments: (1) payments of interest; (2) "amounts not received as an annuity"; and (3) annuities.

The first category is the simplest; interest payments are taxable in full. I.R.C. § 72(j). All payments that are not interest or annuities are "amounts not received as an annuity." Typically, these include policy dividends, lump sum cash settlements of cash surrender values and endowment maturity proceeds, and cash withdrawals and amounts received upon partial surrender of the policy. Reg. § 1.72–11.

Proceeds received during the insured's life are taxed under what is called the "cost recovery rule," which means that the proceeds are included in gross income only to the extent they exceed the investment in the contract, except that proceeds received from a life insurance policy that fails the "seven pay test" of I.R.C. § 7702A(b) and is therefore classified as a "modified endowment contract" (MEC) are taxed under different rules. There are some exceptions to the cost recovery rule, which relate to cash distributions received as a result of certain kinds of changes in the benefits of a contract. See I.R.C. § 7702(f)(7). The seven-pay test is complex: A life insurance contract will fail the "seven pay test" and become an MEC if the accumulated amount paid under the policy at any time during the first seven contract years exceeds the sum of the net level premiums that would have been paid on or before such time if the contract provided for paid-up future benefits after the payment of the seven level payments. I.R.C. § 7702A(b). Generally speaking, distributions from a MEC are treated as if the policy were a typical tax-deferred investment or retirement vehicle. For example, in much the same manner as an IRA where earnings are taxed at the time of distribution, distributions from a MEC are taxable as income at the time received to the extent the cash value of the contract immediately before the payment exceeds the investment in the contract. I.R.C. § 72(e)(10). As in the case of a tax-deferred annuity, except in special circumstances (e.g., the taxpayer becomes disabled, etc.), a 10% penalty tax is imposed on any amount received by a taxpayer under a MEC before the taxpayer reaches age 59½. The purpose of this rule is to prevent sellers of investment vehicles from disguising their products as insurance contracts in order to obtain tax advantages not otherwise available.

[¶ 7,200]

j. Dividends and interest on cash value

All dividends paid or credited before the maturity or surrender of a life insurance contract are tax exempt as a return of capital until the taxpayer has received an amount equal to the premiums paid. When the aggregate dividends plus any other amounts received tax-free under the contract exceed aggregate gross premiums, the excess is taxable as ordinary income. I.R.C. § 72(e)(5).

Interest on life insurance or endowment proceeds left with the insurer after maturity under an interest-only option is taxable as ordinary income at the time the interest is paid or credited. I.R.C. § 72(j).

[¶ 7,205]

k. Special rules for viatical settlements

If a death benefit (or any portion thereof) under a life insurance contract on the life of a terminally or chronically ill insured is sold or assigned to a viatical settlement provider, the amount received on the sale or assignment is treated as an amount paid under the life insurance contract by reason of the insured's death and is excluded from gross income. I.R.C. § 101(a), (g)(2)(A). A viatical settlement provider is defined as "any person regularly engaged in the trade or business of purchasing, or taking assignments of, life insurance contracts on the lives of insureds" who are terminally or chronically ill, provided that certain licensing and other requirements are met. I.R.C. § 101(g)(2)(B). A terminally ill person is one who has been certified by a physician as having an illness or physical condition that can reasonably be expected to result in death within 24 months following the certification. I.R.C. § 101(g)(4)(A). A chronically ill person is one who is not terminally ill but who has been certified by a licensed health care practitioner as being unable to perform, without substantial assistance, at least two "activities of daily living" (i.e., eating, toileting, transferring, bathing, dressing, and continence) for at least 90 days, or a person with a similar level of disability, or a person who requires substantial supervision to protect himself from threats to his health and safety due to severe cognitive impairment and this condition has been certified by a health care practitioner within the previous twelve months. I.R.C. §§ 101(g)(4)(B), 7702B(c)(2). There are various special rules that also apply to chronically ill insureds.

[¶ 7,210]

6. Estate and Gift Tax Treatment of Life Insurance

There are several situations where life insurance proceeds are included in the insured's gross estate for estate tax purposes. First, the proceeds are includible if they are payable directly or indirectly to the insured's estate. I.R.C. § 2042(1). For example, if the owner-insured arranges for the proceeds to be paid to a person other than her personal representative and that person is required to use the proceeds to pay obligations of the estate (e.g., debts, taxes, or administration expenses), the proceeds are deemed to be payable to the estate and are therefore includible in the insured's gross estate. Second, the proceeds are includible in the insured's gross estate if the insured held any of the "incidents of ownership" in the policy at the time of death. I.R.C. § 2042(2). An "incident of ownership" includes the right to any of the economic benefits of the policy, such as the right to change the beneficiary, to surrender or cancel the policy, to assign the policy, or to pledge the policy as security for a loan. Reg. § 20.2042–1(c)(2). Third, even if the insured did not hold any incidents of ownership in the policy at death, the proceeds are includible in the gross estate if the insured transferred the policy (or any incidents of ownership in the policy) within three years before death. I.R.C. § 2035(a). Taken together, the effect of §§ 2042 and 2035(a) is to draw life insurance proceeds into the insured's gross estate if the insured possessed any incidents of ownership in the policy at death or at any time during the three-year period before death.

With a bit of advance planning, it is usually possible to keep life insurance proceeds out of the insured's gross estate. If the insured already owns a policy on his or her own life, the owner-insured should consider transferring all incidents of ownership in the policy to another person. The transfer will result in a completed gift of the value of the policy, but the resulting taxable gift is likely to be considerably less than the proceeds that would otherwise be includible in the insured's gross estate at death. As long as the insured lives for at least three years after relinquishing all incidents of ownership (and assuming the proceeds are not payable to his or her estate), the proceeds will avoid the reach of the estate tax. This is true even if the insured continues to pay the premiums on the policy as they come due, since the premium payments are treated as gifts of cash to the new policy owner (and not as gifts of ownership interests in the policy).

If the insured assigns the policy directly to the intended beneficiary (e.g., the insured's spouse or child), there is a risk that the assignee might die before the insured and retransfer the policy to the insured, thereby incurring an unnecessary estate tax and frustrating the insured's original plan. To avoid this unwelcome outcome, the owner-insured should consider creating an irrevocable inter vivos trust so that the trustee can hold the policy and collect and distribute the proceeds at the insured's death. The terms of the trust should be carefully structured to make sure that the insured cannot reacquire any incidents of ownership in the policy. Thus, for example, the insured should be expressly prohibited from serving as trustee and from holding any powers or beneficial interests that might constitute incidents of ownership in the life insurance policy. However, the insured may continue to pay premiums on the policy. Both the initial transfer of the policy and any subsequent premium payments will be completed gifts for gift tax purposes, and may qualify for one or more annual exclusions if the trust beneficiaries are given appropriate withdrawal powers. (See ¶¶ 4,150 and 4,370).

If there is no policy presently in existence, the insured should consider arranging for the policy to be taken out by another person—either the intended beneficiary or the trustee of an irrevocable trust, as described above. The advantage of this approach is that the insured can avoid possessing or transferring any incidents of ownership in the policy. As a result, even if the insured dies within three years after the policy is taken out, and even if all of the premiums were paid by the insured, the proceeds will not be includible in the insured's gross estate. See Estate of Perry v. Commissioner, 927 F.2d 209 (5th Cir. 1991).

When the owner of a life insurance policy transfers the policy during life (or at death, in the case of an owner other than the insured), the value of the policy is its replacement cost. In the case of a newly-issued policy, the policy is valued at the full amount of the original premium, which may be considerably greater than the initial cash surrender value. See Guggenheim v. Rasquin, 312 U.S. 254 (1941). If the policy has been outstanding for some time, the value is generally equal to: (1) the unexpired premium at the date of the transfer, in the case of a term policy; or (2) the "interpolated terminal reserve" (i.e., the amount the insurance company is required to set aside under the policy to cover the risk of death) plus an adjustment for the unearned portion of the most recent premium at the date of the transfer. Reg. § 25.2512–6. If an employee makes a gift of his or her rights under a group term life insurance plan, the value is determined by using the lower of the cost determined under a table in I.R.C. § 79 or the actual cost of the insurance to the employer, provided the plan does not disproportionately favor key employees.

Note that § 2042 applies only to proceeds of insurance on the decedent's own life. If the decedent died owning a policy on the life of another person who survived the decedent, the value of the policy (determined as described above) is includible in the gross estate along with all the decedent's other property owned at death.

For more detailed discussions of the estate and gift tax treatment of life insurance proceeds, see Stephens et al., Federal Estate and Gift Taxation ¶ 4.14 (8th ed. 2002); Miner et al., 2004 Tax Facts on Insurance & Employee Benefits (2004).

[¶ 7,215]

7. Other Sources of Life Insurance

As noted above, private ownership of life insurance in the United States is substantial, but there is a program of public life insurance embedded in the Social Security system. In effect, the survivor benefit constitutes an annuity for eligible surviving family members of a deceased worker who was fully insured under the Social Security system. The private analog for this coverage is a life insurance policy that pays the face value of the proceeds at death but gives the beneficiary a settlement option in the form of an annuity. The survivor benefit under the Social Security system is discussed in ¶ 8,120.

If a worker dies as a results of a workplace accident, some limited benefits will be provided under the state workers' compensation program, which essentially mandates a range of insurance protections for workers. In several states, if the death occurs in an automobile accident, the mandatory first-party insurance will provide some minimum benefits to the decedent's family. Like the survivor benefit in Social Security, these are essentially government-mandated, limited life insurance protections that are financed privately.

[¶ 7,220]

8. Buying Life Insurance

Ironically, many people do a prodigious amount of research when they purchase a television or a mobile phone contract, but do little to inform themselves about a much more economically significant transaction—the purchase of insurance. The materials below explore several of the most important considerations in the purchase of a life insurance contract. First, however, it is helpful to understand the steps in the process of acquiring a life insurance contract.

[¶ 7,225]

a. *Steps in the process*

If, after the *initial contact* between the consumer and an insurance agent, the consumer desires to purchase insurance, the consumer will submit an *application* to the insurer. The application is normally a form prepared by the insurer. On the application, the consumer will be asked to make representations regarding matters that the insurer deems material to the risk. Frequently the agent will fill out the form after asking the consumer for answers to the questions, but the applicant must always sign the application, representing that the answers on the form are truthful, accurate, and complete. The application will usually be accompanied by the applicant's payment of the first premium.

At the time the agent takes the insured's application, the agent, if authorized to do so, will commonly issue a *binder* to the applicant. This document is also referred to as a "conditional receipt" or "temporary binding receipt." The binder forms a temporary contract of insurance between the insurer and the applicant immediately upon submission of the application; the formal policy documents will not be created and issued until a later date (and perhaps never, if the application is rejected). Ordinarily the binder states that the applicant is covered in accordance with the terms of the formal policy (which the applicant at this point has not seen) until such time as the insurer makes a decision on whether to issue the policy. If the insurer later decides to assume the risk, a policy will be issued dated as of the day of the application. If the application is rejected, the binder terminates and the applicant's first premium payment, if any, is returned. If the applicant dies while the application is pending, proceeds will ordinarily be paid in accordance with the terms of the binder. The insurer's purpose in giving the binder is to give the applicant something of value at the time of the application in the hope that this will deter the insured from withdrawing the application prior to the insurer's making a decision upon it. In contract law terms, the application is an offer (made by the applicant on the insurer's form) that the insurer can choose to accept or reject; until the insurer accepts the offer, there is no binding contract between the applicant and insurer—except for the temporary contract of insurance created by the binder.

After the application is submitted, the insurer will *evaluate* the application. This will ordinarily occur at the insurer's home office, and the purpose of the evaluation is to allow the insurer to determine whether it wants to issue a policy and assume the risk. The insurer will consider the information on the application, perhaps following up on any answers that raise special concerns. In individual life insurance, the insurer is likely to require the applicant to obtain a medical examination, which often will be conducted by a paramedic employed by the insurer who will make a visit to the insured's home. In some cases, more elaborate physical examinations are conducted.

If after investigation the insurer decides to assume the risk, it will *issue* the policy and arrange for it to be *delivered* to the insured. The policy's effective date will be stated on the face of the document; this date is ordinarily retroactive to the date of the application. Most of the documents will be standardized forms.

[¶ 7,226]

Problem

Maria has applied for a policy of permanent insurance on her own life in the amount of $50,000. She submitted the application on February 4, 2004, and she has since successfully passed the medical examination and has been approved for the best rate the company offers on the coverage. On March 13, 2004, Maria had her 28th birthday. It is now April 4, 2004, and the insurer wishes to issue the policy to her now, but with an effective date of February 4, 2004. Maria contends that this is disadvantageous to her, because she has lived through the last two months and feels that she would be paying a premium for two months of coverage that she clearly does not need. Is Maria correct?

[¶ 7,230]

b. *Choosing a company*

When purchasing a lifetime contract, the financial strength of the other party to the contract is of enormous importance. Life and disability insurance contracts may be in force for 30 years or more, so it is extremely important that the insurer have long-term financial stability. State-regulated guaranty funds exist to help bail out insurance companies that fail, but the uncertainty inherent in such relief efforts is well worth avoiding, and in some situations there is a very real possibility that insureds will receive less than the full benefits promised by their policies. Also, weaker insurance companies are unlikely to be able to give the insured the same value for her purchase as a stronger insurer can.

The most widely-known insurance company rating service is the Alfred M. Best Company, which publishes annual reviews of insurers.

Best's rating scale for insurers runs from A+ + for superior to D for poor. Much information, including rating information, is available on the A.M. Best website (www.ambest.com). Many academic and public libraries also subscribe to publications distributed by A.M. Best. Other rating services are Moody's Investors Services (www.moodys.com), Standard and Poor's Insurance Ratings Service (www.standardandpoor.com), and Weiss Research (www.weissratings.com). Sometimes, these other services will give an insurance company a higher rating than the Best rating. If, for example, an agent markets a policy and publicizes a high rating from a service other than Best, it is possible that the Best rating was omitted because it was lower, and thus it would be prudent to take a closer look at the company's financial strength. The company giving the consumer a quote should be willing to provide this information, as should any agent representing or recommending the company.

[¶ 7,235]

c. *Purchasing through an agent*

Through the 1990's, the predominant method of purchasing insurance involved intermediaries—either agents or brokers—who arranged the insurance purchase on behalf of the consumer. These intermediaries typically fit one of two categories: "captive agents" who sell the products of only one company, or "independent agents" (or brokers) who represent several companies at once and, therefore, sell the products of many insurers. Brokers typically have more limited authority to bind the insurance company, but the presumed benefit is that they have some incentive to place a consumer's business with the company that offers the most favorable terms. Both kinds of agents are "agents" in the legal sense (i.e., under the law of principals and agents), but captive agents typically have more extensive actual authority. Companies that use captive agents and direct-sales methods to reach consumers are called "direct writers," and companies that use independent agents are called "agency writers." In 2000, according to the Insurance Information Institute, the average independent insurance agency represented 4.8 life and health insurance carriers. However, almost half of all life insurance is placed by career insurance agents who work for one company only.

Like lawyers, doctors, engineers, and other professionals, insurance agents vary widely in competence. Some are excellent, and others are poorly informed about insurance in general and the nature of the products they sell. Relatively few agents know the content of the coverage of the insurance products they sell; this is because most insurance agents are trained to be salespersons, not to be technical experts in the products they market. An agent who is designated as a "Chartered Life Underwriter" (CLU) has passed a fairly difficult exam administered by the American College of Life Underwriters (www.amercoll.edu). This does not mean that the agent is a good choice, but it does show that the agent has put some extra effort into his or her work and should understand the business and the products better than the average agent. Other professional designations bestowed by the American College include "Life Underwriter Training Council Fellow" (LUTCF) and "Chartered Financial Consultant" (ChFC). Some agents also earn a financial planning certification, such as the "Certified Financial Planner" (CFP) designation from the Certified Financial Planner Board of Standards, Inc. (www.cfp.net).

Finding a good insurance agent is not easy, but a reference from business associates is often helpful. One approach is to choose the company first, and then identify an agent that represents that company, giving preference to the CLU designation. It is usually preferable to work with an agent who specializes in life insurance, as opposed to one who also sells automobile and homeowner's insurance. If a particular agent is recommended, a conversation with the agent about the consumer's own views on insurance should be revealing on whether the agent is compatible with the consumer.

Even if one finds a good agent, one should not expect the agent to be forthcoming about other financial investments which compete with insurance and may be better choices for the consumer. This is because commissions are central to insurance agents' compensation, and the commission method of compensation tends to skew agents' objectivity. When insurance agents are employees of individual companies, they are sometimes paid a salary but almost always receive a commission in addition to the salary—or sometimes in lieu of any salary. Brokers are compensated by commissions. To illustrate, commissions with term life insurance are typically small relative to whole life insurance, and this causes agents to try to sell whole life when term may be a better choice for the consumer. Also, commissions are "front loaded," meaning that a significant portion of a first-year premium on a whole life policy—often most of it—serves as agent compensation. This is one reason the cash value generated in the first year after a policy's issuance is very small, because much of the premium has gone to the agent who sold the policy.

[¶ 7,240]

d. *Other insurance distribution channels*

Most insurance is sold through agents, but a significant amount of insurance is sold through other distribution channels, specifically mail-order, telephone, and now the internet. Mail-order insurance has been around for many years, as some insurers sought to avoid paying for agents, which could enable the insurer to offer a better value to the consumer or make a higher profit. Of course, unless the policy is carefully evaluated, it is not possible to know whether the policy is a good deal or not. Telephone solicitations are predominantly used to generate leads, which are followed by written communication.

There are signs that growth in e-commerce and internet-based transactions may have a significant impact on twenty-first century life insurance marketing. At the very least, the advent of the internet has caused companies to reconsider their past marketing practices. As a result, companies that previously used only captive agents are now investigating direct writing techniques, the use of independent agents, and the selling of insurance through banks, employers, and various kinds of associations. As the distinctions among financial services institutions become blurred, banks are becoming more involved in insurance marketing than ever before (just as insurance companies are more involved in the banking business). Many studies forecast significant declines in the percentage of life insurance sold through traditional agents and a significant increase in the number of consumers who purchase insurance through the internet or who use the internet to get quotes on-line and follow up with offline purchases.

Indeed, there are dozens of websites that offer life insurance quotes. In 2004, a few examples included www.insurance.com, www.relia-quote.com, and www.intelliquote.com, but there are many others as well.

[¶ 7,245]

e. Calculating the need for life insurance

Determining how much life insurance one needs is not an effortless exercise. Indeed, because the future is uncertain, there is no absolutely correct answer to the question "how much insurance" one should purchase. Accordingly, some of the simple formulas that are sometimes recommended are not particularly helpful. One simple formula suggests multiplying one's annual salary by seven or eight, but this formula does not take into account one's special needs or obligations (or lack thereof) which can raise or lower the answer produced by the "salary multiplication" approach. Another approach focuses on income expected to be earned from the present until retirement age, including an annual increase for predicted salary increases, but this formula, like the salary multiplication approach, does not account for the special needs of beneficiaries. Purchasing enough insurance to cover current debts fails to consider the need for coverage to meet future expenses for items such as child care and college tuitions.

A somewhat more elaborate approach estimates short- and long-term needs and subtracts current resources to determine the amount of insurance needed. Short-term needs include end-of-life medical care, funeral expenses, and estate administration costs, as well as outstanding short- and medium-term debts (e.g., credit card balances, auto loans, and college loans) and a reserve for emergency expenses (e.g., repair of a car, home, or other items). While it may be easy to determine the outstanding amount of existing debt, estimating future medical expenses is highly speculative. To short-term needs must be added long-term debts, such as a home mortgage and the cost of children's college education. Estimating the cost of a future college education is another exercise in speculation, based on factors such as the type of institution (public or private), the annual rate of increase in tuition, room and board, and the length of time for which other assets might be accumulated or invested. Long-term needs include the cost of supporting a family over time (e.g., items such as food, clothing, utilities, recreation, etc.), which may vary quite a bit depending on one's personal situation. One approach starts with one year's worth of expenses and multiplies it by the number of years such support will be needed. This approach could be refined to include an assumed rate of inflation.

From the short- and long-term needs should be subtracted one's current resources (e.g., savings, mutual funds, stocks, bonds, existing life insurance, etc.). The calculation should include only assets that are liquid in the sense that they could be easily sold in the event of death. Total resources are subtracted from total needs to arrive at the amount of insurance that should be purchased. In many calculations, the resulting figure will be very high, which may indicate the importance of reviewing one's needs carefully to determine which needs are essential and which ones can be dispensed with if necessary to reduce costs.

[¶ 7,246]

Problem

Jack, age 42, and Jill, age 40, are husband and wife. They have three children: Beth, age 13; Mike, age 10; and Ginny, age 8. Jack is a computer technician with an annual salary of $60,000, and Jill is a junior high social studies teacher with an annual salary of $40,000. Both have excellent employer-provided health insurance and retirement plans. Also, as a fringe benefit at work, each employer provides Jack and Jill with life insurance coverage equal to one year's salary. Jack and Jill wish to provide sufficient resources in the event of either spouse's premature death to enable the survivor to maintain their current standard of living, pay the decedent's end-of-life expenses, and pay for a four-year college education for each child at State University, where the tuition is currently $6,000 per year. If any of the children wants to attend a more expensive private university, Jack and Jill feel that the child should bear the additional cost through summer work, loans, or scholarships. Jack and Jill currently have $15,000 in a checking account, another $20,000 in money market funds, and $100,000 in 401(k) retirement accounts and IRAs. They live in a $300,000 home with an outstanding mortgage of $220,000. Jack and Jill ask you whether they should purchase life insurance and, if so, how much. What advice would you give them?

[¶ 7,250]

9. Claims Processing in Life Insurance

When a life insurance policy matures at the death of the insured, the procedure for submitting a claim and receiving payment of the proceeds is normally quite simple. Depending on the terms of the policy, the insurance proceeds may be payable to the beneficiary in a lump sum or may be payable in periodic installments under a settlement option.

[¶ 7,255]

a. *Submitting a claim*

Knowing whether a loss has occurred in life insurance is one of the most unambiguous situations in all of insurance. Whether the insured is dead is usually easy to determine; the exceptions involve relatively rare situations where the insured's existence is prolonged through some kind of life support (so that the determination of death requires the exercise of medical judgment), or where the insured is missing and his or her whereabouts are unknown. In almost all cases, a death certificate is conclusive on the question of whether the insurer's obligation to pay proceeds is due. Normally, the beneficiary under the life insurance policy submits a proof of death (ordinarily the death certificate) to the insurer, and the insurer will pay the proceeds upon receipt of this proof.

Occasionally a question may arise about a beneficiary designation or whether a particular beneficiary is qualified to receive the proceeds (as is the situation where there is reason to think that the beneficiary might have deliberately brought about the insured's death). In these cases, the insurer will need to conduct additional investigation. If there are multiple claims to the proceeds, the insurer may choose to file an *interpleader*. This is a form of complaint where the insurer essentially sues every party making a claim to the proceeds, pays the proceeds to the court which then holds them in trust, and then asks the court for a judgment discharging the insurer from liability, leaving the disputing claimants before the court to sort out who is entitled to the proceeds.

[¶ 7,260]

b. *Amount payable*

In life insurance, calculating the amount of the proceeds is very simple. The insurer pays the face value of the policy, although with permanent insurance the outstanding amount of any policy loan will be deducted from the proceeds. If the insured dies during the grace period while a premium remains unpaid, the amount of the unpaid premium will be deducted from the proceeds. If the policy has an accidental death endorsement and the insured dies in an accident, the insurer will pay an additional sum in accordance with the endorsement's terms, which usually means the insurer pays twice the face value of the policy. One caveat is that permanent insurance can have a death benefit exceeding the face value if the policy has been in force for a sufficient period of time. This is because, as discussed earlier, in some policies the cash value may grow to an amount that exceeds the policy's face value.

Depending on the policy's terms, the beneficiary may have several options on how to receive the death benefits. The most common options include: (a) lump sum, where the insurer issues a check to the beneficiary for the full amount of the death benefit; (b) fixed payments, where the insurer makes periodic equal payments to the beneficiary until the proceeds are completely paid out, with interest accumulating on the unpaid balance; (c) fixed period, where the beneficiary chooses a period over which to receive payments, and equal payments are made to the beneficiary over that time, with interest accumulating on the unpaid balance; (d) annuity, where the beneficiary receives proceeds in equal payments for life, with the size of the payments based on the beneficiary's life expectancy; (e) retained account, where the insurer keeps the proceeds on account and pays interest on the funds, which can be withdrawn later by the beneficiary at any time.

In life insurance, the amount payable is not offset by sums received from other sources, such as claims against third parties, payments of proceeds under other insurance policies, or payments from the government. Similarly, the insurer is not subrogated to claims the insured might have against third parties. In contrast, in property insurance, if a third party causes the loss of an insured's property and the insurer pays for the loss, the insurer upon paying the loss ordinarily succeeds to the insured's claims against the third party and can pursue that party to secure reimbursement for its payment to the insured. In life insurance, if a third party causes the death of the insured, the insurer is not subrogated to any rights against third parties.

C. DISABILITY INSURANCE

[¶ 7,265]

1. Reasons for Purchasing Disability Insurance

The risk of losing earned income due to disability is generally quite high, and the reasons for purchasing disability insurance are correspondingly strong. However, the vast majority of workers in the United States do not have adequate coverage.

[¶ 7,270]

a. The purpose of disability insurance

Disability insurance is intended to compensate a person who, due to an accident or illness, is unable to earn all or part of his or her former income. In other words, the insurance payments are a substitute for part or all of the income lost due to an accident or illness. Interestingly, this purpose has a close nexus to life insurance. Disability insurance was first offered in the form of a waiver of premium payments under life insurance policies; if an insured under a life policy became disabled, the obligation to make periodic premium payments was waived. Shortly thereafter, life insurers added a periodic income benefit. Eventually, insurers separated the income benefit from the life policy, so that it became possible to purchase a policy of disability insurance.

[¶ 7,275]

b. Comparing life, disability, and health insurance

As discussed above, life insurance is designed to protect the insured's beneficiaries against the economic loss associated with the insured's premature death. At its core, life insurance covers the economic value of a human life, which is a function of the insured's earning capacity and the financial dependence of other persons on that capacity. In addition, as discussed above, life insurance can be structured as an investment vehicle. This function is very different from protecting against the risk that a dependent will suffer economic losses, and it is not something one can do with disability or health insurance. Similarly, one can use life insurance to make an end-of-life gift to a dependent that exceeds the dependent's reliance on the insured's earning capacity. In contrast, disability and health insurance indemnify loss and have no collateral investment or quasi-testamentary function.

The purpose of health insurance is to cover the costs of hospitalization or medical care resulting from illness or accident. Unlike the economic value of a life or a person's earning capacity, hospital and medical expenses are finite and easily measurable. Health insurance, at least as it originated as a commercial insurance product, indemnifies the insured against these losses by reimbursing the insured's out-of-pocket expenses. (Most modern health insurance plans function very differently; much of twenty-first century health "insurance" represents prepayment of expected medical services, as opposed to the insuring of unexpected, fortuitous losses.) In contrast, life insurance makes no similar effort to match proceeds paid with actual losses.

Disability insurance is similar to health insurance in that the same perils—illness or accident—are covered, but the two products cover different manifestations of those perils. Whereas health insurance compensates for the out-of-pocket expenses associated with hospital or medical services, disability insurance compensates for the insured's *loss of income* due to illness or accident. Life insurance is related to disability insurance in the sense that death is the most severe of all disabilities, but in life insurance, the principle of indemnity is weak. In disability insurance, the principle of indemnity is strong; insurers contract to pay less than a person's lost income, which helps ensure that the principle of indemnity (i.e., the benefit may not exceed the loss) is not violated. Many other provisions in disability insurance contracts can be explained as insurers' efforts to make sure that they do not pay proceeds for undeserving claims.

[¶ 7,280]

c. The nature of the risk

Every person eventually dies, but not every person becomes disabled. This does not mean, however, that the risk of death is greater than the risk of disability. At any given age during one's working years, the chances of becoming disabled and losing the ability to earn an income are much greater than the chance of dying at that age. Yet disability insurance is much less prevalent than life insurance (or, for that matter, health insurance). As Table 7–3 shows, an average worker at age 25 has a 44% chance of being disabled for three months or longer sometime during his working years, but the probability that this worker (if male; females have lower mortality) will die between the ages of 25 and 65 is only 15.3%. NAIC Mortality Tables, in ACLI Life Insurance Fact Book 2004, at 148–50. Moreover, the average duration of a disability lasting more than 90 days and starting at age 30 is 4.7 years, and the average duration increases for older workers. According to one estimate by the U.S. Department of Housing and Urban Development, 46% of all foreclosures on conventional mortgages are caused by disability, as compared to only two percent caused by the homeowner's death. ACLI Life Insurance Fact Book 2000, at 53.

The following tables, based on data from the 1985 Commissioners Individual Disability Tables B (85CIDB), illustrate these probabilities:

Table 7–3. Probability of Being Disabled for Three Months or Longer at Particular Ages Before Age 65

Age	Chances of Being Disabled for Three Months or Longer
25	44%
35	41%
45	36%
55	27%

Upon reflection, these numbers are sobering. A young person at the outset of a working career that may last 40 or more years has nearly a one in two chance of being disabled for three months or more sometime in his or her career. The 55–year–old may have a 10– to 15–year retirement horizon, but even this worker faces a more than one in four chance of being disabled for three months or more at some point before retirement. When the calculation is done for a partnership, the probability increases. For example, imagine three business partners, all 40 years of age. The probability that at least one of them will suffer a disability lasting three months or more before age 65 is nearly 80%. A three-month disability can cause extreme financial hardship; when longer disabilities occur, the financial consequences can be catastrophic. Consider the following:

Table 7–4. Probability of a One–Year Disability Lasting Longer

Age	Lasting 1 More Year	Lasting 2 More Years	Lasting 3 More Years
25	67%	57%	47%
35	76%	67%	57%
45	79%	72%	62%
55	81%	73%	62%

Table 7–5. Probability of a Three–Month Disability Lasting for Life

Age	Probability of Lifetime Disability
25	25%
35	28%
45	33%
55	40%

[¶ 7,285]

d. *Measuring the need for disability insurance in a household*

In assessing an individual's need for disability insurance, the objective is to ensure that if a disability should occur, the consumer will have sufficient assets to avoid significant financial dislocation, such as being required to sell her home, giving up plans to pay for a college education for her children, or abandoning her role as the provider for minor children, elderly parents, or other dependents. If the consumer has significant independent personal wealth, disability insurance may be unnecessary. If a household relies on one income, there is a need to insure that income unless the at-home spouse is in a position to begin work at nearly the same earnings level in the event the working spouse becomes disabled. If the at-home spouse is needed to care for the disabled spouse (or wishes to undertake this role), entering the work force may not be an option (or may be an undesirable option). In a two-income household, disability insurance may not be necessary if the family can survive on either of the two incomes, but there are risks in following this strategy. If both income earners become disabled in the same accident (an improbable but not inconceivable outcome), no family income is insured. If one spouse is disabled and that spouse is uninsured (even if the other is insured), the nondisabled spouse may wish to quit his or her employment to care for the disabled, uninsured spouse. This may be impossible, however, if the household depends on the earned income of the nondisabled spouse. Also, if the nondisabled spouse should die without a significant life insurance policy in force or become unemployed, the disabled spouse may become impoverished.

At-home spouses (or "homemakers") add great value to a household. If the at-home spouse becomes disabled, the economic disruption to a family is considerable when the services provided by that person must be purchased on the market. Some states with no-fault automobile insurance plans recognize the economic value of the homemaker and require auto insurance sold in those states to provide coverage in the event a homemaker becomes disabled. But most insurance companies do not sell policies that compensate a household for the services lost when a homemaker becomes disabled.

It is rare that a disability insurance policy fully replaces all of a disabled insured's lost income. If other sources of coverage (e.g., Social Security) or other assets are not adequate to make up the difference, some changes in spending habits will be necessary after the onset of the disability. How much disruption in lifestyle and economic aspirations a household is willing to tolerate, how much risk of that disruption is acceptable, and how much the household is willing to spend to be free of the risk are all questions that need to be asked and answered in determining how much disability insurance should be purchased. In making this determination, it is important to recognize the role, albeit limited, that disability insurance can play in preventing households from becoming destitute.

[¶ 7,290]

e. America's most underinsured risk

Of all the major causes of financial loss that can be managed, either fully or partially, through the purchase of insurance (premature death with surviving dependents; medical and hospital bills; legal liability to third parties; destruction of property, including one's home and personal belongings; lost income due to a disabling illness or accident), most consumers make a reasonable effort to insure against all of these perils except disability. Most consumers "underinsure" for the risk of disability.

Part of the reason that disability is an underinsured risk is that employers are less likely to offer disability insurance as a fringe benefit to their employees. In 1997, among medium and large employers, 87% offered life insurance and 76% offered health insurance as a fringe benefit, but only 55% offered a short-term disability insurance benefit, and only 43% offered a long-term disability insurance benefit. For large- and medium-sized employers of blue collar and service workers, the percentage offering life insurance fell to 81% and the percentage offering health insurance fell to 74%, while the percentage offering long-term disability insurance fell to 28%. As for small employers, in 1996 only 62% offered life insurance and only 64% offered health insurance, while the figure for short-term disability insurance was 29% and the figure for long-term disability insurance was 22%. U.S. Dep't of Commerce, Statistical Abstract of the United States tbl. 703, 704 (2000). (The reason the short-term disability coverage percentage is usually higher is that the category includes sick leave policies, where coverage can range from a few days to as much as a year.) The total proceeds paid by private disability insurance contracts has been approximately $6 billion annually, a relatively low number given the size of the U.S. workforce. ACLI Life Insurance Fact Book 2000, at 53. In contrast, life insurers paid approximately $102 billion in payments to beneficiaries, surrender values, policyholder dividends, and other payments in 2003. ACLI Life Insurance Fact Book 2004, at 104.

Part of the reason U.S. workers are underinsured for disability is that social insurance programs (such as Social Security and veteran's benefits) provide minimum, subsistence benefits when a person becomes disabled. These programs have deterred insurance companies from offering products to low and middle income consumers, which has the overall effect of depressing the supply of available coverage. Because government programs have significant gaps in coverage (as discussed below), the population as a whole tends to be underinsured.

Another factor is that the coverage seems expensive to most consumers, particularly because many people underestimate the likelihood that one day they will be disabled due to illness or accident. (Death and illness, in contrast, seem much more probable, which makes consumers much more likely to purchase coverage against these risks.) But consumers are not mistaken about the cost of the coverage. Disability insurance is, in fact, expensive, and this fact alone deters many consumers from purchasing it.

The reasons for the high cost of disability insurance relative to other insurance products is a function of the particularly acute moral hazard and adverse selection pressures in disability insurance. First, it is not easy for insurers to determine whether a person is able to return to work once disabled; denying or terminating benefits is a litigation-inviting strategy for an insurer, and this probably results in some doubtful claims being fully paid. Second, there are, unfortunately, insureds who perceive a claim upon a disability insurance policy as an easy way to fund an early retirement program. Indeed, history shows that disability claims rise during economic recessions. Feigned claims are not uncommon, and the transaction costs associated with addressing them drive up prices for all insureds. Unlike life insurance, in disability insurance the insured may have considerable control over whether a claim exists and on how long the period of disability will last.

[¶ 7,295]

2. Sources of Disability Insurance

There are several sources of disability insurance, both public and private. Among the most important of these are state workers' compensation programs, Social Security, employer-sponsored group plans, and private individual disability policies.

[¶ 7,300]

a. Workers' compensation

Many workers receive some disability insurance through workers' compensation programs. These provide compensation to a worker, or his or her family, for disability due to workplace accidents. Workers' compensation does not cover illness or non-workplace accidents, so this program cannot be viewed as full protection for the employee. When workers' compensation is available and applicable, the worker receives full payment of medical costs and a percentage of lost wages up to a specified ceiling. In the more generous programs, the percentage is likely to be around two-thirds of a worker's income, but every program has a maximum allowable benefit, which means that workers' compensation emphasizes protection of lower- and middle-income workers. Some injuries give rise to a lump-sum payment, and the survivors of a worker killed on the job will receive benefits as well. In some states, the amount of benefits rises with the number of the worker's dependents. The programs are coordinated with Social Security disability payments so that Social Security is the primary payor, with those payments being offset against any amount due under the workers' compensation program. Because workers compensation is administered by the states, the rules governing payment, benefit levels, and duration of coverage vary significantly depending on the state in which one lives; in fact, it is fair to say that there are 51 different workers' compensation programs in the United States (one in each of the 50 states plus the District of Columbia).

[¶ 7,305]

b. Social Security disability insurance

There is a public version of disability insurance provided through the Social Security system that is designed to provide benefits for workers who become disabled before they reach retirement age. In 1958, Congress enacted legislation to provide disability benefits under the Social Security program for individuals who became disabled after age 60. In 1965, Congress extended this protection to all participants in the program, subject to a one-year elimination period. In 1972, Congress enacted a built-in inflation factor for disability benefits, and this ultimately had the effect of eliminating the private market for low- and middle-income disability insurance. Total disability insurance benefits paid under the program in 2001 were $59.6 billion, which is nearly ten times more than private disability insurance proceeds paid during the same period. See 2002 OASDI Trustees Report (available at www.ssa.gov, the Social Security Administration website).

Before receiving benefits, a worker must satisfy the eligibility requirements. Although not particularly difficult to meet, the worker typically must be employed for 10 years before becoming eligible for the benefits. A worker earns up to four credits per year and needs 40 credits for eligibility; also, 20 of the credits must have been earned in the 10 years prior to the onset of the disability, although younger workers may qualify with fewer credits. The disability must be one that is severe enough to prevent the worker from being employed for at least one year, and the definition of what is a disability is strict; if the worker can adjust to other work while having the medical condition, the worker is not disabled. This is a stricter definition of disability than that which exists under most disability insurance policies purchased in the private market. The benefits paid under the Social Security disability program depend on one's prior earning history and the age at which the worker became disabled, as illustrated by the following chart:

Table 7–6. Disabled Worker's Annual Benefit Payments in 2003 at Various Salaries and Ages at which Disability Began, in Dollars

Salary on Date of Disability	$20,000	$40,000	$60,000	$80,000	$100,000	$200,000
Worker disabled at age 30	$ 9,828	$15,456	$19,572	$22,212	$ 23,676	$ 23,700
Worker disabled at age 40	9,420	14,616	18,984	21,420	23,292	23,712
Worker disabled at age 50	9,036	13,872	18,456	20,712	22,608	23,424
Worker disabled at age 60	8,628	12,960	17,448	19,932	21,624	22,224

Source: Calculations using formula provided at SSA website, www.ssa.gov.

The figures in this chart change annually, depending on the cost-of-living adjustments in the Social Security program.

Eligible children may also receive a monthly payment of up to one-half of the worker's disability amount, and there are also benefits for spouses and divorced spouses. Family maximums also exist, and these are in the range of 150% to 180% of the worker's benefit. As the table shows, disability benefits under the Social Security program are modest; without other savings, insurance, or investments, a worker and his or her family would have severe difficulty subsisting on these payments.

One program that, among other things, provides disability coverage is the Supplemental Security Income (SSI) program, which is administered by the Social Security Administration but is funded with general tax revenues. This program provides assistance for aged, blind, and disabled persons, providing cash to meet basic needs for food, clothing, and shelter. But SSI is very limited due to strict means testing and eligibility requirements. Even if one is eligible, the payments are minimal; the basic SSI payment in 2003 was $552/month for one person and $829/month per couple. Some states add funds to enhance this basic rate, but the amount can be reduced if someone else helps to pay for food and shelter.

[¶ 7,310]

c. *Other disability programs*

In a few states (e.g, California, New York, Rhode Island, New Jersey, Hawaii), there are programs that mandate short-term disability benefits for workers whose illness or injury is not caused on the job. These programs vary substantially from state to state.

Beginning in the 1970's, a minority of states enacted no-fault automobile insurance, which typically requires automobile insurance policies issued in the state to cover certain losses related to bodily injury (as opposed to property damage) incurred by the insured, without regard to fault (or lack thereof) on the part of the insured. These statutes typically mandate the payment of disability benefits to insureds who are disabled as a result of an automobile accident. In some of these states, the coverage extends to at-home spouses who are disabled, under the logic that the household will have to purchase services to substitute for those that would have been provided by the disabled at-home spouse.

There are some other discrete government programs that provide disability benefits in limited situations. The federal black lung program provides disability insurance to some miners; the national vaccine injury program provides some disability protection to persons injured by the receipt of a vaccine; some veterans' benefits programs provide compensation for service-related disabilities; civil service employees receive federal benefits under a separate program; railroad workers receive disability benefits under a program similar to Social Security; and some additional discrete programs can be found in various states and municipalities.

[¶ 7,315]

d. Group insurance

Some employers provide or offer disability insurance to their employees through a group policy. Disability insurance as a fringe benefit is much less prevalent than health insurance, and short-term disability coverages (up to two years) are more prevalent in the employment setting than long-term policies. If the employer provides the coverage as a fringe benefit, the benefits of this kind of coverage are taxable to the employee. Also, the coverage is not portable, meaning that if the employee changes jobs, the coverage disappears. One advantage of the coverage is that there is little or no underwriting involved in getting the coverage; the fact that the employee is well enough to work full-time is the crucial factor, and this means that even an employee who is in relatively poor health can qualify for the coverage.

Some group plans are offered through associations or organizations, such as a professional organization, a labor union, or a fraternal benefit organization. These policies tend to be cheaper than individual policies available in the private market, but some medical underwriting is typically required before the policy is issued.

Creditors sometimes market disability insurance, which will provide funds to pay off a loan in the event of the insured's long-term disability. Like life insurance sold in this situation, this kind of coverage is expensive and should generally be avoided unless the insured cannot qualify for coverage in the standard market. Because no underwriting occurs with these policies (and those who are unhealthy tend to purchase them in disproportionate numbers), the premiums can be several times higher than for other similar products. They are also not a substitute for protecting a family's comprehensive financial needs, as the policy will only serve to make payments on a specific loan in the event of disability and thus will only cover a portion of the family's monthly living expenses.

[¶ 7,320]

e. Private individual disability insurance

Today only about 20 insurance companies are active in the private disability insurance market, and it is hard for other companies to enter this market because it is difficult to obtain data on risk and loss experience. But having access to disability insurance is important for most families. Unless a family has sufficient assets or investment income to meet its cash-flow needs indefinitely, or unless an employee has adequate disability coverage through his or her employer, obtaining disability insurance in the private market is important.

A small portion of the individual market represents policies purchased by business owners. For example, a business owner may insure a key employee against disability, so that the owner can continue to pay the person's salary in the event of disability. Alternatively, the business might purchase the coverage to protect itself from a sudden loss of income or profits in the event of a key employee's disability. Businesses frequently buy a disability policy to cover business overhead expenses, including wages, in case the owner becomes disabled. Sometimes the coverage is in the nature of declining term coverage, which is designed to assist with loan repayments, salary contracts, and other similar expenses.

[¶ 7,325]

3. Common Terms of Disability Insurance

In discussing disability insurance, it is important to understand what constitutes a disability, as well as several other key terms that affect coverage and benefits.

[¶ 7,330]

a. Defining disability

It is a prerequisite to eligibility for benefits that the insured be "disabled," and this raises one of the fundamental difficulties in disability insurance. A professional football player who suffers a career-ending knee injury cannot play on the field, but there is much that he can do either in football—perhaps as, for example, a coach or in a management position—or in other endeavors, although probably at an income far below what he earned as an athlete. A concert pianist who loses a finger would be unable to perform the full classical repertoire, although the artist would presumably be able to teach music or engage in other remunerative activities. Neither the football player nor the concert pianist is completely disabled, but each person has suffered serious, disabling injuries that make it impossible for that person to pursue his or her original career. Determining at what point a person becomes "disabled" within the meaning of a disability insurance policy is frequently a difficult question.

Disability insurance's coverage provisions are defined in terms of the loss of one's capacity to work, not one's loss of income, and there are two basic kinds of disability coverage relating to capacity to work. Most disability policies are "occupational disability" policies, which provide coverage if the insured is disabled from transacting duties of the particular occupation in which the insured is then engaged. This is to be contrasted with the "general" disability policy, which provides that the insured must be unable to pursue any occupation for profit for which the insured is reasonably suited by education, training, or experience. Obviously, total helplessness is not required to demonstrate that the insured is entitled to coverage under an occupational disability policy because the test is whether the insured can perform the material and substantial duties of the job. If the insured after suffering an injury or illness is unable to perform the material duties of her actual occupation in substantially the same manner as before, the insured may recover under the policy. Conversely, if the only activities the insured can no longer perform are not material aspects of the business, the insured cannot recover. Thus, a teacher who suffers dermatitis is not totally disabled, but a surgeon who must terminate her practice of surgery due to dermatitis may well be totally disabled, even though the surgeon can do other work in the medical profession.

Of course, if the surgeon collects proceeds on account of her inability to practice surgery and then earns a substantial salary as a general practitioner, there is a possibility that the advent of the disability will enhance the physician's overall income. This kind of generous coverage is expensive, and thus it may be that the insured will want to tailor the insurance package so that the size of the premiums are reduced. A more cost-effective package might provide the "own occupation" coverage for a five-year term; at that point, the benefits would continue if the insured could not perform another occupation for which she is reasonably suited based on her education, training, and experience. Thus, the benefits would cease for the surgeon who could still practice medicine. If, however, the disability involved a brain injury that prevented the surgeon from engaging in the practice of medicine altogether, the benefits would continue after the "own occupation" period of coverage terminated. Thus, a common configuration of coverage in disability policies is to combine occupational disability coverage for the first 12, 24, or 60 months of the policy with general disability coverage coming into effect thereafter. This kind of policy eventually switches the more generous occupational coverage to the more strict general coverage. Part of the logic of this arrangement is that during the initial period the insured will have enough time to find employment for which the insured is reasonably suited, despite being disabled from the prior employment.

With respect to general disability coverage, most courts have also concluded that total helplessness is not required to establish total disability under a general disability policy, and thus the fact that the insured continues to do some work in order to subsist does not, by itself, bar the insured's recovery. The focus is on whether the insured can or cannot perform the material and substantial acts necessary for any occupation. Courts look at all the circumstances, including the insured's occupation, education, training, and the nature of the injury.

Some policies, particularly older ones, require that the disability be "total and permanent." The permanency requirement is not as prevalent today, but where it exists most courts have interpreted the test to require that the disability be one that will persist for a long, indefinite period of time. A few decisions have insisted that the disability be one that is likely to continue for the remainder of the insured's life.

[¶ 7,335]

b. *Elimination period*

It is common for disability policies to have what is called an "elimination period" of six months, or perhaps even a year. Once a disability begins, the insured will not collect payments until the elimination period expires. It may be possible for the insured to elect a shorter elimination period, but this will come at the price of a higher premium. This period functions much like a deductible in property insurance. The insured essentially self-insures for the initial months of disability, just as an insured must pay the first dollars of a property loss out of his or her own pocket. Because the elimination period is a cost incurred by the insured, it functions to deter the insured from voluntarily incurring a loss in order to collect insurance proceeds.

[¶ 7,340]

c. *Renewability*

Disability insurance comes in one of two forms with respect to the renewability of the coverage—noncancellable policies and guaranteed renewable policies. Under both forms, the insured can renew to age 65, but noncancellable policies also promise not to raise the rates up to age 65. In other words, noncancellable policies give insureds the right to continue coverage by continuing to pay premiums, meaning that the insurer cannot unilaterally change the premiums or benefits. Guaranteed renewable policies are automatically renewed with the same benefits, but the insurer can increase the premium charged if the premium changes for the entire class of insureds. Noncancellable policies are more prevalent in the market, but sales of guaranteed renewable policies have increased in recent years relative to noncancellable policies. The premiums for guaranteed renewable policies are lower, and their increasing popularity no doubt reflects the current conditions in the market for disability insurance.

[¶ 7,345]

d. Benefit period

Unlike a life insurance contract, a disability contract will have a provision stating how long benefits are to be paid. This may be a term of years (e.g., one year, two years, five years, ten years), the period of years until the insured reaches age 65 (or another age, such as 65 or 70), or the rest of the insured's lifetime. Obviously, the longer the period selected, the higher will be the premium. If cost of the coverage is a concern for the policyholder, one might consider a five-year benefit period, instead of a policy that provides coverage for a lifetime. The rationale is that most disabilities resolve themselves within five years; the insured either recovers or dies. Of course, should one opt for the five-year benefit period and survive it without recovering, the financial consequences can be severe, although the insured and his or her family will have had at least some period of time to prepare for this contingency. Shortening the benefit period to two years in order to save premium dollars is a questionable strategy because a large percentage of disabilities last beyond two years.

[¶ 7,350]

e. Recurrent disability

Most disability policies will have some kind of provision that addresses how the insurer will cover disabilities that recur from the same accident or illness. Normally, this clause states the length of time that must elapse between disabilities from the same accident or illness in order for the disability to be considered a separate disability for purposes of the coverage. This can be favorable for the insured in cases where the insured is disabled, seems to recover, and returns to work for a few days only to discover that he or she is not ready to work. The recurrent disability clause will prevent a second elimination period from being applied to the employee's second period of inability to work. The clause can be favorable to the insurer in those instances where a worker under a policy with, say, a two-year benefit period collects benefits for a full two years, returns to work for a few days, and then goes off work again due to the same disability, claiming that a new two-year period has commenced.

[¶ 7,355]

f. Waiver of premium

Just as life insurance policies may waive premiums while the insured is disabled, disability policies also typically contain a waiver of premium provision that eliminates the insured's need to pay premiums during the period of disability.

[¶ 7,360]

g. Residual disability

In most disability policies, disability is an "either-or" proposition; either the insured is totally disabled, or the insured is not disabled. Some policies, however, include the equivalent of a "partial disability" clause that pays a percentage of lost income in the event that the insured is prevented from working a full-time job but is still able to work on a limited basis. One advantage of this provision is that it encourages a disabled insured to return to the workplace even if he or she is unable to work sufficient hours to earn the same income that was received during the pre-disability period. It also protects against a total loss of disability insurance benefits if the insured is able to work only one or two days a week after recovering from an illness or accident.

[¶ 7,365]

h. Exclusions

Like most health insurance policies, disability insurance policies often contain an exclusion for preexisting conditions. Most policies provide for a period of two years (although the length of the period can vary) during which benefits will not be payable for disabilities that arise from illnesses or health conditions that first manifested themselves prior to the policy's effective date. In other words, coverage extends to disabilities arising from conditions that become manifest after the policy becomes effective. Many policies limit the preexisting condition exclusion through the use of a "look-back" provision, which means that if the condition was manifest prior to the look-back period but not during the look-back period, a disability arising from that condition after the policy's effective date will not be excluded from coverage. Assume, for example, that the look-back period is two years. Any disability that appears after the policy's effective date and arises from a condition that existed up to two years before the effective date is presumed to be the same condition, i.e., it is presumed that the condition was operative on the policy's effective date and is therefore outside the coverage. However, conditions that existed prior to the two-year period but were inoperative during that period are presumed to be unrelated to a disability arising after the policy's effective date. As one might expect, this exclusion is fertile ground for disputes between the insurer and insured.

Many policies contain standard exclusions for disabilities incurred as a result of an "act of war." Some contracts exclude coverage for disability due to suicide or self-inflicted injury, disability resulting from the use of drugs or alcohol, and disabilities resulting from criminal conduct. Some contracts have a provision limiting coverage for disabilities associated with mental illness unaccompanied by a physical illness, and some policies make clear that incarceration for a crime is not the equivalent of a disability. Other exclusions are possible as well.

[¶ 7,370]

i. *Optional provisions*

Most insurers offer several optional benefit provisions that may be helpful to particular insureds. One option that should be considered is the *future purchase option*. Under this endorsement, the insured is guaranteed the option to increase the amount of coverage at predetermined intervals. If the applicant expects to need more coverage in the future (e.g., because of increased financial obligations arising from additional dependents, larger debts, etc.) or desires some protection against future health complications that would make adding new coverage more difficult, this is an option that the applicant should consider.

Some policies have a provision that reduces the length of the elimination period if the insured is confined in a hospital. This helps the insured with his or her additional expenses due to the hospitalization. In addition, because the elimination period is designed to discourage false claims, the hospital-confinement provision recognizes that a false claim is probably not being made if the insured is confined to the hospital.

Just as life insurance sometimes includes additional benefits in the event that the insured perishes in an accident, disability insurance sometimes includes additional benefits if dismemberment or a loss of bodily function (such as sight, hearing, etc.) occurs. The benefit will normally be based on a multiple of the monthly payment provided under the policy. Sometimes a disability policy will also contain an accidental death benefit, which is payable to the insured's designated beneficiary.

Some companies offer a cost-of-living rider, which increases the amount of the benefit according to a formula designed to offset the impact of inflation. If one is purchasing a policy at a young age which is designed to stay in force until retirement, this rider is an important provision to preserve the real value of the policy later in life. If one is purchasing a policy with a short benefit period or if one expects to be able to tap other resources later in life to help with family finances (such as a spouse's rising income or an inheritance), this rider is less important.

[¶ 7,371]

Problems

1. Tiffany is a brain surgeon, and she has a disability policy issued by Ace Insurance Company. By all appearances, Tiffany looks healthy, but she is discovered to be a carrier of the hepatitis B virus, and under the rules of the medical licensing authority in her state, she is barred from performing surgery without a patient's informed consent, which has never been given to a doctor in her situation. She is physically able to perform the duties of a surgeon. Is she disabled and entitled to proceeds under her disability policy?

2. Bart, formerly a lawyer, has been disbarred for misuse of client funds. Bart now claims that he was disbarred because he was disabled by attention deficit disorder and chemical dependencies, all of which impaired his ability to practice law. Bart has a disability policy. Is Bart entitled to proceeds under the policy?

3. Modern disability policies define disability in terms of the insured's capacity to do work, instead of in terms of the insured's loss of income. Because the purpose of the coverage is to replace lost income, would it make better sense to define disability in terms of lost income instead of capacity to do work?

4. Kara is a recent law school graduate who is beginning her career as a lawyer with the State Attorney General's Office. She will have a heavy caseload and expects to try at least fifteen cases in each of the next two years. She is interested in disability insurance. She is single, with no dependents, and has no expectation that this will change soon. What kind of disability coverage terms would best serve her interests?

[¶ 7,375]

4. Tax Consequences of Disability Insurance

Disability payments are not subject to federal income tax if the individual insured pays the premium, but the benefit is taxable as ordinary income to the employee if the employer provides and pays for the coverage as a tax-exempt fringe benefit.

[¶ 7,380]

5. Procuring Disability Insurance

The process of obtaining a disability insurance policy is very similar to the process for individual life insurance. The applications will be very similar, and will seek information about the insured's income, occupation, health status and medical history, gender, and other coverage sought or in existence. The individual disability market requires extensive underwriting. The applicant's medical information will be reviewed for the purpose of assessing the individual's risk of becoming disabled. The applicant will be asked to supply medical information and will usually be required to undergo a medical examination. As one would expect, persons with chronic conditions are typically charged higher premiums or are issued policies that exclude coverage for disabilities caused by the existing condition.

The insurer will be more interested in the applicant's income than is typically the case in life insurance. In life insurance, the applicant is presumed to have an unlimited insurable interest in his own life, and thus the maximum coverage that the insurer is willing to issue will be substantially larger than the insured's present income or net worth. Moreover, although there are exceptions to this generalization, most applicants for life insurance do not procure policies at a time when they are contemplating self-destruction. In disability insurance, the policy is designed to replace lost income in the event of disability, and it is thus important that the insurer have an accurate sense of this potential loss. In some instances, the insurer may seek to review the insured's tax returns in order to assess information shown on the application. Note also that the kind of income which the insurer is willing to insure is *earned* income. Unearned income, such as income on investments and returns on property, continues in the event of the insured's disability and is therefore not insurable.

Because of strict underwriting in the individual market, it is often easier to obtain coverage under a group disability insurance policy. Such coverage typically has fewer limitations and exclusions. Employers offering the coverage may purchase the group plan from an insurer for the benefit of their employees, but some large employers self-insure their employee groups for the disability risk.

What factors should the insured consider in purchasing disability insurance? First, determine the amount of coverage that the insured (and his or her spouse) will need if the insured becomes disabled by adding up monthly expenses that must be covered. The resulting amount should be reduced to reflect other sources of income (such as through an employer-provided disability benefit or the Social Security system). Second, determine how long the insured will need the benefits. If, for example, the insured has a spouse whose income will go up in future years or if the insured expects to receive an inheritance, the term may not be as long as a lifetime. Third, determine how long the insured can wait for payments to begin. Accumulated assets may make it possible to have a longer elimination period. Fourth, evaluate the importance of residual coverage and guaranteed renewability. For many people, paying an extra premium to purchase a noncancellable contract is a worthwhile investment, as is purchasing coverage that pays proportionate benefits in the event of partial disability. Fifth, evaluate the importance of a future purchase option and a cost-of-living rider. This will depend in large part on the age of the applicant and expected future coverage needs.

[¶ 7,385]

6. Claims Processing in Disability Insurance

The process for submitting a claim and receiving payment of proceeds is more complicated in disability insurance than the equivalent process in life insurance. Life insurance has a maximum of one loss event per policy, whereas disability insurance may involve multiple claims submitted over a longer period. Also, unlike the determination of death in life insurance, determining whether a disability exists involves the application of contract language to what may be a complex set of facts, and this will ultimately require some subjective assessments.

[¶ 7,390]

a. Submitting the claim

The procedures that an insured should follow in submitting a claim are set forth in the disability insurance policy. Notice of the disability must first be given to the company, and the policy will contain deadlines for when this notice must be given as well as other procedures that must be followed in submitting the claim for benefits. Typically, the notice must include information identifying the insured, the dates and nature of the disability, information on treatment received by physicians and other health care providers, the expected duration of the disability, and other information. At some point, a physician's certification and examination may be required. The insurer will investigate this submission and may ask for additional information.

[¶ 7,395]

b. Amount payable

Once the finding of disability is made, the calculation of benefits is relatively straightforward. The amount of the proceeds will ordinarily be determined by a formula based on a specified percentage of the insured's income at the time of the disability or by resort to a schedule of benefits based on the nature of the disability. Where the amount turns on income, the amount of the insured's monthly benefit is typically the lesser of a percentage of the insured's income (usually 50% to 80%) or a specified dollar amount. If the percentage is 100%, the insurance is very expensive due to the "moral hazard" problem, i.e., the increased risk to the insurer that dubious claims will be presented. If reimbursement is less than 100%, becoming disabled will entail some economic hardship; insureds will try harder to stay in the workforce if they can earn more money by doing so. Similarly, if the insured becomes disabled, the insured will have an incentive to recover and resume work promptly so that the insured's full income will be restored.

Unlike life insurance, some disability insurance policies have provisions that prevent combining the coverage of multiple policies. In some formulations, the clause allows the insurer to reduce the amount of the coverage if the insured is found to have more disability insurance than is justified by his or her current earnings. The point of these clauses is to eliminate the risk that a person might receive a windfall from being disabled, which, if it were possible, would encourage false claims (or encourage the procuring of multiple policies with the intent to submit a false claim at a later time in order to profit at the insurer's expense).

Disability policies vary as to whether benefits are coordinated with payments received from other sources of coverage, such as government disability programs. Under some policies, the insurer pays benefits in addition to whatever is recovered under other forms of protection and the availability of other benefits does not reduce the insurer's obligation. Other policies, however, coordinate payments with Social Security disability benefits and workers' compensation payments, and may even require claimants to apply for Social Security disability benefits. To the extent a claimant obtains benefits under other programs, the payments under the long-term policy are reduced dollar-for-dollar by such benefits. As one would expect, the offset provision reduces the insurer's risk and should result in some reduction in the premium charged for the coverage.

It is common for policies to link the definition of disability to the insured's continued receipt of medical care for the disabling condition. If the disability ends, the payment of proceeds should also end; by requiring the insured to continue to consult with a physician, the insurer has some protection against the insured recovering and nevertheless continuing to collect benefits. An interesting question is whether the insured should be required to submit to particular medical procedures in order to cure the disability. In Heller v. Equitable Life Assurance Society, 833 F.2d 1253 (7th Cir. 1987), the Seventh Circuit held that a board-certified cardiovascular surgeon who had developed carpal tunnel syndrome could not be compelled to undergo surgery on his hand as a condition for continued payment of disability benefits. The policy's requirement that the insured be under the regular care and attendance of a physician, a common clause in disability policies, did not require the insured to undergo what the court viewed as an invasive and somewhat risky procedure. It was also important to the court that the policy did not by its terms specifically require the insured to submit to treatment in order to receive benefits. *Heller* did not address the question of the extent to which an insurer can require medical treatment under the terms of the policy as a condition for the payment of proceeds. It seems reasonable to allow an insurer to condition benefits on the insured submitting to routine, low-risk medical care. Whether an insurer could insist on the insured submitting to more risky, invasive procedures is more troublesome. On the one hand, public policy considerations suggest that the insured's contract rights should not be so conditioned, but on the other hand it is not unreasonable to argue that insurers who commit to pay substantial sums of money should be allowed to condition benefits on substantial efforts by insureds to mitigate losses.

Chapter 8

RETIREMENT PLANNING

A. INTRODUCTION

[¶ 8,000]

1. Overview

Most people in industrialized nations tend to think of age 65 as the normal time for retirement, the stage in life when work is put aside and life enjoyed. These are, we are told, one's "golden years," a time to travel, to enjoy children and grandchildren, to read and write, to play bridge and play golf, a time to do volunteer work and visit with old friends, a time to reflect on life and life's journey. But for many people this vision of retirement is a chimera, for it is a vision of retirement that must be paid for, and the money to pay for it must be accumulated during the forty or fifty years that most people spend in the workforce as an employee or a self-employed worker.

Some of that money, of course, will come from Social Security, and, for many Americans, some of it will come from home equity. But Social Security, even if combined with home equity, will not replace a sufficient portion of pre-retirement income to allow most people to continue to enjoy their pre-retirement standard of living after they stop work. Thus, most people will have to supplement Social Security with other income. Indeed, a popular metaphor to describe the income sources for retirement is a "three-legged stool," with Social Security being just one of the legs. The other two legs are private savings (which includes home equity) and benefits from employer-sponsored retirement plans.

We will see in this chapter, however, that the three-legged stool is not a particularly apt metaphor for many Americans. For one thing, the private savings leg is pretty wobbly for most Americans, who are not noted for being among the world's great savers. Thus, for people with retirement plan income and Social Security, a better metaphor might be a pair of stilts. But less than 50% of Americans will reach retirement age with meaningful benefits from retirement plans. For these Americans, who rely primarily on Social Security, the appropriate metaphor might be the pogo stick or perhaps more apt, one financial crutch. But in this chapter we will also see that metaphorical retirement-income furniture may have more than just three legs: retired people may derive financial support from part-time employment, from family, from church, from government, from private programs for the elderly, and even from discounts for goods and services. But of all the messages in this chapter, one stands out: workers should save a significant part of their income during their working years for retirement, and employer-sponsored retirement savings plans should be the backbone of that savings plan.

One can think of retirement planning as involving three tasks: assessing retirement financial targets and formulating a plan to meet those targets; accumulating assets to meet the financial targets; and drawing down those assets during retirement. We can view these tasks as three legs in a journey, taken one at a time; indeed, the idea of three separate legs of a journey provides much of the organizing structure for this chapter. But this is a bit misleading, for the legs of the journey need not follow in a sequence but may, like time and space in Einstein's universe, overlap: accumulation often begins before meaningful assessment of retirement needs, and for some can continue after retirement has started; moreover, retirement needs, goals and strategies must be reassessed periodically in light of changing circumstances—again, sometimes after retirement has started.

[¶ 8,010]

2. A Policy Perspective on Retirement Planning in the United States

The Employee Benefits Research Institute in Washington, D.C. conducts an annual Retirement Confidence survey. The 2004 survey shows that most Americans are confident that they can retire comfortably. But the survey also shows that only about 60% of working Americans are currently saving for retirement and many of the savers are far behind where most financial experts think they should be. Perhaps even more alarming, the survey found that only 40% of Americans have attempted to calculate how much they need to save to live comfortably in retirement and approximately one third of these did not know or could not remember the result of their calculation. In other words, by and large Americans have an optimistic view of their financial prospects in retirement even though the actual picture is discouraging.

Why do Americans think things are so good when they are in fact so bad? Perhaps the primary reason is that they are using what some people have called the "looking around" model of retirement planning. What this means is that they look around at their parents and older co-workers and friends who are entering retirement now and they see that they are doing okay even without extensive planning. But the generation they are watching spent their working years in a different environment, one in which many employers sponsored mandatory pension plans (with benefits in the form of an annuity) and health care programs for retirees.

They were a generation that saw home equity values rapidly rise. And they were a generation that could receive unreduced Social Security benefits at age 65 and that have had their Social Security benefits annually indexed to a formula that probably overstates the effects of inflation on retirement income.

The world for today's workers is different. Fewer employers sponsor traditional pension plans and fewer still provide retiree health benefits. The minimum age at which a retired worker becomes eligible for unreduced Social Security benefits is rising, and Social Security's indexation formula will likely be modified to limit future benefit increases. Today's workers will probably not see housing values increase as much as they did during their parents' working lives.

What does all this mean? Do all workers need to plan for retirement? Whom should we be concerned about and what should we be doing?

We can start answering these questions by observing that there are two groups of people who do not need to save for retirement: those with substantial assets from inheritance or through extraordinary good fortune in the labor market (think of professional athletes, performers, executives at major corporations), and habitual savers who even without special savings goals such as retirement income will invest substantial portions of their income during their working lives. It is not that such people do not need to engage in financial planning for retirement but rather that they will be reasonably well prepared for retirement even without much planning.

We also may not need to worry about those people who have consciously opted to live for today and risk a reduced standard of living in their retirement years. We might call this Travis–McGee syndrome, after the boat-bum hero of John D. McDonald's great mystery novels, who takes his retirement in chunks whenever he is financially flush and takes on new jobs when he runs out of money. Some such people may anticipate dying before retirement or may make a rational choice to accept a lower standard of living in their retirement years in exchange for a higher standard of living during their working years. Arguably, public policy should not focus on trying to persuade such people to make different decisions, although the possible future societal burden of providing even minimal public assistance to such people in old age may be sufficient reason to be concerned about this group's failure to save for retirement.

Finally, there are the working poor, many of whom are simply too impoverished to save much for retirement. Rather than plan for retirement, many of the working poor cope with old age. Carol Stack, an urban anthropologist who teaches at the University of California at Berkeley, recently testified before the Department of Labor that in her ethnographic studies she

> observed people who have see-sawed in and out of low-skilled jobs in the service sector, immigrants who have competed for those same jobs, and

divorced mothers who have toggled back and forth between work and welfare. For these hard working people there may be no place in their lives for a vocabulary of retirement, no word for it, no room to even think about it. The idea of retirement itself, and certainly the idea of planning for it, are alien to their experiences.... Rather than planning for retirement, they worry about how to cope with old age and the illness and the declining opportunities and immobility that aging brings. [U.S. Dept. of Labor Advisory Council on Employee Welfare and Pension Benefit Plans, Report of the Working Group on Retirement (2001).]

Assuming that there should be a societal response to the problem of lack of financial preparedness for retirement, what should the response be? At one end of a continuum of possible responses is the expansion of Social Security or a mandate that all employers adopt retirement benefit plans for all of their employees. At the other end of the continuum is some sort of governmental effort to educate working people about the importance of planning and saving for retirement. The former solution does not seem in keeping with current political trends. We are currently experimenting with the latter solution, and although there is some evidence that education helps at the margins, there is also evidence that education is simply not sufficient to cajole or scare many people into adequate planning and saving. And as the baby-boom generation rapidly approaches retirement without adequate savings, it may be too late to rely on education and voluntary savings, at least for members of that generation who lack the means to provide for a comfortable retirement.

At any rate, politics, ideology, and public policy all play important roles in the shifting governmental responses to the financial problems of supporting the elderly in retirement. And perhaps somewhere in the intersection of politics, ideology, and public policy, we will discover a solution to this stubborn problem, a problem that will only get worse as our scientific ingenuity extends life expectancy. As a society, or perhaps as a species, we will need to develop commensurate social ingenuity.

[¶ 8,020]

3. ERISA

Some of this chapter will discuss the Employee Retirement Income Security Act of 1974 (ERISA), a comprehensive federal law regulating the provision of employee benefits by private-sector employers. Prior to ERISA, regulation of pension and other employee benefits was a hodge-podge of federal law—mostly tax and collective bargaining law—and state contract, trust, and labor law.

Congress began considering broad pension legislation in 1967, when Senator Jacob Javits of New York introduced a bill addressing several problems, including inadequate funding of pension plans, misuse of pension assets, and pension plan provisions that resulted in long-tenured employees forfeiting or never qualifying for pension benefits despite, in some cases, working 25 or more years for the employer maintaining the plan.

ERISA is a complex piece of social legislation. It introduced minimum substantive standards for pension plans, including standards for funding and vesting. It established mandatory pension survivorship rights for spouses, although such rights can be waived. It set up an agency to insure certain benefits from insolvent pension plans. It established federal standards for the behavior of people who administer plans or manage plan assets. It federalized jurisdiction over pension cases and preempted most state laws regulating employee benefit plans.

ERISA by and large respected the voluntary nature of employer sponsorship of pension plans, but in essence said that if an employer makes a decision to sponsor a pension plan, the plan has to meet minimum requirements to ensure that it is fairly administered and adequately funded, and that its terms and limitations are honestly disclosed to employees. ERISA was not, however, intended to increase employer sponsorship of retirement plans, nor was it designed to educate employees about the importance of planning and saving for retirement. Indeed, the expanded federal regulatory regime for pension plans may have dampened the enthusiasm of some employers to sponsor pension plans. At any rate, pension coverage for the private-sector workforce has remained virtually static since ERISA's enactment more than a quarter century ago.

B. ASSESSING AND PLANNING FOR RETIREMENT FINANCIAL NEEDS

[¶ 8,030]

1. Assessing Retirement Savings Needs

Many types of savings begin with a specific goal: to purchase a car, to make a down-payment on a home, to finance a vacation, to put children through college. In such goal-oriented savings, the ultimate aim can generally be translated into an estimated dollar target. Although assumptions have to be made—how much will the return on investment be, how much will the object of the savings plan increase in cost prior to purchase—the assumptions are generally few and the time horizon is generally not a long one.

In most important ways retirement savings is a type of goal-oriented savings: the goal is a stream of lifetime income to replace wages when a person stops working. And like other types of goal-oriented savings, it is possible to quantify that goal in terms of an estimated dollar amount accumulated by a certain future date. But the calculation of both the date and the dollar amount are considerably more complex, involving more variables, than most other types of goal-oriented savings.

Consider just some of the most basic questions that a person must consider in estimating a dollar amount:

1. *Desired income stream at retirement.* For most people, the purpose of financial planning for retirement is to provide sufficient income so that they can maintain their pre-retirement standard of living. In thinking about retirement income requirements, financial planners and policy thinkers speak in terms of a wage "replacement" rate, i.e., the percentage of pre-retirement income that is needed to maintain the pre-retirement standard of living. We will explore competing ideas of wage replacement later in this chapter, but ignoring the effects of inflation and health-related contingencies, most financial plans suggest aiming for a wage replacement rate of between 65% and 80% of income at the time of retirement. Thus, a person planning to retire must estimate how much she will be earning at retirement and multiply this by the desired wage replacement rate to determine her annual income needs during retirement.

Determining a wage replacement rate itself raises a number of details which are considered more fully in ¶ 8,050. For example, housing costs and recreational activities in retirement vary widely among retirees. In a sense, a wage replacement rate is a proxy for these details, and as one approaches retirement and it becomes possible to project a realistic retirement budget, such budgeting will produce a more accurate assessment of a desired income stream at retirement.

2. *Retirement date.* The later a person retires, the smaller the amount she will need to accumulate to provide a desired stream of income. This simply reflects the reality that a person who retires later will live fewer years in retirement than a person who retires sooner. See Appendix D. Take, for example, a male who wants a $50,000 annual income. One strategy to provide such income would be to purchase a $50,000 life annuity contract from an insurance company. Based on current annuity rates, the premium for such an annuity commencing at 60 would be approximately $750,000; at age 65, $550,000; and at age 70, $350,000. Note that a delayed retirement date results in a longer savings period and a lower savings target.

3. *Date of death.* Unless a person uses her retirement savings to purchase an annuity, which will provide a stream of income for life, she will have to estimate life expectancy, since the longer she expects to live, the longer the period in which her savings will have to provide an income stream. Moreover, if she is married, she may also have to predict her husband's date of death. A number of life expectancy calculators are available on the internet.

Exercise: Using each of the following two internet life expectancy calculators, calculate your own life expectancy:

(1) http://www.livingto100.com/sign_in.cfm;

(2) http://moneycentral.msn.com/investor/calcs/n_expect/main.asp.

What do you think accounts for the difference?

4. *Social security and employer–provided pension benefits.* Social Security and employer-sponsored pension plans are paid in the form of an annuity and thus provide a direct source of wage replacement. Thus, annual retirement income will equal the sum of Social Security benefits, distributions from employer-sponsored pension plans, and withdrawals from accumulated retirement savings. To achieve a desired level of retirement income, the greater the amounts available from Social Security and private pension plans, the less the amounts needed from accumulated savings. As a result, in formulating a retirement savings plan, it is necessary to estimate the amount of income a person will receive from Social Security and private pension plans.

5. *Inflation.* Even a low rate of inflation can substantially erode purchasing power over a person's retirement years. For example, a 2% rate of inflation will reduce a person's purchasing power by 30% by the end of a 20–year retirement. Put in dollar terms, a person who begins with an annual income of $50,000 would, by the 20th year, require annual income of almost $73,000 to maintain the same real purchasing power she had in her first year of retirement.

The inflation issue becomes more acute if a person's expected retirement assets include an annuity from an employer-sponsored pension plan, since such annuities are rarely indexed to inflation and the loss in the annuity's purchasing power will have to be made up with other assets (if the loss in purchasing power is to be made up at all). In effect, this means that a careful retirement planner will need to save additional amounts of money to compensate for the declining purchasing power of the annuity in the later years of retirement.

Thus, a person who wishes to ensure a consistent standard of living will have to consider the possible effects of post-retirement inflation; any dollar savings target should reflect this.

6. *Future health care and assisted care costs.* For many people, health will decline as they age. A decline in health can have two adverse financial effects: (i) it can increase medical costs; and (ii) it can increase homecare services that an individual will need to purchase. Anna Rappaport, a prominent research actuary, illustrated this phenomenon in a short essay, "Story of Joan." Joan is a married woman who begins retirement in good health and with her husband still alive. They are able to continue doing much of what they did before retirement (other than work). But she and her husband find it increasingly difficult to take care of their home and eventually have to hire someone to do yard work and other home maintenance tasks. A few years into her retirement, her husband dies. Joan can still drive but she can no longer prepare meals, so she has to hire someone to help her cook. A few years later she is diagnosed with Parkinson's disease and incurs still further medical expenses. Her condition also results in her no longer being able to drive. Within a few years she cannot manage her own bills and finances, handle her medication, or deal with her phone answering machine. Her problems continue: a year later she cannot bathe or dress herself,

although she can still feed herself. Finally, she has difficulty walking and trouble feeding herself and is moved into a nursing home.

The uncertainty of future health-related problems can, to a large extent, be hedged through various forms of insurance. Some employers, for example, provide retiree health care, although the actual availability of such care is generally contingent on the employer remaining in business and not canceling (or reducing) coverage.

Medicare covers many but not all expenses of health care and some predict that the scope of Medicare coverage may have to be reduced in the future because of financing issues. Individuals can purchase their own health insurance and long-term care insurance, but products from reputable insurance companies are expensive.

7. *Part-time work.* Some people anticipate working part-time in retirement. People who anticipate this as a source of income, however, must estimate the amount of income such work will generate and how long they will continue to work part-time. In addition, the income stream from part-time work may have to be discounted by the possibility that health or other issues will interfere with part-time work.

8. *Domestic status.* Domestic status at the time of retirement has an impact on how much retirement income is needed to maintain a particular lifestyle. There are economies of scale in a multi-member household: in some cases, two can live almost as cheaply as one, particularly since a two-member household will have twice the human resources to provide domestic service while both household members are healthy. Moreover, when one spouse or domestic partner becomes ill or incapacitated, the other can often provide many of the services they need and would otherwise have to purchase. (Similarly, geographically proximate children can help in providing such care.)

In addition, spouses generally pool their economic resources. As we will see later in this chapter, divorce can upset retirement plans.

9. *Amount of retirement debt.* A person will need a higher income replacement rate if she has accumulated substantial debt when she begins retirement.

10. *Support obligations.* Some people enter retirement with obligations to support children, parents or other dependents. Indeed, some people have referred to baby-boomers as a "sandwich" generation, because many of them will enter retirement still supporting both young adult children and aged parents. These support obligations, which are generally informal in nature, should also be considered in assessing financial needs in retirement.

11. *Mortality risk.* We have already noted that in estimating a dollar target for retirement, an individual must estimate her life expectancy. There is, however, a risk that a person will outlive her life expectancy and the cost of meeting this risk should be considered in assessing retirement financial needs.

12.   *One-time expenses.* Some people anticipate one or more one-time, non-recurring expenses in retirement, such as a one-time membership in a club, a wedding for a child, or an expensive overseas vacation.

[¶ 8,035]

Problem

There are several websites that are designed to help people assess their financial needs in retirement. See, for example, the Motley Fool website   (http://partners.financenter.com/motleyfool/calculate/us-eng/retire01.fcs). Consider the following example of projected retirement needs:

Monthly costs that may be reduced at retirement		
	Current	**Estimated**
Housing	$1,700	$1,200
Life Insurance	50	40
Transportation	200	100
Clothing	250	100
Debt payments	400	2,100
Education	350	0
Other	300	200

Monthly costs that may increase at retirement		
	Current	**Estimated**
Medical	$ 80	$200
Food	200	400
Recreation	60	150
Property Insurance	20	30
Years until you retire:		20
Inflation rate:		3.0%

What variables does this website fail to capture?

[¶ 8,040]

2.   Formulating a Retirement Savings Plan and the Value of Saving Early

In a simple world, a person would assess her financial savings needs, determine the future dollar figure necessary to satisfy those needs at retirement, and develop a savings and investment plan to produce those future dollars. For example, a person might develop a plan under which she would contribute a fixed percentage of her annual compensation to a 401(k) plan, with larger contributions occurring as her salary increases. To create such a plan, a person would need only to assume a particular rate of return on investments and a salary scale, i.e., how much her salary would increase each year.

But such a savings plan cannot run on automatic pilot, since estimates of retirement income needs on the one hand, and assumptions about investment return and salary scale on the other, will constantly be in flux. Thus, a retirement plan is a work in progress that must be re-evaluated periodically.

Moreover, in some ways it makes little sense for a relatively young person to try to assess retirement needs, since an assessment at a young age will almost certainly be wildly inaccurate. But the importance of beginning to save for retirement at an early age cannot be overstated. Because of the compounding of investment return, a dollar saved at any age is worth more at retirement than a dollar saved at any later age. Consider this from two perspectives: (i) a person who saves $1,000 per year, beginning at age 20; and (ii) a person who saves 10% of his salary per year, beginning at age 20.

First let us consider the case of an individual who contributes a flat dollar amount each year to a retirement fund over a working career. To determine what annual contributions of $1,000 will be worth in the future, we need to specify a time period and an assumed rate of investment return. The following chart shows what annual contributions of $1,000 beginning at ages 20, 40 and 60 will be worth at age 65, at various assumed rates of return.

Rate of Return	Age 20	Age 40	Age 60
5%	$168,685	$51,113	$6,802
6%	226,508	59,156	6,975
7%	306,752	68,676	7,153
8%	418,426	79,954	7,336

Notice that the value of savings increases geometrically as the time period becomes longer and the rate of return increases. At a 5% rate of return, savings over a 45–year period (beginning at age 20) are worth more than three times as much as savings over a 25–year period (beginning at 40) and nearly 25 times as much as savings over a 5–year period (beginning at age 60). The differences are even more pronounced at higher rates of return.

Now let us consider the case of an individual who contributes a percentage of her salary each year to a retirement fund during her working career. An additional variable goes into the calculations when comparing the value of saving a percentage of wages at different ages, since we expect wages to increase over time. The following three charts assume that an employee begins work at age 20 at an initial annual salary of $20,000 and saves 5% of his salary each year beginning either at age 20, 40 or 60. Assuming annual salary increases of 2%, 3% and 4%, the charts show what the 5% annual contributions will be worth at age 65, at various assumed rates of return.

2% Salary Scale

Rate of Return	Age 20	Age 40	Age 60
5%	$231,588	$ 93,231	$15,746
6%	302,597	106,838	16,138
7%	399,720	122,856	16,541
8%	533,125	141,733	16,955

3% Salary Scale

Rate of Return	Age 20	Age 40	Age 60
5%	$276,961	$126,345	$23,820
6%	356,515	144,055	24,407
7%	464,439	164,842	25,010
8%	611,581	189,272	25,628

4% Salary Scale

Rate of Return	Age 20	Age 40	Age 60
5%	$335,944	$171,609	$35,900
6%	425,783	194,672	36,776
7%	546,593	221,660	37,674
8%	709,982	253,287	38,595

Note that the higher the salary scale, the smaller the age differential at any given rate of return. High salary scales, however, generally occur during periods of inflation and inflation generally also increases the rate of return on investments. At least historically speaking, the rate of return on investments has in the long run exceeded salary scale.

An argument can be made that it becomes easier to save as we grow older and our compensation increases, because increased compensation gives us more discretionary income, i.e., income after expenditures for basic shelter, food, clothing, transportation, and other necessities. Thus, later saving may entail less sacrifice than earlier saving, since more disposable income means that one can save and still see a rising standard of living. Although this may be an argument for increasing savings as a percentage of compensation as our compensation increases, it is not a compelling argument against beginning a meaningful retirement savings program early in one's work-life.

How much should one put aside annually for retirement? There is no single right answer to that question, but certainly anyone who participates in a 401(k) or similar plan should contribute enough to qualify for the maximum employer matching contribution. Financial modeling suggests that within a realistic range of assumptions about salary scale and rate of return on investments, an annual contribution to a 401(k) plan equal to 10% of compensation will replace between 60% and over 100% of retirement-age compensation if a person begins contributing at age 20 and continues through age 65. (For purposes of this calculation, retirement-age compensation is reduced by the amount of the 401(k) contribution in the year prior to retirement.) A contribution rate of 5% will replace between 30% and over 100% of retirement-age compensation over the same savings horizon. The lower part of the range assumes a 4% salary scale and a 5% rate of return; the higher part of the range assumes a 2% salary scale and an 8% rate of return.

If we run the same numbers for someone who begins saving at 10% annually beginning at age 40, the resulting savings will be sufficient to replace only between 30% and 60% of compensation. And if the savings program is deferred until age 60, the resulting savings would only replace about 6% of compensation.

Let's consider one final set of comparative numbers. Suppose that a person does not begin saving until 40, but begins saving at a rate equal to 15% of compensation. The range of replacement rates (again assuming the same range of assumptions concerning salary scale and rate of return) would be between about 45% and 90%.

Keep in mind that the above figures do not consider Social Security, employer sponsored retirement plans, or other income-generating or expense-saving assets, such as owner-occupied housing.

The message in all of this is that beginning a periodic savings program early is important. As the saying goes, a stitch in time saves nine.

[¶ 8,050]

3. Replacement Rate

Financial planners and policy thinkers often conceptualize retirement financial planning in terms of a targeted wage replacement rate designed to maintain an individual's standard of living immediately before retirement. As we have already observed, such a replacement rate is, in a sense, a surrogate for a careful budgeting process in which recurring expenses in retirement are catalogued and tabulated. Such a budget is difficult to prepare and will generally not be accurate if prepared many years before retirement.

Financial planners differ on what an adequate replacement rate is, but there is broad agreement that (except perhaps for the very wealthy) it is less than 100%, with the literature suggesting anywhere from 65% to 85% as an adequate replacement rate to sustain a pre-retirement standard of living.

Why does the literature suggest a targeted replacement rate of less than 100%? There are several reasons:

- A retiree no longer has job-related expenses, such as commuting and work clothing expenses.

- A retiree stops paying payroll taxes.

- A retiree can reduce, perhaps to zero, the amount that she saves from income.

- A retiree's marginal income tax rate often drops upon leaving the job market.

- Housing costs will often decline in retirement, since it is often in retirement that a mortgage is paid off.

On the other hand, there are some expenses that increase in retirement, most notably health care. A recent study prepared by researchers at Georgia State University and Aon Consulting indicates that expenses for household operations also tend to increase for most retirees. Some individuals will find that their expenditures for items such as entertainment and travel increase, while others may find that they decrease during retirement. Moreover, whether some expenses increase or decrease may be sensitive to the aging process, with some expenses decreasing in the early years of retirement and increasing in the late years. Again, the most notable example is health care.

What do financial planners and policy analysts consider to be an adequate replacement rate? Most financial planners have traditionally suggested that a replacement rate of 65% to 70% of real income is needed to maintain a pre-retirement standard of living. Of course, one replacement rate does not fit all workers. A person with relatively low income will ordinarily require a relatively high replacement rate, because she will not have had much discretionary income prior to retirement. Rather, she would have spent almost all of her income on nondiscretionary items, such as food, shelter and clothing. In line with this reality, a study conducted by the American Society of Pension Actuaries suggests a replacement rate equal to 85% of pre-retirement income up to three times the poverty rate, and a 70% higher replacement rate for pre-retirement income above three times the poverty rate.

The benefit structure of Social Security is consistent with this insight: its replacement rate declines as income rises. The chart below illustrates Social Security replacement rates for the year 2004 at full retirement age, for individuals at various monthly income levels. Except for the highest income levels, the chart assumes that the individual had a consistent wage history with respect to the national average wage in each of his or her highest 35 years of earning history.

Income in 2004	Replacement Rate
$ 612	90.00%
2,000	65.70%
3,000	43.80%
5,000	35.00%
7,325	28.40%
10,000	20.80%
15,000	13.90%
25,000	7.50%

It should also be noted that these replacement rates are further skewed toward the bottom because more affluent individuals are required to include a portion of their Social Security benefits in their taxable income.

Moreover, at least one group of researchers has suggested that the traditional wage replacement rates may rest on an overly optimistic view of expenses in retirement. The Georgia State/Aon study previously mentioned suggests that adequate replacement rates should range from between 74% and 87%, with the recommended replacement rate increasing with income level except for individuals with poverty and near-poverty income levels. One explanation for the study's conclusion is that since 1986, when the highest marginal tax rates were substantially reduced, aggregate tax rates do not appreciably decline for individuals with high levels of income.

One can also construct a personalized replacement rate, although in one sense this amounts to little more than creating a budget for retirement. A formula for such a rate might look something like the following:

(1) begin with pre-retirement income;

(2) subtract pre-retirement tax burden;

(3) subtract pre-retirement job-related expenses;

(4) subtract pre-retirement annual savings, including contributions to 401(k) plan;

(5) add estimated additional living, transportation, health and entertainment expenses that are expected in retirement;

(6) add estimated annual retirement tax burden;

(7) divide the total of steps 1 through 6 by pre-retirement income.

The idea of a replacement rate as the key to retirement financial planning can have a serious shortcoming if not corrected for the income-eroding power of inflation and the probability that health care and assisted living expenses will increase in the later stages of retirement. A person can plan for inflation and health-care by the purchase of insurance contracts (health care, assisted care, and annuities indexed to increases in the cost of living), or through saving in the early years of retirement to cover the costs of future inflation and future health care costs. If the latter course is selected, the formula for determining an adequate income replacement rate (see above) would add into the formula a retirement savings rate.

[¶ 8,060]

4. Retirement Plans as Tax Shelters for the Affluent

The orthodox treatment of wages and savings is immediate taxation. The Internal Revenue Code, however, favorably varies this treatment in the case of certain retirement plans, known as "qualified plans." In a qualified plan, participants do not pay tax when contributions are made to a plan on their behalf and neither the plan nor its participants are taxed on plan investment income as it is earned. The participant pays tax only when benefits are actually distributed. This scheme results in tax deferral, which over time has substantial benefit, a benefit whose value correlates with a person's marginal tax rate.

Individuals with high marginal tax rates often do not need to focus specially on saving for retirement if they either have substantial assets or regularly save a substantial part of their income, for their wealth or regular savings habits will provide them with income to support themselves when they retire. For these individuals, retirement planning may mean something else: maximizing the tax benefits of qualified plans, which are heavily regulated under the Internal Revenue Code. For a discussion of how wealthy individuals can use qualified plans in general wealth management, see ¶ ¶ 8,580–8,670.

C. SOCIAL SECURITY BENEFITS

[¶ 8,070]

Social Security benefits are, in one sense, the basic component of retirement income for Americans, to be supplemented with employer-provided pensions and private savings. Thus, it is important to understand the basic coverage, eligibility requirements, benefit structure, and tax treatment of Social Security in formulating a savings strategy for financing retirement.

[¶ 8,080]

1. Coverage and Eligibility

Social Security provides retirement, disability and survivor benefits to workers and their families, based on each worker's earnings record in "covered employment." Today, virtually all employees, including part-time and self-employed individuals, are covered by Social Security if their annual wages exceed a modest threshold amount ($1,400 in 2005). There are a few exceptions. For example, Social Security does not cover certain categories of workers who are covered by a separate retirement system (e.g., federal government employees hired before 1984, employees of state or local governments that have not elected coverage). Also exempt from coverage are students employed by the educational institution they attend, as well as employees of certain established sects that object to insurance on religious grounds.

Social Security benefits are financed primarily through a flat 12.4% payroll tax on the wages of workers in covered employment. Half of this tax is paid directly by the employer and half is paid by the employee through wage withholding. The payroll tax is imposed on each individual worker's wages up to a fixed amount known as the Social Security "wage base." The wage base is indexed each year to reflect increases in national average wages. The wage base for 2005 is $90,000. Most workers earn less than the wage base, with the result that all of their wages are fully subject to the payroll tax. For high earners, however, wages in excess of the wage base are exempt from the payroll tax.

Eligibility for Social Security benefits is based on "quarters of coverage." In general, a worker who has 40 quarters of coverage (i.e., ten years) is "fully insured" and therefore eligible for retirement benefits. Each worker who earns a specified dollar amount of wages in covered employment during the calendar year is credited with up to four quarters of coverage for the year. The dollar amount is indexed each year to reflect increases in national average wages. In 2005, a worker was credited with one quarter of coverage for each $920 of wages, up to a maximum of four quarters for wages of at least $3,680. For example, if Adam earned $1,500 in March and $1,300 in November of 2005, he would have three quarters of coverage for the year; if Betsy earned $5,000 per month (an annual salary of $60,000), she would have four quarters of coverage for the year.

[¶ 8,090]

2. Retirement Benefits

An individual worker's retirement benefit is payable in the form of a monthly annuity for the worker's life. The amount of the monthly payment is calculated based on the worker's "primary insurance amount" (PIA), which in turn reflects the worker's lifetime earnings record. If the worker begins receiving benefits at "full retirement age," the monthly benefit is initially equal to the PIA and is subsequently indexed to reflect annual increases in the cost of living. Actuarial adjustments are required, however, if the worker elects to begin receiving benefits as early as age 62 or to defer benefits until after full retirement age.

In addition to the worker's own retirement benefit, Social Security provides separate benefits for the spouse, children, and certain other family members of a retired or deceased worker. These benefits are often referred to as "derivative" benefits because they are based on the worker's own PIA and are payable to eligible recipients based on their relationship to the worker.

[¶ 8,100]

a. Worker's own retirement benefit

The starting point for calculating a worker's own retirement benefit is the PIA, which is initially determined in the year when the worker reaches age 62 (i.e., when the worker first becomes eligible for benefits). The PIA is calculated as follows:

1. Determine the worker's 35 highest years of covered earnings, up to the amount of the Social Security wage base in each year. (If the worker has less than 35 years of covered earnings, the remaining years are counted at zero.)

2. Index each year's covered earnings to subsequent average national wage growth through age 60. The Social Security Administration publishes a table showing the multiple for prior years' earnings. Add these amounts together and divide by 35 to compute the worker's average indexed annual earnings. Then divide the resulting number by 12 to compute the worker's "average indexed monthly earnings" (AIME).

3. The PIA is calculated under a three-tiered formula which applies different percentages (90%, 32% and 15%) to incremental amounts of the worker's AIME. The "bend points" at which these percentages apply are indexed annually to average national wage growth. For example, the PIA for a worker who reached age 62 in 2005 is equal to 90% of the first $627 of AIME, plus 32% of AIME over $627 but not exceeding $3,779, plus 15% of AIME over $3,779. The resulting amount, rounded down to the nearest whole dime, is the worker's PIA. The larger a worker's AIME, the higher the PIA.

Example: Abigail reaches age 62 in 2005 and has AIME of $4,000. Her PIA is calculated as follows:

90% of first $627	$ 564.30
32% of AIME over $627 but not exceeding $3,779	1,008.64
15% of AIME over $3,779	33.15
Total	$1,606.09

The total is rounded down to $1,606. This is Abigail's PIA.

If the worker continues to work after reaching age 62, her subsequent earnings will be taken into account if this results in higher AIME, but the bend points in the three-tiered formula do not change after the initial calculation. The amount of the monthly benefit is indexed in subsequent years to reflect increases in the cost of living.

Under a special rule, benefits must be reduced for individuals who have some covered employment but are also covered by a state or local governmental plan outside the Social Security system.

As noted above, the worker's retirement benefit is equal to her PIA if she retires at her "full retirement age." Full retirement age varies depending on the year of the worker's birth, ranging from 65 years (for workers born before 1938) to 67 years (for workers born after 1959), as shown in the following chart:

Year of Birth	Full Retirement Age
1937 or earlier	65 years 0 months
1938	65 years 2 months
1939	65 years 4 months
1940	65 years 6 months
1941	65 years 8 months
1942	65 years 10 months
1943–1954	66 years 0 months
1955	66 years 2 months
1956	66 years 4 months

1957	66 years 6 months
1958	66 years 8 months
1959	66 years 10 months
1960 and later	67 years 0 months

A worker may elect to begin receiving Social Security retirement benefits as early as age 62. Indeed, most workers do so. Early retirement, however, results in a reduction in the amount of the monthly benefit, based on the number of months before full retirement age that benefits commence. The reduction is equal to 5/9 of 1% per month for the first 36 months and 5/12 of 1% for each subsequent month. Thus, for example, a worker born in 1943 who retires in 2005 at age 62 (four years before full retirement age) would receive a monthly benefit equal to 75% of her PIA. The purpose of the benefit reduction is to reflect the higher cost of paying out benefits over a longer period. (See ¶ 8,810 for a discussion of the financially optimal time to commence Social Security benefits.)

On the other hand, if a worker delays the commencement of benefits until after full retirement age, benefits are increased to compensate for the shorter payout period. For workers born after 1942, the increase is equal to 2/3 of 1% per month for each month of delayed retirement up to age 70. (A different formula applies to workers born before 1943.) There is no additional increase for workers who delay retirement beyond age 70.

The Social Security Administration's website includes a Social Security benefit calculator and other information on calculating benefits, at http://www.ssa.gov/OACT/ANYPIA/.

[¶ 8,105]

Problem

Martha was born in 1943 and has a PIA of $1,000 per month. Calculate Martha's monthly Social Security benefit, assuming that she elects to begin receiving Social Security benefits at age 62. What difference does it make if she elects to begin receiving benefits at age 66? at age 70?

[¶ 8,110]

b. Benefits for spouses, children and other family members

If a married worker is receiving retirement benefits, the worker's spouse may be entitled to a separate benefit based on the worker's earnings record. To be eligible, the spouse must either have reached age 62 or be taking care of a child of the worker who is under age 16 or disabled. The spouse's benefit at full retirement age is generally equal to 50% of the worker's PIA (with annual cost-of-living adjustments), but the spouse's benefit is reduced if payments commence before the spouse reaches full retirement age unless the spouse is taking care of a child of the worker who is under 16 or disabled.

If the spouse is already eligible for benefits based on his or her own earnings record, those benefits give rise to a dollar-for-dollar reduction in the spousal benefit. In effect, the spouse is entitled to the greater of his or her own benefit or the spousal benefit.

In addition, one or more dependent children of a retired worker may be entitled to separate benefits based on the worker's earnings record. To be eligible, a child must be under age 18, or not more than age 19 and still in elementary or secondary school, or at least age 18 and subject to a disability that began before age 22. The child's benefit is generally equal to 50% of the worker's PIA (with annual cost-of-living adjustments). In certain circumstances, a worker's dependent grandchild or dependent parent may also be entitled to benefits.

The total benefits payable to a retired worker and to the worker's spouse and children based on the worker's earnings record are subject to an overall "family maximum." The family maximum is initially determined when the worker reaches age 62 by applying a four-tiered formula to the worker's PIA, and is indexed to annual cost-of-living increases. For workers who reached age 62 in 2005, the family maximum is equal to 150% of the first $801 of the worker's PIA, plus 272% of PIA between $801 and $1,156, plus 134% of PIA between $1,156 and $1,508, plus 175% of PIA over $1,508, with the result rounded down to the nearest whole dime. The family maximum does not affect the worker's own benefit. However, the derivative benefits payable to the worker's spouse and children will be proportionately reduced to the extent necessary to ensure that those derivative benefits, when combined with the worker's own benefit, do not exceed the family maximum.

Finally, a worker's former spouse may be entitled to separate benefits based on the worker's earnings record. To be eligible, the former spouse must have been married to the worker for at least 10 years, must be at least age 62, and must not be married to someone else. In addition, the worker must also be at least age 62 but need not be currently receiving a retirement benefit. (Special rules apply if the worker died before age 62.) The former spouse's benefit is generally equal to 50% of the worker's PIA (with annual cost-of-living adjustments), although it will be reduced if payments commence before the former spouse reaches full retirement age. Note that a worker who has been married more than once can generate separate spousal benefits for each eligible divorced spouse. A former spouse who has been divorced from two or more workers, however, will only receive a single benefit (the highest of the benefits). The former spouse's benefit is not subject to the family maximum.

[¶ 8,120]

c. *Survivor benefits*

Upon the death of a fully insured worker, the worker's surviving spouse, former spouse, and dependent children may become entitled to survivor benefits based on the deceased worker's earnings record. The survivor benefits supersede any benefits that were payable to these family members before the worker's death.

The decedent's widowed spouse is entitled to the full amount of the decedent's benefit commencing at full retirement age, or, at the spouse's option, to a reduced benefit beginning as early as age 60. (The widowed spouse may be entitled to a survivor benefit before age 60 if the spouse is at least 50 years old and disabled, or is taking care of a child of the decedent who is under age 16 or disabled.) Moreover, if the widowed spouse qualifies for Social Security based on her own earnings record, she can begin receiving the survivor benefit at age 60 and then at full retirement age switch over to her own full retirement benefit (if it is larger than the survivor benefit). Alternatively, the widowed spouse may begin to receive her own benefit before full retirement age and then switch over to a survivor benefit at full retirement age.

In general, the widowed spouse loses the survivor benefit upon remarriage, but this rule does not apply if the remarriage occurs after age 60. Thus, a widowed spouse who remarries after age 60 will be entitled to receive the survivor benefit based on her deceased spouse's earnings record, the spousal benefit based on her new spouse's earnings record, or the retirement benefit based on her own earnings record, whichever is larger.

In addition, each dependent child of a deceased worker is entitled to a survivor benefit equal to 75% of the decedent's PIA as long as the child is under age 18, or not more than age 19 and still in elementary or secondary school, or at least age 18 and subject to a disability that began before age 22. The survivor benefits payable to the spouse and children of a deceased worker are subject to the same family maximum described above.

A surviving former spouse who was married to the decedent for at least 10 years is also entitled to a survivor benefit beginning at age 60. This benefit is computed in the same manner and is subject to the same limitations (including termination on remarriage before age 60) as the benefit payable to the decedent's widowed spouse, except that it is not subject to the family maximum.

[¶ 8,130]

d. *Effect of earnings during retirement*

What happens if a person continues to work after Social Security benefits have commenced? The answer depends on whether the work occurs before or after the worker reaches full retirement age. Beginning at full retirement age, earnings from work have no effect on Social Security benefits. But earnings from a job or self-employment can result in a reduction of Social Security benefits received before full retirement age. For purposes of the retirement earnings test, earnings from personal services are taken into account, but investment income and earnings from other sources are not. Deferred compensation is also excluded to the extent it is attributable to services performed before the worker began receiving retirement benefits.

Benefits received before full retirement age are reduced only if earned income exceeds a threshold called the "exempt amount." Both the exempt amount and the benefit reduction formula depend on whether the worker will attain full retirement age during the current calendar year.

For workers who will not reach full retirement age during the current year, the exempt amount is a dollar amount, and retirement benefits are reduced by $1 for every $2 of earnings above that amount. The exempt amount is indexed to annual average national wage growth. In 2005 the exempt amount is $12,000 ($1,000 per month).

Example: Alma's full retirement age is 66. She begins receiving retirement benefits at age 62, in 2005. In 2005 she earns wages of $14,000. Her benefits will be reduced by $1,000 (50% of $2,000, the amount by which Alma's earnings exceed the exempt amount for the current year.)

For workers who reach full retirement age during the current year, the exempt amount is another dollar amount, and retirement benefits are reduced by $1 for every $3 of earnings above that amount. Only earnings in months prior to attaining full retirement age are taken into account. The exempt amount is indexed to annual average national wage growth. In 2005 the exempt amount is $31,800 ($2,650 per month).

The benefit reduction affects not only the worker's own retirement benefits but also any derivative benefits received by a spouse (but not a former spouse) or a dependent child. The benefit reduction is not necessarily permanent. Upon reaching full retirement age, the retired worker is entitled to recoup the benefit reduction through increased benefits over the worker's remaining life expectancy.

[¶ 8,140]

3. Taxation of Social Security Benefits

Social Security benefits are subject to special income tax treatment. Such benefits may be partially includible in the recipient's gross income or fully excludable, depending on the taxpayer's income level. See I.R.C. § 86. To determine whether, and to what extent, Social Security benefits are taxable, the taxpayer must first calculate "modified adjusted gross income," which for this purpose is defined as adjusted gross income augmented by certain otherwise non-taxable items (e.g., tax-exempt interest and certain foreign-source income). Modified adjusted gross income is then increased by 50% of the taxpayer's Social Security benefits to arrive at what is sometimes called "provisional income." If the taxpayer's provisional income does not exceed the "base amount," the Social Security benefits are fully excludable from gross income. The base amount is $25,000 for taxpayers filing singly, $32,000 for married couples filing jointly, and zero for married taxpayers filing separately unless they live apart for the entire year.

If provisional income exceeds the base amount but does not exceed the "adjusted base amount," 50% of the excess over the base amount (but not more than 50% of the Social Security benefits) is includible in gross income. The adjusted base amount is $34,000 for taxpayers filing singly, $44,000 for married couples filing jointly, and zero for married couples filing separately unless they live apart for the entire year.

Example: Andrew and Beata, a married couple who file jointly, have modified adjusted gross income of $30,000 and Social Security benefits of $16,000. Thus their provisional income is $30,000 + (50% × $16,000), or $38,000. The taxable portion of their benefits under the first tier is 50% × ($38,000 − $32,000), or $3,000.

If provisional income exceeds the adjusted base amount, the includible portion of the Social Security benefits is equal to the sum of: (1) 50% of the difference between the adjusted base amount and the base amount (or 50% of the Social Security benefits, if less), and (2) 85% of the excess of provisional income over the adjusted base amount. In no event, however, can the includible amount exceed 85% of the Social Security benefits.

Example: The facts are the same as in the above example, except that Andrew and Beata have modified adjusted gross income of $46,000. Thus their provisional income is $46,000 + (50% × $16,000), or $54,000. The taxable portion of their benefits is $13,600, determined as follows:

50% × ($44,000 − $32,000),	
but not more than 50% × $16,000	$ 6,000
85% × ($54,000 − $44,000)	8,500
total	$14,500
limit on includible portion (85% × $16,000)	$13,600

[¶ 8,150]

4. Future of Social Security

Social Security faces two demographic issues: first, life expectancy continues to increase; and second, the ratio of active workers to retirees continues to decrease. As a result, most observers believe that unless the Social Security program is modified, the Social Security trust fund will, at some point in the future, have insufficient revenues to meet all of its benefit obligations. (It should be stressed that under the Social Security

Administration's 2004 intermediate projections, Social Security will be able to continue paying 100% of its promised benefits until 2042 and even then it would still have sufficient funds to pay 73% of those benefits.) One of the questions, then, in retirement planning is to what extent it is reasonable to rely on the current Social Security benefit structure.

There are two competing approaches to address the problem of future Social Security shortfalls. In the first approach, Social Security would remain a system that pays an earnings-based benefit weighted in favor of lower-wage workers, but with changes to either its benefit structure or its funding mechanism. Among the changes that seem most likely under this approach are further increases in the full retirement age, a shift in the inflation-indexation criteria from the consumer price index to some less favorable index, and reductions in spousal benefits. It is also possible that the tax rules could be altered to subject a greater portion of benefits to income taxation.

The second approach to addressing the potential shortfall is so-called privatization, in which a portion of the payroll tax contributions to Social Security would be diverted to individual investment accounts and a portion of the guaranteed Social Security benefit would be replaced with funds (including investment earnings) from those accounts. Such a system would obviously have a major impact on financial planning for retirement. It would end indexation of benefits and result in the level of benefits being keyed partly to investment performance rather than simply to earnings. Depending on how such a system is designed, it would probably at least partially reduce the current progressive nature of the benefit structure which produces a higher wage replacement rate for lower-wage workers and would reduce survivor, disability, and family benefits. Will such a system be implemented?

Although there are many elected governmental officials who advocate such a shift in the nature of the Social Security system, few observers think that such a system would be politically palatable unless it preserved the baby boomers' expectations for retirement. But it is the obligation to pay these benefits that is placing financial stress on the system's solvency, and privatization, even partial privatization aimed at relatively youthful workers, would exacerbate rather than ameliorate the system's financial problems by redirecting some payroll taxes away from the Social Security trust funds into private accounts. For this reason, it is unlikely that the system will experience more than some minor experimentation with privatization at the margins, at least in the near future.

D. TAX–SHELTERED RETIREMENT SAVINGS VEHICLES

[¶ 8,180]

1. Overview

The Internal Revenue Code provides a number of tax-sheltered retirement vehicles. Most of the vehicles must be sponsored by a business for its employees (or by a self-employed person for himself and his employees, if any), although the Internal Revenue Code also permits individuals to establish more limited tax-sheltered vehicles, such as an individual retirement account (IRA), outside the employment relationship. This section will first discuss the tax benefits of using tax-sheltered retirement vehicles. The section will then contrast the two basic formats for employer-sponsored plans, the defined benefit and defined contribution plan; describe the different types of defined contribution plans; discuss some special issues in defined benefit plans, including the cash balance and other so-called hybrid defined benefit plans; and finally consider individual savings vehicles that can be created outside the employment relationship.

[¶ 8,190]

2. Benefits of Saving in Tax–Sheltered Retirement Plans

We have already noted that tax-sheltered retirement plans offer significant income tax advantages compared to ordinary savings vehicles. A person who saves for retirement outside a qualified retirement plan is taxed currently on wage or self-employment income when it is earned and then is taxed on any investment income subsequently generated by the amount saved. In contrast, an employee who makes contributions to a qualified plan is not subject to immediate taxation on those contributions, and the qualified plan itself is exempt from tax on investment income. The employee pays tax only on distributions as they are made from the plan.

This tax regime offers two advantages to employees: their marginal tax rates may be lower in retirement than during their working years, resulting in lower taxes on both wage and investment income. More important is the benefit of tax deferral, which can have great value over a long savings horizon such as retirement.

To illustrate, consider two scenarios in which an employee receives $10,000 of compensation. In the first scenario, this amount is received as a taxable cash bonus at year-end, and the amount remaining after tax is invested for 4 years, subject to annual tax on the investment income. In the second scenario, the $10,000 is contributed to a qualified profit-sharing plan, where it is invested for 4 years and then distributed to the employee. Assume that the employee has a 40% marginal tax rate (state and federal taxes combined), and that the invested funds earn 10%

annually before tax. The 10% figure is on the high side, but it simplifies the explanation of the advantage of tax deferral. At the end of this section, we will look at the results of simulations using different interest assumptions and longer time periods.

Scenario One: Immediate Taxation. In year 1, the employee receives $10,000 at year-end, pays $4,000 in tax, leaving $6,000 to invest. In year 2, the employee receives $600 in investment income (10% of $6,000), and pays $240 in tax on that income, leaving $360 in investment income. In year 3, the employee begins with $6,360, earns $636 in investment income (10% of $6,360), and pays $254.40 in tax, leaving $381.60 in investment income. At the start of the year 4, the employee has $6,741.60.

Scenario Two: Deferred Taxation. In year 1, the employer contributes $10,000 at year-end to a profit-sharing account. Because the employee does not pay immediate tax on the contribution, the profit-sharing plan has $10,000. In year 2, the profit-sharing plan earns $1,000 (10% of $10,000), and starts year 3 with $11,000. In year 3, the profit-sharing plan earns $1,100 (10% of $11,000), and starts year 4 with $12,100. In year 4, the profit-sharing plan distributes the $12,100 to the employee, who pays income tax on the distribution. The income tax, at the employee's 40% marginal tax rate, is $4,840, leaving the taxpayer with $7,260.

Thus, comparing the two results, the employee ends up with $6,741.60 in scenario one and $7,260 in scenario two. The use of the profit-sharing plan over this short period increases the employee's after-tax savings by $518.40, or 7.7%. If we allow for 40 years of investment return, the employee would accumulate $61,714 in scenario one and $271,556 in scenario two.

What explains the resulting tax benefits? There are three ways of conceptualizing the tax benefits, which are described below.

1. *Interest-Free Loan from Government.* The first way of conceptualizing the tax benefit is to think of the amount of each year's tax deferral as an interest-free loan from the government, which can be invested by the employee. The employee will have to "repay" the total of these loans when she receives distributions from the plan and pays tax on those distributions. To understand this explanation, complete the following chart:

	Year 1	Year 2	Year 3	Year 4
Account Balance at Start of Year	$ 0	$10,000	$11,000	$12,100
Contribution	10,000	0	0	0
Investment Income	0	1,000		n/a
Interest–Free Loan for Year	4,000	400		n/a
Cumulative Total of Interest–Free Loans	4,000	4,400		n/a

Note that the tax due on the $12,100 distribution is precisely equal to the cumulative total of "interest-free loans." This model produces this result if the employee's marginal tax rate is constant throughout the deferral period.

2. *Reduction in Effective Tax Rate.* A second way of understanding the tax benefit of deferral is that the taxpayer is in effect paying an annual tax on income, but at a reduced effective rate. In our example, the effective tax rate for the deferral period turns out to be 35.88%. Again, complete the following chart:

	Year 1	Year 2	Year 3	Year 4
Account Balance at Start of Year	$ 0	$6,412	$6,823	$
Income During Year 1 Contribution, Years 2 and 3 Investment Income	10,000	641		n/a
Less 35.88% Tax	3,588	230		n/a
After–Tax Income	6,412	411		n/a
Year–End Account Balance	6,412	6,823		n/a

3. *Tax-Free Yield.* A third way of understanding the deferral is to conceptualize it as equivalent to paying tax on the contribution and then receiving a tax-free investment return during the deferral period, i.e., the employee would pay a 40% tax on the $10,000 contribution and then pay no tax on the subsequent investment income. Thus, the employee would pay $4,000 in tax on the contribution, leaving $6,000 to invest. In the second year, the employee would earn $600 in investment income and pay no tax. Once again, complete the following chart:

	Year 1	Year 2	Year 3	Year 4
Account Balance at Start of Year	$ 0	$6,000	$6,600	$7,260
Income During Year 1 Contribution, Years 2 and 3 Investment Income	10,000	600		n/a
Less Tax (40% on contribution, zero on investment income)	400	0	0	n/a
After–Tax Income	6,000	600		n/a
Year–End Account Balance (after tax)	6,000	6,600		n/a

The tax-free yield explanation holds if the employee's marginal tax rate remains constant through the deferral period.

As already noted, the above illustrations assume a 10% rate of return on investment, which is probably unrealistic. The following chart illustrates the accumulations for both a $10,000 immediately taxable cash bonus and a $10,000 tax-deferred profit-sharing plan contribution for various interest rates, after 5 years, 10 years, 25 years, and 45 years of investment accumulation. Note that the chart reduces the profit-sharing contribution at each age by a 40% tax on the accumulation.

	5 Years	10 Years	25 Years	45 Years
5% Rate of Return				
Cash Bonus	$6,956	$8,063	$12,563	$22,690
Plan Contribution	$7,658	$9,773	$20,318	$53,910
6% Rate of Return				
Cash Bonus	$7,161	$8,546	$14,526	$29,467
Plan Contribution	$8,029	$10,745	$25,751	$82,588
8% Rate of Return				
Cash Bonus	$7,585	$9,589	$19,372	$49,478
Plan Contribution	$8,816	$12,954	$41,091	$191,523

To further illustrate the value of the tax deferral, assume that an employee works for 40 years and that the employer makes a $10,000 year-end contribution for each year of employment. Assuming a 6% annual rate of return on investments, the employee's tax-deferred profit-sharing account will have a value of $1,547,620 at the end of 40 years. If that amount is then distributed to the employee and the employee pays a 40% tax, the employee will be left with $928,772.

Compare this to the employee who receives $10,000 annual cash bonuses and invests them in taxable investment vehicles with a 6% before-tax rate of return. After 40 years, the employee will have $519,199. The tax-deferred profit-sharing plan increases the employee's wealth by almost 80%. And it should be noted that with the profit-sharing plan, the benefit of tax deferral can be extended if the employee either takes distributions in the form of annuity payments or transfers a lump sum distribution to an individual retirement account.

It should be emphasized that the tax advantages of a qualified plan may be greater for some types of investments than for others, depending on the after-tax rate of return that would be realized outside the plan. For instance, equities held outside a qualified plan receive three tax benefits that enhance the after-tax rate of return: (1) deferral of gain until stock is sold; (2) capital gains tax rates on sale of stock; and (3) preferential tax rates on qualified dividend income. Accordingly, the examples given above may overstate the tax benefits of a qualified plan that is heavily invested in equities; the examples are more realistic for a plan that is weighted toward fixed-income investments that would not be eligible for tax-favored treatment outside the plan.

[¶ 8,200]

3. Defined Benefit Plans and Defined Contribution Plans

Employer-sponsored pension plans come in two basic varieties: defined benefit and defined contribution plans. These two types of plans are briefly described and compared below.

[¶ 8,210]

a. Defined contribution plans

A defined contribution plan, also known as an individual account plan, is a plan in which each participant has a separate account. The employer (and/or the employee) makes contributions to the plan, which are then allocated among individual accounts for each employee. The plan invests the contributed amounts for each employee and the investment return is credited to the employee's account. The benefit under the plan is always equivalent to the account's value. Some plans permit the employee to take the benefit in the form of an annuity, but this is not common.

Employer contributions to an account are commonly based solely on compensation, but the employee's age and/or seniority may also be taken into account.

Example: Employer contributes 10% of compensation for each employee.

Example: Employer contributes $1,000,000 to the plan. The contribution is allocated among participants based on a point system, with each employee assigned points for compensation level, age, and seniority. The allocation of the contribution to an employee's account is based on the ratio of the employee's points to the aggregate number of points for all participants.

The reason that these plans are called defined contribution plans is that the plan *defines* the employer's *contribution* and the way in which the contributions are allocated among the participants. A 401(k) plan is a defined contribution plan.

[¶ 8,220]

b. Defined benefit plans

In contrast, a defined benefit plan does not define the employer's contribution to the plan; rather, it *defines* the *benefit* that the plan participant will be entitled to receive at retirement. The Internal Revenue Code provides that the normal form of benefit in a defined benefit plan is a life annuity commencing at normal retirement age, which is typically age 65. (For a married employee, the normal form of benefit is a form of joint-and-survivor annuity that has at least equivalent value to the life annuity for the employee alone. The joint-and-survivor annuity is discussed in ¶ 8,690.) Some common types of benefit formulas are: (a) x% times years of service times final pay; (b) x% times years of service times average career pay; (c) $x times years of service; and (d) x% of final pay, reduced by 1% for each year less than 25.

Employees do not have individual accounts in defined benefit plans; they have only a right to receive the promised benefit. This raises the question of how the employer funds a defined benefit plan. Basically, the employer (and in a few plans the employees as well) must pay enough into the plan over time so that the contributions, plus investment income earned thereon, will be sufficient to pay benefits as they come due. The contributions are generally made over the expected life of the plan. An actuary determines how much the employer is required to contribute each year. To make this determination, the actuary must estimate both how much the promised benefits will cost and how much investment income will be earned on contributions. The employer, through the actuary, has considerable flexibility in determining how much will be contributed each year. Thus, for example, a start-up business may decide to contribute as little as possible during the early years of the business, when there is a pressing need for cash. On the other hand, an employer with significant taxable income may wish to contribute as much as possible to the plan, in order to maximize the available tax deferral.

Minimum funding rules (under I.R.C. § 412) ensure that at least a minimum amount is contributed by the employer; maximum deduction rules (under I.R.C. § 404) limit the maximum amount that the employer is permitted to contribute in a particular year without incurring adverse tax consequences.

[¶ 8,230]

c. *Comparing defined benefit plans and defined contribution plans*

1. *Investment of plan assets.* In a defined benefit plan, the investment risk (at least nominally) is on the employer; in a defined contribution plan, the investment risk is on the employee. The converse is also true: if investments do well in a defined benefit plan, the employer can reduce future contributions. In a defined contribution plan, the employee reaps the rewards of good investment performance.

Most defined contribution plans today permit employees to direct the investment of funds in their individual accounts, often providing them with a menu of mutual funds to choose from. Some financial planners and academics have criticized plans that permit self-directed investments because many employees lack the requisite skills and interests to invest their accounts optimally.

A defined benefit plan is prohibited from investing more than 10% of its assets in employer stock or employer real property. This restriction typically does not apply to defined contribution plans.

2. *Participation, benefit accruals and employee incentives.* Defined contribution plans can allow employees to elect annually whether and at what level to participate. The 401(k) plan is the best known example of this type of plan. Although employers may sponsor voluntary participation defined benefit plans, to which the employee contributes a portion of his or her salary, these are rare and the extent of the employee's election is limited to the decision to participate or not.

In a "final pay" defined benefit plan, benefits are indexed to inflation (assuming that wages rise in more or less parallel fashion to inflation) so long as an employee continues to work for the employer maintaining the plan. If the employee leaves employment, however, benefits are frozen based on the employee's compensation at the time the employee leaves. A defined benefit plan with a final pay formula is good for employees who stay with an employer until retirement age; it is not nearly so good for employees who leave long before retirement age. Thus, an employer who wants to tie employees to the firm will generally prefer a defined benefit plan over a defined contribution plan. And employees who frequently change jobs—which is probably the way the economy is now headed—are better off with a defined contribution plan, except perhaps for their final job.

Problem: P begins work at age 25 for an employer with a defined benefit plan that provides a benefit equal to 2% of final pay times years of service. P's pay is $50,000 at age 35, $100,000 at age 45, $150,000 at age 55, and $200,000 at age 65. P retires at age 65. What is his benefit? Alternatively, suppose that P has the same salary history but works for four different employers for 10 years each, and each employer sponsors a defined benefit plan that provides a benefit equal to 2% of final pay times years of service. What is the sum of P's four benefits at age 65?

Because the present value of a dollar's worth of benefit commencing at retirement age (age 65 in most plans) increases as an employee approaches retirement age, annual benefit accruals under traditional defined benefit plans become more valuable as the employee ages (and correspondingly more expensive for the employer to fund). This is true irrespective of whether the plan has a final pay formula, although the final pay formula will accentuate this effect. Accrual patterns in defined benefit plans and defined contribution plans are discussed in more detail in ¶ 8,240.

From the employer's perspective, a defined benefit plan is superior to a defined contribution plan as a vehicle for managing superannuated employees. For example, an employer can design a plan to provide enhanced benefits for employees who leave work at certain times preferred by the employer. This is a particularly important feature of the defined benefit formula for some employers, given the broad restrictions of the Age Discrimination in Employment Act (29 U.S.C. §§ 621 et seq.) on mandatory age-based retirement.

Example: ABC amends its retirement plan to provide that participants who elect to retire during 2005 will receive credit for an additional five years of service.

A defined benefit plan may provide benefits related to years before the plan was adopted by awarding past service credits. For example, P works for Employer Z for 5 years. Employer Z adopts a defined benefit plan, with a benefit formula equal to 1% of final pay times years of service. Employer Z can, if it wishes, draft the plan to provide A with credit for his 5 years of pre-existing service. Similarly, Z can amend an existing defined benefit plan to increase benefits based on years of service before the amendment. (In some cases, the Internal Revenue Code limits the permissible amount of past service credits to prevent overly favoring highly-compensated employees, who generally have longer service tenures than lower-paid employees.) Past service credits are not available in defined contribution plans.

3. *Benefit insurance, plan termination and disposition of plan assets.* Defined benefit plans are insured by the Pension Benefit Guaranty Corporation (PBGC). This gives the employees protection in the event of plan insolvency, but the employer must pay insurance premiums. There is no guarantee program for defined contribution plans.

Defined benefit plans are generally more costly for an employer to administer and maintain, in part because of the need to engage the services of an actuary and pay insurance premiums to the PBGC.

It is relatively easy for an employer to terminate a defined contribution plan and distribute account balances to employees. In contrast, an employer's termination of a defined benefit plan is complex, expensive to undertake, and heavily regulated by the PBGC.

Employers generally cannot have any sort of property interest in the assets of a defined contribution plan, since the assets are allocated to accounts that belong to individual employees. An employer may have a residual stake in any surplus assets of a defined benefit plan, however, since in such plans the employees have only a right to receive promised benefits from the plan and do not own the assets themselves. In a sense, the employer owns the assets, and if the employer terminates the plan at a time when the plan is overfunded (i.e., the value of the plan's assets is greater than its liabilities to pay promised benefits), the asset overage is considered "surplus" which may revert to the employer. In addition, if an ongoing plan is overfunded, the asset overage may be viewed as an employer asset dedicated to paying future payroll costs, since the overage will pay for benefits earned by employees in the future. It should be noted, however, that to discourage reversions, Congress enacted a steep excise tax on reversions. The excise tax, which is paid in addition to income tax, is reduced if the employer agrees to use some of the surplus assets for new employee benefits.

4. *Benefit distributions and loans.* The most common mode of distributing benefits from a defined contribution plan is a lump sum distribution; many defined contribution plans do not offer true annuity

options. (If the plan offers an annuity option, the plan account balance will be converted to an actuarially equivalent annuity or used to purchase an annuity.) In a defined benefit plan, the normal form of benefit is a joint-and-survivor annuity (for a married employee) or a single life annuity (for an unmarried employee). Many defined benefit plans, however, offer other options, including a lump sum distribution equal to the present value of a single life annuity for the employee.

Another difference relating to benefit distributions is that employers can design defined contribution plans that allow employees to receive distributions while they are still working and before retirement age. A defined benefit plan cannot make a distribution to a current employee before retirement age. (The employer can, however, design a defined benefit plan to make distributions to a former employee even though the employee has not reached retirement age.)

A defined contribution plan can be designed to permit employees to take out loans against their account balances. This cannot be done in a defined benefit plan.

[¶ 8,240]

d. *Patterns of benefit growth in defined benefit plans and defined contribution plans*

We have already seen in ¶ 8,230 that the benefit accrual patterns in defined benefit plans favor older employees and, in plans with final pay benefit formulas, employees with greater seniority. We will now illustrate the pattern of benefit growth in a final pay defined benefit plan over a worker's career and compare it with the pattern in a defined contribution plan that produces an approximately equivalent benefit at retirement.

The formula in the defined benefit plan is an annuity, payable at age 65, equal to 2% of final pay times years of service. (To simplify our example, final pay is the pay a person earns in his last year of employment.) An employee, Paul, begins work at age 25 with a starting annual salary of $25,000. Paul works until age 65 and experiences a 5% annual increase in compensation. We will assume an interest rate of 8%, a discount rate of 8% for determining the present value of each year's growth in benefits, and an annuity conversion formula of 11:1 (that is, the cost of providing a $100 annuity at age 65 is $1,100).

In the first year of Paul's career, he accrues an annuity benefit of $500 per year (2% × $25,000 × 1), beginning at age 65. To provide this benefit, the plan will need to have $5,500 when Paul retires at age 65. Using an 8% discount rate, that benefit has a present value of approximately $273. That is, if you invest $273 at 8% interest for 39 years, it will grow to $5,500, the amount needed to purchase the $500 annuity at retirement age.

In the second year, Paul's compensation increases by 5% to $26,250. The accrued annuity benefit is now $1,050 (2% × $26,250 × 2). Thus,

Paul has accrued an additional $550 benefit in the second year (total benefit of $1,050, less previously accrued benefit of $500). The present value of this $550 annuity—payable in 38 years—is approximately $325.

In the last year of employment, Paul's salary has grown to $167,619, which yields an accrued annuity benefit of $134,095 (2% × $167,619 × 40). The portion of that annuity accrued in the 40th year is $9,578, which has a present value of $105,360.

In effect, the present value of the annuity benefit grows larger, both in dollar amount and as a percentage of salary, as the employee ages. The accrued benefit and present value calculations are summarized as follows:

	Year 1	*Year 2*	*Year 40*
Benefit Accrual (current year)	$500	$550	$ 9,578
Present Value	$273	$325	$105,360

As we have already noted, Paul's age–65 annuity, earned over the 40–year period, is $134,095. Under our assumed 11:1 annuity conversion formula, the present value of this benefit at age 65 is $1,475,045.

Now compare the pattern of benefit growth in a defined contribution plan. Assume the same facts as above, except that instead of a defined benefit plan with a 2% final pay formula, Paul's employer sponsors a defined contribution plan to which the employer contributes 12% of annual compensation at the end of each year. If the contributions are invested at an 8% annual rate of return over Paul's 40 years of employment, this plan will result in an accumulated account balance at retirement of $1,468,453. Thus, this defined contribution plan has almost the same value at age 65 as the value of the annuity in the defined benefit plan at age 65. But the pattern of growth in the value of each year's additional benefit in the defined contribution plan is different.

In Paul's first year of employment, the employer contributes 12% of his $25,000 compensation to the plan, or $3,000. In the second year, Paul's compensation increases to $26,250 and the employer's contribution to $3,150. In his last year of employment, Paul's compensation has increased to $167,619 and the employer's contribution to $20,114. Note that the contributions to the defined contribution plan are greater in the early years than the present value of the new benefit accruals in the defined benefit plan, but are less than the present value of the new benefit accruals in the later years. While the employer's contributions increase each year to reflect salary increases, the pattern of growth in contributions as a dollar amount is on a much flatter curve than the growth of the benefits in the defined benefit plan. And as a percentage of pay, the contribution growth pattern is flat.

The following graphs illustrate the patterns of growth in the defined benefit plan and the defined contribution plan. The first graph compares the present value of each year's new benefit accrual in the defined benefit plan with the present value of each year's contribution to the defined contribution plan. The second graph compares the accumulated value of the benefit accruals in the defined benefit plan with the accumulated value of the contributions in the defined contribution plan.

Present Values of Defined Benefit Accruals and Defined Contribution Amounts

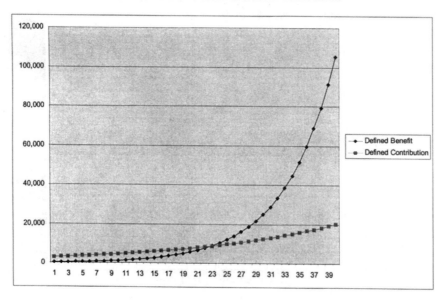

Accumulated Values of Defined Benefit Accruals and Defined Contribution Amounts

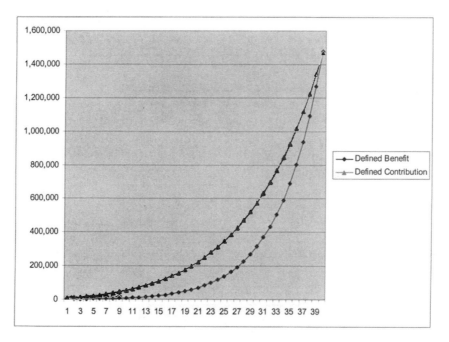

[¶ 8,250]

4. A Closer Look at Defined Contribution Plans

This section will describe the maximum annual limits on contributions to defined contribution plans; describe the major types of employer-sponsored defined contribution plans; and provide an overview of how a defined contribution plan can be "integrated" with Social Security.

[¶ 8,260]

a. *Maximum annual contributions*

Section 415 of the Internal Revenue Code imposes limitations on the amount that can be added to a defined contribution plan during a year. Annual additions include three amounts: employer contributions to a plan; employee contributions to a plan; and forfeitures from other accounts. The maximum addition to a defined contribution plan is the lesser of 100% of compensation or, for 2004, $41,000. The dollar figure is indexed to increases in the cost of living.

A special provision in the Internal Revenue Code (I.R.C. § 414(v)) allows employees who are over age 50 to elect to contribute an additional amount, known as a "catch-up" elective deferral. This amount, which was $3,000 in 2004 and will increase by $1,000 each year until it reaches

$5,000—after which it will be indexed to increases in the annual cost of living—is not subject to the § 415 limitation.

Note that in addition to the § 415 limitation, there is a separate limit on the amount that an employer may deduct annually for aggregate contributions to a defined contribution plan. The limit is generally 25% of the compensation of all participants. I.R.C. § 404(a)(3)(A).

[¶ 8,270]

b. *Plan typology*

There are several categories of defined contribution plans, some of which overlap. The most important of these are the following:

1. *Profit-sharing plans.* In its original conception early in the 20th century, a profit-sharing plan was just what it name suggests: a plan in which an employer would share a portion of its profits with its employees. The plan might, for example, require the employer to contribute a certain percentage of its profits annually, or it could provide that the employer would determine each year how much, if any, to contribute, although the contributions themselves had to come from profits. Thus, an employer could not make contributions in years in which there were no profits. However, Congress amended the Internal Revenue Code in 1986 so that employers can now contribute to profit-sharing plans without regard to whether they have profits. Indeed, after the 1986 legislation, a non-profit organization can sponsor a profit-sharing plan even though by definition it will never have a profit.

The employer's contribution to a profit-sharing plan is allocated to the accounts of employees. A profit-sharing plan can allocate contributions on the basis of compensation, age and seniority (and other factors), but a majority of plans base allocations on compensation alone. Some plans have annual allocations that are heavily weighted toward older employees. Such age-weighted plans are typically adopted by small businesses that wish to provide large benefits for older owners and small benefits for other (predominantly younger) employees. Another variant of this type of plan is the "new comparability plan," which generally has different (and better) benefit formulas for higher-paid employees, regardless of age. When contributions are allocated on some basis other than salary, the I.R.S. may become concerned that age and seniority are being used as a surrogate to discriminate in favor highly compensated employees, who are typically older and more senior than rank-and-file workers. These plans are discussed further in ¶ 8,630.

Profit-sharing plans have considerable flexibility in terms of distributions to employees. Unlike defined benefit plans and certain other types of defined contribution plans, such as money-purchase pension plans (described below), a profit-sharing plan is not required to distribute benefits in annuity form; instead, profit-sharing plans may be designed to provide lump sum payouts to employees (and may do so without spousal consent, in the case of married employees). Profit-sharing plans are also permitted in many circumstances to make distributions to current employees, something that defined benefit plans and certain other types of defined contribution plans generally cannot do.

2. *Money-purchase pension plans.* This type of plan requires the employer to contribute a specified amount to the plan each year. Generally, the employer will contribute a percentage of pay for each employee. These plans are pension plans, that is, plans designed to provide retirement benefits. All pension plans, whether of the defined benefit or defined contribution variety, are required to offer an annuity as the normal form of benefit, and in the case of a married employee, the benefit must be in the form of a qualified joint-and-survivor annuity unless the spouse consents to another form of distribution. (In effect, the account balance is used to purchase an annuity, hence the name "money-purchase pension plan.") Money-purchase pension plans generally cannot make distributions until an employee quits, is laid off or fired, or retires.

One might query why an employer would adopt a money-purchase pension plan rather than a profit-sharing plan, since the profit-sharing plan does not impose a mandatory contribution requirement and has more flexibility with respect to benefits. The answer to this question has to do with a former provision of the Internal Revenue Code, which limited deductions for contributions to profit-sharing plans to 15% of participant compensation. The deductible limit applicable to defined contribution plans, generally, however, was (and remains today) 25%. Thus, if an employer wanted to contribute more than 15% of participant compensation to a defined contribution plan, it was required to adopt a money-purchase pension plan. Indeed, it was common for employers to adopt both a money-purchase pension plan which required the employer to contribute 10% of participant compensation and a separate profit-sharing plan which permitted but did not require additional contributions of up to 15%.

Under 2001 amendments to the Internal Revenue Code, the deductible limit for contributions to profit-sharing plans was increased to 25%. Thus, some observers predict that few employers will adopt or continue to sponsor money-purchase pension plans in the future.

3. *Target benefit plans.* This is a form of money-purchase pension plan in which the employer sets a "target benefit" for each employee under a defined-benefit-type formula and then funds it using actuarial assumptions and factors stated in the plan. The employer contributions are allocated to the accounts of employees, as are the plan's actual investment gain and loss. Thus, the employee bears the risk that the account will be insufficient to purchase the target benefit. The formulas used by target benefit plans provide larger contributions (as a percentage of pay) for employees as they age, because the present value of a given dollar of target benefit increases as employees age. This feature made target benefit plans attractive to some small firms with owners who were older than most other employees. Today, firms that want to favor older

employees are more likely to adopt an age-weighted profit-sharing plan (described below).

4. *Stock bonus plans and ESOPs.* A stock bonus plan is a plan established and maintained by an employer to provide benefits similar to those of a profit-sharing plan, except that the plan pays benefits in the form of stock (or cash, so long as the employee may elect to be paid in stock). One type of stock bonus plan is the "employee stock ownership plan," commonly referred to as an ESOP. An ESOP can borrow money in order to purchase stock of the employer, and the stock is then allocated to the accounts of employees as the loan is paid down. ESOPs can also offer several other unusually generous tax and business advantages to an employer and its owners.

5. *401(k) plans.* A 401(k) plan, also referred to as a "cash or deferred arrangement," is a type of profit-sharing plan that permits an employee to elect to receive an amount as cash compensation or to have the same amount contributed to her account in the plan. Often, the employer will match all or a portion of the employee's contributions. The 401(k) plan is popular with employers because the employer is not required to make contributions for employees who prefer immediate to deferred compensation, as is often the case in other types of defined contribution plans.

For the year 2004, employees may elect to defer up to $13,000 of compensation. This will rise to $14,000 in 2005 and $15,000 in 2006, after which the limit will be indexed to increases in the cost of living. (An employee who makes an elective contribution is immediately vested in that contribution.) In addition, employees who have reached age 50 may make an additional catch-up contribution of $3,000 in 2004, $4,000 in 2005, and $6,000 in 2006, after which the catch-up contribution amount will be indexed to increases in the cost of living. Note that the employee's basic elective 401(k) contribution (but not the catch-up contribution) counts toward the § 415 limit on annual additions to the account ($41,000 in 2004).

Beginning in 2006, an employer can design a 401(k) plan to include a "Roth" feature, which allows the employee to elect to include a 401(k) contribution in taxable income in the year of contribution in exchange for a permanent income tax exclusion for qualified distributions from the plan. The Roth feature is discussed in connection with Roth IRAs in ¶ 8,400.

6. *403(b) plans.* Educational institutions, 501(c)(3) organizations, and ministers may establish 403(b) annuity plans, which are in many respects similar to 401(k) plans. The employee can defer a portion of her salary to a 403(b) plan and the employer can contribute through either direct or matching contributions. The maximum elective deferral for a 403(b) plan is the same as for a 401(k) plan. Moreover, if an employee participates in both a 403(b) annuity plan and a 401(k) plan, the employee's combined contributions to the two plans cannot exceed the maximum deferral amount.

7. *457 plans.* Named for the Internal Revenue Code section that regulates them, 457 plans are certain nonqualified plans established by a government or non-church tax-exempt organization for its employees. (Because governments and tax-exempt organizations do not pay tax, the effects of a non-qualified plan maintained by such entities are similar to those of a qualified plan.) Section 457 imposes the same limit on elective deferrals that applies to 401(k) plans. A major advantage of a 457 plan is that a deferral for such a plan does not reduce the maximum deferral amount for a 401(k) or 403(b) plan.

8. *Keogh (H.R. 10) plans.* Keogh plans (also known as H.R. 10 plans) are adopted by self-employed persons for themselves and their employees, if any. There are no longer significant legal differences between such plans and other qualified retirement plans, but the distinctive name (after the Congressman who sponsored the authorizing legislation) is still sometimes used to describe them.

9. *Self-directed investment plans.* Most defined contribution plans, and virtually all 401(k) plans, offer employees a choice of several investment options. If the plan satisfies certain requirements (found in section ERISA § 404(c)), the plan fiduciaries are exempt from liability for the investment choices made by the employees. Thus, self-directed plans are often known as 404(c) plans. Note that some defined contribution plans continue to follow the more traditional model in which one or more professional investment managers invest the plan's funds as a single pool and each employee's account is credited with a pro-rata share of investment gain or debited with a pro-rata share of investment loss.

[¶ 8,280]

c. *Integration with Social Security*

The Internal Revenue Code enforces a nondiscrimination principle, which attempts to ensure that qualified retirement plans do not discriminate in favor of highly compensated employees in contributions or benefits. Nominally, the nondiscrimination norm enforces a proportionality principle: highly compensated employees should not receive greater contributions, as a percentage of compensation, than non-highly compensated employees. Under a strict application of this principle, if a plan allocated 10% of a highly compensated employee's compensation to his account in a defined contribution plan, at least 10% of all other employees' compensation would have to be allocated to their accounts as well. Nevertheless, there are several ways in which highly compensated employees can receive higher proportionate benefits. Integrating a plan with Social Security is one such way. When a defined contribution plan integrates, it essentially tests for discrimination by counting contributions both to the plan and to Social Security as part of a single retirement program.

Under the Social Security system, the employer pays 6.2% of an employee's wages, up to the Social Security wage base, into the OASDI

Trust Fund. (This trust fund pays retirement benefits, survivor benefits, and disability benefits.) For purposes of Social Security integration, we assume that the portion of the employer's contribution that pays for retirement benefits equals 5.7% of the employee's compensation. For 2005, the Social Security wage base is $90,000.

Thus, in a pure integration regime, a plan could provide that employees receive no plan contributions on compensation up to $90,000, since the employer is contributing 5.7% of such compensation to Social Security; the employer's contribution to the plan could be equal to 5.7% of compensation above $90,000. All employees, then, would receive an employer contribution of 5.7% to a retirement plan on all compensation. But the effect of this scheme would be that the employer would make no contribution to the defined contribution plan for employees earning less than $90,000.

Until changes made by the Tax Reform Act of 1986, an employer was permitted to integrate a defined contribution plan in the way just described. But in 1986, Congress changed the rules to ensure that an integrated defined contribution plan allocates a portion of the employer's contribution to each plan participant. Under the new rules, the contribution above the Social Security wage base can be no more than the lesser of 5.7% or twice the contribution rate below the Social Security wage base.

Problem: A plan provides for a 3% contribution rate below the Social Security wage base. What is the maximum contribution it can provide above the Social Security wage base? What difference does it make if the contribution rate below the Social Security wage base is 5.7%? 10%?

Note that a plan's allocation formula can satisfy the Internal Revenue Code's nondiscrimination rules even if does not formally conform to the above requirements, so long as the plan's allocation formula does not result in greater disparity than would be permitted under those requirements. The methodology for determining "permitted disparity" under the nondiscrimination regulations is complex, however, and most integrated plans are written to comply with the formal integration requirements.

[¶ 8,290]

5. A Closer Look at Defined Benefit Plans

This section will describe the basic classification of defined benefit formulas; Social Security integration of defined benefit plans; permissible offsets against benefits in defined benefit plans; actuarial principles that apply to early retirement benefits under defined benefit plans; "hybrid" defined benefit plans, such as "cash-balance" plans; changes in defined benefit formulas; union-negotiated defined benefit plans; and termination of defined benefit plans.

[¶ 8,300]

a. Defined benefit formulas

We have already seen some examples of benefit formulas that are used in defined benefit plans. In this section, we will explore the two basic categories of defined benefit formulas: (1) unit credit plans; and (2) flat benefit plans.

Unit credit plans. A unit credit plan is one in which the benefit formula is based on a specified benefit unit multiplied by years of service. The benefit unit may be based on compensation or other factors such as a flat dollar amount. Although not commonly done, it is permissible for a plan to impose a cap on the number of years of service that are counted (e.g., 30 years of service). It is not permissible, however, to stop counting years of service when an employee reaches a certain age. The three most common types of formulas in unit credit plans are final pay, career average pay, and dollar amounts.

In a "final pay" plan, benefits are based on the employee's average annual salary for a specified period of time—typically 3 to 5 years—ending in the year the employee stops working. Benefits are earned ("accrued") in units linked to the employee's service (e.g., 1% of final pay for each year of service), so that employees with longer service receive relatively higher benefits in comparison to their pay because their entire benefit is based on their final pay, which is usually their highest pay. Final pay plan formulas are particularly advantageous for employees because benefits are linked to pay and grow automatically as pay increases. Assuming that compensation keeps pace with inflation, final pay plans help to maintain the real value of the benefit, at least as long as the employee continues to work for the employer. They also tend to reward long-service employees, who generally receive substantial productivity-related pay increases during their careers.

A "career average" plan typically pays less than a final pay plan because the benefits earned each year are equal to a percentage of the employee's compensation for that year. For example, a plan might provide for 1% of current pay each year. The total benefit is essentially the sum of the annual accruals. Unlike a final pay plan, which generally keeps pace with inflation as compensation is updated, a career average plan freezes each year's accrual as it is earned. If an employer wishes to assure that the benefit actually replaces an adequate amount of pre-retirement compensation, the employer must periodically amend its plan to increase the compensation used to determine benefits for earlier service.

Unlike the other types of unit credit plans, a "fixed dollar" plan does not base its benefit formula on pay at all. Instead, it provides benefits based on fixed dollar amounts times years of service (e.g., a monthly pension of $10 for each year of service). These plans are most common for plans negotiated between employers and labor organizations. Again, it is not uncommon in these types of plans to see retroactive amendments of the dollar amount to account for inflation.

Flat benefit plans. In a flat benefit plan, the benefit is not determined by multiplying a benefit unit by years of service. Instead, the plan states the benefit as a flat amount. For example, it may provide that the benefit is a flat percentage—say 50%—of final or career average pay. Or it may provide that the benefit is a specified dollar amount. In its purest form, such a plan provides the same benefit to all employees regardless of length of service. Formulas of this sort are rare and typically are found only in small plans where the employer wishes to provide adequate replacement income for all employees (on the assumption that short-term employees will not receive retirement benefits from other employers).

Many flat benefit plans reduce the flat benefit for employees who work less than a specified number of years. Employees who do not work the minimum number of years will have their benefits decreased pro rata to reflect the number of years actually worked divided by the number of years needed to earn the full benefit. For example, a plan might provide a benefit equal to 50% of final pay for employees who have at least 20 years of service. P has only 10 years of service. P will receive a benefit equal to 25% of final pay (10/20 × 50% of final pay). Note that this type of benefit formula is functionally equivalent to a unit credit plan with a cap on allowable service.

Other flat benefit plans use a fractional accrual approach, where the flat benefit is multiplied by a fraction with a numerator equal to a participant's actual years of service and a denominator equal to the number of years of participation the employee would have had if the employee participated in the plan until normal retirement age under the plan. Note that this approach also resembles a unit credit method, although each employee accrues a different annual benefit.

Example: A plan provides a benefit equal to 50% of final pay multiplied by a fraction with a numerator equal to years of service and a denominator equal to years from initial participation in the plan until normal retirement age under the plan (age 65). Nancy began participating in the plan at age 25; the denominator of her fraction will always be 40. Nancy works until she is 35, when her compensation under the plan's final pay formula is $50,000. Nancy's benefit is calculated as follows:

$$(50\% \times \$50,000) \times 10/40 = \$6,250.$$

Owen began participating in the plan at age 55; the denominator of his fraction will always be 10. Owen works until age 65, when his compensation is $50,000. Owen's benefit is calculated as follows:

$$(50\% \times \$50,000) \times 10/10 = \$25,000.$$

This kind of formula, known as a fractional rule formula, was particularly popular when the owner/employee of a small firm would establish a defined benefit plan shortly before his retirement. Nondiscrimination regulations promulgated in 1993, however, impose limits on the permitted disparity between benefits for highly compensated and other employees in plans that use this type of benefit formula.

Definitions of compensation. Most defined benefit formulas include a compensation variable. The method of calculating compensation for plan purposes can be significant. For example, some plan formulas include bonuses and/or commissions while others do not. The Internal Revenue Code's rules limiting discrimination in favor of highly-compensated employees place some restrictions on how a plan can define compensation.

[¶ 8,310]

b. *Integration with Social Security*

In an earlier section we considered the integration of a defined contribution plan with Social Security and saw how employer contributions to Social Security can be aggregated with contributions to the employer's plan. A defined benefit plan can also be integrated with Social Security, but here it is not the contributions but the benefits— Social Security retirement benefits and the defined benefit from the employer plan—that are integrated (unless the defined benefit plan is tested on a contribution basis, as discussed in ¶ 8,630). The methodology for integrating defined benefit plans is extraordinarily complex and this section will only summarize the two basic permissible approaches, the "excess" (or "step-rate") method and the "offset" method.

Central to both methods is the concept of "covered compensation." Covered compensation is the average of the Social Security wage bases for each year in the 35–year period ending with the year in which the employee attains Social Security retirement age. (However, the annual wage bases are not indexed to future increases in either average wage or cost of living.) The I.R.S. periodically publishes tables showing covered compensation, based on the employee's year of birth; it also publishes a table that groups certain people born in different years and provides rounded averages that can be used in lieu of the regular table. Some plans, for simplicity, standardize the definition of covered compensation by using the oldest plan participant's covered compensation (or some lesser specified dollar amount) for all plan participants.

The integration rules also require that integrated plans define compensation in accordance with a statutory definition of "average annual compensation."

Excess Method. Under the excess method, a defined benefit plan can have a higher benefit formula for compensation above a designated integration level. The benefit formula can provide up to ¾% greater benefit for the compensation in excess of the Social Security wage base, but in no event more than twice the percentage for compensation below the wage base. For example, a plan formula might provide a benefit equal to 1% of compensation up to covered compensation, determined separately for each employee, and 1.75% for compensation above covered compensation, times years of service. The plan uses the I.R.S. table of rounded covered compensation. Nora and Henry were each born in 1939, and covered compensation for them in 2004 under the I.R.S. table is $45,000.

Nora has worked for 20 years and has average annual compensation of $40,000. Her benefit is 20% of $40,000, or $8,000 per year. Henry has also worked for 20 years, but he has average annual compensation of $80,000. Henry's annual benefit is calculated as follows:

$$
\begin{array}{ll}
1\% \times 20 \times \$45{,}000 & \$\ 9{,}000 \\
+\ 1.75\% \times 20 \times \$35{,}000 & \underline{12{,}250} \\
& \$21{,}250
\end{array}
$$

Note that even though Henry's compensation exceeds Nora's by 100%, his benefit exceeds Nora's benefit by 166%.

Offset Method. A defined benefit plan using the offset method calculates an employee's benefits under a formula and then reduces that benefit by an offset amount. The offset amount can be no greater than the lesser of: (1) ¾% per year of service, or (2) half the regular plan accrual rate. The maximum offset can reflect no more than 35 years. A plan using the offset method must calculate compensation for the offset on the basis of the 3–year period ending with the current year, but no more than covered compensation. For purposes of the following example, we will assume that compensation for purposes of the offset and compensation for purposes of the basic benefit formula are the same.

Example: The plan formula provides a benefit equal to 1.75% of final average compensation, reduced by 0.75% for each year of service (up to 35 years). Consider Nora and Henry again. Henry's benefit is calculated as follows:

$$
\begin{array}{ll}
1.75\% \times 20 \times \$40{,}000 & \$14{,}000 \\
-\ 0.75\% \times 20 \times \$40{,}000 & \underline{6{,}000} \\
& \$\ 8{,}000
\end{array}
$$

Nora's benefit is calculated as follows:

$$
\begin{array}{ll}
1.75\% \times 20 \times \$80{,}000 & \$28{,}000 \\
-\ 0.75\% \times 20 \times \$45{,}000 & \underline{6{,}750} \\
& \$21{,}250
\end{array}
$$

As is the case with a defined contribution plan, a defined benefit plan can impute "permitted disparity" (i.e., the disparity that would have been permissible if the plan formally complied with the integration rules) to benefit accruals for purposes of nondiscrimination testing.

It should also be noted that before the Tax Reform Act of 1986, plans were subject to looser integration rules. A person with a long period of plan participation may thus find that part of her benefit is calculated under different integration principles.

[¶ 8,320]

c. Benefit offsets other than Social Security

A defined benefit plan may also integrate with factors other than Social Security benefits. These are usually referred to as offsets, since they generally provide for an offset against the plan's benefit formula. Such offsets are generally permitted so long as the offset reflects a benefit of the same character as the benefit provided by the plan. For example, the I.R.S. has ruled that a plan cannot offset benefits by unemployment insurance payments, since such payments are not of the same character as retirement benefits.

The most common types of offset arrangements are the following:

1. *Worker's compensation offsets.* Some pension plans, particularly plans covering industrial workers, include provisions reducing pension benefits by worker's compensation payments.

Example: The plan provides as follows: "In the event a participant is awarded any worker's compensation benefits deemed by the plan administrative committee to be of the same general character as a benefit provided by the plan, only the excess, if any, of the benefit amount prescribed in the plan above the amount of such worker's compensation payment, shall be payable." Peter has accrued a benefit of $1,000 per month under the plan formula and retires early after suffering a job-related injury. Peter files for worker's compensation and is awarded $800 per month. Peter's benefit will be reduced to $200 per month.

The I.R.S. has consistently ruled that such offsets are permissible, except to the extent an award is specifically designated as a medical payment or to compensate for loss of bodily function, such as the loss of an eye or limb. An open issue is whether the offset is reduced for fees the employee pays to an attorney to file the worker's compensation claim.

2. *Floor offset arrangements.* In a floor offset arrangement, a defined benefit plan is essentially integrated with a defined contribution plan of the employer. The defined benefit plan includes a basic benefit formula, but then reduces the benefit so calculated by multiplying a defined contribution account by an annuity conversion factor specified in the plan.

Example: Employer sponsors a defined contribution plan and a defined benefit plan. The defined benefit plan provides a benefit equal to 1% of final pay times years of service. Phil, age 65, has 20 years of service and his final pay is $50,000. He also has a defined contribution account with a balance of $100,000. Phil retires. Under the defined benefit plan's offset provision, the plan calculates the annuity benefit that the defined contribution plan would purchase. Assume that under the interest rate and mortality assumptions specified in the plan, the

$100,000 account balance would purchase a $9,000 age–65 annuity benefit at the time of Phil's retirement. Phil's benefit is determined as follows:

$$1\% \times 20 \times \$50,000 \quad \begin{array}{r} \$10,000 \\ - \quad\underline{9,000} \\ \$\ 1,000 \end{array}$$

It should be said that in some floor offset plans, the timing of retirement can be critical. For example, delaying retirement might result in a substantially larger account balance, so that the employee receives a smaller defined benefit than she would have received at normal retirement age.

Problem: Some people have argued that a floor offset arrangement penalizes good investment performance when the employee has a choice of investment options. Explain why this is so. Other people have argued that a floor offset arrangement can counter the reluctance of some employees to invest substantially in equities, which are riskier than fixed income investments. How can a floor offset arrangement increase an employee's tolerance for investment risk?

3. *Sales commission offsets.* When insurance sales employees retire, they sometimes receive continuing commissions on renewals of policies they sold in previous years. Some defined benefit plans covering such employees offset the defined benefit by all or a portion of the residual commissions paid during retirement. See Bonovich v. Knights of Columbus, 146 F.3d 57 (2d Cir. 1998), for a discussion of the legality of sales commission offsets in particular and offsets generally.

[¶ 8,330]

d. *Actuarial equivalence and early retirement benefits*

Some defined benefit plans permit employees to retire before normal retirement age, which can raise complex plan design and financial planning issues. To illustrate, assume a plan provides an annuity benefit at age 65 equal to 1% of final pay times years of service. Assume also that the plan permits an employee to retire as early as age 55 if the employee has worked at least 20 years. Employee Andy is 55, has 20 years of service, and his compensation is $50,000. Under the benefit formula, Andy's accrued benefit is an annuity equal to 20% of $50,000, or $10,000 per year. If Andy retires this year and begins receiving his benefit, what benefit should he receive? If he receives the full $10,000 per year, his benefit is worth more than if the same $10,000 benefit began at age 65, for the benefit will be paid for an additional ten years (assuming Andy lives to age 65). To compensate for this, plans generally provide for an actuarial reduction in early retirement benefits so that the present values of the age 55 benefit and the age 65 benefit are equivalent.

Some plans, however, provide subsidized early retirement benefits for some employees, where the early retirement benefit is worth more than the normal retirement benefit. In the example given, a fully subsidized benefit would be $10,000 per year, with no reduction. A plan might, however, only partly subsidize the benefit, reducing the benefit amount by some amount less than a full actuarial reduction.

Employers generally require long service for such fully or partly subsidized early retirement benefits. One common subsidized benefit requirement is age 62 plus 30 years of service. Some employers also provide subsidized early retirement benefits for a limited period of time, known as "window" benefits, to encourage older people to retire during periods of corporate downsizing. Sometimes window benefits are made available only to particular classes of employees.

The concept of actuarial equivalence also applies to other benefit forms—for example, a plan might offer a lump sum alternative to the normal life annuity benefit. The lump sum must be at least the actuarial equivalent of the retirement annuity payable at normal retirement age. Section 417 of the Internal Revenue Code provides rules for determining actuarial equivalence. These rules are discussed in ¶ 8,820, which considers post-retirement planning, including the form of benefit payouts from a retirement plan.

[¶ 8,340]

e. *Cash balance and other "hybrid" defined benefit plans*

A cash balance plan is a type of defined benefit plan. The benefit in a cash balance plan, however, is stated as a hypothetical individual account rather than as an annuity. Each employee has such an account (although no dollars are actually allocated to it); the defined benefit to which the employee is entitled, and which the employer funds, is the account balance. The account balance is determined under a plan formula, which describes the employer's deemed contributions and a deemed interest rate. For example, the plan might provide that each year the employee's benefit is increased by a deemed employer contribution equal to 5% of pay, and a deemed interest rate on the previous account balance of 6%. The employee gets the account balance regardless of the plan's investment performance. In theory, because cash balance plans are defined benefit plans and the normal form of benefit in a defined benefit plan must be an annuity, the "normal" form of benefit in a cash balance plan is an annuity (in effect, the account balance is used to purchase an annuity under assumptions stated in the plan). However, cash balance plans are almost always designed to allow an employee to take a lump sum rather than an annuity and virtually all employees who participate in cash balance plans take the benefit as a lump sum.

It is important to keep in mind that cash balance plans are defined benefit plans, even though the benefit promise has the look and feel of an individual account. Although an employee's cash balance benefit is defined in terms of an account balance, there are no true individual accounts. What the employee has is a promise that the plan will pay the account balance on retirement. At any given moment, the cash balance plan may have assets in excess of, or below, the value of the aggregate amounts promised to the employees.

Most cash balance plans result from "conversions" of traditional defined benefit plans into cash balance plans. Conversions generally harm older employees. In part, this is because annual benefit accruals in traditional defined benefit plans increase in value as an employee ages. (See ¶ 8,240.) In contrast, cash balance plans have accrual patterns that resemble allocations in a ordinary defined contribution plan, which do not weight benefits for older employees. Thus, older employees typically earn lower future benefits in the cash balance plan than under the traditional defined benefit formula. And in some cash balance conversions, older, longer-service employees go through a period in which they earn no new benefits at all through a process known as wear-away (see ¶ 8,350).

The legal status of cash-balance plans is currently unsettled. One district court has held that the cash balance form itself violates ERISA's accrual requirements. Cooper v. IBM Personal Pension Plan, 274 F.Supp.2d 1010 (S.D. Ill 2003). Moreover, the legality of wear-away may violate age discrimination rules since the adverse effects of the wear-away tend to correlate with age.

The cash balance form is not the only type of hybrid defined benefit plan in which benefits are stated as lump sum amounts. Another common example is the "pension equity plan" (PEP), which generally provides a benefit equal to a dollar amount multiplied by years of service. For example, a PEP might provide a benefit equal to $5,000 times years of service. An employee with 20 years of service would thus have a benefit of $100,000, which the employee could elect to take in a lump sum or an annuity of equivalent value. (In some plans, the dollar amount increases for older employees with greater seniority.) The legal status of PEPs, like that of cash balance plans, is currently unclear.

[¶ 8,350]

f. *Wear-away of benefits following a change in benefit formula*

Employers sometimes amend a plan to change its benefit formula. ERISA, however, prevents a retroactive reduction in the plan's primary benefits. Thus, benefits already earned as of the date of the amendment cannot be reduced, but they can in effect be frozen as of the date of plan amendment. The employee will accrue a benefit in the future under the revised benefit formula and at retirement will receive the greater of the frozen benefit or the benefit under the revised formula. Note that the frozen benefit will be the benefit under the old formula, calculated with respect to years of service and compensation as of the date of the amendment.

Example: Employer sponsors a final pay defined benefit plan, which provides an age–65 annuity benefit equal to 1% of final pay times years of service. Greg, an employee, has 20 years of service, and under the plan's final pay formula his compensation is $100,000. Greg's benefit is thus an annuity of $20,000 per year. Employer now amends the plan to change the formula to 1% of *career average compensation* times years of service. On the date of the amendment, Greg's career average compensation is $50,000 and his benefit is thus $10,000. If Greg retired today, he would be entitled to the greater of the two benefits.

In the above example, note that it may be several years before Greg's benefit under the new formula will exceed his frozen benefit under the old formula. In the interim, he will in effect earn no new benefits under the plan. The period during which the frozen benefit exceeds the new benefit is often referred to as the wear-away period.

Wear-away is especially controversial with respect to amendments that reduce a subsidized early retirement benefit or convert a traditional defined benefit plan formula to a cash-balance formula, since it can upset a participant's expectations about future benefits. Those who defend wear-away argue that the employee does no worse during a wear-away period than if the employer had terminated the plan, which the employer is permitted to do. But wear-away periods (and plan terminations) do frustrate employee benefit expectations.

[¶ 8,355]

Problem

ABC sponsors a defined benefit plan. The plan's benefit formula provides that an employee will receive an annuity at age 65 equal to 1% of final pay times years of service. Lena, age 55, has worked for ABC for 20 years and has an annual salary of $100,000.

ABC amends its plan to convert to a cash balance formula. Under the amendment, Lena's benefit under the old benefit formula is frozen. The amendment provides that Lena will receive at retirement the greater of the frozen benefit or the amount in a cash balance account, which on the date of the amendment is set at $50,000. The cash balance account will be credited with annual additions equal to 5% of compensation and interest of 6% per year.

What do you need to know to determine whether Lena will be subject to wear-away?

[¶ 8,360]

g. Negotiated defined benefit plans

The majority of retirement plans are sponsored by single employers for their employees. Although these plans are generally negotiated between the employer and the employees' bargaining representative, they are usually drafted and administered by the employer. In such plans, it is important to review not only the plan but also the bargaining agreement, which usually provides the general eligibility and benefit accrual standards for the plan.

In some industries, however, unions negotiate a plan—almost always a defined benefit plan—in which several employers participate. Accordingly, an employee can change jobs and still accrue benefits and vesting credit in the same plan, assuming the new employer is a signatory to the plan. These plans are especially prevalent in industries in which employees typically work for several companies during their careers. The United Mine Workers and the Teamsters, for example, sponsor this type of plan with their employer partners in collective bargaining. Multiemployer plans are subject to special funding rules and separate PBGC provisions (with benefit guarantees that are less generous than those applicable to single-employer plans).

[¶ 8,370]

h. *Terminations of defined benefit plans*

A defined benefit plan may terminate for a myriad of reasons: (1) the employer may decide to end the defined benefit program, perhaps replacing it with a defined contribution plan; (2) the employer may merge with another company that does not wish to continue the defined benefit plan; (3) the employer may become insolvent; or (4) the Pension Benefit Guaranty Corporation, the federally chartered agency that insures benefits in defined benefit plans and regulates the termination of defined benefit plans, may decide to terminate the plan because the plan's benefit obligations substantially exceed the value of the plan's assets.

The termination process for defined benefit plans can be exceedingly complex, and some lawyers specialize exclusively in matters involving the PBGC. For our purposes, we will outline the basic mechanics of terminating a plan whose assets exceed the plan's liabilities (a "sufficient termination") or a plan whose liabilities exceed its assets (an "insufficient termination").

1. *Sufficient termination.* The Internal Revenue Code provides that in a plan termination, all accrued benefits become fully vested to the extent funded. Thus, a sufficient termination always results in immediate vesting of all employees in their accrued plan benefits.

The terminating plan must satisfy benefits in the form prescribed by the plan. To provide benefits in the form of an annuity, the plan is required to secure a commitment from an insurance company to satisfy the plan's benefit obligations as they come due. There are two situations in which a plan may make a lump sum distribution in lieu of the normal annuity benefit. A plan will generally pay a lump sum (equal to the present value of the annuity) if the annuity has a present value of $5,000 or less. Also, if the plan provides for an elective lump sum distribution option, the plan will pay a lump sum (equal to the present value of the annuity) if the participant so elects.

In a sufficient termination, the plan will probably have assets remaining after satisfying the plan's benefit obligations. If the plan permits the employer to recover those assets, the employer may generally do so. However, if the plan was "contributory" (i.e., employees were required to make contributions to the plan from their salary), federal law requires that excess assets be shared with the employees. In addition, to minimize an excise tax on asset reversions, the employer often takes advantage of an excise tax provision that reduces the tax if a portion of the residual plan assets is used to establish a replacement plan or to increase benefits.

2. *Insufficient termination.* Some plans terminate with insufficient assets to pay all promised plan benefits. When this occurs, the Pension Benefit Guaranty Corporation takes over the plan and assumes responsibility for payment of benefits. From the standpoint of a plan participant, the key question in an insufficient termination is whether he will receive his benefits.

There are two steps in determining whether a participant's benefits will be paid: (1) the allocation of plan assets to different categories of benefits; and (2) the PBGC guarantees for any benefits that remain unfunded after the allocation.

Federal law allocates plan assets to six categories of benefits in order of priority. The first two categories consist of benefits attributable to voluntary or mandatory employee contributions, which are relatively unusual features in defined benefit plans. The third category consists of benefits that have been, or could have been, in pay status for at least three years on the date of the event that triggers plan termination (the "insured event"). As a practical matter, in a plan with benefit obligations that exceed PBGC guarantees, this is the most important category for older participants, since plan assets are often sufficient to fund most, if not all, of these benefits. In effect, this means that in most terminations, retirees and other participants who could have retired at least three years before the insured event will be paid their full benefits, even though the benefits exceed PBGC guarantee levels. Other participants who are not yet eligible for retirement or who became eligible less than three years before the insured event are limited to the amount guaranteed by the PBGC.

The amount of the annuity benefit guaranteed by the PBGC was originally $750 per month, but that amount is indexed to the cost of living; for plans terminating in 2005, the guarantee is $3,801.14 per month, or $45,613.68 annually. The benefit is reduced, however, if a participant elects a survivor benefit or retires before age 65. In addition, there are some limits on the guaranteed benefit itself (e.g., guarantees for benefit increases resulting from plan amendments made within five years of the insured event are ratably phased in over the five years). The PBGC also does not guarantee subsidized early retirement benefits, except for individuals who satisfied the eligibility conditions for the subsidy before the insured event. Moreover, the PBGC generally will pay benefits only in annuity form; thus, even if the plan provides for a lump sum distribution option, individuals will not be eligible to receive a lump sum distribution if their plan terminates with insufficient assets to satisfy plan benefits.

[¶ 8,380]

6. Non–Employment Based Retirement Vehicles

We will now consider three tax-sheltered retirement vehicles that exist outside the employment relationship: the individual retirement account (IRA); the Roth IRA; and the health savings account (HSA), which was introduced by the 2003 Medicare overhaul legislation.

[¶ 8,390]

a. *Individual retirement accounts*

ERISA created the "individual retirement account," or IRA. The tax treatment of the individual retirement account is similar to that of a qualified plan: an individual who contributes to an IRA receives an immediate deduction for his contribution; income earned by the IRA is exempt from tax; and the individual is not taxed until amounts are distributed from the IRA.

An individual can contribute to an IRA in a year if: (1) she is under age 70½ at all times during the year; (2) has earned income; and (3) is neither an active participant in an employer-sponsored qualified plan nor the spouse of an active participant. (As discussed below, a person who is an active participant or the spouse of an active participant may be entitled to make a contribution or a reduced contribution if his or her income does not exceed a specified amount.) The contribution limit is the lesser of earned income or a fixed dollar amount. The dollar amount is $3,000 in 2004, $4,000 in 2005 through 2007, and $5,000 in 2008. After 2008, the dollar limit is indexed to increases in the cost of living. (Special rules limit contributions by a person who is an active participant in an employer-sponsored qualified plan.)

In addition, an individual can increase her contribution by a "catch-up" amount if she is at least 50 years of age. The catch-up amount is an additional $500 through the year 2005, and $1,000 for 2006 and subsequent years.

A person filing a joint return can generally aggregate her own compensation with a higher-earning spouse's compensation, less any IRA deduction taken by the spouse. Thus, a person who has no earned income of her own can often contribute to an IRA if her spouse has earned income and they are otherwise eligible to contribute.

Problem: John and Joan are married and file a joint return. Joan and John live primarily off the income from a trust fund, but Joan is a part-time accountant and has $8,000 in earned income in 2006. Joan is 45 and John is 50. Joan contributes $4,000 to an IRA. How much, if any, may John contribute to an IRA? How much could John contribute if the facts were the same but Joan had $10,000 in earned income?

A person who is an active participant in an employer-sponsored qualified plan (or a federal, state or local government plan) is subject to a special limitation on contributions. The limitation is based on whether the participant's modified adjusted gross income (MAGI) exceeds a specified dollar level and if so, by how much. (For this purpose, MAGI has the same meaning as under the rules for taxing Social Security benefits. See ¶ 8,140.) The dollar limits for individuals who are active participants in an employer-sponsored plan are as follows:

Year	Married, filing joint return	Single
2004	$65,000	$45,000
2005	70,000	50,000
2006	75,000	50,000
2007 and thereafter	80,000	50,000

(The applicable limit for married individuals filing separately is zero, unless the spouses live apart for the entire year, in which case the single table is used.)

The contribution limit is zero if an individual's MAGI exceeds the applicable amount by $10,000 or more, with a proportionate reduction in the contribution limit if her MAGI exceeds the applicable amount by less than $10,000.

Example: In 2006, Eve, who is over 50 and is an active participant in an employer-sponsored retirement plan, has modified adjusted gross income of $55,000. Eve is single. Eve's contribution limit is calculated as follows:

	$ 5,000	(amount by which MAGI exceeds applicable limit)
÷	$10,000	
×	$ 5,000	(contribution limit for 2006, including catch-up amount)
=	$ 2,500	

(Beginning in the year 2007, the $10,000 figure will increase to $20,000 for married individuals filing joint returns.)

A special rule applies to a married individual who is not an active participant in an employer-sponsored plan but whose spouse is an active participant. The applicable amount is increased to $150,000.

Example: John and Joan are married and have MAGI of $156,000 in 2005. Joan is an active participant in a qualified plan and has earned income of $50,000. John is self-employed and is 45 years of age. But for

Joan's status as John's wife, John's deductible contribution limit would be $4,000. John's contribution limit is calculated as follows:

$ 6,000 (amount by which MAGI exceeds applicable limit)
÷ $10,000
× $ 4,000 (contribution limit for 2006)
= $ 2,400

[¶ 8,400]

b. *Roth IRAs*

From the enactment of ERISA in 1974 through 1997, there was only one type of IRA, as described above. In 1997, Congress authorized an alternative type of IRA which was named after its principal sponsor, the late Senator William Roth of Delaware. Today, an individual often has a choice of contributing to a traditional IRA or a Roth IRA, although we shall see that there are some instances when an individual is eligible only to contribute to a Roth IRA.

The most important difference between a regular IRA and a Roth IRA lies in the income tax treatment of the respective vehicles. In a traditional IRA, contributions are generally deductible when made and distributions are subject to tax as ordinary income. In a Roth IRA, the tax treatment is reversed: no deduction is allowed for contributions (which are accordingly made from after-tax dollars), but distributions are generally excluded from the recipient's gross income.

The contribution limits described in ¶ 8,390 are in fact an aggregate limit on total annual contributions to both traditional IRAs and Roth IRAs.

Example: In the year 2005, Tom, age 45, contributes $1,000 to a traditional IRA. Tom can also contribute up to $3,000 to a Roth IRA.

We will now explore some key differences between traditional IRAs and Roth IRAs and consider the factors that an individual should take into account in choosing between them.

[¶ 8,410]

(1) Differences between Roth IRAs and traditional IRAs

1. *Maximum contribution limits.* The contribution limit for a Roth IRA is nominally the same as the deductible contribution limit for a traditional IRA: $3,000 in 2004, $4,000 in 2005 through 2007, and $5,000 in 2008. Nevertheless, in almost all cases, the effective contribution limit is higher for a Roth IRA due to its tax treatment. Why is this so?

In the abstract, it is because a dollar contributed to a traditional IRA is a dollar with a built-in income tax liability; in effect, the government has a future claim on a portion of each dollar contributed to a traditional IRA (and on the investment income it earns), and this tax liability reduces the value of the account. In contrast, each dollar contributed to a Roth IRA has already been taxed, and the government has no further claim on that dollar or on the investment income it earns while it is held in the Roth IRA.

Another way of explaining this is that the real cost of contributing a dollar to a Roth IRA should reflect the fact that the contribution is made with after-tax funds. To make a contribution of one dollar to a Roth IRA, an individual must start with an amount sufficient to leave one dollar after paying income tax on the initial amount.

Put another way, a $3,000 contribution to a traditional IRA costs $3,000, while a $3,000 contribution to a Roth IRA made by an individual in the 36% tax bracket really costs $4,687.50—the amount of pre-tax funds that will leave the individual with $3,000 to contribute after paying tax at a 36% rate ($1,687.50).

In theory, assuming a constant tax rate, the net value of a traditional IRA, after paying tax on amounts distributed, should be equivalent to the net proceeds of a Roth IRA over a given period of time, although the timing of taxes will be different. To illustrate the comparison, consider two 40–year-olds, Ted and Ray, each of whom begins with funds of $4,687.50 before tax. Assume that each pays tax at a combined federal and state rate of 36% and that the annual rate of return on investments is 6%. If Ted contributes $4,687.50 to a traditional IRA, the account balance will grow to $20,118 at age 65. Upon receiving a distribution of this amount, Ted must pay a tax of $7,242, leaving Ted with $12,876 after tax. In contrast, Ray pays a tax of $1,687.50 up front and contributes $3,000 to a Roth IRA. (The contribution thus "costs" $4,687.50, the amount contributed to the traditional IRA.) At age 65, the account balance in the Roth IRA will grow to $12,876, which can be withdrawn without paying any additional tax. Thus, Ted and Ray will each end up with $12,876 after tax.

2. *Income eligibility.* With a traditional IRA, an individual who is an active participant in certain employer-sponsored retirement plans is not eligible to make deductible contributions up to the maximum IRA contribution limit if her MAGI exceeds a specified dollar figure, which in 2005 is $70,000 for married individuals filing a joint return and $50,000 for single individuals. The Roth IRA has a higher contribution limit, but the limit applies to all individuals, regardless of whether they are active participants in an employer-sponsored retirement plan. The applicable limit is $150,000 for married individuals filing a joint return, and $95,000 for single individuals.

The contribution limit is zero if an individual's MAGI exceeds the applicable amount by $15,000 or more, with a proportionate reduction in the contribution limit if her MAGI exceeds the applicable amount by less than $15,000.

3. *Contributions permitted after age 70½.* An individual cannot contribute to a regular IRA in or after the year in which he or she

attains age 70½. This provision does not apply to individuals contributing to a Roth IRA.

4. *Minimum distribution rules.* As will be explored in ¶¶ 8,750–8,790, the Internal Revenue Code imposes minimum distribution rules on distributions from qualified plans and IRAs. There are two sets of minimum distribution rules: those that apply during the participant's life and those that apply after the participant's death. The lifetime minimum distribution rules, as they apply to traditional IRAs, require that distributions commence by April 1 of the year following the year in which the IRA holder reaches age 70½. The Roth IRA, however, is not subject to the lifetime distribution rules, although it is subject to the minimum distribution rules that apply after the death of the IRA owner.

[¶ 8,420]

(2) Considerations in deciding whether to use a Roth IRA or a traditional IRA

1. *Earnings limitation.* An individual who is an active participant in a qualified plan is subject to contribution phaseout rules if he or she has MAGI in excess of the applicable dollar amount, which in 2005 is $70,000 for married individuals filing a joint return and $50,000 for single individuals. The applicable limits for Roth IRAs are considerably higher, $150,000 and $95,000. Thus, some individuals can only contribute to a Roth IRA.

But it should also be noted that an individual who exceeds the Roth applicable limit and is not an active participant in an employer-sponsored plan can contribute to a traditional IRA but not to a Roth IRA.

2. *Individuals over 70½.* An individual cannot contribute to a regular IRA if she will be at least age 70½ by the end of the year. Such an individual can, however, contribute to a Roth IRA.

3. *Timing of taxes.* An individual who contributes funds to a traditional IRA receives an immediate income tax deduction and defers tax liability until funds are subsequently withdrawn. In contrast, an individual who uses a Roth IRA must pay an immediate tax on amounts contributed but all investment earnings will be exempt from further income tax liability.

4. *Tax rate at retirement.* An individual who anticipates having a higher tax rate at retirement will benefit from using a Roth IRA rather than a traditional IRA. Accordingly, educated younger people, who generally expect to see their incomes rise in the course of their careers, will often be best served by contributing to a Roth IRA. In contrast, an individual who anticipates a lower tax rate at retirement may benefit from using a traditional IRA.

5. *Distribution flexibility and estate planning.* With a traditional IRA, the owner must begin taking required distributions in the year following the year in which she reaches age 70½. In contrast, the owner

of a Roth IRA is not required to take any distributions during his or her lifetime. Thus, Roth IRAs are better vehicles for building an estate. (The accumulated balance in a Roth IRA will be subject to estate tax at the owner's death but will not be subject to income tax when distributed to the successor beneficiaries.)

[¶ 8,430]

c. Health Savings Accounts

A new savings vehicle called the Health Savings Account (HSA) was created by the Medicare Prescription Drug, Improvement, and Modernization Act of 2003. Although nominally part of a health care program, the HSA is in fact a health-care/retirement savings hybrid. Indeed, from one perspective, an HSA is essentially a special IRA-type savings vehicle for individuals covered by high deductible health insurance policies. In this section, we will consider eligibility for HSAs, contribution limits, tax treatment of contributions and distributions, and use of the HSA as a vehicle for retirement savings.

1. *Eligibility to contribute to HSA.* Only an "eligible" individual can open an HSA. An eligible individual is one who is covered by a "high-deductible health plan" and who is not covered by a non-high-deductible health plan that duplicates the benefits covered in the high-deductible plan. See I.R.C. § 223(c)(1). (Certain types of "permitted coverage" are allowed in addition to the high-deductible health plan, including insurance for dental care, vision care, disability, and accidental injury.)

Note that a person who is covered by a non-high-deductible plan is not eligible to open an HSA if that person is also covered by a high-deductible plan. Thus, a person can lose eligibility to open and contribute to an HSA if, for example, his or her spouse has a non-high-deductible plan that provides family coverage. Moreover, an individual who can be claimed as a dependent on another person's tax return is not eligible to contribute to an HSA.

An individual who becomes eligible for Medicare coverage automatically loses his or her eligibility to make contributions to an HSA.

2. *Definition of high-deductible health plan.* A high-deductible health plan (HDHP) is a health care plan (which can be insured or self-insured) that meets two requirements: a minimum deductible amount and a maximum limit on out-of-pocket expenses. See I.R.C. § 223(c)(2). The minimum deductible for individual coverage is $1,000 and for family coverage $2,000. The maximum limit on out-of-pocket expenses for individual coverage is $5,000 and for family coverage is $10,000. In plans with family coverage, the plan may not pay benefits until the family incurs $2,000 in deductible expense. Thus, the plan may not provide benefits for a particular family member, even though that family member has individually incurred more than $1,000 in expenses. Several health policy analysts have criticized this aspect of the definition of a

HDHP. The minimum deductible and maximum out-of-pocket limits are indexed to the cost of living.

In order to encourage first-dollar coverage for preventive care, a plan will remain a HDHP even though the deductible does not apply to preventive care. Preventive care includes periodic health evaluations, routine prenatal and well-child care, immunizations, screening services and certain diagnostic procedures, and smoke-cessation programs.

3. *Annual contribution limits.* The Internal Revenue Code limits annual contributions to an HSA to the lesser of the deductible amount under the HDHP or a dollar amount, which is indexed to the cost of living. For 2004, the dollar amount is $2,600 for a single-coverage HDHP and $5,150 for a family-coverage HDHP. In addition, eligible individuals who reach age 55 before the end of a year may contribute an additional catch-up amount. The catch-up amount for 2004 is $500, and will increase by $100 each year until it reaches $1,000 in 2009. See I.R.C. § 223(b).

Because an employer is permitted to make HSA contributions on behalf of an eligible employee, the annual contribution limit applies to the aggregate of employer and employee contributions.

4. *Taxation of HSA contributions.* If an eligible individual makes a direct contribution to an HSA (or if a family member makes a contribution on behalf of the individual), the individual may deduct the contribution (up to the limits described above) as an above-the-line deduction.

If an employer makes a contribution on behalf of an employee, either directly or through a flexible health spending account, the contribution is excluded from the employee's income and neither the employer nor the employee pays FICA or FUTA taxes on the contribution.

An eligible individual may not deduct contributions to the extent they exceed the limits applicable to the individual in a particular year. Also, employer contributions in excess of the limits are included in the employee's taxable income. In addition, a 6% excise tax is imposed on the excess contributions unless the contributions and the net income attributable to the contributions are returned to the individual before the last day for filing his income tax return (including extensions).

5. *Taxation of HSA distributions.* Distributions to pay for "qualified medical expenses" (QME) for an HSA account owner, his or her spouse, or dependents, are excluded from gross income. In general, a QME is an amount paid for "medical care" as defined in I.R.C. § 213(d) relating to the medical expense deduction. Health insurance premiums are QMEs in only a few instances: qualified long-term care insurance, COBRA health care continuation coverage, and health care coverage while an individual is receiving unemployment compensation. In addition, distributions to pay for Medicare Part A or Part B, for a Medicare HMO, and for the employee's share of premiums for employer-sponsored insurance (including retiree health insurance) are considered qualified medical expenses. However, premiums for a Medigap policy do not

qualify. Other distributions—that is, distributions that are not for QMEs—are taxed similarly to distributions from individual retirement accounts: they are included in the income of the account owner. And such distributions are also subject to a 10% excise tax unless they are made after the beneficiary dies, becomes disabled, or becomes eligible for Medicare. See I.R.C. § 223(f).

6. *Death or divorce of HSA account owner.* When the owner of an HSA dies, the account passes to the decedent's designated beneficiary (or, if none, to his or her estate). If the designated beneficiary is a spouse, the account is treated as an HSA of the spouse. Any other beneficiary must include the fair market value of the account in gross income, subject to a reduction for any amounts paid within one year after death for QMEs of the decedent. See I.R.C. § 223(f)(8).

The division of an HSA on divorce is not treated as a taxable event, and the portion of the HSA transferred to the spouse becomes the spouse's HSA. See I.R.C. § 223(f)(7).

7. *HSA as retirement savings vehicle.* The primary purpose of the HSA is to stimulate an approach to health care finance known as "consumer driven health care." This concept generally refers to an employer health insurance program that combines catastrophic (i.e., high-deductible) health insurance with a health care reimbursement account for each employee. Health care plans that are structured in this way give the employee a financial stake in how he spends medical dollars: until the employee hits the high deductible limit, his health care expenditures will be made first from his HSA and when his HSA is exhausted, from other resources. Congress enacted the HSA to stimulate this kind of arrangement.

For a relatively healthy person who qualifies as an "eligible" individual, however, the HSA can provide an especially valuable retirement savings vehicle. If the annual contributions to the account exceed the individual's normal non-preventive health care expenses, the individual can create a retirement account that has the following advantages over an individual retirement account or a qualified plan: (1) tax-free distributions to the extent they are used for health care; and (2) no minimum lifetime distribution requirements.

E.   VESTING AND ACCRUAL OF BENEFITS

[¶ 8,440]

1.   Overview

Since the enactment of ERISA in 1974, federal law has provided that a participant obtains a nonforfeitable right in her "accrued benefit" after a certain number of years of service. To understand the concept of vesting, it is also necessary to understand the separate but related concept of benefit accrual. Benefit accrual refers to the growth of a plan benefit over time; vesting refers to the point at which a participant's accrued benefit becomes nonforfeitable.

Example: Ed participates in a defined benefit plan, which provides an age–65 annuity benefit equal to 1% of final pay times years of service. After three years, Ed has accrued a benefit of 3% of final pay. This does not, however, mean that Ed is vested in this benefit. The plan might, for example, provide that Ed's benefit becomes nonforfeitable only when he has five years of service. Thus, if Ed leaves employment in his fourth year, he will forfeit his benefit.

[¶ 8,450]

2. Minimum Vesting Standards

An individual must be immediately vested in benefits derived from the employee's own contributions. But the plan may delay vesting in the accrued benefit funded by employer contributions.

The basic minimum vesting standards today allow a plan to choose between two types of vesting schedules, "cliff vesting" and "graded vesting," for benefits funded by employer contributions.

[¶ 8,460]

a. Cliff vesting

Cliff vesting refers to a type of vesting schedule in which an employee's accrued benefits remain forfeitable until the employee has a specified number of years of service, at which point 100% of the accrued benefits become nonforfeitable. ERISA originally provided that to meet the requirements for cliff vesting, a plan had to provide a participant with a nonforfeitable interest in her accrued benefit after no more than ten years of service. In 1986, the required period was reduced to five years of service.

Example: Same facts as above, but Ed completes five years of service. Ed now has a nonforfeitable interest in a benefit equal to 5% of final pay.

[¶ 8,470]

b. Graded vesting

Graded vesting refers to a schedule under which a participant increases his vested percentage gradually as he accumulates years of service. Under graded vesting, an employee must be at least 20% vested after three years of service, 40% after four years, 60% after five years, 80% after six years, and 100% after seven years. (ERISA's original graded vesting standard prescribed a a 15–year period over which benefits gradually vested.)

Example: Same facts as above, but the plan provides for a seven-year graded vesting schedule. After three years, Ed has a 20% nonforfeitable interest in an annuity equal to 3% of his final pay. Assume that his final pay, as calculated under the plan at the end of three years is $100,000. Ed would be entitled to a $600 annuity (20% × 3% × $100,000) commencing at age 65.

Example: Same facts as above, except that Ed has worked for seven years. Ed now has a 100% nonforfeitable interest in his benefit (i.e., an annuity equal to 7% of his final pay).

Example: Ed has a defined contribution balance of $50,000 and has three years of service. The plan has been funded entirely by the employer and uses the statutory seven-year graded vested schedule. If Ed leaves employment now, he will receive 20% of his account balance, or $10,000. The $10,000 will be distributed to Ed in accordance with the plan's terms.

[¶ 8,480]

c. *Year of service*

Both ERISA and the Internal Revenue Code define a year of service as a 12–month period designated by the plan in which an employee works at least 1,000 hours. Note that 1,000 hours is approximately half of a full year's work.

Because some employers might have difficulty in keeping track of actual hours, the Department of Labor has promulgated alternative methods of counting hours of service, known as "hour equivalencies." For example, a plan can count weeks, instead of hours, of service; if the employer uses this method, an employee must be credited with 45 hours for each week in which the employee works at least one hour. Similarly, there are hour equivalencies for days (an employee receives 9 hours of service for each day worked), months (an employee receives 185 hours for each month worked), and others.

Regulations have also approved a more controversial method of counting years of service, which dispenses with the counting of hours. Under the "elapsed time" method, an employee is credited with one year of service for each full 12-month period the employee works, beginning from date of hire. Under this rule, an employee can have five years of more than 1,000 hours and not vest in her benefits.

Example: Ed is hired on January 1, 2000. Ed's employer sponsors a plan using the elapsed time rule for determining years of service. Ed works 2,000 hours each calendar year for the next five years, but Ed is terminated from employment on December 1, 2005. Although Ed has five calendar years in which he has worked more than 1,000 hours, he is not credited with five years of service under the elapsed time rule because he did not work for the full year in 2005.

The rules governing years of service, and particularly the rules governing the consequences of a person returning to work after a period of absence, are complex and beyond the scope of this chapter.

[¶ 8,490]

d. Benefit accrual

The benefit in which a plan participant vests is the "accrued benefit." In a defined contribution plan, the accrued benefit is the employee's account balance. In a defined benefit plan, the accrued benefit is the benefit set forth in the plan, expressed in the form of an annual benefit commencing at normal retirement age. Courts have sometimes been asked to map out the contours of this definition. In one case, a plan benefit was indexed to the cost of living once benefits commenced. The employer amended the plan to eliminate this feature retroactively. The plan participants sued, arguing that the feature might be eliminated for post-amendment accruals, but could not be removed from benefits already accrued, because ERISA provides that an accrued benefit cannot be reduced or eliminated by plan amendment and, in any event, the participants were already vested in these benefits. The court agreed with the employees. Shaw v. International Ass'n of Machinists & Aerospace Workers Pension Plan, 750 F.2d 1458 (9th Cir. 1985).

But not all benefits are accrued benefits. For example, subsidized early retirement benefits or disability benefits are not accrued benefits. ERISA, however, prohibits a plan amendment that would reduce or eliminate an early retirement benefit (or retirement-type subsidy) or eliminate an optional form of benefit (such as a lump sum distribution option). In the case of a subsidized benefit, the participant can qualify for the benefit only if he or she meets the pre-amendment conditions for the benefit and only to the extent the benefit was accrued prior to the amendment.

Example: A defined benefit plan provides for a subsidized early retirement benefit for employees who retire on or after their 55th birthday with 25 years of service. Ed is 50 and has 20 years of service when the employer amends the plan to eliminate the subsidy. If Ed works until age 55, he will qualify for the subsidy but his subsidized benefit will be based on 20 (not 25) years of service.

The Treasury Department has promulgated regulations on what types of benefits are protected against reduction or elimination through plan amendment. The most important of the non-protected benefits include certain ancillary benefits such as health, life, or accident insurance, and certain temporary enhanced benefits for retired participants who have not yet reached Social Security retirement age.

[¶ 8,500]

e. Minimum standards for benefit accrual

Vesting rules would provide scant protection for employees if there were no rules governing the annual growth of the plan's accrued benefit. For example, assume that before ERISA a defined benefit plan provided an annuity benefit equal to $100 per month times years of service, with a

25–year vesting requirement. After ERISA was enacted, the longest permissible vesting period became ten years. Suppose, however, that the employer amended the plan to provide the following benefit formula: $.01 per month times years of service for the first 24 years of service, and $2,499.76 for the 25th year of service. After ten years, an employee would be 100% vested in a meaningless benefit. To prevent this kind of backloading, Congress adopted minimum accrual rules governing the accrual of benefits over time. There are three alternative rules, each with its own complexities. The most common rule provides that a benefit in a given year cannot exceed a benefit in any prior year by more than one-third.

Example: If a plan provides a benefit of $100 per month for one period of employee service, it cannot provide more than $133.33 per month for any later period of employee service. Thus, a plan could provide a $100 per month accrual for the first ten years of service, and $133 for each year of service thereafter.

Example: If a plan provides for a benefit of 1% of final pay for one period of service, it cannot provide more than 1.33% of final pay for any later period of service. Thus, a plan could provide a benefit equal to 1% of final pay for the first ten years of service and 1.33% for each year of service thereafter.

Problem: Both of the above examples prevent nominal backloading of benefits. But does either of the formulas permit substantial backloading of benefits?

It should be noted that a plan sponsor generally can amend a plan to increase the future rate of benefit accrual.

Example: A plan is adopted in the year 2000 with a benefit formula equal to $100 per month times years of service. In 2005, the sponsor amends the plan to provide that beginning with that year, employees will accrue a benefit equal to $150 per month.

[¶ 8,510]

f. Limitations on vesting

1. *Forfeiture at death.* ERISA does not provide complete protection against forfeiture on the death of the participant. But ERISA does impose on defined benefit plans, as well as money-purchase plans and target benefit plans, a requirement that they offer a pre-retirement survivor annuity for the spouse of a married participant. Other defined contribution plans must either provide that the spouse is entitled to a deceased participant's account balance (unless she waives that right) or provide for a pre-retirement survivor annuity. The amount of the pre-retirement survivor annuity is equal to the survivor annuity that would have been paid if the participant had elected a "qualified joint and survivor annuity" the day before his earliest retirement date under the plan. A qualified joint and survivor annuity is a life annuity for the

participant and a spousal survivor annuity equal to at least 50% of the participant's annuity. The qualified joint and survivor annuity must be at least actuarially equivalent to the participant's single life annuity under the plan. (Further explanation of the qualified joint and survivor annuity, with examples, is provided in ¶ 8,690.)

A plan is permitted to make the pre-retirement survivor annuity elective, with slightly reduced normal retirement benefits for participants who elect that form of benefit. Most defined benefit plans, however, fully subsidize the pre-retirement survivor annuity and provide it automatically to all married participants.

Note that a plan is permitted to provide for forfeiture of the accrued benefit on death for an unmarried participant. Such forfeitures are not uncommon in defined benefit plans, but most defined contribution plans provide for distribution of a deceased participant's account balance to the participant's beneficiary even if the participant is unmarried.

2. *Retiree health and other non-retirement benefits.* ERISA does not provide minimum vesting standards for non-retirement benefits. This means that a participant's rights to such benefits can generally be eliminated unless the plan itself provides that the benefit is nonforfeitable (or forfeitable only under limited circumstances). Under most employee benefit plans, however, the plan sponsor reserves the right to terminate the plan or modify or eliminate benefits under the plan, and courts have generally held that such clauses permit the employer to eliminate benefits unless the plan has clear and unambiguous language providing for the vesting of benefits. See, e.g., Sprague v. General Motors Corp., 133 F.3d 388 (6th Cir. 1998). Moreover, most courts have held that oral representations that benefits will not be reduced or eliminated are not binding and do not protect employees from a subsequent change in the plan.

[¶ 8,520]

g. *Special vesting rules*

1. *Top-heavy plans.* In 1986, Congress became concerned that despite the Internal Revenue Code's nondiscrimination rules, benefits in some plans were excessively weighted toward owners and relatively high-paid employees. In response, Congress enacted I.R.C. § 416, which regulates "top-heavy" plans. A plan is generally be considered top-heavy if more than 60% of the plan's accrued benefits belong to "key employees," which includes 5% owners and certain officers and highly-paid employees. The determination of a plan's top-heaviness is quite complex and beyond the scope of this chapter.

If a plan is top-heavy, it is subject to special vesting requirements for non-key employees. If the plan uses a cliff vesting schedule, the plan must provide that benefits become nonforfeitable after three years rather than five years. Similarly, for plans that use graded vesting, the plan must use a five-year graded vesting schedule rather than a seven-year schedule.

2. *Vesting in employer matching contributions.* A defined contribution plan must provide for no more than three-year vesting in employer matching contributions.

3. *Vesting on plan termination.* I.R.C. § 411(d)(2) provides that a terminating plan must provide 100% vesting of accrued benefits, to the extent funded. For participants in defined contribution plans, this results in full vesting on plan termination. In a defined benefit plan, the extent of plan-termination vesting is tied to how well funded the plan is on termination.

The Code also provides for immediate vesting on a partial plan termination. A partial termination can occur when a large number of nonvested employees cease participating in a plan, generally because of layoffs or corporate restructuring. A partial termination can also occur if a plan sponsor amends the plan to reduce the rate of future benefit accruals and in so doing increases a potential reversion to the employer.

F.   SOURCES OF INFORMATION ABOUT PLANS AND BENEFITS

[¶ 8,530]

Under ERISA, a participant in an employee benefit plan has the right to obtain copies and/or examine various plan documents, and to receive annually a statement of benefits. The most important of these documents are described below.

1. *Plan and trust documents.* A participant can request a copy of the plan and trust documents. Pension plans are generally lengthy and technical documents, filled with boilerplate language and written in legalese.

2. *Summary plan description and summary of material modification.* Recognizing that most participants will not find the plan documents easy or comprehensible reading, ERISA also requires that the plan administrator provide each plan participant and beneficiary a copy of a summary plan description (SPD) within 90 days of becoming a member of the plan. The summary plan description, which is generally in booklet form, is intended to explain the plan rules in language an average plan participant can understand.

The SPD must be complete and accurate and must meet the following other criteria:

- It must provide basic information, including the name of the plan, the plan's employer identification number (EIN), where the plan is located, and the name, address and telephone number of the plan administrator. It must also provide the names, titles and addresses of the plan trustees, if they are different from the administrator.

- It must describe how to become eligible to receive benefits and provide a description or summary of participants' and survivors' benefits.

- It must describe how benefits become vested (nonforfeitable).

- It must specify the type of plan (e.g., defined benefit, defined contribution, single-employer, multiemployer, etc.) and the source of financing. If benefits are provided through another entity (e.g., an insurance company), the SPD must provide the name and address of the entity and describe its functions.

- It must detail how rights to benefits can be lost.

- It must explain how to get other plan documents.

- It must explain how to apply for benefits and how to appeal to the plan any denial of benefits.

- It must explain that the participant has the right to pursue a claim in court if the plan denies the participant's appeal.

- It must give the name and address of the person who has been designated by the plan as its agent for purposes of service of process.

The SPD must be updated every five years if there have been important changes in plan rules. In addition, every time important plan changes are made, participants must receive a "Summary of Material Modification" (SMM) which describes in simple language what has been changed and what the effect of the change will be.

3. *Individual benefit statements.* Participants may request to receive once every twelve months a statement telling them whether they have earned a nonforfeitable right to a pension, and, if so, how much they would be entitled to receive under the plan at retirement age if they stopped working on the date of the statement. If the participant is not vested, the plan must indicate the earliest date on which benefits will vest. If the participant is married and at least 35 years old, the statement must describe the benefits that are available to a surviving spouse and the effect of this protection on the participant's own benefits.

Some plans send out these benefit statements automatically each year, but they are not required to do so. There is currently no prescribed format for benefit statements, and statements from defined benefit plans can be misleading if not read carefully. For example, the benefit statement of some plans may be based on the assumption that the employee has terminated employment and thus the benefit would reflect years of service as of the date of the statement. Other plans, however, project the benefit for current participants to normal retirement age, showing what the benefit would be worth if the employee continued to work until then.

It should be said that benefit statements are largely irrelevant in defined contribution plans in which employees can select investments, since the plan or investment vehicles themselves will generally send the participant periodic account balance statements. Moreover, in many such plans, participants can access this information online.

4. *Deferred vested statement.* If a participant stops working for an employer after earning vested benefits, the plan must send a similar statement after the participant leaves. This is called a "deferred vested statement" and it must show the participant's exact benefits on reaching normal retirement age.

5. *Annual Report (Form 5500).* Each year large plans must file a comprehensive and detailed financial report with the government. Small plans (those with no more than 100 participants) file these financial reports every three years. The reports are called "Form 5500" and are filed with the Internal Revenue Service. The I.R.S. shares the forms with the U.S. Department of Labor (DOL) and the Pension Benefit Guaranty Corporation (PBGC), who use the information for enforcement purposes.

Among the types of information that are required to be included with Form 5500 are: (1) financial statements and a statement by the qualified certified public accountant who audits the plan that the plan records are being kept in accordance with generally accepted accounting standards; (2) in the case of a defined benefit plan, actuarial statements and a statement by the enrolled actuary certifying that the assumptions used by the plan are reasonable; and (3) bank or insurance information if necessary.

Participants can request a copy of the Form 5500 from the plan (which may charge a copying fee) or they can look at the document in the plan's main office. Form 5500s are also available at the Department of Labor's Public Disclosure Room, although the Department of Labor sometimes misplaces forms.

6. *Summary annual reports.* The summary annual report is a one or two page summary of the information in Form 5500. It is a quick and not especially thorough overview of a plan's financial condition. ERISA requires plans to send each participant a copy of the summary annual report.

7. *Other notices and reports.* Federal law requires plans to provide participants with other notices and reports in certain circumstances, including notices when a plan fails to satisfy ERISA funding rules, and information about spousal survivor benefits when participants reach certain ages.

G.   RETIREMENT PLANS AND MARITAL DISSOLUTION

[¶ 8,540]

An individual's interest in a retirement plan is often among his or her most valuable assets. On divorce, then, benefits under a retirement plan are often one of the most important components of marital property subject to division.

Two legal regimes—one federal and one state—regulate the division of retirement plan benefits on divorce and separation. Federal law requires that the division of benefits be effected through a qualified domestic relations order, or QDRO. The purpose of the QDRO is two-fold: to ensure that the plan administrator receives clear instructions about how benefits are to be divided, and to prohibit (with a few exceptions) the division of property in a way that violates the terms of the plan itself. In contrast, state law furnishes the legal rules governing the spouses' respective rights in each other's retirement benefits on divorce. In a sense, federal law protects the plan, while state law dictates the respective rights of the divorcing spouses.

[¶ 8,550]

1. Qualified Domestic Relations Orders

As noted, ERISA requires that the division of retirement benefits on divorce or legal separation be effected through a QDRO. The rules relating to QDRO serve two functions: first, they describe the technical form and content of the QDRO; second, they impose certain limits on the actual division of property under state law.

The technical requirements concerning the form and content of a QDRO are set forth in ERISA § 206(d)(3). In general, a qualified domestic relations order is a state court order that:

(1) relates to child support, alimony payments or marital property rights for a spouse or former spouse, child or other dependent (these individuals are referred to as "alternate payees");

(2) contains the name and last known mailing address of the participant and each alternate payee;

(3) identifies the plan or plans to which the order applies;

(4) describes the rights of alternate payees, including the amount or percentage of the participant's benefits that is to be paid to each alternate payee (or a formula or method for determining such amount or percentage) and the number of payments or the period to which the order applies.

In addition, a QDRO must not do any of the following:

(1) order a plan to provide greater benefits than would ordinarily be required by the plan's terms;

(2) require the plan to provide any type or form of benefit or benefit option that is not available to the participant (for example, if a plan provides for benefits only in annuity form, a QDRO may not require the plan to pay benefits to an alternate payee in a lump sum); or

(3) require payment to an alternate payee of benefits that are already required to be paid to another alternate payee under a previous QDRO.

One exception to these rules is that a QDRO may require that benefits be paid to the alternate payee when the participant reaches the "earliest retirement age," which is defined as the earlier of age 50 or the earliest date a participant could begin to receive benefits if he or she stopped working for the employer.

[¶ 8,560]

2.   Division of Rights in Employee Benefit Plans Under State Law

As noted, state domestic relations law determines how a judge will divide an interest in an employee benefit plan between divorcing or separating spouses. We do not attempt here to summarize the applicable legal standards under the laws of the various states, but we will note some basic recurring issues. It should also be stressed that parties to a divorce or separation generally can reach a private settlement agreement that divides an interest in a retirement plan in any manner that does not violate the QDRO rules, even if the division departs from the standards of otherwise applicable state law.

In the case of a defined contribution plan, a QDRO generally divides the plan account balance between the spouses as of the date of the divorce. In rare cases, a QDRO might also provide for a division of plan contributions made after the divorce.

In the case of a defined benefit plan, drafting a QDRO is considerably more complex, especially when the plan is based on final pay and thus includes implicit indexation of benefits to salary increases. There are three basic approaches to dividing benefits in a defined benefit plan: (1) divide the accrued benefit as of the date of divorce; (2) divide the accrued benefit as of the date of divorce, but increase the benefit to reflect post-divorce salary increases; or (3) divide the accrued benefit as of the date of retirement.

[¶ 8,565]

Problem

Apply the three regimes described in the preceding paragraph to the following facts. Don and Abby are getting divorced. Don participates in a defined benefit pension plan with a benefit equal to 1% of final pay times years of service. Don has 10 years of service at the time of the divorce and his final pay, under the plan's definition, is then $100,000. When Don eventually leaves employment ten years later, he has 20 years of service and his final pay is $150,000. Note the effect that Don's career decision has on the benefits payable to Abby in the second and third approach to dividing benefits.

H. INVESTING FOR RETIREMENT

[¶ 8,570]

Many defined contribution plans allow employees to determine how their account balances should be invested, typically giving them a menu of options. In most cases, the options consist of mutual funds with different risk and return characteristics, and in many plans there is also an opportunity to invest in stock of the employer. Research has shown that many employees who direct their own investments make poor choices: some are too conservative; some are too aggressive; some fail to diversify; and few employees revisit their initial choices.

Basic investment strategy for retirement is based on three central ideas: first, that diversification reduces risk without sacrificing expected return (this is the basic tenet of modern portfolio theory); second, that returns on equity investments have been substantially higher than returns on bonds and other fixed-income securities, at least historically speaking; and third, that an individual's tolerance for risk, and thus investment in equity, should decline as she ages, since she has less time to recover from a period of loss (assuming, as most people do, that the stock market will eventually recover from a period of loss).

The substantial decline in equity values in 2001 and 2002 vividly illustrates this last idea. Some older individuals, who had become accustomed to substantial appreciation in stock values during the previous decade, retained substantial portions of their portfolio in stock. Faced with a dramatic decline in the stock market, many of these people were forced to delay retirement or to retire at a lower-than-anticipated standard of living.

What is the proper ratio of equities to safer, fixed-income investments? Younger investors should certainly allocate a much higher percentage of their retirement investment portfolio to equities than older investors, but by how much? One rule of thumb for asset allocation, sometimes referred to as the rule of 100, calls for the percentage of equities held in a retirement investment portfolio to equal 100 less the investor's age. Thus, the portion of the portfolio invested in stock would be 75% in the case of a 25–year–old, or 40% in the case of a 60–year–old. There are also several on-line calculators that provide suggested allocation ratios that incorporate an individual's tolerance for risk.

The last decade has produced significant research and thought on the investment decisions of participants in self-directed defined contribution plans. Not surprisingly, given that few Americans have received meaningful education in how to manage investments, the research has revealed numerous problems. The following are among the most serious:

1. *Investing in money.* Studies have shown that some individuals invest substantial portions of their portfolio in a money-market fund, a fund whose assets are invested in short-term, safe, fixed-income, low-interest securities. Investing in a money market for long-term returns—

the goal of retirement savings—is imprudent, virtually akin to stuffing savings under a mattress. It may be safe, but assets so invested will not grow into an adequate fund to support retirement.

2. *Investing by dividing.* Research has also shown that a common investment "strategy" is to allocate plan contributions ratably among the available investment alternatives. Thus, if a 401(k) plan offered participants five investment options, a participant would allocate 20% of her contributions to each investment option. This is a random approach to investing that will seldom produce an appropriate portfolio.

3. *Investing in employer stock.* Many 401(k) plans offer participants the opportunity to invest in employer stock. We know empirically that many employees will choose to invest a substantial portion of their account balance in employer stock when it is offered as an investment option. Indeed, in some plans, such as the Proctor & Gamble 401(k) plan, more than 90% of aggregate plan assets are invested in Proctor & Gamble stock (at least as of 2002).

Investing a substantial portion of retirement assets in any single asset violates the basic tenet of modern portfolio theory, which teaches that diversification is essentially a costless way to reduce risk. Moreover, an employee's human capital is already heavily invested in the employer. Thus, if the employer fails, employees who have invested retirement plan assets in employer stock may lose not only their jobs but their retirement savings as well. The opinion of financial advisers is virtually unanimous that an individual should not invest retirement assets in employer stock.

Why, then, do so many employees invest in employer stock? Researchers have suggested a number of reasons. Some employees may want to show loyalty to the employer by investing in employer stock. In some work environments, employees may be subject to pressure from their peers, their supervisors, or both, to invest in employer stock. Some employees may invest in employer stock because they feel they have a special understanding of their employer's business (which does not, of course, mean, that the employer stock is undervalued or less risky than other available investments). Behavioral psychologists believe that there is an "endorsement effect" when employer stock is an available investment option, since employees may believe that the employer would not offer it unless it was a good investment. Finally, when employer stock is offered as one of many investment options, its familiarity to the employee almost always results in some contributions being allocated to it.

4. *Investing without reallocating.* A participant should periodically evaluate her portfolio and adjust it by reallocating assets. In part, this is because allocation strategies might change: as an individual ages, she should consider reducing her equity holdings. But market performance may also cause the composition of a portfolio to depart from the investor's intended allocation.

Example: Tom, age 50, wishes to invest 60% of his portfolio in equities. At the start of the year, Tom's portfolio conforms to this allocation, with $60,000 invested in an equity fund and $40,000 invested in a diversified bond fund. Over the next two years, the equity fund experiences 20% growth and is now worth $86,400, while the bond fund experiences 4% growth and is now worth $43,264. The portion of Tom's portfolio allocated to equities has now risen to 67%.

If Tom continues to believe that the appropriate allocation for his portfolio is 60% equities, he can either restructure his portfolio by selling some of his units in the equity fund or by restructuring his future contribution allocations to favor the bond fund.

I. RETIREMENT PLANS AS TAX SHELTERS FOR THE WEALTHY

[¶ 8,580]

We have already observed that qualified plans offer substantial tax benefits in the form of tax deferral (see ¶ 8,190). What are the policy reasons for providing these tax benefits to participants in qualified plans? The orthodox explanation is that the tax benefits are designed to foster retirement savings among those who would otherwise be reluctant savers. At first glance, it may not seem obvious how the benefits of tax deferral—which correlate with marginal tax rates and thus favor the most affluent individuals—will help reluctant savers (who we can assume are less affluent) to save for retirement. But the theory is that the tax benefits of qualified plans will induce business owners and managers to establish qualified plans so that they can capture valuable tax benefits for themselves and that the plans, once established, will then provide meaningful benefits to rank-and-file employees. Or put another way, the justification for the favorable tax treatment of highly-paid participants in qualified plans is one of trickle-down retirement benefits.

Congress has determined that two sets of rules are necessary to make this trickle-down scheme work efficiently. First, we need rules that ensure that rank-and-file employees will participate in and earn meaningful benefits from qualified plans. The rules that effect these goals are often referred to collectively as the nondiscrimination rules.

Second, we need rules that limit the tax expenditure for qualified plans because Congress, like any prudent shopper, does not want to spend more than necessary when it goes shopping. And in the qualified plan area, Congress is, in effect, shopping for the social good of increasing retirement savings for reluctant savers. So how does Congress limit the tax expenditure for qualified plans? Principally by placing limits on the maximum amount of benefits that highly paid participants can receive from qualified plans. These limits are often referred to as the § 415 limits, after the section of the Internal Revenue Code that imposes them.

The nondiscrimination rules and § 415 limits may be good ideas from the perspective of tax and retirement policy, but business owners and managers—especially in small businesses—sometimes view them as obstacles to the goals they wish to accomplish in adopting qualified plans. Those goals often include allowing highly paid individuals to shelter substantial amounts of income from taxation while minimizing benefits for rank-and-file employees (who may value retirement benefits at less than their cost to the employer). As a result, some businesses hire lawyers and other consultants to help them design plans that deliberately minimize benefits for rank-and-file employees while maximizing benefits for owners and highly paid employees. We will summarize some of the strategies used to create plans that have these effects, without endorsing their use.

The reader should note that the nondiscrimination rules and § 415 limits are among the most complex provisions in the Internal Revenue Code and we can do no more here than provide a basic overview of the rules themselves and the strategies used to cope with them.

[¶ 8,590]

1. Nondiscrimination Rules

The nondiscrimination rules dance a two-step: first, the minimum coverage rules (in I.R.C. § 410(b)) ensure that some of the employer's "non-highly compensated employees" participate in the plan; second, the benefit nondiscrimination rules (in I.R.C. § 401(a)(4)) ensure that the plan benefit formula does not discriminate in favor of "highly compensated employees." In effect, the minimum coverage rules get non-highly compensated employees into the plan and the benefit nondiscrimination rules make sure that the plan's benefit formula treats them fairly once they do get in. Key to both of these rules is the division of employees into highly compensated and non-highly compensated employees.

[¶ 8,600]

a. Definition of highly compensated employees

Section 414(q) of the Internal Revenue defines the term "highly compensated employee." Under this provision, an employee can be considered highly compensated in either of two ways: (1) by being (or having been in the previous year) a 5% owner of the employer sponsoring the plan; or (2) by having compensation in the previous year in excess of a dollar figure, which in 2004 is $90,000 (this figure is indexed to changes in the cost of living). The employer may elect to limit the latter group of employees to those with compensation in the top 20%.

[¶ 8,605]

Problem

XYZ Corporation has 100 employees and a three-tier salary scale. In the previous year, the 20 employees in the top tier (E1 to E20) each received $100,000 of compensation; the 10 employees in the middle tier (E21 to E30) each received $90,000 of compensation; and the 70 employees in the lowest tier (E31 to E100) each received $50,000 of compensation. E21 and E31 each own 50% of the stock of XYZ Corporation. How many highly compensated employees are employed by XYZ Corporation?

[¶ 8,610]

b. *Minimum coverage test*

As noted, the purpose of the minimum coverage test is to ensure that plans cover at least some rank-and-file employees. The minimum coverage test, which appears in I.R.C. § 410(b), provides two alternative sets of rules for compliance: one set of rules uses a strict mathematical formula for determining whether a plan covers an adequate number of non-highly compensated employees; the second set of rules is both more flexible and, as a price for that flexibility, more complex.

The mathematical test, which is often referred to as the ratio percentage test, compares the percentage of the highly compensated employees covered by the plan with the percentage of non-highly compensated employees covered by the plan. The test is satisfied if the coverage rate for non-highly compensated employees is at least 70% of the coverage rate of the highly compensated employees.

Problem: A plan has 10 highly compensated employees and 100 non-highly compensated employees. The plan covers four highly compensated employees. How many non-highly compensated employees must the plan cover to satisfy the ratio percentage test?

Problem: A law firm has the following employees, all of whom have worked for more than one year and are older than age 21:

20 partners, each earning over $100,000 per year.

20 associates, each earning at least $80,000 per year, but less than any partner.

60 other employees, each earning less than $80,000 per year.

The law firm wishes to adopt a profit-sharing plan. If the law firm wishes to exclude the associates from the plan, how many other employees can it exclude under the ratio percentage test? If the law firm wishes to include the associates in the plan, how many other employees can it exclude under the ratio percentage test?

The second and more flexible minimum coverage test, which is referred to as the "average benefits test," has two parts: a "reasonable classification" test and an "average benefits" test. A plan satisfies these tests if: (1) the plan benefits employees who qualify under a classification that is found not to discriminate in favor of highly compensated employees; and (2) the average benefit percentage for non-highly compensated employees is at least 70% of the average benefit percentage for highly compensated employees.

Under Treasury regulations, the reasonable classification test itself has two parts. The first part requires that the classification by which employees are sorted in or out of the plan have a reasonable business justification, e.g., the plan covers salaried but not hourly employees. The second part requires that a less demanding variation of the ratio percentage test be satisfied.

If the plan satisfies the reasonable classification test, the employer's plan as a whole must satisfy an "average benefits test." To satisfy this test, each employee's benefit is expressed as a percentage of pay and the benefit percentages are then separately averaged for the highly compensated employees and the non-highly compensated employees. The average benefit of the non-highly compensated employee group must be at least 70% of the average benefit of the highly compensated employee group.

I.R.C. § 401(a)(26) includes a second rule dealing with plan coverage, known as the minimum participation rule. This rule provides that a defined benefit plan must cover at least the lesser of 40% of all employees or 50 employees. As a practical matter, this test does not constrain the defined benefit plans of most large and medium-sized businesses, since the plans of such employers generally cover at least 50 employees.

[¶ 8,620]

c. *Nondiscrimination in contributions or benefits*

Since 1942, federal tax law has prohibited pension and profit-sharing plans from favoring highly compensated employees in benefits or contributions. See I.R.C. § 401(a)(4). Of course, this does not mean that higher paid employees cannot accrue greater dollar benefits than other employees. Indeed, one of the most important principles underlying the nondiscrimination rules is found in I.R.C. § 401(a)(5), which explicitly provides that the nondiscrimination rules are not violated merely because benefits are proportionate to compensation. For example, assume a firm with two employees, Bob who earns $100,000 and Sam who earns $10,000. The plan allocates $30,000 to Bob's account (30% of his compensation) and $3,000 to Sam (30% of his compensation). This does not violate the nondiscrimination rules. This is sometimes referred to as the rule of proportionality.

As we shall see, however, the rule of proportionality is a weak principle; plans can be designed to provide levels of benefits or contributions that favor highly compensated employees.

[¶ 8,630]

d. *Strategies to favor highly paid employees*

As just suggested, the nondiscrimination rules do not mandate strict fidelity to the underlying principle of proportionality. Here we will look at six tools that planners sometimes use to favor highly compensated employees in benefits or contributions.

1. *Social Security integration ("permitted disparity")*. The Internal Revenue Code permits firms sponsoring defined contribution plans to provide higher contribution rates for compensation above the Social Security wage base (which in 2005 is $90,000); firms sponsoring defined benefit plans can provide larger benefit accrual rates for benefits based on compensation above the wage base or can reduce benefits by a percentage of Social Security benefits. In effect, these rules mean that higher levels of benefits can be provided for individuals whose compensation exceeds the Social Security wage base.

2. *Forfeitures for short tenures*. As we have already seen, a firm may design a plan that conditions receipt of benefits on the employee achieving a specified minimum tenure with the firm. The Internal Revenue Code constrains firms in the design of forfeiture conditions; under current law, a firm generally may require no more than five years of service before benefits become nonforfeitable. In some businesses, however, the distribution of completed job tenures is substantially more skewed toward shorter tenures among rank-and-file employees than among highly compensated employees. In such firms, a smaller percentage of rank-and-file employees than highly compensated employees will ultimately receive benefits.

3. *Providing past service credits and retroactive benefit increases*. When a firm adopts a defined benefit plan, it can credit participants with benefit credits for service prior to the time the plan was adopted. Similarly, a firm may amend an existing defined benefit plan to improve the plan's benefit formula and the enhancements may, at the firm's option, apply to credits based on earlier years of service. The firm's highly compensated employees will benefit disproportionately from such enhancements if they have longer past service, as is often the case, especially in smaller firms. The nondiscrimination regulations limit the award of past service credits in certain situations in which they would be too generous to highly compensated employees, but some discrimination remains possible because the regulations indicate that an award of up to five years of past service credit will not be considered discriminatory no matter how severe the discriminatory effects.

4. *Choice of plan format*. When a firm's highly paid employees are older than rank-and-file employees, which is commonly the case in smaller enterprises, the firm can favor the highly paid employees by adopting a defined benefit plan, in which the present value of benefits will generally correlate with age. Moreover, a plan can base benefits on the fractional accrual rule (see ¶ 8,300), which provides larger annual accruals for employees who are closer to retirement age at the time the plan is adopted.

5. *Discrimination in favor of lower-paid "highly compensated" employees*. In some businesses, there are employees who fall within the statutory definition of "highly compensated employees" but are not highly compensated in the overall structure of the firm. For example, an associate in a law firm might earn $100,000 but be closer in pay to the

non-attorney employees of the firm than to the higher-paid lawyers. The plan may provide lower benefits for these employees or may exclude them from the plan altogether. Moreover, if they are excluded from the plan, the operation of the minimum coverage rules will permit the plan to exclude a greater percentage of non-highly compensated employees from participation.

6. *Coverage rules.* As we have already seen, the ratio percentage test permits a plan to exclude at least 30% of a firm's non-highly compensated employees. And, as noted above, a plan can exclude more than 30% of a firm's rank-and-file employees if it does not cover 100% of the firm's highly compensated employees or it is able to use the average benefits test.

7. *Cross-testing.* I.R.C. § 401(a)(4) prohibits discrimination in favor of highly compensated employees in benefits *or* contributions. The I.R.S., at least since 1993, has taken the position that this means that contributions to a defined contribution plan can be tested on either a "contributions" or a "benefits" basis. Testing a defined contribution plan on a "benefits" basis requires that contributions be converted into the hypothetical benefits that they would purchase at retirement age. In effect, this means that contributions are credited with an assumed rate of interest through retirement age under the plan. Thus, a dollar contribution for a younger employee will purchase a larger benefit than the same dollar contribution for an older employee. As a result, testing a defined contribution plan on a "benefits" basis will permit much larger contributions for older employees. Because in many firms the favored employees are on average older than younger employees, testing on a "benefits" basis can result in larger contributions (as a percentage of salary) for the favored employees.

Example: An incorporated medical practice employs Dave, a 55–year–old doctor and Nick, a 25–year–old nurse. Dave has $150,000 of compensation and Nick has $25,000 of compensation. The medical practice sponsors a profit-sharing plan, with a formula that weights benefits in favor of older employees. The plan provides Dave with a $40,000 contribution, which is approximately 27% of Dave's cash compensation, and Nick with a $750 contribution, which is 3% of Nick's cash compensation. This will satisfy the nondiscrimination rules if the plan is cross-tested.

In the last five years, some aggressive plan designers have combined cross-testing with other planning techniques and have designed defined contribution plans in which highly paid employees, regardless of age, receive higher contribution rates than rank-and-file employees. These plans are sometimes referred to as new comparability plans.

[¶ 8,640]

2. Section 415 Limits

Section 415 includes two limits: one that limits annual additions to defined contribution plans, and one that limits the maximum benefit that can be paid from a defined benefit plan. The statutory limits have been adjusted from time to time, sometimes reducing the limits and sometimes increasing them, depending on national revenue needs and other political considerations. Most recently, the limits were increased in 2001 to their highest levels since their initial introduction in 1974. We will summarize the limits and briefly discuss some strategies for maximizing benefits.

[¶ 8,650]

a. *Limit on annual additions to defined contribution plans*

I.R.C. § 415(c) limits the amount of annual additions to an employer's defined contribution plans to $40,000 (or 100% of compensation, if lower). The $40,000 figure is indexed to increases in the cost of living (rounded down to the next lowest $1,000), and in 2005 is $42,000.

The term "annual additions" includes employer contributions, employee contributions (such as 401(k) plan contributions), and forfeitures of former participants that are allocated to other accounts. The term does not, however, include investment income.

Moreover, participants who are at least age 50 are permitted to make "catch-up" elective contributions to 401(k) plans. The catch-up contributions can be up to $3,000 in 2004 and will rise to $4,000 in 2005 and $5,000 in 2006 (after which the limit will be increased in $100 increments to reflect changes in the cost of living). Thus, for an individual over age 50, the effective contribution limit in 2005 will be $45,000 if the employee participates in a 401(k) plan.

The following chart indicates how much an individual can accumulate at age 65 if she begins making maximum contributions to a defined contribution plan beginning at ages 25, 35, 45, or 55, assuming an annual return on investments of 5%, 6% or 8%. The chart assumes no future changes in the cost of living, so that the § 415 limit on annual additions is $41,000 through age 49 and $46,000 thereafter.

	Age 25	*Age 35*	*Age 45*	*Age 55*
5%	$5,359,718	$3,019,480	$1,582,777	$653,512
6%	6,895,318	3,605,231	1,768,064	688,696
8%	12,255,035	5,208,802	2,218,961	765,692

[¶ 8,660]

b. *Limit on maximum benefit from defined benefit plan*

I.R.C. § 415(b) provides that a defined benefit plan cannot provide a retirement benefit in excess of the greater of $160,000 or 100% of a participant's high three-year average compensation. The dollar figure is indexed to inflation (in $5,000 increments, rounding to the next lowest $5,000), and in 2005 is $170,000. The dollar limitation continues to reflect post-retirement increases in the cost of living, so in some circumstances the benefit can increase after retirement.

To prevent the accrual of a maximum annuity benefit in a single year, § 415(b)(5) phases in the dollar limitation over a period of ten years of plan participation. Thus, the largest benefit accrual possible in a single year (based on the indexed limitation in effect in 2005) is $17,000.

When benefits are paid in a form other than a life annuity or a joint-and-survivor annuity, the benefit is actuarially converted to a straight life annuity using prescribed interest rates and mortality tables. Moreover, the § 415(b) limitation is reduced if the benefit commences prior to age 62.

The present value of a $170,000 life annuity is dependent on the discount rate and life expectancy at commencement. A plausible range of present values for such an annuity at age 65 would be between $1,500,000 and $2,300,000; at age 62, between $1,900,000 and $2,750,000.

[¶ 8,670]

c. *Strategies for maximizing benefits under § 415*

Section 415 also included a third limit, prior to its repeal in 1996, which applied when an employer maintained both a defined contribution plan and a defined benefit plan, either separately or in combination. The combined limit, as it was sometimes called, was designed to permit an employer who sponsored both types of plans to provide greater benefits to its employees than an employer who sponsored only one type of plan. The increased benefits under the combined limit, however, were less than the total benefits that could have been provided using the full limits for each type of plan. A complex formula was used to reduce partly either or both of the applicable limitations. When the combined limit was in effect, tax planning focused on when to adopt a defined benefit plan and how to allocate the combined limit's restrictions between the separate defined contribution and defined benefit limitations.

As noted, the combined limit no longer applies. As a result, an employer can provide maximum annual additions to defined contribution plans and still provide a maximum benefit under a defined benefit plan. This has substantially reduced the complexity of planning under § 415.

It should be noted that most planning involving § 415 occurs in owner-dominated firms. Providing maximum benefits can be expensive in a firm with many rank-and-file employees, but this may not be a major issue in small, owner-dominated firms, either because there are few if any rank-and-file employees or because aggressive planning around the nondiscrimination rules can result in relatively small benefits for such employees.

The following concepts play an important role in planning to maximize benefits under § 415:

1. *Maximize annual contributions.* Because the primary tax benefit of qualified plans is based on tax deferral, and because the tax deferral

begins when contributions are made to the plan, the optimal strategy under § 415 is to participate to the extent possible in both a defined contribution plan and a defined benefit plan and to make the largest permissible deductible contributions. As explained below, however, a firm should not adopt a defined benefit plan until favored employees are receiving the maximum annual contributions to a defined contribution plan ($42,000 in 2005 for those under 50).

2. *Defer adoption of defined benefit plan until favored employees are receiving maximum annual additions to defined contribution plan.* A firm seeking to favor a particular employee generally should defer adoption of a defined benefit plan until the firm is able to make maximum additions to a defined contribution plan. There are two reasons for this. First, defined contributions are less costly to sponsor because they do not require the services of an actuary or payment of premiums to the PBGC. Second, and more important, the defined benefit maximum itself is a fixed dollar annuity that can be created and funded at any time. It does not make sense to create and fund this annuity until doing so will increase aggregate deferred compensation, and this will not occur until annual additions to a defined contribution plan reach the § 415(c) limit in effect for the year.

3. *Establish 401(k) plan to permit catch-up contributions.* As already noted in ¶ 8,260, an individual who is at least 50 years of age is permitted to make "catch-up" contributions to a 401(k) plan. The § 415(c) limits on annual additions do not apply to catch-up contributions.

4. *Make age 62 normal retirement age for defined benefit.* The § 415 limit is not reduced for benefits unless they commence before age 62. Thus, the most valuable benefit under a defined benefit plan is a benefit commencing at age 62.

5. *Roth 401(k) plans.* Beginning in 2006, I.R.C. § 402A will permit 401(k) plans to offer a participants a "Roth" option, under which their elective contributions will be subject to immediate income tax but subsequent qualified distributions will be exempt from tax. As discussed earlier in ¶ 8,410, the Roth feature effectively increases contribution limits.

J. DISTRIBUTIONS FROM RETIREMENT PLANS

[¶ 8,680]

We will now consider four issues involving distributions from retirement plans: (1) mandatory and permissible forms of benefit payouts from pension and profit-sharing plans, including the qualified joint-and-survivor annuity for married participants; (2) taxation of distributions; (3) timing of distributions, including the minimum distribution rules which require that benefits be paid out over specified time periods; and (4) financial planning in retirement.

At the outset, however, it may be useful to note three basic principles that inform the regulation and tax treatment of distributions from qualified plans. All three principles are derived from the idea that the tax subsidy for qualified plans is designed to encourage employers to sponsor, and employees to participate in, plans that will provide participants with a source of retirement income after they leave the labor market.

The first principle is that individuals should be encouraged to preserve plan benefits until they actually retire. Thus, we have tax and regulatory rules that discourage pre-retirement consumption of retirement assets. For example, the Internal Revenue Code imposes a 10% penalty tax on early withdrawal of retirement plan assets.

The second principle is that individuals should use tax-favored plan savings to support themselves in retirement and not to build tax-advantaged estates. Thus, we have minimum distribution rules that generally require that plan distributions commence by the time an individual reaches age 70½ or, if later, retires.

Finally, we generally favor pension assets lasting for the life of the participant or, if married, the joint lives of the participant and his or her surviving spouse. Thus, the normal form of pension benefit for a married participant is a joint-and-survivor annuity and for an unmarried participant a life annuity.

1. Forms of Benefit

[¶ 8,690]

a. *Pension plans*

Approximately 75 years ago, the Treasury Department issued regulations that defined a pension plan as "a plan established and maintained by an employer to provide systematically for the payment of definitely determinable benefits to his employees over a period of years, usually for life, after retirement." Although this regulation is still extant (Treas. Reg. § 1.401–1(b)), it has largely been superseded by ERISA, which provides that the normal form of benefit in a defined benefit plan is a life annuity for a single participant and a "qualified joint-and-survivor annuity" (QJSA) for a participant who has been married for at least one year. A QJSA is a life annuity for the participant and a spousal survivor annuity equal to at least 50% (but not more than 100%) of the participant's annuity; the spousal survivor annuity is commonly set at 50% of the participant's life annuity. The QJSA must be at least actuarially equivalent to a single life annuity for the participant's life, but may be subsidized if the employer so designs its plan.

Example: Ben is married to Sue when he retires. Under the plan's formula, Ben would be entitled to a life annuity of $1,000 per month if he were single. But because he is married, Ben's normal form of benefit is a QJSA. Assume that the actuarial reduction leaves Ben with a life annuity of $800 per month. If Ben dies, survived by Sue, the plan will pay $400 per month to Sue for her life. Note that if Sue dies first, Ben will continue to receive the $800 benefit for his life.

The QJSA requirements also apply to defined contribution plans whose form of benefit is an annuity, such as a money-purchase pension plan.

Despite these requirements, a pension plan may offer alternative forms of benefit distribution. The most common alternative form is a lump sum distribution, but some plans offer additional options, such as: (1) a joint-and-survivor annuity that does not require that the spouse be designated as a beneficiary; (2) an annuity with payments guaranteed for a fixed term of years (so that if the participant dies during the fixed term, the annuity continues to be paid to a designated beneficiary for the rest of the fixed term); or (3) a partial lump sum payment and a reduced annuity.

Optional benefit forms must be actuarially equivalent to the plan's normal form of benefit. Section 417(e) of the Code specifies the interest rates that must be used to determine actuarial equivalence, and authorizes the Secretary of the Treasury to prescribe mortality tables used for this purpose.

Under the original provisions of ERISA, a married participant could simply elect an alternative benefit and cut off any benefits for his or her surviving spouse. In 1984, in order to help married couples make more informed choices and to protect the spouse's interest in the benefit, Congress amended ERISA to require that a spouse consent in writing to any form of benefit other than a QJSA. The consent, which follows notice from the plan about the various available forms of benefits, must be either notarized or witnessed by the plan administrator.

[¶ 8,700]

b. *Profit-sharing and stock bonus plans*

Fewer restrictions apply to profit-sharing plans. Indeed, a profit-sharing plan may require that participants take their benefits in a lump sum distribution, although most profit-sharing plans provide other options as well. Other common distribution options provide for periodic distributions over the participant's life expectancy, over the life expectancy of the participant and spouse (or other beneficiary), or over a fixed term of years. Some profit-sharing plans allow participants to use their account balances to purchase an annuity from an insurance company.

Profit-sharing and stock bonus plans are exempt from the QJSA rules for an individual participant if they satisfy three requirements: (1) the plan provides that the full account balance remaining at the participant's death will be paid to his or her surviving spouse, unless the spouse consents to a different beneficiary designation; (2) the plan does not offer a life annuity benefit option (or a life annuity option, if available, is not selected by the participant); and (3) the plan is not a direct or indirect transferee of a plan that would have been required to provide a QJSA form of benefit.

Special distribution requirements apply to stock bonus plans. Generally speaking, such plans must at least offer an option to receive benefits in the form of employer securities, although they may also offer a cash option. In cases where by-law or charter restrictions limit stock ownership to employees, a plan may distribute cash in lieu of employer securities. Moreover, if the employer distributes securities that are not publicly traded on an established securities market, the employer must provide the participant with a put option to sell the securities to the employer or plan at a fair price.

[¶ 8,710]

2. Taxation of Benefits

Our discussion of the taxation of benefits includes three parts: (1) the normal tax rules applicable to distributions from qualified plans and IRAs; (2) the rules regulating rollovers and transfers to individual retirement plans or other qualified plans; and (3) penalty taxes for distributions prior to the year in which a participant reaches age 59½.

[¶ 8,720]

a. *Normal income tax rules*

The general rule for distributions from qualified plans is simple: distributions are includible in the participant's gross income, unless they are rolled over or directly transferred to another qualified plan (see ¶ 8,730). There are, however, exceptions to the general rule where the participant contributed after-tax dollars to the plan; in that case, the tax treatment turns on whether the contributions were regular contributions or Roth contributions.

If the contributions were not Roth contributions, the participant recovers her investment in the contract ratably, without imposition of tax, over the expected time period for the distributions. For benefits paid in the form of an annuity, the expected time period is based on the annuitant's age at the annuity starting date, with the expected number of payments determined under charts set forth in I.R.C. § 72(d). There are two charts, one for single life annuities and one for annuities payable over more than one life. The charts are as follows:

Annuity Payable Over One Life

Age at Annuity Starting Date	Number of Expected Payments
Not more than 55	360
More than 55 but not more than 60	310
More than 60 but not more than 65	260
More than 65 but not more than 70	210
More than 70	160

Annuity Payable Over More Than One Life

Combined Age of Annuitants	Number of Expected Payments
Not more than 110	410
More than 110 but not more than 120	360
More than 120 but not more than 130	310
More than 130 but not more than 140	260
More than 140	210

Problem: Brad participates in a qualified plan and has made $26,000 in nondeductible (after-tax) contributions to the plan. Brad and his wife Joan will receive a joint-and-survivor annuity of $1,000 per month from the plan for as long as either spouse is alive. Brad is 66 and Joan is 65 at the annuity starting date. How much of each monthly payment is includible by Brad and Joan in their gross income? How much of the 261st monthly payment is includible in their gross income?

If the participant (or the participant's surviving spouse, in the case of a joint-and-survivor annuity) dies before fully recovering his investment in the annuity, the rest of the investment can be deducted on his final income tax return.

If a participant receives benefits in a form other than an annuity (for example, a non-periodic distribution from a profit-sharing plan), the rules for recovery of the investment in the contract are more complex. Each distribution is multiplied by a fraction, with a numerator equal to the investment in the contract at the time of distribution and a denominator equal to the vested portion of the account balance. For reasons of administrative convenience, the plan is allowed to use a uniform valuation date (such as the last day of the preceding plan year) in determining the account balance. I.R.S. Notice 87–13, Q & A 11.

Example: In 2005, when Will has a $5,000 investment in the contract and a $25,000 vested account balance, he receives a $10,000 distribution. The non-taxable portion of the distribution is calculated as follows: $10,000 × $5,000/$25,000, or $2,000. The $8,000 balance of the distribution is taxable. Will now has an account balance of $15,000 and a remaining investment in the contract of $3,000.

In 2006, Will's account is credited with $1,000 of investment income, bringing the account total to $16,000. Will receives a $10,000 distribution. The non-taxable portion of the distribution is calculated as follows: $10,000 × $3,000/$16,000, or $1,875. The $8,125 balance of the distribution is taxable.

In most cases, a participant's account will reflect both employer and employee contributions and investment earnings thereon. Under I.R.C. § 72(d)(2), the employer can divide the account into one portion consisting of employer contributions (and investment earnings thereon) and another portion consisting of employee contributions (and investment earnings thereon). The employee may then treat each portion as a separate contract and direct that distributions be made first from the portion funded with his own contributions, thereby accelerating the recovery of his investment in the contract. (This would be true regardless of the payment method under which the account is paid.)

In contrast to these rules, distributions from Roth accounts (whether a Roth 401(k) plan or a Roth IRA) are fully excludable from gross income if two conditions are met: (1) the distribution is made at or after the time the participant reaches age 59½, or after the participant becomes disabled or dies; and (2) the distribution occurs at least five years after the first contribution to the Roth 401(k) plan or Roth IRA. If a distribution does not satisfy these conditions, the distributions are still non-taxable to the extent they do not exceed the participant's contributions to the Roth 401(k) plan or Roth IRA.

[¶ 8,730]

b. *Rollovers and direct transfers to IRAs or other qualified plans*

As we have already observed, the great tax advantage of qualified plans consists of tax deferral. An individual who receives a distribution can continue the tax deferral by "rolling over" the distribution to an IRA or another qualified plan, or by having the plan transfer the distribution directly to an IRA or another qualified plan. (In the case of a rollover or direct transfer to a qualified plan, the qualified plan must permit such rollovers or transfers.)

At one time, rollovers were limited to certain "lump sum distributions" (a term specially defined by statute). Today, any distribution may be rolled over unless it falls within one of the following categories: (1) a payment that is part of substantially equal annuity payments from the plan; (2) a payment that is part of substantially equal installment payments over a period of ten or more years; (3) a required minimum distribution (see ¶¶ 8,750–8,790); or (4) a hardship distribution (i.e., certain distributions made to current employees from a 401(k) plan or 403(b) annuity because of "hardship"). To make a rollover, an individual must transfer all or a portion of the distribution to an IRA or another qualified plan within 60 days of receipt, although the I.R.S. can waive the 60–day requirement in cases of unavoidable hardship beyond the control of the individual.

An individual can also make a direct transfer of a distribution by requesting that the trustee of the plan make the distribution directly to an IRA or another qualified plan.

An individual does not have to rollover or transfer the full amount of the distribution, but only the portion rolled over or transferred will be exempt from tax.

An advantage of the direct transfer is that it avoids the mandatory 20% income tax withholding that applies to distributions made to the participant. Thus, an individual who receives a distribution and wishes to make a complete rollover must reach into her own pocket to make up the withheld amount, although she will ultimately be credited with the withheld amount when she files her tax return.

Example: Fred has a $100,000 account balance in a profit-sharing plan. Fred requests a lump sum distribution. The plan withholds $20,000 for income tax purposes pays Fred $80,000. Since Fred's distribution is $100,000 (even though part of the distribution was withheld), he must deposit $100,000 in an IRA or another qualified plan within 60 days after receiving the $80,000 distribution.

Generally speaking, an individual cannot rollover any portion of a distribution that is otherwise exempt from taxation (e.g., a return of contributions made with before-tax dollars). But this rule is subject to exceptions in two cases: (1) a direct transfer to a qualified defined contribution plan that accounts separately for the includible and excludable portions of the distribution; and (2) a rollover or direct transfer to an IRA.

There are three categories of individuals who may make rollovers or direct transfers of distributions from a qualified plan: (1) a participant in the plan; (2) the spouse of a deceased participant; and (3) an alternate payee, who is treated for rollover purposes as if she herself were a participant in the plan.

[¶ 8,740]

c. *Penalty taxes for early distributions*

Section 72(t) of the Code imposes a 10% excise tax on distributions made from a qualified plan or an IRA before an employee reaches age 59½, other than distributions made after the employee's death or attributable to disability. The tax applies only to the portion of a distribution that would otherwise be includible in the employee's gross income; thus, the tax does not apply to amounts that are rolled over to an IRA or qualified plan. There are also several exceptions to the penalty tax, including: (1) distributions that are part of a series of substantially equal periodic annual (or more frequent) payments made for the life or life expectancy of the employee or the joint lives of the employee and a designated beneficiary; (2) distributions made from a qualified plan to an individual over age 55 after a separation from service; (3) distributions used to pay certain medical expenses; and (4) distributions from an IRA for certain first-time home purchases or higher education expenses. Note that in some cases the penalty tax exemption applies only to distributions from an IRA. In such cases, an individual who receives a distribution from a qualified plan should consider having the distribution transferred first to an IRA and then withdrawn from the IRA.

[¶ 8,750]

3. Minimum Distribution Rules

To prevent a never-ending story of tax deferral through the use of qualified plans and IRAs, Congress included minimum distribution rules when it enacted ERISA. The minimum distribution rules are found in I.R.C. § 401(a)(9). In broad terms, the rules are designed to ensure that qualified plan participants and IRA owners will begin to take distributions upon leaving the labor market, and after their death any remaining benefits will be distributed to their beneficiaries. Failure to comply with the minimum distribution rules can result in a penalty tax equal to 50% of the amount that should have been but was not distributed, as well as potential loss of the plan's tax qualified status in egregious cases.

At the direction of Congress, the I.R.S. promulgated substantially revised regulations on the minimum distribution rules, which went into effect in 2002. The regulations generally attempted to simplify the rules and to soften their impact. We will look first at the rules governing distributions during the life of the participant (or IRA owner) and then at the rules governing distributions to beneficiaries after the death of the participant (or IRA owner). Despite the simplifying changes made by the regulations, the minimum distribution rules remain inordinately complex; we can provide only an overview here. As a matter of convenience, the following discussion will use the term "participant" to include not only participants in qualified plans but also owners of individual retirement accounts.

[¶ 8,760]

a. *Lifetime distributions*

The rules regulating lifetime distributions involve two basic questions: at what times must distributions be made and how much must be distributed?

Key to the first question is the concept of the "required beginning date" (RBD). In general, the RBD is the first day of April following the year in which a participant reaches age 70½. This is the date by which distributions must commence, with one exception. A participant in a qualified plan (but not an IRA owner) who continues working after age 70½ can defer distributions until she actually retires (unless she is a 5%

owner of the plan sponsor). In that case, the RBD is the first day of April following the year of retirement, and distributions must commence on or before that date. Subsequent distributions must occur by December 31 of each year. Thus, in the first year it is possible to have two required distributions, one on April 1 and one on December 31. To avoid income bunching in a single year, it is often advisable to take the first distribution by December 31 of the year in which the participant attains age 70½.

The second question involves the amount of the required distributions. The minimum distribution is equal to the account balance as of the last valuation date in the previous year divided by the number of years in a distribution period. (For most plans and all IRAs, the valuation date is December 31.)

A table in the regulations shows the distribution period, which is based on the joint life expectancy of the participant and a hypothetical beneficiary (ten years younger than the participant) in the distribution year. The distribution period under this "uniform lifetime" table changes each year, to reflect the advancing age and shorter life expectancy of the participant and the deemed beneficiary. The uniform lifetime table provides, in part, as follows:

Participant's Age	Distribution Period
70	27.4
71	26.5
72	25.6
* * *	* * *
80	18.7
* * *	* * *
85	14.8
* * *	* * *
100	6.3

Although the distribution period is generally determined under the uniform lifetime table, there is one important exception. In the case of a married participant whose spouse is more than ten years younger than the participant, the distribution period is based on the actual life expectancies of the participant and his or her spouse, as set forth in a joint life expectancy table in the regulations. This produces a longer distribution period, smaller annual required distributions, and enhanced opportunities for tax deferral.

It should also be noted that the regulations do not allow a participant who receives more than the required distribution in one year to apply the excess amount against the required distribution in a subsequent year.

Finally, one should keep in mind that Roth vehicles are not subject to the minimum distribution rules, which makes Roth IRAs especially valuable for individuals who are primarily concerned with accumulating an estate rather than with generating income during retirement.

[¶ 8,765]

Problems

1. Pam owns an IRA, which has an account balance of $100,000 on December 31, 2005. Pam's 70th birthday is March 1, 2006. How much must Pam withdraw from the IRA by April 1, 2007, to satisfy the minimum distribution rules?

2. On December 31, 2006, Pam's account balance is $110,000. How much must Pam withdraw from the IRA by December 31, 2007?

3. Why might Pam consider taking the first distribution in 2006 rather than in 2007?

[¶ 8,770]

b. Distributions after death

The rules governing distributions after the participant's death depend on whether there is a designated beneficiary and, if so, whether the beneficiary is the participant's surviving spouse. As might be expected, benefits payable to a surviving spouse receive more favorable treatment. A trust qualifies as a designated beneficiary only if it meets certain technical requirements, and a decedent's estate is categorically disqualified. I.R.C. § 401(a)(9)(E); Reg. § 1.401(a)(9)–4.

[¶ 8,780]

(1) Beneficiary other than spouse

If the beneficiary is a person other than the participant's surviving spouse, the determination of required distributions depends primarily on two variables: first, whether the participant is living on the required beginning date; and second, whether there is a "designated beneficiary" to whom distributions are payable.

Participant dies on or after the required beginning date; designated beneficiary. Generally speaking, distributions will be made over the life expectancy of the beneficiary, which is initially determined as of the beneficiary's birthday in the year after the participant's death. For years thereafter, the beneficiary's remaining life expectancy is reduced by one year. However, if the beneficiary is older than the participant, distributions continue to be made over the participant's remaining life expectancy in the year of death, determined as of the participant's birthday in that year. Again, the initial life expectancy is reduced by one year for each year following the participant's death. Life expectancy is determined under tables set forth in the regulations under I.R.C. § 79.

Example: Participant (Jim) dies after his required beginning date, survived by a designated beneficiary (Ella). In the year after Jim's death, Ella has a life expectancy of 25 years. If Jim's account balance was $100,000, Ella's minimum required distribution for the year is $4,000

($100,000 ÷ 25). In the following year, the minimum required distribution would be the remaining account balance divided by 24.

Note that if there is more than one beneficiary of a single account, the age of the oldest beneficiary is used.

Participant dies on or after the required beginning date; no designated beneficiary. Distributions will be made over the participant's remaining life expectancy in the year of death, determined as of the participant's birthday in that year. The initial life expectancy is reduced by one year for each year following the participant's death.

Participant dies before the required beginning date; designated beneficiary. The beneficiary will receive distributions over her life expectancy, which is initially determined as of her birthday in the year after the participant's death and reduced by one year for each year thereafter. However, a plan may permit a participant to elect distributions under a "five-year" rule which requires only that the entire account balance be distributed by the end of the fifth year after the year of the participant's death. This option may be useful in the case of a very elderly beneficiary with a life expectancy of less than five years, or where the account balance is small and the beneficiary expects that her marginal tax rate will decline within five years after the participant's death.

Note that a plan sponsor may design the plan to make the five-year rule mandatory.

Participant dies before required distribution date; no designated beneficiary. The five-year rule applies automatically. Thus, the entire account balance must be distributed by the end of the fifth year after the year of the participant's death.

[¶ 8,790]

(2) Beneficiary is surviving spouse

If the participant dies on or after the required beginning date, distributions to the surviving spouse must begin by the end of the year after the participant's death, as in the case of any other beneficiary.

However, if the participant dies before the required beginning date and the surviving spouse is the sole beneficiary, the surviving spouse is not required to begin receiving distributions until the later of the end of the year following the participant's death or the end of the year in which the participant would have reached age 70½. Distributions are made over the spouse's life expectancy, which is recalculated annually using the life expectancy tables in the regulations under I.R.C. § 79. The spouse is also generally permitted to rollover the account balance to an IRA, which is treated as the spouse's own IRA. This effectively permits the spouse to defer distribution until the year following the year in which the spouse reaches age 70½.

[¶ 8,800]

4. Financial Planning in Retirement

In this section, we are concerned with the use of wealth to provide retirement income rather than to build an estate to pass on at death. Of necessity, this focus is somewhat artificial, for most people with the means to do so wish both to maintain their standard of living in retirement and to pass on some wealth to their offspring. But our primary focus here is on methods of generating income during retirement.

We have already examined the importance of projecting assets and needs during retirement. Up until retirement, such projections are highly speculative as to both assets and needs, but the forecasts are likely to become more reliable, especially as to assets, as retirement approaches. At retirement age, an individual generally knows, or can calculate, her Social Security benefits, her annuity or lump sum equivalent from a defined benefit retirement plan, the balance in defined contribution accounts, net equity in a personal residence, and any outside savings. And she will have some idea of her store of human capital, including her ability to earn income from part-time employment or consulting. But the value of these assets in the future is still subject to risks. For example, the rate of return on investments cannot be projected with certainty, and a person cannot generally know exactly how much she will earn from part-time employment (or how long she will be able to work).

Similarly, it becomes easier to quantify financial needs in retirement as retirement draws near; but again, a prediction is merely an informed guess. For example, it is generally impossible to predict with certainty future rates of inflation, health care needs, living expenses, or the sequence and timing of deaths—all of which bear on projected retirement needs.

Against this backdrop of uncertainty, the individual must make financial decisions in planning for retirement. We will look here at some of the most basic decisions: (1) when to start receiving Social Security benefits; (2) what form of benefit to take from a defined benefit pension plan (and when to begin taking it); (3) how to invest assets during retirement; and (4) how to draw down assets during retirement.

[¶ 8,810]

a.   When to start Social Security benefits?

We have already seen that an individual can begin to start receiving Social Security benefits as early as age 62, albeit with an actuarial reduction to reflect the increased payout period. Does it make sense to take benefits before reaching full Social Security retirement age? What factors should the individual consider in making the decision? (Of course, an individual may have no real choice if she needs to claim early benefits to support herself before the full retirement age.)

The most important considerations are the individual's life expectancy and whether she expects to earn income between early and full retirement age. A person with a shorter-than-average life expectancy generally does considerably better by electing early retirement, but this may not be true if she continues to earn income because her earnings can substantially reduce the benefits received up to full retirement age.

The issue can be analyzed in terms of present value using a financial model. Suppose a person whose full retirement age is 65½ begins receiving early Social Security retirement benefits at age 62, invests them until full retirement age, and then purchases an annuity based on standard insurance pricing. Assuming a 3% annual increase in the consumer price index and an annual after-tax rate of return on investments of 7.2%, one analysis found that a person with a normal life expectancy would do better to delay receiving retirement benefits until full retirement age. (The analysis was done by Thomas G. Walsh, then a visiting scholar at the TIAA–CREF Institute. The analysis is available on-line at: http://www.tiaa-crefinstitute.org/Publications/wkpapers/wp_pdfs/wp7–2002.pdf.) If the after-tax interest rate exceeded 8%, however, the person would do better to begin receiving benefits early.

Given the relatively low rates of return available in recent years, people who anticipate regular or longer-than-average life expectancies generally should delay receiving Social Security benefits until full retirement age. The advantage of such delay will be even more pronounced if the economy experiences high rates of inflation.

Similar considerations apply to an individual whose spousal benefits exceed the benefits for which she is eligible based on her own earnings record. Indeed, because the actuarial adjustment is larger for spousal benefits than for a worker's own primary benefits, a spouse generally should delay receiving benefits until full retirement age. There is one important caveat, however. If the spouse's own benefits exceed the spousal benefits, the spouse can begin taking the spousal benefits at age 62 and then shift over to her own benefits upon reaching full retirement age. Under present law, the early receipt of spousal benefits does not produce any reduction in the worker's own benefits at full retirement age.

[¶ 8,820]

b. *What form of benefit to take from a defined benefit plan*

The normal form of benefit for an unmarried participant in a defined benefit plan is an annuity for life, commencing at normal retirement age under the plan. For a married participant the normal form of benefit is a qualified joint-and-survivor annuity. Most defined benefit plans, however, provide optional benefit forms, which a participant may elect in lieu of the normal form of benefit. (As noted above in ¶ 8,690, the spouse of a married participant must consent to such an election.) The most common form of alternative benefit is a lump sum benefit, but many plans also offer additional annuity choices (e.g., an annuity with a death benefit). Participants typically must consider whether to elect a lump sum benefit in lieu of an annuity and whether to elect a single-life annuity rather than a joint-and-survivor annuity. It should be noted, however, that a plan may be drafted to provide the normal form of benefit as the only available option.

1. *Annuity vs. lump sum benefit.* An annuity has a singular advantage over a lump sum benefit: it provides periodic income that will continue as long as the annuitant lives. In contrast, an individual who receives a lump sum and rolls it over into an IRA must decide each year how much to withdraw and how to invest the remaining balance. This can require considerable investment acumen and planning to ensure that the individual will not outlive her assets. In addition, a participant's creditors generally cannot reach a benefit that is payable in the form of an annuity, but such protection may not be available for a lump sum benefit. An annuity therefore has considerable value, and the annuity offered by the plan is likely to be larger than an annuity purchased from an insurance company with the proceeds of a lump sum benefit. Accordingly, disinterested financial experts routinely recommend that most individuals should take the annuity option offered by a plan. Individuals should be wary of financial advisors who recommend lump sum payouts, since such financial advisors often receive fees for managing the lump sum payouts.

In some cases, however, a lump sum may be the more attractive benefit option. This could occur, for example, in the following circumstances:

1. A short life expectancy makes a lump sum option attractive. A few plans make a lump sum benefit available only to participants who qualify for unrated life insurance premiums, but most plans allow a participant with a short life expectancy simply to choose a lump sum payout.

2. Individuals with substantial personal wealth may not be concerned about outliving their assets and may therefore not need the security of a stream of annuity payments. Moreover, in calculating the lump sum value of benefits, a plan is required to use the interest rate on 30–year Treasury bonds. Those rates have been relatively low in recent years, averaging around 5%. If an individual believes that she can achieve a higher rate of return and does not need the security of a lifetime annuity, she should consider taking her benefit in a lump sum.

3. Individuals with large consumer debt may find in certain circumstances that using a lump sum benefit to pay off that debt (which typically carries a high interest rate) can improve their financial position in retirement.

4. Individuals who expect high levels of inflation might consider taking a lump sum benefit, since inflation will erode the value of fixed annuity payments during retirement. But this would make sense only if

the individual has the resources and expertise to invest successfully in an inflationary economy.

Even in the situations mentioned above, however, a participant should be cautious in choosing a lump sum benefit. Some plans provide subsidies for certain forms of annuities but not for lump sum benefits. This commonly occurs in two situations. In one situation, a plan offers a subsidized early retirement annuity for participants who satisfy certain age and/or service requirements; such plans often provide a lump sum benefit equivalent to a life annuity at normal retirement age which does not reflect the subsidy. In the second situation, a plan subsidizes the qualified joint-and-survivor annuity benefit; such subsidies are rarely, if ever, reflected in an alternative lump sum benefit. In each case, the value of the subsidy will generally outweigh other considerations unless the subsidy is small or the participant (and, if relevant, his or her spouse) has a short life expectancy.

2. *Single-life annuity vs. joint-and-survivor annuity.* Often one spouse has a defined benefit pension and the other spouse does not, or both spouses have defined benefit plans but one spouse's benefits are substantially greater. In such cases, it may make sense to choose a joint-and-survivor annuity rather than a single-life annuity, to protect the spouse with the lower benefits.

One criticism of the existing qualified joint-and-survivor annuity rules is that the survivor annuity may be as low as 50% of the annuity payable during the participant's life. By contrast, if the participant outlives the spouse, there is no reduction in the participant's benefit. Arguably it is irrational to have a steep benefit reduction if the participant dies first but no reduction if the non-participant spouse dies first, since the surviving spouse's living expenses are likely to be more or less the same regardless of which spouse dies first. Accordingly, there have been legislative proposals to allocate the QJSA more equally between the spouses and to provide a more uniform benefit for the surviving spouse regardless of the order of deaths.

Although ERISA provides for a QJSA with a survivor annuity as low as 50% of the annuity payable during the participant's life, some plans offer other QJSA options with larger benefits for the participant's surviving spouse. Selecting such an option will result in a lower benefit during the participant's life, but the larger survivor benefit may be attractive, especially if the participant's surviving spouse is a woman, since women typically have longer life expectancies than men. (The value of a survivor annuity payable to a woman tends to be less under the unisex mortality tables that are used in determining actuarial equivalence than would be the case under sex-differentiated mortality tables.)

In some cases, however, a single-life annuity makes good sense. The most common situation is where the non-participant spouse has a shorter life expectancy than the participant. Another situation is where the participant carries sufficient life insurance on his or her own life to provide an adequate income for the surviving spouse. Even in these situations, however, it is important to compare the present values of the plan's single-life and joint-and-survivor annuities, since the plan may subsidize the latter.

3. *When to commence benefits.* All defined benefit plans have a normal retirement age, but many plans also permit participants to begin receiving benefits at an earlier age. As discussed above in ¶ 8,330, if a participant elects to begin receiving benefits before normal retirement age, the plan generally reduces the amount of the monthly benefit payments to reflect the longer payout period, in accordance with actuarial factors stated in the plan.

In some cases, the plan may subsidize the early benefit, either by providing unreduced monthly benefit payments or by requiring less than a full actuarial reduction. In general, when a plan provides a substantial subsidy, the employee must meet certain eligibility criteria, including age and/or service requirements. For example, some plans provide that participants with at least 25 years of service who work through at least age 60 can retire with no reduction in benefits. Another common formula found in many union-negotiated plans permits employees to retire with unreduced benefits at any age after completing 30 years of service. There are many variations on eligibility requirements for subsidized early retirement benefits.

In general, an employee who is eligible for a subsidized early retirement benefit will have to decide whether to retire or continue working. In most cases, a person who continues working will earn additional benefit accruals, so the comparison is often between retiring immediately with a subsidized benefit or retiring later with an increased benefit due to additional years of service.

Example: ABC Retirement Plan provides a benefit equal to 1% of final pay times years of service, beginning at age 65. The plan also provides that a person with 25 years of service may retire at age 62 with no reduction in benefits. Mike has 25 years of service and is 62 years old. His final pay under the plan's formula is $100,000. If Mike retires now, he will receive an annual benefit of $25,000. If Mike continues working until age 65, he will have 28 years of service and his final pay amount might have increased as well. Thus, in determining whether he should retire now or continue working, Mike should compare the value of three additional years of benefit payments, plus the personal value to him of early retirement (which might, of course, include compensation from a different job), with the additional salary he will earn if he stays with ABC and the larger benefit payments he will receive if he retires at age 65.

Not all subsidized early retirement benefits are fully subsidized; in some plans, benefits are reduced but by an amount less than a full actuarial reduction. Determining whether an early retirement benefit is truly subsidized generally requires the assistance of an actuary, who will compare the value of the early retirement benefit under the plan with a benefit that reflects appropriate interest and mortality factors. Nevertheless, the following chart (reproduced from a standard actuarial text) provides approximate full actuarial reductions (based on benefits earned to the date of early retirement):

Age at Retirement	Benefit Percentage
64	89.6%
63	80.5%
62	72.5%
61	65.5%
60	59.3%
59	53.8%
58	48.9%
57	44.5%
56	40.6%
55	37.1%

The above chart reflects a 6% interest rate and a mortality table known as UP–1984. In general, if a plan's early retirement reduction factors yield a larger benefit, the benefit enjoys at least some subsidy (assuming that 6% is the correct interest rate).

[¶ 8,830]

c. *Investing and drawing down assets at retirement*

For most retired individuals with retirement savings, the primary financial goal is to make their savings last through retirement, i.e., not to outlive their savings. To achieve this goal, an individual should have both an investment strategy and a spending strategy. Of necessity, the primary focus of the investment strategy during retirement is on preserving and producing regular income rather than on asset growth (in contrast with the investment strategy for retirement savings during the individual's working life).

We have already explored the basic principles of investment portfolio management and asset allocation: diversification and a shift from equity investments to fixed income investments as a person ages. As described earlier, a common rule of thumb for equity allocation is 100% less the investor's age. A more conservative strategy is arguably appropriate, however, once a person is retired and solely dependent on private savings and Social Security for support, because a retiree will find it more difficult to make up investment losses when she is already drawing down assets to support herself. Indeed, some experts suggest that no more than 20% of a retiree's assets be allocated to equity investments, to protect against periods of investment loss.

Nevertheless, some financial advisors and academics continue to suggest that the minimum allocation to equity should be between 50% and 75%, even in retirement. This is based on the historical rates of return to equity investments compared to fixed income investments. But because there is no assurance that investment returns on different asset categories will adhere to historical patterns, many independent advisors are skeptical of equity allocations that exceed 50% after retirement. Some financial advisors also suggest that a retiree's equity holdings should be weighted toward safer, less volatile industries, such as regulated utilities.

An individual might also consider investing some retirement savings in a financial instrument with insurance features, such as an annuity contract, especially if the individual is not receiving a life annuity from a qualified plan. An annuity contract is both an investment vehicle and, by virtue of its periodic payments, a tool for managing the drawing down of assets in retirement. Some insurance companies (e.g., Metropolitan Life and TIAA–CREF) now offer or are developing annuity products with payments indexed to increases in the cost of living.

Another insurance product that can protect an individual against the risk of living too long is an endowment policy, which is a mirror image of life insurance: the policy pays proceeds to an individual who lives to an age specified in the contract. An endowment contract can provide a target age for an individual to use in drawing down assets, while providing partial replenishment of assets if the individual outlives the target age.

The main problem with such individual insurance contracts is that the market for such products is currently thin and premiums tend to be relatively high. It is possible, however, that the commercial annuity market may be invigorated as large numbers of baby boomers approach retirement age. Moreover, some defined contribution plans allow participants to convert the balance in their accounts into an annuity contract at group rate premiums.

In addition, some individuals have opportunities to invest in unorthodox annuity arrangements. For example, an individual may transfer cash or property to a family member in exchange for a promised stream of annuity payments. (Such "private annuity" arrangements may be subject to various requirements under state law.) Or an individual may assign the remainder interest in her home to another person in exchange for the assignee's promise to pay the individual a stream of annuity payments for life. In essence, this "reverse mortgage" is an annuity arrangement in which the annuitant's cost (in effect, the premium) is the remainder interest in the home, which vests in possession at the annuitant's death. The market for private insurance arrangements, however, may be poorly regulated under state law, and individuals contemplating such an arrangement should make sure that the arrangement is legitimate and that the party promising to make lifetime annuity payments is reliable and adequately bonded. Individuals generally should not enter into such private arrangements without the advice of competent and independent counsel.

Recognizing that successful portfolio management for retirees would be advanced through the development of investment products and counseling addressed to the particular needs of retirees, several large mutual fund companies, including Vanguard, Fidelity, and T. Rowe Price, have established divisions to market such products and provide such counseling.

Formulating a strategy to draw down assets in retirement is also important, but research suggests that many retirees have no very clear understanding of how much they can withdraw each year without exhausting their savings before death. For example, assume that a person with accumulated retirement savings of $1,000,000 wishes to have a fixed annual income and anticipates an investment return of 8% (in a portfolio allocated toward equity). Many individuals (and their financial advisors) might believe that a conservative, principal-conserving strategy would be to withdraw $80,000 annually (i.e., the expected rate of return). But this strategy is in fact aggressive and unwise, for three reasons. First, of course, there is a substantial risk that the average investment return over time will turn out to be less than 8%. A second, more subtle risk is that even if the average rate of return is 8%, the actual rate of return will almost certainly be less during some periods and more during others. If the periods of low return occur during the early years of retirement—especially if there are periods of steep market loss (which occurred as recently as 2001)—the portfolio will suffer disproportionate losses (because it is also being depleted by the $80,000 withdrawals) and will not recover its initial value even if the average return eventually turns out to be 8%. Third, retirees may need an increasing stream of payments as they age, because of inflation and rising medical and home care costs.

Several studies have examined the "success" rate of different withdrawal patterns over various time horizons, with success being defined as a portfolio that is not exhausted before the end of the relevant time period. These studies use historical data and provide success rates for different portfolio asset mixes (with success rates depending primarily on when a person retires). For example, one thoughtful study by three finance professors at Trinity College in Texas (http://www.aaii.com/promo/mstar/feature.shtml), based on historical data from 1926 through 1995, shows that a portfolio with a 50% equity allocation will have only a 51% success rate at the end of 30 years if withdrawals are set at 8% of the initial principal amount; using a shorter historical period (1946 through 1995), the success rate is only 48%. A greater equity allocation yielded more favorable success rates for both historical periods (a 100% equity portfolio with a 7% withdrawal rate yielded a 100% success rate for the period 1946 through 1995), but higher equity allocations carry much higher risk and, as we have already noted, there is no guarantee that future rates of return will match historical rates of return. Indeed, some financial analysts predict a decline in future rates of return on equity investments compared to historical rates of return. (Several papers on withdrawal rates, including the Trinity study, are collected at http.www. bylo.org/saferetr.html.)

Based on historical data, then, a withdrawal rate of 7% of initial value might seem plausible with a 50% equity portfolio over an expected payout period of 30 years. (With a 25% equity allocation, the study suggests a 6% withdrawal rate.) But such a withdrawal rate might nevertheless be imprudent, even if the historical rate of return was an accurate predictor of future returns.

First, there is the problem of inflation. What happens if the annual dollars withdrawn from savings are adjusted annually to reflect inflation? Here, the initial withdrawal rate would have to be set at 4% to have a success rate above 80% (for both 50% and 25% equity allocations).

Second, there is the problem of rising health and home care expenses as a person ages. Thus, a portion of the portfolio's initial value might be held in reserve (or invested in appropriate protective insurance policies).

Third, the option of early retirement and the advance of medical science make it likely that many retirees will live beyond 30 years.

As a result, some financial researchers suggest that the most prudent approach to drawing down retirement savings is to structure inflation-sensitive portfolios and to withdraw a fixed percentage of the portfolio's current value at the start of each year. This approach would result in higher annual payments following periods of inflation if the portfolio's design accomplished its purpose, and would produce an acceptable portfolio success rate over a 40–year time horizon.

There are different views on the appropriate strategy for drawing down assets in retirement. It seems clear, however, that in determining a withdrawal rate an individual should consider several factors: (1) the individual's own life expectancy (or the joint life expectancy of both spouses, in the case of a married couple), as well as the possibility of outliving that life expectancy; (2) risk tolerance (which, as noted above, is relevant not only for asset allocation but also for withdrawal rates); (3) the possibility of inflation and escalating living and medical costs as a person ages; and (4) a range of expected rates of return. Additional considerations are also relevant, including the individual's desire to leave property at death to his or her heirs and the individual's ability to compensate for portfolio failure (for example, by working or by relying on the generosity of children or others.)

K. CONCLUSION

[¶ 8,840]

Financial planning for retirement is a project that spans a person's entire adult life. In this chapter, we have suggested that this project involves three tasks: assessing retirement needs and setting retirement financial targets; accumulating assets while in the workforce; and spending down—some might say rationing—those assets after leaving the workforce. The tasks are not entirely sequential, and often overlap. The process of assessing retirement needs, for example, is a continuous one since a person's personal and financial circumstances are constantly changing. One might, for example, move, marry, divorce, change careers, or suffer illness or injury. And one's savings strategy might be upset by inflation, volatile investment returns, changes in the tax laws or in Social Security, and by other unpredictable events.

We have noted the common (and perhaps overworked) metaphor of retirement savings as a "three-legged stool" based on on Social Security, private savings, and employer-sponsored retirement plans. The future of Social Security will be shaped by political, economic and demographic forces that no individual worker can control, which means that in planning for retirement individuals should concentrate their efforts primarily on the other two legs of the stool. In this connection, two points deserve special emphasis.

First, employer plans are generally a preferred means of saving for retirement. Such plans enjoy substantial tax benefits that are not generally available through other savings vehicles. Moreover, employer plans generally make it easier to follow through with a regular savings program because contributions are made automatically by the employer. Such plans also make it easier to resist the temptation to tap retirement savings for personal consumption, and they are generally immune to claims by creditors and third parties.

Second, it is important to begin saving for retirement at an early age. Due to the compounding of interest, the earlier a dollar is saved the more it will be worth at retirement. A young person should not put off saving for retirement simply because the idea of retirement seems distant. At the very least, any person who is eligible to participate in a 401(k) plan should be sure to make sufficient contributions to qualify for the maximum employer match, and should resist the temptation to consume retirement plan payouts upon changing jobs. Such payouts should be preserved, generally in an individual retirement account.

We have also noted that the three-legged stool metaphor is incomplete and that other sources of retirement income, such as part-time work, may be available.

The chapter also focused on the challenges of investment and drawing down assets after a person leaves the workforce. Most financial planners suggest that individuals should, during the course of their lives, move from a well-diversified portfolio weighted toward riskier but potentially high-yield equity investments when they are young to a safer, well-diversified portfolio weighted toward relatively secure fixed-income investments as they age. Finally, the chapter emphasized both the importance and the difficulty of ensuring that a person does not outlive his or her retirement assets. In this connection, a person should consider investing a portion of retirement savings in insurance products that protect against the risk of outliving one's assets, particularly inflation-graded annuity products and long-term care insurance.

Long ago the poet Robert Burns wrote, "come grow old with me, the best is yet to be." When Burns wrote those lines, life expectancies were short and people were generally supported by their families when they became infirm and unable to work. We live in different times, but with prudent planning and regular and thoughtful saving, retirement can still be looked forward to as the best period of life.

Chapter 9

ELDER LAW

A. OVERVIEW

[¶ 9,000]

This chapter explores the important subject of "elder law," which covers a broad range of legal issues faced by Americans as they live longer. Some major elder law issues have already been covered in previous chapters. For example, Social Security benefits and the options and alternatives available under that important program are considered in Chapter 8. That chapter also addresses withdrawals and distributions from employer-based pension systems, as well as the range of self-directed retirement arrangements, including individual retirement accounts, 401(k) plans, and the like. Similarly, the tax provisions that pertain to the sale of a principal residence, a major financial transaction for many older people, are examined in Chapters 3 and 5. Chapter 5 also looks at reverse mortgages, an increasingly popular financial mechanism that enables older homeowners to utilize the equity in their residences without requiring them to move.

Among the purposes of elder law is the effectuation of a client's wishes to the maximum extent possible. Client autonomy and respect demand nothing less. To this end, various devices have been developed to enable an older person to control his or her medical destiny and to have someone handle the older person's financial matters. These mechanisms, do not, however, supplant a client's power to take charge of daily activities, as long as the client has both the mental understanding (often called "legal capacity") and the willingness to do so. To that end, Part B of this chapter considers when a person no longer has the requisite "legal capacity" and the various means by which that person's wishes can be implemented when that capacity is lacking.

The remainder of this chapter deals with two of the most significant issues in elder law, especially when they are intertwined—namely, how to pay for medical care and where to live. Accordingly, Part C examines the Medicare program, the federal government's response to the increasingly expensive health care costs of persons age 65 and over, as well as

Americans of any age who are disabled. As that Part will show, Medicare's focus is on acute care in hospitals and similar settings. Its coverage of long-term care costs is very limited. When such care is required, therefore, the cost of such care is financed in one of three ways: by the individual with or without assistance from family members (usually known as self-pay); through private long-term care insurance; or through the Medicaid program, a joint effort of the federal and state governments to pay medical costs of impoverished Americans of any age. Parts D and E of this chapter consider these last two sources of long-term care financing.

For further discussion of issues involving older persons, see Frolik & Kaplan, Elder Law (3d ed.2003).

B. PLANNING FOR POSSIBLE INCAPACITY

[¶ 9,100]

As noted above, a number of legal mechanisms have been developed to make certain medical decisions and handle the financial affairs of a person who lacks the legal capacity to do so directly. These mechanisms do not apply, however, when a person has such capacity. Although these topics are regularly subsumed within the rubric of "elder law," they can apply with equal force to adults of any age whose capacity has been impaired. This section begins, therefore, with an examination of when a person's legal capacity is impaired. It then proceeds to the various mechanisms that apply to that situation, beginning with formal guardianship and proceeding to less formal means of surrogate decision-making.

[¶ 9,110]

1. Legal Capacity

In general, "legal capacity" can be understood to mean that the client comprehends the options being presented and can communicate the decision that this person is making. Communication in this context need not necessarily be verbal; raising a limb or making some other physical gesture might be sufficient. While the law presumes that an adult has legal capacity, in some cases that presumption might be problematic. Nonetheless, legal capacity is a prerequisite to signing legal documents, transferring property, or making any of the arrangements described later in this section. A person who lacks such capacity may do none of those things, and a guardianship must be sought to enable some other person to take over that person's decision-making responsibilities. See ¶ 9,120.

At the outset, it must be noted that legal capacity, or "competency" as it is sometimes styled, is not a single construct. A person whose mental faculties have declined may still have enough capacity to sign checks and pay bills but not enough to make investment decisions or make a will. Moreover, the notion of legal capacity is often very difficult to determine. It is not like reading a person's blood pressure or measuring a glucose level. A person's legal capacity may vary with the physical setting, the time of day, the complexity of the task at hand, or even the interaction of particular medications. Accordingly, a person's legal capacity might be enhanced by familiar surroundings, optimal scheduling, breaking down a given project into smaller tasks, or altering the combination or sequencing of specific medications. Even cognitively debilitating conditions, like Alzheimer's disease, often progress slowly and do not entirely eliminate a person's capacity until the later stages of these conditions.

Too often, a person's legal capacity is questioned merely because that person is depressed or is withdrawing from family and friends. Those are serious problems, to be sure, but they do not necessarily indicate a diminution of mental ability. Similarly, an unwillingness to agree with the recommendations of family members—or even of professional advisors—does not indicate mental impairment. After all, most credit card holders roll over their monthly balances by not paying the entire amount billed, even though every available source of financial advice indicates that this practice is unsound. But those credit card holders are not deemed to be mentally incapacitated simply because they fail to manage their finances in the most prudent manner. Similarly, wealthy individuals often spend enormous amounts of money on frivolous ventures, ranging from lavish accommodations or exotic entertainment to multi-million-dollar political campaigns. People have a right to make silly decisions or act eccentrically without having their legal capacity challenged. Legal capacity, in other words, is not the same as rationality according to some other person's standards.

The only guidance on this subject provided by the Model Rules of Professional Conduct (MRPC) advises lawyers to "consider and balance such factors as: the client's ability to articulate reasoning leading to a decision, variability of state of mind and ability to appreciate consequences of a decision; the substantive fairness of a decision; and the consistency of a decision with the long-term commitments and values of the client." MRPC 1.14, cmt. 6. Obviously, this is not an easy question to resolve.

But the central significance of a client's legal capacity requires that this issue be resolved. To that end, some advisors rely on their personal observations of the client or the observations of family members and friends. These approaches, however, are potentially subject to bias or various conflicts of interest. Some advisors choose instead to administer simple "mental status" tests that evaluate attention span, memory, and language comprehension. These tests, however, have their own problems, including cultural bias, which can undermine their reliability in some cases.

Still other advisors engage professional assistance in making legal capacity determinations, and the Model Rules specifically recommend this approach. See MRPC 1.14, cmt. 6. But this approach is not a panacea either, since medical professionals often employ very different techniques to assess a person's mental functioning. In one comprehensive study employing six methodologies for diagnosing dementia, the proportion of subjects so diagnosed ranged from 3.1% to 29.1%—a tenfold difference—depending upon the specific approach being used. Indeed, only 20 subjects out of a total of 1,879 tested were found to be demented according to all six methodologies. See Erkinjuntti et al., The Effect of Different Diagnostic Criteria on the Prevalence of Dementia, 337 New Eng. J. Med. 1667 (1997).

Such imprecision notwithstanding, determining a client's capacity is crucially important. Some advisors take the following steps to maximize their clients' abilities: (1) shortening client meetings even if doing so makes more meetings necessary; (2) speaking to the client more slowly; (3) reducing extraneous noise during office interviews; (4) using open-ended questions rather than yes-or-no inquiries; (5) preparing documents in large type and sending those documents to the client in advance. Moreover, some advisors videotape their sessions to document the level of a client's capacity at the time an action is taken, although other advisors eschew this practice entirely.

In any case, the Model Rules require that a lawyer "maintain a normal client-lawyer relationship" to the extent possible. MRPC 1.14(a). Accordingly, these advisors will follow a client's instructions as long as doing so poses no harm to the client or to any other person. A lawyer may act in an emergency, however, whenever a client's "health, safety, or financial interest . . . is threatened with imminent or irreparable harm." MRPC 1.14, cmt. 9. Otherwise, if a client lacks sufficient capacity, appointment of a guardian may be necessary, as explained below.

[¶ 9,115]

Problems

1. Whenever Louise hears that a storm is expected, she drives to the nearest convenience store and buys several days' worth of toilet paper and ready-to-eat meals. At the present time, she has enough such supplies to last three weeks. Does this behavior suggest that Louise's capacity to make rational decisions is becoming impaired? What if her garage has enough of these items to last six months? Six years?

2. Though Bruce is still able to write checks legibly, he no longer records these checks in his checkbook and never opens his monthly bank statements when they arrive in the mail. Do these practices suggest that Bruce is starting to suffer from diminished capacity? What if his checking account has an average balance of $275? $27,500?

[¶ 9,120]

2. Guardianship

Every state has some procedure for designating a surrogate decision-maker for a person who lacks legal capacity. These statutes vary considerably from state to state, but they share certain key elements. For example, most states require that some person ask a court to appoint a surrogate for the person in question. The person making this request is called the "petitioner," the person appointed is called a "guardian" or sometimes a "conservator," and the person for whom the surrogate is appointed is called the "ward" or the "incapacitated person." The guardian so appointed may make a variety of decisions affecting the health care and the financial affairs of the ward, though these two general areas are often assigned to different persons. For example, some financial institutions and nonprofit organizations serve as financial overseers but typically do not deal with health care issues. In any case, the appointment of a guardian is a court-supervised procedure that secures a decision-maker in place of the incapacitated person.

While guardianships are based on a person's legal incapacity rather than age, the vast majority of guardianships in this country involve persons over age 60. This process is not an inevitable accompaniment to aging, however. Many alternatives to guardianship exist, but they must all be created while the older person still has sufficient legal capacity. See ¶ 9,200. In addition, modern banking practices can be employed to reduce somewhat the need for certain activities that are typically performed by guardians. For example, income receipts from Social Security, pension plans, bank certificates of deposit, bond funds, and stock dividends can all be deposited automatically into a person's bank account without requiring some person to handle these items. Similarly, recurring expenses such as mortgage payments, electricity bills, and telephone service can be set up as automatic withdrawals from a client's checking account, thereby ensuring continuity of basic services without the need for a guardian to be involved in the bill-paying process.

[¶ 9,125]

a. *Procedural Aspects of Guardianship*

A guardianship begins with a petition to the probate court or a similar tribunal (sometimes called the surrogate's court or orphans' court). While guardianship petitions are most often filed by the putative ward's family or friends, most states also allow social service agencies and medical facility employees to file for guardianship when no family member is available.

The specific contents of the guardianship petition are governed by state practice and procedure, but at a minimum, the petition must allege facts that demonstrate the need for a guardian and state whether that person is to have control over the ward's finances or health care matters.

The petition must also provide the name of someone, not necessarily the petitioner, who is willing and able to serve as guardian. Courts are often loath to create a guardianship unless someone is willing and able to fulfill this function. This requirement can become a serious stumbling block, because many people do not want to accept the responsibilities of acting as a guardian for an incapacitated adult.

Beyond these essentials, some states require a list of the putative ward's income and assets. Others require an explanation why no alternative arrangement will suffice. In that connection, some petitions are required to set forth a proposed course of action that the guardian intends to take. In any case, the petition must be provided to the putative ward on a timely basis, presumably to give that person an opportunity to object. Most states also require that notice of the petition be provided to the putative ward's family and anyone else who lives with that person.

Within a short time after notice is given, a hearing is usually held to determine whether the petition seeking the guardianship should be granted. The putative ward may attend this hearing, but this is often unnecessary according to local court practices. In some circumstances, the court might hold the hearing off-site, perhaps where the putative ward lives, to enable that person to participate in the proceedings despite a physical inability to go to court.

Almost all hearings are held before a judge, although many states allow the alleged incapacitated person to request a jury trial. Many courts employ "visitors" who physically inspect the putative ward in that person's regular place of residence and then report back to the court about what they found. These visitors may also interview the petitioner, and perhaps the proposed guardian as well, to get a better sense of the need for a guardianship and the suitability of the person who has been nominated to serve in that capacity. As is the case with judicial proceedings generally, legal counsel may represent the putative ward, though some states employ a guardian ad litem for this purpose.

[¶ 9,130]

b. *Financial Implications of Guardianship*

Guardianship is not cheap, at least for wards who have resources. Costs encompass the one-time expenses of securing the guardianship, as well as ongoing expenses of the guardian once that person has been appointed. Some of the one-time expenses include the following:

1. Legal fees, which can be several thousand dollars for an uncontested guardianship. A contested guardianship costs even more, and an appeal will cost more still.

2. Expenses for a physician or other qualified professional to assess the putative ward's incapacity. In-court testimony by such a person will involve further costs.

3. Fees for social workers who may be engaged to devise a proposed plan of care for the ward.

4. Expenses of court visitors and guardians ad litem.

5. Court fees, though they are usually quite modest.

All of these costs are charged against the ward's assets.

In addition, after court approval, a guardian is entitled to compensation for that person's time and effort. Financial institutions and nonprofit organizations that serve as guardians also charge for their services, sometimes as flat fees, sometimes at hourly rates, and sometimes as a percentage of the assets involved. Family members and friends typically do not receive fees for serving as guardians, but they are reimbursed from the ward's assets for any out-of-pocket costs incurred in the course of the guardianship.

[¶ 9,135]

c. *Responsibilities of a Guardian*

The responsibilities of a guardian depend on the nature of the guardianship that the court approves. (For a discussion of an alternative known as "limited guardianship," see Frolik, Promoting Judicial Acceptance and Use of Limited Guardianship, 31 Stetson L. Rev. 735 (2002).) A guardian for medical matters, sometimes called a "guardian of the person," customarily begins by assessing the ward's living conditions and preparing a plan to respond to the inadequacies that motivated the court to grant the guardianship petition. Thereafter, the guardian may be required to provide written reports on a regular basis to the court that is supervising the guardianship.

A guardian of the person may make whatever medical decisions are required, including whether the ward should be moved into a nursing home or similar facility. State law may require judicial approval for certain actions, such as terminating life support, but guardians generally have broad discretion to do whatever they think the situation demands. The applicable standard in most cases is the "best interests of the ward," which considers the way that the incapacitated person lived before the guardianship was created. If the guardian is unable to ascertain what that standard would require in a particular instance, the test generally becomes whatever a "reasonable person" would do under the same circumstances. Some courts utilize "visitors" to see what the guardian has done and to report those findings to the supervising court.

A guardian for financial matters, sometimes called a "guardian of the estate" or a "conservator," typically begins the guardianship by preparing an inventory of the ward's assets and assessing that person's financial condition. The guardian then collects the ward's income, pays bills, and generally gets that person's financial affairs in order. To that end, the guardian might make changes in the ward's investment holdings and arrange for the disposition of specific properties, including the ward's residence. The guardian may also apply for public assistance on behalf of the ward and obtain insurance benefits to which the ward is entitled.

The guardian must provide a report to the court, usually styled an "accounting," on a regular basis, typically at least once a year. These reports must show income received and expenditures paid during the period covered by the accounting. In addition, when the ward dies, the guardianship terminates, and the guardian must render a final accounting of the financial transactions undertaken on behalf of the ward. The guardian may be held personally liable for any losses resulting from improper transactions, and the court may impose additional penalties in cases of egregious misconduct.

In any event, the powers of a guardian are not unlimited. For example, a guardian is not allowed to vote in a political election, consent to a marriage or divorce, or make a will on behalf of the ward.

[¶ 9,140]

Problems

1.   Patricia is often confused about world events and has lost interest in maintaining her once fastidious home. Some neighbors have noticed the change in her behavior and have petitioned for a guardian to be appointed for her. She claims that she can handle her finances just fine and that she is afraid that a guardian might make her leave her home, which she really does not want to do. She has asked you to resist the guardianship petition but is petrified of appearing in court. She tells you that the only time she was in a courtroom was 38 years ago when she was divorced, and she still has nightmares about the experience. What special request might you make on her behalf to improve her chances of resisting a guardianship?

2.   You have just been appointed a guardian for Victor and are starting to prepare an inventory of his assets. In doing so, you notice that he has no fewer than 62 chess sets of various styles, most of which are still in their packing material. A quick perusal of his credit card statements reveals that Victor has been purchasing chess sets, often several at a time, whenever they are offered on one of the television shopping networks. As guardian, what steps should you take to best preserve Victor's assets?

[¶ 9,150]

3.   Advance Medical Directives

One of the defining characteristics of modern medicine is continuous progress in the treatment of illnesses that were formerly regarded as untreatable. In some cases, however, the process of providing such treatments may not accord with a particular client's wishes. While most people want to be cured, certain treatments seem to offer only a postponement of the inevitable, often accompanied with unacceptable limitations and restrictions. Since the 1970's, therefore, a growing movement has developed various means by which a client can decline medical treatment under specified conditions.

Two general points should be made at the outset. First, none of these means is required when a client is competent. That is, as long as the client/patient has sufficient legal capacity (see ¶ 9,110), that person has the right to refuse medical treatment without further ado. But if the client either cannot understand the nature of the options being presented or is unable to communicate which option the client desires, it may become necessary to consult some sort of document to ascertain the client's wishes. These documents are often described as "advance medical directives," and they provide guidance on medical decisions when a client cannot do so directly. In any case, even if a client has an advance medical directive, the client is not obliged to follow that document as long as the client has sufficient legal capacity. These documents apply, in other words, only when a client cannot make his or her own medical decisions.

Second, the subject of advance medical directives seems to have been subsumed as part of elder law or occasionally as part of a comprehensive estate plan, but it is not exclusively an older person's issue. After all, the most prominent cases that established a patient's right to determine his or her own care involved women in their twenties. See Matter of Quinlan, 355 A.2d 647 (N.J. 1976) (22–year–old in a persistent vegetative state); Cruzan v. Director, Missouri Dept. of Health, 497 U.S. 261 (1990) (25–year-old in same). Thus, this subject should be of interest to everyone, though older people tend to be more familiar with some of these issues and often have fairly specific ideas of what they want and do not want.

There are two basic types of advance medical directives: living wills, and health care proxies (often known as durable powers of attorney for health care). Every state has one or the other of these two basic formats, and most states recognize both types of documents. The forms themselves are often available from the websites of state medical societies and from various consumer-oriented websites as well, such as healthdirectives.org, legalzoom.com, and willsforamerica.com, to name just a few. In addition, major religious organizations have developed advance medical directives that incorporate the teachings of their faith into these documents.

In any case, as a matter of federal law, the Patient Self–Determination Act requires that health care providers furnish written information to patients describing their right to make health care decisions and document the existence of advance health care directives. See 42 U.S.C. §§ 1395cc(f), 1396a(w). Many health care providers routinely furnish blank forms of living wills and health care proxies to patients on admission to a facility. The Act applies to all Medicare- and Medicaid-certified hospitals, nursing homes, home health care agencies, and pre-paid care organizations. While the Act requires providers to make available information about advance medical directives, it does not require patients to actually prepare a directive. In fact, most people have no advance medical directive, though there are considerable variations by age: one study found that only 9% of persons under age 30, but 35% of persons over age 75, have an advance medical directive. See U.S. Gen. Accounting Office, Patient Self–Determination Act: Providers Offer Information on Advance Directives but Effectiveness Uncertain 9 (GAO/HEHS–95–135, 1995).

What then happens to the vast majority of people, namely, those without any advance medical directive? In three out of four states, the legislatures have created an advance medical directive for them. Clients are not stuck with these state-created directives, of course. They may always prepare their own. But these so-called health care surrogacy statutes do provide an alternative to the court system, a process that is often cumbersome, costly, and prone to delays. In effect, these health care surrogacy statutes are the medical care equivalent of intestate succession: a default arrangement that applies when the client has not left individualized instructions. See ¶ 2,100. Accordingly, this section begins with an examination of these health care surrogacy statutes before considering the two alternative forms of advance medical directives.

[¶ 9,155]

a. *Health Care Surrogacy Statutes*

Although there are variations among the states, the general thrust of health care surrogacy statutes is the same: to designate some person who will act as the client's decision-maker for health care in certain specified circumstances. The specified circumstances often pertain to fairly dire medical conditions, such as terminal illness, permanent unconsciousness, and the like. In situations other than those listed, the surrogacy statutes do not apply.

Typically, the persons designated as decision-makers may direct that certain life-sustaining procedures (usually involving assistance with breathing, eating, hydration, or similar functions) be withheld. Some statutes provide more detailed lists, including surgery and renal dialysis, while others are less specific and allow the surrogate to make whatever medical decisions that the client could make directly. Many of these laws specifically provide that the health care provider may rely on the decision of the designated surrogate, regardless of any conflicting interests that person may have.

The heart of these surrogacy statutes is a categorized list of prioritized decision-makers. While the specifics vary from one state to another, high priority is reserved for a patient's spouse, followed by the patient's adult children or parents. Other relatives are often listed as well, such as siblings or adult grandchildren. Sometimes, domestic partners can be included as spousal equivalents or as "close friends," but the latter category usually has a fairly low priority.

In any case, none of the persons listed in the surrogacy statute is obligated to serve as decision-maker. That is, a person who is entitled to priority under the statute may simply decline the office of surrogate and refuse to make a decision. After all, since the client never prepared an advance medical directive, the persons listed in the statute may be very uncomfortable with the scope of responsibility that has been foisted upon them, often quite fortuitously.

Moreover, the need for urgent action may determine which person becomes the surrogate. Most statutes require that a surrogate be "available," though to what extent or within what time frame is generally not set forth. Most of these statutes contemplate telephonic communication; facsimile transmissions are less frequently mentioned, and e-mail is almost totally unconsidered. In any case, if a putative surrogate is not "available" within the parameters required, most statutes dictate that the next highest ranked person or category of persons be contacted for this purpose.

One potential problem relates to multiple persons in a given category. That is, if a patient has three children and they disagree on the appropriate course of action, what happens? Most statutes advise that consensus should be reached, but what if the persons involved cannot reach a consensus? Does majority vote govern? If so, what if there is a tie, such as when there are four children, or two siblings, for example? Does the statute then look to the next category down?

The point here is not to denigrate surrogacy statutes, which, after all, seek only to fill a void that the client has left. Rather, it is important for clients to be aware of the statutory default procedure, so they can make an informed decision about whether to accept that procedure or to use one of the means described below to make their own arrangements instead.

[¶ 9,160]

b. *Living Wills*

Living wills are the older of the two standard forms of advance health care directives. These documents are generally quite brief and respond directly to what concerns many people the most—namely, the provision of medical care that delays death but provides little real hope of recovery or improvement. In short, living wills respond to the dread that many Americans have about being "tied to machines" to maintain an existence that some regard as not life in any true sense. The exact phrasing varies by state, but the essence of a living will is that the maker of the document orders that death-delaying procedures be discontinued when that person is terminally ill or permanently unconscious.

Some statutes expand on what procedures are contemplated by this instruction, but most living wills themselves are straightforward declarations unburdened by that level of detail. Thus, many people completing living wills may not realize, for example, that these documents often do not permit the withdrawal of food and water if death would result from the consequent starvation or dehydration.

The formalities of executing the document also vary by state, but all states require that the maker sign the document. Most states require at least one witness, sometimes specifying that this person must have no pecuniary interest in the estate of the person making the living will. Some states require notarization, but others do not, recognizing that many living wills are prepared in medical settings where a notary public might not be on hand. Finally, some states are more accepting of alterations to their statutory forms than are other jurisdictions.

As this brief overview suggests, living wills are very limited documents. They have no application unless the patient has a medical condition described in the authorizing statute. Statutory definitions often require that death be "imminent," a status that can be very problematic to assess in many real life situations. Moreover, even if the living will applies, it may be effective to block only certain types of procedures.

[¶ 9,165]

c. *Health Care Proxies*

In response to the limitations of living wills, most state legislatures recognize the health care proxy as an alternative form of advance medical directive. The health care proxy designates one person with general authority to make medical decisions on behalf of an incapacitated client. Formats vary by state, but most forms allow a client to name whomever that person wants, without regard to the designee's relationship to the client. The watchword here is maximum flexibility. Thus, a domestic partner, a particular relative who has medical training, or anyone else in whose judgment the client has confidence, can be the designated decision-maker under a health care proxy.

The scope of health care proxies, moreover, is not limited to terminal illness. The named agent can typically withhold or withdraw any medical procedure, including food and water, and make any other medical decision that the person executing the proxy would be able to make directly. Many statutes provide a standard form that enables the maker of the document to limit the agent's authority if that is desired. Absent such restrictions, the agent is charged with doing whatever he or she thinks is best under the circumstances. After all, it was the client who chose the designated decision-maker, not some state legislature. In that connection, a client should also designate a successor agent under the health care proxy in case the client's first choice is unavailable or for any reason unable or unwilling to serve.

Formalities of execution typically include signing by the document's maker and at least one witness. Notarization is usually not required. Many states require that the named agent sign the document as well, thereby providing a sample of that person's signature. In addition, such signing acknowledges that the agent knows about the responsibility of being a health care decision-maker and agrees to accept that burden. This agent may subsequently change his or her mind in this regard, perhaps because of medical crises or other events that have arisen during the intervening years, but the agent's signature indicates that the agent at least initially was willing to serve.

Some clients prefer to execute a health care proxy in conjunction with a living will. The agent then has broad decision-making authority regarding the client's health care, but the client's specific concerns about death-delaying procedures are covered in the living will. This practice is not common, no doubt because of potential conflict between the two directives. That is, what happens if the agent under the health care proxy decides not to follow the client's living will? As a practical matter, no one may even know about the client's living will, unless the agent produces it, which may explain the absence of reported cases dealing with this situation. Nevertheless, this combination of advance medical directives is an option for those clients who want to designate a particular decision-maker but also want to indicate their personal preferences regarding end-of-life care.

[¶ 9,170]

d. *Issues Common to Advance Medical Directives*

Even if a client has prepared an advance medical directive, at least three general issues must be confronted:

1. *Portability:* Given that advance medical directives are creatures of state law, what is their effectiveness when the client is outside the state that authorized the directive in question? Some states grant full reciprocity to out-of-state directives, while other states impose certain conditions that parallel their own requirements. Still other states recognize only their own forms. Clients who spend a major portion of the year in a different state should probably prepare advance medical directives in both their home state and their other state of residence.

2. *Accessibility:* Where should advance medical directives be kept? Common locations are lawyers' offices or central registries of religious organizations. These facilities are often closed, however, when medical emergencies arise, thereby weakening the usefulness of the directives. At a minimum, whoever is designated as agent under a health care proxy should have a copy of the pertinent advance medical directive. Further, whoever is likely to accompany the client to the hospital should know where the directive is kept and should be able to locate it readily. After all, if a directive cannot be produced promptly in an emergency, why have one? Some Internet-based services offer to maintain 24–hour availability via facsimile transmission and to provide a

wallet-sized card that would identify registrants. See, e.g., http://www.uslivingwillregistry.com.

3. *Enforceability:* Can a client depend upon the directive being honored as prepared? Most states permit health care providers to refuse to follow a patient's advance medical directive for reasons of "conscience." In those circumstances, however, the provider is usually required to transfer the patient to a facility or health care provider who will carry out the instructions provided in the directive. Only a small minority of states impose any penalty on health care providers who refuse to follow a patient's advance medical directive, though some states refer such refusals to the state licensing authorities for possible disciplinary action. See Note, Enforcement Problems Arising from Conflicting Views of Living Wills in the Legal, Medical and Patient Communities, 62 U. Pitt. L. Rev. 793, 800–01 (2001).

[¶ 9,175]

Problems

1.   Jennifer has been in a relationship with Christine for the past 23 years. Jennifer is concerned about what might happen if she is unable to make medical decisions for herself. Despite the length of their relationship, Jennifer's state of residence does not recognize Christine as anything more than a "close friend." Jennifer's parents have never approved of her relationship with Christine and have had little contact with her for the past 15 years. If Jennifer does not prepare an advance medical directive, who will make medical decisions on her behalf when she is unable to do so? What can Jennifer do to make sure that Christine is her medical decision-maker?

2.   Brad has two adult children from his former marriage to Britney. Those two children have diametrically opposite religious views about the sanctity of life, and Brad doubts that the two of them could ever agree on any medical decision affecting such matters. Brad's brother, Jason, has not spoken to Brad since Jason's marriage 12 years ago when Brad refused to be Jason's best man because Jason married someone of a different religion. Brad's only other blood relative is his 19–year old grandson, Patrick, who dropped out of college last year because of severe medical problems related to his cocaine addiction. In terms of health care decision-making for Brad, what is Britney's status? Should Brad consider a health care proxy under these circumstances, and who should he designate as the agent if he prepares such a document?

3.   Max recently witnessed the full treatment regimen of modern medicine when his only sibling spent five weeks in a hospital hooked up to various medical devices and was never able to communicate with Max. As Max is filing insurance claims to cover the nearly $150,000 of medical costs incurred by his brother, he is worried about what might happen to him in a similar situation. Max has no remaining relatives, but he wants the bulk of his estate to go to his college, rather than "down the drain of some hospital," as he puts it. What should Max do now to accomplish his goal?

4. Late in life, Rebecca had a change in outlook and now believes that life should never be halted before God so determines. Her entire extended family feels otherwise, so Rebecca wants her friend from church, Vanessa, to make sure that the "doctors don't kill me before my time" and that they "let nature take its course." How might Rebecca implement her desires in this regard?

[¶ 9,200]

4. Financial Arrangements

Clients who want to avoid guardianship have several devices available that empower other people to handle their financial affairs. These devices are: joint ownership of property, a durable power of attorney for property, and a living trust. Each of these devices will be considered in this section, but they all have two very important elements in common:

1. These devices must be created while the client still has sufficient legal capacity. That is, these forms of surrogate decision-making must be established before the client needs them. By the time the client needs someone else to manage his or her financial affairs, it is usually too late to make the necessary arrangements, and guardianship is the only alternative available. See ¶ 9,120.

2. Each device requires that the client be completely comfortable with at least one other person. The person designated to handle the client's financial affairs has enormous control over that client's money, and there is always a significant potential for abuse or misuse of the funds. There are legal remedies in most instances, of course, but they are necessarily after-the-fact and are often rather cumbersome and costly. The best way to combat financial abuse is to prevent it from occurring in the first place.

In any case, using one of these mechanisms for a particular asset does not preclude using different mechanisms for other assets. Thus, a client might have her checking account in joint ownership while holding her real estate in a living trust. Moreover, the mechanisms described below can also be utilized by a client who has full legal capacity but wishes to delegate responsibility for handling that person's financial matters to some trusted individual. Thus, these mechanisms have relevance beyond the specific context of avoiding a possible future guardianship.

[¶ 9,210]

a. *Joint Ownership*

Of the three guardianship alternatives considered in this section, joint ownership is the easiest to create and the simplest to operate. Joint ownership can take various formats, but the most typical is "joint tenancy with a right of survivorship." Creating a joint tenancy often involves nothing more than adding another person to an existing bank account or brokerage account, though it may require retitling property in two or more persons' names. Once the joint tenancy is created, the rights of the owners depend on the type of asset involved. In the case of a joint account in a bank or other financial institution, each co-owner may have access to all of the funds in the account, subject to a liability to account to the other owners for any withdrawals in excess of his or her net contributions. See ¶ 2,320. In the case of other property such as real property, each co-owner may be able to convey his or her interest, but a conveyance of the underlying property requires joint action on the part of all of the owners. See ¶ 2,315. There are also testamentary implications in these arrangements, because property held in joint tenancy passes automatically to the surviving joint tenant without going through the probate process. See ¶ 2,310.

For many clients, this arrangement will be all that is needed to make sure that bills are paid, certificates of deposit are cashed or rolled over, dividend checks are cashed or reinvested, and so forth. Many married couples place much, if not all, of their property in joint tenancy, but this form of property ownership is not restricted to married couples. Any two (or more) persons, regardless of family relationship, may hold property as joint tenants or as tenants in common; a tenancy by the entirety, however, is available only to married couples. In the elder law context, the most common arrangement has an older person holding property in joint tenancy with an adult child, or niece or nephew, if the older person has no children.

Joint tenancy generally gives each co-owner immediate access to the underlying property and at least partial control over the disposition of the property. This feature can be both an advantage and a disadvantage. On the one hand, joint tenancy is simple to understand and easy to implement. Since almost all married couples have at least some property in joint tenancy, most people are already somewhat familiar with this form of holding property. And no special forms or legal fees are required. Very wealthy clients might have some gift and estate tax consequences when property is transferred into joint tenancy with someone other than a spouse, but in many cases there are no gift or estate tax consequences involved in making this arrangement. See ¶ 4,230.

The downside is that each co-owner's interest in joint tenancy property is subject to the claims of his or her creditors. Thus, there is always a possibility that a joint tenancy may be severed if one co-owner's interest is reached to satisfy debts arising from business or student loans, divorce settlements, gambling losses, or the like. One response to this concern is to use different co-tenants for different assets. For example, a client might have a joint checking account with her son and hold her stock investments in joint tenancy with her daughter. And her apartment buildings could be jointly owned with a niece or nephew, especially if that niece or nephew has special expertise in real estate or lives near the properties in question.

There may be income tax consequences to holding property in joint tenancy. For tax purposes, income earned on joint tenancy property is reportable by each joint tenant according to that person's proportionate ownership interest in the property. And if the new joint tenant pays tax at a higher rate than did the original owner, the total tax paid on the income generated by this property will increase. On the other hand, when a joint tenant dies, the surviving joint tenant will receive the property with a tax "basis" that is determined, in whole or in part, by the property's fair market value when the deceased joint tenant died. See ¶ 4,030.

[¶ 9,215]

Problem

Marta has $65,000 in her checking account at the present time. She wants to add her son, Chet, to her account so he can handle her routine financial transactions. Marta is concerned, however, about Chet's money management skills. For example, he often purchases items on impulse and then needs to "roll over" his credit card bills instead of paying them in full every month, as Marta does. How might she limit her financial exposure but still have Chet on her bank account?

[¶ 9,220]

b. Durable Powers of Attorney

A very different alternative to guardianship is the durable power of attorney (DPOA). This legal document designates a specific person, known as the "attorney-in-fact" or the "agent," to handle the financial aspects of a wide range of transactions for another person, often called the "principal" or the "maker." The "durable" feature of a DPOA means that the authorization that it provides continues even if the client loses legal capacity and becomes unable to change the document. But as long as a client has the requisite legal capacity, that person may revoke or modify any existing DPOA. Upon a client's death, the DPOA no longer has any effect.

The DPOA is a very flexible instrument that enables the agent to handle the maker's finances when the maker is unable or unwilling to do so. It does not, however, convey any property ownership in specific assets. Accordingly, a DPOA does not require retitling of assets or new signature cards. Nor does it have any immediate tax consequences, because there is no change of ownership. Similarly, a DPOA has no direct impact on a maker's testamentary plans or the probate process when the maker passes away.

The cost of preparing a DPOA depends entirely on its intended scope and the degree to which the client seeks customization. That is, standard forms are available under most state statutes and on certain websites, such as legalzoom.com and willsforamerica.com. These forms typically cover a broad range of financial transactions, from taxes and checking accounts to certificates of deposit, mutual funds, real estate, stocks, and other more exotic investments as well.

But in particular cases, these standard forms may not best effectuate a client's wishes. For example, while a client might want her son to handle most financial matters, the client's out-of-state real estate might be better managed by a niece who lives near that property. In that case, the client would want two DPOAs: one, naming the son as agent and covering all assets other than the out-of-state real estate; and another, naming the niece as agent and covering only that real estate. Or a client who has a brokerage account with sophisticated investments, such as stock options and straddles, might want her daughter, the investment banker, to handle that account. Once again, a DPOA that names the daughter as agent for a particular asset might be appropriate. As is the case with legal documents generally, the more customized the product, the higher the preparation cost.

The scope of a DPOA is further implicated in the decision whether to allow an agent to make gifts. The typical DPOA does not include this power, because a "gifting" power is generally antithetical to an agent's fiduciary duty to act solely for the benefit of the maker. The potential for abuse in this situation is huge, since a gift—by definition—benefits the donee rather than the donor. Nevertheless, some clients want their agents to make gifts for family occasions, for estate planning purposes, in connection with a Medicaid application, or otherwise. In that circumstance, the DPOA must include a specific authorization for gifts.

This authorization can be tailored to minimize the potential for abuse. Some possible steps in this direction include the following:

1. Name a different agent under a separate DPOA for the sole purpose of making gifts.

2. Authorize the named agent under the DPOA to make gifts to anyone other than the agent or the agent's family.

3. Allow the agent to make gifts to himself or herself, but only with the consent of another person.

4. Restrict gifts to specific amounts, specific maximums, named donees, or for enumerated purposes.

5. Restrict gifts to recognized charities only.

These provisions obviously limit the agent's ability to accommodate changes in family circumstances, applicable law, or property values, but they might enable the maker to feel more comfortable with the enormous power being conveyed under a DPOA that allows gifts.

Discomfort with the scope of power granted in a DPOA can also be addressed in the DPOA's effective date. As noted previously, a client must have sufficient legal capacity when the DPOA is created. But some clients still want to maintain control of their finances at that time. In other words, the maker might be willing to execute a DPOA but does not want it to take effect right away. One response to this dilemma is a delayed or "springing" DPOA, whereby the DPOA is not effective until certain specified conditions occur. The "springing" provision might refer to a judicial determination of impaired capacity, a medical determination of same by one or more named physicians, or some other occurrence that might (or might never) occur in the future. Until those conditions are met, the DPOA in question does not take effect.

While a "springing" provision may resolve the maker's discomfort with the DPOA's power, it can undercut that document's usefulness by raising potential questions about whether it is currently in effect. For example, a bank with no previous relationship with the named agent might question whether the conditions specified in the DPOA regarding the maker's incapacity have in fact occurred. As a result, some delays or confusion might be encountered in actually using a "springing" DPOA that contains a triggering mechanism.

Using a less formal approach, the maker can execute a DPOA that is effective immediately and leave the executed document with a trusted advisor (someone other than the agent named in the DPOA). When this trusted advisor deems the time appropriate, this person can deliver the DPOA to the named agent, thereby enabling the agent to assume the powers granted in the DPOA. This procedure, however, assumes that the trusted advisor will be available whenever the need for assistance arises and will fulfill this person's duties as contemplated. Other alternatives to a "springing" provision include creating co-agents or using different DPOAs for different assets.

While individual formats vary considerably, most DPOAs contain the following provisions:

1. Reimbursement of out-of-pocket expenses of the agent in performing the designated functions. Compensation for the agent's time is generally not authorized, but most forms allow a maker to authorize such payments.

2. Requirement that the DPOA be notarized. If real estate is to be subject to the DPOA, some states require that the DPOA be in recordable form, even though DPOAs are generally not recorded.

3. Designation of a possible successor agent in case the named agent dies, loses legal capacity, or refuses to serve. If the original agent cannot exercise the powers granted by the DPOA and no successor agent has been designated, the maker may be forced into a guardianship, which is what the DPOA was intended to prevent.

4. Signature blank for the designated agent. Though usually not mandatory, signature blanks evidence an agent's acknowledgment of the responsibilities involved in this process, at least at the time that the DPOA was executed.

[¶ 9,225]

Problems

1. Steve prepared a DPOA that named his daughter Karen as agent. A gifting provision that was added to the standard DPOA form allows Karen to make gifts of no more than $11,000 per year to any of Steve's four grandchildren. One of Steve's grandchildren, Thomas, claims that Steve told him many years ago that if Thomas went to an Ivy League college, Steve would "cover" the tuition costs. Thomas plans to attend Dartmouth this coming year and wants Karen to pay this year's $32,000 tuition bill. May she do so?

2. Assuming that Thomas in the preceding problem is not happy with your conclusion, should he ask Steve to replace Karen as the agent under the DPOA?

[¶ 9,230]

c. *Living Trusts*

A revocable or "living" trust is the most intricate of the guardianship alternatives considered in this section. Of course, living trusts can also function as will substitutes that detail how assets are to be divided after the trust's settlor dies. Accordingly, these trusts are often a major fixture of the estate planning process. See ¶ 2,350. In this section, however, they are considered only in the context of handling a person's financial affairs while that person is alive.

A living trust enables another person or persons, the trustees, to invest and manage a client's assets and to disburse funds as that client has directed. For example, a settlor might prefer a private room instead of a semi-private room in the hospital or the nursing home, even when there is no medical necessity for a private room. This preference typically increases the daily charge at the facilities in question, but if a living trust authorizes such payments, they are appropriate expenditures. Similarly, if a client wants to provide care for a favored pet, the trustee under a living trust may pay for such care, however frivolous such an expenditure might seem. In this manner, a living trust enables the client/settlor to effectuate his or her spending preferences as if that person were spending the funds directly.

Such individualization does not come cheap, however. Creating a living trust requires a trust instrument that is tailored to the client's needs, because most state statutes do not contain standard forms for living trusts as they do for DPOAs. But the legal fees for drafting such a trust are just the beginning. The new trust must be funded with property, and this process may involve retitling of certain assets and perhaps even recording new deeds if real estate is involved. Indeed, clients often make the mistake of setting up a living trust—usually at a seminar devoted to "beating the probate trap" or some other objective—

and then failing to transfer their assets to the new trust. Even clients who transfer some assets to the trust often fail to make similar transfers of assets acquired subsequently (inheritances, for example). For this purpose, a DPOA might be helpful, but the point remains that a living trust can provide the intended benefits only for assets that are actually held in the trust.

By definition, a revocable trust can be revoked by the client who created it. The usual caveats regarding legal capacity, however, apply here as well: the client/settlor must have sufficient legal capacity both when the trust is first created and when the assets are transferred to the trust. After that time, the trust can be revoked, but only if the client has sufficient legal capacity. If the client subsequently becomes incapacitated, the trust in effect becomes irrevocable. Until that point, however, the client may transfer assets to or from the trust, change the trustee, alter the trust's instructions, or cancel the entire arrangement. Indeed, while a client retains capacity, he or she may serve as sole trustee or as co-trustee, thereby minimizing the loss of control, at least for the time being.

Regardless of whether the settlor, a close friend, or a relative serves as trustee, many living trusts also name a financial institution as co-trustee. Banks and many investment companies have designated departments that service such trusts. These institutions provide record-keeping, asset management, and even related tax planning services, all for a fee, of course. Those fees represent an additional expense of operating a living trust and often are scaled according to the value of the assets under trust management. But the point remains that the ability to obtain professional investment expertise is one of the distinct advantages of the living trust format.

On the other hand, a living trust might be a cumbersome mechanism for holding certain assets. If real estate is held in a living trust, for example, it may be more difficult to obtain a mortgage due to the lender's inability to sell mortgages on trust-held property in the secondary mortgage market. Similarly, automobiles held in a trust often cause problems in obtaining appropriate insurance due to automobile insurers' unfamiliarity with this form of property ownership for vehicles.

In any case, there is no income tax advantage to establishing a living trust. A living trust's very revocability makes it a "grantor trust," meaning that its income is taxed to the client/grantor. I.R.C. § 676(a). And when the trust is no longer revocable due to a client's subsequent incapacity, it retains its status as a "grantor trust" because its income may be used for the client's benefit. I.R.C. § 677(a)(1).

[¶ 9,235]

Problem

Daria wants to set up a living trust to manage her property, which consists of a portfolio of stocks and bonds worth $350,000 and a residence worth $450,000. She also owns a collection of antique dolls worth $50,000. Since the bank that Daria intends to name as trustee imposes an annual charge of 1.8% of assets under management, should Daria transfer ownership of all her assets to the new trust?

C. MEDICARE

[¶ 9,300]

Medicare is a governmental program that pays for the health care of most persons age 65 years and older as well as disabled persons of any age. It has several distinct parts that are usually referred to by letter (Part A, Part B, etc.) and are financed by very different means. Part A pays for hospital charges and nonphysician expenses and is funded by a 2.9% payroll tax on a person's wages, salary, and income from self-employment. In the case of an employee, half of this payroll tax is withheld from the employee's paycheck and half is collected directly from the employer, but the total is the same. Although the mechanics of this payroll tax mirror those of the Social Security payroll tax that was discussed in ¶ 8,080, there is one very important difference: Medicare's payroll tax has no annual cap. Thus, an executive earning $500,000 per year would pay Medicare 2.9% of the entire $500,000, even though her contribution to the Social Security program was limited by that program's annual wage cap ($87,900 in 2004).

Medicare Part B covers doctors' charges and is financed by a combination of monthly premiums paid by enrollees ($66.60 in 2004) and general tax revenues. In fact, the monthly premium is calculated to cover only 25% of Medicare Part B's costs. General tax revenues, in other words, provide the remaining 75% of Medicare Part B's expenses. (Beginning in 2007, higher-income enrollees—those whose adjusted gross income plus tax-exempt interest exceeds $80,000 ($160,000 for married couples)—will pay augmented Part B premiums to offset part of this subsidy.)

Medicare Part C encompasses a variety of managed care alternatives to Medicare Parts A and B (often called "traditional" Medicare), with the precise funding mechanism depending upon the specific plan selected. Finally, Medicare Part D provides coverage of prescription drugs beginning in 2006. This drug benefit will be financed by enrollee-paid premiums, which are expected to be approximately $35 per month, and general tax revenues.

[¶ 9,310]

1. Eligibility

There are several routes to Medicare eligibility, but the most common pathway is being 65 years old and eligible for Social Security retirement benefits. As considered in Chapter 8, eligibility for Social

Security retirement benefits requires earning at least 40 "quarters of coverage" or being the spouse (or former spouse) of someone who did. See ¶ 8,080. Once that requirement is satisfied, a person can receive Medicare Part A benefits without any further cost. Note that this person need not actually be receiving Social Security retirement benefits; mere eligibility for such benefits is sufficient.

Medicare's eligibility age of 65 years is generally absolute. It does not change according to the "full retirement age" of the person in question, which in turn depends upon that person's year of birth. See ¶ 8,100. Each person must meet this age requirement even if that person's eligibility for benefits derives from a spouse's work history. For example, assume that Ray is 67 years old and eligible for Social Security retirement benefits. His wife, Linda, is 62 years old. Ray is currently eligible for Medicare, but Linda must wait until she reaches age 65, even though she intends to qualify on the basis of Ray's work record. Furthermore, receiving Social Security retirement benefits prior to reaching age 65 (see ¶ 8,100) does not entitle the recipient to Medicare Part A benefits.

Persons who are at least 65 years old but who have not earned 40 quarters of coverage may purchase Medicare Part A for a stipulated monthly premium that changes annually. In 2004, that amount was $343. While this cost is not inexpensive, Medicare is often a bargain because it accepts *all* potential enrollees, regardless of pre-conditions, medical history, or related factors. There is one legal requirement, however: potential enrollees must reside in the United States and be either citizens or resident aliens who have lived in this country for the preceding five years. In addition, they must also enroll in Part B, which ordinarily is voluntary.

Though less common, another important pathway to Medicare eligibility is receiving Social Security disability payments for at least 24 months. See ¶ 7,305. Such persons receive Medicare benefits regardless of their age. A final category of eligible recipients is patients with "end stage renal disease," once again regardless of their age.

Medicare Part B eligibility is generally tied to eligibility for Medicare Part A. Indeed, when a person is first enrolled in Part A, that person is enrolled in Part B automatically. Due to the significant federal subsidy described earlier, most Medicare enrollees keep that coverage. Some people, however, decline Medicare Part B, because they are still part of the employed workforce and are covered by their employer's health plan for employees. When these people do retire, they may purchase Part B coverage at that time without any penalty. But any other person who delays enrollment in Part B faces an increased premium of 10% for each 12–month period during which that person could have enrolled in Part B. For example, assume that Jack delays enrolling in Part B for 55 months after first enrolling in Part A. There are four 12–month periods during those 55 months. Accordingly, Jack will pay face a premium increase of 40% (10% times four 12–month periods) of his monthly

Medicare Part B premium when he enrolls in Part B. This 40% factor, moreover, will be applied to *all* of Jack's future Part B premiums—a permanent penalty, in other words.

2. Coverage Under Part A

Coverage under Medicare Part A has four major components: hospital charges, skilled nursing facility (SNF) care, home care, and hospice care. Each of these components has its own set of limitations, restrictions, and medical requirements. Physicians' charges and most medical care that is received as an outpatient are covered by Medicare Part B. See ¶ 9,370.

a. Hospital Charges

Medicare pays all relevant services for the first 60 days in a hospital during a single "spell of illness," subject to two general limitations. First, Medicare pays for care only in semi-private rooms unless a private room is "medically necessary." But if a hospital has no semi-private rooms at all or none is immediately available, Medicare will pay for a private room. Second, Medicare imposes a single deductible per "spell of illness" that increases annually. In 2004, that amount was $876. This charge is the patient's responsibility, unless that patient has supplemental "medigap" insurance that covers this expense. See ¶ 9,400.

Obviously, a critical factor in assessing a client's potential financial exposure to hospital charges is this phrase, "spell of illness." This period begins when a patient is admitted to the hospital and ends when that patient has been out of a hospital, SNF, or other rehabilitative facility for 60 consecutive days, counting the day of discharge. After a "spell of illness" concludes, a new hospital admission requires a new deductible, regardless of the medical reason for the new admission. For example, assume that Anita enters the hospital on March 15 and leaves on March 22. If she returns before 60 days have passed, Anita will be within the same "spell of illness" and will not owe another deductible. But if she is admitted after that 60–day period has elapsed (say, on June 1), then she will be responsible for another deductible, even if this second admission is due to a recurrence of the same medical condition that required her hospitalization on March 15.

Within the "spell of illness" parameter, Medicare pays all costs, including room charges, special diets, laboratory tests, special care units (e.g., intensive care), diagnostic procedures, and pharmaceuticals used while in the hospital. Blood transfusions are covered as well, other than the first three pints of blood, for which the patient is responsible. After the first 60 days in a "spell of illness," Medicare pays costs according to a more limited schedule:

1. For days 61 through 90, Medicare pays all costs after a per-day deductible that is equal to one-fourth of the per-"spell of illness" deductible. For 2004, that amount was $219 (one-fourth of $876).

2. After the first 90 days, Medicare pays all costs for up to 60 additional days after a per-day deductible that is equal to one-half of the per-"spell of illness" deductible. For 2004, that amount was $438 (one-half of $876). But each day of coverage after the first 90 days counts against a 60–day "lifetime reserve" which cannot again be used during a subsequent hospitalization. (For inpatient care in a psychiatric hospital, lifetime coverage is limited to 190 days.)

These co-payment requirements on days after the first 60 days are less consequential to most clients for two reasons: first, the per-day deductibles are covered in all "medigap" policies (see ¶ 9,410); and second, the average length of a hospital stay for patients 65 years and older is only six days, according to the most recent data available. There are lengthier stays, of course, but cost controls mandated since the 1980's have sharply limited hospital stays.

[¶ 9,335]

Problem

Yassim has had a difficult year medically: he was in the hospital on January 6–10, again on March 2–5, then on May 26–28, again on September 22–23, and finally on November 28–20. Assuming that Medicare will cover these hospital stays, for how many deductibles is Yassim responsible?

[¶ 9,340]

b. *Skilled Nursing Facilities*

Medicare covers some costs of care received in a skilled nursing facility (SNF), or nursing homes, as they are commonly called. But this coverage is limited by four significant requirements, *all* of which must be met or else Medicare will pay no portion of the bill. In that case, the patient must turn to his or her own resources, private long-term care insurance (see ¶ 9,500), or Medicaid, the government's health care program for poor people (see ¶ 9,700). The four requirements of Medicare's SNF coverage are as follows:

1. The facility itself must be approved by Medicare and must agree to be a participating institution. Among other things, such an agreement includes a willingness to accept Medicare's "reimbursement" rates in full satisfaction of its charges. In addition, participating institutions must comply with numerous federal mandates regarding health and safety, residents' rights, and quality of care. Even those facilities that participate in Medicare typically limit the number of "Medicare beds" that they will

maintain. Thus, even a Medicare-approved SNF may not have a bed available for a specific patient at any given time.

2. Admission into the SNF must be preceded by a hospital stay within the preceding 30 days. Patients who go directly from their homes, for example, to a SNF without requiring hospitalization—a situation common in many circumstances involving older persons—are not covered by Medicare when they get to the SNF.

3. The preceding hospital stay must have been at least three days in duration, not counting the day of discharge. Current hospital practices, which sharply limit the length of permissible stays, make this requirement much more onerous than it was when Medicare was created in 1965. Be that as it may, assume that Peter falls in his apartment and is taken to the hospital for emergency care. Assume further that Peter broke no bones and was admitted into the hospital overnight merely for observation. The next morning, he is discharged from the hospital directly to a SNF for recuperative therapy. Because Peter's hospital stay was less than three days, Medicare will not pay his expenses in the SNF.

4. The patient must receive "skilled nursing care" for a condition that was treated in the hospital or is medically related to that condition. This type of care consists of services that require trained personnel, such as a licensed practical nurse, registered nurse, or physical therapist; e.g., most injections, gastronomy feedings, catheters, and the like. Furthermore, a medical professional must certify that the patient requires such care on a daily basis. Patients receiving this level of care actually represent a small minority of all nursing home residents, most of whom require only assistance with such daily activities as eating, bathing, and toileting. Such care is often called "custodial care," and Medicare does not cover its cost.

Even if a patient satisfies all four of these conditions, Medicare's coverage is limited to 20 days of all costs, and up to 80 additional days of partial coverage within a single "spell of illness." That crucial phrase has the same meaning in this context as it did with respect to hospital stays. See ¶ 9,330. Regarding the partial coverage for days 21 through 100, Medicare pays all costs after a per-day deductible that is equal to one-eighth of the hospital per-"spell of illness" deductible. In 2004, therefore, that amount was $109.50 (one-eighth of $876). This per-day deductible is often covered by private "medigap" policies (see ¶ 9,415), but costs incurred beyond the first 100 days of a SNF stay are not. While many SNF stays are essentially recuperative in nature and last less than 100 days, many others relate to chronic conditions and exceed that limit by several years or more. With regard to those stays, Medicare's SNF coverage provides little real benefit.

[¶ 9,345]

Problems

1. Martha was in the hospital during March 16–20 for surgery to replace her hip. She then transferred to a nursing home to receive intensive rehabilitative therapy of the sort that can be provided only in a nursing home. She was in this facility a total of 28 days at a cost of $250 per day. How much of this expense will Medicare cover?

2. Eric recently suffered a stroke that left him unable to feed himself or control his bladder. As a result, he moved into a nursing home where he receives assistance with these essential functions. If he stays in this facility three years at a cost of $140 per day, how much of this expense will Medicare cover?

[¶ 9,350]

c. Home Health Care

Medicare provides certain home-based health services to persons who are confined to their homes. To qualify, these persons must be unable to leave their homes except with assistance from other people or by using devices such as wheelchairs, walkers, or canes. Moreover, they must rarely leave their homes except to obtain medical treatment.

The services provided include various therapies (occupational, speech, physical), medical supplies, and "part-time or intermittent" nursing care. This last item, however, is sharply limited to care of no more than eight hours per day, with a maximum of 28 hours per week (or up to 35 hours per week in individually-reviewed circumstances). Thus, it does not encompass 24–hours-a-day nursing care provided at home. In addition, the nursing care must be provided (or supervised) by a licensed nurse who is employed by a Medicare-approved home health agency pursuant to a written plan of care that was prepared by a physician and reviewed by that physician at least once every two months. Informal care by friends, church groups, or relatives does not qualify. Nor do meal preparation, homemaking or other nonmedical services.

When Medicare's coverage does apply, it pays the entire cost of these home-based health services with no deductibles or co-payments required. One exception applies to Medicare's coverage of "durable medical equipment," such as wheelchairs, hospital beds, traction equipment, and walkers. For such items, the patient must pay 20% of the cost.

[¶ 9,360]

d. Hospice Care

Hospice care refers to a comprehensive package of services that are provided to persons near the end of their lives. To qualify for Medicare coverage, the patient must be certified by a physician as having a remaining life expectancy of no more than six months. To that end, Medicare provides hospice care for two separate periods of 90 days each, plus additional 60–day periods as needed. Predicting a patient's remaining life expectancy is often very difficult, especially for certain medical conditions. As a result, many patients do not enter hospice care until they are well within sight of the end. On the other hand, some patients stabilize in hospice care and beat all life expectancy predictions.

While in hospice care, a patient forgoes any right to the curative services that Medicare typically provides, except for conditions that are unrelated to the patient's terminal illness. Instead, hospice care provides extended home care benefits, including homemaking services, pharmaceuticals, medical supplies, custodial care items, and even counseling. Doctors' and nurses' charges are included as well, all with the goal of providing pain relief and symptom control, rather than medical intervention that addresses the patient's underlying illness. These services are typically provided by an organization that does this type of work as its primary mission. Hospices are generally not distinct facilities.

Medicare covers all costs of hospice care without deductibles or co-payments. As is so often the case, some exceptions exist. Here, there are two:

1. Outpatient drugs are provided, but the patient must pay 5% of their cost, or $5 per prescription, whichever is less.

2. The patient must pay 5% of the cost of "respite care," which consists of very short-term institutionalization (usually no more than five consecutive days) to provide relief to the patient's regular caregivers. Medicare sets the rate for such care by geographic region.

[¶ 9,370]

3. Coverage Under Part B

Coverage under Medicare Part B deals primarily with outpatient expenses, particularly doctors' charges. Doctors' charges, moreover, are covered by Part B even when the charges pertain to treatment provided in a hospital setting. In that case, Part A pays for the hospital bill, but Part B pays for the doctors' fees. This is an important distinction from the patient's perspective, because Part B has a very different payment regime. In general, Part B imposes a per-year deductible of $100 that increases annually. In 2004, that deductible was $100. After that deductible is satisfied, Medicare pays 80% of all covered charges, and the patient pays the remaining 20%. This co-payment expense, however, is often covered by "medigap" insurance policies. See ¶ 9,410.

[¶ 9,375]

a. Benefits Provided

Medicare Part B covers office visits of physicians, diagnostic tests performed in doctors' offices or in hospitals on an outpatient basis, outpatient blood transfusions, and drugs that cannot be self-administered. Ambulance services are covered as well, but only if any other form of transportation would endanger the patient's health. Even then, the ambulance benefit relates only to trips between the patient's home and a hospital or SNF; i.e., trips to a physician's office are not included. Medical supplies, such as splints and casts, are covered, as are durable medical equipment and outpatient therapy.

Numerous details fill voluminous program manuals with distinctions that baffle most nonmedical—and even some medical—personnel. For example, so-called "routine" examinations by physicians and dentists are not covered, unless they are required as part of a larger treatment plan. Similarly, Medicare covers podiatric care for foot injuries and diseases, including treatment of ingrown toenails and bunion deformities, but not corn and callus removal or nail trimming. Cosmetic surgery is generally not covered, but if such surgery is performed in connection with an accident or to improve a bodily function, Medicare will pay the cost. Thus, breast prostheses are covered following a mastectomy but not otherwise, in most cases. Similarly, corrective lenses are usually not covered, but if they are needed after a cataract operation, Medicare will cover the cost of those lenses.

With respect to equipment, the distinctions are even finer. For example, if a person needs to use a seat lift chair, the cost of the lift mechanism—but not the cost of the chair itself—may be covered. Similarly, orthopedic shoes are not covered unless they are an "integral part" of leg braces. Even then, a physician's prescription is necessary for these items, as well as for electrical nerve stimulators, wheelchairs, and similar items.

[¶ 9,380]

b. *Patients' Financial Obligations*

As noted above, enrollees in Medicare Part B are responsible for the first $100 of covered charges each year and then 80% of the subsequent costs. A crucially important provision, however, affects the enrollee's obligation for the remaining 20%: these percentages are applied *not* to the physicians' actual charges, but rather to Medicare's "reasonable charge" for the services provided. And since these official rates have generally lagged behind increases in health care costs, the Medicare enrollee's financial obligations regarding Part B's coverage are often much less than they might appear at first.

For example, assume that Jocelyn has already satisfied her annual deductible this year and now visits her gastroenterologist, who bills her $155 for his examination. Under Medicare Part B, Jocelyn must pay 20% of Medicare's "reasonable charge" for this service, which—we will assume—is $100. Thus, Jocelyn owes $20 (20% of Medicare's "reasonable charge" of $100). Her doctor will also receive $80 (80% of $100) directly from Medicare. In other words, he collects only $100 for his examination of Jocelyn—$80 from Medicare and $20 from Jocelyn. The remaining charge of $55 (bill of $155 less $100 received) is not collected.

Needless to say, Jocelyn's physician is less than pleased with this arrangement, but that is how Medicare Part B works. He might write off the uncollected $55, or he might raise his rates to non-Medicare patients (often called "cost-shifting"). Other alternatives include limiting the number of Medicare enrollees that he will see or restricting his practice to non-Medicare patients.

Another alternative is terminating his relationship with Medicare as a "participating provider." (In some states, however, participation in Medicare is required as a condition of being licensed as a physician.) He could still see Medicare patients, including Jocelyn, but he would not be limited to Medicare's "reasonable charges" for his services. Even as a "nonparticipating provider," however, he would not be able to charge Jocelyn whatever he wanted. The differential that a nonparticipating provider may charge a Medicare enrollee (sometimes called "balance billing") is limited to 15% of Medicare's "reasonable charge" for the service in question.

Returning to the preceding example, assume all of the same facts, except that Jocelyn's physician is a "nonparticipating provider." Medicare will still pay the doctor only $80, representing 80% of Medicare's "reasonable charge" of $100. But Jocelyn can now be billed for $15 (15% of $100) of so-called "excess charges" in addition to her regular co-payment of $20 that represents 20% of Medicare's "reasonable charge." As a result, Jocelyn will owe her doctor a total of $35 (regular co-payment of $20 plus the "excess charges" of $15).

Jocelyn's doctor has still not collected his entire fee, however. Instead, he received $80 from Medicare and $35 from Jocelyn, a total of $115 compared to his bill of $155. In any case, her doctor's status as a Medicare provider had financial significance to Jocelyn, because she owed $15 of "excess charges." Some "medigap" insurance policies will cover her liability for these "excess charges," depending upon the specific policy package that she selects. See ¶ 9,410.

The cost-sharing scheme described above applies to most services covered by Medicare Part B, but there are some exceptions. Clinical diagnostic laboratory tests are covered in full, with no reference to the annual deductible or any co-payments by the enrollee. This same treatment applies to second opinions regarding surgery (or third opinions if the first two disagree), expenses of pneumococcal vaccine, and kidney donation costs. On the other hand, costs of outpatient treatment for mental, psychoneurotic, or personality disorders are subject to a 50% (rather than 20%) co-payment obligation. In that case, the patient pays half of Medicare's approved rates for the services provided.

[¶ 9,385]

Problem

Henry requires a medical procedure that can be done on an outpatient basis. Each of two doctors is willing to perform the procedure on Henry for the same fee, namely $655. He heard from a friend who had the procedure done last week that Medicare's "reasonable charge" for this procedure is $300. One of the physicians is listed in Medicare's directory of "participating providers," but the other doctor is not. What financial difference will it make to Henry which physician he chooses?

[¶ 9,390]

4. General Programmatic Exclusions

Part A and Part B of Medicare are subject to general exclusions that apply to all of their coverages, in addition to the specific limitations that pertain to individual items, some of which have been described above. The major programmatic exclusions of Medicare are as follows:

1. Services must be provided in the United States. This is an important constraint for Americans who are considering lengthy periods of time or permanent relocation outside this country. In short, their Medicare benefits will not accompany them overseas, so they must make alternative arrangements (such as travel health insurance) for medical care wherever they are going to live. (Nevertheless, emergency hospital services and related physicians' charges and ambulance costs are covered in Canada and Mexico for persons residing on the respective U.S. borders.)

2. Most routine care is not covered, including dental services, eye and ear examinations, eyeglasses, hearing aids, and annual physical check-ups. Indeed, this absence of medical maintenance coverage is one of the reasons that some older Americans are attracted to the managed care options in Medicare. See ¶ 9,460.

3. Care is not covered by Medicare if it is provided by "immediate relatives" of the enrollee or members of that person's household. 42 U.S.C. § 1395y(a)(11). This exclusion pertains to most of the usual suspects, including a person's spouse, parents, children, siblings, grandchildren, and one's in-laws.

In addition, Medicare generally covers only services that are "reasonable and necessary" for the diagnosis and treatment of illness or injury. 42 U.S.C. § 1395y(a)(1). This standard moves as the state of the art progresses, but it excludes procedures that are currently considered experimental, such as acupuncture, transsexual surgery, and cellular therapy, to name just a few.

Nevertheless, a patient may not be liable for services that fail to meet this standard if the patient did not know, or could not have been expected to know, that Medicare would not cover the services in question. Under this "waiver of liability" provision, the patient is relieved of liability unless, prior to the performance of the services, the physician gave the patient a written notice of the reason why Medicare would not cover these services and the patient agreed in writing to pay the applicable charges.

[¶ 9,400]

5. "Medigap" Insurance Options

To cope with the array of deductibles and co-payments in Medicare Parts A and B, many clients secure a private insurance policy to fill Medicare's gaps. Accordingly, such insurance policies are known collectively as "medigap" insurance. Federal law requires that only certain packages of benefits may be offered as medigap insurance, and these packages are labeled A through J, with plan A being the most basic and plan J being the most extensive. Although the contents of the packages are fixed to facilitate consumer choice, the premiums for these packages are not stipulated, and clients (and their advisors) need to determine the most appropriate policy for the money. No one is required to purchase any medigap policy, and many Medicare beneficiaries rely instead on retiree health benefit plans that are provided by their former employers instead of purchasing a medigap policy. But retiree health benefits have increasingly been curtailed in recent years, leaving more retirees to secure their own insurance to supplement Medicare's coverages. In any case, there is no governmental subsidy for this insurance, so purchasers bear the entire cost of their policies.

[¶ 9,405]

a. *Consumer Protection Provisions*

There are several advantageous features of medigap insurance. First, all such policies are "guaranteed renewable," meaning that the insurance company must renew the policy unless the insured fails to pay the premiums when they are due or made a material misrepresentation on the insurance application. Premiums can, and usually do, increase regularly as the cost of health care rises, and Medicare's dollar-denominated deductibles rise annually. But as long as a client pays her bill, the policy must be renewed.

Second, federal law provides that an applicant for a medigap policy cannot be rejected for medical reasons if that person applies within six months of first obtaining coverage under Medicare Part B. (Claims relating to pre-existing conditions may, however, be denied if they occur within the policy's first six months.) 42 U.S.C. § 1395ss(s)(2)(A). After that, a person is at the mercy of the insurance market and may find that certain packages are either unavailable or unaffordable because of that person's medical profile.

Finally, federal law prohibits an insurance company from selling more than one medigap policy to any buyer, and premiums paid for a duplicative policy must be refunded. See 42 U.S.C. § 1395ss(d)(3). In practice, insurance sellers usually obtain a written commitment from a buyer who currently has medigap insurance that he or she intends to cancel that policy when the new medigap policy takes effect. That way, the client is protected by her existing policy until the new medigap policy is issued.

[¶ 9,410]

b. Benefit Packages

The ten standardized medigap packages are set forth graphically at ¶ 9,415, but several features merit specific attention.

Plan A includes five "core" or basic benefits. This package must be offered in every state and by every insurance company that sells medigap policies in that state. Those "core" benefits include the following items:

1. The hospital per-day deductible for days 61 through 90.

2. The hospital per-day deductible for the 60 "lifetime reserve" days.

3. An additional "lifetime reserve" of 365 hospital days with no deductible.

4. The first three pints of blood that are not covered by Medicare.

5. The 20% co-payment obligation under Part B.

Thereafter, various benefits are mixed and matched in packages that are generally more inclusive as they proceed down the alphabet. Moreover, plans F and J come in two different versions: one as shown, and the other with an annual deductible that is increased annually. In 2004, it was $1,690.

A client who frequently visits nonparticipating providers may want to look closely at the "excess charges" benefit in plans F, G, I, and J. Note that plan G pays only 80% of the "excess charges," while the other three plans cover the entire amount. For example, if Jocelyn in the earlier example incurred $15 of "excess charges" from her nonparticipating physician, plan G would cover $12 of those costs (80% of $15), while plans F, I, and J would cover the entire $15.

Some features are less appealing than they might appear at first. For example, the "at-home recovery" benefit pays for short-term assistance with bathing, dressing, and personal hygiene following an illness or injury. But the maximum amount is $40 per visit with a cap of $1,600 per year. Similarly, the "preventive medical care" benefit covers a range of important screenings and tests, as well as influenza shots and physical examinations, but it also is subject to an annual cap—in this case, only $120.

Be that as it may, the medigap dilemma is the same as insurance generally: clients must balance the cost of the protection obtained against the financial exposure avoided. And the more risks that an insured shifts to an insurance company, the higher that person's premiums will be. In other words, the customary insurance trade-off of cost versus risk applies in this context. Clients also need to consider the financial strength of the insurance company, its reputation for customer service, and perhaps its underwriting criteria if a client's medical history warrants such concern.

[¶ 9,415]

10 Standard Medicare Supplement Benefit Plans										
BASIC BENEFITS	Plan A	Plan B	Plan C	Plan D	Plan E	Plan F	Plan G	Plan H	Plan I	Plan J
Part A Hospital (Days 61-90)	X	X	X	X	X	X	X	X	X	X
Lifetime Reserve Days	X	X	X	X	X	X	X	X	X	X
365 Life Hosp. Days — 100%	X	X	X	X	X	X	X	X	X	X
Blood (first 3 pints)	X	X	X	X	X	X	X	X	X	X
Part B 20% Coinsurance	X	X	X	X	X	X	X	X	X	X
ADDITIONAL BENEFITS	A	B	C	D	E	F	G	H	I	J
Skilled Nursing Facility Coinsurance (Days 21-100)			X	X	X	X	X	X	X	X
Part A "Spell of Illness" Deductible		X	X	X	X	X	X	X	X	X
Part B Annual Deductible			X			X				X
Part B Excess Charges						100%	80%		100%	100%
Foreign Travel Emergency			X	X	X	X	X	X	X	X
At-Home Recovery				X			X		X	X
Prescription Drugs								1	1	2
Preventive Medical Care					X					X

Two prescription drug benefits are offered:

1. A "basic" benefit with $250 annual deductible, 50% coinsurance, and a $1,250 maximum annual benefit (Plans H and I above); and

2. An "extended" benefit (Plan J above) containing a $250 annual deductible, 50% coinsurance, and a $3,000 maximum annual benefit.

[¶ 9,420]

Problems

1.   Returning to the problems at ¶ 9,345, which medigap policies would cover Martha's and Eric's financial exposure?

2.   Returning to the problem at ¶ 9,385, what amount will Henry be required to pay if he has a medigap policy that is plan D? Plan F? Plan G?

[¶ 9,430]

6.   Managed Care Alternatives Under Part C

Approximately one in eight Medicare beneficiaries is enrolled in a managed care alternative, often referred to as Medicare Part C or "Medicare Advantage." These arrangements usually consist of Medicare health maintenance organizations (HMO), though more recent entrants such as the Preferred Provider Organization (PPO) also exist. All of these plans purport to provide a seamless health care plan without the segmentation of Medicare Part A, Medicare Part B, and a medigap policy. Counterparts to these managed care arrangements predominate the health insurance market for persons under age 65, and many of the considerations that are applicable to them apply in this context as well.

[¶ 9,435]

a.   Medicare HMOs

The overwhelmingly most common alternative to "traditional" Medicare is the Medicare HMO. In exchange for the standard Medicare Part B premium and typically some additional amount per month, a Medicare HMO provides its enrollees with all of the benefits of Medicare Parts A and B but with no deductibles or co-payments. As a result, enrollees in a Medicare HMO have no need for medigap insurance. To be sure, Medicare HMOs usually restrict a client's choice of physicians, hospitals, and other health care providers to those in the HMO's network, but that is the trade-off in managed care generally.

Most Medicare HMOs offer various benefits that Medicare has never included, the most common being prescription drugs. Indeed, the availability of pharmaceuticals with only a nominal co-payment per prescription has historically been the primary attraction of Medicare HMOs to many senior citizens. Some Medicare HMOs also provide eyeglasses, hearing aids, chronic care management programs, and nutrition guidance, among other features. Each organization sets the terms of its own package with a view to what its target market most wants and the applicable cost constraints. To that end, many Medicare HMOs maintain restricted formularies, whereby certain medications are not available or are available only at a substantial additional cost. Finally, Medicare HMOs radically simplify the paperwork involved in securing medical care. There are no patient obligations to calculate and monitor, so most claim forms are unnecessary.

Almost all HMOs provide physical examinations on a regular basis to enable them to manage medical problems before they become severe. That is, after all, the foundational premise of managed care generally. The downside, of course, is that when the sponsoring organization does not receive additional funds for services actually rendered, there is a financial incentive to limit care or deny coverage for certain more expensive treatments.

For that reason, Medicare HMOs are required to offer an appeals procedure for enrollees to challenge care denials and similar claims. 42 U.S.C. § 1395mm(c)(5)(B). Under this procedure, a HMO must notify the enrollee within 60 days if the claim is denied. Appeals then follow to an independent review organization, then to an administrative law judge, and eventually to a U.S. district court, if need be. But an expedited review within 72 hours can be obtained if a longer wait would seriously jeopardize the enrollee's life or health. See 42 U.S.C. § 1395w–22(g)(3).

[¶ 9,440]

b. *Leaving Medicare Managed Care*

Medicare enrollees also have the option of leaving the HMO entirely and rejoining traditional Medicare at the beginning of the next month, but this option generally exists only once during the first three months of the year. There are some situations, however, that allow an enrollee to "disenroll" from a Medicare HMO at other times. Those situations include the following:

1. A beneficiary may switch plans during the annual re-enrollment period that begins on November 1 of each year. This change takes effect the following January.

2. An enrollee may switch plans whenever that person moves out of the managed care plan's service area.

3. Anyone who enrolls in a managed care plan when he or she first became eligible for Medicare benefits at age 65 may leave that plan and enroll in traditional Medicare at any time during that person's *first* year of enrollment. See 42 U.S.C. § 1395w–21(e)(4) (final sentence).

[¶ 9,445]

c. *Other Options*

Managed care options beyond the Medicare HMO are being developed, though most are still in their infancy. The Preferred Provider Organization, or PPO, operates much like a Medicare HMO, except that it allows its members to use health care providers who are outside its network of designated providers. In that case, however, the member must typically pay an additional fee or co-payment for the service provided. Thus, there is still an economic incentive to stay within the PPO's network, but there is no prohibition against using out-of-network providers. (Some Medicare HMOs also offer this feature, known as a "point of service" option, for an additional premium.)

Other plans may be offered by "religious fraternal benefit societies" exclusively to members of a church or an association of churches. 42 U.S.C. § 1395w–28(e)(2)(A). The sponsoring "society" may not, however, limit enrollment based on health status, and the plans must provide health coverage to members who are not entitled to Medicare benefits. Other arrangements include Provider Sponsored Organizations, which essentially mimic Medicare HMOs but are run by health care providers rather than by insurance companies.

[¶ 9,450]

d. *Medigap Insurance and Medicare Managed Care*

An important consideration for persons in a Medicare managed care plan is what happens if they "disenroll" from that plan. That is, should they maintain (or obtain) a medigap policy, even when the Medicare HMO makes such a policy superfluous, in case they subsequently decide to leave the HMO? The same issue presents itself if a Medicare HMO drops out of the Medicare program, as an increasing number of such plans have done in recent years. The former HMO members may now want a medigap policy, but they are beyond the six-month window during which they could not be rejected for medical reasons. See ¶ 9,405.

Federal law makes several provisions for persons in this situation. First, anyone who joined a managed care plan when that person first became eligible for Medicare at age 65 cannot be rejected for medical reasons, if that person leaves the managed care plan during the first year of enrollment. This rule encourages new Medicare beneficiaries to try managed care when they first join Medicare, without forfeiting the ability to obtain their choice of medigap policies. The one requirement is that the person must apply for the medigap policy within 63 days of losing coverage under the managed care plan. For example, Melonie joined a Medicare HMO on her 65th birthday, which was February 22. After several months, she decides to leave this plan effective September 30. She must apply for a medigap policy within 63 days (i.e., by December 2) to be assured that her application will not be rejected for medical reasons.

For persons beyond the first year of Medicare eligibility, different rules apply. If a person owned a medigap policy but terminated it upon joining a managed care plan, this person can re-instate that medigap policy, but only if this person left the managed care plan during the *first* year of such enrollment. Application for the replacement policy must occur within 63 days of losing coverage under the managed care plan.

For Medicare beneficiaries in all other situations, the law provides that medigap plans A, B, C, and F remain available. 42 U.S.C. § 1395ss(s)(3)(A), (B)(iii), (C)(i). Once again, application for the new policy must be made within 63 calendar days of losing coverage under the Medicare managed care plan. If this requirement is not satisfied, or if any other medigap plan is sought, acceptance is subject to the underwriting criteria of the insurance companies. No federal protection applies.

[¶ 9,455]

Problem

Greta, age 68, has received a notice from her Medicare HMO that it will not participate in the Medicare program after this year. No other Medicare HMOs operate within 300 miles of Greta's home, so she intends to return to traditional Medicare and wants a medigap policy to supplement Medicare's coverage. If she applies for her new policy by January 15, is she assured of getting a medigap plan H policy? If she waits until April 15, is she assured of getting a plan C policy?

[¶ 9,460]

7. Prescription Drug Coverage

Medicare has historically not covered outpatient pharmaceuticals. For that reason, coverage of prescription drugs is one of the main attractions of Medicare HMOs and other managed care arrangements. See ¶ 9,435. Retirees can also obtain such coverage by purchasing certain medigap policies—specifically, plans H, I, and J. See ¶ 9,420. In addition, some older people have prescription drug coverage through retiree health benefit plans that are provided by their former employers. Moreover, many state governments offer financial assistance in purchasing pharmaceuticals, though these programs are often restricted to lower-income individuals. Finally, some drug manufacturers provide senior citizens with proprietary discount cards that apply to certain of their products. Despite these possibilities, Congress amended the Medicare program in December of 2003 to provide special drug discount cards for 2004–2005 and a more substantial drug benefit beginning in 2006.

[¶ 9,465]

a. Drug Discount Cards

Medicare's drug discount cards are offered by various providers and require an annual fee of no more than $30. These cards differ widely in terms of the discounts that they provide, the drug manufacturers that participate, and the drugs that they cover. Consequently, clients must compare each package of offered discounts against their personal drug needs.

This task may be relatively straightforward for older persons with chronic ailments. Their drug regimens usually call for regular dosages of specific medicines, and the resulting drug expense is therefore fairly predictable. Nevertheless, as a person's medical condition changes or as new drugs become available, that person's drug expenses may change dramatically from one year to the next. Be that as it may, the Medicare drug discount card program will disappear when the Part D prescription drug benefit commences in 2006.

[¶ 9,470]

b. Drug Coverage Under Part D

Medicare Part D coverage is available to any Medicare enrollee who wants it. Many key details have not yet been formulated, including an enrollee's premium costs, though current estimates are about $35 per month initially. Benefits apply to any prescription drug, regardless of manufacturer, subject to the following financial parameters (in 2006; all dollar amounts to be indexed thereafter):

1. Annual deductible of $250.

2. Co-payment of 25% for the next $2,000 of annual drug expenditures (i.e., for drug costs above $250 but below $2,250 per year).

3. No coverage for the next $2,850 of annual drug costs (i.e., for drug costs above $2,250 but below $5,100).

4. Co-payment of 5% for annual drug costs above $5,100.

For example, an enrollee in Part D who has annual drug expenditures of $3,100—the approximate average annual drug costs for persons age 65 years and older—would pay the first $250 as the annual deductible, $500 as the 25% co-payment of the next $2,000 of annual costs, and all of the remaining drug costs in excess of $2,250, or $850. As a result, this person's out-of-pocket drug expenses would be $1,600 under this program—more than one-half of her total drug expense—without even considering the Part D premium of $35 per month (estimated). (More generous benefits are provided for enrollees with very low annual income and assets of no more than $10,000 for singles and $20,000 for married couples.)

Faced with this convoluted benefit structure, many older clients will need to assess the likely benefit of participating in Medicare Part D. That is, the estimated monthly premium of $35 translates into an annual cost of $420, which when combined with the annual deductible of $250, means that an older client with less than $670 of expected annual drug expenses will receive no benefit from this program and therefore may decide not to enroll. Complicating this decision further is a provision of the 2003 enactment that terminates the drug coverage feature in medigap plans H, I, and J when Medicare Part D begins. Current holders of such policies, however, may continue to renew their existing policies, including their drug coverage, after that date.

On the other hand, a person who chooses not to enroll in Medicare Part D and later changes her mind pays for that delay. The premium charged a person in this circumstance will be increased by a late enrollment penalty equal to 1% of the monthly premium for each month during which that person was eligible for Medicare Part D but did not enroll in that program. Moreover, this penalty continues as long as that person is enrolled in Part D. It does not apply, however, if the late enrollee had comparable drug coverage through a managed care plan, a medigap policy, a retiree health plan, or certain governmental programs, such as veterans' benefits.

[¶ 9,475]

Problems

1. Anna–Maria has a heart condition that she controls with prescription medications costing $100 per month. If she enrolls in Medicare Part D, what will be her annual savings after considering the Part D premiums that she would need to pay?

2. Larry has several chronic ailments and as a result, his drug expenses are twice the national average for older Americans—namely, $6,200 per year. What percentage of his drug costs will be covered by Part D, after considering the Part D premiums?

D. LONG–TERM CARE INSURANCE

[¶ 9,500]

1. The Need for Long–Term Care

One of the major issues faced by Americans as they age is how to finance long-term care if the need for such care arises. Of course, there is no assurance that such care will ever be necessary. The majority of older persons live in their own homes until very near the end of their lives. Moreover, the largest amount of long-term care is provided without charge by the older person's spouse or adult children (and their spouses).

But societal forces are increasing the likelihood that such care will be provided on a more formal basis by nonfamily members, with corresponding financial implications. Some of those forces include the following:

1. Americans are living longer and experiencing medical conditions that accompany old age, such as physical and mental impairments and certain degenerative diseases.

2. Some medical conditions that previously were either untreatable or required hospitalization can now be treated or at least ameliorated in a less intensive setting, such as a nursing home.

3. These conditions, however, often require more technical expertise than many family members can provide.

4. Finally, family members are increasingly unavailable to provide informal care, because they have family obligations of their own, are employed outside the home as part of the compensated workforce, or are located too far away to provide care on a regular basis.

As a result, the challenge of financing long-term care is becoming a major aspect of retirement planning.

[¶ 9,505]

a. *Long–Term Care Settings*

The term "long-term care" encompasses a broad spectrum of possible care settings, ranging from home health services brought into a person's residence to a medically oriented residential institution that is often termed a "nursing home." The latter has significant cost implications in light of the national average cost of $57,700 per year for such facilities. This cost can vary considerably from region to region or even among facilities within a given area, and charges exceeding twice the national average are common in certain communities. Yet the cost of a nursing home, averaging $148 per day, pales in comparison to the cost of home care provided on an around-the-clock basis: home health care at $15 per hour for 24 hours amounts to $360 per day.

These two possibilities, 24–hour home care and a nursing home, are by no means the only possibilities. Home care, for example, might be appropriate for less than 24 hours per day, if a client's condition does not require around-the-clock availability, or if family members are willing and able to provide coverage for part of the day or night. Moreover, other less medically oriented settings have developed to accommodate seniors with less intensive needs. The older versions are often called "board and care" homes or "homes for the aged," and they provide minimal assistance beyond meal preparation and basic personal care. Newer variations on this theme, often called "assisted living facilities," provide some medical attention and assistance with daily living activities but at a level below that of traditional nursing homes and at a lower cost. These facilities typically consist of apartments that are geared to the needs of older persons, with pull-cords and alert buttons in the restrooms, and generally provide a number of meals per week in a communal setting. Still other variations, such as continuing care retirement communities, offer independent living arrangements but with a conventional nursing home on the premises in case the residents ever need those services.

[¶ 9,510]

b. *Who Bears the Financial Burden of Long-term Care*

As explained at ¶ 9,340, the government's health care program for older Americans, Medicare, covers the cost of nursing homes but under several severe constraints: the client must require "skilled nursing care" for a condition that was initially treated during a hospital stay that lasted at least three days and occurred within 30 days of entering the nursing home. Even then, Medicare pays full charges for only the first 20 days and then part of the costs for the next 80 days. After 100 days in the same "spell of illness," Medicare's coverage ceases. Similarly, medigap insurance policies limit their coverage to that part of that daily cost that Medicare does not pay during days 21–100. See ¶ 9,415. Beyond that point, medigap policies provide no coverage either.

With respect to home health care, Medicare's coverage is also very limited. As explained in ¶ 9,350, patients may receive certain therapies and "part-time or intermittent" nursing care, but such care is limited to eight hours per day with a weekly cap of 28 hours in most circumstances. That is only four hours per day, and such care must be ordered by a physician and reviewed by that physician every two months.

Other long-term care settings, such as assisted living facilities, board and care homes, and continuing care retirement communities, are completely outside the scope of the Medicare program. That leaves the financial burden for long-term care to the older adult and his or her family, or to the Medicaid program, but only if the rather strict financial eligibility standards of that poverty-oriented program are satisfied. See ¶ 9,700. With the patient (and perhaps the patient's family) at financial risk for the cost of long-term care, more Americans are turning to long-term care insurance to cover this uncertain but potentially significant cost.

[¶ 9,520]

2. Nature of the Product

Long-term care insurance is an entirely private product with no direct governmental subsidy and no statutory requirement that it even be offered. In other words, there is no guarantee of acceptance comparable to medigap policies sought during the first six months of eligibility for Medicare Part B. See ¶ 9,405. At the present time, most long-term care insurance policies are purchased by individuals, but many membership organizations and affinity groups, such as AARP or professional societies, include long-term care insurance among their benefits. In these circumstances, acceptance is often guaranteed though some age-based restrictions may apply. Some large employers are also making long-term care insurance available to their employees on a group (i.e., guaranteed acceptance) basis, but usually without any financial contribution on the employer's part.

There is no standardization of terms or policy provisions in long-term care insurance, unlike the situation with medigap insurance and its ten standard packages. See ¶ 9,415. Most policies issued in recent years are so-called "tax-qualified" policies, meaning that they meet certain minimum standards that are set forth in the federal tax code. See ¶ 9,580. For the most part, therefore, long-term care insurance policies are very much products of their specific contracts, and different companies offer different benefits under different conditions. Some generalizations are possible, however.

For example, long-term care insurance usually covers *all* levels of care in nursing homes, not just the "skilled nursing care" that Medicare covers. The vast majority of nursing home residents, in fact, receive either "custodial" or "intermediate" care. These care levels concentrate on the so-called "activities of daily living" (ADLs)—namely, eating, bathing, dressing, toileting, transferring from bed to chair, and controlling continence. Patients with Alzheimer's Disease, who comprise about half of the nursing home population, typically require only "custodial care."

Most long-term care insurance policies also cover home health care, though many older policies cover only nursing home expenses. Even then, home health care coverage is usually limited to a specified number of hours per day, or a percentage of the policy's nursing home coverage. For example, a policy that pays $200 per day for nursing home costs might limit its coverage of home health care to one-half of that amount, or $100 per day. The home health care benefit, in other words, does not envision around-the-clock care.

Most newer policies also cover assisted living facilities, either explicitly or via language providing that benefits can cover a less intensive institution if the resources of a nursing home are not medically required for the particular patient. In addition, some policies cover respite care; i.e., expenses incurred in providing a break to the patient's regular caregiver. Expenses of independent living in a continuing care retirement community are not covered by long-term care insurance, but the cost of care in the facility's nursing home unit would usually be covered.

[¶ 9,530]

3. Financial Components of Coverage

There are three major financial components that determine the coverage provided by a long-term care insurance policy: the amount that the policy will pay per day, the length of time the policy will pay that amount, and the "elimination" period before the policy will start to pay its benefits. The usual insurance trade-off applies here: the greater the coverage obtained, the higher the premium cost of the insurance. Clients, therefore, need to balance their desire for extensive coverage with their ability and willingness to pay for such coverage. In other words, the more risk that is shifted to the insurance company, the more expensive the resulting premium will be. This is a very important consideration, because an ability to afford the insurance premium is essential if the insurance is to provide the coverage expected. Moreover, some insurance companies have increased premiums on existing policies at the time of their annual renewal, raising concerns about their continuing affordability.

[¶ 9,535]

a. Daily Dollar Maximum

Most long-term care insurance coverage is based on a specified benefit per day, and this benefit level is selected when a policy is first obtained. This amount can range from $40 to $300 or more, depending upon the issuing company. The cost of coverage correlates pretty closely with the amount of coverage; i.e, a benefit of $200 per day costs twice as much as a benefit of $100 per day. Accordingly, clients can choose to cover all or only a portion of their expected long-term care expenses and self-insure for the remaining portion of those costs.

An important consideration involved in any type of insurance that defines its benefits in terms of dollar amounts is the impact of future inflation. Long-term care insurance policies are generally obtained many years before the insured event occurs, so inflation over a long period of time can substantially erode the value of the coverage obtained. One alternative is for the client to simply self-insure for the balance not covered by that person's insurance, a potential liability that effectively increases each passing year. A different approach adjusts the benefit payable every year via an inflation protection "rider."

Such a rider typically increases the daily benefit level in one of two ways:

1. The benefit can be increased by a stipulated *amount* every year. This increase is usually expressed as a percentage of the initial daily benefit. For example, a 5% rider would increase a daily benefit of $100 by $5 (5% of $100) each year. Thus, the benefit would be $100 the first year, $105 the next year, $110 the next year, and $5 more each year thereafter.

2. The benefit is increased by a stipulated *percentage* every year, thereby compounding the increase and more closely matching the actual impact of inflation. A 5% compounding rider on a $100 daily benefit, for example, would yield benefits of $100 the first year, $105 ($100 plus 5% of $100) the second year, $110.25 ($105 plus 5% of $105) the next year, and increasing by 5% each year thereafter. This alternative shows significant differences compared to the 5% noncompounded rider after about 15 years or so.

Whatever mechanism is employed, an inflation rider is one of the two most expensive riders (the other being inclusion of home health care benefits) that a long-term care insurance policy can have, and it can easily increase a policy's premium by 100% or more, depending upon the age of the insured when a policy is first secured.

[¶ 9,540]

b. Duration of Coverage

Another key financial component of long-term care insurance is the length of time that benefits are payable, usually measured in years. The benefit period is also closely correlated with premium cost, so that the premium for a three-year policy will be about one-half of the cost of a six-year policy. Lifetime coverage is also available, at least for younger clients.

Clients generally do not know, of course, whether they will ever require long-term care, let alone how long they will need such care. Some statistics suggest that there is a 43% chance that a person age 65 years will spend some time in a nursing home, but how much long-term care they will require *before* entering a nursing home is anyone's guess. Moreover, many nursing home stays are relatively short: three to six months. Persons who spend more than one year in a nursing home, however, tend to face multi-year stays, often three to five years. Whether previous years' patterns of nursing home utilization will hold in the future is also unknowable at the present time.

Instead of a benefit that is expressed in terms of years, some long-term care insurance policies employ a "pooling of benefits" concept that makes a policy's entire benefit payout available for the client to use. For example, assume that Bernice has a four-year policy that pays $100 per day. Four years of benefits translate into a benefit "pool" of $146,000 (365 days for 4 years is 1,460 days, times $100 per day). If Bernice is able to live in an assisted living facility that charges only $80 per day, her benefit "pool" of $146,000 will pay for 1,825 days, a total of five years. Alternatively, if the specific nursing home that Bernice needs charges $125 per day, her benefit "pool" will pay for 1,168 days, or only 3.2 years. The "pooling of benefits" approach, in other words, provides a maximum amount of money to be used as the insured chooses.

[¶ 9,545]

c. *Elimination Period*

Recognizing that many nursing home stays are relatively short, almost all long-term care insurance policies employ a time-based deductible, usually called an "elimination" or "waiting" period. The idea is that the policy will pay benefits only after a client has received long-term care in a covered setting for a specified number of days. Thus, the first 60 days, for example, would be at the client's expense, with the policy benefits not starting until after that point. Some policies require that each episode of long-term care have its own elimination period, while other policies calculate a person's long-term care utilization on a cumulative basis. Under that regimen, once a client has required long-term care for the requisite number of days, even if those days were accumulated in several stays over more than one year, the policy's benefits commence.

[¶ 9,550]

Problems

1.   Three years ago, Anthony acquired a long-term care insurance policy that pays $100 per day for five years with no elimination period. Anthony's policy has an inflation protection rider that increases the daily benefit by $5 each year; i.e., no compounding. What is the daily benefit that Anthony can receive in this, the fourth year of his policy?

2.   Anthony from the previous problem has now entered a nursing home that charges $125 per day at the present time, but increases its daily charge by $10 every six months. How much will Anthony pay out of pocket if he stays in this nursing home for the entire current year? How much will Anthony pay out of pocket if he stays in this nursing home for the entire next year?

3.   Janice has a long-term care insurance policy that pays $150 per day for three years with no inflation protection rider. If this policy employs the "pool of benefits" approach, how long would her policy pay benefits if Janice goes to a nursing home that charges $125 per day? For her benefits to last four years, what is the maximum daily charge that Janice can pay?

4.   Jacob has a long-term care insurance policy that pays $140 per day for five years with a 90–day elimination period. He enters an assisted living facility that charges $85 per day. How much will Jacob pay out of pocket before his policy begins to pay benefits?

[¶ 9,560]

4. Other Key Policy Provisions

The range of possible policy options is great and ever-expanding as insurance companies continue to refine their products to enhance their appeal. Some of the more common such provisions are as follows:

1. Most policies are "guaranteed renewable," meaning that the policy cannot be cancelled by the insurance company except for nonpayment of premiums. To further guard against the possibility of unintended lapse due to nonpayment, some policies have a grace period after a policy's renewal date wherein a renewal payment will ensure continued coverage. Other policies allow an insured to name someone to receive a notice or copy of the renewal invoice, if a policy renewal payment has not been received by a certain date. None of these provisions, however, prevents an insurance company from raising its rates, but it must do so for an entire "class" of policyholders within a given state, rather than an individual policyholder.

2. Many policies provide that once long-term care benefits have started, no further premiums need to be paid to keep the policy in force. This "waiver of premiums" rider usually increases the policy's premium cost, though some issuers include it without an extra charge.

3. Because the likelihood of ever needing long-term care is so unknowable, some policies include a "premium refund" clause that refunds some of the premiums that the insured paid if no (or only a few) months of long-term care benefits were claimed under the policy. The refunded premiums often go to some designatee, generally one of the client's heirs, thereby serving as a possible incentive for that person to care for the client directly. This provision, in other words, speaks to two vital concerns of many clients: first, that the premiums paid will be lost if long-term care is never needed; and second, that families might choose not to provide care themselves if a client has long-term care insurance.

4. A "nonforfeiture of benefits" rider provides that even a lapsed policy will provide some long-term care benefits. The exact amount of that coverage will depend on how long a policy was in effect, and ten years is a common minimum. Some riders provide that full daily benefits are payable for a reduced time period, while others indicate that only a portion of the policy benefit amount is available.

5. An alternative to the "nonforfeiture of benefits" rider allows a policy to be paid up after a specified number of years, usually at least ten. No further premiums are required, and future rate increases are irrelevant.

5. Medical Limitations on Benefits

[¶ 9,570]

a. *Pre–Existing Conditions*

The single most significant medical limitation regarding long-term care insurance involves "pre-existing conditions." Most people purchase this insurance initially when they are in their sixties or later, although the age of initial purchase has been dropping in recent years. By that point in their lives, many people have developed some sort of medical profile and often a chronic, though not life-threatening, condition as well. Accordingly, how that medical profile will affect their long-term care insurance is a major issue.

Individual insurance companies employ their own medical underwriting criteria and alter these proprietary criteria from time to time as the state of medicine progresses and their field experience changes. Accordingly, a given applicant may confront very different results from different issuers. In any case, the principal possibilities are as follows:

1. A client's health history may be so severe that an insurance company refuses to issue a policy at all. As already noted, there is no statutory requirement that long-term care insurance be offered to anyone. Indeed, the likelihood of being denied long-term care insurance is a major reason why individuals are often advised to purchase this insurance at younger ages before their

health begins to deteriorate. After certain ages, long-term care insurance may be unobtainable even for persons in good medical condition.

2. A company might issue a long-term care insurance policy but will exclude the specific condition from coverage under the policy. Alcoholism and drug addiction are just two examples of the sort of ailments that often receive this treatment.

3. Another possibility is that a company will issue a policy but will charge a higher than standard rate for that policy or will limit the amount of benefits that the insured can purchase. For example, an insured may be able to obtain coverage for a maximum of only two years, even though that person desires and is able to afford the premium for a longer benefit period.

4. In other cases, a company will issue a policy but will stipulate that benefits will not be provided for a "pre-existing condition" if that condition requires care during some period—often the first six months—of the policy's effectiveness. Many policies preclude benefits only during the specified period, but some group plans preclude *any* coverage if the medical condition in question requires long-term care during that period. The exact terms are set forth in the policy itself, sometimes subject to state law or regulation. A "pre-existing condition" is frequently defined as one for which the insured sought (or should have sought) treatment during some period of time preceding the policy's effective date.

Some companies request physical examinations or certain diagnostic tests (usually blood work) before making their decision, or may calibrate their response depending upon the exact nature of the client's condition and how well controlled it may be.

[¶ 9,575]

b. *Other Medical Limits*

Beyond pre-existing conditions, most long-term care insurance policies limit the payment of benefits via "case management." Under this provision, a client seeking benefits under a policy is examined by a caseworker who is under contract, perhaps even a full-time employee, of the insurance company. This person performs a gatekeeping function to assess the policyholder's condition and determine the best accommodation for that condition. The initial assessment may be reviewed after a period of time, depending upon the insurance company's policies and the client's exact condition. If the client disagrees with the case manager's recommendation or chooses some other course of action, the insurance company will generally deny coverage for the costs incurred in that alternative treatment plan.

Most policies also limit the types of facilities that are eligible for benefits, typically referring to some sort of state licensure requirements.

Some older policies that are still in force also restrict institutional care to nursing homes, though more modern policies include assisted living facilities as well.

In addition, some policies require that a policyholder must have been hospitalized before needing long-term care, a provision that mimics Medicare's approach to long-term care. The majority of states prohibit this sort of restriction, and a smaller number also prohibit a requirement that patients must have received a higher level of care in a nursing home before coverage for a lower level of care will be provided.

[¶ 9,580]

6. Tax–Qualified Policies

A subset of long-term care insurance policies was created in 1997 under the rubric of "tax-qualified." This subset now constitutes the majority of new policies issued, even though many policies that are not "tax-qualified" are still in force. From a planning perspective, therefore, this category of long-term care insurance is the predominant model. The essence of a "tax-qualified" long-term care insurance policy is that it meets certain requirements set forth in the Internal Revenue Code and has certain federal tax benefits as a result.

[¶ 9,585]

a. Policy Requirements

Section 7702B(b) of the Internal Revenue Code sets forth a number of specific requirements, often cross-referencing particular provisions of the long-term care insurance model act and model regulations that have been promulgated by the National Association of Insurance Commissioners. Some of the more significant of these requirements are as follows:

1. "Tax-qualified" policies must be "guaranteed renewable." See ¶ 9,560.

2. Such policies need not include "nonforfeiture of benefits," but such a provision must be available if a prospective policyholder wants to pay for it. See ¶ 9,560.

3. Similarly, inflation protection need not be included, but it must be offered. See ¶ 9,535.

4. These policies may not require a client to enter a hospital before being covered for long-term care benefits or require a client to use a higher level of nursing home care before receiving benefits for a lower level of such care. See ¶ 9,575.

5. Policies must allow insureds to designate someone to receive a notice of policy termination due to nonpayment of premiums at least 30 days before such termination is effective. This provision seeks to prevent "unintentional lapse" when an insured inadvertently misses a premium payment.

Other requirements relate to mandatory disclosures and similar consumer protections.

[¶ 9,590]

b. Federal Tax Treatment

Long-term care insurance policies that satisfy the criteria to be "tax-qualified" have two principal tax features:

1. Any benefits that are paid by these policies are not taxed to the policyholders. This provision has a cap that is adjusted annually for inflation, and in 2004, this amount was $230 per day. But if an insured's actual cost of long-term care is higher, then that higher amount is allowed. For example, assume that Fred's long-term care insurance policy pays up to $275 per day, and the nursing home in which he resides charges $270 per day. That entire $270 is tax-free to Fred, despite the applicable per-day cap.

2. Premiums paid for this insurance are deductible against an insured's federal income tax.

This last feature, however, is subject to several caveats that effectively limit and in many cases negate entirely the purported tax benefit. First, only a portion of the premiums are deductible depending upon the age of the insured in the current year. The deductible amounts are adjusted for inflation annually, and in 2004, they were as follows:

Age	Amount
Under 41	$ 260
41–50	$ 490
51–60	$ 980
61–70	$2,600
Over 70	$3,250

Any premium in excess of these limits is not deductible. So, if a 65–year old client paid $3,500 on long-term care insurance, only $2,600 (in 2004) of that amount is deductible. The remaining $900 ($3,500 less $2,600) is ignored for tax purposes.

In any case, once the tax-deductible limit is determined, this amount is a "medical expense" for federal income tax purposes. The tax code allows such expenses to be deducted only to the extent that they exceed 7.5% of a taxpayer's "adjusted gross income" (AGI). See ¶ 3,190. Accordingly, a taxpayer must total all of his or her out-of-pocket medical costs (other than any long-term care insurance premiums in excess of the applicable limit), and reduce that amount by 7.5% of the taxpayer's AGI. In all likelihood, some portion of this person's long-term care insurance premium will be rendered nondeductible by this provision.

For example, assume that Lashonda is the 65–year old–client referred to above and that she has the following medical expenses this year in addition to her long-term care insurance policy: Medicare Part B premiums (see ¶ 9,300) of $66.60 per month for 12 months, or $799; medigap insurance premiums of $1,100 per year; and prescription drug expenses of $600. Her AGI is $50,000, and her medical expense deduction is computed as follows:

Long-term care insurance (limited)	$2,600
Medicare Part B	799
Medigap insurance	1,100
Prescription drugs	600
Total medical costs	$5,099
7.5% of AGI ($50,000)	(3,750)
Deduction	$1,349

The financial benefit of this deduction is further constrained by the classification of "medical expenses" as "itemized deductions." As a result of this designation, many older clients may be unable to claim any deduction for medical expenses unless the total of their "itemized deductions" exceeds their so-called "standard deduction." Moreover, the standard deduction increases annually for inflation and is augmented for persons age 65 years and older. See I.R.C. § 63(f)(1), (3). In 2004, that amount was $5,800. As a result, many clients may find that they are unable to deduct *any* of their long-term care insurance premiums.

[¶ 9,595]

Problems

1. Thomas pays $2,900 per year for a long-term care insurance policy that pays $300 per day for life, with inflation protection, nonforfeiture of benefits, and several other optional provisions. How much can he deduct if Thomas is 58 years old? How much if he is 68 years old? How much if he is 78 years old?

2. Assume that Thomas from the preceding problem is 78 years old and that his wife, Julie, is 68 years old. She also has a long-term care insurance policy, but she bought her policy several years ago and her premium is $1,500 per year. They both have Medicare Part B, and they pay $1,800 per year for two medigap policies. Their "adjusted gross income" this year is $63,000. How much can they deduct as medical expenses?

[¶ 9,600]

7. Planning Considerations

Planning for the cost of long-term care is similar to planning for other major life expenses: many variables are unknown and unknowable in advance, and there is more than one approach that can work. The approach considered in this section is shifting the risk of this expenditure via long-term care insurance. Within this approach, several key considerations appear.

[¶ 9,605]

a. The Client's Age

A client's age is a very significant factor because it directly affects the premium charged. In fact, premiums for long-term care insurance are much more age-sensitive than are other forms of insurance, including medical or even life insurance. Premiums are lower for younger people because they are less likely to need long-term care any time soon and tend to be healthier. As noted at ¶ 9,570, a client's health status can restrict the coverage that can be obtained, or raise the cost of obtaining that coverage, or even preclude obtaining this coverage at all.

Take, for example, a somewhat "standard" package that is offered by a major long-term care insurance carrier: $100 per day for nursing homes and for home health, four years of coverage, a 100–day elimination period, and no inflation protection. The annual premiums for such coverage are:

Age	Amount
55	$ 510
65	$ 990
75	$2,830

Clearly, the younger applicants have a significant cost advantage over a 75–year-old applicant.

For younger applicants, however, the issue of inflation adjustments looms large. All other things being equal, the 55–year-old applicant will not need the insurance benefits for a much longer period than will the 75–year-old applicant. During that time, the erosion of those benefits by inflation can be significant. Adding a 5% compounded inflation adjustment rider to the package described above yields the following premiums:

Age	Amount
55	$1,090
65	$1,740
75	$4,230

Perhaps, the 75–year-old applicant will forgo inflation protection and simply go with the package outlined previously. In that case, that person's premium is still $2,830, a substantial increase over what the 55–year old applicant and even the 65–year old applicant must pay.

More sophisticated analyses might consider the time value of money and might determine the present value amount that is needed to fund the premiums in question. But even those calculations ignore the impact of two very important points:

    1. While younger applicants will presumably pay their premiums for more years, they also have long-term care coverage throughout

that period in case the need for long-term care arises earlier than anticipated.

    2. Younger applicants are more likely to qualify for a long-term care insurance policy, as noted previously.

The point remains that the client's age is a major determinant of the premium charged.

[¶ 9,610]

Problem

Using the website of a long-term care insurance company, determine the premium charged for a policy paying $100 per day for nursing home care, $50 per day for home health, for five years with a 90–day elimination period for persons aged 35, 45, and 55 years. Then add an inflation protection rider to these policies and determine the new premiums.

[¶ 9,620]

b. *Financial Strength of the Insurance Company*

Another key planning consideration in long-term care insurance is the financial strength of the company itself. This factor is vitally important for three major reasons:

    1. A long-term care insurance company that experiences financial stress is more likely to raise premiums on current policies at their annual renewal dates. As noted at ¶ 9,560, rates can be increased even on policies that are "guaranteed renewable." If those rates are increased too high, the insurance may become unaffordable, causing the client to drop this coverage precisely when it is likely to be needed.

    2. If a long-term care insurance company fails, the client may be unable to secure replacement insurance because of medical conditions that have arisen since the first policy was obtained. Moreover, even if replacement insurance is obtainable, the client is presumably older than he or she was when the original policy was purchased, so the new premium would reflect that increased age. As shown in ¶ 9,605, premiums rise dramatically with age, so the new premium might be unaffordable.

    3. Long-term care insurance has no federal guarantee comparable to what the Federal Deposit Insurance Corporation provides on bank deposits. Some states have guarantee funds, but not all do. Even those states with such funds typically protect policyholders only if they reside in the state in question, and those guarantees are further limited to benefit amounts of $100,000 or less. This figure would cover less than three years of benefits of $100 per day and even less for policies with higher daily benefit levels.

The financial strength of an insurance company can be assessed using certain insurance company rating systems, but the long-term care insurance industry is still fairly young, and these ratings may have less reliability in this context than they do for other insurance products.

[¶ 9,625]

c. *Alternative Approaches: Investment Assets*

Many clients recognize the possibility of needing long-term care but do not want insurance to cover their potential liability. Persons with significant assets may simply decide to self-insure. Such clients may nevertheless want long-term care insurance for three reasons:

1. A client's assets may be illiquid. That is, substantial ownership interests in real estate or closely held businesses might not generate the cash needed to pay monthly bills for long-term care. Borrowing against those assets may be feasible if there is sufficient equity available to support such loans. With respect to residences, a reverse mortgage might be employed to cover the long-term care expenses of the client, especially if the client is receiving home care in the residence. See ¶ 5,790 regarding such mortgages. A home equity loan might also serve this purpose, though such loans usually require repayment on a schedule that is less favorable than a reverse mortgage.

2. Assets that might be sold to pay for long-term care might trigger taxes on their previously unrealized appreciation. As noted in ¶ 3,550, gains on investment assets are generally not subject to income tax until the assets are sold. Furthermore, a client may have intended to eliminate the income tax on those gains by holding the properties until his or her death, thereby allowing the properties' basis to be stepped up to their fair market value in the hands of the new owners. See ¶ 3,510. Those plans could be jeopardized if the assets are sold during the client's lifetime to pay for long-term care.

3. A client may have testamentary plans for the specific assets in question, and those bequest intentions would be upset by the need to dispose of these assets before the client dies. See ¶ 2,275.

Alternatively, some clients may choose to save the insurance premiums and invest those funds themselves to cover this potential expense. The following example illustrates the task that they have undertaken. Assume that a client is unmarried and is 65 years old, no nursing home stay is needed until the client is 80 years old, the client has an effective federal and state income tax rate of 26%, and the client cannot deduct the long-term care insurance premium. This client's goal is to replicate the long-term care insurance policy described at ¶ 9,605—namely, four years at $100 per day with a 100–day elimination period and a 5% compounded inflation protection rider. This policy has an annual premium of $1,740. (This example assumes that the insurance company does not raise its rates during the period in question.)

The first step is determining what the daily benefit will be 15 years from now, when the client is 80 years old: $100 per day after 15 years of 5% annually compounded increases produces a daily benefit of $208, or $6,240 for a 30–day month. The next step is determining the lump sum that is needed to generate four years of benefits of $6,240 per month, assuming a 6% annual rate of return. That amount is $265,699.

This, then, is the amount that the client must obtain by making annual investments of $1,740 for 15 years. To do so, however, requires that the client earn 28.9% compounded annually *after* tax. This result requires pre-tax annual returns of 39.1%. (If the amount is saved in a tax-deferred account, the effective tax rate will be closer to 30%, since withdrawals from these accounts are taxed as ordinary income, so the required annual investment return becomes 41.3%.) Furthermore, this rate of return must be earned not just for one "great" year, but year after year for 15 consecutive years. Not exactly a slam dunk in any market.

[¶ 9,630]

d. *Alternative Approaches: Life Insurance*

Some clients currently have life insurance that they could access to pay for long-term care. Many life insurance contracts have so-called "accelerated benefits" or "living benefits" riders that allow an insured to obtain a stipulated percentage of the policy's death benefit prior to dying. The precise requirements are determined by the specific insurance policy, but a common requirement is that the insured have a fairly short remaining life expectancy, often as little as six months. See ¶ 7,135.

In any case, as long as the insured has "an illness or physical condition which can reasonably be expected to result in death" within 24 months, the receipt of these accelerated benefits is free of federal income tax. I.R.C. § 101(g)(1)(A), (4)(A). These benefits can also be obtained tax-free by someone who is "chronically ill," which means that the insured requires "substantial assistance" to perform at least two activities of daily living. I.R.C. §§ 101(g)(1)(B), (4)(B), 7702B(c)(2). In that circumstance, the amount that qualifies for tax-free treatment is limited to the same amount that applies to long-term care insurance benefits. In 2004, that amount was $230 per day. As with those benefits, higher amounts can be received tax-free as long as they do not exceed the actual cost of long-term care. See ¶ 9,590.

For clients without an "accelerated benefits" rider on their life insurance, one alternative is to sell the life insurance policy itself and then use the proceeds of that sale to pay for long-term care. Such sales are often called "viatical settlements" and allow a policyholder to obtain part of a policy's death benefit prior to dying. Different "viatical settlement providers" employ different valuation methodologies for determining the amount that they will pay for any given policy, but generally, the shorter a policyholder's life expectancy, the higher the sale proceeds will be. And as long as that life expectancy is two years or less when the sale is made, the proceeds of the sale are received free of federal income tax.

E. MEDICAID

[¶ 9,700]

Medicaid is the health care component of this nation's welfare system. As such, it pays for the medical expenses of poor people, regardless of their age. The vast majority of Medicaid recipients, in fact, are *not* old. They span the entire age range, though older recipients do account for a disproportionately large share of Medicaid's expenditures. It may seem somewhat incongruous to discuss this poverty-oriented program in a volume concerned with "wealth management," but Medicaid is the largest financing source for nursing home care in this country and is a substantial funder of home health care as well. (Medicaid also funds a very small number of assisted living arrangements, primarily as demonstration projects that substitute for more expensive nursing home placements.) Poor people look to Medicaid for their health care needs generally, not just the costs of long-term care. But many families that have never before relied on public assistance find that the costs of long-term care overwhelm their resources and they then need such assistance. It is in connection with the financing of long-term care, therefore, that this chapter considers the Medicaid program.

[¶ 9,710]

1. General Overview of Medicaid Long–Term Care

Enacted at the same time as Medicare, Medicaid is very different from that program. Whereas Medicare is an age-based entitlement, Medicaid is a means-tested program. That is, strict limits are applied to the income and assets of a potential Medicaid recipient. Special allowances are made, however, for the spouse of a Medicaid recipient if that spouse is not institutionalized—the "community spouse" in Medicaid's argot. (By federal law, Medicaid recognizes only marriages between a man and a woman. 1 U.S.C. § 7.) But unmarried recipients must expend all of their income, except for a small monthly allowance of less than $50, and all of their assets that are not "exempt resources" before Medicaid benefits are available. And when a Medicaid recipient dies, Medicaid seeks reimbursement from any assets in that person's estate for the expenditures that Medicaid made for that person's care. In short, Medicaid is a welfare program that is intended to cover the medical costs of persons who lack the means to pay these costs themselves.

[¶ 9,715]

a. Financing and Eligibility Determinations

Medicaid has no dedicated revenue source, unlike Medicare Part A's payroll tax or Medicare Part B's monthly premium payments from its enrollees. Instead, Medicaid is financed out of general tax revenues and is therefore vulnerable to budgetary pressures whenever tax receipts decline. Moreover, Medicaid is a joint undertaking of the federal and state governments. The federal government pays at least half of the program's costs and as much as 83% of those costs for states with very low per capita income. The states pay the balance of these costs, and for most states, Medicaid represents one of their largest expenditures after education.

Because both levels of government (i.e., federal and state) pay Medicaid's costs, both levels of government determine the contours of this program. Accordingly, many aspects of Medicaid, from determining who is eligible for Medicaid benefits to the scope of the benefits being provided, are governed by both federal and state rules and regulations. Many state provisions, moreover, are not readily accessible by persons outside the public aid bureaucracy that administers welfare programs. For practical purposes, therefore, this chapter will focus primarily on the *federal* Medicaid provisions, but advisors should be aware that many key issues are informed by state, and often by local, practices and procedures.

In any case, Medicaid benefits are obtained by a client's applying for such benefits at the local office of the department that administers the program, often the department of public aid or assistance. There, intake workers may accept or deny the application without further ado. Appeals can be taken, of course, to higher ranked officials within the department and ultimately to a court if need be. If an application is found to have been improperly denied, Medicaid benefits are paid retroactive to the date of the initial application. But while these appeals are pending, Medicaid is not paying for the applicant's long-term care. That reality often puts the Medicaid applicant at risk of being discharged from the nursing facility for lack of payment.

[¶ 9,720]

b. Medicaid Status and the Client

There are other ramifications of applying for Medicaid benefits as well. It is an open secret that persons seeking a nursing home placement have more difficulty securing that placement if they receive or are eligible for Medicaid benefits, rather than paying for such care themselves or via long-term care insurance. Some nursing homes do not accept Medicaid recipients at all, and others drop out of the Medicaid program, largely in response to declining payments received from Medicaid. These payments, usually styled "reimbursement rates," have generally failed to keep up with the rising costs of operating a nursing facility, including rapidly escalating premiums for liability insurance. In many areas, these rates do not even cover the out-of-pocket costs of caring for a patient. The nursing home, in those circumstances, loses money every day on every Medicaid recipient. The only way that these facilities can stay in business is from the higher charges that they collect from patients who pay privately or have long-term care insurance. Thus, many nursing homes—and other health care providers as well—"monitor their census," meaning that they restrict the number of money-losing Medicaid recipients that they accept. (Nevertheless, when a nursing facility leaves the Medicaid program, federal law protects the current residents of that facility who are Medicaid recipients from being involuntarily discharged. 42 U.S.C. § 1396r(c)(2)(F)(i)(I).)

From the perspective of the client, these realities have at least three major implications:

1. One's status as a Medicaid recipient can have an adverse effect on the chances of being admitted to the nursing home of one's choice. That factor is a vital issue for many clients who are accustomed to securing the treatment they want, in medical care and in other aspects of their lives. Instead, they must settle for a facility that is willing to accept the lower reimbursement rates that Medicaid pays. Moreover, some private-pay residents will exhaust their resources and eventually require Medicaid assistance, so nursing homes are even less likely to accept clients who already qualify for Medicaid benefits.

2. Facilities that do accept Medicaid recipients may be less desirable in various respects, one of which may be their location vis-à-vis a client's family. That is, if the only facility that "has a Medicaid bed," as the expression goes, is located some distance from the client's relatives, those relatives may be unable to visit the client on a regular basis. And it is another open secret that the care and attention that one receives in a nursing home is often affected by how regularly family members visit the resident.

3. If the level of care in a client's current nursing facility declines to the point that the client wants to transfer to a different facility, that person's status as a Medicaid recipient might restrict the choices that are available. Medicaid status, in other words, reduces the client's flexibility to change facilities as circumstances warrant.

[¶ 9,730]

2. Income Eligibility

Medicaid eligibility begins with a prospective applicant's income. For this purpose, income includes all economic receipts without regard to their specific source. Even gifts and bequests are counted, as is all interest income and all Social Security benefits. In other words, Medicaid does not recognize the various distinctions made in the federal tax code that exclude gifts, bequests, municipal bond interest, and all or part of a person's Social Security benefits. See ¶¶ 3,030–3,100. Nor are capital gains treated any differently than any other form of income. For purposes of Medicaid, income is income.

Having determined an applicant's income, Medicaid employs two very different pathways to eligibility, denominated "medically needy" and "income cap" in the typical shorthand. Those states that use the "medically needy" standard compare an applicant's income to the amount of that person's medical bills. If this income is not sufficient to meet those needs, this person is eligible for Medicaid regardless of the amount of that person's income per se. For example, assume that William's monthly income consists of $3,000 from his former employer's pension plan and $800 from Social Security, a total of $3,800. His nursing home expense, Medicare Part B premium, and prescription drugs cost $4,500 per month. Under the "medically needy" standard, William is eligible for Medicaid because his monthly medical expenses of $4,500 exceed his monthly income of $3,800. He can keep a personal monthly allowance that ranges from $20 to $50 depending on state regulations, and will apply the rest of his income to his medical bills. Medicaid will then pay the remaining costs directly to the health care providers involved. At the present time, 30 states utilize the "medically needy" standard or some approximate variant of that approach.

A different group of states use the "income cap" standard whereby an applicant's income is tested against a fixed amount that increases annually for inflation. In 2004, that amount was $1,692 per month. If an applicant's income exceeds this amount, that person is not eligible for Medicaid, regardless of the level of his or her medical expenses. Thus, William from the preceding example would be ineligible for Medicaid in an "income cap" state even though he cannot pay his medical bills, because his monthly income of $3,800 exceeds the current "income cap" level. Moreover, the "income cap" approach does not concern itself with the amount by which that person's income exceeds the applicable cap. *Any* excess triggers ineligibility.

Because this approach is so restrictive, most "income cap" states allow prospective applicants to transfer their income in excess of the applicable cap to a "qualified income trust" and thereby gain Medicaid eligibility. Such trusts are authorized under 42 U.S.C. § 1396p(d)(4)(B) and are sometimes referred to as "*Miller* trusts" in reference to the court case that sanctioned their use: Miller v. Ibarra, 746 F.Supp. 19 (D. Colo. 1990). This mechanism enables many people who would not otherwise qualify for Medicaid, such as William in the preceding example, to gain access to Medicaid benefits. These trusts have one very significant drawback, however: when the Medicaid recipient dies, any funds that remain in the trust must revert to the state to the extent of the expenditures that Medicaid paid on that recipient's behalf.

[¶ 9,735]

Problems

1. Michelle receives monthly income from the following sources: Social Security benefits of $900; pension plan distributions of $600; dividends of $100; and tax-free municipal bond interest of $700. Her nursing home costs $3,400 per month. If Michelle lives in a state that applies the "medically needy" standard in determining income eligibility for Medicaid, is Michelle eligible for Medicaid benefits?

2. If Michelle from the preceding problem lives in a state that applies the "income cap" standard in determining income eligibility for Medicaid, is Michelle eligible for Medicaid benefits? If not, what might you suggest to her?

[¶ 9,740]

3. Exempt Resources

Medicaid allows recipients to own certain "exempt" or "noncountable" assets and still receive benefits under the program, including long-term care. Any assets, or "resources" in Medicaid's argot, that do not fit within these categories or exceed the dollar limits for these categories must be "spent down." Only after these assets have been exhausted will Medicaid benefits begin.

There is, however, a general exemption, often styled the "asset disregard." This exemption applies to $2,000, or $3,000 for a married couple if both the husband and the wife are seeking Medicaid benefits. These amounts are not adjusted for inflation and have not increased since Medicaid was created in 1965. All investment properties, stocks, bonds, certificates of deposit, individual retirement accounts, and other retirement-oriented holdings are subject to this single limit. There is a specific exclusion for life insurance, but it applies *only if* the life insurance policy's death benefit does not exceed $1,500. If the death benefit exceeds this ridiculously low figure, the entire cash surrender value of the insurance policy is counted. (Term insurance is ignored for this purpose, because it has no cash surrender value.)

[¶ 9,745]

a. Personal Property

Certain types of tangible personal property are exempted, often with specific dollar limits applied. Any amounts in excess of these limits are counted toward the "asset disregard" explained in ¶ 9,740, and assets not protected by that allowance must presumably be sold and the sale proceeds "spent down" before Medicaid benefits will begin. As with almost all aspects of Medicaid, enforcement of its provisions varies from state to state and often within a state. Be that as it may, personal property is exempted as follows:

1. Wedding and engagement rings, regardless of their value.

2. Personal effects and household goods, subject to a cap of $2,000 based on the "fair market value" of these assets. This $2,000 limit, moreover, is applied to the sum of these assets, not item by item. But if a community spouse is present, the $2,000 limit is ignored.

3. One automobile, subject to a cap on its "fair market value" of $4,500. If a community spouse is present, however, this limitation is ignored. And if the vehicle has been modified for use by a handicapped person, it is exempt without regard to its value.

[¶ 9,750]

b. *Burial Arrangements*

Medicaid exempts one burial space, without limit as to its value, and a separate and identifiable "burial fund" that is set aside in a prepaid plan, bank account, or trust, of up to $1,500. If a community spouse is present, another burial space and burial account are allowed for that person.

Some states define "burial spaces" to include caskets, vaults, urns, headstones, and even contracts for the opening and closing of the gravesite. This treatment essentially removes any dollar limit for purchases of these items. Generally, this treatment requires that the money must be held in trust for the item in question or be specified in a prepaid burial plan.

[¶ 9,755]

c. *Residence*

The single largest "exempt resource" is an applicant's residence. Medicaid allows an applicant to own one residence, "regardless of its value." 20 C.F.R. § 416.1212(b). For this purpose, it does not matter how large the home is, what improvements have been made, or whether there is any mortgage debt outstanding. Persons who rent have no comparable allowance. The only significant requirement is that the Medicaid applicant must "intend to return" to the residence in question. 42 U.S.C. § 1382b(a)(1). This element is essentially a subjective inquiry, but some states begin to question the likelihood of an applicant's returning home after some period of time, typically six months. If a Medicaid applicant's medical condition suggests that returning home is improbable, which is likely to be the case for many older persons, the home loses its status as an "exempt resource" and must be sold and the sale proceeds "spent down" before Medicaid benefits will begin. Other states simply attach liens after an applicant has been institutionalized for some period of time, often three months or less, and foreclose upon the home at some later date, perhaps after the applicant has died.

If a community spouse is present, the residence is an "exempt resource" and retains that status regardless of the Medicaid applicant's condition. (A home remains exempt even when there is no community spouse, if a sibling or a disabled child of the Medicaid applicant lives there.) Should that community spouse decide to sell the home, the Medicaid exemption remains in effect as long as the sale proceeds are reinvested in a new residence that is acquired within three months of the prior sale. 20 C.F.R. § 416.1212(d). Any sale proceeds that are not so reinvested, however, become an "available resource" subject to the usual "spend down" requirement.

For example, assume that Jack and Jill own a residence that is worth $165,000, but Jill decides to sell this home when Jack is admitted to a nursing home due to a cognitive impairment that is likely to increase over time. Jill sells the home on March 1 and acquires a condominium that is closer to Jack's nursing home in May. This condominium, however, cost only $135,000. The remaining $30,000 ($165,000 less $135,000) represents available resources that Jill must spend on Jack's care.

As this example shows, Medicaid has no counterpart to the federal tax code's $250,000 gain exclusion on principal residences. See ¶ 5,710. To take an extreme example, if Jill sold the residence for $800,000 and realized a gain of $650,000, the entire $800,000 could be an "exempt resource" as long as Jill's new residence costs at least $800,000. The tax law, however, would subject some portion of that $650,000 gain to taxation. As with many other assets, the treatment of the home is not the same under Medicaid as it is under the tax law.

[¶ 9,760]

d. Trusts

Medicaid's rules relating to trusts reflect the variety of forms that these instruments can take. In general, any trust that a Medicaid applicant can access, regardless of restrictions on the timing or use of distributions, is an "available resource" and is therefore not exempt. Accordingly, a revocable trust is not exempt, because the essence of a revocable trust is that the settlor (here, the Medicaid applicant) can dissolve the trust and obtain its assets. See ¶ 2,350.

An irrevocable trust, in contrast, cannot be dissolved by the Medicaid applicant and is therefore generally an "exempt resource." But if any portion of the trust's corpus can be distributed to the Medicaid applicant or used for that person's benefit, that portion of the trust is an "available resource." In any case, establishing and funding such a trust is a transfer of assets that is potentially subject to a penalty period of ineligibility for Medicaid benefits. See ¶ 9,770.

With trusts, of course, there are always exceptions. One exception is the *Miller* trusts in "income cap" states for Medicaid applicants with excess monthly income. See ¶ 9,730. A more broadly applicable exception applies to "pooled account" trusts under 42 U.S.C. § 1396p(d)(4)(C). This type of trust must be established for a disabled individual by a nonprofit organization that maintains a separate account for that individual, but pools the resources of similar accounts for investment and management. Any funds remaining in the separate account after the beneficiary dies may be retained by the nonprofit organization that serves as the trustee for the trust. Otherwise, those funds must be paid to the state to reimburse it for medical expenses paid by Medicaid when the beneficiary in question was alive.

Another type of exempt trust is one created for the benefit of a disabled individual, if the trust was established *before* that individual's 65th birthday by the individual's parent, grandparent, or legal guardian using assets of that individual. See 42 U.S.C. § 1396p(d)(4)(A). These trusts are often called "disability trusts," "special needs trusts," or "supplemental needs trusts." When the trust beneficiary dies, the trust must reimburse the state for medical expenses paid by Medicaid during the beneficiary's lifetime. In any case, the requirement that the beneficiary must be younger than 65 years old when the trust is established makes these trusts less useful in the context of elder law. (Also exempt are trusts that are established by third parties from their own assets, rather than from resources of the trust beneficiary. Such trusts are most often used by parents of disabled *children* and are therefore beyond the scope of this chapter.)

[¶ 9,765]

Problems

1. In each of the following cases, determine the extent of the exempt and countable assets:

   a. Andrew owns a home that is worth $135,000 with no mortgage balance, and a bank account with $15,000.

   b. Betty owns a home that is worth $155,000 with an outstanding mortgage of $75,000, and a bank account with $70,000.

   c. Cathy rents her apartment at a cost of $800 per month and has mutual funds that are worth $150,000.

   d. Daniel has a prepaid burial plan that cost $20,000, as well as life insurance with a face amount of $10,000 and a cash surrender value of $7,000.

   e. Elizabeth has a prepaid burial plan that cost $5,000, as well as life insurance with a face amount of $25,000 and a cash surrender value of $17,500.

2. James will enter a nursing home soon and is interested in obtaining Medicaid benefits for his care. He and his wife, Julia, own a home that is worth $250,000 with no mortgage, and a late model Mercedes automobile that is worth $70,000. They have no life insurance or burial plans, but they do have investment assets that are worth $140,000. What is the amount of

their exempt assets? What if they use $30,000 of their investment assets to put a new roof on the house? To install a heated swimming pool? To purchase prepaid burial plans? To invest in an apartment building for low-income tenants?

[¶ 9,770]

4.　Asset Transfers

Prospective Medicaid applicants who have countable assets in excess of the "asset disregard" amounts have basically two choices: spend down those excess resources, typically on the cost of long-term care; or transfer those assets to someone else. This section examines Medicaid's treatment of such transfers. In a nutshell, Medicaid looks back 36 months from the date on which a person applies for Medicaid benefits and imposes an ineligibility penalty for the "uncompensated value" of any transfers made during that time. (If more than one transfer was made during the "look-back" period, the total "uncompensated value" of all such transfers is used in determining the ineligibility period.) This 36–month period is called the "look-back" period. For transfers to a trust, however, the "look-back" period is 60 months. In either case, the ineligibility penalty is the number of months that Medicaid will not provide long-term care benefits, and it is equal to the number of months of care that the "uncompensated value" would have paid for. 42 U.S.C. § 1396p(c)(1)(E)(i).

[¶ 9,775]

a.　*Uncompensated Value*

The "uncompensated value" is simply the excess of the asset's value that a Medicaid applicant transferred over the value of any money or property that the applicant received in exchange for that asset. Thus, when a Medicaid applicant purchases something of value, there is usually no "uncompensated value," although a countable asset might result. For example, assume that Michael bought a motorboat for $35,000. That purchase would, in all likelihood, not involve any "uncompensated value," because Michael received a motorboat that is presumably worth the $35,000 that he paid. That motorboat, however, is a countable asset.

But a countable asset does not result from all purchases. If the item purchased is an "exempt asset" as delineated in ¶ 9,740, there are no immediate Medicaid consequences from the transaction. For example, if Michael had used the $35,000 to buy a condominium, that home would be an exempt asset under the provisions analyzed in ¶ 9,755. Moreover, some purchases do not result in any assets at all. If Michael had used the $35,000 to purchase an around-the-world cruise for him and his wife, there would be no asset after they returned (at least not in the financial sense) and therefore no "uncompensated value" to consider.

The most common circumstance of "uncompensated value" is an outright gift, the transfer of money or property made without receiving anything in exchange. It can also occur when a person sells an asset for less than its fair market value. For example, assume that Michael sold stock or a residential lot that is worth $50,000 to his daughter for $15,000. In that case, the $35,000 difference between what he received and what he gave up is "uncompensated value" for Medicaid purposes. Determining the property's fair market value may be a challenge in some situations, of course, but the principle remains the same: a sale for less than full fair market value produces "uncompensated value."

[¶ 9,780]

b. *Penalty Period Divisor*

Once the "uncompensated value" has been determined, this amount is divided by the cost of care to derive the Medicaid ineligibility period. Some states employ state-wide or county-specific cost-of-care averages that reflect the private pay rate at facilities within the applicable jurisdiction at the time of the Medicaid application. See 42 U.S.C. § 1396p(c)(1)(E)(i)(II). Other states use different formulas, including the private pay rate at the particular facility in which the Medicaid applicant is residing. Whatever divisor is employed, the penalty period is then calculated and imposed beginning with the date that the assets were transferred.

For example, assume that Carol transferred $200,000 on March 1, 2005 and applied for Medicaid on September 15, 2006. Looking back 36 months from the September 15 application date, the March 1 transfer is within the penalizable period. The "uncompensated" amount of $200,000 is then divided by the average cost-of-care rate that Carol's state is using, say $4,000, to derive a period of ineligibility of 50 months. Medicaid, in other words, will not cover any of Carol's long-term care needs for 50 months starting on March 1, 2005—until May 1, 2009, in other words.

In any case, transfers that precede the "look-back" period have no Medicaid consequences. That is, Medicaid would not have imposed *any* period of ineligibility if Carol had waited 36 months after making her transfer of assets—i.e, until March 2, 2008—before applying for Medicaid benefits. This rule applies, it should be noted, regardless of the amount transferred. Of course, most people do not know that they will be needing long-term care 36 months in advance and are unwilling to part with substantial assets based on that possibility. Moreover, people inclined to make such transfers need to retain sufficient resources to pay for their own care during this "look-back" period.

One further caveat applies: the 36–month "look-back" period is a creature of statutory law and can be altered whenever Congress chooses. In fact, the "look-back" period was originally 24 months and was then extended to 30 months and most recently to 36 months in 1993. The "look-back" rule of 60 months for transfers to a trust was created at that time as well. And the relevant "look-back" period is the one that is in effect when an applicant applies for Medicaid, *not* when the asset was transferred. As a result, transfers that appear to be beyond the "look-back" period when made might nevertheless produce an ineligibility penalty, if that period was lengthened between the time that transfer was made and the date when Medicaid benefits are sought.

To illustrate this situation, assume that Carol in the preceding example did not apply for Medicaid benefits until April 2, 2008; i.e., more than 36 months after her March 1, 2005 asset transfer. Assume further that Congress changed the "look-back" period to 42 months during this interim. As a result, the applicable "look-back" period starts 42 months before April 2008, which is October 2004, so the transfer of March 1, 2005 is *within* the "look-back" period. Accordingly, a period of ineligibility will be imposed even though the "look-back" period that was in effect when Carol made the transfer—namely, 36 months—expired one month before she applied for Medicaid benefits.

[¶ 9,785]

c. *Exempt Transfers*

Although an ineligibility period applies to most asset transfers that involve "uncompensated value," certain transfers are exempted from this rule:

1. Transfers that take place before the applicable "look-back" period: currently 36 months, or 60 months in the case of most transfers in trust.

2. Transfers to a "community spouse" of exempt assets (home, automobile, household goods) and additional assets that are needed for the special "community spouse" allowances. See ¶ 9,800.

3. Transfers (including a residence) to a blind or disabled child of the Medicaid applicant, or in trust for the benefit of that child.

An asset transfer is also exempt from Medicaid penalties if the applicant can prove to the state's satisfaction that the transfer was "exclusively for a purpose other than to qualify" for Medicaid. 42 U.S.C. § 1396p(c)(2)(C)(ii).

In addition to the situations just described, a Medicaid applicant's residence may be transferred without penalty to the following relatives:

1. A minor child.

2. An adult child who lived in the home and enabled the applicant to live there during the two years prior to entering a nursing facility.

3. A brother or sister of the Medicaid applicant, if this sibling has an "equity interest" in the home and lived there during the entire year prior to the Medicaid applicant's entering a nursing facility. 42 U.S.C. § 1396q(c)(2)(B).

[¶ 9,790]

Problems

1.   Pauline sold some undeveloped land that was worth $300,000 to her son Charles for $200,000 on June 1, 2004. On September 27, 2006, Pauline entered a nursing home and applied for Medicaid benefits. The private pay rate at her facility, which her state uses to calculate ineligibility periods, is $4,000 per month. When will Medicaid benefits be available to Pauline?

2.   Norman put $400,000 on March 1, 2005 into an irrevocable trust that distributes all of its income to his grandchildren. To avoid an ineligibility period, what is the earliest date on which Norman can apply for Medicaid benefits? If he applies for such benefits before that date, when will the ineligibility period expire if the county average of private pay nursing home rates in his county is $5,000 per month?

3.   Danielle entered a nursing home on October 1, 2006. One month earlier, she had transferred $275,000 in trust for the benefit of her permanently disabled child. On that same date, Danielle deeded her home, worth $225,000, to her other child, who has lived with Danielle for the past three years and has functioned as a full-time caregiver to Danielle during this period. If the state uses $4,500 as its divisor to calculate ineligibility periods, how long will Danielle be ineligible for Medicaid benefits?

4.   Alan has $80,000 in his checking account as well as a $2,000 savings account, but no other assets. He has just entered a nursing home and plans to give $40,000 to his granddaughter, Stephanie. Assume that his state of residence uses $4,000 as its penalty divisor. When will Alan be eligible for Medicaid nursing home benefits? What are Stephanie's financial obligations toward Alan?

[¶ 9,800]

5. Allowances for the Community Spouse

Medicaid authorizes special allowances for the spouse of a Medicaid recipient who is receiving long-term care benefits under that program. These allowances are intended to enable the spouse to continue living in the community (hence the term, "community spouse") and thereby avoid "spousal impoverishment." To that end, a community spouse may retain a portion of the couple's "countable assets" and receive a specified level of monthly income. Moreover, these allowances are *in addition* to the various "exempt assets" examined previously—namely, a residence, one automobile, household goods, and a prepaid burial arrangement. See ¶¶ 9,745, 9,750, and 9,755. These assets are subject to Medicaid's estate recovery provisions, however, after the Medicaid applicant and the community spouse have died. See ¶ 9,820.

[¶ 9,805]

a. Asset Allowance

The assets that a community spouse is allowed to retain make up the "community spouse resource allowance," sometimes referred to as the CSRA. This amount is set by each state from within a range that is established by the federal government and adjusted annually for inflation. In 2004, this range was $18,552 to $92,760. Some states use the low point of this range, while others use the high point. Some states set a statutory limit within the specified range, such as $40,000, and do not change this amount annually.

Still other states provide that the CSRA is half of a couple's "countable assets," but not less than the low point of the range or more than the high point of that range. To illustrate this statutory pattern, assume that Fred and Ginger live in such a state and have assets that are worth $100,000 in addition to their home (including furnishings), one automobile, and prepaid burial plans. If Fred applies for Medicaid long-term care benefits, Ginger's CSRA will be $50,000, half of their combined assets of $100,000. If their assets were worth only $30,000, half would be $15,000, which is less than the CSRA range's low point, so Ginger's CSRA would be the CSRA range's low point. On the other hand, if they owned assets worth $300,000, half of that amount would be $150,000, which exceeds the CSRA range's high point, so Ginger's CSRA would be the CSRA range's high point.

In addition, a state may allow a higher CSRA to generate the income that is needed for the community spouse's monthly income allowance. See ¶ 9,810.

[¶ 9,810]

b. Monthly Income Allowance

Generally, a community spouse is entitled to keep his or her own income. 42 U.S.C. § 1396r–5(b)(1). This so-called "name on the check" rule means that a community spouse retains the Social Security benefits, pension distributions, and other items that are paid to that person alone. Income that is paid to both spouses is allocated according to their ownership interests, which in most circumstances means that the income is split equally. But in the generation that is currently receiving long-term care, a couple's income is likely to be paid disproportionately to the husband, reflecting the societal employment patterns that prevailed during their working lives. As a result, the wife often has relatively little income in her own name. And if the husband enters a nursing home, most of the couple's income will go to pay his bills, leaving the wife with very little income on which to live in the community at large.

Medicaid allows the community spouse in this situation to retain a specified amount of monthly income, an amount that bears the tongue-twisting moniker of the "minimum monthly maintenance needs allowance," or MMMNA. Like the CSRA, states may set the amount of the MMMNA from within a range that is established by the federal government and adjusted annually for inflation. In 2004, this range was $1,515 to $2,319. If a community spouse's income is less than the MMMNA that the state uses, additional income will be transferred from the institutionalized spouse, typically the husband, to that community spouse.

This so-called "income first" method can best be illustrated with an example. Assume that Matthew and Melinda have "countable assets" of $180,000, providing Melinda a CSRA of $90,000 under their state's formula (see ¶ 9,805). Their monthly income derives from the following sources:

Sources of Income	Matthew	Melinda
Social Security	($1,000)	$500
Private Pension	940	0
Total Income	$1,940	
Personal Needs Allowance	(40)	
Net Income	$1,900	

Matthew's income of $1,900 will be applied to his nursing home costs, and Medicaid will pay the balance that is due to the facility. But Melinda has monthly income of only $500 from Social Security, plus $150 per month from investing her CSRA, a total of $650. (A CSRA of $90,000 invested at 2% yields $1,800 per year, or $150 per month.) Assume that the state in which Melinda resides has a MMMNA of $1,950, meaning that she is short by $1,300 ($1,950 less $650). Accordingly, $1,300 of Matthew's income will be transferred to Melinda. That leaves only $600 ($1,900 less $1,300) of Matthew's income for the nursing home, so Medicaid will pay more of Matthew's long-term care bills.

If the institutionalized spouse's income is insufficient to bring the community spouse's income up to the state's MMMNA, the state must increase the CSRA to generate the additional income. So, in the preceding example, if Matthew's income was less than the $1,300 that is needed to bring Melinda's income up to $1,950, some additional "countable assets" would be transferred to her. In today's low interest environment, that additional CSRA might be substantial. After all, a deficiency of, say $300 per month, translates into required additional income of $3,600 per year, which at 2% necessitates an additional investment amount of $180,000.

A community spouse may also request a "fair hearing" to seek additional income. This proceeding is conducted by employees of the agency that administers the Medicaid program but not any official who participated in the initial determination. 42 C.F.R. § 431.240(a)(3). Further appeals can be taken to state or federal courts. In any case, the standard for seeking additional income is somewhat forbidding: the community spouse must prove that he or she needs additional income "due to exceptional circumstances resulting in significant financial duress." 42 U.S.C. § 1396r–5(e)(2)(B).

This "income first" method has one very serious shortcoming: it ignores the possibility that some of the income that is being transferred to the community spouse will cease when the institutionalized spouse dies. For example, Social Security benefits to the couple will usually decline when one spouse dies, and many pension plans provide for reduced payments when the former employee passes away. At that point, the community spouse will receive less income than was anticipated when Medicaid funded that person's MMMNA. To counter this possibility, many advisors suggest that assets should be transferred first to generate the income that is needed to fund a community spouse's MMMNA. That source of income, after all, will not be affected by the death of the institutionalized spouse. Only a minority of states utilize this so-called "resources first" approach, and even those states may switch to the "income first" approach, because the U.S. Supreme Court has ruled that states may transfer income instead of providing an increased CSRA. Wisconsin Department of Health and Family Services v. Blumer, 534 U.S. 473 (2002).

[¶ 9,815]

Problems

1. Henry and Hannah own a home that is worth $130,000, an automobile that is worth $18,000, prepaid burial plans that cost $8,700, a bank account with $45,000 and various mutual funds that are worth $115,000. Hannah requires long-term care and applies for Medicaid assistance. What can Henry retain if the state in which he and Hannah reside split a couple's assets in determining the CSRA?

2. Assume the same facts as in the preceding problem, except that the state in which Henry and Hannah reside provides that the CSRA is a couple's entire assets up to $40,000. Under this law, what would be Henry's CSRA?

3. Ralph has monthly income from Social Security of $1,000 and from an employer-provided pension of $2,500. His wife Rose has Social Security income of $500 per month and receives $700 per month in dividends from a diversified portfolio of stocks. If Ralph receives Medicaid nursing home benefits, how much income will be available to Rose? Assume that their state of residence has set a MMMNA of $2,100 and a personal needs allowance of $35 per month.

4. Assume the same facts as in the preceding problem, except that Ralph's pension income is $835 per month. The state assumes a 3% rate of return in community spouse applications for additional resources. How much additional CSRA can Rose receive?

[¶ 9,820]

6. Estate Recovery

Unlike any other welfare program, Medicaid has a reimbursement feature whereby a Medicaid recipient is required to reimburse the state for expenditures that were made on his or her behalf out of any assets owned at the beneficiary's death. This feature, which states have been required to implement since 1993, transforms Medicaid from a welfare program into a quasi-loan program in certain respects. On the other hand, Medicaid does not impose any interest charges for the often substantial time lag between the payments made by Medicaid to the nursing home and the reimbursement by the recipient's estate.

Under this so-called "estate recovery" program, a former Medicaid recipient's liability is limited to what Medicaid actually paid. The former recipient will receive the advantage, therefore, of Medicaid's generally lower daily rates. For example, assume that Peg resides in a nursing home where the private pay rate is $107 per day, but Medicaid pays only $82 per day. When Peg dies, her estate will owe Medicaid only what it paid, in this case $82 per day. Moreover, the Medicaid rate (here $82) applies as long as Medicaid pays *any* portion of a Medicaid recipient's bill. So if Peg has sufficient income to pay the nursing facility $65 per day, the nursing home will collect that amount from her and receive $17 per day from the Medicaid program ($82 less $65). When Peg dies, her estate's liability to Medicaid is the $17 per day that Medicaid actually paid.

Although Medicaid has been considered in this chapter primarily in connection with nursing home care, the estate recovery mandate encompasses other expenses as well. If a former recipient was at least 55 years old when Medicaid benefits were received, the state must recover its costs for home-and community-based health services and for prescription drugs as well. In any case, estate recovery is postponed until after the former Medicaid recipient's spouse or blind or disabled child has passed away.

At that time, any assets in a Medicaid recipient's probate estate are subject to estate recovery. 42 U.S.C. § 1396p(b)(4)(A). The definition of a person's probate estate is a function of state law, which necessarily governs this area. But states have been granted federal authorization to expand their own definitions of the "probate estate" for this limited purpose. This expansion does not happen automatically, but states may include nonprobate assets in which a deceased Medicaid recipient had "any legal title or interest at the time of [that person's] death," such as property that is held in a joint tenancy, a living trust, a life estate, "or other arrangement." 42 U.S.C. § 1396p(b)(4)(B).

Estate recovery is generally implemented when the Medicaid recipient dies. But if that person is survived by a community spouse, no recovery claim is collected as long as that spouse is alive. 42 U.S.C. § 1396p(b)(2). Only when the community spouse passes away may Medicaid proceed with estate recovery. So, if Arnold dies while receiving Medicaid benefits, his wife Maria may continue to live in their home, regardless of its value, without any time limit. This procedure effectively amplifies the protections that Medicaid affords for a community spouse in the form of resources and monthly income allowances. See ¶¶ 9,805 and 9,810.

In implementing the Medicaid estate recovery program, most states utilize liens on real property, especially on the recipient's residence. State employees also watch death lists, do property checks at local courthouses, and file probate claims. Some states require that banks and nursing homes send funds of a deceased Medicaid recipient to the state immediately upon that person's death. States are allowed to waive estate recovery to avoid "undue hardship," but many states have not yet implemented this provision.

[¶ 9,825]

Problems

1. Medicaid paid $77,000 towards the long-term care of Ellen before she died. Her estate consists of a home that is worth $62,000 and a savings account with $2,000. Her will names her niece Tonya as sole beneficiary. What will Tonya receive from her aunt's estate? Can Medicaid seek reimbursement from Tonya for any amount?

2. Assume the same facts as in the preceding problem, except that Ellen received an inheritance of $30,000 from her sister Kimberly one month before Ellen died. How much will Tonya receive from her aunt Ellen's estate?

3. Assume the same facts as in the first problem, except that Ellen and Tonya owned the home in question as joint tenants with a right of survivorship. How much will the state be able to collect from Ellen's estate? If the state of Ellen's residence utilizes an expanded definition of the "probate estate" for Medicaid purposes that includes jointly held real estate, how much will the state collect from Ellen's estate?

Chapter 10

CREDIT, DEBT, AND ASSET PROTECTION

A. INTRODUCTION

[¶ 10,000]

1. Statistics on Debt

As the New York Times reported on May 4, 2004, "household debt climbed at twice the pace of household income from the beginning of 2000 through 2003; Americans, enticed by low interest rates, took on $2.3 trillion in new mortgage debt during this period, an increase of nearly 50 percent; consumer credit rose 33 percent, rising to $2 trillion in 2003 from $1.5 trillion in 2003."

[¶ 10,005]

2. Thinking About Debt and Credit

For starters, think about the words "credit" and "debt." Credit has a positive connotation—"I have good credit" or "I can get credit if I need it." Debt, on the other hand, has a negative connotation—"Epstein has too much debt." Credit, properly used, can result in productive personal investments—home ownership, new cars, memorable family vacations, etc. Debt, improperly incurred, can result in foreclosure, bankruptcy, etc.

Debt can result from either borrowing or buying, and "purchase money" loans somewhat blur any distinction between the two. D buys furniture on credit from F Furniture Store—debt from buying. Or D borrows money from B Bank to buy furniture from F Furniture Store and uses the loan proceeds to buy the furniture—debt from "purchase money" borrowing.

"Secured" and "unsecured" are different forms of debt (or credit). Most secured loans to individuals are "purchase money loans," i.e., loans made to finance the purchase of an item which is then used as security or collateral for the loan. Car loans and home mortgages are the most

738

common examples of secured loans to individuals. Credit card debt is now the most common form of unsecured credit to an individual.

As common experience and common sense would suggest, the cost of a secured loan such as a car loan or a home loan is generally less than the cost of an unsecured loan. The cost of credit reflects the risk that the creditor is taking in extending the credit. And, by taking collateral for the loan and adding to debt collection rights, the creditor is reducing its risk and thus can reduce the cost of credit.

"Open-end" and "closed-end" are other terms for classifying consumer debt (credit). Credit card debt is the most common example of "open-end" debt—i.e., the individual gets a line of credit that contemplates an indefinite series of separate credit extensions and repayments with a finance charge computed from time to time on the outstanding balance.

"Closed-end" debt describes a single extension of credit to be repaid in a number of payments agreed upon at the time of the credit extension. Car financing is the most common example of closed-end debt.

"Prime" and "subprime" are still other terms for describing consumer debt. The subprime lending market extends credit to borrowers who do not meet the standards for borrowing in the prime market and therefore might not otherwise have access to credit. These individuals and households may have high debt in comparison to their income, little or no credit history, few assets, or impaired credit.

The subprime industry follows the same basic principles as other lenders in determining the cost of credit. Because lenders assess subprime loans as higher risk, loan amounts in the subprime market are generally smaller than those in the prime market, lenders spend more to originate subprime loans, subprime loans are generally prepaid at faster rates than prime loans, and subprime borrowers are charged significantly higher fees and rates than prime borrowers. All of that is obvious; it is less obvious why the rate charged in subprime deals which is higher than the rate charged in the prime market is called the subprime rate.

There is a broad spectrum of subprime credit transactions—pawns, payday loans, etc. While loan amounts in the subprime market are generally smaller than those in the prime market, there has been a significant increase in recent years in subprime lending involving automobiles and home mortgages. Moreover, there is a broad spectrum of practices in the subprime lending market, ranging from those that legitimately protect the subprime lender who takes a relatively high risk in lending to practices that are "predatory." These predatory practices include (1) excessive prepayment penalties, (2) scheduled balloon payments (i.e., a final payment significantly larger than prior installment payments), (3) negative amortization (i.e., initial payments are so low that the amount owed increases notwithstanding the debtor's making all scheduled payments), and (4) flipping (i.e., repeated refinancing of loans).

Obviously, there is no disagreement about the need to curtail these predatory practices. There is, however, presently a strong disagreement as to whether state legislatures or federal agencies should take the lead in curtailing predatory practices.

B. INCURRING DEBT

1. Availability of Credit

[¶ 10,100]

a. *Credit reports and the Fair Credit Reporting Act*

Before extending credit to a consumer, the creditor will often obtain the consumer's credit report. Most creditors rely on credit reports generated by local or national credit bureaus.

Nationally, there are three major credit bureaus: Equifax, Experian and TransUnion. These credit bureaus, along with other national and local bureaus, compile credit information for subscribers. The subscribers not only use the bureaus to obtain credit reports, but also provide the bureaus with information which may be used by other merchants.

A bad credit report may cause a consumer to be unable to purchase a car, a house, or even a television on credit. Because credit reports are so easy to obtain and widely used, consumers should be aware of inaccuracies in their reports.

A number of states have enacted legislation attempting to regulate credit bureaus and protect consumers. However, because of the large size and scope of the operations of credit bureaus, federal regulation has preempted much of the law in this area. In 1970, Congress passed the Fair Credit Reporting Act, Title VI of the Consumer Credit Protection Act, 15 U.S.C. §§ 1681 et seq.

Section 609 of the Fair Credit Reporting Act allows consumers access to all information in a consumer's file, including the sources of the information and the identification of each person that obtained a consumer report. Additionally, the agency must also include a summary of the consumer's rights with the disclosure, including the right to dispute material in the report. If a consumer finds an inaccurate statement, section 611 details the procedures that a consumer reporting agency must take upon receiving notice of a dispute concerning a report. All inaccurate or incomplete information must be promptly deleted, and all incomplete information must be promptly deleted or corrected. If the dispute is left unresolved, the consumer may file a brief statement setting forth the nature of the dispute. The consumer's statement, or the agency's clear and accurate summary of the statement must then be presented in any subsequent consumer report containing the information in dispute. Furthermore, at the consumer's request, the reporting agency is required to give "notification" that an item has been deleted or that the statement or summary has been added "to any person designated by the consumer" who has received a consumer report within the past two years for employment purposes or within the past six months for any other purpose.

[¶ 10,105]

b. *Discrimination in credit*

Credit scoring is used by credit companies which handle a large volume of consumer debt and which screen a large volume of applicants. It is a statistical method of assessing credit risk that rates the likelihood that an individual will pay back the loan considering factors such as the consumer's past delinquencies, type of credit, and how often credit is applied for and number of inquiries.

Creditors use a statistical program to compare the information they receive from one applicant with the credit performance of other consumers with similar profiles. Thus, points are awarded for each factor that serves as an indication that the individual is likely to repay the debt. A total number of points helps creditors predict whether an individual is credit worthy.

Generally credit bureaus provide risk scores to their subscribers who then use the score to evaluate objectively an applicant's credit worthiness. Each lender uses the scores differently. The scores only become meaningful and useful within the context of a particular lender's own cutoff points and risk guidelines. The Equal Credit Opportunity Act insures that all applicants are treated equally. Credit scoring systems cannot consider characteristics such as race, sex, marital status, national origin or religion. § 701.

Regulation B issued by the Federal Reserve Board under the Equal Credit Opportunity Act applies to all extensions of credit, including commercial credit, and generally prohibits discrimination based on race, color, religion, national origin, sex, marital status, age, status as public assistance recipient, etc., and specifically prohibits a creditor from requiring the signature of the applicant's spouse except where necessary or reasonably believed to be necessary to make specific property available to satisfy the debt.

[¶ 10,110]

Problems and Questions

1. You are representing Anne in her divorce action against Henry. Anne has not been employed outside the home since she worked to put Henry through medical school. Henry has a very successful medical practice and your evaluation leads you to believe that Anne will be financially secure after the divorce.

When Anne applied for a new telephone in her own name, the phone company asked for her marital status on the application and then asked for a

$200 security deposit before providing her with a new phone number and listing in her own name. Anne is upset because Henry obtained a new telephone number and listing without providing a security deposit.

You discover that the phone company requires that all individuals make a security deposit unless they meet at least two of the following three requirements: (1) record of steady income, (2) own their home or have a lease of at least one year, and (3) have had a prior phone and made consistent payments on that account. Has the telephone company violated the Equal Credit Opportunity Act?

2. Borrower is 70 years old. Lender turns down Borrower's application for a 20-year 80% mortgage loan on a home that Borrower wants to purchase for a retirement home. If it can be shown that Lender would grant a 30-year 90% mortgage to an applicant 35 years of age with the same asset and income position as Borrower's, is there a violation of the Equal Credit Opportunity Act?

2. Regulation of Cost of Credit

[¶ 10,115]

a. *State usury laws*

The word "usury" has a long history going back at least to biblical times. Originally, prohibitions on usury were prohibitions on charging interest on loans—any interest. It was considered morally wrong—sinful—to charge interest.

Not only have we changed our attitudes about what is sinful, we have also changed the meaning of the word "usury." Today, usury laws prohibit charging excessive interest.

Whitworth & Yancey v. Adams, 26 Va. 333 (1827) provides the following reason for usury laws: "These statutes were made to protect needy and necessitous persons from the oppression of usurers and monied men who are eager to take advantage of the distress of others."

"Protection of needy and necessitous persons." The more that people use credit for convenience, lifestyle and stuff we just want, the harder it is to base a defense of usury laws on protection of borrowers who go into debt as a result of necessity. Admittedly, as any parent understands, the distinction between wants and needs can become a point of dispute. And the literature is rich with disputes over the moral, social and economic predicates of usury laws.

Nonetheless, every state has usury laws. Plural. Typically, these laws provide different maximum rates for different forms of consumer credit: e.g., a general rate with higher rates for small loans, lower rates for credit sale finance charges, etc.

[¶ 10,120]

(1) Which state's rates apply?

And these different rates differ from state to state. Therefore, when a transaction involves a contact with more than one state, conflict of laws questions may arise. Suppose, for example, that a buyer who resides in State Y (where the maximum rate of interest is 7%) finances the purchase of an automobile with a seller in State X (where the maximum rate of interest is 12%). Which state's interest rate applies? Can the seller charge 12% interest without violating any usury laws?

The general rule is the same as the rule under contract law, i.e., the rights and duties of the contracting parties are governed by the law of the state with the most significant relationship to the transaction and the parties. Restatement (Second) Contracts § 188. When addressing usury, specifically, the court should consider (1) the place of the contracting, (2) the place of any negotiations which occurred, (3) the place of performance, (4) the location of the subject matter and (5) the domicile or residence of the parties. Restatement (Second) Conflict of Laws § 203. In applying these factors, the courts generally look to the law of the state with the most significant relationship to the transaction that would uphold the agreement. In the above example, without more facts, the answer would most likely be "yes."

Some consumer credit contracts include a choice of law provision specifying by which state's laws the parties want the transaction to be governed. Again, the general rule is the same as the rule under contract law; the inclusion of such a clause does not always mean that the courts will apply the law of the state chosen by the parties.

Another important question of which state's rates apply depends on an interpretation of § 85 of the National Banking Act of 1863, rather than an application of contracts or conflicts rules. Under § 85, a national bank can charge the highest rate of interest allowed by the state in which it is located. In the 19th century, § 85 protected national banks from discrimination by state legislatures. In the late 20th century and now in the 21st century, § 85 results in state legislatures' discriminating against state banks and other local lenders.

Consider the problem that the United States Supreme Court addressed in Marquette National Bank v. First of Omaha Service Corp., 439 U.S. 299 (1978), involving the first nationwide credit card. In 1966 Bank of America created the first nationwide credit card, BankAmericard (later renamed Visa). BankAmericard's network of merchants that agreed to honor any BankAmericard card, wherever issued, enabled a bank in Omaha, Nebraska to make consumer loans to Minnesota residents by issuing cards to them.

A bank located in Minneapolis sought to enjoin First of Omaha Service Corporation and First National Bank of Omaha (Omaha Bank), a

Nebraska-chartered national bank, from making credit card loans to residents of Minnesota at interest rates that exceeded Minnesota's usury rates. Nebraska law permitted interest rates to be charged at a rate of 18% for the first $999.99, and 12% for any amount owed of $1000 or more. The Minnesota rate was a flat 12%. Both Marquette Bank and Omaha Bank were enrolled in the BankAmericard program that allowed purchases of goods and services at participating merchants wherever the merchants were located. The Minnesota trial court enjoined First of Omaha from using Nebraska rates in Minnesota, and First of Omaha appealed. The Minnesota Supreme Court reversed and the United States Supreme Court affirmed the Minnesota Supreme Court, stating: "Section 85 ... plainly provides that a national bank may charge interest 'on any loan' at the rate allowed by the laws of the State in which the bank is 'located.' The question before us is therefore narrowed to whether Omaha Bank and its BankAmericard program are 'located' in Nebraska and for that reason entitled to charge its Minnesota customers the rate of interest authorized by Nebraska law." The Court held that "Omaha Bank cannot be deprived of this location merely because it is extending credit to residents of a foreign State" and the Court explicitly rejected Marquette Bank's argument that Omaha Bank's marketing of its card to Minnesota residents should subject it to Minnesota usury laws. The Court stated, "Minnesota residents were always free to visit Nebraska and receive loans in that State. It has not been suggested that Minnesota usury laws would apply to such transactions."

After the *Marquette* decision, every bank, state and national, located in Minnesota was at a competitive disadvantage compared to Omaha Bank and every other national bank located in Nebraska. Minnesota amended its usury laws, and many other states amended their usury laws to allow banks in their state to compete effectively with out-of-state national banks.

Regardless of what type of rate regulation a state imposes, in order for a debtor, attorney or judge to determine if a transaction is usurious, she must be able to determine what charges are considered interest. Generally, any compensation, remuneration or other benefit exacted by the lender will be deemed interest unless the charge is to reimburse or compensate the seller for a specific expenditure or service other than extending credit.

Loan Origination and Closing Expenses. These are expenses generally charged by banks or mortgage companies to do an appraisal, obtain a credit report and record the mortgage. Absent a specific statute providing otherwise, most jurisdictions consider these to be reasonable expenses incurred by the lender in preparing a loan, and therefore are not interest. Loan origination fees, however, which are expressed as points (a point is one percent of the principal) are often considered interest in the usury test because the charge for points varies with the size of the principal.

Commitment Fees. These are charges paid to a lender in exchange for a promise to make a loan in the future. Courts disagree as to the treatment of these fees. Some courts consider a commitment fee to be interest because it is nothing more than an overhead cost or the lender's passing off the risk to the borrower that interest rates might go up, after the lender has committed to a fixed rate. Therefore, the commitment fee serves as a discount or the taking of interest in advance. Other courts decide whether a commitment fee is interest by determining whether the fee is a legitimate "reasonable" cost to the buyer. The determination of what is reasonable is answered by looking to customary and acceptable practices in the trade on a case by case basis.

Charges Payable by the Debtor on Default. These charges are generally foreclosure costs or other types of expenses incurred in the collection of the debt. Courts generally do not consider these charges to be interest.

Prepayment Penalties. According to common law, a lender is not obligated to accept prepayment of a loan prior to its maturity date. By paying the loan off early, the debtor is able to stop the running of interest and the lender loses money. Loan agreements often provide for prepayment penalties. Generally, these prepayment penalties are not considered as interest; instead, courts view prepayment penalties as consideration given in exchange for early termination of the loan.

[¶ 10,125]

(2) How is interest computed?

The method of computing interest varies from one state to another, and from one type of credit transaction to another. Most usury statutes are based on an "add-on" rate method.

Under the add-on method, interest is computed by using an I = PRT formula (Interest = Principal × Rate × Time) which figures interest on the full original term, disregarding the fact that repayments will be made in monthly installments. To illustrate, Creditor lends Borrower $100 for 1 year at 8%. At the end of the year Creditor will collect the entire principal of $100 plus $8.00 of interest.

Now, if Creditor required Borrower to pay in monthly installments, the computation is a little different. The same formula is used, but now the $8.00 is "added on" to the $100, making the amount owed $108 payable over 12 months or $9.00 per month.

Clearly, Creditor receives more by Borrower's paying in installments because now Creditor is charging interest on the principal already paid back in each month's installment. How much more is less clear without using software programs or tables similar to the following Federal Reserve Board table.

Conversion of Add-on Rate to Annual Percentage Rate

Add-on Rate	6 Months	12 Months	24 Months	36 Months	60 Months	120 Months
	Payment Schedule					
6%	10.21%	10.90%	11.13%	11.08%	10.85%	10.21%
8%	13.59%	14.45%	14.68%	14.55%	14.13%	13.12%
10%	16.949%	17.97%	18.16%	17.92%	17.27%	15.86%
12%	20.29%	21.46%	21.57%	21.20%	21.21%	18.49%

For example, assume that a borrower takes out a $100 loan with an stated annual interest rate of 6% which is to be repaid over a one-year term in 12 monthly installments. Under the add-on method, the amount of each monthly installment is calculated as $106 ÷ 12, or $8.83. This stream of monthly payments reflects an annual percentage rate of 10.9%, as shown in the table for a loan with a 6% add-on rate and a 12–month payment schedule.

Multi-year, variable interest loans raise additional problems in computing the interest rate for purposes of applying a usury statute. Variable rate loans are one way that lenders can make longer term loans in an inflationary economy. Lenders do this by tying interest rates to economic indicators.

In *Arneill Ranch v. Petit*, 134 Cal.Rptr. 456 (Cal. Ct. App. 1976), the creditor charged an interest rate of "7½ percent per annum, or at the prime rate plus 2 percent . . . whichever is greater." The maximum legal interest rate was 10%. Hence, the interest on the loan would exceed the maximum legal interest rate only if the prime rate exceeded 8%. The prime rate did eventually rise above 8%, causing the interest rate to be 10.08% for one period and 11.46% for another period. So the debtor sued, claiming the loan was usurious.

The California court held that a variable interest rate agreement, although it provides under certain conditions for interest charges in excess of 10%, does not violate the 10% usury rate if the parties contracted in good faith and without intent to avoid usury laws. The court stated that "[w]hen payment of full legal interest is subject to a contingency, so that the lender's profit is wholly or partially put in hazard, the interest so contingently payable need not be limited to the legal rate, providing the parties are contracting in good faith without the intent to avoid the statute against usury." The determinative question was whether the variable interest rate was used "as a colorable device to obtain greater profit than was permissible under (the usury) laws."

All states provide the debtor with some remedy for violations of usury statutes. Again, the states vary significantly as to the remedy, ranging from forfeiture of the excessive interest to avoidance of the entire loan.

[¶ 10,130]

Problems and Questions

1. Hawkins borrows $10,000 from Harnecker. The relevant usury rate is 10%. The loan agreement provides for 10% interest and also provides for 15% interest on all late payments. Hawkins defaults. Harnecker sues. Should Hawkins have a usury defense?

2. One statistical and historical study suggests that usury laws are a "primitive means of social insurance" meant to ensure "low interest rates" for those who suffer financial adversity. Glaeser & Scheinkman, Neither a Borrower Nor a Lender Be: An Economic Analysis of Interest Restrictions and Usury Laws, 41 J. Law & Econ. 1, 26 (1998). Do you agree?

[¶ 10,135]

b.   Credit life insurance

The sale of credit insurance and other add-ons can be extremely profitable for lenders and credit sellers. Lenders and retailers who are able to sell credit insurance to consumers receive significant compensation through retention of a part of the premiums. The credit insurance industry is often described as a place where there is "reverse competition" because the higher the price of the insurance, the higher the premium that is shared with the creditor who chooses the insurance.

Credit life insurance pays off the credit obligation in the event of the debtor's death. The most common type of credit life insurance is decreasing term, where the amount of the coverage declines as the loan balance is reduced over the life of the credit transaction.

The majority of the states allow the premium to be based on what is called "gross coverage." Gross coverage is written on the "total of payments" in a precomputed installment loan, where the total of payments includes both the principal and interest on the loan. If coverage can only be set to cover the principal on the loan, the term "net coverage" is used.

If gross coverage is permitted by law, there is an economic overcharge in most cases. If a debtor dies during the term of the loan, the creditor is entitled to be paid the unpaid balance on the principal and that portion of the interest that *has been earned*, but not paid. But in almost no case, where death occurs during the loan term, would the creditor be entitled to be paid the principal and *all* of the precomputed interest. Therefore, setting the initial credit insurance premium on the total principal and precomputed interest overinsures the creditor's interest. Recognizing that gross coverage overinsures the loan, some states allow only net coverage.

3.   Disclosure of Credit Terms and the Truth in Lending Act

"Truth in Lending Act," or "TILA," is the popular name for Title I of the Consumer Credit Protection Act of 1968, and is codified at 15 U.S.C. §§ 1601 et seq. TILA is essentially a disclosure statute. Congress empowered the Board of Governors of the Federal Reserve Board to prescribe regulations to carry out the purposes of TILA. The Federal Reserve Board published a comprehensive set of regulations commonly known as "Reg. Z."

For TILA to cover a consumer credit transaction, the transaction must be "primarily for personal, family, or household purposes." For example, if a consumer buys an automobile and occasionally uses it for business purposes, TILA still applies.

Precisely what must be disclosed depends on whether the consumer credit transaction is open-end or closed-end and whether it is a loan or credit sale. There are, however, some general requirements that apply to all TILA disclosures.

The disclosure of the cost of credit in dollars and cents, as well as a percentage, is probably the most important requirement in TILA. The finance charge is the cost of credit as a dollar amount, whereas the annual percentage rate ("APR") reflects that cost on an annual percentage basis. The basic definition of a "finance charge" is broad. A finance charge is: (1) the sum of all charges, (2) payable directly or indirectly by the consumer, (3) imposed directly or indirectly by the creditor, (4) as an incident to or a condition of the extension of credit. 15 U.S.C. § 1605(a).

The other item that is required to be disclosed more conspicuously than other terminology is the APR. The APR reflects the effective cost of credit when declining balances are taken into account. Its disclosure must be more conspicuous than any other required disclosure.

Most consumer credit transactions are multiple installment transactions. For example, suppose Bob and Dan both borrow $1,000 for one year. Both agree to pay a $100 finance charge. Bob is to repay the loan at the end of the year; Dan is to pay in 12 equal monthly installments. Using $R = I/PT$ to compute the annual percentage rate, the rate in the two transactions would be identical.

The comparison would be misleading in Dan's transaction, however. The formula fails to take into account the fact that Dan is paying installments over the 12 months of the loan and that each installment payment reduces the amount of credit. Dan, unlike Bob, does not have the use of the entire $1,000 for the entire year. After the first month, Dan only has the use of less than the full $1,000. After the second month, Dan only has the use of even less. Accordingly, the annual percentage rate disclosed to Dan should be higher than the annual percentage rate disclosed to Bob. Therefore, something more "sophisticated" than R = I/PT must be used to compute the true cost of the credit in transactions in which the debtor pays in installments. The Federal Reserve Board has created special tables in Reg. Z.

Enforcement of TILA is through a combination of administrative actions, criminal prosecution, and private litigation. For private litigation, consumers act as their own "private attorney general" seeking three types of damages: actual damages, statutory damages, and attorney's fees. A claim of actual damages, to which there is no cap, may be recovered for any violation assuming the plaintiff can show actual injury. In open-end transactions, statutory damages may be imposed for inadequate initial disclosure or periodic statements. In closed-end transactions, statutory damages may be awarded if the credit company fails to disclose the amount financed, the finance charge, the annual percentage rate, or the number of payments. Statutory damages are twice the amount of any finance charge involved in the transaction, with a $200 minimum and a $2,000 maximum.

[¶ 10,145]

Problems and Questions

1. Harry's Health Club (HHC) offers "lifetime memberships" for $500, payable all at once or in 25 monthly payments of $20. Not surprisingly, all of the club's members chose the monthly payment alternative and sign notes agreeing to make the 25 monthly payments. Should HHC provide a Truth in Lending disclosure? What if HHC tenders the notes to a finance company which buys the notes, after checking on the creditworthiness of the member/maker, at a discount of $100?

2. How should the disclosures for open-end credit differ from the disclosures for closed-end credit?

3. Have you ever received a Truth in Lending disclosure? If so, did you read any of it?

4. A recent law review article concludes, "To date, Truth in Lending has not lived up to its potential. The challenge for consumer advocates is to rhetorically recapture disclosure law from industry lobbyists. To do so, consumer advocates must recast the goal of disclosure law as aiming not merely to truthfully describe contracts, but as aiming to create practical contractual understanding on the part of vulnerable debtors. Anything less risks wasting the historically unique opportunity of credit disclosure law as yet another demobilizing illusion of debtor protection." Peterson, Truth, Understanding and High Cost Consumer Credit, 55 Fla. L. Rev. 807 (2003). Do you agree? What more can be done "to create practical contractual understanding on the part of vulnerable debtors"?

C. NOT PAYING DEBT

[¶ 10,200]

1. Credit Card Billing Problems and the Credit Billing Act

The Fair Credit Billing Act (FCBA), 15 U.S.C. §§ 1601 et seq., sets forth an orderly procedure for identifying and resolving disputes between a card-holder and a card issuer as to the amount due at any time. Basically, the FCBA billing error provisions (1) establish procedures for consumers to use in complaining about certain billing errors and (2) require creditors to provide explanations or corrections for the alleged errors. The FCBA allows consumers to dispute a creditor's statement of accounts in the consumer's name and to seek correction and resolution of the dispute in a timely and orderly manner.

Section 1637(b)(10) requires the issuer to disclose on its periodic billing statements the address to which the cardholder may send billing inquiries. Additionally, § 1637(b)(7) requires that at the time that the consumer opens the account and at semi-annual intervals thereafter, the credit issuer must furnish to the consumer a statement in the form prescribed in Reg. Z § 226.7(a)(9) explaining the consumer's rights and obligations under the FCBA.

This information is particularly important as the billing error provisions of the Act are triggered only by a communication from the consumer that meets the following six requirements of § 1666:

(1) the notice must be in writing;

(2) the notice must be received at the address indicated by the issuer;

(3) the notice must enable the creditor to identify the name and account number of the obligor;

(4) the notice must indicate the obligor's belief that the statement contains a billing error;

(5) the notice must set forth the amount of the billing error; and

(6) the notice must set forth the reasons for the obligor's belief that the statement contains a billing error.

After the creditor receives a proper claim of error, the creditor has thirty days to provide either a written acknowledgment of receipt or a written response. If the creditor issues a written acknowledgment of receipt, then it must provide a written response no later than 90 days after the receipt of the notice of a claim of error. 15 U.S.C. § 1666(a)(3)(A), (B).

Until the creditor provides a "response," there are a number of restrictions placed on the creditor. First, the creditor may not take any action to collect the disputed amount. Second, the creditor may not restrict or close the account solely because of the refusal to pay the amount in dispute. The creditor may, however, apply the disputed amount against the credit limit on the account. Third, the creditor cannot report to a third party that the disputed amount is delinquent. If a creditor fails to comply with these requirements, the creditor loses his right to collect the amount in dispute.

[¶ 10,205]

2. Informal Collection Efforts

When a debtor defaults in paying an obligation, the creditor will first remind the debtor of the obligation and attempt through extrajudicial "persuasion" to get the debtor to pay it "voluntarily." Typically, they will privately negotiate, compromise, and settle. Occasionally, the creditor or its agent becomes overzealous.

[¶ 10,210]

a. *Judicial constraints*

Courts have sought to moderate the conduct of creditors by allowing debtors to recover actual and punitive damages for abusive collection activities under the following common law tort concepts: defamation, invasion of right to privacy, and intentional infliction of mental anguish. Actual recoveries on these theories, however, are relatively rare. It is difficult to match the facts of debt collection with the elements of these torts.

[¶ 10,215]

b. *Fair Debt Collection Practices Act*

More important, a number of states statutorily regulate the collection of consumer debts. The Federal Trade Commission has published a proposed trade regulation rule relating to the collection of consumer debts. And, Congress has enacted the Fair Debt Collection Practices Act, FDCPA.

FDCPA does not apply to all consumer credit collection efforts. It governs the conduct of "debt collectors," i.e., persons who regularly collect debts owed to someone else, including lawyers. FDCPA does not apply to the lender or credit seller that is attempting to collect its own debts. It does apply to a creditor who "in the process of collecting his own debts, uses any name other than his own which would indicate that a third person is collecting or attempting to collect the debts." FDCPA § 803(6).

FDCPA severely limits "debt collector" contacts with third parties. A "debt collector" may contact a person other than a consumer, the consumer's spouse (or the consumer's parents if the consumer is a minor) and the consumer's attorney only for the purpose of finding the debtor. Section 804 sets out specific guidelines which a "debt collector" must follow when contacting third parties to learn a debtor's whereabouts. The "debt collector" may not volunteer that she is a "debt collector"; such information may be furnished only if "expressly requested." Even if expressly requested, a "debt collector" may not tell a third party that the debtor owes a debt.

Once the debtor has been located and contacted, the "debt collector" must give the debtor the opportunity to require verification of the debt. No later than five days after first communicating with the debtor, the "debt collector" must send the debtor a written notice setting out the amount of the debt, the name of the creditor, the debtor's right to dispute the accuracy or existence of the debt, and the debt collector's duty to obtain verification of the debt if it is disputed by the debtor within 30 days.

FDCPA does not expressly limit the number of times that a "debt collector" may contact a debtor in attempting to collect a debt. Section 805, however, governs such contacts. The contact must not be at a time or place "which should be known to be inconvenient." All "debt collector" contact with the debtor must cease when the debt collector learns that the debtor is represented by an attorney, receives a written refusal to pay, or receives a written communication from the debtor requesting that such contacts end.

In addition to the above rules limiting contacts by "debt collectors," FDCPA also generally forbids any conduct by "debt collectors" which is abusive, deceptive, misleading, or unfair. Sections 806 through 808 contain "laundry lists" of illustrative practices which are specifically forbidden.

A "debt collector" who violates the FDCPA is civilly liable for damages. A violation of FDCPA is also considered an unfair or deceptive act or practice, in violation of § 814 of the Federal Trade Commission Act. The Federal Trade Commission may thus seek a variety of remedies against a "debt collector" that violates the FDCPA.

[¶ 10,220]

c. *"The Gong Show"*

Here is an example of how other countries deal with individual debt and debt collectors.

Chinese Deadbeats Cringe at the Sound of Mr. Li's Gong; He Appears at Their Doors, Shouting "Pay Your Debts"; Shame Is Better Than Law

Wall Street Journal (Sept. 21, 2000)

Armed with a large bronze gong and clad in a cherry-red vest emblazoned with the words "Debt Collector," Li Qiuzhong steps into a dimly lit beverage store and bellows, "I'm here to collect your debts!"

Inside is Li Lanying, the heavyset owner of the concrete building, which also serves as her home. Ms. Li (no relation to Mr. Li) peeks out the front door to see if her neighbors are watching, then beckons the debt collector to her private quarters in back. "OK, OK," she mumbles. "Please come inside."

Ms. Li is one of China's growing legion of debtors. She has built her business on credit but freely acknowledges that she often ducks paying her bills—in this case, a $1,900 tab for a batch of Chinese liquor she sold nearly five years ago. Now, confronted with Mr. Li's gong and foghorn voice, she pleads for a few minutes' time to look up the exact amount.

Across China, a flawed legal system has left individuals and companies caught in a rising tide of debt, leaving almost everyone owing something to someone. Although the government doesn't publish personal-debt statistics, the crunch has clearly created a financial logjam that could, if left unchecked, derail Beijing's efforts to give the private sector a larger role in the economy. China lacks the usual mechanisms for dunning deadbeats. It has no small-claims courts, for starters. And though individuals can file civil claims at about 2,000 local courts, there's no limit on the size of these claims. The upshot: Cases can drag on for years, with the outcome sometimes dependent on good relations with judges, according to lawyers and former court officials. Even when a ruling is issued, the government doesn't do much to enforce it.

Enter Mr. Li, a straight-talking, 62–year–old former railway worker who bills himself "China's No. 1 Debt Collector." His cacophonous street theater can shame even the most brazen borrowers into paying up.

"My method isn't just effective: It's extremely effective," says the sprightly Mr. Li, who boasts an 80% success rate for the more than 1,000 debt-collection cases he has handled since he first donned his now-famous red vest three years ago. "The Chinese don't like to lose face," he says. "But if they don't pay their bills, that's exactly what I do to them."

Not long ago, all of this would have been unthinkable. But the last three years have seen an explosion of private debt collectors in China's biggest cities. These small operators work without explicit government approval, making it impossible to gauge how big a dent they are making in the mountain of debt. Yet the demand for such unofficial bailiffs is strong, says Charles Qin, a senior partner with Llinks Law Firm in Shanghai. And it all began with Mr. Li.

Fear of public humiliation has always been strong in China, where some criminals are still paraded through town in trucks. It took Mr. Li to realize the power of shame in debt collection.

The epiphany struck three years ago, when his son came to him with a problem: A family acquaintance had borrowed nearly $2,000 but refused to pay it back. Newly retired, Mr. Li took on the project himself. But when he politely requested payment, he too was rebuffed.

Incensed, Mr. Li decided to fight back. First, he bought his 2–foot–wide gong. Then he had a seamstress make his red vest and stitch across the front the Chinese characters tao zhai—literally, "chasing debt."

Armed for embarrassment, he confronted the borrower at a department store where she worked—and threatened to stay put until she paid up. Within minutes, the borrower capitulated, Mr. Li says.

"I could tell she had money from the rings and clothes she wore," he recalls. "She just didn't want to pay it."

That encounter gave birth to Wanbang Debt Collection Co., China's best-known private collection agency. In his home city of Zibo in northeastern Shandong province, Mr. Li soon became a celebrity. Even the city's vice mayor has passed business to him, he says, though the city government declines to comment on the matter. Nationally, he has inspired nearly a dozen copycat debt collectors, who have offered to pay him $600 a year to name their companies after him.

Mr. Li's advertising technique is as direct as his collection method: Cruising around town on a red motorcycle with a red "Debt Collector" flag attached to his rearview mirror, he stops randomly to solicit new customers. On a recent afternoon, Mr. Li leaps off his motorcycle near the Zibo train station and starts handing out his name card, a flimsy piece of photocopied paper. Within minutes, he is surrounded by more than 100 people and his supply is exhausted. "The market is unlimited," Mr. Li says, breaking away from the mushrooming crowd.

Back in his office—a three-room apartment that doubles as his home—Mr. Li sifts through a metal basket filled with more than 100 handwritten requests for his services, some from as far away as Tibet. "I never imagined that so many other people have the same problem that my son had," Mr. Li says.

The job has some drawbacks. With business booming, Mr. Li hasn't taken a vacation in three years. His typical workday stretches from 5 a.m. to midnight. He worries, too, that what he does is technically illegal. China officially banned debt collectors in the mid–1990s, after some agencies linked to organized crime sprang up. Mr. Li says the government tolerates his business because it knows he is filling a void and because he doesn't resort to blackmail or violence.

Local officials in the Zibo city government decline to comment on Mr. Li's business. But just to be on the safe side, Mr. Li follows a few common-sense ground rules. He rarely collects debts owed by state enterprises, and he won't touch cases that are pending before China's courts, for fear of angering officialdom. To ward off any talk of favoritism, he never deviates from his standard collection fee, regardless of the customer: 10% for debts one year old, 20% for two years, 30% for three years, 40% for four years and 50% for five years or more.

He also has avoided going out at night ever since one late-night foray last year ended when he was detained by angry villagers. Police intervened, getting Mr. Li released after a couple of hours.

One recent evening, Mr. Li sat at the dining-room table that serves as his desk. Across from him was Cao Hengbo, a 33–year–old manager of a private Chinese liquor maker that enlisted the debt collector's help to extract the $1,900 payment from Ms. Li, the store owner.

Mr. Cao and his colleagues had been chasing Ms. Li for years. Once, Mr. Cao says, they hired local thugs to bully her into paying, but friends of Ms. Li scared off the toughs. The courts were never an option, he says. "It would cost us more in dinners, gifts and money than the debt we're owed, and even then it would be hard to enforce the ruling," he says.

At dawn the next day, they were off to Ms. Li's store in remote Changyi. Though she eventually agreed to pay up, she said she needed to confer first with her husband, who was away on a business trip. Mr. Li agreed to give her a few days, but reminded her on the way out that he would soon be back.

"It's psychological warfare," Mr. Li said a little later as he slid into the back of a taxi. "And I know that if she doesn't pay tomorrow, then she'll pay the next day or the next after that, because she doesn't want to be embarrassed."

Three weeks later, Mr. Li returned to Changyi and collected the debt in full.

[¶ 10,225]

3. Judicial Collection of Unsecured Debts

If out-of-court collection efforts are unsuccessful, the creditor will resort to the remedies provided by law or contract whereby property of the debtor is seized and applied in satisfaction of the obligation. Some of these remedies are creatures of the common law; others are statutory animals. Most are hybrids. Almost all of them, regardless of their source in law, are parented by the states, not by the federal government.

To a large extent, the states agree on the kinds and general nature of remedies available to creditors; but they disagree widely on the particulars of the remedies. So creditors' remedies, in name and broad substance, are much the same in every state. Yet, the details, especially procedural details, of creditors' remedies differ significantly among the states.

This chapter focuses not on these differences, but on the general design of the creditors' remedies that are common throughout the country and also on some of the most significant issues associated with these remedies. Just remember to study local law carefully, and pay close attention to all the unique detail, when working in the real world on a debtor-creditor case.

At the broadest level, the law of non-bankruptcy creditors' remedies involves only two issues:

1. when and how a creditor gets rights (usually, a lien) in the property of the debtor; and

2. the lien priority in relation to third parties' rights to the property, including other creditors' liens and other claims and the claims of transferees.

These two issues are common and most important to every kind of non-bankruptcy creditors' remedy.

The most general rule of the law of creditors' remedies is that a creditor cannot hold, take, apply, or otherwise in any sense grab any property of the debtor unless and until the creditor gets some kind of legal or equitable claim to the property itself. Debt alone creates personal obligation, not necessarily any property claim.

Typically, the claim to property that a creditor gets and enforces against the debtor and other persons is a lien, which is a property interest that gives the creditor defined rights to the property against the debtor and other persons.

Generally, a creditor does not acquire a lien on the debtor's property, i.e., the creditor cannot seize property of the debtor in satisfaction of the obligation, until the creditor reduces her claim to judgment and then enforces the judgment through a process called execution.

A judgment is, first, a debt: a new, substituted form of the obligation that the debtor owes the creditor. The tort, contract, or other claim that powered the lawsuit is gone. In place of this claim is the judgment that is itself a form of debt.

A judgment is, second, the state's recognition of the legitimacy of the creditor's claim against the debtor. Along with this recognition comes willingness by the state to use its coercive power to collect the judgment debt forcibly from the debtor's property (both real and personal) if the judgment is not voluntarily paid.

To begin with, the judgment or some formalization of the judgment gives the creditor a lien on the debtor's interests in real property.

Next, the judgment supports the process of execution whereby the state, at the creditor's request, levies on the debtor's property—both real and personal—and applies the property in satisfaction of the judgment. The actual process or mechanics of execution involve a sheriff or other state or local government official, often with gun at side, actually or constructively impounding and later selling as much of the debtor's property as is necessary to satisfy the judgment.

Execution and the remedies in aid of it are available to satisfy almost any money judgment, and every creditor has access to the courts and thus can get a judgment. So execution is a remedy or right that is available to creditors generally, without regard to the basis of the debtor's obligation and without the need for the debtor's consent. In this sense, execution is the law's standard, general creditors' remedy.

To reach property of a debtor held by third persons, and to collect debts owed to the creditor, there is a special judicial proceeding in the nature of an adversary suit against the person who holds the debtor's property or owes it money: garnishment. Garnishment is in essence a special form of execution—designed for reaching property of the debtor held by a third party. For example, when a creditor wishes to levy or execute upon a bank account, it seeks to obtain property of the debtor held by a third person. In this context, the proper nomenclature regarding what occurs when, for example, the Internal Revenue Service tries to go against a bank account of delinquent taxpayer, is that the Service is garnishing the bank account.

Most lawyers do not like to do judicial collecting; most creditors do not like to pay for this kind of legal work. Obtaining a judgment and getting a sheriff to seize and sell property of a debtor (read "voter", read "neighbor" . . .) can be difficult, time consuming, expensive, stressful—and often unsuccessful.

From a creditor's viewpoint, judicial debt collection is not a preferred method of debt collection because of the time and money involved in pursuing it. There is no guarantee that the debtor will have assets with which to satisfy a judgment if and when one is obtained. Even if the debtor's estate is not depleted when a creditor finally gets a judgment, the property by that time may have been subjected to other creditors' liens having priority.

[¶ 10,230]

Problems and Questions

1. If Mr Li opened a branch office in San Francisco, would he be subject to the Fair Debt Collection Practices Act? Would he be in violation of the Fair Debt Collection Practices Act if he used the same collection practices in the United States that he used in China?

2. Jane owes Kate $10,000. Kate has obtained a judgment against Jane. Through the discovery process, Kate has learned that Jane's assets include a painting valued at $15,000, a bank account with a $15,000 balance, and three racing greyhounds valued at $15,000. How should Kate attempt to collect her judgment? What if any additional information do you need?

3. Why do most law school courses on "creditors rights" spend little, if any, time on judicial collection law and most, if not all, of the time on bankruptcy?

[¶ 10,235]

4. Collection of Secured Debt

Generally, those other creditors' liens will be consensual liens. Consensual liens form the largest exception to the rule that execution is the law's standard creditors' remedy. Indeed, this exception practically swallows the rule in the sense that sizable credit is rarely extended by a seller or lender without the security of a consensual lien.

Liens of judgment, execution, attachment and the like arise solely by force of law in connection with judicial proceedings against the debtor without the debtor's consent. A consensual lien arises from an agreement between creditor and debtor providing that, upon the debtor's default, whatever property the parties have identified in their agreement can be applied to satisfy whatever obligations the parties have described in their agreement.

A consensual lien can be created in real estate or personalty of any kind, including goods and intangibles. When the creditor is a lender of money, or a supplier of property or services on credit, the lien is usually created at the inception of the debtor-creditor relationship. Yet, a consensual lien can be created at any time during such a relationship. Moreover, a debtor can create a consensual lien in favor of any kind of creditor, not just a lender or seller, to secure any kind of fresh or preexisting obligation, not just a loan or an extension of purchase-money credit.

There are various devices for creating consensual liens on real property, including the mortgage, the deed of trust, and the land-sale contract. The differences in these various devices and in the laws of the various states largely concern (a) the mechanics of applying the collateral in satisfaction of the secured obligation, and (b) the procedures for safeguarding the debtor's rights and interests.

When the creditor and debtor set about to create a consensual lien on personal property, the governing law in almost every case is Uniform Commercial Code Article 9. Every state other than Louisiana has adopted Uniform Commercial Code Article 9. Article 9 provides only one device for creating consensual liens in personal property: the Article 9 security interest. "Security interest" is Article 9's name for lien. A "secured party" is a creditor in whose favor a security interest exists. The obligation owed to the secured party is the secured debt.

The basic rights of a secured party (i.e., a creditor who has an Article 9 security interest, that is, a consensual lien on personal property or fixtures of the debtor) are the rights upon the debtor's default (1) to repossess (i.e., to seize) the collateral (the property subject to the lien), (2) to dispose of it (usually by sale), and (3) to apply the proceeds in satisfaction of the secured debt. The secured party need not file a lawsuit, get the sheriff involved, or otherwise invoke state action. The secured party can grab the collateral herself, without giving the debtor notice or an opportunity for a hearing, and dispose of the collateral herself through a sale she arranges and conducts. It's called self-help repossession, and the only two limitations are that (1) the debtor must be in default and (2) the secured party can't breach the peace.

Default is a term which the debtor and the secured party themselves define in their agreement creating the security interest. Typically the definition is dictated by the secured party—typically "default" is defined to cover far more than just nonpayment. The following excerpt from a security agreement is illustrative:

The occurrence of any of the following shall, at the option of Secured Party, be an Event of Default:

1. Debtor's failure to make any payments required by the Loan Agreement or perform any of the other obligations under the Loan Agreement;

2. Debtor's failure to comply with any of the provisions of, or the incorrectness of any representation or warranty contained in, this Security Agreement, the Note, or in any of the other Obligations;

3. Transfer or disposition of any of the Collateral, except as expressly permitted by this Security Agreement;

4. Attachment, execution or levy on any of the Collateral;

5. Debtor voluntarily or involuntarily becoming subject to any proceeding under (a) the Bankruptcy Code or (b) any similar remedy under state statutory or common law.

A secured party determines if and when a default occurs based on its interpretation of the agreement and circumstances. A disgruntled debtor can later ask a court to review the secured party's determination of default but a secured party does not need prior judicial approval before deciding that a default has occurred and taking the debtor's property that is collateral.

A secured party does need to avoid a "breach of the peace" in taking the property. "Breach of the peace" is not defined by the UCC but has been explained by numerous reported cases. Breach of the peace means not only conduct that actually breaches the peace, but also conduct that threatens breaching the peace even though the peace is not actually breached. It clearly means that the secured party cannot break and enter into the debtor's premises, but—within limits—quietly entering the debtor's open space is okay. It is frequently said the peace is breached if the debtor is present and objects to the repossession.

After repossession the secured party can always sell or otherwise dispose of the property upon reasonable, prior notice to the debtor and apply the proceeds as far as they'll go in satisfaction of the secured debt. The UCC requires that all aspects of the sale must be "commercially reasonable." The UCC does not define the phrase "commercially reasonable" but does establish safe harbors and guidelines.

If the sale produces more than necessary to satisfy the expenses and obligations, the surplus is paid to the debtor. If a commercially reasonable sale produces less than is necessary to satisfy the obligations secured by the collateral, the debtor is liable for the deficiency. To satisfy the deficiency the secured party either grabs other property subject to an existing lien or sues the debtor in court for the deficiency. The debtor commonly counterclaims for damages based on an allegation that the repossession resulted in a breach of the peace or that some aspect of the disposition was not commercially reasonable.

Sometimes, the secured party keeps the property in complete or partial satisfaction of the secured debt. It's called strict foreclosure and requires an acceptance or acquiescence by the debtor.

Complete satisfaction means that the secured party herself keeps the collateral in full satisfaction of the secured debt. Therefore, regardless of the value of the collateral, even if the value is less than the secured debt, the debtor is no longer liable for the secured debt. The secured party keeping the collateral herself totally wipes out the secured debt. In commercial transactions, but not in consumer transactions, partial satisfaction is possible, too, which means that the parties can agree that the secured party herself will keep the collateral with some or partial credit against the secured debt and with the debtor remaining liable for the balance.

Example 1. Chris loaned Dana $3,000 in a consumer transaction. The loan is secured by a security interest in Dana's Norwich Terrier, Winky. Dana defaults, having paid almost nothing on the secured debt. Chris takes Winky from Dana's front yard. Winky is worth only $2,000 but is very cute. Chris decides she wants Winky herself. So, Chris sends Dana a proposal that Chris will accept the collateral in full satisfaction of the secured debt. Within 20 days after sending the proposal Chris has not received from Dana an objection to Chris's proposal. The secured debt is satisfied. Dana's liability is ended for this debt.

Example 2. Same facts as Example 1, except that secured party Chris wants to keep Winky with only a $2,000 credit against the secured debt. She cannot do it.

In theory, consensual liens encourage lending and other extensions of credit, and also reduce the price of credit, partly because they significantly reduce the costs and time involved in forcibly satisfying obligations that debtors are unwilling to pay voluntarily. In practice, consensual liens encourage credit largely because the rights that accompany the liens give creditors considerable leverage in persuading debtors to pay up "voluntarily."

[¶ 10,240]

Problems and Questions

1. Mike owes Judy $15,000. Judy has a security interest in Mike's car. Mike is in default. From Mike's perspective what are the advantages and disadvantages to objecting to Judy's repossessing the car?

2. Kate owes Sam $200,000. Sam has a security interest in Kate's boat. Kate defaults. Sam repossesses and resells the boat. The boat sells for $80,000. Sam incurs costs of $5,000 in repossessing and reselling. What are Sam's further collection rights, if any?

3. Should the answer to Problem 2 be different if the collateral is Kate's house, instead of her boat?

[¶ 10,245]

5. Meaning and Importance of Exemptions Under Nonbankruptcy Law and in Bankruptcy

The common law subjects all of a debtor's property to the payment of her debts. By constitution or statute, however, all states immunize some of a debtor's personal property and, to a limited extent, the interest in her home from certain claims of creditors.

A state constitutional or statutory provision that so protects a debtor's property is known as an exemption law. Property covered by such a law is said to be exempt. Unsecured creditors cannot reach exempt property through judicial collection efforts. Exempt property is generally not exempt from the liens and other remedies of secured creditors.

Exemption laws normally apply only in favor of debtors who are natural persons, and typically protect only property used for personal rather than business purposes. They were originally intended to protect the tax base: debtors could not produce taxable wealth if they were left destitute. Today, exemption laws serve multiple purposes, including:

- providing the debtor with property necessary for his physical survival;

- protecting the dignity and the cultural identity of the debtor;

- enabling the debtor to rehabilitate himself financially and earn income in the future;

- protecting the debtor's family from the adverse consequences of impoverishment;

- shifting the burden of providing the debtor and his family with minimal support from society to the debtors' creditors.

Bankruptcy law has long provided exemptions for individual debtors because the reasons for exemptions are most compelling when a debtor is in bankruptcy. In bankruptcy, *all* of a debtor's creditors will collectively and simultaneously reach for her property to satisfy their claims. The value of the bankruptcy estate almost never equals her debts. The debtor would thus lose everything, literally everything, without the protective exemptions. Also, a pre-eminent goal of bankruptcy law is to provide the debtor with a financial fresh start, and this new beginning is most meaningful if the debtor is permitted to keep some of her old assets.

Under the Bankruptcy Code, a debtor in bankruptcy can exempt property that was exempt under local law and nonbankruptcy federal law. Bankruptcy law simply imports these exemptions.

The Bankruptcy Code also gives the debtor the option of exempting, alternatively, the property described in § 522(d). The property listed there is exempted solely as matter of federal bankruptcy law but *only if* the debtor elects the § 522(d) exemptions and forgoes nonbankruptcy exemptions otherwise available to her. In theory, therefore, the debtor can freely choose between these two sources of law (en masse)—either § 522(d) *or* state and nonbankruptcy federal law—for her exemptions. She will naturally choose the source that protects more of her property.

There is a kicker. The debtor is denied the choice if her state has legislated that local debtors cannot assert the bankruptcy law exemptions of § 522(d). In this event, which is commonly described as the state having "opted out," the debtor is stuck with the nonbankruptcy exemptions available to her under state law and nonbankruptcy federal law. She cannot choose the § 522(d) exemptions.

Most states have opted out. So, outside of bankruptcy and in most bankruptcy cases, the source of the debtor's exemptions is nonbankruptcy law, mainly state statutes.

Federal nonbankruptcy law similarly shields certain property from certain claims of creditors. Most of the federal provisions relate to payments under federal social programs such as Social Security benefits and veterans' benefits.

Additionally, the Employee Retirement Income Security Act of 1974 (ERISA) requires that private retirement plans include a provision prohibiting alienation of plan benefits. These anti-alienation provisions protect plan assets from the claims of creditors (other than certain governmental claims and claims for alimony or child support).

Individual retirement accounts (IRAs) as well as "simplified employee pension plans" (SEPs) are exempt from ERISA coverage. This means that there is no federal anti-alienation protection for these types of plans, and no federal protection from creditors (other than a § 522(d) exemption, where state law does not preclude the use of federal bankruptcy law exemptions). Instead, to the extent that there will be any protection from creditors, the protection will have to come from state law. Some, but by no means all, state exemption statutes provide various levels of protection from creditors for IRAs and SEPs.

There are two notable characteristics of state exemption statutes: (1) obsolescence, and (2) extreme variety. Nevertheless, certain generalizations are possible. All states exempt certain personal property from creditor process. In some jurisdictions, the exempt property is identified by type (e.g., the family Bible, the family rifle); in others, by value (e.g., personal property of a value of $5,000); in still others, by both type and value (e.g., an automobile with a value of not more than $2,000).

The procedure for asserting rights under an exemption statute also varies from state to state. The burden usually is on the debtor to claim the exemption, and usually the statute sets a time limit on assertion of an exemption. Where the statute is of a "value" type (e.g., personal property of a value of $5,000), the statute generally provides for the appointment of appraisers who value property selected as exempt by the debtor. Where the statute specifies items of property that are exempt, courts are often confronted with the problem of applying a 19th century statute to 21st century "property" e.g., whether a television set is a "musical instrument" or whether an automobile is a salesman's "tool of trade."

[¶ 10,250]

a. *Life insurance*

Interests in, or rights under, life insurance policies are everywhere protected to some degree from creditors' process, but the states widely disagree on the extent and effect of life insurance exemptions. Differences exist with regard to (1) the classes of persons who can claim the exemption, (2) the classes of creditors against whom the exemption is effective, and (3) the nature and amount of the interests and rights that are shielded from process. The basic issues that arise in connection with life insurance exemptions are more easily understood by dealing separately with matured and unmatured policies.

A life insurance policy matures when the insured dies. At that time, quite naturally, the insured loses interest in the availability of an exemption for the proceeds of the policy. The beneficiary's interest increases dramatically. Before the policy matured, the beneficiary's rights under the policy amounted to little more than an expectancy, nothing she could count on and thus nothing of much value to anyone. Now she has a certain and definite right to the proceeds of the policy. More than one set of creditors may try to take the proceeds from her.

The easiest case to consider in reviewing the scope of life insurance exemption laws is that of a person who, as a named beneficiary, is paid the proceeds of a policy covering the life of a deceased relative such as a spouse or parent. The beneficiary must defend the proceeds not only against the claims of her own creditors, but also from the claims of the insured's creditors. The insured's creditors will argue that their debtor's money was used to pay the premiums on the insurance policy and that, therefore, they can in effect trace the contributions and the proceeds of the policy into the hands of the beneficiary. This argument usually fails because most states explicitly exempt proceeds of life insurance paid to a beneficiary from the claims of the insured's creditors.

Modern exemption laws, either by their express terms or as construed by the courts, also shield life insurance proceeds from the claims of the beneficiary's own creditors.

Whether or not insurance proceeds paid to an insured's estate are exempt from claims of her creditors depends upon the wording of the applicable exemption laws. Ordinarily, the insured's creditors can reach such proceeds unless an exemption law specifically shields the property from them. Because few states have exemption laws shielding insurance proceeds paid to an insured's estate, the creditors of an insured can reach such proceeds in most states.

If a debtor owns an unmatured insurance policy on her own life, the policy can have present value that her creditors may want to seize and apply to their claims. For example, the policy may have a cash surrender value. This means that the insured can demand of the insurer a sum of money, up to to the policy's cash surrender value, which can take the form of either a loan secured by the policy and its proceeds or a liquidating payment upon surrender of the policy and termination of coverage. If the insured borrows against the cash surrender of the policy and then dies while the policy is still in force (and before the loan is repaid), the insurer is entitled to collect the outstanding amount of the loan before paying the remaining proceeds to the beneficiary.

Unsecured creditors of a debtor-policyowner whose life is insured by a policy having a present cash surrender or loan value may view that feature of the policy as a leviable asset. In many states, however, on one theory or another, the cash surrender value of an insurance policy is exempt from unsecured creditors' claims. The exemption results not only under statutes explicitly protecting an insured's interest in a life insurance policy, but also under laws protecting a beneficiary's claim, however contingent, to the proceeds of such a policy.

A principal reason for exempting the cash surrender value of such a life policy is that, if the insured's creditors could force the debtor to cash in the policy, the beneficiary—who is usually a close relative and often a dependent—would be left unprotected if the insured died before reinstating the policy's coverage. Creditors have been unable to overcome the exemption even in cases where the insured debtor-policyowner retained the right willy nilly to change the beneficiary or surrender the policy for its present cash value. An interesting question, on which there is surprisingly little law, is whether the exemption that prevents creditors from forcing an insured to cash in a life policy also prevents them from seizing the money that an insured debtor-policyowner receives upon voluntarily cashing in the policy for some purpose other than paying her creditors. Probably not. The reason for preventing a forced surrender does not apply in the case of a surrender freely effected. Moreover, the usual rule applicable to exemptions generally is that proceeds of exempt property are not themselves exempt.

An increasingly important problem is whether a product marketed as, or labeled in form, a life insurance policy is, in substance, a life insurance policy within the meaning of exemption laws. A debtor's savings account, a certificate of deposit belonging to her, or her portfolio of stocks, per se, is usually not exempt from the claims of creditors. In most states, however, a policy of insurance covering her life is exempt in and of itself. Does this insurance exemption apply if the policy also serves as an investment vehicle for the insured? The answer is usually "yes" if the investment feature is merely a cash surrender value. If the investment features are more extensive, however, substance will control over form in determining the applicability of insurance exemptions.

[¶ 10,255]

b. Homestead

Almost all states also have homestead laws designed to protect the family home from the reach of certain classes of creditors. The amount of property protected by such homestead laws varies significantly from one state to another, with the Florida and Texas statutes providing the most generous protection to debtors.

Homestead laws protect only real property interests of the debtor and so are of no aid to renters. Moreover, not all real property interests of the debtor may be the subject of a homestead claim. Common statutory limitations include the requirements that the debtor have a family, that the property be occupied and used as a residence (an almost universal limitation), that the owner have a specified (usually present, possessory) interest in the property, and (in a few states) that there be a formal declaration that the property is a homestead.

[¶ 10,260]

c. Exceptions from exemptions

The protection afforded by an exemption statute is not absolute. The federal tax lien reaches and may be satisfied from "exempt property." A number of states make similar exceptions for state taxes, claims for alimony and child support, and materialmen's and mechanics' liens.

More important, by statute in most states and case law in others, mortgages and security interests are generally not affected by an exemption statute. Thus, the bank that finances the purchase of a home or car will be able to seize and sell the property notwithstanding the fact that the property is covered by an exemption statute. Or, if Debbie gives Chip a second lien on her car to secure a Chanukah loan, Chip can, on Debbie's default, foreclose on Debbie's car.

In other words, the property itself is not exempt, but only the debtor's interest or equity in that property.

[¶ 10,265]

d. Applying value limitations on exemptions

Recall that personal property exemptions and homestead exemptions commonly carry value limitations. For example, "one motor vehicle to the extent of a value not exceeding $2,000."

In applying this or any other exemption, whether it covers personal or real property, remember that the property itself is not exempt. Rather, the subject of the exemption is the debtor's interest in the property. Creditors can only reach their debtor's interest when they grab property in satisfaction of their claims; and exemption laws thus protect only the debtor's interest in property.

Thus, value limitations on exemptions apply to the debtor's interest in property, not to the property itself. The debtor's interest is measured by her equity in the property. Her equity is determined by subtracting from the worth of the property itself, determined by its fair market value free and clear of all claims, the amount of liens and security interests that encumber it and are superior in rank to the lien (actual or potential) of the creditor attempting to execute on the property.

For example, suppose that Diane owns an automobile worth about $5,500. Bank has a perfected security interest in the vehicle to secure a $3,500 loan. An unsecured creditor, Carla, wins a $2,000 judgment against Diane and is set to enforce the judgment through execution, levy and sale.

If state law permits Diane to exempt a motor vehicle to the extent of $2,000 in value, this law actually means that $2,000 of Diane's equity in the property is exempt. Carla cannot touch the car if there is no excess equity, that is, no equity exceeding $2,000.

Diane's equity in this case is exactly $2,000, which is computed as follows: $5,500 (vehicle's value free of liens and encumbrances) minus $3,500 Bank security interest (which is superior to Carla's claim) = $2,000. This amount is fully protected by the $2,000 exemption statute, so Carla cannot touch the car. There is no free value to apply against her claim. The larger part of the value, $3,500, is claimed by the Bank, a superior encumbrancer (the holder of the perfected security interest). The balance which the debtor owns is protected from Carla's reach by the exemption law.

When the debtor's equity in exempt property exceeds the value limitation of the exemption law, the consequence is not to deprive the debtor of the exemption altogether. Rather, the property is seized and sold under creditors' process, the debtor gets so much of the equity that is exempted, and the creditor gets the balance of the equity actually produced by the sale.

[¶ 10,270]

Problems and Questions

1. State law allows an individual to exempt one motor vehicle to the extent of a value not exceeding $3,000. Debtor Don owns a 1973 Cadillac that he claims is worth only $2,500. Cleo has a judgment against Don for $10,000. Is the Cadillac subject to execution to enforce Cleo's $10,000 judgment?

2. Same facts as Problem 1, except that Cleo has a security interest in the car. Can Don prevent Cleo from repossessing the Cadillac by asserting that it is exempt?

3. Denise owns a home with a market value of $450,000. Denise owes Mark $200,000, and Mark has a mortgage on Denise's home. Denise owes other various other creditors a total of $300,000. Denise is in default on all of

her debts. If the homestead statute in Denise's state provides for a homestead of a value not exceeding $40,000 what are Mark's collection rights? What are the collection rights of Denise's other creditors?

4. Why do states such as Florida and Texas have virtually unlimited homestead exemptions? Why should the amount of property that a debtor can claim as exempt differ significantly from state to state?

D. AVOIDING COLLECTION OF DEBT

[¶ 10,300]

1. Fraudulent Transfers

Rather than see their property seized by creditors, debtors sometimes transfer their property to friends or relatives for no or little consideration or with the understanding that after the transfer the debtor can continue to use and benefit from the property. Assume for example that Debtor owes Creditor $100,000. Debtor owns Greenacre which is worth $100,000. Debtor gives Greenacre to Third Party with the understanding that Third Party will later return Greenacre. Or, Debtor owes Creditor $100,000. Debtor sells Greenacre to Third Party for $1 with the understanding that Debtor can continue to use Greenacre as if she owned it. Without knowing anything about fraudulent transfer law, you know that Debtor probably cannot get away with either of these transactions.

And, without knowing anything about fraudulent transfer law, you know that it is probably not a good thing for a transaction to be regarded as a "fraudulent transfer." You just need to know three more things about fraudulent transfer law:

(1) what is fraudulent transfer law;

(2) what transfers are fraudulent transfers;

(3) what are the practical consequences of the determination that a transaction is a fraudulent transfer under fraudulent transfer law.

[¶ 10,305]

a. *What is fraudulent transfer law?*

The purpose of fraudulent transfer law is to protect creditors from a debtor's transfers of property that unfairly reduce that debtors' assets—assets to which creditors may have to look for repayment. As the United States Court of Appeals for the Third Circuit explained, "Such transactions operated as a fraud against the debtor's creditors because the debtor's estate was depleted without exchanging property of similar value from which creditors' claims could be satisfied." Mellon Bank v. Metro Communications, Inc., 945 F.2d 635, 645 (3d Cir. 1991).

[¶ 10,310]

(1) Statute of Elizabeth

The basis of the modern law of fraudulent conveyances is the Statute of Elizabeth, enacted in 1570. It provides that "covinous and fraudulent feoffments, gifts, grants, alienations, conveyances, bonds, suits, judgments and executions, as well of lands and of tenements as of goods and chattels, ... devised and contrived of malice, fraud, covin, collusion or guile, to the end, purpose and intent, to delay, hinder or defraud creditors and others ... shall be utterly void, frustrate and of no effect...."

The law of fraudulent conveyances soon became something other than the language of the statute. The statute of Elizabeth says that fraudulent conveyances are "void," but void only as to persons "hindered, delayed or defrauded." In other words, a fraudulent conveyance is valid as between the grantor and the grantee; in other words, a fraudulent conveyance is not void but rather is voidable by certain creditors of the grantor. The language of the statute also indicates that it is a penal statute with the remedy being the delivery of half the fraudulently transferred property to the crown and the other half to the defrauded creditor. Courts, however, since Mannocke's Case (1572) have taken the position that the judgment creditor need not rely on the remedy provided in the statute but can ignore the transfer and proceed directly against the property in the grantee's hands.

[¶ 10,315]

(2) "Badges of Fraud"

Note also that the Statute of Elizabeth requires "intent to delay, hinder or defraud." Since proof of a particular intent is a difficult task, courts soon developed the concept of "badges of fraud," i.e., circumstances indicative of intent to defraud. The first such case was Twyne's Case (1601). There P was indebted to T for £400 and to C for £200. C sued P and, while the action was pending, P secretly conveyed to T by deed of gift all of his chattels (worth £300) in satisfaction of T's claim. P, however remained in possession of some of his property—some sheep—and treated them as his own. C obtained a judgment against P, but when the sheriff sought to levy on the sheep, friends of P prevented him from doing so, asserting that the sheep belonged to T. Thereupon C sued T to set aside the conveyance from P to T as a fraudulent, noting the following "badges of fraud": (1) the conveyance is general, i.e., of all P's (the debtor's) assets; (2) the debtor continues in possession and deals with the property as his own; (3) the conveyance is made while a suit against the debtor is pending; (4) the transaction is secret; and (5) T (the transferee) takes the property in trust for the debtor.

In virtually every American jurisdiction, the Statute of Elizabeth has been either recognized as part of the inherited common law or expressly adopted or enacted in more or less similar terms. The concept of "badges of fraud" has also been generally adopted, although what constitutes a "badge of fraud" varies from jurisdiction to jurisdiction. Among the most commonly recognized "badges of fraud" are those mentioned in Twyne's Case; intra-family transfers; voluntary transfers (i.e., transfers of property without consideration); and transfers of all or a substantial amount of property immediately prior to anticipated litigation. Not only do states differ as to what facts constitute "badges of fraud," there is also no uniformity as to what weight is to be given to a particular "badge"— whether it is conclusive of fraud, prima facie evidence of fraud, or merely admissible evidence of fraud.

The "badge of fraud" rule that is most uniformly recognized is that preferring one creditor over others is not a badge of fraud. It is not a badge of fraud for debtor, D, to pay creditor, X, in full and pay nothing to other creditors, Y and Z. Obviously, D's payment to X hinders and delays the other creditors. If, however, Y or Z were permitted to set aside the payment to X, there would merely be a substitution of one preference for another. Fraudulent conveyance law is intended to ensure only that some deserving creditor receives the debtor's reachable assets. Allocation of assets among creditors is determined by state judicial collection law or by the bankruptcy statutes.

[¶ 10,320]

(3) Uniform Fraudulent Transfer Act

Today, fraudulent conveyance law is still statutory but modern statutes are based on the Uniform Fraudulent Transfer Act (UFTA) promulgated by the National Conference of Commissioners on Uniform State Laws, not the Statute of Elizabeth.

As of May 2004, 43 states had adopted the UFTA, and two more states were considering it. The following are the key sections of the UFTA: §§ 1, 2 and 3, which are definitional; §§ 4 and 5, which answer the question which transfers are fraudulent transfers; and §§ 7 and 8, which answer the question what are the consequences of determining that a transaction is a fraudulent transfer. The key to understanding the UFTA is to understand that the UFTA in essence recognizes two kinds of fraudulent transfers—(1) transfers made with actual intent to defraud and (2) transfers that are constructively fraudulent—and two categories of protected creditors—(1) present creditors and (2) future creditors.

[¶ 10,325]

b. *Which transfers are fraudulent transfers?*

The UFTA, like the Statute of Elizabeth, reaches transfers made with "an actual intent to hinder, delay or defraud any creditor of the debtor." UFTA § 4(a)(1). And, the UFTA in § 4(b) identifies a number of possible "badges of fraud" [although it does not use that phrase] that are relevant in determining whether there was any such "actual intent to hinder, delay or defraud."

More important, the UFTA reaches some transfers in which the debtor was completely free from fraudulent intent—transfers of the property of an insolvent or financially troubled debtor for which the debtor receives less than "reasonably equivalent value." UFTA § 5(a). Accordingly, if D sells Greenacre and it can be shown that (i) D was insolvent at the time of the sale and (ii) the amount D received was less than the "reasonably equivalent value" of Greenacre, the transfer is a § 5(a) fraudulent transfer, regardless of D's intent.

"Reasonably equivalent value" under the UFTA is different from "consideration" under common law contracts. A mere peppercorn is not enough. The UFTA inquires into the adequacy of consideration; it is in essence a comparative value standard.

And, note that the reasonably equivalent value must be received by the debtor/transferor. If, for example, D grants C a mortgage on Greenacre to secure a $100,000 loan that C makes to T and it can be shown that D was insolvent at the time of the mortgage, the mortgage is a § 5 fraudulent transfer. C may well have provided "reasonably equivalent value" but that value went to T, not the debtor/transferor D.

Section 2 defines "insolvency." Insolvency depends on a comparison of the debtor's debts and assets. Under § 2(a), if the amount of the debts is greater than the fair valuation of the assets, the debtor is insolvent— regardless of whether she is currently paying her debts. While nonpayment of debts creates a presumption of insolvency pursuant to § 2(b), that presumption can be rebutted by showing that the fair valuation of the assets is greater than the amount of the debts.

In determining the fair valuation of the debtor's "assets" in § 2, it is important to check the definition of "asset" in § 1 and note that "exempt property" is excluded from the term "asset." In states with "liberal" exemption statutes, most of an individual's property will be exempt. In such states, most individuals will be "insolvent" for UFTA purposes.

Not all transfers by an insolvent debtor are fraudulent transfers. Section 5 looks at both whether the debtor was insolvent and whether the debtor received "reasonably equivalent value." While the phrase "reasonably equivalent value" is not statutorily defined, the term "value" is. The § 3 definition of value includes "antecedent" debt. Accordingly, repayment of a debt is not a fraudulent transfer under § 5(a).

For example, Dawn owes $10,000 to Alice, $20,000 to Bert, and $30,000 to Cora. Dawn uses her last $20,000 to pay Bert. This debt repayment is not a § 5(a) fraudulent transfer.

However, with two additional facts, this debt repayment might be a § 5(b) fraudulent transfer. If (1) Bert is a relative of Dawn or other "insider" as that term is defined in § 1, and (2) Bert has reasonable cause to believe that Dawn is insolvent, then and only then will a debt repayment be a fraudulent transfer.

[¶ 10,330]

c. *What are the consequences of determining that a transaction is a fraudulent transfer?*

Answering questions about the practical consequences of a determination that a transaction is a fraudulent transfer requires answering two basic questions: (1) who has a remedy? and (2) what are the remedies?

[¶ 10,335]

(1) Who has a remedy?

The UFTA confers remedies only on creditors. The heading of § 7 of the UFTA is "Remedies of *Creditors*" (emphasis added). Both UFTA § 7(a) and UFTA § 7(b) provide that "a creditor ... may.... "

The debtor/transferor does not have any remedy either under the UFTA or under case law, even where the transferee has promised to reconvey. Various reasons have been given for this rule: pari delicto, unclean hands, discouraging fraudulent conveyances.

Assume, for example, that D transfers Greenacre to X who promises to reconvey. If the Greenacre transaction is a fraudulent transfer under the UFTA, creditors of D have remedies under UFTA. Creditors of D can recover Greenacre.

Only D's creditors have remedies under the UFTA. D cannot recover Greenacre from X even though X promised to reconvey it.

And, under the UFTA, not every creditor of the debtor/transferor has remedies with respect to every fraudulent transfer. Compare the headings of UFTA § 4 ("Transfers Fraudulent As to Present and Future Creditors") and § 5 ("Transfers Fraudulent As to Present Creditors"). As is suggested by the headings of the sections and stated by the text in the sections, a transaction that is a "fraudulent transfer" under § 5 ("without receiving a reasonably equivalent value") results in remedies only for present creditors.

The definitions of UFTA § 1 do not include phrase "present creditor." UFTA § 5 explains that a "present creditor" is a "creditor whose claim arose before the transfer was made."

Use the following hypothetical to review:

On January 15, D borrows $100,000 from P. On March 3, D transfers Greenacre to T. On April 5, D borrows $200,000 from F. P is a present creditor. P thus has UFTA remedies if the April 5 transaction meets the requirements of either UFTA § 4 or § 5. F is a future creditor. F has remedies under the UFTA only if the April 5 transaction meets the requirements of UFTA § 4.

[¶ 10,340]

(2) What are the remedies?

Once it has been determined that a transaction is a fraudulent transfer under UFTA §§ 4 or 5, look to §§ 7 and 8 for the remedies. Creditors can file a complaint against the person to whom the property was fraudulently transferred and recover either the transferred property or money damages measured by the lesser of the amount of the creditor's claim or the value of the transferred property as of the time of the transfer.

Fraudulent transfer law is a significant factor in all of the various actions that a debtor might take in avoiding collection of debts—bankruptcy, maximizing exemptions, and asset protection trusts. And so we will be considering fraudulent transfer law again. And again. And again.

[¶ 10,345]

Problems and Questions

1. Determine if the following might be fraudulent under the Uniform Fraudulent Transfer Act:

(a) At the time his daughter started law school, Dick promised her a new car if she finished first in her class. She graduates first in her class. Dick buys her a new car even though he had sustained financial reverses that he had not anticipated at the of his promise and is now insolvent.

(b) While insolvent, Dave sells his match box and hot wheels car collection to his sister Sally for $20,000, about its fair market value. Dave then hides the $20,000 in foreign bank accounts under various aliases.

2. While unable to pay their creditors all of what they owe, Husband and Wife pay the Harvard Museum of Natural History $85,900 and reserve two places on the Harvard Museum of Natural History's Legendary Places Around the World by Private Jet travel program. What can Husband and Wife's creditors do?

[¶ 10,400]

2. Bankruptcy

Why are there so many bankruptcy cases?

The following chart shows the number of bankruptcy filings from 1980–2003.

U.S. Bankruptcy Filings 1980–2003
(Business, Non–Business, Total)

Year	Total Filings	Business Filings	Non-Business Filings	Consumer Filings as a Percentage of Total Filings
1980	331,264	43,694	287,570	86.81%
1981	363,943	48,125	315,818	86.78%
1982	380,251	69,300	310,951	81.78%
1983	348,880	62,436	286,444	82.10%
1984	348,521	64,004	284,517	81.64%
1985	412,510	71,277	341,233	82.72%
1986	530,438	81,235	449,203	84.69%
1987	577,999	82,446	495,553	85.74%
1988	613,465	63,853	549,612	89.59%
1989	679,461	63,235	616,226	90.69%
1990	782,960	64,853	718,107	91.72%
1991	943,987	71,549	872,438	92.42%
1992	971,517	70,643	900,874	92.73%
1993	875,202	62,304	812,898	92.88%
1994	832,829	52,374	780,455	93.71%
1995	926,601	51,959	874,642	94.39%
1996	1,178,555	53,549	1,125,006	95.46%
1997	1,404,145	54,027	1,350,118	96.15%
1998	1,442,549	44,367	1,398,182	96.92%
1999	1,319,465	37,884	1,281,581	97.12%
2000	1,253,444	35,472	1,217,972	97.17%
2001	1,492,129	40,099	1,452,030	97.31%
2002	1,577,651	38,540	1,539,111	97.56%
2003	1,660,245	35,037	1,625,208	97.89%

A legitimate question is why are there so many bankruptcy filings. An equally legitimate question is why are there so few bankruptcy filings.

There is not much a debtor can do outside of bankruptcy to fix her debt problems. At least not much that a debtor can do without the help and support of her creditors.

Recall that when the debtor is an individual, state and federal laws exempt certain property of the debtor from the collection efforts of certain creditors. At most, these exemption statutes enable a debtor to keep some of his or her property from some of his or her creditors; exemption statutes do not enable a person with debt problems to "fix" the problems.

A debtor can try to work out some sort of debt repayment agreement with her creditors. Law professors who teach first year contracts courses call these agreements "compositions" and "extensions." Real lawyers and people in business call these agreements "workout agreements."

Whatever you call them, they are "agreements" and only bind the creditors who agree. If even one creditor refuses to participate in the workout agreement, that creditor can in essence, "blow up" any deal by suing on its debt and using the execution process to levy on and sell assets of the debtor that are essential to the debtor's performing its workout obligations.

Assume, for example, that Epstein has reached an agreement with nine out of ten of his largest creditors to pay 90% of their claims over three years at a new, higher interest rate. That tenth, non-assenting creditor is not bound. And, that non-assenting creditor can sue on its debt, obtain a judgment, and levy on and cause the sale of property important to Epstein.

Recall that when a debtor does not pay a debt despite the requests (and then demands) of a creditor, the creditor can go to court—sue on the debt. Such a suit usually results in a default judgment; that is, in most cases the debtor will not defend or show up, and the creditor will get everything it asked for in its complaint "by default." A creditor with a judgment against Epstein can then obtain an "execution lien" from the court that issued the judgment. And, with an execution lien, the creditor can get the sheriff to "levy on," or take physical possession of, Epstein's property. The sheriff will then sell the property at an execution sale.

At least that is what can happen unless Epstein is one of the more than 1.5 million people who files for bankruptcy each year. An Epstein bankruptcy filing will stop ("stay") all such creditor collection action.

[¶ 10,405]

a. What is different about bankruptcy?

Initially, four basic differences between bankruptcy and state debt-or-creditor law should be noted.

First, bankruptcy law is federal law. Congress enacted the present version of the Bankruptcy Code, title 11 of the United States Code, in 1978, and has since amended it frequently but not significantly.

Second, the vocabulary of bankruptcy law is different from the vocabulary of state collection law. The Bankruptcy Code uses technical terms such as "automatic stay" and "preference" that are not a part of state law. And, the Bankruptcy Code uses terms such as "debtor" and "redemption" with different meanings than those terms have under state law.

Third, state law focuses on individual action by a particular creditor and puts a premium on prompt action by a creditor. Under state law, the first creditor to attach the debtor's property, the first creditor to execute on the property, etc., is the one most likely to be paid. Bankruptcy, on the other hand, compels collective creditor collection action and emphasizes equality of treatment, rather than a race of diligence. While bankruptcy law does not require equal treatment for all creditors, the claims of all unsecured creditors receive equivalent distributions.

After the commencement of a bankruptcy case, the "automatic stay" bars a creditor from improving its position vis-à-vis other creditors by obtaining payment from the debtor or seizing assets of the debtor or filing a lien against the debtor's property. The instant that the debtor files for bankruptcy the debtor and her assets are protected by the automatic stay—creditors are barred from extrajudicial and judicial collection actions against the debtor and her property, and creditors' actions in violation of this statutory stay will be ineffective.

The Bankruptcy Code even limits a creditor's ability to improve its possession vis-à-vis other creditors by payment from the debtor or seizing assets of the debtor or filing a lien against the debtor's property before the bankruptcy filing. Some pre-bankruptcy payments to creditors and pre-bankruptcy liens obtained by creditors that are valid outside of bankruptcy can be invalidated in bankruptcy. The Bankruptcy Code provides for the recovery of certain pre-bankruptcy "transfers." The Bankruptcy Code's definition of "transfer" includes liens. Accordingly, these avoidance provisions reach both payments and liens.

Consider the avoidance of a pre-bankruptcy payment. When the bankruptcy trustee avoids a pre-bankruptcy payment to a creditor, the trustee recovers that payment from that creditor and the recovery becomes available for pro rata distribution to all unsecured creditors.

Assume, for example, that Debtor owes Creditor $10,000. Debtor repays Creditor $8,000 of the $10,000 debt. Debtor later files for bankruptcy. At the time of bankruptcy, Creditor has a $2,000 claim against Debtor, and the $8,000 belongs only to Creditor. If the bankruptcy trustee is able to void the payment, the $8,000 will be distributed to all unsecured creditors pro rata, and Creditor will again have a $10,000 claim against Debtor.

The various invalidation provisions reflect certain basic bankruptcy policies. The most significant such provision is § 547, designed to advance the bankruptcy policy of equal treatment of similar claims.

Remember that outside of bankruptcy, each creditor is left to its own devices. Common law does not condemn a preference. Under common law, a debtor, even an insolvent debtor, may treat certain creditors more favorably than other similar creditors. Although D owes X, Y, and Z $1,000 each, D may pay X's claim in full before paying any part of Y's claim or Z's claim. And, each creditor may use its own powers of persuasion or the judicial process to collect its claim in full even though the debtor lacks sufficient funds or property to pay all creditors in full.

The Bankruptcy Code treats creditors collectively, and provides for equal treatment of similar claims: The Bankruptcy Code's preference provision, § 547, is intended to provide an orderly transition from the non-bankruptcy approach of "first come, first served" to the bankruptcy policy of equal treatment of similar claims. The legislative history of the Code explains the rationale for § 547 as follows:

The purpose of the preference section is twofold. First, by permitting the trustee to avoid pre-bankruptcy transfers that occur within a short period before bankruptcy, creditors are discouraged from racing to the courthouse to dismember the debtor during his slide into bankruptcy. The protection thus afforded the debtor often enables him to work his way out of a difficult financial situation through cooperation with all of his creditors. Second, and more important, the preference provisions facilitate the prime bankruptcy policy of equality of distribution among creditors of the debtor. Any creditor that received a greater payment than others of his class is required to disgorge so that all may share equally. [House Report 95–595 at 117–18.]

Let's consider first the principles of preference law and then the practical significance of preference law to a debtor. Under § 547(b), the bankruptcy trustee may avoid any transfer of property of the debtor:

(1) to or for the benefit of a creditor;

(2) for or on account of an antecedent debt owed by the debtor before such transfer was made;

(3) made while the debtor was insolvent [for purposes of this provision there is a rebuttable presumption that the debtor was insolvent during the 90 days preceding the date of the filing of the bankruptcy petition];

(4) made—

(A) on or within 90 days before the date of the filing of the petition; or

(B) between ninety days and one year before the date of the filing of the petition, if such creditor at the time of such transfer was an insider [for purposes of this provision an "insider" includes relatives of an individual debtor and directors of a corporate debtor]; and

(5) that enables such creditor to receive more than such creditor would receive [in a bankruptcy case under Chapter 7] if . . . the transfer had not been made. . . .

Use the following examples to test your understanding of the principles of preference law.

Example 1. D owes C $10,000. D pays C $7,000 on January 15. D files for bankruptcy on April 5. Unless C can rebut the presumption that D was insolvent on January 15, the bankruptcy trustee can recover the $7,000 from C.

Example 2. On January 15, D buys a new car on credit from C, making a $7,000 down payment to C and financing the $20,000 balance. D files for bankruptcy on April 5. The $7,000 down payment is not recoverable from C under § 547(b). It was not made for an "antecedent debt." Any monthly car payments made after January 15 and before April 5, however, would be for an "antecedent debt."

Now let's consider the practical significance of preference law to a debtor like D. What are the negative economic consequences to the debtor of a bankruptcy court's determining that a payment made by the debtor prior to bankruptcy is a preference? None. In Example 1, D did not have the $7,000 before she filed for bankruptcy. The fact that in bankruptcy all of D's creditors share in the $7,000 instead of C alone having the $7,000 is not a negative economic consequence to the debtor D. Just a negative economic consequence to the creditor C.

Now think about a possible positive economic consequence to the debtor. Take another look at Example 1. What if D waited another couple of weeks before filing for bankruptcy so that the gap between the payment of the $7,000 and the bankruptcy filing was more than 90 days? No preference; C keeps the $7,000. As that question and answer suggest, a debtor who has made a substantial payment to an existing creditor on an antecedent debt can sometimes obtain additional credit from that creditor to avoid or at least defer filing for bankruptcy.

Fourth, and most important, the prospects for debtor relief are much greater in bankruptcy than under state law. As the Supreme Court has stated:

> The federal system of bankruptcy is designed not only to distribute the property of the debtor, not by law exempted, fairly and equally among his creditors, but as a main purpose of the act, intends to aid the unfortunate debtor by giving him a fresh start in life, free from debts, except of a certain character, after the property which he owned at the time of bankruptcy has been administered for the benefit of creditors. Our decisions lay great stress upon this feature of the law—as one not only of private but of great public interest in that it secures to the unfortunate debtor, who surrenders his property for distribution, a new opportunity in life. [Stellwagen v. Clum, 245 U.S. 605, 617 (1918).]

And, the phrase "fresh start" nowhere appears in the Bankruptcy Code. Courts and commentators, however, consistently connect the bankruptcy "fresh start" policy with the bankruptcy discharge. The term "discharge" does appear in the Bankruptcy Code. A lot. And this chapter will discuss discharge a lot. Later.

There are two general forms of bankruptcy relief: (1) liquidation, and (2) rehabilitation or reorganization. The Bankruptcy Code provides for these two forms of relief in five separate kinds of bankruptcy cases: (1) Chapter 7 cases, (2) Chapter 9 cases, (3) Chapter 11 cases, (4) Chapter 12 cases, and (5) Chapter 13 cases. This book does not deal with Chapters 9 and 12. Chapter 9 cases involve governmental entities as debtors, and it is infrequently used. Chapter 12 is limited to family farmer bankruptcy. This chapter will deal briefly with the three basic forms of bankruptcy relief: Chapter 7, Chapter 11, and Chapter 13.

[¶ 10,410]

b. *What happens in Chapter 7*

Chapter 7 is presently available to all individuals. No eligibility tests—no statutory requirement of inability to pay debts or any form of insolvency. Recent legislative proposals, however, would restrict the use of Chapter 7 by individuals. Specifically, Congress is considering imposing a statutory means test which would require individuals who are financially able to pay creditors to use Chapter 11 or Chapter 13 rather than Chapter 7. Chapter 11 is available to all individuals but most Chapter 11 debtors are business entities. There is more for lawyers to do in Chapter 11 than in Chapter 7 or Chapter 13, and the professional fees are correspondingly higher. Chapter 13 can be used only by individuals with a "regular income" (as defined in § 101(27)) who have debts within the statutory debt limits. In 2004, these limits were $871,550 for secured debts and $290,525 for unsecured debts.

Chapter 7 is entitled "Liquidation." The title is descriptive. In a Chapter 7 case, the trustee collects the non-exempt property the debtor had when she filed her bankruptcy petition, converts that property to cash, and distributes the cash to the creditors. In essence, the debtor gives up all of the non-exempt property she owns at the time of the filing of the bankruptcy petition in the hope of obtaining a discharge. A discharge releases the debtor from any further personal liability for her pre-bankruptcy debts.

The costs of Chapter 7 bankruptcy are thus (1) a filing fee now set at $155, (2) attorneys fees which typically run around $1,000, and (3) loss of any interest in non-exempt property owned *at the time the debtor filed for bankruptcy.*

Note the italicized time limit. If Moira files a bankruptcy petition on January 30, she keeps her earnings for February, and March, and April and so forth. Bankruptcy costs Moira only what she had at the time she filed for bankruptcy. And, if Moira finds a lottery ticket on February 2 and wins $1,000,000 in the lottery, she keeps that too. Assuming that her Chapter 7 case ends in a discharge.

Discharge is the main benefit of Chapter 7 bankruptcy for an individual debtor. Assume, for another example, that another debtor, Fran, owes various creditors $200,000. Fran files a Chapter 7 petition on April 5. The Chapter 7 trustee takes and sells the various nonexempt assets that Fran owned as of April 5. And, assume further that creditors only receive $3,000 from the liquidation of Fran's assets. If Fran receives a bankruptcy discharge, the pre-bankruptcy creditors will be precluded from pursuing Fran for the remaining $197,000.

As the preceding paragraph implies, not every Chapter 7 case under the bankruptcy laws results in a discharge. Section 727(a) lists a number of grounds for withholding a discharge. Most of these statutory objections have as their foundation some form of dishonesty or lack of cooperation of the debtor in bankruptcy. For example, certain fraudulent transfers can be the basis for an objection to discharge. Section 727(a)(2) denies a discharge to a Chapter 7 debtor who transferred property "with an intent to hinder, delay or defraud" within 12 months immediately preceding the filing of the bankruptcy petition or after filing a bankruptcy petition.

As the example of Fran's bankruptcy in which creditors received 1.5% of what they owed suggests, the amount—or lack of amount—that creditors receive from the liquidation of the debtor's nonexempt assets is irrelevant in determining whether a Chapter 7 debtor receives a discharge. Indeed, empirical studies show that in more than 95% of Chapter 7 cases, unsecured creditors receive nothing.

Nothing for unsecured creditors in Chapter 7?

Think about what you have right now. Do you own a house? For most Chapter 7 debtors, as for most students, the answer to that question is "no." Do you own a car? If so, could you sell that car for more than you still owe on the car? Again, for most Chapter 7 debtors, as for most students, the answer again is "no." What else do you own that could be sold for real money? Your used clothes? Your used appliances? Your used furniture?

In sum, for most debtors, the only out of pocket costs of filing for bankruptcy under Chapter 7 are the $155 filing fee and whatever their bankruptcy attorney charges. Not surprisingly, the vast majority of bankruptcy cases are Chapter 7 cases. The term "bankruptcy" is often used to describe Chapter 7 liquidation cases.

[¶ 10,415]

c.   *What happens in Chapter 11*

Cases under Chapters 11 and 13 are often described as "chapter proceedings." Chapters 11 and 13 generally deal with debtor rehabilitation or reorganization, not liquidation, of the debtor's assets. In a Chapter 11 or 13 case, creditors usually look to future earnings of the debtor, not the property of the debtor at the time of the initiation of the bankruptcy proceeding, to satisfy their claims. The debtor retains his assets and makes payments to creditors, usually from post-petition earnings, pursuant to a court approved plan.

While Chapter 11 is available to individual debtors, very few individuals avail themselves of Chapter 11. Too complicated—too expensive. Chapter 11 contemplates that:

1. there will be a plan of debt repayment approved by both creditors and the court;

2. the debtor's creditors will form a committee which will participate in the plan process and vote on whether to accept the plan; and

3. the debtor will pay not only for her own attorney but also for the attorney representing the committee of creditors.

[¶ 10,420]

d.   *What happens in Chapter 13*

By contrast, in a Chapter 13 case, there is no creditor participation in the plan process; no creditors' committee; and no attorney representing the creditors' committee for the debtor to pay. In Chapter 13 cases, the Bankruptcy Code and the bankruptcy judge protect creditors by requiring that the debtor's plan commit all "disposable income", as defined by the Code and determined by the court, for the payment of creditors.

Again, the primary advantage of Chapter 11 or Chapter 13 to an individual debtor is that he gets to keep his "stuff"—his house, his car, his bass boat, etc. The disadvantage of Chapter 11 or 13 is the continuing legal obligation to make payments to creditors as provided in the court-approved plan of reorganization.

Individual debtors in Chapter 11 cases and Chapter 13 cases, like debtors in Chapter 7 cases, can qualify for a bankruptcy discharge. The time of the discharge, however, is different.

The general rule for Chapter 13 is that a debtor must complete all payments under the plan before she receives a discharge. By contrast, a Chapter 11 debtor is discharged from all obligations, other than her obligations to make plan payments, at the time the plan is approved by the court, i.e., confirmed. The difference between the Chapter 13 and the Chapter 11 discharge rules are illustrated by the following three examples:

Example 1. In 2001, Debtor files for relief under Chapter 13 of the Bankruptcy Code. His plan provides for payments to holders of unsecured claims over 36 months. Under Debtor's Chapter 13 plan, each unsecured creditor will have been paid 75% of what it was owed. Debtor owed Creditor $40,000. The court approves, i.e., confirms the plan. Debtor makes all of the plan payments and receives a discharge. Creditor will have received only $30,000 of its $40,000 debt over 3 years, but is barred by the discharge from pursuing Debtor for the remaining $10,000.

Example 2. Same facts as Example 1, except that Debtor defaults after making payments to holders of unsecured claims totaling 10% of the amount of their claims. Creditor has received only $4,000. Debtor did not receive a discharge and so Creditor can now pursue Debtor for the remaining $36,000.

Example 3. In 2001, Debtor files for relief under Chapter 11 of the Bankruptcy Code. Debtor's Chapter 11 plan provides for payments to holders of unsecured claims over 24 months. At the end of the 24th and final monthly payment, each unsecured creditor will have been paid 50% of what it was owed. Debtor owed Creditor $40,000. The court approves, i.e., confirms the plan. Debtor makes only one plan payment and defaults. Since this is a Chapter 11 case, Debtor receives his bankruptcy discharge as soon as the plan was confirmed. The most that Creditor can collect from Debtor is $20,000 (50% of $40,000 as provided in the plan), including the payment already made under the plan.

Remember that most individual debtors are able to choose their form of bankruptcy—Chapter 7, Chapter 11 or Chapter 13. And, remember that most individuals choose Chapter 7.

A leading bankruptcy empiricist lamented the lack of empirical studies explaining the reasons for the choosing Chapter 7:

We also remain largely ignorant of how a client chooses Chapter 7 versus Chapter 13. We have every reason to think that the lawyer makes the choice for the client or at least strongly influences that choice. Yet we have little idea how lawyers arrive at their conclusions or what processes they use to do so. [Westbrook, Empirical Research in Consumer Bankruptcy, 12 J. Bankr. L. & Prac. 3 (2003).]

Even without a detailed empirical demonstration, it seems likely that both debtors and their lawyers prefer the immediate relief in a Chapter 7 case to the years of supervised payments in a Chapter 13. Proceedings under Chapter 7 are not only quicker but cheaper. A bankruptcy administrator reports that "about 70% of the consumer cases are filed under Chapter 7. This is because the Bankruptcy Code permits debtors to choose between Chapter 7 and Chapter 13, and under Chapter 7 most debtors are not obligated to repay anything. Although Chapter 7 cases are referred to as liquidations, the reality is that in 96% of Chapter 7 cases, creditors do not receive anything." Landry, The Policy and Forces Behind Consumer Bankruptcy Reform: A Classic Battle Over Problem Definition, 33 U. Memphis L. Rev. 509 (2003).

Some law professors have suggested that filing under Chapter 13 instead of Chapter 7 will protect a debtor's credit rating. There are no empirical studies that support that suggestion. Most credit bureaus simply enter "bankruptcy" in the debtor's file, regardless of whether it is a Chapter 7 case or a Chapter 13 case.

Indeed, some creditors seem to believe that filing a Chapter 7 bankruptcy improves a debtor's creditworthiness. There are creditors that specialize in granting credit to debtors who have filed for bankruptcy. For example, the website, http://www.after-bankruptcy-credit-card.com advertises credit cards to rehabilitate credit after bankruptcy with the pitch : "Did you know that the fact that you filed bankruptcy stays on your credit report for ten years. As time goes it becomes less significant. The interesting truth is that you are probably a better credit risk after bankruptcy than before."

Section 727(a)(8) which limits the frequency of a Chapter 7 discharge, provides some legal support for the pitch. An individual who has received a discharge in a Chapter 7 bankruptcy case cannot receive another Chapter 7 discharge for six years. Consider the following example.

Example. In January 2004, Dave files a Chapter 7 bankruptcy and receives a discharge in April 2004. Dave applies for a credit card in June 2004. That credit card issuer knows that Dave cannot obtain a discharge in any Chapter 7 case filed before January 2010.

[¶ 10,425]

Problems and Questions

1. Dale owes $100,000 on educational loans, $50,000 in credit card debts, $40,000 on his car loan (2003 BMW), $30,000 in back taxes, and

$20,000 to various other unsecured creditors. Dale is single and does not own a home. His salary is $80,000 a year. Dale is considering bankruptcy. What are the advantages and disadvantages to Dale of bankruptcy? If Dale files for bankruptcy, should he file for Chapter 7 or Chapter 13?

2. Donna owes Chad $200,000. Chad realizes that Donna has severe financial problems and so agrees to release Donna from any further liability if Donna pays $120,000. Over the next month, Donna pays Chad $120,000. Two weeks later, Donna files for bankruptcy. Would Chad be affected by Donna's bankruptcy?

3. What property is exempt in bankruptcy? What is the practical significance, if any, of exempt property in bankruptcy?

4. Is there a "stigma" of bankruptcy? Should there be a stigma of bankruptcy?

[¶ 10,430]

e. *Discharge*

Because discharge is the focal point of most individual bankruptcy cases, let's focus more closely on the bankruptcy concept of discharge. A debtor who receives a bankruptcy discharge is protected from any further personal liability on his dischargeable debts. Reread this sentence and notice the limitations on the concept of discharge.

First, as previously noted, not every person who is a debtor in a bankruptcy case receives a discharge. A Chapter 7 debtor must contend with the § 727 objections to discharge based on "misdeeds" before or during the bankruptcy case. A Chapter 11 or Chapter 13 debtor must perform her plan obligations.

Second, "discharge" is not a magic word—it's not like "abracadabra." A discharge does not make the debt disappear. The debt is still there. Even after the discharge. All that a discharge does is protect the debtor who has received the discharge from any further personal liability on the debt. To illustrate:

Example 1. Duane owes Connie $10,000. George guaranteed payment. Duane defaults, files for bankruptcy and receives a bankruptcy discharge. Because of Duane's discharge, Connie cannot sue Duane or take any other action to collect that debt from Duane individually. Notwithstanding Duane's discharge, Connie can still sue George on the guaranty. Duane's discharge does not affect George's guarantee of Duane's debt. The debt has not been vaporized.

Example 2. Dan owes Mary $20,000. Mary has a mortgage on land owned by Dan, Blackacre, as collateral for the debt. Dan defaults, files for bankruptcy, and receives a discharge. Again, because of Dan's discharge, Mary cannot sue Dan or take any other action to collect that debt from Dan individually. And, again, notwithstanding Dan's discharge, neither Dan's debt nor the mortgage securing that debt has been vaporized. Mary can still foreclose her mortgage—evict Dan from Blackacre and sell Blackacre. If, however, the net proceeds from the sale of

Blackacre are less than the unpaid debt, Mary cannot obtain a deficiency judgment against Dan individually.

Third, and most important, even if the debtor is able to obtain a discharge, she will not necessarily be freed from all creditors' claims. Certain obligations are not affected by a bankruptcy discharge. Section 523 sets out 18 exceptions to discharge. Some of these 18 statutory exceptions are based on the conduct of the debtor in incurring a particular debt. Most are based on the nature of the debt. For example, under § 523, most educational loans, most tax claims, and most family obligations such as alimony and child support are excepted from discharge.

It is very important to understand the difference between § 727(a) objections to discharge and § 523(a) exceptions to discharge. If an objection to discharge has been established, all creditors may attempt to collect the unpaid balance of their claims from the debtor. If a creditor establishes an exception to discharge, only that creditor may attempt to collect the unpaid portion of its claim from the debtor; all other prepetition claims remain discharged. Proof of an objection to discharge benefits all creditors; proof of an exception to discharge benefits only the creditor that establishes the exception. To illustrate:

Example 1. Ben files for bankruptcy. Ben's creditors include John, Kate and Lily. As a result of the liquidation of Ben's assets in the Chapter 7 case, creditors are paid 10% of what they are owed. If an objection to Ben's discharge is established and Ben does not receive a discharge, then John, Kate, Lily, and Ben's other creditors can resume their efforts to collect the remaining 90% of their debts.

Example 2. Ben files for bankruptcy. Ben's creditors include John, Kate and Lily. As a result of the liquidation of Ben's assets in the Chapter 7 case, creditors are paid 10% of what they are owed. If John is able to establish that his debt is one of the types of debt excepted from discharge under § 523, then John—but not Kate, Lily or Ben's other creditors—can resume his efforts to collect the remaining 90% of his claim.

And, for too many law students and graduate students, it is important to be aware of the educational loan exception to discharge in § 523(a)(8), which provides as follows:

A discharge . . . does not discharge an individual debtor from any debt . . . for an educational benefit overpayment or loan made, insured, or guaranteed by a governmental unit, or made under any program funded in whole or in part by a governmental unit or nonprofit institution, or for an obligation to repay funds received as an educational benefit, scholarship, or stipend, unless excepting such debt from discharge under this paragraph will impose an undue hardship on the debtor and the debtor's dependents.

What is an "undue hardship"? It is pretty much up to the bankruptcy judge. In In re Berscheid, 309 B.R. 5 (Bankr. D. Minn. 2002), the court held that Mr. Berscheid was not entitled to an undue hardship discharge of $42,657.30 in student loans. Mr. Berscheid was 47 years old; he had two young children with serious medical conditions, and his wife was pregnant with their third child; he worked as a family therapist at the Christian Recovery Center. In Judge Dreher's words:

> The Berscheid family lives modestly. They own one vehicle, which is in the shop because they cannot afford repair. They are using a vehicle loaned by a family member. The family spends virtually nothing on clothes, entertainment and dental expenses, for which they have no insurance. They have no life insurance. The balance in the 403(b) retirement plan is about $1,200. They purchased their home for $118,000. The home is 45 miles from Berscheid's place of work. They could not find affordable housing closer to Berscheid's workplace. Had they remained in an apartment, their rent would have been roughly equal to their current mortgage payment.

> Berscheid took his current employment because he believed that he was "called" to help people. His current position with a nonprofit allows him to serve a public which cannot pay. He is an educated, principled man who is devoted to his family and his work. His work with a nonprofit, however, keeps him from entering private practice where he would make more money. The Berscheids' commitment to home schooling their children means that Lisa, who is otherwise able and employable, will not want to work outside the home.

> A vocational rehabilitation expert testified that if Berscheid left the nonprofit sector and entered private practice he would be able to earn, conservatively, $60,000 per year, and perhaps quite a bit more. He has not tried to find more gainful employment. He wants to stay where he is. I find that ... if Berscheid left the nonprofit sector, it is very likely that he could make more money than he does now.

Take note, law and business students: public interest work is not the way to avoid paying your education loans. At least not in Judge Dreher's court.

And, in no bankruptcy judge's court can a person use bankruptcy to discharge unpaid taxes. Section 523(a)(1) excepts from the bankruptcy discharge all income taxes for the three tax years immediately preceding bankruptcy. And even taxes more than three years old are not discharged if (a) a return was not filed, or (b) the return for these taxes more three years old was filed late and within two years of the bankruptcy filing, or (3) a return was timely filed but it was "fraudulent." Moreover, a debt incurred to pay taxes that would have been nondischargeable is itself excepted from the discharge.

Example. In March 2004, Doris uses her American Express card to pay the $1,200 she owes for 2003 taxes. In June, Doris files for bankruptcy with her American Express bill unpaid and receives a bankruptcy discharge. The bankruptcy discharge does not affect American Express's right to collect the $1,200 attributable to the payment of taxes described in § 523(a)(1).

As this example suggests, there is no blanket exception from discharge for credit card debts. But the credit card industry is spending "big bucks" lobbying for bankruptcy protection.

[¶ 10,435]

Problems and Questions

1.   Chuck makes a loan to Dana. Chuck requires that Greg guarantee the loan. Dana later files for bankruptcy. Can Dana obtain a bankruptcy discharge even though Chuck has not been paid? If Dana obtains a bankruptcy discharge, can Chuck still collect from Greg?

2.   The law is that a person can not contract away her right to a discharge. Is the law "right"? Should a creditor be able to offer a loan at a lower rate in exchange for the borrower's reducing the lender's risk by contracting away her right to a bankruptcy discharge?

3.   Dennis obtains a bankruptcy discharge. One of the debts discharged is a $5,000 debt owed to Dr. Payne for braces for Denis's kids. Dr. Payne refuses to continue to treat Dennis's kids. Dennis offers to pay in advance, and Dr. Payne still refuses. What can Denis do?

[¶ 10,440]

3.   Converting Non–Exempt Property to Exempt Property

It is not unusual for a debtor contemplating bankruptcy to increase her exempt property before filing. There are two different ways for a debtor to increase her exempt property before filing for bankruptcy.

First, the debtor can relocate. Move to a state that has a more generous exemption statute. Recall that a debtor in bankruptcy can take advantage of state exemption laws. More specifically, the debtor can use the exemption law of the state "in which the debtor's domicile has been located for the 180 days immediately preceding the date of filing of the bankruptcy petition or for a longer portion of such 180 day period than in any other place." 11 U.S.C. § 522(b).

Example. Danielle, a New Jersey resident, sells her $1,300,000 home in New Jersey and moves to Florida, where she buys a new house for at least $1,300,000. If she had filed for bankruptcy while living in New Jersey, creditors would get her house. New Jersey's homestead exemption is nominal. If she is able to delay bankruptcy for 91 days, then she can take advantage of the much more generous Florida homestead statute and keep the house. Just ask Bowie Kuhn. (After you ask your dad or some other older baseball fan, "Who was Bowie Kuhn?")

Second, she can convert nonexempt property to exempt property on the eve of bankruptcy by swapping (directly or indirectly) one kind for the other or by conveying solely-owned property to a form of joint ownership with a spouse that will put the property beyond creditor's reach. The debtor's lawyer may have advised her to do so as prudent "bankruptcy planning." The debtor's unsecured creditors who are thereby affected call it something else: actual fraud.

There is no simple answer whether such a conversion is right or wrong, permitted or damned in bankruptcy. The complexity begins in deciding where to look for an answer. The technically proper source of law on the propriety of a conversion may be different depending on how the issue arises, that is, on the remedy that is sought. Three different remedies are possible for a conversion that is wrongful: it can amount to a fraudulent transfer that is avoidable under Bankruptcy Code § 548 or § 544(b) and state fraudulent conveyance law, or can serve as a reason for denying an exemption provided by state or federal law or as the basis for denying a bankruptcy discharge. Properly, state law will control if the object is to avoid a transfer under local fraudulent conveyance law or to deny a state exemption. Denial of discharge, however, is always an issue that federal bankruptcy law controls. For the most part, however, essentially the same analysis is followed in answering the ultimate question which is at the bottom of each remedy: did the conversion amount to actual fraud.

The larger problems that complicate the question are that the doctrine is soft and the issue in every case is highly fact-intensive. The traditional doctrine on whether or not converting assets to exempt property is actually fraudulent is easily and often stated: the conversion of nonexempt to exempt property on the eve of bankruptcy, thereby placing the property out of the reach of creditors, does not in itself support a finding of actual fraudulent intent "even if the debtor acts with the express purpose of placing property beyond the reach of creditors and even though the debtor is insolvent at the time." The reason is that the debtor is entitled to make legitimate, full use of the exemptions to which the law entitles her, and is free to engage in a certain amount of "bankruptcy exemption planning."

The debtor is not allowed, however, to convert assets for fraudulent purposes. Thus, a conversion is a fraudulent transfer if extrinsic evidence, beyond the conversion itself, establishes that the debtor acted with intent to hinder, delay or defraud her creditors.

It is usually rather difficult to distinguish between a valid conversion, by which a debtor properly fully uses her legal exemptions, and an avoidable conversion which is motivated by the debtor's intent to defraud her creditors. The debtor's intention is always the ultimately decisive fact, but there is seldom direct evidence of it.

The courts typically consider a set of key circumstances that are commonly reflective of intention, that is, the courts hunt among the facts and circumstances of the case for "badges" or "indicia of fraud" which suggest actual fraudulent intent, as they usually do in any kind of case in which actual fraud is an issue. A non-exclusive list of these badges in conversion cases would include, for example:

1. whether the debtor paid fair consideration for the exempt property she acquired, and whether the transferee of the nonexempt property paid fair value for it;

2. whether the money used to acquire the exempt property was borrowed or was proceeds of collateral;

3. the debtor's financial condition at the time of acquiring the exempt property and as a result of the acquisition;

4. whether the debtor accomplished the conversion openly or secretly, and whether she lied to or misled creditors;

5. the amount and value of the exempt property;

6. the length of time between acquiring the exempt property and filing bankruptcy;

7. whether the exempt property was acquired about the time a creditor began, or threatened to begin, collection activities;

8. the amount of the debtor's nonexempt property involved in the conversion and remaining after it.

There are many, many reported cases. Reliably reconciling them is impossible because, even though the courts' analysis is basically the same, the cases differ substantially in five very relevant respects.

1. the facts;

2. the distribution of weight to various facts in the balancing process that determines the presence or absence of fraud;

3. the object of finding actual fraud (e.g., to avoid a transfer as fraudulent, to deny exemptions, or to prevent a discharge);

4. the source of law (state or federal); and,

5. the procedural posture.

We nevertheless are tempted to generalize that the most important facts seem to be whether the debtor effected the conversion openly in the ordinary course of business, and (especially if the exemption lacks any value cap) whether the type and amount of exempt property the debtor acquired is unusual for exemption purposes. The former is important for the obvious reason that sneaky, odd conduct naturally smacks of actual fraud.

The large importance of the type and amount of exempt property is made clear by two cases decided differently by the same court on the denial of discharge. The debtor, a physician, got into financial trouble because of soured investments. In contemplation of bankruptcy, and upon his lawyer's advice, the debtor liquidated almost all of his nonexempt property (cash, IRA, profit-sharing plan, house, and everything else) at market value and converted the proceeds into exempt life insurance or annuity contracts worth $700,000. These contracts were issued by a fraternal benefit association, and the applicable local exemption law exempted any and all money or other benefits payable by such an association. Because the exemption was unlimited as to value it carried "the potential for unlimited abuse," and the Eighth Circuit agreed with the lower court that the debtor had abused the exemption to the extent of losing his right to a discharge: the debtor-doctor "did not want a mere *fresh* start, he wanted a *head* start." In the end he got no start at all. Norwest Bank Nebraska v. Tveten, 848 F.2d 871 (8th Cir. 1988).

The contrasting companion case is Hanson v. First Nat'l Bank, 848 F.2d 866 (8th Cir. 1988), which the Eighth Circuit decided along with *Tveten*. The debtors in Hanson also converted property on their lawyer's advice shortly before bankruptcy, but on a much smaller scale. They did not sell everything they owned. Rather, the conversion involved about $34,000 in property. With the proceeds they bought two life insurance policies with cash values totalling $20,000 and paid $11,000 on their existing home mortgage. The applicable local law limited the insurance exemption to $20,000, and exempted the homestead. The Eighth Circuit agreed with the bankruptcy court that there were "no indicia of fraud." The debtors merely "sold the property for its fair market value and then used this money to take advantage of some of the limited exemptions available under [applicable] law on the advice of counsel."

In truth, the only material differences between these two cases, *Tveten* and *Hanson*, are the form of the exempt property the debtors acquired and its value. Subsequently, the Eighth Circuit conceded that the cases establish that "where an exemption, other than a homestead exemption, is not limited in amount, the amount of property converted into exempt forms and the form taken may be considered in determining whether fraudulent intent exists." The effect is judicially to limit in value the size of otherwise unlimited exemptions, taking into account the purpose of exemptions to provide "property to the debtor useful to his continuing survival." In re Johnson, 880 F.2d 78 (8th Cir. 1989).

Thus, the amount of exempt property that a debtor can legitimately acquire is directly related to the property's usefulness to the debtor's survival and other exemption purposes. In *Tveten*, the exempt property was functionally equivalent to cash.

Presumably, the courts will rarely, in this manner, limit exemptions that the legislature has already capped in value. With respect to these exemptions, a policy decision has already been made as to their appropriate size. Funding them by conversion of nonexempt assets is likely to be fraudulent only if the debtor acts under cover or otherwise extraordinarily so that creditors are misled or otherwise directly harmed. There must be evidence of fraudulent intent beyond and apart from the form and value of the exempt property.

Recall that *Tveten* suggested that a debtor's use of nonexempt property to acquire or enhance his homestead might be treated differently by the Eighth Circuit. It would certainly be treated differently by the courts of the states with the most generous homestead exemptions— Texas and Florida.

Under Texas law, a debtor has an absolute right to acquire, improve, or pay down a lien against homestead property, even if the debtor does so with actual intent to hinder, delay, or defraud creditors. Thus, the use of otherwise exempt property to acquire, improve, or pay down a lien against a homestead may not be set aside, or the homestead exemption denied, regardless of the debtor's state of mind or the effect on creditors. If a Texas debtor channeled nonexempt assets into exempt homestead property with actual intent to hinder, delay, or defraud creditors, the proper remedy in bankruptcy is to deny the debtor's discharge, not to avoid the transaction or deny the exemption.

A fraudulent transfer of nonexempt assets may not be used as a basis for disallowing a Florida homestead exemption. If the debtor obtained the funds channeled into the homestead property by dishonest means, however, a bankruptcy court may make use of subrogation, a constructive trust, an equitable lien, or any other equitable remedy that may be appropriate under the circumstances. Such a step would be for the benefit of the victim, however, not for the benefit of all creditors.

[¶ 10,445]

Problems and Questions

1.   Dave borrows $10,000 from Carlos in an unsecured loan. Dave uses the $10,000 to prepay an exempt life insurance policy. When Dave defaults on his loan to Carlos, what are Carlos's legal rights?

2.   Is "exemption planning" different from tax planning? How can you distinguish a debtor's taking advantage of state exemption laws from a taxpayer taking advantage of a "loophole" in the Internal Revenue Code?

[¶ 10,450]

4. Owning Property in Tenancy by the Entirety

About half of the states still recognize tenancy by the entirety. And, in about half of those states, a husband and wife can protect property from the claims of certain creditors by owning that property in tenancy by the entirety.

Tenancy by the entirety began in England for reasons unrelated to debt and avoiding payment of debt. It was a way for a husband and wife to own property jointly—a way of avoiding the wife's common law legal disabilities. For present purposes, you should be aware of two unique characteristics of tenancy by the entirety: (1) only married couples can own property in tenancy by the entirety, and (2) neither the husband nor the wife can dispose of any part without the assent of the other, but the whole must remain to the survivor. Pennsylvania Supreme Court Justice Musmanno once remarked:

> Husband and wife own an estate in entireties as if it were a living tree, whose fruits they share together. To split the tree in two would be to kill it and then it would not be what it was before when either could enjoy

its shelter, shade, and fruit as much as the other. [Sterrett v. Sterrett, 166 A.2d 1, 2 (Pa. 1960).]

Tenancy by the entirety today permits a husband and wife to keep creditors from enjoying the fruit or even the shade—to own property free from certain creditors' collection efforts. About half of the states still recognize tenancy by the entirety, and in about half of those states a creditor of only one spouse cannot reach tenancy by the entirety property because one spouse alone cannot assign his or her interest. Consider the following examples:

Example 1. Husband and Wife own Greenacre in tenancy by the entirety. Husband negligently injures Victim. Victim obtains a $100,000 judgment against Husband. Victim will not be able to collect that judgment by levying on Greenacre.

Example 2. Husband and Wife own Greenacre in tenancy by the entirety. Husband wants to borrow $200,000. Louis, the lender, requires both Husband and Wife to sign the promissory note. Husband defaults. Louis will be able to look to Greenacre to collect his claim.

As the above examples suggest, tenancy by the entirety permits a husband and wife to protect property from the claims of only certain creditors. A creditor of both spouses is able to reach entirety property. And, a recent Supreme Court decision looked to the language of the Federal Tax Lien Act to conclude that the Internal Revenue Service could collect federal taxes owed by a husband from entirety property. United States v. Craft, 535 U.S. 274 (2002).

By way of comparison to homestead, tenancy by the entirety is available only to married couples. And, unlike a homestead, tenancy by the entirety is not limited to the family home. An unlimited amount of commercial or investment property can be held by the entirety and thus inaccessible to creditors of only the husband, or only the wife.

A more positive view of tenancy by the entirety is that it encourages the creation of marital property controlled by both spouses. Protection from creditors is provided to one spouse only if the other spouse is given equal ownership rights in the underlying property.

[¶ 10,455]

Problems and Questions

1. Husband and Wife own substantial real estate in tenancy by the entirety. Husband applies for a loan at First Bank. What can First Bank do to maximize its right to collect the loan?

2. Why is tenancy by the entirety available only to married couples? Why is tenancy by the entirety available only in about half of the states?

[¶ 10,460]

5. Asset Protection Trusts

A recent newspaper article discusses the growing use of asset protection trusts:

Litigation Boom Spurs Efforts to Save Assets

Wall Street Journal (Oct. 14, 2003)

The drumbeat of litigation against doctors, accountants, business executives and other professionals is prompting a growing number of people to play defense: They're putting their money where creditors can't get to it. A key technique is the so-called asset-protection trust. The idea is to put a big chunk of your money in an irrevocable trust. The trust is run by an independent trustee, who may opt to give you payments from time to time. If done correctly, the trust—which has to be located in a jurisdiction that has passed special laws—generally can't be touched by creditors if you're sued or file for bankruptcy protection. . . .

Nobody tracks exactly how many asset-protection trusts are drafted each year, especially since many are located in exotic offshore jurisdictions. But lawyers and trust companies say interest in them seems to be increasing. National City Corp's Delaware-based trust company, which started only 10 months ago, expects to pull in $200 million in asset-protection trust business in its first two years. . . .

Most asset protection trusts are located offshore, in locales like the Cook Islands, Nevis and Gibraltar, which have attracted sizable trust business by enacting laws that protect trusts from U.S. creditor claims.

But the number of U.S.-based trusts is now picking up as states change their laws, partly to lure people who are worried about putting their wealth abroad. Alaska, Delaware, Rhode Island, Nevada, and as of this year, Utah, now permit these trusts for both residents and nonresidents. About 1,500 domestic asset protection trusts holding more than $2 billion in assets have been created since 1997, estimates Richard Nenno, managing director and trust counsel, Wilmington Trust Co., Del. . . .

A recent survey of individuals with more than $1 million in assets found that 35% had some form of asset-protection plan, compared with just 17% of respondents in 2000. And more than 61% of the respondents who didn't have an asset-protection plan were interested in creating one, up from only 43% in 2000, found the study by Prince & Associates, Redding, Conn., a market research and consulting firm.

Domestic asset-protection trusts are controversial, because they haven't yet been tested in court and it is still unclear how well they'll hold up. Article IV of the Constitution says that each state should have "full faith and credit" in the legal judgments made in other states.

Lawyers, therefore, worry that a plaintiff who wins a judgment in a New York court might be able to enforce the ruling against an asset-protection trust created in Delaware. . . .

People setting up asset-protection trusts have to pay attention to avoid running afoul of the law. While creating an offshore asset-protection trust may sound sketchy, they're legal as long as they're not used to evade income taxes; you have to disclose the assets and income in the trust to the Internal Revenue Service.

Another caveat: People shouldn't set up an asset-protection trust if you know you have a potential legal action looming on the horizon. Courts are likely to rule against such a trust, calling it a "fraudulent conveyance," if it is set up right before a lawsuit, bankruptcy or divorce.

Brian D. and Elizabeth G. Weese, the owners of a now-defunct Baltimore bookstore chain, recently faced several lawsuits charging that they fraudulently moved nearly $20 million in assets to a Cook Islands trust called "Book Worm II" to avoid creditors ahead of bankruptcy. Several months ago, the Weeses settled the case for more than $12 million; the money was provided by Ms. Weese's father, Rite Aid Corp. founder Alexander Grass. . . .

Asset-protection trusts don't come cheap. Offshore asset-protection trusts can cost anywhere from $20,000 to $50,000 to set up, plus annual administrative fees of $2,000 to $5,000 and asset-management fees of about 1% on the assets placed in the trust. Domestic asset-protection trusts cost less, running anywhere from $3,000 to $10,000 in attorney's fees, plus asset-management fees of roughly 1%.

Because of the high fees, asset-protection trusts generally don't make sense unless you're willing to put at least $1 million in them.

—————————

An asset protection trust is a special form of spendthrift trust—a self-settled spendthrift trust. To understand the previous sentence and the possibilities and problems with asset protection trusts, it is necessary to recall the basic concepts of a trust and spendthrift trusts.

In order to create a trust, there must be a settlor (property owner who created the trust), a trustee, and a beneficiary. The settlor transfers assets to the trustee by means of a trust agreement setting out the terms of the trust. Although the trustee is strictly speaking the "owner" of the trust assets, the trustee owns those assets not for the trustee's own benefit, but for the benefit of the beneficiaries, for whom the trustee is a fiduciary. The rights and obligations of the trustee and the beneficiaries are established by the terms of the trust instrument and through a body of trust law that has developed principally through decisions by courts defining and enforcing the interests of trust beneficiaries.

Since the late 19th century, spendthrift provisions have been a part of the body of court-developed trust law. A spendthrift provision prevents the beneficiary's creditors from seizing the trust assets and the beneficiary from assigning his interest in the trust assets. A typical spendthrift trust provision might read "The interest of any trust beneficiary can not be assigned or seized by legal process."

The Massachusetts Supreme Judicial Court explained the rationale for judicial enforcement of spendthrift trust provisions as follows:

> The founder of this trust was the absolute owner of his property. He had the entire right to dispose of it, either by an absolute gift to his brother, or by a gift with such restrictions or limitations, not repugnant to the law, as he saw fit to impose.... His intentions ought to be carried out, unless they are against public policy.... He has the entire jus disponendi, which imports that he may give it absolutely, or may impose any restriction or fetters not repugnant to the nature of the estate which he gives. Under our system, creditors may reach all the property of the debtor not exempted by law, but they cannot enlarge the gift of the founder of the trust, and take more than he has given. [Broadway National Bank v. Adams, 133 Mass. 170, 173–74 (1882).]

There are limitations on the protection that can be achieved through spendthrift trust provisions.

First, certain creditors can collect their claims from trust assets, notwithstanding spendthrift trust provisions. For example, § 157 of the Restatement (Second) of Trusts provides that a claim is enforceable against the interest of the beneficiary: (1) by the spouse or child of the beneficiary for support or alimony; (2) for necessary services or supplies provided to the beneficiary (i.e., necessities of life such as food, clothing, lodging, and medical care); (3) for services rendered and materials furnished that preserve or benefit the beneficiary's interest; and (4) by the United States or a state governmental entity.

Second, and more important, there has been a longstanding rule that a spendthrift provision for the settlor's own benefit is unenforceable. To illustrate:

Example 1. Settlor transfers property to Trustee in trust for Beneficiary. A trust agreement provision that Beneficiary's creditors cannot seize the trust property to satisfy debts owed by Beneficiary will generally be enforceable.

Example 2. Settlor transfers property to Trustee in trust for herself, Settlor. A trust agreement provision that Settlor's creditors cannot seize the trust property to satisfy debts owed by Settlor will generally not be enforceable.

While the rule against self-settled spendthrift trusts is easy to state and easy to apply, the rationale for the rule is neither easy to state nor easy to explain. The leading treatise on trusts simply states that "it is against public policy to permit the owner of property to create for his own benefit an interest in that property that cannot be reached by creditors." 2 Scott & Fratcher, The Law of Trusts § 156, at 168 (4th ed. 1987). For critical commentary on the judicial rule against self-settled trusts, see Hirsch, Spendthrift Trusts and Public Policy: Economic and Cognitive Perspectives, 73 Wash. U. L.Q. 1 (1995); Danforth, Rethinking the Law of Creditors' Rights in Trusts, 53 Hastings L.J. 287 (2002).

Of greater practical significance are legislative actions taken in several small island jurisdictions and in several states to validate self-settled spendthrift trusts. These laws have spawned a new term ("asset protection trust"), a new law journal (the Journal of Asset Protection), at least one new multi-volume treatise (Osborne, Asset Protection: Domestic and International Law and Tactics (1995)), and new offshore financial industries—more than a trillion dollars is now held in offshore asset protection trusts.

At a November 2003 American Law Institute–American Bar Association program on planning techniques for large estates, Duncan Osborne, lawyer and author of the multi-volume treatise on asset protection, compared domestic and offshore opportunities and concluded that "those states cannot match offshore jurisdictions when it comes to the primary reason for creating such a trust: shelter from the claims of creditors." One of Osborne's reasons is also set out in the *Wall Street Journal* article set out above: "Domestic asset-protection trusts are controversial, because they haven't yet been tested in court and it is still unclear how well they'll hold up. Article IV of the Constitution says that each state should have 'full faith and credit' in the legal judgments made in other states. *Lawyers, therefore, worry that a plaintiff who wins a judgment in a New York court might be able to enforce the ruling against an asset-protection trust created in Delaware.*"

Let's consider that italicized example more carefully.

Example 1. In 2004, Settlor, a New York resident, creates a Delaware asset protection trust. The trust agreement contains spendthrift provisions, specifies Delaware law as the controlling law, names Settlor as beneficiary, and names a Delaware trust company as trustee. Settlor transfers significant assets to the trustee, and the trustee takes possession of the assets in Delaware. Subsequently Creditor obtains a large judgment against Settlor in a New York court. Creditor then brings a collection action in the same New York court, claiming that the assets of the Delaware asset protection trust should be made available to satisfy its claim.

The New York court would have to consider the following questions:

(1) Is the Delaware trustee a necessary party?

(2) If so, does the New York court have jurisdiction over the Delaware trustee?

(3) In determining the validity of the Delaware asset protection trust, should the New York court apply the trust law of Delaware as designated in the trust instrument, or should the court apply New York trust law because the relevant Delaware trust law permitting self-settled spendthrift trusts violates the public policy of the State of New York which does not recognize self-settled spendthrift trusts?

And, even assuming that a New York court answered those questions so as to decide that the assets in the Delaware trust could be used to satisfy the judgement, then we get to the earlier referenced "full faith and credit" questions. There would have to be recourse to the Delaware courts to enforce the New York court decision. Under the Full Faith and Credit clause of the U.S. Constitution, would the Delaware court have to give effect to the New York judgment, even if that judgment violates the Delaware public policy allowing the use of self-settled spendthrift trusts?

Now, let's move the trust to an offshore location.

Example 2. In 2004, Settlor, a New York resident, creates an asset protection trust in the Cook Islands. The trust agreement contains spendthrift provisions, specifies the law of the Cook Islands as the controlling law, names Settlor as beneficiary, and names a Cook Islands trust company as trustee. Settlor transfers significant assets to the trustee and the trustee takes possession of the assets in the Cook Islands. Subsequently Creditor obtains a large judgment against Settlor in a New York court. Creditor then brings a collection action in the same New York court, claiming that the assets of the Cook Islands asset protection trust should be made available to satisfy its claim.

Same three questions as above. Except now it is harder to answer these questions so as to decide that the assets in the Cook Islands trust can be used to satisfy the judgment. And, even if the New York court so decides, there will have to be an action in the Cook Islands courts to enforce the New York court decision.

The Cook Islands courts, unlike Delaware courts, are not bound by the Full Faith and Credit clause of the U.S. Constitution. And, the Cook Islands International Trusts Act of 1984 expressly provides that a Cook Islands court need not recognize the judgment of a court from another jurisdiction.

Understanding the risks and rewards of asset protection trusts requires an understanding of not only the law of spendthrift trusts but also the law of fraudulent transfers. Even if a creditor's challenge to the validity of a self-settled asset protection trust is unsuccessful, the creditor can always claim that the settlor's transfer to the asset protection trust was fraudulent under relevant fraudulent transfer laws. If a fraudulent transfer claim is successful, the usual remedy is an order setting the transfer aside. Thus, with a fraudulent transfer claim, the effectiveness of a self-settled asset protection trust is essentially irrelevant; if a debtor makes a fraudulent transfer within the meaning of the fraudulent transfer laws, the transfer can be set aside and the transferred assets recovered by a creditor, without regard to the identity of the transferee.

Will a settlor's transfer to an asset protection trust be fraudulent under relevant fraudulent transfer law? It depends, of course, on the facts and the law. Probably the most important fact is whether the transfer is made with a specific creditor or credit problem in mind or with the more general goal of shielding assets from possible future claims. And, the greater the time gap between the transfer and the accrual of the claim, the less likely that a court will find that an earlier transfer was fraudulent with respect to that future creditor.

Example 1. Penny sues Dr. Payne for malpractice. While the law suit is pending, Dr. Payne creates and transfers significant assets to a new asset protection trust. This seems like the Weeses in the *Wall Street Journal* article—this seems like a fraudulent transfer.

Example 2. Dr. Sawbones creates and transfers significant assets to a new asset protection trust. Two years later, Sally sues Dr. Sawbones for malpractice. It seems unlikely that a court will find that the transfer was a fraudulent transfer.

The governing law can also be important. Most of the laws, foreign and domestic, that recognize self-settled spendthrift trusts also weaken the ability of creditors to reach the assets under fraudulent transfer law. For example, under the International Trusts Act of 1984, a transfer of assets to a Cook Islands asset protection trust is a fraudulent transfer only if a creditor can prove beyond a reasonable doubt all of the following: (1) the transfer was made "with the principal intent to defraud the creditor"; (2) as a result of the transfer, the settlor was "insolvent or without property by which the creditor's claim could have been successful"; and (3) "the creditor's cause of action accrued" before the transfer occurred. In sum, only present creditors can challenge the transfer, and in challenging the transfer a creditor must show both actual intent to defraud and insolvency. Moreover, the Cook Islands International Trusts Act of 1984 has a very short statute of limitations for fraudulent transfer challenges: the creditor must bring the action within one year of the date of the transfer. And, most important, creditors have to bring their action in the Cook Islands. The Act provides that Cook Islands courts shall not recognize a foreign judgment against a Cook Islands asset protection trust.

There are still other laws that are important in dealing with asset protection trusts. Recall that one of the grounds for withholding a bankruptcy discharge is that the debtor transferred assets with an "intent to hinder, delay or defraud creditors." Transfers of assets to an asset protection trust can cost a debtor her bankruptcy discharge. See In re Portnoy, 201 B.R. 685 (Bankr. S.D.N.Y. 1996).

Or her freedom. For example, a couple, the Andersons (no, not Jim and Margaret), spent five months in jail for refusing to retrieve assets held in a Cook Islands asset protection trust. See FTC v. Affordable Media, 179 F.3d 1228 (9th Cir. 1999), cert. denied, 534 U.S. 1042 (2001). See generally Rothschild & Rubin, Asset Protection After *Anderson*, 26 Estate Planning 466 (Dec. 1999).

A recent continuing legal education presentation on asset protection planning concludes:

1. Asset protection planning is an essential element of estate planning. Estate planners cannot simply refrain from doing it. But there are lines that never should be crossed.

2. You know for sure that you are beyond a line if creditors already are circling, or any form of dishonesty is involved in the planning.

3. Asset protection planning is best viewed as a form of risk management. The goal should be peace of mind, and the assumption should be that present creditors cannot be avoided.

Roth, Protecting Assets From Creditors, Legally, Ethically and Morally, SG062 ALI–ABA 75 (Feb. 22, 2002). For additional background and commentary on asset protection trusts, see Sterk, Asset Protection Trusts: Trust Law's Race to the Bottom?, 85 Cornell L. Rev. 1035 (2000); Marty–Nelson, Offshore Asset Protection Trusts, 47 Rutgers L.Rev. 11 (1994); Sullivan, Gutting the Rule Against Self–Settled Trusts: How the New Delaware Trust Law Competes with Offshore Trusts, 23 Del. J. Corp. L. 423 (1998).

[¶ 10,465]

Problems and Questions

1. Which of the following would be an appropriate candidate for an asset protection trust?

Derwood, a doctor who has just been sued for $10,000,000 for medical malpractice;

Wendy, a wealthy woman who is planning to marry impecunious Henry;

Ricardo, a successful real estate investor.

2. Why did Alaska, Delaware, and other states enact laws permitting self-settled asset protection trusts?

3. Why would a lawyer recommend a domestic asset protection trust instead of an offshore asset protection trust?

E. POSTSCRIPT

[¶ 10,475]

As this volume was going to press, Congress passed and the President signed into law legislation that, in one form or another, had been considered since the mid–1990's. The principal impact of that legislation is to make it more difficult for individuals to avail themselves of Chapter 7 and to force them into Chapter 13. The key provisions of the law as they affect the matters discussed in this chapter are:

- Most individuals will not be allowed to file for Chapter 7 and will be relegated to Chapter 13, if their income exceeds their state's median income and, using a formula, the bankruptcy judge determines that the individual can afford to pay 25% of her "nonpriority" unsecured debt (e.g., credit card debt). The court will then determine how much of her debt the debtor should be required to pay under Chapter 13, based on standards used by the I.R.S. in measuring a debtor's ability to pay tax deficiencies. If the debtor could pay at least $100 per month for 60 months under these standards, then she would be barred from filing under Chapter 7 and would most likely find that Chapter 13 offered the only available bankruptcy option.

- Homestead exemptions are limited in several ways. A debtor who has not lived in a state for at least two years must use the exemption of the state that he lived in for a majority of the 180–day period preceding his move, if that exemption is less than that of the debtor's current state of residency. Also, even if a filer lived for more than two years in a state, such as Florida, with a very liberal homestead exemption, the amount of his homestead exemption would be limited to $125,000 if he acquired his residence less than 40 months before filing for bankruptcy. The $125,000 limit also applies to a filer, regardless of his period of residence in a particular home, who has violated certain securities laws or who has been convicted of certain crimes.

- Individuals who intend to file for bankruptcy protection must meet with a credit counselor within six months prior to filing a petition in bankruptcy. Moreover, debtors who file in bankruptcy must attend and pay for mandatory credit counseling and money management classes before any of their debts will be discharged.

- Attorneys who represent filers in a bankruptcy proceeding may be subject to monetary penalties if information that is provided about the case is found to be inaccurate.

Time will be needed to determine the full impact of the new legislation on the economy and on individuals who find it necessary to file for relief in bankruptcy.

Appendix A

DISCOUNTED PRESENT VALUE OF $1, PAYABLE AT END OF FIXED TERM OF YEARS, AT SPECIFIED DISCOUNT RATES

Term (Years)	Discount Rate							
	3%	4%	5%	6%	7%	8%	10%	12%
1	0.97087	0.96154	0.95238	0.94340	0.93458	0.92593	0.90909	0.89286
2	0.94260	0.92456	0.90703	0.89000	0.87344	0.85734	0.82645	0.79719
3	0.91514	0.88900	0.86384	0.83962	0.81630	0.79383	0.75131	0.71178
4	0.88849	0.85480	0.82270	0.79209	0.76290	0.73503	0.68301	0.63552
5	0.86261	0.82193	0.78353	0.74726	0.71299	0.68058	0.62092	0.56743
6	0.83748	0.79031	0.74622	0.70496	0.66634	0.63017	0.56447	0.50663
7	0.81309	0.75992	0.71068	0.66506	0.62275	0.58349	0.51316	0.45235
8	0.78941	0.73069	0.67684	0.62741	0.58201	0.54027	0.46651	0.40388
9	0.76642	0.70259	0.64461	0.59190	0.54393	0.50025	0.42410	0.36061
10	0.74409	0.67556	0.61391	0.55839	0.50835	0.46319	0.38554	0.32197
11	0.72242	0.64958	0.58468	0.52679	0.47509	0.42888	0.35049	0.28748
12	0.70138	0.62460	0.55684	0.49697	0.44401	0.39711	0.31863	0.25668
13	0.68095	0.60057	0.53032	0.46884	0.41496	0.36770	0.28966	0.22917
14	0.66112	0.57748	0.50507	0.44230	0.38782	0.34046	0.26333	0.20462
15	0.64186	0.55526	0.48102	0.41727	0.36245	0.31524	0.23939	0.18270
16	0.62317	0.53391	0.45811	0.39365	0.33873	0.29189	0.21763	0.16312
17	0.60502	0.51337	0.43630	0.37136	0.31657	0.27027	0.19784	0.14564
18	0.58739	0.49363	0.41552	0.35034	0.29586	0.25025	0.17986	0.13004
19	0.57029	0.47464	0.39573	0.33051	0.27651	0.23171	0.16351	0.11611
20	0.55368	0.45639	0.37689	0.31180	0.25842	0.21455	0.14864	0.10367
25	0.47761	0.37512	0.29530	0.23300	0.18425	0.14602	0.09230	0.05882
30	0.41199	0.30832	0.23138	0.17411	0.13137	0.09938	0.05731	0.03338
40	0.30656	0.20829	0.14205	0.09722	0.06678	0.04603	0.02209	0.01075
50	0.22811	0.14071	0.08720	0.05429	0.03395	0.02132	0.00852	0.00346

Appendix B

FUTURE VALUE OF $1, PAYABLE AT END OF FIXED TERM OF YEARS, AT SPECIFIED DISCOUNT RATES, COMPOUNDED ANNUALLY

Term (Years)	Interest Rate							
	3%	4%	5%	6%	7%	8%	10%	12%
1	1.0300	1.0400	1.0500	1.0600	1.0700	1.0800	1.1000	1.1200
2	1.0609	1.0816	1.1025	1.1236	1.1449	1.1664	1.2100	1.2544
3	1.0927	1.1249	1.1576	1.1910	1.2250	1.2597	1.3310	1.4049
4	1.1255	1.1699	1.2155	1.2625	1.3108	1.3605	1.4641	1.5735
5	1.1593	1.2167	1.2763	1.3382	1.4026	1.4693	1.6105	1.7623
6	1.1941	1.2653	1.3401	1.4185	1.5007	1.5869	1.7716	1.9738
7	1.2299	1.3159	1.4071	1.5036	1.6058	1.7138	1.9487	2.2107
8	1.2668	1.3686	1.4775	1.5938	1.7182	1.8509	2.1436	2.4760
9	1.3048	1.4233	1.5513	1.6895	1.8385	1.9990	2.3579	2.7731
10	1.3439	1.4802	1.6289	1.7908	1.9672	2.1589	2.5937	3.1058
11	1.3842	1.5395	1.7103	1.8983	2.1049	2.3316	2.8531	3.4785
12	1.4258	1.6010	1.7959	2.0122	2.2522	2.5182	3.1384	3.8960
13	1.4685	1.6651	1.8856	2.1329	2.4098	2.7196	3.4523	4.3635
14	1.5126	1.7317	1.9799	2.2609	2.5785	2.9372	3.7975	4.8871
15	1.5580	1.8009	2.0789	2.3966	2.7590	3.1722	4.1772	5.4736
16	1.6047	1.8730	2.1829	2.5404	2.9522	3.4259	4.5950	6.1304
17	1.6528	1.9479	2.2920	2.6928	3.1588	3.7000	5.0545	6.8660
18	1.7024	2.0258	2.4066	2.8543	3.3799	3.9960	5.5599	7.6900
19	1.7535	2.1068	2.5270	3.0256	3.6165	4.3157	6.1159	8.6128
20	1.8061	2.1911	2.6533	3.2071	3.8697	4.6610	6.7275	9.6463
25	2.0938	2.6658	3.3864	4.2919	5.4274	6.8485	10.8347	17.0001
30	2.4273	3.2434	4.3219	5.7435	7.6123	10.0627	17.4494	29.9599
40	3.2620	4.8010	7.0400	10.2857	14.9745	21.7245	45.2593	93.0510
50	4.3839	7.1067	11.4674	18.4202	29.4570	46.9016	117.3909	289.0022

Appendix C

PRESENT VALUE OF LIFE ESTATE, REMAINDER AND SINGLE–LIFE ANNUITY IN $1, AT SPECIFIED AGES AND DISCOUNT RATES

Age	Life Estate	Remainder	Annuity	Age	Life Estate	Remainder	Annuity
	3% Discount Rate				6% Discount Rate		
0	0.87049	0.12951	29.0163	0	0.96767	0.03233	16.1278
10	0.83990	0.16010	27.9967	10	0.96210	0.03790	16.0350
20	0.78985	0.21015	26.3283	20	0.93865	0.06135	15.6441
30	0.72790	0.27210	24.2632	30	0.90468	0.09532	15.0780
40	0.64828	0.35172	21.6092	40	0.84987	0.15013	14.1646
50	0.54909	0.45091	18.3029	50	0.76498	0.23502	12.7497
60	0.43668	0.56332	14.5560	60	0.64967	0.35033	10.8279
70	0.32032	0.67968	10.6773	70	0.50993	0.49007	8.4988
80	0.20953	0.79047	6.9842	80	0.35604	0.64396	5.9340
90	0.11985	0.88015	3.9948	90	0.21508	0.78492	3.5847
100	0.06813	0.93187	2.2709	100	0.12678	0.87322	2.1130

Age	Life Estate	Remainder	Annuity	Age	Life Estate	Remainder	Annuity
	4% Discount Rate				7% Discount Rate		
0	0.92537	0.07463	23.1342	0	0.97567	0.02433	13.9381
10	0.90569	0.09431	22.6422	10	0.97405	0.02595	13.9150
20	0.86605	0.13395	21.6513	20	0.95582	0.04418	13.6546
30	0.81373	0.18627	20.3432	30	0.92873	0.07127	13.2676
40	0.74082	0.25918	18.5206	40	0.88209	0.11791	12.6013
50	0.64274	0.35726	16.0685	50	0.80510	0.19490	11.5014
60	0.52414	0.47586	13.1036	60	0.69500	0.30500	9.9286
70	0.39424	0.60576	9.8560	70	0.55544	0.44456	7.9348
80	0.26403	0.73597	6.6006	80	0.39503	0.60497	5.6433
90	0.15396	0.84604	3.8490	90	0.24252	0.75748	3.4646
100	0.08864	0.91136	2.2159	100	0.14454	0.85546	2.0649

Age	Life Estate	Remainder	Annuity	Age	Life Estate	Remainder	Annuity
		5% Discount Rate				8% Discount Rate	
0	0.95309	0.04691	19.0619	0	0.98027	0.01973	12.2534
10	0.94171	0.05829	18.8343	10	0.98133	0.01867	12.2666
20	0.91119	0.08881	18.2238	20	0.96687	0.03313	12.0859
30	0.86871	0.13129	17.3741	30	0.94517	0.05483	11.8146
40	0.80484	0.19516	16.0968	40	0.90553	0.09447	11.3191
50	0.71244	0.28756	14.2488	50	0.83612	0.16388	10.4515
60	0.59376	0.40624	11.8751	60	0.73206	0.26794	9.1507
70	0.45675	0.54325	9.1350	70	0.59460	0.40540	7.4325
80	0.31260	0.68740	6.2519	80	0.43015	0.56985	5.3768
90	0.18563	0.81437	3.7125	90	0.26814	0.73186	3.3518
100	0.10817	0.89183	2.1633	100	0.16151	0.83849	2.0188

Age	Life Estate	Remainder	Annuity	Age	Life Estate	Remainder	Annuity
		10% Discount Rate				12% Discount Rate	
0	0.98484	0.01516	9.8484	0	0.98688	0.01312	8.2240
10	0.98897	0.01103	9.8897	10	0.99254	0.00746	8.2712
20	0.97921	0.02079	9.7921	20	0.98529	0.01471	8.2108
30	0.96485	0.03515	9.6485	30	0.97529	0.02471	8.1274
40	0.93589	0.06411	9.3589	40	0.95357	0.04643	7.9464
50	0.87963	0.12037	8.7963	50	0.90753	0.09247	7.5628
60	0.78804	0.21196	7.8804	60	0.82732	0.17268	6.8944
70	0.65796	0.34204	6.5796	70	0.70636	0.29364	5.8863
80	0.49061	0.50939	4.9061	80	0.54053	0.45947	4.5044
90	0.31453	0.68547	3.1453	90	0.35535	0.64465	2.9613
100	0.19322	0.80678	1.9322	100	0.22229	0.77771	1.8524

Source: I.R.S. Pub. 1457.

Appendix D

LIFE EXPECTANCY OF PERSON
AT SPECIFIED AGES

Age	Life Expectancy	Age	Life Expectancy	Age	Life Expectancy
0	82.4	38	45.6	76	12.7
1	81.6	39	44.6	77	12.1
2	80.6	40	43.6	78	11.4
3	79.7	41	42.7	79	10.8
4	78.7	42	41.7	80	10.2
5	77.7	43	40.7	81	9.7
6	76.7	44	39.8	82	9.1
7	75.8	45	38.8	83	8.6
8	74.8	46	37.9	84	8.1
9	73.8	47	37.0	85	7.6
10	72.8	48	36.0	86	7.1
11	71.8	49	35.1	87	6.7
12	70.8	50	34.2	88	6.3
13	69.9	51	33.3	89	5.9
14	68.9	52	32.3	90	5.5
15	67.9	53	31.4	91	5.2
16	66.9	54	30.5	92	4.9
17	66.0	55	29.6	93	4.6
18	65.0	56	28.7	94	4.3
19	64.0	57	27.9	95	4.1
20	63.0	58	27.0	96	3.8
21	62.1	59	26.1	97	3.6
22	61.1	60	25.2	98	3.4
23	60.1	61	24.4	99	3.1
24	59.1	62	23.5	100	2.9
25	58.2	63	22.7	101	2.7
26	57.2	64	21.8	102	2.5
27	56.2	65	21.0	103	2.3
28	55.3	66	20.2	104	2.1
29	54.3	67	19.4	105	1.9
30	53.3	68	18.6	106	1.7
31	52.4	69	17.8	107	1.5
32	51.4	70	17.0	108	1.4
33	50.4	71	16.3	109	1.2
34	49.4	72	15.5	110	1.1
35	48.5	73	14.8	111 and over	1.0
36	47.5	74	14.1		
37	46.5	75	13.4		

Source: I.R.S. Pub. 590.

Appendix E

HUD SETTLEMENT STATEMENT

A. Settlement Statement

U.S. Department of Housing
and Urban Development

OMB Approval No. 2502-0265
(expires 6/30/2009)

B. Type of Loan

1. ☐ FHA   2. ☐ FmHA   3. ☐ Conv. Unins.
4. ☐ VA   5. ☐ Conv. Ins.

6. File Number:	7. Loan Number:	8. Mortgage Insurance Case Number:

C. Note: This form is furnished to give you a statement of actual settlement costs. Amounts paid to and by the settlement agent are shown. Items marked "(p.o.c.)" were paid outside the closing; they are shown here for informational purposes and are not included in the totals.

D. Name & Address of Borrower:	E. Name & Address of Seller:	F. Name & Address of Lender:

G. Property Location:	H. Settlement Agent:
	Place of Settlement:
	I. Settlement Date:

J. Summary of Borrower's Transaction		K. Summary of Seller's Transaction	
100. Gross Amount Due From Borrower		**400. Gross Amount Due To Seller**	
101. Contract sales price		401. Contract sales price	
102. Personal property		402. Personal property	
103. Settlement charges to borrower (line 1400)		403.	
104.		404.	
105.		405.	
Adjustments for items paid by seller in advance		**Adjustments for items paid by seller in advance**	
106. City/town taxes to		406. City/town taxes to	
107. County taxes to		407. County taxes to	
108. Assessments to		408. Assessments to	
109.		409.	
110.		410.	
111.		411.	
112.		412.	
120. Gross Amount Due From Borrower		**420. Gross Amount Due To Seller**	
200. Amounts Paid By Or In Behalf Of Borrower		**500. Reductions In Amount Due To Seller**	
201. Deposit or earnest money		501. Excess deposit (see instructions)	
202. Principal amount of new loan(s)		502. Settlement charges to seller (line 1400)	
203. Existing loan(s) taken subject to		503. Existing loan(s) taken subject to	
204.		504. Payoff of first mortgage loan	
205.		505. Payoff of second mortgage loan	
206.		506.	
207.		507.	
208.		508.	
209.		509.	
Adjustments for items unpaid by seller		**Adjustments for items unpaid by seller**	
210. City/town taxes to		510. City/town taxes to	
211. County taxes to		511. County taxes to	
212. Assessments to		512. Assessments to	
213.		513.	
214.		514.	
215.		515.	
216.		516.	
217.		517.	
218.		518.	
219.		519.	
220. Total Paid By/For Borrower		**520. Total Reduction Amount Due Seller**	
300. Cash At Settlement From/To Borrower		**600. Cash At Settlement To/From Seller**	
301. Gross Amount due from borrower (line 120)		601. Gross amount due to seller (line 420)	
302. Less amounts paid by/for borrower (line 220)	( )	602. Less reductions in amt. due seller (line 520)	( )
303. Cash ☐ From ☐ To Borrower		603. Cash ☐ To ☐ From Seller	

Section 5 of the Real Estate Settlement Procedures Act (RESPA) requires the following: • HUD must develop a Special Information Booklet to help persons borrowing money to finance the purchase of residential real estate to better understand the nature and costs of real estate settlement services; • Each lender must provide the booklet to all applicants from whom it receives or for whom it prepares a written application to borrow money to finance the purchase of residential real estate; • Lenders must prepare and distribute with the Booklet a Good Faith Estimate of the settlement costs that the borrower is likely to incur in connection with the settlement. These disclosures are mandatory.

Section 4(a) of RESPA mandates that HUD develop and prescribe this standard form to be used at the time of loan settlement to provide full disclosure of all charges imposed upon the borrower and seller. These are third party disclosures that are designed to provide the borrower with pertinent information during the settlement process in order to be a better shopper.

The Public Reporting Burden for this collection of information is estimated to average one hour per response, including the time for reviewing instructions, searching existing data sources, gathering and maintaining the data needed, and completing and reviewing the collection of information.

This agency may not collect this information, and you are not required to complete this form, unless it displays a currently valid OMB control number.

The information requested does not lend itself to confidentiality.

L. Settlement Charges

			Paid From Borrowers Funds at Settlement	Paid From Seller's Funds at Settlement
700. Total Sales/Broker's Commission based on price $	@	% =		
Division of Commission (line 700) as follows:				
701. $	to			
702. $	to			
703. Commission paid at Settlement				
704.				
800. Items Payable In Connection With Loan				
801. Loan Origination Fee	%			
802. Loan Discount	%			
803. Appraisal Fee	to			
804. Credit Report	to			
805. Lender's Inspection Fee				
806. Mortgage Insurance Application Fee to				
807. Assumption Fee				
808.				
809.				
810.				
811.				
900. Items Required By Lender To Be Paid In Advance				
901. Interest from	to	@$ /day		
902. Mortgage Insurance Premium for		months to		
903. Hazard Insurance Premium for		years to		
904.		years to		
905.				
1000. Reserves Deposited With Lender				
1001. Hazard insurance	months@$	per month		
1002. Mortgage insurance	months@$	per month		
1003. City property taxes	months@$	per month		
1004. County property taxes	months@$	per month		
1005. Annual assessments	months@$	per month		
1006.	months@$	per month		
1007.	months@$	per month		
1008.	months@$	per month		
1100. Title Charges				
1101. Settlement or closing fee	to			
1102. Abstract or title search	to			
1103. Title examination	to			
1104. Title insurance binder	to			
1105. Document preparation	to			
1106. Notary fees	to			
1107. Attorney's fees	to			
(includes above items numbers:		)		
1108. Title insurance	to			
(includes above items numbers:		)		
1109. Lender's coverage	$			
1110. Owner's coverage	$			
1111.				
1112.				
1113.				
1200. Government Recording and Transfer Charges				
1201. Recording fees: Deed $	; Mortgage $	; Releases $		
1202. City/county tax/stamps: Deed $	; Mortgage $			
1203. State tax/stamps: Deed $	; Mortgage $			
1204.				
1205.				
1300. Additional Settlement Charges				
1301. Survey	to			
1302. Pest inspection to				
1303.				
1304.				
1305.				
1400. Total Settlement Charges (enter on lines 103, Section J and 502, Section K)				

*

Topical Index

All references are to paragraph numbers

A

Accounting and Taxation
Accrual method, 3,880
Annual accounting period, 3,860
Cash method, 3,870
Installment method, 3,890
Inventory, 3,880

Advance Medical Directives
Accessibility, 9,170
Enforceability, 9,170
Generally, 9,150
Health care proxies, 9,165
Living wills, 9,160
Patient Self–Determination Act, 9,150
Portability, 9,170
Surrogacy statutes, 9,155

Adverse Selection, 7,020, 7,060

Alternative Minimum Tax, 3,900

Asset Protection
Asset protection trusts, 10,460
Bankruptcy vs. non-bankruptcy election, 10,245
Converting non-exempt property to exempt property, 10,440
Exemption laws, 10,245, 10,260, 10,265
Life insurance, 10,250
Homestead, 10,255
Self-settled trusts, 2,535
Spendthrift trusts, 2,525
Tenancy by the entirety, 10,460
Value limitations on exemptions, 10,265

Assignment of Income
Income from property, 3,780
Income from services, 3,770

Automobile Leases, 5,850

B

Basis
Adjustments to basis, 3,520
Cost basis, 3,490

Basis—Cont'd
Gifted property, 3,500
Inherited property, 3,510
Spousal transfers of property, 3,530

Bankruptcy
See also Asset Protection, Credit Issues, Debt
Chapter 7, generally, 10,410
Chapter 11, generally, 10,415
Chapter 13, generally, 10,420
Comparison with state law, 10,405
Discharge, 10,430
Number of, 10,400

Bonds
Callable bonds, 1,290
Convertible bonds, 1,300
Current yield, 1,230
Credit risk, 1,230
Effective yield, 1,220
Face value, 1,220
Generally, 1,220
High yield (junk) bonds, 1,270
Interest rate risk, 1,240
Junk bonds, 1,270
Maturity, 1,220
Principal, 1,220
Taxation of, 3,820
Tax-exempt bonds, 1,270
Yield, 1,220
Yield curve, 1,250
Yield to maturity (YTM), 1,220
Zero coupon bonds, 1,260

Business Expenses
Carrying on requirement, 3,320
Clothing, 3,340
Commuting, 3,340
Education expenses, 3,360, 6,130
Employee business expenses limit, 3,330
Entertainment, 3,340
Meals and lodging, 3,340
Ordinary and necessary requirement, 3,310
Public policy issue, 3,370
Reasonable compensation limit, 3,350
Trade or business requirement, 3,320
Travel, 3,340